William

OXFORD

The Australian
PRIMARY
DICTIONARY
Third Edition

William Sandefur

OXFORD

OXFORD

The Australian PRIMARY DICTIONARY
Third Edition

Compiled by
Maureen Brooks and Joan Ritchie

Edited by
Ken and Lesley Wing Jan

OXFORD
UNIVERSITY PRESS

OXFORD
UNIVERSITY PRESS

253 Normanby Road, South Melbourne, Victoria 3205, Australia.

Oxford University Press is a department of the University of Oxford. It furthers the University's objective of excellence in research, scholarship, and education by publishing worldwide in

Oxford New York

Auckland Bangkok Buenos Aires Cape Town Chennai
Dar es Salaam Delhi Hong Kong Istanbul Karachi Kolkata
Kuala Lumpur Madrid Melbourne Mexico City Mumbai
Nairobi São Paulo Shanghai Singapore Taipei Tokyo Toronto

OXFORD is a trade mark of Oxford University Press
in the UK and in certain other countries

© Oxford University Press 1984, 1995, 2001

First published 1984
Second edition published 1995
Third edition published 2001
Reprinted 2001, 2002

This book is copyright. Apart from any fair dealing for the purposes of private study, research, criticism or review as permitted under the Copyright Act, no part may be reproduced, stored in a retrieval system, or transmitted, in any form or by any means, electronic, mechanical, photocopying, recording or otherwise without prior written permission. Enquiries to be made to Oxford University Press.

First edition complied by A.J. Augarde and Angela M. Ridsdale
Second edition complied by Maureen Brooks and Joan Ritchie
Third edition (based on the second edition) edited by Ken and Lesley Wing Jan

National Library of Australia
Cataloguing-in-Publication data:
Wing Jan, Ken
　The Australian Primary Dictionary.
　ISBN 0 19 551451 3.

　1. English language—Dictionaries, Juvenile. 2. English language—
　Pronunciation—Dictionaries, Juvenile. I. Wing Jan, Lesley, 1946- .
　II. Title. III. Title: The Oxford Junior Dictionary.

Cover designed by Olga Lavecchia
Typeset by Egan-Reid Ltd, Auckland
Printed through Bookpac Production Services, Singapore

OWLS
OXFORD
DICTIONARY
WORD AND
LANGUAGE
SERVICE

Do you have a query about words, their origin, meaning, use, spelling, pronunciation, or any other aspect of international English? Then write to OWLS at the Australian National Dictionary Centre, Australian National University, Canberra ACT 0200 (email ANDC@anu.edu.au). All queries will be answered using the full resources of The Australian National Dictionary and The Oxford English Dictionary.
The Australian National Dictionary Centre and Oxford University Press also produce OZWORDS, a biannual newsletter which contains interesting items about Australian words and language. Subscription is free – please contact the OZWORDS subscription manager at Oxford University Press, GPO Box 2784Y, Melbourne, VIC 300, or ozwords@oup.com.au

Contents

Introduction		vii
Origins of words		vii
How the dictionary is set out		ix
How the information about each word is set out		x
The Australian Primary Dictionary		1
Appendix 1	Some common prefixes	499
Appendix 2	Some common suffixes	500
Appendix 3	Floral Emblems of Australian States and Territories	501
Appendix 4	English terms	502
Appendix 5	Mathematical terms	503
Appendix 6	Computers and technology	504
Appendix 7	Aboriginal words	505
Appendix 8	Human body	506
Appendix 9	Civics and citizenship	507
Map showing the Aboriginal languages referred to in tnis dictionary		508

Introduction

This dictionary provides information that should help you develop a better understanding of how words are used in the English language.

It contains the following information about words:

- *Their meanings* (definitions)
- *Their part/s of speech* (how they are used in sentences). Please remember that the part of speech is determined by the way the word is used in a piece of text. The part of speech indicated for each headword only applies to the definition provided. There are times when a particular word may be used in a different context and therefore the part of speech may be different.
- *How they are pronounced.* There are no simple rules that tell you how to pronounce Australian words from the way that they are written. A pronunciation guide is provided to help you work out how to pronounce some difficult or unfamiliar words. It tells you how many syllables the word has and that the stress is on the syllable in bold type. Putting stress on a syllable means pronouncing it more strongly than the rest of the word. For example, for the headword '**impromptu**' the pronunciation guide is as follows: (*say* im-**promp**-tyoo).
- *Their spelling.*
- *Associated words* (word building).
- *Additional information* (shaded usage boxes).

The appendices include lists of words grouped under specific headings. Beside each word is a number that refers to a particular page in the dictionary where additional information about the word can be found.

Origins of words

English words are written using an alphabet of twenty-six letters: five of the letters are called vowels (a, e, i, o, u) and the rest are consonants (b, c, d, f, g, h, j, k, l, m, n, p, q, r, s, t, v, w, x, y, z).

The words that we use today come from many sources. Some have been in the English language since the time of the Angles and Saxons 1500 years ago (we say that these words come from Old English) while others are comparatively new. Many words have been borrowed from other languages and there are some words the origin of which we do not know. There are even some words that have changed over time through common usage and others that have developed from the manipulation of existing words. The following diagram shows some of the sources of words in Australian English.

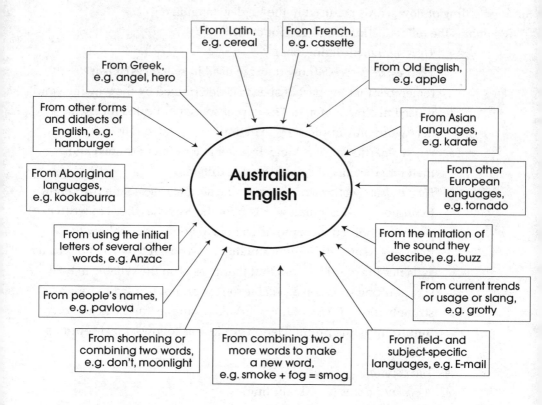

How the dictionary is set out

Alphabetical order

The words are arranged in alphabetical order. Down the side of each page is an alphabet strip to help you with the alphabetical order.

Guide words

At the top of each page spread there are two guide words. These help you work out which words will be on the page.

How the information about each word is set out

Each word listed in the dictionary is called a **headword**. The information after each headword is called an **entry**.

The **entry** (information) about each listed word (**headword**) may be set out in the following way.

Headword
The word that you look up is printed in blue, bold print.

Part of speech
This tells you the work that the word usually does in a sentence.

Pronunciation guide
This helps you work out how to say the word. It tells you how many syllables there are in the word. The parts in **bold print** are the parts that you emphasise when you say the word.

Definition
This explains what the word means. Sometimes a word has more than one meaning so each new meaning (definition) is given a number.

formal *adjective* **faw**-muhl
1 strictly following the accepted rules or customs, as in *You will receive a formal invitation to the wedding.* 2 to do with a special ceremony, as in *The formal opening of the new school takes place tomorrow.*
formally *adverb*

Usage Do not confuse **formal** with the adjective **former**, which means earlier or of past times.

Sentence
Sometimes a sentence is written to help you better understand the word's meaning and how it can be used.

Word building
This shows other words that can be built from the headword or other words that are related to it.

Some entries include shaded boxes that provide information which helps clarify the use and meaning of a headword.

Aa

a *adjective* (called the *indefinite article*)
1 one; any, as in *Can you lend me a book?*
2 each; every, as in *I go there twice a month.*

abacus *noun* **abacuses** or **abaci**
a frame for counting with beads sliding on wires.

abalone *noun* (*say* ab-uh-**loh**-nee)
an edible type of shellfish.

abandon *verb* **abandons, abandoning, abandoned**
to give up; to leave something without intending to return, as in *Abandon ship!*

abattoir or **abattoirs** *noun*
(*say* **ab**-uh-twah)
a place where animals are slaughtered for food.

abbey *noun* **abbeys**
1 a group of buildings where monks or nuns live and work. 2 a community of monks or nuns.

abbot *noun* **abbots**
the head of an abbey of monks.

abbreviate *verb* **abbreviates, abbreviating, abbreviated**
to shorten something.

abbreviation *noun* **abbreviations**
something shortened, especially a word, as in *'TV' is an abbreviation of 'television'.*

ABC *noun*
the alphabet, as in *We know our ABC.*

abdomen *noun* **abdomens**
1 the part of the body that contains the stomach. 2 the rear part of the body of an insect, spider, etc.
abdominal *adjective*

abduct *verb* **abducts, abducting, abducted**
to carry off or kidnap illegally.

abide *verb* **abides, abiding, abode** or **abided**
1 to tolerate, as in *I can't abide noise.*
2 (*old-fashioned use*) to stay or remain, as in *Abide with me.*
abide by, to keep a promise, etc., as in *You must abide by the rules.*

able *adjective* **abler, ablest**
1 having the power, skill, or opportunity to do something. 2 skilful, as in *an able musician.*
ability *noun*, **ably** *adverb*

-able *suffix*
able to have a particular action done to it; suitable for a particular purpose, as in *The wardrobe is nearly too heavy to be movable. Is this dress fashionable?*

abnormal *adjective*
not normal; most unusual, as in *These high temperatures are abnormal for April.*
abnormality *noun*

aboard *adverb*
on a ship or an aircraft.

abode *noun* **abodes**
the place where someone lives.

abode past tense and past participle of **abide.**

abolish *verb* **abolishes, abolishing, abolished**
to get rid of a law, custom, etc.

abolition *noun* **abolitions**
(*say* ab-uh-**lish**-uhn)
the act of abolishing something, especially capital punishment or slavery.
abolitionist *noun*

abominable *adjective*
1 (*colloquial*) very bad. 2 causing loathing, as in *an abominable crime.*
abominable snowman, a yeti.

a
b
c
d
e
f
g
h
i
j
k
l
m
n
o
p
q
r
s
t
u
v
w
x
y
z

aborigines

aborigines *plural noun*
the people who were the first to live in a country.
Aborigines, the people who were the first to live in Australia.
aboriginal *adjective* and *noun*

abortion *noun* **abortions**
the removal of a foetus from a woman's womb before it has developed fully enough to live.

abound *verb* **abounds, abounding, abounded**
to be plentiful.

about *preposition*
1 on the subject of; in connection with, as in *This film is about the police.* 2 all round, as in *They ran about the playground. Toys lay about the room.* 3 near to, as in *She's about twenty years of age.*
about to, going to, as in *He was about to sing.*

about *adverb*
1 in various directions or places, as in *They were running about.* 2 somewhere near by, as in *There were wild animals about.*

above *preposition*
1 higher than. 2 more than.
above-board, honest.

above *adverb*
at or to a higher place.

abrasive *adjective*
to do with scraping or grazing, as in *The abrasive steel wool cleaned the burnt pan.*
abrasion *noun*

abreast *adverb*
side by side, as in *They walked three abreast.*
abreast of something, keeping up with something, as in *We must be abreast of modern discoveries.*

abroad *adverb*
in or to another country.

abrupt *adjective*
1 sudden, as in *What caused his abrupt departure?* 2 rather rude because of saying little, as in *an abrupt reply.*

abscess *noun* **abscesses**
a swollen place in or on the body containing pus, as in *tooth abscess.*

abscond *verb* **absconds, absconding, absconded**
to leave or run away, especially to avoid arrest, as in *He absconded from the remand centre.*

abseil *verb* **abseils, abseiling, abseiled**
(*say* **ab**-sayl)
to descend a cliff, etc., using ropes tied around the body.

absence *noun* **absences**
not being in a place, especially not being at school, work, etc.

absent *adjective*
not present; away.

absentee *noun* **absentees**
someone who is not at school, work, etc.
absenteeism *noun*

absent-minded *adjective*
forgetful; not attentive, as in *an absent-minded pupil.*
absent-mindedly *adverb*

absolute *adjective*
1 complete, as in *She had absolute trust in her friend.* 2 not restricted, as in *The king had absolute power.*

absolutely *adverb*
1 completely. 2 (*colloquial*) definitely, as in *'Are you going to Beth's party?' 'Absolutely!'*

absorb *verb* **absorbs, absorbing, absorbed**
1 to soak up. 2 to be very interesting to someone, as in *The book absorbed him.*
be absorbed in something, to be giving something all your attention.
absorbent *adjective,* **absorption** *noun*

abstract *adjective* (*say* **ab**-strakt)
concerned with ideas, not with things, as in *Happiness is abstract.*
abstract noun, a word which names things like qualities, conditions, etc., not a concrete object, as in *'Love' and 'thought' are abstract nouns; 'dog' and 'cake' are not.*

abstract *verb* **abstracts, abstracting, abstracted** (*say* uhb-**strakt**)
to take away, as in *Moisture was abstracted from the sponge.*

abstract *noun* **abstracts** (*say* **ab**-strakt)
a summary.

abstract noun *noun* **abstract nouns**
a word which names qualities, actions, states of mind, or ideas which are not physical things, as in *'Bravery', 'joy' and 'love' are abstract nouns.*

absurd *adjective*
ridiculous, as in *an absurd hat.*
absurdity *noun*

abundance *noun*
plenty, as in *an abundance of good things.*

abundant *adjective*
large in amount.

abuse *verb* **abuses, abusing, abused** (*say* uh-**byooz**)
1 to misuse. 2 to say unpleasant things about someone.

accompany

abuse *noun* **abuses** (*say* uh-**byoos**)
1 misuse of something.   2 unpleasant words said about someone.   3 physical harm done to someone.

abusive *adjective*
saying unpleasant things about someone.

abysmal *adjective*
(*colloquial*) very bad, as in *an abysmal meal. The weather was abysmal.*

abyss *noun* **abysses**
a hole so deep that it seems to have no bottom.

acacia *noun* **acacias**
any plant belonging to the largest Australian plant family, as in *The wattle is a well-known acacia.*

academic *adjective*
1 concerned with learning.   2 not practical; full of theory, as in *The architect's plans were too academic to work.*

academy *noun* **academies**
1 a college or school, as in *She attends the music academy.*   2 a society concerned with art or learning, as in *a writers' academy.*

accelerate *verb* **accelerates, accelerating, accelerated**
to move more quickly.
acceleration *noun*

accelerator *noun* **accelerators**
a pedal that you press down to make a motor vehicle go faster.

accent *noun* **accents** (*say* **ak**-sent)
1 the way that you pronounce words.
2 the way that people in different parts of a country pronounce words differently, as in *He has a New Zealand accent.*   3 pronouncing part of a word more strongly than the rest, as in *The accent in 'spider' is on the first syllable.*   4 a mark put over a letter to show its pronunciation, as in *The word 'café' has an accent on the 'e'.*

accent *verb* **accents, accenting, accented** (*say* ak-**sent**)
to pronounce part of a word more strongly than the rest.

accentuate *verb* **accentuates, accentuating, accentuated** (*say* uhk-**sen**-tyoo-ayt *or* uhk-**sen**-choo-ayt)
to stress or emphasise, as in *She accentuated her lines in the play by highlighting them.*

accept *verb* **accepts, accepting, accepted**
1 to take something which is offered.
2 to agree with something, as in *I accept that idea.*
acceptance *noun*

Usage Do not confuse **accept** with **except**, which is a preposition meaning not including.

acceptable *adjective*
1 worth accepting, as in *an acceptable offer.*   2 satisfactory, as in *an acceptable standard of work.*

access *noun* **accesses**
a way to reach something, as in *This road is the only access to the house.*
give access to something, to allow something to be reached, as in *These stairs give access to the attic.*

Usage Do not confuse **access** with **excess**, which means too much of something.

access *verb* **accesses, accessing, accessed**
(*in Computing*) to gain access to something, as in *access a file.*

accessible *adjective*
easy to reach.
accessibility *noun*

accessory *noun* **accessories**
1 an extra or spare part; things like shoes and handbags that go with clothes.   2 a person who assists in committing a crime, as in *an accessory to murder.*

accident *noun* **accidents**
an unexpected event, especially one in which someone is killed or injured.
by accident, not on purpose.

accidental *adjective*
not done on purpose, as in *accidental damage.*
accidentally *adverb*

acclaim *verb* **acclaims, acclaiming, acclaimed**
to welcome or applaud someone enthusiastically.

acclimatise or **acclimatize** *verb* **acclimatises, acclimatising, acclimatised**
to get used to, or to make someone or something become used to a new climate, environment, etc.
acclimatisation *noun*

accommodate *verb* **accommodates, accommodating, accommodated**
1 to provide a room or lodging for someone.   2 to change or fit in with, as in *She will accommodate herself to the new work timetable.*
accommodation *noun*

accompany *verb* **accompanies, accompanying, accompanied**
1 to go somewhere with someone.   2 to play music that supports a singer, etc.
accompaniment *noun*, **accompanist** *noun*

a
b
c
d
e
f
g
h
i
j
k
l
m
n
o
p
q
r
s
t
u
v
w
x
y
z

accomplish

accomplish *verb* accomplishes, accomplishing, accomplished
to do something successfully.
accomplishment *noun*

accomplished *adjective*
skilful, as in *an accomplished pianist*.

accord *noun*
agreement or consent, as in *The government had an accord with the unions over wages*.
of your own accord, without being asked or told to do something.

according *adverb*
according to someone, in the opinion of someone; as stated by someone, as in *According to him, we are stupid*.
according to something, in a way that suits something, as in *Price the apples according to their size*.

accordingly *adverb*
1 consequently; therefore, as in *His name was called and accordingly he left the room*.
2 in a suitable way, as in *Silence is necessary, so please act accordingly*.

accordion *noun* accordions
a portable musical instrument like a large concertina; a squeezebox.
accordionist *noun*

account *noun* accounts
1 a description or story. 2 an arrangement to keep money in a bank, etc. 3 a statement of money owed, spent, or received; a bill. 4 consideration, as in *Take it into account*.
on account of, because of.
on no account, certainly not.

account *verb* accounts, accounting, accounted
to record how money has been spent.
account for something, to make it clear why something happens.

accountant *noun* accountants
a person trained in preparing and examining financial accounts.
accountancy *noun*

accumulate *verb* accumulates, accumulating, accumulated
to collect; to pile up, as in *He accumulated a large number of football cards. Dark clouds began to accumulate*.
accumulation *noun*

accurate *adjective*
correct; exact, as in *an accurate total*.
accuracy *noun*

accuse *verb* accuses, accusing, accused
to say that someone has committed a crime, etc.
accusation *noun*

accustomed *adjective*
usual or customary, as in *I sat in my accustomed chair*.
accustomed to, being used to, as in *I am accustomed to having lunch at twelve o'clock*.

ace *noun* aces
1 the card of highest or lowest value in each suit of a pack of cards. 2 a very skilful person or thing, as in *Christopher is an ace at swimming*.

ache *noun* aches
a dull or continuous pain.

ache *verb* aches, aching, ached
to feel a dull or continuous pain.

achieve *verb* achieves, achieving, achieved
to accomplish, as in *She achieved her ambition*.
achievement *noun*

acid *noun* acids
1 (*in Science*) a substance that contains hydrogen and neutralises alkalis. 2 the drug LSD (lysergic acid diethylamide).
acidic *adjective*, **acidity** *noun*

acid *adjective*
sour, as in *This fruit has an acid taste*.
acid rain, rain that contains harmful acids because it has absorbed waste gases from the air.

acknowledge *verb* acknowledges, acknowledging, acknowledged
1 to admit that something is true. 2 to say that you have received a letter, etc. 3 to express thanks for something.
acknowledgment *noun*

acne *noun* (*say* **ak**-nee)
inflamed red pimples on someone's face.

acorn *noun* acorns
the seed of the oak-tree.

acoustics *plural noun* (*say* uh-**koo**-stiks)
1 the qualities of a place which make it good or bad for sound, as in *This hall has bad acoustics*. 2 the science of sound.

acquaint *verb* acquaints, acquainting, acquainted
to tell someone about something, as in *Acquaint him with the facts*.
be acquainted with someone, to know someone slightly.

acquaintance *noun* acquaintances
someone you know slightly.
make someone's acquaintance, to get to know someone.

acquire *verb* acquires, acquiring, acquired
to obtain, as in *She acquired computer skills at her course*.
acquisition *noun*

acquit *verb* acquits, acquitting, acquitted
to decide that someone is not guilty.
acquittal *noun*

acre *noun* acres (*say* **ay**-kuh)
a piece of land measuring about half a hectare.

acrobat *noun* acrobats
a person who gives displays of jumping and balancing as entertainment.
acrobatic *adjective*, **acrobatics** *plural noun*

acronym *noun* acronyms
a word formed from the initial letters of other words, as in *'AIDS' is an acronym from the words 'Acquired Immune Deficiency Syndrome'.*

across *adverb* and *preposition*
1 from one side of a thing to the other, as in *The table measures 1.5 metres across.* 2 to or on the other side of something, as in *How can we get across the busy road?*

act *noun* acts
1 an action. 2 a short performance in a program of entertainment, as in *a juggling act.* 3 a pretence, as in *She is only putting on an act.* 4 one of the main parts of a play or opera, as in *An act can include several scenes.* 5 a law passed by parliament, as in *The government has passed many acts on land rights.*

act *verb* acts, acting, acted
1 to do something. 2 to have an effect, as in *Drugs act on the brain.* 3 to take a part in a play, film, etc. 4 to behave, as in *He acted wisely in the crisis.*

action *noun* actions
1 doing something; something that has been done. 2 a battle; fighting, as in *He was killed in action.* 3 the part that makes a gun, musical instrument, etc. work. 4 energy, as in *She is a woman of action.*
out of action, not working properly.
take action, to do something.

activate *verb* activates, activating, activated
to start something working.

active *adjective*
1 taking part in activities. 2 functioning, as in *an active volcano.* 3 to do with the type of verb in which the subject performs the action, as in *In 'He hit me' the verb is active; in 'I was hit' the verb is passive.*

activity *noun* activities
1 being active or lively, as in *The baby was full of activity.* 2 an action or occupation, as in *outdoor activities.*

actor *noun* actors
a performer in a play, film, etc.

actress *noun* actresses
a female performer in a play, film, etc.

actual *adjective*
real, as in *The film showed actual events.*
actually *adverb*

acupuncture *noun*
a Chinese medical procedure in which parts of the body are pricked with needles to relieve pain or cure disease.

acute *adjective* acuter, acutest
1 sharp, as in *acute pain.* 2 severe, as in *an acute shortage of trained staff.*
acute accent, the mark ´ put over a letter, as in *café.*

acute angle *noun*
an angle less than 90 degrees.

AD short for *Anno Domini*, used with dates that come after the birth of Jesus, as in *Cook reached Australia in AD 1770.*

adamant *adjective*
determined in what you decide, say, etc., as in *She was adamant she would leave now.*

Adam's apple *noun* Adam's apples
the lump at the front of a man's neck.

adapt *verb* adapts, adapting, adapted
to become suited to something; to make something suitable for a new purpose, as in *Can you adapt to your new situation? They adapted the car for driving in the desert.*
adaptable *adjective*, **adaptation** *noun*

adaptor *noun* adaptors
a device to connect pieces of electrical or other equipment.

add *verb* adds, adding, added
to put one thing with another.
add to, to increase.
add up, to make or find a total; (*colloquial*) to make sense, as in *Add up the figures. It just doesn't add up—why should he do such a thing?*

adder *noun* adders
a small poisonous snake, especially the common European viper.

addict *noun* addicts
someone who does or uses something that he or she cannot give up, as in *a drug addict.*
addicted *adjective*, **addiction** *noun*, **addictive** *adjective*

addition *noun* additions
1 the act of adding numbers together. 2 something added, as in *An addition was built on the house.*
in addition, also.
additional *adjective*

additive *noun* additives
something added to food, etc. in small amounts.

address

address *noun* **addresses**
1 the details of the place where someone lives, as in *My address is 4 Collins Street, Melbourne.* 2 a speech.

address *verb* **addresses, addressing, addressed**
1 to write an address on a letter, parcel, etc. 2 to make a speech, remark, etc. to someone, as in *The judge addressed the prisoner.*

adenoids *plural noun*
the spongy flesh at the back of your nose, which may hinder breathing.

adequate *adjective*
enough; suitable, as in *adequate water supplies; an adequate response to the problem.*

adhere *verb* **adheres, adhering, adhered**
to stick to something.
someone adheres to something, someone follows a plan, rule, etc.

adhesive *adjective*
causing things to stick together.
adhesion *noun*

adhesive *noun* **adhesives**
a glue.

adjacent *adjective*
near or next, as in *Her house is adjacent to the shop. We were in an adjacent room.*

adjective *noun* **adjectives**
a word that describes a noun or adds to its meaning, as in *Adjectives are words like 'big', 'honest', and 'strange'.*

adjourn *verb* **adjourns, adjourning, adjourned** (*say* uh-**jern**)
1 to break off a meeting, etc. until a later time. 2 to move to another place.
adjournment *noun*

adjudicate *verb* **adjudicates, adjudicating, adjudicated** (*say* uh-**joo**-duh-kayt)
to act as judge in a competition, debate, etc.
adjudication *noun*, **adjudicator** *noun*

adjust *verb* **adjusts, adjusting, adjusted**
to put something into its proper position or order.
adjuster *noun*, **adjustment** *noun*

administer *verb* **administers, administering, administered**
1 to look after, manage, or govern after, as in *The principal administers the school.* 2 to give formally, as in *He administered the punishment.*

administration *noun*
management of a business, or government.
administrator *noun*, **administrative** *adjective*

admirable *adjective*
worth admiring; excellent, as in *an admirable piece of work. This is an admirable place for a holiday.*
admirably *adverb*

admiral *noun* **admirals**
a naval officer of high rank.

admire *verb* **admires, admiring, admired**
1 to think someone or something is very good, beautiful, etc. 2 to look at something and enjoy it.
admiration *noun*

admirer *noun* **admirers**
someone who thinks that a particular person or thing is very good, beautiful, etc.

admission *noun* **admissions**
1 agreeing or confessing, as in *He is guilty by his own admission.* 2 entering, as in *Admission to the show is by ticket only.*

admit *verb* **admits, admitting, admitted**
1 to let someone come in. 2 to agree or confess.

admittance *noun*
entering, as in *The sign read: 'No admittance'.*

Usage **Admission** means entering a public place, usually after paying some money. **Admittance** is a more formal word and often refers to entering a place that is private.

admittedly *adverb*
as an agreed fact; without denying it, as in *Admittedly I was teasing the dog, but I didn't expect him to bite.*

adolescence *noun*
the time between being a child and being an adult.
adolescent *noun* and *adjective*

adopt *verb* **adopts, adopting, adopted**
1 to take someone into your family and treat him or her as your child. 2 to accept something, as in *They adopted a strict fitness routine.*
adoption *noun*, **adoptive** *adjective*

adore *verb* **adores, adoring, adored**
to love very much.
adorable *adjective*, **adoration** *noun*

adorn *verb* **adorns, adorning, adorned**
to decorate, as in *The house was adorned with balloons for his birthday.*
adornment *noun*

adrenalin or **adrenaline** *noun*
a hormone that stimulates your nervous system and makes you feel excited.

aeronautics

adrift *adverb* and *adjective*
drifting, as in *The boat was adrift.*

adult *noun* **adults**
a person or animal that is fully grown.

adulterate *verb* **adulterates, adulterating, adulterated**
to spoil something by adding other substances, as in *She adulterated the orange juice by adding too much water.*

adultery *noun* **adulteries** (*say* uh-**dul**-tuh-ree)
being unfaithful to your wife or husband by having another lover.
adulterer *noun*, **adulterous** *adjective*

advance *verb* **advances, advancing, advanced**
1 to move or put forward, as in *The enemy advanced. He advanced the clock.* **2** to make progress, as in *She is advancing in maths.* **3** to pay or lend money, as in *His pocket money was advanced.*

advance *noun* **advances**
1 a forward movement. **2** progress. **3** a loan.
in advance, beforehand.
in advance of, before.

advanced *adjective*
1 far on in progress, life, etc., as in *an advanced age.* **2** not basic, as in *an examination at advanced level.*

advantage *noun* **advantages**
something useful or helpful.
take advantage of something, to use something profitably; to use something unfairly, as in *Take advantage of our introductory offer! They took advantage of our generosity, and tricked us.*
to your advantage, profitable or helpful to you.
advantageous *adjective*

Advent *noun*
1 the coming of Jesus. **2** the period before Christmas in the Christian calendar.
advent, the arrival of an important person or thing.

adventure *noun* **adventures**
1 an exciting or dangerous experience. **2** taking risks; danger, as in *He likes adventure.*
adventurous *adjective*

adverb *noun* **adverbs**
a word that tells you how, when, where, or why something happens, as in *Adverbs are words like 'easily', 'indoors', and 'soon'.*
adverbial *adjective*

adversary *noun* **adversaries**
(*say* **ad**-vuh-suh-ree)
an opponent or enemy.

adverse *adjective*
unfavourable; harmful, as in *The drug had adverse effects.*

adversity *noun* **adversities**
misfortune; trouble, as in *In adversity he showed strength of character.*

advertise *verb* **advertises, advertising, advertised**
1 to praise goods hoping that people will buy them. **2** to make something publicly known, as in *Have you advertised the concert?*
advertiser *noun*

advertisement *noun* **advertisements**
a public notice that advertises something.

advice *noun*
1 something said to someone to help him or her decide what to do. **2** a piece of information, as in *We received advice on the weather.*

advisable *adjective*
sensible; worth doing.
advisability *noun*

advise *verb* **advises, advising, advised**
to give someone advice; to recommend something.
adviser *noun*, **advisory** *adjective*

Usage Do not confuse **advice**, which is a noun, with **advise**, which is a verb.

advocate *noun* **advocates**
(*say* **ad**-vuh-kuht)
a person who speaks in favour of someone or something.

advocate *verb* **advocates, advocating, advocated** (*say* **ad**-vuh-kayt)
to speak in favour of something, as in *He advocated that daylight saving be kept.*

aerial *adjective*
to do with or existing in the air, as in *an aerial photograph of our offices; aerial acrobatics.*

aerial *noun* **aerials**
a wire, rod, etc. for receiving or transmitting radio or television signals; an antenna.

aerobatics *plural noun*
an exciting display by flying aircraft.
aerobatic *adjective*

aerobics *plural noun*
exercises which strengthen your heart and lungs.

aerodrome *noun* **aerodromes**
a small airport or airfield.

aeronautics *plural noun*
the study of aircraft and flying.
aeronautic *adjective*, **aeronautical** *adjective*

aeroplane

aeroplane *noun* **aeroplanes**
a flying machine with wings.

aerosol *noun* **aerosols**
a device that holds a liquid under pressure and lets it out in a fine spray.

aesthetic *adjective*
1 to do with beauty; valuing beauty, as in *an art critic with high aesthetic values; an aesthetic young poet.* 2 pleasing to look at, as in *These chairs have aesthetic appeal rather than practical use.*

affair *noun* **affairs**
1 a thing, a matter, or an event, as in *Her bank balance was her affair. The funeral was a sad affair.* 2 a temporary sexual relationship between two people who are not married to each other.
affairs, business, as in *money affairs.*

affect *verb* **affects, affecting, affected**
1 to have an effect on; to harm, as in *The sun affected her skin.* 2 to pretend or pose, as in *He affected to understand when he was really confused.*

Usage Do not confuse **affect** with **effect**, which is a noun meaning something that happens or an impression.

affection *noun* **affections**
love or liking, as in *I have a great affection for my nephew.*
affectionate *adjective*

affirm *verb* **affirms, affirming, affirmed**
to state strongly, as in *He affirmed his faith in his employer.*
affirmation *noun*

affirmative *adjective*
approving or agreeing, as in *an affirmative answer.*

afflict *verb* **afflicts, afflicting, afflicted**
to cause someone distress.
affliction *noun*

affluent *adjective* (*say* **af-loo-uhnt**)
rich, as in *an affluent country.*
affluence *noun*

afford *verb* **affords, affording, afforded**
1 to have enough money to pay for something. 2 to have enough time, etc. to do something.

afforestation *noun*
the covering of an area with trees.

afloat *adjective* and *adverb*
floating; on a boat, as in *The boat is afloat. Do you enjoy life afloat?*

afraid *adjective*
frightened.

I'm afraid, I am sorry; I regret, as in *I'm afraid I've burnt the cakes.*

afresh *adverb*
again; in a new way, as in *We must start afresh.*

aft *adverb* (*say* ahft)
at or towards the back of a ship or plane.

after *preposition*
1 later than, as in *Come after dinner.* 2 in spite of, as in *After all I've done for him, he never thanked me.* 3 behind, as in *He came in after me.* 4 pursuing, as in *Run after him.* 5 in imitation or honour of, as in *She was named after her aunt.*

after *adverb*
1 later, as in *It came a week after.* 2 behind, as in *Jill came tumbling after.*

afternoon *noun* **afternoons**
the time from noon or lunchtime to evening.

afterwards *adverb*
at a later time.

again *adverb*
1 once more; another time, as in *Try again.* 2 as before, as in *You will soon be well again.*
again and again, often.

against *preposition*
1 touching or hitting, as in *He leant against the wall.* 2 not on the side of; not in favour of, as in *Are you against smoking?*

age *noun* **ages**
1 how old someone or something is. 2 (*colloquial*) a very long time, as in *We've been waiting for ages.* 3 a period of history, as in *the Stone Age.* 4 the last part of someone's life, as in *She had the wisdom that comes with age.*

age *verb* **ages, ageing, aged**
to become old; to cause to become old, as in *She aged when she was ill. The weatherboard house aged in the salt air of the coast.*

aged *adjective* (*say* ayjd)
1 having the age of, as in *a girl aged 9.* (*say* **ay**-jid) 2 very old, as in *an aged man.*

agency *noun* **agencies**
the office or business of someone who organises things, as in *employment agency.*

agenda *noun* **agendas** (*say* uh-**jen**-duh)
a list of things to be done or discussed, as in *May I see the agenda for the Parent-Teachers' meeting?*

agent *noun* **agents**
1 someone who organises things for other people, as in *a travel agent.* 2 a spy, as in *a*

secret agent. **3** a person or thing that has power or produces an effect, as in *The scientist was an agent for change. Bleach is a good cleaning agent.*

aggravate *verb* aggravates, aggravating, aggravated
 1 to make something worse. **2** to annoy.
 aggravation *noun*

aggression *noun* aggressions
 starting a war, attack, etc.; the act of being aggressive.
 aggressor *noun*

aggressive *adjective*
 1 (of a person) using or likely to use violence. **2** forceful, as in *an aggressive campaign against smoking.*

aggro *noun*
 (*colloquial*) trouble, especially fighting, as in *tough young men looking for aggro.*
 aggro *adjective*

agile *adjective*
 moving quickly or easily.
 agility *noun*

agitate *verb* agitates, agitating, agitated
 1 to make someone disturbed or anxious.
 2 to campaign for something, as in *They agitated for a better hospital system.*
 3 to shake or stir something quickly, as in *The washing machine agitated the clothes.*
 agitation *noun*

agitator *noun* agitators
 a person who campaigns for something.

agnostic *noun* agnostics (*say* ag-**nos**-tik)
 someone who believes that we cannot know for sure whether there is a God.

ago *adverb*
 in the past, as in *She died long ago.*

agony *noun* agonies
 severe pain or suffering.
 agonising *adjective*

agree *verb* agrees, agreeing, agreed
 1 to think the same as someone else. **2** to say that you are willing, as in *She agreed to go with him.*
 agree with someone, to suit someone, as in *Spicy food doesn't agree with her.*
 agree with something, to match something, as in *His story doesn't agree with theirs.*

agreeable *adjective*
 1 willing, as in *We shall go if you are agreeable.* **2** pleasant, as in *an agreeable place.*

agreement *noun* agreements
 1 agreeing, as in *Are we in agreement?*
 2 an arrangement that people have agreed

on, as in *An agreement was reached between the employer and employees.*

agriculture *noun*
 farming.
 agricultural *adjective*

aground *adverb*
 stranded on the bottom in shallow water, as in *The ship ran aground.*

ah *interjection*
 an exclamation of surprise, pity, admiration, etc.

ahead *adverb*
 forwards; in front, as in *Dorothy went ahead to show us the way.*

aid *noun* aids
 1 help. **2** money, food, etc. sent to another country to help it, as in *overseas aid.*
 3 something that helps, as in *a hearing aid.*
 in aid of something, to help something.

AIDS or **Aids** *noun*
 a disease caused by a virus called HIV, that greatly weakens a person's resistance to other diseases and eventually causes death. [from the first letters of the words *Acquired Immune Deficiency Syndrome*]

ailment *noun* ailments
 an illness, usually a slight one.
 ailing *adjective*

aim *verb* aims, aiming, aimed
 1 to try or intend to do something, as in *The team aimed to win.* **2** to point a gun, etc. at someone or something. **3** to throw, kick, or shoot something in a particular direction.

aim *noun* aims
 1 purpose; intention, as in *Their aim is to reach the top of the mountain.* **2** the act of pointing a gun, etc.

aimless *adjective*
 with no aim or purpose, as in *an aimless life.*
 aimlessly *adverb*

air *noun* airs
 1 the mixture of gases which surrounds the earth and which everyone breathes. **2** a tune. **3** an appearance or impression of something, as in *an air of mystery.*
 airs, haughty, affected behaviour, as in *He puts on airs.*
 by air, in a plane.
 in the air, uncertain; spreading about, as in *All our plans are still in the air. Rebellion was in the air.*
 on the air, on radio or television.

air

air *verb* **airs, airing, aired**
1 to expose clothes, a room, etc. to fresh air or warmth to remove damp or stale smells. 2 to express, as in *He aired his opinions*.

airborne *adjective*
1 flying. 2 carried by the air, as in *airborne freight; airborne pollen*.

air-conditioning *noun*
a system for controlling the temperature, purity, etc. of the air in a room or building.
air-conditioned *adjective*

aircraft *noun* **aircraft**
1 an aeroplane or a helicopter, as in *Two aircraft landed together*.
aircraft-carrier, a large ship with a flat deck on which aircraft can take off and land.

airfield *noun* **airfields**
a place where aircraft can take off and land.

air force *noun* **air forces**
a large group of people and aircraft organised for fighting.

airlift *noun* **airlifts**
emergency transport of supplies, etc. by air, especially in a famine, war, etc., as in *An airlift of medicine and food was arranged for Bosnia*.

airline *noun* **airlines**
a company that provides a regular transport service by aircraft.

airlock *noun* **airlocks**
1 a bubble of air that stops liquid flowing through a pipe. 2 a compartment with airtight doors at each end.

airmail *noun*
mail carried by plane.

airport *noun* **airports**
an airfield, especially one for passengers and cargo.

air raid *noun* **air raids**
an attack by aircraft.

airstream *noun* **airstreams**
a current of air, especially one that affects the weather.

airstrip *noun* **airstrips**
a strip of land prepared for aircraft to take off and land.

airtight *adjective*
not letting air get in or out.

airy *adjective* **airier, airiest**
1 with plenty of fresh air. 2 light-hearted; insincere, as in *airy promises*. 3 light as air.
airily *adverb*

aisle *noun* **aisles**
(rhymes with *mile*)
1 a part at the side of a church. 2 a passage between or beside rows of seats or pews.

ajar *adverb* and *adjective*
slightly open, as in *Leave the door ajar*.

akimbo *adverb*
with your hands on your hips and your elbows turned outwards.

Akubra *noun* **Akubras**
(*trademark*) a wide-brimmed Australian hat.

alarm *noun* **alarms**
1 a warning sound or signal. 2 fright or anxiety, as in *He cried out in alarm*.
alarm clock, a clock that can be set to make a sound to wake a sleeping person.

alarm *verb* **alarms, alarming, alarmed**
to make someone frightened or anxious.

albatross *noun* **albatrosses**
a large sea bird with very long wings and a stout body.

album *noun* **albums**
1 a book in which you can keep photographs, stamps, autographs, etc. 2 a long-playing record.

Alcheringa or **Alchuringa** *noun*
(*say* Al-**chuh**-ringuh)
another word for the Aboriginal Dreamtime.

alcohol *noun*
1 a colourless liquid made by fermenting sugar or starch. 2 a drink containing this liquid, that can make people drunk.

alcoholic *adjective*
to do with alcohol, as in *alcoholic drink*.

alcoholic *noun* **alcoholics**
someone who is ill from continually drinking too much alcohol.
alcoholism *noun*

alcove *noun* **alcoves**
part of a room, etc. where the wall is set back from the main part.

alderman *noun*
an elected local government councillor in some Australian states, as in *The alderman was asked to look at the dog problem in the local council area*.

ale *noun* **ales**
beer.

alert *adjective*
watching for something; ready to act.

alert *noun* **alerts**
an alarm, as in *cyclone alert*.
on the alert, on the lookout against danger or attack.

algebra *noun* (*say* **al**-juh-bruh)
mathematics in which letters and symbols are used to represent numbers.
algebraic *adjective*

algorithm or **algorism** *noun* **algorithms**
(*in Mathematics*) the process or set of rules used for doing a sum.

alias *adverb*
also named, as in *Robin of Locksley alias Robin Hood*.

alias *noun* **aliases** (*say* **ay**-lee-uhs)
a false or different name.

alibi *noun* **alibis** (*say* **al**-uh-buy)
1 evidence that an accused person was not present when a crime was committed.
2 (*colloquial*) an excuse.

alien *adjective* (*say* **ay**-lee-uhn)
foreign, as in *The immigrant's alien customs were not understood by the child.*
alien to, very different from, as in *Lying was alien to his nature.*

alien *noun* **aliens**
1 someone who is not a citizen of the country where he or she is living.   2 a being from another world, as in *The aliens entered the spaceship.*

alienate *verb* **alienates, alienating, alienated**
to make someone unfriendly, as in *The unreliable politician alienated his supporters.*
alienation *noun*

alight *adjective*
on fire; burning, as in *The bush was alight.*

alight *verb* **alights, alighting, alighted**
1 to descend from a vehicle, horse, etc.
2 to come to earth; to settle, as in *The cockatoos alighted on the gum.*

alike *adjective*
similar; like each other, as in *The sisters are very much alike.*

alike *adverb*
in the same way, as in *He treats everybody alike.*

alimentary canal *noun* **alimentary canals**
the tube along which food passes through the body.

alive *adjective*
living; existing, as in *Is he alive?*
alive to something, aware of something, as in *She is alive to the dangers.*
alive with something, full of living or moving things.

alkali *noun* **alkalis** (*say* **al**-kuhl-luy)
a substance that neutralises or reduces acids or that combines with acids to form salts.
alkaline *adjective*, **alkalinity** *noun*

all *adjective*
the whole number or amount of, as in *All my books are in the desk.*

all *noun*
1 everything, as in *That is all I know.*
2 everyone, as in *All were agreed.*

all *adverb*
1 completely, as in *She was dressed all in white.*   2 very much, as in *He was all excited.*   3 to each team or competitor, as in *The score is four goals all.*
all-clear, a signal that a danger has passed.
all out, using all your ability, as in *Go all out to win.*
all right, satisfactory; safe and sound.
all there, (*colloquial*) mentally alert; intelligent.
all the same, nevertheless; making no difference, as in *It was raining but I went out all the same. It's all the same to me.*
all together, all at once; all in one place or in a group, as in *They came all together.*

Allah
the Muslim name for God.

allege *verb* **alleges, alleging, alleged** (*say* uh-**lej**)
to say, usually without proof, that someone has done something, as in *He alleged that I stole the ring.*
allegation *noun*, **alleged** *adjective*, **allegedly** *adverb*

allegiance *noun* **allegiances** (*say* uh-**lee**-juhns)
loyalty, as in *New citizens must promise allegiance to their adopted country.*

allegory *noun* **allegories**
a simple story, poem, etc. which is really about something different from what it seems to be, as in *Aesop's Fables are allegories.*
allegorical *adjective*

allergic *adjective*
very sensitive to something, which may make you ill, as in *He is allergic to pollen, which gives him hay fever.*
allergy *noun*

alley *noun* **alleys**
1 a narrow street or passage.   2 a place where you can play tenpin bowling.

alliance *noun* **alliances**
a friendly connection or association between countries, etc.

alligator

alligator *noun* **alligators**
a large reptile of the crocodile family but having a broader head and found mainly in South America.

alliteration *noun*
repeating the same letter or sound at the beginning of adjacent or closely connected words, as in *The wicked witch was waiting while the wily wolf ran away.*

allot *verb* **allots, allotting, allotted**
to distribute portions, jobs, etc.

allotment *noun* **allotments**
1 a small piece of land; a building block. 2 a share, as in *Her allotment of the inheritance was small.*

allow *verb* **allows, allowing, allowed**
1 to permit, as in *Smoking is not allowed.* 2 to give or provide, as in *She was allowed $100 for books.*

allowance *noun* **allowances**
a sum of money given regularly to someone.
make allowances for something, to be considerate on account of something, as in *We must make allowances for the fact that he was the youngest in the competition.*

alloy *noun* **alloys**
a metal formed from a mixture of metals, as in *Bronze is an alloy of copper and tin.*

all right *adjective*
satisfactory; in good condition or safe, as in *He fixed my bike, so it's all right. She is all right now despite being lost in the bush overnight.*

all right *interjection*
yes; I consent, as in *All right, I'm coming!*

all-round *adjective*
in all respects; having all sorts of abilities, as in *a good all-round athlete.*
all-rounder *noun*

alluvial *adjective*
to do with soil, sand, etc. left behind by a flood, especially in a river valley or delta.

ally *noun* **allies** (*say* **al**-uy)
1 a country in alliance with another country. 2 a person who helps or cooperates with you.
allied *adjective*

almighty *adjective*
1 having complete power. 2 (*colloquial*) very great, as in *an almighty crash.*
the Almighty, God.

almond *noun* **almonds** (*say* **ah**-muhnd)
an oval, edible nut.

almost *adverb*
very nearly, as in *I am almost ready.*

aloft *adverb*
high up or overhead, as in *The hot-air balloons were aloft.*

alone *adjective* and *adverb*
without any other people or other things.

along *preposition* and *adverb*
1 from one end of something to the other. 2 on; onwards, as in *Move along, please!* 3 accompanying someone, as in *I have brought my brother along.*

alongside *preposition* and *adverb*
next to something.

aloud *adverb*
in a voice that can be heard.

alps *plural noun* **alps**
a range of high, usually snow-covered, mountains, as in *The Australian Alps and Swiss Alps are good skiing areas.*

alphabet *noun* **alphabets**
the letters used in a language, usually arranged in a set order.
alphabetical *adjective*, **alphabetically** *adverb*

alpine *adjective*
to do with the Alps, as in *The alpine ash is found in the mountains of south-eastern Australia.*

already *adverb*
by or before now, as in *I've already told you once.*

alright *adverb*
all right; in good condition, satisfactory.

> **Usage** To use **alright** instead of **all right** is considered incorrect by many people.

Alsatian *noun* **Alsatians** (*say* al-**say**-shuhn)
a large, strong breed of dog; a German shepherd, as in *Alsatians are often used by the police.*

also *adverb*
as something or someone extra; besides.

altar *noun* **altars**
a table or raised surface used in religious ceremonies.

alter *verb* **alters, altering, altered**
to change, as in *Some trees alter in autumn.*
alteration *noun*

alternate *verb* **alternates, alternating, alternated** (*say* ol-tuh-nayt *or* **awl**-tuh-nayt)
to happen, work, etc. in turns; to cause something to happen, etc. in this way.
alternation *noun*

alternate *adjective* (*say* ol-**ter**-nuht *or* awl-**ter**-nuht)
1 every second one, as in *They work on alternate days.* **2** happening or coming in turns, one after the other, as in *alternate laughter and tears.*
alternately *adverb*

Usage Do not confuse **alternate** with **alternative**. **Alternative** means that you have a choice between two or more things.

alternative *adjective* (*say* ol-**ter**-nuh-tiv *or* awl-**ter**-nuh-tiv)
available instead of something else, as in *We offer an alternative menu for vegetarians.*

Usage Do not confuse **alternative** with the adjective **alternate**. **Alternate** means that first one thing and then the other happens, works, etc.

alternative *noun* **alternatives**
1 any of two or more possibilities, as in *For your project you can choose from four alternatives.* **2** choice, as in *He had no alternative but to go.*

although *conjunction*
though.

altitude *noun* **altitudes**
the height of something, especially above sea-level.

alto *noun* **altos**
1 a female singer with a low voice; a contralto. **2** a male singer with a voice higher than a tenor's.

altogether *adverb*
1 completely, as in *He is altogether wrong.* **2** on the whole, as in *Altogether, it wasn't a bad holiday.*

Usage Do not confuse **altogether** with **all together** which means 'all at once' or 'all in one place'.

aluminium *noun*
a lightweight, silver-coloured metal.

always *adverb*
1 all the time; at all times. **2** often, as in *You are always crying.* **3** whatever happens, as in *You can always sleep on the floor.*

am 1st person singular present tense of **be**.

a.m. short for Latin *ante meridiem* which means 'before midday'.

amalgamate *verb* **amalgamates, amalgamating, amalgamated**
to join together, as in *The groups amalgamated to form a team.*
amalgamation *noun*

amateur *noun* **amateurs** (*say* am-uh-tuh)
1 someone who does something as a hobby, without being paid for it. **2** an athlete who is not paid for playing sport. **3** a person who completes a task without much skill, as in *The lopsided chair was built by an amateur.*
amateur *adjective*

amateurish *adjective*
not having or showing skill, as in *The new band gave an amateurish performance.*

amaze *verb* **amazes, amazing, amazed**
to surprise someone greatly.
amazement *noun*

ambassador *noun* **ambassadors**
someone sent to a foreign country to represent his or her government.

amber *noun*
1 a hard, clear, yellowish substance used for making ornaments. **2** a yellowish colour, especially used in traffic-lights as a signal for caution.

ambidextrous *adjective*
able to use both hands with equal skill.

ambiguous *adjective*
having more than one possible meaning; uncertain, as in *His reply was ambiguous.*
ambiguity *noun*

ambition *noun* **ambitions**
1 a strong desire to achieve something, as in *The student was filled with ambition to do well.* **2** the thing that you want, as in *His ambition is to captain Australia.*
ambitious *adjective*

amble *verb* **ambles, ambling, ambled**
to walk slowly.

ambulance *noun* **ambulances**
a specially equipped vehicle for carrying sick or injured people.

ambush *noun* **ambushes**
a surprise attack from a hidden place.

ambush *verb* **ambushes, ambushing, ambushed**
to attack by surprise from a hidden place, as in *They were ambushed in the underpass.*

amen *interjection*
a word used at the end of a prayer or hymn, meaning 'may it be so'.

amend *verb* **amends, amending, amended**
to change or improve something.
amendment *noun*

amenity *noun* **amenities**
a pleasant or useful feature, as in *The school has many amenities including a swimming pool, gymnasium and tennis courts.*

amiable

amiable *adjective*
friendly; good-tempered, as in *She had an amiable talk with her favourite teacher.*
amiability *noun*, **amiably** *adverb*

amicable *adjective*
friendly, as in *The club members had an amicable meeting.*
amicably *adverb*

amid or **amidst** *preposition*
in the middle of; among, as in *amid the stress of everyday life. They lived amid the trees.*

amino acid *noun* **amino acids**
an acid found in proteins.

ammonia *noun*
a colourless gas or liquid with a strong smell, used especially in cleaning.

ammunition *noun*
explosive objects used in fighting, such as bullets, shells, and grenades.

amnesia *noun* (*say* am-**nee**-zee-uh *or* am-**nee**-*zh*uh)
a loss of memory.

amnesty *noun* **amnesties**
pardoning people who have broken the law, or letting them out of prison.

amoeba *noun* **amoebas** (*say* uh-**mee**-buh)
a tiny, jelly-like creature consisting of one cell.

among or **amongst** *preposition*
1 surrounded by; in, as in *She hid among the bushes.* 2 between, as in *Let's divide the money among ourselves.*

amount *noun* **amounts**
a quantity.

amount *verb* **amounts, amounting, amounted**
to be equal to something, as in *The bill amounted to $55.*

ampere *noun* **amperes** (*say* **am**-pair)
a unit for measuring the rate of flow of an electric current; an amp.

ampersand *noun* **ampersands**
the sign like this &, which means 'and', as in *The ampersand is used in the names of firms like Smith & Co.*

amphibious *adjective*
able to live or move both on land and in water.
amphibian *noun*

amphitheatre *noun* **amphitheatres** (*say* am-fee-**theer**-tuh)
a round building with tiers of seats surrounding an empty space, as in *The ancient Greeks performed plays in amphitheatres.*

ample *adjective* **ampler, amplest**
1 large, as in *This car has an ample boot.* 2 more than enough, as in *We had ample provisions.*
amply *adverb*

amplifier *noun* **amplifiers**
a device, usually electronic, for making something louder.

amplify *verb* **amplifies, amplifying, amplified**
1 to make something louder or stronger. 2 to give more details about something, as in *The rules of the game were amplified for the players' benefit.*
amplification *noun*

amputate *verb* **amputates, amputating, amputated**
to cut off a diseased leg or arm.
amputation *noun*

amuse *verb* **amuses, amusing, amused**
1 to make someone laugh or smile, as in *The clown amused the children.* 2 to make time pass pleasantly for someone, as in *John amused himself by playing with his Lego.*

amusement *noun* **amusements**
1 something that amuses, as in *the amusement provided by the circus.* 2 being amused; laughing or smiling, as in *She showed amusement at the jokes.*

amusing *adjective*
able to make you laugh or smile, as in *an amusing story.*

an *adjective* (called the *indefinite article*)
an (used instead of *a* when the next word begins with a vowel-sound or a silent h), as in *Take an apple. You can hire boats for an hour or more.*

anaemia *noun* (*say* uh-**nee**-mee-uh)
a poor condition of the blood that makes someone look pale.
anaemic *adjective*

anaesthetic or **anesthetic** *noun* **anaesthetics** (*say* an-is-**thet**-ik)
a drug that makes you unable to feel pain, as in *You need an anaesthetic before having surgery.*
anaesthesia *noun*

anaesthetise or **anaesthetize** *verb* **anaesthetises, anaesthetising, anaesthetised**
to give an anaesthetic to a person or an animal.
anaesthetist *noun*

anagram *noun* **anagrams**
a word or phrase made by rearranging the letters of another word or phrase, as in *'Oils' is an anagram of 'soil'.*

anguish

analogue *adjective*
using something like a clock face to indicate numbers, as in *An analogue watch is better than a digital watch for learning to tell the time.*

analogy *noun* analogies
a comparison between two things that are fairly like each other, as in *an analogy between the human heart and a pump.*
analogous *adjective*

analyse *verb* analyses, analysing, analysed
1 to examine something carefully. 2 to divide something into its parts, as in *The chemist analysed the potion.*
analysis *noun*, **analytic** *adjective*, **analytical** *adjective*

analyst *noun* analysts
a person who is trained in analysing the human mind, chemicals, etc., as in *The nervous person visited an analyst. He was employed as an analyst in the laboratory.*

Anangu *noun*
an Aborigine, especially from Central Australia.

Origin This word comes from the Aboriginal Western Desert language: **Anangu** = person. See the Aboriginal Languages map at the back of this dictionary.

anarchist *noun* anarchists
someone who thinks that governments and laws are bad and should be abolished.
anarchism *noun*

anarchy *noun*
1 disorder; confusion, as in *There was anarchy in the classroom when the relief teacher came.* 2 lack of government or control, as in *After the revolution there was anarchy in the streets.*

anatomy *noun*
the science or study of how the body is constructed.
anatomical *adjective*, **anatomist** *noun*

ancestor *noun* ancestors
a relation who lived long ago, as in *Many Australians' ancestors come from Britain.*
ancestral *adjective*, **ancestry** *noun*

anchor *noun* anchors
a heavy object joined to a ship by a chain or rope and dropped to the seabed, etc. to stop the ship from moving.

anchovy *noun* anchovies (*say* an-chuh-vee *or* an-**choh**-vee)
a small, very salty fish.

ancient *adjective*
1 to do with times long past, as in *ancient history.* 2 very old, as in *ancient ruins.*
Ancient Egypt, Egypt when it was ruled by the Pharaohs.
Ancient Rome, Rome, and the empire ruled by it, from early times up to AD 476.

and *conjunction*
1 in addition to, as in *We had pie and chips.* 2 so that; as a result, as in *Work hard and you will pass. Touch that and you'll be burnt.* 3 (*colloquial*) to, as in *Go and buy a pen.*

anecdote *noun* anecdotes
a short amusing account of something that has happened, especially to the person telling it.

anemometer *noun* anemometers
a device for measuring the speed of the wind.

anemone *noun* anemones
(*say* uh-**nem**-uhnee)
1 a small, brightly-coloured, cup-shaped flower. 2 a marine animal with a tube-shaped body and tentacles; a sea anemone.

angel *noun* angels
1 a messenger or attendant of God. 2 a very kind or beautiful person.
angelic *adjective*, **angelically** *adverb*

anger *noun*
a strong feeling that you want to quarrel or fight with someone.

angle *noun* angles
1 the space between two lines or surfaces that meet. 2 a point of view, as in *What is your angle on this?*

angle *verb* angles, angling, angled
1 to put something in a slanting position. 2 to present news, etc. in a particular way, as in *The report was angled so that the terrorists appeared to have done nothing wrong.*

angler *noun* anglers
someone who fishes with a fishing-rod.

Anglican *adjective*
to do with the Anglican Church, previously known as the Church of England, as in *They were married with an Anglican ceremony.*

Anglo-Saxon *noun* Anglo-Saxons
an English person, especially of the time before the Norman Conquest in the 11th Century.

angry *adjective* angrier, angriest
feeling or showing anger.
angrily *adverb*

anguish *noun*
severe suffering; great sorrow or pain.
anguished *adjective*

a
b
c
d
e
f
g
h
i
j
k
l
m
n
o
p
q
r
s
t
u
v
w
x
y
z

angular

angular *adjective*
1 with sharp corners.   2 bony, as in *a thin, angular face.*

animal *noun* **animals**
anything that lives and can move about, as in *Horses, dogs, birds, fish, bees, and humans are all animals.*

animate *verb* **animates, animating, animated**
1 to make lively, as in *The invitation to the party animated her.*   2 to make a film by photographing a series of drawings, etc.
animation *noun*, **animator** *noun*

animated *adjective*
1 lively and interesting, as in *animated conversation.*   2 to do with a film made by animation, as in *animated cartoon.*

animosity *noun* **animosities**
a feeling of being an enemy towards someone, as in *There was a lot of animosity in his voice.*

aniseed *noun*
a seed with a strong, sweet taste like liquorice.

ankle *noun* **ankles**
the part of the leg where it is joined to the foot.
ankle biter, (*colloquial*) a very small child.

annex *verb* **annexes, annexing, annexed**
(*say* uh-**neks**)
to add something to a larger thing, as in *The factory annexed the vacant block next to it.*
annexation *noun*

annexe *noun* **annexes** (*say* **an**-eks)
a building added to another building.

annihilate *verb* **annihilates, annihilating, annihilated** (*say* uh-**nuy**-uh-layt)
to destroy.
annihilation *noun*

anniversary *noun* **anniversaries**
a day when you remember something special that happened on the same date in a previous year.

announce *verb* **announces, announcing, announced**
to make something known; to say something publicly, especially in a broadcast.
announcer *noun*

announcement *noun* **announcements**
something that is made known publicly, especially in a newspaper or on the radio or television.

annoy *verb* **annoys, annoying, annoyed**
to give someone a feeling of not being pleased.

annoyance *noun* **annoyances**
1 the feeling of being irritated, as in *She felt annoyance waiting in the queue.*
2 something that annoys you, as in *Flies were a great annoyance at the picnic.*

annual *adjective*
1 happening or coming every year.
2 lasting only one year or season, as in *annual plants.*
annually *adverb*

annual *noun* **annuals**
1 a book that comes out once a year.   2 a plant that dies when winter comes.

anode *noun* **anodes**
the electrode by which electric current enters a device, as in *The anode is the positive electrode in a cell such as a battery, while the cathode is the negative electrode.*

anon. short for **anonymous.**

anonymous *adjective*
1 with a name that is unknown, as in *an anonymous writer.*   2 by or from someone whose name is unknown, as in *an anonymous letter.*
anonymity *noun*

anorak *noun* **anoraks**
a waterproof jacket, usually with a hood.

anorexia *noun*
an illness that makes someone not want to eat.
anorexic *adjective*

another *adjective*
1 different, as in *Find another cup—that one's dirty.*   2 one more, as in *Take another biscuit.*

another *pronoun*
additional person or thing.

answer *noun* **answers**
1 a reply.   2 the solution to a problem.

answer *verb* **answers, answering, answered**
1 to give or find an answer to.   2 to respond to a signal, as in *Answer the telephone.*
answer back, to reply cheekily.
answer for something, to be responsible for something.

ant *noun* **ants**
a small, usually wingless insect which lives in a family group called a colony.

antagonise or **antagonize** *verb*
antagonises, antagonising, antagonised
to make someone feel you are his or her enemy.

antagonism *noun* **antagonisms**
opposition, active hostility, hatred.
antagonistic *adjective*

anyhow

Antarctic *noun*
the area around the South Pole.

anteater *noun* **anteaters**
an animal with a long tongue that lives by eating ants, as in *Echidnas and numbats are anteaters*.

antelope *noun* **antelope** or **antelopes**
an animal like a deer, found in Africa and parts of Asia.

antenna *noun* **antennae**
1 a feeler on the head of an insect or crustacean. 2 an aerial for radio or television.

anthem *noun* **anthems**
a religious or patriotic song, usually sung by a choir or group of people, as in *'Advance Australia Fair' is our national anthem*.

anthill *noun* **anthills**
a mound of earth over an ants' nest.

anthology *noun* **anthologies**
a collection of poems, stories, songs, etc. in one book.

anthropology *noun*
the study of human beings and their customs, beliefs, etc.
anthropological *adjective*, **anthropologist** *noun*

antibiotic *noun* **antibiotics**
a drug like penicillin which destroys bacteria.

anticipate *verb* **anticipates, anticipating, anticipated**
1 to do something before the proper time. 2 to do something before someone else does it. 3 to look forward to something.

anticipation *noun*
looking forward to doing something.
in anticipation of something, expecting that something will happen, as in *I had taken my umbrella in anticipation of rain*.

anticlimax *noun* **anticlimaxes**
a disappointing end or result.

anticlockwise *adverb* and *adjective*
moving in the opposite direction to clockwise.

anticyclone *noun* **anticyclones**
an area where air pressure is high, usually causing fine weather.

antidote *noun* **antidotes**
something which acts against the effects of a poison or disease.

antifreeze *noun*
a chemical that is added to water to make it less likely to freeze, as in *Canberra drivers need to use antifreeze in the winter*.

antipodes *plural noun* (*say* an-ti-puh-deez)
places directly opposite each other on the earth such as the North and South poles.
the Antipodes, Australia and New Zealand, seen from the point of view of Britain.

antiquated *adjective*
old-fashioned, as in *an antiquated record player*.

antique *noun* **antiques** (*say* an-**teek**)
something that is valuable because it is very old.

anti-Semitic *adjective* (*say* an-tee-suh-**mit**-ik)
unfriendly or hostile to Jews.
anti-Semitism *noun*

antiseptic *noun* **antiseptics**
a substance that kills germs.

antivenene *noun* **antivenenes**
an injection which fights against the poison in the venom of snakes, spiders, etc.; an antivenom.

antler *noun* **antlers**
the long, branching horn of a deer and similar animals.

antonym *noun* **antonyms**
a word that has the opposite meaning to another word, as in *'Sweet' is the antonym of 'sour'*.

anus *noun* **anuses**
the opening at the lower end of the intestines, through which solid waste leaves the body.

anvil *noun* **anvils**
a large block of iron on which hot metal is beaten into a particular shape.

anxiety *noun* **anxieties**
being worried; something that worries you, as in *full of anxiety; the anxiety of illness*.

anxious *adjective*
1 worried. 2 eager, as in *They were anxious to help us*.

any *adjective*
1 one or some, as in *Have you any wool?*
2 no matter which, as in *Come any day you like*. 3 every, as in *Any fool knows that!*

any *adverb*
at all; in some degree, as in *Is it any good?*

anybody *noun* and *pronoun*
anyone.

anyhow *adverb*
1 anyway. 2 (*colloquial*) carelessly, as in *He does his work anyhow*.

a
b
c
d
e
f
g
h
i
j
k
l
m
n
o
p
q
r
s
t
u
v
w
x
y
z

anyone

anyone *noun* and *pronoun*
any person.

anything *noun* and *pronoun*
any thing.

anyway *adverb*
whatever happens; whatever the situation
may be.

anywhere *adverb*
in or to any place.

Anzac *noun* Anzacs
1 a soldier in the Australian and New
Zealand Army Corps during the First
World War (1914–1918). 2 any soldier
from Australia and New Zealand.
[from the first letters of the words
Australian and New Zealand Army Corps]

aorta *noun* aortas (*say* ay-aw-tuh)
the main artery through which the blood
leaves the left side of the heart before
flowing to the rest of the body.

apart *adverb*
1 away from each other; separately, as in
Keep your desks apart. 2 into pieces, as in *It
fell apart.*

apartheid *noun* (*say* uh-**pah**-tayt)
the policy of keeping non-Whites separate
from Whites, as in *Since the recent democratic
elections, South Africa no longer has a policy of
apartheid.*

apartment *noun* apartments
1 a single room or a set of rooms. 2 a flat.

apathy *noun*
lack of interest, as in *His apathy towards
training annoyed the coach.*
apathetic *adjective*

ape *noun* apes
a monkey without a tail, as in *Gorillas,
chimpanzees, and orang-utans are apes.*

apex *noun* apexes
the highest point of something, as in *the
apex of the mountain; the apex of her career.*

aphid or **aphis** *noun* aphids or aphides
a tiny insect that sucks juices from plants.

apiary *noun* apiaries
a place where bees are kept.

apologise or **apologize** *verb* apologises,
apologising, apologised
to say that you are sorry.

apology *noun* apologies
a statement of regret for a mistake,
wrongdoing, etc., as in *He offered an apology
for his rudeness.*
apologetic *adjective*, **apologetically** *adverb*

apostle *noun* apostles
1 one of the twelve men sent out by Jesus
to tell people about God. 2 a person who
believes strongly in an idea, theory, etc., as
in *an apostle for free speech.*

apostrophe *noun* apostrophes
(*say* uh-**pos**-truh-fee)
a punctuation mark like this ' used to show
that letters have been left out (as in *I can't*)
or with *s* to show who owns something (as
in *the boy's books, the boys' books*).

appal *verb* appals, appalling, appalled
(*say* uh-**pawl**)
to shock someone deeply, as in *The violence
appalled everyone.*

apparatus *noun* apparatuses
equipment for a particular experiment, job,
activity, etc., as in *building apparatus; gym
apparatus.*

apparent *adjective*
1 clear; obvious, as in *The answer was
apparent when we had all the information.*
2 that appears to be true, as in *The apparent
reason for his action was not the real one.*
apparently *adverb*

appeal *verb* appeals, appealing, appealed
1 to ask for something that you need, as in
She appealed for funds. 2 to be attractive or
interesting, as in *Tennis doesn't appeal to
me.* 3 to ask for a decision to be changed,
as in *He appealed against the prison sentence.*

appeal *noun* appeals
1 a request for something you need, as in
the Smith Family's blanket appeal.
2 attraction; interest, as in *Skating has little
appeal for him.* 3 a request for a decision to
be changed, as in *His appeal was refused.*

appear *verb* appears, appearing, appeared
1 to come into sight. 2 to seem. 3 to
take part in a play, film, show, etc.

appearance *noun* appearances
1 coming into sight. 2 taking part in a
play, film, show, etc. 3 what someone
looks like. 4 what something seems to be.

appease *verb* appeases, appeasing,
appeased
to make peaceful or calm, especially by
giving in to demands.
appeasement *noun*

appendicitis *noun*
an inflammation or disease of the
appendix.

appendix *noun* appendices or appendixes
1 a small tube leading off from the
intestines. 2 a section added at the end of
a book.

appetite *noun* appetites
desire, especially for food or drink.
appetiser *noun*, **appetising** *adjective*

applaud *verb* applauds, applauding,
applauded
to show that you like something, especially
by clapping.
applause *noun*

apple *noun* apples
a roundish firm red or green fruit with
crisp flesh.
Apple Isle, Tasmania.

appliance *noun* appliances
a device, as in *household electrical appliances.*

applicable *adjective*
1 able to be used, as in *This law is no longer
applicable.* 2 relevant, as in *Cross out any
responses which are not applicable.*

applicant *noun* applicants
someone who applies for something, as in
job applicant.

application *noun* applications
1 a letter, etc. asking for something.
2 great effort and attention to something,
as in *She showed application in her studies.*
3 something put or laid on a surface, as in
an application of paint.

applied *adjective*
put to practical use, as in *Cookery is an
applied science.*

apply *verb* applies, applying, applied
1 to put one thing on another, as in *Apply a
patch to the puncture.* 2 to start using
something, as in *She applied the mouth-to-
mouth method of resuscitation.*
apply for something, to ask for a job, etc.
apply to someone, to concern someone, as
in *Her remarks do not apply to you.*
apply yourself to something, to give all your
attention to something.

appoint *verb* appoints, appointing, appointed
to choose someone for a job or task, as in
*She was appointed principal. He was appointed
to collect the lunch orders.*

appointment *noun* appointments
1 an arrangement to meet or visit someone,
as in *dental appointment.* 2 choosing
someone for a job, as in *appointment as
principal.* 3 a job or position to which a
person is appointed, as in *The appointment
for the superintendent was filled.*

appraise *verb* appraises, appraising,
appraised
to estimate the value or quality of a person
or thing.
appraisal *noun*

appreciate *verb* appreciates, appreciating,
appreciated
1 to enjoy or value. 2 to understand.
3 to increase in value.
appreciation *noun*

appreciative *adjective*
able to enjoy or value something, as in
I enjoy playing to an appreciative audience.

apprehend *verb* apprehends, apprehending,
apprehended
to seize or arrest, as in *The police
apprehended the thief.*

apprehension *noun* apprehensions
fear; worry.
apprehensive *adjective*

apprentice *noun* apprentices
someone who is learning a trade or craft.
apprenticeship *noun*

approach *verb*
1 to come near to. 2 to go to someone
with a request or offer. 3 to tackle a
problem, as in *He approached the difficult
question with care.*

approach *noun* approaches
1 coming near to a place. 2 a request or
offer. 3 a way of tackling a problem.
4 the final part of an aircraft's flight before
landing.

approachable *adjective*
(of a person) easy to speak to; friendly.

appropriate *adjective*
suitable.

approval *noun*
approving someone or something;
permission, as in *She needed her parents'
approval for the party.*
on approval, received by a customer to
examine before buying.

approve *verb* approves, approving, approved
to say or think that someone or something
is good, suitable or permitted, as in *I
approve of good manners. The principal
approved the students' request for a longer
lunch hour.*

approximate *adjective*
not exact, as in *The approximate size of the
playground is half a hectare.*
approximately *adverb*

approximation *noun* approximations
something that is nearly exact.

apricot *noun* apricots
a juicy, orange-coloured fruit with a stone
in it.

April *noun*
the fourth month of the year.

apron

apron *noun* **aprons**
a garment worn over the front of your body to protect your clothes.

apt *adjective*
1 likely, as in *He is apt to be careless.*
2 suitable, as in *an apt comment.* 3 quick at learning, as in *an apt pupil.*

aptitude *noun* **aptitudes**
a talent, as in *He has an aptitude for music.*

aquarium *noun* **aquariums**
a tank or building in which live fish are displayed.

aquatic *adjective*
to do with water, as in *aquatic sports.*

aqueduct *noun* **aqueducts**
a bridge that carries water across a valley.

Arab *noun* **Arabs**
a member of a people inhabiting Arabia and other parts of the Middle East and North Africa.
Arabian *adjective*

Arabic *adjective*
to do with the Arabs or their language.

arabic figures or **arabic numerals** *plural noun*
the figures 1, 2, 3, 4, etc. (compare *Roman numerals*).

arable *adjective*
suitable for growing crops, as in *arable land.*

arbitrary *adjective* (*say* **ah**-buh-truh-ree *or* **ah**-buh-tree)
done or chosen at random or without a proper reason, as in *an arbitrary decision.*
arbitrarily *adverb*

arbitration *noun*
settling a quarrel between two people or two sides.
arbitrate *verb*, **arbitrator** *noun*

arc *noun* **arcs**
1 a curve. 2 bright light made by an electric current passing across a gap between two electrodes.

arcade *noun* **arcades**
a covered passage or area, especially for shopping.

arch *noun* **arches**
a curved part that helps to support a bridge or building.

arch *verb* **arches, arching, arched**
to curve, as in *The gymnast arched her back.*

archaeology *noun* (*say* ah-kee-**ol**-uh-jee)
the study of ancient remains.
archaeological *adjective*, **archaeologist** *noun*

archaic *adjective* (*say* ay-**kay**-ik)
old-fashioned or out of date, as in *an archaic sewing machine.*

archbishop *noun* **archbishops**
a chief bishop.

archer *noun* **archers**
someone who shoots with a bow and arrows.
archery *noun*

architect *noun* **architects** (*say* **ah**-kuh-tekt)
someone who designs buildings.

architecture *noun*
1 designing buildings. 2 a style of building, as in *colonial architecture.*

Arctic *noun*
the area around the North Pole.

arctic *adjective*
1 to do with the North Pole, as in *arctic oceans.* 2 (*colloquial*) very cold, as in *arctic conditions.*

are plural and 2nd person singular present tense of **be.**

area *noun* **areas**
1 part of a country, place, etc. 2 the space occupied by something, as in *The area of this room is 20 square metres.*

arena *noun* **arenas** (*say* uh-**ree**-nuh)
the central part of a stadium, etc. where contests take place, as in *athletic arena*

aren't short for *am not* or *are not.*

argue *verb* **argues, arguing, argued**
1 to quarrel. 2 to give reasons for something, as in *She argued that housework should be shared.*

argument *noun* **arguments**
1 a quarrel. 2 a reason given for something.

argumentative *adjective*
usually ready to disagree or quarrel, as in *The argumentative student was unwelcome in the group.*

aria *noun* **arias** (*say* **ah**-ree-uh)
a solo in an opera.

arid *adjective*
dry and barren.
aridity *noun*

arise *verb* **arises, arising, arose, arisen**
1 to appear; to come into existence.
2 (*old-fashioned use*) to rise; to stand up.

aristocracy *noun* **aristocracies**
the people of the highest social rank.

aristocrat *noun* **aristocrats**
(*say* **a**-ruh-stuh-krat)

a nobleman or noblewoman, as in *Dukes and Duchesses are aristocrats.*
aristocratic *adjective*

arithmetic *noun*
1 the science or study of numbers.
2 calculating with numbers.
arithmetical *adjective*

ark *noun* **arks**
the ship in which Noah and his family escaped the Flood, according to the Bible.

arm *noun* **arms**
1 the part of your body between your shoulder and your hand.   2 a sleeve.
3 something shaped like an arm, especially the side part of a chair.

arm *verb* **arms, arming, armed**
1 to supply with weapons.   2 to prepare for war.
armed forces or **armed services,** the army, navy, and air force.

armada *noun* **armadas** (*say* ah-**mah**-duh)
a fleet of warships, especially the Spanish Armada which attacked England in 1588.

armadillo *noun* **armadillos**
a South American animal with large claws for digging and whose body is covered with a shell of bony plates.

armaments *plural noun*
weapons.

armchair *noun* **armchairs**
a chair with parts on either side to rest your arms on.

armistice *noun* **armistices**
an agreement to stop fighting in a war or battle.

armour *noun*
a metal covering to protect people or things in battle.
armoured *adjective*

armpit *noun* **armpits**
the hollow under the arm at the shoulder.

arms *plural noun*
weapons, as in *Lay down your arms.*
arms race, the competition between nations in building up supplies of weapons.

army *noun* **armies**
1 a large number of people trained to fight on land.   2 a large group, as in *an army of supporters.*

aroma *noun* **aromas** (*say* uh-**roh**-muh)
a smell, especially a pleasant one, as in *the aroma of oranges.*
aromatic *adjective*

arose past tense of **arise.**

around *adverb* and *preposition*
1 round, as in *They stood around the pool.*
2 about, as in *Stop running around.*

arouse *verb* **arouses, arousing, aroused**
1 to bring into existence, as in *The debate aroused strong feelings.*   2 to awake from sleep, as in *The alarm aroused her.*

arrange *verb* **arranges, arranging, arranged**
1 to put into order, as in *The titles were arranged alphabetically.*   2 to plan or provide for, as in *They arranged a farewell party for Bill and Joan.*
arrangement *noun,* **arranger** *noun*

array *noun* **arrays**
a display; a series, as in *an impressive array of books.*

arrears *plural noun*
the amount, especially of work, rent, etc. still owing or incomplete, as in *rent arrears.*

arrest *verb* **arrests, arresting, arrested**
1 to use the power of the law to seize someone.   2 to stop something, as in *Arrest the spread of AIDS.*

arrest *noun* **arrests**
arresting someone or something.
under arrest, seized by the police, etc.

arrive *verb* **arrives, arriving, arrived**
1 to reach the end of a journey; to get somewhere.   2 to come, as in *The great day arrived.*
arrival *noun*

arrogant *adjective*
unpleasantly proud, with little respect for others.
arrogance *noun*

arrow *noun* **arrows**
1 a pointed stick shot from a bow.   2 a sign used to show the way to go.

arsenal *noun* **arsenals**
a place where bullets, shells, etc., and weapons are made or stored.

arsenic *noun*
a very poisonous metallic substance.

arson *noun*
the crime of deliberately burning property.

art *noun* **arts**
1 the production of something that is beautiful, especially by painting or drawing; things produced in this way, as in *the art of portrait painting; Renoir's art.*   2 a subject in which opinion and imagination are more important than exact measurement and calculation, as in *English and history are arts; chemistry and biology are sciences.*   3 a skill, as in *the art of sewing.*

artefact

artefact *noun* artefacts
an object made by humans, especially one studied by archaeologists.

artery *noun* arteries
a tube carrying blood from the heart to parts of the body.

artesian bore *noun* artesian bores
a well bored through a layer of rock which holds water so that natural pressure produces a constant supply of water with little or no pumping.

artful *adjective*
skilled at deceiving people.
artfully *adverb*

arthritis *noun* (*say* ah-**thruy**-tuhs)
a disease that makes joints in the body painful and stiff.
arthritic *adjective*

article *noun* articles
1 an object; a thing. **2** a piece of writing published in a newspaper or magazine. **3** (*in grammar*) the word 'a' or 'an' (called the *indefinite article*) or the word 'the' (called the *definite article*).

articulate *adjective* (*say* ah-**tik**-yuh-luht)
able to speak clearly and fluently.

articulate *verb* articulates, articulating, articulated (*say* ah-**tik**-yoo-layt)
to speak clearly.
articulation *noun*

articulated *adjective*
with parts that are connected by flexible joints, as in *an articulated bus, truck, etc.*

artificial *adjective*
not natural; made by human beings.
artificial respiration, helping someone to start breathing again, especially after an accident.
artificiality *noun*, **artificially** *adverb*

artillery *noun*
1 large guns. **2** the part of the army that uses large guns.

artist *noun* artists
1 someone who creates art, especially a painter. **2** an entertainer.

artistic *adjective*
1 showing skill and beauty, as in *an artistic flower arrangement.* **2** to do with art or artists, as in *artistic exhibition.*

artistry *noun*
the skill of an artist, as in *Look at the artistry of that carving!*

as *adverb*
equally; similarly, as in *This is just as easy.*

as *conjunction*
1 in the way that; how, as in *Leave it as it is.* **2** when; while, as in *She slipped as she got off the bus.* **3** because, as in *Leave him here, as he's cross.*
as ... as, in the same way; to the same extent that, as in *It is not as hard as you think.*
as well, also.

as *preposition*
in the character or role of; like, as in *He was dressed as a pirate.*

asbestos *noun*
a grey substance that is made up of fine, soft fibres, once used as fireproof or insulating material.

ascend *verb* ascends, ascending, ascended
to climb something; to go up.
ascent *noun*

ascertain *verb* ascertains, ascertaining, ascertained (*say* ass-uh-**tayn**)
to find out or confirm.

ash *noun* ashes
1 the powder that is left after something has been burned, as in *cigarette ash.* **2** a tree with silvery bark and hard pale timber.
the Ashes, the prize for which England and Australia play each other at cricket.
ashy *adjective*

ashamed *adjective*
feeling shame or embarrassment.

ashen *adjective*
grey; pale, as in *Her face was ashen.*

ashore *adverb*
towards or on the shore.

ashtray *noun* ashtrays
a small bowl for cigarette ash.

Ash Wednesday *noun* Ash Wednesdays
the first day of Lent.

Asian *adjective*
to do with Asia.

aside *adverb*
to or at one side; away.

aside *noun* asides
something said on the stage by an actor which the other actors are supposed not to hear.

ask *verb* asks, asking, asked
1 to speak so as to find out or get something. **2** to invite, as in *Ask him to the party.*
ask for it or **ask for trouble,** (*colloquial*) to behave in such a way as to get into trouble.
a big ask, (*colloquial*) a difficult task.

asleep *adverb* and *adjective*
sleeping, as in *I fell asleep. She is asleep.*

aspect *noun* aspects
1 one part of a problem or situation, as in *Perhaps the worst aspect of winter is the dark mornings.* 2 the appearance of someone or something. 3 the direction a house, etc. faces, as in *This sunny room has a northern aspect.*

asphalt *noun* (*say* **ash**-felt *or* **as**-felt)
1 a sticky black substance like tar. 2 this substance is mixed with gravel to surface roads, playgrounds, etc.

aspirin *noun* aspirins
a drug used to relieve pain or reduce fever.

ass *noun* asses
a donkey.

assassin *noun* assassins
a person who murders someone.

assassinate *verb* assassinates, assassinating, assassinated
to murder someone, especially a leader, politician, etc.
assassination *noun*

assault *noun* assaults
a violent or illegal attack on someone or something.

assault *verb* assaults, assaulting, assaulted
to make an assault on someone.

assemble *verb* assembles, assembling, assembled
1 to bring people together. 2 to put things together.

assembly *noun* assemblies
1 the act of assembling, as in *the assembly of cars at the factory.* 2 people who regularly meet together; a parliament. 3 a regular meeting, such as when everybody in a school meets together.
assembly line, a series of workers and machines to assemble the parts of a product.

assert *verb* asserts, asserting, asserted
to declare something.
assert yourself, to use firmness or authority.
assertion *noun*

assertive *adjective*
showing or using firmness or authority, as in *The assertive school captain chose the team quickly.*

assess *verb* assesses, assessing, assessed
to decide or test the value of a person or thing.
assessment *noun*, **assessor** *noun*

asset *noun* assets
something useful or valuable, as in *A good education is an asset in life.*
assets, property.

assign *verb* assign, assigning, assigned
1 to give or allot. 2 to tell someone to do a task.

assignment *noun* assignments
something that someone has to do, especially a task given to a journalist, or to a student at school or college.

assimilate *verb* assimilates, assimilating, assimilated
1 to learn and make use of, as in *She quickly assimilated the new ideas on photography.*
2 to become an accepted part of a group, etc., as in *The migrants were soon assimilated into the neighbourhood.*

assist *verb* assists, assisting, assisted
to help.
assistance *noun*

assistant *noun* assistants
someone who helps another person.

associate *verb* associates, associating, associated (*say* uh-**soh**-see-ayt *or* uh-**soh**-shee-ayt)
1 to put things or ideas naturally or regularly together, as in *I associate Christmas with a holiday at the beach.* 2 to work together, as in *Two firms have associated on this project.*

associate *noun* associates
(*say* uh-**soh**-see-uht *or* uh-**soh**-shee-uht)
a colleague or companion, as in *business associate.*

association *noun* associations
1 an organisation, as in *The Parents and Citizens Association.* 2 the relationship between two or more things, as in *the association of koalas and kangaroos with Australia.*

assorted *adjective*
to do with various sorts; mixed, as in *assorted lollies.*
assortment *noun*

assume *verb* assumes, assuming, assumed
1 to accept, without proof or question, that something is true or sure to happen. 2 to take or put on something, as in *He assumed an innocent look.*
assumed, false, as in *an assumed name.*
assumption *noun*

assurance *noun* assurances
1 confidence, as in *She spoke with assurance in the debate.* 2 a promise or guarantee, as in *He gave me an assurance that he would deliver the parcel.*

assure *verb* assures, assuring, assured
1 to tell someone something positively, as in *I can assure you that we will make every*

asterisk

effort to help. **2** to make sure that something will happen, as in *Rain will assure a good crop of vegetables.*
assure yourself, to make yourself feel certain or confident.

asterisk *noun* **asterisks**
a star-shaped sign * used to draw attention to something.

asteroid *noun* **asteroids**
one of the small planets found mainly between the orbits of Mars and Jupiter.

asthma *noun* (*say* **as**-muh)
a disease which makes breathing difficult.
asthmatic *adjective* and *noun*

astonish *verb* **astonishes, astonishing, astonished**
to surprise someone greatly.
astonishment *noun*

astound *verb* **astounds, astounding, astounded**
to amaze or shock someone greatly.

astray *adverb*
away from the right or true path, as in *The foolish child was easily led astray. The letter had gone astray.*

astride *adverb*
with one leg on each side of something.

astrology *noun*
the study of how the planets and stars may affect our lives.
astrologer *noun*, **astrological** *adjective*

astronaut *noun* **astronauts**
someone who travels in a spacecraft.

astronomical *adjective*
1 connected with astronomy. **2** extremely large, as in *The cost was astronomical.*

astronomy *noun*
the study of the sun, moon, planets, and stars.
astronomer *noun*

at *preposition*
in a particular place, time, way, or direction.
at all, in any way.
at it, working at something.
at once, immediately; without any delay.

ate past tense of **eat.**

atheist *noun* **atheists**
someone who believes that there is no God.
atheism *noun*

athlete *noun* **athletes**
someone who takes part in, or is good at, athletics.

athletic *adjective*
1 to do with athletics, as in *an athletic*

competition. **2** physically strong, as in *an athletic build.*

athletics *plural noun*
physical exercises and sports like running and jumping.

atlas *noun* **atlases**
a book of maps.

atmosphere *noun* **atmospheres**
1 the air around the earth. **2** a feeling, as in *There was a happy atmosphere at the party.*
atmospheric *adjective*

atoll *noun* **atolls**
a ring-shaped island of coral in the sea.

atom *noun* **atoms**
a tiny part of something; the smallest possible part of a chemical element, as in *Every atom has a nucleus at its centre.*
atom bomb, an atomic bomb.

atomic *adjective*
to do with atoms; nuclear.
atomic bomb, a bomb that uses atomic energy.
atomic energy, energy created by splitting or joining together the central parts of some atoms.

atone *verb* **atones, atoning, atoned**
to show sorrow by making amends, as in *He atoned for his selfishness by being kind to everyone.*

atrocious *adjective* (*say* uh-**troh**-shuhs)
awful; terrible, as in *an atrocious crime.*
atrocity *noun*

attach *verb* **attaches, attaching, attached**
to fix or fasten.
attached to, fond of.

attachment *noun* **attachments**
1 something fixed or fastened to a device so that it can do a special kind of work, as in *The garden hose has a car-washing attachment.* **2** fondness or friendship.

attack *verb* **attacks, attacking, attacked**
1 to try to hurt or defeat someone or something by using force; to act harmfully on something, as in *He attacked his victim with a knife. Rust attacks metal.* **2** to approach with vigour, as in *She attacked the project with enthusiasm.*

attack *noun* **attacks**
1 an attempt to hurt or harm someone or something. **2** a sudden illness or pain.

attain *verb* **attains, attaining, attained**
to reach or accomplish something, as in *I have attained Grade 3 on the violin.*
attainment *noun*

attempt *verb* **attempts, attempting, attempted**
to make an effort to do something.

attempt *noun* **attempts**
making an effort to do something.

attend *verb* **attends, attending, attended**
1 to be present somewhere; to go to a meeting, place, etc. 2 to look after or serve someone, as in *The mother attended her sick child*. 3 to give care and thought to something, as in *I have some business to attend to*.

attendance *noun* **attendances**
1 being present somewhere. 2 the number of people who are present at a meeting, an event, etc.

attendant *noun* **attendants**
someone who helps or goes with another person, as in *classroom attendant*.

attention *noun*
care or thought given to someone or something.
stand to attention, to stand with your feet together and arms straight downwards, as soldiers do on parade.

attentive *adjective*
paying attention or concentrating.

attic *noun* **attics**
a room in the roof of a house.

attitude *noun* **attitudes**
1 the way you think, feel, or behave, as in *Her attitude to sport was one of loathing*. 2 the position of your body, as in *She flung out her arms in an attitude of surrender*.

attract *verb* **attracts, attracting, attracted**
1 to get someone's attention or interest; to seem pleasant to someone. 2 to pull something by an invisible force, as in *Magnets attract pins*.
attraction *noun*

attractive *adjective*
1 able to get someone's interest, as in *an attractive offer*. 2 (of a person) good-looking.

auburn *adjective*
(of hair) reddish-brown.

auction *noun* **auctions**
a sale when things are sold to the person who offers the most money for them.
auctioneer *noun* .

audible *adjective*
loud enough to be heard.
audibility *noun*

audience *noun* **audiences**
1 the people who have gathered to see or hear something. 2 a formal interview

with an important person, as in *an audience with the Pope*.

audiovisual *adjective*
using both sound and pictures to give information, as in *Audiovisual aids include films and video recordings*.

audition *noun* **auditions**
a test to see if a performer is suitable for a job or a part in a play, etc.

auditorium *noun* **auditoriums**
(*say* aw-duh-**taw**-ree-uhm)
the part of a building where the audience sits.

August *noun*
the eighth month of the year.

aunt *noun* **aunts**
1 the sister of your mother or father.
2 your uncle's wife.

auntie or **aunty** *noun* **aunties**
(*colloquial*) an aunt.

aural *adjective*
to do with hearing, as in *an aural comprehension test*.

> **Usage** Do not confuse **aural** with **oral**, which means spoken, or using your mouth.

Aussie *noun* **Aussies**
(*colloquial*) an Australian.

Aussie Rules *plural noun*
the game of Australian Rules football.

austere *adjective*
1 without comfort or luxury, as in *an austere room*. 2 strict in self-discipline, as in *the austere rules of some religious groups*.
austerity *noun*

authentic *adjective*
genuine, as in *an authentic signature*.
authenticity *noun*

author *noun* **authors**
the writer of a book, play, poem, etc.
authorship *noun*

authorise or **authorize** *verb* **authorises, authorising, authorised**
to give official permission for something.

authority *noun* **authorities**
1 the right or power to give orders to other people. 2 an organisation or person that can give orders to other people, as in *building authority*. 3 a very knowledgeable person; a book, etc. that gives reliable information, as in *an authority on cooking*.

autistic *adjective*
unable to communicate with other people or respond to surroundings.

a
b
c
d
e
f
g
h
i
j
k
l
m
n
o
p
q
r
s
t
u
v
w
x
y
z

autobiography

autobiography *noun* **autobiographies**
the story of someone's life written by himself or herself.
autobiographical *adjective*

autocracy *noun* **autocracies**
government of a country by a person with total power.
autocrat *noun*, **autocratic** *adjective*

autograph *noun* **autographs**
a person's signature.

automatic *adjective*
1 working on its own; not needing continuous attention or control by human beings. 2 done without thinking.
automatically *adverb*

automatic *noun* **automatics**
a car whose gears change automatically, as in *The car salesman asked if I wanted an automatic or manual.*

automation *noun* (*say* aw-tuh-**may**-shuhn)
the use of machines instead of people to do jobs; the production of goods by this method, as in *Automation is now used in the car industry. These cars were produced mainly by automation.*

autumn *noun* **autumns**
the season when leaves fall from deciduous trees, between summer and winter.
autumnal *adjective*

auxiliary *adjective*
helping, as in *auxiliary staff. The yacht has an auxiliary engine.*

auxiliary *noun* **auxiliaries**
a type of verb that is used in forming parts of other verbs; a helping verb, as in *In 'I have finished', the auxiliary is 'have'.*

available *adjective*
able to be obtained or used, as in *Avocados are now available throughout the year. I am available for library duty today.*
availability *noun*

avalanche *noun* **avalanches**
(*say* av-uh-**lahnsh** *or* av-uh-**lansh**)
a sudden fall of rocks or snow down the side of a mountain.

avenge *verb* **avenges, avenging, avenged**
to get revenge, as in *He vowed to avenge his friend's death.*

avenue *noun* **avenues**
a wide street, especially one with trees along both sides at regular intervals.

average *noun* **averages**
1 the usual or ordinary standard, as in *Her work is above the average.* 2 the result of adding several quantities together and dividing the total by the number of quantities, as in *The average of 2, 4, 6, and 8 is 5.*

average *adjective*
1 to do with the usual or ordinary standard, as in *average performance.*
2 worked out as an average, as in *The batsman's average score is 30.*

average *verb* **averages, averaging, averaged**
to work out, produce, or amount to an average.

avert *verb* **averts, averting, averted**
1 to turn something away, as in *People averted their eyes from the accident.* 2 to prevent something, as in *The train driver's quick reaction had averted a disaster.*

aviary *noun* **aviaries**
a place where birds are kept.

aviation *noun*
the practice or science of flying aircraft.
aviator *noun*

avid *adjective*
1 eager, as in *She is an avid reader.*
2 greedy, as in *He was avid for fame.*

avocado *noun* **avocados**
a green- or black-skinned fruit, shaped like a pear, with smooth, oily, edible flesh and a large stone.

avoid *verb* **avoids, avoiding, avoided**
1 to keep yourself away from someone or something, as in *She avoided her enemy.*
2 to find a way of not doing something, as in *He left the country to avoid his debts.*
avoidance *noun*

await *verb* **awaits, awaiting, awaited**
to wait for.

awake *verb* **awakes, awaking, awoke, awoken**
1 to wake up. 2 to become active, as in *His ambition was awoken by early success.*

awake *adjective*
not sleeping.

awaken *verb* **awakens, awakening, awakened**
to wake up.

award *verb* **awards, awarding, awarded**
to give someone a prize, payment, etc., as in *He was awarded the music prize.*

award *noun* **awards**
a thing given officially to a person who has done something successful.
award wage, a wage, fixed by a special court, to be paid to certain workers.

aware *adjective*
knowing; realising, as in *I was aware of his anger*.
awareness *noun*

awash *adjective*
with waves or water flooding over it, as in *The sink has overflowed, and the kitchen floor is awash!*

away *adverb*
1 at or to a distance; not at the place where you usually are, as in *Hilary is away in England at present*.   2 out of existence, as in *The ice-cream melted away*.   3 continuously; persistently, as in *He was working away at his sums*.

away *adjective*
played or gained on an opponent's ground, as in *an away match; an away win*.

awe *noun*
a feeling of respect and amazement that a person has when faced with something wonderful, frightening or completely unknown, as in *The mountains filled him with awe. The child stared at the prime minister in silent awe*.
awe-inspiring, causing awe or wonder; amazing, magnificent, as in *the awe-inspiring sight of snow-capped Cradle Mountain*.

awesome *adjective*
causing awe; awe-inspiring, as in *the awesome force of a tropical cyclone*.

awful *adjective*
1 (*colloquial*) very bad; very great, as in *I've been an awful fool*.   2 causing fear or horror, as in *an awful crime*.
awfully *adverb*

awhile *adverb*
for a short time.

awkward *adjective*
1 not convenient; difficult to use or deal with, as in *an awkward time to visit. The tall boy found the small bike awkward to ride*.
2 clumsy, as in *an awkward young man*.

awning *noun* **awnings**
a sheet of canvas, etc. to give shade to a door, window, etc.

awoke past tense of **awake** *verb*.

awoken past participle of **awake** *verb*.

axe *noun* **axes**
a tool for chopping.
get the axe, (*colloquial*) to be dismissed from a job; to be stopped suddenly, as in *Our project got the axe*.
someone has an axe to grind, someone has his or her own reasons for doing something.

axe *verb* **axes, axing, axed**
(*colloquial*)
1 to dismiss someone from a job.   2 to reduce expenses, wages, etc., as in *The government axed defence spending*.

axis *noun* **axes**
1 a line through the centre of a spinning object.   2 a line dividing something in half.

axle *noun* **axles**
the rod through the centre of a wheel, on which it turns.

axolotl *noun* **axolotls** (*say* aks-uh-**lot**-uhl)
a fish-like creature with short legs and a long tail, found in Mexico.

azalea *noun* **azaleas** (*say* uh-**zay**-lee-uh *or* uh-**zayl**-yuh)
an attractive shrub with colourful flowers that bloom in early spring.

azure *adjective*
sky-blue.

Bb

babble *verb* **babbles, babbling, babbled**
1 to talk in a silly or meaningless way, as in *The toddler babbled to his mother*. 2 to murmur, as in *a babbling brook*.

baboon *noun* **baboons**
a large kind of monkey with a long nose, found in Africa and Arabia.

baby *noun* **babies**
a very young child or animal.
babyish *adjective*

baby *verb* **babies, babied**
to treat like a baby, as in *The worried mother babied her five year old*.

bachelor *noun* **bachelors**
a man who is not married.

back *noun* **backs**
1 the part of your body from your shoulders to your buttocks; the similar part of an animal's body. 2 the part of a thing that faces backwards; the less important side of something, as in *The back of the house is built of timber, while the front is of brick*. 3 the part of a thing or place that is farthest from the front, as in *We had to stand at the back of the hall*. 3 a defending player in football, hockey, etc.

back *adverb*
1 backwards; to the place you have come from, as in *Go back! He looked back*. 2 to an earlier time, as in *Put the clock back*. 3 at a distance, as in *The house stands back from the road*. 4 in return, as in *I paid him back*.

back *verb* **backs, backing, backed**
1 to move backwards or reverse. 2 to bet on something. 3 to give support, as in *He backed my company with his capital. I will back you up in your claim. The guitarist backed the singer*.

back down, to withdraw from a fight, etc.
back off, to draw back or retreat.
back out, to reverse a car, etc.
turn one's back on, to abandon or ignore.

back *adjective*
placed at the back, as in *the back row*.

backache *noun* **backaches**
pain in your back, usually lasting for a long time.

backbone *noun* **backbones**
1 the spine. 2 firmness of character, as in *She has the backbone to survive her loss*.

backfire *verb* **backfires, backfiring, backfired**
1 to explode in the exhaust pipe, etc. because of a fault in the engine, as in *The old car backfired*. 2 to have the opposite effect from the one planned; to go wrong, as in *Their plan backfired*.

background *noun* **backgrounds**
1 the part of a scene, view, etc. that is farthest away from you. 2 the conditions or situation underlying something, as in *The background to the war included famine*. 3 a person's experience, education, etc.
background music, music used to accompany a film, etc.
in the background, not noticeable; not obvious.

backhand *noun* **backhands**
a stroke in games such as tennis, in which the back of your hand faces your opponent.

backing *noun*
1 support, as in *Our firm will give you financial backing*. 2 material that forms a support or back for something. 3 musical accompaniment, especially for a singer.

backlash *noun* **backlashes**
a strong, usually angry reaction.

bake

backlog *noun* backlogs
work that should have been finished but still remains to be done.

backpack *noun* backpacks
a bag carried on the back by school children, bushwalkers, etc.

backstroke *noun*
a swimming stroke where you lie on your back, kick your legs and move your arms back over your head.

backward *adjective*
1 going backwards, as in *a backward step*. 2 not as advanced or developed as others, as in *backward country*.

backward *adverb*
backwards.

backwards *adverb*
1 to or towards the back. 2 in reverse, as in *Count backwards from 10 to 1*.
backwards and forwards, in one direction and back again, many times.

backwater *noun* backwaters
1 a branch of a river that comes to a dead end. 2 a peaceful, secluded or dull place, as in *The little country town was a real backwater*.

backyard *noun* backyards
an open area at the back of a house.

bacon *noun*
smoked or salted meat from the back or sides of a pig.

bacteria *plural noun*
very tiny organisms, as in *Some bacteria cause disease*.
bacterial *adjective*

bad *adjective* worse, worst
1 not good, as in *The television picture is bad. All this drinking is bad for your health*.
2 naughty, as in *You've been a bad boy!*
3 serious, as in *a bad mistake*. 4 decayed, as in *This meat has gone bad*. 5 unhealthy; injured, as in *He had a bad heart. I've got a bad leg*. 6 unhappy, as in *I feel bad about not having phoned her*.
not bad, (*colloquial*) fairly good.

baddy *noun* baddies
(*colloquial*) a villain, especially in a film, story, etc.

badge *noun* badges
something that you wear on your clothes to show people who you are, what school or club you belong to, etc.

badger *noun* badgers
a nocturnal, burrowing animal from the northern hemisphere, with a black and white striped head.

badger *verb* badgers, badgering, badgered
to pester, as in *He badgered me for his pocket money*.

badly *adverb*
1 in a bad way. 2 (*colloquial*) very much, as in *He wants the book badly*.
badly off, poor.

badminton *noun*
a game in which a lightweight object called a *shuttlecock* is hit backwards and forwards with rackets across a high net.

baffle *verb* baffles, baffling, baffled
to puzzle someone completely.

bag *noun* bags
a flexible container made of paper, plastic, cloth, etc.
bags of something, (*colloquial*) plenty of something, as in *There's bags of room*.

bag *verb* bags, bagging, bagged
1 (*colloquial*) to seize or catch, as in *I bagged the best seat*. 2 to put something into bags.

bagel *noun* bagels
a hard, ring-shaped bread roll.

baggage *noun*
luggage.

baggy *adjective* baggier, baggiest
hanging loosely, as in *baggy suit*.

bagpipes *plural noun*
a musical instrument with air squeezed out of a bag into a set of pipes.

bail *noun* bails
1 money paid or promised so that an accused person will not be kept in prison before coming to trial. 2 one of the two small pieces of wood placed on top of the stumps in cricket.

Usage Do not confuse **bail** with **bale** *noun*; **bale** means a large bundle.

bail *verb* bails, bailing, bailed
to scoop water out of a boat.
bailer *noun*

bait *noun*
food put on a hook or in a trap to catch fish or animals.

bait *verb* baits, baiting, baited
1 to torment an animal; to tease someone.
2 to put food on a hook or in a trap, to catch fish or animals.

bake *verb* bakes, baking, baked
1 to cook in an oven. 2 to make something very hot; to become very hot, as in *The bitumen road baked in the sun*. 3 to make something hard by heating it, as in *Pots bake in a kiln*.
baking powder, a special powder used to make cakes rise.

a b c d e f g h i j k l m n o p q r s t u v w x y z

baker

baker *noun* **bakers**
someone who makes or sells bread and cakes.
bakery *noun*

baklava *noun* (*say* **bak**-luh-vuh *or* buh-**klah**-vuh)
a type of rich Greek-Turkish cake made from flaky pastry, honey and nuts.

balaclava *noun* **balaclavas**
a usually woollen, close-fitting hood that covers all your head except your face.
[from the name of the town *Balaclava* in the Crimea where a battle was fought and where soldiers wore this kind of hood]

balance *noun* **balances**
1 a device for weighing things, with two containers hanging from a horizontal bar. 2 steadiness, as in *He lost his balance and fell over.* 3 equality, as in *We must strike a balance between cost and quality.* 4 the difference between money paid into and money taken out of an account. 5 an amount of money that is owed.

balance *verb* **balances, balancing, balanced**
to make something steady or equal; to be steady or equal.
balanced diet, the right sort and amount of food for good health.

balcony *noun* **balconies**
1 a platform sticking out from the outside wall of a building, as in *A balcony usually has railings around it and can be reached from an upstairs room.* 2 the upstairs part of a cinema or theatre.

bald *adjective* **balder, baldest**
without any or much hair on your scalp.

bale *noun* **bales**
a large, tightly bound bundle of wool, cotton, etc.

Usage Do not confuse **bale** with **bail**, a sum of money, or a piece of wood placed on top of cricket stumps.

bale *verb* **bales, baling, baled**
to clear water from the bottom of a boat.
bale out, to jump out of an aircraft with a parachute.

ball *noun* **balls**
1 a round object used in many games.
2 something round, as in *a ball of string.*
3 a grand or formal dance. 4 an enjoyable time, as in *We had a ball at the disco.*

ballad *noun* **ballads**
a simple song or poem, especially one that tells a story.

ballerina *noun* **ballerinas**
(*say* bal-uh-**ree**-nuh)
a female ballet-dancer.

ballet *noun* **ballets** (*say* **bal**-ay)
a type of entertainment performed on stage, telling a story or expressing an idea in graceful dancing and mime.
ballet-dancer *noun*

balloon *noun* **balloons**
1 a small rubber bag inflated with air or gas and used as a toy or for decoration.
2 a large round or pear-shaped bag, often carrying a basket for passengers, inflated with a light gas or hot air, so that it can rise into the air. 3 an outline in a strip cartoon containing spoken words.

ballot *noun* **ballots** (*say* **bal**-uht)
1 a secret method of voting. 2 a piece of paper on which a vote is made.

ball-point or **ball-point pen** *noun* **ball-points** or **ball-point pens**
a pen that writes with a tiny ball round which the ink flows.

ballroom *noun* **ballrooms**
a large room where dances are held.

balsa *noun* (*say* **bol**-suh *or* **bawl**-suh)
a lightweight wood used for making models, etc.

Bama *noun*
an Aborigine, especially from Queensland.

Origin This word comes from many north Queensland Aboriginal languages: **bama** = person, man. See the Aboriginal Languages map at the back of this dictionary.

bamboo *noun* **bamboos**
a tall plant with hard hollow stems which are used for canes, furniture, etc.

ban *verb* **bans, banning, banned**
to forbid.

banana *noun* **bananas**
a long, curved, soft fruit with a yellow skin.

band *noun* **bands**
1 an organised group of people, as in *a band of rock climbers.* 2 a group of musicians, as in *a rock band.* 3 a flat thin strip or loop of paper, metal, cloth, etc. put around something, especially to hold it or decorate it. 4 a strip of colour, light, etc. that contrasts with areas on either side of it, as in *A blue band was painted around the white walls.*

band *verb* **bands, banding, banded**
to join together in a group.

bandage *noun* bandages (*say* ban-dij)
a strip of material for binding a wound.

bandicoot *noun* bandicoots
a cat-sized marsupial with a long pointed head, which feeds at night on insects, plants, etc.

bandit *noun* bandits
an outlaw.

bandy *adjective* bandier, bandiest
having legs that curve outwards at the knees.

bang *noun* bangs
1 a sudden loud noise. 2 a heavy blow or knock.

bang *verb* bangs, banging, banged
1 to hit or shut noisily. 2 to make a loud noise.

banish *verb* banishes, banishing, banished
to punish someone by sending him or her away from a place.
banishment *noun*

banisters *plural noun*
a handrail with upright supports at the side of a staircase.

banjo *noun* banjos
an instrument like a guitar with a round body.

bank *noun* banks
1 sloping ground beside a river. 2 a piece of raised sloping ground. 3 a mass of cloud, fog, snow, etc. 4 a business which looks after people's money.
bankcard, a credit card issued by a bank.

bank *verb* banks, banking, banked
1 to make into a pile or heap, as in *The traffic banked up at peak hour.* 2 to round a curve in a car, aircraft, etc. with one side higher than the other, as in *The plane banked as it turned to fly to Melbourne.* 3 to put money in a bank.
bank on, (*colloquial*) to rely on, as in *'Will he bring me a present?' 'Don't bank on it.'*

banknote *noun* banknotes
a piece of paper money.

bankrupt *adjective*
unable to pay your debts.
bankruptcy *noun*

banksia *noun* banksias
a shrub or tree usually with leathery leaves and flowers of varying colour, shaped in dense spikes, as in *The banksia is a favourite Australian plant.*
[from the name of Joseph **Banks**, the naturalist]

banner *noun* banners
a large flag, piece of cloth, etc., carried on one or two poles in a procession.

banquet *noun* banquets (*say* bang-kwuht)
a great feast.

baptise or **baptize** *verb* baptises, baptising, baptised
to receive someone into the Christian Church by sprinkling him or her with water, or immersing him or her in water, and usually giving him or her Christian names.

baptism *noun* baptisms
the act of baptising.

bar *noun* bars
1 a long piece of a hard substance, as in *a metal bar.* 2 a counter or room where refreshments, especially drinks, are served. 3 one of the small equal sections into which music is divided, as in *A waltz has three beats in a bar.*
the Bar, (*in Law*) barristers as a group; the job of being a barrister.

bar *verb* bars, barring, barred
1 to fasten with a bar. 2 to prevent someone from taking part in something.

barb *noun* barbs
1 a backward-curving point on a fish-hook, spear, etc. 2 a hurtful remark.

barbarian *noun* barbarians
an uncivilised, savage person.

barbaric *adjective*
very cruel.
barbarity *noun*

barbarous *adjective*
uncivilised.
barbarism *noun*

barbecue *noun* barbecues
1 a meal where meat is cooked over charcoal, gas, etc. out of doors. 2 a place or device in which meat is cooked out of doors.

barbed wire *noun*
wire with small spikes on it, used to make fences.

barber *noun* barbers
a men's hairdresser.

bar-code *noun* bar-codes
a code made up of a series of lines and spaces, printed on goods, library books, etc., so that they can be identified by a computer, as in *Supermarket goods have barcodes which are scanned to identify the price.*

bard *noun* bards
(*old-fashioned use*) a poet or minstrel.

a
b
c
d
e
f
g
h
i
j
k
l
m
n
o
p
q
r
s
t
u
v
w
x
y
z

bardi

bardi or **bardie, bardee** *noun*
the edible part of a young beetle, moth, etc.
[from the Aboriginal language Nyungar
and other languages]

bare *adjective* **barer, barest**
1 without clothing or covering, as in *The
trees were bare.* 2 empty or almost empty,
as in *The cupboard was bare.* 3 that is only
just enough, as in *the bare necessities of
life.* 4 plain, as in *the bare facts.*
barely *adverb*

bareback *adjective* and *adverb*
riding on a horse without a saddle.

bargain *noun* **bargains**
1 an agreement to buy or sell something.
2 something bought cheaply.

bargain *verb* **bargains, bargaining, bargained**
to argue over the price of something.
bargain for something, to expect something,
as in *He got more than he bargained for.*

barge *noun* **barges**
a long, flat-bottomed cargo boat used on a
canal or river.

barge *verb* **barges, barging, barged**
to rush or bump heavily into someone.
barge in, to intrude or interrupt rudely, as
in *Must you barge in while I'm having a
private conversation?*

baritone *noun* **baritones**
a male singer with a voice between a tenor
and a bass.

bark *noun* **barks**
1 the sound made by a dog, etc. 2 the
outer covering of a tree's branches or trunk.

bark *verb* **barks, barking, barked**
1 to make the sound of a dog, etc. 2 to
scrape your skin accidentally on something.

barley *noun*
a kind of grain from which malt is made.
barley sugar, a sweet made from boiled
sugar.

bar mitzvah *noun* **bar mitzvahs**
a religious ceremony for Jewish boys who
are 13.

barn *noun* **barns**
a building on a farm where grain, stock
feed, etc. is stored.

barnacle *noun* **barnacles**
a shellfish that attaches itself to rocks and
the bottoms of ships.

barometer *noun* **barometers**
(*say* buh-**rom**-uh-tuh)
an instrument that measures air pressure,
used in forecasting the weather.
barometric *adjective*

baron *noun* **barons**
one of the lowest rank of noblemen.
baronial *adjective*

baroness *noun* **baronesses**
1 a female baron. 2 a baron's wife or
widow.

barrack *verb* **barracks, barracking,
barracked**
1 to loudly cheer and encourage a team,
etc., as in *Bruce barracked for Geelong.* 2 to
shout or jeer at players, a speaker, etc.
barracker *noun*

barracks *noun* **barracks**
a place where soldiers live.

barrage *noun* **barrages** (*say* ba-rahzh)
a concentrated attack on something,
especially of gunfire, as in *a barrage of
bullets; a barrage of questions.*

barramundi *noun*
a large, silvery-grey Australian freshwater
fish highly valued as food.

Origin This word probably comes from a
central Queensland Aboriginal language.
See the Aboriginal Languages map at the
back of this dictionary.

barrel *noun* **barrels**
1 a large cylindrical container with flat
ends. 2 the metal tube of a gun, through
which the shot is fired.

barren *adjective*
not able to produce children, crops, etc.

barricade *noun* **barricades**
a barrier, especially one put up quickly to
block a street.

barricade *verb* **barricades, barricading,
barricaded**
to block or defend a place by using a
barricade.

barrier *noun* **barriers**
1 a fence, railing, etc. to stop people
getting past. 2 an obstacle, as in *Lack of
funds has been a barrier to progress.*

barrister *noun* **barristers**
a lawyer who is allowed to act on behalf of
people in any law court.

barrow *noun* **barrows**
1 a small, two-wheeled cart used especially
by street sellers, as in *The florist sold daffodils
and carnations from a barrow.* 2 a
wheelbarrow.

barter *verb* **barters, bartering, bartered**
to exchange goods for other goods, without
using money.

base *noun* **bases**
1 the lowest part of something; the part on which a thing stands. **2** a basis.
3 headquarters, especially for the army, navy, or air force. **4** (*in Science*) a substance (such as an alkali) that combines with an acid to form a salt. **5** a system of counting and expressing numbers, as in *The decimal system uses the number 10 as its base.* **6** each of the four places which a player runs to in baseball, softball, etc.

base *verb* **bases, basing, based**
to use something to start from, as in *I will base my story on your life.*
base on or **upon,** to use something as a basis, as in *The story is based on actual events.*

baseball *noun* **baseballs**
1 a game played by two teams of nine players with a circuit of four bases which the batting player must complete. **2** the ball used in this game.

basement *noun* **basements**
a room or area of a building below ground level.

bash *verb* **bashes, bashing, bashed**
to hit hard.
bash someone up, (*colloquial*) to beat someone up.

bash *noun* **bashes**
1 a heavy blow. **2** (*colloquial*) an attempt, as in *Have a bash at it.* **3** (*colloquial*) a party or social event, as in *There's a bash to celebrate her birthday.*

bashful *adjective*
shy.

BASIC *noun*
a computer language that is designed to be easy to learn.
[from the first letter of the words *Beginners All-purpose Symbolic Instruction Code*]

basic *adjective*
1 forming a base or basis, as in *a basic knowledge of French.* **2** most important, as in *Food is a basic human need.*
basically *adverb*

basil *noun*
a sweet-smelling herb used to flavour food.

basin *noun* **basins**
1 a deep round dish, as in *a pudding-basin.* **2** a large container to hold water for washing in, as in *a wash-basin.* **3** an enclosed area of water where ships can stay safely. **4** the area of land drained by a river.

basis *noun* **bases**
1 something to start from or add to, as in

These players will be the basis of a new team.
2 the main principle or ingredient, as in *The basis of success is hard work.*

bask *verb* **basks, basking, basked**
to lie or sit comfortably warming yourself, as in *The cat basked in the warmth of the fire.*

basket *noun* **baskets**
a container, often made of woven strips of cane, etc.

basketball *noun* **basketballs**
1 a game in which players try to score points by throwing a ball through a high hoop or basket. **2** the ball used in this game.

bass *noun* **basses** (*say* bays)
the lowest adult male singer, instrument, or part in written music, as in *The part is sung by a bass.*

bass *adjective* (*say* bays)
to do with or forming the lowest sounds in music, as in *a bass note.*

basset or **basset hound** *noun* **bassets** or **basset hounds**
a small breed of dog with large, hanging ears and very short legs.

bassoon *noun* **bassoons**
a bass woodwind instrument.

bastard *noun* **bastards**
(*often insulting*)
1 a person whose parents are not married. **2** (*colloquial*) a person, especially an unpleasant or unfortunate person.

bat *noun* **bats**
1 a wooden implement used to hit the ball in cricket, baseball, and other games.
2 a flying mammal, active at night, that looks like a mouse with wings.
off your own bat, without any help from other people.

bat *verb* **bats, batting, batted**
to use a bat in cricket, etc.

batch *noun* **batches**
persons or things forming a group or dealt with together, as in *this batch of Year 6 students; a batch of letters.*

bated *adjective*
with bated breath, anxiously; hardly daring to speak.

bath *noun* **baths**
1 a large container for water in which to wash your whole body. **2** washing your whole body, as in *I'd like to have a bath.*
3 the water used in washing in this way, as in *Your bath is getting cold.*

bath *verb* **baths, bathing, bathed**
to wash in a bath, especially a baby.

bathe

bathe *verb* bathes, bathing, bathed
1 to go swimming. 2 to wash something gently, as in *Bathe the sore eyes*.
bather *noun*

bathers *plural noun*
a swimming costume; togs; cossie.

bathroom *noun* bathrooms
a room with a shower, bath, washing basin, etc.

batik *noun* (*say* **bah**-teek *or* **bat**-ik)
1 a method of dyeing cloth, etc. by covering with wax the parts not to be coloured. 2 the material treated in this way.

bat mitzvah *noun* bat mitzvahs
a religious ceremony for Jewish girls who are 13.

baton *noun* batons
a short stick, especially one used to conduct an orchestra.

batsman *noun* batsmen
a person who bats, especially in cricket; a batter.

battalion *noun* battalions
an army unit consisting of two or more companies.

batten *noun* battens
a strip of wood, as in *Battens can be used in roofs to support tiles.*

batter *noun*
a beaten mixture of flour, eggs, and milk, for making pancakes, etc.

batter *verb* batters, battering, battered
to hit hard and often.

battering-ram *noun* battering-rams
a heavy pole used to break down gates, walls, etc.

battery *noun* batteries
1 a portable device for storing and supplying electricity. 2 a series of cages in which animals are kept close together on a farm, as in *Free-range hens are not kept in batteries.* 3 a set of devices, especially a group of large guns.

battle *noun* battles
a fight between large organised forces.

battlefield *noun* battlefields
a place where a battle is or was fought.

battlements *plural noun*
the top of a castle wall, usually with notches through which arrows, etc. can be shot.

battler *noun* battlers
a person who struggles against the odds, as in *He was a real battler and stayed on his farm during the years of drought.*

battleship *noun* battleships
a heavily-armoured warship.

baulk *verb* baulks, baulking, baulked (*say* bawk)
to refuse to go on, as in *He baulked at the idea of a shorter lunch break. The horse baulked at the high fence.*

bawl *verb* bawls, bawling, bawled
1 to shout, as in *'Look out!', he bawled.* 2 to cry loudly, as in *The toddler was bawling.*

bay *noun* bays
1 a place where the shore curves inwards. 2 a compartment or area especially marked off, as in *a bomb bay; parking bay; loading bay*.
at bay, prevented from coming near someone, as in *Keep the enemy at bay*.
bay window, a window that sticks out from the wall of a house.

bay *adjective*
a dark reddish-brown colour, as in *bay horse*.

bayonet *noun* bayonets
a dagger fixed to the muzzle of a rifle.

bazaar *noun* bazaars
1 a sale to raise money for a charity, etc. 2 an oriental market.

BC short for *before Christ*, used with dates that come before the birth of Jesus, as in *Julius Caesar came to Britain in 55 BC.*

be *verb* (present tense: singular, 1st person **am**, 2nd person **are**, 3rd person **is**, plural **are**; present participle **being**; past tense: singular, 1st and 3rd persons **was**, 2nd person **were**, plural **were**; past participle **been**)
1 to exist, as in *There is a bus-stop at the corner.* 2 to go or come; to visit, as in *Has the postman been yet? Have you ever been to Africa?* 3 to have a particular description, as in *She is my teacher. You are very tall.* 4 to become, as in *She wants to be a scientist.* 5 used to form parts of other verbs, as in *It is coming. He was killed.*

beach *noun* beaches
the sandy or pebbly part of the shore, especially of the sea.

beacon *noun* beacons
a light used as a warning signal.

bead *noun* beads
1 a small piece of something hard with a hole through it, threaded on a string, cotton or wire to make a necklace, embroider a dress, etc. 2 a small drop of liquid, as in *beads of sweat.*

beady *adjective* **beadier, beadiest**
like beads, especially describing eyes that are small and bright.

beagle *noun* **beagles**
a small, short-haired dog used for hunting.

beak *noun* **beaks**
the hard, horny part of a bird's mouth.

beaker *noun* **beakers**
1 a tall mug or cup. **2** (*in Science*) a glass container for pouring liquids.

beam *noun* **beams**
1 a long, thick bar of wood or metal. **2** a ray of light or other radiation.

beam *verb* **beams, beaming, beamed**
1 to smile very happily. **2** to send out a beam of light, radio waves, etc.

bean *noun* **beans**
1 a kind of plant with seeds growing in pods. **2** the seed or pod of this kind of plant, eaten as food.
spill the beans, (*colloquial*) to reveal a secret.

bear *verb* **bears, bearing, bore, born** or **borne**
1 to carry or support. **2** to have or show, as in *The letter bore her signature.* **3** to produce, especially to give birth to children, as in *She was born in 1950. She has borne three sons.* **4** to endure or tolerate, as in *I can't bear this pain.*
bearable *adjective*

Usage See the note at **born.**

bear *noun* **bears**
a large, heavy, furry animal.

beard *noun* **beards**
hair on the lower part of a man's face.
bearded *adjective*

bearing *noun* **bearings**
1 the way you behave, walk, stand, etc.
2 the direction or relative position of something, as in *That answer has no bearing on the question.*
your bearings, knowing where you are in relation to other things, as in *I have lost my bearings.*

beast *noun* **beasts**
1 any large, four-footed animal.
2 (*colloquial*) a person or thing you dislike.
beastly *adjective*

beat *verb* **beats, beating, beat, beaten**
1 to hit someone or something often, especially with a stick. **2** to make repeated movements, as in *Feel your heart beating.* **3** to do better than someone; to overcome. **4** to stir something briskly.

5 to shape or flatten something by hitting it many times.
beat someone up, to beat someone violently.

beat *noun* **beats**
1 a regular rhythm or stroke, as in *the beat of your heart.* **2** a strong rhythm in pop music, as in *This tune has got a beat.* **3** the regular route of a person, especially a policeman or policewoman.

Beaufort scale *noun* (*say* boh-fuht skayl)
a scale for wind-speed ranging from 0 (calm) to 12 (hurricane).

beaut *adjective* (*say* byoot)
(*colloquial*) excellent; very enjoyable, as in *a beaut concert.*

beauty *noun* **beauties**
1 a quality that gives delight or pleasure, especially to your senses, as in *the beauty of the sunset.* **2** a person or thing that has beauty.
beautiful *adjective*, **beautifully** *adverb*, **beautify** *verb*

beaver *noun* **beavers**
a brown, furry, amphibious North American animal with strong teeth which builds dams in rivers.

becalmed *adjective*
unable to sail on because the wind has dropped.

became past tense of **become.**

because *conjunction*
for the reason that, as in *We were happy because it was a holiday.*
because of, for the reason of; on account of, as in *He limped because of his bad leg.*

beckon *verb* **beckons, beckoning, beckoned**
to make a sign to someone asking them to come.

become *verb* **becomes, becoming, became, become**
1 to come to be; to start being, as in *It became darker.* **2** to be suitable for; to look attractive on someone, as in *That dress becomes you.*
become of, to happen to, as in *What will become of me?*

bed *noun* **beds**
1 something for sleeping on; a place to sleep or rest, as in *I'm going to bed now.*
2 part of a garden where plants are grown. **3** the bottom of the sea or of a river. **4** a flat base; a foundation. **5** a layer of rock.

a
b
c
d
e
f
g
h
i
j
k
l
m
n
o
p
q
r
s
t
u
v
w
x
y
z

bedclothes

bedclothes *plural noun*
sheets, blankets, doonas, etc.

bedding *noun*
things for making a bed, such as sheets, blankets, doonas, mattress etc.

bedlam *noun*
a loud noise or disturbance, as in *There was bedlam at the playgroup.*

bedraggled *adjective* (*say* buh-**drag**-uhld *or* bee-**drag**-uhld)
wet and dirty.

bedridden *adjective* (*say* **bed**-rid-uhn)
too ill to get out of bed.

bedroom *noun* **bedrooms**
a room where you sleep.

bedside *noun* **bedsides**
the space beside a bed, especially the bed of someone who is ill, as in *He sat by his son's bedside all night.*

bedspread *noun* **bedspreads**
a covering put over the top of a bed.

bedtime *noun* **bedtimes**
the time when you go to bed or when you ought to go to bed.

bee *noun* **bees**
a stinging insect that makes honey.
spelling bee, a competition to test spelling skills.
working bee, a group organised to work on a community project.

beech *noun* **beeches**
a tree similar to the European variety with smooth grey bark and glossy leaves.

beef *noun*
the meat of an ox, bull, or cow, as in *roast beef for dinner.*

beehive *noun* **beehives**
a container for bees to live in.

beeline *noun*
make a beeline for something, to go quickly and directly towards something.

been past participle of **be.**

beer *noun* **beers**
an alcoholic drink made from malt and hops.

beetle *noun* **beetles**
an insect with hard, shiny covers over its wings.

beetroot *noun* **beetroot**
a dark red root vegetable.

before *adverb*
earlier; already, as in *Have you been here before?*

before *preposition*
1 sooner or earlier than, as in *the day before yesterday.* 2 in front of, as in *leg before wicket.*

beforehand *adverb*
1 earlier, as in *She had tried to phone me beforehand.* 2 before something happens, as in *Let me know beforehand if you're going to the meeting.*

beg *verb* **begs, begging, begged**
1 to ask to be given money, food, etc. 2 to ask seriously or desperately, as in *He begged me not to tell the teacher.*
I beg your pardon, I didn't hear or understand what you said; I apologise.

began past tense of **begin.**

beggar *noun* **beggars**
1 someone who lives by begging. 2 (*colloquial*) a person, as in *You lucky beggar!; you poor beggar.*

begin *verb* **begins, beginning, began, begun**
to start.

beginner *noun* **beginners**
someone who is just starting to learn or is still learning a subject.

beginning *noun* **beginnings**
the start of something.

begrudge *verb* **begrudges, begrudging, begrudged**
to resent or envy as in *He begrudged paying the bill; She did not begrudge her friend's luck.*

begun past participle of **begin.**

behalf *noun*
on behalf of someone, for someone; done to help someone.
on behalf of something, to help a cause.
on my behalf, for me.

behave *verb* **behaves, behaving, behaved**
1 to act in a particular way, as in *They behaved very badly at the party.* 2 to act in an acceptable way, as in *The polite child always behaved.*
behaviour *noun*

behead *verb* **beheads, beheading, beheaded**
to cut off someone's head.

behind *preposition*
1 at or to the back of; hidden by, as in *She hid behind a tree.* 2 not making such good progress as others, as in *He's behind the rest of the class in Japanese.* 3 supporting, as in *I am wholeheartedly behind the peace talks.*
behind someone's back, without someone knowing or approving.

behind *adverb*
1 at or to the back, as in *The others are a long way behind.* 2 staying after other people have gone, as in *We were left behind when the bus went.* 3 not making good progress; late, as in *I'm behind with my rent.*

behind *noun* **behinds**
1 (*colloquial*) a person's bottom, as in *He kicked me on the behind.* 2 (*in Australian Rules*) a scoring kick equal to one point.

beige *noun* and *adjective* (*say* bayzh)
a fawn colour.

being *noun* **beings**
1 a creature. 2 existence, as in *Experience the joy of being.*

belch *verb* **belches, belching, belched**
1 to let wind noisily out of your stomach through your mouth. 2 to send out smoke, fire, etc.

belch *noun* **belches**
the act or sound of belching.

belfry *noun* **belfries**
a tower, or part of a tower, in which bells hang.

belief *noun* **beliefs**
1 something you accept; a firm opinion, as in *It is my belief that there is life after death.* 2 trust or confidence, as in *I have a strong belief in my teacher.*

believe *verb* **believes, believing, believed**
to think that something is true or that someone is telling the truth.
believe in something, to think that something exists; to think that something is good, as in *Do you believe in ghosts? We believe in sharing our belongings.*
make believe, to pretend.
believable *adjective,* **believer** *noun*

bell *noun* **bells**
a device that makes a ringing sound, especially a cup-shaped, metal device containing a clapper.
bellbird, a small bird with a call like a bell, found in south-eastern forests of Australia.

bellow *verb* **bellows, bellowing, bellowed**
to roar or shout, as in *The bull bellowed. 'Quick march!', bellowed the sergeant.*

bellows *plural noun*
a device for blowing air into a fire, organ-pipes, etc.

belly *noun* **bellies**
the part of the body containing the stomach and the intestines.
belly button, the navel.

belong *verb* **belongs, belonging, belonged**
to have a proper place, as in *The butter belongs in the fridge.*
belong to someone, to be owned by someone, as in *That pencil belongs to me.*

belongings *plural noun*
the things that you own.

beloved *adjective* (*say* buh-**luv**-uhd *or* buh-**luvd**)
greatly loved.
beloved *noun*

below *preposition*
lower than, as in *hitting below the belt.*

below *adverb*
at or to a lower place, as in *I'll have the top bunk; you sleep below.*

belt *noun* **belts**
1 a strip of material, especially one worn round the waist. 2 a region or area, especially a narrow one, as in *a wheatbelt; the coastal belt.*

belt *verb* **belts, belting, belted**
1 to put a belt around; to fasten with a belt. 2 (*colloquial*) to hit hard.
belt out, (*colloquial*) to sing or play music very loudly.
belt up, (*colloquial*) to be quiet.

bench *noun* **benches**
1 a long seat. 2 a long table for working at. 3 (*in Sport*) an area to the side of the playing field where players not taking part can watch the game.
the bench, judges or magistrates.

bend *verb* **bends, bending, bent**
1 to make or become curved or crooked. 2 to move the top of your body downwards; to stoop.
bend over backwards, to try very hard.

bend *noun* **bends**
a curve or turn.
the bends, (*colloquial*) a sickness suffered especially by deep sea divers in which you have bubbles of gas in your blood because you have come too quickly to the surface.

beneath *preposition* and *adverb*
under, as in *Beneath this soil there is clay.*

benefactor *noun* **benefactors**
someone who gives money or other help.
benefaction *noun*

benefit *noun* **benefits**
1 advantage; help, as in *The benefit of exercise is usually good health.* 2 money paid by the government to help people who are sick, out of work, earning very little money, etc., as in *sickness benefit.*

bent

3 a game, concert, etc. to raise money for a particular person or purpose.
the benefit of the doubt, being ready to believe that someone is innocent or correct, when you cannot be sure.
beneficial *adjective*

bent *adjective*
curved or crooked.
bent on something, determined to do something.

bent *noun*
a liking or talent for something, as in *a bent for music.*

bequeath *verb* **bequeaths, bequeathing, bequeathed**
(rhymes with *breathe*)
to leave someone something in a will.
bequest *noun*

bereaved *adjective*
left sad because someone has died.
bereavement *noun*

beret *noun* **berets** (*say* be-ray)
a soft, round, flat cap.

berry *noun* **berries**
a small, juicy fruit, as in *strawberry.*

berserk *adjective*
wild and uncontrolled, as in *The angry child went berserk when the ice-cream was taken from him.*

berth *noun* **berths**
1 a sleeping-place on a ship or train. **2** a place where a ship ties up.

Usage Do not confuse **berth** with **birth**, which means being born.

beside *preposition*
1 next to; close to, as in *beside the lake.*
2 having nothing to do with, as in *That is beside the point.*
beside yourself, very excited or upset, as in *He was beside himself with grief.*

besides *preposition*
in addition to, as in *Who came besides you?*

besides *adverb*
also; in addition to this, as in *That coat costs too much. Besides, it's the wrong colour.*

besiege *verb* **besieges, besieging, besieged**
(*say* buh-**seej** *or* bee-**seej**)
1 to surround a place with troops. **2** to crowd around someone or something, as in *The pop star's hotel was besieged by hundreds of fans.*

best *adjective*, superlative of **good** and **well.**
most excellent; having the highest quality, as in *They ate the best food available.*

best man, the bridegroom's main helper at a wedding.
best seller, a book that sells in very large numbers.

best *adverb*
1 in the best way; most, as in *He did best in the race. I like this novel best.* **2** most usefully; most wisely, as in *He is best ignored.*

best *noun*
1 the best person or thing, as in *She was the best at tennis.* **2** the best people or things, as in *These apples are the best you can buy.* **3** victory, as in *We got the best of the fight.*

bet *verb* **bets, betting, bet** or **betted**
1 to risk a sum of money on the result of a race, contest, etc., as in *She always bets on the Melbourne Cup.* **2** (*colloquial*) to be certain; to predict, as in *I bet I'm right.*

bet *noun* **bets**
1 an agreement that you will pay money, etc. if you are wrong in forecasting the result of a race, contest, etc. **2** the money you risk losing in a bet.

betray *verb* **betrays, betraying, betrayed**
1 to be disloyal to a person, cause, etc., as in *The spy betrayed his country.* **2** to reveal something that should have been kept secret, as in *I betrayed my friend by reading her diary.*
betrayal *noun*

better *adjective*, comparative of **good** and **well.**
1 having a higher quality, usefulness, appeal, etc., as in *This material is better than the cheap variety. This serrated knife is better to use for cutting tomatoes. He is better looking than his brother.* **2** recovered from an illness, as in *Are you better?*

better *adverb*
1 in a better way, as in *She played better yesterday.* **2** more usefully; more wisely, as in *We had better leave now, before it's too late.*
better off, more wealthy; safer, healthier, etc., as in *Ask Rob to pay the bill—he's better off than either of us. You'd be better off if you didn't worry so much.*

better *noun* **betters**
a better person or thing, as in *The kind woman was my better.*
get the better of, to overcome something; to get an advantage over someone.

better *verb* **betters, bettering, bettered**
to improve, as in *He bettered his performance in maths with hard work. She hopes to do better than her rival in the big race.*

between *preposition*
1 within two or more given limits, as in *Call on me between Tuesday and Friday.*
2 when comparing; separating, as in *What is the difference between butter and margarine?* 3 shared among, as in *Divide these lollies between the children.*
4 connecting two or more people, places, or things, as in *The train runs between Brisbane and Sydney.*

between *adverb*
separating or connecting two or more places, etc., as in *These two houses do not touch; there is a gap between. The two towns are about fifty kilometres apart, and there is only one road between.*

beverage *noun* **beverages**
a drink.

beware *verb*
to be careful, as in *Beware of the dog.*

Usage This verb is only used when a command is being expressed and is usually followed by *of.*

bewilder *verb* **bewilders, bewildering, bewildered**
to puzzle someone completely.
bewilderment *noun*

bewitch *verb* **bewitches, bewitching, bewitched**
1 to delight someone very much, as in *Her beauty bewitched him.* 2 to put a magic spell on someone.

beyond *preposition*
1 farther than, as in *Don't go beyond the end of the street.* 2 outside the range of; too difficult for, as in *This car is beyond repair.*

beyond *adverb*
farther on, as in *You can see the next valley and the mountains beyond.*

bias *noun* **biases**
1 a feeling of prejudice or favouritism, as in *A bias against football prevented him from enjoying the game. The teacher chose Sally because of her bias towards girls.* 2 a tendency or direction, as in *The results showed a bias in favour of change.*
biased *adjective*

bib *noun* **bibs**
1 a cloth, etc. put under a baby's chin during meals. 2 the top part of an apron or overalls.

Bible *noun* **Bibles**
the holy book of Christianity and Judaism.
biblical *adjective*

bibliography *noun* **bibliographies**
1 a list of books, etc. read or referred to by a writer of a book, article, project, etc. 2 a list of books on a particular subject, as in *a bibliography on Australia's native animals.*

bicentenary *noun* **bicentenaries**
(*say* buy-suhn-**ten**-uh-ree *or* buy-suhn-**teen**-uh-ree)
a two-hundredth anniversary.
bicentennial *noun* and *adjective*

bicycle *noun* **bicycles**
a two-wheeled vehicle driven by pedals.

bid *verb* **bids, bidding, bid**
to offer an amount of money, as in *She bid $1000 for the antique chair.*

bid *noun* **bids**
1 an amount offered for something, especially at an auction. 2 an attempt, as in *He will make a bid for the world record.*

big *adjective* **bigger, biggest**
1 large. 2 important. 3 elder, as in *my big sister.*

bigamy *noun* **bigamies**
the crime of having two or more wives or husbands at the same time.
bigamist *noun*, **bigamous** *adjective*

bike *noun* **bikes**
(*colloquial*) a bicycle or motor cycle.

bikini *noun* **bikinis**
a woman's two-piece bathing-costume that covers very little of her body.

bilby *noun* **bilbies**
a burrowing marsupial bandicoot found in the woodlands and plains of the drier parts of Australia; a dalgite.

Origin This word comes from Yuwaalaraay, an Aboriginal language of New South Wales: **bilbi**. See the Aboriginal Languages map at the back of this dictionary.

bile *noun*
a bitter, greenish-brown fluid produced in the liver, that helps the body to digest fat.

bilge *noun* **bilges**
1 the bottom of a ship. 2 the filthy water that collects inside the bottom of a ship.

bilingual *adjective*
able to speak two languages; dealing with two languages, as in *a bilingual teacher; a bilingual dictionary.*

bill *noun* **bills**
1 an account showing how much money is owing. 2 the plan for a proposed law.
3 a poster. 4 a program of entertainment, as in *There's a magician on the bill.* 5 a bird's beak.

billabong

billabong *noun* **billabongs**
a creek, pool, lagoon, etc. formed when a river floods or when floodwaters recede.

billiards *noun*
a game played with long sticks (called *cues*) and three balls on a cloth-covered table.

billion *noun* **billions**
1 a thousand millions (1,000,000,000).
2 (*less common*) a million millions (1,000,000,000,000).

billow *noun* **billows**
a large wave, as in *the billows of the sea*.
billowy *adjective*

billow *verb* **billows, billowing, billowed**
to rise up or move like waves on the sea, as in *a yacht with billowing sails*.

billy *noun* **billies** or **billycans**
a can with a lid and wire handle, used especially for boiling water, making tea, etc. over an open fire in the bush.

billycart *noun* **billycarts**
a small four-wheeled cart which you control by ropes attached to the front wheels.

billy-goat *noun* **billy-goats**
a male goat.

bin *noun* **bins**
a large or deep container, as in *garbage bin; wheat bin*.

binary *adjective*
involving sets of two; consisting of two parts.
binary system, a system of expressing numbers by using the digits 0 and 1 only, as in *In the binary system, 21 is written 10101.*

bind *verb* **binds, binding, bound**
1 to tie up or tie together. 2 to make someone do something or promise something. 3 to fasten material round something. 4 to fasten the pages of a book inside a cover.

bindi-eye or **bindy-eye** *noun* **bindi-eyes**
a small prickly weed.

Origin This word comes from the Aboriginal languages Kamilaroi and Yuwaalaraay **bindayaa**. See the Aboriginal Languages map at the back of this dictionary.

bingo *noun*
a game played with cards on which numbered squares are covered or crossed out as the numbers are called out at random.

binoculars *plural noun*
a device with lenses for both eyes, for making distant objects seem nearer.

biodegradable *adjective*
able to be broken down by bacteria in the environment, as in *a biodegradable washing-powder*.

biography *noun* **biographies**
the story of a person's life.
biographer *noun*, **biographical** *adjective*

biology *noun*
the science or study of living things.
biological *adjective*, **biologist** *noun*

biomass *noun*
the total amount or weight of living things in a particular area.

bionic *adjective*
worked by or containing electronic devices, but behaving like a living being, as in *They designed a bionic man*.

biopsy *noun* **biopsies**
the examination of tissue removed from the body to discover whether there is disease.

biosphere *noun*
the parts of the earth's surface and its atmosphere where living things are found.

birch *noun* **birches**
a thin tree with shiny bark and slender branches growing in cool climates.

bird *noun* **birds**
1 a feathered animal with two wings and two legs. 2 (*colloquial*) a young woman.
bird's-eye view, a general view of something, especially from above.

birth *noun* **births**
1 being born. 2 the beginning, as in *the birth of civilisation*.
birth certificate, a document showing where and when you were born.
birth control, ways of avoiding making a baby.
birth rate, the number of children born in one year for every 1,000 of the population.

Usage Do not confuse **birth** with **berth**, which means a sleeping-place, or a place where a ship ties up.

birthday *noun* **birthdays**
the anniversary of the day you were born.

birthmark *noun* **birthmarks**
a mark which has been on your body since you were born.

birthplace *noun* **birthplaces**
where you were born.

biscuit *noun* **biscuits**
a flat, thin cake, usually crisp and
sometimes sweet.

bisect *verb* **bisects, bisecting, bisected**
to divide something into two equal parts.

bishop *noun* **bishops**
1 an important clergyman in charge of all
the churches in a city or district. 2 a
chess-piece shaped rather like a bishop's
mitre.

bison *noun* **bison**
a hairy, buffalo-like creature of the northern
hemisphere, with a large head and
shoulders.

bistro *noun* **bistros**
a small casual restaurant or wine bar.

bit *noun* **bits**
1 a small piece or amount of something.
2 the part of a horse's bridle that is put into
its mouth. 3 the part of a tool that cuts or
grips. 4 (*in Computing*) a unit of
information expressed as a choice between
two possibilities.
a bit, slightly, as in *I'm a bit worried.*
bit by bit, gradually.
bits and pieces, oddments.

bit past tense of **bite** *verb.*

bitch *noun* **bitches**
1 a female dog, fox, or wolf. 2 (*offensive
colloquial*) a spiteful or unpleasant
woman. 3 (*colloquial*) an unpleasant
thing, as in *That was a bitch of a job!*

bitchy *adjective* **bitchier, bitchiest**
(*colloquial*) spiteful, as in *Stop making bitchy
remarks about Joan!*

bite *verb* **bites, biting, bit, bitten**
1 to cut or take with your teeth. 2 to
penetrate, as in *The tyres bit into the mud.*
3 to accept bait, as in *The fish are biting.*
4 to sting or hurt, as in *a biting wind.*
bite the dust, to be killed.

bite *noun* **bites**
1 the act of biting. 2 a mark or spot made
by biting, as in *a snake bite.* 3 a snack.

bitter *adjective*
1 not sweet; tasting unpleasant.
2 resentful; envious, as in *She was bitter
towards the winner.* 3 difficult to accept or
bear, as in *a bitter disappointment.* 4 very
cold, as in *a bitter wind.*

bitumen *noun* (*say* **bich**-uh-muhn)
1 a mixture like tar used for making
roads. 2 a tarred road.

bizarre *adjective* (*say* buh-**zah**)
very strange; eccentric.

black *adjective* **blacker, blackest**
1 having the very darkest colour, like
coal. 2 with very dark skin, especially an
Aborigine or African. 3 dismal; not
hopeful, as in *The outlook is black.* 4 very
dirty. 5 evil, as in *Murder is a black deed.*
black and blue, bruised.
black coffee, coffee without milk or cream.
black eye, an eye with a bruise around it.
black hole, (*in Astronomy*) a region in space
with such strong gravity that no light
escapes.
black market, illegal trading.

black *noun* **blacks**
1 the colour, as in *The mourner was dressed
in black.* 2 a person with very dark skin.

blackberry *noun* **blackberries**
a sweet black berry which grows on a
prickly bush.

blackboard *noun* **blackboards**
a dark board for writing on with chalk.

blacken *verb* **blackens, blackening,
blackened**
to make or become black.

blackmail *verb* **blackmails, blackmailing,
blackmailed**
to get money from someone by threatening
to reveal something that he or she wants to
keep secret.

blackout *noun* **blackouts**
1 losing consciousness or memory for a
short time. 2 a time when there is a
power failure.

blacksmith *noun* **blacksmiths**
someone who makes and repairs things
made of iron, especially someone who
makes and fits shoes for horses.

bladder *noun* **bladders**
1 the bag-like part of the body in which
urine collects. 2 the inflatable bag inside
a football.

blade *noun* **blades**
1 the sharp part of a knife, sword, axe,
etc. 2 the flat, wide part of an oar,
propeller, etc. 3 a long narrow leaf, as in *a
blade of grass.*

blame *verb* **blames, blaming, blamed**
to say that someone or something has
caused what is wrong, as in *My brother
broke the window but Mum blamed me!*
he is to blame, he is the person who caused
what is wrong.

blame *noun*
the responsibility for causing something
bad to happen, as in *I got the blame for what
he did.*

blameless

blameless *adjective*
having done no wrong; innocent.

blank *adjective*
1 not written, drawn, or printed on, as in *blank paper.* 2 without interest or expression, as in *a blank face.* 3 empty, as in *When she asked me what was special about today, my mind went blank.*
blank cartridge, a cartridge which makes a noise but does not fire a bullet.
blank verse, poetry without rhymes.

blank *noun* **blanks**
1 an empty space. 2 a blank cartridge.
draw a blank, not to get the result you wanted, as in *I looked for my gloves in the garage, but drew a blank.*

blanket *noun* **blankets**
a large cloth especially one made from wool, used as a warm covering for a bed.

blare *verb* **blares, blaring, blared**
to make a harsh, loud sound.

blaspheme *verb* **blasphemes, blaspheming, blasphemed**
to talk without respect about sacred things.
blasphemous *adjective*, **blasphemy** *noun*

blast *noun* **blasts**
1 a strong rush of wind or air. 2 a loud noise or explosion, as in *a blast of trumpets; a dynamite blast.*
blast-off, the launching of a spacecraft.

blast *verb* **blasts, blasting, blasted**
1 to blow something up with explosives.
2 (*colloquial*) to criticise severely, as in *The students were blasted for their laziness.*

blatant *adjective*
not hidden in any way; obvious, as in *The thief left blatant clues and was soon caught.*

blaze *noun* **blazes**
a very bright flame, fire, or light.

blaze *verb* **blazes, blazing, blazed**
1 to burn or shine brightly. 2 to feel very strongly, as in *He was blazing with anger.*
blaze a trail, to show the way for others to follow.

blazer *noun* **blazers**
a kind of jacket, often with a badge on the top pocket, as in *The school uniform included a blazer.*

bleach *verb* **bleaches, bleaching, bleached**
to make or become white.

bleach *noun* **bleaches**
a substance to make things white, to clean things, and to kill germs.

bleak *adjective* **bleaker, bleakest**
1 bare and cold, as in *the bleak Monaro plains.* 2 dreary; miserable, as in *The future looks bleak.*

bleary *adjective* **blearier, bleariest**
with eyes that do not see clearly; blurred.

bleat *verb* **bleats, bleating, bleated**
1 to make a bleat, as in *The lamb bleated for its mother.* 2 to speak in a complaining voice, as in *The child bleated about wanting another toy.*

bleat *noun* **bleats**
the cry of a lamb, calf, etc.

bleed *verb* **bleeds, bleeding, bled**
1 to lose blood. 2 to draw blood from someone or an animal.

bleep *noun* **bleeps**
a small, high sound such as some digital watches make.

blemish *noun* **blemishes**
a flaw or imperfection.

blend *verb* **blends, blending, blended**
to mix together smoothly or easily.

blender *noun* **blender**
a machine for liquidising or chopping food.

bless *verb* **blesses, blessing, blessed**
1 to wish or bring someone happiness.
2 to make or call a person or thing holy.

blessing *noun* **blessings**
1 being blessed. 2 a short prayer.
3 something you are glad of, as in *It's a blessing that they are safe.*

blew past tense of **blow** *verb*.

blight *noun* **blights**
1 a plant disease. 2 an evil influence, as in *Drug abuse is a blight on the community.*

blind *adjective* **blinder, blindest**
1 unable to see. 2 without thought or understanding, as in *The selfish person was blind to the needs of others.*
blind alley, a road which has one end closed.

blind *verb* **blinds, blinding, blinded**
1 to take away a person's sight, as in *He was blinded by the car accident. For a moment, I was blinded by the sun.* 2 to deceive, as in *blinded by flattery.*

blind *noun* **blinds**
1 a screen for a window. 2 something used to hide the truth, as in *His story of having been away on a business trip was just a blind.*

blindfold *verb* **blindfolds, blindfolding, blindfolded**
to cover someone's eyes with a cloth so that the person cannot see where he or she is, or what is happening.

blindfold *noun* blindfolds
a piece of cloth used to cover someone's eyes so that the person cannot see where he or she is, or what is happening.

blink *verb* blinks, blinking, blinked
to shut and open your eyes quickly.

bliss *noun*
great happiness.
blissful *adjective*, **blissfully** *adverb*

blister *noun* blisters
a watery swelling like a bubble on your skin, as in *Hot sun can cause blisters on unprotected skin.*

blitz *noun* blitzes
a sudden, violent attack, especially from aircraft, as in *the blitz on London during the war; a police blitz on speeding drivers.*

blizzard *noun* blizzards
a severe snowstorm.

bloated *adjective*
swollen by fat, gas, or liquid.

blob *noun* blobs
a small round mass of something, as in *blobs of paint.*

block *noun* blocks
1 a solid piece of something. 2 an obstruction. 3 a large building or group of buildings with streets all around it. 4 a piece of land on which a house is built.
block letters, capital letters.

block *verb* blocks, blocking, blocked
1 to obstruct, as in *Tall buildings blocked our view.* 2 to stop up, as in *Leaves blocked the drain.*

blockade *noun* blockades
the surrounding or blocking of a place by an enemy to prevent entry and exit especially of supplies, as in *They blockaded the city to prevent food supplies from entering.*

bloke *noun* blokes
(*colloquial*) a man or fellow.

blond or **blonde** *adjective* blonder, blondest
fair-haired.

blonde *noun* blondes
a fair-haired girl or woman.

blood *noun*
1 the red liquid that flows through veins and arteries. 2 your race, descent, or parentage, as in *The cousins were of the same blood.*
blood donor, someone who gives some blood for use in transfusions.
in cold blood, deliberately and cruelly.

bloodbath *noun* bloodbaths
the killing of a large number of people; a massacre

bloodhound *noun* bloodhounds
a large breed of dog used to track people by their scent.

bloodshed *noun*
the killing and injuring of people.

bloodshot *adjective*
having eyes streaked with red.

bloodstream *noun*
the blood flowing round the body.

bloodthirsty *adjective* bloodthirstier, bloodthirstiest
eager to kill; involving a lot of killing, as in *a bloodthirsty film.*

bloody *adjective* bloodier, bloodiest
1 bleeding, as in *a bloody cut.* 2 involving bloodshed, as in *a bloody battle.*
3 (*colloquial*) very great, as in *You're a bloody fool. You're a bloody marvel.*
bloody-minded, deliberately awkward or not helpful.

bloom *noun* blooms
a flower.
in bloom, flowering.

blossom *noun* blossoms
a mass of flowers, especially on a fruit-tree.

blossom *verb* blossoms, blossoming, blossomed
1 to produce flowers. 2 to develop into something, as in *She blossomed into a fine singer.*

blot *noun* blots
1 a spot or blob of ink. 2 a flaw or fault.

blot *verb* blots, blotting, blotted
1 to make a blot on something, as in *She blotted her tunic with paint.* 2 to dry with blotting-paper, tissue, etc., as in *She blotted up the spilt milk with a towel.*
blot out, to take away or delete, as in *She blotted out the awful experience with a holiday.*
blot your copybook, to spoil your good reputation.

blotch *noun* blotches
an untidy patch of colour.
blotchy *adjective*

blouse *noun* blouses
a piece of women's clothing like a shirt.

blow *verb* blows, blowing, blew, blown
1 to move in or with a current of air, as in *Her hat blew off.* 2 to push air from your mouth or nose, as in *He blew out the candles.* 3 to make something by blowing,

blow

as in *Let's blow bubbles.* **4** to make a sound by blowing, as in *Blow the whistle.* **5** to melt with too strong an electric current, as in *A fuse has blown.* **6** (*colloquial*) to waste, as in *He blew $50 on a bet.*
blow up, to destroy by an explosion; to explode; to inflate, as in *Guerrillas blew up the radio station. The store of dynamite blew up. Blow up the balloons.*

blow *noun* **blows**
  1 the act of blowing, as in *Give your nose a blow.* **2** a storm with high winds, as in *The big blow damaged many of Broome's buildings.* **3** a hard knock or hit. **4** a shock; a disaster, as in *His death was a great blow. The disaster was a major blow for the space program.*
  blow-in, (*colloquial*) a person who arrives unexpectedly.
  blowtorch, a device for directing an intense flame at something.

blowfly *noun* **blowflies**
  a large fly which lays eggs in meat, wounds, flesh of animals, etc.
  blowie, (*colloquial*) a blowfly.

blubber *noun* **blubbers**
  whale fat.

blubber *verb* **blubbers, blubbering, blubbered**
  to sob in a noisy way.

bludge *verb* **bludges, bludging, bludged**
  (*colloquial*) to avoid work or live off the efforts of others.
  bludger *noun*

blue *adjective* **bluer, bluest**
  1 blue in colour. **2** miserable; depressed. **3** obscene, as in *blue movies.*
  once in a blue moon, very rarely.
  true-blue, very loyal or genuine.

blue *noun*
  1 a colour like the colour of a cloudless sky. **2** (*colloquial*) a fight or mistake.
  out of the blue, with no warning, as in *Out of the blue, my friend Rob turned up.*

bluebottle *noun* **bluebottles**
  1 a jellyfish with a poisonous sting. **2** a large, bluish-green fly.

blue heeler *noun* **blue heelers**
  a highly intelligent Australian cattle dog with a blue or red flecked coat; a heeler.

blueprint *noun* **blueprints**
  a detailed plan.

blues *plural noun*
  a type of sad song or tune of black American origin.
  the blues, a very sad feeling.

blue-tongue *noun* **blue-tongues**
  a large lizard with a broad blue tongue.

bluff *verb* **bluffs, bluffing, bluffed**
  to deceive someone by pretending, especially by pretending to be able to do something.

bluff *noun* **bluffs**
  something that someone pretends in order to deceive someone else; a threat that someone makes but is unlikely to carry out, as in *He said he'd report us, but that was just a bluff.*
  call someone's bluff, to challenge someone to do what he or she has threatened to do, because you think that he or she will not or cannot do it.

blunder *noun* **blunders**
  a foolish mistake.

blunt *adjective* **blunter, bluntest**
  1 not sharp, as in *blunt knife.* **2** direct, outspoken, as in *The blunt criticism of her project upset the student.*

blur *verb* **blurs, blurring, blurred**
  to make or become unclear or smeared.

blurb *noun* **blurbs**
  a description that praises something, especially a book.

blush *verb* **blushes, blushing, blushed**
  to become red in the face, especially when you are embarrassed.

bluster *verb* **blusters, blustering, blustered**
  1 to blow in gusts. **2** to behave in a noisy or pompous way, as in *He blustered his way through the interview.*
  blustery *adjective*

BMX *noun* **BMXs**
  a bicycle with a strong frame suitable for riding on rough surfaces.
  [from the abbreviation of *bicycle motocross, cross* being represented by an 'X']

boa or **boa constrictor** *noun* **boas** or **boa constrictors**
  a large South American snake that crushes its prey.

boar *noun* **boars**
  a male pig.

board *noun* **boards**
  1 a flat piece of wood. **2** a flat piece of wood set up for a particular purpose, as in *an ironing board; a notice-board.* **3** the provision of regular meals, usually with accommodation, for payment. **4** a committee, as in *school board.*
  board-game, a game played on a board, such as chess or draughts.
  on board, aboard.

board *verb* **boards, boarding, boarded**
1 to go on to a ship, plane, etc.   2 to give or get meals and accommodation.
board over or **up**, to cover something with boards.

boarder *noun* **boarders**
1 a child that lives at a boarding-school during the term.   2 a person who pays for a room and meals.

boarding-school *noun* **boarding-schools**
a school in which children live during the term.

boast *verb* **boasts, boasting, boasted**
to be proud, especially in talking, as in *She boasted about her talented children*.
boastful *adjective*, **boastfully** *adverb*

boat *noun* **boats**
a device built to float and travel on water.
boat people, refugees who leave their country by sea, as in *Many boat people have settled here*.
in the same boat, in the same situation; having the same difficulties.

bob *verb* **bobs, bobbing, bobbed**
to move quickly, especially up and down.

bobcat *noun* **bobcats**
1 a small North American wild cat.   2 a small, four-wheeled, earth-moving machine.

bodice *noun* **bodices**
the upper part of a woman's dress.

bodily *adjective*
to do with your body, as in *bodily functions*.

bodily *adverb*
so as to move the whole of someone or something, as in *He was picked up bodily and bundled into the kidnappers' car*.

body *noun* **bodies**
1 the flesh, bones, etc. of a person or animal.   2 a corpse.   3 the main part of something, as in *the body of the car*.   4 a group of people, things, etc., as in *a body of actors; a body of facts*.   5 a distinct object or piece of matter, as in *Stars and planets are heavenly bodies*.
body-building, making your body strong and muscular by doing things like lifting heavy weights, exercising, and eating special foods.

bodyguard *noun* **bodyguards**
a guard to protect someone's life.

bog *noun* **bogs**
an area of wet, spongy ground.
boggy *adjective*

bog *verb* **bogs, bogging, bogged**
to become stuck, as in *bogged in the mud; bogged down by difficulty*.

bogan *noun* **bogans**
(*colloquial*) a person who is not 'with it' in behaviour, dress, etc. and is seen as not acceptable.

bogey *noun* **bogeys** or **bogies** (*say* **bohg**-gee)
an evil or mischievous spirit.
bogeyman, a real or imagined person causing fear.

bogey *noun*
1 a swim or bath.   2 a swimming hole.

Origin This word comes from the Aboriginal language Dharuk: **bugi** = swim or dive.

bogong *noun* **bogongs** (*say* **boh**-gong)
a large brown moth which breeds on the southern plains, used as a food by Aborigines.

Origin This word comes from the Aboriginal language Ngarigo: **bugung**.

boil *verb* **boils, boiling, boiled**
1 to make or become hot enough to bubble and give off vapour.   2 to cook something in water that is bubbling and giving off steam; to be in that state, as in *I boiled the potatoes. The kettle is boiling*.
be boiling, (*colloquial*) to feel or be very hot.

boil *noun* **boils**
an inflamed spot on the skin.

boiler *noun* **boilers**
1 a container in which water is heated for boiling things, as in *The chef cooked the Christmas pudding in the boiler*.   2 an apparatus for providing a hot water supply, steam and heat.
boiler suit, overalls with sleeves usually worn when a person does dirty work.

boiling-point *noun* **boiling-points**
the temperature at which something boils.

boisterous *adjective*
noisy and lively.

bold *adjective* **bolder, boldest**
1 brave, as in *a bold soldier*.   2 impudent, as in *a bold child*.   3 clear; easy to see, as in *bold outline*.

bollard *noun* **bollards**
1 a short, thick post to direct or keep out traffic.   2 a short, thick post on a ship, quay, etc. to which ropes are attached.

bolster *noun* **bolsters**
a long pillow.

a
b
c
d
e
f
g
h
i
j
k
l
m
n
o
p
q
r
s
t
u
v
w
x
y
z

bolster

bolster *verb* **bolsters, bolstering, bolstered**
to raise or increase something, as in *Her success bolstered her confidence.*
bolster up, to support or encourage someone; to help something that is weak.

bolt *noun* **bolts**
1 a sliding bar for fastening a door. 2 a thick metal pin for fastening things together. 3 a sliding bar that opens and closes the breech of a rifle. 4 a flash of lightning.
a bolt from the blue, a surprise, usually unpleasant.

bolt *verb* **bolts, bolting, bolted**
1 to fasten with a bolt. 2 to run away, as in *The horse bolted.* 3 to swallow food quickly.

bomb *noun* **bombs**
a device that explodes.
the bomb, nuclear weapons.

bomb *verb* **bombs, bombing, bombed**
to attack with bombs.

bombard *verb* **bombards, bombarding, bombarded**
1 to attack with gunfire. 2 to direct a large number of questions, complaints, etc. at someone.
bombardment *noun*

bomber *noun* **bombers**
1 an aircraft built to drop bombs. 2 a person who uses bombs, especially a terrorist.

bond *noun* **bonds**
1 something that binds, restrains, or unites. 2 a document stating an agreement.

bondage *noun*
the condition of belonging to someone else as his or her slave.

bone *noun* **bones**
one of the hard pieces of a skeleton.
have a bone to pick with someone, to want to argue with someone about something.

bonfire *noun* **bonfires**
an outdoor fire to burn rubbish or celebrate something.

bonnet *noun* **bonnets**
1 the hinged cover over a car engine. 2 a round hat usually tied under someone's chin.

bonus *noun* **bonuses**
an extra payment or benefit in addition to what you get or expect.

bony *adjective* **bonier, boniest**
1 thin. 2 with big bones.

bonzer *adjective*
(*colloquial*) excellent, as in *a bonzer holiday.*

boodie *noun* **boodies**
a burrowing rat kangaroo found only on islands off the Western Australian coast.

Origin This word comes from the Aboriginal language Nyungar: **burdi**. See the Aboriginal Languages map at the back of this dictionary.

book *noun* **books**
a set of sheets of paper, usually with printing or writing on, fastened together inside a cover.

book *verb* **books, booking, booked**
1 to reserve a place in a theatre, hotel, plane, etc. 2 to note the personal details of a rule-breaker, etc., as in *He was booked for speeding.*
book in, to record that you have arrived in a place such as a hotel.

bookcase *noun* **bookcases**
a piece of furniture designed to hold books.

bookkeeping *noun*
recording details of buying, selling, etc.

booklet *noun* **booklets**
a small book.

bookmaker *noun* **bookmakers**
a person whose business is taking bets, especially bets made on horse-races.
bookie, (*colloquial*) a bookmaker.

bookmark *noun* **bookmarks**
something to mark a place in a book.

boom *noun* **booms**
1 a deep, hollow sound. 2 prosperity; growth. 3 a long pole at the bottom of a sail to keep it stretched. 4 a long pole carrying a microphone, etc.

boom *verb* **booms, booming, boomed**
1 to make a deep, hollow sound, as in *The guns boomed continually.* 2 to be prosperous, as in *Business is booming.*

boomer *noun* **boomers**
a large adult male kangaroo.

boomerang *noun* **boomerangs**
a curved stick, wooden missile used by Aborigines in hunting, warfare and in recreation and often one which returns in flight to the thrower.

Origin This word comes from the Aboriginal language Dharuk, probably **bumaring**. See the Aboriginal Languages map at the back of this dictionary.

boost *verb* **boosts, boosting, boosted**
to increase the power, value, or reputation of a person or thing.

booster *noun* **boosters**
1 something that increases the power of a system, especially a radio or television transmitter. 2 an additional engine or rocket for a spacecraft, etc. 3 an additional dose of a vaccine.

boot *noun* **boots**
1 a shoe that covers the ankle or leg. 2 the compartment for luggage in a car. 3 (*colloquial*) a firm kick.
the boot is on the other foot, the situation has been reversed.

boot *verb* **boots, booting, booted**
1 to kick. 2 to make a computer ready.
boot out, to get rid of forcefully.

booth *noun* **booths**
a small enclosure for telephoning, voting, etc.

booze *noun*
(*colloquial*) alcoholic drink.
boozer, (*colloquial*) a drinker or the pub a person drinks at.

border *noun* **borders**
1 a boundary, as in *the South Australian border*. 2 an edge, as in *There is a black border around the poster*.

borderline *adjective*
being on the edge of, as in *a borderline pass in the test*.

bore *verb* **bores, boring, bored**
1 to drill a hole. 2 to make someone feel tired and uninterested, as in *The children were bored by the long lecture*.

bore *noun* **bores**
1 a man-made, deep hole, especially to find water. 2 a person who makes you feel tired and uninterested. 3 something uninteresting or annoying.
boredom *noun*

bore past tense of **bear** *verb*.

borer *noun* **borers**
an insect which bores into wood, other plant material, etc.

born or **borne** past participle of **bear** *verb*.

Usage **Born** is used in sentences such as *Their son was born on 17 December. Their second child will have been born by now.* **borne** is used in sentences like *She has borne three children.*

borrow *verb* **borrows, borrowing, borrowed**
to be lent something.

bosom *noun* **bosoms**
a person's breast.

boss *noun* **bosses**
(*colloquial*) a person who controls a business, workers, etc.

bossy *adjective* **bossier, bossiest**
fond of ordering people about.

botany *noun*
the study of plants.
botanical *adjective*, **botanist** *noun*

both *adjective* and *pronoun*
the two; not only one, as in *Are both films good? Both are interesting.*

both *adverb*
both … and, not only … but also, as in *This house is both small and ugly.*

bother *verb* **bothers, bothering, bothered**
1 to cause someone trouble or worry. 2 to take trouble about something; to be concerned.

bother *noun* **bothers**
trouble or worry.

bottle *noun* **bottles**
a narrow-necked container for liquids.

bottle *verb* **bottles, bottling, bottled**
to put something in a bottle or bottles, as in *to bottle wine*.

bottlebrush *noun* **bottlebrushes**
a shrub or small tree whose flowers are shaped like a brush

bottleneck *noun* **bottlenecks**
a place where something, especially traffic, cannot flow freely.

bottom *noun* **bottoms**
1 the base of something. 2 the farthest part of something, as in *Go to the bottom of the garden*. 3 a person's buttocks.

bottomless *adjective*
1 very deep. 2 inexhaustible, as in *a bottomless supply of money*.

bough *noun* **boughs**
(rhymes with *cow*)
a branch of a tree.

bought past tense and past participle of **buy** *verb*.

boulder *noun* **boulders**
a large smooth stone.

bounce *verb* **bounces, bouncing, bounced**
1 to spring back when thrown against something. 2 to make a ball, etc. bounce. 3 to move to and fro; to jump about. 4 (of a cheque) to be sent back by a bank because it is worthless.

bounce

bounce *noun* **bounces**
1 the action of bouncing. 2 liveliness, as in *She was full of bounce after she won lotto.*
bouncy *adjective*

bouncing *adjective*
big and healthy, as in *a bouncing baby.*

bound past tense and past participle of **bind** *verb.*

bound *adjective*
bound for, travelling towards, as in *This train is bound for Kalgoorlie.*
bound to, certain to; obliged to, as in *He is bound to come.*
bound up with, closely connected with, as in *His illness is bound up with smoking.*

bound *verb* **bounds, bounding, bounded**
to leap; to run with leaping steps.

bound *noun* **bounds**
a springy leap, as in *The kangaroo came towards us in a bound.*

boundary *noun* **boundaries**
1 a line that marks a limit. 2 a hit to the outer edge of a cricket field, scoring four or six runs.

bounds *plural noun*
a boundary, as in *beyond the bounds of common sense.*
out of bounds, where you are not allowed to go, as in *The teachers' car park is out of bounds to pupils.*

bountiful *adjective*
generous or more than enough, as in *They grew a bountiful supply of tomatoes in summer.*

bouquet *noun* **bouquets** (*say* boo-**kay** *or* boh-**kay**)
a bunch of flowers.

boutique *noun* **boutiques** (*say* boo-**teek**)
a small shop, especially one that sells fashionable clothes.

bow *noun* **bows**
(rhymes with *go*)
1 a knot made with loops. 2 the stick used for playing a violin, cello, etc. 3 a device for shooting arrows.
bow-legged, bandy.
bow-tie, a necktie tied in a bow.

bow *noun* **bows**
(rhymes with *cow*)
1 the front part of a ship. 2 bowing your body, as in *The waiter gave a bow.*

bow *verb* **bows, bowing, bowed**
(rhymes with *cow*)
to bend your body forwards to show respect or submission, as in *He bowed to the Queen.*

bowel or **bowels** *noun*
the large intestine which carries food from the stomach.

bowerbird *noun* **bowerbirds**
a bird which builds leafy shelters decorated with feathers, shells, etc. during courting with his mate.

bowl *noun* **bowls**
1 a deep, round dish. 2 an object shaped like a bowl, as in *toilet bowl; bowl of a spoon.*
3 a hard heavy ball made to run in a curve.

bowl *verb* **bowls, bowling, bowled**
(*in Cricket*) 1 to send a ball towards a batsman. 2 to get a batsman out by hitting the wicket with the ball.

bowler *noun* **bowlers**
1 a player who bowls to the batter.
2 a bowls-player, as in *tenpin bowler.*
3 a hard felt hat with a rounded top.

bowling *noun*
1 the game of bowls. 2 the game of knocking down skittles with a ball. 3 the action of throwing a cricket ball, as in *His bowling was very fast.*

bowls *plural noun*
a game played by rolling heavy balls towards a target.

box *noun* **boxes**
1 a container made of wood, cardboard, etc. 2 a compartment in a theatre, lawcourt, etc., as in *witness-box.* 3 a hut or shelter, as in *sentry-box.* 4 a type of eucalypt with fibre-like bark, as in *yellow box gum.*
box number, a number to show where answers should be sent to a newspaper advertisement, etc.
box office, a place where you can book seats for a theatre, cinema, etc.
the box, (*colloquial*) television.

box *verb* **boxes, boxing, boxed**
1 to fight with fists.
boxing, fighting with the fists, especially as a sport.

boxer *noun* **boxers**
someone who boxes, especially as a sport.

Boxing Day *noun* **Boxing Days**
the day after Christmas Day.

boy *noun* **boys**
1 a young male person. 2 a son, as in *My boy's just learned to sail.*
boyhood *noun,* **boyish** *adjective*

boycott *verb* **boycotts, boycotting, boycotted**
to refuse to have anything to do with, as in *They boycotted the buses when the fares went up.*

boyfriend *noun* **boyfriends**
a girl's or woman's regular male friend or
lover.

bra *noun* **bras**
underwear worn by women to support the
breasts.
[from an abbreviation of *brassière*]

brace *noun* **braces**
1 a device for holding something in
place. 2 a wire device for straightening
your teeth.
braces straps worn over your shoulders to
hold trousers up.

bracelet *noun* **bracelets**
an ornament worn round the wrist.

brachiosaurus *noun* **brachiosauruses**
(*say* bray-kee-uh-**saw**-ruhs *or*
brak-ee-uh-**saw**-ruhs)
a plant-eating dinosaur with front legs
longer than the back legs.

bracken *noun*
a large coarse fern that is widespread in
cool areas; a mass of these ferns.

bracket *noun* **brackets**
1 a mark used in pairs to enclose words or
figures, as in *There are round brackets ( ) and
square brackets [ ].* 2 a support attached to
a wall, etc., as in *Shelves can be fixed on
brackets.*

brag *verb* **brags, bragging, bragged**
to boast.

braid *noun* **braids**
1 a plait. 2 a decorative band of cloth.

braille *noun*
a system of writing or printing that blind
people can read by touch.

brain *noun* **brains**
1 the part inside the top of the head that
controls the body. 2 the mind or
intelligence, as in *They haven't much brain.*
3 (*colloquial*) an intelligent person, as in *the
brain of the class.*

brainy *adjective* **brainier, brainiest**
intelligent, as in *She's the brainiest child in
the school.*

brake *noun* **brakes**
a device for stopping or slowing down
something.

bramble *noun* **brambles**
a wild thorny shrub, especially the
blackberry.

branch *noun* **branches**
1 a part that sticks out from the trunk of a
tree. 2 part of a railway, river, road, etc.

that leads off from the main part. 3 part
of a large organisation.

branch *verb* **branches, branching, branched**
to form a branch, as in *The new growth
branched from the trunk of the tree.*
branch out, to start something new.

brand *noun* **brands**
1 a particular kind of goods, as in *a cheap
brand of tea.* 2 a mark made by branding,
as in *Brands are used on cattle to show who
owns them.*

brand *verb* **brands, branding, branded**
to mark cattle, sheep, etc. with a hot iron.

brandish *verb* **brandishes, brandishing,
brandished**
to wave something about.

brandy *noun* **brandies**
a kind of strong alcoholic drink.

brass *noun* **brasses**
1 a metal made from copper and zinc.
2 wind instruments made of brass, such as
trumpets and trombones.
brass band, a group of people playing brass
wind instruments.
brass-rubbing, making a picture by rubbing
a piece of paper laid over a brass memorial
tablet on a tomb; a picture made in this way.

brassy *adjective* **brassier, brassiest**
1 coloured like brass. 2 loud and harsh,
as in *a brassy laugh.*

brave *adjective* **braver, bravest**
not afraid; ready to face danger, pain, etc.
bravery *noun*

brawl *noun* **brawls**
a noisy quarrel or fight.

brawn *noun*
1 muscular strength. 2 cooked pork or
veal pressed in a mould setting in its own
jelly.

brawny *adjective* **brawnier, brawniest**
having strong muscles.

bray *verb* **brays, braying, brayed**
to make a harsh noise like a donkey.

brazen *adjective*
1 made of brass. 2 shameless or rude, as
in *The girl was corrected for her brazen
behaviour.*

brazier *noun* **braziers** (*say* bray-zee-uh)
a metal container holding hot coals, etc., as
in *The outdoor party had braziers for warmth
and cooking.*

breach *noun* **breaches**
1 the breaking of an agreement, rule, etc.,
as in *breach of the law.* 2 a gap, as in *a
breach in the wall of the castle.*

bread

bread *noun*
1 food made by baking flour and water, usually with yeast. 2 (*colloquial*) money.

breadth *noun* **breadths**
width.

breadwinner *noun* **breadwinners**
someone who earns the money for a family.

break *verb* **breaks, breaking, broke, broken**
1 to divide into two or more pieces by hitting, pressing, etc. 2 to stop working properly, as in *My watch has broken.* 3 to stop or end, as in *She broke her silence.* 4 to fail to keep a promise, law, etc. 5 to change, as in *After a sunny week, the weather broke.* 6 (of waves) to fall and scatter, as in *The waves were breaking over the rocks.* 7 to go suddenly or with force, as in *They broke through the enemy's defences.* 8 (of a boy's voice) to become deeper, when a boy is around 14 years old. 9 to get or become free, as in *break away; break loose; break open.*
break a record, to do better than anyone has done before.
break down, to stop working properly; to collapse, as in *The machine broke down. The peace talks broke down.*
break off, to detach something; to stop, as in *We broke off, and restarted work an hour later.*
break out, to start suddenly, as in *chicken-pox broke out at the school.*
break the news, to make something known.
break up, to split up; to reach the end of a school term, as in *Emma and her boyfriend have broken up. We break up next Friday.*

break *noun* **breaks**
1 a broken place; a gap, as in *a break in the brick wall; a break in the bad weather.* 2 a sudden dash, as in *a break for freedom.* 3 a short rest from work. 4 (*colloquial*) a piece of luck; a fair chance, as in *Give me a break.*
break of day, dawn.

breakable *adjective*
easily broken, as in *Be careful with that box—there are breakable things in it.*

breakage *noun* **breakages**
a broken thing, as in *All breakages must be paid for.*

break-dancing *noun*
a style of energetic dancing in which the dancers often spin round on their backs, elbows, or heads.

breakdown *noun* **breakdowns**
1 a collapse or failure, as in *a nervous breakdown.* 2 dividing something up into parts to make it easier to understand, as in *a breakdown of the accounts.*

breaker *noun* **breakers**
a wave breaking on the shore.

breakfast *noun* **breakfasts**
the first meal of the day.

breakneck *adjective*
dangerously fast, as in *He drove at breakneck speed.*

breakthrough *noun* **breakthroughs**
an important advance or achievement.

breakwater *noun* **breakwaters**
a wall built out into the sea to protect a harbour or coast against heavy waves.

breast *noun* **breasts**
1 one of the parts of a woman's body where milk is produced. 2 a person's or animal's chest.
breast-stroke, a way of swimming in which you extend both arms forward and sweep them back while kicking like a frog.

breath *noun* **breaths** (*say* breth)
the air that someone breathes.
out of breath, panting.
take someone's breath away, to surprise or delight someone.

breathalyser *noun* **breathalysers**
a device to measure the amount of alcohol in someone's breath.
breathalyse *verb*

breathe *verb* **breathes, breathing, breathed** (*say* breeth)
1 to take air into your lungs through your nose or mouth and send it out again. 2 to be or seem alive, as in *Is she breathing?* 3 to speak, especially softly, as in *Don't breathe a word of this.*

Usage Do not confuse **breathe** with **breath**, which is a noun.

breather *noun* **breathers**
a pause for rest, as in *Let's have a breather.*

breathless *adjective*
short of breath.

breathtaking *adjective*
surprising or delightful.

bred past tense and past participle of **breed** verb.

breech *noun* **breeches**
the part of a gun barrel where the bullets are put in.

breeches *plural noun* (*say* brich-uhz)
trousers, especially trousers that fit tightly at the knee.

breed *verb* **breeds, breeding, bred**
1 to produce offspring. 2 to keep

animals so as to get young ones from them. **3** to create, as in *Poverty breeds illness*.

breed *noun* **breeds**
a variety of similar animals, as in *A Siamese is a breed of cat*.

breeder *noun* **breeders**
someone who breeds animals.

breeding *noun*
1 the mating of animals to produce offspring. **2** good manners resulting from being taught how to behave.

breeze *noun* **breezes**
a gentle wind.
breezy *adjective*

brethren *plural noun*
(*old-fashioned use*) brothers.

brevity *noun*
being brief or short, as in *Not wanting to waste time, Sebastian delivered his important message with brevity*.

brew *verb* **brews, brewing, brewed**
1 to make beer or tea. **2** to start or develop, as in *Trouble is brewing*.

brewery *noun* **breweries**
a place where beer is made.
brewer *noun*

bribe *verb* **bribes, bribing, bribed**
to persuade someone to act incorrectly by a gift of money, etc.
bribery *noun*

bribe *noun* **bribes**
money or a gift offered to someone to influence him or her.

brick *noun* **bricks**
a small, hard block of baked clay, etc. used in building.

bricklayer *noun* **bricklayers**
a worker who builds with bricks.

brick veneer *noun* **brick veneers**
a house with a timber frame and a single brick exterior.

bride *noun* **brides**
a woman on her wedding day.
bridal *adjective*

bridegroom *noun* **bridegrooms**
a man on his wedding day.

bridesmaid *noun* **bridesmaids**
a girl or unmarried woman who assists the bride at a wedding.

bridge *noun* **bridges**
1 a structure built over a river, railway, or road, to allow people to cross it. **2** the high platform above a ship's deck, from where the ship is controlled. **3** the bony upper part of your nose.

bridge *noun*
a card-game for two pairs of players.

bridle *noun* **bridles**
the part of a horse's harness that controls its head.

brief *adjective* **briefer, briefest**
lasting a short time.
in brief, in a few words.

brief *noun* **briefs**
instructions and information, especially given to a barrister.

briefcase *noun* **briefcases**
a flat case for documents, papers, etc.

brigade *noun* **brigades**
1 an army unit usually consisting of three battalions. **2** a group of people in uniform, as in *the fire brigade*.

brigadier *noun* **brigadiers**
an officer who commands a brigade and is higher in rank than a colonel.

brigand *noun* **brigands**
an outlaw, especially one who robs travellers in wild country.

bright *adjective* **brighter, brightest**
1 giving a strong light; shining. **2** clever, as in *He's a bright lad*. **3** cheerful.

brighten *verb* **brightens, brightening, brightened**
to make or become bright.

brilliant *adjective*
1 very bright. **2** very clever. **3** (*colloquial*) excellent or superb, as in *That was a brilliant film!*
brilliance *noun*

brim *noun* **brims**
1 the edge around the top of a container. **2** the projecting edge of a hat.

brimming *adjective*
full, as in *The saucepan was brimming with soup*.
brimming over, overflowing.

brine *noun*
salt water.

bring *verb* **brings, bringing, brought**
to make someone or something come; to lead or carry here, as in *The storm brought rain. Spring brings new growth. I will bring the cake*.
bring about, to cause something to happen.
bring off, to achieve something.

brink

bring round, to make someone conscious again after he or she has fainted.
bring up, to look after and educate a child.

brink *noun* brinks
the edge of a steep or dangerous place.

brisk *adjective* brisker, briskest
quick and lively.

bristle *noun* bristles
a short, stiff hair.
bristly *adjective*

brittle *adjective* brittler, brittlest
likely to break or snap, as in *brittle biscuits.*

broad *adjective* broader, broadest
1 wide. 2 complete; full, as in *in broad daylight.* 3 not detailed, as in *a broad outline.* 4 to do with an accent being very strong, as in *Her broad Scottish accent appealed to many.*
broad bean, a large flat bean.

broadcast *verb* broadcasts, broadcasting, broadcast
to transmit or take part in a radio or television program.
broadcaster *noun*

broadcast *noun* broadcasts
a radio or television program.

broaden *verb* broadens, broadening, broadened
to make something broader; to become broader.

broad-minded *adjective*
tolerant of other people's ways and ideas.

broadside *noun* broadsides
1 firing by all the guns on one side of a ship. 2 a vigorous attack with words.

broccoli *noun*
a vegetable with greenish flower-heads.

brochure *noun* brochures
a pamphlet containing information about travel, equipment, courses, etc.

broke past tense of **break** *verb.*

broke *adjective*
(*colloquial*) having no money left; bankrupt.

broken past participle of **break** *verb.*

broken *adjective*
1 having been broken, out of order, as in *broken plate; broken radio.* 2 interrupted, as in *broken sleep.*
broken English, the English language spoken in an imperfect way.
broken-hearted, very sad.
broken home, a home where the parents have separated.

broker *noun* brokers
someone who buys and sells things for other people, as in *stockbroker.*

brolga *noun*
a large Australian bird with grey feathers and red skin on its head that lives near water in eastern and northern Australia.

Origin This word comes from Kamilaroi, an Aboriginal language of New South Wales. See the Aboriginal Languages map at the back of this dictionary.

bronchitis *noun* (*say* brong-**kuy**-tuhs)
a disease of the lungs.

brontosaurus *noun* brontosauruses
(*say* bron-tuh-**saw**-ruhs)
a large, plant-eating dinosaur with a long tail like a whip.

bronze *noun*
1 a metal made from copper and tin.
2 a yellowish-brown colour.
bronze medal, a medal made of bronze, usually awarded as the third prize.

Bronze Age *noun*
the time in history when tools and weapons were made of bronze.

brooch *noun* brooches
(rhymes with *coach*)
an ornament pinned on to clothes.

brood *noun* broods
young birds that were hatched together.

brood *verb* broods, brooding, brooded
1 to sit on eggs to hatch them. 2 to keep thinking about something, especially resentfully, as in *He brooded over his defeat.*

brook *noun* brooks
a small stream or creek, as in *In Western Australia, creeks are often called brooks.*

broom *noun* brooms
1 a brush with a long handle, for sweeping. 2 a shrub or small tree with drooping, almost leafless branches and masses of usually yellow flowers.

broth *noun* broths
a thin soup.

brother *noun* brothers
a man or boy who has the same parents as another person.
brotherly *adjective*

brother-in-law *noun* brothers-in-law
the brother of your husband or wife.

brought past tense and past participle of **bring.**

brow *noun* **brows**
1 the forehead. 2 an eyebrow. 3 the top of a hill or the edge of a cliff.

brown *adjective* **browner, brownest**
1 having the colour of soil or dark wood, as in *Brown bread is often made from wholemeal flour.* 2 suntanned.

brownie *noun* **brownies**
a small square of chocolate cake with nuts. Brownie, a junior Guide.

browse *verb* **browses, browsing, browsed**
1 to feed on grass or leaves. 2 to read or look at something casually.

bruise *noun* **bruises**
a dark mark on skin made by hitting it.

bruise *verb* **bruises, bruising, bruised**
to give someone a bruise; to get a bruise.

brumby *noun* **brumbies**
a wild unbroken horse.

brunch *noun* **brunches**
breakfast and lunch combined as one meal.

brunette *noun* **brunettes**
a woman with dark brown or black hair.

brush *noun* **brushes**
1 a device for sweeping, scrubbing, painting, etc. 2 the act of brushing, as in *She gave her hair a good brush.* 3 an unpleasant meeting or argument, as in *a brush with the police.*

brush *verb* **brushes, brushing, brushed)**
1 to use a brush on something, as in *Have you brushed your hair?* 2 to touch someone or something gently, as in *She brushed against the wet paint.*
to brush aside, to dismiss.
brush up on, to refresh your knowledge of something.

brussels sprout *noun* **brussels sprouts**
a green vegetable like a small cabbage.

brutal *adjective*
harsh and cruel.
brutality *noun*, **brutalise** *verb*, **brutally** *adverb*

brute *noun* **brutes**
1 a brutal person. 2 an animal.

bubble *noun* **bubbles**
1 a thin transparent ball of liquid filled with air or gas. 2 a small ball of air in a liquid or a solid.
bubble gum, chewing-gum that you can blow up into bubbles.

bubbler *noun* **bubblers**
a drinking fountain.

bubbly *adjective* **bubblier, bubbliest**
1 full of bubbles, as in *Soda water is bubbly.* 2 lively, as in *a child with a bubbly personality.*

buccaneer *noun* **buccaneers**
a pirate.

buck *noun* **bucks**
a male deer, rabbit, or hare.

buck *verb* **bucks, bucking, bucked**
1 (of a horse) to jump with the back arched. 2 to oppose or resist, as in *The rebellious student always bucked the school rules.*
buck up, (*colloquial*) to cheer up; to hurry.

bucket *noun* **buckets**
a container with a handle, for carrying liquids, etc.

buckle *noun* **buckles**
a fastener for a belt or strap.

buckle *verb* **buckles, buckling, buckled**
1 to fasten with a buckle. 2 to crumple or bend, as in *His knees buckled. The plastic tray buckled in the heat.*
buckle up, to put on a seatbelt.

bud *noun* **buds**
a flower or leaf before it has opened.

Buddhism *noun* (*say* **buud**-iz-uhm)
a religion that started in Asia and follows the teachings of Buddha who lived in India in the 5th Century BC.
Buddhist *noun*

budding *adjective*
developing well, as in *a budding singer.*

budge *verb* **budges, budging, budged**
to move slightly, as in *This door is stuck—it won't budge.*

budgerigar *noun* **budgerigars**
(*say* **buj**-uh-ree-gah)
a small, usually green or yellow parrot from dry inland areas, often kept as a pet.

budget *noun* **budgets**
1 the money available for a particular purpose. 2 a plan for spending money wisely.

budget *verb* **budgets, budgeting, budgeted**
to plan a budget.

budgie (*colloquial*) a budgerigar.

buff *noun* **buffs**
1 the dull yellow colour. 2 an enthusiast, as in *a railway buff.*

buffalo *noun* **buffalo** or **buffaloes**
a wild ox of Africa or Asia.

a b c d e f g h i j k l m n o p q r s t u v w x y z

buffer

buffer *noun* **buffers**
1 something that softens a blow, especially a device on a railway engine or wagon or at the end of a railway line. 2 (*in Computing*) a memory in which data can be stored temporarily, especially while being sent from one device to another.

buffet *noun* **buffets** (*say* **buf**-ay)
1 a room or counter where refreshments are sold. 2 a meal where guests serve themselves.

bug *noun* **bugs**
1 an insect. 2 (*colloquial*) a germ or microbe. 3 (*colloquial*) a secret hidden microphone. 4 (*colloquial*) a fault in something, especially a computer program.

bug *verb* **bugs, bugging, bugged**
1 (*colloquial*) to fit with a secret hidden microphone. 2 (*colloquial*) to annoy.

bugle *noun* **bugles** (*say* **byoo**-guhl)
a brass instrument like a small trumpet.
bugler *noun*

build *verb* **builds, building, built**
to make something by putting parts together.
build in, to include, as in *a sink unit with cupboards built in.*
build on, to add, especially an extension to a house.
build up, to accumulate or increase; to cover an area with buildings; to make stronger or more famous, as in *A backlog of work has built up. All the paddocks around the town have been built up. Exercise regularly to build up your health. The tour built up the pop star's reputation.*

build *noun* **builds**
the shape of a person's body, as in *of slender build.*

builder *noun* **builders**
someone who puts up buildings.

building *noun* **buildings**
1 the construction of houses, etc. 2 something built, such as a house or a block of flats.

building society *noun* **building societies**
an organisation, like a bank, that lends money to people who want to buy houses.

built-up *adjective*
densely covered with houses and other buildings, as in *a built-up area.*

bulb *noun* **bulbs**
1 a glass globe with a wire inside to produce electric light. 2 something that looks like an onion, planted in the ground to produce daffodils, tulips, etc.

bulge *noun* **bulges**
a swelling.
bulgy *adjective*

bulge *verb* **bulges, bulging, bulged**
to swell outwards, as in *His stomach bulged over his belt.*

bulimia *noun*
an eating disorder where a person overeats and then causes vomiting.

bulk *noun* **bulks**
1 the size of something, especially when it is large. 2 the majority, as in *The bulk of the work is done.*
in bulk, in large quantities.
bulky *adjective*

bull *noun* **bulls**
a male animal (used in speaking of cattle, elephants, or whales).

bull ant *noun* **bull ants**
a large ant giving a painful bite.

bulldog *noun* **bulldogs**
a breed of dog with a short, thick neck.

bulldozer *noun* **bulldozers**
a heavy vehicle with tracks, with a wide metal blade in front, used to clear or flatten land.
bulldoze *verb*

bullet *noun* **bullets**
a small lump of metal shot from a rifle or pistol.

bulletin *noun* **bulletins**
a short official news report.

bulletproof *adjective*
able to stop bullets, as in *bulletproof vest.*

bullfight *noun* **bullfights**
a contest between men and bulls, presented as public entertainment.
bullfighter *noun*, **bullfighting** *noun*

bullion *noun*
bars of gold or silver.

bullock *noun* **bullocks**
a young bull that has been castrated.

bull's-eye *noun* **bull's-eyes**
the centre of a target.

bully *noun* **bullies**
1 someone who hurts or frightens a weaker person by force or threats. 2 starting play in hockey.

bully *verb* **bullies, bullying, bullied**
to hurt or frighten a weaker person.

bulrush *noun* **bulrushes**
a tall rush with a soft thick top, used for weaving.

bulwark *noun* **bulwarks** (*say* **buul**-wuhk)
a defending wall; a defence, as in *Low interest rates are sometimes seen as a bulwark against inflation*.
bulwarks, a ship's side above the level of the deck.

bum *noun* **bums**
(*colloquial*) a person's bottom.

bumble-bee *noun* **bumble-bees**
a large bee with a loud hum.

bump *noun* **bumps**
1 a dull-sounding blow or collision, as in *We heard a bump as the car backed into the tree*. 2 a swelling or lump, as in *a bump on the head*.
bumpy *adjective*

bump *verb* **bumps, bumping, bumped**
1 to knock against something. 2 to move along with jolts, as in *The cart bumped along the road*.
bump into someone, (*colloquial*) to meet someone unexpectedly.
bump someone off, (*colloquial*) to kill someone.

bun *noun* **buns**
1 a plain or sweet round bread roll. 2 a round bunch of hair at the back of a woman's head.

bunch *noun* **bunches**
a number of things joined or tied together, as in *a bunch of bananas*.

bundle *noun* **bundles**
a number of things tied or wrapped together.

bundle *verb* **bundles, bundling, bundled**
1 to tie or wrap things up together. 2 to put hurriedly or carelessly, as in *They bundled him into a taxi*.

bungalow *noun* **bungalows**
a cottage, shack, or sleepout.

bungee jumping *noun*
the sport of jumping from a height where the person is attached to an elastic cord or rope secured around the ankles.

bungle *verb* **bungles, bungling, bungled**
to do something unsuccessfully or clumsily.
bungler *noun*

bunk *noun* **bunks**
a bed like a shelf, as on a ship.
bunk beds, two single beds, joined one above the other.

bunker *noun* **bunkers**
1 a container for storing fuel. 2 a sand-filled hollow made as an obstacle on a golf-course. 3 an underground shelter.

Bunsen burner *noun* **Bunsen burners**
a device that uses gas to make a flame for scientific experiments, etc.

bunyip *noun* **bunyips**
an imaginary creature in Aboriginal legend which lives in swamps, lagoons, etc.

> **Origin** This word comes from the Aboriginal language Wemba-wemba: **banib**. See the Aboriginal Languages map at the back of this dictionary.

buoy *noun* **buoys** (*say* boi)
1 an anchored floating object used to mark a channel, shallow water, etc. 2 a ring used to help people stay afloat; a lifebuoy.

buoyant *adjective*
1 able to float. 2 cheerful, as in *He was in a buoyant mood*.
buoyancy *noun*

burden *noun* **burdens**
1 a heavy load. 2 something hard to put up with.
burdensome *adjective*

bureau *noun* **bureaux** (*say* **byoo**-roh *or* byoo-**roh**)
1 a writing-desk with drawers. 2 an office or department, as in *weather bureau*.

bureaucracy *noun* **bureaucracies**
a government with a central administration.
bureaucrat *noun*, **bureaucratic** *adjective*

burette *noun* **burettes**
(*in Science*) a tube with a tap at one end, used for measuring exact amounts of liquid.

burglar *noun* **burglars**
someone who breaks into a building to steal things.
burglary *noun*, **burgle** *verb*

burial *noun* **burials**
burying someone who has died; a funeral.

burly *adjective* **burlier, burliest**
big and strong, as in *a burly wrestler*.
burliness *noun*

burn *verb* **burns, burning, burnt** *or* **burned**
1 to damage or destroy something with fire or heat. 2 to be damaged or destroyed by fire or heat. 3 to be on fire. 4 to feel very hot.
burn off, to clear a forest area, farming land, etc. by burning.
burn down, to destroy or be destroyed by burning.

burn *noun* **burns**
an injury caused by fire or heat.

a
b
c
d
e
f
g
h
i
j
k
l
m
n
o
p
q
r
s
t
u
v
w
x
y
z

burner

burner *noun* **burners**
the part of a lamp or gas stove that shapes the flame.

burning *adjective*
1 intense, as in *a burning desire*. 2 hotly discussed, as in *a burning question*.

burp *noun* **burps**
(*colloquial*) a belch.

burp *verb* **burps, burping, burped**
(*colloquial*) to belch or to help to burp, especially by patting the back, as in *Burp the baby after her milk*.

burr *noun* **burrs**
the prickly part of some plants which sticks to fur, clothes, etc.

burrow *noun* **burrows**
a hole dug by a rabbit, fox, etc.

burrow *verb* **burrows, burrowing, burrowed**
1 to dig a burrow. 2 to dig or search deeply, as in *He burrowed in his pockets*.

burst *verb* **bursts, bursting, burst**
1 to break apart. 2 to start something suddenly, as in *He burst out laughing and she burst into tears*. 3 to be very full, excited, etc., as in *bursting with energy*.
burst in, to rush in.

burst *noun* **bursts**
1 a split, as in *There's a burst in one of the pipes*. 2 something short and forceful, as in *a burst of gunfire*.

bury *verb* **buries, burying, buried**
1 to put a person or thing under the ground. 2 to cover up completely, as in *She buried the money in her clothes*.
bury the hatchet, to stop quarrelling or fighting.

bus *noun* **buses**
a large vehicle for passengers to travel in.
bus-stop, a place where a bus regularly stops.

bush *noun* **bushes**
1 a plant like a small tree with many stems or branches. 2 an area of land covered by bush.
bush capital, Canberra.
bushie, a person from the country.
the bush, the country, not the city, as in *We're from the bush*.
bushy *adjective*

bushed *adjective*
1 lost, as in *He was bushed in the strange town*. 2 tired out, exhausted, as in *They were bushed after fighting the fires*.

bushranger *noun* **bushrangers**
a person who robbed others and escaped into and lived in the bush.

bush tucker *noun* **bush tuckers**
traditional Aboriginal food.

bush walking *noun*
a hike in the bush, especially including camping out.

busily *adverb*
in a busy way.

business *noun* **businesses** (*say* biz-nuhs)
1 a person's occupation, as in *My business is publishing*. 2 a person's concerns or responsibilities, as in *Mind your own business*. 3 serious work or discussion, as in *We had better get down to business*. 4 an affair or subject, as in *I am tired of the whole business*. 5 buying and selling, as in *She has made a career in business*. 6 a shop or firm, as in *a successful building business*.

businesslike *adjective*
efficient and practical.

busker *noun* **buskers**
someone who entertains in the street, especially by playing music and who hopes to get money from people passing by.

bust *noun* **busts**
1 a woman's bosom. 2 a sculpture of a person's head and shoulders.

bust *verb* **busts, busting, busted**
1 (*colloquial*) to break or burst. 2 (*colloquial*) to raid and arrest, as in *The drug dealers were busted*.

bust *adjective*
(*colloquial*)
1 broken or burst. 2 bankrupt.

bustle *verb* **bustles, bustling, bustled**
to hurry or be very busy.

busy *adjective* **busier, busiest**
1 doing a lot; having much to do. 2 full of activity, as in *a busy street*. 3 (of a telephone line) engaged.

busybody *noun* **busybodies**
someone who interferes in other people's business.

but *conjunction*
however; nevertheless, as in *I wanted to go but I couldn't*.

but *preposition*
except, as in *There's no one here but me*.

butane *noun* (*say* byoo-**tayn**)
a gas used as fuel.

butcher *noun* **butchers**
1 someone who cuts up meat and sells it. 2 a cruel murderer.

butchery *noun* **butcheries**
unnecessary or cruel killing.

butler *noun* **butlers**
a male servant in charge of other servants.

butt *verb* **butts, butting, butted**
1 to hit someone or something with your head. 2 to place the edges of things together. 3 to jut out, as in *The verandah butted out from the rest of the building*.
butt in, to interrupt or intrude.

butt *noun* **butts**
1 someone who is often ridiculed, as in *Why is he always the butt of your jokes?* 2 the thicker end of a weapon or tool. 3 the stub or end of a cigarette. 4 (*colloquial*) the buttocks.

butter *noun*
a solid food made from cream, used as a spread and in cooking.

butterfly *noun* **butterflies**
an insect with large white or coloured wings.
butterflies, (*colloquial*) nervous feelings in your stomach.

butterfly stroke *noun*
a swimming stroke in which you raise both arms together and throw your body forward.

butterscotch *noun* **butterscotches**
a kind of hard toffee.

buttocks *plural noun*
the part of the body on which a person sits.

button *noun* **buttons**
1 a fastener sewn on clothes. 2 a small knob, as in *She pressed the button to ring the bell.*

button *verb* **buttons, buttoning, buttoned**
button up, to fasten something with a button or buttons; to be fastened in this way, as in *Button up your coat. This jacket buttons up at the front.*

buttonhole *noun* **buttonholes**
1 a slit for a button to pass through. 2 a flower worn on a lapel.

buttress *noun* **buttresses**
a support built against a wall.

buy *verb* **buys, buying, bought**
1 to get something by paying for it, as in *I bought these cards yesterday.* 2 (*colloquial*) to accept; to believe, as in *Nobody will buy that excuse.*
buyer *noun*

buy *noun* **buys**
a purchase, as in *That car was a good buy.*

buzz *noun* **buzzes**
1 a vibrating, humming sound.
2 (*colloquial*) a pleasant, exciting feeling, as in *I really get a buzz from cycling.*
3 (*colloquial*) a telephone call.

buzz *verb* **buzzes, buzzing, buzzed**
to hum.
buzz off, (*colloquial*) to go away.
buzzer *noun*

buzzard *noun* **buzzards**
a bird of prey like a large hawk.

by *preposition*
1 near; beside, as in *Sit by me.* 2 through; along, as in *You can reach it by the path.*
3 using; by means of, as in *cooking by gas.*
4 before, as in *Do your homework by tomorrow.* 5 past, as in *She went by the window.* 6 during, as in *They came by night.* 7 according to, as in *Don't judge by appearances.*
by the way, incidentally; on a different subject.

by *adverb*
1 past, as in *I can't get by.* 2 for future use, as in *Put some money by for the holidays.*
by and by, soon; later on, as in *We'll pass Centennial Park by and by—in fact, there it is now. By and by, Jack turned up.*
by and large, on the whole.

bye *noun* **byes**
a run scored in cricket when the batter has not touched the ball.

bye-bye *interjection*
(*colloquial*) goodbye.

by-election *noun* **by-elections**
an election to fill a vacancy when a member of parliament has died or resigned.

bygone *adjective*
belonging to the past, as in *bygone farming methods.*

by-law *noun* **by-laws**
a law made by a local government authority.

bypass *noun* **bypasses**
1 a road that takes traffic past a congested area. 2 an alternative passage for blood to circulate through while a surgeon is operating on someone's heart.

by-product *noun* **by-products**
something produced while something else is being made, as in *Tar and coke are by-products of making gas from coal.*

bystander *noun* **bystanders**
someone standing near but taking no part when something happens.

byte *noun* **bytes**
a unit of storage in a computer's memory.

Cc

cab *noun* **cabs**
1 a taxi. 2 a compartment for the driver of a truck, crane, etc.

cabaret *noun* **cabarets** (*say* **kab**-uh-ray)
an entertainment, especially performed in a restaurant or night-club.

cabbage *noun* **cabbages**
a round, green, leafy vegetable.

cabin *noun* **cabins**
1 a small house, especially one made of timber. 2 a compartment in a ship, plane, etc.

cabinet *noun* **cabinets**
a cupboard with drawers or shelves.
the Cabinet, a group of senior ministers who control the government.

cable *noun* **cables**
1 a group of insulated wires which carry electricity. 2 thick rope, wire, or chain. 3 a telegram sent overseas.
cable television, a television system in which programs are transmitted by wire instead of through the air.

cackle *noun* **cackles**
1 the clucking of a hen. 2 a loud, silly laugh. 3 stupid chattering.

cactus *noun* **cacti**
a fleshy, water-storing plant that grows in hot, dry places.

caddie *noun* **caddies**
someone who helps a golfer by carrying the clubs.

caddy *noun* **caddies**
a small container for tea-leaves.

cadet *noun* **cadets**
a young person being trained for the armed forces, the police or journalism.

café *noun* **cafés** (*say* **kaf**-ay)
a small restaurant.

cafeteria *noun* **cafeterias**
(*say* kaf-uh-**teer**-ree-uh)
a café where the customers serve themselves.

caffeine *noun*
a drug found in tea and coffee which keeps you awake and makes you feel active.

cage *noun* **cages**
a container made of bars or wires, in which birds or animals are kept.

cagey *adjective* **cagier, cagiest**
(*colloquial*) cautious about giving information, etc.

cake *noun* **cakes**
1 a baked mixture of flour, eggs, butter, etc. 2 a flat, round lump of something, as in *a cake of soap. We ate fish cakes.*
have your cake and eat it, (*colloquial*) to enjoy two alternative good things of which you can usually only have one.
something is a piece of cake, (*colloquial*) something is very easy.

caked *adjective*
covered with dried mud, make-up, etc.

calamity *noun* **calamities**
a disaster.
calamitous *adjective*

calcium *noun*
a greyish-white element contained in teeth, bones, and lime.

calculate *verb* **calculates, calculating, calculated**
1 to work out something. 2 to plan or intend something.
calculation *noun*

calculating *adjective*
shrewd or scheming, as in *The calculating students managed to avoid cleaning duty.*

calculator *noun* **calculators**
a machine for doing sums.

calendar *noun* **calendars**
something that shows the dates of the month or year.

calf *noun* **calves**
1 a young cow, whale, seal, etc. **2** the back part of the leg below the knee.

calico *noun*
cotton cloth.

call *verb* **calls, calling, called**
1 to shout. **2** to telephone. **3** to tell someone to come to you. **4** to make a visit, as in *She called on her grandfather.* **5** to name someone or something, as in *The baby is called Andrew.* **6** to describe, as in *He called his brother a thief.* **7** to wake someone up. **8** to order to take place, as in *The principal called a meeting with the house captains.*
call it a day, to decide that you have done enough work for one day, and stop working.
call off, to cancel.
call someone names, to insult someone.

call *noun* **calls**
1 a shout or cry. **2** a short visit. **3** telephoning someone. **4** a request or invitation.

calligraphy *noun* (*say* kuh-**lig**-ruh-fee)
the art of producing beautiful handwriting.

calling *noun* **callings**
a profession or trade.

calliper *noun* **callipers**
a metal splint used to support an injured arm or leg.

callous *adjective*
not caring about other people's feelings; cruel.

calm *adjective* **calmer, calmest**
1 quiet and still, as in *a calm sea.* **2** not excited or agitated, as in *Please keep calm.*
calmly *adverb*, **calmness** *noun*

calorie *noun* **calories**
a unit for measuring an amount of heat or the energy produced by food.
calorific *adjective*

came past tense of **come**.

camel *noun* **camels**
a large animal with a long neck and one or two humps on its back, as in *Camels are often used for transport in desert areas.*

camera *noun* **cameras**
a device for taking photographs, films, or television pictures.
cameraman *noun*

camouflage *noun* (*say* kam-uh-flah*z*h)
a way of hiding things by making them look like part of their surroundings.

camp *noun* **camps**
a place where people live in tents, huts, campervans, etc. for a short time.

camp *verb* **camps, camping, camped**
to live in a tent, hut, campervan, etc., as in *Let's camp here for the night.*
camper *noun*

campaign *noun* **campaigns**
1 a planned series of actions, especially to arouse interest in something, as in *a campaign for human rights.* **2** a series of battles in one area or with one aim.

campaign *verb* **campaigns, campaigning, campaigned**
to carry out a planned series of actions, especially to arouse interest in something, as in *They are campaigning to stop the destruction of the rainforest.*

campervan *noun* **campervans**
a large motor vehicle especially designed for eating, living and sleeping, as in *We travelled around Kakadu in a campervan.*

campus *noun* **campuses**
the buildings of a college or university and the land around them.

can *verb* present tense **can**; past tense **could**; **cans, canning, canned**
1 to be able to do something; to know how to do something, as in *Can you lift this stone? I could yesterday.* **2** to be allowed to do something, as in *Can I go home?* **3** to put or preserve in a can.
canned music, recorded music.
cannery *noun*

can *noun* **cans**
a metal container for food, drink, etc.
can-opener, a tool for opening cans.

canal *noun* **canals**
1 an artificial waterway. **2** a tube in a human's or animal's body, as in *The semicircular canals in your ears help you balance.*

canary *noun* **canaries**
a small yellow bird that sings.
[from the name of the **Canary** Islands where this bird was first seen]

cancel

cancel *verb* **cancels, cancelling, cancelled**
1 to say that something planned will not be done or not take place. 2 to stop an order for something. 3 to mark a stamp, ticket, etc. so that it cannot be used again.
cancel out, to stop the effect of one another, as in *The arguments cancelled each other out.*
cancellation *noun*

cancer *noun* **cancers**
1 a disease in which a harmful growth forms in your body. 2 a harmful growth in your body.

candid *adjective*
1 honest; not hiding one's thoughts. 2 taken, usually without a person's knowledge, as in *candid photographs.*

candidate *noun* **candidates**
1 someone who wants to be elected or chosen for a particular job, position, etc. 2 someone sitting an examination.

candle *noun* **candles**
a stick of wax with a wick through it, giving light when burning.

candlelight *noun*
light given by a candle or candles.

candlestick *noun* **candlesticks**
a holder for a candle or candles.

cane *noun* **canes**
1 the stem of a reed or tall grass; a thin stick. 2 a thin stick used to beat someone.

cane *verb* **canes, caning, caned**
to beat someone with a cane.

canine *adjective*
to do with dogs.
canine tooth, a pointed tooth.

canine *noun* **canines**
1 a dog. 2 a canine tooth.

cannibal *noun* **cannibals**
1 a person who eats human flesh. 2 an animal that eats animals of its own kind.
cannibalism *noun*

cannon *noun* **cannon** or **cannons**
a large, heavy gun.

cannonball *noun* **cannonballs**
a large ball fired from a cannon.

cannot
can not, as in *I cannot swim.*

canoe *noun* **canoes**
a narrow, lightweight boat.

canoe *verb* **canoes, canoeing, canoed**
(*say* cuh-**noo**)
to travel in a canoe.
canoeist *noun*

canopy *noun* **canopies**
an overhanging cover, as in *a canopy of trees in the rainforest.*

can't short for *can not.*

canteen *noun* **canteens**
1 a cafeteria for workers in a factory, office, etc. 2 a box containing a set of cutlery. 3 a soldier's or camper's water-flask or set of eating utensils. 4 a small shop at school where lunches, snacks, etc. are sold; a tuck shop.

canter *verb* **canters, cantering, cantered**
to go at a gentle gallop.

canvas *noun* **canvases**
1 strong, coarse cloth. 2 a piece of this kind of cloth for painting on.

canvass *verb* **canvasses, canvassing, canvassed**
to visit people to ask for votes, opinions, etc.

Usage Do not confuse **canvass** with **canvas**, which means a kind of material.

canyon *noun* **canyons**
a deep valley, usually with a river running through it.

cap *noun* **caps**
1 a soft hat without a brim but often with a peak. 2 a sign of being chosen to be in a particular sports team, as in *He got his cap in the cricket team.* 3 a cover or top. 4 something that makes a bang when it is fired in a toy pistol.

cap *verb* **caps, capping, capped**
1 to cover something, as in *snow-capped mountains.* 2 to do better than something, as in *Can you cap that joke?*

capable *adjective*
able to do something.
capability *noun,* **capably** *adverb*

capacity *noun* **capacities**
1 ability, as in *He has a great capacity for work.* 2 the amount that something can hold. 3 the position someone occupies, as in *He was successful in his capacity as coach.*

cape *noun* **capes**
1 a piece of high land sticking out into the sea. 2 a cloak.

caper *verb* **capers, capering, capered**
to jump about playfully.

caper *noun* **capers**
a playful leap, as in *The parents were amused at their children's capers.*

capital *noun* **capitals**
1 a capital city, as in *Canberra is our capital.*
2 a capital letter. 3 money or property that can be used to make more wealth.

capital *adjective*
the principal or most important, as in *capital city.*
capital punishment, punishing people by killing them.

capitalism *noun*
an economic system in which the production and distribution of goods depends on private companies and not the government.

Usage Compare this with **communism.**

capitalist *noun* **capitalists**
(*say* **kap**-uh-tuh-list)
someone who uses his or her wealth to make more wealth; a very rich person.

capital letter *noun*
a large letter of the kind used at the start of a name or a sentence, as in *A, B, C, etc. are capital letters.*

cappuccino *noun* **cappuccinos**
(*say* kap-uh-**cheen**-oh)
coffee with milk made frothy by pressurised steam.

capsicum *noun* **capsicums**
a variety of pepper plant with red, green, or yellow fruit, used in salads and to add flavour to other foods.

capsize *verb* **capsizes, capsizing, capsized**
to overturn a boat in the water.

capsule *noun* **capsules**
1 a hollow pill containing medicine. 2 a small spacecraft or pressurised cabin.

captain *noun* **captains**
1 someone in command of a ship, plane, sports team, etc. 2 an officer in the army or navy.

caption *noun* **captions**
1 the words printed with a picture to describe it. 2 a heading in a newspaper or magazine.

captivating *adjective*
charming and attractive.

captive *noun* **captives**
a confined or imprisoned person or animal.

captive *adjective*
imprisoned; unable to escape, as in *to be held captive. The captive rabbit struggled to get free.*
captivity *noun*

capture *verb* **captures, capturing, captured**
1 to catch or imprison an animal or person. 2 (*in Computing*) to put data into a form that a computer can accept.

capture *noun*
1 the act of capturing or imprisoning an animal or person, as in *The police were relieved with the capture of the criminal.*
2 the thing or person captured, as in *The brumby was a fine capture for the stockman.*

car *noun* **cars**
1 a motor car. 2 a railway carriage, as in *a dining-car.*
car phone, a mobile telephone fitted to a car.

caramel *noun* **caramels**
1 burnt sugar used to give a sweet taste to food. 2 a sweet made from butter, milk, and sugar.

carat *noun* **carats**
1 a measure of weight for precious stones. 2 a measure of the purity of gold.

caravan *noun* **caravans**
1 a small house on wheels, used for living in, especially by people on holiday. 2 a group of people travelling together, especially across a desert.

carbohydrate *noun* **carbohydrates**
a compound of carbon, oxygen, and hydrogen, as in *Sugar and starch are carbohydrates.*

carbon *noun*
1 an element found in charcoal, graphite, diamonds, etc. 2 a carbon copy or carbon paper.
carbon copy, a copy made with carbon paper; an exact copy, as in *The attack was a carbon copy of one carried out last month.*
carbon dioxide, a colourless gas made by humans and animals breathing.
carbon monoxide, a colourless, poisonous gas found especially in the exhaust of motor cars, etc.
carbon paper, thin coated paper put between sheets of paper to make a copy on the bottom sheet of what is written on the top sheet.

carburettor *noun* **carburettors**
a device for mixing fuel and air in an internal-combustion engine.

carcass or **carcase** *noun* **carcasses**
the dead body of an animal or bird.

card *noun* **cards**
1 a small, usually oblong, piece of stiff paper or cardboard, as in *birthday card; business card.* 2 a playing-card. 3 a

a
b
c
d
e
f
g
h
i
j
k
l
m
n
o
p
q
r
s
t
u
v
w
x
y
z

cardboard

small, oblong piece of plastic issued by a bank, building society, etc. to a customer enabling him or her to receive credit, or operate the account from an automatic teller machine, as in *bankcard; keycard*.
cards, a game with playing-cards.
something is on the cards, something is likely or possible.

cardboard *noun*
thick, stiff paper.

cardiac *adjective*
to do with the heart, as in *He suffered a cardiac arrest*.

cardigan *noun* **cardigans**
a knitted jacket usually buttoned up the front.

cardinal *noun* **cardinals**
one of the leading priests in the Roman Catholic Church.

cardinal number *noun* **cardinal numbers**
a number for counting things; 1, 2, 3, etc. (compare *ordinal number*).

care *noun* **cares**
1 worry; trouble, as in *She was free from care*. 2 serious thought or attention; caution, as in *Take more care with your homework*. 3 protection; supervision, as in *Leave the child in my care*.
care of ..., at the address of ..., as in *Write to him care of his friend*.
take care, to be careful.
take care of, to look after; to deal with, as in *Please could you take care of the cat while I'm away? That cheque will take care of the gas bill*.

care *verb* **cares, caring, cared**
to feel interested or concerned.
care for, to look after; to be fond of, as in *He cared for his wife when she was ill. I don't care for peanuts*.

career *noun* **careers**
a job or profession; a way of earning a living or making progress.

career *verb* **careers, careering, careered**
to rush along wildly.

carefree *adjective*
without worries or responsibilities.

careful *adjective*
1 giving serious thought and attention to something, as in *She is a careful worker*.
2 avoiding danger or harm, as in *a careful driver. Be careful with that knife!*
carefully *adverb*

careless *adjective*
1 not taking proper care or paying attention. 2 insensitive, as in *Her careless remarks hurt me*.
carelessly *adverb*, **carelessness** *noun*

caress *noun* **caresses** (say kuh-**res**)
a gentle, loving touch.

caretaker *noun* **caretakers**
someone who looks after a school, block of flats, etc.

cargo *noun* **cargoes**
goods carried in a ship or aircraft.

caricature *noun* **caricatures**
an amusing or exaggerated picture or description of someone.

carillon *noun* **carillons** (say kuh-**ril**-yuhn)
a set of bells in a tower sounded from a keyboard or mechanically.

carnation *noun* **carnations**
a flower having white or brightly-coloured blooms with a sweet smell.

carnival *noun* **carnivals**
1 an annual festival, usually with a procession of people in fancy dress, as in *Melbourne's Moomba carnival*. 2 a series of sporting events, as in *swimming carnival; surf carnival*.

carnivore *noun* **carnivores**
an animal that eats meat.
carnivorous *adjective*

carol *noun* **carols**
a joyous song, especially a Christmas hymn.
caroller *noun*, **carolling** *noun*

carp *noun* **carp**
a freshwater edible fish.

carpenter *noun* **carpenters**
someone who makes things, especially parts of buildings, out of wood.

carpentry *noun*
the work of a carpenter; things made by a carpenter.

carpet *noun* **carpets**
a thick, soft, woven covering for a floor.

carriage *noun* **carriages**
1 one of the separate parts of a train where passengers sit. 2 a passenger vehicle pulled by horses. 3 deportment, as in *She has good carriage as she holds her head high when she walks*.

carrot *noun* **carrots**
an orange-coloured root vegetable.

carry *verb* **carries, carrying, carried**
1 to support the weight of something.
2 to take something from one place to

another. **3** to have with you, as in *He is carrying a gun.* **4** to go a long distance, as in *Sound carries in the mountains.*
carried away, very excited.
carry on, to continue; to manage; (*colloquial*) to behave excitedly or strangely, as in *The firm can't carry on with so little money. Stop carrying on!*
carry out, to put something into practice, as in *The plan has been carried out successfully.*

cart *noun* **carts**
a small vehicle for carrying loads.
put the cart before the horse, to do things in the wrong order; to fail to recognise what is most important or urgent.

cart *verb* **carts, carting, carted**
1 to carry something in a cart.
2 (*colloquial*) to carry or transport something heavy or tiring, as in *I've been carting these books around the school all afternoon.*

cartilage *noun* (*say* **kah**-tuh-lij *or* **kaht**-lij) tough, flexible tissue attached to a bone.

carton *noun* **cartons**
a lightweight cardboard box.

cartoon *noun* **cartoons**
1 an amusing drawing. **2** a series of drawings telling a story. **3** an animated film.
cartoonist *noun*

cartridge *noun* **cartridges**
1 the case containing the explosive for a bullet or shell. **2** a container holding film to be put into a camera, ink to be put into a pen, etc.
cartridge paper, strong white paper.

cartwheel *noun* **cartwheels**
1 the wheel of a cart. **2** a somersault done sideways, with your arms and legs spread wide.

carve *verb* **carves, carving, carved**
1 to cut something carefully or artistically, as in *He carves figures into tree trunks.* **2** to cut meat into slices.

cascade *noun* **cascades**
a waterfall.

case *noun* **cases**
1 a container, as in *a case of apples.*
2 a suitcase. **3** an example of something existing or happening, as in *four cases of chicken-pox.* **4** something investigated by the police or by a lawcourt, as in *a case of murder.* **5** the facts or arguments used to support something, as in *She made a good case for equality.* **6** the form of a word that shows how it is related to other words,

Fred's *is the possessive case of* Fred.
in any case, anyway.
in case, because something may happen, as in *Take an umbrella in case it rains.*

cash *noun*
1 money in coins and banknotes.
2 immediate payment for goods, as in *Will you charge it or pay cash?*

cash *verb* **cashes, cashing, cashed**
to change a cheque, etc. into coins and banknotes.
cash in on something, (*colloquial*) to take advantage of something.

cashew *noun* **cashews**
a small, edible, curved nut.

cashier *noun* **cashiers**
someone in charge of the money in a bank, office, or shop.

cask *noun* **casks**
1 a barrel to hold wine, etc. **2** a plastic or foil lined container for wine, etc. enclosed in a cardboard pack to which a small tap-like piece is attached to control flow.

casket *noun* **caskets**
1 a small box for jewellery, etc. **2** a coffin.

casserole *noun* **casseroles**
1 a covered dish in which food is cooked. **2** food cooked in a dish of this kind, as in *a meat and vegetable casserole.*

cassette *noun* **cassettes**
a small sealed case containing recording tape, film, etc.
cassette recorder, a tape recorder that uses cassettes.

cast *verb* **casts, casting, cast**
1 to throw. **2** to shed or throw off. **3** to make a vote. **4** to make something of metal or plaster in a mould. **5** to choose the performers for a play, film, etc.
cast off, to untie a boat; to take stitches off your knitting-needle.
cast on, to put stitches on to your knitting-needle.

cast *noun* **casts**
1 a shape made by pouring liquid metal or plaster into a mould. **2** all the performers in a play, film, etc.

castanets *plural noun*
two pieces of wood, ivory, etc. held in one hand and clapped together to make a clicking sound, usually for Spanish dancing.

castaway *noun* **castaways**
a shipwrecked or marooned person.

caste

caste *noun* **castes** (*say* kahst)
1 one of the classes or divisions in which Hindus are born and whose members have no contact with other classes. 2 a social class or system based on dividing people into groups according to their wealth, etc.

castle *noun* **castles**
1 a large, old building made to protect people in it from attack. 2 a piece in chess, also called a *rook*.

castor or **caster** *noun* **castors** (*say* kah-stuh)
a small wheel on the leg of a table, chair, etc.
castor oil, oil made from the seeds of a tropical plant, used as a medicine.
castor sugar, finely-ground, white sugar.

casual *adjective*
1 not deliberate or planned, as in *a casual remark*. 2 informal; suitable for leisure time, as in *casual clothes*. 3 not regular or permanent, as in *casual work*.
casually *adverb*

casualty *noun* **casualties**
someone killed or injured in war or in an accident.

casuarina *noun* **casuarinas**
(*say* kazh-yuh-**ree**-nuh)
a type of tree or shrub with needle-like leaves and very slender branches.

cat *noun* **cats**
1 a small furry animal, usually kept as a pet and known for catching mice. 2 a lion, tiger, leopard, etc. 3 (*colloquial*) a spiteful girl or woman.
let the cat out of the bag, to reveal a secret.

catacomb *noun* **catacombs**
(*say* kat-uh-**koom** or kat-uh-**kohm**)
a series of underground passages and rooms where bodies used to be buried, especially in Ancient Rome.

catalogue *noun* **catalogues**
a list, especially of goods for sale.

catalyst *noun* **catalysts** (*say* **kat**-uh-luhst)
1 something that starts or speeds up a chemical reaction. 2 something or someone that starts or speeds up change, as in *The assassination of an Austrian archduke was the catalyst that sparked off the First World War*.

catamaran *noun* **catamarans**
a boat with two hulls fixed side by side.

catapult *noun* **catapults**
a device for shooting pellets, small stones, etc.

cataract *noun* **cataracts**
1 a large waterfall. 2 an eye disease which causes blurred vision.

catastrophe *noun* **catastrophes**
(*say* kuh-**tas**-truh-fee)
a great or sudden disaster.
catastrophic *adjective*

catch *verb* **catches, catching, caught**
1 to get hold of someone or something; to stop or intercept something. 2 to surprise or detect someone, as in *He was caught in the act*. 3 to get an illness, as in *She caught a cold*. 4 to be in time to get on a bus or train. 5 to hear or understand. 6 to become entangled; to cause something to be entangled, as in *I caught my sleeve on a rose bush*.
catch fire, to start burning.
catch on, (*colloquial*) to become popular; to understand, as in *a fashion that is catching on. Hasn't he caught on yet?*
catch someone out, to show that someone is wrong or mistaken.
catch up, to get level.

catch *noun* **catches**
1 something caught or worth catching, as in *He took a good catch at cricket. We had a large catch of fish*. 2 a hidden difficulty, as in *The catch in the agreement is you must pay extra*. 3 a device for fastening a door, window, etc.

catching *adjective*
(of a disease) easily caught, and liable to spread quickly, as in *Chicken-pox is catching*.

catchment area *noun* **catchment areas**
(*in Geography*) an area from which water drains into a river or a reservoir.

catch-phrase *noun* **catch-phrases**
a phrase that is used frequently, as in *'Life wasn't meant to be easy' is a well-known catch-phrase*.

catchy *adjective* **catchier, catchiest**
easy to remember; soon becoming popular, as in *a catchy tune*.

category *noun* **categories**
a group or division of people or things, as in *The competition had three categories: fiction, non-fiction, and poetry*.

cater *verb* **caters, catering, catered**
to provide food or entertainment.
caterer *noun*

caterpillar *noun* **caterpillars**
a long, creeping creature that turns into a butterfly or moth.

cathedral *noun* **cathedrals**
a large, important church having a bishop as its chief priest.

cathode *noun* **cathodes**
the electrode by which electric current leaves a device, as in *The cathode is the negative electrode in a cell such as a battery, while the anode is the positive electrode.*

Catholic *adjective*
1 to do with the Roman Catholic church.
2 to do with all Christians, as in *the Holy Catholic Church.*

Catholic *noun* **Catholics**
a Roman Catholic.

cat's-eye *noun* **cat's-eyes**
each of a line of devices containing small pieces of glass or plastic that reflect the lights of vehicles, set in the middle of a road or along its edge to help drivers see their way at night.

cattle *plural noun*
animals such as cows and bulls, especially bred for milk or meat.
cattle dog, a dog bred and trained to work with cattle, as in *Blue Heelers make good cattle dogs.*
cattle station, a large farm, especially in outback areas, where cattle are raised.

catwalk *noun* **catwalks**
a long, narrow platform used in fashion shows, etc.

caucus *noun* **caucuses** (*say* kaw-kuhs)
a meeting of the members of parliament who belong to a particular political party, as in *Labor's caucus voted for a new leader.*

caught past tense and past participle of **catch** *verb.*

cauldron *noun* **cauldrons**
a large, round, metal cooking-pot in which things are boiled.

cauliflower *noun* **cauliflowers**
a kind of cabbage with a large head of white flowers.

cause *noun* **causes**
1 what makes something happen; a reason, as in *You have no cause for complaint.* **2** a purpose for which people work, as in *She worked all her life for the cause of justice.* **3** an organisation or charity, as in *This collection is for a good cause.*

cause *verb* **causes, causing, caused**
to make something happen, as in *He likes to cause trouble.*

caution *noun* **cautions**
1 carefulness. **2** a warning.

cautious *adjective*
careful.
cautiously *adverb*

cavalry *noun*
soldiers who fight on horseback or in armoured vehicles.

cave *noun* **caves**
a large hole in the side of a hill or cliff, or under the ground.

cave *verb* **caves, caving, caved**
to explore caves.
cave in, to collapse.

cavern *noun* **caverns**
a cave, especially a deep or dark cave.

cavewoman *noun* **cavewomen**
a woman who lived in a cave in prehistoric times.

cavity *noun* **cavities**
a hollow or hole, as in *cavity in the wall; tooth cavity.*

CD short for **compact disc.**

CD-ROM short for *compact disc read-only memory,* a system for storing information to be displayed on a VDU screen.

cease *verb* **ceases, ceasing, ceased**
to stop.
cease-fire, an agreement to stop firing guns, etc. made between people who are fighting a war.

ceaseless *adjective*
never-ending.

cedar *noun* **cedars**
an evergreen tree with hard, sweet-smelling wood, as in *Cedar makes fine furniture.*

cede *verb* **cedes, ceding, ceded** (*say* seed)
to give up one's rights to or possession of something, as in *The defeated country ceded land to its enemy.*

ceiling *noun* **ceilings** (*say* see-ling)
1 the flat surface that covers the top of a room. **2** the highest limit that something can reach, as in *The auctioneer put a ceiling of $300 on the antique vase.*

celebrate *verb* **celebrates, celebrating, celebrated**
1 to do something to show that a day or an event is important, as in *We celebrate Christmas and birthdays.* **2** to perform a ceremony, as in *The priest celebrated mass.*
celebrated, famous.
celebration *noun*

celebrity *noun* **celebrities**
a famous person, as in *a TV celebrity.*

celery

celery *noun*
a vegetable with crisp green stems.

celibate *adjective* (*say* sel-uh-buht)
unmarried and not having sexual intercourse.
celibacy *noun*

cell *noun* **cells**
1 a small room, especially in a prison.
2 a very tiny part of a living creature or plant. 3 a device that uses energy from chemicals, heat, or light to produce electricity.

cellar *noun* **cellars**
an underground room.

cello *noun* **cellos** (*say* chel-oh)
a musical instrument with strings, like a very large violin, placed between the knees of the player.

cellular *adjective*
1 consisting of cells, as in *the cellular structure of living things.* 2 using a network of radio stations to allow messages to be sent over a wide area, as in *a cellular telephone.*

cellulite *noun* (*say* sel-yuh-luyt)
lumpy fat, especially on the hips and thighs.

cellulose *noun*
tissue that forms the main part of all plants and trees.

Celsius *adjective*
using a scale for measuring temperature that gives 0 degrees for freezing water and 100 degrees for boiling water.

Celtic *adjective* (*say* kel-tik)
to do with the people descended from those who lived in Britain before the Romans came and now living in Wales, Scotland, and Ireland, as in *a Celtic language.*

cement *noun*
1 a powdery mixture of lime and clay which, when mixed with water, is used in building to make floors, join bricks together, etc. 2 a strong glue.

cemetery *noun* **cemeteries** (*say* sem-uh-tree)
a place where dead people are buried.

cenotaph *noun* **cenotaphs** (*say* sen-uh-tahf)
a tomb-like monument to a person whose body is elsewhere, as in *The cenotaph was a memorial to the soldier killed in war.*

censor *noun* **censors**
someone who looks at films, books, letters, etc. and removes anything that he or she thinks may be harmful.
censorship *noun*

censor *verb* **censors, censoring, censored**
to look at films, books, letters, etc. as your official job, removing anything that you think may be harmful.

censure *noun*
criticising or disapproving of something.

census *noun* **censuses**
an official count or survey of population, traffic, etc.

cent *noun* **cents**
a coin equal to one hundredth of a dollar.

centenary *noun* **centenaries**
the hundredth anniversary of something.

centimetre *noun* **centimetres**
one-hundredth of a metre.

centipede *noun* **centipedes**
a small, long creature with many legs.

central *adjective*
1 to do with the centre. 2 most important, as in *She will have a central role in our plans.*
central heating, a method of heating a building by pipes, radiators, etc. supplied from a central source.
centralise *verb*, **centrally** *adverb*

centre *noun* **centres**
1 the middle of something. 2 an important place, as in *the centre of the country's steel industry.* 3 a place where particular things happen, as in *a shopping centre; a leisure centre.* 4 (*in Sport*) the middle player in a line in some field games.
centre of gravity, the point in an object around which its mass is perfectly balanced.
Red Centre, Central Australia.

centrifugal *adjective*
moving away from the centre; using centrifugal force, as in *a centrifugal pump.*
centrifugal force, a force that appears to make something revolving move out from the centre.

centurion *noun* **centurions**
an officer in the ancient Roman army, originally commanding a hundred men.

century *noun* **centuries**
1 one hundred years. 2 a hundred runs scored by a batter in an innings at cricket.

ceramic *adjective*
made from baked clay, as in *ceramic pots.*

ceramics *plural noun*
the art of making objects out of clay; the items made, as in *Ceramics is studied at art school. Ceramics were sold at the fete.*

cereal *noun* **cereals**
  1 a grass that produces seeds which are used as food, as in *Cereals include wheat, barley, oats, maize, and rye.*   2 a breakfast food made from seeds of this kind.

cerebral *adjective* (*say* **se**-ruh-bruhl)
  to do with the brain.

ceremony *noun* **ceremonies**
  (*say* **se**-ruh-muh-nee)
  the solemn actions carried out at a wedding, funeral, or other important occasion.
  ceremonial *adjective*

certain *adjective*
  1 sure, as in *I am certain of that.*   2 without doubt, as in *It is certain that he is guilty.*
  a certain person or **thing,** someone or something that is known but not named or described.
  for certain, for sure.
  make certain, to make sure.
  certainly *adverb*

certificate *noun* **certificates**
  an official document that can be used to prove something, as in *a birth certificate; a building certificate.*

certify *verb* **certifies, certifying, certified**
  to declare something officially, especially that someone is insane.

cervix *noun* **cervices** (*say* **ser**-viks)
  the neck-like entrance to the womb.

CFC short for *chloro-fluorocarbon,*
  a chemical used in refrigerators and aerosols, thought to be harmful to the ozone layer.

chain *noun* **chains**
  1 a row of metal rings fastened together.   2 a group of associated hotels, shops, restaurants, etc., as in *the McDonald's chain.*   3 a connected series of things, as in *a chain of events.*
  chain gang, a party of convicts who, in earlier times, were chained together and given hard labour.
  chain reaction, a series of happenings, one causing another.
  chain saw, a saw with teeth on a loop of chain driven round by a motor.

chair *noun* **chairs**
  1 a seat, usually with a back, for one person.   2 the person who is in control of a meeting.
  chair-lift, a set of seats hanging from a moving cable, carrying people up a mountain, etc.

chairperson *noun* **chairpersons**
  the person who is in control of a meeting.

chalet *noun* **chalets** (*say* **shal**-ay)
  a small house with a sloping pointed roof, usually built of wood and often used as a holiday house, particularly in the snowfields.

chalk *noun* **chalks**
  1 a kind of soft white rock.   2 a soft white stick of a similar rock, used for writing on blackboards, etc.
  chalky *adjective*

challenge *noun* **challenges**
  something difficult that you have to do, or that you ask someone to do, as in *I accept the challenge to climb the mountain.*

challenge *verb* **challenges, challenging, challenged**
  to ask someone to do something difficult, have a contest, etc.
  challenger *noun*

chamber *noun* **chambers**
  1 (*old-fashioned use*) a room.   2 a hall used for meetings of a parliament, etc.
  chamber music, music for a small group of players.

chambers *plural noun*
  rooms used by a barrister or a judge.

chameleon *noun* **chameleons**
  (*say* kuh-**mee**-lee-uhn)
  a small lizard able to change colour to suit the colour of its surroundings.

champagne *noun* (*say* sham-**payn**)
  a bubbly French wine.

champion *noun* **champions**
  1 the best person in a sport, competition, etc.   2 someone who supports a cause by fighting, speaking, etc., as in *Martin Luther King was a champion of human rights.*

championship *noun* **championships**
  a contest to decide who is the best player, competitor, etc.

chance *noun* **chances**
  1 a possibility; an opportunity, as in *This is your only chance.*   2 a risk, as in *Take a chance.*   3 the way things happen accidentally, as in *It was pure chance that we met.*
  by chance, accidentally; without any planning, as in *By chance, I caught a glimpse of what he was writing. We found the place by chance.*

chandelier *noun* **chandeliers**
  (*say* shan-duh-**leer**)
  a hanging support with branches for several lights.

a
b
c
d
e
f
g
h
i
j
k
l
m
n
o
p
q
r
s
t
u
v
w
x
y
z

change

change *noun* **changes**
1 the act of changing, as in *a sudden change in the weather*. **2** the money that you get back when you give more money than is needed to pay for something. **3** another set of clothes. **4** a variation in your routine, as in *Let's walk home for a change*.

change *verb* **changes, changing, changed**
1 to make something or someone different; to become different. **2** to exchange, as in *I changed my car for a van*. **3** to give coins or notes of small values in exchange for other money, as in *Can you change a $20 note?* **4** to put on different clothes, as in *She changed for her aerobics class*.

channel *noun* **channels**
1 a stretch of water joining two seas, as in *The English Channel is between Britain and France*. **2** a broadcasting wavelength. **3** a method of communication, as in *He approached his boss through the usual channels*. **4** a way for water to flow along, as in *stormwater channel*. **5** the part of a river, sea, etc. that is deep enough for ships.

chant *noun* **chants**
a tune, especially one that is often repeated.

chant *verb* **chants, chanting, chanted**
to say or call words in a rhythm; to sing, as in *They chanted nursery rhymes*.

chaos *noun* (*say* **kay**-os)
complete disorder, as in *The room was in chaos*.
chaotic *adjective*

chap *noun* **chaps**
(*colloquial*) a man or boy.

chapel *noun* **chapels**
1 a place within a church or belonging to a school, etc., used for Christian worship. **2** a small church.

chapped *adjective*
with rough, cracked skin.

chapter *noun* **chapters**
a section of a book.

char *verb* **chars, charring, charred**
to scorch; to blacken with fire.

character *noun* **characters**
1 the characteristics of a person or thing. **2** a person, especially in a story or play. **3** an interesting or eccentric person, as in *Maurice is quite a character*.

characteristic *adjective*
typical.

characteristic *noun* **characteristics**
something that makes a person or thing noticeable or different from others.

charades *plural noun* (*say* shuh-**rahdz**)
a game in which people have to guess a word from other people's acting.

charcoal *noun*
a black substance made by burning wood slowly.

charge *verb* **charges, charging, charged**
1 to ask a particular price. **2** to accuse someone of committing a crime. **3** to rush to attack someone or something. **4** to store electrical energy in something, as in *Please charge the torch batteries*.

charge *noun* **charges**
1 the price asked for something. **2** accusing someone of a crime. **3** rushing to attack. **4** the amount of explosive needed to fire a gun, etc. **5** electricity in something.
in charge of, deciding what shall happen to a person or thing; controlling.

chariot *noun* **chariots**
a horse-drawn vehicle with two wheels, used in ancient times for fighting, racing, etc.
charioteer *noun*

charisma *noun* (*say* kuh-**riz**-muh)
the quality that makes someone special, popular, influential, etc., as in *Most voters seem to prefer a leader with charisma*.
charismatic *adjective*

charity *noun* **charities**
1 giving money, help, etc. to other people. **2** an organisation to help those in need, as in *The Red Cross is a well-known charity*.
charitable *adjective*

charm *noun* **charms**
1 attractiveness. **2** a magic spell. **3** something small worn or carried for good luck.

charm *verb* **charms, charming, charmed**
1 to give pleasure or delight to someone; to attract. **2** to put a spell on; to bewitch.

chart *noun* **charts**
1 a large map used especially to navigate the seas. **2** a diagram, list, etc. giving information in an orderly way.
the charts, (*colloquial*) a list of the records that are most popular.

charter *noun* **charters**
1 an official document giving someone rights, etc., as in *The Magna Carta is a well-known charter*. **2** hiring a plane, vehicle, etc.
charter flight, a flight by a hired plane.

chemical

charter *verb* charters, chartering, chartered
to hire a plane, vehicle, etc.

chase *verb* chases, chasing, chased
to go quickly to try to catch up with someone or something.

chasm *noun* chasms (*say* **kaz**-uhm)
a deep opening in the ground.

chassis *noun* chassis (*say* **shaz**-ee *or* **shas**-ee)
the frame of a vehicle, etc. on which the body is put.

chastise *verb* chastises, chastising, chastised
to rebuke severely or punish, as in *They were chastised for stealing.*

chat *verb* chats, chatting, chatted
to have a friendly or informal talk.
chat up, (*colloquial*) to talk to someone in a friendly way because you are attracted to him or her, as in *Carly was trying to chat up Tim at the party last night.*

chat *noun* chats
a friendly or informal talk with someone.
chatty *adjective*

chatter *verb* chatters, chattering, chattered
1 to talk quickly or stupidly; to talk too much. 2 to make a rattling noise, as in *Her teeth chattered in the cold wind.*

chauffeur *noun* chauffeurs (*say* **shoh**-fuh *or* shoh-**fer**)
someone who is paid to drive a car.

chauvinism *noun* (*say* **shoh**-vuh-niz-uhm)
too much or prejudiced support for a particular cause, group, sex, etc.
male chauvinist, a man who shows prejudice against women.
chauvinist *noun and adjective*

cheap *adjective* cheaper, cheapest
1 low in price; not expensive. 2 having inferior quality.

cheat *verb* cheats, cheating, cheated
1 to trick someone. 2 to try to do well in an examination, game, etc. by breaking the rules.

cheat *noun* cheats
someone who cheats.

check *verb* checks, checking, checked
1 to make sure that something is correct or in good condition, as in *Please check your tyres.* 2 to make something stop or go slower, as in *The train's delay checked their progress.*
check in, to sign your name to show you have arrived at a hotel; to show your ticket at an airport.

check on or **up on something,** to look at something and see whether it is correct or suitable.
check out, to pay your bill and leave a hotel; to check on something.

check *noun* checks
1 checking something. 2 something that stops or slows down, as in *A desire to be fit put a check on their eating junk food.* 3 the situation in chess when a king may be taken. 4 a pattern of squares.

Usage Do not confuse **check** with **cheque,** which means a piece of paper telling your bank to pay money out of your account.

checkmate *noun* checkmates
the winning situation in chess.

checkout *noun* checkouts
the place where you pay in a supermarket or a large shop.

check-up *noun* check-ups
a careful check or examination, especially a medical one.

cheddar *noun*
a kind of hard cheese.

cheek *noun* cheeks
1 the side of the face below the eye. 2 impudence.

cheek *verb* cheeks, cheeking, cheeked
to be cheeky to someone.

cheeky *adjective* cheekier, cheekiest
impudent or bold.
cheekily *adverb*, **cheekiness** *noun*

cheer *noun* cheers
a shout of pleasure; a shout praising or encouraging someone.

cheer *verb* cheers, cheering, cheered
1 to give a cheer. 2 to comfort or encourage someone.
cheer up, to make someone cheerful; to become cheerful.

cheerful *adjective*
happy.

cheese *noun* cheeses
a solid food made from milk curds.
cheesy *adjective*

cheetah *noun* cheetahs
a large, spotted animal of the cat family, that can run very fast.

chef *noun* chefs (*say* shef)
a cook, especially the chief cook in a restaurant, etc.

chemical *adjective*
to do with chemistry.

chemical

chemical *noun* chemicals
a substance used in or obtained by chemistry.

chemist *noun* chemists
1 someone who makes or sells medicines. 2 an expert in chemistry.

chemistry *noun*
1 the way that substances combine and react with one another. 2 the study of these combinations, reactions, etc.

cheque *noun* cheques
1 a written instruction to a bank to pay money out of your account. 2 the form you write this instruction on.
cheque-book, a number of blank cheques fastened together.

Usage Do not confuse **cheque** with **check** *noun*, which means the action of making sure that something is correct or in good condition.

cherish *verb* cherishes, cherishing, cherished
1 to protect lovingly. 2 to be fond of.

cherry *noun* cherries
a small, round, reddish fruit with a stone.

cherub *noun* cherubim
1 an angel that is represented in art as a plump child with wings. 2 a beautiful, innocent, or well-behaved child.

chess *noun*
a game for two players with sixteen pieces each (called **chessmen**) on a board of 64 squares (called a **chessboard**).

chest *noun* chests
1 a big, strong box. 2 the front part of your body between your neck and your waist.
chest of drawers, a piece of furniture with drawers.
get something off your chest, (*colloquial*) to say something that you are anxious to say.

chestnut *noun* chestnuts
1 a European tree or the glossy, hard, edible nut it produces. 2 a horse of reddish-brown colour.

chew *verb* chews, chewing, chewed
to grind food between your teeth.
chewy *adjective*

chewing-gum *noun*
a sticky flavoured substance for chewing.

chic *adjective* (*say* sheek)
stylish and elegant, as in *a chic outfit*.

chick *noun* chicks
a very young bird, especially a very young chicken.

chicken *noun* chickens
1 a young fowl. 2 a fowl's flesh used as food.

chicken *adjective*
(*colloquial*) afraid; cowardly.

chicken *verb* chickens, chickening, chickened
chicken out, (*colloquial*) to stop or withdraw because you are afraid.

chicken-pox *noun*
a disease that produces red itchy spots on your skin.

chief *noun* chiefs
the most important person or leader in a group, as in *chief of the army*.

chief *adjective*
most important, as in *The chief cause of the famine was drought*.

chieftain *noun* chieftains
the chief of a tribe, clan, band of robbers, etc.

chiffon *noun* chiffons (*say* **shif**-on *or* shuh-**fon**)
a light, see-through fabric made from silk, nylon, etc.

chilblain *noun* chilblains
a sore, usually on a hand or foot, caused by cold weather.

child *noun* children
1 a young person; a boy or girl.
2 someone's son or daughter.
child care, the care of children, especially in a crèche, etc.

childhood *noun* childhoods
the time when you are a child.

childish *adjective*
1 suitable for children, as in *a childish game*. 2 immature, as in *Don't be childish!*

childlike *adjective*
having the good qualities of a child, such as innocence, honesty, etc.

childproof *adjective*
not able to be opened or operated by small children, as in *The car has childproof door-locks*.

chill *noun* chills
1 coldness. 2 an illness that makes you shiver, as in *Don't catch a chill in the rain*.

chill *verb* chills, chilling, chilled
to make something or someone cold, as in *Chill the drinks*.

chilli *noun* chillies
a small, hot-tasting, green or red variety of capsicum.

chilly *adjective* **chillier, chilliest**
  1 slightly cold. 2 unfriendly, as in *a chilly welcome*.
  chilliness *noun*

chime *noun* **chimes**
  a sound made by a bell.

chime *verb* **chimes, chiming, chimed**
  to ring, as in *The clock chimes every hour*.

chimney *noun* **chimneys**
  a tall pipe or structure that carries away smoke from a fire.

chimpanzee *noun* **chimpanzees**
  a small African ape.

chin *noun* **chins**
  the part of the face under the mouth.

china *noun*
  thin, delicate pottery.

chink *noun* **chinks**
  1 a narrow opening, as in *He looked through a chink in the curtains*. 2 a clinking sound, as in *They heard the chink of coins*.

chip *noun* **chips**
  1 a small piece cut from something larger. 2 a place where a small piece has been knocked off something. 3 a small piece of potato that is fried. 4 a small counter used in games. 5 a small piece of silicon inside a computer with electric circuits on it which can store information or perform technical operations; a silicon chip.
  to have a chip on your shoulder, (*colloquial*) to have a grievance; to be ready to quarrel or fight, as in *He's got a chip on his shoulder about wealthy people*.

chip *verb* **chips, chipping, chipped**
  to knock small pieces off something, as in *He chipped the cup on the tap*.

chirp *verb* **chirps, chirping, chirped**
  to make short, sharp sounds like a small bird.

chirpy *adjective* **chirpier, chirpiest**
  (*colloquial*) lively and cheerful.

chisel *noun* **chisels**
  a tool with a sharp end for shaping wood, stone, etc.

chisel *verb* **chisels, chiselling, chiselled**
  to shape or cut with a chisel.
  chiseller *noun*

chlorine *noun*
  a chemical used to disinfect water, etc.
  chlorinate *verb*, **chlorination** *noun*

chlorophyll *noun*
  the substance that makes plants green.

chocolate *noun* **chocolates**
  1 a sweet, brown food. 2 a sweet made of or covered with this substance. 3 a sweet powder used for making drinks; a drink made of it.

choice *noun* **choices**
  1 the act of choosing. 2 the power to choose between things, as in *Please make your choice of food*. 3 what you have chosen, as in *This book is my choice*.

choke *verb* **chokes, choking, choked**
  1 to stop someone breathing properly.
  2 to be unable to breathe properly.
  3 to block up something.

choke *noun* **chokes**
  a device in a motor vehicle to control the amount of air mixed with the petrol.

cholesterol *noun* (*say* kuh-**les**-tuh-rol)
  a substance found in all the cells of your body that helps to carry fat and that is thought to be bad for your arteries if you have too much of it.

choose *verb* **chooses, choosing, chose, chosen**
  1 to decide to take one person or thing instead of another. 2 to make a decision about something, as in *He chose not to play football*.

choosy *adjective* **choosier, choosiest**
  (*colloquial*)
  1 hard to please, as in *That cat is getting choosy—she won't eat ordinary cat-food*.
  2 careful and cautious when making a choice.

chop *verb* **chops, chopping, chopped**
  to cut or hit something with a heavy blow.

chop *noun* **chops**
  1 a chopping blow. 2 a small, thick slice of meat with a bone.
  get the chop, (*colloquial*) to be dismissed or killed.

chopper *noun* **choppers**
  1 a small axe. 2 (*colloquial*) a helicopter.

choppy *adjective* **choppier, choppiest**
  full of small waves, as in *a choppy sea*.

chopsticks *plural noun*
  a pair of thin sticks used for eating Chinese, Japanese, Vietnamese, etc. food.

choral *adjective* (*say* **ko**-ruhl)
  to do with a choir or chorus, as in *There was a choral performance at the church*.

chord

chord *noun* **chords** (*say* kawd)
a number of musical notes sounded together.

Usage Do not confuse **chord** with **cord**, which means a piece of thin rope.

chore *noun* **chores** (*say* chaw)
a hard job; a regular task, as in *household chores*.

choreography *noun* (*say* ko-ree-**og**-ruh-fee)
the design or arrangement of a ballet, dancers, etc.

chorus *noun* **choruses** (*say* **kaw**-ruhs)
1 a group of people singing or speaking together. **2** music sung by a group of people. **3** the words repeated after every verse of a song or poem.

christen *verb* **christens, christening, christened**
to baptise someone and give a name to, as in *He was christened John*.
christening *noun*

Christian *noun* **Christians**
someone who believes in the teachings of Christ.
Christianity *noun*

Christian *adjective*
to do with Christ or Christians.
Christian name, a name that someone has besides his or her surname, as in *Her Christian name is Catherine*.

Christmas *noun* **Christmases**
the time of celebrating Jesus's birthday on 25 December or the days around it.
Christmas pudding, a rich pudding eaten at Christmas.
Christmas tree, an evergreen or artificial tree decorated at Christmas.

chromatic *adjective*
to do with colours, especially bright ones.
chromatic scale, a musical scale going up or down in semitones.

chrome *noun*
a shiny, silvery metal.

chromosome *noun* **chromosomes**
the part of an animal cell that carries genes.

chronic *adjective*
1 lasting for a long time, as in *a chronic disease*. **2** (*colloquial*) very bad, as in *a chronic film*.
chronically *adverb*

chronicle *noun* **chronicles**
a record of events.

chronological *adjective*
in the order in which things happen.
chronologically *adverb*

chronology *noun*
the arrangement of events in the order in which they happened, especially in history or geology.

chrysalis *noun* **chrysalises** (*say* **kris**-uh-lis *or* **kris**-uh-luhs)
the cover a caterpillar makes around itself before it turns into a butterfly or moth.

chrysanthemum *noun* **chrysanthemums**
a garden plant with white or brightly-coloured flowers which blooms in autumn.

chubby *adjective* **chubbier, chubbiest**
plump, as in *a chubby baby*.

chuck *verb* **chucks, chucking, chucked**
(*colloquial*) to throw.

chuckle *verb* **chuckles, chuckling, chuckled**
to laugh quietly.

chuckle *noun* **chuckles**
a quiet laugh.

chunk *noun* **chunks**
a thick lump, as in *a chunk of meat*.
chunky *adjective*

church *noun* **churches**
1 a building where Christians worship.
2 Christian worship, as in *Do you go to church?*
the Church, a group or organisation of Christians, as in *the Anglican Church; the Catholic Church*.

churinga *noun*
a sacred Aboriginal object which is normally carved or painted.

Origin This word comes from Aranda, an Aboriginal language of the Northern Territory. See the Aboriginal Languages map at the back of this dictionary.

churn *noun* **churns**
1 a large container for milk. **2** a machine for making butter.

churn *verb* **churns, churning, churned**
1 to make butter in a churn. **2** to stir something vigorously.
churn out, to produce large quantities of something.

chute *noun* **chutes** (*say* shoot)
a steep channel for people or things to slide down, as in *laundry chute*.

chutney *noun*
a strong-tasting mixture of fruit, chillies, sugar, vinegar, etc.

cider *noun*
an alcoholic or non-alcoholic drink made from apples.

cigar *noun* cigars
a roll of compressed tobacco-leaves for smoking.

cigarette *noun* cigarettes
a small, thin roll of shredded tobacco in thin paper for smoking.

cinder *noun* cinders
a small piece of coal, wood, etc. partly burned.

cinema *noun* cinemas
a place where people go to see films.

cinnamon *noun*
a light-brown spice used to flavour food.

circle *noun* circles
1 a round, flat shape; the shape of a coin or wheel, as in *The edge of a circle is always the same distance from the centre.* 2 something like a circle, as in *The players formed a circle around their coach.* 3 a balcony in a cinema or theatre. 4 a number of people with similar interests, as in *She belongs to a writers' circle.*

circle *verb* circles, circling, circled
1 to move in a circle, as in *Vultures circled overhead.* 2 to go around something, as in *The space probe circled Mars.*

circuit *noun* circuits (*say* ser-kuht)
1 a circular line or journey. 2 a racecourse. 3 the path of an electric current.
circuit-breaker, an automatic device for stopping the flow of current in an electric circuit.

circular *adjective*
like a circle; round.

circular *noun* circulars
a letter, advertisement, etc. sent to a lot of people.

circulate *verb* circulates, circulating, circulated
1 to move around and come back to the beginning, as in *Blood circulates in the body.* 2 to send something to people, as in *Has the announcement been circulated?* 3 to move around among guests, as in *The host circulated at his party.*

circulation *noun* circulations
1 the movement of blood around your body. 2 the number of copies of each issue of a newspaper, etc. that is sold.

circumference *noun* circumferences
the line or distance around something, especially around a circle.

circumnavigate *verb* circumnavigates, circumnavigating, circumnavigated
to sail around, as in *The yacht circumnavigated the world.*

circumstance *noun* circumstances
a fact, condition, event, etc. connected with someone or something, as in *He won under difficult circumstances.*

circus *noun* circuses
1 an entertainment with clowns, acrobats, animals, etc., usually performed in a big tent. 2 an area for sports and games in ancient times.

cistern *noun* cisterns
a tank for storing water, as in *toilet cistern.*

citizen *noun* citizens
1 someone born in a city or country, or living there. 2 someone who has full rights in a country.

citizenship *noun*
the status or rights of a citizen.
citizen *noun*

citizenship ceremony *noun* citizenship ceremonies
a special occasion when a person becomes an official member of a country.

citric acid *noun*
a weak acid found in fruits like lemons and limes.

citrus *adjective*
to do with fruits like oranges, lemons, and grapefruit.

city *noun* cities
1 a large, important town. 2 the people who live in a city, as in *Almost the entire city turned out to support its team.*

civic *adjective*
to do with a city, citizens, or their council, as in *civic offices.*

civil *adjective*
1 to do with citizen, as in *civil liberties.* 2 to do with people who are not in the armed forces. 3 polite.
civil engineering, designing and making roads, bridges, and large buildings.
civil rights, the rights of citizens, especially to have freedom, equality, and the right to vote.
civil war, a war fought between groups of people of the same country, such as the English Civil War (1642–51) or the American Civil War (1861–65).

civilian *noun* civilians
someone who is not in the armed services or police force.

a
b
c
d
e
f
g
h
i
j
k
l
m
n
o
p
q
r
s
t
u
v
w
x
y
z

civilisation

civilisation or **civilization** *noun* civilisations
1 the act of making or becoming civilised, as in *Ancient Rome brought civilisation to the provinces it ruled.* 2 a civilised condition or society, as in *The Chinese civilisation is much older than any in Europe.*

civilise or **civilize** *verb* civilises, civilising, civilised
to improve someone's behaviour, manners, education, etc.

clad *adjective*
clothed or covered, as in *a knight clad in armour; a building clad with granite.*

claim *verb* claims, claiming, claimed
1 to ask for something that you think belongs to you. 2 to state or declare, as in *He claims his evidence is accurate.*

claim *noun* claims
1 a demand or request for something you think is your due, as in *an insurance claim.* 2 something claimed, especially a piece of ground claimed or given for mining, etc. 3 the right or title to something, as in *After your patience you have a claim to be heard.*

claimant *noun* claimants
someone who asks for something that he or she thinks should be given to him or her, especially benefit payments.

clam *noun* clams
a large edible shellfish.

clamber *verb* clambers, clambering, clambered
to climb with difficulty, as in *We clambered up the muddy slope.*

clammy *adjective* clammier, clammiest
unpleasantly damp and sticky.

clamour or **clamor** *noun* clamours
a loud or angry shouting or noise, as in *A clamour arose in the classroom when the teacher gave detention at lunchtime.*

clamp *noun* clamps
a device for holding things together.

clamp *verb* clamps, clamping, clamped
to fix with a clamp.
clamp down on something, to stop or try to stop something.

clan *noun* clans
a group sharing the same ancestor, especially among Aboriginal groups and in the Scottish Highlands.

clang *verb* clangs, clanging, clanged
to make a loud ringing sound.

clanger *noun* clangers
(*colloquial*) a mistake.
drop a clanger, to make a mistake.

clap *verb* claps, clapping, clapped
to make a noise by hitting the palms of your hands together, especially as applause.

clap *noun* claps
1 clapping, especially as applause, as in *Give our winning team a good clap!* 2 a sudden sharp noise, as in *a clap of thunder.*

clarify *verb* clarifies, clarifying, clarified
to make something clear.
clarification *noun*

clarinet *noun* clarinets
a woodwind instrument.
clarinettist *noun*

clarity *noun*
clearness, as in *Speak with clarity.*

clash *noun* clashes
1 a loud jarring sound like metal objects struck together. 2 a conflict.

clash *verb* clashes, clashing, clashed
1 to make a loud sound like cymbals banging together. 2 to happen inconveniently at the same time, as in *I missed one of those programs because they clashed.* 3 to differ; to come into conflict, as in *Their views on the book clashed. Gangs of rival supporters clashed outside the football ground.*

clasp *noun* clasps
1 a device for fastening things. 2 a grasp or embrace.

clasp *verb* clasps, clasping, clasped
to hold someone or something tightly.

class *noun* classes
1 a group of similar people, animals, or things. 2 a system of different ranks in society, as in *the working class.* 3 a group of children, students, etc. who are taught together. 4 (*colloquial*) elegant appearance or behaviour, as in *That actor has really got class.* 5 the best quality, as in *They travelled first class.*

class *verb* classes, classing, classed
to put things in classes or groups, as in *The wool was classed as extra fine.*

classic *adjective*
generally agreed to be excellent or important, as in *a classic wine.*

classic *noun* classics
a book, film, writer, etc. that is generally agreed to be excellent or important.
classics, Greek and Latin language or literature.

classical *adjective*
1 to do with Greek or Roman literature, etc. 2 serious or conventional, as in *classical music*.

classified *adjective*
1 put into classes or groups. 2 officially secret, as in *classified information*.
classified advertisements, small advertisements arranged in columns according to their subject.

classify *verb* **classifies, classifying, classified**
to put things in classes or groups.
classification *noun*

classroom *noun* **classrooms**
a room where a class is taught.

clatter *noun*
a rattling or annoying noise.

clatter *verb* **clatters, clattering, clattered**
to make a rattling or annoying noise.

clause *noun* **clauses**
1 part of a contract, treaty, law, etc. 2 (*in grammar*) part of a sentence with its own verb, as in *There are two clauses in 'I'm wearing the T-shirt which you gave me'*.

claustrophobia *noun*
(*say* klos-truh-**foh**-bee-uh *or* klaws-truh-**foh**-bee-uh)
the abnormal fear of being confined in a small place.
claustrophobic *adjective*

claw *noun* **claws**
one of the hard, sharp nails that some birds and other animals have on their feet.

claw *verb* **claws, clawing, clawed**
to grasp or scratch with a claw or hand.

clay *noun*
a sticky kind of earth, as in *Clay is used for making bricks and pottery*.
clayey *adjective*

clean *adjective* **cleaner, cleanest**
1 without any dirt or stains. 2 fresh; not yet used, as in *a clean page*. 3 not rude or obscene, as in *clean jokes*. 4 honest, as in *a clean fight*.
cleanliness *noun*, **cleanly** *adjective and adverb*, **cleanness** *noun*

clean *adverb*
completely, as in *I clean forgot*.
clean bowled, bowled out in cricket without your bat touching the ball.
clean-shaven, without a beard or moustache.

clean *verb* **cleans, cleaning, cleaned**
to make something clean.

cleaner *noun* **cleaners**
1 someone who cleans rooms, etc. 2 something used for cleaning.

cleanse *verb* **cleanses, cleansing, cleansed**
(*say* klenz)
to make clean or pure, as in *Cleanse the cut carefully. Cleanse the system*.
cleanser *noun*

clear *adjective* **clearer, clearest**
1 easy to understand, see, or hear, as in *a clear voice*. 2 free from obstacles or unwanted things, as in *The table is clear*. 3 transparent, as in *clear glass*.
clearly *adverb*, **clearness** *noun*

clear *adverb*
1 clearly, as in *Speak loud and clear*. 2 completely, as in *He got clear away*. 3 at a distance from something, as in *Stand clear of the gates*.

clear *verb* **clears, clearing, cleared**
1 to make or become clear or free from obstacles, as in *His argument was made clear by further explanation. The drain was cleared of tree roots*. 2 to show or check that someone is innocent or reliable, as in *His name was cleared by the new evidence*. 3 to jump over something without touching it.
clear off, (*colloquial*) to go away.
clear out, to empty or tidy something; (*colloquial*) to go away.
clear up, to make things tidy.

clearance *noun* **clearances**
1 the removal of something that obstructs, causes a problem, etc., as in *a clearance of bush to prevent fire*. 2 getting rid of unwanted goods. 3 the space between two things. 4 permission, as in *The plane was given clearance to take off*.

clearing *noun* **clearings**
an open space in the bush, forest, etc.

clef *noun* **clefs**
a sign at the beginning of a line of a written piece of music that shows what musical key it is in.

clench *verb* **clenches, clenching, clenched**
to close your teeth or fingers tightly.

clergy *plural noun*
people who have official permission to conduct services in a Christian church.

clerical *adjective*
1 to do with office workers and clerks. 2 to do with the clergy, as in *clerical collar*.

clerk *noun* **clerks** (*say* klahk)
someone employed to keep records and accounts, deal with papers in an office, etc.

clever

clever *adjective* **cleverer, cleverest**
quick to learn and understand things; skilful.

cliché *noun* **clichés** (*say* klee-shay)
a phrase or idea that is used too often, as in *'She was as pretty as a picture' is a cliché.*

click *noun* **clicks**
a short, sharp sound, as in *She heard a click as someone turned on the light.*

client *noun* **clients**
someone who gets help or advice from a lawyer, architect, accountant, etc.; a customer.

cliff *noun* **cliffs**
a steep rock-face, especially on the coast.

cliff-hanger *noun* **cliff-hangers**
something like a story or a sports match that is exciting because you do not know how it will finish.

climate *noun* **climates**
the normal weather conditions in a particular area as observed over a long period.
climatic *adjective*

climax *noun* **climaxes**
the most important or exciting part of a story, series of events, etc., as in *The climax of the game was when the winning goal was scored.*
climactic *adjective*

climb *verb* **climbs, climbing, climbed**
1 to go up or down something. 2 to grow upwards. 3 to rise.
climb down, to admit that you have been wrong.
climber *noun*

cling *verb* **clings, clinging, clung**
to hold on tightly, as in *The child clung to its mother.*

clinic *noun* **clinics**
a place where people see doctors, etc. for treatment or advice, as in *dental clinic.*

clink *verb* **clinks, clinking, clinked**
to make a short ringing sound.

clip *noun* **clips**
1 a fastener for keeping things together.
2 a trimming. 3 a short part from a film, video, etc. 4 the amount of wool from a sheep, flock, etc., as in *The season's clip was good.*

clip *verb* **clips, clipping, clipped**
1 to fasten with a clip. 2 to cut something with shears or scissors.

clipboard *noun* **clipboards**
a board that you can carry around, with a clip at the top to hold papers.

clipper *noun* **clippers**
an old type of fast sailing-ship.

clippers *plural noun*
an instrument for clipping hedges, hair, nails, etc.

clipping *noun* **clippings**
a piece cut off or out, especially from a newspaper or magazine.

cloak *noun* **cloaks**
a piece of clothing, usually without sleeves, that hangs loosely from your shoulders.

cloakroom *noun* **cloakrooms**
a place where you can leave coats, hats, bags, etc.

clock *noun* **clocks**
a device that shows what the time is.

clockwise *adverb* and *adjective*
moving around a circle in the same direction as a clock's hands.

clockwork *adjective*
worked by a spring which you wind up.
like clockwork, smoothly and regularly, as in *Our plans went like clockwork.*

clog *noun* **clogs**
1 a shoe with a wooden sole.

clog *verb* **clogs, clogging, clogged**
to block something up, as in *Fat clogged the drain.*

cloister *noun* **cloisters**
1 a covered path around a courtyard or along the side of a cathedral, monastery, etc. 2 a monastery or convent where monks and nuns live in a secluded way.

clone *noun* **clones**
an animal or plant made from the cells of another animal or plant.

clone *verb* **clones, cloning, cloned**
to produce a clone.

close *adjective* **closer, closest** (*say* klohs)
1 near. 2 careful; detailed, as in *with close attention.* 3 tight; with little empty space, as in *a close fit.* 4 in which competitors are nearly equal, as in *a close race.* 5 stuffy, as in *It's very close in this room.*
closely *adverb*, **closeness** *noun*

close *adverb* **closer, closest** (*say* klohs)
at only a short distance; closely, as in *Follow close behind.*

close *noun* **closes** (*say* klohs)
a street closed at one end.

coach

close *verb* **closes, closing, closed** (*say* klohz)
1 to shut. 2 to end or finish.
close in, to get nearer or shorter, as in *The police closed in around the house. The evenings close in as winter gets nearer.*

close-up *noun* **close-ups** (*say* **klohs**-up)
a photograph or film taken at short range.

closure *noun* **closures** (*say* kloh-*zhuh*)
the closing of something, as in *The government was responsible for several school closures.*

clot *noun* **clots**
1 a mass of blood, cream, etc. that has nearly become solid. 2 (*colloquial*) a stupid person.

clot *verb* **clots, clotting, clotted**
to form into clots.

cloth *noun* **cloths**
1 material woven from wool, cotton, nylon, etc. 2 a piece of this material.

clothe *verb* **clothes, clothing, clothed**
to put clothes on.

clothes *plural noun*
things worn to cover your body.
clothes-line, a line on which clothes are hung to dry or air.
clothes-peg, a device to hold clothes on a clothes-line.

clothing *noun*
clothes.

cloud *noun* **clouds**
a mass of water-vapour, smoke, dust, etc. floating in the air.
cloudless *adjective*

cloud *verb* **clouds, clouding, clouded**
to fill or darken with clouds or trouble, as in *The sky clouded over. Disappointment clouded her face.*

cloudy *adjective* **cloudier, cloudiest**
1 full of clouds. 2 hard to see through, as in *a cloudy liquid.*

clout *verb* **clouts, clouting, clouted**
to give someone or something a hard blow.

clove *noun* **cloves**
the dried bud of a tropical tree, used to flavour apple pies, etc.

clover *noun*
a small wild plant, usually with three leaves, as in *Most lawns contain some clover.*

clown *noun* **clowns**
1 someone in a circus who makes people laugh. 2 an amusing or foolish person.
clown about or **clown around,** to act foolishly or playfully.

club *noun* **clubs**
1 a heavy stick. 2 a stick for playing golf. 3 a group of people who meet together because they are interested in the same thing. 4 an organisation which offers food, entertainment etc. to its members. 5 a playing-card with a black clover leaf printed on it.

club *verb* **clubs, clubbing, clubbed**
to hit with a heavy stick.
club together, to join with other people in doing something, especially raising money.

cluck *verb* **clucks, clucking, clucked**
to make a noise like a hen.

clue *noun* **clues**
something that helps you to solve a puzzle or a mystery.
not have a clue, to be ignorant or helpless.

clueless *adjective*
(*colloquial*) stupid; having no idea of how to do something.

clump *noun* **clumps**
a cluster of trees, shrubs, etc.

clumsy *adjective* **clumsier, clumsiest**
likely to knock things over, drop things, or do something stupid.
clumsily *adverb,* **clumsiness** *noun*

clung past tense and past participle of **cling.**

cluster *noun* **clusters**
a group of people or things close together.

clutch *verb* **clutches, clutching, clutched**
to grasp or snatch at something.

clutch *noun* **clutches**
1 a tight grasp. 2 a device for disconnecting the engine of a motor vehicle from its gears and wheels.
clutches, cruel grasp or control, as in *He was in the clutches of debt because of his gambling.*

clutter *noun*
a lot of things left around untidily.

clutter *verb* **clutters, cluttering, cluttered**
to make something untidy or confused.

cm short for **centimetre** or **centimetres.**

Co. short for **company.**

c/o short for **care of.**

coach *noun* **coaches**
1 a comfortable bus, usually with one deck, used for long journeys. 2 a carriage pulled by horses. 3 a carriage of a railway train. 4 an instructor in athletics, sports, etc.

coach *verb* **coaches, coaching, coached**
to instruct or train someone in athletics, sports, etc.

a
b
c
d
e
f
g
h
i
j
k
l
m
n
o
p
q
r
s
t
u
v
w
x
y
z

coal

coal *noun*
a hard, black mineral used as fuel.

coarse *adjective* **coarser, coarsest**
1 not delicate or smooth.   **2** rough, as in *coarse humour*.

coast *noun* **coasts**
the seashore and the land close to it.
coastal *adjective,* **coastline** *noun*

coast *verb* **coasts, coasting, coasted**
to ride downhill without using power, as in *They stopped pedalling and coasted down the slope.*
coast along, to make progress without much effort.

coastguard *noun* **coastguards**
someone whose job is to keep watch on coasts, prevent smuggling, illegal fishing, etc.

coat *noun* **coats**
1 a piece of clothing with sleeves, worn over other clothes.   **2** a coating, as in *a coat of paint.*   **3** an animal's fur or hair.
coat-hanger, a shaped piece of wood, wire, or plastic for hanging a piece of clothing on.
coat of arms, a design on a shield, etc. representing a family, town, etc.

coat *verb* **coats, coating, coated**
to cover with a coating.

coating *noun* **coatings**
a covering; a layer, as in *a coating of chocolate.*

coax *verb* **coaxes, coaxing, coaxed**
to persuade someone gently or patiently.

cobalt *noun*
a silvery-white metal whose pigment gives a deep-blue colour to pottery, etc.

cobbler *noun* **cobblers**
(*old-fashioned use*) someone who mends shoes.

cobble-stone *noun* **cobble-stones**
a smooth, round stone, as in *Streets used to be paved with cobble-stones.*

cobra *noun* **cobras** (*say* **kob**-ruh *or* **kohb**-ruh)
a poisonous hooded snake of Africa and Asia.

cobweb *noun* **cobwebs**
a thin, sticky net spun by a spider to trap insects.

cock *noun* **cocks**
a male bird, especially a male fowl.

cock *verb* **cocks, cocking, cocked**
1 to turn something upwards or in a particular direction, as in *He cocked his eye at me.*   **2** to make a gun ready to fire.

cockatoo *noun* **cockatoos**
a parrot with a crest and a powerful beak, as in *Some well-known cockatoos are the sulphur-crested, the galah and the gang-gang.*

cockeyed *adjective*
(*colloquial*) crooked or absurd, as in *cockeyed hat; cockeyed idea.*

cockle *noun* **cockles**
1 an edible shellfish found in Europe.
2 (in South Australia) the name given to the pipi.

cockney *noun* **cockneys**
1 someone born in London, especially in east London.   **2** a kind of English spoken by cockneys.

cockpit *noun* **cockpits**
the place for the pilot or driver in a plane, racing car, etc.

cockroach *noun* **cockroaches**
a dark brown insect which lives in kitchens, bathrooms, etc.

cocky *adjective* **cockier, cockiest**
(*colloquial*) conceited; cheeky.

cocky *noun* **cockies**
1 (*colloquial*) a cockatoo.   **2** a farmer, especially one who owns a small farm.

cocoa *noun* **cocoas**
1 a hot drink that tastes of chocolate.
2 the powder from which you make this drink.

coconut *noun* **coconuts**
a large, round nut that grows on a palm tree, containing a sweet white lining and a milky juice.

cocoon *noun* **cocoons**
the silky protective case spun by the larvae of moths and other insects before they become adult.

cod *noun* **cod**
a large, edible freshwater or marine fish.

code *noun* **codes**
1 a set of signs, letters, etc. for sending messages secretly or quickly, as in *Morse code.*   **2** a set of rules, as in *the legal code.*

code *verb* **codes, coding, coded**
to put into code, as in *The message was coded to keep it secret.*

coeducation *noun*
the education of boys and girls together.
coeducational *adjective*

coffee *noun* **coffees**
1 a hot drink made from the roasted and crushed beans of a tropical shrub.   **2** the powder from which you make this drink.

coffin *noun* **coffins**
the long box in which a corpse is buried or cremated; a casket.

cog *noun* **cogs**
one of a number of pieces sticking out from the edge of a wheel and allowing it to drive another wheel, chain, etc.

coherent *adjective*
1 clear and easy to understand, as in *a coherent explanation*. **2** sticking together, as in *coherent materials*.
cohesion *noun*

coil *verb* **coils, coiling, coiled**
to wind something into circles or spirals.

coil *noun* **coils**
a circle or spiral of rope, wire, etc.

coin *noun* **coins**
a piece of metal money.
coinage *noun*

coin *verb* **coins, coining, coined**
1 to manufacture money. **2** to invent, especially a new word.

coincide *verb* **coincides, coinciding, coincided**
to happen at the same time as something else, as in *The end of term coincides with my birthday*.

coincidence *noun* **coincidences**
the way that two things can happen accidentally at the same time; a case of this happening.

coke *noun*
a solid fuel made out of coal.

colander *noun* **colanders** (*say* kol-uhn-duh)
a strainer for vegetables, etc.

cold *adjective* **colder, coldest**
1 not hot or warm; to do with or at a low temperature. **2** not kind or emotional; unfriendly.
cold war, a situation where nations are enemies without actually fighting.
give someone the cold shoulder, to be unfriendly to someone.
coldly *adverb*, **coldness** *noun*

cold *noun* **colds**
1 cold weather or temperature. **2** an illness that makes your nose run, gives you a sore throat, etc.

cold-blooded *adjective*
1 having blood that changes temperature according to the surroundings. **2** ruthless or without pity.

coleslaw *noun*
a salad made of chopped raw cabbage, etc. covered in dressing.

collaborate *verb* **collaborates, collaborating, collaborated**
to work with someone on a job; to help, as in *He was said to have collaborated with the enemy*.
collaboration *noun*, **collaborator** *noun*

collage *noun* **collages** (*say* kuh-**lahzh** *or* kol-ahzh)
a picture made by fixing small objects to a surface.

collapse *verb* **collapses, collapsing, collapsed**
1 to fall to pieces; to break. **2** to become very weak or ill. **3** to fall down.

collapsible *adjective*
able to be folded up, as in *a collapsible table*.

collar *noun* **collars**
1 the part of a garment that goes around your neck. **2** a band that goes around the neck of a dog, cat, horse, etc.

collate *verb* **collates, collating, collated**
to collect and arrange something in an organised way, as in *Collate the results, showing them on a graph*.

colleague *noun* **colleagues**
someone that you work with.

collect *verb* **collects, collecting, collected**
1 to get things together from various places, especially as a hobby, as in *She collects stamps; I collect coins*. **2** to go and get someone or something. **3** to gather money, as in *I am collecting for the Red Cross*.
collector *noun*

collection *noun* **collections**
1 things you have collected as a hobby, as in *stamp collection*. **2** money given by people at a meeting, church service, etc.

collective *adjective*
including or using many or all people or things, as in *a collective effort*.

collective noun *noun*
a singular noun that is a name for a group of things or people, as in *In 'a pack of dogs', 'pack' is a collective noun*.

college *noun* **colleges**
1 a place where people can continue learning something after they have left school. **2** accommodation for students in a university. **3** an upper secondary school. **4** a private school.

collide *verb* **collides, colliding, collided**
to crash into something, as in *The bicycle collided with the car*.
collision *noun*

collie

collie *noun* **collies**
a breed of dog with a long, pointed muzzle and long hair.

colloquial *adjective*
suitable for conversation but not for formal speech or writing, as in *'Chuck' is a colloquial word for 'throw'.*

colon *noun* **colons**
a punctuation mark (:), as in *Colons are often used to introduce lists like this: red, blue, green.*

colonel *noun* **colonels** (*say* **ker**-nuhl)
an army officer, usually in charge of a regiment.

colonial *adjective*
to do with a colony or colonies, as in *colonial ruler; colonial architecture.*

colonist *noun* **colonists**
a person who settles in a place and lives in a colony there, as in *When white settlement began in Australia there were few free colonists.*

colony *noun* **colonies**
1 a settlement or settlers in a new country fully or partly controlled by another country, as in *Australia was once a colony of Britain.* 2 a group of people or animals living together, as in *an artists' colony; a colony of possums.*

colossal *adjective*
huge; great.

colour or **color** *noun* **colours**
1 the effect produced by rays of light of a particular wavelength, as in *Red, blue, and yellow are colours.* 2 the use of all colours, not just black and white, as in *Is this film in colour?* 3 the colour of someone's skin. 4 a substance used to give colour to things. 5 the special flag of a ship or regiment.

colour or **color** *verb* **colours, colouring, coloured**
1 to give something a colour or colours. 2 to influence, as in *Her tastes in food were coloured by overseas travel.* 3 to blush.
colouring *noun*

colour-blind or **color-blind** *adjective*
unable to see or distinguish between some colours.

coloured or **colored** *adjective*
1 having a particular colour. 2 with a dark skin.

Usage The word **coloured**, used to describe people, is often considered to be insulting; it is better to use **black**.

colourful or **colorful** *adjective*
full of colour; lively, as in *a colourful story of life on the goldfields.*

colourless or **colorless** *adjective*
1 without colour, as in *Many gases are colourless.* 2 uninteresting, as in *a colourless town.*

colt *noun* **colts**
a young male horse.

column *noun* **columns**
1 a pillar. 2 something long and narrow. 3 a vertical part of a page, as in *Newspapers are printed in columns.* 4 a regular feature in a newspaper, as in *a gardening column.*
columnist *noun*

coma *noun* **comas** (*say* **koh**-muh)
an unnatural deep sleep caused by illness or injury.

comb *noun* **combs**
1 a device for making hair tidy. 2 the red, fleshy crest on a fowl's head.

comb *verb* **combs, combing, combed**
1 to tidy with a comb. 2 to search carefully, as in *They combed the bush for the lost child.*

combat *noun* **combats**
a fight or struggle.
combatant *noun*

combat *verb* **combats, combating, combated**
to struggle against something.

combination *noun* **combinations**
1 the act of joining or mixing. 2 a series of numbers or letters used to open a combination lock.
combination lock, a lock that is opened by setting a dial or dials to positions shown by numbers or letters.

combine *verb* **combines, combining, combined** (*say* kuhm-**buyn**)
to join or mix together.

combustion *noun*
the process of burning.
combustible *adjective* and *noun*

come *verb* **comes, coming, came, come**
1 to move towards a person or place, as in *Come here!* 2 to arrive; to reach a place, as in *Has that letter come yet?* 3 to become, as in *Dreams can come true.* 4 to occur, as in *It comes on the next page.* 5 to amount, as in *The bill came to $10.*
come about, to happen.
come across someone, to meet someone.
come by something, to get something.

commercialised

come round or **come to,** to become conscious, after being unconscious.
have it coming to one, (*colloquial*) to be about to get what you deserve.
how come?, (*colloquial*) how did it happen?

comeback *noun* **comebacks**
a return to the success that someone had at an earlier time, as in *Some pop stars have had several comebacks.*

comedian *noun* **comedians**
someone who entertains people by making them laugh.

comedy *noun* **comedies**
1 a play, film, etc. that makes people laugh. 2 an amusing incident or series of incidents, as in *The interview turned into a comedy.*

comet *noun* **comets**
an object moving across the sky with a bright tail of light.

comfort *noun*
freedom from worry or pain.

comfort *verb* **comforts, comforting, comforted**
to make a person feel less grief, pain, or worry.

comfortable *adjective*
1 pleasant to use or wear, as in *a comfortable chair.* 2 free from worry or pain, as in *The nurse made the patient comfortable.*
comfortably *adverb*

comic *adjective*
funny.
comic strip, a series of drawings telling a funny story or a story in several parts.
comical *adjective,* **comically** *adverb*

comic *noun* **comics**
1 a comedian. 2 a paper or small magazine full of comic strips.

coming *adjective*
to do with the future or next, as in *in the coming years; the coming week.*

coming *noun* **comings**
arrival, as in *comings and goings.*

comma *noun* **commas**
a punctuation mark (,) used to mark a pause in a sentence or to separate items in a list.

command *verb* **commands, commanding, commanded**
1 to tell someone to do something. 2 to be in charge of, as in *A centurion commanded a hundred soldiers.* 3 to deserve and get sympathy, respect, etc., as in *Her skill commands admiration.*
commandant *noun,* **commander** *noun*

command *noun* **commands**
1 an instruction, as in *a command to run.* 2 authority; control, as in *He is in command of these soldiers.* 3 ability, as in *She has a good command of Japanese.*

commandment *noun* **commandments**
a sacred command, especially one of the Ten Commandments of Moses.

commando *noun* **commandos**
a soldier trained for making dangerous raids.

commemorate *verb* **commemorates, commemorating, commemorated**
to be a celebration or reminder of some past event, person, etc.
commemoration *noun,* **commemorative** *adjective*

commence *verb* **commences, commencing, commenced**
to start.
commencement *noun*

commend *verb* **commends, commending, commended**
1 to praise, as in *He was commended for bravery.* 2 to recommend, as in *I commend this recipe for bread as being always successful.*
commendable *adjective,* **commendation** *noun*

comment *noun* **comments**
a remark or opinion.

commentary *noun* **commentaries**
a description of an event, especially while it is happening.

commentator *noun* **commentators**
a person who gives a commentary on events, especially sports.
commentate *verb*

commerce *noun*
business operations, especially the buying and selling of goods on a large scale; trade.

commercial *adjective*
1 connected with trade or commerce. 2 intended to make a profit, as in *a commercial design studio.* 3 financed by advertisements, as in *commercial radio.*
commercially *adverb*

commercial *noun* **commercials**
an advertisement, especially on television or radio.

commercialised or **commercialized** *adjective*
altered so as to make money, or more money than before, usually with a loss of quality, as in *A lot of holiday resorts are very commercialised.*

a
b
c
d
e
f
g
h
i
j
k
l
m
n
o
p
q
r
s
t
u
v
w
x
y
z

commission

commission *noun* **commissions**
1 the authority to perform a certain task and the persons given such authority, as in *a commission to investigate crime.* 2 an order for something, especially art work to be produced, as in *a commission to paint the prime minister's portrait.* 3 a warrant giving the rank of officer in the armed forces, as in *a commission as captain.*
4 money, usually in addition to wages, paid to a salesperson on every sale made.

commit *verb* **commits, committing, committed**
1 to do something, as in *She committed the crime.* 2 to put a person or thing into a particular place, as in *He was committed to prison.* 3 to place in someone's care, as in *The parent committed his young son to the teacher on the excursion.*
to commit yourself, to promise or decide to do something.
commitment *noun*

committee *noun* **committees**
a group of people appointed to organise or discuss something.

commodity *noun* **commodities**
a product that is bought and sold, especially a mineral or a farm product.

common *adjective* **commoner, commonest**
1 ordinary; usual; happening often, as in *The gum is a common tree.* 2 to do with all or most people, as in *It was common knowledge.* 3 shared, as in *Music was their common interest.* 4 lacking good taste, as in *common taste in clothes.*

common noun *noun*
a name representing a class of objects or a concept, not a particular individual, thing or object.

commonplace *adjective*
ordinary, as in *a commonplace remark about the weather.*

common-room *noun* **common-rooms**
a room for the social use of teachers or pupils at a school, college, etc.

commonwealth *noun* **commonwealths**
an independent nation or community, especially a democratic one.
the Commonwealth, an association of Britain and various other countries, such as Canada, Australia, New Zealand, and India.

commotion *noun* **commotions**
an uproar.

communal *adjective*
shared by several people, as in *a communal bathroom at a college.*

commune *noun* **communes**
a group of people sharing housing, food, etc.

communicate *verb* **communicates, communicating, communicated**
to pass news, information, opinions, etc. to other people.
communicative *adjective*

communication *noun* **communications**
1 communicating or the passing of news, information, opinions, etc. 2 something communicated; a message. 3 a way of communicating, as in *Communications include radio, television, and telephones.*

communion *noun* **communions**
the sharing of thoughts, interests, ideas, etc., as in *The painter enjoys communion with other artists.*
Communion, the Christian ceremony in which holy bread and wine, being or representing the body and blood of Christ, are given to worshippers.

communism *noun*
a system where property is shared by the community.
Communism, a political system where the state controls property, production, trade, etc.; the belief in this sort of system.

Communist *noun* **Communists**
someone who believes in Communism.

community *noun* **communities**
a group of people living in one area, district or country, as in *the school community; the Australian community.*

commuter *noun* **commuters**
someone who regularly travels to work, especially by train or bus.
commute *verb*

compact *adjective*
small and neat.

compact disc *noun* **compact discs**
a smooth disc on which digital signals are recorded, and from which the signals are read by a laser beam; a CD, as in *a recording of Beethoven on compact disc.*
compact-disc player, a device for reproducing sound recorded on a compact disc.

companion *noun* **companions**
1 a friend who is with you, or who shares something with you. 2 a thing that matches another, as in *The companion to this glove is lost.*
companionship *noun*

company *noun* **companies**
1 a group of people doing something together. 2 having people with you, as in

I am lonely: I need company. **3** visitors, as in *We've got company.* **4** an army unit consisting of two or more platoons.

comparable *adjective*
(*say* **kom**-puh-ruh-buhl)
similar.

comparative *adjective*
1 judged or estimated by comparison, as in *The comparative qualities of cotton and wool were discussed by the tailor.* **2** to do with comparisons, as in *a comparative survey.*
comparatively *adverb*

comparative *noun* **comparatives**
the form of an adjective or an adverb that expresses 'more', as in *The comparative of 'big' is 'bigger'; the comparative of 'bad' is 'worse'.*

compare *verb* **compares, comparing, compared**
to work out or say how things are similar, as in *Compare your answers.*
compare with, to be similar to; to be as good as, as in *How does his car compare with ours? Our football oval cannot compare with the Melbourne Cricket Ground.*

comparison *noun* **comparisons**
the action of comparing.

compartment *noun* **compartments**
a part or division of something, especially of a railway carriage.

compass *noun* **compasses**
an instrument with a magnetic needle that shows you where north is.
compass or **compasses** a device for drawing circles.

compassion *noun*
pity; mercy.
compassionate *adjective*

compatible *adjective*
1 able to live or exist together without trouble. **2** (*to do with equipment, herbicides, etc.*) able to be used together, as in *This computer and that printer are compatible.*

compel *verb* **compels, compelling, compelled**
to force someone to do something.

compensate *verb* **compensates, compensating, compensated**
to give someone something to make up for a loss, injury, etc.
compensation *noun*

compère *noun* **compères** (*say* **kom**-pair)
someone who introduces the performers in a show or broadcast.

compete *verb* **competes, competing, competed**
to take part in a competition.

competent *adjective*
able to do a particular thing, as in *He is a competent musician.*
competence *noun*

competition *noun* **competitions**
1 a game, race, etc. in which you try to do better than other people. **2** the person or group being competed against; the opposition, as in *The competition looks too good.*
competitive *adjective*, **competitor** *noun*

compile *verb* **compiles, compiling, compiled**
to collect and arrange information, quotations, etc., as in *She compiled a collection of bush ballads.*
compilation *noun*, **compiler** *noun*

complacent *adjective*
satisfied with the way you are, with what you do, etc., and not worried about what is wrong with your situation, as in *Nobody should be complacent about wasting resources.*

complain *verb* **complains, complaining, complained**
1 to say that you are not pleased about something. **2** to say that you are suffering from an illness, pain, etc., as in *He complained of a toothache.*

complaint *noun* **complaints**
1 the act of complaining; a grievance, as in *There were many complaints against the early starting time.* **2** an illness.

complement *noun* **complements**
the amount needed to fill or complete something, as in *This ship has a full complement of sailors.*

complement *noun*
a word or words used after a verb to complete the meaning; in *'She is brave'* and *'He was made king'*, the complements are *'brave'* and *'king'.*
complementary *adjective*

Usage Do not confuse **complement** with **compliment**, which means words or actions that show approval.

complete *adjective*
1 having all its parts, as in *a complete jigsaw puzzle.* **2** finished, as in *The work is complete.* **3** in every way, as in *It came as a complete surprise.*
completely *adverb*

a
b
c
d
e
f
g
h
i
j
k
l
m
n
o
p
q
r
s
t
u
v
w
x
y
z

complete

complete *verb* completes, completing, completed
to make something complete.
completion *noun*

complex *adjective*
complicated.
complexity *noun*

complex *noun* complexes
1 a group of related things, especially a group of buildings. 2 a fixed idea or set of attitudes, as in *inferiority complex*.

complexion *noun* complexions
the colour or appearance of your skin, especially of your face.

complicated *adjective*
1 made of a lot of different parts, as in *a complicated machine*. 2 difficult, as in *a complicated problem*.

complication *noun* complications
1 a complicated situation or condition.
2 a difficulty, especially a new one.

compliment *noun* compliments
words or actions that show you approve of a person or thing.
complimentary *adjective*

Usage Do not confuse **compliment** with **complement**, which means the amount needed to complete something, or the words after some kinds of verb.

compo *noun*
(*colloquial*) payment to a worker to compensate for an injury received at work or travelling to and from work.

component *noun* components
a part, especially of a machine.

compose *verb* composes, composing, composed
1 to write music. 2 to make or build up something.
composer *noun*

composite *adjective*
made up of different parts, types, etc., as in *composite class*.

composition *noun* compositions
1 the act or method of putting something together, as in *The composition of the project on the environment was completed by a small group*. 2 a thing composed, especially a piece of music. 3 an essay, as in *a composition on your favourite animal*.

compost *noun*
manure made of decayed leaves, grass, vegetable peelings, etc.

compound *noun* compounds
1 a compound substance, as in *Water is a compound of hydrogen and oxygen*. 2 a word made up of two or more existing words, as in *spaceship*. 3 a fenced area containing buildings, especially where the entry and exit of people is controlled, as in *an embassy compound*.

compound *adjective*
made of two or more parts or ingredients.

comprehend *verb* comprehends, comprehending, comprehended
1 to understand. 2 to include; take in, as in *This documentary will comprehend many aspects of Australia's native fauna*.

comprehension *noun* comprehensions
1 understanding. 2 an exercise that tests or helps your understanding of a language.

comprehensive *adjective*
including all or many kinds of people or things.
comprehensive school, a secondary school for children of all abilities.

compress *verb* compresses, compressing, compressed
1 to press or squeeze together. 2 to get something into a small space.
compression *noun,* **compressor** *noun*

comprise *verb* comprises, comprising, comprised
to include; to consist of.

Usage Do not use **comprise** with 'of'. It is incorrect to say *The group was comprised of twenty men*; the correct way to say this is: *The group was composed of twenty men*.

compromise *noun* compromises
(*say* **kom**-pruh-muyz)
settling a dispute by accepting less than you wanted.

compromise *verb* compromises, compromising, compromised
(*say* **kom**-pruh-muyz)
to accept less than you wanted in order to settle a dispute.

compulsory *adjective*
1 required by law or a rule, as in *The wearing of seatbelts is compulsory*.
2 necessary, as in *compulsory fees; compulsory attendance*.

compute *verb* computes, computing, computed
to calculate.
computation *noun*

computer *noun* **computers**
a machine that quickly and automatically does calculations, solves problems, etc.
computer science, the study of how computers work and are used.
computer virus, a program written deliberately to disrupt the working of a computer system.

computerise or **computerize** *verb*
computerises, computerising, computerised
to equip with computers; to do something by computer, as in *Has your office been computerised yet? The bookings were computerised.*

comrade *noun* **comrades**
a friend or companion.
comradeship *noun*

con *verb* **cons, conning, conned**
(*colloquial*) to deceive or trick, as in *Some ads try to con you.*

concave *adjective*
curved like the inside of a circle or ball.

conceal *verb* **conceals, concealing, concealed**
to hide someone or something.
concealment *noun*

concede *verb* **concedes, conceding, conceded** (*say* kuhn-**seed**)
1 to admit that something is true, as in *He conceded that he was wrong.* **2** to admit defeat, as in *The prime minister conceded defeat as the votes were counted in the election.*

conceit *noun*
vanity; pride.
conceited *adjective*

conceive *verb* **conceives, conceiving, conceived**
1 to become pregnant. **2** to form an idea, plan, etc.

concentrate *verb* **concentrates, concentrating, concentrated**
1 to give your full attention to something; to think hard about one thing. **2** to bring or come together in one place, as in *The crowd concentrated in the city square.* **3** to make a liquid stronger by removing water, etc. from it, as in *Some fruit juices have been concentrated.*

concentration *noun* **concentrations**
1 giving your full attention to something.
2 condensing a liquid. **3** the strength of a liquid, etc., as in *Test the effect of acid in different concentrations.*
concentration camp, a place where political prisoners, etc. are held.

concentric *adjective*
having the same centre, as in *A stone thrown in a pool makes concentric ripples.*

concept *noun* **concepts**
an idea, as in *The concept of time travel is often found in science fiction novels.*

conception *noun* **conceptions**
1 the act of conceiving, as in *There is usually a time of nine months between the conception of a child and his or her birth.* **2** an idea, as in *The plan was brilliant in its conception.*

concern *verb* **concerns, concerning, concerned**
1 to be important or interesting to someone, as in *I am more concerned with health than money.* **2** to be about a particular subject, as in *This story concerns a shipwreck.* **3** to worry someone, as in *Your bad behaviour concerns me.*

concern *noun* **concerns**
1 something that is of interest, importance or anxiety, as in *concern over unemployment.*
2 a business, as in *the large wool concern.*

concerning *preposition*
on the subject of; in connection with.

concert *noun* **concerts**
a musical entertainment.

concertina *noun* **concertinas**
a portable musical instrument that you squeeze to push air past reeds.

concerto *noun* **concertos** (*say* kuhn-**cher**-toh or kuhn-**sher**-toh)
a piece of music for one instrument and an orchestra.

concession *noun* **concessions**
something that someone lets you have or do, as in *As a special concession, parents may park in the teachers' car park on wet days.*

conciliate *verb* **conciliates, conciliating, conciliated**
to try and end disagreement between two people or groups.
conciliation *noun*

concise *adjective*
giving a lot of information in a few words.

> **Usage** Do not confuse **concise** with **precise**, which means exact.

conclude *verb* **concludes, concluding, concluded**
1 to finish. **2** to decide, as in *The jury concluded that he was not guilty.*

a
b
c
d
e
f
g
h
i
j
k
l
m
n
o
p
q
r
s
t
u
v
w
x
y
z

concrete

concrete *adjective*
1 made of concrete, as in *concrete path*. 2 existing in material form or real; definite, as in *A ball is a concrete object. The police need concrete evidence.*

concrete *noun*
cement mixed with gravel, etc. and used in building.

concrete noun *noun*
a word which names physical things, as in *'House', 'smoke', 'book' and 'cake' are concrete nouns.*

concussion *noun*
an injury to the brain caused by a hard knock.

condemn *verb* **condemns, condemning, condemned**
1 to say that you strongly disagree with something. 2 to convict or sentence a criminal, as in *He was condemned to death*. 3 to declare that houses, etc. are not fit to be used.
condemnation *noun*

condense *verb* **condenses, condensing, condensed**
1 to make liquid, etc. stronger or thicker, as in *condensed milk*. 2 to make something smaller or shorter, as in *a condensed report*. 3 to change into water or other liquid, as in *Steam condenses on cold windows*.
condensation *noun*, **condenser** *noun*

condition *noun* **conditions**
1 the character or state of a person or thing; how someone or something is, as in *This bike is in good condition. The athlete is in excellent condition for the Olympics.*
2 something that must happen if something else is to happen, as in *Learning to swim is a condition of going sailing.*
on condition or **on condition that,** only if.

condition *verb* **conditions, conditioning, conditioned**
1 to put something into a proper or fit state, as in *Condition your hair*. 2 to train or accustom, as in *They have been conditioned to obey unquestioningly.*

condom *noun* **condoms**
a rubber sheath to cover a man's penis, used as a contraceptive and as protection against disease.

condone *verb* **condones, condoning, condoned**
to forgive or overlook, as in *The teacher condoned the student's carelessness because the child was unwell.*

conduct *noun* (*say* **kon**-dukt)
behaviour.

conduct *verb* **conducts, conducting, conducted** (*say* kuhn-**dukt**)
1 to lead or guide. 2 to organise or manage something. 3 to behave, as in *Conduct yourself properly*. 4 to direct the performance of an orchestra, etc. 5 to allow electricity, heat, etc. to pass along, as in *Copper conducts electricity well.*

conduction *noun*
the conducting of electricity, heat, etc., as in *Heat can be transferred by conduction, convection, or radiation.*

conductor *noun* **conductors**
1 someone who sells tickets on a bus, etc. 2 someone who conducts an orchestra, etc. 3 something that conducts electricity, heat, etc.

cone *noun* **cones**
1 an object which is circular at one end and pointed at the other end. 2 something shaped like a cone, as in *ice-cream cone*. 3 the fruit of a pine, fir, cedar, etc.

confectioner *noun* **confectioners**
someone who makes or sells sweets.
confectionery *noun*

confer *verb* **confers, conferring, conferred**
1 to give someone a title, honour, etc. 2 to have a discussion.

conference *noun* **conferences**
a meeting for discussion, as in *a peace conference.*

confess *verb* **confesses, confessing, confessed**
to admit that you have done something wrong.

confession *noun* **confessions**
1 an act of admitting that you have done wrong, as in *The burglar made a confession of all his crimes*. 2 (*in the Roman Catholic Church*) an act of telling a priest your sins.

confetti *plural noun*
tiny bits of coloured paper thrown at a bride and bridegroom.

confide *verb* **confides, confiding, confided**
to tell someone a secret.
confide in someone, to trust someone; to talk to someone about something secret.

confidence *noun*
1 trust; faith. 2 believing that you are right or that you can do something.
in confidence, as a secret.
confidence trick, deceiving someone after persuading him or her to trust you.

confident *adjective*
showing or feeling confidence or certainty about something, as in *The confident swimmer was unafraid when the boat capsized.*

confidential *adjective*
1 to be kept secret, as in *This information is confidential.* 2 trusted to keep secrets, as in *a confidential secretary.*
confidentially *adverb*

confine *verb* confines, confining, confined
1 to restrict something, as in *She confines her training to running one kilometre daily.* 2 to keep someone in a place, as in *The prisoner was confined in jail for years.*
confinement *noun*

confirm *verb* confirms, confirming, confirmed
1 to prove that something is true. 2 to make something definite, as in *Please write to confirm your booking.* 3 to make someone a full member of the Christian Church in a special ceremony conducted by a bishop.
confirmation *noun*

confiscate *verb* confiscates, confiscating, confiscated
to take something away from someone as a punishment.
confiscation *noun*

conflict *noun* conflicts (*say* **kon**-flikt)
a struggle against a person, idea, interests, etc.

conflict *verb* conflicts, conflicting, conflicted (*say* kuhn-**flikt**)
to disagree; not to match or fit with something else, as in *Their ideas about how to complete the project conflicted.*

conform *verb* conforms, conforming, conformed
1 to follow accepted rules, other people's wishes, etc., as in *He always conforms with school rules.* 2 to follow a particular idea, fashion, etc., as in *His short hairstyle conforms to today's fashion.*
conformist *noun*, **conformity** *noun*

confront *verb* confronts, confronting, confronted
1 to come face to face with someone, as in *The armies confronted each other.* 2 to face up to something, as in *We need to confront the problem of drug abuse.* 3 to challenge someone, as in *The government is confronted by the need to look after the unemployed.*
confrontation *noun*

confuse *verb* confuses, confusing, confused
1 to make someone puzzled or muddled. 2 to mistake one thing for

another, as in *She confused the small orange with the mandarin.*
confusion *noun*

congeal *verb* congeals, congealing, congealed
to make or become semi-solid by cooling, as in *Cooking fat congeals when it cools.*

congested *adjective*
overcrowded; too full of something, as in *roads congested with traffic.*
congestion *noun*

congratulate *verb* congratulates, congratulating, congratulated
to tell someone how pleased you are about something that has happened to him or her, or that he or she has done.
congratulations *plural noun*

congregate *verb* congregates, congregating, congregated
to collect or gather into a crowd or mass, as in *People congregated at the scene of the accident.*

congregation *noun* congregations
the people who take part in a church service.

congress *noun* congresses
a formal meeting or a conference, as in *A congress of doctors discussed the issue of transplants.*

congruent *adjective*
(*in Mathematics*) having exactly the same shape and size, as in *The two triangles are congruent.*
congruence *noun*

conical *adjective*
shaped like a cone, as in *a conical spire on the church.*

conifer *noun* conifers (*say* **kon**-uh-fuh)
an evergreen tree that bears cones, as in *A pine tree is a conifer.*
coniferous *adjective*

conjugate *verb* conjugates, conjugating, conjugated
to give the different forms of a verb.
conjugation *noun*

conjunction *noun*
a joining word, as in *The most common conjunctions are: 'after, 'in order that', 'that', 'although', 'like', 'though', 'and', 'now', 'till', 'as', 'once', 'unless', 'because', 'or', 'until', 'before', 'since', 'when', 'but', 'so', 'where', 'for', 'so that', 'whether', 'if', 'than', 'while'.*

conjure *verb* conjures, conjuring, conjured
to perform tricks that look like magic.
conjurer *noun*

connect

connect *verb* **connects, connecting, connected**
1 to join together, as in *Connect the two wires.* 2 to put or go naturally together; to be associated with, as in *Bondi is connected with sun and surf.*
connection *noun*, **connective** *adjective*, **connector** *noun*

conning tower *noun* **conning-towers**
the part on top of a submarine, containing the periscope.

conquer *verb* **conquers, conquering, conquered**
to defeat; to overcome, as in *He managed to conquer his fear.*
conqueror *noun*

conquest *noun* **conquests**
the defeat of someone or something, as in *the conquest of your enemy; the conquest of his stutter by speech therapy.*

conscience *noun* (*say* **kon**-shuhns)
knowing what is right or wrong.

conscientious *adjective*
(*say* kon-shee-**en**-shuhs)
1 careful and honest, as in *conscientious work.* 2 guided by your conscience, as in *He was a conscientious objector to joining the army.*
conscientiously *adverb*

conscious *adjective* (*say* **kon**-shuhs)
1 awake and aware of one's surroundings, etc. 2 aware or knowing about something, as in *Are you conscious of the danger you are in?*
consciously *adverb*, **consciousness** *noun*

conscript *verb* **conscripts, conscripting, conscripted** (*say* kuhn-**skript**)
to make someone join the armed forces.
conscription *noun*

conscript *noun* **conscripts** (*say* **kon**-skript)
a person who has been made to join the armed forces.

consecutive *adjective*
following one after another.

consensus *noun*
1 the agreement of everyone, as in *Can we reach a consensus on this issue?* 2 the opinion of most people, as in *There was a consensus that the law should be changed.*

consent *noun*
agreement or permission.

consent *verb* **consents, consenting, consented**
to agree; to permit something.

consequence *noun* **consequences**
1 something which happens because of an event or action, as in *His illness was the consequence of smoking.* 2 importance, as in *It is of no consequence.*
consequently *adverb*

conservation *noun*
the keeping of something, especially natural surroundings, in its original form and protecting it from change, loss, damage, etc.
conservationist *noun*

conservative *adjective*
not liking rapid change; moderate or avoiding extremes in dress, tastes, etc., as in *The conservative architect continued to design old-fashioned houses. He is a conservative dresser.*
conservatism *noun*

conservative *noun* **conservatives**
a person who dislikes change or who is careful.

conservatory *noun* **conservatories**
a greenhouse made mainly of glass, often attached to a house, where plants needing special care can be grown.

conserve *verb* **conserves, conserving, conserved**
1 to prevent something being changed, spoilt, or wasted. 2 to make fruit into jam.

consider *verb* **considers, considering, considered**
1 to think carefully about or give attention to something. 2 to have an opinion; to believe, as in *We consider that people should be allowed to follow their own religion. I consider her intelligent.*

considerable *adjective*
large; important.
considerably *adverb*

considerate *adjective*
kind and thoughtful.

consideration *noun* **considerations**
1 careful thought or attention. 2 being thoughtful about other people. 3 something that needs careful thought; a reason, as in *Money is a major consideration in this plan. Good weather was the main consideration in choosing a camping holiday.*

considering *preposition*
in view of; with regard to, as in *This car runs well, considering its age.*

consist *verb* **consists, consisting, consisted**
consist of, to be made of.

consistency *noun* consistencies
 1 thickness, especially of a liquid. 2 being in agreement.

consistent *adjective*
 1 matching or agreeing with something; reasonable. 2 (of a person) always acting in the same way.
 consistently *adverb*

consolation *noun* consolations
 comfort or sympathy given to someone.
 consolation prize, a prize given to someone who does not win a main prize.

console *verb* consoles, consoling, consoled
 to give someone comfort or sympathy.

consonant *noun* consonants
 a letter that is not a vowel, as in *In 'table', the consonants are t, b, and l.*

conspicuous *adjective*
 noticeable; remarkable, as in *conspicuous red hair; conspicuous courage.*

conspiracy *noun* conspiracies
 plotting to do something evil or illegal.
 conspirator *noun*, **conspire** *verb*

constable *noun* constables
 a police officer.

constant *adjective*
 1 not changing; continuous, as in *constant temperature; constant supply of water.* 2 (of a person) reliable, as in *constant friend.*
 constancy *noun*, **constantly** *adverb*

constant *noun* constants
 (*in Science and Mathematics*) a number or quantity that does not change.

constellation *noun* constellations
 a group of stars.

constipated *adjective*
 unable to empty the bowels easily or regularly.
 constipation *noun*

constituency *noun* constituencies
 a district that elects a member of parliament; an electorate.

constituent *noun* constituents
 1 a part of something, as in *A constituent of milk is fat.* 2 someone who lives in the district of a particular member of parliament.
 constituent *adjective*

constitute *verb* constitutes, constituting, constituted
 to form or make up something, as in *the States and Territories that constitute Australia.*

constitution *noun* constitutions
 1 the principles or laws by which a country is governed. 2 the condition or health of someone's body.
 constitutional *adjective*

constrict *verb* constricts, constricting, constricted
 to make narrow or squeeze tightly, as in *After a snake bite you must constrict the flow of poison to the heart.*

construct *verb* constructs, constructing, constructed
 to build.

construction *noun* constructions
 1 building, as in *The construction of a shopping centre took a long time.*
 2 something built, as in *The house was a sturdy construction.*

constructive *adjective*
 helpful, as in *constructive criticism.*

consul *noun* consuls
 1 an official representative of one country, living in another country. 2 in Ancient Rome, an elected chief ruler.

consult *verb* consults, consulting, consulted
 to go to a person, book, etc. for information, advice, etc., as in *Consult your dictionary for help with spelling.*
 consultation *noun*

consultant *noun* consultants
 1 a person who provides professional advice. 2 a senior hospital doctor.

consume *verb* consumes, consuming, consumed
 1 to eat or drink something. 2 to destroy, as in *The building was consumed by fire.* 3 to use up something, as in *The world consumes a lot of fossil fuels.*

consumer *noun* consumers
 someone who buys or uses goods, services, etc.

consumption *noun*
 eating, drinking, or using up something, as in *The consumption of oil has increased.*

contact *noun* contacts
 1 touching someone or something.
 2 communication, as in *contact by phone.* 3 a person to communicate with, as in *a business contact.*
 contact lens, a small lens worn against your eyeball instead of spectacles.

contact *verb* contacts, contacting, contacted
 to get in touch with someone.

contagious *adjective* (say kuhn-**tay**-juhs)
 caught by contact with infected people or things, as in *a contagious disease.*

contain

contain *verb* **contains, containing, contained**
to have something inside; to include, as in *This book contains a great deal of information.*

container *noun* **containers**
something designed to contain things, especially a large box-shaped container for transporting goods by sea.

contaminate *verb* **contaminates, contaminating, contaminated**
to make something dirty, impure, diseased, etc., as in *Asbestos fibres contaminated his lungs.*
contamination *noun*

contemplate *verb* **contemplates, contemplating, contemplated**
1 to look at something. 2 to think about something. 3 to intend or plan to do something.
contemplation *noun*

contemporary *adjective*
1 belonging to the same period, as in *Henry Lawson was contemporary with Banjo Paterson.* 2 modern; up-to-date, as in *We like contemporary furniture.*

contempt *noun*
a feeling of despising someone.
contemptible *adjective*

contemptuous *adjective*
despising someone, as in *contemptuous of her cruel ways.*

Usage Do not confuse **contemptuous**, which describes a person's attitude, with **contemptible**, which describes someone or something that is despised, as in *a contemptible crime.*

contend *verb* **contends, contending, contended**
1 to struggle or compete. 2 to maintain or declare, as in *We contend that the company was guilty of negligence.*
contender *noun*

content *noun* (*say* **kon**-tent)
1 what is contained in something. 2 the amount of a substance found in something, as in *milk with a low fat content.*

content *adjective* (*say* kuhn-**tent**)
happy, satisfied, as in *Are you content with your wages?*
contentment *noun*

contents *plural noun* (*say* **kon**-tents)
what something contains.

contest *noun* **contests** (*say* **kon**-test)
a competition.

contest *verb* **contests, contesting, contested** (*say* kuhn-**test**)
to compete; to argue about something, as in *Carlton and Essendon contested the Grand Final. After her death, relatives contested her will.*

contestant *noun* **contestants** (*say* kuhn-**test**-uhnt)
someone in a contest.

context *noun* **contexts**
the words that come before or after a particular word or phrase and help to fix its meaning, as in *Words taken out of context can change the original meaning.*

continent *noun* **continents**
one of the main masses of land in the world, as in *The continents are Africa, Antarctica, Asia, Australia, Europe, North America, and South America.*
the Continent, the mainland of Europe, not including the British Isles.
continental *adjective*

continual *adjective*
happening often, as in *his continual coughing.*
continually *adverb*

continue *verb* **continues, continuing, continued**
to go on doing something.
continuation *noun*

continuous *adjective*
going on all the time; without a break, as in *a continuous line.*
continuity *noun,* **continuously** *adverb*

Usage Do not confuse **continuous** with **continual**, which sometimes has the same meaning, but more usually means happening often but with breaks in between.

contour *noun* **contours**
1 an outline. 2 a line on a map joining points that are the same height above sea level.

contraception *noun*
preventing women from becoming pregnant.

contraceptive *noun* **contraceptives**
something that is used to prevent women from becoming pregnant.

contract *noun* **contracts** (*say* **kon**-trakt)
a formal agreement.

contract *verb* **contracts, contracting, contracted** (*say* kuhn-**trakt**)
1 to make or become smaller, as in *Heated*

conventional

metal contracts as it cools. **2** to make a contract. **3** to get an illness, as in *She contracted pneumonia.*
contraction *noun*

contractor *noun* **contractors**
a company or firm that does an agreed piece of work for someone else, especially in the building industry, as in *We have employed a contractor to install all the windows in the new office.*

contradict *verb* **contradicts, contradicting, contradicted**
to say that something is not true or that someone is wrong.
contradiction *noun*, **contradictory** *adjective*

contralto *noun* **contraltos**
a female singer with a low voice.

contraption *noun* **contraptions**
a device or machine that looks strange.

contrary *adjective*
1 (*say* **kon**-truh-ree) opposite; unfavourable, as in *My view of the book was contrary to his.* **2** (*say* kuhn-**trair**-ree) obstinate, as in *a contrary child.*

contrary *noun* **contraries** (*say* **kon**-truh-ree)
the opposite, as in *Good is the contrary of evil.*
on the contrary, the opposite is true.

contrast *noun* **contrasts** (*say* **kon**-trahst)
1 the act of contrasting. **2** a clear difference, as in *He's a complete contrast to his brother.* **3** the degree of difference between colours or tones, as in *The contrast between cream and white is slight.* **4** a comparison showing differences, as in *the contrast between good and evil.*

contrast *verb* **contrasts, contrasting, contrasted** (*say* kuhn-**trahst**)
1 to show that two things are clearly different. **2** to be clearly different.

contribute *verb* **contributes, contributing, contributed**
1 to give money, help, etc. to a cause, fund, etc. **2** to help to cause something, as in *His tiredness contributed to the accident.* **3** to write something for a magazine, newspaper, etc.
contribution *noun*, **contributor** *noun*

contrive *verb* **contrives, contriving, contrived**
1 to devise or invent, as in *He contrived a watering system for his garden.* **2** to manage or plan cleverly, as in *She contrived to be there at the same time as her boss.*

control *noun* **controls**
1 making someone or something do what you want; authority, as in *She has excellent*

control of her class. **2** a way of making someone or something do what you want, as in *price controls on petrol; volume control.*
control tower, the building at an airport where people control air traffic by radio.
in control, controlling.
out of control, no longer having power over something.

control *verb* **controls, controlling, controlled**
1 to be able to make someone or something do what you want. **2** to regulate prices, flow of gas, etc.
controller *noun*

controversial *adjective*
causing a controversy, as in *Daylight saving is a controversial issue.*

controversy *noun* **controversies** (*say* **kon**-truh-ver-see or kuhn-**trov**-uh-see)
a long argument or disagreement.

conundrum *noun* **conundrums**
a riddle.

convalescent *adjective*
recovering from an illness.
convalescence *noun*

convection *noun*
heating by air, liquid, etc. that moves.
convector *noun*

convenience *noun* **conveniences**
1 being convenient or suitable, as in *the convenience of automatic teller machines.* **2** something that is useful, as in *The house has every modern convenience, such as central heating, a fitted kitchen, built-in cupboards, etc.* **3** a public toilet.
at your convenience, as it suits you.
convenience foods, foods that are easy to use and usually have been partly prepared, only requiring heating.

convenient *adjective*
easy to use or reach; suitable, as in *Our house is convenient to the school. A convenient time for the meeting was arranged.*
conveniently *adverb*

convent *noun* **convents**
1 a place where nuns live and work.
2 a school run by nuns.

convention *noun* **conventions**
1 an accepted way of doing things.
2 a conference of people with a common interest, as in *a musicians' convention.*

conventional *adjective*
1 done in the accepted way; traditional.
2 to do with weapons that are non-nuclear.
conventionally *adverb*

a
b
c
d
e
f
g
h
i
j
k
l
m
n
o
p
q
r
s
t
u
v
w
x
y
z

converge

converge *verb* **converges, converging, converged**
1 to come together, as in *The two roads converge.* **2** to approach from different directions, as in *Thousands of fans converged on the football ground.*

conversation *noun* **conversations**
talk between two or several people.
conversational *adjective*

converse *verb* **converses, conversing, conversed** (*say* kuhn-**vers**)
to speak, as in *They conversed in low voices.*

converse *noun* (*say* **kon**-vers)
the opposite, as in *The converse of 'good' is 'evil'.*

conversion *noun* **conversions**
the act of converting or changing; the process of being converted, as in *a house conversion; the conversion of water to steam.*

convert *verb* **converts, converting, converted** (*say* kuhn-**vert**)
1 to change. **2** to make someone change his or her beliefs. **3** to kick a goal after scoring a try in Rugby.
converter *noun*, **convertible** *adjective*

convert *noun* **converts** (*say* **kon**-vert)
someone who has changed his or her beliefs.

convex *adjective*
curved like the outside of a circle or ball.

convey *verb* **conveys, conveying, conveyed**
1 to transport. **2** to communicate a message, idea, etc.

conveyor belt *noun* **conveyor belts**
a belt, chain, etc. carrying goods in a factory, etc.

convict *verb* **convicts, convicting, convicted** (*say* kuhn-**vikt**)
to prove or declare that someone is guilty of a crime.

convict *noun* **convicts** (*say* **kon**-vikt)
a person found guilty of a crime, as in *English convicts were sent to the early Australian colonies.*

conviction *noun* **convictions**
1 being found guilty of a crime. **2** a firm belief, as in *She has a strong conviction in the existence of God.*

convince *verb* **convinces, convincing, convinced**
to persuade.

convoy *noun* **convoys**
a group of ships, vehicles, etc. travelling together.

convulsion *noun* **convulsions**
an uncontrollable spasm of the muscles; a fit.
in convulsions, uncontrollable laughter.

cooee *noun* **cooees**
(*colloquial*) a long, loud call used to attract attention, especially in the bush.

cook *verb* **cooks, cooking, cooked**
to prepare food by heating it.

cook *noun* **cooks**
someone who cooks.

cookery *noun*
the practice or skill of cooking food.

cool *adjective* **cooler, coolest**
1 to do with or at a fairly low temperature; fairly cold. **2** not emotional or excited. **3** fashionable, as in *He's only wearing those sun-glasses in order to look cool.*
coolly *adverb*, **coolness** *noun*

cool *verb* **cools, cooling, cooled**
to make someone or something cool; to become cool.
cooler *noun*

coolamon *noun*
a basin-like vessel made of wood or bark used by Aborigines to hold water, liquids and for a variety of other purposes such as carrying a baby.

Origin This word comes from Kamilaroi, an Aboriginal language of New South Wales. See the Aboriginal Languages map at the back of this dictionary.

coolibah *noun* **coolibahs**
a type of gum tree found in central and northern Australia.

Origin This word comes from the Aboriginal language Yuwaaliyaay: **gulabaa**. See the Aboriginal Languages map at the back of this dictionary.

cooped up *adjective*
having to stay in a place which is too small or in which you feel trapped, as in *We were cooped up in the plane for two hours, waiting for permission to take off.*

cooperate *verb* **cooperates, cooperating, cooperated** (*say* ko-**op**-uh-rayt)
to work helpfully with other people.
cooperation *noun*, **cooperative** *adjective*

coordinate *verb* **coordinates, coordinating, coordinated** (*say* koh-**aw**-duhn-ayt)
to get people or things working properly together, as in *She coordinated the school fete. The young children could not coordinate their dance movements.*
coordination *noun*, **coordinator** *noun*

coronation

coordinate *noun* **coordinates**
(*say* koh-**aw**-duhn-uht)
one of a pair of numbers or letters that show a particular point on a map or graph.

cop *noun* **cops**
(*colloquial*) a policeman.
cop shop, a police station.
not much cop, not very good.

cop *verb* **cops, copping, copped**
to get or receive something, as in *The politician copped a lot of criticism.*
cop it, to get into trouble.

cope *verb* **copes, coping, coped**
to deal with something successfully, as in *How did you cope with your homework?*

copper *noun*
a reddish-brown metal, as in *Copper is used for making wire, coins, etc.*
copper cups, a Western Australian shrub with orange, cup-shaped flowers.
copper sulphate, blue crystals that are a compound of copper, sulphur, and oxygen.
coppery *adjective*

copulate *verb* **copulates, copulating, copulated** (*say* **kop**-yoo-layt)
to have sexual intercourse.
copulation *noun*

copy *noun* **copies**
1 something made to look exactly like something else. 2 something written out a second time. 3 one newspaper, magazine, book, etc., as in *We each have a copy of 'Seven Little Australians'.*

copy *verb* **copies, copying, copied**
1 to make a copy of something. 2 to do exactly the same as someone else.
copycat, (*colloquial*) a person who copies another.
copier *noun*, **copyist** *noun*

copyright *noun* **copyrights**
the right by law of an author, composer, publisher, etc. to be the only person allowed to reproduce a book, piece of music, recording, etc.

coral *noun*
a hard substance made of the skeletons of tiny marine creatures, as in *The Barrier Reef is made of coral.*

cord *noun* **cords**
1 thin rope; a piece of thin rope. 2 the covered wire used to connect an electrical item to the power outlet, as in *cord of the iron.* 3 ribbed fabric, especially corduroy.

Usage Do not confuse **cord** with **chord**, which means a number of musical notes sounded together.

cordial *adjective*
warm and friendly, as in *a cordial welcome.*
cordiality *noun*, **cordially** *adverb*

cordial *noun* **cordials**
a fruit-flavoured drink.

corduroy *noun* (*say* **kaw**-duh-roi)
thick cotton cloth with raised lines across it.

core *noun* **cores**
the part in the middle of something.

corella *noun* **corellas**
a type of Australian parrot.

Origin This word comes from the Aboriginal language Wiradhuri probably from **garila**. See the Aboriginal Languages map at the back of this dictionary.

corgi *noun* **corgis**
a small breed of dog with short legs and large, upright ears.

cork *noun* **corks**
1 the lightweight bark of a kind of oak-tree. 2 a piece of this bark used to seal a bottle.

corkscrew *noun* **corkscrews**
a device for removing corks from bottles.

cormorant *noun* **cormorants**
a large diving sea bird.

corn *noun*
grain; cereal plant, as in *Cornflakes are made from corn.*

corn *noun* **corns**
a small, hard lump on your toe or foot.

corned *adjective*
preserved with salt, as in *corned beef.*

corner *noun* **corners**
the point where two lines, roads, or walls meet.

corner *verb* **corners, cornering, cornered**
1 to trap someone, as in *The police cornered the escaped prisoner.* 2 to go around a corner, as in *His car cornered badly.*

cornet *noun* **cornets**
a brass musical instrument rather like a small trumpet.

cornflour *noun*
fine flour used for making custards, sauces, etc.

corny *adjective* **cornier, corniest**
(*colloquial*) repeated so often that people are bored, as in *corny jokes.*

coronary *noun* **coronaries** (*say* ko-ruhn-ree)
a sudden and sometimes fatal heart attack.

coronation *noun* **coronations**
the crowning of a king or queen.

coroner

coroner *noun* coroners
an official who holds an inquiry into the cause of an unnatural death.

corporal *noun* corporals
a soldier just below sergeant in rank.

corporal *adjective*
to do with the human body.
corporal punishment, beating or whipping someone.

corporation *noun* corporations
a group of people acting or working together, especially in business, as in *the Australian Broadcasting Corporation.*

corps *noun* corps (*say* kaw)
1 a large unit of soldiers. 2 a group of people involved in a special activity, as in *diplomatic corps; press corps.*

Usage Do not confuse **corps** with **corpse**, which is the next word in this dictionary.

corpse *noun* corpses
a dead body.

corpuscle *noun* corpuscles
(*say* kaw-puh-suhl)
one of the red or white cells in the blood.

correct *adjective*
1 true; accurate; without any mistakes, as in *Your sums are all correct.* 2 proper, as in *Is that the correct way to talk to your parents?*
correctly *adverb*, **correctness** *noun*

correct *verb* corrects, correcting, corrected
to make something correct; to mark the mistakes in something.
correction *noun*

correspond *verb* corresponds, corresponding, corresponded
1 to agree with; to match, as in *Your story corresponds with what I heard.* 2 to exchange letters with someone.

correspondence *noun*
1 similarity; agreement, as in *There is a close correspondence between oranges and mandarins. There was close correspondence between the two reports on the environment.* 2 letters; writing letters. 3 letters sent or received.

correspondent *noun* correspondents
1 someone who writes letters to you.
2 someone employed to send news or articles to a newspaper, etc.

corridor *noun* corridors
1 a long, narrow way from which doors open into rooms or compartments.
2 a permitted route, as in *an air corridor.*

corroboree *noun* corroborees
an Aboriginal dance ceremony with song and music.

Origin This word comes from the Aboriginal language Dharuk: **garabari** = a style of dancing. See the Aboriginal Languages map at the back of this dictionary.

corrode *verb* corrodes, corroding, corroded
to wear away by rust, chemical action, etc.
corrosion *noun*, **corrosive** *adjective*

corrugated *adjective*
shaped into folds or ridges, as in *corrugated iron.*

corrupt *adjective*
1 wicked. 2 liable to give or accept bribes.
corruption *noun*

corset *noun* corsets
a close-fitting piece of underwear worn to shape the body or to support it after injury.

cosmetics *plural noun*
substances for making your skin or hair look better or different, as in *Lipstick and face powder are cosmetics.*

cosmic *adjective* (*say* koz-mik)
to do with the universe.
cosmic rays, very strong radiation from outer space.

cosmonaut *noun* cosmonauts
an astronaut.

cossie *noun* cossies (*say* koz-ee)
(*colloquial*) a swimming costume; bathers; togs.

cost *verb* costs, costing, cost
to have a certain price, as in *That book cost $15 last year. The car accident cost many lives.*

cost *noun* costs
the price of something.
at all costs, or **at any cost**, no matter what the cost or difficulty may be.
cost of living, the average amount each person in a country spends on food, clothing, and housing.

costly *adjective* costlier, costliest
expensive.

costume *noun* costumes
clothes, especially for a particular purpose or of a particular period, as in *gym costume; colonial costume.*

cosy *adjective* cosier, cosiest
warm and comfortable.

cot *noun* **cots**
a baby's bed with high sides.

cottage *noun* **cottages**
a small house, especially in the country.
cottage cheese, soft, white, lumpy cheese
made from curdled milk.
cottage pie, minced meat covered with
mashed potato and baked.

cotton *noun*
1 a soft white substance covering the seeds
of certain plants. 2 the thread or cloth
made from this substance.
cotton on, to begin to understand.

cotton wool *noun*
a soft, fluffy, cotton-like material used for
putting cream on skin, cleaning wounds, etc.

couch *noun* **couches**
a long, soft seat, usually with one end
raised; a lounge.
couch potato, *(colloquial)* a person who
spends too much time watching television
or videos.

cough *verb* **coughs, coughing, coughed**
(say kof*)*
to push air suddenly out of your lungs
with a sharp sound.
cough up, *(colloquial)* to give someone
money, information, etc., as in *Where's my
change? Cough it up!*

cough *noun* **coughs** *(say* kof*)*
1 the act or sound of coughing. 2 an
illness which makes you cough frequently.

council *noun* **councils**
a group of people chosen or elected to
organise or discuss something, especially to
plan the affairs of a town, as in *school
council; land council; local council.*
councillor *noun*

Usage Do not confuse **council** with
counsel, which is the next word in this
dictionary.

counsel *noun* **counsels**
1 advice. 2 the barrister or barristers
involved in a case in a lawcourt.

counsel *verb* **counsels, counselling,
counselled**
to give advice to someone.
counsellor *noun*

count *verb* **counts, counting, counted**
1 to use numbers to find out how many
people or things there are in a place; to add
up. 2 to say numbers in their proper
order. 3 to include someone or something
in a total, as in *There are 30 in the class, not
counting the teacher.* 4 to have a particular

value or importance, as in *Qualifications
must count for something.*
count on, to rely on.

count *noun* **counts**
1 counting; a total, as in *The final count of
votes was taken.* 2 one of the things that
someone is accused of, as in *He was found
guilty on all counts.* 3 a nobleman from
Europe.

countenance *noun* **countenances**
someone's face; the expression on
someone's face.

counter *noun* **counters**
1 a long table where customers are served
in a shop, restaurant, bank, etc. 2 a small,
round, flat piece of plastic, etc. used in
games, especially board games.
counter lunch, a usually cheap, but filling
midday meal in a hotel.

counter *verb* **counters, countering, countered**
to oppose or contradict, as in *In chess, she
successfully countered my moves.*

counterfeit *adjective (say* **kown**-tuh-fuht *or*
kown-tuh-feet*)*
copied so as to deceive or swindle people,
as in *counterfeit money.*

country *noun* **countries**
1 part of the world where a nation of
people lives. 2 the rural area beyond a
town or city. 3 the people who live in
a country, as in *The country voted for peace.*

coup *noun* **coups** *(say* koo*)*
a violent or illegal seizing of power, as in
*The government was overthrown in a military
coup.*

couple *noun* **couples**
two people or things.

couple *verb* **couples, coupling, coupled**
to join things together.
coupling *noun*

coupon *noun* **coupons**
a piece of paper that gives you the right to
receive or do something.

courage *noun*
the ability to ignore fear; bravery.

courageous *adjective*
brave; ready to face danger, pain, etc.

courier *noun* **couriers** *(say* **koo**-ree-uh*)*
1 someone who carries a message.
2 someone employed to guide and help
people on holiday.

course *noun* **courses**
1 the direction in which something goes or
moves, as in *the ship's course; the wind
changing course.* 2 a series of lessons,

court

exercises, etc., as in *a science course.* **3** part of a meal, as in *the main course.* **4** a stretch of land or water for races, as in *the Randwick course.*
in due course, eventually; at the expected time.
in the course of, during.
of course, certainly, as in *Of course they will help us. 'Will you help us?' 'Of course!'*

court *noun* **courts**
1 a lawcourt. **2** an enclosed place for games like tennis or netball. **3** a courtyard. **4** the place where a king or queen lives.

court *verb* **courts, courting, courted**
to try to get someone's love or support.
courtship *noun*

courteous *adjective* (*say* **ker-tee-uhs**)
polite.
courteously *adverb*, **courtesy** *noun*

court martial *noun* **courts martial**
1 a court for trying offenders against military law. **2** a trial in this court.

courtyard *noun* **courtyards**
a space surrounded by walls or buildings.

cousin *noun* **cousins**
a child of your uncle or aunt.

cove *noun* **coves**
a small bay.

cover *verb* **covers, covering, covered**
1 to put one thing over or around another; to hide something. **2** to travel a certain distance, as in *We covered many kilometres in a day.* **3** to deal with or include, as in *This book covers stamp collecting.* **4** to be enough money for something, as in *$2 will cover my fare.* **5** to aim a gun at or near someone, as in *I've got you covered.*
cover up, not to let anyone know about something wrong or illegal.

cover *noun* **covers**
1 something used for covering something else; a lid, wrapper, envelope, etc.
2 something that hides or shelters you, as in *We ran for cover as the storm started.*

cover-up *noun* **cover-ups**
the act of hiding something that is wrong or illegal, as in *There has been a cover-up of the accident at the chemical plant.*

cow *noun* **cows**
1 a female animal kept by farmers for its milk and beef. **2** a female of many large animals, such as the elephant, whale, etc.

coward *noun* **cowards**
someone who is not brave.
cowardice *noun*, **cowardly** *adjective*

cowboy *noun* **cowboys**
1 a man who rides around looking after the cattle on a large farm in America.
2 (*colloquial*) a person who uses dishonest methods in business, organisations, etc., as in *Those cowboys who put in the double glazing never sealed the gaps around the window frames!*

cox *noun* **coxes**
someone who steers a boat.

coxswain *noun* **coxswains** (*say* **kok**-swayn *or* **kok**-suhn)
a cox.

coy *adjective*
shy; pretending to be shy or modest.
coyly *adverb*, **coyness** *noun*

crab *noun* **crabs**
a shellfish with ten legs, the first pair being pincers.

crab-apple *noun* **crab-apples**
a small, sour apple.

crack *noun* **cracks**
1 a sudden sharp noise, as in *the crack of a pistol shot.* **2** a sudden knock, as in *a crack on the head.* **3** a line on the surface of something where it has broken but not come completely apart; a narrow gap, as in *There's a crack in this cup.*

crack *verb* **cracks, cracking, cracked**
1 to make a crack in something; to get a crack, as in *The plate has cracked.* **2** to make a sudden sharp noise, as in *He cracked the whip.* **3** to surrender, especially under pressure, torture, etc. **4** (*colloquial*) to tell a joke, as in *He cracked some old jokes.* **5** to find the solution or answer, as in *cracked the code.*
get cracking, (*colloquial*) to get busy; to start some work.

cracker *noun* **crackers**
1 a paper tube which bangs when two people pull it apart; a bon-bon, as in *Christmas crackers.* **2** a thin, savoury biscuit. **3** a loud firework.

crackle *verb* **crackles, crackling, crackled**
to make small cracking sounds, as in *The fire crackled in the grate.*

cradle *noun* **cradles**
1 a cot for a baby. **2** a supporting frame, as in *The painters needed a cradle to paint the tall building.*

cradle *verb* **cradles, cradling, cradled**
to hold gently.

craft *noun* **crafts**
1 a job which needs skill with the hands; a skill, as in *Pottery is a craft.* **2** a boat,

craftsman *noun*
a skilled worker or person who practises a craft.
craftsmanship *noun*

plane, or spacecraft.   **3** cunning or deceit, as in *He used craft to trick the buyer into paying more.*

craftsman *noun*
a skilled worker or person who practises a craft.
craftsmanship *noun*

crafty *adjective* **craftier, craftiest**
cunning; clever.
craftily *adverb*, **craftiness** *noun*

crag *noun* **crags**
a steep piece of rough rock, as in *The cliffs around the beach had many crags.*
craggy *adjective*

cram *verb* **crams, cramming, crammed**
1 to push a lot of things into a space.
2 to fill something very full.

cramp *noun* **cramps**
pain caused by a muscle tightening suddenly.

cramp *verb* **cramps, cramping, cramped**
1 to keep someone or something in a very small space.   **2** to hinder someone's freedom, growth, etc.

crane *noun* **cranes**
1 a machine for lifting and moving heavy objects.   **2** a large wading bird with long legs, neck and bill.

crane *verb* **cranes, craning, craned**
to stretch your neck so that you can see something.

crank *noun* **cranks**
1 an L-shaped rod used to turn or control something.   **2** a person with strange or fanatical ideas, as in *a health-food crank.*
cranky *adjective*

crank *verb* **cranks, cranking, cranked**
to turn something by using an L-shaped rod, as in *I had to crank the car's engine to get it to start.*

cranny *noun* **crannies**
a crevice; a narrow hole or space.

crash *verb* **crashes, crashing, crashed**
1 to make a loud, smashing noise, as in *Crash the cymbals.*   **2** to move with a loud noise, as in *The elephants crashed through the jungle.*   **3** to collide or cause a vehicle to collide, as in *Kerrie crashed the car.*

crash *noun* **crashes**
1 the loud noise of something falling or breaking.   **2** a violent collision or fall.

crash-helmet *noun* **crash-helmets**
a padded helmet worn by motor-cyclists, cyclists etc.

crash landing *noun* **crash landings**
an emergency landing of an aircraft, which usually damages it.

crate *noun* **crates**
a container in which goods are transported, as in *a crate of milk.*

crater *noun* **craters**
1 the mouth of a volcano.   **2** a hole in the ground made by a bomb, etc.

crave *verb* **craves, craving, craved**
to desire something strongly.

crawl *verb* **crawls, crawling, crawled**
1 to move on your hands and knees.
2 to move slowly, as in *The traffic crawled.*   **3** to be full of or covered with insects, etc., as in *This room's crawling with cockroaches.*   **4** (*colloquial*) to be too nice or flattering to a person to gain favour, as in *A person who crawls to the teacher is called a crawler.*

crawl *noun*
1 a crawling movement.   **2** a swimming stroke with the arms hitting the water alternately while the legs kick; freestyle.

crayfish *noun*
1 a small freshwater animal, like a lobster, which is highly valued as food, as in *Yabbies and marron are crayfish.*   **2** a medium-sized, marine shellfish, as in *The rock lobster is a marine crayfish.*

crayon *noun* **crayons**
a stick or pencil of coloured wax for drawing, colouring, etc.

craze *noun* **crazes**
an enthusiastic and brief interest in something.

crazy *adjective* **crazier, craziest**
mad.
crazy about, (*colloquial*) very enthusiastic; in love with.
crazily *adverb*, **craziness** *noun*

creak *noun* **creaks**
a harsh scraping or squeaking sound.
creaky *adjective*

creak *verb* **creaks, creaking, creaked**
to make a creaking noise, as in *Old floorboards creak at night.*

cream *noun*
1 the richest part of milk.   **2** a yellowish-white colour.   **3** a substance that looks like cream, as in *face cream.*
the cream, the best part of something, as in *The cream of the country's athletes are in the Olympics.*
creamy *adjective*

crease

crease *noun* **creases**
1 a line made in something by folding, pressing, or squashing it. 2 a line on a cricket pitch showing where a batter should stand and a bowler bowl.

crease *verb* **creases, creasing, creased**
to make a crease or creases in something; to develop creases, as in *Crease the trousers. Linen creases easily.*

create *verb* **creates, creating, created**
1 to make something that no one else has made or can make. 2 to give rank to, as in *He was created a general.*
creation *noun*, **creative** *adjective*, **creativity** *noun*

creative *adjective*
1 able to make or invent things, as in *a creative pastime.* 2 showing imagination and thought as well as skill, as in *You don't have to do something that has been done before; be creative!*

creator *noun* **creators**
someone who makes or invents something.
the Creator, God.

creature *noun* **creatures**
a living animal or person.

crèche *noun* **crèches** (*say* kraysh *or* kresh)
a place where babies or small children are looked after while their parents are busy.

credibility *noun*
being credible or believable, as in *After continually lying, he lost credibility with his friends.*

credible *adjective*
able to be believed; trustworthy.
credibly *adverb*

Usage Do not confuse **credible** with **creditable**, which means deserving praise.

credit *noun*
1 honour; approval, as in *Give her credit for her honesty.* 2 belief or trust, as in *I place no credit in his promises.* 3 the amount of money in someone's account at a bank, etc. 4 trusting someone to pay for something later on, as in *Do you want cash now or can I have it on credit?* 5 the amount of money a person is allowed to spend or borrow, as in *My credit is good.*
credits or **credit titles,** the list of people who have helped to produce a film, television program, etc.
something does you credit, something that you have done is good and you deserve praise for it, as in *Your project work does you credit.*

credit *verb* **credits, crediting, credited**
1 to believe, as in *Can you credit that?* 2 to enter something as a credit in an account, as in *We will credit you with $100.*

credit card *noun* **credit cards**
a card allowing someone to buy goods on credit.

creed *noun* **creeds**
a set or statement of beliefs, as in *a religious creed.*

creek *noun* **creeks**
a small stream.
up the creek, (*colloquial*) in trouble.

creep *verb* **creeps, creeping, crept**
1 to move along close to the ground. 2 to move quietly or secretly, as in *They crept up on the enemy.* 3 to come gradually, as in *Doubt crept into her mind.*

creep *noun* **creeps**
1 a creeping movement. 2 (*colloquial*) an unpleasant person.
give someone the creeps, (*colloquial*) to make someone feel afraid or very uncomfortable.

creeper *noun* **creepers**
a plant that grows close to the ground, or climbs walls, fences, etc.

creepy *adjective* **creepier, creepiest**
feeling or causing horror or fear, as in *a creepy film.*

cremate *verb* **cremates, cremating, cremated**
to burn a corpse to ashes.
cremation *noun*

crematorium *noun* **crematoria**
(*say* krem-uh-**taw**-ree-uhm)
a place where corpses are cremated.

crêpe *noun* **crêpes** (*say* krayp)
1 cloth with a wrinkled surface. 2 a kind of thin French pancake.

crept past tense and past participle of **creep** *verb.*

crescendo *noun* **crescendos**
(*say* kruh-**shen**-doh)
music that gets gradually louder.

crescendo *adjective* and *adverb*
increasing in loudness or force.

crescent *noun* **crescents**
1 a narrow curved shape, pointed at both ends, as in *The new moon is a crescent.* 2 a curved street.

cress *noun*
a green, leafy herb used in salads and sandwiches.

crest *noun* **crests**
1 a tuft of hair, feathers, or skin on an animal's head. 2 the top of a hill, wave, etc. 3 the part above the coat of arms or on a badge, etc., as in *the school crest*.

crevasse *noun* **crevasses**
a deep crack in a glacier.

crevice *noun* **crevices**
a crack or narrow opening in rock, wall, etc.

crew *noun* **crews**
the people who work on a ship, aircraft, etc.

crib *noun* **cribs**
1 a baby's cot. 2 a framework containing fodder for animals.

cricket *noun*
a game played outdoors by two teams of eleven players, some members of one team taking turns to bowl at a wicket defended by a batting player of the other team.
cricketer *noun*

cricket *noun* **crickets**
an insect like a grasshopper which makes a loud, chirping noise.

cried past tense and past participle of **cry** *verb*.

crime *noun* **crimes**
an action that breaks the law.

criminal *noun* **criminals**
someone who has committed one or more crimes.

criminal *adjective*
to do with crime or criminals, as in *criminal behaviour*.

crimson *adjective*
dark red.

crinkle *verb* **crinkles, crinkling, crinkled**
to crease or wrinkle.
crinkly *adjective*

cripple *noun* **cripples**
someone who cannot walk properly.

cripple *verb* **cripples, crippling, crippled**
1 to make someone a cripple. 2 to damage something seriously, as in *Flood can cripple a farmer*.

crisis *noun* **crises** (*say* **kruy**-suhs)
1 an important, dangerous, or very difficult time or situation. 2 a turning point, especially during an illness.

crisp *adjective* **crisper, crispest**
1 very dry so that it breaks easily. 2 firm and fresh, as in *a very crisp apple*. 3 frosty. 4 quick and precise, as in *crisp movements*.

crisp *noun* **crisps**
a potato chip.

criss-cross *adjective* and *adverb*
with crossing lines.

critic *noun* **critics**
1 a person who disapproves or finds mistakes. 2 someone who gives opinions on books, plays, films, music, etc., as in *film critic for a newspaper*.

critical *adjective*
1 criticising or finding mistakes. 2 to do with critics or criticism, as in *a critical review*. 3 to do with a crisis; very serious, as in *The spread of disease reached a critical point*.
critically *adverb*

criticise or **criticize** *verb* **criticises, criticising, criticised** (*say* **krit**-uh-suyz)
to say that someone or something is bad, unsatisfactory, etc.

criticism *noun* **criticisms**
(*say* **krit**-uh-siz-uhm)
what a critic says; the work of a critic.

croak *noun* **croaks**
a deep, hoarse sound, like that of a frog.

crochet *noun* (*say* **kroh**-shay)
a kind of needlework done with a hooked needle.

crockery *noun*
cups, saucers, plates, etc.

crocodile *noun* **crocodiles**
a large, carnivorous reptile with a thick skin, long tail and huge jaws, living in water and on land in hot countries.

croissant *noun* **croissants** (*say* **krwa**-sawn)
a crescent-shaped roll of rich pastry, first made in France and usually eaten for breakfast.

crook *noun* **crooks**
1 (*colloquial*) someone who cheats or robs people; a criminal. 2 a bend or curve, as in *the crook of your arm*. 3 a shepherd's stick with a curved end.

crook *adjective*
(*colloquial*)
1 unwell or injured, as in *feeling crook; crook back*. 2 bad or unpleasant, as in *crook weather; crook job*.

crooked *adjective* (*say* **kruuk**-uhd)
1 bent; twisted; not straight. 2 (*colloquial*) dishonest.

croon *verb* **croons, crooning, crooned**
to sing softly or sentimentally.
crooner *noun*

crop

crop *noun* **crops**
1 something grown for food, as in *a good crop of wheat*. 2 the handle of a whip.

crop *verb* **crops, cropping, cropped**
1 to cut off hair, grass, etc. 2 to sow or plant land with a crop.
crop up, to happen or appear unexpectedly.

croquet *noun*
a game played on a lawn, in which wooden balls are driven through hoops with a mallet.

cross *noun* **crosses**
1 a mark or shape like + or ×. 2 an upright post with another post across it, used in ancient times for crucifixions. 3 a mixture of two different things, as in *This cat is a cross between a Persian and Siamese.*
the Cross, the cross on which Jesus was crucified, used as a symbol of Christianity.

cross *verb* **crosses, crossing, crossed**
1 to go across something, as in *Cross the road*. 2 to draw one or more lines across something, as in *Cross the cheque.* 3 to make the sign or shape of a cross with something, as in *Cross your fingers for good luck.*
cross something out, to draw a line across something because it is unwanted, wrong, etc.

cross *adjective*
1 angry; bad-tempered. 2 going from one side to another, as in *cross winds.*
crossly *adverb,* **crossness** *noun*

cross-country *adjective*
across the country, not on roads, as in *a cross-country race through the pine forest.*

cross-examine *verb* **cross-examines, cross-examining, cross-examined**
to question someone carefully, especially in a lawcourt.
cross-examination *noun*

cross-eyed *adjective*
with eyes that look or seem to look in different directions.

crossing *noun* **crossings**
1 a place where people can cross a road, railway, etc. 2 a journey across an area, especially water, as in *We had a smooth crossing to Tasmania.*

cross-legged *adverb* and *adjective*
with legs crossed.

cross section *noun* **cross sections**
1 a solid figure cut at right angles to an axis. 2 a drawing of this cut.

crossword *noun* **crosswords**
a puzzle in which you have to guess words from clues and write them on a chequered square or diagram.

crotchet *noun* **crotchets** (*say* **kroch**-uht)
a musical note equal to half a minim and usually one beat, written ♩.

crouch *verb* **crouches, crouching, crouched**
to lower your body, with your arms and legs bent.

crow *noun* **crows**
a large black bird with a powerful beak.
as the crow flies, in a straight line.

crow *verb* **crows, crowing, crowed**
1 to make a noise like a rooster.
2 to boast; to be proudly triumphant.

crowbar *noun* **crowbars**
an iron bar used as a lever.

crowd *noun* **crowds**
a large number of people in one place.

crowd *verb* **crowds, crowding, crowded**
1 to make a crowd, as in *The students crowded around the visitor.* 2 to cram; to fill uncomfortably full, as in *Darling Harbour is crowded with tourists.*

crown *noun* **crowns**
1 an ornamental head-dress worn by a king or queen. 2 the highest part of something, as in *She bumped the crown of her head. Winning the gold medal was the crown of her sporting achievement.*

crown *verb* **crowns, crowning, crowned**
1 to make someone a king or queen. 2 to reward; to end something successfully, as in *Their efforts were crowned with success.*

crow's-nest *noun* **crow's-nests**
a lookout position at the top of a ship's mast.

crucial *adjective* (*say* **kroo**-shuhl)
most important, as in *a crucial stage in the experiment.*

crucifix *noun* **crucifixes**
a model of the Cross or of Jesus on the Cross.

crucify *verb* **crucifies, crucifying, crucified**
1 to put to death by nailing a person to a cross. 2 (*colloquial*) to defeat thoroughly in an argument, match, etc.; to humiliate, as in *My team was crucified in the final. The critics crucified the performer.*
crucifixion *noun*

crude *adjective* **cruder, crudest**
1 natural; not refined, as in *crude oil.*
2 rough; not finished properly, as in *a crude hut.* 3 vulgar; rude, as in *crude jokes.*

cubic

cruel *adjective* **crueller, cruellest**
1 pleased at, or not caring about, the pain and suffering of others, as in *a cruel tyrant*. 2 causing pain and suffering, as in *a cruel war*.
cruelly *adverb*, **cruelty** *noun*

cruise *verb* **cruises, cruising, cruised**
1 to sail or travel at a slow or moderate speed. 2 to have a cruise on a ship or yacht.

cruise *noun* **cruises**
a holiday at sea.

crumb *noun* **crumbs**
a tiny piece of bread, cake, etc.

crumble *verb* **crumbles, crumbling, crumbled**
to break or fall into small pieces.
crumbly *adjective*

crumpet *noun* **crumpets**
a soft, flat cake of yeast mixture, eaten toasted with butter.

crumple *verb* **crumples, crumpling, crumpled**
1 to make or become very creased. 2 to collapse, as in *She crumpled on the ground after the attack*.

crunch *verb* **crunches, crunching, crunched**
to make a crunching sound in walking, moving, chewing, etc., as in *The skaters crunched on the ice. Julia crunched a carrot*.

crunch *noun* **crunches**
the noise made by chewing hard food, walking on gravel, etc.
the crunch, (*colloquial*) a crucial event; a crisis.
crunchy *adjective*

crusade *noun* **crusades**
1 a military expedition by Christian Europeans made in the Middle Ages to Palestine to recover the Holy Land from the Muslims. 2 a campaign against something that you think is bad, as in *a crusade against crime*.
crusader *noun*

crush *verb* **crushes, crushing, crushed**
1 to press something so that it gets broken or harmed. 2 to defeat.

crush *noun* **crushes**
1 a crowd; a crowded situation. 2 (*colloquial*) a temporary strong liking for someone; an infatuation.

crust *noun* **crusts**
1 the hard outside part of something, especially of bread. 2 the rocky outer part of the planet Earth.

crustacean *noun* **crustaceans**
(*say* krus-**tay**-shuhn)
a shellfish, as in *Crabs, lobsters, crayfish and yabbies are crustaceans*.

crutch *noun* **crutches**
a long walking-stick that fits under a lame or injured person's arm to help him or her to walk.

cry *verb* **cries, crying, cried**
1 to shout. 2 to let tears fall from your eyes.
cry out for something, to need something urgently, as in *The front door is crying out for a coat of paint*.

cry *noun* **cries**
1 a loud shout. 2 a period of weeping, as in *a good cry about her loss*.

crypt *noun* **crypts**
a room underneath a church, as in *People were often buried in the crypt*.

crystal *noun* **crystals**
1 a transparent, colourless mineral, rather like glass. 2 a small, solid piece of a substance with a symmetrical shape, as in *crystals of snow and ice*.
crystalline *adjective*

crystallise or **crystallize** *verb* **crystallises, crystallising, crystallised**
1 to form into crystals. 2 to cover with sugar, as in *The grapes were crystallised*.

cub *noun* **cubs**
a young lion, tiger, fox, bear, etc.
Cub, a junior Scout.

cubby-hole *noun* **cubby-holes**
a small compartment; a snug place.

cubby-house *noun* **cubby-houses**
a child's playhouse.

cube *noun* **cubes**
1 something that has six square sides, as in *Dice and sugar lumps are cubes*. 2 the result of multiplying something by itself twice, as in *The cube of 3 is $3 \times 3 \times 3 = 27$*.
cube root, what gives a particular number if it is multiplied by itself twice, as in *The cube root of 8 is 2*.

cube *verb* **cubes, cubing, cubed**
1 to multiply a number by itself twice, as in *4 cubed is $4 \times 4 \times 4 = 64$*. 2 to cut something into small cubes.

cubic *adjective*
to do with or shaped like a cube.
cubic metre, the volume of a cube with sides that are one metre long.

a
b
c
d
e
f
g
h
i
j
k
l
m
n
o
p
q
r
s
t
u
v
w
x
y
z

cubicle

cubicle *noun* **cubicles**
a small division of a room, especially one where people change their clothes.

cuboid *adjective*
an object shaped like a cube.

cuckoo *noun* **cuckoos**
a bird that makes a sound like 'cuck-oo', as in *Cuckoos lay their eggs in other birds' nests*.

cucumber *noun* **cucumbers**
a long or round green salad vegetable.

cud *noun*
half-digested food that a cow, etc. brings back from its first stomach to chew again.

cuddle *verb* **cuddles, cuddling, cuddled**
to put your arms closely around a person or animal that you love.
cuddly *adjective*

cue *noun* **cues**
1 something said or done that acts as a signal for an actor, etc. to say or do something, as in *Your cue is: 'Here's the detective!'* 2 a long stick used to strike the ball in billiards, snooker, etc.

cuff *noun* **cuffs**
the end of a sleeve that fits around the wrist or the part turned up at the legs of trousers.

cuff *verb* **cuffs, cuffing, cuffed**
to hit someone with your hand.

cul-de-sac *noun* **cul-de-sacs**
a dead end road or street.

cull *verb* **culls, culling, culled**
1 to select or gather, as in *to cull facts from books*. 2 to select an animal, especially for killing to control the population, as in *culling kangaroos*.

culminate *verb* **culminates, culminating, culminated**
to reach the highest or last point, as in *a long struggle that culminated in victory*.
culmination *noun*

culprit *noun* **culprits**
a person who has done wrong.

cult *noun* **cults**
a religion; being devoted to someone or something, as in *The cult of basketball is popular with teenagers*.

cultivate *verb* **cultivates, cultivating, cultivated**
1 to use land to grow crops. 2 to try to make something grow or develop, as in *to cultivate a taste for reading*.
cultivated, (of a person) with good manners and education.
cultivation *noun*, **cultivator** *noun*

culture *noun* **cultures**
1 development of the mind, body, arts, music, etc. 2 customs and traditions, as in *Aboriginal culture*.
cultural *adjective*, **cultured** *adjective*

cunning *adjective*
1 clever at deceiving people.
2 ingenious, as in *a cunning plan*.

cup *noun* **cups**
1 a small container from which you drink liquid, as in *Cups usually have handles and are used with saucers*. 2 an ornamental cup given as a prize, as in *a silver cup for the premiership*.

cup *verb* **cups, cupping, cupped**
to put into the shape of a cup, as in *She cupped her hands*.

cupboard *noun* **cupboards** (*say* **kub**-uhd)
a recess or piece of furniture with a door, in which things may be stored.

curator *noun* **curators** (*say* kyoo-**ray**-tuh)
someone in charge of a museum, art gallery, etc.

curb *verb* **curbs, curbing, curbed**
to restrain or hold back, as in *Curb your anger*.

curd *noun* **curds**
a thick substance like a jelly, formed when milk turns sour.

curdle *verb* **curdles, curdling, curdled**
to form into curds, as in *Milk curdles in the heat*.
curdle someone's blood, to horrify or terrify someone.

cure *verb* **cures, curing, cured**
1 to get rid of someone's illness. 2 to stop something bad. 3 to treat something so as to preserve it, as in *Fish can be cured in smoke*.

cure *noun* **cures**
something that cures a person or thing, as in *They are trying to find a cure for cancer*.

curfew *noun* **curfews**
a time or signal after which people must stay indoors until the next day.

curiosity *noun* **curiosities**
1 a desire to know about things. 2 an unusual or strange person or thing, as in *The old woman was a curiosity to the young children*.

curious *adjective*
1 wanting to find out about things.
2 strange.
curiously *adverb*

curl *verb* **curls, curling, curled**
to form into a spiral or curve, as in *The waves curled onto the beach*.
curl up, to sit or lie with your knees drawn up.

curl *noun* **curls**
a curve or coil, especially of hair.

curly *adjective* **curlier, curliest**
full of curls; curling, as in *She had curly hair*.

currant *noun* **currants**
1 a small, black, dried grape. **2** a small, round, juicy berry; the shrub that produces this berry.

Usage Do not confuse **currant** with **current**, which means a movement of water, air, or electricity.

currawong *noun* **currawongs**
a large bird with mainly black or grey feathers, yellow eyes and a loud ringing call.

Origin This word probably comes from the Aboriginal language Yagara: **garrawan**. See the Aboriginal Languages map at the back of this dictionary.

currency *noun* **currencies**
money, as in *foreign currency*.

current *adjective*
happening or used now, as in *current events*.
currently *adverb*

current *noun* **currents**
a movement of water, air, or electricity.

Usage Do not confuse **current** with **currant**, which means a dried grape or berry or the shrub itself.

curriculum *noun* **curricula**
a course of study, as in *the grade six curriculum*.

curry *noun* **curries**
food cooked with spices that make it taste hot.

curry *verb* **curries, currying, curried**
to groom a horse by brushing or combing it.
curry favour, to try to get someone's favour or approval.

curse *noun* **curses**
1 a call or prayer for someone to be harmed or killed. **2** something very unpleasant, as in *the curse of drought*. **3** an angry word or swear word.

curse *verb* **curses, cursing, cursed**
to make a curse; to use a curse against someone.
be cursed with something, to suffer because of something.

cursor *noun* **cursors**
a movable indicator (often a flashing light) on a VDU screen, showing where the next keystroke will be.

curtain *noun* **curtains**
a piece of cloth hung at a window, door, or across the front of a stage.

curtsy *noun* **curtsies**
putting one foot behind the other and bending the knees, a mark of respect made by women, as in *The girl made a curtsy to the Queen*.

curvature *noun* **curvatures**
curving, as in *the curvature of the earth*.

curve *noun* **curves**
a line that is not straight or flat but bends smoothly.

curve *verb* **curves, curving, curved**
to put something in a curve; to be in a curve, as in *The river curved gently*.

cuscus *noun*
a furry marsupial, like a possum, which is active at night and found in northern Australia and New Guinea.

cushion *noun* **cushions**
a bag, usually of cloth, filled with soft material so that it is comfortable to sit on or rest against.

cushion *verb* **cushions, cushioning, cushioned**
1 to supply with cushions, as in *cushioned seats*. **2** to protect from shock or harm, as in *People should not be cushioned from the truth*.

custard *noun*
a thick, sweet, yellow liquid eaten with pudding, fruit, etc.

custody *noun*
1 protective care, as in *in her mother's custody after the divorce*. **2** imprisonment, as in *The prisoner was taken into custody by the police*.

custom *noun* **customs**
1 the usual way of doing things, as in *It is the custom to go on holiday in the summer*.
2 regular business from customers.
customs, taxes paid on goods brought into a country; the place at a port, airport, etc. where officials examine your luggage.

customary

customary *adjective*
usual, as in *It is customary to thank your host.*
customarily *adverb*

customer *noun* **customers**
someone who uses a shop, bank, business, etc.

cut *verb* **cuts, cutting, cut**
1 to use a knife, axe, scissors, etc. to divide, separate, or shape something. 2 to make something shorter or smaller; to remove part of something, as in *They are cutting all their prices.* 3 to divide a pack of playing-cards. 4 to hit a ball with a chopping movement. 5 to go sideways or across something, as in *The driver cut the corner.* 6 to stay away from something deliberately, as in *She cut her music lesson.*
cut and dried, already decided.
cut a tooth, to have a new tooth coming.
cut off, to interrupt; to isolate, as in *She cut me off before I had finished what I was saying. We were nearly cut off by the tide.*
cut out, to shape something by cutting; (*colloquial*) to stop doing something, as in *Cut out the joking!*
cut short, to stop something before it should end.

cut *noun* **cuts**
1 the act of cutting; the result of cutting, as in *She made a cut in the wood. Lamb chops are a delicious cut of meat.* 2 a small wound.
3 a reduction in prices, wages etc.
4 (*colloquial*) a share, as in *I want a cut of the profits.*

cute *adjective* **cuter, cutest**
(*colloquial*)
1 attractive. 2 clever, as in *a cute move in chess.*

cuticle *noun* **cuticles** (*say* **kyoo**-tik-uhl)
the skin at the base of a fingernail or toenail.

cutlass *noun* **cutlasses**
a short sword with a wide curved blade.

cutlery *noun*
knives, forks, and spoons used at the table.

cutlet *noun* **cutlets**
a small thick slice of veal or lamb on a bone.

cut-price *adjective*
sold at a reduced price, as in *a cut-price pack of eight toilet rolls.*

cutting *noun* **cuttings**
1 a clipping, as in *She collected newspaper cuttings about her team.* 2 a piece cut off a plant to grow as a new plant. 3 a steep-sided passage cut through high ground for a railway or road.

cycle *noun* **cycles**
1 a bicycle. 2 a series of events that are regularly repeated, as in *Rainfall is part of the water cycle. The tadpole is a stage in the life cycle of a frog.*

cycle *verb* **cycles, cycling, cycled**
to ride a bicycle.
cyclist *noun*

cyclone *noun* **cyclones**
a wind rotating around a calm central area, especially a violent wind of this kind in tropical areas, as in *A cyclone once destroyed Darwin.*
cyclonic *adjective*

cygnet *noun* **cygnets** (*say* **sig**-nuht)
a young swan.

cylinder *noun* **cylinders**
1 an object with straight sides and circular ends. 2 part of an engine in which a piston moves.

cylindrical *adjective*
shaped like a cylinder.

cymbal *noun* **cymbals**
a round, slightly hollowed metal plate that is hit to make a ringing sound, as in *The drummer clashed the cymbals together.*

cynic *noun* **cynics** (*say* **sin**-ik)
someone who doubts that anything can be good.
cynical *adjective*, **cynically** *adverb*, **cynicism** *noun*

cypress *noun* **cypresses**
an evergreen tree with dark leaves and hard wood.

cyst *noun* **cysts** (*say* sist)
a growth containing liquid that appears inside your body or under your skin.

Dd

dab *verb* **dabs, dabbing, dabbed**
to touch gently with something soft, as in
I dabbed my eyes with a handkerchief.

dab *noun* **dabs**
a gentle touch with something soft.

dabble *verb* **dabbles, dabbling, dabbled**
1 to splash something about in water.
2 to do something as a hobby, as in *He is a scientist, but he dabbles in music.*

dachshund *noun* **dachshunds**
(*say* **daks**-huund *or* **dash**-huund)
a small breed of dog with a long body and
very short legs.

daddy-long-legs *noun*
1 a small spider with very long
legs.   2 (*colloquial*) a tall person.

daffodil *noun* **daffodils**
a yellow, trumpet-shaped flower that
grows from a bulb.

daft *adjective* **dafter, daftest**
(*colloquial*) silly; mad.

dagger *noun* **daggers**
a short pointed knife with two sharp edges,
used as a weapon.

daily *adjective*
happening or done every day, as in *daily lessons.*

dainty *adjective* **daintier, daintiest**
delicate, pretty, and small.
daintily *adverb*, **daintiness** *noun*

dairy *noun* **dairies**
a place where milk, butter, cheese, etc. are
made or sold.
dairy farm, a farm that produces mainly
milk, butter, and cheese.

dais *noun* (*say* **day**-uhs)
a low platform at the end of a hall, used to
support a speaker, lectern, etc.

daisy *noun* **daisies**
a small flower with white petals and a
yellow centre.

dalgite or **dalgyte** *noun* **dalgites**
the Western Australian name for the bilby,
a small burrowing marsupial.

> **Origin** This word comes from the
> Aboriginal language Nyungar: **dalgaj**. See
> the Aboriginal Languages map at the back
> of this dictionary.

Dalmatian *noun* **Dalmatians**
a large breed of dog that is white with
black or brown spots.
[from the name of the *Dalmatia* region on
the eastern Adriatic coast]

dam *noun* **dams**
1 a wall built to hold water back, especially
across a river to make a reservoir.   2 an
artificial waterhole that provides water for
farm animals.

dam *verb* **dams, damming, dammed**
to hold water back with a dam.

damage *noun*
injury; harm.

damage *verb* **damages, damaging, damaged**
to injure or harm.

damages *plural noun*
money paid to someone to make up for an
injury or loss.

Dame *noun* **Dames**
the title of a lady who has been given the
equivalent of a knighthood, as in *Dame Joan Sutherland.*
dame, a comic middle-aged woman in a
pantomime, usually played by a man.

a
b
c
d
e
f
g
h
i
j
k
l
m
n
o
p
q
r
s
t
u
v
w
x
y
z

damn

damn *verb* **damns, damning, damned**
1 to curse, as in *Damn this awful weather!*
2 to condemn, as in *His book was damned by the critics.*
damn!, a swear word or curse.

damned *adjective*
(*colloquial*) hateful; annoying, as in *damned flies!*

damp *adjective* **damper, dampest**
slightly wet; not quite dry.
dampness *noun*

damper *noun* **dampers**
a simple kind of bread which is usually baked in the ashes of an outdoor fire.

dance *verb* **dances, dancing, danced**
to move about in time to music.
dancer *noun*

dance *noun* **dances**
1 a piece of music or set of movements for dancing. 2 a party or gathering where people dance.

dandelion *noun* **dandelions**
a yellow wildflower with a thick stalk and jagged leaves.

dandruff *noun*
tiny white flakes of dead skin in a person's hair.

danger *noun* **dangers**
something that is dangerous.

dangerous *adjective*
likely to kill or harm you.

dangle *verb* **dangles, dangling, dangled**
to hang or swing loosely.

dappled *adjective*
marked with patches or spots of colour or shade, as in *a dappled horse; dappled light.*

dare *verb* **dares, daring, dared**
1 to be brave enough or rude enough to do something, as in *I daren't dive in. How dare you speak to me like that!* 2 to challenge someone to do something brave, as in *I dare you to climb that tree.*

daredevil *noun* **daredevils**
a reckless, daring, or brave person.

daring *adjective*
not afraid to take risks; brave, as in *a daring plan to rescue the hostages.*

dark *adjective* **darker, darkest**
1 with little or no light, as in *a dark night.* 2 not light in colour, as in *a dark green coat.*
dark horse, a person about whom you know little but who you think might do something unexpected and impressive.
darkly *adverb*, **darkness** *noun*

dark *noun*
1 absence of light, as in *Cats can see in the dark.* 2 sunset, as in *She went out after dark.*

darken *verb* **darkens, darkening, darkened**
to make something dark; to become dark.

darkroom *noun* **darkrooms**
a room kept dark for processing photographs.

darling *noun* **darlings**
someone who is loved very much.

darn *verb* **darns, darning, darned**
to mend a hole by sewing across it.

dart *noun* **darts**
1 a small pointed missile. 2 a sudden, rapid movement.
darts, a game where darts are thrown at a dartboard to score points.

dartboard *noun* **dartboards**
a round target at which you throw darts.

dash *verb* **dashes, dashing, dashed**
1 to rush. 2 to throw something violently; to shatter, as in *The ship was dashed against the rocks.*

dash *noun* **dashes**
1 a rush; a hurry. 2 a short line (—) used in writing or printing.

dashboard *noun* **dashboards**
a panel with dials and controls in front of the driver of a car, aircraft, etc.

data *plural noun* (*say* **day**-tuh *or* **dah**-tuh)
a collection of information or facts, as in *The survey contained data on school leavers.*

Usage The singular form of **data** is **datum,** but it is not often used.

database *noun* **databases**
a store of information held in a computer.

date *noun* **dates**
1 the day of the month, or the year, when something happens. 2 an appointment to meet someone. 3 a small, sweet, brown fruit that grows on a palm tree.

date *verb* **dates, dating, dated**
1 to give a date to something. 2 to have existed from a particular time, as in *The church dates from 1820.* 3 to seem old-fashioned, as in *Some clothes styles date very quickly.*

date-line *noun*
an imaginary line running north-south which passes through the Pacific Ocean, to the east of which the date is a day earlier than to the west.

daub *verb* daubs, daubing, daubed
(*say* dawb)
to spread roughly, a usually thick sticky
substance on a surface, as in *The artist
daubed the wall with oil paint.*

daughter *noun* daughters
a girl or woman who is the child of a
particular person.

daughter-in-law *noun* daughters-in-law
the wife of your son.

daunting *adjective*
able to discourage or overwhelm, as in *the
daunting task of cataloguing the library.*

dawdle *verb* dawdles, dawdling, dawdled
to go or act too slowly.

dawn *noun* dawns
the time when the sun rises.

day *noun* days
1 the 24 hours between midnight and the
next midnight. 2 the light part of the day.

daybreak *noun*
the first light of day.

day-dream *verb* day-dreams, day-dreaming,
day-dreamed
to have pleasant dream-like thoughts.

daylight *noun*
1 the light of day. 2 dawn, as in *We must
start before daylight.*

daylight saving *noun*
a system which involves putting the clock
forward one or more hours to obtain extra
daylight during summer.

day-to-day *adjective*
ordinary; happening every day, as in *the
routine of day-to-day life.*

daze *noun*
in a daze, unable to think or see clearly.

dazed *adjective*
unable to think or see clearly.

dazzle *verb* dazzles, dazzling, dazzled
1 to make someone dazed with bright
light, as in *Her eyes were dazzled by the
sun.* 2 to impress or amaze, as in *Everyone
was dazzled by the student's knowledge of
computers.*

dead *adjective*
1 not alive; not lively or active, as in *This
place is really dead at the weekend.*
2 complete; sure, as in *a dead certainty.*
3 (*colloquial*) very tired or unwell.
4 numb, as in *The snow made his fingers and
toes feel dead.*
dead end, a street or passage with an
opening at only one end.

dead heat, a race in which two or more
winners finish exactly together.

deaden *verb* deadens, deadening,
deadened
to make pain, noise, etc. weaker.

deadline *noun* deadlines
a time-limit for the completion of a job,
application, etc.

deadlock *noun*
1 a situation in which people cannot agree.
2 a lock which needs a key to open or close
it.

deadly *adjective* deadlier, deadliest
able or likely to cause death or serious
damage, as in *deadly poison; a deadly weapon.*

deadpan *adjective*
(*colloquial*) appearing to be serious when in
fact you are joking or teasing someone, as
in *He was an expert in deadpan humour.*

deaf *adjective* deafer, deafest
unable or unwilling to hear, as in *born deaf;
deaf to my request.*
deafness *noun*

deafen *verb* deafens, deafening, deafened
to make deaf by loud noise, as in *The band
deafened the audience.*

deal *verb* deals, dealing, dealt
1 to hand out something, as in *Deal out the
certificates.* 2 to trade or do business, as in
*He deals in scrap metal. Our company deals
with many factories.* 3 to give out cards for
a card-game.
deal with, to be concerned with something;
to do something that needs doing, as in
*This book deals with sharks. Various jobs need
to be dealt with.*
dealer *noun*

deal *noun* deals
1 an agreement; a bargain. 2 someone's
turn to give out cards for a card-game.
a good deal or **a great deal,** a large
amount.

dean *noun* deans
1 an important clergyman in a cathedral,
etc. 2 an important official in a college or
university.
deanery *noun*

dear *adjective* dearer, dearest
1 loved very much. 2 the usual way of
beginning a letter, as in *Dear Sir; Dear
John.* 3 expensive.

death *noun* deaths
1 the end of life or the process of dying or
being killed, as in *death from pneumonia.*

a
b
c
d
e
f
g
h
i
j
k
l
m
n
o
p
q
r
s
t
u
v
w
x
y
z

debate

108

2 the ending or destruction of something, as in *the death of our plans*.
deathly *adjective*

debate *verb* **debates, debating, debated**
to discuss or argue something, especially in an organised manner.

debate *noun* **debates**
1 a discussion in a parliament or where two teams of speakers put their views on a particular topic, as in *parliamentary debate; a school debate on 'Speeding is a health hazard'*. **2** a discussion, as in *The view that drugs should be legalised is open to debate*.

debris *noun* (*say* **deb**-ree *or* **day**-bree *or* duh-**bree**)
scattered fragments; wreckage, as in *The debris of the crashed plane was spread over a wide area*.

debt *noun* **debts** (*say* det)
something that you owe someone.

debtor *noun* **debtors** (*say* **det**-uh)
someone who owes you money.

debug *verb* **debugs, debugging, debugged** (*colloquial*)
1 to remove faults from a computer program. **2** to remove listening devices from a room.

début *noun* **débuts** (*say* **day**-byoo *or* **day**-boo *or* duh-**boo**)
the first public appearance of a performer, player, etc.

decade *noun* **decades**
a period of ten years, as in *The war lasted for a decade*.

decaffeinated *adjective*
with most of the stimulant caffeine removed, as in *Many people prefer decaffeinated coffee*.

decagon *noun*
a ten-sided, two-dimensional shape.

decahedron *noun*
a ten-sided solid shape.

decant *verb* **decants, decanting, decanted**
to pour a liquid from one container into another without disturbing any solid matter that was in the first container.
decanter, a container used for serving wine, water, juice, etc.

decapitate *verb* **decapitates, decapitating, decapitated**
to remove a person's head.

decathlon *noun* **decathlons**
an athletic contest consisting of ten events.

decay *verb* **decays, decaying, decayed**
to go bad; to rot.

decay *noun*
decaying; the result of decaying, as in *tooth decay*.

deceased *adjective* (*say* duh-**seest**)
dead, as in *He was remembered in his deceased aunt's will*.

deceit *noun* (*say* duh-**seet**)
dishonesty, especially by hiding the truth from someone.
deceitful *adjective*, **deceitfully** *adverb*

deceive *verb* **deceives, deceiving, deceived** (*say* duh-**seev**)
to make someone believe something that is not true.

December *noun*
the last month of the year.

decent *adjective*
1 respectable, as in *Not many of his jokes are decent*. **2** proper; suitable, as in *I hope to earn a decent wage*.
decency *noun*, **decently** *adverb*

deception *noun*
deceiving someone.

deceptive *adjective*
able or likely to mislead, as in *Appearances are often deceptive*.

decibel *noun* **decibels**
a unit for comparing and measuring the different levels of sound.

decide *verb* **decides, deciding, decided**
1 to make up your mind; to make a choice. **2** to settle a contest or argument.
decidedly *adverb*

decided *adjective*
1 definite or unquestionable, as in *a table with a decided tilt*. **2** to do with having firm clear opinions, as in *The athlete was decided about the need for daily exercise*.

deciduous *adjective*
to do with a tree that loses its leaves in autumn, as in *Most Australian native trees are not deciduous*.

decimal *adjective*
to do with using tens or tenths.
decimalisation *noun*, **decimalise** *verb*

decimal *noun* **decimals**
a decimal fraction.

decimal fraction *noun*
any fraction shown as a decimal, as in *0.1, 0.48*.

decimal number *noun*
a number made up of a whole number and a decimal fraction, as in *3.65*.

decimal point *noun* the dot in a decimal fraction.

a
b
c
d
e
f
g
h
i
j
k
l
m
n
o
p
q
r
s
t
u
v
w
x
y
z

decipher *verb* **deciphers, deciphering, deciphered** (*say* duh-**suy**-fuh)
1 to decode something. 2 to work out the meaning of something written badly, as in *handwriting difficult to decipher.*

decision *noun* **decisions**
1 the act or process of deciding, as in *an easy decision.* 2 a point reached after thought or consideration, as in *I have made my decision.* 3 a tendency to be firm in what a person says, thinks or does, as in *The cricket captain acted with decision when he chose his team.*

decisive *adjective*
1 settling or ending something, as in *a decisive battle.* 2 determined; resolute, as in *a decisive person.*
decisively *adverb*

deck *noun* **decks**
1 a floor on a ship or bus. 2 a pack of cards. 3 an outdoor, usually wooden platform attached to a house, unit, etc.
deck-chair, a folding chair with a seat of canvas or plastic material.

declaration *noun* **declarations**
1 the act of saying something clearly or firmly; an official statement, as in *a declaration of peace.* 2 the act of declaring an innings in cricket closed.

declare *verb* **declares, declaring, declared**
1 to say something clearly or firmly.
2 to end a cricket innings before all the batters are out.
declare war, to say that you have started a war against someone.

decline *verb* **declines, declining, declined**
1 to become weaker or smaller.
2 to refuse something.

decode *verb* **decodes, decoding, decoded**
to find the meaning of something written in code.

decompose *verb* **decomposes, decomposing, decomposed**
to decay; to rot, as in *Bodies decompose after death.*
decomposition *noun*

decompression *noun*
the gradual reduction of air pressure of a person who has experienced high pressure, especially under deep water, as in *The diver had to undergo decompression to stop him from getting the bends.*

decontaminate *verb* **decontaminates, decontaminating, decontaminated**
to remove contamination, especially infection or radioactivity, as in *The hospital ward was decontaminated after the cholera outbreak.*

decorate *verb* **decorates, decorating, decorated**
1 to make something look more beautiful or colourful. 2 to give someone a medal.
decorative *adjective*

decoration *noun* **decorations**
1 things like paint, ornaments, carpets, and pictures that make a place look more beautiful. 2 making something look more beautiful or colourful. 3 a medal, as in *decoration for bravery.*

decorum *noun*
polite or proper behaviour.

decoy *noun* **decoys** (*say* **dee**-koi)
something used to tempt a person or animal into a trap.

decrease *verb* **decreases, decreasing, decreased** (*say* duh-**krees**)
to make something or a group of people smaller or fewer; to become smaller or fewer.

decrease *noun* **decreases** (*say* **dee**-krees)
the amount by which something decreases.

decree *noun* **decrees**
an official order or decision, as in *a decree that the school should close.*

decree *verb* **decrees, decreeing, decreed**
to make a decree.

decrepit *adjective*
old and weak, as in *The decrepit man suffered a lot of pain. The decrepit building was bulldozed.*

dedicate *verb* **dedicates, dedicating, dedicated**
1 to devote, as in *She dedicated her life to nursing.* 2 to mention someone's name at the beginning of a book, etc., as a sign of friendship or thanks.
dedication *noun*

deduce *verb* **deduces, deducing, deduced**
to work out something by reasoning.

Usage Do not confuse **deduce** with **deduct**, which is the next word in this dictionary.

deduct *verb* **deducts, deducting, deducted**
to subtract part of something.
deductible *adjective*

deduction *noun* **deductions**
1 something worked out by reasoning.
2 something subtracted, as in *a deduction of 10 per cent.*

a
b
c
d
e
f
g
h
i
j
k
l
m
n
o
p
q
r
s
t
u
v
w
x
y
z

deed

deed *noun* **deeds**
1 something special that someone has done, as in *a good deed for a friend*. 2 a legal document, as in *deeds of ownership for a new house*.

deep *adjective* **deeper, deepest**
1 going down a long way from the top, as in *deep sea*. 2 wide, as in *a deep bookshelf*. 3 measured from top to bottom or from front to back, as in *a hole two metres deep*. 4 intense; strong, as in *deep feelings*.
deepen *verb*, **deeply** *adverb*

deer *noun* **deer**
a fast-running, graceful animal with four legs, the male usually having antlers.

deface *verb* **defaces, defacing, defaced**
to spoil the appearance of something.

de facto *adjective* (*say* dee-**fak**-toh *or* day-**fak**-toh)
existing in a way that is not legal or official, as in *a de facto ruler; de facto wife*.

defame *verb* **defames, defaming, defamed**
to attack the good reputation of a person, as in *The politician said he was defamed by the journalist*.
defamation *noun*, **defamatory** *adjective*

default *noun* **defaults**
1 a failure to appear, pay a debt, or act as one should, as in *The team was fined because of a default*. 2 (*in Computing*) what a computer does if you do not give it instructions to do something different, as in *The default is to save the data on the disk on which the last save was made*.

defeat *verb* **defeats, defeating, defeated**
to beat someone in a game or battle.

defeat *noun* **defeats**
a lost game or battle.

defecate *verb* **defecates, defecating, defecated**
to get rid of solid waste from the body through the bowel.
defecation *noun*

defect *noun* **defects** (*say* dee-fekt)
a fault or flaw.

defect *verb* **defects, defecting, defected** (*say* duh-**fekt**)
to desert a country or cause; to join the enemy.
defection *noun*, **defector** *noun*

defective *adjective*
having flaws or faults, as in *The defective goods were returned to the shop*.

Usage Do not confuse **defective** with **deficient**, which means lacking something.

defence *noun* **defences**
1 the act of defending or resisting attack, as in *Her defence in a difficult situation was to remain silent*. 2 something that defends, as in *The high wall was a defence against the enemy*.
defenceless *adjective*

defend *verb* **defends, defending, defended**
1 to protect, especially from attack. 2 to try to prove, especially in a lawcourt that a person is innocent, as in *The lawyer defended the accused man in court*.
defender *noun*, **defensible** *adjective*

defendant *noun* **defendants**
a person accused of something in a lawcourt.

defensive *adjective*
1 able to defend, as in *defensive weapons*. 2 to do with a person who seems to expect criticism, and is eager to avoid it.

defer *verb* **defers, deferring, deferred**
to postpone, as in *She deferred her departure*.
deferment *noun*

defiance *noun*
the act of resisting or disobeying a rule, law, request, etc., as in *The child's defiance of the teacher amazed the rest of the class*.
defiant *adjective*, **defiantly** *adverb*

deficiency *noun* **deficiencies**
a shortage; a lack, as in *a vitamin deficiency*.
deficient *adjective*

deficit *noun* **deficits** (*say* def-uh-suht)
the amount by which something is less than what is required or expected, especially the amount by which the total money received is less than the total money spent, as in *The tuckshop accounts showed a deficit because of increased costs*.

defile *verb* **defiles, defiling, defiled**
to make a thing dirty or impure.

define *verb* **defines, defining, defined**
1 to explain what a word means. 2 to show clearly what something is, as in *First define the problem*.

definite *adjective*
fixed or certain; exact, as in *Can you be definite about that? Choose a definite date for your holiday*.

definitely *adverb* and *interjection*
certainly.

definition *noun* **definitions**
something defined, especially what a word means.

deflate *verb* **deflates, deflating, deflated**
1 to let air out of a tyre, balloon, etc. 2 to

delicate

make someone less proud or confident, as in *The runner felt deflated when she lost the race.* **3** to lower or reduce the cost of goods or value of money, as in *The cost of sugar was deflated when growers produced too much.*
deflation *noun*, **deflationary** *adjective*

deflect *verb* **deflects, deflecting, deflected**
to make something turn aside.
deflection *noun*

defoliate *verb* **defoliates, defoliating, defoliated**
to destroy the leaves of trees or plants, as in *Severe frost can defoliate some plants.*

deforestation *noun*
the loss of trees from an area, as in *Deforestation can occur as towns and cities grow bigger.*

deformed *adjective*
not properly or naturally shaped, as in *a deformed animal with one eye; a deformed tree.*
deformation *noun*, **deformity** *noun*

defrost *verb* **defrosts, defrosting, defrosted**
1 to remove ice or frost from a refrigerator. **2** to unfreeze frozen food.

deft *adjective*
skilful and quick, as in *deft fingers playing the piano.*
deftly *adverb*

defuse *verb* **defuses, defusing, defused**
1 to remove the fuse from a bomb, explosive, etc. **2** to make a situation less tense, dangerous, etc., as in *She defused the argument with an apology.*

defy *verb* **defies, defying, defied**
1 to say or show that you will not obey. **2** to challenge, as in *I defy you to do that.* **3** to prevent something being done, as in *The door defied all attempts to open it.*

degenerate *verb* **degenerates, degenerating, degenerated**
to become worse or lower in standard, as in *The game degenerated into a succession of brawls.*
degeneration *noun*

degrade *verb* **degrades, degrading, degraded**
to humiliate someone.
degradation *noun*

degree *noun* **degrees**
1 a unit for measuring temperature, as in *Water boils at 100 degrees centigrade, or 100°C.* **2** a unit for measuring angles, as in *There are 90 degrees (90°) in a right angle.* **3** extent, as in *to some degree.* **4** an award to someone at a university, institute

of technology, etc. who has successfully finished a course, as in *She has a degree in English.*

dehydrated *adjective*
with all its moisture removed, as in *dehydrated peas.*
dehydration *noun*

deity *noun* **deities** (*say* **dee**-uh-tee *or* **day**-uh-tee)
a god.

dejected *adjective*
sad or gloomy, as in *a dejected expression after the loss.*
dejection *noun*

delay *verb* **delays, delaying, delayed**
1 to make someone or something late, as in *Cold weather can delay the growth of plants.* **2** to postpone something.

delay *noun* **delays**
a postponement or stoppage, as in *a delay of the meeting till next week; a delay in the game due to injury.*

delegate *noun* **delegates** (*say* **del**-uh-guht)
a representative, as in *The vice-captain was a delegate for the school captain.*

delegate *verb* **delegates, delegating, delegated** (*say* **del**-uh-gayt)
to choose or send another person to act on your behalf, as in *The principal delegated her duties to her deputy when she was away.*
delegation *noun*

delete *verb* **deletes, deleting, deleted**
to cross something out; to erase something.
deletion *noun*

deliberate *adjective* (*say* duh-**lib**-uh-ruht)
1 done on purpose, as in *It was a deliberate insult.* **2** slow and careful, as in *a slow, deliberate way of talking.*
deliberately *adverb*

deliberate *verb* **deliberates, deliberating, deliberated** (*say* duh-**lib**-uh-rayt)
to discuss or think carefully, as in *The students deliberated over electing their class representative.*
deliberation *noun*

delicacy *noun* **delicacies**
1 being delicate; frail, as in *Her delicacy meant she needed constant rest.* **2** a delicious food.

delicate *adjective*
1 fine; soft; fragile, as in *as delicate as a spider's web.* **2** becoming ill easily, as in *a delicate child.* **3** using or needing great care, as in *delicate peace negotiations.*
delicately *adverb*

a
b
c
d
e
f
g
h
i
j
k
l
m
n
o
p
q
r
s
t
u
v
w
x
y
z

delicatessen
112

delicatessen *noun* **delicatessens**
a shop or part of a supermarket that sells cooked meats, cheeses, etc.

delicious *adjective*
tasting or smelling very pleasant.
deliciously *adverb*

delight *verb* **delights, delighting, delighted**
to please someone greatly.

delight *noun* **delights**
great pleasure.
Turkish delight, a square of jelly coated in icing sugar or sometimes chocolate.
delightful *adjective*, **delightfully** *adverb*

delinquent *noun* **delinquents**
someone, especially a young person, who breaks the law.
delinquency *noun*

delirious *adjective*
1 affected by a high fever, as in *delirious with malaria*. **2** extremely excited or enthusiastic, as in *delirious over her win*.
deliriously *adverb*

delirium *noun* **deliriums**
the confused state of mind of people who are drunk or who have a high fever.

deliver *verb* **delivers, delivering, delivered**
1 to bring things like letters, milk, or newspapers to someone's house. **2** to give a speech, lecture, etc. **3** to help with the birth of a baby. **4** to rescue, as in *He was delivered from death by a blood transfusion*.
deliverance *noun*, **delivery** *noun*

delta *noun* **deltas**
the area (usually triangular) between the branches of a river at its mouth.
delta wing, a triangular swept-back wing on an aircraft.

delude *verb* **deludes, deluding, deluded**
to make someone believe something that is not true, as in *I had been deluded into thinking that everything was going well*.

deluge *noun* **deluges**
1 a large flood. **2** a heavy fall of rain. **3** something coming in great numbers, as in *a deluge of questions*.

deluge *verb* **deluges, deluging, deluged**
to fall in a deluge on someone, as in *He was deluged with questions*.

delusion *noun* **delusions**
a false belief or opinion; a false belief that is a sign of mental illness, as in *The thin girl dieted constantly under the delusion that she was fat*.

Usage Do not confuse **delusion** with **illusion**, which means an imaginary thing.

de luxe *adjective*
being of very high quality, as in *de luxe, gold-plated bath-taps*.

demand *verb* **demands, demanding, demanded**
to ask for something firmly or forcefully.

demand *noun* **demands**
1 something demanded, as in *a demand for complete obedience*. **2** a desire to have something, as in *There's a great demand for old furniture*.
in demand, wanted; popular.

demanding *adjective*
1 asking for many things, as in *Toddlers can be very demanding*. **2** needing skill or effort, as in *She has a demanding job*.

demean *verb* **demeans, demeaning, demeaned**
to make others have less respect, as in *He demeaned himself by lying to his friend*.

demeanour or **demeanor** *noun* **demeanours**
the way a person outwardly behaves, as in *The friendly boy was known for his happy demeanour*.

demist *verb* **demists, demisting, demisted**
to remove condensation from a windscreen, window, etc.

demo *noun* **demos**
(*colloquial*) a demonstration.

democracy *noun* **democracies**
1 government of a country by leaders who have been elected by the people. **2** a country governed in this way, as in *Every adult has the right to vote in a democracy*. **3** the belief that everyone is equal in a society.

democrat *noun* **democrats**
a person who believes in or supports democracy.

democratic *adjective*
to do with or connected with democracy, as in *democratic elections*.
democratically *adverb*

demolish *verb* **demolishes, demolishing, demolished**
to knock something down and break it up.
demolition *noun*

demon *noun* **demons**
1 a devil. **2** a forceful, skilful person, as in *a demon player on the football field*.

demonstrate *verb* **demonstrates, demonstrating, demonstrated**
1 to show something, as in *She has clearly*

demonstrated her ability. **2** to take part in a demonstration, as in *a rally to demonstrate against school closures.*
demonstrator *noun*

demonstration *noun* **demonstrations**
1 showing how to do or work something.
2 a march, meeting, rally, etc. to show everyone what you think about something, as in *a demonstration against the new freeway.*

demoralise or **demoralize** *verb*
demoralises, demoralising, demoralised
to make someone lose confidence or courage.
demoralisation *noun*

demote *verb* **demotes, demoting, demoted**
to reduce someone to a lower rank, as in *The sergeant was demoted to the rank of a private.*

den *noun* **dens**
1 a lair, as in *a lion's den.* **2** a place where something illegal happens, as in *a gambling den.* **3** a small private room, as in *He is reading in his den.*

denial *noun* **denials**
denying or refusing something, as in *a denial of the charges; self-denial.*

denim *noun* **denims**
strong cotton cloth, as in *Jeans are made out of denim.*

denomination *noun* **denominations**
1 a particular church or religious group, especially in the Christian Church, as in *Catholic denomination; Anglican denomination.* **2** the range of units within a set of numbers, weights, money, etc., as in *The five cent coin is the smallest denomination in our currency.*

denominator *noun* **denominators**
the number below the line in a fraction, as in *In ¹/₄ the 4 is the denominator.*

denote *verb* **denotes, denoting, denoted**
to indicate; to mean, as in *A tick denotes that the goods have been checked.*

denounce *verb* **denounces, denouncing, denounced**
to speak against something; to accuse someone.
denunciation *noun*

dense *adjective* **denser, densest**
1 thick, as in *The fog was getting denser.*
2 packed close together, as in *dense forest.* **3** (*colloquial*) stupid.
densely *adverb*

density *noun* **densities**
1 thickness, as in *The density of the fog made it hard to drive.* **2** (*in Science*) the mass of something per unit of volume, as in *Water has greater density than air.*

dent *noun* **dents**
an impression or hollow made in a surface by hitting it.

dental *adjective*
to do with teeth or dentists, as in *dental appointment.*

dentist *noun* **dentists**
a person who cares for other people's teeth.
dentistry *noun*

denture *noun* **dentures**
a set of false teeth.

deny *verb* **denies, denying, denied**
to say that something is not true; to refuse, as in *He denied hitting his friend. The prisoners were denied light and exercise.*

deodorant *noun* **deodorants**
something that is put on the body or sprayed into the air to hide or prevent smells.
deodorise *verb*

depart *verb* **departs, departing, departed**
to go away; to leave.
departure *noun*

department *noun* **departments**
part of a big organisation, as in *The Department of Education is a part of the Public Service.*
department store, a large shop that sells many kinds of goods.

depend *verb* **depends, depending, depended**
depend on or **upon someone,** to rely on someone, as in *He depended on them for help.*
depend on or **upon something,** to be decided by something else, as in *Whether we can have a barbecue depends on the weather.*

dependable *adjective*
able to depend upon; reliable, as in *a dependable helper.*

dependant *noun* **dependants**
a person who depends on another, as in *We have two dependants, a son and a daughter.*

dependent *adjective*
depending or relying, as in *He was dependent on her wages.*
dependence *noun*

depict *verb* **depicts, depicting, depicted**
1 to paint or draw. **2** to describe.

deplorable *adjective*
extremely bad; shocking, as in *a deplorable lack of manners.*
deplorably *adverb*

a
b
c
d
e
f
g
h
i
j
k
l
m
n
o
p
q
r
s
t
u
v
w
x
y
z

deplore

deplore *verb* deplores, deploring, deplored
to be very upset or annoyed by something.
deplorable *adjective*

deport *verb* deports, deporting, deported
to send someone out of a country, as in *The overseas visitor was deported for drug smuggling.*
deportation *noun*

deportment *noun*
the way you hold your body, as in *Keeping your back and shoulders straight will improve your deportment.*

deposit *noun* deposits
1 an amount of money paid into a bank.
2 a first payment for something, as in *Pay a deposit on the new house.* 3 a layer of solid matter in or on the earth, as in *gold deposits.*

depot *noun* depots (*say* **dep**-oh)
1 a place where things are stored; a place where buses, trains, etc. are kept when they are not in use. 2 the headquarters of an army regiment.

depress *verb* depresses, depressing, depressed
to make someone very sad.

depressed *adjective*
1 very sad. 2 having economic difficulties, as in *a depressed area with high unemployment.*

depression *noun* depressions
1 a great sadness. 2 an area of low air pressure which may bring rain. 3 a long period when there is less trade and business than usual and many people have no work. 4 a shallow hollow in the ground.

deprive *verb* deprives, depriving, deprived
to take something away from someone, as in *Prisoners are deprived of their freedom.*
deprivation *noun*

depth *noun* depths
how deep something is, as in *the depth of the river.*
in depth, thoroughly, as in *They studied the goldrushes in depth.*

deputation *noun* deputations
a group of people selected to represent other people, as in *A deputation of students represented their school at the science fair.*

deputy *noun* deputies
a substitute or chief assistant for someone.
deputise *verb*

derail *verb* derails, derailing, derailed
to cause a train to leave the track.

derelict *adjective* (*say* de-ruh-likt)
1 abandoned, as in *a derelict ship.*
2 ruined, as in *a derelict house with crumbling walls.*

derision *noun*
scorn, as in *They treated the cheat with derision.*
deride *verb*, **derisive** *adjective*, **derisory** *adjective*

derivation *noun* derivations
where a word comes from, as in *The derivation of 'boomerang' comes from the word 'bumaring' in the Dharuk Aboriginal language.*

derive *verb* derives, deriving, derived
to obtain a thing from another person or thing, as in *I derive great pleasure from music.*
derivation *noun*, **derivative** *adjective* and *noun*

derrick *noun* derricks
1 a crane for hoisting heavy things.
2 a tower that holds the drill when a well is being drilled, especially for oil.

descant *noun* descants
a tune sung or played above another tune.
descant recorder, a high-pitched recorder.

descend *verb* descends, descending, descended
to go down.
be descended from someone, to be in the same family as someone but living at a later time than him or her.
descent *noun*

descendant *noun* descendants
a person who is in the same family as you, was born after you, and is your child, or a child of your child, etc.

descent *noun* (*say* duh-**sent**)
1 the act or way of going down, as in *Their descent from the mountain was slow.* 2 a downward slope, as in *a steep descent.*
3 the origins of your family, as in *This family is of convict descent.*

describe *verb* describes, describing, described
to say what someone or something is like.
description *noun*, **descriptive** *adjective*

desert *noun* deserts (*say* **dez**-uht)
a large area of very dry, often sandy, land with little or no vegetation.

Usage Do not confuse **desert** with **dessert**, which means food eaten at the end of a meal.

detain

desert *verb* **deserts, deserting, deserted**
(*say* duh-**zert**)
to abandon someone; to leave something
without intending to return.
desertion *noun*

deserter *noun* **deserters**
someone who leaves the armed forces
without permission.

deserts *plural noun* (*say* duh-**zerts**)
what someone deserves, as in *He got his just
deserts*.

deserve *verb* **deserves, deserving, deserved**
to be worthy of a reward, punishment, etc.,
as in *The winner deserves a prize. The rude
child deserved a reprimand*.
deservedly *adverb*

design *noun* **designs**
1 a plan or pattern for something, as in *the
design for a new school*. 2 the way that
something is made or planned; an
arrangement or pattern, as in *an imaginative
design*.

design *verb* **designs, designing, designed**
to draw a design; to plan a building,
machine, etc.
designer *noun*

designate *verb* **designates, designating,
designated**
to mark or describe as something
particular, as in *The river was designated as
the State boundary*.

desirable *adjective*
1 worth having, as in *a desirable house*.
2 worth doing; advisable, as in *It is
desirable for you to come with us*.
desirability *noun*

desire *verb* **desires, desiring, desired**
to want something very much.
desirous *adjective*

desk *noun* **desks**
1 a kind of table, often with drawers, used
for writing or reading at. 2 the counter in
a hotel, bank, etc., as in *information desk*.

desktop *adjective*
small enough to be put on top of someone's
desk, as in *a desktop computer*.
desktop publishing, using a desktop
computer and printer to arrange words and
pictures so that they are ready to be made
into a book.

desolate *adjective*
1 having nobody living there, as in *a
desolate island*. 2 sad; lonely, as in *He was
desolate after his wife's death*.
desolation *noun*

despair *noun*
a feeling of hopelessness.

desperate *adjective*
1 violent; dangerous, as in *a desperate
criminal*. 2 hopeless; extremely bad, as in
a desperate situation.
desperately *adverb*, **desperation** *noun*

despise *verb* **despises, despising, despised**
to think someone is inferior or worthless.
despicable *adjective*

despite *preposition*
in spite of.

dessert *noun* **desserts** (*say* di-**zert**)
sweet food eaten at the end of a meal.

Usage Do not confuse **dessert** with **desert**,
which means an area of very dry land.

dessertspoon *noun* **dessertspoons**
a medium-sized spoon used for eating
dessert and as a measurement in cooking.

destination *noun* **destinations**
the place you are travelling to.

destined *adjective*
intended; already determined or fated, as
in *They felt they had been destined to meet*.
be destined to, to definitely happen, as in
She was destined to become school captain.

destiny *noun* **destinies**
fate or something meant to happen, as in
His destiny was to become famous.

destitute *adjective*
without food, clothing, shelter, money, etc.

destroy *verb* **destroys, destroying, destroyed**
to ruin or put an end to something.
destruction *noun*, **destructive** *adjective*

destroyer *noun* **destroyers**
a fast warship.

detach *verb* **detaches, detaching, detached**
to unfasten; to separate, as in *Detach the
trailer from the car*.
detachable *adjective*, **detachment** *noun*

detached *adjective*
not prejudiced; not involved, as in *a
detached observer*.

detail *noun* **details**
1 a tiny part of something, as in *Every detail
in the dress was perfect*. 2 a small piece of
information, as in *The student examined the
details of the timetable*.
in detail, describing or covering each part
fully.

detain *verb* **detains, detaining, detained**
1 to keep someone at a place, as in *detained
for questioning*. 2 to keep someone
waiting, as in *detained at the doctor's surgery*.

a
b
c
d
e
f
g
h
i
j
k
l
m
n
o
p
q
r
s
t
u
v
w
x
y
z

detect

detect *verb* **detects, detecting, detected**
to discover.
detectable *adjective*, **detection** *noun*,
detector *noun*

detective *noun* **detectives**
a person who investigates crimes.

detention *noun* **detentions**
being made to stay in a place, especially
being made to stay late at school as a
punishment.

deter *verb* **deters, deterring, deterred**
to put someone off doing something.

detergent *noun* **detergents**
a powder or liquid used with water to
clean dishes, clothes, carpet, windows, etc.

deteriorate *verb* **deteriorates, deteriorating,
deteriorated**
to become worse in condition or quality, as
in *Paintwork deteriorates when it is exposed to
the weather.*
deterioration *noun*

determined *adjective*
with your mind firmly made up; resolute,
as in *He is determined to leave now.*
determination *noun*

deterrent *noun* **deterrents**
something intended to stop people from
acting in a certain way, as in *Burglar alarms
can act as a deterrent to thieves.*
deterrence *noun*

detest *verb* **detests, detesting, detested**
to hate, as in *She detested noise.*
detestable *adjective*, **detestation** *noun*

detonate *verb* **detonates, detonating,
detonated**
to set off an explosion.
detonation *noun*, **detonator** *noun*

detour *noun* **detours**
a route used instead of the normal route.

deuce *noun*
a tennis score when both sides have 40
points.

devastate *verb* **devastates, devastating,
devastated**
to ruin or destroy something; to make a
place impossible to live in, as in *The wheat
crop was devastated by a mice plague. Darwin
was devastated by a cyclone in 1974.*
devastation *noun*

devastated *adjective*
very shocked and upset, as in *I was
absolutely devastated to hear that he had lost
his job.*

devastating *adjective*
crushing; overwhelming, as in *the
devastating effects of war; a devastating defeat.*

develop *verb* **develops, developing,
developed**
1 to make or become bigger or better, as in
*to develop the business; to develop your mind
with reading.* 2 to put up new buildings
on a piece of land, as in *Several blocks have
been developed in the last year.* 3 to treat
photographic film with chemicals so that
pictures can be seen.
developing country, a poor country that is
building up its industry and trying to
improve its people's living conditions.

development *noun* **developments**
1 something that has happened, as in *Have
there been any further developments in the
situation since I last saw you?* 2 putting up
new buildings; a group of these buildings,
as in *Extensive development has taken place in
Canberra. New developments surround the old
town.*

device *noun* **devices**
something made for a particular purpose.
leave someone to his or her own devices, to
leave someone to do as he or she likes,
without help or advice.

Usage Do not confuse **device**, which is a
noun, with **devise**, which is a verb meaning
to invent or plan something.

devil *noun* **devils**
an evil person.
devil-devil, an evil spirit in Aboriginal
belief.
the Devil, Satan.
devilish *adjective*, **devilry** *noun*

devious *adjective*
1 using unfair and dishonest methods; not
showing what he or she intends to do, as in
*They thought up a devious plan to remove the
president from power. He's devious, and you
can't trust him.* 2 not direct, as in *We took a
devious route to avoid the traffic-jam.*

devise *verb* **devises, devising, devised**
to invent something; to plan something, as
in *We devised a way of keeping out burglars.*

devoid *adjective*
lacking or free from something, as in *devoid
of commonsense; a garden devoid of weeds.*

devote *verb* **devotes, devoting, devoted**
to give something or yourself completely,
as in *They devote all their free time to sport.
Mother Theresa devoted herself to helping the
poor.*
devotee *noun*, **devotion** *noun*

devoted *adjective*
1 loving and loyal, as in *a devoted parent*.
2 very enthusiastic, as in *He's a devoted supporter of the local football team*.
devotedly *adverb*

devour *verb* **devours, devouring, devoured**
to eat or swallow something greedily.

dew *noun*
tiny drops of water that form during the night on surfaces out of doors.
dewy *adjective*

dexterity *noun*
skill or cleverness in using the hands or mind, as in *The carpenter showed dexterity in making the table. The student's mental dexterity helped him finish the crossword*.

diabetes *noun* (*say* duy-uh-**bee**-teez)
a disease in which there is too much sugar in a person's blood.
diabetic *adjective* and *noun*

diabolical *adjective*
1 like a devil, as in *diabolical cruelty*.
2 extremely bad, clever or annoying, as in *diabolical behaviour; diabolical weather*.

diagnose *verb* **diagnoses, diagnosing, diagnosed**
to find out what disease someone has, as in *The doctor diagnosed appendicitis*.
diagnosis *noun*, **diagnostic** *adjective*

diagonal *noun* **diagonals**
a straight line joining opposite corners of a rectangle.
diagonally *adverb*

diagram *noun* **diagrams**
a picture or plan that explains something.

diagrammatic *adjective*
in the form of a diagram, as in *diagrammatic information*.

dial *noun* **dials**
1 the face of a clock or watch marked to show the hours, minutes, etc. 2 a similar flat plate marked with a scale for measuring weight, volume, speed etc., as in *radio dial; speedo dial*. 3 (*colloquial*) a person's face, as in *Wipe that smile off your dial*.

dial *verb* **dials, dialling, dialled**
to telephone a number by turning a telephone dial or by pressing keys.

dialect *noun* **dialects**
the way people speak in a particular region or social group.

dialogue *noun* **dialogues**
1 a conversation between two or more people, groups, etc. 2 written conversation in a book, play, etc.

diameter *noun* **diameters**
1 the width of a circle. 2 a line drawn from one side of a circle to the other, passing through the centre.

diamond *noun* **diamonds**
1 a very hard jewel that looks like clear glass. 2 a shape which has four equal sides but which is not a square. 3 a playing-card with a red diamond shape on it.

diaphragm *noun* **diaphragms**
(*say* **duy**-uh-fram)
1 the muscular part inside the body between the chest and the abdomen, used in breathing. 2 a thin sheet or membrane that keeps things apart.

diarrhoea *noun* (*say* duy-uh-**ree**-uh)
too frequent emptying of waste matter that is too watery, from the bowels.

diary *noun* **diaries**
a book where you can write down what happens each day.

dice *plural noun*
small cubes marked with dots (1 to 6) on their sides, used in games.

Usage The correct singular form of **dice** is **die**, as in *The die is cast*.

dictate *verb* **dictates, dictating, dictated**
1 to speak or read something aloud for someone else to write down. 2 to tell someone what to do; to give orders.
dictation *noun*

dictator *noun* **dictators**
a ruler who has unlimited power.
dictatorial *adjective*, **dictatorship** *noun*

dictionary *noun* **dictionaries**
a book where you can find out what a word means and how to spell it, as in *Dictionaries usually give words in alphabetical order*.

did past tense of **do**.

didn't short for *did not*.

didgeridoo *noun* **didgeridoos**
(*say* dij-uh-ree-**doo**)
a long, wooden, tube-like Aboriginal wind instrument that makes a low vibrating sound.

die *verb* **dies, dying, died**
to stop living; to come to an end, as in *He died from hunger. The fire died*.

die *noun* **dice**
one of a set of dice.

diesel *noun* **diesels**
1 an engine that works by burning oil not petrol. 2 fuel for this kind of engine.

diet

diet *noun* **diets**
1 special meals that someone eats to be healthy or to lose weight.   2 the food you normally eat, as in *A healthy diet includes fruit and vegetables.*

differ *verb* **differs, differing, differed**
1 to be different, as in *The shrubs and trees differ in size.*   2 to disagree, as in *The two writers differ on this point.*

difference *noun* **differences**
how different something is from something else.

different *adjective*
unlike; not the same, as in *Her hat is different from mine.*
differently *adverb*

difficult *adjective*
not easy.

difficulty *noun* **difficulties**
1 not being easy; trouble, as in *I had difficulty in climbing up the slippery slope.*
2 something that causes a problem, as in *We faced many difficulties when travelling across the Nullarbor.*

diffuse *adjective* (*say* duh-**fyoos**)
spread out; not concentrated, as in *diffuse light.*

diffuse *verb* **diffuses, diffusing, diffused**
1 to spread something widely or thinly, as in *The light was diffused by the dense wattle trees.*   2 to mix slowly, as in *diffusing gases.*
diffusion *noun*

dig *verb* **digs, digging, dug**
1 to move soil; to make a hole in the ground.
2 to poke, as in *He dug me in the ribs.*
digger *noun*

dig *noun* **digs**
1 a place where archaeologists are looking for ancient remains.   2 a sharp thrust or poke, as in *She gave me a dig in the ribs with her elbow.*   3 (*colloquial*) an unpleasant remark, as in *What he said was clearly a dig at my failure.*

digest *verb* **digests, digesting, digested**
1 to soften and change food in the stomach and intestine so that the body can absorb its goodness.   2 to take in and understand information.
digestible *adjective*, **digestion** *noun*

digestive *adjective*
to do with the digestion of food, as in *the digestive juices of the body.*
digestive system, the parts of the body used in digesting food.

digger *noun* **digger**
1 a miner, especially a gold-digger of the Australian goldfields.   2 an Australian soldier, especially one who fought in the First World War.

digit *noun* **digits** (*say* **dij**-uht)
any of the numbers from 0 to 9.

digital *adjective*
to do with or using digits, as in *A digital clock shows the time with a row of figures, not on a dial as an analogue clock does.*

dignified *adjective*
having or showing dignity, as in *a dignified appearance; a dignified speech at the funeral.*

dignity *noun* **dignities**
1 a serious or noble manner.   2 a high rank.

dilemma *noun* **dilemmas**
a difficult choice.

diligent *adjective*
hard-working; showing care and effort, as in *a diligent student; a diligent piece of work.*

dill *noun*
a herb with strong-smelling leaves and seeds used to flavour food.

dill *noun* **dills**
(*colloquial*) a foolish or unintelligent person.

dilute *verb* **dilutes, diluting, diluted**
to make a liquid weaker by mixing it with water.
dilution *noun*

dim *adjective* **dimmer, dimmest**
not bright.
dimly *adverb*

dimension *noun* **dimensions**
measurement; size.
dimensional *adjective*

diminish *verb* **diminishes, diminishing, diminished**
to make something smaller; to become smaller.

dimple *noun* **dimples**
a small hollow on the skin.

din *noun*
a loud noise.

dine *verb* **dines, dining, dined**
to have dinner.
diner *noun*

dinghy *noun* **dinghies** (*say* **ding**-gee)
a small boat, sometimes an inflatable one made of rubber.

disadvantage

dingo *noun* **dingoes**
the yellowish, wild native dog of mainland Australia.

Origin This word comes from the Aboriginal language Dharuk: **dingu**. See the Aboriginal Languages map at the back of this dictionary.

dingy *adjective* **dingier, dingiest** (*say* **din**-jee)
shabby; dirty-looking, as in *the dingy room in the old house.*

dinner *noun* **dinners**
the main meal of the day.

dinosaur *noun* **dinosaurs**
a large prehistoric animal.

dip *verb* **dips, dipping, dipped**
1 to put or lower briefly into liquid, etc., as in *Dip the brush in the paint. The farmer is dipping his sheep to protect them from parasites.*   2 to go below a surface or level, as in *The sun dipped below the horizon.*   3 to lower or be lowered, especially the beam of headlights.
dip into a book, to read small parts of a book from time to time.

dip *noun* **dips**
1 the act of dipping.   2 a slope downward as in *The road has a dip in it.*   3 a quick swim.   4 a liquid for dipping, as in *sheep dip.*   5 a creamy mixture into which you dip biscuits, vegetables, etc. before eating them.

diphtheria *noun* (*say* dif-**theer**-ree-uh)
a serious disease of the throat.

diploma *noun* **diplomas**
a certificate awarded for skill in a particular subject, as in *cooking diploma.*

diplomacy *noun*
keeping friendly with other nations or other people.
diplomat *noun*, **diplomatic** *adjective*, **diplomatically** *adverb*

dire *adjective* **direr, direst**
1 urgent, as in *The refugees are in dire need of food and shelter.*   2 causing fear of what will happen, as in *dire warnings of disaster.*   3 (*colloquial*) very bad, as in *His latest record's really dire.*
in dire straits, in a very bad situation, as in *We were in dire straits, with no money and nowhere to live.*

direct *adjective*
1 as straight or quick as possible.
2 straightforward; frank.
direct object, the word that receives the

action of a verb, as in *The direct object is 'him' in the sentence, 'She hit him'.*
directly *adverb*, **directness** *noun*

direct *verb* **directs, directing, directed**
1 to show someone the way.   2 to control; to manage, as in *Direct the traffic flow. She directed the meeting efficiently.*
director *noun*

direction *noun* **directions**
1 the way you go to get somewhere.
2 directing something, as in *The direction of the play was done well.*
directions, information on how to use or do something.
directional *adjective*

director *noun* **directors**
1 a person who is in charge of something, especially one of a group of people managing a company.   2 a person who decides how a film or play should be made or performed.

directory *noun* **directories**
a list of people or businesses with their telephone numbers, addresses, etc.

direct speech *noun*
the actual words spoken by the subject of a sentence, as in *Darren said, 'We won the game'. The actual words spoken by Darren are 'We won the game'.*

dirt *noun*
1 earth, soil, as in *The child was playing happily in the dirt.*   2 anything that is not clean, as in *dirt on the towel.*

dirty *adjective* **dirtier, dirtiest**
1 not clean.   2 rude; obscene, as in *Someone has written dirty words on the wall.*   3 unfair; mean, as in *It was a dirty trick to steal my pencils.*
dirtily *adverb*, **dirtiness** *noun*

disability *noun* **disabilities**
something that prevents someone from using his or her body in the usual way, as in *a sight disability.*

disable *verb* **disables, disabling, disabled**
1 to make someone unable to use his or her body properly.   2 to make something unable to work, as in *The telephone system had been disabled by the earthquake.*

disabled *adjective*
having a disease or injury that makes it difficult for someone to use his or her body in the usual way.

disadvantage *noun* **disadvantages**
something that hinders you or makes things difficult.

disagree

be at a disadvantage, to be hindered by something, as in *He was at a disadvantage because he had missed a term's work while he was ill.*
disadvantaged *adjective*

disagree *verb* **disagrees, disagreeing, disagreed**
1 to have or express a different opinion from someone else. 2 to have a bad effect on someone, as in *Rich food disagrees with me.*
disagreement *noun*

disagreeable *adjective*
1 unpleasant, as in *Cleaning the oven is a disagreeable task.* 2 bad-tempered.

disappear *verb* **disappears, disappearing, disappeared**
to stop being visible; to vanish.
disappearance *noun*

disappoint *verb* **disappoints, disappointing, disappointed**
to fail to do what someone hopes for.
disappointing *adjective*, **disappointment** *noun*

disapprove *verb* **disapproves, disapproving, disapproved**
not to approve of someone or something.
disapproval *noun*, **disapproving** *adjective*, **disapprovingly** *adverb*

disarm *verb* **disarms, disarming, disarmed**
1 to reduce the size of your army, air force, etc. 2 to take away someone's weapons.
3 to make less angry; to charm or win over, as in *He disarmed his critics with a smile.*
disarmament *noun*

disaster *noun* **disasters**
1 a very bad accident or misfortune.
2 (*colloquial*) a complete failure, as in *The meal was a disaster.*
disastrous *adjective*, **disastrously** *adverb*

disbelieve *verb* **disbelieves, disbelieving, disbelieved**
to be unable or unwilling to believe; to doubt.

disc *noun* **discs**
1 any round, flat object. 2 a round, flat piece of plastic on which sound or data is recorded, as in *computer disc.*
disc brake, a brake using pads of fireproof material pressing against a flat plate.
disc jockey, someone who introduces and plays recorded pop music.

discard *verb* **discards, discarding, discarded**
to get rid of something.

discharge *verb* **discharges, discharging, discharged**
1 to release someone. 2 to send something out, as in *Vehicles must not discharge excessive fumes.* 3 to dismiss from a position or job. 4 to unload, as in *a ship discharging cargo.* 5 to fire a gun, etc.

disciple *noun* **disciples**
a follower of a political or religious leader, especially one of Jesus's first twelve followers.

discipline *noun*
orderly and obedient behaviour.

disclose *verb* **discloses, disclosing, disclosed**
to make known or reveal.
disclosure *noun*

disco *noun* **discos**
(*colloquial*) a place where people dance to recorded pop music; a discothèque.

discolour *verb* **discolours, discolouring, discoloured**
to spoil or change the colour of something.

discomfort *noun*
uneasiness or slight pain, as in *discomfort in the presence of her enemy; discomfort from the plaster cast on her arm.*

disconnect *verb* **disconnects, disconnecting, disconnected**
to break a connection; to detach something, as in *Disconnect the telephone. Disconnect the hose.*
disconnection *noun*

discontented *adjective*
not contented; dissatisfied.
discontent *noun*, **discontentedly** *adverb*

discothèque *noun* **discothèques**
(*say* **dis-kuh-tek**)
a nightclub, party, etc. for dancing to recorded pop music.

discount *noun* **discounts**
an amount deducted from the full or normal price, especially for prompt or early payment

discourage *verb* **discourages, discouraging, discouraged**
1 to take away someone's enthusiasm or confidence, as in *Don't get discouraged: try again.* 2 to try to persuade someone not to do something, as in *You should discourage him from going out in the rain.*
discouragement *noun*, **discouraging** *adjective*

discover *verb* **discovers, discovering, discovered**
1 to find something. 2 to find something out, as in *We only discovered the truth later.*
discoverer *noun*, **discovery** *noun*

discreet *adjective*
being careful in what you say and do, especially when you have a secret to keep.
discreetly *adverb*

dislocate

discrepancy *noun* discrepancies
the difference between two or more things,
as in *the discrepancy between the two students' accounts of the accident.*

discretion *noun*
1 being discreet, as in *She showed discretion when dealing with personal information.*
2 the ability or freedom to act on your own judgment, as in *I leave the planning to your discretion.*

discriminate *verb* discriminates, discriminating, discriminated
1 to notice the differences between things; to prefer one thing to another. 2 to treat people differently or unfairly because of their race, sex, or religion.
discrimination *noun*, **discriminatory** *adjective*

discus *noun* discuses (*say* dis-kuhs)
a thick, heavy disc thrown in an athletic contest.

discuss *verb* discusses, discussing, discussed (*say* dis-**kus**)
to talk with other people about a subject.

discussion *noun* discussions
1 a conversation between two people with different opinions. 2 a piece of writing that presents more than one view on a topic.
discuss *verb*, **discusses** *verb*, **discussing** *verb*, **discussed** *verb*

disease *noun* diseases
an illness; sickness, as in *The disease of hepatitis spread quickly in the refugee camp.*
diseased *adjective*

disembark *verb* disembarks, disembarking, disembarked
to put or go ashore; get off a plane, bus, etc.

disgrace *noun*
1 a loss of reputation; shame, as in *He suffered disgrace when he was dismissed for theft. It's no disgrace to be poor.* 2 a person or thing that causes shame or disapproval, as in *The slums are a disgrace.*
in disgrace, disapproved of, as in *He is in disgrace for telling lies.*
disgraceful *adjective*, **disgracefully** *adverb*

disgrace *verb* disgraces, disgracing, disgraced
to cause disgrace to someone or something.

disguise *verb* disguises, disguising, disguised
to change the appearance, voice, etc. of a person or thing so as to become unrecognisable.

disguise *noun* disguises
something used to disguise a person or thing.

disgust *noun*
a strong feeling of dislike.

disgust *verb* disgusts, disgusting, disgusted
to cause disgust, as in *His greed disgusted us.*
disgusted *adjective*

disgusting *adjective*
causing a strong feeling of dislike.
disgustingly *adverb*

dish *noun* dishes
1 a plate or bowl for food. 2 food served on a dish, as in *Curry is a delicious dish.*

dishevelled *adjective*
untidy in appearance, as in *dishevelled hair.*

dishonest *adjective*
deceitful or insincere.
dishonesty *noun*

dishwasher *noun* dishwashers
a machine for washing crockery, cutlery, etc.

disinfect *verb* disinfects, disinfecting, disinfected
to clean something to destroy germs, especially with disinfectant.
disinfectant *noun*

disintegrate *verb* disintegrates, disintegrating, disintegrated
to break up into small pieces.
disintegration *noun*

disinterested *adjective*
not prejudiced; not favouring one side more than the other, as in *We will need to find a disinterested person to judge the competition.*

Usage Do not confuse **disinterested** with **uninterested**, which means that you are bored by something or do not want to know anything about it.

disjointed *adjective*
not connected or fitting together, as in *a disjointed conversation.*

disk *noun* disks
a disc, especially one used to store computer data.

dislike *verb* dislikes, disliking, disliked
not to like someone or something.

dislike *noun* dislikes
a feeling of not liking someone or something.

dislocate *verb* dislocates, dislocating, dislocated
1 to dislodge a bone from its proper place in the body, as in *He dislocated his wrist.*
2 to disrupt, as in *The flood dislocated rail services.*
dislocation *noun*

dislodge

dislodge *verb* dislodges, dislodging, dislodged
to move something from its place.

disloyal *adjective*
not loyal; unfaithful, as in *Her unkind comments were disloyal to her friend.*

dismal *adjective*
gloomy.
dismally *adverb*

dismantle *verb* dismantles, dismantling, dismantled
to take something to pieces; to pull down.

dismay *noun*
discouragement or despair.
dismayed *adjective*

dismiss *verb* dismisses, dismissing, dismissed
1 to send someone away, and especially to stop employing them. 2 to reject an idea, etc., as in *The teacher dismissed our suggestion.* 3 to get a batter out in cricket.
dismissal *noun*

dismount *verb* dismounts, dismounting, dismounted
to get off a horse, bicycle, etc.

disobey *verb* disobeys, disobeying, disobeyed
to refuse or fail to obey.
disobedience *noun*, **disobedient** *adjective*

disorder *noun* disorders
1 confusion; disturbance. 2 an illness, as in *stomach disorder.*
disorderly *adjective*

disorganised or **disorganized** *adjective*
badly organised; untidy.

dispatch or **despatch** *noun* dispatches
a report or message.

dispatch or **despatch** *verb* dispatches, dispatching, dispatched
1 to send a person or thing off somewhere. 2 to kill.

dispensary *noun* dispensaries
an area in a chemist or hospital where medicines are prepared and given out.

dispense *verb* dispenses, dispensing, dispensed
1 to distribute or to hand out, as in *The Red Cross dispensed blankets to the needy.* 2 to prepare medicine.
dispense with, to do without something.

dispenser *noun* dispensers
a device that distributes something, as in *a soap dispenser.*

disperse *verb* disperses, dispersing, dispersed
to scatter, as in *The police dispersed the crowd.*
dispersal *noun*, **dispersion** *noun*

displace *verb* displaces, displacing, displaced
1 to force something out of its present place or position, as in *Solar power may well displace fossil fuels in the future.* 2 to move a person or a group of people, often by force, from an area where they live, work, etc., as in *Many people are displaced in war and become refugees.*

displacement *noun*
1 displacing, as in *the displacement of the old heating system with the new improved one.* 2 the amount of water displaced by a ship, etc. floating in it.

display *verb* displays, displaying, displayed
to show something; to arrange something so that it can be clearly seen.

display *noun* displays
1 an exhibit or show, as in *the flower display.* 2 the showing of information on a VDU screen.

displease *verb* displeases, displeasing, displeased
to annoy.
displeasing *adjective*, **displeasure** *noun*

disposable *adjective*
made to be thrown away after it has been used, as in *a disposable towel.*

disposal *noun*
the act of getting rid of something.
at your disposal, for you to use; ready for you.

dispose *verb* disposes, disposing, disposed
to make someone willing or ready to do something, as in *I am not disposed to help him.*
dispose of, to get rid of.

disposition *noun* dispositions
a person's character or qualities, as in *a cheerful disposition.*

disprove *verb* disproves, disproving, disproved
to prove that something is not true.

dispute *noun* disputes
a quarrel or disagreement.

disqualify *verb* disqualifies, disqualifying, disqualified
to remove someone from a race or competition because he or she has broken the rules.
disqualification *noun*

disregard *verb* disregards, disregarding, disregarded
to ignore, as in *She disregarded my feelings.*

disrespect *noun*
lack of respect.
disrespectful *adjective*, **disrespectfully** *adverb*

disrupt *verb* disrupts, disrupting, disrupted
to put into disorder, as in *Floods disrupted traffic.*
disruption *noun*, **disruptive** *adjective*

dissatisfied *adjective*
not satisfied; discontented.
dissatisfaction *noun*

dissect *verb* dissects, dissecting, dissected
to cut something up so as to examine it.
dissection *noun*

dissent *verb* dissents, dissenting, dissented
to think differently on something; to disagree, as in *She dissented from her mother's idea of dress.*

dissolve *verb* dissolves, dissolving, dissolved
to mix something with a liquid so that it becomes part of the liquid.

dissuade *verb* dissuades, dissuading, dissuaded
to persuade someone not to do something, as in *I will dissuade him from giving up his job.*

distance *noun* distances
the amount of space between two places.
in the distance, far away.

distant *adjective*
1 far away. **2** not friendly or sociable, as in *After the argument she was distant with her friend.*

distaste *noun* distastes
a strong dislike, as in *a distaste for ill-mannered behaviour.*

distil *verb* distils, distilling, distilled
to purify a liquid by boiling it and condensing the vapour.

distillery *noun* distilleries
a place where spirits such as whisky are produced.
distiller *noun*

distinct *adjective*
1 easily heard or seen; definite, as in *a distinct improvement.* **2** clearly separate or different, as in *A wallaby is distinct from a kangaroo.*
distinctly *adverb*

distinction *noun* distinctions
1 a difference. **2** excellence; honour, as in *He was a scientist of distinction.* **3** an award for excellence, as in *She received a distinction in music.*

distinctive *adjective*
distinguishing one thing from another, as in *She has a distinctive voice which is very husky.*

distinguish *verb* distinguishes, distinguishing, distinguished
1 to mark or notice the differences between things. **2** to see or hear something clearly.

distinguished *adjective*
1 famous, as in *a distinguished historian.* **2** having dignity, as in *She kept her distinguished manner despite her loss.*

distort *verb* distorts, distorting, distorted
1 to change something into an abnormal shape, as in *His face was distorted with anger.* **2** to change something so that it is untrue, as in *Newspapers sometimes distort the facts.*
distorted *adjective*, **distortion** *noun*

distract *verb* distracts, distracting, distracted
to take someone's attention away from something, as in *Don't distract me from my work.*
distracting *adjective*, **distraction** *noun*

distress *noun*
great sorrow, pain, trouble, or danger.
distressing *adjective*, **distressingly** *adverb*

distribute *verb* distributes, distributing, distributed
1 to deal or share out, as in *The teacher distributed textbooks to the class.* **2** to sell or deliver goods to customers. **3** spread or scatter around, as in *She distributed the wheat to the hens.*
distribution *noun*, **distributive** *adjective*

distributor *noun* distributors
someone who distributes goods, as in *a stationery distributor.*

district *noun* districts
1 an area marked off for a special purpose, as in *a central business district.* **2** a particular area or region, as in *a wine-growing district.*

distrust *noun*
lack of trust; suspicion.
distrustful *adjective*

disturb *verb* disturbs, disturbing, disturbed
1 to spoil someone's peace or rest; to worry someone. **2** to dislodge something, as in *The cleaner disturbed the papers on the desk.*
disturbance *noun*

disused *adjective*
no longer used, as in *a disused warehouse.*

ditch *noun* ditches
a narrow trench to hold or carry away water; a channel.

a b c d e f g h i j k l m n o p q r s t u v w x y z

dither

dither *verb* **dithers, dithering, dithered**
to hesitate, as in *If you're going to cross the road, wait till there is no traffic, then cross; don't dither.*

ditto marks *plural noun*
the same as before, as in *Twenty bottles of red wine, $260; ditto white, $170.*

Usage Ditto marks (") are sometimes used in lists, bills, etc., to show where something is repeated.

divan *noun* **divans**
a bed or couch without back or sides.

dive *verb* **dives, diving, dived**
1 to go into water head first. 2 to go under water. 3 to move downwards quickly, as in *The plane dived.*

diver *noun* **divers**
1 a swimmer who dives. 2 someone who works under water wearing a wet suit, as in *police diver.*

diverse *adjective*
varied; being of several different kinds, as in *the diverse colours of a rainbow.*
diversify *verb*, **diversity** *noun*

diversion *noun* **diversions**
1 diverting of attention, as in *The fight in the playground created a diversion.* 2 a different way for traffic to go while the usual road is temporarily closed.

divert *verb* **diverts, diverting, diverted**
1 to change the direction of something. 2 to distract attention from, as in *The mother used a toy to divert her child when he was given an injection.* 3 to entertain or amuse someone, as in *They were diverted by her many jokes.*

divide *verb* **divides, dividing, divided**
1 to separate or break into smaller parts; to share out, as in *We divided the money between us.* 2 (*in Mathematics*) to find out how many times one number is contained in another, as in *Six divided by two equals three ($6 \div 2 = 3$).*

dividend *noun* **dividends**
1 (*in Mathematics*) an amount to be divided. 2 a share of the profits of a business.

divider *noun* **dividers**
a partition, as in *The screen formed a divider in the large room.*

divine *adjective*
1 to do with God; coming from God. 2 more than humanly excellent, as in *divine talent.* 3 (*colloquial*) excellent; extremely beautiful, as in *divine weather.*
divinely *adverb*, **divinity** *noun*

divine *verb* **divines, divining, divined**
to discover by guessing, inspiration or magic, as in *The farmer used a Y-shaped stick to divine the presence of water in the sandy soil.*

division *noun* **divisions**
1 dividing, especially in mathematics. 2 something that divides, as in *a division of opinion.* 3 a part of something, as in *He plays football in the under 12 division.* 4 an army unit made up of two or more brigades or regiments.
divisible *adjective*

divorce *noun* **divorces**
the legal ending of a marriage.

divorce *verb* **divorces, divorcing, divorced**
to end a marriage to someone by legal means, as in *She divorced her husband.*
divorced *adjective*, **divorcee** *noun*

dizzy *adjective* **dizzier, dizziest**
giddy and feeling confused.
dizzily *adverb*, **dizziness** *noun*

DJ short for **disc jockey.**

do *verb* **does, doing, did, done**
1 to perform an action; to carry out something, as in *I have done my job.* 2 to deal with something; to solve a problem, as in *I can't do this sum.* 3 to be suitable or enough, as in *This room will do for two people.* 4 to manage or progress; to get on, as in *She is doing well at school.* 5 used in questions like *Do you want this?* and in statements with 'not' like *I do not want it.*
someone could do with something, someone needs or wants something, as in *I could do with a bath.*
do away with, to get rid of or kill.
do something up, to fasten something, as in *Do up your coat.*
do without something, to manage without having something.

dob *verb* **dobs, dobbing, dobbed**
dob in, (*colloquial*)
1 to give someone an unwanted job, etc., as in *I dobbed her in for washing the dishes.* 2 to give money towards something, as in *Everyone dobbed in a few dollars for the present.*
dob on, (*colloquial*) to tell on someone, as in *The students dobbed on those who started the fight.*
dobber *noun*

Dobermann *noun* **Dobermanns**
a large, muscular breed of dog, often kept to protect people or buildings.

docile *adjective*
willing to obey, as in *a docile child.*

dock *noun* **docks**
1 a place where ships are loaded, unloaded, or repaired; a shipyard.
2 a place where goods are loaded on or unloaded from a truck; a loading dock.

dock *verb* **docks, docking, docked**
1 to come into a dock. 2 to join two spacecraft together in orbit.

dock *noun* **docks**
a place for the prisoner in a criminal court.

dock *verb* **docks, docking, docked**
to cut an animal's tail short; to take money away from someone's pay, as in *Your wages will be docked if you are late for work.*

doctor *noun* **doctors**
1 a person trained to heal sick people.
2 a person who has received the highest degree from a university, as in *Doctor of Philosophy.*

doctrine *noun* **doctrines**
a religious or political belief.
doctrinal *adjective*

document *noun* **documents**
something important written or printed.
documentation *noun*

documentary *noun* **documentaries**
a film or a television program showing real events or situations.

dodecagon *noun*
a 12-sided, two-dimensional shape.

dodecahedron *noun*
a solid shape that has twelve identical faces.

dodge *verb* **dodges, dodging, dodged**
to move quickly to avoid someone or something.

dodgem *noun* **dodgems**
a small, electrically-driven car at a fair, carnival, etc. which you have to drive around an enclosure, dodging other cars.

dodgy *adjective* **dodgier, dodgiest**
(*colloquial*)
1 not safe; involving risk, as in *a dodgy plan.* 2 dishonest or unreliable, as in *a dodgy trader.*

doe *noun* **does**
a female deer, rabbit, or hare.

does 3rd singular present tense of **do**.

doesn't short for *does not*, as in *He doesn't understand.*

dog *noun* **dogs**
a four-legged animal that barks, often kept as a pet.

dog-eared *adjective*
(of a book) having the corners of its pages turned down through use.

dogged *adjective* (*say* **dog**-uhd)
not giving up in spite of difficulties; obstinate.
doggedly *adverb*

dogmatic *adjective*
being convinced that you are right and not considering others' opinions.

do-it-yourself *adjective*
able to be made by an amateur handyman, as in *a do-it-yourself kit for making a desk.*

doldrums *plural noun*
the parts of the ocean, near the equator, where there is little or no wind.
in the doldrums, not active; bored and sad.

dole *noun*
(*colloquial*) money paid by the government to an unemployed person, as in *They're on the dole.*

doll *noun* **dolls**
a small model, especially of a baby or a child, used as a toy.
doll's house, a tiny toy house.

dollar *noun* **dollars**
the main unit of money in Australia since 1966.

dollop *noun* **dollops**
a shapeless lump of something soft, as in *a dollop of cream.*

dolly *noun* **dollies**
a child's name for a doll.

dolphin *noun* **dolphins**
a large sea mammal like a porpoise with a slender nose, as in *Dolphins are intelligent and playful mammals.*

domain *noun* **domains**
an area ruled by one person.

dome *noun* **domes**
a roof shaped like the top half of a ball, as in *the dome of the Australian War Memorial.*

domestic *adjective*
1 to do with the home, as in *Domestic science includes subjects like cookery and needlework.* 2 tame, as in *Cats and dogs are domestic animals.*
domesticate *verb*, **domesticity** *noun*

domesticated *adjective*
1 trained to live with people, as in *Dogs are domesticated animals.* 2 enjoying household work and home life, as in *He has become quite domesticated since he got married.*

dominant *adjective*
1 most powerful or important, as in *Money is a dominant force in our society.* 2 highest; towering, as in *the dominant landmark of the Rialto Tower.*
dominance *noun*

dominate

dominate *verb* **dominates, dominating, dominated**
to command or control.
domination *noun*

dominion *noun* **dominions**
1 rule or authority, as in *In ancient times the Romans had dominion over the known world.*
2 an area of land that is controlled by a ruler, as in *Australia was once a dominion of Britain.*

domino *noun* **dominoes**
a small, flat, oblong piece of wood or plastic with dots (1 to 6) or a blank space at each end, used in a game.
dominoes, the game played with these pieces.

donate *verb* **donates, donating, donated**
to give something, especially money, to a charity or an organisation.
donation *noun*

done past participle of **do.**

donkey *noun* **donkeys**
an animal that looks like a small horse with long ears.

donor *noun* **donors**
someone who gives something, as in *a blood donor.*

don't short for *do not*, as in *Don't cycle on the pavement.*

doodle *verb* **doodles, doodling, doodled**
to scribble or draw, especially in an absent-minded way.

doodle *noun* **doodles**
a drawing or scribble done absent-mindedly.

doom *noun*
ruin; death.
doom and gloom, unpleasant or gloomy things, news, etc., as in *The newspapers always seem to be full of doom and gloom nowadays.*

doom *verb* **dooms, dooming, doomed**
to destine something or someone to suffer damage, harm, or death, as in *The plan was doomed to fail. Many animals living in the rainforest could be doomed for extinction.*
doomed *adjective*

doona *noun* **doonas**
a thick soft quilt with a removable cover, used instead of blankets; a duvet.

door *noun* **doors**
something that opens and closes the entrance to a room, building, cupboard, etc.

doorstep *noun* **doorsteps**
the step or piece of ground outside a door.

doorway *noun* **doorways**
the opening which a door fits.

dope *noun* **dopes**
(*colloquial*)
1 a narcotic drug. 2 a fool.
3 information.

dopey *adjective* **dopier, dopiest**
(*colloquial*)
1 half asleep. 2 stupid.

dormant *adjective*
not active; sleeping, as in *a dormant volcano; dormant plants in winter.*

dormitory *noun* **dormitories**
a room, especially in a boarding school, for several people to sleep in.

DOS short for *disk operating system*, a computer program that allows you to work with data on a computer disc.

dose *noun* **doses**
an amount of medicine taken at one time.

dossier *noun* **dossiers** (*say* **dos**-ee-uh *or* **dos**-ee-ay)
a set of pieces of information about a person, event, etc.

dot *noun* **dots**
a tiny spot.

dot *verb* **dots, dotting, dotted**
to mark with dots.

dotty *adjective* **dottier, dottiest**
(*colloquial*) stupid or slightly mad.
dottiness *noun*

double *adjective*
1 twice as much; twice as many, as in *a double helping of dessert.* 2 having two of something, as in *a double-barrelled shotgun.* 3 suitable for two people, as in *a double bed.*
double bass, a musical instrument with strings, like a large cello.
double-decker, a bus with two floors, one above the other.
double glazing, windows with two layers of glass to keep noise out and heat in.
doubly *adverb*

double *noun* **doubles**
1 twice the amount, cost, etc., as in *You could pay double for this carpet elsewhere.*
2 someone who looks exactly like someone else.

double *verb* **doubles, doubling, doubled**
1 to make something twice as big; to become twice as big. 2 to fold something.
on the double, quickly; hurrying.

double-cross *verb* double-crosses, double-crossing, double-crossed
to trick or betray someone whom you are supposed to be helping.

doubt *noun* doubts
not feeling sure about something; uncertainty.
doubtful *adjective*, **doubtless** *adverb*

doubt *verb* doubts, doubting, doubted
not to feel sure about something, as in *I doubt whether he is telling the truth. Is he telling the truth? I doubt it.*

dough *noun*
1 a thick mixture of flour, etc. and liquid used for making bread, buns, etc.
2 (*colloquial*) money.
doughy *adjective*

doughnut *noun* doughnuts
a usually ring-shaped cake that has been fried and covered with sugar.

douse *verb* douses, dousing, doused
(*say* dows)
to throw water over, as in *They doused the fire before going to bed.*

dove *noun* doves
1 a kind of pigeon. 2 a peaceful person.

dovetail *noun* dovetails
a wedge-shaped joint used to join two pieces of wood together.

dovetail *verb* dovetails, dovetailing, dovetailed
1 to join two pieces of wood with a dovetail. 2 to fit neatly together, as in *My plans dovetailed with hers.*

dowdy *adjective* dowdier, dowdiest
unattractive, dull or unfashionable, as in *dowdy clothes.*

dowel *noun* dowels
a headless wooden or metal pin for holding together two pieces of wood, stone, etc.

down *adverb* and *preposition*
1 to or in a lower place, as in *Jack fell down.*
2 along, as in *Walk down the road with me.*

down *noun* downs
a change in luck, etc., as in *the ups and downs of life.*
have a down on someone, (*colloquial*) to have a prejudice or grudge against someone.

down *noun*
very soft feathers or hair, as in *Ducklings are covered with down.*
downy *adjective*

downfall *noun* downfalls
1 ruin; ceasing to have fortune or power.
2 a heavy fall of rain, snow, etc.

downhill *adverb*
down a slope.
going downhill, getting worse in quality or condition, as in *His handwriting is going downhill.*

downpour *noun* downpours
a time when rain falls heavily.

downright *adjective* and *adverb*
thorough; thoroughly, as in *That's a downright lie. I felt downright angry about it.*

downs *plural noun*
open rolling country, as in *the Darling Downs of Queensland.*

downstairs *adverb* and *adjective*
to or on a lower floor.

downstream *adverb*
in the direction that a river or stream flows.

downward or **downwards** *adverb*
towards a lower place.

doze *verb* dozes, dozing, dozed
to sleep lightly.
dozy *adjective*

dozen *noun* dozens
a set of twelve.
dozens of, (*colloquial*) lots of, as in *dozens of mistakes.*

Dr short for **Doctor.**

drab *adjective* drabber, drabbest
1 not colourful, as in *drab clothes.*
2 boring, as in *He lived a drab existence.*

draft *noun* drafts
a rough sketch, plan or piece of writing.

Usage Do not confuse **draft** with **draught**, which means a current of air.

draft *verb* drafts, drafting, drafted
to make a draft or plan.

drag *verb* drags, dragging, dragged
1 to pull something heavy along. 2 to search a river, lake, etc. with nets and hooks.

drag *noun*
(*colloquial*) something that hinders or annoys you, as in *Having to take him everywhere is a drag.*

dragon *noun* dragons
a fierce monster in stories.

dragonfly *noun* dragonflies
an insect with a long body and two pairs of transparent wings.

a
b
c
d
e
f
g
h
i
j
k
l
m
n
o
p
q
r
s
t
u
v
w
x
y
z

drain

drain *verb* **drains, draining, drained**
1 to get rid of water with drains or pipes. 2 to flow or trickle away. 3 to empty liquid out of a container, as in *He drained his glass.* 4 to exhaust, as in *drained of strength.*
drainage *noun*

drain *noun* **drains**
1 a pipe, channel, etc. for taking away water or sewage. 2 something that uses up your strength, as in *Looking after her friend's children has been a real drain on her.*
something has gone down the drain, (*colloquial*) something has been lost or wasted, as in *If we can't go on holiday, all our planning will have gone down the drain.*

drake *noun* **drakes**
a male duck.

drama *noun* **dramas**
1 a play performed on stage, radio or television in which there is conflict or sadness. 2 an oral or written text that is meant to be acted out. 3 a sudden, exciting or interesting event.
dramatist *noun*

dramatic *adjective*
1 to do with drama, as in *a dramatic production.* 2 exciting; impressive, as in *A dramatic change has taken place.*
dramatically *adverb*

dramatist *noun* **dramatists**
someone who writes plays.

dramatise or **dramatize** *verb* **dramatises, dramatising, dramatised**
1 to make something into a play, as in *We dramatised a Paul Jennings story for our school play.* 2 to exaggerate, as in *He always dramatised any illness.*
dramatisation *noun*

drank past tense of **drink** *verb*.

drape *verb* **drapes, draping, draped**
to hang cloth over something.

drastic *adjective*
having a strong or violent effect, as in *Bleach has a drastic effect on coloured material.*
drastically *adverb*

draught *noun* **draughts**
(rhymes with *craft*)
a current of usually cold air in a room, chimney, etc.
draughty *adjective*

Usage Do not confuse **draught** with **draft**, which means a rough sketch or plan.

draughts *noun*
a game played with 24 round pieces on a chessboard.

draughtsman *noun* **draughtsmen**
1 someone who makes drawings of buildings, roads, etc. 2 a piece used in the game of draughts.

draw *verb* **draws, drawing, drew, drawn**
1 to make a picture, diagram, etc. with a pencil, crayon, pen, etc., as in *I have drawn a map of Australia.* 2 to pull, as in *She drew her chair up to the table.* 3 to attract, as in *The fair drew large crowds.* 4 to end a game or contest with the same score on both sides, as in *They drew 2–2 last Saturday.* 5 to come, as in *The ship was drawing nearer. The winter is drawing to a close; spring is nearly here.*

draw *noun* **draws**
1 an attraction, as in *The famous pianist will be a big draw at the concert. We all feel the draw of the beach in summer.* 2 a raffle or similar competition in which the winner is chosen by chance. 3 a game that ends with the same score on both sides.

drawback *noun* **drawbacks**
a disadvantage.

drawbridge *noun* **drawbridges**
a bridge that may be raised or lowered over a moat.

drawer *noun* **drawers**
a sliding container in a piece of furniture.

drawing *noun* **drawings**
something drawn with a pencil, crayon, etc.
drawing-pin, a short pin with a large flat top.

drawl *verb* **drawls, drawling, drawled**
to speak very slowly or lazily.

dread *verb* **dreads, dreading, dreaded**
to fear something very much.

dread *noun*
great fear or terror.

dreadful *adjective*
1 awful; terrible, as in *a dreadful disease.* 2 very annoying or very bad, as in *We had a dreadful time at the party.*
dreadfully *adverb*

dream *noun* **dreams**
1 things that you seem to see while you are asleep. 2 something imagined; an ambition or ideal, as in *Her dream is to own a farm.*
dreamy *adjective*

dream *verb* **dreams, dreaming, dreamt** or **dreamed**
1 to have a dream or dreams. 2 to have an ambition, as in *She dreams of being a ballet-dancer.* 3 to think something may happen, as in *I never dreamt she would leave.*

Dreamtime *noun*
the Aboriginal belief in a collection of events which, before time began, shaped the world as it exists today.

dreary *adjective* **drearier, dreariest**
gloomy; boring.
drearily *adverb*, **dreariness** *noun*

dredge *verb* **dredges, dredging, dredged**
to drag up something, especially mud from the bottom of a river or the sea.
dredger *noun*

drench *verb* **drenches, drenching, drenched**
to soak, as in *They got drenched in the rain.*

dress *verb* **dresses, dressing, dressed**
1 to put clothes on. 2 to put a bandage on a wound. 3 to prepare food for cooking or eating, as in *The chef dressed the salad with oil and lemon juice.*

dress *noun* **dresses**
1 a garment with a skirt and blouse together. 2 clothes; a costume, as in *fancy dress.*
dress rehearsal, a rehearsal at which the actors in a play wear their costumes.

dresser *noun* **dressers**
a sideboard with shelves at the top.

dressing *noun* **dressings**
1 a mixture of oil, vinegar, etc. for a salad. 2 a covering for a wound; a plaster.

dressing-gown *noun* **dressing-gowns**
a loose garment worn over pyjamas, etc.

dressmaker *noun* **dressmakers**
a person whose job is to make clothes for women and children.

drew past tense of **draw** *verb.*

dribble *verb* **dribbles, dribbling, dribbled**
1 to let saliva trickle out of your mouth. 2 to flow or allow to flow in drops, as in *Dribble the hose on the ferns.* 3 to kick a ball as you run along, so that the ball stays close to your feet.

dried past tense and past participle of **dry** *verb.*

drier or **dryer** *noun* **driers**
something that dries hair, clothes, etc.

drift *noun* **drifts**
1 a slow movement, as in *the drift of country people to the cities.* 2 a mass of sand, etc. piled up by the wind. 3 the general meaning of a speech, etc., as in *I don't follow your drift.*

drift *verb* **drifts, drifting, drifted**
1 to be carried gently along by water or air. 2 to move or live aimlessly, as in *He drifted from town to town when he lost his job.*

driftwood *noun*
wood washed ashore from the sea.

drill *noun* **drills**
1 a tool for making holes, as in *an electric drill.* 2 repeated exercises in military training, gymnastics, etc. 3 a procedure or routine, as in *fire-drill.*

drill *verb* **drills, drilling, drilled**
1 to make a hole with a drill. 2 to do repeated exercises, as in *Watch the soldiers drilling.*

drink *verb* **drinks, drinking, drank, drunk**
1 to swallow liquid. 2 to drink alcoholic drinks, as in *Don't drink and drive.*
drinkable *adjective*, **drinker** *noun*

drink *noun* **drinks**
1 a liquid for drinking. 2 a drink that contains alcohol.
the drink, (*colloquial*) the sea.

drip *verb* **drips, dripping, dripped**
1 to fall in drops. 2 to let liquid fall in drops, as in *The tap was dripping.*
drip-dry clothes, clothes that do not need ironing.

drip *noun* **drips**
1 a falling drop of liquid. 2 (*colloquial*) a dull person.

dripping *noun*
the solid fat which comes from roasting meat.

drive *verb* **drives, driving, drove, driven**
to make something or someone move; to make someone go into a particular state, as in *That child will drive me mad!*
be driving at something, to be trying to say something, as in *What is he driving at?*
driver *noun*

drive *noun* **drives**
1 a journey in a vehicle. 2 energy; enthusiasm, as in *The new manager has great drive.* 3 a road, especially one leading to a large house. 4 a powerful stroke in cricket, golf, tennis, etc.

drive-in *adjective*
able to be used without getting out of your car, as in *a drive-in bottle-shop.*

drizzle *noun*
gentle rain.

drone *noun* **drones**
1 a deep humming sound. 2 a male bee.

drone *verb* **drones, droning, droned**
1 to make a low humming sound. 2 to talk in a boring voice.

drool

drool *verb* **drools, drooling, drooled**
to let saliva run out of your mouth.
drool over, to look at something with great pleasure, as in *He's been drooling over car catalogues all afternoon.*

droop *verb* **droops, drooping, drooped**
to hang down weakly.

drop *noun* **drops**
1 a tiny amount of liquid. 2 a fall; a decrease, as in *a drop in prices.*
droplet *noun*

drop *verb* **drops, dropping, dropped**
1 to fall or let something fall. 2 to sink or fall to the ground from tiredness, a blow, etc. 3 to stop or abandon, as in *They dropped the project when it became too expensive.* 4 (*colloquial*) to break off a friendship, as in *She dropped her boyfriend.*
drop in, to visit someone.
drop out, (*colloquial*) to stop taking part in something.

drought *noun* **droughts**
(rhymes with *out*)
a long period of dry weather.

drove past tense of **drive** *verb.*

drown *verb* **drowns, drowning, drowned**
1 to die because of being under water and unable to breathe. 2 to kill someone or an animal by forcing them to stay under water, stopping them from breathing.
3 to make so much noise that another sound cannot be heard, as in *The drums drowned out the piano.*

drowsy *adjective* **drowsier, drowsiest**
sleepy.
drowsily *adverb*, **drowsiness** *noun*

drug *noun* **drugs**
1 a substance that kills pain or cures a disease. 2 a substance that affects your senses or your mind, as in *Heroin is a harmful drug.*

drug *verb* **drugs, drugging, drugged**
to use a drug to make someone unconscious, etc.

drum *noun* **drums**
1 a musical instrument made of a cylinder with a thin sheet of material such as skin stretched over one end or both ends. 2 a cylindrical container, as in *an oil drum.*

drum *verb* **drums, drumming, drummed**
1 to play a drum or drums. 2 to tap or thump on something, as in *He drummed his fingers on the table.*
drum up, to get something by vigorous effort, as in *He's drumming up money for a new playground.*
drummer *noun*

drumstick *noun* **drumsticks**
1 a stick used for hitting a drum. 2 the lower part of a roast leg of chicken, etc.

drunk *adjective*
lacking control from drinking too much alcohol.

drunk *noun* **drunks**
someone who is drunk.
drunkard *noun*

drunk past participle of **drink** *verb.*

dry *adjective* **drier, driest**
1 not wet; not damp. 2 boring; dull, as in *a dry book.*
dry dock, a dock which can be emptied of water, for repairing ships.
dry ice, carbon dioxide frozen solid.
the Dry, the rainless season in northern and central Australia.
dryly *adverb*, **dryness** *noun*

dry *verb* **dried, drying**
to make or become dry.
dry up, to become dry; to make something dry.

dry-clean *verb* **dry-cleans, dry-cleaning, dry-cleaned**
to clean clothes with chemicals instead of water.
dry-cleaning *noun*, **dry-cleaner** *noun*

dual *adjective*
double.
dual carriageway, a road with at least four lanes, with two or more in each direction.

Usage Do not confuse **dual** with **duel,** which is a noun meaning a fight between two people.

dub *verb* **dubs, dubbing, dubbed**
to change or add new sound to the sound on a film or magnetic tape.

dub *verb* **dubs, dubbing, dubbed**
to give someone a name or title.

dubious *adjective* (*say* **dyoo**-bee-uhs)
doubtful or unsure, as in *The scientist was dubious about the result of the experiment.*

duchess *noun* **duchesses**
1 a duke's wife or widow. 2 a woman holding the rank of duke.

duck *noun* **ducks**
1 a web-footed bird with a flat beak.
2 a batter's score of nought at cricket.
duckbill or **duck-billed platypus,** a platypus.

duck *verb* **ducks, ducking, ducked**
1 to bend down quickly to avoid something. 2 to get under water quickly; to push someone under water quickly.

duckling *noun* **ducklings**
a young duck.

duct *noun* **ducts**
a tube or channel for carrying bodily fluids, cable, home heating, etc., as in *tear duct; electrical duct*.

dud *noun* **duds**
(*colloquial*) something that is useless or that fails to work, as in *The firework was a dud*.

due *adjective*
1 expected at a certain time, as in *The train is due in five minutes*. 2 owing; to be paid, as in *Your subscription is due*. 3 suitable, right or proper, as in *The old soldier was given due respect in the Anzac parade*.
in due course, eventually; at the expected time.

due *adverb*
directly, exactly, as in *The camp is due north*.
due to, because of, as in *His lateness was due to an accident*.

duel *noun* **duels**
a fight between two people, especially with pistols or swords.

Usage Do not confuse **duel** with **dual**, which is an adjective meaning double.

duet *noun* **duets**
a piece of music for two players or two singers.

duffle-coat *noun* **duffle-coats**
a thick overcoat with a hood.

dug past tense and past participle of **dig** *verb*.

dugong *noun* **dugongs** (*say* **doo**-gong *or* **dyoo**-gong)
an Asian marine mammal; a sea cow, as in *the dugongs of north-west Australian waters*.

duke *noun* **dukes**
a very high-ranking nobleman or a prince who rules a small nation.

dull *adjective* **duller, dullest**
1 not bright; gloomy, as in *a dull day*. 2 not sharp, as in *a dull pain*. 3 stupid, as in *a dull boy*. 4 boring, as in *a dull TV program*.
dully *adverb*, **dullness** *noun*

duly *adverb*
rightly or properly; as expected, as in *She was duly given credit for the new invention. Having promised to come, they duly arrived*.

dumb *adjective* **dumber, dumbest**
1 unable to speak; silent. 2 (*colloquial*) stupid.

dumbfounded *adjective*
unable to say anything because you are so astonished.

dummy *noun* **dummies**
1 something made to look like a person or thing; an imitation. 2 an imitation teat for a baby to suck.

dump *noun* **dumps**
1 a place where something, especially rubbish, is left or stored. 2 (*colloquial*) an unpleasant or untidy place.

dump *verb* **dumps, dumping, dumped**
1 to get rid of something you don't want. 2 to put something down carelessly, as in *He dumped his schoolbag on the bench*.

dumpling *noun* **dumplings**
a lump of boiled or baked dough.

dune *noun* **dunes**
a mound of loose sand shaped by the wind.

dung *noun*
the waste matter from the bowel of an animal.

dungarees *plural noun*
a pair of work trousers or overalls made from coarse cotton cloth.

dungeon *noun* **dungeons** (*say* **dun**-juhn)
an underground prison cell.

duo *noun* **duos**
a pair of people, especially playing music.

duplex *noun* **duplexes** (*say* **dyoo**-pleks)
a building consisting of two flats, units or houses which share a common wall, as in *Sometimes a duplex is called a semi-detached house*.

duplicate *noun* **duplicates**
(*say* **dyoo**-pluh-kuht)
something exactly the same as something else.

duplicate *verb* **duplicates, duplicating, duplicated** (*say* **dyoo**-pluh-kayt)
to make a copy of something, as in *She duplicated the important document*.
duplication *noun*, **duplicator** *noun*

durable *adjective*
lasting or hard-wearing.
durability *noun*

duration *noun*
the time something lasts.

during *preposition*
while something else is going on.

dusk *noun*
the time of fading light between day and night; twilight.

dust

dust *noun*
tiny particles of dry earth or other material.

dust *verb* **dusts, dusting, dusted**
1 to clear dust away. **2** to sprinkle with dust or powder, as in *Dust the cake with icing sugar*.
duster *noun*

dustbin *noun* **dustbins**
a container for household rubbish.

dustpan *noun* **dustpans**
a pan into which dust is brushed from the ground, floor, etc.

dusty *adjective* **dustier, dustiest**
covered with dust.

dutiful *adjective*
doing your duty; obedient.
dutifully *adverb*

duty *noun* **duties**
1 what you ought to do or must do. **2** a kind of tax, as in *stamp duty*.
on (or **off**) **duty,** working (or not working).

duty-free *adjective*
having no tax charged on it by the customs authorities, as in *Duty-free goods can be bought at airports and on ships and planes*.

duvet *noun* **duvets** (*say* **doo**-vay)
a kind of quilt used instead of other bedclothes; a doona.

dux *noun*
the top pupil in a class or in a school.

dwarf *noun* **dwarfs** or **dwarves**
a very small person or thing.

dwarf *verb* **dwarfs, dwarfing, dwarfed**
to make something seem very small, as in *The new skyscraper dwarfs all the buildings around it*.

dwell *verb* **dwells, dwelling, dwelt**
to live somewhere.

dwell on something, to think or talk about something for a long time.
dweller *noun*, **dwelling** *noun*

dwindle *verb* **dwindles, dwindling, dwindled**
to get smaller gradually, as in *His savings dwindled away during his holiday*.

dye *noun* **dyes**
something used to dye fabrics, hair, etc.

dye *verb* **dyes, dyeing, dyed**
to colour something by putting it in a special liquid.

Usage Do not confuse **dyeing** with **dying** which is the present participle of the verb **to die**.

dyke or **dike** *noun* **dykes**
an embankment built to prevent flooding.

dynamic *adjective*
energetic; active, as in *The dynamic new business succeeded quickly*.

dynamite *noun*
1 a powerful explosive. **2** (*colloquial*) something very exciting, dangerous, etc., as in *Just wait till we publish that story—it's dynamite!*

dynamo *noun* **dynamos**
1 a machine that makes electricity. **2** an energetic person, as in *She's a real dynamo— he has two jobs*.

dynasty *noun* **dynasties** (*say* **din**-uh-stee)
a line of rulers who belong to the same family.

dyslexia *noun* (*say* dis-**lek**-see-uh)
a problem in reading and spelling, caused by difficulty in recognising the shapes of letters in the alphabet.
dyslexic *adjective*

dystrophy *noun* (*say* **dis**-truh-fee)
a disease that severely weakens your muscles, as in *muscular dystrophy*.

Ee

each *adjective*
every, as in *Each child had a cake.*

each *pronoun*
every one, as in *Each of you may have a sweet.*
each other, said of something done by each of two or more people to the other one or other ones, as in *They were yelling at each other.*

eager *adjective*
strongly wanting to do something; enthusiastic.
eagerly *adverb*, **eagerness** *noun*

eagle *noun* **eagles**
a large powerful bird of prey with very good eyesight.

ear *noun* **ears**
1 the part of the head that you hear with.
2 hearing ability, as in *She has a good ear for music.*

ear *noun* **ears**
the cluster of seeds at the top of a stalk of corn.

eardrum *noun* **eardrums**
a membrane in the ear that vibrates when sound reaches it.

earl *noun* **earls**
a British nobleman.

early *adverb* and *adjective* **earlier, earliest**
1 before the usual or correct time.
2 near the beginning, as in *early spring.*
earliness *noun*

earmark *verb* **earmarks, earmarking, earmarked**
to decide that something shall be used for a particular purpose, as in *Funds have been earmarked for setting up a computer room.*

earn *verb* **earns, earning, earned**
to get something by working for it or as a reward, as in *He is earning $50 a day. They earned a holiday after their hard work.*

earnest *adjective*
very serious; determined.
in earnest, seriously.
earnestly *adverb*

earnings *plural noun*
money that is earned.

earphone *noun*
a device for listening to recorded or broadcast sound that fits over or into your ear.

earring *noun* **earrings**
an ornament for your ear.

earth *noun* **earths**
1 the planet that we live on.
2 soil; dirt, as in *Dig the earth.*
3 dry land; the ground, as in *I fell to the earth.*
4 connection to the ground to complete an electric circuit, as in *The dangerous power point didn't have an earth.*
on earth, (*colloquial*) at all, as in *Why on earth did you say that?*
cost the earth, (*colloquial*) to cost a huge amount of money.
earthly *adjective*, **earthy** *adjective*

earthenware *noun*
crockery made of baked clay.

earthquake *noun* **earthquakes**
a sudden violent shaking of the ground.

earthworm *noun* **earthworms**
a small wriggling creature that lives in the soil.

earwig *noun* **earwigs**
an insect with a pair of small, claw-like pincers at the rear end of its body.

ease

ease *noun*
relief or freedom from difficulty or discomfort.
at ease, comfortable or free from anxiety, as in *at ease in the company of good friends.*

ease *verb* **eases, easing, eased**
1 to relieve from pain or worry, as in *The medicine eased her pain.* **2** to relax; to begin to take it easy, as in *The students asked the teacher to ease up on the homework.* **3** to move something slowly and carefully, as in *The mirror was eased into the frame.*

easel *noun* **easels**
a stand for holding a blackboard or a painting.

easily *adverb*
1 without difficulty. **2** without doubt; very possibly, as in *She is easily the best runner. He could easily be lying.*

east *noun*
the area where the sun rises.

east *adjective*
1 coming from the east, as in *an east wind.* **2** situated in the east, as in *the east coast.*
easterly *adjective*, **eastern** *adjective*

east *adverb*
towards the east, as in *We looked east.*
eastward *adjective and adverb,* **eastwards** *adverb*

Easter *noun*
the period when the resurrection of Jesus is remembered; this time as a holiday, as in *We went to Sydney for Easter.*
Easter egg, a sweet artificial egg, usually made of chocolate, eaten at or near Easter.

easy *adjective* **easier, easiest**
1 able to be done or understood without any trouble. **2** comfortable; giving ease, as in *an easy chair.*
easiness *noun*

easy *adverb* **easier, easiest**
with ease; comfortably, as in *Take it easy.*

easygoing *adjective*
calm and tolerant.

eat *verb* **eats, eating, ate, eaten**
1 to take food into the mouth and swallow it. **2** to use up something; to destroy something, as in *The sea air has eaten away the ironwork.*

eatable *adjective*
fit to be eaten; edible.

eaves *plural noun*
the overhanging edges of a roof.

eavesdrop *verb* **eavesdrops, eavesdropping, eavesdropped**
to listen to a private conversation.

ebb *noun*
the tide when it is going out.
at a low ebb, in a low or weak condition.

ebb *verb* **ebbs, ebbing, ebbed**
1 to go down, as in *The tide was ebbing.* **2** to weaken or lessen, as in *His strength ebbed away.*

ebony *noun* **ebonies**
1 a hard black wood, as in *The black keys on a piano are often made of ebony.* **2** a deep black colour.

eccentric *adjective*
(*say* uhk-**sen**-trik *or* ek-**sen**-trik)
1 behaving strangely. **2** not always at the same distance from the centre; (of a pivot, hub, etc.) not placed in the centre, as in *The spacecraft was in an eccentric orbit.*
eccentric *noun*, **eccentricity** *noun*

echidna *noun* **echidnas** (*say* uh-**kid**-nuh)
a spiny mammal with a long snout and claws, found in Australia and New Guinea; the spiny anteater.

echo *noun* **echoes**
a sound that is heard again as it bounces off something.

echo *verb* **echoes, echoing, echoed**
1 to make an echo. **2** to repeat a sound or saying.

éclair *noun* **éclairs** (*say* ay-**klair**)
a finger-shaped cake made from a type of pastry which is iced and filled with cream.

eclipse *noun* **eclipses**
1 a time when the moon comes between the sun and the earth, so that all or part of the sun is hidden. **2** a time when the earth comes between the sun and the moon, so that all or part of the moon is in shadow.

ecological *adjective*
to do with ecology, as in *The oil spillage was an ecological disaster.*

ecology *noun* (*say* uh-**kol**-uh-jee *or* ee-**kol**-uh-jee)
the science concerned with living creatures and plants studied in their surroundings.
ecologist *noun*

economic *adjective* (*say* ee-kuh-**nom**-ik *or* e-kuh-**nom**-ik)
1 to do with economics. **2** profitable, as in *It is not economic to run buses on a Sunday.*

economical *adjective*
(*say* ee-kuh-**nom**-ik-uhl *or* e-kuh-**nom**-ik-uhl)
careful in using money, goods, etc.; not

effort

wasteful, as in *economical in planning the budget; an economical car.*
economically *adverb*

economics *noun* (*say* ee-kuh-**nom**-iks *or* e-kuh-**nom**-iks)
the study of how money is used and how goods, etc. are made, sold, and used.

economist *noun* **economists**
(*say* uh-**kon**-uh-mist)
an expert in economics.

economise or **economize** *verb*
economises, economising, economised
(*say* uh-**kon**-uh-muyz)
to be economical.

economy *noun* **economies**
(*say* uh-**kon**-uh-mee)
1 the careful spending or use of things in order to save money, etc., as in *During the drought, water had to be used with economy.*
2 the wealth that a country gets from business and industry, as in *The Australian economy used to rely strongly on the wool industry.*

ecosystem *noun* **ecosystems**
a group of plants and animals that are connected because of where or how they live.

ecstasy *noun* **ecstasies**
a feeling of great delight or joy.
ecstatic *adjective*

eczema *noun* (*say* **ek**-suh-muh)
a skin disease causing rough, itching patches.

edge *noun* **edges**
1 the part along the side or end of something.   **2** the sharp part of a knife, axe, etc.
on edge, nervous; irritable.

edge *verb* **edges, edging, edged**
1 to move slowly, as in *She edged towards the door.*   **2** to give something an edge.

edgeways *adverb*
with the edge outwards or forwards.
not get a word in edgeways, not to be able to interrupt a talkative person.

edgy *adjective* **edgier, edgiest**
tense and easily annoyed.

edible *adjective*
not poisonous; eatable.

edit *verb* **edits, editing, edited**
1 to get a newspaper, book, magazine, etc. ready for publishing.   **2** to put a film, tape-recording, etc. in the order you want.

edition *noun* **editions**
1 the form in which something is published, as in *a paperback edition.*   **2** all the copies of a newspaper, book, etc. issued at the same time, as in *The first edition of the novel sold out.*

editor *noun* **editors**
someone who edits, especially the main person responsible for a newspaper, magazine, etc.

editorial *noun* **editorials**
a newspaper article giving the editor's opinion on current affairs.

educate *verb* **educates, educating, educated**
to give someone knowledge or skill.
educator *noun*

education *noun*
the process of training people's minds and abilities so that they can learn things and develop skills; the training that is given to someone, as in *She has had a good education.*
educational *adjective*

eel *noun* **eels**
a long fish that looks like a snake.

eerie *adjective* **eerier, eeriest**
frighteningly strange; weird.
eerily *adverb*, **eeriness** *noun*

effect *noun* **effects**
1 something that happens because of something else, as in *The sun had a painful effect on her pale skin.*   **2** a general impression, as in *The colourful lights created a cheerful effect.*

Usage Do not confuse **effect** with **affect**, which is a verb meaning to have an effect on, or to harm.

effective *adjective*
producing an effect; impressive.
effectively *adverb*, **effectiveness** *noun*

effeminate *adjective* (*say* uh-**fem**-uh-nuht *or* ee-**fem**-uh-nuht)
having some of the characteristics of a woman, as in *an effeminate man.*

effervescent *adjective* (*say* ef-uh-**ves**-uhnt)
fizzy, as in *an effervescent drink.*
effervescence *noun*

efficient *adjective*
doing work well; effective.
efficiency *noun*, **efficiently** *adverb*

effort *noun* **efforts**
1 hard work; using energy, as in *Digging the ditch required a lot of effort.*   **2** an attempt, as in *a good effort to finish.*
effortless *adjective*

a
b
c
d
e
f
g
h
i
j
k
l
m
n
o
p
q
r
s
t
u
v
w
x
y
z

e.g. for example, as in *He teaches many subjects, e.g. music, geography, and maths.*

egg *noun* **eggs**
1 an oval or round object with a thin shell, laid by birds, insects, fishes, etc., in which their offspring develop. 2 a hen's or duck's egg used as food.

egg *verb* **eggs, egging, egged**
egg on, to encourage someone, usually to do something bad.

eggplant *noun* **eggplants**
a purple, egg-shaped fruit with white flesh, used as a vegetable.

ego *noun* **egos** (*say* **ee**-goh)
1 the self; the part of the mind that makes you an individual. 2 the sense of self importance, as in *The constant winner soon had a swollen ego. Losing the job was a blow to my ego.*

egotist *noun* **egotists** (*say* **eg**-uh-tuhst *or* **eeg**-e-tuhst)
a person who talks and thinks about him or herself all the time.
egotistical *adjective*

eiderdown *noun* **eiderdowns**
(*say* **uy**-duh-down)
a quilt filled with down or feathers.

eight *noun* **eights**
the number 8, one more than seven.
eighth *adjective* and *noun*

eighteen *noun* **eighteens**
the number 18, one more than seventeen.
eighteenth *adjective* and *noun*

eighty *noun* **eighties**
the number 80, eight times ten.
eightieth *adjective* and *noun*

eisteddfod *noun* **eisteddfods**
(*say* uh-**sted**-fuhd)
a competition for singers, musicians, dancers, etc.

either *adjective* and *pronoun* (*say* **uy**-thuh *or* **ee**-thuh)
1 one of two, as in *Either team can win.* 2 both of two, as in *Put chairs at either end of the table.*

either *adverb*
also; similarly, as in *If you won't play, I won't either.*

either *conjunction*
either ... or, one thing or another, but not both, as in *You can choose either red or blue. Either come in or go out.*

ejaculate *verb* **ejaculates, ejaculating, ejaculated**
1 to exclaim suddenly, especially when you are surprised. 2 to discharge semen from the penis.

eject *verb* **ejects, ejecting, ejected**
1 to send something out forcefully. 2 to make someone leave a place.
ejection *noun*

elaborate *adjective* (*say* uh-**lab**-uh-ruht *or* ee-**lab**-uh-ruht)
complicated; carefully planned.

elaborate *verb* **elaborates, elaborating, elaborated** (*say* uh-**lab**-uh-rayt *or* ee-**lab**-uh-rayt)
to describe or work out something in detail.
elaboration *noun*

elastic *adjective*
able to go back to its normal shape after being stretched, as in *elastic band.*
elasticity *noun*

elastic *noun*
elastic material or cord.

elated *adjective*
delighted, as in *She was elated by her win.*
elation *noun*

elbow *noun* **elbows**
the joint in the middle of your arm.
elbow-grease, (*colloquial*) vigorous rubbing or polishing; hard work.

elbow *verb* **elbows, elbowing, elbowed**
to push with your elbow or elbows, as in *She elbowed me aside and took my place in the queue. I elbowed my way to the front of the crowd.*

elder *adjective*
older, as in *his elder brother.*

elderly *adjective*
rather old.

eldest *adjective*
oldest, as in *my eldest sister.*

elect *verb* **elects, electing, elected**
to choose someone by voting.

election *noun* **elections**
1 the act of electing or being elected, as in *the election of school captain; her election as captain.* 2 a time when someone is elected, especially to be a Member of Parliament.

elector *noun* **electors**
someone who votes in an election.
electoral *adjective*, **electorate** *noun*

electorate *noun* **electorates**
an area represented by one member of parliament.

electric *adjective*
to do with or worked by electricity, as in *electric plug; electric lawnmower.*
electric chair, a chair which electrocutes criminals.
electrical *adjective*, **electrically** *adverb*

electrician *noun* **electricians**
someone whose job is to deal with electrical equipment, especially the installation of such equipment.

electricity *noun*
a kind of energy used for lighting, heating, and making machines work.

electrify *verb* **electrifies, electrifying, electrified**
1 to charge something with electricity.
2 to make something work with electricity. 3 to excite or startle someone, as in *Her acting electrified the audience.*
electrification *noun*

electrocute *verb* **electrocutes, electrocuting, electrocuted**
to kill someone by electricity.
electrocution *noun*

electrode *noun* **electrodes**
a conductor through which electricity enters or leaves something.

electrolysis *noun*
the breaking up of a substance by passing electricity through it, as in *Water can be broken down into oxygen and hydrogen by electrolysis.*

electromagnet *noun* **electromagnets**
a magnet worked by electricity.
electromagnetic *adjective*

electron *noun* **electrons**
a particle of matter that is smaller than an atom, has a negative electric charge, and carries electricity.

electronic *adjective*
using devices such as transistors, silicon chips, diodes, etc., which are worked by electrons, as in *electronic typewriter.*
electronic mail, the use of a computer system to send or receive messages over long distances.
electronic music, music made by instruments such as synthesisers.
electronically *adverb*, **electronics** *noun*

elegant *adjective*
tasteful; smart, as in *elegant clothes.*
elegance *noun*, **elegantly** *adverb*

element *noun* **elements**
1 (*in Science*) a substance that cannot be split up into simpler substances, as in *Copper, oxygen, and sulphur are elements.*
2 a part of something. 3 a principle, as in *Learn the elements of algebra.* 4 the wire or coil that gives out heat in an electric heater, oven, etc.
be in your element, to be in a situation that you like, or doing something that you enjoy, as in *I'm in my element when talking about video games.*
the elements, the weather, especially bad weather.

elementary *adjective*
dealing with the first or simplest stages of something; easy, as in *elementary arithmetic.*

elephant *noun* **elephants**
a very big animal from Africa or India with a trunk, ivory tusks, and large ears.

elevate *verb* **elevates, elevating, elevated**
to lift something up; to put something high up.
elevation *noun*, **elevator** *noun*

eleven *noun* **elevens**
1 the number 11, one more than ten.
2 a team of eleven people in cricket, hockey, etc.
eleventh *adjective* and *noun*

elf *noun* **elves**
a small or mischievous fairy.

eligible *adjective*
qualified or suitable for something; being a suitable person to marry, as in *eligible to compete in the Commonwealth Games; an eligible bachelor.*
eligibility *noun*

Usage Do not confuse **eligible** with **legible**, which means clear enough to read.

eliminate *verb* **eliminates, eliminating, eliminated**
to get rid of someone or something.
elimination *noun*

élite *noun* **élites**
a group of people who are thought of as better than others in some way and are given special advantages because of this.

Elizabethan *adjective*
to do with the time of Queen Elizabeth I (1558–1603), as in *Elizabethan architecture.*

elk *noun* **elk** or **elks**
a large kind of deer.

ellipse *noun* **ellipses**
an oval shape.

a
b
c
d
e
f
g
h
i
j
k
l
m
n
o
p
q
r
s
t
u
v
w
x
y
z

elliptical

elliptical *adjective*
1 oval-shaped. 2 with some words left out, as in '*One moment, please' is an elliptical sentence from the sentence, 'one moment if you please'*.

elm *noun* **elms**
a tall, deciduous, European tree with rough leaves.

elocution *noun*
the skill of speaking clearly and expressively.

elongated *adjective*
lengthened.
elongation *noun*

elope *verb* **elopes, eloping, eloped**
to go away secretly to marry, usually without the parents' permission.

eloquence *noun*
speaking effectively or skilfully.
eloquent *adjective*

else *adverb*
besides; instead, as in *Nobody else knows*.
or else, otherwise; (*colloquial*) or there will be trouble, as in *Give me the money or else!*

elsewhere *adverb*
somewhere different.

elude *verb* **eludes, eluding, eluded**
to avoid being caught by someone; to escape from someone.

elusive *adjective*
difficult to find, catch, remember, or describe, as in *The platypus is an elusive animal. Some memories are elusive.*

E-mail short for **electronic mail**.

emancipate *verb* **emancipates, emancipating, emancipated**
to set someone free.
emancipation *noun*

embankment *noun* **embankments**
a wall or mound of earth to hold back water or to support a road or railway.

embark *verb* **embarks, embarking, embarked**
to go on board a ship.
embark on or **upon,** to begin something.
embarkation *noun*

embarrass *verb* **embarrasses, embarrassing, embarrassed**
to make someone feel shy or awkward.
embarrassment *noun*

embassy *noun* **embassies**
the building where an ambassador lives and works.

embedded *adjective*
fixed firmly into something, as in *an embedded splinter in her finger.*

embers *plural noun*
small pieces of burning coal or wood in a dying fire.

emblem *noun* **emblems**
a symbol, as in *The dove is an emblem of peace.*

embrace *verb* **embraces, embracing, embraced**
1 to put your arms around someone; to hug someone. 2 to include something, as in *The musical concert embraced a range of instruments.*

embrace *noun*
the act of embracing; a clasp.

embroider *verb* **embroiders, embroidering, embroidered**
to decorate cloth with sewn designs or pictures.
embroidery *noun*

embryo *noun* **embryos**
a baby or young animal in the very early stages of development before it is born.
embryonic *adjective*

emerald *noun* **emeralds**
1 a green jewel. 2 a bright green colour.

emerge *verb* **emerges, emerging, emerged**
to come out; to appear.
emergence *noun*

emergency *noun* **emergencies**
a sudden dangerous or serious event or situation.

emery-board *noun*
a nail-file made from a gritty paper like sandpaper.

emigrate *verb* **emigrates, emigrating, emigrated**
to go and live in another country.
emigrant *noun*, **emigration** *noun*

Usage Do not confuse **emigrate** with **immigrate**, which means to come into a country to live there.

eminent *adjective*
1 famous, as in *an eminent scientist*. 2 outstanding, as in *She is known for her eminent kindness*.
eminence *noun*

emission *noun* **emissions**
the act of sending something out into the atmosphere; something that is sent out, especially pollution, as in *There will be stricter controls on exhaust emissions of vehicles.*

emit *verb* **emits, emitting, emitted**
to send something out, as in *The volcano emitted smoke and lava.*

emotion *noun* **emotions**
  1 a strong feeling, as in *Fear and hate are dangerous emotions.* **2** being excited or upset, as in *Her voice trembled with emotion as she accepted her prize.*

emotional *adjective*
  1 to do with strong feelings, as in *The missing child's parents have been under great emotional stress.* **2** having or expressing strong feelings, as in *They said an emotional farewell and wept a lot.*
  emotionally *adverb*

emperor *noun* **emperors**
  a man who rules an empire.

emphasis *noun* **emphases**
  special importance given to something, as in *The emphasis on homework at the school was very clear.*
  emphatic *adjective*, **emphatically** *adverb*

emphasise or **emphasize** *verb*
  emphasises, emphasising, emphasised
  to give emphasis to something.

empire *noun* **empires**
  1 a group of countries ruled by one person or group of people, as in *the Roman Empire.* **2** a large business, organisation, etc. owned or directed by one person or group, as in *The Coles-Myer empire owns many stores.*

employ *verb* **employs, employing, employed**
  1 to pay someone to work for you. **2** to use something, as in *Fighter planes were employed by the enemy force.*

employee *noun* **employees** (*say* em-**ploi**-ee)
  someone who is employed by someone else.

employer *noun* **employers**
  someone who employs people.

employment *noun*
  1 employing someone; being employed.
  2 a job, as in *He has secure employment.*

empress *noun* **empresses**
  1 a female emperor. **2** the wife of an emperor.

empty *adjective* **emptier, emptiest**
  with nothing inside or on it.
  emptiness *noun*

empty *verb* **empties, emptying, emptied**
  to make something empty; to become empty.

emu *noun* **emus** (*say* ee-myoo)
  a large, Australian, grey-brown bird which cannot fly but is able to run at high speed.

emulate *verb* **emulates, emulating, emulated** (*say* em-yoo-layt)
  to try to copy or be similar to, as in *She tried to emulate her friend's calmness.*

emulsion *noun* **emulsions**
  1 a creamy mixture, especially medicine, paint, chemicals, etc., as in *an emulsion for soothing chickenpox; emulsion for developing photographs.*

enable *verb* **enables, enabling, enabled**
  to make something possible for someone, as in *This calculator enables you to multiply and divide.*

enamel *noun* **enamels**
  1 a shiny, glassy substance for coating metal, pottery, etc. **2** a hard, shiny paint. **3** the hard, shiny surface of teeth.

encamp *verb* **encamps, encamping, encamped**
  to settle in a camp.
  encampment *noun*

enchant *verb* **enchants, enchanting, enchanted**
  1 to delight someone. **2** to put a magic spell on someone.
  enchantment *noun*, **enchantress** *noun*

enchanting *adjective*
  able to delight someone, as in *She has an enchanting smile.*
  enchantingly *adverb*

enclose *verb* **encloses, enclosing, enclosed**
  1 to put something in a box, envelope, etc. **2** to put a fence, wall, etc. around something.
  enclosure *noun*

encore *noun* **encores**
  an extra item performed at a concert, show, etc. after the applause.

encounter *verb* **encounters, encountering, encountered**
  to come across someone or something unexpectedly.

encourage *verb* **encourages, encouraging, encouraged**
  to give someone confidence or hope; to support something.
  encouragement *noun*

encyclopaedia or **encyclopedia** *noun*
  encyclopaedias or **encyclopedias**
  a book or set of books containing all sorts of information.
  encyclopaedic, encyclopedic *adjective*

end *noun* **ends**
  1 the last part of something; the point where something stops. **2** the part that is

end

left after something has been used, as in *a cigarette end*. **3** an aim or purpose, as in *Her end is to win the debating competition*.
make ends meet, to spend no more money than you earn.
no end, (*colloquial*) very many; a great deal.
on end, upright; continuously, as in *His hair stood on end. She spoke for two hours on end*.

end *verb* **ends, ending, ended**
to finish.

endanger *verb* **endangers, endangering, endangered**
to put someone or something in a dangerous situation, as in *His foolish behaviour on the boat endangered the children's safety*.

endangered species *noun*
a species in danger of extinction, as in *The bilby is an endangered species*.

endeavour or **endeavor** *verb* **endeavours, endeavouring, endeavoured**
to try, as in *He endeavoured to please her*.

ending *noun* **endings**
the last part of something, as in *The story's ending was sad*.

endless *adjective*
1 never stopping, as in *endless patience*.
2 (*colloquial*) too many to be numbered, as in *endless complaints; endless debts*.
endlessly *adverb*

endorse *verb* **endorses, endorsing, endorsed**
to give your name or support to, as in *He endorsed his cheque. The generous person endorsed many charities*.

endure *verb* **endures, enduring, endured**
1 to bear or put up with pain, suffering, etc. **2** to continue; to last, as in *Your luck will not endure forever*.
endurance *noun*

enemy *noun* **enemies**
someone who hates you or wants to harm you.
the enemy, the nation or army that is at war with your country.

energetic *adjective*
1 full of energy, as in *an energetic puppy*.
2 done with energy, as in *an energetic dance*.
energetically *adverb*

energy *noun* **energies**
1 strength to do things; liveliness. **2** the ability to do work, as in *Solar energy heats the pool*.

enforce *verb* **enforces, enforcing, enforced**
to make people obey a law, order, etc.
enforceable *adjective*, **enforcement** *noun*

engage *verb* **engages, engaging, engaged**
1 to occupy or use. **2** to employ someone, as in *He engaged an assistant*.
3 to start a battle against someone. **4** to interlock, as in *The car moved when the gears engaged*.
engage in something, to take part in something.

engaged *adjective*
1 having promised to marry someone.
2 already being used, as in *Her telephone number is engaged*.

engagement *noun* **engagements**
1 being engaged. **2** an appointment to meet someone or do something, as in *an engagement for lunch*. **3** a battle.

engine *noun* **engines**
1 a motor. **2** a vehicle that pulls a railway train.

engineer *noun* **engineers**
an expert in engineering.

engineering *noun*
designing, building, or controlling engines, machines, bridges, docks, etc.

English *noun*
the language of England, now used in the United Kingdom, the United States, Australia and most Commonwealth countries.

engrave *verb* **engraves, engraving, engraved**
to carve lines, words, etc. on a hard surface.
engraver *noun*

engrossed *adjective*
with all your attention taken up, as in *I was engrossed in my work*.

engulf *verb* **engulfs, engulfing, engulfed**
to swallow up; to swamp, as in *The house was engulfed by fire*.

enhance *verb* **enhances, enhancing, enhanced**
to add to a thing's value or attractiveness, as in *The school play was enhanced by the wonderful costumes*.
enhancement *noun*

enjoy *verb* **enjoys, enjoying, enjoyed**
to get pleasure from something.
enjoyable *adjective*, **enjoyment** *noun*

enlarge *verb* **enlarges, enlarging, enlarged**
to make something bigger.
enlargement *noun*

enlist *verb* **enlists, enlisting, enlisted**
1 to join the armed forces; to bring someone into the armed forces. **2** to persuade someone to help or support you, as in *She enlisted my support in organising the fair*.
enlistment *noun*

enmity *noun* **enmities**
being someone's enemy; hatred, as in *The enmity between the two countries ended in war. The argument caused enmity between them.*

enormous *adjective*
huge.
enormously *adverb*

enough *adjective, noun,* and *adverb*
as much or as many as required, as in *There is enough food. I've had enough. He sings well enough to join the choir.*

enquire *verb* **enquires, enquiring, enquired**
to ask, as in *He enquired if I was well.*
enquiry *noun*

enrage *verb* **enrages, enraging, enraged**
to make a person or an animal very angry.
enraged *adjective*

enrich *verb* **enriches, enriching, enriched**
to make richer or improve the quality of something, as in *Profits enriched the company. Compost will enrich the soil.*
enrichment *noun*

enrol *verb* **enrols, enrolling, enrolled**
to make or become a member of a society, class, etc.
enrolment *noun*

en route *adverb* (*say* on-**root**)
on the way, as in *We stopped at Gundagai en route to Melbourne.*

ensemble *noun* **ensembles**
(*say* on-**som**-buhl)
1 a group of things that go together. 2 a group of musicians.

ensue *verb* **ensues, ensuing, ensued**
to happen afterwards; to follow, as in *After the teacher's absence from the classroom a fight ensued.*

en suite *noun* (*say* on **sweet**)
a small bathroom attached to a bedroom, as in *a house with an en suite.*

ensure *verb* **ensures, ensuring, ensured**
to make sure.

> **Usage** Do not confuse **ensure** with **insure**, which means to protect yourself or your goods with insurance.

entangle *verb* **entangles, entangling, entangled**
to tangle, as in *Her scarf became entangled in the bush.*
entanglement *noun*

enter *verb* **enters, entering, entered**
1 to come or go in. 2 to write something in a list, book, etc.; to put something into a computer, as in *Enter the data.* 3 to enrol; to go in for a contest, examination, etc.

enterprise *noun* **enterprises**
1 a challenging task or project, especially one that needs courage, as in *the ambitious enterprise of raising funds for refugees.* 2 the skill and willingness you need for such a task, as in *Her enterprise made her an excellent organiser.*

enterprising *adjective*
adventurous; courageous.

entertain *verb* **entertains, entertaining, entertained**
1 to amuse someone. 2 to have people as guests and give them food and drink.
entertainer *noun*, **entertainment** *noun*

enthusiasm *noun* **enthusiasms**
a strong liking for, or interest in, someone or something.

enthusiast *noun* **enthusiasts**
a person who has an enthusiasm for something, as in *a football enthusiast.*

enthusiastic *adjective*
full of enthusiasm, as in *She is very enthusiastic about her new hobby.*
enthusiastically *adverb*

entice *verb* **entices, enticing, enticed**
to attract with a promise of pleasure, reward, etc., as in *The window display enticed him to buy the cream cakes.*

entire *adjective*
whole, as in *The entire class went on an excursion.*
entirely *adverb*, **entirety** *noun*

entitle *verb* **entitles, entitling, entitled**
to give you a right to something, as in *You are entitled to three attempts in the long-jump event.*
entitled, having the title, as in *a book entitled 'The Magic Pudding'.*

entrance *noun* **entrances** (*say* **en**-truhns)
1 the way into a place. 2 the act of entering, as in *The actor made a grand entrance.*

entrance *verb* **entrances, entrancing, entranced** (*say* en-**trahns** or en-**trans**)
to enchant, as in *They were entranced when she played the violin.*

entrant *noun* **entrants**
someone who goes in for a contest, examination, etc.

entreat *verb* **entreats, entreating, entreated**
to ask someone seriously or desperately; to beg.
entreaty *noun*

entrée *noun* **entrées** (*say* **on**-tray)
the dish served before the main course of a meal.

entrust

entrust *verb* **entrusts, entrusting, entrusted**
to trust someone with something; to give
someone a thing to look after, as in *She
entrusted her necklace to me.*

entry *noun* **entries**
1 an entrance. 2 something written in a
list, diary, etc.

envelop *verb* **envelops, enveloping,
enveloped** (*say* en-**vel**-uhp)
1 to wrap something up. 2 to cover
someone or something completely, as in *a
mountain enveloped in mist.*

envelope *noun* **envelopes** (*say* en-vuh-lohp
or **on**-vuh-lohp)
a wrapper or covering, especially for a
letter.

envious *adjective*
feeling envy or having a strong desire for
another person's belongings, talents,
success, etc., as in *She was envious of her
friend's ability to swim well.*
enviously *adverb*

environment *noun* **environments**
surroundings, especially as they affect
people and other living things, as in *Some
animals and plants can die out if their
environment is damaged.*
environmental *adjective*

environmentalist *noun* **environmentalists**
a person who wants to protect or improve
the environment.

envy *noun*
a discontented feeling you have when
you want something that someone else
has got.

envy *verb* **envies, envying, envied**
to feel discontent or jealousy about a
person's possessions, talents, etc.

enzyme *noun* **enzymes**
a chemical substance that causes changes
such as digestion.

epic *noun* **epics**
a book, poem, or film which tells a story of
heroic deeds.

epic *adjective*
very impressive or heroic, as in *the sailor's
epic voyage around the world in a small yacht.*

epidemic *noun* **epidemics**
a disease spreading quickly through a
community.

epilepsy *noun*
a nervous disorder that makes a person's
body move uncontrollably, and which can
make the person become unconscious.
epileptic *adjective* and *noun*

epilogue *noun* **epilogues** (*say* ep-uh-log)
words written or spoken at the end of
something, especially a story or a play.

episode *noun* **episodes**
1 an incident in a series of events. 2 one
program in a radio or television serial.

epistle *noun* **epistles**
the Epistles, the letters written by Jesus's
apostles that are books in the New
Testament.

epitaph *noun* **epitaphs**
the words, in memory of a dead person,
written on a tomb or gravestone.

epoch *noun* **epochs** (*say* ee-pok)
an era or a long period in history, especially
one marked by notable events.
epoch-making, very important.

equal *adjective*
the same in amount, size, value, etc.
be equal to something, to be able to do
something, as in *He was equal to the task.*
equality *noun*, **equally** *adverb*

equal *noun* **equals**
a person or thing that is equal to another, as
in *The eminent heart surgeon had no equal.*

equal *verb* **equals, equalling, equalled**
to be the same in amount, size, value, etc.

equalise or **equalize** **equalises, equalising,
equalised**
to make things equal, as in *The scores were
equalised.*

equaliser or **equalizer** *noun* **equalisers**
a goal, etc. that makes the score equal.

equation *noun* **equations**
(*say* uh-**kway**-zhuhn *or* ee-**kway**-zhuhn)
(*in Mathematics*) a statement that two
amounts are equal, as in *In the equation
$x + 1 = 3$, x equals 2.*

equator *noun*
(*say* uh-**kway**-tuh *or* ee-**kway**-tuh)
an imaginary line round the earth at an
equal distance from the North and South
Poles, as in *Countries on or near the equator
have a very hot climate.*
equatorial *adjective*

equestrian *adjective*
to do with horse-riding, as in *an equestrian
event.*

equidistant *adjective*
at an equal distance, as in *The centre of a
circle is equidistant from all the points around
its circumference.*

equilateral *adjective*
(*say* eek-wuh-**lat**-uh-ruhl)
having all sides equal, as in *an equilateral
triangle.*

especially

equilateral triangle *noun*
a triangle that has three equal sides and three equal angles.

equilibrium *noun* **equilibria**
(*say* eek-wuh-**lib**-ree-uhm *or* ek-wuh-**lib**-ree-uhm)
balance; being balanced, as in *The scales were kept in equilibrium. Change can disturb some people's equilibrium.*

equinox *noun* **equinoxes**
each of the two times in the year when the day and night are of equal length (about 22 September and 20 March).

equip *verb* **equips, equipping, equipped**
to supply someone or something with what is needed, as in *Are you equipped for rock climbing?*

equipment *noun*
the things needed for a particular purpose, as in *sports equipment.*

equivalent *adjective*
equal in value, importance, meaning, etc.
equivalent fractions, fractions that have the same value, as in $^1/_2$, $^4/_8$, *and* $^5/_{10}$ *are equivalent fractions.*
equivalence *noun*

era *noun* **eras** (*say* **eer**-ruh)
a period in history, as in *the Elizabethan era; the post-war era.*

eradicate *verb* **eradicates, eradicating, eradicated**
to destroy completely, as in *Farmers have tried to eradicate rabbits.*

erase *verb* **erases, erasing, erased**
1 to rub out something.   2 to wipe out a recording on magnetic tape.
eraser *noun*

erect *adjective*
vertical; standing on end, as in *The soldier has an erect posture.*

erect *verb* **erects, erecting, erected**
1 to build.   2 to make something upright; to raise, as in *The goal posts were erected at the beginning of the football season.*
erection *noun*

ermine *noun* **ermine**
1 a kind of weasel with brown fur in summer and white fur in winter.   2 this white fur.

erode *verb* **erodes, eroding, eroded**
to wear away, as in *Water eroded the rocks.*

erosion *noun*
wearing something away, especially the destruction and removal of rock, soil, sand, etc. by the action of water or wind, as in

The removal of forests has made erosion a major problem for farmers.

errand *noun* **errands**
a short journey to take a message, fetch goods, etc.

erratic *adjective* (*say* uh-**rat**-ik)
not reliable or regular.
erratically *adverb*

error *noun* **errors**
a mistake.
in error, by mistake; mistaken.
erroneous *adjective*

erupt *verb* **erupts, erupting, erupted**
to burst or break out suddenly; to explode, as in *The crowd erupted into applause. The volcano erupted.*
eruption *noun*

escalate *verb* **escalates, escalating, escalated**
to get or make gradually greater or more serious, as in *The riots escalated into a war.*
escalation *noun*

escalator *noun* **escalators**
a staircase with an endless line of steps moving up or down.

escape *verb* **escapes, escaping, escaped**
1 to get free; to get away.   2 to avoid something, as in *He escaped punishment.*

escape *noun* **escapes**
1 the act of escaping, as in *The great escape from prison made headlines.*   2 a way to escape from something, as in *Holidays are the best escape from work.*

escort *noun* **escorts** (*say* **es**-kawt)
1 a person who accompanies someone, especially to give protection.   2 a group of ships, aircraft, etc. accompanying someone or something.

escort *verb* **escorts, escorting, escorted** (*say* uhs-**kawt**)
to act as an escort to someone or something.

Eskimo *noun* **Eskimos** *or* **Eskimo**
one of the people who live in very cold parts of North Canada, Alaska, Greenland, and eastern Siberia.

Usage The official name of the people who live in the far north of the North American continent is *Inuit.*

esky *noun* **eskies**
trademark a portable container with special insulation for keeping food and drink cool.

especially *adverb*
chiefly; more than anything else, as in *I like cakes, especially cream cakes.*

a b c d e f g h i j k l m n o p q r s t u v w x y z

espionage

espionage *noun* (*say* es-pee-uh-nahzh)
spying or the use of spies, especially by a government.

esplanade *noun* **esplanades**
a long, open, level area or street for walking on, especially by the sea, as in *the esplanade at St Kilda in Melbourne*.

espresso or **expresso** *noun*
strong black coffee made under steam pressure.

Esq. short for **Esquire**.

Esquire *noun*
an old-fashioned title put after a man's name in addressing formal letters, etc., as in *To Sam Browne, Esquire*.

essay *noun* **essays**
a short piece of writing about a particular subject.

essence *noun* **essences**
1 the most important quality or ingredient of something, as in *The essence of success is usually hard work*. 2 a concentrated liquid, as in *vanilla essence*.

essential *adjective*
necessary, as in *Water is essential to life*.
essentially *adverb*

essential *noun* **essentials**
an essential thing, as in *A passport is an essential when travelling overseas*.

establish *verb* **establishes, establishing, established**
to start a business, government, relationship, etc.

establishment *noun* **establishments**
1 setting up something, as in *the establishment of a new school*. 2 a place where business is carried on; an organisation, as in *a banking establishment*.
the Establishment, people in positions of power and influence.

estate *noun* **estates**
1 an area of land with lots of houses or factories on it. 2 a large area of land belonging to one person. 3 everything that a person owns when he or she dies.

estate agent *noun* **estate agents**
someone whose business is selling or renting buildings and land.

esteem *verb* **esteems, esteeming, esteemed**
to think that a person or thing is excellent.

estimate *noun* **estimates** (*say* es-tuh-muht)
a calculation or guess about the amount or value of something.

estimate *verb* **estimates, estimating, estimated** (*say* es-tuh-mayt)
to make an estimate or calculation, as in *The crowd was estimated at 80,000*.
estimation *noun*

estuary *noun* **estuaries** (*say* es-tyoo-uh-ree *or* es-choo-uh-ree)
the mouth of a large river where it flows into the sea.

etc. short for *et cetera*.

et cetera and other similar things; and so on.

etch *verb* **etches, etching, etched**
1 to make a picture by engraving on a metal plate or glass with an acid. 2 to impress deeply, especially on the mind, as in *The beautiful scene was etched in her memory*.
etching *noun*

eternal *adjective*
lasting for ever; not ending or changing.
eternally *adverb*, **eternity** *noun*

ether *noun* (*say* ee-thuh)
a colourless liquid made from alcohol, used as an anaesthetic or a solvent.

ethics *plural noun*
a set of beliefs and rules about our ideas of right and wrong, as in *His ethics prevented him from cheating*.

ethnic *adjective*
to do with a national, racial, or tribal group, as in *The Australian population consists of many ethnic groups*.
ethnic cleansing, the mass killing or removal of one ethnic group by another.

etymology *noun* **etymologies**
1 the study of words and where they come from. 2 a description of where a word came from and how it developed.

eucalypt *noun* **eucalypts**
a gum tree.

eucalyptus *noun* **eucalyptuses** (*say* yoo-kuh-**lip**-tuhs)
a mainly Australian evergreen tree from which timber and an oil is obtained.

euphemism *noun* **euphemisms**
a word or phrase which is used instead of an impolite or less tactful one, as in *'Pass away' is a euphemism for 'die'*.
euphemistic *adjective*

euro *noun* **euros** (*say* **yoo**-roh)
1 a short-haired type of kangaroo from the drier parts of Australia. 2 currency of Europe.

Origin This word comes from the Aboriginal language Adnyamathanha: **yuru, thuru**. See the Aboriginal Languages map at the back of this dictionary.

European *adjective*
to do with Europe, as in *a European holiday*.
European Community or **European Economic Community**, a group of countries in Europe that trade freely together.

euthanasia *noun*
(*say* yoo-thuh-**nay**-zhee-uh)
causing someone to die gently and painlessly when he or she is suffering from an incurable disease.

evacuate *verb* **evacuates, evacuating, evacuated**
to move people away from a dangerous place.
evacuation *noun*, **evacuee** *noun*

evade *verb* **evades, evading, evaded**
to avoid.
evasion *noun*, **evasive** *adjective*

evaluate *verb* **evaluates, evaluating, evaluated**
to estimate the value of something.
evaluation *noun*

evangelist *noun* **evangelists**
someone who tells people about the Christian gospel.
evangelical *adjective*, **evangelism** *noun*

evaporate *verb* **evaporates, evaporating, evaporated**
1 to change from liquid into steam or vapour. 2 to remove moisture by heating a liquid.
evaporated milk, milk that has been thickened by evaporating water from it.
evaporation *noun*

eve *noun* **eves**
1 the day or evening before an important day, as in *Christmas Eve*. 2 the time just before an event, as in *the eve of the election*.

even *adjective*
1 equal, as in *Our scores were even*.
2 smooth; level, as in *He has an even temper*. 3 (*in Mathematics*) that can be divided exactly by two, as in *Six and fourteen are even numbers*.
get even with someone, to take revenge on someone, as in *I'll get even with him*.
evenly *adverb*, **evenness** *noun*

even *adverb*
1 so much as, as in *You haven't even started your work!* 2 still more so, as in *I ran fast, but Nick ran even faster*. 3 remarkably enough, as in *She even ignored her mother*.

even if, although.
even now, at this moment.
even so, nevertheless.

even *verb* **evens, evening, evened**
to make something even; to become even.

evening *noun* **evenings**
the time at the end of the day before most people go to bed.
evening dress, formal clothes worn to an official function, ball, etc.

event *noun* **events**
1 something that happens, especially something important. 2 an item in a sports program, as in *the diving event*.
at all events or **in any event**, anyway.

eventful *adjective*
full of happenings, especially remarkable or exciting ones, as in *The cyclist made an eventful journey across the Nullarbor*.

eventual *adjective*
happening at last or as a result, as in *Many failures preceded his eventual success*.

eventually *adverb*
1 finally, as in *Eventually, after many failures, he succeeded*. 2 sooner or later, as in *Don't worry, we'll get there eventually*.

ever *adverb*
1 at any time, as in *It's the best present I've ever had*. 2 always, as in *ever hopeful*.
3 at all, as in *Why ever didn't you tell me?*
ever since, through the time since, as in *Ever since she was chosen as captain, she has ignored her old friend*.

evergreen *adjective*
having green leaves all through the year, as in *evergreen trees*.

everlasting *adjective*
lasting for ever or for a long time.
everlasting daisy, a brightly-coloured flower with stiff, papery petals.

every *adjective*
all the people or things of a particular kind; each, as in *Every child should learn to swim*.
every bit as ... as, exactly as good, bad, etc. as someone or something.
every other day, week, etc., each alternate one; every second one.

everybody *pronoun*
everyone.

everyday *adjective*
happening or used every day; ordinary, as in *an everyday occurrence*.

everyone *pronoun*
every person; all people, as in *Everyone likes her*.

a
b
c
d
e
f
g
h
i
j
k
l
m
n
o
p
q
r
s
t
u
v
w
x
y
z

everything

everything *pronoun*
1 all things; all, as in *Everything you need is here.* 2 the only or most important thing, as in *Beauty is not everything.*

everywhere *adverb*
in all places.

evict *verb* **evicts, evicting, evicted**
to make someone move out of a house, flat, etc.
eviction *noun*

evidence *noun*
anything that gives people reason to believe something, as in *A cough is evidence of a cold. The evidence convicted the criminal.*
in evidence, clearly seen.

evident *adjective*
obvious, as in *It is evident that he is lying.*
evidently *adverb*

evil *adjective*
wicked; harmful.
evilly *adverb*

evil *noun* **evils**
something evil; a sin, as in *Slavery was a great evil.*

evolution *noun* (*say* eev-uh-**loo**-shuhn *or* ev-uh-**loo**-shuhn)
1 gradual change into something different. 2 the development of animals and plants from earlier or simpler forms of life.
evolutionary *adjective*

evolve *verb* **evolves, evolving, evolved**
to develop gradually or naturally.

ewe *noun* **ewes** (*say* yoo)
a female sheep.

exact *adjective*
1 correct, as in *exact change.* 2 giving all the details, as in *an exact description.*
exactly *adverb*, **exactness** *noun*

exaggerate *verb* **exaggerates, exaggerating, exaggerated**
to make something seem bigger, better, worse, etc. than it really is.
exaggeration *noun*

exalt *verb* **exalts, exalting, exalted**
1 to make higher or greater. 2 to praise someone highly.

exam *noun* **exams**
an examination.

examination *noun* **examinations**
1 a test of someone's knowledge or skill.
2 a close inspection of something, as in *A chest examination can detect lung disease.*

examine *verb* **examines, examining, examined**
to look into, test, or check something.

examiner *noun* **examiners**
a person who sets and marks an examination to test students' knowledge.

example *noun* **examples**
1 a single thing or event that shows what a group of things or an event is like, as in *Hepatitis is an example of a contagious disease.* 2 a person or thing that you should copy or learn from, as in *Parents like to set a good example for their children.*
for example, as an example.

exasperate *verb* **exasperates, exasperating, exasperated**
to make someone very annoyed.
exasperation *noun*

excavate *verb* **excavates, excavating, excavated**
to make a hole or uncover by digging, as in *They excavated the site for the new office block. The ancient city was excavated by the archaeologists.*
excavation *noun*, **excavator** *noun*

exceed *verb* **exceeds, exceeding, exceeded**
1 to be greater than something else. 2 to do more than you need or ought to do, as in *The driver was exceeding the speed limit.*

exceedingly *adverb*
extremely; very much, as in *I am exceedingly grateful for your help.*

Usage Do not confuse **exceedingly** with **excessively,** which means too much or too greatly.

excel *verb* **excels, excelling, excelled**
excel at something, to be very good at something.

excellent *adjective*
extremely good.
excellence *noun*

except *preposition*
not including; apart from, as in *Everyone got a prize except me.*

Usage Do not confuse **except** with **accept,** which is a verb meaning to take something which is offered, or to agree with something.

exception *noun* **exceptions**
something that does not follow the normal rule or something not included, as in *Everyone wore school uniform with the exception of the new student. Everything was free with the exception of drinks.*
take exception to something, to be offended by something.

exceptional *adjective*
unusual or outstanding, as in *Permission will be granted only in very exceptional circumstances. She has exceptional computing skills.*
exceptionally *adverb*

excerpt *noun* **excerpts**
a piece taken from a book, play, film, etc.

excess *noun* **excesses**
too much of something, as in *We have an excess of food.*

Usage Do not confuse **excess** with **access**, which means a way to reach something.

excessive *adjective*
too much or too great.
excessively *adverb*

Usage Do not confuse **excessively** with **exceedingly**, which means extremely or very much.

exchange *verb* **exchanges, exchanging, exchanged**
to give something and receive something else for it.

exchange *noun* **exchanges**
1 the act of exchanging, as in *the exchange of Christmas gifts.* 2 a place where telephone lines are connected to each other when a call is made. 3 a place where company shares, etc. are bought and sold, as in *the stock exchange.*
exchange program, an arrangement in which groups of pupils from two schools, usually in different countries, each go for a while to the other school.

excite *verb* **excites, exciting, excited**
1 to make someone feel strongly, as in *Racism excites anger in many people.* 2 to make someone lively, active, etc., as in *The child was excited by the new toy.*
excitable *adjective*, **excitedly** *adverb*

excitement *noun* **excitements**
1 being excited, as in *She felt excitement on her birthday.* 2 something that excites you, as in *the excitement of the circus for children.*

exclaim *verb* **exclaims, exclaiming, exclaimed**
to shout or cry out.

exclamation *noun* **exclamations**
1 the act of exclaiming. 2 a word or phrase that expresses surprise, pain, delight, etc.

exclamation mark *noun*
the punctuation mark '!' placed after an exclamation.

exclude *verb* **excludes, excluding, excluded**
to shut or keep someone or something out.
exclusion *noun*

exclusive *adjective*
1 used or owned by only one person or group and not shared with anyone else, as in *Guests have exclusive use of the hotel pool.* 2 not allowing many people to be involved, as in *an exclusive club for very wealthy people.*
exclusively *adverb*

excrete *verb* **excretes, excreting, excreted**
to pass waste matter out of your body.
excrement *noun*, **excretion** *noun*, **excretory** *adjective*

excursion *noun* **excursions**
a short journey made for pleasure, study, etc.

excuse *verb* **excuses, excusing, excused**
(*say* ek-**skyooz** *or* uhk-**skyooz**)
1 to forgive. 2 to allow someone not to do something, or to leave a room, etc., as in *Please may I be excused from swimming?*
excuse me, a polite apology for interrupting, disagreeing, etc.
excusable *adjective*, **excusably** *adverb*

excuse *noun* **excuses** (*say* ek-**skyoos** *or* uhk-**skyoos**)
a reason given to explain why something wrong has been done.

execute *verb* **executes, executing, executed**
1 to kill someone as a punishment. 2 to perform or produce something, as in *She executed a perfect somersault on the trampoline.*
execution *noun*, **executioner** *noun*

executive *noun* **executives**
a senior person in a business or government organisation.

exempt *adjective*
not having to do something, as in *The injured student was exempt from sport.*
exemption *noun*

exercise *noun* **exercises**
1 activity needing physical effort to make your body strong and healthy. 2 a piece of work done for practice, as in *piano exercises.*
exercise book, a book for writing in.

exercise *verb* **exercises, exercising, exercised**
1 to do exercises. 2 to give exercise to an animal, etc. 3 to use something, as in *You will have to exercise patience.*

Usage Do not confuse **exercise** with **exorcise**, which means to get rid of an evil spirit.

a
b
c
d
e
f
g
h
i
j
k
l
m
n
o
p
q
r
s
t
u
v
w
x
y
z

exert

exert *verb* **exerts, exerting, exerted**
to use power, influence, etc., as in *He exerted all his strength to bend the bar. She exerted her influence to get her friend a job.*
exert yourself, to make an effort.
exertion *noun*

exhale *verb* **exhales, exhaling, exhaled**
to breathe out; to send out something with your breath.
exhalation *noun*

exhaust *verb* **exhausts, exhausting, exhausted**
1 to make someone very tired.   2 to use up something completely, as in *The food supplies were soon exhausted by the hungry campers.*
exhaustion *noun*

exhaust *noun* **exhausts**
1 the waste gases from an engine.   2 the pipe these gases are sent out through.

exhibit *verb* **exhibits, exhibiting, exhibited**
to display or show something in public.
exhibitor *noun*

exhibit *noun* **exhibits**
something displayed in public, as in *an art exhibit.*

exhibition *noun* **exhibitions**
a collection of things arranged for people to look at.

exile *verb* **exiles, exiling, exiled**
to be sent away from your country so that you must live somewhere else, especially for political reasons.

exile *noun* **exiles**
1 a person who has been forced to live in another country.   2 the long absence from your own country, as in *He was in exile for ten years.*

exist *verb* **exists, existing, existed**
1 to be; to be real, as in *Do ghosts exist?*
2 to stay alive, as in *They existed on biscuits and water.*

existence *noun* **existences**
1 the fact of existing or being, as in *Dinosaurs are no longer in existence.*
2 staying alive, as in *a struggle for existence.*

exit *noun* **exits**
1 the way out of a building, hall, etc.
2 going off the stage, as in *The actress made her exit.*

exit *verb* **exits, exiting, exited**
to leave the stage, a room, etc., as in *The narrator exits.*

exodus *noun*
a mass departure of people or things, as in *a population exodus to avoid the floods.*

exorcise or **exorcize** *verb* **exorcises, exorcising, exorcised**
to get rid of an evil spirit.
exorcism *noun*, **exorcist** *noun*

> **Usage** Do not confuse **exorcise** with **exercise**, which means to do exercises, to give exercise to an animal, etc., or to use something.

exotic *adjective*
unusual; foreign or not native to your own country, as in *She loved to cook exotic food. The exotic plant needed special care in our climate.*

expand *verb* **expands, expanding, expanded**
to make or become larger.
expansion *noun*

expanse *noun* **expanses**
a wide area, as in *an expanse of desert.*

expect *verb* **expects, expecting, expected**
1 to think that something will probably happen or that someone will come, as in *We expected it would rain.*   2 to think that something ought to happen, as in *She expects us to be obedient.*   3 to be pregnant, as in *She is expecting.*

expectant *adjective*
1 pregnant, as in *an expectant mother.*
2 full of expectation or hope.
expectantly *adverb*

expectation *noun* **expectations**
1 a strong hope that something will happen or that you will get something that you want, as in *the expectation of a party on your birthday.*   2 a strong belief that something is likely to happen, as in *The dark clouds brought an expectation of rain.*

expecting *adjective*
pregnant, as in *an expecting mother.*

expedition *noun* **expeditions**
a journey made in order to do something, as in *a climbing expedition.*

expel *verb* **expels, expelling, expelled**
1 to send or force something out, as in *This fan expels stale air.*   2 to make someone leave a school, country, etc., as in *He was expelled for bullying.*

expenditure *noun*
spending, as in *We must reduce our expenditure.*

expense *noun* **expenses**
the cost of something, as in *We bought the house at great expense. The war was won at the expense of many lives.*

expenses, money used or claimed for something particular, as in *travelling expenses.*

expensive *adjective*
costing a lot of money.

experience *noun* **experiences**
1 what you learn from doing and seeing things. **2** something that has happened to you.

experience *verb* **experiences, experiencing, experienced**
to have something happen to you, as in *This is the hottest summer I have ever experienced.*

experienced *adjective*
1 having much experience, as in *She is an experienced traveller.* **2** skilled and knowledgeable, as in *an experienced teacher.*

experiment *noun* **experiments**
a test made in order to study what happens.
experimental *adjective*, **experimentally** *adverb*

experiment *verb* **experiments, experimenting, experimented**
to carry out experiments.
experimentation *noun*, **experimenter** *noun*

expert *adjective*
skilful; knowledgeable, as in *an expert driver.*

expert *noun* **experts**
someone who has skill or special knowledge in a particular subject, as in *an expert in heart surgery.*

expertise *noun*
the knowledge or skill that an expert has.

expire *verb* **expires, expiring, expired**
1 to come to an end; to stop being usable, as in *Your driver's licence has expired.* **2** to die.
expiry *noun*

explain *verb* **explains, explaining, explained**
1 to make something clear to someone else, as in *The teacher explained the rules.* **2** to show why something happens, as in *Please explain your lateness.*
explanatory *adjective*

explanation *noun* **explanations**
an oral or written text that tells how or why something took place.

explode *verb* **explodes, exploding, exploded**
1 to burst or suddenly release energy with a loud bang. **2** to set off a bomb. **3** to increase suddenly or quickly, as in *Food prices exploded during the shortage.*

exploit *noun* **exploits** (*say* **eks**-ploit)
a brave or exciting deed, as in *the exploits of astronauts.*

exploit *verb* **exploits, exploiting, exploited**
(*say* ek-**sploit** *or* uhk-**sploit**)
1 to use or develop resources, as in *The oil resources were exploited to provide necessary fuel.* **2** to use something or someone selfishly, as in *She exploited the good nature of her friend.*
exploitation *noun*

explore *verb* **explores, exploring, explored**
1 to travel through a country, etc. in order to learn about it. **2** to examine something, as in *He explored his body for signs of the disease.*
exploration *noun*, **exploratory** *adjective*, **explorer** *noun*

explosion *noun* **explosions**
1 the exploding of a bomb, petrol tank, etc. **2** a sudden or quick increase, as in *the population explosion.*

explosive *adjective*
likely to explode; able to cause an explosion, as in *an explosive situation caused by the meeting of old enemies; explosive fireworks.*
explosively *adverb*

explosive *noun* **explosives**
an explosive substance, as in *Dynamite is an explosive.*

export *verb* **exports, exporting, exported**
(*say* ek-**spawt** *or* ek-spawt)
to send goods overseas to be sold.
exporter *noun*

export *noun* **exports** (*say* **ek**-spawt)
something that is sent overseas to be sold.

expose *verb* **exposes, exposing, exposed**
1 to reveal or uncover something, as in *She exposed her skin to the sun.* **2** to show that someone has done wrong; to make someone's crimes known. **3** to put at risk, as in *The fireman exposed himself to danger when he rescued the child.* **4** to let light reach a film in a camera, so as to take a picture.

exposition *noun* **expositions**
1 an oral or written text that gives one view about a topic. **2** a large public exhibition.

exposure *noun* **exposures**
1 revealing or uncovering; being uncovered and being harmed by the weather, as in *The exposure of his secrets*

express
150

embarrassed him. *The mountaineers were suffering from exposure.* **2** letting light reach a film in a camera; a section of film used for making one picture, as in *This film has 24 exposures.*

express *verb* **expresses, expressing, expressed**
to put an idea or feeling into words.

express *adjective*
going or sent very quickly, as in *an express train; express mail.*

express *noun* **expresses**
a fast train or bus stopping at few stations.

expression *noun* **expressions**
1 the look on a person's face. **2** a word or phrase. **3** a way of speaking, playing music, etc. that conveys feelings.
expressionless *adjective,* **expressive** *adjective*

expulsion *noun* **expulsions**
the act of expelling or being expelled, as in *expulsion of air from tyres; the student's expulsion from school for stealing.*

exquisite *adjective*
very delicate or beautiful.
exquisitely *adverb*

extend *verb* **extends, extending, extended**
1 to stretch out, as in *The property extended to the coast.* **2** to make something longer or large, as in *The new owner plans to extend the house.* **3** to offer or give, as in *Extend a welcome to your friends.*

extension *noun* **extensions**
1 the act of extending, as in *an extension of friendship to the new neighbours.*
2 something added on, as in *We are building an extension at the back of the house.* **3** an extra telephone in an office, house, etc.

extensive *adjective*
wide or large, as in *extensive gardens.*
extensively *adverb*

extent *noun* **extents**
1 the area or length of something.
2 amount or level, as in *The extent of the damage was enormous.*

exterior *noun* **exteriors**
the outside of something.

exterminate *verb* **exterminates, exterminating, exterminated**
to destroy or kill.
extermination *noun*

external *adjective*
outside, as in *Some houses in the bush have external toilets.*
externally *adverb*

extinct *adjective*
1 not existing any more, as in *The dodo is an extinct bird.* **2** not active, as in *an extinct volcano.*
extinction *noun*

extinguish *verb* **extinguishes, extinguishing, extinguished**
to put out a fire or light.
extinguisher *noun*

extra *adjective*
more than usual; added, as in *There is an extra charge for sauce with your pie.*

extra *noun* **extras**
1 an extra person or thing, as in *We have one extra for dinner.* **2** someone acting as part of the crowd in a film or play. **3** a run in cricket scored without the bat hitting the ball.

extract *verb* **extracts, extracting, extracted**
(*say* ek-**strakt** *or* uhk-**strakt**)
to remove; to take something out of something else, especially by effort or force
extraction *noun,* **extractor** *noun*

extract *noun* **extracts** (*say* **eks**-trakt)
1 a piece taken from a book, play, film, etc. **2** something obtained from something else, as in *a plant extract.*

extraction *noun*
1 taking something out, as in *the extraction of minerals from rock.* **2** the removal of a tooth. **3** the place or people that you come from, as in *She is of Irish extraction.*

extraordinary *adjective*
unusual; very strange.
extraordinarily *adverb*

extraterrestrial *adjective*
existing beyond the planet Earth, as in *extraterrestrial worlds.*

extraterrestrial *noun* **extraterrestrials**
a living thing from somewhere outside the planet Earth.

extravagant *adjective*
spending too much; stupidly wasteful, as in *an extravagant use of resources.*
extravagance *noun,* **extravagantly** *adverb*

extreme *adjective*
1 very great or strong, as in *extreme cold.*
2 farthest away, as in *the extreme edge of the playground.*
extremity *noun*

extreme *noun* **extremes**
1 something very great, strong, or far away, as in *extremes in distance.* **2** either end of something, as in *the extremes of the swimming pool.*

a b c d e f g h i j k l m n o p q r s t u v w x y z

eyewitness

in the extreme, extremely.
to extremes, to extreme or unreasonable behaviour, as in *He was driven to extremes.*

extremely *adverb*
as much or as far as possible; very much.

exuberant *adjective*
very cheerful or lively.
exuberance *noun*

exult *verb* **exults, exulting, exulted**
to rejoice; to be very pleased about a victory, as in *The ex-prisoner exulted in his freedom.*
exultant *adjective,* **exultation** *noun*

eye *noun* **eyes**
1 the part of the head used for seeing. 2 the small hole in a needle.

eye *verb* **eyes, eyeing, eyed**
to look at someone or something closely.

eyeball *noun* **eyeballs**
the ball-shaped part of the eye.

eyebrow *noun* **eyebrows**
a curved fringe of hair growing above your eye.

eyelash *noun* **eyelashes**
one of the short hairs that grow on an eyelid.

eyelid *noun* **eyelids**
the upper or lower cover of the eyeball.

eye-opener *noun* **eye-openers**
(*colloquial*) something that surprises or shocks you, as in *Hearing about the number of homeless people was an eye-opener for me.*

eyepiece *noun* **eyepieces**
the lens of a telescope, microscope, etc. that you put to your eye.

eyesight *noun*
the ability to see.

eyesore *noun* **eyesores**
something ugly to look at, as in *That rubbish tip is an eyesore.*

eyewitness *noun* **eyewitnesses**
someone who actually saw an accident, crime, etc.
eyewitness account, a description of something that happened, made by someone who saw it happen.

Ff

fable *noun* **fables**
a story which teaches a lesson connected with right and wrong, as in *the fable of 'The Boy who Cried Wolf'.*

fabric *noun* **fabrics**
cloth, as in *woollen fabric.*

fabricate *verb* **fabricates, fabricating, fabricated**
1 to make something, especially in a factory. 2 to invent a story, etc., as in *He fabricated an excuse.*

fabulous *adjective*
1 incredibly great, as in *fabulous wealth.*
2 (*colloquial*) wonderful; marvellous.
3 spoken of or described in myths, as in *Dragons are fabulous creatures.*

face *noun* **faces**
1 the front part of your head. 2 the look on a person's face, as in *She had a sour face.* 3 the front of something, as in *Put the cards face down.* 4 a surface, as in *A cube has six faces.*
face to face, looking directly at someone.
in the face of something, in spite of something.
face washer, a cloth for washing the face.
facial *adjective*

face *verb* **faces, facing, faced**
1 to look in a certain direction; to have the front in a particular direction, as in *The church faces the school.* 2 to meet or deal with someone or something confidently or bravely, as in *You will have to face the facts.*

faces *noun*
the surfaces of a solid shape.

facet *noun* **facets** (*say* **fas**-uht)
1 one aspect or view of something. 2 one side of a many-sided object like a diamond.

facetious *adjective* (*say* fuh-**see**-shuhs)
trying to be funny when you should not.
facetiously *adverb*

facilitate *verb* **facilitates, facilitating, facilitated**
to make something easier, as in *Computerisation greatly facilitated the work of the post office.*

facility *noun* **facilities** (*say* fuh-**sil**-uh-tee)
1 something that helps you to do things, as in *The youth club has facilities for dancing and sport.* 2 easiness; skill, as in *They all learned to read and write with great facility. He has a facility for languages and was soon fluent in Japanese.*

fact *noun* **facts**
something that is true or certain.
as a matter of fact or **in fact**, really.
the facts of life, knowledge of how humans have sex and produce babies.

faction *noun* **factions**
1 a small group within a larger group who hold different opinions, etc., especially in politics. 2 (in Western Australia) a sports house or team within a school or club, as in *Red faction won the carnival.*

factor *noun*
1 something that helps to bring about a result or situation, as in *Good publicity was a factor in our firm's success.* 2 a whole number that when multiplied with another whole number produces a given result, as in $2 \times 3 = 6$: *'2' and '3' are factors of '6'.*

factory *noun* **factories**
a large building where machines are used to make things.

facts and figures *plural noun*
the precise details of something.

factual *adjective*
based on fact; real.
factually *adverb*

fad *noun* **fads**
1 a craze, as in *The fad for hoops comes and goes.* 2 someone's particular like or dislike, as in *He has a fad about what food he will and will not eat.*

fade *verb* **fades, fading, faded**
1 to lose colour, freshness, or strength. 2 to disappear gradually. 3 to make a sound, etc. become gradually weaker or stronger.

faeces *plural noun* (*say* **fee**-seez)
solid waste that is sent out of the body.

Fahrenheit *adjective* (*say* **fa**-ruhn-huyt)
using a scale for measuring temperature that gives 32 degrees for freezing water and 212 degrees for boiling water.

fail *verb* **fails, failing, failed**
1 to try to do something but not being able to do it. 2 to become weak or useless; to come to an end, as in *Her eyesight is failing. The crops failed.* 3 not to do something, as in *He failed to warn me.*

fail *noun* **fails**
not being successful in an examination, etc., as in *She has five passes and one fail.*
without fail, definitely, as in *I'll be there without fail.*

failing *noun* **failings**
a fault or weakness, as in *Laziness is his main failing.*

failure *noun* **failures**
1 not being a success. 2 someone or something that has failed.

faint *adjective* **fainter, faintest**
1 weak; not clear or distinct. 2 nearly unconscious; exhausted, as in *She felt faint in the heat.*
faintly *adverb,* **faintness** *noun*

faint *verb* **faints, fainting, fainted**
to become unconscious for a short time.

faint-hearted *adjective*
lacking in courage and confidence.

fair *adjective* **fairer, fairest**
1 right or just; honest, as in *It's not fair! Fair prices were maintained.* 2 light in colour, as in *fair hair.* 3 moderate; quite good, as in *a fair number of offers. I've got a fair idea of what is needed.* 4 fine; favourable, as in *fair weather.*
fair dinkum, true, genuine.
fair go, (*colloquial*) a reasonable chance.
fairness *noun*

fair *noun* **fairs**
1 a group of outdoor entertainments like rides, sideshows, and stalls. 2 an exhibition or market, as in *a book fair; a trade fair.*

fairly *adverb*
1 honestly; justly. 2 moderately; quite, as in *It is fairly hard.*

fairy *noun* **fairies**
an imaginary small creature who can do magic.
fairy bread, bread buttered and sprinkled with hundreds and thousands.
fairy godmother, someone who helps you by magic.
fairy story or **fairy tale,** a story about fairies; an unbelievable story.
fairyland *noun*

fairy penguin *noun* **fairy penguins**
a small penguin with a steel-blue back and a white front, found on the southern coasts of Australia.

faith *noun* **faiths**
1 strong belief or trust. 2 a religion, as in *the Christian faith.*
in good faith, honestly; trustingly.
faithless *adjective*

faithful *adjective*
reliable; trustworthy.
faithfully *adverb,* **faithfulness** *noun*

fake *noun* **fakes**
a copy of something made to deceive people.

fake *verb* **fakes, faking, faked**
1 to make something that looks real so as to deceive people. 2 to pretend, as in *He faked illness in order to miss sport.*
faker *noun*

falcon *noun* **falcons**
a small kind of hawk with a keen eye for hunting its prey.
falconry *noun*

fall *verb* **falls, falling, fell, fallen**
1 to come down; to drop down, especially suddenly. 2 to decrease, as in *Prices fall during sales.* 3 to be captured or overthrown, as in *The city fell after a long siege.* 4 to die in battle, as in *Many soldiers fell in the battle of Long Tan.* 5 to happen, as in *Silence fell.*
6 to become, as in *She has fallen ill.* 7 to come or be directed at, as in *His glance fell on me.*
fall back on, to use for support or in an emergency.
fall down, to fail.

fall

fall for, to be attracted or convinced by.
fall out, to quarrel; to leave your place in a military line.
fall through, to fail.

fall *noun* **falls**
the act of falling or dropping, as in *She had a nasty fall*.
falls, a waterfall.

fallacy *noun* **fallacies**
a false idea or belief.
fallacious *adjective*

fall-out *noun*
radioactive dust, etc. from a nuclear explosion, especially when carried by the wind.

fallow *adjective*
ploughed but not sown with crops, as in *The field was left fallow every three years*.

false *adjective* **falser, falsest**
1 untrue; incorrect. 2 artificial; fake, as in *false teeth. He tried to use a false passport but was caught.* 3 treacherous; deceitful, as in *a false friend*.
falsely *adverb*, **falseness** *noun*, **falsity** *noun*

falsehood *noun* **falsehoods**
a lie.

falter *verb* **falters, faltering, faltered**
to hesitate when you move or speak.

fame *noun*
the state of being famous, as in *Her fame as a writer spread when her stories were adapted for television*.
famed *adjective*

familiar *adjective*
1 well-known; often seen or experienced, as in *a familiar sight.* 2 knowing something well, as in *Are you familiar with Shakespeare's plays?*
familiarity *noun*, **familiarly** *adverb*

family *noun* **families**
1 parents and their children, sometimes including grandchildren and other relations. 2 a group of things that are alike in some way, as in *a tree belonging to the eucalypt family*.
family allowance, government financial assistance to help in the cost of rearing children.
family planning, deciding how many babies to have and when to have them; birth control.
family tree, a diagram showing how people in a family are related.

famine *noun* **famines**
a very bad shortage of food.

famished *adjective*
very hungry.

famous *adjective*
known to a lot of people; very well known, as in *a famous scientist*.

fan *noun* **fans**
1 a device for making the air move about, so as to cool people or things. 2 an enthusiast, as in *a football fan*.

fan *verb* **fans, fanning, fanned**
to send a draught of air at something, as in *She fanned her face with her hand*.
fan out, to spread out.

fanatic *noun* **fanatics** (*say* fuh-**nat**-ik)
someone who is too enthusiastic about something, as in *The athlete became a fanatic about body building*.
fanatical *adjective*, **fanatically** *adverb*

fan belt *noun* **fan belts**
a belt driving the fan that cools a vehicle's radiator.

fancy *noun* **fancies**
1 a liking or desire for something, as in *a fancy for a cream cake*. 2 something existing in the imagination, as in *The fancy of holidays on the moon was the story's plot*.

fancy *adjective* **fancier, fanciest**
decorated; not plain, as in *fancy cakes*.
fancy dress, unusual costume worn to parties, dances, etc.

fancy *verb* **fancies, fancying, fancied**
1 (*colloquial*) to want or desire something, as in *I fancied an ice-cream*. 2 to imagine or think of something, as in *Just fancy him riding a horse!*
fancy yourself, to be conceited.

fanfare *noun* **fanfares**
a short piece of loud music on trumpets.

fang *noun* **fangs**
1 a long, sharp tooth, especially of a dog.
2 the tooth of a venomous snake.

fantastic *adjective*
1 (*colloquial*) marvellous; excellent.
2 strange; ridiculous, as in *fantastic furniture.* 3 imaginary, as in *the fantastic idea of a city under the sea*.
fantastically *adverb*

fantasy *noun* **fantasies**
something imaginary or fantastic, as in *He had the fantasy of being captain of the Australian cricket team*.

far *adverb* **farther, farthest**
1 a long way, as in *We didn't go far*.
2 much, as in *She's a far better singer than I am*.

far and wide, over a large area.
far out, (*colloquial*) excellent or fantastic.
so far, up to now.

far *adjective* **farther, farthest**
distant; opposite, as in *on the far side of the river*.
a far cry, very different, as in *Conditions here are a far cry from what you are used to*.

far-away *adjective*
1 distant, as in *far-away places*. 2 dreamy or distant, as in *a far-away look in her eyes*.

farce *noun* **farces**
1 a ridiculous comedy. 2 ridiculous and disorganised events, as in *My tennis lessons were a farce, I learnt nothing*.
farcical *adjective*

fare *noun* **fares**
the money you pay to travel on a bus, train, ship, aircraft, etc.

fare *verb* **fares, faring, fared**
to get on; to progress, as in *How did you fare in your test?*

farewell *noun* **farewells**
a goodbye; a parting, as in *tearful farewell*.

far-fetched *adjective*
unlikely; difficult to believe.

farm *noun* **farms**
a property where someone grows crops and keeps animals for food.

farm *verb* **farms, farming, farmed**
1 to grow crops and raise animals for food. 2 to use land for growing crops, as in *They farm a thousand hectares near Yass*.

farmer *noun* **farmers**
someone who owns or looks after a farm.

farther *adverb* and *adjective*
at or to a greater distance; more distant, as in *She lives farther from the school than I do. He sat on the farther side of the river.*

farthest *adverb* and *adjective*
at or to the greatest distance; most distant.

fascinate *verb* **fascinates, fascinating, fascinated**
to be very attractive or interesting to someone.
fascination *noun*

Fascism *noun* (*say* fash-iz-uhm)
a dictatorial type of government; a belief in this type of government.
Fascist *noun* and *adjective*

fashion *noun* **fashions**
1 the style of clothes or other things that most people like at a particular time. 2 a way of doing something, as in *He works in a quick fashion*.

fashion *verb* **fashions, fashioning, fashioned**
to make something in a particular shape or style, as in *He fashioned a toy from the pine cone*.

fashionable *adjective*
1 following the fashion, as in *fashionable young people*. 2 popular among smart people, as in *a fashionable drink*.
fashionably *adverb*

fast *adjective* **faster, fastest**
1 rapid; quick, as in *He's a fast runner*.
2 firmly fixed, as in *Make the boat fast*.
3 showing a time later than the correct time, as in *Your watch is fast*. 4 finished in a short time, as in *He ran a fast race to break the world record*.

fast *adverb*
1 quickly. 2 firmly.
fast asleep, deeply asleep.

fast *verb* **fasts, fasting, fasted**
to go without food.

fasten *verb* **fastens, fastening, fastened**
to join one thing firmly to another.
fastener *noun*, **fastening** *noun*

fat *noun* **fats**
1 the white, greasy part of meat. 2 an oily or greasy substance used in cooking, as in *Butter, margarine, and lard are fats*. 3 an energy-rich food, as in *Milk, cheese, and cream contain fat*.
the fat of the land, the best food.

fat *adjective* **fatter, fattest**
1 with a very thick, round body, as in *a fat man*. 2 plump, ready for killing, as in *fat lamb*.

fatal *adjective*
able to cause death or disaster, as in *a fatal accident*.
fatality *noun*, **fatally** *adverb*

fate *noun* **fates**
1 the power that makes things happen, as in *Fate determined that he would die*. 2 what has to happen and cannot be altered; what happens to someone in the end, as in *Her fate was to become famous*.

father *noun* **fathers**
1 a male parent. 2 the title given to priests in the Catholic and Anglican church.

father-in-law *noun* **fathers-in-law**
the father of your husband or wife.

fathom *noun* **fathoms**
a unit of almost 2 metres, used in measuring the depth of water.

fathom

fathom *verb* fathoms, fathoming, fathomed
to understand, as in *I can't fathom how you did it.*

fatigue *noun* (*say* fuh-**teeg**)
1 tiredness. 2 weakness in metals, etc. caused by repeated stress.
fatigued *adjective*

fatten *verb* fattens, fattening, fattened
to make or become fat.

fattening *adjective*
likely to make you fat, as in *Cakes with a lot of sugar and cream in them are fattening.*

fatty *adjective* fattier, fattiest
1 like fat, as in *wax is a fatty substance.*
2 full of fat, as in *fatty sausages.*

fault *noun* faults
something wrong that spoils a person or thing; a flaw or mistake.
at fault, wrong; responsible for a mistake, as in *The fuel system was at fault. We don't know who was at fault.*
faultless *adjective*

fault *verb* faults, faulting, faulted
to find faults in something, as in *The judges couldn't fault the gymnast who scored a perfect 10.*

faulty *adjective* faultier, faultiest
having a fault or faults; wrong.

fauna *noun* (*say* **faw**-nuh)
the animals of an area, or of a period in the past, as in *The best known Australian fauna are the koala and the kangaroo.*
faunal emblem, an animal officially adopted as the symbol of a country, State or Territory.
faunal *adjective*

favour or **favor** *noun* favours
1 something kind that you do for someone, as in *Will you do me a favour?* 2 approval; goodwill, as in *The good student was looked on with favour.*
in favour of someone or something, liking or supporting someone or something.
in your favour, to your advantage.

favour or **favor** *verb* favours, favouring, favoured
1 to like or support someone or something.
2 to be kinder to one person than to others, as in *You favour her and not me.*

favourable or **favorable** *adjective*
helpful; approving.
favourably *adverb*

favourite or **favorite** *adjective*
liked most or preferred above all others, as in *my favourite book.*

favourite or **favorite** *noun* favourites
a person or thing that someone likes most.

favouritism or **favoritism** *noun*
the unfair favouring of one person, cause, etc. at the expense of another, as in *The ballet teacher showed favouritism to the talented dancer.*

fawn *noun* fawns
1 a young deer. 2 a light brown colour.

fax *noun* faxes
1 the process of sending copies of documents by electronic means, using the same wires as the telephone system. 2 a copy made by this process.

fax *verb* faxes, faxing, faxed
to send a copy of something by fax.

fear *noun* fears
a feeling that something unpleasant may happen to you.
for fear of something, because of the risk of something.
fearless *adjective*, **fearlessly** *adverb*

fear *verb* fears, fearing, feared
1 to be afraid of someone or something.
2 to be anxious or sad about something, as in *She feared for her child's life.*

fearful *adjective*
1 frightened, as in *I am fearful I will fall.*
2 awful, as in *a fearful storm.*
fearfully *adverb*

fearsome *adjective*
frightening, as in *a fearsome monster.*

feast *noun* feasts
a large, splendid meal.

feast *verb* feasts, feasting, feasted
to have a large, splendid meal.
feast your eyes on something, to look at something and enjoy it, as in *Feast your eyes on these pictures.*

feat *noun* feats
a brave or clever deed.

feather *noun* feathers
one of the very light coverings that grow from a bird's skin.
feathery *adjective*

feature *noun* features
1 any part of the face, as in *He has sharp features.* 2 an important or noticeable part of something; a characteristic, as in *The glass walls were a feature of the house.* 3 a long or important film, broadcast program, or newspaper article.

feature *verb* features, featuring, featured
to make something an important or noticeable part of something; to be an

fence

important or noticeable part of something, as in *The meal featured a delicious dessert. Sport features a lot in the Sunday papers.*

February *noun*
the second month of the year.

fed past tense and past participle of **feed** *verb.*

federal *adjective*
to do with a system in which several states are ruled by a central government but make some of their own laws.

federation *noun*
the joining of a number of states to form a single nation; the states give some of their powers to the central government.
federal *adjective*

fed up *adjective*
discontented; very annoyed.

fee *noun* **fees**
a payment, charge, or subscription, as in *the doctor's fee.*

feeble *adjective* **feebler, feeblest**
weak, as in *a feeble body; feeble light.*
feebly *adverb*

feed *verb* **feeds, feeding, fed**
1 to give food to a person or animal. 2 to eat, as in *Sheep feed on grass.* 3 to supply to, as in *Oil feeds the machine. Feed the fire with wood.*
feeder *noun*

feed *noun* **feeds**
1 (*colloquial*) a meal, as in *a good feed at the restaurant.* 2 food for animals, as in *Stocks of feed were low in the drought.*

feedback *noun*
1 a response, as in *Is there any feedback from our customers?* 2 something being returned to where it came from, especially a signal in an electronic device.

feel *verb* **feels, feeling, felt**
1 to touch something to find out what it is like. 2 to experience something; to have a feeling.
feel like something, to want something.

feeler *noun* **feelers**
1 a long, thin part that sticks out from an insect's body, used for feeling. 2 a cautious question, suggestion, etc. to test people's reaction, as in *I put out feelers to see what they thought of my plan.*

feeling *noun* **feelings**
1 a mental or physical experience; what you feel. 2 the power to feel things, as in *the feeling for music.* 3 sympathy or understanding, as in *He shows no feeling for*

my suffering. 4 someone's opinion, as in *What's your feeling about this change?*

feet plural of **foot.**

feign *verb* **feigns, feigning, feigned** (*say* fayn)
to pretend or invent, as in *He feigned illness to avoid homework.*

feline *adjective*
belonging to the cat family; like a cat, as in *The dancer moved with feline grace.*

fell *verb* **fells, felling, felled**
1 to cut down a tree. 2 to knock someone down.

fell past tense of **fall** *verb.*

fellow *noun* **fellows**
1 a friend or companion; someone who belongs to the same group. 2 (*colloquial*) a man or boy, as in *He's a good fellow.*

fellow *adjective*
to do with the same group, class, kind, etc., as in *Her fellow teachers supported her.*

fellowship *noun* **fellowships**
1 friendship. 2 a group of friends; a society, as in *a fellowship of writers.*

felon *noun* **felons**
a criminal.

felt *noun*
thick woollen material.
felt-tip or **felt-tipped pen,** a pen with a tip made of felt or fibre.

felt past tense and past participle of **feel.**

female *adjective*
to do with the sex that gives birth to offspring, as in *Women, girls, cows, and hens are all female.*

female *noun* **females**
a female person or animal.

feminine *adjective*
1 to do with or like a woman, as in *feminine dress; feminine appearance.* 2 having qualities thought to be associated with a woman, as in *Gentleness and care are often regarded as feminine qualities.*
femininity *noun*

feminist *noun* **feminists**
a supporter of women's claims to be given rights equal to those of men.
feminism *noun*

fen *noun* **fens**
a low-lying area of marshy or flooded land, especially in Tasmania.

fence *noun* **fences**
1 a barrier around a garden, paddock, etc. or beside a road, railway, etc., as in *Fences are usually made of wood or posts and*

a
b
c
d
e
f
g
h
i
j
k
l
m
n
o
p
q
r
s
t
u
v
w
x
y
z

fence

158

wire. **2** (*colloquial*) someone who buys stolen goods and sells them again.
sit on the fence, to avoid committing yourself to either side in a contest, argument, etc.

fence *verb* **fences, fencing, fenced**
1 to put a barrier around or along something. **2** to fight with thin swords called *foils,* as a sport.
fencer *noun,* **fencing** *noun*

fend *verb* **fends, fending, fended**
fend for yourself, to take care of yourself.
fend off, to keep a person or thing away from yourself.

ferment *noun* (*say* **fer**-ment)
1 the act of fermenting, as in *The ferment of yeast in bread dough makes it rise.* **2** an excited or agitated condition; unrest, as in *The crowd was in ferment at the demonstration.*

ferment *verb* **ferments, fermenting, fermented** (*say* fer-**ment** *or* fuh-**ment**)
to bubble and change chemically by the action of a substance like yeast.
fermentation *noun*

fern *noun* **ferns**
a plant with feathery leaves and no flowers.

ferocious *adjective*
fierce; savage; cruel.
ferociously *adverb,* **ferocity** *noun*

ferret *noun* **ferrets**
a small animal used for catching rabbits and rats.

ferret *verb* **ferrets, ferreting, ferreted**
1 to hunt with ferrets. **2** to search for, as in *The detective ferreted for clues.*

ferry *noun* **ferries**
a boat or plane used for carrying people or things across a river, harbour, etc.

ferry *verb* **ferries, ferrying, ferried**
to carry people or things across a river, channel, etc.

fertile *adjective*
1 producing good crops. **2** able to produce offspring.
fertility *noun*

fertilise *or* **fertilize** *verb* **fertilises, fertilising, fertilised**
to make fertile or productive, as in *I fertilise the garden with compost. The female egg is fertilised by the male sperm to begin new life.*
fertilisation *noun*

fertiliser *or* **fertilizer** *noun* **fertilisers**
a substance added to the soil to make it more fertile.

fervent *adjective*
very enthusiastic; passionate, as in *a fervent supporter of forest conservation; a fervent plea for justice.*
fervently *adverb,* **fervour** *noun*

festival *noun* **festivals**
a time when people arrange special celebrations, performances, processions, etc., as in *the festival of Easter; a music festival.*

festive *adjective*
joyful, as in *the festive season of Christmas.*
festivity *noun*

festoon *verb* **festoons, festooning, festooned**
to decorate a place with flowers, ribbons, etc.

feta *noun*
a soft, white, salty cheese from Greece.

fetch *verb* **fetches, fetching, fetched**
1 to go and get someone or something.
2 to be sold for a particular price, as in *The bookcase fetched $100.*

fete *noun* **fetes** (*say* fayt)
an outdoor entertainment with the sale of goods, amusements, etc., especially to raise funds for a charity, school, etc.

fetlock *noun* **fetlocks**
the part of a horse's leg above and behind its hoof.

fetter *noun* **fetters**
a chain around a prisoner's ankles.
fetters, something which restricts or prevents you from doing what you want.

fettuccine *noun* (*say* fe-tuh-**chee**-nee)
wide strips of pasta.

feud *noun* **feuds**
a long-lasting quarrel or feeling of hatred.

feudal *adjective*
to do with the medieval system in which people could farm land in exchange for work done for the landowner.
feudalism *noun*

fever *noun* **fevers**
1 an unusually high body-temperature, usually with an illness, as in *scarlet fever.*
2 excitement; agitation, as in *The fans were in a fever before the siren went.*
fevered *adjective,* **feverish** *adjective,* **feverishly** *adverb*

few *adjective* **fewer, fewest**
not many.

few *noun*
a small number of people or things.
a good few or **quite a few,** a fairly large number.

fez *noun* **fezzes**
a round, flat-topped hat with a tassel, worn especially by Muslim men.

fiancé *noun* **fiancés** (*say* fee-**on**-say)
a man engaged to be married.

fiancée *noun* **fiancées** (*say* fee-**on**-say)
a woman engaged to be married.

fiasco *noun* **fiascos** (*say* fee-**as**-koh)
a complete failure, as in *The party turned into a fiasco*.

fib *noun* **fibs**
a lie, usually about something unimportant.
fibber *noun*

fibre *noun* **fibres** (*say* **fuy**-buh)
1 a very thin thread.   2 a substance made up of thin threads.   3 the part of food that is not easily digested, as in *Bran is good fibre*.
fibrous *adjective*

fibreglass *noun*
a kind of plastic containing glass fibres, used in building, etc., as in *Surfboards are made from fibreglass*.

fibro *noun* **fibros**
a house made from sheets of asbestos and cement.

fickle *adjective*
often changing; (of a person) not loyal, as in *a fickle supporter*.

fiction *noun* **fictions**
1 writings about events that have not really happened; stories and novels.
2 something imagined or untrue.
fictional *adjective*, **fictitious** *adjective*

fiddle *noun* **fiddles**
1 a violin.   2 a fraud or illegal scheme.

fiddle *verb* **fiddles, fiddling, fiddled**
1 to play the violin.   2 to play about with something with your fingers.
3 (*colloquial*) to cheat; to get or change something dishonestly.
fiddler *noun*

fiddly *adjective*
(*colloquial*) small and awkward to handle, use, or do.

fidelity *noun* (*say* fuh-**del**-uh-tee)
1 faithfulness, as in *the fidelity of true friends*.   2 the exactness with which sound is reproduced, as in *Compact discs are known for their high fidelity*.

fidget *verb* **fidgets, fidgeting, fidgeted**
to move about restlessly.
fidgety *adjective*

field *noun* **fields**
1 an area of open land, as in *a field of clover; a football field*.   2 an area of knowledge, as in *an important development in the field of science*.   3 those taking part in a race, etc., as in *The field for the Melbourne Cup is excellent*.
field events, athletic events other than races, as in *The long jump is a field event*.

field *verb* **fields, fielding, fielded**
1 to stop or catch the ball in cricket, softball, etc.   2 to be in the team that is not batting in cricket, etc.
fielder *noun*

fieldwork *noun*
practical work or research done in various places, not in a school, library, laboratory, etc., as in *We went to the coast to do some geography fieldwork*.

fiend *noun* **fiends** (*say* feend)
1 a devil.   2 a nuisance or an annoying person.
fiendish *adjective*, **fiendishly** *adverb*

fierce *adjective* **fiercer, fiercest**
1 angry and violent or cruel.   2 very intense, as in *She is a fierce supporter of the anti-smoking campaign*.
fiercely *adverb*, **fierceness** *noun*

fiery *adjective* **fierier, fieriest**
1 full of flames or heat.   2 very emotional; easily made angry, as in *He had a fiery temper*.

fiesta *noun* **fiestas** (*say* fee-**est**-uh)
a holiday, celebration or religious festival.

fife *noun* **fifes**
a small, shrill flute.

fifteen *noun* **fifteens**
1 the number 15, one more than fourteen.
2 a team in Rugby Union football.
fifteenth *adjective* and *noun*

fifth *adjective*
next after the fourth.

fifty *noun* **fifties**
the number 50, five times ten.
fiftieth *adjective* and *noun*

fifty-fifty *adjective* and *adverb*
shared equally between two people or groups, as in *We have fifty-fifty shares in the fireworks. Let's split the lollies fifty-fifty*.

fig *noun* **figs**
a small, soft fruit full of small seeds.

fight *verb* **fights, fighting, fought**
1 to struggle against someone or something, especially by using hands,

fight 160

weapons, etc. **2** to try to stop something, as in *They fought the fire*.
fighter *noun*

fight *noun* **fights**
1 a struggle against someone, using hands, weapons, etc. **2** an attempt to overcome or destroy something, as in *the fight against poverty*.

figurative language *noun*
using words in ways that are different from their usual meanings, as in '*He is up to his ears in debt' is a figurative use of the phrase 'up to his ears'*.

figure *noun* **figures**
1 one of the signs we use for numbers, such as 1, 2, and 3. **2** the shape of someone's body. **3** a diagram or illustration. **4** a pattern or shape, as in *a figure of eight*.
figure of speech, a special way of using words that makes someone's speech or writing interesting, such as a metaphor or a simile.
figures, arithmetic, as in *Are you good at figures?*

figure *verb* **figures, figuring, figured**
1 to appear or take part in something, as in *His name does not figure in the list of entrants*.
2 to imagine, as in *I figure he'll turn up later*. **3** to work out, as in *We figured that we had enough money for the holiday*.

filament *noun* **filaments**
a thread or thin wire.

file *noun* **files**
1 a metal tool with a rough surface that is rubbed on things to make them smooth.
2 a folder, box, etc. to keep papers in; the collection of such papers in an orderly way. **3** a line of people one behind the other. **4** (*in Computing*) a collection of data that has been given a particular name.

file *verb* **files, filing, filed**
1 to make something smooth with a file.
2 to arrange in a file. **3** to walk one behind the other.

fill *verb* **fills, filling, filled**
1 to make something full; to become full. **2** to occupy, as in *She filled the advertised position of coach*.
fill in, to complete a document; to act as a substitute, as in *Fill in this form. I'll fill in for Sam while he's on holiday*.
fill up, to fill something completely.
filler *noun*

fill *noun* **fills**
1 enough to fill a person or thing, as in *Eat your fill*. **2** earth, rocks, etc. to fill a hole in the ground; landfill.

fillet *noun* **fillets**
a piece of fish or meat without bones.

filling *noun* **fillings**
something used to fill a hole or gap, especially a substance put in a tooth to replace a decayed part.

filly *noun* **fillies**
a young mare.

film *noun* **films**
1 a moving picture that tells a story, such as those shown in cinemas. **2** a roll or piece of thin plastic, etc. put in a camera for taking photographs. **3** a very thin layer of something, as in *a film of oil on the lake*.
filmy *adjective*

film *verb* **films, filming, filmed**
to make a film of something.

filo pastry *noun*
very thin pastry in leaf-like layers.

filter *noun* **filters**
a device for removing dirt or other unwanted things from liquid, gas, etc. which passes through it.

filter *verb* **filters, filtering, filtered**
1 to pass through a filter. **2** to move gradually, as in *They filtered into the hall*.
filtration *noun*

filth *noun*
disgusting dirt.
filthy *adjective*

fin *noun* **fins**
1 one of the thin, flat parts sticking out from a fish's body and helping it to swim. **2** a thin, flat part sticking out on the outside of a plane, car, surfboard, etc.

final *adjective*
1 coming at the end; last. **2** able to put an end to argument or doubt, as in *I say you must not go, and that's final!*
finality *noun*, **finally** *adverb*

final *noun* **finals**
the last of a series of contests, as in *My team is in the final*.
finalist *noun*

finale *noun* **finales** (*say* fuh-**nah**-lee)
the last part of a show, piece of music, etc.

finance *noun*
the use or management of money.
financial *adjective*

a
b
c
d
e
f
g
h
i
j
k
l
m
n
o
p
q
r
s
t
u
v
w
x
y
z

finance *verb* finances, financing, financed
to supply money for something, as in *How will you finance your expedition?*
financier *noun*

finch *noun* finches
a small, brightly-coloured bird with a short, thick beak.

find *verb* finds, finding, found
1 to see or get something. **2** to learn or experience something, as in *He found that digging is hard work.*
find fault, to think or say that someone or something is not satisfactory.
find out, to come to know something for the first time; to catch someone doing something wrong.
finder *noun*

findings *plural noun*
things you have found out, as in *The committee's findings were written up in a report.*

fine *adjective* finer, finest
1 dry and sunny; bright, as in *fine weather.* **2** very thin; delicate, as in *fine material.* **3** excellent, as in *a fine picture.* **4** healthy, as in *I'm fine despite my cough.* **5** thin or sharp, as in *a fine needle.*
finely *adverb*

fine *noun* fines
money which has to be paid as a punishment.

fine *verb* fines, fining, fined
to make someone pay money as a punishment.

finger *noun* fingers
1 one of the separate parts of your hand. **2** a narrow piece of something, as in *fish fingers.*

finger *verb* fingers, fingering, fingered
to touch and feel something with your fingers.

fingernail *noun* fingernails
the hard covering at the end of a finger.

fingerprint *noun* fingerprints
a mark made by the tip of a person's finger, as in *Detectives identified the criminal by his fingerprints.*

finicky *adjective*
1 very fussy, as in *She has always been finicky about what she eats.* **2** small and awkward to handle, use, or do, as in *Sewing on sequins is a finicky job.*

finish *verb* finishes, finishing, finished
to come to an end; to bring something to an end.

finish *noun* finishes
the end of something.

finite *adjective*
having limits, as in *There is a finite amount of money to spend on the present.*

fiord *noun* fiords (*say* fee-**awd**)
an inlet of the sea between high cliffs, as in *There are many fiords in Norway.*

fir *noun* firs
an evergreen tree with leaves like needles, as in *Firs are used as Christmas trees.*

fire *noun* fires
1 burning; the heat and bright light that come from burning things. **2** fuel burning in a fireplace or furnace to give heat. **3** a bushfire. **4** great enthusiasm, as in *His speech on freedom was full of fire.*
fire-ban, the official forbidding of lighting fires in the open on days of high fire risk.
firebreak, a strip of land deliberately burned to kill vegetation to prevent a bushfire, etc. spreading
fire-drill, practising what to do if a building etc. is on fire.
fire-escape, a special staircase or ladder by which you can leave a building that is on fire.
fire extinguisher, a device containing a substance that puts out fires, such as water, and a means of sending this towards the fire.
fire hazard, something that is likely to catch fire or to burn easily, as in *Petrol is a fire hazard.*
fire hydrant, a place in the street where fire-fighters can connect hoses to the water main.
on fire, burning.
set fire to something, to start something burning.

fire *verb* fires, firing, fired
1 to start something burning. **2** to bake pottery, bricks, etc. in an oven. **3** to shoot a gun. **4** (*colloquial*) to dismiss someone from his or her job. **5** to fill with enthusiasm, as in *The coach's speech fired his team to victory.*

firearm *noun* firearms
a small gun; a rifle or pistol.

fire brigade *noun* fire brigades
a team of people organised to fight fires.

fire-engine *noun* fire-engines
a large vehicle that carries firemen and equipment to fight fires.

firefighter *noun* fire-fighters
a member of a team employed to put out fires, especially bushfires.

a
b
c
d
e
f
g
h
i
j
k
l
m
n
o
p
q
r
s
t
u
v
w
x
y
z

fireman

fireman *noun* **firemen**
a man who is a member of a fire brigade.

fireplace *noun* **fireplaces**
the part of a room where the fire and hearth are.

fireproof *adjective*
able to stand great heat and not burn, as in *Asbestos is a fireproof substance.*

fire station *noun* **fire stations**
the headquarters of a fire brigade.

firewood *noun*
wood suitable for fuel.

fireworks *plural noun*
cardboard or paper tubes containing chemicals that burn attractively or noisily.

firm *noun* **firms**
a business, as in *She works for a clothing firm.*

firm *adjective* **firmer, firmest**
1 fixed or solid so that it will not move.
2 definite; not likely to change, as in *a firm belief in the future.*
firmly *adverb*, **firmness** *noun*

first *adjective*
1 coming before all others. 2 the most important, as in *He plays in the First Eleven.*
firstly *adverb*

first *noun*
a person or thing that is first.
at first, at the beginning; to start with.

first *adverb*
before everything else.

first aid *noun*
treatment given to an injured person before a doctor comes.

First Australian *noun* **First Australians**
an Aborigine.

first class *adjective*
excellent and of the highest quality, as in *first class seats; first class service.*

firsthand *adjective and adverb*
got directly, rather than from other people or from books, as in *It was firsthand information. She received the news firsthand.*

first-rate *adjective*
excellent.

fish *noun* **fish or fishes**
an animal that always lives and breathes in the water.

fish *verb* **fishes, fishing, fished**
1 to try to catch fish. 2 to search for something; to try to get something, as in *He is only fishing for praise.*
fish out to pull out something.

fisherman *noun* **fishermen**
someone who tries to catch fish.

fishmonger *noun* **fishmongers**
a shopkeeper who sells fish.

fishy *adjective* **fishier, fishiest**
1 smelling or tasting of fish. 2 (*colloquial*) suspicious; doubtful, as in *a fishy story.*

fission *noun* (say fish-uhn)
splitting something, especially splitting the central part of an atom.

fist *noun* **fists**
a tightly closed hand.

fit *adjective* **fitter, fittest**
1 suitable; good enough, as in *a meal fit for a king.* 2 healthy; strong, as in *Keep fit with exercises.*
see fit or **think fit to do something,** to decide or choose to do something.
fitness *noun*

fit *verb* **fits, fitting, fitted**
1 to be the right size and shape. 2 to put something into place. 3 to be suited to something, as in *Her speech fitted the occasion perfectly.*
fit in, to be suitable or agreeable.
fitter *noun*

fit *noun* **fits**
1 the way something fits, as in *This coat is a good fit.* 2 a sudden illness, especially one that makes you move violently or become unconscious. 3 an outburst, as in *a fit of rage.*
in fits and starts, not regularly; in short bursts.

fitted *adjective*
made to fit something exactly, as in *a fitted sheet.*

fitting *noun* **fittings**
a trying on of clothes so that a dressmaker, tailor, etc. can check for a correct fit.

fitting *adjective*
suitable; proper, as in *The barbecue was a fitting end to the school camp.*

five *noun* **fives**
the number 5, one more than four.

fix *verb* **fixes, fixing, fixed**
1 to join something firmly to something else; to put something where it will not move. 2 to decide or settle, as in *We have fixed a date for the party.* 3 to mend, as in *She's fixing my bike.*
fix up, to arrange or organise something; to make better, as in *Fix up the mess. Aspirin will fix up your headache.*

fix noun fixes
1 (colloquial) an awkward situation, as in *I'm in a fix*. 2 finding the position of something, especially by using a compass. 3 (colloquial) a dose of an addictive drug.

fixture noun fixtures
1 something fixed in its place. 2 a sporting event especially a match, race, etc. planned for a particular day.

fizz verb fizzes, fizzing, fizzed
1 to make a hissing, spluttering sound. 2 to produce a lot of small bubbles, as in *The soda water fizzed as I poured it out*.
fizzy adjective

fizzer noun fizzers
(colloquial) a failure.

fizzle verb fizzles, fizzling, fizzled
to make a small hissing sound.
fizzle out, to end in a disappointing or unsuccessful way.

flab noun
(colloquial) unwanted fat on someone's body, as in *You'll have to get rid of some of the flab you put on over Christmas!*

flabbergasted adjective
(colloquial) extremely surprised.

flabby adjective flabbier, flabbiest
fat and soft; not firm.

flag noun flags
a piece of material with a coloured pattern or shape on it, used as a sign or signal.

flag verb flags, flagging, flagged
1 to become weak; to droop, as in *The runner flagged in the heat*. 2 to signal with a flag, as in *The ships flagged messages to each other*.

flagpole noun flagpoles
a pole to which a flag is attached.

flagship noun flagships
a ship that carries the naval officer in charge of a fleet of ships.

flagstaff noun flagstaffs
a flagpole.

flagstone noun flagstones
a flat slab of paving stone.

flake noun flakes
a very light, thin piece of something, as in *a flake of pastry*.
flaky adjective

flake verb flakes, flaking, flaked
to come off in light, thin pieces.
flake out, (colloquial) to faint or fall asleep.

flame noun flames
fire that is shaped like a tongue; a quantity of burning gas.

flame verb flames, flaming, flamed
to burn or blaze.

flan noun flans
a pastry case with a savoury or sweet filling.

flank noun flanks
the side of something.

flannel noun flannels
1 a piece of soft cloth used for washing yourself; a face washer. 2 a kind of soft material, as in *These trousers are made of flannel*.

flap verb flaps, flapping, flapped
1 to move up and down or from side to side, as in *The bird flapped its wings. The yacht's sail was flapping*. 2 (colloquial) to panic or fuss.

flap noun flaps
1 a part that hangs down from one edge of something, usually to cover an opening, as in *Stick down the flap of the envelope*. 2 the act or sound of flapping, as in *the flap of a bird's wing*. 3 (colloquial) a panic or fuss, as in *Don't get in a flap*.

flare verb flares, flaring, flared
1 to burn with a sudden, bright flame. 2 to become angry suddenly. 3 (of skirts or trousers) to get gradually wider.

flare noun flares
1 a sudden, bright flame. 2 a bright light used as a signal. 3 a gradual widening, especially in skirts or trousers.

flash verb flashes, flashing, flashed
1 to make a sudden, bright burst of light. 2 to appear suddenly; to move quickly, as in *The answer flashed into his head. The train flashed past*.

flash noun flashes
1 a sudden, bright burst of light. 2 a device for making a brief, bright light by which to take photographs inside or at night. 3 a sudden display of anger, wit, etc. 4 a short item of news.
in a flash, immediately; very quickly.

flashback noun flashbacks
going back in a film or story to something that happened earlier, as in *The hero's childhood was shown in flashbacks*.

flashy adjective flashier, flashiest
unpleasantly showy and bright.

flask

flask *noun* **flasks**
a bottle with a narrow neck.

flat *adjective* **flatter, flattest**
1 with no curves or bumps; smooth and level. 2 spread out; lying at full length, as in *Lie flat on the ground.* 3 uninteresting; boring, as in *a flat voice.* 4 complete; not changing, as in *a flat refusal.* 5 not fizzy, as in *This beer is flat.* 6 below the proper musical pitch, as in *The clarinet was flat.* 7 punctured; with no air inside, as in *a flat tyre.* 8 not high, as in *flat country; flat shoes.* 9 not glossy, as in *flat paint.*
flat feet, feet without the normal arch.
flat out, as fast as possible.
flatly *adverb*, **flatness** *noun*

flat *noun* **flats**
1 the flat part of anything or something flat, as in *the flat of her hand.* 2 the note that is a semitone below a particular musical note; the sign (♭) that indicates this. 3 a set of rooms for living in, usually on one floor of a building.

flatten *verb* **flattens, flattening, flattened**
to make something flat; to become flat.

flatter *verb* **flatters, flattering, flattered**
1 to praise someone more than he or she deserves. 2 to make someone seem better or more attractive than he or she really is, as in *The artist has flattered his subject.*
flatterer *noun*, **flattery** *noun*

flaunt *verb* **flaunts, flaunting, flaunted**
to display something too proudly.

flautist *noun* **flautists** (*say* **flaw**-tuhst)
a person who plays the flute.

flavour or **flavor** *noun* **flavours**
the taste and smell of something.

flavour or **flavor** *verb* **flavours, flavouring, flavoured**
to give something a particular taste and smell.
flavouring *noun*

flaw *noun* **flaws**
something that makes a person or thing imperfect, as in *The diamond with a flaw sold at a lower price.*
flawed *adjective*, **flawless** *adjective*

flax *noun*
a plant that produces fibres from which cloth is made and seeds from which oil is made.

flea *noun* **fleas**
a small insect without wings that sucks blood.

flee *verb* **flees, fleeing, fled**
to run away.

fleece *noun* **fleeces**
the wool that covers a sheep or other animal's body.
fleecy *adjective*

fleece *verb* **fleeces, fleecing, fleeced**
1 to shear a sheep. 2 to cheat someone, as in *The greedy salesperson fleeced his customers.*

fleet *noun* **fleets**
a number of ships, aircraft, or vehicles, owned by one country or company, as in *naval fleet; a fleet of taxis.*

fleeting *adjective*
very brief, as in *I caught a fleeting glimpse of him.*

flesh *noun*
1 the soft substance between the skin and bones of people and animals. 2 the pulp of a fruit or vegetable.
fleshy *adjective*

flew past tense of **fly** *verb.*

flex *noun* **flexes**
flexible insulated wire for electric current.

flex *verb* **flexes, flexing, flexed**
to move your muscles; to bend your arms, legs, etc.

flexible *adjective*
1 easy to bend. 2 easy to change or adapt, as in *Our working hours are flexible.*
flexibility *noun*

flexitime *noun*
a system of working a set number of hours with the starting and finishing times chosen by the employees, as long as they work the correct number of hours in total.

flick *noun* **flicks**
a quick, light hit or movement.

flick *verb* **flicks, flicking, flicked**
to hit or move with a flick, as in *She flicked the hair from her jacket.*

flicker *verb* **flickers, flickering, flickered**
to burn or shine unsteadily.

flight *noun* **flights**
1 the act of flying through the air. 2 a journey in an aircraft, rocket, etc. 3 a group of flying birds, aircraft, etc. 4 a series of stairs. 5 running away; an escape, as in *flight from the enemy.*

flimsy *adjective* **flimsier, flimsiest**
light and thin; fragile, as in *flimsy fabric; a flimsy folding table.*

flora

flinch *verb* **flinches, flinching, flinched**
1 to feel or show fear. **2** to wince, as in *flinched in pain*.

fling *verb* **flings, flinging, flung**
to throw something violently or carelessly, as in *He flung his shoes under the bed*.

fling *noun* **flings**
a time of pleasure or wild behaviour, as in *The students had a fling after the exams*.
give it a fling, to make an attempt at.

flint *noun* **flints**
1 a very hard kind of stone. **2** a piece of this stone or hard metal used to produce sparks.
flinty *adjective*

flip *verb* **flips, flipping, flipped**
to flick, as in *Flip the coin. Flip through the magazine*.

flippant *adjective*
not showing proper seriousness, as in *Don't be flippant about his illness*.

flipper *noun* **flippers**
1 a limb that water-animals use for swimming. **2** a device that you wear on your feet to help you swim. **3** (*in cricket*) a tricky ball from a spin bowler which appears to go to the leg side but in fact goes straight, as in *Shane Warne bowls lots of flippers*.

flirt *verb* **flirts, flirting, flirted**
to behave towards someone as though you wanted to gain his or her love, to amuse yourself.
flirtation *noun*

flit *verb* **flits, flitting, flitted**
to fly or move lightly and quickly, as in *A moth flitted across the room*.

float *verb* **floats, floating, floated**
1 to stay or move on the surface of a liquid or in the air. **2** to make something stay on the surface of a liquid.

float *noun* **floats**
1 a device designed to rest on the surface of a liquid. **2** a trailer to transport horses. **3** a vehicle carrying a display in a parade, etc. **4** a small amount of money kept for paying small bills or giving change.

flock *noun* **flocks**
a group of sheep, goats, or birds.

flock *verb* **flocks, flocking, flocked**
to gather in a large crowd; to move in a large crowd.

flog *verb* **flogs, flogging, flogged**
1 to beat someone severely with a whip or stick. **2** (*colloquial*) to sell, as in *He flogged me his watch*. **3** (*colloquial*) to steal, as in *Who flogged my pencils?*

flogger *noun* **floggers**
(*in Australian Rules*) masses of streamers in team colours, attached to a pole and waved in support.

flood *noun* **floods**
1 a large amount of water spreading over a place that is usually dry. **2** a great amount of something, as in *a flood of requests*.
flood-plain, the flat area beside a river that becomes covered with water when the river floods.

flood *verb* **floods, flooding, flooded**
1 to cover something with a large amount of water. **2** (of a river) to flow over its banks. **3** to arrive in large amounts, as in *Letters flooded in*.

floodlight *noun* **floodlights**
a lamp that makes a broad, bright beam.
floodlit *adjective*

floor *noun* **floors**
1 the part of a room that people walk on. **2** all the rooms on the same level in a building; a storey, as in *Her office is on the top floor*.

floor *verb* **floors, flooring, floored**
1 to put a floor into a building. **2** to knock someone down. **3** (*colloquial*) to confuse or baffle someone, as in *Some of the exam questions floored everyone*.

floorboard *noun* **floorboards**
one of the boards forming the floor of a room.

flop *verb* **flops, flopping, flopped**
1 to fall or sit down suddenly. **2** to flap or droop. **3** (*colloquial*) to be a failure.

flop *noun* **flops**
1 the movement or sound of sudden falling or sitting down. **2** (*colloquial*) a failure.

floppy *adjective* **floppier, floppiest**
hanging loosely or heavily, as in *a floppy T-shirt; a dog with floppy ears*.

floppy disc *noun* **floppy discs**
a round, flat piece of magnetic material, used with computers to store information.

flora *noun* (*say* **flaw**-ruh)
the plants of a particular area or period, as in *Australia's flora includes gums and wattles*.

floral

floral *adjective*
to do with flowers, as in *a floral display*.
floral emblem, a plant officially adopted by a country, State or Territory as a symbol.

florist *noun* **florists**
a person who deals in or sells flowers.

flounder *verb* **flounders, floundering, floundered**
to move or behave awkwardly or helplessly, as in *I was floundering, trying desperately to think of an answer*.

flounder *noun*
a kind of flat edible fish.

flour *noun*
a white or brown powder made from wheat, corn, etc. and used for making bread, cakes, pastry, etc.
floury *adjective*

flourish *verb* **flourishes, flourishing, flourished**
1 to grow or develop strongly; to be successful, as in *Her business flourished, and gained a large share of the market*. 2 to wave something about, as in *She rushed in flourishing her music award*.

flow *verb* **flows, flowing, flowed**
1 to move along smoothly like a river.
2 to hang loosely or easily, as in *She has flowing hair. The silk dress flows as she walks*.

flow *noun* **flows**
1 a flowing movement or mass, as in *the swift flow of the river*. 2 the tide when it is coming in, as in *ebb and flow*.
flow chart, a diagram with special shapes connected by lines showing the order in which a series of actions or processes happen, especially a diagram of a computer program.

flower *noun* **flowers**
1 the part of a plant from which seed or fruit develops, as in *Most flowers have coloured petals*. 2 a plant that has this kind of part.
in flower, producing flowers.
flowery *adjective*

flower *verb* **flowers, flowering, flowered**
to produce flowers.

flowery *adjective*
1 decorated with flowers, or pictures of them, as in *flowery wallpaper*. 2 sounding very grand, as in *a flowery style of writing*.

flown past participle of **fly** *verb*.

flu *noun* short for **influenza**.

fluctuate *verb* **fluctuates, fluctuating, fluctuated**
to rise and fall irregularly, as in *The price of petrol fluctuates*.
fluctuation *noun*

flue *noun* **flues**
a pipe that takes smoke and fumes away from a stove, a central-heating boiler, etc.

fluent *adjective*
skilful at speaking, especially at speaking a foreign language, as in *fluent in Japanese*.
fluency *noun*, **fluently** *adverb*

fluff *noun*
a light, soft substance that comes off blankets, cloth, etc., as in *woollen fluff*.
fluffy *adjective*

fluid *noun* **fluids**
a substance that flows easily; any liquid or gas.

fluke *noun* **flukes**
1 an unexpected piece of good luck that makes you able to do something you thought you could not do. 2 one of the flat halves of a whale's tail.

fluke *verb* **flukes, fluking, fluked**
to achieve by a fluke, as in *He fluked the goal*.

flung past tense and past participle of **fling**.

fluorescent *adjective*
creating light from radiation, as in *a fluorescent lamp*.
fluorescence *noun*

fluoridation *noun*
adding fluoride to drinking-water.

fluoride *noun*
a chemical that is thought to help prevent tooth-decay.

flush *verb* **flushes, flushing, flushed**
1 to blush. 2 to clean or remove something with a fast flow of liquid, as in *Flush the toilet*.

flush *adjective*
1 level; without any part sticking out, as in *The doors are flush with the walls*.
2 (*colloquial*) having plenty of money.

flustered *adjective*
nervous and confused.

flute *noun* **flutes**
a musical instrument consisting of a long pipe with holes that are covered by fingers or keys.

flutter *verb* **flutters, fluttering, fluttered**
1 to move with a quick flapping of wings, as in *A butterfly fluttered in through the open*

folk

window. **2** to move or flap quickly and irregularly, as in *The flags fluttered in the breeze. My heart fluttered with anxiety.*

flutter *noun* **flutters**
1 a fluttering movement. **2** a nervously excited condition, as in *Mum was in a flutter about the flight to Bali.* **3** (*colloquial*) a small bet.

fly *verb* **flies, flying, flew, flown**
1 to move through the air with wings or in an aircraft, as in *I have flown from Melbourne to Sydney.* **2** to wave in the air, as in *Flags were flying.* **3** to make something move through the air, as in *They flew model planes.* **4** to move quickly, as in *Time flies. I flew down the corridor.*

fly *noun* **flies**
1 the front opening of a pair of trousers. **2** a small flying insect with two wings. **3** a real or artificial insect used as bait in fishing.
fly-fishing, fishing with a real or artificial insect as bait.

flying doctor *noun* **flying doctors**
a doctor who uses aircraft to visit patients, especially in the outback.

flying fox *noun* **flying foxes**
1 a large, fruit-eating bat. **2** an overhead cable used to carry materials, supplies, etc. over a river, rough country, etc. **3** a piece of playground equipment.

flying saucer *noun* **flying saucers**
a saucer-shaped flying object, believed to come from a planet other than Earth.

flyleaf *noun* **flyleaves**
a blank page at the beginning or end of a book.

foal *noun* **foals**
a young horse.

foam *noun*
1 froth or very small bubbles. **2** a spongy substance made from rubber or plastic.
foamy *adjective*

foam *verb* **foams, foaming, foamed**
to froth or bubble.

focaccia *noun* **focaccias** (*say* fuh-**kah**-chuh)
a type of flat bread from Italy, usually flavoured with herbs, olives, capsicum, etc.

focus *noun* **focuses** or **foci**
1 the distance at which something appears most clear to an eye or a lens. **2** the point at which rays, etc. meet. **3** the most important or interesting part of something.

in focus, appearing clearly.
out of focus, not appearing clearly.
focal *adjective*

focus *verb* **focuses** or **focusses, focusing** or **focussing, focused** or **focussed**
1 to use or adjust a lens so that objects appear clearly. **2** to concentrate, as in *She focused her attention on the problem.*

fodder *noun*
food for horses and farm animals.

foe *noun* **foes**
(*old-fashioned use*) an enemy.

foetus or **fetus** *noun* **foetuses** (*say* fee-tuhs)
a developing human or animal in its mother's womb, especially eight weeks after conception.
foetal *adjective*

fog *noun* **fogs**
thick mist.
foggy *adjective*

foghorn *noun* **foghorns**
a loud horn for warning ships in fog.

fogy *noun* **fogies**
a dull person with old-fashioned ideas.

foil *noun* **foils**
1 a very thin sheet of metal, as in *aluminium foil.* **2** a person or thing that makes another look better in comparison. **3** a thin sword used in fencing.

foil *verb* **foils, foiling, foiled**
to frustrate, as in *We foiled his evil plan.*

fold *verb* **folds, folding, folded**
1 to bend or move so that one part lies on another part. **2** to blend one ingredient into another, as in *Fold the milk into the flour.*
folding, made so that it can be folded to take up less space, as in *a folding chair.*
fold your arms, to wrap your arms round each other and hold them in front of your body.

fold *noun* **folds**
1 a line where something is folded. **2** an enclosure for sheep, etc.

folder *noun* **folders**
a folding cover for loose papers, as in *Keep your homework in this folder.*

foliage *noun*
the leaves of a tree or plant.

folk *plural noun*
people in general or a specific group, as in *Many folk gathered in the park. The townsfolk voted.*
folk-dance, a traditional dance of a country or a group of people.

folklore

folk-song, a traditional song of a country or a group of people.

the folks, your parents or relatives.

folklore *noun*
old beliefs and legends.

follow *verb* **follows, following, followed**
1 to come or go after. **2** to do a thing after something else. **3** to take someone or something as a guide or example. **4** to support or take an interest in a pastime, sports team, etc., as in *Which football team do you follow?* **5** to understand, as in *Do you follow me?* **6** to result, as in *Who knows what trouble may follow?*
follow up, to follow one thing with another; to do more work, research, etc. on something.

follower *noun* **followers**
1 a person who follows or supports a religion, a leader, a political party, etc.
2 (*in Australian Rules*) one of the two players, who does not have a fixed position on the field, but follows the play.

following *preposition*
1 after, as in *Following the motor-cycle outriders came the president's car.* **2** as a result of, as in *Following our visit to Darwin, we have decided to go there for our next holiday.*

fond *adjective* **fonder, fondest**
loving, as in *fond embraces.*
fond of, liking very much, as in *I'm fond of chocolate.*
fondly *adverb*, **fondness** *noun*

font *noun* **fonts**
a basin in a church which holds water for baptism.

font or **fount** *noun*
a set of printing type with the same appearance and size.

food *noun* **foods**
anything that a plant or animal can take into its body to make it grow or give it energy.
food-chain, a series of plants and animals, each of which serves as food for the next one.

fool *noun* **fools**
1 a stupid or unwise person. **2** a jester or clown, as in *Stop playing the fool.*

fool *verb* **fools, fooling, fooled**
1 to behave like a fool. **2** to trick or deceive someone, as in *She fooled them when she wore a wig.*
fool about or **fool around**, to behave stupidly.

foolhardy *adjective* **foolhardier, foolhardiest**
reckless or foolishly rash.
foolhardiness *noun*

foolish *adjective*
stupid or unwise.
foolishly *adverb*, **foolishness** *noun*

foolproof *adjective*
easy to use or do correctly.

foot *noun* **feet**
1 the lower part of a leg. **2** the lowest part of something, as in *at the foot of the hill.* **3** an old-fashioned measure of length, equal to about 30 centimetres.
on foot, walking.

football *noun* **footballs**
1 a game played by two teams which try to kick or throw an inflated ball, as in *Australian Rules, soccer, Rugby League and Rugby Union are all football games.* **2** the ball used in this game.
footballer *noun*

foothill *noun* **foothills**
a low hill near the bottom of a mountain or range of mountains.

foothold *noun* **footholds**
1 a place to put your foot when climbing, etc. **2** a firm position, as in *Winning the first three matches has given us a strong foothold in the championship.*

footing *noun*
1 having your feet placed on something; what your feet are standing on, as in *He lost his footing and fell down.* **2** a position or status, as in *We are on a friendly footing with that country.*

footlights *plural noun*
a row of lights along the front of the stage in a theatre.

footnote *noun* **footnotes**
a note printed at the bottom of a page.

footpath *noun* **footpaths**
a path for people to walk along.

footprint *noun* **footprints**
a mark made by a foot or shoe.

footsteps *plural noun*
the sound or marks your feet make when you walk or run.
follow in someone's footsteps, to do as someone did before you.

footy or **footie** *noun*
1 a game of football, especially Australian Rules. **2** a football, especially the oval ball used in Australian Rules.

for *preposition*
1 intended to be received or used by, as in *This letter is for you.* 2 towards; in the direction of, as in *They set out for home.* 3 in order to have or get, as in *Go for a walk.* 4 as far as; as long as, as in *We've been waiting for hours.* 5 at the price of, as in *She bought it for $2.* 6 instead of; in place of, as in *We exchanged stamps for coins.* 7 because of, as in *He was punished for swearing.* 8 concerning; in respect of, as in *She has a good ear for music.* 9 in defence or support of, as in *Are you for or against the government?* 10 in spite of, as in *For all his wealth, he is unhappy.*
for ever, always.

forbid *verb* **forbids, forbidding, forbade, forbidden**
1 to tell someone not to do something, as in *I forbid you to go.* 2 not to allow something, as in *Smoking is forbidden here.*

forbidding *adjective*
looking stern or unfriendly.

force *noun* **forces**
1 strength; power. 2 (*in Science*) an influence that can be measured and that tends to cause things to move, as in *wind force.* 3 an organised group of police, soldiers, etc. 4 being active or effective, as in *Is that law still in force?*
the forces, the army, navy, and air force.

force *verb* **forces, forcing, forced**
1 to use your power or strength to make someone do something. 2 to break something open.

forceful *adjective*
strong and effective, as in *a forceful speaker.*
forcefully *adverb*

Usage See the note at **forcible.**

forceps *noun* **forceps** (*say* **faw**-seps)
pincers used by a dentist, surgeon, etc.

forcible *adjective*
done by force.
forcibly *adverb*

Usage **forcible** can also mean strong and vigorous, but the more usual word for this is **forceful.**

ford *noun* **fords**
a shallow place where you can wade or drive across a river.

fore *adjective*
at or towards the front, as in *the fore wings of the dragonfly.*

fore *noun*
to the fore, to or at the front; in a leading position, as in *First class is in the fore of the plane. Our firm has always been to the fore in using new technology.*

forecast *verb*
to say what you think is going to happen before it happens.

forecast *noun* **forecasts**
a statement of what you think is going to happen before it happens, especially what the weather is going to be.

forecourt *noun* **forecourts**
an open space, often enclosed, in front of a large building, as in *Parking is not allowed on the hotel forecourt.*

forefathers *plural noun*
ancestors.

forefinger *noun* **forefingers**
the finger next to your thumb.

foregone *adjective*
foregone conclusion, an inevitable or obvious result.

foreground *noun* **foregrounds**
the part of a scene, view, etc. that is nearest to you.

forehead *noun* **foreheads** (*say* **fo**-ruhd *or* **faw**-hed)
the part of your face above your eyebrows.

foreign *adjective*
1 to do with another country. 2 strange; unnatural, as in *Lying is foreign to her.*

foreigner *noun* **foreigners**
a person from another country.

foreman *noun* **foremen**
someone in charge of a group of other workers.

foremost *adjective*
most important.

foresee *verb* **foresees, foreseeing, foresaw, foreseen**
to know what is going to happen before it happens; to expect something, as in *He foresaw trouble from the prisoners.*
foreseeable *adjective*, **foresight** *noun*

forest *noun* **forests**
a lot of trees growing together.
forested *adjective*, **forester** *noun*

forester *noun* **foresters**
1 a person managing a forest or skilled in forestry. 2 a grey kangaroo from eastern Australia.

forestry

forestry *noun*
planting forests and looking after them.

foretell *verb* **foretells, foretelling, foretold**
to predict, as in *She foretold their defeat.*

forever *adverb*
continually, as in *He is forever complaining.*

forfeit *noun* **forfeits**
something that you lose or have to pay as a
penalty.

forfeit *verb* **forfeits, forfeiting, forfeited**
to lose something as a penalty, as in *The
team that failed to turn up forfeited match
points.*

forgave past tense of **forgive.**

forge *verb* **forges, forging, forged**
1 to shape metal by heating and
hammering. 2 to copy something so as to
deceive people, as in *These ten-dollar notes
are forged.*
forge ahead, to get ahead by making a
strong effort.

forge *noun*
a place where metal is heated and shaped;
a blacksmith's workshop.

forgery *noun* **forgeries**
the act of copying something so as to
deceive people; a copy made to deceive
people, as in *That's not the real painting; it's a
forgery!*

forget *verb* **forgets, forgetting, forgot, forgotten**
1 to fail to remember, as in *I forgot my
homework.* 2 to stop thinking about
something, as in *We have forgotten our
quarrels.*
forget yourself, to behave rudely or
thoughtlessly.

forgetful *adjective*
tending to forget things.
forgetfulness *noun*

forget-me-not *noun* **forget-me-nots**
a small blue flower.

forgive *verb* **forgives, forgiving, forgave,
forgiven**
to stop being angry with someone about
something, as in *I forgave his rudeness when
he apologised.*
forgiveness *noun*

forgo or **forego** *verb* **forgoes, forwent,
forgone**
to go without.

fork *noun* **forks**
1 a small device with prongs for lifting
food to your mouth. 2 a large device with
prongs used for digging or lifting things.
3 a place where a road, river, etc. divides
into two or more parts.

fork *verb* **forks, forking, forked**
1 to dig or lift with a fork. 2 to divide
into two or more branches, as in *Go left
where the road forks.*
fork out, (*colloquial*) to pay out money.

forklift *noun* **forklifts**
a truck with two metal bars at the front for
lifting and moving heavy loads.

forlorn *adjective*
unhappy; not cared for, as in *a forlorn voice;
the bare and forlorn house.*

form *noun* **forms**
1 the shape, appearance, or condition of
something, as in *The dark form of a tree stood
out against the sunset.* 2 the way in which
something exists; a kind of thing, as in *Ice is
a form of water.* 3 a long seat without a
back. 4 a printed paper with spaces
where you give answers. 5 a class in
school, as in *Form one is the same as Year
seven.*

form *verb* **forms, forming, formed**
1 to shape or construct something; to
create something. 2 to develop, as in
Algae formed in the lake.

formal *adjective* **faw-muhl**
1 strictly following the accepted rules or
customs, as in *You will receive a formal
invitation to the wedding.* 2 to do with a
special ceremony, as in *The formal opening of
the new school takes place tomorrow.*
formally *adverb*

Usage Do not confuse **formal** with the
adjective **former**, which means earlier or of
past times.

formality *noun* **formalities**
1 formal behaviour. 2 something done to
obey a rule or custom, as in *The result was
known so the announcement was just a
formality.*

format *noun* **formats**
1 the shape and size of a book, a magazine,
etc. 2 the way something is arranged, as
in *What will the format of the lesson be?*

format *verb* **formats, formatting, formatted**
(*in Computing*) to prepare a computer disc
to take data, including removing old data
from it.

formation *noun* **formations**
1 the act of forming or making something. 2 something formed or made, as in
formations of rock. 3 a special pattern or
arrangement, as in *flying in formation.*

former *adjective*
earlier; of past times, as in *in former days*.
formerly *adverb*

Usage Do not confuse **former** with **formal**, which means strictly following the accepted rules, or ceremonial.

former *noun*
the former, the first of two people or things just mentioned, as in *Brown and Jones came in; the former looked happy*.

formidable *adjective*
(*say* **faw**-muh-duh-buhl *or* faw-**mid**-uh-buhl)
frightening; very difficult to deal with or do, as in *a formidable task*.
formidably *adverb*

formula *noun* **formulas** or **formulae**
1 a set of chemical symbols showing what a substance consists of, as in H_2O *is the formula for water*. 2 a rule or statement expressed in symbols or numbers. 3 a list of what is needed for making something, as in *The formula for paste is flour and water*.

formulate *verb* **formulates, formulating, formulated**
to express something clearly and exactly, as in *They formulated a plan*.
formulation *noun*

forsake *verb* **forsakes, forsaking, forsook, forsaken**
to abandon, as in *She forsook her children*.

fort *noun* **forts**
a fortified building.
hold the fort, to care for something or a situation while someone is absent.

forte *noun* (*say* **faw**-tay)
a person's strong point; something in which a person excels, as in *His forte is cooking*.

forte *adjective* and *adverb* (*say* **faw**-tay)
(*in music*) loud; loudly, as in *This piece is to be played forte*.

forthright *adjective*
direct and outspoken.

fortify *verb* **fortifies, fortifying, fortified**
1 to make a place strong against attack.
2 to strengthen something, as in *A good breakfast will fortify you for the day's work*.
fortification *noun*

fortnight *noun* **fortnights**
two weeks.
fortnightly *adverb* and *adjective*

fortress *noun* **fortresses**
a large fort; a fortified town.

fortunate *adjective*
lucky.
fortunately *adverb*

fortune *noun* **fortunes**
1 luck; chance. 2 a lot of money, property, etc., as in *a fortune in shares*.
fortune-teller, someone who tells you what will happen to you in the future.

forty *noun* **forties**
the number 40, four times ten.
forty winks, a short sleep.
fortieth *adjective* and *noun*

forward *adjective*
1 going forwards; placed in the front, as in *The leader sent a forward party of trained troops*. 2 bold, as in *The conceited student spoke in a forward manner to the teacher*.

forward *adverb*
forwards, as in *Please move forward*.

forward *noun* **forwards**
a player in the front line of a team at football, hockey, etc.

fossil *noun* **fossils**
the remains of a prehistoric animal or plant that has been in the ground for a very long time and become hard like rock.
fossil fuel, fuel such as coal, oil, etc., that was formed from living things a very long time ago.
fossilised *adjective*

foster *verb* **fosters, fostering, fostered**
1 to bring up someone else's child as if he or she were your own. 2 to encourage or promote the growth of something, as in *He fostered his pupil's painting talent*.
foster-child *noun*, **foster-mother** *noun*

fought past tense and past participle of **fight** *verb*.

foul *adjective* **fouler, foulest**
1 disgusting; filthy, as in *a foul smell*.
2 unfair; breaking the rules, as in *Foul play spoiled the game*.
foully *adverb*, **foulness** *noun*

foul *noun* **fouls**
an action that breaks the rules of a game.

found *verb* **founds, founding, founded**
1 to get something started; to establish something, as in *She founded a hospital*.
2 to base, as in *This novel is founded on fact*.

found past tense and past participle of **find**.

foundation

foundation *noun* foundations
1 the solid base on which a building is built. **2** a base or basis, as in *The rumour has no foundation. The foundation of good business is efficiency.* **3** the beginning of something, as in *The school's foundation occurred in the last century.*

founder *noun* founders
someone who starts something, as in *The founder of the Royal Flying Doctor Service was John Flynn.*

founder *verb* founders, foundering, foundered
to fill with water and sink, as in *The ship foundered.*

foundry *noun* foundries
a place where metal or glass is made or moulded.

fountain *noun* fountains
a device that makes water shoot up into the air.

fountain pen *noun* fountain pens
a pen that can be filled with a supply of ink.

four *noun* fours
the number 4, one more than three.
on all fours, crouching on hands and knees.

fourteen *noun* fourteens
the number 14, one more than thirteen.
fourteenth *adjective* and *noun*

fourth *adjective*
next after the third.
fourthly *adverb*

four-wheel drive *noun* four-wheel drives
a vehicle with all four wheels being driven by the engine and used for travelling over rough country, muddy areas, etc.

fowl *noun* fowls
a bird that is kept for its eggs or meat.

fox *noun* foxes
1 a wild animal that looks like a small dog with a long, furry tail. **2** a cunning or sly person.
foxy *adjective*

foyer *noun* foyers (*say* **foi**-uh)
the entrance hall of a cinema, theatre, hotel, etc.

fraction *noun* fractions
1 a number that is not a whole number, as in $^1\!/_2$ and $^3\!/_5$ *are fractions.* **2** a tiny part of something, as in *You have heard only a fraction of what happened.*
fractional *adjective*, **fractionally** *adverb*

fracture *verb* fractures, fracturing, fractured
to break something, especially to break a bone.

fracture *noun* fractures
the breaking of something, especially a bone.

fragile *adjective* (*say* **fra**-juyl)
easy to break or damage; delicate, as in *fragile glass; fragile health.*
fragility *noun*

fragment *noun* fragments
1 a small piece broken off something, as in *a fragment of rock.* **2** a small part, as in *She overheard fragments of conversation.*
fragmentary *adjective*, **fragmentation** *noun*, **fragmented** *adjective*

fragrant *adjective* (*say* **fray**-gruhnt)
with a sweet or pleasant smell.
fragrance *noun*

frail *adjective* frailer, frailest
weak; fragile, as in *The old man was very frail after his fall.*
frailty *noun*

frame *noun* frames
1 something that fits around the outside of a picture. **2** a rigid structure that supports something, as in *I've broken the frame of my glasses. This bicycle has a light frame.* **3** a human body, as in *He has a small frame.*
frame of mind, the way you think or feel for a while, as in *Wait till he's in a better frame of mind.*

frame *verb* frames, framing, framed
1 to put a frame on or around. **2** to form or construct, as in *They were framing new laws.* **3** (*colloquial*) to make an innocent person seem to be guilty.

frame-up *noun* frame-ups
(*colloquial*) making an innocent person seem to be guilty.

framework *noun* frameworks
1 a frame supporting something, as in *the framework of the new building.* **2** a basic plan or system, as in *the framework for the new primary school syllabus.*

franchise *noun* franchises
1 the right to vote in elections. **2** a licence to sell a firm's goods or services in a certain area.

frank *adjective* franker, frankest
honest; making your thoughts and feelings clear to people.
frankly *adverb*, **frankness** *noun*

frank *verb* franks, franking, franked
to mark something with a postmark to show that postage has been paid.

frankfurt *noun* **frankfurters**
a type of spicy smoked sausage first made in Frankfurt, Germany.

frantic *adjective*
wildly agitated or excited.
frantically *adverb*

fraud *noun* **frauds**
1 the act of cheating; dishonesty.
2 someone who is not what he or she pretends to be.
fraudulent *adjective*

frayed *adjective*
worn and ragged at the edge, as in *Your shirt collar is frayed.*

freak *noun* **freaks**
1 a very strange or abnormal person, animal, or thing. 2 (*colloquial*) someone who is very enthusiastic about a particular thing, as in *She is a fitness freak.*
freakish *adjective*

freckle *noun* **freckles**
a small brown spot on the skin caused by the sun.
freckled *adjective*

free *adjective* **freer, freest**
1 able to do what you want to do or go where you want to go. 2 not costing anything, as in *a free ride.* 3 available; not being used or occupied, as in *His afternoons are free.* 4 generous, as in *She is very free with her money.*
free of something, not having something; not affected by something, as in *The roads are free of traffic on Sundays.*
do something of your own free will, to do something without being asked, told, or forced to do it.
freely *adverb*

free *verb* **frees, freeing, freed**
to make someone or something free, as in *She freed the caged bird.*

freebie *noun* **freebies**
(*colloquial*) something provided free of charge.

freedom *noun*
being free; independence.

freehand *adjective* and *adverb*
without using any help (such as compasses) when drawing, as in *Draw a circle freehand.*

free-range *adjective*
to do with animals that are not caged but roam free; the produce from these animals, as in *free-range chickens; free-range eggs.*

freestyle *noun*
a fast swimming stroke in which the body is lying face downwards, the arms reach forward alternately in an overarm action and pull back through the water while the legs keep kicking.

free verse *noun*
a poem without either rhyme or a regular rhythm.

freeway *noun* **freeways**
a main road with several lanes for fast traffic.

freeze *verb* **freezes, freezing, froze, frozen**
1 to turn into ice or another solid; to become covered with ice, as in *The lake froze last night.* 2 to make or be very cold, as in *My hands are frozen.* 3 to keep wages, prices, etc. at a fixed level. 4 to stand completely still; suddenly.

freezer *noun* **freezers**
a large refrigerator for keeping food very cold, as in *You can keep food in freezers for months.*

freezing point *noun* **freezing points**
the temperature at which a liquid freezes.

freight *noun* (*say* frayt)
1 goods carried in a truck, ship, plane, etc. 2 the cost of transporting something.

freighter *noun* **freighters**
a ship or plane carrying mainly goods.

French *adjective*
to do with France.
French fries, thin strips of fried potato; chips.
French horn, a brass musical instrument made of a tube that goes around in a circle.
French window, a long window that serves as a door, opening on to a garden or balcony.

frenzy *noun* **frenzies**
wild excitement; madness.
frenzied *adjective*

frequency *noun* **frequencies**
1 happening often, as in *the frequency of rain in winter.* 2 the rate at which something happens, as in *the frequency of a heartbeat.* 3 the number of to-and-fro movements made each second by a wave of sound, light, etc., as in *radio stations on certain frequencies.*

frequent *adjective* (*say* free-kwuhnt)
happening often.
frequently *adverb*

frequent

frequent *verb* **frequents, frequenting, frequented** (*say* fruh-**kwent**)
to be in or go to a place often, as in *They frequented the youth club.*

fresh *adjective* **fresher, freshest**
1 not old, tired, or used, as in *fresh bread; fresh after her sleep.* **2** not tinned or preserved, as in *fresh fruit.* **3** cool and clean, as in *fresh air.* **4** not salty, as in *fresh water.*
freshly *adverb*, **freshness** *noun*

freshen *verb* **freshens, freshening, freshened**
to make something fresh; to become fresh.

freshwater *adjective*
to do with fresh water; living in rivers or lakes, as in *freshwater crocodile.*

fret *verb* **frets, fretting, fretted**
to worry or be upset about something.
fretful *adjective*, **fretfully** *adverb*

fretsaw *noun* **fretsaws**
a very narrow saw used for making fretwork.

fretwork *noun*
1 the skill of cutting decorative patterns in wood. **2** wood cut in this way.

friar *noun* **friars**
a man belonging to a religious order such as the Franciscans who has vowed to live a life of poverty and prayer.
friary *noun*

friction *noun*
1 the action of one thing rubbing against another. **2** disagreement; quarrelling, as in *friction between two friends.*
frictional *adjective*

Friday *noun* **Fridays**
the sixth day of the week.

fridge *noun* **fridges** short for **refrigerator.**

friend *noun* **friends**
1 someone you like who likes you. **2** a helpful or kind person.
make friends, to become someone's friend.
friendless *adjective*

friendly *adjective* **friendlier, friendliest**
behaving like a friend; kind and helpful.
friendliness *noun*

friendship *noun* **friendships**
being friends.

frieze *noun* **friezes** (*say* freez)
a strip of designs or pictures along the top of a wall.

frigate *noun* **frigates**
a fast warship.

fright *noun* **frights**
1 sudden, great fear. **2** a person or thing that looks ridiculous, as in *Her hair looked a fright.*

frighten *verb* **frightens, frightening, frightened**
to cause someone fright or fear.

frightful *adjective*
1 awful, as in *frightful storm.* **2** (*colloquial*) very bad, as in *frightful plan.*
frightfully *adverb*

frill *noun* **frills**
1 a decorative edging, usually pleated, on a dress, curtain, etc. **2** an unnecessary extra, as in *a simple life with no frills.*
frilled *adjective*, **frilly** *adjective*

fringe *noun* **fringes**
1 a decorative edging for fabric, with many threads hanging down loosely. **2** a straight line of short hair hanging down over your forehead. **3** the edge of something, as in *He stood on the fringe of the crowd.*
fringe benefit, an extra benefit on top of a wage or salary.
fringed *adjective*

frisk *verb* **frisks, frisking, frisked**
1 to jump or run around playfully. **2** to search someone by moving your hands over his or her clothes.

frisky *adjective* **friskier, friskiest**
playful; lively.
friskily *adverb*, **friskiness** *noun*

fritter *noun* **fritters**
a slice of fruit, meat, etc. fried in batter, as in *banana fritter.*

fritter *verb* **fritters, frittering, frittered**
fritter away, to waste something gradually; to spend money or time on trivial things, as in *He frittered away his money on gambling.*

frivolous *adjective*
1 not behaving seriously, as in *Don't be frivolous! This is an important matter.*
2 trivial, as in *frivolous pleasures.*
frivolity *noun*, **frivolously** *adverb*

frizzy *adjective* **frizzier, frizziest**
tightly curled, as in *She has frizzy hair.*

frock *noun* **frocks**
(old-fashioned use) a girl's or woman's dress.

frog *noun* **frogs**
a small jumping animal with webbed feet that can live both in water and on land.
have a frog in your throat, to be hoarse.

frogman *noun* **frogmen**
a swimmer equipped with a wet suit, flippers and breathing apparatus for swimming under water.

frolic *verb* **frolics, frolicking, frolicked**
to spend time in lively, cheerful games or pastimes.

frolic *noun* **frolics**
a lively, cheerful game or pastime, as in *The children had a frolic in the pool*.
frolicsome *adjective*

from *preposition*
1 out of, as in *She comes from Perth*.
2 measured with reference to, as in *We are a kilometre from home*. 3 starting at, as in *Say the poem from the beginning*. 4 because of, as in *I suffer from headaches*. 5 as opposed to, as in *Can you tell margarine from butter?*

front *noun* **fronts**
1 the part of a person or thing that faces forwards; the most important side of something, as in *The front of the house is brick*. 2 the part of a thing or place that is furthest forward, as in *Go to the front of the class*. 3 a road along the seashore, lake, etc., as in *Our holiday home is on the beach front*. 4 the place where fighting is happening in a war, as in *More troops were moved to the front*. 5 the forward edge of an advancing mass of hot or cold air, as in *A cold front is headed for Canberra*.
in front, at or near the front.
frontal *adjective*

frontier *noun* **frontiers**
the boundary between two countries or regions.

frost *noun* **frosts**
1 powdery ice that forms on things in freezing weather. 2 weather with a temperature below freezing point.
frosty *adjective*

frost *verb* **frosts, frosting, frosted**
to become covered with frost, as in *The windscreen frosted up on the cold morning. The lake frosted over during winter*.
frosted glass, glass that has a rough surface so that you cannot see through it.

frostbite *noun*
harm done to the skin by very cold weather.
frostbitten *adjective*

frosting *noun*
icing for cakes.

froth *noun*
a white mass of tiny bubbles on or in a liquid; foam.
frothy *adjective*

froth *verb* **froths, frothing, frothed**
to form a froth or foam.

frown *verb* **frowns, frowning, frowned**
to wrinkle your forehead because you are angry or worried.

frown *noun* **frowns**
wrinkling your forehead, or your expression when you have a wrinkled forehead because you are angry or worried.

froze past tense of **freeze**.

frozen past participle of **freeze**.

frugal *adjective* (*say* **froo**-guhl)
1 very economical and careful, as in *a frugal housekeeper*. 2 costing little money, as in *a frugal meal of rice*.
frugality *noun*

fruit *noun* **fruit** or **fruits**
1 the seed-container that grows on a tree or plant and is often used as food, as in *Apples, oranges, and bananas are fruit*. 2 the result of doing something, as in *He lived to see the fruits of his efforts*.
fruit salad, a mixture of raw fruit cut up for eating.
fruity *adjective*

fruitful *adjective*
1 successful; having good results, as in *Their talks were fruitful*. 2 producing fruit, as in *a fruitful blackberry bush*.
fruitfully *adverb*

fruitless *adjective*
unsuccessful; having no results.
fruitlessly *adverb*

frustrate *verb* **frustrates, frustrating, frustrated**
to prevent someone from doing something; to disappoint someone.
frustration *noun*

fry *verb* **fries, frying, fried**
to cook something in very hot fat or oil.

frying-pan *noun* **frying-pans**
a shallow pan in which things are fried.
out of the frying-pan into the fire, from a bad situation to something worse.

fudge *noun*
a soft sweet made with milk, sugar, butter, etc.

fuel *noun* **fuels**
something that is burnt to make heat or power, as in *Gas and oil are fuels*.

fuel *verb* **fuels, fuelling, fuelled**
to supply something with material to burn to make heat or power, as in *Gas fuelled the central heating*.

fugitive *noun* **fugitives** (*say* **fyoo**-juh-tiv)
a person who is running away from something, especially the law.

a
b
c
d
e
f
g
h
i
j
k
l
m
n
o
p
q
r
s
t
u
v
w
x
y
z

fugue

fugue *noun* **fugues** (*say* fyoog)
a piece of music in which themes are repeated in a pattern.

fulcrum *noun* **fulcra** or **fulcrums**
the point on which a lever rests or balances.

fulfil *verb* **fulfils, fulfilling, fulfilled**
to accomplish something; to do what is required, as in *He fulfilled his early promise as a painter by winning the Archibald Prize. She fulfilled the requirements for the job.*
fulfilment *noun*

full *adjective*
1 containing as much or as many as possible, as in *The box was full of pencils.*
2 having many people or things, as in *full of ideas.* 3 complete, as in *the full story.*
4 the greatest possible, as in *Full speed ahead!* 5 fitting loosely; with many folds, as in *a full skirt.*
in full, not leaving out anything.
to the full, completely; thoroughly.
fullness *noun*, **fully** *adverb*

full *adverb*
completely; very, as in *You knew full well what I wanted.*

full blood *noun* **full bloods**
1 a person of unmixed race, especially an Aborigine. 2 a pure-bred animal.

full moon *noun* **full moons**
the moon when you can see the whole of it as a bright circle.

full stop *noun* **full stops**
the dot used as a punctuation mark at the end of a sentence or after the letters of some abbreviations.

full-time *adjective* and *adverb*
to do with the normal working hours of the day, as in *a full-time job. She works full-time.*

fumble *verb* **fumbles, fumbling, fumbled**
to hold or handle something clumsily.

fume *verb* **fumes, fuming, fumed**
1 to give off strong-smelling smoke or gas. 2 to be very angry.

fumes *plural noun*
strong-smelling smoke or gas.

fun *noun*
amusement; enjoyment.
make fun of, to make people laugh at someone; to make a person or thing seem ridiculous.

function *noun* **functions**
1 what someone or something does or ought to do, as in *The function of a doctor is to cure sick people.* 2 an important event, party, etc., as in *The prime minister attends many functions.* 3 any of the basic operations of a computer, calculator, etc.

function *verb* **functions, functioning, functioned**
to work properly, as in *These scissors won't function.*

functional *adjective*
1 working properly, as in *The machine is fully functional again.* 2 practical, as in *a car with a simple, functional design.*
functionally *adverb*

fund *noun* **funds**
money collected or kept for a special purpose, as in *They started a fund for refugees.*

fundamental *adjective*
basic, as in *The fundamental rules of good behaviour should be followed in the classroom.*
fundamentally *adverb*

funeral *noun* **funerals**
the ceremony when a dead body is buried or burnt.

fungus *noun* **fungi**
a plant without leaves or flowers, growing on other plants or on decayed material, as in *Mushrooms and toadstools are fungi.*

funnel *noun* **funnels**
1 a chimney on a ship or steam engine.
2 a tube with one very wide end to help you pour things into bottles or other containers.

funnel-web *noun* **funnel-webs**
an aggressive, black, poisonous spider found in eastern Australia.

funny *adjective* **funnier, funniest**
1 able to make you laugh or smile, as in *a funny joke.* 2 strange; odd, as in *a funny smell.*
funnybone, part of your elbow which gives you a strange tingling feeling if it is hit.
funnily *adverb*

fur *noun* **furs**
1 the soft hair that covers some animals.
2 animal skin with the hair on it, used for clothing, as in *Furs are warm to wear.*

furious *adjective*
very angry; raging, as in *furious with the naughty child; furious storm.*
furiously *adverb*

furl *verb* **furls, furling, furled**
to roll up and fasten a sail, flag, or umbrella.

furlong *noun* **furlongs**
an old-fashioned measure of distance equal to about 201 metres.

furnace *noun* **furnaces**
a device in which great heat can be produced for making glass, manufacturing metals and heating buildings, etc.

furnish *verb* **furnishes, furnishing, furnished**
to provide furniture, fittings, etc. for a house, office, etc.

furniture *noun*
tables, chairs, beds, cupboards, and other movable things that you need inside a house, school, office, etc.

furrow *noun* **furrows**
1 a long cut in the ground made by a plough. 2 a deep wrinkle on the skin.

further *adverb* and *adjective*
1 at or to a greater distance; more distant, as in *I can't walk any further.* 2 more, as in *We need further information.*

Usage **Farther** can also be used when referring to physical distance, as in *I can't walk any farther*, though **further** is preferred by many people even in this sense.

further *verb* **furthers, furthering, furthered**
to help something progress, as in *We want to further the cause of peace.*

further education *noun*
education for people above school age.

furthermore *adverb*
also; moreover.

furthest *adverb* and *adjective*
at or to the greatest distance; most distant, as in *I travelled furthest. The furthest points from the equator are the north and south poles.*

Usage **Farthest** is used especially when referring to physical distance, as in *He walked farthest*, though **furthest** is preferred by many people even in this sense.

furtive *adjective*
cautious, as though you were about to do something wrong, as in *He gave a furtive glance around the shop, then slipped some lollies into his pocket.*

fury *noun* **furies**
wild anger; a rage.

fuse *verb* **fuses, fusing, fused**
1 to stop working because a fuse has melted, as in *The lights have fused.* 2 to blend together, especially through melting.

fuse *noun* **fuses**
1 a safety device containing a short piece of wire that melts if too much electricity passes through it. 2 a device for setting off an explosive.

fuselage *noun* **fuselages**
(*say* **fyoo**-zuh-lah*zh*)
the body of an aircraft, as in *Wings and tail are fitted to the fuselage.*

fusion *noun* (*say* **fyoo**-*zh*uhn)
1 the act of blending or joining together.
2 the joining together of the central parts of atoms, usually releasing energy.

fuss *noun* **fusses**
unnecessary excitement or worry about something that is not important.
make a fuss of someone, to treat someone with much kindness and attention.

fuss *verb* **fusses, fussing, fussed**
to be unnecessarily excited or worried about something that is not important.

fussy *adjective* **fussier, fussiest**
1 fussing; inclined to make a fuss. 2 full of unnecessary details or decorations, as in *She prefers plain to fussy clothes.*
fussily *adverb*, **fussiness** *noun*

futile *adjective* (*say* **fyoo**-tuyl)
useless; having no result, as in *The injured bird made a futile attempt to fly.*
futility *noun*

future *noun*
1 the time that will come, as in *Next year is the future.* 2 what is going to happen in the time that will come, as in *Many victories will certainly happen in the talented club's future.*

future tense *noun*
the form of a verb that shows that something is going to happen in the time that will come, as in *In English, the future tense uses 'will' and 'shall' in front of the verb.*
in future, from now onwards.

fuzz *noun*
1 fluffy or frizzy hair. 2 (*colloquial*) the police.

fuzzy *adjective* **fuzzier, fuzziest**
1 blurred; not clear. 2 like fuzz, fluffy, as in *a fuzzy jumper.*
fuzzily *adverb*, **fuzziness** *noun*

Gg

g short for **gram** or **grams**.

gabble *verb* gabbles, gabbling, gabbled
to talk so quickly that it is difficult for people to understand what you are saying.

gaberdine *noun* gaberdines
a smooth, heavy, hard-wearing cotton or woollen cloth.

gable *noun* gables
the three-sided part of a wall between two sloping roofs.
gabled *adjective*

gadget *noun* gadgets (*say* **gaj**-uht)
a small, useful device, as in *a gadget for opening tins*.
gadgetry *noun*

Gaelic *noun* (*say* **gay**-lik)
a Celtic language that is spoken in some parts of Ireland and Scotland.

gag *noun* gags
1 something put over someone's mouth to stop him or her from speaking. 2 a joke.

gag *verb* gags, gagging, gagged
to put something over someone's mouth so that he or she cannot speak.

gaggle *noun*
a flock of geese.

gaiety *noun*
being cheerful; amusement.

gaily *adverb*
in a cheerful way.

gain *verb* gains, gaining, gained
to get something that you did not have before.
gain on or **gain upon,** to come closer to someone or something you are chasing.

gain *noun* gains
something you have got that you did not have before; profit.

gala *noun* galas (*say* **gah**-luh)
a festival or special occasion, as in *A gala was held to celebrate the bicentenary of the nation*.

galah *noun*
1 a grey-backed, pink-breasted cockatoo found in most parts of Australia. 2 a person who makes a fool of himself or herself, as in *The man made a galah of himself when he ran onto the football field and stopped the game*.

Origin **Galahs** comes from Yuwaalaraay, an Aboriginal language of New South Wales. See the Aboriginal Languages map at the back of this dictionary.

galaxy *noun* galaxies (*say* **gal**-uhk-see)
a very large group of stars, as in *You can see three galaxies without a telescope*.
galactic *adjective*

gale *noun* gales
a very strong wind.

gallant *adjective*
1 brave. 2 polite and helpful, especially towards women.
gallantly *adverb*, gallantry *noun*

galleon *noun* galleons
a large Spanish sailing-ship used from the 15th to the 17th Century.

gallery *noun* galleries
1 a building or room where works of art are displayed. 2 a platform sticking out from the inside wall of a building, as in *a gallery in a church for the choir*. 3 a long room or passage, as in *a shooting gallery*.

galley *noun* galleys
1 an ancient type of long ship propelled by oars. 2 the kitchen in a ship or plane.

gallon *noun* **gallons**
an old-fashioned measure of liquid equal to about 4$^1/_2$ litres.

gallop *noun* **gallops**
1 the fastest pace a horse can go. 2 a fast ride on a horse.

gallop *verb* **gallops, galloping, galloped**
to ride at the fastest pace a horse can go, as in *The cattlemen galloped away.*

gallows *noun*
a framework on which criminals were hanged.

Gallup poll *noun* **Gallup polls**
questioning a number of people so as to estimate how many people think in a certain way, as in *A Gallup poll showed that 60% of people were in favour of a ban on smoking.*

galore *adjective*
in large amounts, as in *There was food galore at the party.*

galvanise or **galvanize** *verb* **galvanises, galvanising, galvanised**
1 to coat iron with zinc to protect it from rust. 2 to stimulate or shock someone into doing something, as in *The bad report galvanised the student into doing more work.*

gamble *verb* **gambles, gambling, gambled**
1 to play a game for money. 2 to take great risks, as in *He is gambling with his life.*
gambler *noun*

game *noun* **games**
1 something that you can play, usually with rules, as in *Football, chess, and dominoes are games.* 2 one section of a long game like tennis or whist, as in *In tennis, you must win at least 6 games to win a set.* 3 wild animals or birds hunted for sport or food, as in *Some people shoot game like quail and duck.*
play the game, to behave fairly according to the rules.
the game is up, a fraud or secret has been revealed.

game *adjective*
1 able and willing to do something, as in *He's game for all kinds of tricks.* 2 brave, as in *The game player did not complain about the injury.*
gamely *adverb*

gander *noun* **ganders**
a male goose.

gang *noun* **gangs**
1 a group of young people who go about together. 2 a group of people who work together, as in *a gang of road workers.* 3 a group of gangsters, as in *a gang of thieves.*

gangplank *noun* **gangplanks**
a plank for walking on to or off a ship.

gangrene *noun*
rotting flesh caused by a stop in blood circulation.

gangster *noun* **gangsters**
a violent criminal.

gangway *noun* **gangways**
1 a gap left for people to move along between rows of seats or through a crowd. 2 a gangplank or other structure for getting on or off a ship.

gaol *noun* **gaols** (*say* jayl)
a prison; a jail.
gaoler *noun*

Usage Do not confuse **gaol** with **goal**, which means the posts on a sports field, or a point scored in sports, or something that you try to do.

gaol *verb* **gaols, gaoling, gaoled**
to put someone in prison.

gap *noun* **gaps**
an opening or break in something; an interval in time or space, as in *a gap in the wall; a gap in the program.*

gape *verb* **gapes, gaping, gaped**
1 to open wide, as in *The front door gaped open.* 2 to stare in amazement, especially with an open mouth.

garage *noun* **garages** (*say* ga-rahzh or ga-rahj or guh-**rahzh** or guh-**rahj**)
1 a building in which motor vehicles are kept. 2 a place where petrol is sold or cars, etc., are repaired.
garage sale, the sale of various household goods from the garage of a house.

garbage *noun*
rubbish.

garbled *adjective*
difficult to understand; mixed-up, as in *a garbled message.*

garden *noun* **gardens**
a piece of ground where flowers, fruit, or vegetables are grown.
gardener *noun*, **gardening** *noun*

gargle *verb* **gargles, gargling, gargled**
to wash your throat by moving liquid around inside it, without swallowing.

gargoyle *noun* **gargoyles**
an ugly or amusing carving on a building, especially one of a head that sticks out from a gutter and sends out rainwater through its mouth.

garish

garish *adjective* (*say* **gair**-rish *or* **gah**-rish)
very bright or gaudy, as in *Hot pink and bright orange are garish colours.*

garland *noun* **garlands**
a wreath of flowers for decoration.

garlic *noun*
a plant rather like an onion, with a strong-smelling bulb used for flavouring food.

garment *noun* **garments**
something you wear; a piece of clothing.

garnish *verb* **garnishes, garnishing, garnished**
to decorate food to make it taste or look better.

garrison *noun* **garrisons**
troops who defend a town or fort.

garter *noun* **garters**
a band of elastic to hold up socks or stockings.

gas *noun* **gases**
1 a substance like air, as in *Oxygen and hydrogen are gases.* **2** a gas that burns and is used for heating or cooking, as in *Gas is used for gas stoves and gas heaters.*
gaseous *adjective*

gas *verb* **gasses, gassing, gassed**
to overcome or harm someone with a poisonous gas.

gash *noun* **gashes**
a long, deep cut or wound.

gasket *noun* **gaskets**
a flat ring or strip of soft material for sealing a joint between metal surfaces.

gasp *verb* **gasps, gasping, gasped**
1 to breathe quickly and noisily when you are tired, ill, or astonished. **2** to say something or to speak in a breathless way, as in *'Is this the right train for Brisbane?', he gasped.*

gastric *adjective*
to do with the stomach, as in *gastric juices.*

gastroenteritis *noun*
an illness in which your stomach and intestines become inflamed.

gate *noun* **gates**
1 something that opens and closes the entrance to a garden, paddock, etc. **2** a place where you wait before you get on a plane, etc. **3** the number of people attending a football match, etc.

gateau *noun* **gateaux** (*say* **gat**-oh)
a rich cake, usually made in several layers with cream in between.

gateway *noun* **gateways**
1 an opening containing a gate. **2** a way to reach something, as in *the gateway to success.*

gather *verb* **gathers, gathering, gathered**
1 to come together; to bring things or people together, as in *The children gathered to watch the fireworks. Gather the material on the elastic.* **2** to collect or pick fruit, nuts, berries, etc. **3** to understand, decide, or learn, as in *I gather that you are on holiday.*
gather speed, to get faster gradually.

gathering *noun* **gatherings**
an assembly or meeting of people; a party.

gaudy *adjective* **gaudier, gaudiest**
too showy and bright, as in *She wore a gaudy hat to the Melbourne Cup.*

gauge *noun* **gauges** (*say* gayj)
1 one of the standard sizes of something. **2** the distance between a pair of railway lines. **3** a measuring instrument, as in *a pressure gauge.*

gauge *verb* **gauges, gauging, gauged**
1 to measure. **2** to estimate; to judge, as in *Try to gauge how many people are likely to respond.*

gaunt *adjective*
1 thin and looking ill or tired, as in *gaunt after illness.* **2** grim and desolate, as in *a gaunt stretch of land.*

gauntlet *noun* **gauntlets**
a glove with a wide covering for the wrist.

gauze *noun*
thin, net-like material of wire, silk, cotton, etc.

gave past tense of **give**.

gay *adjective* **gayer, gayest**
1 cheerful. **2** brightly coloured. **3** (*colloquial*) homosexual.

gaze *verb* **gazes, gazing, gazed**
to look at something or someone for a long time, as in *He gazed at the sunset.*

gaze *noun* **gazes**
a long, steady look.

gazelle *noun* **gazelles**
a small graceful antelope.

gear *noun* **gears**
1 equipment; clothes, as in *mountaineering gear; trendy gear.* **2** a set of toothed wheels working together in a machine, especially those transmitting power from an engine to the wheels of a vehicle.
in gear, with the gears connected.
out of gear, with the gears not connected.

gecko *noun* **geckos**
a small tropical lizard.

geese plural of **goose**.

Geiger counter *noun* Geiger counters
a device that detects and measures
radioactivity.

gel *noun* gels
a jelly-like substance, especially one used
on your hair to give it a particular style.

gelatine *noun* (*say* jel-uh-**teen**)
a clear, tasteless substance used to make
jellies, etc.
gelatinous *adjective*

gelding *noun* geldings
a male horse that has been desexed.

gem *noun* gems
1 a jewel. **2** a person or thing of great
beauty or worth, as in *What a gem she is! We
bought the house; it's a real gem.*

gemfish *noun*
an edible fish found off the coast of New
South Wales and Victoria; hake.

gender *noun* genders (*say* jen-duh)
1 the group in which a noun or pronoun
belongs in some languages, as in *The gender
of 'he' is masculine, the gender of 'she' is
feminine, and the gender of 'it' is neuter.* **2** a
person's sex.

gene *noun* genes (*say* jeen)
one of the factors in your body that
controls what characteristics you inherit
from your parents.

genealogy *noun* genealogies
the study of the history of families; a list of
the people who are or were members of a
particular family.

general *adjective*
1 to do with all or most people or things,
as in *the general population; general
knowledge.* **2** not detailed; not specialised,
as in *a general science course.*
general election, electing Members of
Parliament for the whole country.
general practitioner, a doctor who is not a
specialist or consultant.
general store, a shop which stocks a wide
range of goods, especially in a country
town.
in general, usually.

general *noun* generals
a high-ranking army officer.

generalise or **generalize** *verb* generalises,
generalising, generalised
to talk about general things, not particular
things; to state principles, as in *Some young
people are safe drivers and some are not; you
can't generalise.*
generalisation *noun*

generally *adverb*
usually.

generate *verb* generates, generating,
generated
to produce or create something, as in
*Hydroelectric power is generated from the
Snowy Mountains.*
generator *noun*

generation *noun* generations
1 a single stage in a family, as in *Three
generations were included: grandparents,
parents, and children.* **2** all the people born
about the same time, as in *His generation
grew up during the war.* **3** the production
of something, especially electricity.
generation gap, parents and children
failing to understand or communicate with
each other.

generous *adjective*
ready to give or share what you have.
generosity *noun*, **generously** *adverb*

genesis *noun*
the origin; the beginning of something, as
in *The genesis of the modern Olympic Games
came from Greece.*
Genesis, the first book of the Bible, telling
the story of the creation of the world.

genetic *adjective* (*say* juh-**net**-ik)
to do with genes.
genetic engineering, the science of altering
the genes of a living thing in order to make
it stronger or more suitable for a particular
purpose.
genetically *adverb*

genetics *noun*
the science that examines how the
characteristics of living things are passed
on to their offspring by means of genes.

genial *adjective*
kind, pleasant, and cheerful, as in *a genial
host. His genial smile made us feel welcome.*
genially *adverb*

genie *noun* genies
a magical being in stories who can make
your wishes come true, as in *The genie
appeared whenever Aladdin rubbed the lamp.*

genitals *plural noun*
the parts of the body used for sexual
intercourse.

genius *noun* geniuses
an unusually clever person.

genocide *noun* (*say* **jen**-uh-suyd)
the deliberate killing of a people or a
nation.

genre

genre *noun*
a type or form of written, visual or oral texts used for a specific purpose.

gent *noun* gents
(*colloquial*) a gentleman; a man.
the Gents, (*colloquial*) men's public toilets.

gentile *noun* gentiles
a person who is not Jewish.

gentle *adjective* gentler, gentlest
kind and quiet; not rough or severe.
gentleness *noun*, **gently** *adverb*

gentleman *noun* gentlemen
1 a man, as in *Good evening, ladies and gentlemen!* **2** a well-mannered or honest man, as in *He's a real gentleman.*
gentlemanly *adverb*

genuine *adjective*
real; not faked or pretending, as in *This diamond is genuine. She looked at me in genuine astonishment.*
genuinely *adverb*

genus *noun* genera (*say* **jee**-nuhs)
a group of similar animals or plants, as in *The blue gum belongs to the 'Eucalyptus' genus.*

geography *noun*
the science or study of the world and its climate, peoples, and products.
geographer *noun*, **geographical** *adjective*, **geographically** *adverb*

geology *noun* (*say* jee-ol-uh-jee)
the science or study of the earth's crust, its rocks, etc.
geological *adjective*, **geologically** *adverb*, **geologist** *noun*

geometry *noun*
the science or study of lines, angles, surfaces, and solids.
geometric *adjective*, **geometrical** *adjective*, **geometrically** *adverb*

geranium *noun* geraniums
(*say* juh-**ray**-nee-uhm)
a plant with mainly red, pink, or white flowers that is often grown in a pot.

geriatric *adjective*
to do with old people's health and care, as in *geriatric hospital.*

germ *noun* germs
a tiny living thing, especially one that causes a disease.

German measles *plural noun*
a disease caught by contact with infected people, that gives you a cough, a sore throat, and red spots, and that can harm an unborn baby if its mother catches the disease; rubella.

German shepherd *noun* German shepherds
a large, wolf-like dog often used as a police or guard dog; an Alsatian.

germinate *verb* germinates, germinating, germinated
to start growing and developing.
germination *noun*

gestation *noun*
the time when a foetus is growing in its mother's womb, as in *Elephants have a long period of gestation.*

gesticulate *verb* gesticulates, gesticulating, gesticulated
to make movements with your hands and arms while you are talking.

gesture *noun* gestures (*say* jes-chuh)
a movement or action which expresses what you feel.

get *verb* gets, getting, got
1 to become, as in *Are you getting angry?* **2** to obtain or receive something, as in *He got four years in prison. I got a new bike yesterday.* **3** to reach a place, as in *We'll get there by midnight.* **4** to put or move, as in *I can't get my shoe on.* **5** to prepare, as in *Shall I get the tea?* **6** to persuade or order, as in *Get him to wash up.* **7** to succeed in bringing, placing, etc., as in *I'll get you to the airport on time. Get into the box.* **8** (*colloquial*) to understand, as in *Do you get what I mean?* **9** to harm, injure, etc., as in *I'll get you for that.*
get away with, to escape punishment, etc., as in *They got away with the robbery.*
get by, to manage.
get off, to stop riding on a bus, horse, etc.; to avoid being punished.
get on, to start riding on a bus, horse, etc.; to make progress; to be friendly with someone.
get on with, to work at something.
get out of, to avoid something.
get over, to recover from an illness, shock, etc.
get there, (*colloquial*) to succeed.
get through to someone, (*colloquial*) to make someone understand something, as in *I've tried to explain, but I just can't get through to him.*
get your own back, to have your revenge.
have got to, must.

getaway *noun* getaways
an escape.

get-together *noun* get-togethers
(*colloquial*) a social gathering.

geyser *noun* **geysers** (*say* gee-zuh *or* guy-zuh)
a natural spring that shoots up columns of hot water.

ghastly *adjective* **ghastlier, ghastliest**
horrible; awful, as in *a ghastly crime*.

ghetto *noun* **ghettos** (*say* get-oh)
a part of a city where a minority group live, such as people from another country.

ghost *noun* **ghosts**
1 the spirit of a dead person seen by a living person. 2 a shadow or show, as in *My team hasn't a ghost of chance of winning*. 3 blurred vision on a television screen.
ghostly *adjective*

ghoul *noun* **ghouls**
1 an evil spirit in Muslim folklore that eats dead bodies. 2 (*colloquial*) a person who is unpleasantly interested in death or injury, as in *A crowd of ghouls had gathered at the scene of the car crash*.

giant *noun* **giants**
1 a huge man. 2 a person or thing of great size, ability, courage, etc., as in *a political giant; a business giant*.
giantess *noun*

giant *adjective*
huge.

giddy *adjective* **giddier, giddiest**
having the feeling that everything is turning around in circles; causing this feeling, as in *I'm feeling giddy; a giddy dance*.
giddily *adverb*, **giddiness** *noun*

gidgee *noun* **gidgees**
1 an unpleasant-smelling wattle tree.
2 an Aboriginal spear.

Origin This word comes from the Aboriginal language Yuwaalaraay: **gijir**. See the Aboriginal Languages map at the back of this dictionary.

gift *noun* **gifts**
1 a present. 2 a talent, as in *She has a gift for music*.

gifted *adjective*
with a natural ability for doing something well.

gig *noun* **gigs**
(*colloquial*) an occasion when a musician or band plays rock music, jazz, etc. in public.

gigantic *adjective*
huge.
gigantically *adverb*

giggle *verb* **giggles, giggling, giggled**
to laugh in a silly way.

giggle *noun* **giggles**
1 a silly laugh. 2 (*colloquial*) something amusing; a joke, as in *We did it for a giggle*.
the giggles, (*colloquial*) a fit of giggling.

gild *verb* **gilds, gilding, gilded**
to cover something with a thin layer of gold paint or gold; to gilt.

Usage Do not confuse **gild** with **guild**, which is a noun meaning a society of people with similar skills.

gilgie or **jilgie** *noun* **gilgies** (*say* jil-gee)
a Western Australian name for a yabby

Origin This word comes from the Aboriginal language Nyungar: **jilgi**. See the Aboriginal Languages map at the back of this dictionary.

gill *noun* **gills**
one of the parts on a fish's side that it breathes through.

gilt *adjective*
gold-coloured or thinly covered with gold, as in *a gilt frame*.

gilt *noun*
gold or golden material used in gilding.

gimmick *noun* **gimmicks**
something unusual done or used to attract people's attention, as in *Some shops use gimmicks to sell their products*.
gimmicky *adjective*

gin *noun*
a colourless alcoholic drink.

ginger *noun*
1 a flavouring that makes food taste spicy. 2 a reddish-yellow colour, as in *ginger hair*.
ginger beer, a sweet, fizzy drink that tastes of ginger.
gingery *adjective*

gingerbread *noun*
a cake or biscuit flavoured with ginger.

gingerly *adverb*
cautiously.

ginormous *adjective*
(*colloquial*) enormous.

gipsy or **gypsy** *noun* **gipsies**
a member of a group of people with Indian ancestors but now found mainly in Europe, who wander from place to place rather than having a settled home.

giraffe

giraffe *noun* **giraffes**
a tall African animal with spotted skin, a very long neck and long legs.

girder *noun* **girders**
a metal beam supporting part of a building or bridge.

girdle *noun* **girdles**
1 a belt or piece of clothing worn around your waist. 2 a corset.

girl *noun* **girls**
1 a young female person. 2 a daughter, as in *My girl's in the netball team.*
girlhood *noun*, **girlish** *adjective*

girlfriend *noun* **girlfriends**
1 a boy's or man's regular female friend or lover. 2 a girl's or woman's regular female friend.

girth *noun* **girths**
1 the measurement around something, as in *The inflated plastic figure had a wide girth.* 2 a band fastened around a horse's belly to keep its saddle in place.

gist *noun* (*say* jist)
the main points or general meaning of a speech, argument, etc.

give *verb* **gives, giving, gave, given**
1 to let someone have something, as in *She has given me a lolly.* 2 to make; to do something suddenly, as in *He gave a laugh.* 3 to present or perform, as in *They gave a concert.* 4 to bend or go downwards; to collapse, as in *Will this branch give if I sit on it?* 5 to pay, as in *He will give hundreds of dollars for those books.*
give away, to sacrifice something; to reveal a secret, as in *He gave all his wealth away. They've given away our plans!*
give in, to surrender.
give off, to send out something.
give out, to hand out something; to become worn out, as in *Which government department gives out grants? I think the engine will give out soon.*
give up, to stop doing or trying something; to surrender, as in *They gave up trying to get in. Most of the soldiers gave up without a struggle.*
give way, to collapse; to let someone go before you, as in *The bridge gave way. I gave way to a woman pushing a pram.*
giver *noun*

given *adjective*
definite; stated; agreed, as in *Meet at a given time.*
given to, tending to; having a particular habit, as in *He is given to boasting.*

glacial *adjective* (*say* **glay**-seeuhl *or* **glay**-shuhl)
1 to do with ice; icy, as in *glacial wind.*
2 formed by glaciers, as in *a glacial valley.*
3 ice in a mass, as in *glacial drift.*

glaciation *noun*
the action of glaciers, as in *This valley was formed by glaciation.*

glacier *noun* **glaciers** (*say* **glay**-see-uh *or* gla-see-uh)
a river of ice moving slowly along a mountain valley.

glad *adjective* **gladder, gladdest**
pleased; happy.
glad of something, grateful for something.
gladden *verb*, **gladly** *adverb*, **gladness** *noun*

gladiator *noun* **gladiators**
in Ancient Rome, a man who fought with a sword or other weapons at public shows.

glamour *or* **glamor** *noun*
1 the attractive, exciting appearance of something, as in *The glamour of a career in television attracted her.* 2 a person's beauty or attractiveness.
glamorise *verb*

glamorous *adjective*
attractive and exciting; beautiful, as in *Port Douglas is a glamorous place to spend a holiday. People expect film stars to be glamorous.*

glance *verb* **glances, glancing, glanced**
1 to look at something briefly. 2 to hit and slide off something, as in *The ball glanced off his bat.*

glance *noun* **glances**
a brief look.

gland *noun* **glands**
an organ of the body that produces substances which are sent into the blood, or sent out of the body.

glandular *adjective*
to do with the glands, as in *Glandular problems caused ill health.*
glandular fever, a disease that gives you a fever and makes some of your glands painful and swollen.

glare *verb* **glares, glaring, glared**
1 to shine with a very bright or dazzling light. 2 to look angrily at someone.

glare *noun* **glares**
1 very strong light. 2 an angry stare.

glaring *adjective*
1 very bright, as in *glaring sunlight.*
2 very obvious, as in *That's a glaring error!*

glossary

glass *noun* **glasses**
1 a hard, brittle, usually clear substance, as in *Glass is used for making windows, mirrors, dishes, etc.* 2 a cup made of this material, usually without a handle.
glasses, spectacles; binoculars.
glassful *noun*

glasshouse *noun* **glasshouses**
a light structure with the sides and roof made mainly of glass which traps the heat from the sun, and used for growing plants; a greenhouse.

glassy *adjective* **glassier, glassiest**
1 like glass. 2 dull; without liveliness or expression, as in *a glassy stare.*

glaze *verb* **glazes, glazing, glazed**
1 to fit or cover something with glass.
2 to give a shiny surface to pottery, etc. 3 to become glassy, as in *Her eyes glazed and she fainted.*

glazier *noun* **glaziers**
someone who fits glass into window frames.

gleam *noun* **gleams**
1 a beam of soft light, especially one that comes and goes. 2 a small amount, as in *a gleam of hope.*

gleam *verb* **gleams, gleaming, gleamed**
to shine with beams of soft light.

glee *noun*
delight; joy.
gleeful *adjective*, **gleefully** *adverb*

glen *noun* **glens**
a narrow valley, especially in Scotland.

glide *verb* **glides, gliding, glided**
1 to fly or move smoothly. 2 to fly without using an engine.

glider *noun* **gliders**
a plane that does not use an engine.

glimmer *verb* **glimmers, glimmering, glimmered**
to shine faintly.

glimmer *noun* **glimmers**
1 a faint shine. 2 a small sign, as in *a glimmer of success.*

glimpse *noun* **glimpses**
a brief view or look.

glimpse *verb* **glimpses, glimpsing, glimpsed**
to see something briefly.

glint *verb* **glints, glinting, glinted**
to flash or sparkle.

glisten *verb* **glistens, glistening, glistened**
to shine like something wet or polished.

glitter *verb* **glitters, glittering, glittered**
to sparkle.

gloat *verb* **gloats, gloating, gloated**
to show unpleasant pleasure about your success or about harm that has happened to someone else.

global *adjective*
to do with the whole world, as in *Pollution is a global concern.*
global warming, a gradual increase in the average temperature of the earth's climate, caused by the greenhouse effect.
globally *adverb*

globe *noun* **globes**
1 something shaped like a ball. 2 a ball with a map of the whole world on it.
the globe, the world, as in *a company with branches all over the globe.*

glockenspiel *noun* **glockenspiels**
a musical instrument made of metal bells, tubes, or especially bars of different sizes that you hit with small hammers.

gloom *noun* **glooms**
a depressed condition or feeling, as in *He was filled with gloom at the thought of losing his job.*

gloomy *adjective* **gloomier, gloomiest**
1 almost dark; not lighted, as in *a gloomy room.* 2 depressed; sad, as in *a gloomy expression.*
gloomily *adverb*, **gloominess** *noun*

glorify *verb* **glorifies, glorifying, glorified**
1 to praise someone highly. 2 to make something seem better or more splendid than it is.
glorification *noun*

glorious *adjective*
having glory; wonderful, as in *a glorious morning in autumn.*
gloriously *adverb*

glory *noun* **glories**
1 fame and honour; praise, as in *She covered herself in glory at the gymnastics competition.*
2 splendour; beauty, as in *the glories of the Barrier Reef.*

gloss *noun* **glosses**
1 the shine on a smooth surface.
2 a paint that makes surfaces shiny.
glossy *adjective*

glossary *noun* **glossaries**
a list of words with their meanings explained, as in *Your Science book has a glossary at the back.*

a
b
c
d
e
f
g
h
i
j
k
l
m
n
o
p
q
r
s
t
u
v
w
x
y
z

glove

glove *noun* **gloves**
a covering for your hand.

glow *verb* **glows, glowing, glowed**
1 to be bright and warm without flames.
2 to be in a cheerful or excited condition.

glow *noun*
1 brightness and warmth without flames.
2 a cheerful or excited condition, as in *a glow of enthusiasm*.

glower *verb* **glowers, glowering, glowered**
to look bad-tempered.

glow-worm *noun* **glow-worms**
an insect whose tail gives out a green light.

glucose *noun*
a type of sugar that is found in plants and which animals and people make in their bodies from the food they eat, as in *Glucose gives your body energy*.

glue *noun* **glues**
a thick liquid for sticking things together.
gluey *adjective*

glue *verb* **glues, gluing, glued**
to stick something with glue.

glum *adjective* **glummer, glummest**
depressed; sad.
glumly *adverb*

glut *noun*
an over-supply of something, as in *A glut of oranges forced their price down*.

glutton *noun* **gluttons**
someone who eats too much.
gluttonous *adjective*, **gluttony** *noun*

gnarled *adjective* (*say* nahld)
twisted and lumpy, like an old tree.

gnash *verb* **gnashes, gnashing, gnashed**
(*say* nash)
to strike your teeth together.

gnat *noun* **gnats** (*say* nat)
a tiny fly that bites.

gnaw *verb* **gnaws, gnawing, gnawed**
(*say* naw)
to keep biting something that is hard, as in *The dog gnawed the bone*.

gnome *noun* **gnomes** (*say* nohm)
a kind of dwarf in fairy tales that usually lives underground.

go *verb* **goes, going, went, gone**
1 to move in any direction, as in *Where are you going?* 2 to leave; to set out, as in *We shall go in a minute.* 3 to lead; to extend, as in *This road goes to Alice Springs.* 4 to become, as in *The milk went sour.* 5 to work properly, as in *My watch isn't going.* 6 to have a proper place; to belong, as in

Plates go on that shelf. 7 to happen or proceed, as in *The show went well.* 8 to make a particular movement or sound, as in *The gun went bang.* 9 to be finished or lost, as in *My money has gone.* 10 to be sold, as in *The house went very cheaply.* 11 to pass, as in *Time goes slowly when you are waiting.*
go along with, to agree.
go back on, not to keep a promise.
go in for, to do or take part in something.
go missing, (*colloquial*) to be lost.
go off, to explode; to become stale; to stop liking someone or something, as in *The whole box of fireworks went off at once. That milk has gone off. I've gone off him ever since he ruined my bike.*
go on, to happen; to do something more than once, as in *What's going on? Unless you stop him now, he'll go on stealing things.*
go one better, to do better than someone else.
go out, to leave a house, home, etc.; to go to entertainments; to stop burning or shining, as in *I went out and locked the door. We go out twice a week to the cinema. The fire's gone out.*
go out with someone, to be someone's regular girlfriend or boyfriend.

go *noun* **goes**
1 (*colloquial*) a turn or try, as in *May I have a go?* 2 (*colloquial*) a success, as in *They made a go of it.* 3 energy; liveliness, as in *She's full of go.*
all the go, (*colloquial*) fashionable.
on the go, always working or moving.

go-ahead *noun*
permission to do something, as in *The principal has given us the go-ahead to organise a class excursion.*

go-ahead *adjective*
adventurous and keen to try out new methods, as in *a modern, go-ahead company developing new electronic products.*

goal *noun* **goals**
1 something that you try to do or to achieve, as in *Her goal was to become prime minister.* 2 the two posts that the ball must go between to score a point in football, hockey, etc. 3 a point scored in football, hockey, netball, etc.

> **Usage** Do not confuse **goal** with **gaol**, which means prison.

goalie *noun* **goalies**
(*colloquial*) a goalkeeper.

goalkeeper *noun* **goalkeepers**
the player in soccer, hockey, etc. who stands in the goal and guards it.

goalposts *plural noun*
the upright posts of a goal in sports.

goanna *noun* **goannas**
any of a number of large, fast-moving
Australian lizards.

goat *noun* **goats**
an animal with horns, belonging to the
same family as sheep.

gobble *verb* **gobbles, gobbling, gobbled**
to eat something quickly and greedily.

gobbledegook or **gobbledygook** *noun*
complicated technical or official language
that is difficult or impossible for most
people to understand.

go-between *noun* **go-betweens**
a person who takes messages between
people who are unable or unwilling to
meet each other.

goblet *noun* **goblets**
a glass that you drink from, with a long
stem and a base.

goblin *noun* **goblins**
a mischievous, ugly, dwarf-like elf.

god *noun* **gods**
someone or something that is worshipped.
God, the creator of the Universe in
Christian, Jewish, and Muslim belief.
godless *adjective*, **godly** *adjective*

godparent *noun* **godparents**
someone who promises, when a child is
baptised, to see that it is brought up as a
Christian.
godchild *noun*, **god-daughter** *noun*, **godfather**
noun, **godmother** *noun*, **godson** *noun*

godsend *noun* **godsends**
something that arrives unexpectedly and
helps you very much, as in *The lotto win was
a godsend for the unemployed family.*

goggles *plural noun*
large spectacles to protect the eyes from
wind, water, dust, etc.

going *noun*
1 departure, as in *comings and goings.*
2 the condition of the ground for walking,
riding, etc., as in *We had a hard going
travelling across the desert.* 3 speed of
working or moving, as in *It was good going
to get there by noon.*

going *adjective*
1 working well; prosperous, as in *a going
concern.* 2 existing, as in *What is the going
rate for delivering newspapers?*
going to, ready or likely to do something.

go-kart or **go-cart** *noun* **go-karts**
a type of very small racing car.
go-karting *noun*

gold *noun*
1 a precious yellow metal. 2 a bright
yellow colour.
gold medal, a medal made of gold,
awarded as the first prize.
goldrush, a sudden movement of people to
a place where gold has been found.

golden *adjective*
1 made of gold, as in *golden chain.*
2 coloured like gold, as in *golden hair.*
3 precious; important, as in *a golden
opportunity.*
golden wedding, the 50th anniversary of a
wedding.

goldfield *noun* **goldfields**
an area where gold is found or mined.

goldfish *noun* **goldfish**
a small red or orange fish, often kept as a
pet.

golf *noun*
an outdoor game played by hitting a small
ball with a club into a series of small holes,
around a set course.
golfer *noun*, **golfing** *noun*

gondola *noun* **gondolas** (*say* **gon**-duh-luh)
a boat with high pointed ends, used on the
canals in Venice.
gondolier *noun*

gone past participle of **go** *verb.*

gong *noun* **gongs**
a large metal disc that makes a deep,
hollow sound when it is hit.

good *adjective* **better, best**
1 having the quality people like, want, or
praise, as in *a good book.* 2 kind, as in *It
was good of you to help us.* 3 well-behaved,
as in *Be a good boy.* 4 healthy; giving
benefit, as in *Exercise is good for you.*
5 thorough; large enough, as in *Have a good
drink.* 6 quite large; considerable, as in *It's
a good distance to the station.* 7 useful;
suitable, as in *This desk is good enough for
me.* 8 competent or skilful, as in *a good
driver.*
as good as, nearly.
good evening, a polite way of greeting
someone in the evening.
good morning, a polite way of greeting
someone in the morning.
good night, a polite way of saying goodbye
to someone at night.

a
b
c
d
e
f
g
h
i
j
k
l
m
n
o
p
q
r
s
t
u
v
w
x
y
z

good

good *noun*
1 something good or right, as in *Do good to others*. 2 benefit; profit, as in *I'm telling you for your own good*.
for good, for ever.
no good, useless.

goodbye *interjection*
a word you use when you leave someone, or at the end of a telephone call.

Good Friday *noun*
the Friday before Easter, when Christians remember Jesus's death on the Cross.

good-looking *adjective*
attractive; handsome.

good-natured *adjective*
kind; easygoing.
good-naturedly *adverb*

goodness *noun*
1 the state of being good or virtuous, as in *The kind doctor's goodness was clear to all*. 2 the good part of something, as in *Vegetables with the goodness boiled out are tasteless*.
goodness gracious, goodness me, or **my goodness,** ways of expressing surprise.

goods *plural noun*
1 things that are bought and sold. 2 things that are carried on trains, trucks, etc.; freight.
someone delivers the goods, someone does or supplies what is needed, as in *You can rely on her; she always delivers the goods*.

goodwill *noun*
1 being friendly, as in *They have shown us a lot of goodwill*. 2 approval, as in *My plan has the principal's goodwill*.

goose *noun* **geese**
1 a large bird that is kept for its meat and eggs, as in *Geese have webbed feet*. 2 (*colloquial*) a silly or simple person, as in *Don't be a goose*.

gooseberry *noun* **gooseberries**
a small green fruit that grows on a prickly bush.

goose-pimples *plural noun*
your skin when it is covered in small bumps, with all the hairs standing on end, because you are cold or afraid; goose-bumps.

gore *verb* **gores, goring, gored**
to wound with a horn or tusk, as in *The bull gored the matador*.

gorge *noun* **gorges**
a narrow valley with steep sides.

gorge *verb* **gorges, gorging, gorged**
to eat too much in a greedy way.

gorgeous *adjective*
magnificent; beautiful, as in *A peacock has gorgeous colours*.
gorgeously *adverb*

gorilla *noun* **gorillas**
a large, strong African ape.

Usage Do not confuse **gorilla** with **guerrilla**, which means someone who fights by means of ambushes and surprise attacks.

gory *adjective* **gorier, goriest**
covered in blood; involving a lot of killing, as in *gory sights at the battle; a gory film*.

gosh *interjection*
an exclamation of surprise.

gosling *noun* **goslings**
a young goose.

go-slow *noun* **go-slows**
a way of protesting by deliberately working slowly.

gospel *noun* **gospels**
1 the teachings of Jesus. 2 something that you can safely believe, as in *You can take what she says as gospel*.
the Gospels, the first four books of the New Testament.

gossip *noun* **gossips**
1 talk, especially rumours, about other people. 2 someone who likes talking about other people.

gossip *verb* **gossips, gossiping, gossiped**
1 to talk a lot about other people. 2 to talk a lot in a friendly way.

got past tense and past participle of **get**.

gouge *verb* **gouges, gouging, gouged**
(*say* gowj)
to press or scoop out something, as in *The cook gouged the flesh from the melon*.

gourd *noun* **gourds**
1 the hard-skinned fruit of a climbing plant. 2 this fruit hollowed out to make a bowl or container.

gourmet *noun* **gourmets** (*say* **goor**-may)
a person who is very knowledgeable about good food.

govern *verb* **governs, governing, governed**
to be in charge of a country or organisation.
governor *noun*

government *noun* **governments**
the group of people who are in charge of a country.
governmental *adjective*

governor *noun* **governors**
a representative of the Crown in each Australian State.

Governor-General *noun*
the main representative of the Crown in Australia and some other countries in the British Commonwealth.

gown *noun* **gowns**
a loose, flowing garment, especially for a woman.

GP short for **general practitioner.**

grab *verb* **grabs, grabbing, grabbed**
to take hold of something suddenly, firmly, or greedily.

grace *noun* **graces**
1 beauty, especially in movement.
2 goodwill; favour, as in *They prayed, asking for God's grace.* 3 a short prayer before or after a meal.

graceful *adjective*
beautiful, especially in movement, as in *a graceful dancer.*
gracefully *adverb*, **gracefulness** *noun*

gracious *adjective*
1 kind; pleasant to other people.
2 merciful, as in *gracious in defeat.* 3 used as an exclamation of surprise, as in *Good gracious! Gracious me!*
graciously *adverb*

grade *noun* **grades**
1 a step in a scale of quality, value, or rank; a standard, as in *The grade of timber used for the table was first class. He received high grades for his assignments. She reached grade five in music.* 2 a class in school.
make the grade, (*colloquial*) to reach the proper standard.

grade *verb* **grades, grading, graded**
to sort or divide things or people according to quality, value, or rank.

gradient *noun* **gradients** (*say* gray-dee-uhnt)
1 a slope. 2 the amount that a road or railway slopes.

gradual *adjective*
happening slowly but steadily.
gradually *adverb*

graduate *noun* **graduates** (*say* grad-yoo-uht)
someone who has been to a university or college and got a degree.

graduate *verb* **graduates, graduating, graduated** (*say* grad-yoo-ayt)
1 to get a university degree. 2 to divide something into graded sections; to mark

something so that it can be used for measuring, as in *The ruler was graduated in millimetres and centimetres.*
graduation *noun*

graffiti *plural noun* (*say* gruh-**fee**-tee)
words or drawings scribbled on a surface, usually in a public place.

graft *noun* **grafts**
1 a shoot from one plant inserted into a slit in another from which it receives sap to feed it. 2 a piece of living tissue, etc., transplanted to another part of the body by a surgeon, as in *skin graft.*

grain *noun* **grains**
1 cereals when they are growing or after they have been harvested. 2 the seed of a cereal; a small, hard seed or piece. 3 the pattern of lines on a piece of wood, cloth, etc.
grainy *adjective*

gram *noun* **grams**
a unit of weight equal to a thousandth of a kilogram.

grammar *noun* **grammars**
1 the rules for using words. 2 a book that gives the rules for using words.

grammatical *adjective*
to do with grammar; according to the rules of grammar, as in *This sentence is grammatical.*
grammatically *adverb*

gramophone *noun* **gramophones**
a machine for reproducing sound that has been recorded on discs.

Usage **Gramophone** is a rather old-fashioned word; the machine is now usually called a **record-player.**

grand *adjective* **grander, grandest**
1 great; splendid, as in *a grand house.*
2 complete, as in *the grand total.*
3 the main or most important, as in *the grand final.*
grand piano, a large piano with horizontal strings.
grandly *adverb*

grandad *noun* **grandads**
(*colloquial*) grandfather.

grandchild *noun* **grandchildren**
a child of your son or daughter.
granddaughter *noun*, **grandson** *noun*

grandeur *noun*
greatness; splendour, as in *the grandeur of the Great Ocean Road along the Victorian coast.*

grandma

grandma *noun* **grandmas**
(*colloquial*) grandmother.

grandparent *noun* **grandparents**
the parent of your father or mother.

grandstand *noun* **grandstands**
a structure with rows of seats for spectators at a racecourse or sports ground.

granite *noun*
a very hard kind of rock.

grant *verb* **grants, granting, granted**
to give or allow someone what he or she has asked for.
take something for granted, to assume that something is true or will always be available.

grant *noun* **grants**
something given, especially a sum of money.

granulated *adjective*
in grains, as in *granulated sugar*.

grape *noun* **grapes**
a small green or purple berry that grows in bunches on a vine, used as fruit and in making wine.

grapefruit *noun* **grapefruit**
a large, round, yellow citrus fruit with a soft, juicy flesh.

grapevine *noun* **grapevines**
a climbing plant on which grapes grow.
hear something on the grapevine, to hear something unofficially from other people who have passed on the information from one to another, as in *There's going to be a new teacher next week; I heard it on the grapevine*.

graph *noun* **graphs**
a diagram that shows how two amounts are related.
graph paper, paper covered with small squares, used for making graphs.

graphic *adjective*
1 to do with drawing or painting, as in *a graphic artist*. 2 short and lively, as in *The sports commentator gave a graphic account of the race*.
graphically *adverb*

graphics *plural noun*
diagrams, lettering, and drawings, especially pictures that are produced by a computer.

graphite *noun*
a soft kind of carbon used for the lead in pencils, for lubricating, etc.

grapple *verb* **grapples, grappling, grappled**
1 to struggle or wrestle. 2 to hold

something firmly, as in *The gymnast grappled the horizontal bars*.
grapple with something, to try to deal with a problem, etc.

grasp *verb* **grasps, grasping, grasped**
1 to hold tightly. 2 to understand.

grasp *noun*
1 a firm hold or grip. 2 the power to understand things, as in *She has a good grasp of mathematics*.

grasping *adjective*
greedy for money or possessions.

grass *noun* **grasses**
1 a green plant with thin stalks.
2 ground covered with grass; lawn.
3 (*colloquial*) marijuana. 4 (*colloquial*) an informer, especially a police informer.
grassy *adjective*

grasshopper *noun* **grasshoppers**
a jumping, plant-eating insect that makes a shrill noise.

grassland *noun* **grasslands**
a large open area covered with grass, used especially for grazing cattle.

grate *noun* **grates**
1 a metal framework that keeps fuel in the fireplace. 2 a fireplace.

grate *verb* **grates, grating, grated**
1 to shred something into small pieces, as in *He grated some cheese*. 2 to make an unpleasant noise by rubbing something, as in *The chalk grated on the blackboard*.

grateful *adjective*
feeling glad that someone has done something for you, as in *I am grateful for your help*.
gratefully *adverb*

grating *noun* **gratings**
a framework of metal bars placed across an opening, as in *a grating over a drain*.

gratitude *noun*
being grateful.

grave *noun* **graves**
the place where a dead body is buried.

grave *adjective* **graver, gravest**
serious; solemn; important, as in *grave news*.
gravely *adverb*

gravel *noun*
small stones mixed with coarse sand, as in *Gravel is often used to make paths*.
gravelled *adjective*, **gravelly** *adjective*

gravestone *noun* **gravestones**
a stone monument over a grave.

graveyard *noun* **graveyards**
a place where dead bodies are buried; a cemetery.

gravity *noun*
1 the force that pulls all objects in the universe towards each other. **2** the force that pulls everything towards the earth. **3** seriousness, as in *The prime minister spoke with gravity when referring to the war.*
gravitation *noun*, **gravitational** *adjective*

gravy *noun*
a hot brown liquid made from meat-juice, flour and water.

graze *verb* **grazes, grazing, grazed**
1 to hurt your skin by rubbing against something; to scrape something as you pass it, as in *I grazed my arm on the wall. My bike grazed the side of the parked car.* **2** to eat grass as it grows, as in *The cows were grazing in the field.*

grazier *noun* **graziers**
the owner of a very large property on which sheep or cattle are raised.

grease *noun*
thick fat or oil.
greasy *adjective*

great *adjective* **greater, greatest**
1 very large. **2** very important; extremely clever or talented, as in *a great composer.* **3** (*colloquial*) very good or enjoyable, as in *We had a great time.* **4** older by one generation, as in *Your great-grandfather is the grandfather of one of your parents.*
greatly *adverb*, **greatness** *noun*

Grecian *adjective*
to do with Greece, as in *a Grecian vase.*

greed *noun*
great desire, especially for food or money.

greedy *adjective* **greedier, greediest**
wanting more food or money than you need.
greedily *adverb*, **greediness** *noun*

green *adjective* **greener, greenest**
1 having the colour of grass, leaves, etc. **2** to do with protecting the environment, as in *the green movement.*
someone has green fingers, someone is skilled or successful at growing plants.

green *noun* **greens**
1 green colour. **2** an area of grass, used for a special purpose especially on a golf course, as in *a putting-green.*
Green, a person who belongs to a political party or group favouring a way of life which does not damage the earth or its people; a conservationist.

greenery *noun*
green leaves or plants.

greenfinch *noun* **greenfinches**
a small bird with green and yellow feathers introduced into Australia.

greengrocer *noun* **greengrocers**
someone who keeps a shop that sells fruit and vegetables.
greengrocery *noun*

greenhouse *noun* **greenhouses**
a glass building which traps the sun's heat and used for growing plants; a glasshouse.
greenhouse effect, the bad effect of large amounts of gases such as methane and carbon dioxide in the earth's atmosphere, trapping heat and causing the earth to become too warm.

greenie *noun* **greenies**
(*colloquial*) a person who thinks that our environment should be protected by restricting the use of chemicals, preventing the overuse of natural resources, etc.; a conservationist.

greenish *adjective*
rather green.

greens *plural noun*
green vegetables, such as beans and spinach.

greet *verb* **greets, greeting, greeted**
to welcome; to receive, as in *The singer was greeted with applause.*

greeting *noun* **greetings**
words or actions used to greet someone.
greetings, good wishes.

grenade *noun* **grenades**
a small bomb usually thrown by hand.

grevillea *noun* **grevilleas**
any tree or shrub of a large, mainly Australian family, many of which have very brightly-coloured flowers and are widely grown.

grew past tense of **grow.**

grey *noun*
the colour between black and white, like ashes or lead.

greyhound *noun* **greyhounds**
a fast, slim breed of dog used in racing.

grey nurse *noun*
a common shark in the south-eastern waters of Australia.

grid *noun* **grids**
1 a framework or pattern of bars or lines crossing each other, as in *a security grid on the window.* **2** a network of lines, electric-power connections, gas-supply lines, etc.

grief

grief *noun*
deep sadness.
come to grief, to have an accident or misfortune.
grief stricken, to be overcome with sadness.

grievance *noun* **grievances**
something that you are discontented about, as in *The workers' main grievance was poor pay.*

grieve *verb* **grieves, grieving, grieved**
1 to feel very sad. 2 to make someone feel very sad, as in *Your behaviour grieves me.*

grievous *adjective*
1 able to cause great pain and suffering, as in *a grievous injury.* 2 serious, as in *a grievous mistake.*
grievously *adverb*

grill *noun* **grills**
1 a device for grilling food; a griller. 2 grilled food.

grill *verb* **grills, grilling, grilled**
1 to cook something over or under a griller or a heated surface. 2 to question someone closely and severely, as in *He was grilled by the police.*

grille *noun* **grilles**
a grating or lattice-like screen, as in *The grille on a car protects the radiator. Grilles were installed on the office windows to prevent theft.*

grim *adjective* **grimmer, grimmest**
1 stern; severe, as in *The judge looked grim.* 2 frightening; unpleasant, as in *Travelling through the violent storm was a grim experience.*
grimly *adverb*, **grimness** *noun*

grimace *noun* **grimaces**
a strange or twisted expression on your face, as in *The bystander grimaced with horror at the car accident.*

grime *noun*
dirt, especially in a thin layer, as in *grime on the carpet.*
grimy *adjective*

grin *verb* **grins, grinning, grinned**
to give a smile showing your teeth.
grin and bear it, to endure something without complaining.

grin *noun* **grins**
a smile showing your teeth.

grind *verb* **grinds, grinding, ground**
1 to crush something into tiny pieces, as in *The wheat was ground into flour.* 2 to sharpen, smooth or polish something by rubbing it on a rough surface, as in *Grind the knife on a sharpening stone.* 3 to move

with a harsh rubbing sound, as in *The brakes of the old bus ground to a halt.* 4 rub or rub together in a grating manner, as in *grinding your teeth.* 5 to impose difficult or boring work, life, etc., as in *Poverty ground down the family's spirit.*
grinder *noun*

grindstone *noun* **grindstones**
a rough, round, revolving stone used for grinding things.
keep someone's nose to the grindstone, to make someone work hard without stopping.

grip *verb* **grips, gripping, gripped**
1 to hold tightly. 2 to keep someone's attention, as in *The story gripped the audience.*

grip *noun* **grips**
1 a way of holding tightly. 2 the power of holding attention, as in *She has a firm grip on her audience.* 3 a good control of your own behaviour, emotions, etc., as in *She lost her grip when she was sacked.*

grisly *adjective* **grislier, grisliest**
horrible, as in *the grisly remains of a dead sheep.*

gristle *noun*
the tough, rubbery part of meat; cartilage.
gristly *adjective*

grit *noun*
1 tiny pieces of stone or sand. 2 (*colloquial*) courage; endurance.
gritty *adjective*

grit *verb* **grits, gritting, gritted**
1 to close your teeth tightly. 2 to put grit on a road or path.

grizzle *verb* **grizzles, grizzling, grizzled**
to complain or whine, as in *The tired toddler grizzled to her mother.*

grizzly bear *noun* **grizzly bears**
a large, fierce bear of North America.

groan *verb* **groans, groaning, groaned**
to make a long, deep sound of pain or distress.

groan *noun* **groans**
a long, deep sound of pain or distress.

grocer *noun* **grocers**
someone who keeps a shop that sells food, drink, and other goods for the house.

grocery *noun* **groceries**
a grocer's shop.
groceries, goods sold by a grocer.

grog *plural noun*
(*colloquial*) beer and other alcoholic drinks.

groggy *adjective* **groggier, groggiest**
dizzy, especially because you are ill, injured, etc.

groin *noun* **groins**
the hollow between your belly and your thigh.

groom *noun* **grooms**
1 someone whose job is to look after horses. 2 a bridegroom.

groom *verb* **grooms, grooming, groomed**
1 to clean and brush a horse or other animal. 2 to make neat and trim, as in *a well-groomed beard*. 3 to prepare or train a person for a particular purpose, as in *She was groomed to take over the manager's position*.

groove *noun* **grooves**
a long narrow cut in the surface of something, as in *Records have grooves in them*.

grope *verb* **gropes, groping, groped**
to feel about for something you cannot see.

gross *adjective* **grosser, grossest**
1 overfed; bloated, as in *The pig was gross*. 2 with bad manners, as in *gross behaviour*. 3 very bad or shocking, as in *gross stupidity*. 4 total; without anything deducted, as in *gross income*.
Gross Domestic Product, the value of all the goods produced and services provided in a country in one year.
grossly *adverb*, **grossness** *noun*

gross *noun* **gross**
144; twelve dozen of something.

grotesque *adjective* (*say* groh-**tesk**)
very strange; ridiculous.
grotesquely *adverb*

grotty *adjective* **grottier, grottiest**
(*colloquial*) unpleasant; dirty.

grouch *noun* **grouches**
(*colloquial*) a discontented person.
grouchy *adjective*

ground *noun* **grounds**
1 a position, area, or distance on the earth's surface, as in *The runner covered a lot of ground*. 2 soil or earth, as in *stony ground*. 3 an area of a special kind or for a special use, as in *fishing-grounds; cricket-ground*.
grounds, reasons, as in *Have you any grounds for suspicion?*
the grounds, the gardens of a large house.
to get off the ground, (*colloquial*) to make a successful start.
to lose ground, to retreat or give way.

ground past tense and past participle of **grind**.

grounded *adjective*
1 prevented from flying, as in *The planes were grounded because of fog*. 2 (*colloquial*) kept indoors by your parents, usually for misbehaving.

ground floor *noun* **ground floors**
in a building, the floor that is level with the ground.

groundsheet *noun* **groundsheets**
a piece of waterproof material for spreading on the ground; the floor of a tent.

groundsman *noun* **groundsmen**
someone whose job is to look after a sports ground.

groundwork *noun*
work that forms the basis for further work, etc., as in *The groundwork for maths is learning your tables*.

group *noun* **groups**
a number of people, animals, or things that belong together in some way.

group *verb* **groups, grouping, grouped**
to make a group; to collect people, animals, or things together.

groupie *noun* **groupies**
(*colloquial*) a keen follower or fan of a pop star, sports star, etc.

grove *noun* **groves**
a group of trees; a small wood.

grovel *verb* **grovels, grovelling, grovelled**
1 to act as though you were very unimportant to try to please someone important, or to try to prevent him or her from being annoyed with you; to apologise a lot. 2 to crawl on the floor, as in *He was grovelling under his desk for his locker key*.

grow *verb* **grows, growing, grew, grown**
1 to become bigger, as in *He has grown a lot*. 2 to develop, as in *The seeds are growing*. 3 to plant something in the ground and look after it, as in *She grows lovely roses*. 4 to become, as in *He grew rich*.
grow on, to become more attractive or more natural to someone, as in *This music grows on you*.
grow out of, to get too big or too old for something.
grow up, to develop; to become an adult, as in *The legend grew up over the centuries. They want to be actors when they grow up*.
grower *noun*

growl *verb* **growls, growling, growled**
to make a deep, rough sound, as in *Angry dogs growl*.

growl

growl *noun* **growls**
a deep, rough sound, as in *the growl of the lion*.

grown-up *noun* **grown-ups**
an adult.

growth *noun* **growths**
1 the act of growing; development, as in *The boy's growth surprised his grandparents*. 2 something that has grown, as in *spring growth on the bushes*.

grub *noun* **grubs**
1 a tiny creature that will become an insect. 2 (*colloquial*) food.

grubby *adjective* **grubbier, grubbiest**
rather dirty.

grudge *noun* **grudges**
a dislike of someone because you think he or she has harmed you, or because you are jealous.

grudge *verb* **grudges, grudging, grudged**
to resent letting someone have something.
grudgingly *adverb*

gruelling *adjective*
exhausting, as in *a gruelling race*.

gruesome *adjective*
horrible, as in *The dead soldiers were a gruesome sight*.

gruff *adjective* **gruffer, gruffest**
with a rough, unfriendly voice or manner.
gruffly *adverb*

grumble *verb* **grumbles, grumbling, grumbled**
1 to complain continually or with a bad temper. 2 to make a deep, heavy sound, as in *We could hear thunder grumbling in the distance*.
grumbler *noun*

grumpy *adjective* **grumpier, grumpiest**
bad-tempered.
grumpily *adverb*, **grumpiness** *noun*

grunt *noun* **grunts**
the sound a pig makes.

grunt *verb* **grunts, grunting, grunted**
to make the sound a pig makes.

guarantee *noun* **guarantees**
1 a promise to do something, especially to repair something if it goes wrong. 2 something which acts as a guarantee, as in *An alarm is no guarantee against a robbery*.

guarantee *verb* **guarantees, guaranteeing, guaranteed**
to promise to do something, especially to repair something if it goes wrong, as in *I guarantee I will be there. The new car was guaranteed against any defect for three years*.

guard *verb* **guards, guarding, guarded**
1 to protect something or someone. 2 to prevent someone from escaping.
guard against, to be careful to prevent something.

guard *noun* **guards**
1 a careful watch, as in *Keep a close guard on the cash register*. 2 someone who protects a person or place, as in *bodyguard*. 3 a group of soldiers or policemen protecting something or someone, or preventing someone from escaping. 4 a protecting device, as in *a fire guard; mouth guard*.
on guard, protecting; preventing someone from escaping.

guardian *noun* **guardians**
1 someone who protects something, as in *The Wilderness Society is seen as the guardian of endangered species*. 2 someone who is legally in charge of a child whose parents cannot look after him or her.
guardianship *noun*

guerrilla *noun* **guerrillas** (*say* guh-**ril**-uh)
someone who fights by means of ambushes and surprise attacks.

Usage Do not confuse **guerrilla** with **gorilla,** which is a kind of ape.

guess *verb* **guesses, guessing, guessed**
to give an opinion or an answer about something you are not sure of.

guess *noun* **guesses**
an opinion or answer that you give about something you are not sure of.
guesswork *noun*

guest *noun* **guests** (*say* gest)
1 a person who is invited to visit or stay at someone's house. 2 someone staying at a hotel. 3 someone taking part in a show which he or she does not usually appear in.
guest house, a kind of small hotel.

guide *noun* **guides**
1 someone who shows people the way, helps them, or points out interesting sights. 2 a book that tells you about a place.
Guide, a member of the Girl Guides Association, an organisation for girls.
guide dog, a dog specially trained to show a blind person the way.

guide *verb* **guides, guiding, guided**
to show someone the way, to help someone, or to show someone interesting sights.
guided missile, a kind of rocket that is controlled while it is in flight.

guideline *noun* **guidelines**
a suggestion for how something should be

guild *noun* **guilds** (*say* gild)
a society of people, especially in the Middle Ages, with similar skills or interests, as in *the quilters guild*.

Usage Do not confuse **guild** with **gild**, which is a verb meaning to cover something with a thin layer of gold paint or gold.

guillotine *noun* **guillotines** (*say* gil-uh-teen)
1 a device used in France in the past for cutting off people's heads. 2 a device with a sharp blade for cutting paper.

guilt *noun*
1 the fact that you have done something wrong, as in *The prisoner's guilt was proved by the evidence*. 2 a feeling that you have done something wrong, as in *All the class carried the guilt of being rude to the relief teacher*.
guilty *adjective*

guinea-pig *noun* **guinea-pigs**
1 a small furry animal without a tail, as in *Guinea-pigs are often kept as pets*. 2 a person who is used in an experiment, as in *In testing the drug, they used him as a guinea-pig*.

guitar *noun* **guitars**
a musical instrument with strings that you pluck.
guitarist *noun*

gulf *noun* **gulfs**
1 a large bay, as in *the Gulf of Carpentaria*. 2 a great difference, as in *A vast gulf existed between the rich and poor*.

gull *noun* **gulls**
a seagull.

gullet *noun* **gullets**
the tube from the throat to the stomach.

gullible *adjective*
easily deceived or tricked.

gully *noun* **gullies**
1 a small narrow valley made by running water. 2 a gutter or drain. 3 (*in Cricket*) a fielding position between point and slips.

gulp *verb* **gulps, gulping, gulped**
1 to swallow something quickly or greedily. 2 to make a loud swallowing noise; to gasp, as in *He gulped in fright when he saw the snake on the path*.

gum *noun* **gums**
1 the fleshy part of the mouth that holds the teeth. 2 a sticky substance used as glue. 3 chewing-gum. 4 a gum-tree, as in *flowering gum; red gum*.
gummy *adjective*

gum *verb* **gums, gumming, gummed**
to cover or stick something with gum.

gumboot *noun* **gumboots**
a rubber boot.

gum-tree *noun* **gum-trees**
any tree of the large, mainly Australian eucalyptus family.
up a gum-tree, (*colloquial*) in great difficulties.

gun *noun* **guns**
1 a weapon that fires shells or bullets from a metal tube. 2 a pistol fired to signal the start of a race. 3 a device that forces a substance out of a tube, as in *a grease-gun*.
gunfire *noun*, **gunshot** *noun*

gunman *noun* **gunmen**
a man armed with a gun.

gunpowder *noun*
a type of explosive.

gunyah *noun* **gunyahs**
a temporary shelter of the Aborigines, usually made from branches, bark, leaves, or grass.

Origins This word comes from the Aboriginal language Dharuk: **ganyi**. See the Aboriginal Languages map at the back of this dictionary.

gurgle *verb* **gurgles, gurgling, gurgled**
to make a bubbling sound, as in *The water gurgled as it flowed out of the bath*.

gurgler *noun* **gurglers**
(*colloquial*) a plughole in a sink; a drain.
down the gurgler, (*colloquial*) lost forever.

guru *noun* **gurus**
a respected teacher who has great influence.

gush *verb* **gushes, gushing, gushed**
1 to flow quickly. 2 to talk too enthusiastically or emotionally.

gust *noun* **gusts**
a sudden rush of wind, rain, smoke, etc.
gusty *adjective*

gut *noun* **guts**
the lower alimentary canal from the stomach to the anus; the intestine.
guts, (*colloquial*) courage, the stomach or a greedy person, as in *the guts to fight on; kicked in the guts; greedy guts*.

gut

gut *verb* **guts, gutting, gutted**
1 to remove the insides from a dead fish or other animal. 2 to remove or destroy the inside of something, as in *The factory was gutted by fire.*

gutless *adjective*
(*colloquial*) without courage; cowardly.

gutter *noun* **gutters**
a long, narrow channel at the side of a street or along the edge of a roof to carry away rain water.

guy *noun* **guys**
(*colloquial*) a man.
guys, (*colloquial*) any person, female or male.

guy or **guy-rope** *noun* **guys** or **guy-ropes**
a rope used to hold something in place, as in *Slacken the guy-ropes of your tent at night.*

guzzle *verb* **guzzles, guzzling, guzzled**
to eat or drink greedily.
guzzler *noun*

gym *noun* **gyms** (*say* jim)
(*colloquial*)
1 a gymnasium, as in *a workout at the gym.* 2 gymnastics, as in *We do gym at school.*

gymkhana *noun* **gymkhanas**
(*say* jim-**kah**-nuh)
a series of horse-riding contests.

gymnasium *noun* **gymnasiums**
a place designed for gymnastics and sport.

gymnastics *plural noun*
exercises and movements that demonstrate strength, skill, and agility.
gymnast *noun*

gynaecology or **gynecology** *noun* (*say* guy-nuh-**kol**-uh-jee)
the branch of medical science that deals with diseases and medical conditions that only women have.

gyroscope *noun* **gyroscopes**
a device that keeps steady because of a heavy wheel spinning inside it.
gyroscopic *adjective*

Hh

ha short for **hectare** or **hectares**.

habit *noun* **habits**
something that you do without thinking, because you have done it so often.
habitual *adjective*, **habitually** *adverb*

habitat *noun* **habitats**
where an animal or plant lives naturally.

hack *verb* **hacks, hacking, hacked**
to chop or cut roughly.

hack *noun* **hacks**
1 a horse let out for hire. 2 a weak old horse. 3 a person hired to do dull routine work, especially writing.
hack it, to put up with.

hacker *noun* **hackers**
someone who uses a computer to get access to a company's or government's computer system without permission.

had past tense and past participle of **have**.

hadn't short for *had not*.

haemorrhage or **hemorrhage** *noun*
haemorrhages (*say* **hem**-uh-rij)
a large flow of blood from a burst blood vessel.

hag *noun* **hags**
an ugly old woman.

haggard *adjective*
looking unwell or very tired, especially from worry, suffering, etc.

haggle *verb* **haggles, haggling, haggled**
to argue about a price or agreement.

haiku *noun*
a Japanese three-lined poem that usually has 17 syllables.

hail *noun*
1 frozen drops of rain. 2 a large number of objects falling with great force at one time, as in *killed in a hail of bullets*.
hailstone *noun*, **hailstorm** *noun*

hail *verb* **hails, hailing, hailed**
1 to rain hailstones, as in *It is hailing*. 2 to call out to someone, as in *She hailed the captain*.

hair *noun* **hairs**
1 a soft covering that grows on the heads and bodies of people and animals, as in *Her hair is black*. 2 one of the threads that makes up this soft covering, as in *I found a hair in the soup*.
in your hair, (*colloquial*) annoying you.
hairbrush *noun*, **haircut** *noun*

hairdresser *noun* **hairdressers**
someone whose job is to cut and style people's hair.

hairpin *noun* **hairpins**
a pin for keeping your hair in place.
hairpin bend, a very sharp bend in a road.

hair-raising *adjective*
terrifying.

hairy *adjective* **hairier, hairiest**
1 having a lot of hair, as in *a hairy man*.
2 (*colloquial*) frightening, dangerous, as in *a hairy ride on a roller-coaster*.

hake *noun*
a marine fish that can be eaten; gemfish.

hakea *noun* **hakeas** (*say* **hay**-kee-uh)
an Australian shrub or tree having spiny, usually very attractive flowers and woody fruits.

half *noun* **halves**
one of the two equal parts that something is or can be divided into, as in *Two halves make a whole*.

half *adverb*
partly; not completely, as in *This meat is only half cooked*.

a
b
c
d
e
f
g
h
i
j
k
l
m
n
o
p
q
r
s
t
u
v
w
x
y
z

half-baked

half-baked *adjective*
(*colloquial*) not properly planned; foolish, as in *a half-baked idea*.

half-hearted *adjective*
not very enthusiastic.
half-heartedly *adverb*

half-mast *noun*
at half-mast, flying a flag half-way down its flagpole, usually as a sign that someone important has died.

half-time *noun*
the time half-way through a game.

half-way *adverb* and *adjective*
at a point half the distance or amount between two places or times.

hall *noun* **halls**
1 the first room or passage inside the front door of a house. 2 a very large room for meetings, concerts, etc., as in *the school hall*. 3 a large, important building or house, as in *the Town Hall*.

Halloween *noun*
the night of 31 October, when some people think that magic things happen.

hallucination *noun* **hallucinations**
thinking that you can see or hear something that is not really there.
hallucinate *verb*

halo *noun* **haloes**
1 a circle of light, especially shown round the head of a saint in a picture. 2 a circle of white or coloured light around a planet, especially the sun or moon.

halt *verb* **halts, halting, halted**
to stop.

halter *noun* **halters**
a rope or strap put around a horse's head so that it can be controlled.

halve *verb* **halves, halving, halved**
1 to divide something into halves. 2 to reduce something to half its size, as in *If the shop had another checkout it would halve the queues*.

ham *noun* **hams**
1 meat from a pig's leg. 2 (*colloquial*) an actor or performer who is not very good. 3 (*colloquial*) someone who sends and receives radio messages as a hobby.

hamburger *noun* **hamburgers**
a flat cake of seasoned minced beef, usually fried or grilled and eaten in a soft bread bun.

hammer *noun* **hammers**
a heavy tool used for hitting nails, breaking rocks, etc.

hammerhead, a shark with a flattened head shaped like a hammer.

hammer *verb* **hammers, hammering, hammered**
1 to hit something with a hammer. 2 to knock loudly, as in *He hammered on the door*. 3 (*colloquial*) to treat roughly; to defeat.
hammer out, to agree on something after a long discussion.

hammock *noun* **hammocks**
a bed made of a strong net or piece of cloth hung up above the ground or floor.

hamper *noun* **hampers**
a big basket with a lid, often used to carry food or picnic things.

hamper *verb* **hampers, hampering, hampered**
to get in the way of someone or something; to make it difficult for someone to do something.

hamster *noun* **hamsters**
a small animal with brown fur, as in *Hamsters are often kept as pets in England*.

hand *noun* **hands**
1 the part of your body at the lower end of your arm. 2 a pointer on a clock or dial. 3 a worker. 4 one of a ship's crew, as in *All hands on deck!* 5 the cards held by one player in a card-game. 6 side or direction, as in *on the other hand*.
at first hand, directly from the person concerned.
at hand, near.
by hand, using your hand or hands.
hands down, winning easily or completely.
in hand, in your possession; being dealt with.
on hand, available.
out of hand, out of control.

hand *verb* **hands, handing, handed**
to give or pass something to someone.
hand down, to pass something on from one generation to another, as in *a skill that has been handed down from father to son for centuries*.

handbag *noun* **handbags**
a small bag carried, especially by a woman.

handbook *noun* **handbooks**
a book that gives useful facts about something, as in *The school handbook began with a map of the school*.

handcuffs *plural noun*
a pair of metal rings joined by a chain, used for locking a person's wrists together.

hangover

handful *noun* **handfuls**
1 what you can carry in one hand. 2 a small number of people or things. 3 (*colloquial*) a troublesome person or task, as in *The spoilt child was a real handful.*

handicap *noun* **handicaps**
1 a disadvantage that makes progress or success difficult, as in *His chief handicap is his shyness.* 2 a physical or mental disability. 3 a disadvantage given to a stronger competitor to make the chances more equal; the race, etc. in which this disadvantage is given, as in *That golfer always plays with a handicap. The horses ran in the three year-old handicap at Caulfield.*

handicapped *adjective*
1 suffering from a disadvantage. 2 suffering from a mental or physical handicap.

handicraft *noun* **handicrafts**
artistic work done with your hands, as in *Handicrafts include needlework, woodwork, and pottery.*

handiwork *noun*
something done or made by your hands.

handkerchief *noun* **handkerchiefs**
(*say* **hang**-kuhr-cheef)
a square piece of material for wiping your nose, forehead, etc.

handle *noun* **handles**
the part of a thing by which you can hold or control it.

handle *verb* **handles, handling, handled**
1 to touch or feel or use something with your hands, as in *Handle the goods with care. He handled the saw like an expert.* 2 to manage or deal with something.
handler *noun*

handlebars *plural noun*
the steering bar of a bicycle, etc.

hand-out *noun* **hand-outs**
1 a thing given free to someone who needs it. 2 notes given out in a class, etc.

hand-picked *adjective*
carefully chosen for a particular purpose, as in *A hand-picked squad of commandos led the raid.*

handrail *noun* **handrails**
a narrow rail for holding as a support.

handsome *adjective* **handsomer, handsomest**
1 attractive; good-looking, as in *a handsome man.* 2 generous, as in *a handsome gift.*
handsomely *adverb*

hands on or **hands-on** *adjective*
involving actual experience of doing something, as in *a hands on computer training course.*

handstand *noun* **handstands**
balancing on your hands with your feet in the air.

handwriting *noun*
writing done by hand.
handwritten *adjective*

handy *adjective* **handier, handiest**
1 useful. 2 conveniently placed, as in *His house is handy for the station.* 3 clever with the hands, as in *He's very handy, he built a cubby-house.*

handyman *noun* **handymen**
someone who does small jobs or repairs.

hang *verb* **hangs, hanging, hung**
1 to fix the top part of something to a hook, nail, etc. 2 to stick wallpaper to a wall. 3 to float in the air. 4 (in this sense, the past tense and past participle are **hanged**) to kill someone by hanging him or her from a rope that tightens around the neck.
hang around, to loiter; *A gang of youths was hanging around outside the club.*
hang in, (*colloquial*) to keep at, persevere.
hang on, to hold tightly; (*colloquial*) to wait, as in *Hang on to the rope. Hang on! I'm not ready yet.*
hang out, (*colloquial*) to be at a place often.
hang up, to end a telephone conversation; to hang from a hook, rail, etc., as in *Please hang up your school blazer.*

hangar *noun* **hangars**
a large shed where aircraft are kept.

Usage Do not confuse **hangar** with **hanger**, which is the next word in this dictionary.

hanger *noun* **hangers**
a device on which you hang things, as in *a coat-hanger.*

hang-glider *noun* **hang-gliders**
a device on which a person can glide through the air.
hang-gliding *noun*

hangman *noun* **hangmen**
a man whose job is to kill people by hanging them.

hangover *noun* **hangovers**
1 an unpleasant feeling after drinking too much alcohol. 2 something left over from the past.

a
b
c
d
e
f
g
h
i
j
k
l
m
n
o
p
q
r
s
t
u
v
w
x
y
z

hang-up

hang-up *noun* **hang-ups**
(*colloquial*) something that makes you unhappy or frustrated, as in *He has a hang-up about his squeaky voice.*

hank *noun* **hanks**
a coil or piece of wool, thread, etc.

hanky *noun* **hankies**
(*colloquial*) a handkerchief.

Hanukkah *noun*
a Jewish festival held in December.

haphazard *adjective* (*say* hap-**haz**-uhd)
accidental; done or chosen at random.
haphazardly *adverb*

happen *verb* **happens, happening, happened**
to take place; to occur.
happen to do something, to do something without planning to, as in *I happened to see what he had written.*

happening *noun* **happenings**
something that happens; an unusual event, as in *We've heard of strange happenings at the deserted house.*

happy *adjective* **happier, happiest**
pleased; glad; contented; enjoying yourself.
happily *adverb*, **happiness** *noun*

happy-go-lucky *adjective*
having a cheerful attitude to life and not worrying about the future.

harass *verb* **harass, harassing, harassed** (*say* ha-ruhs or huh-**ras**)
to annoy or trouble someone often.
harassed *adjective*, **harassment** *noun*

harbour or **harbor** *noun* **harbours**
a place where ships can shelter or unload.

harbour or **harbor** *verb* **harbours, harbouring, harboured**
to give shelter to someone, especially a criminal, etc.

hard *adjective* **harder, hardest**
1 firm; solid; not soft, as in *hard ground.*
2 difficult, as in *hard sums.* 3 severe; harsh, as in *a hard winter; a hard heart.*
4 energetic; using great effort, as in *a hard worker.*
hard and fast, not able to be changed, as in *There are no hard and fast rules about when you should take a break.*
hard hat, a helmet worn especially by building workers.
hard of hearing, slightly deaf.
hard up, short of money.
hard water, water containing minerals that prevent soap from making much lather.
hard yakka, hard, boring work.
hardness *noun*

hard *adverb* **harder, hardest**
1 with great effort, as in *Work hard.*
2 with difficulty, as in *hard-earned money.* 3 so as to be solid, as in *The lake froze hard.*

hard-boiled *adjective*
1 boiled until it is hard, as in *a hard-boiled egg.* 2 (*colloquial*) tough; not sympathetic, as in *a hard-boiled salesman.*

hard disc *noun* **hard discs**
a round, flat, rigid piece of magnetic material, used with computers to store information.

harden *verb* **hardens, hardening, hardened**
to make something hard; to become hard, as in *He hardened the timber by painting it. The glue hardened. His heart was hardened by war.*
hardener *noun*

hard-hearted *adjective*
having no feelings.

hardly *adverb*
only just; only with difficulty, as in *She was hardly able to walk.*

hardship *noun* **hardships**
something that causes suffering or discomfort.

hardware *noun*
1 metal implements and tools; machinery.
2 the machinery of a computer.

hard-wearing *adjective*
able to stand a lot of wear, as in *Denim is a hard-wearing cloth.*

hardwood *noun* **hardwoods**
wood from a eucalypt or deciduous trees, as in *Oak and Tasmanian ash are hardwoods.*

hardy *adjective* **hardier, hardiest**
1 strong; able to endure difficult conditions. 2 able to grow outdoors all the year round, as in *hardy plants.*

hare *noun* **hares**
an animal like a large rabbit, as in *Hares can run very fast.*

hark *verb* **harks, harking, harked**
(*old-fashioned use*) to listen.
hark back, to return to an earlier subject.

harm *noun*
injury; damage.
harmful *adjective*

harm *verb* **harms, harming, harmed**
to hurt someone; to damage something.

harmless *adjective*
not dangerous or offensive.
harmlessly *adverb*

harmonica *noun* **harmonicas**
a mouth-organ.

harmonise or **harmonize** *verb* **harmonises, harmonising, harmonised**
to produce harmony or agreement, as in *The violin harmonised with the piano. The bold pattern of the curtains did not harmonise with the floral carpet.*
harmonisation *noun*

harmony *noun* **harmonies**
1 a pleasant combination of musical notes. 2 agreement; friendship.
harmonic *adjective*, **harmonious** *adjective*, **harmoniously** *adverb*

harness *noun* **harnesses**
the straps put over a horse's head and around its neck to control it.

harness *verb* **harnesses, harnessing, harnessed**
1 to put a harness on a horse. 2 to use something to produce power, etc., as in *They harnessed the fast-flowing water of the river to make electricity.*

harp *noun* **harps**
a musical instrument made of strings stretched across a frame and plucked by your fingers.
harpist *noun*

harp *verb* **harps, harping, harped**
to keep on talking about something in a boring way, as in *He keeps harping on his misfortunes.*

harpoon *noun* **harpoons**
a spear-like missile with a rope attached for catching whales, etc.

harpsichord *noun* **harpsichords**
a musical instrument like a piano but with the strings plucked and not struck.

harsh *adjective* **harsher, harshest**
rough and unpleasant; cruel, as in *harsh weather; a harsh government.*
harshly *adverb*, **harshness** *noun*

harvest *noun* **harvests**
1 the time when farmers gather in the corn, fruit, or vegetables they have grown.
2 the crop that is gathered in.

harvest *verb* **harvests, harvesting, harvested**
to gather in the crops.
harvester *noun*

has 3rd person singular of **have**.

hash *noun* **hashes**
1 a mixture of small pieces of meat and vegetables, usually fried. 2 a mess.
make a hash of, (*colloquial*) to make a mess of something; to bungle.

hasn't short for *has not*.

hassle *noun* **hassles**
(*colloquial*) a difficulty; a disagreement, as in *a hassle about who should borrow the car.*

haste *noun*
a hurry.

hasten *verb* **hastens, hastening, hastened**
to hurry; to speed something up, as in *What can we do to hasten the work?*

hasty *adjective* **hastier, hastiest**
hurried; done too quickly.
hastily *adverb*, **hastiness** *noun*

hat *noun* **hats**
a covering for your head.
hat trick, getting three goals, wickets, victories, etc. one after the other or in one game.
under your hat, secret, as in *Keep it under your hat.*

hatch *noun* **hatches**
an opening in a floor, wall, or door, usually with a covering.

hatch *verb* **hatches, hatching, hatched**
1 to break out of an egg, as in *These chicks hatched this morning.* 2 to keep an egg warm until a baby bird is born. 3 to plan, as in *They were hatching a plot.*

hatchback *noun* **hatchbacks**
a car with a sloping back door, hinged at the top.

hatchet *noun* **hatchets**
a small axe.

hate *verb* **hates, hating, hated**
to dislike very much.

hate *noun* **hates**
1 a great dislike. 2 (*colloquial*) someone or something that you dislike very much.

hateful *adjective*
hated; very nasty.
hatefully *adverb*

hatred *noun* (say **hay**-truhd)
a great dislike.

haughty *adjective* **haughtier, haughtiest**
(*say* **haw**-tee)
too proud of yourself; thinking other people are inferior or worthless.
haughtily *adverb*, **haughtiness** *noun*

haul *verb* **hauls, hauling, hauled**
to pull something, using a lot of power or strength.

haul *noun* **hauls**
an amount of something that someone has gained, as in *The thieves made a haul worth over $20,000. The trawler brought home a large haul of fish.*

a
b
c
d
e
f
g
h
i
j
k
l
m
n
o
p
q
r
s
t
u
v
w
x
y
z

haunt

haunt *verb* **haunts, haunting, haunted**
1 to visit a place often. **2** (of ghosts) to appear often in a place or to a person. **3** to stay in your mind, as in *The memory haunts me.*

have *verb* **has, having, had**
1 to own; to possess, as in *We have all we need.* **2** to contain, as in *This tin had lollies in it.* **3** to enjoy, as in *We had a good party.* **4** to experience or suffer, as in *She has had an accident.* **5** to be forced to do something, as in *We had to wash up.* **6** to get something done, as in *I'm having my watch mended.* **7** to receive; to get, as in *I had a letter from her.* **8** forming the past tenses of verbs, as in *She has gone. I have counted. We had eaten them.*
have someone on, (*colloquial*) to fool someone.

haven *noun* **havens** (*say* **hay**-vuhn)
1 a harbour. **2** a safe place.

haven't short for *have not.*

haversack *noun* **haversacks**
a strong canvas bag carried on the back or over the shoulder.

havoc *noun*
great destruction, as in *The cyclone created havoc in Darwin.*

hawk *noun* **hawks**
1 a bird of prey with very strong eyesight. **2** a warlike person.

hawk *verb* **hawks, hawking, hawked**
to go around selling things.
hawker *noun*

hay *noun*
dried grass for feeding to animals.
hay fever, irritation of the nose, throat, and eyes caused by pollen or dust.

haywire *adjective*
(*colloquial*) out of control.

hazard *noun* **hazards**
a danger; a risk.
hazard warning lights, a car's indicator lights arranged so that they all flash at once to show that the car has had to stop in a dangerous place.
hazardous *adjective*

haze *noun* **hazes**
thin mist.

hazel *noun* **hazels**
1 a type of small nut-tree. **2** a nut from this tree. **3** a light brown colour.

hazy *adjective* **hazier, haziest**
1 misty. **2** obscure; uncertain, as in *She has a hazy idea of astronomy.*
hazily *adverb*, **haziness** *noun*

H-bomb *noun* **H-bombs**
a hydrogen bomb.

he *pronoun*
the male person or animal being talked about.

he *noun*
a male animal, as in *This cat is a he.*

head *noun* **heads**
1 the part of the body containing the brains, eyes, and mouth. **2** brains; intelligence, as in *Use your head!* **3** a talent or ability, as in *He has a head for sums.* **4** the side of a coin on which someone's head is shown. **5** a person, as in *It costs $3 per head.* **6** the top or front of something, as in *a pinhead.* **7** the chief; the person in charge of something, as in *She's the head of this school.* **8** a crisis, as in *Things came to a head.*
keep your head, to stay calm.
off the top of your head, (*colloquial*) without preparation or careful thought, as in *He simply gave an estimate off the top of his head.*
over your head, too difficult for you; without asking your opinion, as in *Advanced mathematics is over my head. The decision was taken over my head.*

head *verb* **heads, heading, headed**
1 to be at the top or front of something. **2** to hit a ball with your head. **3** to move in a particular direction, as in *They headed for the coast.*
head off, to get in front of someone in order to turn them aside.

headache *noun* **headaches**
1 a pain in the head that goes on hurting. **2** (*colloquial*) a problem or difficulty.

headdress *noun* **headdresses**
a decorative covering for the head.

head first *adverb*
with your head at the front, as in *I dived in head first.*

heading *noun* **headings**
a word or words at the top of a piece of printing or writing.

headland *noun* **headlands**
a piece of high land sticking out into the sea.

headlight *noun* **headlights**
a strong light at the front of a car, train, etc.

headline *noun* **headlines**
a heading in a newspaper.
the headlines, the main points of the news.

headlong *adverb* and *adjective*
1 falling head first. 2 in a hasty or thoughtless way.

headmaster *noun* **headmasters**
the male teacher in charge of a school.

headmistress *noun* **headmistresses**
the female teacher in charge of a school.

head-on *adverb* and *adjective*
with the front parts colliding, as in *trucks meeting head-on; a head-on collision.*

headphones *noun*
a set of earphones that fit over the head for listening to music, the radio, etc.

headquarters *plural noun*
the place from which an organisation is controlled.

headstand *noun* **headstands**
balancing upside down on your head and hands.

headstone *noun* **headstones**
a stone set up at the head of a grave.

headstrong *adjective*
being determined to have your own way; obstinate.

headway *noun*
progress, as in *They made no headway in their talks.*

heal *verb* **heals, healing, healed**
1 to make someone healthy; to become healthy. 2 to cure a disease.
healer *noun*

health *noun*
1 the condition of a person's body or mind, as in *His health is bad.* 2 being healthy, as in *in sickness and in health.*
health food, food that has been altered little from its natural condition and is thought to be good for your health.

healthy *adjective* **healthier, healthiest**
1 free from illness; having good health. 2 producing good health, as in *Fresh air is healthy.*
healthily *adverb*, **healthiness** *noun*

heap *noun* **heaps**
1 a pile, especially an untidy pile. 2 (*colloquial*) an old, worn out vehicle, as in *My car is a heap.*
heaps, (*colloquial*) a large amount, as in *We've got heaps of time.*

heap *verb* **heaps, heaping, heaped**
1 to make into a pile, as in *They heaped the wood for the bonfire.* 2 to put on large amounts, as in *She heaped his plate with food.*

hear *verb* **hears, hearing, heard**
1 to take in sounds through the ears. 2 to receive news or information.
hear! hear!, words that people say to show that they agree with what the speaker is saying.

hearing *noun* **hearings**
1 the ability to hear. 2 a chance to be heard; a trial in court.
hearing-aid, a device to help partially deaf people to hear.

hearsay *noun*
rumour; gossip, as in *It's only hearsay that the principal has resigned.*

hearse *noun* **hearses**
a vehicle for taking the coffin to a funeral.

heart *noun* **hearts**
1 the part of the body that makes the blood circulate. 2 your feelings or emotions; sympathy. 3 courage or enthusiasm. 4 the middle or most important part of something. 5 a curved shape representing a heart; a playing-card with this shape on it.
break someone's heart, to make someone very unhappy.
by heart, by using your memory.
heart attack or **heart failure**, a time when the heart stops working properly.

hearten *verb* **heartens, heartening, heartened**
to encourage or cheer up, as in *The news of her mother's recovery heartened her.*

hearth *noun* **hearths** (*say* hahth)
the floor of a fireplace, or the area in front of it.

heartless *adjective*
cruel.

hearty *adjective* **heartier, heartiest**
1 strong; vigorous, as in *a hearty athlete.* 2 enthusiastic; sincere, as in *Hearty congratulations!*
heartily *adverb*, **heartiness** *noun*

heat *noun* **heats**
1 being hot; great warmth. 2 a race or contest to decide who will take part in the final.
heat wave, a long period of hot weather.

heat *verb* **heats, heating, heated**
to make something hot; to become hot.
heater *noun*

heath *noun* **heaths**
1 an area of uncultivated land with low shrubs. 2 the plant growing on such an area, especially heather, as in *the coastal heath of Western Australia.*

heathen

heathen *noun* **heathens**
someone who does not believe in one of the world's chief religions, especially one which proclaims there is only one God.

heather *noun*
a low European bush with small purple, pink, or white flowers.

heave *verb* **heaves, heaving, heaved**
1 to lift or move something heavy.
2 (*colloquial*) to throw. 3 to rise and fall, as in *The boat heaved in the wild seas.* 4 to vomit.

heaven *noun*
1 the place where God and angels are thought to live. 2 a very pleasant place or condition.
good heavens! or **heavens!,** an exclamation of surprise.
the heavens, the sky.

heavenly *adjective*
1 in the sky, as in *heavenly bodies.*
2 (*colloquial*) very nice, as in *This cake is heavenly.*

heavy *adjective* **heavier, heaviest**
1 weighing a lot; hard to lift or carry.
2 strong; important; severe, as in *A heavy emphasis is placed on practical experience. The job carries a heavy responsibility. Heavy rain fell.* 3 hard; difficult, as in *heavy work. The book made heavy reading.*
heavy metal, (*in Music*) a type of loud rock music with a strong rhythm.
with a heavy heart, unhappily, as in *I left my home town with a heavy heart.*
heavily *adverb,* **heaviness** *noun*

heavy *noun* **heavies**
1 (*colloquial*) a person holding the top position in business, an organisation, etc., as in *All the military heavies were there for the ceremony.* 2 (*colloquial*) a large violent person; a thug.

heavy-duty *adjective*
able to stand hard use, as in *heavy-duty batteries last longer than ordinary ones.*

heavyweight *noun* **heavyweights**
1 a heavy person. 2 a boxer or wrestler of the heaviest weight.

Hebrew *noun*
an ancient language with a modern form that is the official language of Israel.

heckle *verb* **heckles, heckling, heckled**
to interrupt or annoy a public speaker.

hectare *noun* **hectares** (*say* **hek**-tair)
a unit of area equal to 10,000 square metres or nearly 2½ acres.

hectic *adjective*
very active or busy, as in *Monday morning is a hectic time in the office.*

he'd short for *he had, he should,* or *he would.*

hedge *noun* **hedges**
a row of bushes forming a barrier.

hedge *verb* **hedges, hedging, hedged**
1 to make or trim a hedge. 2 to surround something with a hedge. 3 to avoid being too definite.

hedgehog *noun* **hedgehogs**
a small insect-eating mammal with a pig-like snout and a coat of spines, which is able to roll itself into a small ball when attacked.

heed *verb* **heeds, heeding, heeded**
to pay attention to something.

heed *noun*
careful attention given to something.
heedless *adjective*

heel *noun* **heels**
1 the back part of your foot. 2 the part of a sock, shoe, etc. around or under the back part of your foot.
down at heel, shabby in dress etc.; poor.
take to your heels, to run away.

heel *verb* **heels, heeling, heeled**
to mend the heel of a shoe.

heeler *noun* **heelers**
a blue heeler dog.

hefty *adjective* **heftier, heftiest**
big and strong.

heifer *noun* **heifers** (*say* **hef**-er)
a young cow.

height *noun* **heights**
1 how high someone or something is.
2 a high place. 3 the highest or most important part of something.

heighten *verb* **heightens, heightening, heightened**
1 to make something higher; to increase something. 2 to become higher, as in *Their excitement heightened as the kick-off approached.*

heir *noun* **heirs** (*say* air)
someone who inherits something.
heiress *noun*

heirloom *noun* **heirlooms** (*say* **air**-loom)
a piece of personal property that has been in a family for several generations.

held past tense and past participle of **hold** *verb.*

helicopter *noun* **helicopters**
a kind of aircraft without wings, lifted by a large, horizontal, revolving propeller on top.

heredity

heliport *noun* **heliports**
a place for helicopters to take off and land.

helium *noun* (*say* **hee**-lee-uhm)
a light, colourless gas that does not burn.

helix *noun* **helices**
a three-dimensional spiral.

hell *noun*
1 a place where people are thought to be punished after they die. **2** a very unpleasant place or condition.
for the hell of it, (*colloquial*) for no particular reason.
Hell!, an exclamation of anger.
hellish *adjective*

he'll short for *he will*.

hello or **hallo, hullo** *interjection*
a word used to greet someone or to attract someone's attention.

helm *noun* **helms**
the handle or wheel used to steer a ship.
helmsman *noun*

helmet *noun* **helmets**
a strong covering to protect your head.

help *verb* **helps, helping, helped**
1 to do something useful for someone, as in *The teacher helped me with my work. I helped my mother on with her coat.* **2** to assist in reducing a pain or difficulty, as in *Medicine helps cure sickness.* **3** to be of use or service to, as in *Does this information help?*
helper *noun*, **helpful** *adjective*, **helpfully** *adverb*

help *noun*
1 doing something useful for someone.
2 someone who does something, especially housework, for someone.

helping *noun* **helpings**
a portion of food.

helpless *adjective*
not able to do things or look after yourself.
helplessly *adverb*, **helplessness** *noun*

hem *noun* **hems**
the edge of a piece of cloth that is folded over and sewn down.

hem *verb* **hems, hemming, hemmed**
to fold over and sew down the edge of something.
hem in, to surround a place; to restrict someone's movements.

hemisphere *noun* **hemispheres**
1 half a sphere. **2** half of the globe, as in *Australia is in the southern hemisphere.*

hemp *noun*
a plant that produces coarse fibres from which cloth, ropes, etc. are made.

hen *noun* **hens**
a female bird, especially a chicken or fowl.

hence *adverb*
1 from this time on. **2** therefore.

henceforth *adverb*
from now on; from this time on.

hepatitis *noun*
a disease which inflames the liver and causes the skin to turn yellow.

heptagon *noun*
a seven-sided, two-dimensional shape.

her *pronoun*
a word used for *she*, usually when it is the object of a sentence, or when it comes straight after a preposition, as in *I can see her. He took the books from her.*

her *adjective*
of her; belonging to her, as in *That is her book.*

herald *noun* **heralds**
a person or thing that carries official messages or announces future events, as in *The herald brought a message to the Queen. Spring is the herald of summer.*

herald *verb* **heralds, heralding, heralded**
to say that someone or something is coming.

heraldry *noun*
the study of coats of arms.
heraldic *adjective*

herb *noun* **herbs**
a plant used for flavouring, or for making medicines.
herbal *adjective*

herbivore *noun* **herbivores**
an animal that eats plants.

herd *noun* **herds**
1 a group of cattle that feed together.
2 a mass of people; a mob.

herd *verb* **herds, herding, herded**
to gather animals together or move them in a large group.

here *adverb*
in or at or to this place, as in *Come here. Sit here.*
here and there, in or to various places.

hereafter *noun*
1 the future. **2** life after death.

heredity *noun* (*say* huh-**red**-uh-tee)
the inheritance of characteristics from your parents or ancestors, as in *Heredity determines hair and eye colour.*
hereditary *adjective*

a
b
c
d
e
f
g
h
i
j
k
l
m
n
o
p
q
r
s
t
u
v
w
x
y
z

heretic

heretic *noun* **heretics**
a person who has beliefs or opinions that most people think are wrong because they disagree with beliefs that are generally accepted.

heritage *noun* **heritages**
1 what you have inherited. **2** things passed from one generation to another, as in *Folk music is part of our cultural heritage.*

hermit *noun* **hermits**
someone who lives alone and keeps away from everyone else.
hermitage *noun*

hero *noun* **heroes**
1 a person who is admired for his or her courage, outstanding achievements, etc. **2** the most important man or boy in a story, play, etc.
heroic *adjective*, **heroically** *adverb*, **heroism** *noun*

heroin *noun*
a dangerous and addictive drug made from morphine, as in *The use of heroin is illegal.*

heroine *noun* **heroines**
1 a woman or girl who has done something very brave. **2** the most important woman or girl in a story, play, etc.

heron *noun* **herons**
a wading bird with long legs and a long S-shaped neck.

hero-worship *verb* **hero-worships, hero-worshipping, hero-worshipped**
to admire very much; to idolise, as in *He hero-worships the captain of his team.*

herring *noun* **herring** or **herrings**
1 an edible marine fish from North Atlantic waters. **2** The edible Australian marine or freshwater fish.

hers *pronoun*
of her; belonging to her, as in *Those books are hers. That house is hers.*

herself *pronoun*
her and nobody else, as in *She hurt herself. She has good reason to feel proud of herself.*
by herself, on her own; alone, as in *She did the work all by herself. She was standing by herself at the party.*

he's short for *he is* and (before a verb in the past tense) *he has.*

hesitant *adjective*
uncertain or reluctant to act, speak, etc.; hesitating, as in *She spoke in a hesitant voice about her past.*
hesitantly *adverb*

hesitate *verb* **hesitates, hesitating, hesitated**
to be slow or uncertain in speaking, moving, etc.
hesitation *noun*

hessian *noun* (*say* hesh-uhn)
strong coarse cloth used to make wheat bags, potato sacks, etc.

heterosexual *noun* **heterosexuals**
having sexual attraction to persons of the opposite sex.

hexagon *noun* **hexagons**
a flat shape with six sides.
hexagonal *adjective*

hey *interjection*
an exclamation used to express surprise or to call someone's attention.

hi *interjection*
an exclamation used to greet someone or to call someone's attention.

hibernate *verb* **hibernates, hibernating, hibernated** (*say* huy-buh-nayt)
to sleep for a long time during cold weather, as in *Bears hibernate in winter.*
hibernation *noun*

hibiscus *noun*
a shrub or small tree with large bright-coloured flowers.

hiccup or **hiccough** *noun* **hiccups**
a high gulping sound made when your breath is briefly interrupted.

hide *verb* **hides, hiding,** *past tense* **hidden** or **hid,** *past participle* **hidden**
1 to get into a place where you cannot be seen, as in *I hid behind a tree.* **2** to keep someone or something from being seen, as in *The gold was hidden in a cave.* **3** to keep something secret, as in *Are you hiding the truth from me?*

hide-and-seek *noun*
a game in which one person looks for others who are hiding.

hideous *adjective*
1 very ugly, revolting, as in *hideous appearance; hideous crime.* **2** (*colloquial*) unpleasant, as in *a hideous film.*
hideously *adverb*

hide-out *noun* **hide-outs**
a hiding-place, especially used by a person on the run from the law; a refuge.

hiding *noun*
being hidden, as in *She went into hiding.*
hiding-place, a place where someone or something is hidden.

hiding *noun* **hidings**
   1 a beating, as in *Give him a good hiding.*
   2 a convincing defeat in a game, as in
   Collingwood gave Geelong a hiding.

hieroglyphics *plural noun*
   (*say* huy-uh-ruh-**glif**-iks)
   pictures used especially in ancient Egypt to
   represent words.

hi-fi *noun* **hi-fis** (*say* **huy**-fuy)
   stereo equipment which reproduces sound
   very close to the original.
   [from *high fidelity*]

high *adjective* **higher, highest**
   1 reaching a long way up, as in *a high
   building.*   2 far above the ground or above
   sea-level, as in *high clouds.*   3 measuring
   from top to bottom, as in *two metres high.*
   4 very good, as in *high quality food; high
   standard of production.*   5 very large;
   greater than normal, as in *high prices.*
   6 lively; happy, as in *She is in high spirits.*
   7 made by a sound wave that oscillates
   rapidly; at the top end of a musical scale, as
   in *a high note.*   8 going bad, as in *This meat
   is high.*
   high jump, an athletic contest of jumping
   over a horizontal bar.
   high time, when you should do something
   at once, as in *It's high time you started work.*

higher education *noun*
   education after the completion of
   secondary school.

high explosive *noun* **high explosives**
   a very strong explosive.

high fidelity *noun*
   reproducing sound with very little
   distortion.

highlands *plural noun*
   mountainous country, especially in
   Tasmania.
   highlander *noun*

highlight *noun* **highlights**
   the most interesting part of something.

highlighter *noun* **highlighters**
   a pen with bright, coloured ink that you
   spread over words on paper to draw
   attention to them.

highly *adverb*
   1 in a high degree; extremely, as in *highly
   amusing.*   2 favourably, as in *He thinks
   highly of her.*

highly-strung *adjective*
   very sensitive or nervous.

highness *noun*
   the state of being high, as in *the highness of
   taxation charges.*
   Highness, a title for a prince or princess, as
   in *His Royal Highness, the Prince of Wales.*

high-pitched *adjective*
   high in sound.

high-rise *noun* **high-rises**
   a building with many storeys, as in *There
   are many high-rises around Circular Quay.*

high school *noun* **high schools**
   a secondary school.

highway *noun* **highways**
   an important road or route.

highwayman *noun* **highwaymen**
   a robber, usually on horseback, who stole
   from highway travellers.

hijack *verb* **hijacks, hijacking, hijacked**
   to seize control of a plane or vehicle during
   a journey.
   hijacker *noun*

hike *noun* **hikes**
   1 a long walk, especially in the country for
   pleasure.   2 a rise in prices, etc., as in
   another hike in the petrol price.

hike *verb* **hikes, hiking, hiked**
   to go for a long walk in the country.
   hiker *noun*

hilarious *adjective*
   very funny or merry, as in *an hilarious joke;
   hilarious atmosphere at the party.*
   hilariously *adverb*, **hilarity** *noun*

hill *noun* **hills**
   a piece of ground that is higher than the
   ground around it.
   hillside *noun*, **hilly** *adjective*

hilt *noun* **hilts**
   the handle of a sword, dagger, etc.
   to the hilt, completely.

him *pronoun*
   a word used for *he*, usually when it is the
   object of a sentence, or when it comes
   straight after a preposition, as in *I like him.
   I gave it to him.*

himself *pronoun*
   him and nobody else, as in *He hurt himself.
   He ought to be ashamed of himself.*
   by himself, on his own; alone, as in *He did
   the work all by himself. He was sitting by
   himself.*

hind *adjective* (*say* huynd)
   at the back, as in *the hind legs of a donkey.*

hind *noun* **hinds** (*say* huynd)
   a female deer.

a
b
c
d
e
f
g
h
i
j
k
l
m
n
o
p
q
r
s
t
u
v
w
x
y
z

hinder

hinder *verb* **hinders, hindering, hindered**
(*say* **hin**-duh)
to get in someone's way; to make it difficult for a person to do something, as in *The thick scrub hindered the progress of the search party.*
hindrance *noun*

Hindu *noun* **Hindus**
someone who believes in Hinduism, the main religion of India.

hinge *noun* **hinges**
a joining device on which a door, gate, lid, etc. turns or swings when it opens.

hinge *verb* **hinged, hinging, hinged**
to attach or be attached by a hinge, as in *The cupboard door was hinged to the frame.*
hinge on something, to depend on something.

hint *noun* **hints**
1 a slight indication or suggestion, as in *Give me a hint of what you want.* 2 a useful idea, as in *household hints.*

hip *noun* **hips**
1 the bony part at the side of the body between the waist and the thigh. 2 the fruit of the wild rose.

hippo *noun* **hippos** (*colloquial*) short for **hippopotamus.**

hippopotamus *noun* **hippopotamuses**
an African mammal with short legs and thick skin that lives by rivers, lakes, etc.

hire *verb* **hires, hiring, hired**
to pay for the use of something.

hire purchase *noun*
buying something by paying in instalments.

his *adjective*
to do with him; belonging to him, as in *his house; his own business.*

hiss *verb* **hisses, hissing, hissed**
to make a sound like an *s, The snakes were hissing.*

historian *noun* **historians**
someone who writes or studies history.

historic *adjective*
famous or important in history, as in *The federation of the colonies was an historic event for Australia.*

history *noun* **histories**
1 what happened in the past. 2 the study of what happened in the past. 3 a description of important events.
historical *adjective*, **historically** *adverb*

hit *verb* **hits, hitting, hit**
1 to come against someone or something with force; to knock or strike. 2 to have a bad effect on someone or something, as in *Famine hit the poor countries.* 3 to reach, as in *I can't hit that high note.*
hit it off with someone, to become friendly with someone the first time you meet him or her.
hit on something, to think of an idea, an answer, etc. suddenly.

hit *noun* **hits**
1 a knock or stroke. 2 a shot that hits the target, as in *The archer had many good hits in the competition.* 3 a success, especially a successful song or record.

hitch *verb* **hitches, hitching, hitched**
1 to fasten with a loop, hook, etc.
2 (*colloquial*) to hitch-hike.
hitch up, to pull something up quickly or with a jerk, as in *He hitched up his trousers.*

hitch *noun* **hitches**
1 a sudden, hasty pull or push, as in *He gave me a hitch up into the tree.* 2 a knot. 3 a slight difficulty or delay, as in *There was a hitch in our travel when the train was late.*

hitchhike *verb* **hitchhikes, hitchhiking, hitchhiked**
to travel by getting lifts in other people's vehicles.
hitchhiker *noun*

hi-tech *adjective*
to do with high technology equipment, such as electronic devices, computers, and other modern machines or knowledge, as in *a new hi-tech computer system for the school office.*

HIV short for *human immunodeficiency virus,* a virus that weakens a person's resistance to disease; the virus that causes AIDS.

hive *noun* **hives**
1 a beehive. 2 a very busy place, as in *The office was a hive of activity.*

hoard *noun* **hoards**
a secret store of money, treasure, food, etc.

Usage Do not confuse **hoard** with **horde,** which means a large crowd, a gang, or an army.

hoard *verb* **hoards, hoarding, hoarded**
to store things away, especially more things than you need.
hoarder *noun*

hoarding *noun* **hoardings**
1 a temporary fence around a building site. 2 a tall fence covered with advertisements.

Holy Land

hoarse *adjective* **hoarser, hoarsest**
having a rough or croaking voice, as in *He was hoarse from shouting.*
hoarsely *adverb,* **hoarseness** *noun*

hoax *noun* **hoaxes**
a trick played on someone.
hoax *verb*

hobble *verb* **hobbles, hobbling, hobbled**
to walk with difficulty; to limp.

hobby *noun* **hobbies**
something that you do for pleasure in your spare time, as in *Gardening and stamp-collecting are popular hobbies.*

hockey *noun*
a game played, on a field or ice, by two teams using curved sticks and a small hard ball.

hoe *noun* **hoes**
a long-handled garden tool with a blade, used for weeding, etc.

hoe *verb* **hoes, hoeing, hoed**
to weed, loosen earth, or dig with a hoe.

hog *noun* **hogs**
1 a male pig. 2 (*colloquial*) a greedy person.
go the whole hog, (*colloquial*) to do something completely or thoroughly.

hog *verb* **hogs, hogging, hogged**
(*colloquial*) to take more than your fair share of something.

hoist *verb* **hoists, hoisting, hoisted**
to lift something up, especially using ropes or pulleys.

hold *verb* **holds, holding, held**
1 to have something in your hands. 2 to have; to possess or keep, as in *She holds the high jump record.* 3 to keep steady; to stop someone or something moving, as in *They held the thief until help arrived.* 4 to contain, as in *This jug holds a litre.* 5 to support, as in *This plank won't hold my weight.* 6 to stay unbroken; to continue, as in *Will this good weather hold?* 7 to believe; to value, as in *She holds strong opinions on animal rights.* 8 to stop, as in *Hold everything!* 9 to celebrate or conduct, as in *A party was held at the end of the term.*
hold it, stop; wait a minute.
hold on, to keep holding something; to wait, as in *Hold on as tightly as you can. Hold on! I'm not ready yet.*
hold out, to last or continue.
hold up, to hinder something or someone; to rob someone with threats or force, as in *Roadworks in the town centre are holding up the traffic. He was held up by a man with a knife.*

hold *noun* **holds**
1 influence or power, as in *She has a strange hold over me.* 2 the way of holding something, as in *a firm hold on the rail; a secure hold on her job.* 3 the part of a ship or aircraft where cargo is stored.
get hold of, to grasp; to get; to make contact with someone, as in *Get hold of the handle. We couldn't get hold of any pineapples. I've phoned several times, but can't get hold of her.*

hold-up *noun* **hold-ups**
1 a delay. 2 a robbery with threats or force.

hole *noun* **holes**
1 a gap or opening made in something. 2 an animal's burrow, as in *a wombat's hole.* 3 (*colloquial*) a small unpleasant place, town, etc.
holey *adjective*

holiday *noun* **holidays**
a day or time when you do not go to work or school; a time when you go away to enjoy yourself.
on holiday, having a holiday.

hollow *adjective* **hollower, hollowest**
with an empty space inside; not solid, as in *a hollow chocolate Easter egg.*

hollow *noun* **hollows**
1 a hollow place; a hole. 2 a small valley.

hollow *verb* **hollows, hollowing, hollowed**
to make something hollow; excavate.

holly *noun* **hollies**
an evergreen bush with shiny, prickly leaves, as in *Holly often has red berries in winter.*

holocaust *noun* **holocausts**
(*say* **hol**-uh-kawst *or* **hol**-uh-kost)
an immense destruction, especially by fire, as in *the threat of a nuclear holocaust.*
the Holocaust, the mass murder of Jews by the Nazis from 1942 until 1945.

hologram *noun* **holograms**
an image like a photograph made by laser beams, that appears to have depth as well as height and width.

holster *noun* **holsters**
a leather case for a pistol, usually attached to a belt.

holy *adjective* **holier, holiest**
1 treated with religious respect; to do with God, as in *holy Scripture.* 2 devoted to God or a religion, as in *a holy priest.*
holiness *noun*

Holy Land *noun*
an area between the River Jordan and the Mediterranean Sea.

home

home *noun* **homes**
 1 the place where you live.   2 the place where you were born or where you feel you belong.   3 a place where people are looked after, as in *a home for the elderly*.
 4 the finishing point in a game, race, etc., as in *She made a run for home in softball*.
 feel at home, to feel comfortable and happy.
 home economics, the study of how to manage a household.
 homeless *adjective*

home *adverb*
 1 to or at the place where you live, as in *Go home! Is she home yet?*   2 to the place aimed at or intended, as in *Push the bolt home. Try to get the message home that smoking isn't good for him*.
 bring something home to someone, to make someone realise something.

homely *adjective* **homelier, homeliest**
 simple; ordinary, as in *a homely meal*.
 homeliness *noun*

home-made *adjective*
 made at home; not bought from a shop.

homesick *adjective*
 sad because you are away from home.
 homesickness *noun*

homestead *noun* **homesteads**
 the main house on a large farm, sheep, or cattle station.

home unit *noun* **home units**
 a self-contained apartment usually privately-owned, being one of several in the same building or on the same block of land.

homeward or **homewards** *adverb*
 towards home.

homework *noun*
 school work that a pupil has to do at home.

homicide *noun* **homicides**
 (*say* **hom**-uh-suyd)
 the killing of a human being by another.

homing *adjective*
 trained to fly home, as in *a homing pigeon*.

homograph *noun* **homographs**
 a word spelt like another but with different meaning, for example *pole* (each of the ends of the earth's axis) and *pole* (a long, thin, round piece of wood, etc.).

homonym *noun* **homonyms**
 a word spelt or pronounced like another but having a different meaning, for example *bear* (the animal) and *bear* to endure; *peal* (to ring) and *peel* (the skin of fruit).

homophone *noun* **homophones**
 a word pronounced like another but having a different meaning for example *pair* (two) and *pear* (the fruit).

homosexual *adjective*
 (*say* hoh-moh-**sek**-shoo-uhl *or* hom-uh-**sek**-shoo-uhl)
 to do with loving or being attracted only to people of the same sex as yourself.
 homosexual *noun*

honest *adjective*
 1 fair and just; not cheating or stealing, as in *an honest shopkeeper*.   2 truthful, as in *an honest reply*.
 honestly *adverb*, **honesty** *noun*

honey *noun*
 a sweet, sticky food made by bees.

honeycomb *noun* **honeycombs**
 a wax structure made by bees to hold their honey and eggs.

honeyeater *noun* **honeyeaters**
 an Australian bird with a long tongue for feeding on nectar, etc.

honeymoon *noun* **honeymoons**
 a holiday spent together by a newly-married couple.

honeysuckle *noun*
 1 a climbing plant with sweet-smelling yellow or pink flowers.   2 an Australian tree or shrub having flowers rich in nectar, as in *The banksia is a common honeysuckle*.

honk *noun* **honks**
 a loud sound like the one made by a car horn or a wild goose.

honour or **honor** *noun* **honours**
 1 great respect for someone.   2 something given to a deserving person, as in *the Order of Australia honour*.   3 good reputation, as in *a person of honour*.   4 a person or thing that brings approval and respect, as in *She is an honour to the police force*.

honour or **honor** *verb* **honours, honouring, honoured**
 1 to feel or show respect for someone or something, as in *Honour your parents. Honour the flag.*   2 to accept and pay a cheque, bill, etc.

honourable or **honorable** *adjective*
 honest or loyal.
 honourably *adverb*

hood *noun* **hoods**
 1 a covering of soft material for your head and neck.   2 a folding roof or cover for a car, etc.
 hooded *adjective*

horror

hoof *noun* **hoofs**
the horny part of the foot of a horse, deer, etc., as in *You could hear the horses' hoofs.*

hook *noun* **hooks**
a piece of bent or curved metal for hanging things on or catching hold of something.
hooked *adjective*

hook *verb* **hooks, hooking, hooked**
1 to catch something, especially a fish, with a hook. 2 to fasten with or on a hook, as in *Hook the rope of the boat onto the mooring.* 3 to send a ball in a curve, as in *The batter hooked the ball and scored one run.*

hooligan *noun* **hooligans**
a young, rough, noisy person, as in *The hooligans caused trouble at the shopping centre.*

hoop *noun* **hoops**
a large ring made of metal, wood, etc.

hooray *interjection*
a shout of joy or approval; a cheer.

hoot *noun* **hoots**
1 a sound like the one made by an owl, car horn, etc. 2 a shout of disapproval, as in *The team's poor play was greeted with loud hoots.* 3 (*colloquial*) laughter and its cause.
someone doesn't care a hoot or **two hoots**, (*colloquial*) someone doesn't care at all.

hoot *verb* **hoots, hooting, hooted**
1 to make a sound like an owl, car horn, etc. 2 to scorn or mock, as in *The audience hooted the pathetic performance.*
3 (*colloquial*) to laugh in a loud noisy way, as in *They hooted with laughter.*
hooter *noun*

hop *verb* **hops, hopping, hopped**
1 to jump on one foot. 2 to move in jumps, as in *The kangaroo hopped away.*
3 (*colloquial*) to move quickly, as in *Here's the car; hop in!*
hop into, (*colloquial*) to begin a meal, activity, etc. with enthusiasm.
hopping mad, (*colloquial*) very angry.

hop *noun* **hops**
1 a jump made on one foot. 2 a climbing plant used to give beer its bitter flavour, as in *The hops of Tasmania are exported to many countries.*

hope *noun* **hopes**
1 the feeling of wanting something to happen, and thinking that it will happen.
2 a person or thing that makes you feel like this, as in *A change in the weather was their only hope of survival.*

hope *verb* **hopes, hoping, hoped**
to want something to happen, and to think

that it will; to expect something, as in *I hope that she will get better. We are hoping for better weather.*

hopeful *adjective*
1 having or feeling hope. 2 likely to be good or successful, as in *The small child made a hopeful attempt to climb the tree.*
hopefully *adverb*

hopeless *adjective*
1 without hope. 2 very bad at something, as in *I'm hopeless at cricket.*
hopelessly *adverb*, **hopelessness** *noun*

horde *noun* **hordes**
a large crowd; a gang or army.

Usage Do not confuse **horde** with **hoard**, which means a secret store of something.

horizon *noun* **horizons** (*say* huh-**ruy**-zuhn)
the line where the sky and the land or sea seem to meet.

horizontal *adjective* (*say* ho-ruh-**zon**-tuhl)
level; flat; going from left to right or right to left, as in *a horizontal line.*
horizontally *adverb*

hormone *noun* **hormones**
a substance made in glands in the body, sent directly into the blood, and affecting other organs in the body.

horn *noun* **horns**
1 a kind of pointed bone that grows on the heads of bulls, cows, rams, etc. 2 a brass musical instrument that you blow. 3 a device for making a warning sound.

hornet *noun* **hornets**
a large insect of the wasp family which can cause a harmful sting.

horoscope *noun* **horoscopes**
a forecast of a person's future from a diagram showing the relative positions of the stars and planets at his or her birth.

horrible *adjective*
terrible; nasty.
horribly *adverb*

horrid *adjective*
horrible; nasty, as in *horrid weather.*

horrific *adjective*
horrifying, as in *Murder is an horrific crime.*
horrifically *adverb*

horrify *verb* **horrifies, horrifying, horrified**
to cause horror or shock in someone.

horror *noun* **horrors**
1 great fear, dislike, or shock, as in *the horror of snakes.* 2 a horrifying person or thing, as in *the horror of famine.*

a
b
c
d
e
f
g
h
i
j
k
l
m
n
o
p
q
r
s
t
u
v
w
x
y
z

horse

3 (*colloquial*) a bad or mischievous person, as in *The toddler was a little horror*.

horse *noun* **horses**
1 a four-legged mammal with a flowing mane and tail used for riding, and to carry and pull loads. **2** a framework, as in *clothes-horse*. **3** a structure to jump over in gymnastics.
look a gift horse in the mouth, to complain about a gift or to be ungrateful for it.
on horseback, mounted on a horse.

horsepower *noun* **horsepower**
a unit for measuring the power of an engine, equal to 746 watts.

horse-radish *noun* **horse-radishes**
a plant with a strong-smelling root used in making a sauce.

horseshoe *noun* **horseshoes**
a U-shaped piece of metal nailed to a horse's hoof to protect it from wear.

horticulture *noun*
the art of planning and looking after gardens.

hose *noun* **hoses**
a long flexible tube through which water travels.

hose *verb* **hoses, hosing, hosed**
to water, spray, or drench with a hose, as in *Hose the garden*.

hosiery *noun*
stockings, socks, etc.

hospice *noun* **hospices** (*say* hos-puhs)
a special kind of hospital where people go when they are dying.

hospitable *adjective*
welcoming; liking to give hospitality, as in *a hospitable inn. They are a hospitable family*.
hospitably *adverb*

hospital *noun* **hospitals**
a place where sick or injured people are looked after.

hospitality *noun*
friendly and generous treatment given to guests.

host *noun* **hosts**
1 someone who has guests and looks after them. **2** a large crowd, as in *a host of people*.
hostess *noun*

hostage *noun* **hostages**
someone who is held as a prisoner or is threatened with death until some demand is met.

hostel *noun* **hostels**
a place where travellers, students, etc. can stay for a low price.

hostile *adjective*
to do with an enemy; unfriendly, as in *The hostile forces attacked us. Peter used to be a shy, almost hostile person. The desert is a hostile place*.
hostility *noun*

hot *adjective* **hotter, hottest**
1 very warm; to do with or at a high temperature. **2** having a burning taste like pepper or mustard. **3** excited; angry, as in *a hot temper*.
hot air, (*colloquial*) nonsense; boastful words.
hot line, a direct telephone line by which important people can communicate with each other, or by which you can get information quickly.
hot water, (*colloquial*) trouble.
not so hot, (*colloquial*) ordinary; not very good.
hotly *adverb*

hot *verb* **hots, hotting, hotted**
hot up, (*colloquial*) to become hotter, more exciting or dangerous; to make something hotter, more exciting or dangerous, as in *The war's hotting up. He hotted up the engine of the car*.

hot cross bun *noun* **hot cross buns**
a spicy bun with a cross marked on it, eaten at Easter.

hot dog *noun* **hot dogs**
(*colloquial*) a hot frankfurt in a soft roll.

hotel *noun* **hotels**
a building where people pay to have meals and stay for the night.

hothead *noun* **hotheads**
a person who acts hastily; or is easily angered.

hothouse *noun* **hot-houses**
a heated, mainly glass, building for growing tender plants.

hound *noun* **hounds**
any dog, especially one used for racing or hunting.

hound *verb* **hounds, hounding, hounded**
to chase or harass someone, as in *The family was hounded by newspaper reporters*.

hour *noun* **hours**
1 one of the twenty-four parts into which a day is divided. **2** a particular time, as in *Why are you up at this hour?*

hours, the period of time that a business is open or a person works, as in *She works irregular hours.*

hour-glass *noun* **hour-glasses**
an old-fashioned device for telling the time, having two vertically connected glass bulbs containing sand that takes an hour to pass from the top to the bottom bulb.

hourly *adjective* and *adverb*
every hour; done once an hour.

house *noun* **houses** (*say* hows)
1 a building where people live, usually designed for one family. **2** a building used for a special purpose, as in *opera-house; hen-house*. **3** a building for a government assembly; the assembly itself, as in *Parliament House; The House of Representatives*. **4** one of the divisions in some schools for sports competitions, etc. **5** the audience in a theatre, as in *a full house*.

house *verb* **houses, housing, housed** (*say* howz)
to provide a house or room for someone or something.

houseboat *noun* **houseboats**
a boat that you can live in.

household *noun* **households**
all the people who live together in the same house.

householder *noun* **householders**
someone who owns or rents a house.

house-husband *noun* **house-husbands**
a man who does the housekeeping for his family.

housekeeper *noun* **housekeepers**
a person employed to look after a household.

housekeeping *noun*
1 management of a household. **2** the money for a household's food and other supplies.

House of Representatives *noun*
the lower house of the federal parliament of Australia.

house-proud *adjective*
very careful to keep a house clean and tidy.

house-trained *adjective*
trained not to leave faeces and urine in the house, as in *This dog is not house-trained.*

house-warming *noun* **house-warmings**
a party to celebrate moving to a new home.

housewife *noun* **housewives**
a woman who does the housekeeping for her family.

housework *noun*
the work like cooking and cleaning that has to be done in a house.

housing *noun* **housings**
1 accommodation; houses, as in *The government provided more housing for low income earners*. **2** a cover or guard for a piece of machinery, as in *The strong housing for the motor prevented accidents occurring.*

hovel *noun* **hovels**
a small miserable place to live.

hover *verb* **hovers, hovering, hovered**
1 to stay in one place in the air. **2** to wait near someone or something; to loiter.

hovercraft *noun* **hovercraft**
a vehicle that travels just above the surface of water or land, supported by a strong current of air.

how *adverb*
1 in what way, as in *How did you do it?* **2** to what extent, as in *How sure are you?* **3** in what condition, as in *How are you?*
how about, would you like?, as in *How about a game of football?*
how do you do?, something said when you meet someone.
how many, what total.
how much, what amount; what price.
how's that?, what is your opinion or explanation of that?
howzat?, the way to ask a cricket umpire if a batter is out.

however *adverb*
1 in whatever way; to whatever extent, as in *You will never catch him, however hard you try*. **2** nevertheless, as in *It was pouring; however, he went out.*

however *conjunction*
in any way, as in *You can do it however you like.*

howl *noun* **howls**
a long, loud cry like an animal in pain.

howl *verb* **howls, howling, howled**
to make a long, loud cry like an animal in pain.

howler *noun* **howlers**
(*colloquial*) a silly, obvious mistake.

HQ short for **headquarters.**

hub *noun* **hubs**
1 the centre of a wheel. **2** a centre of interest, activity, etc., as in *The office is the hub of the school.*
hub-cap, a cover for the centre of a vehicle's wheel.

huddle

huddle *verb* huddles, huddling, huddled
to crowd together with other people for warmth, comfort, etc.

hue *noun* hues
a colour; variety or shade of colour, as in *the different hues of the sea*.

hue and cry *noun*
widespread alarm or protest.

huff *noun* huffs
an annoyed or offended mood, as in *She's in a huff*.

hug *verb* hugs, hugging, hugged
1 to clasp someone tightly in your arms.
2 to keep close to something, as in *The ship hugged the shore*.

hug *noun* hugs
clasping someone tightly in your arms, usually lovingly.

huge *adjective* huger, hugest
extremely large.
hugely *adverb*

huh *interjection*
an exclamation of questioning or scorn.

hulk *noun* hulks
1 an old decaying ship, as in *Before convicts were transported to Australia they were often kept in hulks*. 2 a large, clumsy person or thing.
hulking *adjective*

hull *noun* hulls
the main part or framework of a ship.

hullabaloo *noun* hullabaloos
an uproar.

hum *verb* hums, humming, hummed
1 to sing a tune with your lips closed.
2 to make a low, continuous sound like a bee.

hum *noun* hums
a humming sound.

human *noun* humans
any man, woman, or child.

human *adjective*
to do with humans; belonging to the human species, as in *human biology; a human being*.

humane *adjective* (*say* hyoo-**mayn**)
kind; merciful.
humanely *adverb*

humanitarian *adjective*
(*say* hyoo-man-uh-**tair**-ree-uhn)
concerned with helping people and relieving suffering.

humanity *noun* humanities
1 all the people in the world. 2 the possession of human qualities, as in *Slaves are denied their humanity by being treated as property*. 3 being humane; kind-heartedness, as in *The volunteer medical staff showed their humanity by helping the famine victims*.
humanities, arts subjects such as history and literature, not sciences.

humble *adjective* humbler, humblest
modest; not proud.
humbly *adverb*

humid *adjective* (*say* **hyoo**-muhd)
damp; moist.
humidity *noun*

humiliate *verb* humiliates, humiliating, humiliated
to lower the pride or self-respect of someone.
humiliation *noun*

humility *noun*
being humble.

hummingbird *noun* hummingbirds
a small tropical bird that makes a humming sound with its wings.

hummus *noun*
a dip or paste made from ground chick peas, sesame oil, lemon, and garlic.

humour or **humor** *noun*
1 the quality of being amusing; what makes people laugh. 2 the ability to enjoy funny or comical things, as in *He has a good sense of humour*. 3 a mood, as in *Keep him in a good humour*.
humorist *noun*, **humorous** *adjective*

humour or **humor** *verb* humours, humouring, humoured
to please someone by doing what he or she wants.

hump *noun* humps
a round lump, especially one on a person's or camel's back.
humpback *noun*, **humpbacked** *adjective*

hump *verb* humps, humping, humped
1 to carry something on your back. 2 to form a round shape or lump, as in *The children humped the bedclothes to pretend someone was in the bed*.

humpy *noun* humpies
1 a temporary Aboriginal bush shelter made from saplings, boughs etc. 2 any rough bush hut.

Origin This word comes from Yagara, an Aboriginal language of Queensland. See the Aboriginal map at the back of this dictionary.

humus *noun* (*say* **hum**-uhs) (*say* **hyoo**-muhs) rich earth made by decayed plants.

hunch *verb* hunches, hunching, hunched
to bend something into an arched shape, as in *He hunched his shoulders.*

hunch *noun* hunches
1 a feeling that you can guess what will happen, as in *I have a hunch that she won't come.* 2 a hump.

hunchback *noun* hunchbacks
a person with a hump on his or her back.
hunchbacked *adjective*

hundred *noun* hundreds
the number 100, ten times ten.
hundreds and thousands, tiny coloured, sweet-tasting decorations for a cake.
hundredth *adjective*

hung past tense and past participle of **hang.**

hunger *noun*
the feeling that you want to eat; the lack of food.
hunger strike, refusing to eat as a way of making a protest.

hungry *adjective* hungrier, hungriest
feeling hunger.
hungrily *adverb*

hunk *noun* hunks
1 a large piece cut or torn off, as in *a hunk of bread.* 2 (*colloquial*) a very attractive young man.

hunt *verb* hunts, hunting, hunted
1 to go after a wild animal because you want to kill it. 2 to search for something, as in *He hunted for his lost keys.*
hunter *noun,* **huntsman** *noun*

hunt *noun* hunts
1 the act of hunting, as in *a wild pig hunt.* 2 a search, as in *the police hunt for escaped prisoners.*

hurdle *noun* hurdles
1 a frame that you jump over in hurdling. 2 an obstacle or difficulty, as in *Poor health was a hurdle for the student.*

hurdling *noun*
a race in which you run and jump over obstacles.
hurdler *noun*

hurl *verb* hurls, hurling, hurled
to throw something as far as you can.

hurricane *noun* hurricanes
a very severe storm with a violent wind, especially a cyclone wind.

hurry *noun*
moving quickly; doing something quickly.
in a hurry, hurrying; impatient, as in *They were in a hurry to catch their train. He's always in a hurry and hates waiting.*

hurry *verb* hurries, hurrying, hurried
1 to move quickly; to do something quickly. 2 to try to make someone be quick, as in *The teacher hurried the dawdling students along.*
hurriedly *adverb*

hurt *verb* hurts, hurting, hurt
1 to cause pain or harm to a person or animal. 2 to suffer pain, as in *My arm hurts.*
hurtful *adjective*

hurtle *verb* hurtles, hurtling, hurtled
to move very quickly, as in *The train hurtled along.*

husband *noun* husbands
the man that a woman has married.

hush *verb* hushes, hushing, hushed
to make something or someone silent; to become silent, as in *Hush the crying baby. The crowd hushed as the speaker approached the platform.*

hush-hush *adjective*
(*colloquial*) very secret, as in *They're planning a surprise party—it's all very hush-hush.*

husk *noun* husks
the dry outer covering of some fruits or seeds.

husky *adjective* huskier, huskiest
1 hoarse, as in *She has a husky voice.* 2 big and strong.
huskily *adverb,* **huskiness** *noun*

husky *noun* huskies
a breed of dog used by the Inuit, especially to pull sledges.

hustle *verb* hustles, hustling, hustled
1 to hurry. 2 to make someone move quickly, often by bumping them or pulling and pushing them along, as in *The children were hustled out of the classroom.*

hut *noun* huts
a small house or shelter.

hutch *noun* hutches
a box or cage for a pet rabbit, etc.

hyacinth *noun* hyacinths
a sweet-smelling flower that grows from a bulb.

a b c d e f g h i j k l m n o p q r s t u v w x y z

hybrid

hybrid *noun* **hybrids**
an animal or plant that combines two different species, as in *A mule is a hybrid of a donkey and a horse.*

hydrangea *noun* **hydrangeas**
(*say* huy-**drayn**-juh)
a deciduous shrub with large pink, blue, or white flowers and large leaves.

hydrant *noun* **hydrants**
an outlet, especially in a street, where a hose can be connected to the main water system.

hydraulic *adjective*
worked by the movement of water or other liquid, as in *hydraulic brakes.*
hydraulically *adverb*

hydrochloric acid *noun*
a colourless acid containing hydrogen and chlorine.

hydroelectric *adjective*
using water-power to make electricity.

hydrofoil *noun* **hydrofoils**
a boat designed to skim over the surface of the water.

hydrogen *noun*
a very light gas without colour, taste, or smell.
hydrogen bomb, a very powerful bomb using energy from the joining of hydrogen nuclei.
hydrogen peroxide, a colourless liquid that is used as a bleach.

hydroponics *plural noun*
growing plants without soil, in sand, gravel, or liquid with special fertilisers added.

hydrosphere *noun*
all the water on the surface of the earth and in its atmosphere.

hyena or **hyaena** *noun* **hyenas**
(*say* huy-**ee**-nuh)
a dog-like, flesh-eating mammal.

hygiene *noun* (*say* **huy**-jeen)
conditions, especially cleanliness necessary for maintaining health.
hygienic *adjective,* **hygienically** *adverb*

hymn *noun* **hymns**
a religious song, especially one praising God.
hymn book *noun*

hyperactive *adjective*
unable to relax and always moving about or doing things.

hyphen *noun* **hyphens**
a short dash used to join words or parts of words together, as in *There is a hyphen in the word 'hide-out' but not in 'hydrogen bomb'.*
hyphenated *adjective,* **hyphenation** *noun*

hypnosis *noun* (*say* hip-**noh**-suhs)
a condition like a deep sleep in which someone's actions may be controlled by someone else.

hypnotism *noun* (*say* **hip**-nuh-tiz-uhm)
the study or practice of hypnosis, as in *She underwent hypnotism to give up smoking.*
hypnotic *adjective,* **hypnotist** *noun,* **hypnotise** *verb*

hypochondriac *noun* **hypochondriacs**
(*say* huy-puh-**kon**-dree-ak)
a person who continually worries about his or her health for no good reason.

hypocrite *noun* **hypocrites** (*say* **hip**-uh-krit)
someone who pretends to be a better person than he or she really is.
hypocrisy *noun,* **hypocritical** *adjective*

hypodermic *adjective*
(*say* huy-puh-**der**-mik)
to do with something injected under the skin, as in *A hypodermic syringe was used to treat the patient.*

hypotenuse *noun* **hypotenuses**
(*say* huy-**pot**-uh-nyooz)
the side opposite the right angle in a right-angled triangle.

hypothermia *noun*
the condition of having a very low body temperature, which is harmful.

hypothesis *noun* **hypotheses**
(*say* huy-**poth**-uh-sis)
a suggestion that tries to explain something; a theory that has not been tested or proved, as in *We tested John's hypothesis to see if it was correct.*
hypothetical *adjective*

hypothesise or **hypothesize** *verb*
hypothesises, hypothesising, hypothesised
to put forward a hypothesis; to accept something temporarily and use it as a hypothesis.

hysterical *adjective*
1 uncontrollably wild with excitement or emotion, as in *She became hysterical with the news of her friend's accident.* **2** (*colloquial*) extremely funny.
hysterically *adverb,* **hysteria** *noun,* **hysterics** *plural noun*

Ii

I *pronoun*
a word used by someone to speak about himself or herself.

ibis *noun* **ibises** (*say* **uy**-buhs)
a wading bird with a curved beak, long neck and long legs.

ice *noun* **ices**
frozen water.
ice age, a time in the past when ice covered large areas of the earth.

ice *verb* **ices, icing, iced**
1 to make something icy; to become icy.   **2** to put icing on a cake.

iceberg *noun* **icebergs**
a large mass of ice floating in the sea.

ice-breaker *noun* **ice-breakers**
a ship with strong bows for breaking through ice.

ice-cream *noun* **ice-creams**
a sweet, creamy, frozen food, usually flavoured.

ice-hockey *noun*
a game like hockey played on ice by skaters.

icicle *noun* **icicles**
a thin, pointed piece of ice that hangs down.

icing *noun*
a sugary substance for decorating cakes.

icon *noun* **icons**
1 a picture or statue, especially one used for religious purposes.   **2** a symbol used in a computer system to represent a program, choice, window, etc.

icy *adjective* **icier, iciest**
like ice; very cold, as in *icy weather*.
icily *adverb*

icy pole *noun* **icy poles**
a piece of flavoured ice on a small stick; an iceblock.

ID *noun* **IDs**
something that proves who you are, such as a passport, as in *The security man asked to see my ID.*

I'd short for *I had, I should,* or *I would.*

idea *noun* **ideas**
something that someone has thought of; a plan.

ideal *adjective*
perfect, as in *The spacious house was ideal for the large family.*
ideally *adverb*

ideal *noun* **ideals**
something or someone that you think is perfect or worth trying to be like, as in *Happiness for all people is an ideal that can never be reached.*

identical *adjective*
exactly the same.
identically *adverb*

identify *verb* **identifies, identifying, identified**
to discover who someone is or what something is, as in *The police have identified the car used in the robbery.*
identify with, to think that you share another person's feelings, another group's beliefs, etc.
identification *noun*

identikit *noun* **identikits**
a picture of someone built up from descriptions of him or her.

identity *noun* **identities**
who someone is; the typical features of a place, as in *He revealed his identity by signing his name. Harbour views are part of the identity of Sydney.*

a
b
c
d
e
f
g
h
i
j
k
l
m
n
o
p
q
r
s
t
u
v
w
x
y
z

idiom

idiom *noun* **idioms** (*say* id-ee-uhm)
a phrase that means something different from the meanings of the words in it, as in *'over the moon' and 'on your last legs' are idioms*.
idiomatic *adjective*, **idiomatically** *adverb*

idiot *noun* **idiots**
1 a very stupid person. **2** a person with very limited intelligence.
idiot box, (*colloquial*) a television set.
idiocy *noun*, **idiotic** *adjective*, **idiotically** *adverb*

idle *adjective* **idler**, **idlest**
1 doing nothing; lazy, as in *idle workers*.
2 useless; with no particular purpose, as in *idle gossip*.
idly *adverb*

idol *noun* **idols**
a person or thing that people worship or treat as if he, she, or it were a god.
idolatry *noun*, **idolise** *verb*

i.e. short for the Latin *id est*, which means 'that is', as in *I like racket sports best, i.e. badminton, squash, and tennis. He was a hypocrite, i.e. someone who pretends to be better than he really is.*

if *conjunction*
1 supposing that; on condition that, as in *I'll tell you what happened if you promise to keep it secret.* **2** although; even though, as in *I'll finish this job if it kills me!*
3 whenever, as in *I get a headache if I don't wear my glasses.* **4** whether, as in *Tell me if you're hungry.*
if only, I wish, as in *If only I were rich!*

igloo *noun* **igloos**
an Inuit's round house made of blocks of hard snow.

igneous *adjective* (*say* ig-nee-uhs)
formed by volcanoes, as in *igneous rocks*.

ignite *verb* **ignites**, **igniting**, **ignited**
to set fire to something; to catch fire.

ignition *noun*
1 the action of igniting, as in *The ignition of the bonfire proved difficult because the wood was wet.* **2** the system that starts the fuel in an engine burning so as to drive a vehicle or machine.

ignorant *adjective*
1 not knowing about something; knowing very little, as in *ignorant of mathematics; ignorant of good manners.* **2** having no education, as in *The ignorant people could not read or write.*
ignorance *noun*, **ignorantly** *adverb*

ignore *verb* **ignores**, **ignoring**, **ignored**
to take no notice of someone or something.

iguanodon *noun* **iguanodons**
(*say* i-**gwah**-nuh-don)
a large, plant-eating dinosaur with small fore-limbs.

I'll short for *I shall* or *I will*.

ill *adjective*
1 not well; in bad health. **2** bad; harmful, as in *There were no ill effects*.

ill *adverb*
badly, as in *She was ill-treated*.

illegal *adjective*
not legal; against the law.
illegally *adverb*

illegible *adjective* (*say* i-**lej**-uh-buhl)
not clear enough to read.
illegibly *adverb*

illegitimate *adjective* (*say* il-i-**jit**-i-muht)
1 not lawful. **2** (*old-fashioned use*) born when the parents are not married to each other, as in *an illegitimate child*.

illiterate *adjective* (*say* i-**lit**-uh-ruht)
unable to read or write.
illiteracy *noun*

illness *noun* **illnesses**
1 the state of being ill. **2** something that makes people ill; a disease, as in *Cancer is a dreadful illness*.

illogical *adjective*
against the rules of orderly thinking; not logical, as in *It is illogical to accuse her—she was nowhere near the scene of the crime*.
illogically *adverb*

illuminate *verb* **illuminates**, **illuminating**, **illuminated**
1 to light something up; to decorate streets, etc. with lights. **2** to make something clear; to explain something.
illumination *noun*

illusion *noun* **illusions**
an imaginary thing; something that looks like one thing in appearance but really is another thing, or not there at all.

Usage Do not confuse **illusion** with **delusion**, which means a false belief or opinion, or a sign of mental illness.

illustrate *verb* **illustrates**, **illustrating**, **illustrated**
1 to show something by pictures, examples, etc. **2** to put pictures in a book.
illustrative *adjective*, **illustrator** *noun*

illustration *noun* **illustrations**
1 a picture in a book, as in *The illustrations*

immune

in the book were black and white. **2** an example that explains something, as in *Fruit and vegetables are good illustrations of healthy food.* **3** the explanation of something by pictures, examples, etc., as in *He gave illustrations of the new swimming techniques.* **4** making pictures for a book, as in *The illustration of the book was expensive.*

illustrious *adjective* (*say* i-**lus**-tree-uhs)
famous, as in *illustrious writer.*

I'm short for *I am.*

image *noun* **images**
1 a picture or statue of a person or thing.
2 what you see in a mirror, through a lens, etc. **3** a person who looks very much like another. **4** the way that people think of a person or thing, as in *A common image of Australia is one of suntanned swimmers at the beach.*

imagery *noun*
the skilful use of words to produce pictures in the mind of the reader.

imaginary *adjective*
not real; imagined.

Usage Do not confuse **imaginary** with **imaginative**, which means able to imagine things.

imagination *noun*
the ability to imagine things.

imaginative *adjective*
able to imagine things; showing an ability to imagine things, as in *an imaginative child; an imaginative design for a book of ghost stories.*

Usage Do not confuse **imaginative** with **imaginary**, which means imagined or not real.

imagine *verb* **imagines, imagining, imagined**
to make pictures in your mind of things and people that you cannot see.
imaginable *adjective*

imbecile *noun* **imbeciles** (*say* **im**-buh-seel)
(*colloquial*) a very stupid person.

imitate *verb* **imitates, imitating, imitated**
to copy.
imitation *noun*, **imitator** *noun*

immaculate *adjective*
pure or spotless, as in *The pale carpet was in immaculate condition.*

immature *adjective*
not fully grown or developed.
immaturity *noun*

immediate *adjective*
1 happening or done without any delay.
2 nearest, as in *our immediate neighbours.*

immediately *adverb*
without any delay; at once.

immense *adjective*
huge.
immensely *adverb*, **immensity** *noun*

immerse *verb* **immerses, immersing, immersed**
to put something completely into a liquid.
be immersed in something, to be very interested or involved in something.

immersion *noun*
the act of immersing something; being immersed.
immersion heater, a device that heats water with an electric element immersed in the water.

immigrant *noun* **immigrants**
someone who has come to a new country to live.

immigrate *verb* **immigrates, immigrating, immigrated**
to come into a country to live there.
immigration *noun*

Usage Do not confuse **immigrate** with **emigrate**, which means to go and live in another country.

immobile *adjective*
not moving.
immobility *noun*

immobilise or **immobilize** *verb*
immobilises, immobilising, immobilised
to stop something moving or working.

immodest *adjective*
1 conceited or boastful. **2** not decent, as in *Some cultures believe it is immodest for women to wear short skirts.*

immoral *adjective*
not following the accepted standards of right and wrong; wicked, as in *Cheating is immoral.*
immorality *noun*

immortal *adjective*
living for ever; never dying.
immortality *noun*

immune *adjective*
safe from danger or attack, especially from disease, as in *The confident student was immune to criticism. She was immune to measles.*
immunity *noun*

immunise

immunise or **immunize** *verb* immunises, immunising, immunised
to make someone safe, especially from disease.
immunisation *noun*

imp *noun* imps
1 a small devil. 2 a naughty child.
impish *adjective*

impact *noun* impacts
1 a collision; the force of a collision. 2 a strong influence or effect, as in *The impact of computers on education has been dramatic.*

impair *verb* impairs, impairing, impaired
to harm or weaken, as in *The wound impaired his health.*
impairment *noun*

impale *verb* impales, impaling, impaled
to fix something on to a sharp object; to pierce someone or something.

impartial *adjective*
not favouring one side more than the other; fair, as in *We prefer an impartial umpire.*
impartiality *noun*, impartially *adverb*

impassable *adjective*
unable to be passed or got through, as in *The entrance was made impassable by the avalanche.*

impatient *adjective*
not patient; in a hurry.
impatience *noun*, impatiently *adverb*

imperative *noun* imperatives
1 a command. 2 the form of a verb that expresses a command, as in *'Go!' and 'stop!' are imperatives.*

imperceptible *adjective*
difficult or impossible to see, as in *The tiny flaws in the glass were imperceptible.*
imperceptibly *adverb*

imperfect *adjective*
not perfect; not complete.
imperfection *noun*, imperfectly *adverb*

imperial *adjective*
to do with an empire or its ruler, as in *China was once an imperial power.*
imperial unit, one of the official units of weight or measurement, such as the ounce or the gallon, once used in Australia for all goods before the introduction of the metric system.

impersonal *adjective*
1 not affected by personal feelings; showing no emotion, as in *The doctor showed an impersonal approach to his work.*
2 not referring to a particular person, as in *an impersonal letter.*
impersonally *adverb*

impersonate *verb* impersonates, impersonating, impersonated
to pretend to be someone else.
impersonation *noun*, impersonator *noun*

impertinent *adjective*
not respectful; rude.
impertinence *noun*

impetuous *adjective* (*say* im-**pet**-yoo-uhs)
acting or done in a rash and thoughtless way.

implement *noun* implements
(*say* im-pluh-muhnt)
a tool; a device for working with.

implement *verb* implements, implementing, implemented (*say* im-pluh-**ment**)
to put a plan, idea, etc. into action.

implore *verb* implores, imploring, implored
to beg someone to do something.

imply *verb* implies, implying, implied
to suggest something without actually saying it, as in *Asking what time it is implies that you are in a hurry.*
implication *noun*

Usage Do not confuse **imply** with **infer**, which means to guess or to reach an opinion from something that is suggested but not actually said.

impolite *adjective*
without good manners; not respectful and thoughtful towards other people.

import *verb* imports, importing, imported
(*say* im-**pawt**)
to bring in goods from another country.
importer *noun*

import *noun* imports (*say* **im**-pawt)
something brought in from another country.

important *adjective*
1 worth considering seriously; having a great effect, as in *an important decision.*
2 powerful or influential, as in *an important politician.*
importance *noun*, importantly *adverb*

impose *verb* imposes, imposing, imposed
1 to force something on to one or more people, as in *The plans to build a freeway were imposed on the suburb against the wish of the residents.* 2 to officially put on a tax, set a new law, etc., as in *The government imposed a further tax on cigarettes. A new traffic regulation was imposed at the busy inter-section.*
impose on someone, to take unfair advantage of someone.

inability

imposing *adjective*
looking important; impressive, as in *a large and imposing house.*

imposition *noun* **impositions**
something that someone is made to suffer, especially as a punishment.

impossible *adjective*
1 not possible. 2 (*colloquial*) very annoying, as in *He is impossible!*
impossibility *noun*, **impossibly** *adverb*

impostor *noun* **impostors**
someone who is not what he or she pretends to be.

impotent *adjective*
not having the power to do things; ineffective.

impracticable *adjective*
unable to be done or used, as in *The idea of digging a tunnel under the river proved impracticable because of its very high cost.*

Usage Do not confuse **impracticable** with **impractical**, which is the next word in this dictionary.

impractical *adjective*
1 not good at making or doing things, as in *He is impractical, and can't tackle any household repair jobs.* 2 not likely to work or be useful; not seeing things as they really are, as in *an impractical invention. Their ideas are impractical.*

impress *verb* **impresses, impressing, impressed**
to make someone think you are very good at something.
impress something on someone, to remind someone strongly about something.

impression *noun* **impressions**
1 a vague idea, as in *I got the impression she was unwell.* 2 an effect on your mind or feelings, as in *The film made a great impression on him.* 3 an imitation of a person or a sound, as in *He gave an impression of a kookaburra.*

impressive *adjective*
able to create respect, admiration, approval, etc., as in *an impressive piece of writing.*
impressively *adverb*

imprint *verb* **imprints, imprinting, imprinted**
to impress firmly, especially on the mind, as in *Images of the bushfires were imprinted on her memory forever.*

imprison *verb* **imprisons, imprisoning, imprisoned**
to put someone in prison.
imprisonment *noun*

improbable *adjective*
unlikely.
improbability *noun*, **improbably** *adverb*

impromptu *adjective* and *adverb*
(*say* im-**promp**-tyoo)
done without any rehearsal or preparation.

improper *adjective*
1 not proper; wrong, as in *improper behaviour.* 2 indecent, as in *improper language.*
improperly *adverb*, **impropriety** *noun*

improve *verb* **improves, improving, improved**
to make something better; to become better.
improvement *noun*

improvise *verb* **improvises, improvising, improvised**
1 to do something without rehearsal or preparation, especially to play music without rehearsing, as in *Jazz players improvise a lot.* 2 to make something quickly with what is available, as in *We improvised when we used sheets for curtains.*
improvisation *noun*

impudent *adjective*
not respectful; rude or cheeky.
impudence *noun*

impulse *noun* **impulses**
1 a sudden desire to do something, as in *an impulse to leave the room.* 2 a push; a driving force, as in *The impulse to improve road safety came from the high accident rate.*
impulsive *adjective*, **impulsively** *adverb*

impure *adjective* **impurer, impurest**
not pure; dirty, as in *Impure water can cause disease.*
impurity *noun*

in *preposition*
1 at; inside, as in *in Adelaide; in the box.* 2 during, as in *We ski in winter.* 3 into, as in *She has fallen in the water.* 4 arranged as; consisting of, as in *a serial in four parts.*
in all, coming to a total of, as in *$4 for the oranges, and $5 for the bananas—that makes $9 in all.*

in *adverb*
1 inwards; inside, as in *Get in.* 2 at home; indoors, as in *Is anybody in?* 3 batting, as in *Which team is in?*
in for, likely to get, as in *You're in for a shock.*
in on, taking part in something, as in *I want to be in on this game.*

in *adjective*
fashionable, as in *Teenagers like to wear in clothes.*

inability *noun*
being unable to do something.

a b c d e f g h i j k l m n o p q r s t u v w x y z

inaccessible

inaccessible *adjective*
unable to be reached, as in *an inaccessible mountain path.*

inaccurate *adjective*
not accurate.
inaccuracy *noun,* **inaccurately** *adverb*

inactive *adjective*
not active.
inaction *noun,* **inactivity** *noun*

inadequate *adjective*
not enough, as in *the inadequate water supplies of the desert.*
inadequacy *noun,* **inadequately** *adverb*

inanimate *adjective* (*say* in-**an**-uh-muht)
not living or moving, as in *inanimate stones.*

inappropriate *adjective*
not appropriate; unsuitable.
inappropriately *adverb*

inattention *noun*
not being attentive; not listening.
inattentive *adjective*

inaudible *adjective*
unable to be heard.
inaudibility *noun,* **inaudibly** *adverb*

incapable *adjective*
unable to do something, as in *He is incapable of work.*

incarnate *adjective*
with a human body, as in *He was so cruel he seemed like a devil incarnate.*
incarnation *noun*

incendiary *adjective*
able to start a fire, as in *an incendiary bomb.*

incense *noun* (*say* in-sens)
a substance that makes a spicy smell when it is burnt.

incense *verb* **incenses, incensing, incensed**
(*say* in-**sens**)
to make someone very angry, as in *The unfair decision incensed the players.*

incentive *noun* **incentives**
an encouragement to do something, especially to work harder.

incessant *adjective*
continual; not stopping, as in *The incessant noise prevented her from sleeping.*
incessantly *adverb*

incest *noun*
sexual intercourse between close relations.

inch *noun* **inches**
a measure of length equal to about $2^1/_2$ centimetres.
within an inch of his life, so that he almost died.

incident *noun* **incidents**
an event.

incidental *adjective*
not important.
incidental music, music used to accompany a film, etc.
incidentally *adverb*

incinerator *noun* **incinerators**
a device in which rubbish is burnt to ashes.

inclination *noun* **inclinations**
a tendency, as in *He had an inclination to eat too many sweets.*

incline *verb* **inclines, inclining, inclined**
(*say* in-**kluyn**)
to lean or bend.
be inclined to do something, to feel like doing something; to tend to do something, as in *I'm not inclined to help them. He is inclined to be lazy.*

incline *noun* **inclines** (*say* in-kluyn)
a slope.

include *verb* **includes, including, included**
to make or consider something as part of a group of other things.
inclusion *noun*

inclusive *adjective*
including everything; including all the things mentioned, as in *The fully inclusive price covers accommodation, travel, and food. Stay from Monday to Thursday inclusive.*

incoherent *adjective*
not clear; confused, as in *His speech was incoherent after his stroke.*

income *noun* **incomes**
the money that you get regularly.
income tax, tax charged on the money that you get regularly.

incompatible *adjective*
1 not able to live or exist together without trouble, as in *The incompatible couple separated.* 2 (*in Computing*) not able to be used together, as in *This computer and that printer are incompatible.*

incompetent *adjective*
unable to do a job properly.
incompetence *noun,* **incompetently** *adverb*

incomplete *adjective*
not complete; unfinished.
incompletely *adverb*

incomprehensible *adjective*
unable to be understood, as in *an incomprehensible legal document.*

indicate

incongruous *adjective*
(*say* in-**kong**-groo-uhs)
not suitable; out of place, as in *the incongruous sight of an elephant in the back garden.*
incongruity *noun*, **incongruously** *adverb*

inconsiderate *adjective*
not considerate; thoughtless.
inconsiderately *adverb*

inconsistent *adjective*
not consistent.
inconsistency *noun*, **inconsistently** *adverb*

inconspicuous *adjective*
not noticeable or remarkable.
inconspicuously *adverb*

inconvenient *adjective*
not convenient; awkward, as in *It was inconvenient to call at dinner time.*
inconvenience *noun*, **inconveniently** *adverb*

incorporate *verb* **incorporates, incorporating, incorporated**
to include, as in *The principal incorporated many of the students' suggestions in the new rules.*
incorporation *noun*

incorrect *adjective*
not correct; wrong.
incorrectly *adverb*

increase *verb* **increases, increasing, increased** (*say* in-**krees**)
to make something bigger; to become bigger, as in *She increased her weight by several kilograms. His wage increased.*
increasingly *adverb*

increase *noun* **increases** (*say* **in**-krees)
1 growth or enlargement as in *an increase in prices.* **2** the amount by which something is made or becomes bigger as in *There was an increase of five cents per litre in the price of petrol.*

incredible *adjective*
unbelievable, as in *She told an incredible story about space aliens landing in the school grounds.*
incredibly *adverb*

Usage Do not confuse **incredible** with **incredulous**, which is the next word in this dictionary.

incredulous *adjective*
unable to believe, as in *She gave an incredulous look when she heard of her lotto win.*
incredulity *noun*, **incredulously** *adverb*

incriminate *verb* **incriminates, incriminating, incriminated**
to make a person appear to be guilty, as in *His fingerprints on the safe incriminated him in the robbery.*

incubate *verb* **incubates, incubating, incubated**
to hatch eggs by keeping them warm.
incubation *noun*

incubator *noun* **incubators**
1 an apparatus for keeping alive very small babies, especially babies born sooner than usual. **2** an apparatus for hatching eggs.

indebted *adjective*
owing something to someone.

indecisive *adjective*
not decisive; hesitating, as in *The indecisive captain was replaced.*

indecent *adjective*
not decent; obscene, as in *indecent language.*
indecency *noun*, **indecently** *adverb*

indeed *adverb*
really; truly, as in *He was very wet indeed.*

indefinite *adjective*
not definite; vague.
indefinite article, the word 'a' or 'an'.

indefinitely *adverb*
for an indefinite or unlimited time.

indelible *adjective*
impossible to rub out or remove, as in *She used an indelible marker to label her clothes.*
indelibly *adverb*

indent *verb* **indents, indenting, indented**
1 to make notches or recesses in something. **2** to print or write the beginning of a line further to the right than usual.
indentation *noun*

independent *adjective*
not controlled or influenced by any other person or thing.
independence *noun*, **independently** *adverb*

index *noun* **indexes**
1 a list of names, subjects, titles, etc., especially at the end of a book.
2 a number showing how prices or wages have changed.
index finger, the finger next to your thumb.

Indian *noun* **Indians**
1 a Native American, as in *Cowboys and Indians.* **2** an inhabitant or native of India.

indicate *verb* **indicates, indicating, indicated**
1 to point out or show something, as in *He indicated where to go for a passport.* **2** to be

a
b
c
d
e
f
g
h
i
j
k
l
m
n
o
p
q
r
s
t
u
v
w
x
y
z

indicator

a sign of something, as in *Dark clouds can indicate a storm*.
indicative *adjective*, **indication** *noun*

indicator *noun* **indicators**
1 something that tells you what is happening. 2 one of the lights on the corners or sides of a vehicle that are used to show which way the driver wants to turn.

indifferent *adjective*
1 not caring about something; not interested. 2 not very good; ordinary, as in *He is an indifferent cricketer who will not make the team*.
indifference *noun*, **indifferently** *adverb*

indigestible *adjective*
not easy to digest.

indigenous *adjective*
native to or belonging to a particular place, as in *The indigenous people of Australia are the Aborigines. Australia's indigenous plants include the banksia and the eucalypt*.

indigestion *noun*
pain caused by difficulty in digesting food.

indignant *adjective*
angry at something that seems unfair or wicked.
indignantly *adverb*, **indignation** *noun*

indigo *noun*
a deep blue colour.

indirect *adjective*
not direct or not going straight to the point, as in *I was unable to follow her indirect instructions*.

indirect question *noun*
a question reported in indirect speech, as in *'She asked whether it was time to go' is an indirect question; the question she actually asked was 'Is it time to go?'*

indirect speech *noun*
someone's words given in an altered, reported form, instead of being written down exactly in the way they were said (*direct speech*), as in *'He said that he was sure' is indirect speech; 'I am sure' is direct speech*.
indirectly *adverb*

indispensable *adjective*
essential.

indisposed *adjective*
slightly unwell, as in *indisposed by headache*.

indistinct *adjective*
not clear, as in *His speech was indistinct because he mumbled*.
indistinctly *adverb*

indistinguishable *adjective*
1 impossible to tell apart from something else. 2 impossible to see or hear clearly.

individual *adjective*
1 to do with one person, as in *an individual personality*. 2 single; separate, as in *individual servings*.
individually *adverb*

individual *noun* **individuals**
one person.

individuality *noun*
the things that make one person or thing different from another.

indoctrinate *verb* **indoctrinates, indoctrinating, indoctrinated**
to fill someone's mind with particular ideas or beliefs.
indoctrination *noun*

indoor *adjective*
placed or done inside a building, as in *indoor furniture; indoor sports*.

indoors *adverb*
inside a building, as in *We moved indoors when rain started*.

induce *verb* **induces, inducing, induced**
1 to persuade. 2 to start the birth of a baby artificially.
inducement *noun*

indulge *verb* **indulges, indulging, indulged**
to let someone have or do what he or she wants.
indulge in something, to have something that you like to eat, drink, etc.
indulgence *noun*, **indulgent** *adjective*

industrial *adjective*
to do with industry, as in *an industrial worker*.
industrial action, ways for workers to protest, such as striking or working to rule.
Industrial Revolution, the expansion of industry using machines in the late 18th and early 19th Century.
industrialist *noun*, **industrially** *adverb*

industrialise or **industrialize** *verb*
industrialises, industrialising, industrialised
to increase or develop the industry in a country.
industrialisation *noun*

industrious *adjective*
hard-working, as in *an industrious pupil*.
industriously *adverb*

industry *noun* **industries**
1 the production or manufacture of things, as in *the mining industry*. 2 a large business enterprise, as in *the tourism industry*.

inferior

3 conscientious work; diligence, as in *The student's industry gave her an excellent report.*
heavy industry, making iron, steel, large machines, and other large or heavy products.
light industry, making small or light products.

inedible *adjective*
unable to be eaten, as in *The burnt chicken was inedible.*

ineffective *adjective*
not getting the desired result or effect, as in *The dye used on the cloth was ineffective.*
ineffectively *adverb*

ineffectual *adjective*
not effective; not confident or convincing, as in *The player made an ineffectual effort to reach the ball.*
ineffectually *adverb*

inefficient *adjective*
not doing work well; wasteful of energy, as in *an inefficient secretary; inefficient use of natural resources.*
inefficiency *noun,* **inefficiently** *adverb*

inequality *noun* **inequalities**
the condition of not being equal, as in *the inequality between the rich and poor.*

inert *adjective*
not moving or reacting.

inertia *noun* (*say* in-**er**-shuh)
lack of energy; lethargy, as in *The tourists were filled with inertia in the tropical heat of Cairns.*

inevitable *adjective*
unavoidable; sure to happen.
inevitability *noun,* **inevitably** *adverb*

inexhaustible *adjective*
unable to be used up completely; never-ending, as in *The world's energy supplies are not inexhaustible.*

inexpensive *adjective*
not expensive; cheap.
inexpensively *adverb*

inexperience *noun*
not having experience, knowledge or skill, as in *The young girl's inexperience prevented her from getting the job.*
inexperienced *adjective*

inexplicable *adjective*
impossible to explain.
inexplicably *adverb*

infallible *adjective*
never wrong; never-failing, as in *Teachers are not infallible. Sleep is an infallible cure for a tired child.*
infallibility *noun,* **infallibly** *adverb*

infamous *adjective* (*say* **in**-fuh-muhs)
wicked; thought to be wicked.
infamy *noun*

infant *noun* **infants**
a baby or young child.
infancy *noun*

infantile *adjective*
1 to do with babies or young children.
2 annoyingly childish, as in *The grade six class was accused of infantile behaviour when they sprayed water everywhere.*
infantile paralysis, poliomyelitis.

infantry *noun*
soldiers trained to fight on foot.
infantryman *noun*

infatuated *adjective*
(*say* in-**fat**-choo-ay-tuhd)
filled with foolish or blind love, as in *She was infatuated with the pop singer.*

infect *verb* **infects, infecting, infected**
1 to give someone a disease. **2** to influence others, as in *The gifted teacher infected her class with an enthusiasm for history.*

infection *noun* **infections**
1 the act of infecting, as in *There was little chance of infection after the family was inoculated.* **2** an illness caused by an infectious disease, as in *Her chest infection was eventually cleared up by antibiotics.*

infectious *adjective*
able to be spread from one person to another, as in *Hepatitis is an infectious disease. Her infectious laughter soon had everyone laughing.*

infer *verb* **infers, inferring, inferred**
to reach an opinion from something that is suggested but not actually said; to guess, as in *He inferred from her silence that she agreed.*
inference *noun*

Usage Do not confuse **infer** with **imply,** which means to suggest something without actually saying it.

inferior *adjective*
less good or important; low or lower in position, quality, etc., as in *inferior film; inferior rank; inferior goods.*
inferiority *noun*

inferior *noun* **inferiors**
a person who is lower in position, rank, etc. than another.

a
b
c
d
e
f
g
h
i
j
k
l
m
n
o
p
q
r
s
t
u
v
w
x
y
z

infernal

infernal *adjective*
1 to do with hell.   2 (*colloquial*) awful; very annoying, as in *an infernal nuisance*.
infernally *adverb*

inferno *noun* **infernos** (*say* in-**fer**-noh)
a fierce fire.

infested *adjective*
full of troublesome things like insects, rats, etc.

infiltrate *verb* **infiltrates, infiltrating, infiltrated**
to get into a place or organisation without being noticed.
infiltration *noun*, **infiltrator** *noun*

infinite *adjective* (*say* **in**-fuh-nuht)
endless; too large to be measured or imagined, as in *the infinite distances of space*.
infinitely *adverb*

infinitive *noun* **infinitives** (*say* in-**fin**-uh-tiv)
the form of a verb that does not change to indicate a particular tense, etc., as in *The infinitive usually occurs with 'to', as in 'to go'*.

infinity *noun* **infinities** (*say* in-**fin**-uh-tee)
an infinite number or distance.

infirm *adjective*
weak because of being old or ill.
infirmity *noun*

infirmary *noun* **infirmaries**
a type of hospital.

inflame *verb* **inflames, inflaming, inflamed**
1 to make a part of your body red and sore.   2 to make someone angry.
inflammation *noun*, **inflammatory** *adjective*

inflammable *adjective*
able to be set alight, as in *Synthetic materials are very inflammable*.

Usage The opposite of **inflammable** is **non-flammable**. The word **flammable** means the same as **inflammable**.

inflate *verb* **inflates, inflating, inflated**
1 to fill something with air or gas.   2 to raise or exaggerate something too much, as in *Inflated claims have been made for this product*.
inflatable *adjective*

inflation *noun*
1 filling something with air or gas.
2 a general rise in prices.
inflationary *adjective*

inflexible *adjective*
unable to be bent or changed, as in *inflexible timber; inflexible rules*.
inflexibility *noun*, **inflexibly** *adverb*

inflict *verb* **inflicts, inflicting, inflicted**
to make someone suffer something, as in *She inflicted a severe blow on him*.

influence *noun* **influences**
the power to affect someone or something, as in *She is a good influence on her less confident friend*.
influential *adjective*

influence *verb* **influences, influencing, influenced**
to have an effect on the way someone behaves; to affect something, as in *Hot weather influenced everyone's temper. The tides are influenced by the moon*.

influenza *noun* (*say* in-floo-**en**-zuh)
an infectious disease that causes fever, soreness in your nose and throat, and pain.

influx *noun*
a flowing of people or things into a place, usually in large numbers, as in *an influx of people into the arena; an influx of letters*.

inform *verb* **informs, informing, informed**
to tell someone something.
inform against or **on someone,** to tell the police about someone.

informal *adjective*
1 not formal; relaxed, as in *informal dress at the barbecue; an informal party*.   2 to do with language that is used for everyday speech; colloquial.   3 incorrect or invalid, as in *an informal vote*.
informality *noun*, **informally** *adverb*

informant *noun* **informants**
a person who tells you something.

information *noun*
facts; knowledge; what someone tells you.
information technology, ways of storing, arranging, and giving out information, especially the use of computers and telecommunications.

information report *noun*
an oral or written text that provides factual information about a topic.

informative *adjective* (*say* in-**faw**-muh-tiv)
with a lot of helpful information, as in *an informative booklet*.

informed *adjective*
knowing about something; educated, as in *informed listeners*.

informer *noun* **informers**
a person who tells the police about someone else.

infrequent *adjective*
not often.
infrequency *noun*, **infrequently** *adverb*

infuriate *verb* infuriates, infuriating, infuriated
to make someone very angry.

ingenious *adjective*
clever, especially at thinking of new ways
to do things, as in *an ingenious builder*.
ingeniously *adverb*, **ingenuity** *noun*

ingot *noun* ingots
a lump of metal after it has been cast,
usually shaped like a brick.

ingrained *adjective*
deep in the surface of something, as in
ingrained dirt.

ingratitude *noun*
a lack of gratitude or thanks for something
that has been done for you, as in *The parents
were upset by the ingratitude of their children
after giving them so much help*.

ingredient *noun* ingredients
(*say* in-**gree**-dee-uhnt)
1 one of the parts of a mixture. 2 one of
the things used in a recipe.

inhabit *verb* inhabits, inhabiting, inhabited
to live in a place.
inhabitable *adjective*, **inhabitant** *noun*

inhale *verb* inhales, inhaling, inhaled
to breathe in.
inhaler *noun*

inhaler *noun* inhalers
a device that someone uses for taking
medicine, especially for asthma, into his or
her lungs.

inherent *adjective* (*say* in-**heer**-ruhnt *or*
in-**he**-ruhnt)
naturally or permanently part of something,
as in *There are dangers inherent in bushwalking
if you are unprepared*.
inherently *adverb*

inherit *verb* inherits, inheriting, inherited
1 to receive money, property, a title, etc.
when its previous owner dies. 2 to get
certain characteristics from your parents or
ancestors.
inheritance *noun*, **inheritor** *noun*

inhibited *adjective*
resisting or holding back emotions,
instincts, or impulses, as in *He felt inhibited
in a room of strangers*.

inhospitable *adjective*
(*say* in-hos-**pit**-uh-buhl)
1 unfriendly to visitors. 2 giving no
shelter, as in *an inhospitable rocky island*.

inhuman *adjective*
cruel; without pity or kindness.
inhumanity *noun*

initial *adjective*
first; of the beginning, as in *the initial stages
of the work*.

initial *noun* initials
the first letter of a word or name, especially
of someone's first name.

initiate *verb* initiates, initiating, initiated
(*say* i-**nish**-ee-ayt)
1 to start something. 2 to admit someone
as a member of a society or group, often
with special ceremonies.
initiation *noun*

initiative *noun* initiatives
(*say* i-**nish**-ee-uh-tiv)
1 the action that starts something, as in *He
took the initiative in making peace*. 2 ability
or power to start things or to get them done
on your own, as in *She showed great initiative
and was soon promoted to manager*.

inject *verb* injects, injecting, injected
to put a medicine or drug through
someone's skin into his or her body using a
hollow needle.
injection *noun*

injure *verb* injures, injuring, injured
to harm or hurt someone.
injurious *adjective*, **injury** *noun*

injustice *noun* injustices
1 unfairness or lack of justice in a situation,
as in *Unemployment causes a lot of injustice in
society*. 2 an unjust or unfair act, as in *The
accusation of theft was an injustice to the honest
student*.

ink *noun* inks
a black or coloured liquid used for writing
and printing.
inky *adjective*

inkling *noun*
a slight idea or suspicion, as in *I had an
inkling that she would win the race*.

inland *adverb*
in or to a place on land and away from the
coast, as in *We live inland*.
the inland, the Australian outback and its
inhabitants, as in *Much of the inland is desert
country. All the inland listened to the election
broadcast*.

in-law *noun* in-laws
a member of someone's husband's or wife's
family, as in *We're going to visit the in-laws at
Easter*.

inlet *noun* inlets
a strip of water reaching into the land from
a sea, river, or lake.

inn

inn *noun* **inns**
a small hotel, especially for travellers, as in *an outback inn.*
innkeeper *noun*

innate *adjective*
born with; natural, as in *He had an innate talent for drawing.*

inner *adjective*
inside; nearest the centre.
inner tube, the inflatable tube inside a tyre.
innermost *adjective*

innings *noun* **innings**
the time when a cricket team or player is batting.

innocent *adjective*
1 not guilty; not wicked. 2 harmless, as in *innocent fun.*
innocence *noun*, **innocently** *adverb*

innocuous *adjective*
harmless, as in *She made an innocuous comment, not intended to hurt.*

innovation *noun* **innovations**
1 the invention or use of new things, as in *The last ten years have seen great innovations in computer technology.* 2 something new that you have just invented or started using, as in *Email is a recent innovation for communicating with others.*
innovative *adjective*, **innovator** *noun*

innumerable *adjective*
too many to be counted.

inoculate *verb* **inoculates, inoculating, inoculated**
to inject someone as protection against a disease.
inoculation *noun*

in-patient *noun* **in-patients**
someone who stays at a hospital for treatment.

input *noun* **inputs**
what you put into something, especially data sent to a computer.

input *verb* **inputs, inputting, input**
(*in Computing*) to put data or programs into a computer, as in *When the symbol '?—' appears, input the number you have chosen.*

inquest *noun* **inquests**
an official investigation to decide why someone died.

inquire *verb* **inquires, inquiring, inquired**
1 to ask; to enquire. 2 to make an official investigation.

inquiry *noun* **inquiries**
an official investigation.

inquisitive *adjective*
always trying to find out things, especially about other people's business.
inquisitively *adverb*

insane *adjective* **insaner, insanest**
mad.
insanely *adverb*, **insanity** *noun*

insanitary *adjective*
not clean or healthy.

inscribe *verb* **inscribes, inscribing, inscribed**
to write or carve something, as in *The cup was inscribed with the winning team's name.*
inscription *noun*

insect *noun* **insects**
a small animal with six legs and no backbone, as in *Flies, ants, butterflies, and bees are insects.*

insecticide *noun* **insecticides**
a poison for killing unwanted insects.

insecure *adjective*
1 not secure or safe, as in *The unlocked house is insecure.* 2 not feeling safe or confident, as in *I felt insecure at the party without my friends.*
insecurely *adverb*, **insecurity** *noun*

insensitive *adjective*
not sensitive; unfeeling, as in *The selfish person was insensitive to other people's needs.*
insensitively *adverb*, **insensitivity** *noun*

inseparable *adjective*
unable or unwilling to be separated, especially friends.
inseparably *adverb*

insert *verb* **inserts, inserting, inserted**
to put a thing into something else.
insertion *noun*

inside *noun* **insides**
the middle or centre of something; the part nearest to the middle.
inside out, with the inside turned so that it faces outwards.
insides, (*colloquial*) your stomach and bowels, as in *I've something wrong with my insides.*

inside *adjective*
placed in or coming from the centre of something; in or nearest to the middle, as in *an inside page.*

inside *adverb*
1 to the part nearest the centre of something; indoors, as in *Come inside.* 2 (*colloquial*) in prison, as in *He's inside for ten years.*

inside *preposition*
in or to the middle or centre of something, as in *It's inside that box.*

instrument

insight *noun* **insights**
an accurate or good understanding of a person's character, a situation or problem, as in *The teacher's report showed impressive insight into the child's character. The community worker had insight into the difficulties of the unemployed.*

insignificant *adjective*
not important; not influential.
insignificance *noun*

insincere *adjective*
not sincere; faked, as in *She showed insincere concern when her opponent tripped.*
insincerely *adverb*, **insincerity** *noun*

insist *verb* **insists, insisting, insisted**
to be very firm in asking or saying something, as in *He insisted that he was innocent.*
insistence *noun*, **insistent** *adjective*

insolent *adjective*
very rude; insulting.
insolence *noun*

insoluble *adjective*
1 impossible to solve, as in *an insoluble problem.* 2 impossible to dissolve, as in *an insoluble chemical.*
insolubility *noun*

insolvent *adjective*
unable to pay your debts; bankrupt.

insomnia *noun* (*say* in-**som**-nee-uh)
the inability to sleep.

inspect *verb* **inspects, inspecting, inspected**
to look carefully at people or things; to check that something is doing its work correctly, as in *The Health Minister inspected the hospital.*
inspection *noun*

inspector *noun* **inspectors**
1 someone employed to inspect things or people. 2 an officer in the police, above the rank of sergeant.

inspire *verb* **inspires, inspiring, inspired**
to fill someone with good or useful thoughts or feelings, as in *The applause inspired her with confidence.*
inspiration *noun*

install *verb* **installs, installing, installed**
1 to put something in position and ready to use, as in *They installed central heating.* 2 to put someone into an important position with a ceremony, as in *He was installed as captain of the school.*
installation *noun*

instalment *noun* **instalments**
one of the parts into which something is divided so as to spread it over a period of time, as in *He is paying for his bike in monthly instalments.*

instance *noun* **instances**
an example, as in *You need to eat healthy food —for instance, fruit and vegetables.*

instant *adjective*
1 happening immediately, as in *instant success.* 2 able to be made very quickly, as in *instant coffee.*

instant *noun* **instants**
1 a moment, as in *I don't believe it for an instant.* 2 an exact time, as in *Come here this instant!*

instantaneous *adjective*
happening or done in an instant, or without any delay.
instantaneously *adverb*

instantly *adverb*
without any delay.

instead *adverb*
in place of something else; as a substitute, as in *There were no potatoes, so we had bread instead.*

instep *noun* **insteps**
the inner arch of your foot between your toes and your ankle.

instinct *noun* **instincts**
a natural tendency to do or feel something, as in *Spiders spin webs by instinct. She has an instinct for good music.*
instinctive *adjective*, **instinctively** *adverb*

institute *noun* **institutes**
1 a society or organisation, as in *the Institute of Architects.* 2 a building used by a society.

institute *verb* **institutes, instituting, instituted**
to establish or start something.

institution *noun* **institutions**
1 an institute. 2 a habit or custom; a well-known person or thing, as in *Going for a Sunday bike ride was a family institution. The senior teacher was an institution at the school.*

instruct *verb* **instructs, instructing, instructed**
1 to educate someone. 2 to inform someone, as in *My client instructs me that you have not acted upon her request.* 3 to tell someone what to do.
instruction *noun*, **instructional** *adjective*, **instructive** *adjective*, **instructor** *noun*, **instructress** *noun*

instrument *noun* **instruments**
1 a device for making musical sounds. 2 a device for delicate or scientific work, as in *surgical instrument.*

instrumental

instrumental *adjective*
  1 to do with or using musical instruments, as in *an instrumental group of guitar, drums and clarinet.*   **2** being one of the causes of something, as in *She was instrumental in getting him a job.*

instrumentation *noun*
  the use or arrangement of instruments in music.

insubordinate *adjective*
  (*say* in-suh-**baw**-duh-nuht)
  disobedient.

insufficient *adjective*
  not enough.
  insufficiently *adverb*

insulate *verb* **insulates, insulating, insulated**
  to cover something so as to stop the movement of heat, cold, electricity, etc., as in *We insulated the house to reduce the heating bills. Electric cords must be insulated.*
  insulation *noun*, **insulator** *noun*

insulin *noun*
  a chemical that controls how much sugar you have in your blood, as in *The illness of diabetes is caused by having abnormal levels of insulin in the body.*

insult *verb* **insults, insulting, insulted**
  (*say* in-**sult**)
  to speak or behave in a way that hurts someone's feelings or pride.

insult *noun* **insults** (*say* **in**-sult)
  a remark or action that hurts someone's feelings or pride.

insurance *noun*
  an agreement to pay regular amounts of money to a firm which, in return, will pay you a large amount of money if you suffer a loss, injury, etc.

insure *verb* **insures, insuring, insured**
  to protect yourself or your goods with insurance.

  Usage Do not confuse **insure** with **ensure**, which means to make sure.

intact *adjective*
  not damaged; complete, as in *Despite the storm our tent was still intact.*

intake *noun* **intakes**
  1 the act of taking something in, as in *an intake of knowledge; intake of food.*   **2** the number of people or things taken in, as in *The school had a high intake of pupils.*

integer *noun* **integers** (*say* **in**-tuh-juh)
  a negative or positive whole number, such as –2, –1, 0, 1, 2, 3, etc.

integral *adjective* (*say* **in**-tuh-gruhl *or* in-**teg**-ruhl)
  1 necessary to a whole of something, as in *Your heart is an integral part of your body.*
  2 whole; complete, as in *an integral design.*
  integrally *adverb*

integrate *verb* **integrates, integrating, integrated** (*say* **in**-tuh-grayt)
  1 to make parts into a whole; to connect things together, as in *The bus routes were integrated to improve the transport system.*
  2 to join people together into a single community; to get people of different races to live happily together.
  integrated circuit, a very small piece of material with many electric circuits on it, such as a silicon chip.
  integration *noun*

integrity *noun* (*say* in-**teg**-ruh-tee)
  honesty, as in *The lawyer was respected particularly for his integrity.*

intellect *noun* **intellects**
  the ability to think and reason.

intellectual *adjective*
  1 appealing to the mind, as in *She has intellectual tastes in reading.*   **2** able to think effectively; keen to study and learn, as in *an intellectual writer.*
  intellectually *adverb*

intellectual *noun* **intellectuals**
  an intellectual person.

intelligence *noun*
  1 the ability to learn, understand, reason, etc., as in *Her intelligence enabled her to understand the difficult theory.*
  2 information, especially of military value; the people who collect and study this information.

intelligent *adjective*
  good at thinking and learning; clever.
  intelligently *adverb*

intelligible *adjective*
  able to be understood, as in *The confused message was barely intelligible.*
  intelligibility *noun*, **intelligibly** *adverb*

intend *verb* **intends, intending, intended**
  1 to have in mind what you plan to do; to plan, as in *She was intending to go swimming.*
  2 to have something as a plan for someone else, as in *I intend you to do this job.*

intense *adjective*
  1 very strong or great, as in *intense heat.*
  2 having or showing strong feelings, as in *a very serious, intense woman.*
  intensely *adverb*

interminable

intensify *verb* **intensifies, intensifying, intensified**
to make something more intense or stronger; to become more intense or stronger, as in *Intensify the volume. The heat intensified towards noon.*
intensification *noun*

intensity *noun* **intensities**
the strength, greatness of something, as in *intensity of heat; intensity of pleasure.*

intensive *adjective*
with a lot of effort; thorough, as in *intensive farming. We made an intensive search.*
intensively *adverb*

intent *noun* **intents**
intention; purpose, as in *My intent was to finish the work.*

intent *adjective*
eager; very interested, as in *He was intent on winning.*
intent on, eager to do something; determined to do something, as in *They're intent on their work. She's intent on buying her own house.*
intently *adverb*

intention *noun* **intentions**
what you intend to do; a plan.

intentional *adjective*
deliberate; planned.
intentionally *adverb*

interact *verb* **interacts, interacting, interacted**
to have an effect on one another, as in *It is interesting to watch how two competitive people interact. Observe how acids and metals interact.*
interaction *noun*

interactive *adjective*
(*in Computing*) allowing information to be sent immediately in either direction between a computer system and its user.

intercept *verb* **intercepts, intercepting, intercepted**
to stop or catch a person or thing going from one place to another, as in *The teacher intercepted the note being passed around the classroom.*
interception *noun,* **interceptor** *noun*

interchange *verb* **interchanges, interchanging, interchanged**
1 to put two things in each other's place.
2 to give and receive something; to exchange things.
interchangeable *adjective,* **interchangeably** *adverb*

interchange *noun* **interchanges**

exchange between two people, etc., as in *the interchange of gifts at Christmas; the interchange of roster duties.*

intercom *noun* **intercoms**
(*colloquial*) a device for communicating by radio, telephone, etc.

intercourse *noun*
1 communication or dealings between people. 2 sexual intercourse.

interest *noun* **interests**
1 the feeling a person has when his or her attention is fixed on something; curiosity, as in *a great interest in ancient civilisations.*
2 a thing that interests someone, as in *His interests are fishing and Aussie Rules.*
3 money paid regularly in return for money loaned or deposited.

interest *verb* **interests, interesting, interested**
to make someone want to look, listen, help with something, etc.

interface *noun* **interfaces**
(*in Computing*) the place where two systems or devices are connected, as in *My laptop computer has an interface for connecting it to the college's network.*

interfere *verb* **interferes, interfering, interfered**
1 to take part in something that has nothing to do with you, as in *Don't interfere in my business.* 2 to get in the way, as in *Television interferes with my reading.*
interference *noun*

interior *noun* **interiors**
the inside of something, as in *The interior of the house was painted while the vine-covered exterior was not.*
the interior, the land far from the coast; the inland.

interjection *noun* **interjections**
an exclamation, as in *Interjections are words like 'ah' and 'oh'.*

interlock *verb* **interlocks, interlocking, interlocked**
to fit into one another, as in *The building blocks interlocked.*

interlude *noun* **interludes**
1 an interval or short period of time.
2 music played during an interval.

intermediate *adjective*
coming between two things in place, order, time, etc.

interminable *adjective*
(*say* in-**ter**-min-uh-buhl)
seeming to go on forever; endless, as in *interminable speech.*
interminably *adverb*

intermission

intermission *noun* **intermissions**
an interval in a play, film, etc.

intermittent *adjective*
happening at intervals, as in *Intermittent showers spoiled the game but didn't stop it.*
intermittently *adverb*

intern *noun* **interns**
a junior doctor living and working in a hospital while completing further training.

intern *verb* **interns, interning, interned**
to imprison someone in a special camp or building, usually during a war.
internee *noun*, **internment** *noun*

internal *adjective*
to do with the inside of something, as in *She suffered internal injuries in the accident.*
internally *adverb*

international *adjective*
to do with more than one country, as in *Interpol is an international police organisation.*
internationally *adverb*

interplanetary *adjective*
between planets, as in *interplanetary travel.*

interpret *verb* **interprets, interpreting, interpreted**
1 to explain what something means. 2 to translate from one language into another.
interpretation *noun*, **interpreter** *noun*

interrogate *verb* **interrogates, interrogating, interrogated**
to question someone closely, as in *The police interrogated the suspects.*
interrogation *noun*, **interrogator** *noun*

interrupt *verb* **interrupts, interrupting, interrupted**
1 to stop someone talking. 2 to stop something going on, as in *Rain interrupted play.*
interruption *noun*

intersect *verb* **intersects, intersecting, intersected**
to cross or divide something, as in *intersecting lines.*

intersection *noun* **intersections**
1 a place where lines or roads, etc. cross each other. 2 (*in Mathematics*) the items that are shared by two or more sets.

interstate *adjective*
between states, as in *interstate football matches.*

interstate *adverb*
in, into or from a state other than that in which a person normally lives, as in *They moved interstate.*

interstellar *adjective*
between the stars.

interval *noun* **intervals**
1 a time between two events or between two parts of a play, film, etc. 2 a space between two things, as in *Buttons were sewn on the jacket at even intervals.*
at intervals, with some time or distance between each one; not continuously.

intervene *verb* **intervenes, intervening, intervened**
1 to interrupt an argument, fight, etc. and try to stop it or change its result. 2 to come between a particular event or time and the present, as in *Ten years had intervened since she had last seen her sister.*
intervention *noun*

interview *noun* **interviews**
a meeting with someone to ask him or her questions or to discuss something.

interview *verb* **interviews, interviewing, interviewed**
to have an interview with someone.
interviewer *noun*

intestine *noun* or **intestines** *plural noun*
the long tube along which food passes from the stomach.
intestinal *adjective*

intimate *adjective* (*say* in-tuh-muht)
1 very friendly. 2 private; personal, as in *intimate thoughts.* 3 detailed; close, as in *She has an intimate knowledge of dog breeds.*
intimacy *noun*, **intimately** *adverb*

intimate *verb* **intimates, intimating, intimated** (*say* in-tuh-mayt)
to tell someone or give someone a hint, as in *He has not yet intimated what his plans are.*
intimation *noun*

intimidate *verb* **intimidates, intimidating, intimidated**
to frighten someone so as to make him or her do something.
intimidation *noun*

into *preposition*
1 to the inside of somewhere; to a place inside, as in *Go into the house.* 2 to a particular condition, situation, job, etc., as in *He got into trouble. She got into acting.* 3 saying how many times one number is included in another, as in *3 into 12 goes 4 times.*

intolerable *adjective*
unbearable, as in *intolerable noise; intolerable heat.*
intolerably *adverb*

inverted commas

intolerant *adjective*
not tolerant, especially of other people's beliefs or behaviour.
intolerance *noun*, **intolerantly** *adverb*

intonation *noun* intonations
1 the pitch or tone of a voice or musical instrument. **2** (*in grammar*) using the pitch of your voice to alter the meaning of what you are saying, for example when asking a question.

intoxicate *verb* intoxicates, intoxicating, intoxicated
1 to make someone drunk. **2** to make someone very excited, as in *She is intoxicated by the thought of overseas travel.*
intoxication *noun*

intrepid *adjective*
brave; fearless.
intrepidly *adverb*

intricate *adjective*
complicated, as in *an intricate pattern.*
intricacy *noun*, **intricately** *adverb*

intrigue *verb* intrigues, intriguing, intrigued
(*say* in-**treeg**)
1 to interest someone very much. **2** to make secret plans.

introduce *verb* introduces, introducing, introduced
1 to make someone known to other people. **2** to announce a broadcast, speaker, etc. **3** to start something being used or considered, as in *New traffic laws were introduced by the police force.*

introduction *noun* introductions
1 the act of introducing someone or something, as in *The introduction of rabbits to Australia has created many problems.* **2** a piece at the beginning of a book, speech, etc.
introductory *adjective*

intrude *verb* intrudes, intruding, intruded
to come in or join in without being wanted.
intrusion *noun*, **intrusive** *adjective*

intruder *noun* intruders
1 someone who intrudes. **2** a burglar.

intuition *noun* (*say* in-tyoo-**ish**-uhn *or* in-choo-**ish**-uhn)
the power to know or understand things without having to think hard, as in *His intuition told him what the next move should be.*
intuitive *adjective*

Inuit *noun* Inuit *or* Inuits
one of the people who live in very cold parts of North America.

inundate *verb* inundates, inundating,

inundated
to flood something; to overwhelm, as in *Rising waters inundated the low-lying land. The speaker was inundated with questions.*
inundation *noun*

invade *verb* invades, invading, invaded
to attack and enter a country, place, etc.
invader *noun*

invalid *noun* invalids (*say* in-vuh-leed *or* in-vuh-lid)
someone who is ill or weakened by a long illness.

invalid *adjective* (*say* in-**val**-uhd)
not valid, especially legally, as in *This passport is invalid and cannot be used.*

invaluable *adjective*
very valuable; priceless, as in *invaluable information; an invaluable diamond ring.*

invariable *adjective*
unchangeable; always the same, as in *An invariable temperature had to be kept in the premature baby's humidicrib.*

invariably *adverb*
always.

invasion *noun* invasions
the act of attacking and entering a place.

invent *verb* invents, inventing, invented
to be the first person to make or think of a particular thing.
invention *noun*, **inventive** *adjective*, **inventor** *noun*

inverse *adjective*
reversed; opposite, as in *The poor result was inverse to the big effort the team gave.*
inverse proportion, a relation between two quantities in which one quantity grows smaller as the other grows larger.
inversely *adverb*

inverse *noun*
1 the opposite of something. **2** (*in Mathematics*) an operation that produces the opposite effect to another, as in *Division is the inverse of multiplication.*

invert *verb* inverts, inverting, inverted
to turn something upside down.
inversion *noun*

invertebrate *noun* invertebrates
(*say* in-**ver**-tuh-bruht)
an animal without a backbone, as in *Amoebas, worms, and jellyfish are invertebrates.*

inverted commas *noun*
punctuation marks, " " or ' ', put before and after spoken words.

invest

invest *verb* **invests, investing, invested**
  1 to use money so as to earn interest or make a profit. **2** to devote time, energy, etc. to something, as in *He invested a lot of time in playing Nintendo.*
investment *noun*, **investor** *noun*

investigate *verb* **investigates, investigating, investigated**
to find out as much as you can about something, especially about a crime.
investigation *noun*, **investigator** *noun*

invigorate *verb* **invigorates, invigorating, invigorated**
to give someone strength or vigour, as in *Exercise invigorates me.*

invincible *adjective*
unable to be defeated.
invincibly *adverb*

invisible *adjective*
unable to be seen.
invisibility *noun*, **invisibly** *adverb*

invite *verb* **invites, inviting, invited**
  1 to ask someone politely to do something, especially to come to a party, etc. **2** to bring something on yourself, as in *You are inviting trouble by making rude jokes about the principal.*
invitation *noun*

inviting *adjective*
attractive; tempting, as in *an inviting job offer.*
invitingly *adverb*

in vitro *adjective* (*say* in-**vit**-roh)
taking place in a test tube or artificial environment, as in *In vitro fertilisation occurs when an egg is fertilised by a sperm in a test tube rather than a womb.*

invoice *noun* **invoices**
a list of goods sent or of work done, with the prices charged.

involuntary *adjective*
not deliberate; done without thinking, as in *The startled student gave an involuntary squeal of surprise.*
involuntarily *adverb*

involve *verb* **involves, involving, involved**
  1 to mean; to result in, as in *The job involved great effort.* **2** to affect; to make someone part of something, as in *Changes in the duty roster don't involve us. We are involved in charity work.*
involvement *noun*

involved *adjective*
  1 complicated, as in *a long and involved explanation.* **2** concerned or interested, especially romantically, as in *He is involved with a new girlfriend.*

inward *adjective*
  1 on the inside, especially in your mind, as in *her inward happiness.* **2** going or facing inwards.
inwardly *adverb*

inward *adverb*
inwards, as in *He moved inward to the centre of the room.*

inwards *adverb*
towards the inside.

iodine *noun* (*say* **uy**-uh-deen *or* **uy**-uh-duyn)
a chemical used to kill germs.

IOU *noun* **IOUs** (*say* I owe **you**)
a piece of paper on which you write that you owe someone money.

IQ *noun* **IQs**
a measure of someone's intelligence, calculated from the results of a special test.

irate *adjective*
very angry.

iris *noun* **irises**
  1 the coloured part of the eyeball. **2** a flower with long, pointed leaves.

iron *noun* **irons**
  1 a strong, heavy metal. **2** a device that is heated for smoothing clothes or cloth. **3** a tool made of iron, as in *a branding iron.*
irons, chains round a prisoner's ankles.

iron *verb* **irons, ironing, ironed**
to smooth clothes or cloth with an iron.
iron out, to solve a difficulty, as in *The worst faults in the computer program have now been ironed out.*

Iron Age *noun*
the time in history when iron began to be used for tools and weapons.

ironbark *noun* **ironbarks**
a gum tree with a thick, hard usually black bark and hard dense timber.

ironic *adjective* (*say* uy-**ron**-ik)
using irony; full of irony.
ironical *adjective*, **ironically** *adverb*

irony *noun* **ironies** (*say* **uy**-ruh-nee)
  1 saying the opposite of what you mean so as to emphasise it, as in *You use irony if you say 'What a lovely day' when it is pouring with rain.* **2** an unexpected or strange event or situation.
ironic *adjective*, **ironically** *adverb*

irrational *adjective*
not rational; absurd.
irrationality *noun*, **irrationally** *adverb*

irregular *adjective*
1 not regular or even; not usual, as in *irregular floorboards; irregular heartbeat.*
2 against the rules, as in *It was irregular not to wear school uniform.*
irregularity *noun*, **irregularly** *adverb*

irrelevant *adjective* (*say* i-**rel**-uh-vuhnt)
having nothing or little to do with what is being talked about, as in *Don't ask irrelevant questions—it wastes time.*
irrelevance *noun*, **irrelevantly** *adverb*

irresistible *adjective*
unable to be resisted because something is too strong, delightful, or convincing, as in *the irresistible force of the cyclone; the irresistible chocolate cake; the irresistible arguments against smoking.*
irresistibly *adverb*

irresponsible *adjective*
not trustworthy; not sensible, as in *An irresponsible student cannot be elected class captain.*
irresponsibility *noun*, **irresponsibly** *adverb*

irreverent *adjective*
not respectful, especially towards holy things.
irreverence *noun*, **irreverently** *adverb*

irrigate *verb* **irrigates, irrigating, irrigated**
to supply land with water through channels, etc. so that crops can grow.
irrigation *noun*

irritable *adjective*
easily annoyed, as in *The child became irritable in hot humid weather.*
irritability *noun*, **irritably** *adverb*

irritate *verb* **irritates, irritating, irritated**
1 to annoy someone. 2 to make part of your body itch or feel sore, as in *The sun irritated her fair skin.*
irritant *noun*, **irritation** *noun*

is 3rd person singular present tense of **be.**

Islam *noun* (*say* iz-lahm *or* iz-lam)
the religion of Muslims.
Islamic *adjective*

island *noun* **islands**
a piece of land surrounded by water.
islander *noun*

isle *noun* **isles**
a small island.

isn't short for *is not.*

isobar *noun* **isobars** (*say* **uy**-suh-bah)
a line on a map connecting places that have the same atmospheric pressure.

isolate *verb* **isolates, isolating, isolated**
1 to separate a chemical, as in *Marie Curie succeeded in isolating radium.* 2 to put someone or something apart from others, as in *The disruptive student was isolated from his class.*
isolation *noun*

isosceles *adjective* (*say* uy-**sos**-uh-leez)
(of a triangle) with two sides equal.

isotope *noun* **isotopes** (*say* **uy**-suh-tohp)
(*in Science*) a form of an element that is different from other forms in the structure of its nucleus, but has the same chemical properties as the other forms.

issue *noun* **issues**
1 something sent or given out, published, or put into circulation, as in *an issue of blankets for the refugees; a Christmas issue of stamps; the latest issue of banknotes.* 2 a magazine or newspaper brought out at a particular time, as in *Tuesday's issue of the Age.* 3 a subject for discussion or concern, as in *What are the real issues?*

issue *verb* **issues, issuing, issued**
1 to send or give out; to supply, as in *They issued blankets to the refugees.* 2 to publish; to put into circulation, as in *The dictionary was issued in parts. These banknotes have just been issued.* 3 to come out, as in *Smoke was issuing from the chimney.*

it *pronoun*
1 the thing being talked about. 2 the player in a game who has to catch other people, as in *You're it now!*

italic *adjective* (*say* i-**tal**-ik)
printed sloping, as in *like this.*
italicise *verb*

italics *plural noun* (*say* i-**tal**-iks)
italic letters.

itch *noun* **itches**
1 a tickling feeling in your skin that makes you want to scratch it. 2 a longing to do something, as in *He has an itch to go to Tasmania.*
itchy *adjective*

itch *verb* **itches, itching, itched**
1 to have an irritation on your skin which you want to scratch. 2 to desire very much, as in *I itch to dance.*

item *noun* **items**
one thing in a list or group of things, especially a piece of news.

itinerant *adjective*
travelling from place to place, as in *Shearers are itinerant workers.*

a
b
c
d
e
f
g
h
i
j
k
l
m
n
o
p
q
r
s
t
u
v
w
x
y
z

itinerary

itinerary *noun* **itineraries**
(*say* uy-**tin**-uh-ruh-ree *or* uy-**tin** uh-ree)
a list of places to be visited on a journey; a route.

it'll short for *it will*.

its *pronoun*
to do with it; belonging to it, as in *The problem is difficult, its solution will be hard. The cat hurt its paw.*

it's short for *it is* and (before a verb in the past tense) *it has*, as in *Can you see if it's raining? It's been raining.*

itself *pronoun*
it and nothing else.
by itself, without help, attention, etc. from anybody; alone, as in *This machine works by itself. His house stands by itself in the bush.*

I've short for *I have*.

ivory *noun*
1 the hard, creamy-white substance that forms elephants' tusks. 2 a creamy-white colour.
ivories, (*colloquial*) the keys of a piano.

ivy *noun*
a climbing evergreen plant with shiny leaves.

Jj

jab *verb* jabs, jabbing, jabbed
1 to poke someone or something. **2** to stab or pierce someone or something.

jab *noun* jabs
1 a poking, stabbing, or piercing movement. **2** (*colloquial*) an injection.

jabiru *noun* jabirus (*say* jab-uh-**roo**)
a type of large Australian stork with glossy greenish-black and white feathers and red legs, found along the north and east coast.

jacaranda *noun* jacarandas
a tropical tree with blue or purple trumpet-shaped flowers.

jack *noun* jacks
1 a device for lifting something heavy off the ground. **2** a playing-card with a picture of a young man on it. **3** a small white ball that you aim at in the game of bowls.

jack *verb* jacks, jacking, jacked
to lift something with a jack, as in *The mechanic jacked up the car to fix the tyre.*
jack up, to refuse to cooperate.

jackal *noun* jackals
a wild animal from Africa or Asia rather like a dog.

jackass *noun* jackasses
1 a male donkey. **2** a stupid person.
laughing jackass, a kookaburra.

jackeroo or **jackaroo** *noun* jackeroos
a young person gaining experience by working as a trainee on a sheep or cattle station.

jacket *noun* jackets
1 a coat which covers the top half of the body. **2** a cover for a book; a dust-jacket. **3** the skin of a potato that is cooked without being peeled.

jack-in-the-box *noun* jack-in-the-boxes
a toy figure that springs out of a box when you lift the lid.

jackknife *verb* jackknifes, jackknifing, jackknifed
to go out of control, as in *The semi-trailer jackknifed when its trailer skidded round towards the cabin.*

jackpot *noun* jackpots
an amount of prize-money that increases until someone wins it.

jade *noun*
a green stone which is carved to make ornaments.

jaded *adjective*
tired and bored.

jaffle *noun* jaffles
a sandwich with a savoury or sweet filling, sealed and toasted between two hot metal plates.

jagged *adjective* (*say* **jag**-uhd)
uneven and sharp.

jaguar *noun* jaguars
a large, fierce animal rather like a leopard.

jail *noun* jails
a prison.
jailer *noun*

jam *verb* jams, jamming, jammed
1 to make or become fixed and difficult to move, as in *The door has jammed.* **2** to squeeze or wedge, as in *I jammed my fingers in the door.*

jam *noun* jams
1 a lot of people, cars, logs, etc. crowded together so that it is difficult to move, as in *a traffic jam.* **2** (*colloquial*) a difficult situation, as in *He's in a jam.* **3** a sweet food made of fruit boiled with sugar until it

a
b
c
d
e
f
g
h
i
j
k
l
m
n
o
p
q
r
s
t
u
v
w
x
y
z

jamboree

is thick. **4** a Western Australian wattle tree with a scent like raspberry jam, as in *The raspberry jam wattle is commonly called the jam tree.*

jamboree *noun* **jamborees**
a large party or celebration, especially a large gathering of Scouts.

jam-packed *adjective*
(*colloquial*) full of people or things so that there is no room for anything else, as in *a jam-packed hall.*

jangle *verb* **jangles, jangling, jangled**
to make a harsh ringing sound.

January *noun*
the first month of the year.

jar *noun* **jars**
a container usually made of glass.

jar *verb* **jars, jarring, jarred**
1 to make a harsh sound. **2** to strike with a painful force or jolt, as in *He jarred his neck.* **3** to have an unpleasant effect on your feelings, as in *His cruel comments jarred on her.*

jargon *noun*
the language used by a particular group or profession, as in *medical jargon; computer jargon.*

jarrah *noun* **jarrahs**
a tall Western Australian gum tree with hard, dark red wood.

jaundice *noun*
a disease that makes your skin yellow.

jaunt *noun* **jaunts**
a short journey which you make for pleasure.

javelin *noun* **javelins**
a light spear thrown in sport.

jaw *noun* **jaws**
1 the lower part of the face. **2** one of the two bones that hold the teeth.

jazz *noun*
a kind of music with strong rhythm, often played without rehearsing.
jazzy *adjective*

jealous *adjective*
unhappy or resentful because you feel that someone rivals you or is better or luckier than you.
jealously *adverb*, **jealousy** *noun*

jeans *plural noun*
trousers made of denim or other strong material.

jeep *noun* **jeeps**
a small, sturdy, especially military vehicle with four-wheel drive.

jeer *verb* **jeers, jeering, jeered**
to laugh or shout at someone rudely or scornfully.

jelly *noun* **jellies**
a soft, sweet food that melts in your mouth; any similar soft, slippery substance, as in *ice-cream and jelly; petroleum jelly.*
jellied *adjective*

jellyfish *noun* **jellyfish**
a marine animal with a body like jelly and stinging tentacles.

jeopardise or **jeopardize** *verb* **jeopardises, jeopardising, jeopardised** (*say* jep-uh-duyz)
to risk or put in danger.
jeopardy *noun*

jerk *noun* **jerks**
1 a sudden sharp movement.
2 (*colloquial*) a fool.
jerks, (*colloquial*) exercises, as in *physical jerks.*
jerkily *adverb*, **jerkiness** *noun*, **jerky** *adjective*

jerk *verb* **jerks, jerking, jerked**
to make a sudden sharp movement.

jest *noun* **jests**
a joke.
in jest, joking; not seriously.

jester *noun* **jesters**
a professional entertainer at a king's court in the Middle Ages.

jet *noun* **jets**
1 a stream of liquid, gas, flame, etc. forced out of a narrow opening. **2** a narrow opening from which a jet comes out, as in *a gas jet.* **3** a jet plane.
jet engine, an engine that works by sending out a jet of hot gas at the back.
jet lag, very great tiredness that someone feels after a long air journey because he or she has not got used to the differences in time in different parts of the world.
jet-propelled *adjective*, **jet-propulsion** *noun*

jet *verb* **jets, jetting, jetted**
1 to come out in a strong stream.
2 (*colloquial*) to send or travel in a jet plane.

jet *noun*
1 a hard black mineral. **2** a deep glossy black colour.

jetty *noun* **jetties**
a long pier extending out in a river, sea, etc. to which boats, ships, etc. can be moored.

Jew *noun* **Jews**
1 a member of the race of people descended from the ancient tribes of Israel.
2 someone who believes in Judaism.
Jewess *noun*, **Jewish** *adjective*

jewel *noun* **jewels**
a precious stone; an ornament including one or more precious stones.
jewel beetle, an Australian beetle with brilliant colours.
jewelled *adjective*

jeweller *noun* **jewellers**
someone who sells or makes jewellery.

jewellery *noun*
jewels or ornaments that you wear.

jib *noun* **jibs**
1 a triangular sail stretching forward from the mast. **2** the projecting arm of a crane.

jib *verb* **jibs, jibbing, jibbed**
to stop and refuse to go on, as in *The horse jibbed at the gate. The class jibbed at the extra homework.*

jig *noun* **jigs**
1 a lively dance. **2** a device that holds something in place while you work on it with tools.

jig *verb* **jigs, jigging, jigged**
1 to dance a jig. **2** to move up and down quickly and jerkily, as in *Alf was jigging up and down, trying to get warm.*

jigsaw *noun* **jigsaws**
1 a saw that can cut curved shapes. **2** a jigsaw puzzle.
jigsaw puzzle, a puzzle made of shapes that you fit together to make a picture.

jilleroo or **jillaroo** *noun* **jilleroos**
a female worker on a sheep or cattle station.

jingle *noun* **jingles**
1 a tinkling or clinking sound. **2** a verse or group of words with repetitive sounds, especially a simple song used in an advertisement on radio or television.

jingle *verb* **jingles, jingling, jingled**
to make a tinkling or clinking sound.

jinx *noun*
(*colloquial*) a person or thing that seems to cause bad luck.

job *noun* **jobs**
1 work that someone does regularly to earn a living, as in *He got a job as a postman.* **2** a particular task, as in *We shall have tea when we finish this job.* **3** (*colloquial*) a difficult task, as in *You'll have a job to lift that box.* **4** (*colloquial*) a situation; a state of affairs, as in *It's a good job you're here.* **5** (*colloquial*) a crime, especially a robbery.

jobless *adjective*
unemployed.

jockey *noun* **jockeys**
someone who rides horses in races.

jodhpurs *plural noun* (*say* **jod**-puhz)
trousers for horse-riding, fitting closely from the knee to the ankle.

joey *noun* **joeys**
a young kangaroo or wallaby.

jog *verb* **jogs, jogging, jogged**
1 to run slowly, especially for exercise. **2** to give something a slight knock or push.
jog someone's memory, to help someone remember something.
jogger *noun*, **jogging** *noun*

join *verb* **joins, joining, joined**
1 to put things together; to come together; to fasten or unite things. **2** to become a member of an organisation, group, etc.
join in, to take part in something.

join *noun* **joins**
a place where things join.

joiner *noun* **joiners**
someone whose job is to make furniture and other things out of wood.
joinery *noun*

joint *noun* **joints**
1 a place where things are fixed together. **2** the place where two bones fit together. **3** a large piece of meat.

joint *adjective*
shared or done by two or more people, countries, etc.
jointly *adverb*

joist *noun* **joists**
a long beam supporting a floor or ceiling.

joke *noun* **jokes**
1 something said or done to make people laugh. **2** a trick.
no joke, something serious.

joke *verb* **jokes, joking, joked**
to make jokes or tease.
jokingly *adverb*

joker *noun* **jokers**
1 someone who jokes. **2** a playing-card with a picture of a jester on it, used in some games as the card having the highest value. **3** (*colloquial*) a person; a fool, as in *Who's this joker?*

jolly *adjective* **jollier, jolliest**
happy; cheerful.
jollity *noun*

jolt *verb* **jolts, jolting, jolted**
to move something or someone suddenly and sharply; to move along with sudden sharp movements.

jolt

jolt *noun* jolts
1 a sudden sharp movement.
2 a surprise or shock.

jostle *verb* jostles, jostling, jostled
to push someone roughly.

jot *verb* jots, jotting, jotted
to write something quickly.

joule *noun* joules
(*in Science*) a unit of work or energy.

journal *noun* journals
1 a newspaper or magazine. 2 a diary.

journalist *noun* journalists
someone who writes for a newspaper or
magazine.
journalism *noun*, **journalistic** *adjective*

journey *noun* journeys
1 going from one place to another. 2 the
distance you travel or the time you take to
travel somewhere, as in *Sydney to
Melbourne is about a day's journey by car*.

journey *verb* journeys, journeying, journeyed
to go from one place to another.

joust *verb* jousts, jousting, jousted
to fight on horseback with lances, as in
*Knights in the Middle Ages used to joust as a
sport*.

jovial *adjective*
cheerful; good-humoured, as in *A jovial
Father Christmas greeted the children*.
joviality *noun*, **jovially** *adverb*

joy *noun*
great happiness or pleasure.

joyful *adjective*
very happy.
joyfully *adverb*

joyless *adjective*
without joy; miserable.

joyous *adjective*
very happy.
joyously *adverb*

joy ride *noun* joy rides
(*colloquial*) a ride in a motor car, usually
without its owner's permission.

joystick *noun* joysticks
1 (*colloquial*) the lever that controls the up-
and-down and (together with the rudder)
the turning movements of a plane. 2 a
lever that controls the movements of a
computer's cursor.

jubilant *adjective* (*say* **joo**-buh-luhnt)
extremely happy; joyful, as in *a jubilant
celebration of the victory*.
jubilantly *adverb*, **jubilation** *noun*

jubilee *noun* jubilees
(*say* **joo**-buh-lee)
a time of celebrating, especially for an
anniversary, as in *A silver jubilee is the
25th anniversary; a golden jubilee is
the 50th anniversary; and a diamond jubilee
is the 60th anniversary*.

Judaism *noun* (*say* **joo**-day-iz-uhm)
the religion of the Jewish people.

judge *noun* judges
1 someone appointed to hear cases in a
lawcourt and decide what should be
done. 2 someone appointed to decide
who has won a contest or competition.
3 someone who is good at forming
opinions or making decisions about things,
as in *She's a good judge of musical skills*.

judge *verb* judges, judging, judged
1 to act as judge for a law case or a
contest. 2 to estimate or guess
something. 3 to form an opinion, as in
*The teacher judged the student as being very
unhappy*.

judgment or **judgement** *noun* judgments
1 the decision made in a court case,
contest, etc. 2 ability to estimate things or
to make decisions wisely. 3 someone's
opinion or conclusion, as in *In my judgment,
the food is too salty*. 4 something
considered as a punishment from God, etc.

judicial *adjective* (*say* joo-**dish**-uhl)
to do with lawcourts, judges, or decisions
made in lawcourts.
judicially *adverb*

judicious *adjective* (*say* joo-**dish**-uhs)
having or showing good sense, as in *They
made judicious use of the computer in the
classroom*.
judiciously *adverb*

judo *noun* (*say* **joo**-doh)
a Japanese method of wrestling and self-
defence based on ju-jitsu.

jug *noun* jugs
a container for liquids, with a handle and
lip.

juggle *verb* juggles, juggling, juggled
to keep a number of objects moving in the
air without dropping any.
juggler *noun*

juice *noun* juices
1 the liquid from fruit, vegetables, or other
food. 2 liquid in your body, as in *digestive
juices*.
juicy *adjective*

ju-jitsu *noun*
a Japanese method of unarmed self-defence.
[from the Japanese **jujitsu** = gentle skill]

jukebox *noun* jukeboxes
a machine that plays a record when you put a coin in.

July *noun*
the seventh month of the year.

jumble *verb* jumbles, jumbling, jumbled
to mix things up in a confused way.

jumble *noun* jumbles
a confused mixture; a muddle.
jumble sale, a sale of second-hand goods to raise money for charity, etc.

jumbo *noun* jumbos
a huge jet airliner, for several hundred passengers; jumbo jet.

jumbuck *noun* jumbucks
a sheep.

jump *verb* jumps, jumping, jumped
1 to move suddenly from the ground into the air.   2 to go over something by jumping, as in *The horse jumped the fence.*   3 to move quickly or suddenly, as in *He jumped out of his seat.*   4 to change rapidly, as in *She jumped from one subject to another.*
jump at something, to accept something eagerly.
jump the gun, (*colloquial*) to start before you should.
jump the queue, not to wait for your proper turn.

jump *noun* jumps
1 a sudden movement into the air.   2 an obstacle to jump over.   3 a sudden rise in amount, price, value, etc., as in *House prices jumped.*
jump suit, a piece of clothing made in one piece and covering your whole body.

jumper *noun* jumpers
1 a person or animal that jumps.   2 a knitted pullover.

jumpy *adjective* jumpier, jumpiest
nervous.

junction *noun* junctions
a place where roads or railway lines join.

June *noun*
the sixth month of the year.

jungle *noun* jungles
a thick, tangled forest, especially in a tropical country.

junior *adjective*
1 younger, as in *The junior members of the family had little say in choosing holidays.*

2 for young children, as in *a junior school.*   3 lower in rank or importance, as in *a junior employee.*

junior *noun* juniors
1 a younger person.   2 a person of lower rank or importance, as in *a junior in the company.*

junk *noun*
1 rubbish.   2 things that are worth little or nothing, as in *I'm not paying good money for that junk!*
junk food, food of poor quality, usually containing a lot of sugar and starch.
junk mail, advertisements that you do not want, delivered with newspapers or with the post.

junk *noun* junks
a Chinese sailing-boat with a flat bottom.

junket *noun* junkets
a sweet, soft food made from milk.

junkie *noun* junkies
(*colloquial*) a drug addict.

jurisdiction *noun*
the legal right to deal with situations.

jury *noun* juries
1 a group of people appointed to make a decision about a case in a lawcourt, as in *There are usually 12 people in a jury.*   2 a group of people who award prizes in a competition.
juror *noun*, **juryman** *noun*, **jurywoman** *noun*

just *adjective*
1 fair; right; giving proper consideration to everybody, as in *There were no favourites in the just teacher's class.*   2 deserved, as in *He got his just reward.*
justly *adverb*

just *adverb*
1 exactly, as in *It's just what I wanted.*
2 only; simply, as in *I just wanted another cake.*   3 hardly; barely; by only a short distance, as in *just missed the plane.*   4 a very short time ago, as in *She has just gone.*

justice *noun*
1 fairness; being just, as in *a strong sense of justice.*   2 the law, as in *The criminal was brought to justice.*
do justice to something, to be fair to something; to show or use something in the best way possible, as in *To do the film justice, it had to cover a huge story in a very short time. We did his cooking justice, and ate every last scrap of food.*

justify *verb* justifies, justifying, justified
to show that something is fair, reasonable,

jut

or acceptable, as in *Do you think that you were justified in taking such a risk?*
justifiable *adjective*, **justifiably** *adverb*, **justification** *noun*

jut *verb* **juts, jutting, jutted**
to stick out.

juvenile *adjective* (*say* **joo**-vuh-nuyl)
1 to do with young people, as in *juvenile detention centre*. **2** immature, as in *juvenile behaviour*.
juvenile delinquent, a young person who breaks the law.

juxtapose *verb* **juxtaposes, juxtaposing, juxtaposed**
to place side by side, as in *The garage was juxtaposed to the house.*

Kk

kaleidoscope *noun* **kaleidoscopes**
(*say* kuhl-**luy**-duh-skohp)
a tube that you look through to see brightly-coloured patterns which change as you turn the end of the tube.
kaleidoscopic *adjective*

kanga cricket *noun*
a game of cricket with the rules and equipment changed slightly to suit young players.

kangaroo *noun* **kangaroos**
an Australian animal with short front limbs and a large thick tail that jumps on its strong back legs, as in *Female kangaroos have pouches in which they carry their joeys, or babies.*

Origin This word comes from the Aboriginal language Gungu Yimidhirr: **gangurru**. See the Aboriginal Languages map at the back of this dictionary.

kangaroo paw, a Western Australian plant with woolly flowers having a large range of colours and shaped like the paw of a kangaroo, as in *The floral emblem of Western Australia is a red and green kangaroo paw.*

karaoke *noun* (*say* ka-ruh-**oh**-kee)
1 a machine that plays recorded pop music without words, so that people can sing the words. **2** singing to music from this machine, as in *We had karaoke at the party.*

karate *noun* (*say* kuh-**rah**-tee)
a Japanese method of self-defence using the hands, arms, and feet.
[from the Japanese, = empty hand]

karri *noun*
a tall Western Australian gum tree highly valued for its timber.

Origin This word probably comes from the Aboriginal language Nyungar. See the Aboriginal Languages map at the back of this dictionary.

kayak *noun* **kayaks** (*say* **ky**-ak)
a long, thin canoe with a covering over the top, especially the kind the Inuit use.

kebab *noun* **kebabs**
small pieces of meat, vegetables, etc. grilled on a skewer; shish kebab.

keel *noun* **keels**
the long piece of wood or metal along the bottom of a boat.
on an even keel, steady or steadily.

keel *verb* **keels, keeling, keeled**
to tilt or overturn, as in *The ship keeled over.*

keen *adjective* **keener, keenest**
1 enthusiastic; very interested, as in *She is keen on swimming.* **2** sharp, as in *a keen knife.* **3** very cold, as in *a keen wind.*
keenly *adverb*, **keenness** *noun*

keep *verb* **keeps, keeping, kept**
1 to have something and not get rid of it. **2** to stay; to remain, as in *Keep still!* **3** to make someone or something stay in the same position or condition, as in *The fire kept us warm.* **4** to stay in good condition, as in *Will the milk keep until tomorrow?* **5** to prevent, as in *How can we keep the teacher from knowing?* **6** to do something continually, as in *She kept laughing.* **7** to be faithful to something; not to break something, as in *He kept his promise.* **8** to look after; to give a home and food to people or animals, as in *The children keep rabbits.*
keep up, to make the same progress as others; to continue something, as in *They walked so fast that we couldn't keep up. Keep up the good work!*

a
b
c
d
e
f
g
h
i
j
k
l
m
n
o
p
q
r
s
t
u
v
w
x
y
z

keep

keep *noun* **keeps**
1 the food or money that you need to live, as in *She earns her keep.* 2 a strong tower in a castle.
for keeps, (*colloquial*) to keep; permanently, as in *Is this football mine for keeps?*

keeper *noun* **keepers**
1 someone who looks after an animal, place, building, etc. 2 the player who minds the goal, wicket, etc.

keeping *noun*
care; looking after something, as in *The key is in his safe keeping.*
in keeping with something, agreeing with or suiting something.

keepsake *noun* **keepsakes**
something kept to remember a person or occasion, as in *The photo was a keepsake of their friendship.*

keg *noun* **kegs**
a small barrel, as in *a keg of beer.*

kelp *noun*
large brown seaweed suitable for fertiliser.

kelpie *noun* **kelpies**
an Australian breed of sheep-dog with short hair and short, pointed ears.

kennel *noun* **kennels**
a small shelter for a dog.

kept past tense and past participle of **keep** *verb.*

kerb or **curb** *noun* **kerbs**
the edge of a pavement.

kerfuffle *noun* **kerfuffles**
(*colloquial*) a fuss.

kernel *noun* **kernels**
the edible part in the middle of a nut.

ketchup *noun*
a thick sauce made from tomatoes.

kettle *noun* **kettles**
a container with a spout and handle, used for boiling water in.
another kettle of fish, a totally different matter.
a pretty kettle of fish, a strange or difficult situation.

kettledrum *noun* **kettledrums**
a drum made of skin stretched over a hollow, bowl-shaped metal part.

key *noun* **keys**
1 a piece of metal shaped so that it opens a lock. 2 a device for winding up a clockwork train, clock, etc. 3 a small lever that you press with your finger, as in

Typewriters and pianos have keys. 4 a scale of musical notes related to each other, as in *This piece is written in the key of C major.*
5 a thing that explains or solves something, as in *Use a key to identify the tree. Detectives searched for months before finding the key to the crime.*

keyboard *noun* **keyboards**
the set of keys on a piano, typewriter, computer, etc.

keycard *noun* **keycards**
a plastic card that enables the holder to withdraw money from an automatic teller machine.

keyhole *noun* **keyholes**
the hole through which a key is put into a lock.

keynote *noun* **keynotes**
1 the main idea in something said, written, or done. 2 the note on which a key in music is based, as in *The keynote of C major is C.*

kg short for **kilogram** or **kilograms.**

khaki *noun* (*say* **kah**-kee *or* kah-**kee**)
a dull, yellowish-brown colour, as in *Soldiers wear a uniform of khaki.*

kibbutz *noun* **kibbutzim**
a group of people in Israel, sharing a home, food, etc. and working especially as farmers.
[from the Hebrew, = gathering]

kick *verb* **kicks, kicking, kicked**
1 to hit someone or something with your foot. 2 to move your legs about vigorously. 3 to move backwards sharply, as in *The gun kicked into his shoulder when he fired.* 4 (*colloquial*) to give up, as in *He kicked the smoking habit.*
kick off, to start a football match; (*colloquial*) to start doing something, as in *The party kicked off with a puppet show.*
kick out, to get rid of someone; to dismiss someone.
kick up, (*colloquial*) to make a noise or fuss.

kick *noun* **kicks**
1 a kicking movement. 2 a sudden backwards movement, especially of a gun when fired. 3 (*colloquial*) a thrill; a bit of excitement or pleasure. 4 (*colloquial*) an interest or activity, as in *He's on a health kick.*

kick-off *noun* **kick-offs**
the start of a football match.

kid *noun* **kids**
1 a young goat. 2 (*colloquial*) a child.

kid *verb* **kids, kidding, kidded**
(*colloquial*) to deceive or tease someone.

kidnap *verb* **kidnaps, kidnapping, kidnapped**
to take someone away and keep him or her prisoner until you get what you want.
kidnapper *noun*

kidney *noun* **kidneys**
one of two organs in the body that remove unwanted substances from the blood and send them out of the body in urine.
kidney machine, a machine that does what the kidneys should do, used by someone with kidney disease.

kill *verb* **kills, killing, killed**
1 to make someone or an animal die.
2 to destroy something; to put an end to something, as in *The bad news killed the party.*
killer *noun*

killjoy *noun* **killjoys**
a gloomy person.

kiln *noun* **kilns**
an oven for hardening or drying pottery, bricks, hops, etc.

kilogram *noun* **kilograms**
a unit of weight equal to 1,000 grams; a kilo.

kilometre *noun* **kilometres**
(*say* kil-uh-mee-tuh *or* kuh-lom-uh-tuh)
a unit of length equal to 1,000 metres.

kilowatt *noun* **kilowatts**
a unit of electrical power equal to 1,000 watts.

kilt *noun* **kilts**
a kind of pleated skirt worn especially by Scotsmen.
kilted *adjective*

kin *noun*
your family or relatives.
next of kin, your closest relative.

kind *noun* **kinds**
a type or sort of something, as in *What kind of food do you like?*
kind of, (*colloquial*) vague; vaguely, as in *I had a kind of idea that this would happen. We kind of hoped you would come.*

kind *adjective* **kinder, kindest**
ready to help and love other people; friendly.
kind-hearted *adjective*, **kindness** *noun*

kindergarten *noun* **kindergartens**
(*say* kin-duh-gah-tuhn)
a school or class for very young children.
[from the German **kindergarten** = children's garden]

kindle *verb* **kindles, kindling, kindled**
1 to set light to something. 2 to start burning.

kindling *noun*
small pieces of wood for lighting fires.

kindly *adverb*
1 in a caring and sympathetic way, as in *She behaved kindly to the lost child.*
2 please, as in *Kindly close the door.*

kindly *adjective* **kindlier, kindliest**
kind or kind-hearted, as in *She gave a kindly smile.*
kindliness *noun*

kindred *adjective*
1 related by blood or marriage. 2 similar, as in *The friends have kindred tastes in music.*

kinetic *adjective* (*say* kuh-**net**-ik *or* kuy-**net**-ik)
to do with or produced by movement, as in *A hammer makes use of kinetic energy to bang in a nail.*

king *noun* **kings**
1 a man who has been crowned as the ruler of a country. 2 a most powerful person or thing, as in *cattle king; the lion as king of the jungle.* 3 a piece in chess. 4 a playing-card with a picture of a king on it.
king brown, a large, brown, very venomous snake found in drier parts of Australia.
kingly *adjective*

kingdom *noun* **kingdoms**
a country that is ruled by a king or queen.

kingfisher *noun* **kingfishers**
a brightly-coloured bird that lives near water and catches fish.

king-size or **king-sized** *adjective*
larger than the usual size, as in *a king-size packet of breakfast cereal.*

kink *noun* **kinks**
1 a short twist in a rope, wire, piece of hair, etc. 2 something peculiar or eccentric, as in *She soon learned their individual habits and kinks.*
kinky *adjective*

kiosk *noun* **kiosks** (*say* kee-osk)
a small stall, shop, etc. where newspapers, sweets, tobacco, souvenirs, etc. are sold.

kipper *noun* **kippers**
a fish, especially a herring which has been salted, dried and usually smoked.

kiss *verb* **kisses, kissing, kissed**
to touch with the lips especially as a sign of love, affection, greeting, or respect.

kiss

kiss *noun* **kisses**
1 a touch with the lips. **2** a light touch, as in *the kiss of the sun*.
kiss of life, blowing air from your mouth into someone else's to help him or her to start breathing again, especially after an accident.

kit *noun* **kits**
1 equipment; clothes, as in *first aid kit; hockey kit*. **2** a set of parts sold to be fitted together, as in *a cubby-house kit*.

kitchen *noun* **kitchens**
a room where food is prepared and cooked.

kite *noun* **kites**
a light frame covered with cloth, paper, etc. and flown in the wind at the end of a long piece of string.

kitten *noun* **kittens**
a very young cat.
kittenish *adjective*

kitty *noun* **kitties**
1 an amount of money that you can win in a game. **2** an amount of money put aside for a special purpose.

kiwi *noun* **kiwis** (*say* **kee**-wee)
a New Zealand bird that cannot fly.
Kiwi, (*colloquial*) a person from New Zealand.

kiwi fruit *noun* **kiwi fruits**
an oval fruit with soft, juicy, green flesh and a hairy skin.

knack *noun* **knacks**
a special skill.

knave *noun* **knaves**
(*old-fashioned use*)
1 a dishonest man. **2** the jack in a pack of playing-cards.
knavery *noun*, **knavish** *adjective*

knead *verb* **kneads, kneading, kneaded**
to press and stretch something soft, especially dough, with your hands.

knee *noun* **knees**
the joint in the middle of your leg.

kneecap *noun* **kneecaps**
the bony part at the front of your knee.

kneel *verb* **kneels, kneeling, knelt**
to be or get into a position on your knees.

knew past tense of **know**.

knickers *plural noun*
underpants worn by women or girls.

knick-knack or **nick-nack** *noun* **knick-knacks**
a small object, dainty ornament, etc., as in *The old house was full of interesting but useless knick-knacks*.

knife *noun* **knives**
a cutting instrument made of a short blade set in a handle.

knife *verb* **knifes, knifing, knifed**
to stab someone with a knife.

knight *noun* **knights**
1 a man who has been given the honour that lets him put 'Sir' before his name. **2** a warrior who had been given the rank of a nobleman, in the Middle Ages. **3** a piece in chess, with a horse's head.

knit *verb* **knits, knitting, knitted**
1 to make something by looping together threads of wool or other material, using long needles or a machine. **2** to briefly wrinkle the forehead. **3** to become joined or healed, as in *The broken bones knitted eventually*.
knitter *noun*, **knitting-needle** *noun*

knives plural of **knife** *noun*.

knob *noun* **knobs**
1 the round handle of a door, drawer, etc. **2** a small piece of butter, etc. **3** a control to adjust a radio, television set, etc.
knobbly *adjective*, **knobby** *adjective*

knock *verb* **knocks, knocking, knocked**
1 to hit something hard or by accident. **2** (*colloquial*) to criticise something unfavourably.
knock back, (*colloquial*) to eat or drink, especially quickly; to refuse, as in *The hungry man knocked back three pies. She knocked back my offer of help.*
knock off, (*colloquial*) to stop working; to deduct something from a price; to steal something, as in *Let's knock off, it's time to go home. He knocked $20 off the price because we paid in cash. They knocked off several paintings from the art gallery.*
knock out, to hit someone so as to make him or her unconscious.

knock *noun* **knocks**
the act or sound of hitting something.

knocker *noun* **knockers**
1 a device for knocking on a door. **2** a critic, as in *I'm sick of all these knockers.*

knockout *noun* **knockouts**
1 the act of knocking someone out. **2** a contest in which competitors have to drop out one by one. **3** (*colloquial*) an excellent person or thing.

knot *noun* **knots**
1 a fastening made with string, rope, ribbon, etc. **2** a tangle; a lump, as in *knots*

in the hair. **3** a round spot on a piece of wood where there was a branch. **4** a unit for measuring the speed of ships and aircraft, as in _One knot equals 1,852 metres per hour._

knot _verb_ **knots, knotting, knotted**
to tie with string, rope, ribbon, etc.

knotty _adjective_ **knottier, knottiest**
1 full of knots. **2** difficult; puzzling, as in _a knotty problem._

know _verb_ **knows, knowing, knew, known**
1 to have something in your mind that you have learnt or discovered, as in _I knew she was honest._ **2** to recognise or be familiar with a person or place, as in _I have known him for years._

know-all _noun_ **know-alls**
(_colloquial_) someone who thinks he or she knows everything.

know-how _noun_
skill; ability for a particular job.

knowing _adjective_
showing that you know something; cunning, as in _He gave me a knowing look._

knowingly _adverb_
1 in a knowing way, as in _He winked at me knowingly._ **2** deliberately, as in _She would never have done such a thing knowingly._

knowledge _noun_ (_say_ **nol**-ij)
what someone or everybody knows, as in _a good knowledge of Australian history; common knowledge._

knowledgeable _adjective_
(_say_ **nol**-ij-uh-buhl)
having much knowledge; clever, as in _a knowledgeable teacher._
knowledgeably _adverb_

knuckle _noun_ **knuckles**
any one of the joints in your fingers.

koala _noun_ **koalas**
a furry, tree-dwelling Australian animal with a stout body, thick grey-brown fur, rounded furry ears, a leathery nose, and strong claws, as in _Koalas eat gum leaves._

kookaburra _noun_ **kookaburras**
a large Australian kingfisher that makes a laughing or shrieking noise; the laughing jackass.

Origin This word comes from the Aboriginal language Wiradhuri: **guguburra**. See the Aboriginal Languages map at the back of this dictionary.

Koori _noun_ (_say_ **kuu**-ree _or_ **koor**-ree)
an Aborigine, especially from New South Wales and Victoria.

Origin This word comes from the Aboriginal language Awabakal: **gurri** = Aboriginal person. See the Aboriginal Languages map at the back of this dictionary.

Koran _noun_ (_say_ kaw-**rahn** _or_ kuh-**rahn**)
the holy book of the Muslims.

kosher _adjective_ (_say_ **koh**-shuh _or_ **kosh**-uh)
to do with food prepared according to Jewish religious law.

kowari _noun_
a small, yellowish-brown, meat-eating marsupial with a black brushy tail found in the deserts of central Australia.

Origin This word comes from Diyari, an Aboriginal language of South Australia. See the Aboriginal Languages map at the back of this dictionary.

kowtow _verb_ **kowtows, kowtowing, kowtowed**
to behave very humbly towards a person and try to please him or her, especially because you hope to get something for yourself, as in _She kowtowed to the new boss because she wanted a promotion._
[from the Chinese, = knock the head]

kudos _noun_ (_say_ **kyoo**-dos)
(_colloquial_) glory; fame, as in _He got great kudos from winning a gold medal._

kung fu _noun_ (_say_ kuung-**foo**)
a Chinese method of self-defence rather like karate.

kurrajong _noun_ **kurrajongs**
an evergreen Australian tree with glossy leaves and cream and red flowers.

Origin This word comes from the Aboriginal language Dharuk: **garrujung**. See the Aboriginal Languages map at the back of this dictionary.

kylie _noun_ **kylies**
a boomerang.

Origin This word comes from the Aboriginal language Nyungar: **garli**. See the Aboriginal Languages map at the back of this dictionary.

Ll

L short for **learner driver**.
L plates, as in *The L plates were attached to the learner's car.*

lab short for **laboratory**.

label *noun* **labels**
a piece of paper, cloth, etc. fixed on or beside something to show what it is, whose it is, how much it costs, or where it is going.

label *verb* **labels, labelling, labelled**
1 to put a label on something. 2 to assign to a category, as in *The class was labelled as uncontrollable.*

laboratory *noun* **laboratories**
(*say* luh-**bo**-ruh-tuh-ree *or* luh-**bo**-ruh-tree)
a room or building where scientific work is done.

laborious *adjective*
needing a lot of effort; very hard, as in *laborious work.*
laboriously *adverb*

labour *or* **labor** *noun*
1 hard work. 2 the process of childbirth. 3 people employed to do work, as in *The labour force demanded increased pay.*
Labor Party, the political party.

labourer *noun* **labourers**
someone who does hard work with his or her hands, especially out of doors, as in *brickie's labourer.*

Labrador *noun* **Labradors**
a large dog with a black or golden coat, often trained as a guide-dog for the blind.
[from the name of the *Labrador* coast in Newfoundland]

labyrinth *noun* **labyrinths**
a complicated network of passages; a maze.

lace *noun* **laces**
1 a fine, open material or trimming, made by weaving thread in patterns. 2 a piece of thin cord used to tie up a shoe, a football, etc.
lacy *adjective*

lacerate *verb* **lacerates, lacerating, lacerated**
(*say* **las**-uh-rayt)
to injure flesh by cutting or tearing it; to wound.
laceration *noun*

lack *noun*
being without something, as in *There was a lack of water for the crops.*

lack *verb* **lacks, lacking, lacked**
to be without something, as in *He lacks intelligence.*

lacklustre *adjective*
to be without vitality; dull, as in *a lacklustre performance.*

laconic *adjective* (*say* luh-**kon**-ik)
using few words to say something, as in *The farmer, not wanting to waste words, gave a laconic reply.*
laconically *adverb*

lacquer *noun*
1 a hard, glossy varnish. 2 a substance sprayed on the hair to keep it in place.

lacrosse *noun*
a game like hockey but using a long-handled stick with a net on it to catch and throw the ball.
[from the French **la crosse** = the cross.]

lactate *verb* **lactates, lactating, lactated**
to produce milk, as in *The sow lactates to feed her piglets.*

lad *noun* **lads**
1 a boy; a youth. 2 (*colloquial*) a male.

ladder *noun* **ladders**
1 a set of horizontal bars fixed between two uprights and used for climbing up or down. 2 a vertical ladder-like flaw in a stocking, etc. where a stitch has come undone. 3 a graded structure especially in a career or sport, as in *Essendon is at the top of the AFL ladder*.

laden *adjective*
heavily loaded.

ladle *noun* **ladles**
a large, deep spoon used for serving soup or other liquids.

lady *noun* **ladies**
1 a polite name for a woman. 2 a well-mannered woman.
Lady, the title of a noblewoman.
ladylike *adjective*

ladybird *noun* **ladybirds**
a small flying beetle, usually red with black spots.

lag *verb* **lags, lagging, lagged**
1 to make less progress than others because you are going too slowly, as in *He's lagging behind again*. 2 to wrap pipes, boilers, etc. with insulating material to keep them warm.

lag *noun* **lags**
1 a delay; a falling behind. 2 (*colloquial*) a convict especially one who repeatedly breaks the law, as in *the old lag*.

lager *noun* **lagers** (*say* **lah**-guh)
a light type of beer.

lagoon *noun* **lagoons**
1 a saltwater lake separated from the sea by sandbanks or reefs. 2 an area of fresh water, usually shallow and often stagnant, as in *During the wet season, lagoons form in tropical Australia*.

lah or **la** *noun*
the sixth note of the musical scale.

laid past tense and past participle of **lay** *verb*.

Usage Do not confuse **laid**, as in *I laid the table* with **lain**, as in *The weary girl has lain on the bed*.

laid-back *adjective*
relaxed; easy-going.

lain past participle of **lie** *verb*.

Usage Do not confuse **lain**, as in *The weary girl has lain on the bed* with **laid**, as in *I laid the table*.

lair *noun* **lairs**
1 the place where a wild animal lives. 2 (*colloquial*) a youth or man who dresses showily; a larrikin.

lake *noun* **lakes**
a large area of water surrounded by land.

lama *noun* **lamas**
a Buddhist priest or monk in Tibet and Mongolia.

lamb *noun* **lambs**
1 a young sheep. 2 the meat from young sheep.

lame *adjective* **lamer, lamest**
1 unable to walk properly. 2 weak; not convincing, as in *a lame excuse*.
lamely *adverb*, **lameness** *noun*

lament *verb* **laments, lamenting, lamented**
to express grief or regret about death etc.
lamentation *noun*, **lamentable** *adjective*

laminated *adjective*
1 made of layers joined together, as in *The knife had a laminated handle*. 2 permanently covered in a kind of plastic for protection, as in *a laminated wall-chart*.

lamington *noun* **lamingtons**
a small, square sponge cake coated with chocolate and coconut.
lamington drive, the sale of lamingtons for fundraising.

lamp *noun* **lamps**
a device for producing light from electricity, gas, or oil.
lampshade *noun*

lamppost *noun* **lampposts**
a tall post in a street, etc., with a lamp at the top.

lance *noun* **lances**
a long spear, especially one used by a horseman.

lance *verb* **lances, lancing, lanced**
to prick or cut open with a sharp instrument, as in *Lance the boil*.

lance-corporal *noun* **lance-corporals**
a soldier who comes between a corporal and a private in rank.

land *noun* **lands**
1 all the dry parts of the world's surface. 2 the ground used for farming, building, etc. 3 a country.

land *verb* **lands, landing, landed**
1 to set or go ashore, as in *The First Fleet landed in Botany Bay*. 2 to bring an aircraft to the ground or other surface. 3 to reach the ground after jumping or falling, as in

a
b
c
d
e
f
g
h
i
j
k
l
m
n
o
p
q
r
s
t
u
v
w
x
y
z

land claim

The parachutist landed on rocky ground. **4** to bring a fish out of the water, as in *He landed a big salmon.* **5** to obtain, as in *She landed the job.* **6** to find oneself in a certain situation or place, as in *The disobedient students landed in trouble.*

land claim *noun* **land claims**
a claim to land by Aborigines based on their traditional link with that land, as in *Aboriginal people won their land claim at Uluru.*

land council *noun* **land councils**
a body appointed to represent Aborigines in Aboriginal land.

landing *noun* **landings**
1 the level area at the top or bottom of stairs. **2** bringing or coming to land, as in *The first moon landing took place in 1969.* **3** a place where people, ships, etc. land.

landlady *noun* **landladies**
a woman who rents out land, houses, flats or rooms.

landlord *noun* **landlords**
a man who rents out land, houses, flats or rooms.

landlubber *noun* **landlubbers**
a person unused to the sea.

landmark *noun* **landmarks**
1 an object on land that you can easily see from a distance. **2** an important event in history, as in *The Gallipoli campaign is seen as a landmark in our history.*
landmark decision, an important decision.

land rights *plural noun*
the right of Aborigines to own land they have occupied or had traditional association with over a period of time.

landscape *noun* **landscapes**
1 a view of a particular area of town or countryside. **2** a picture of the countryside.

landscape *verb* **landscapes, landscaping, landscaped**
to lay out a garden according to a set pattern.

landslide *noun* **landslides**
1 a mass of earth or rocks sliding down the side of a hill or mountain. **2** a great victory for one side, especially in an election.

lane *noun* **lanes**
1 a narrow road. **2** a division in a road for a single line of traffic. **3** a strip of track or water for one runner or swimmer in a race.

language *noun* **languages**
1 words spoken or written. **2** the words used in a particular country or by a particular group of people. **3** a system of signs or symbols to convey information, as in *computer language.*

languid *adjective* (*say* **lang**-gwuhd)
slow because of tiredness, weakness or laziness.
languidly *adverb*.

lanky *adjective* **lankier, lankiest**
awkwardly tall and thin.
lankiness *noun*

lanolin *noun*
the fat found on a sheep's wool and used in cosmetics, etc.

lantana *noun* **lantanas**
a plant with bright, strongly-scented flowers regarded as a weed in warmer areas.

lantern *noun* **lanterns**
a transparent case for holding a light and shielding it from the wind.

lap *noun* **laps**
1 the part from the waist to the knees of a person sitting down. **2** a circuit of a sports track or length of a pool.

lap *verb* **laps, lapping, lapped**
1 to get a lap or more ahead of a competitor in a race. **2** to drink with the tongue, as in *The cat lapped up the milk.* **3** to make a gentle splash, as in *Small waves were lapping against the rocks.*

lapel *noun* **lapels** (*say* luh-**pel**)
the flap folded back at the front edge of a coat, jacket, etc.

lapse *noun* **lapses**
1 a slight mistake or fault, as in *lapse of memory.* **2** the passing of time, as in *After a lapse of three months work began again.*

lapse *verb* **lapses, lapsing, lapsed**
1 to fail to maintain a standard or state, as in *He lapsed into bad habits.* **2** to be no longer valid because of not being renewed, as in *My driver's licence lapsed.*

laptop *noun* **laptops**
a computer small enough to be held and used on your lap.

larceny *noun* **larcenies** (*say* **lah**-suh-nee)
the theft of personal property.

lard *noun*
white fat from pigs, used in cooking.

large *adjective* **larger, largest**
greater than average size or amount; big.

laugh

at large, free to roam about, not captured, as in *The escaped prisoners are still at large*; in general, as a whole, as in *Fred Hollows was respected by the country at large*.
largeness *noun*

largely *adverb*
mainly; mostly.

lark *noun* **larks**
1 a small bird of the northern hemisphere known for its sweet song.   **2** (*colloquial*) something amusing; a bit of fun, as in *They tied their shoelaces together for a lark*.

larrikin *noun* **larrikins**
a person, usually young, who behaves in a rough, wild way; a hooligan.

larva *noun* **larvae**
an insect in the first stage of its life, after it comes out of the egg.

lasagne *noun* (*say* luh-**sahn**-yuh)
pasta in the form of sheets or wide ribbons; the meal using this type of pasta.

laser *noun* **lasers** (*say* **lay**-zuh)
a device that makes a very narrow beam of intense light.

lash *verb* **lashes, lashing, lashed**
1 to beat with a whip, etc.   **2** to beat or strike, as in *Rain lashed against the window*. **3** to tie something tightly, as in *They lashed it to the mast*.

lash *noun* **lashes**
1 a stroke with a whip.   **2** the cord of a whip.   **3** an eyelash.

lass *noun* **lasses**
a girl; a young woman.

lasso *noun* **lassos** (*say* la-**soo**)
a rope with a loop at the end which tightens when you pull the rope, as in *The stockman used a lasso to catch the brumby*.

last *adjective*
1 coming after all the others; final, as in *the last bus*.   **2** most recent; the latest, as in *last night*.
at last, finally; at the end.
the last straw, a final or added thing that makes something unbearable.

last *adverb*
after all others, as in *My team came last*.

last *verb* **lasts, lasting, lasted**
1 to go on or continue, as in *The journey lasts two hours*.   **2** to go on without being used up, as in *How long will our supplies last?*

latch *noun* **latches**
a bar with a catch and lever used to keep a door or gate closed.

latch *verb* **latches, latching, latched**
to fasten with a latch.
latch on to, to understand, as in *The students quickly latched on to the new computer program*.

late *adjective* **later, latest**
1 coming after the proper or expected time. **2** near the end of a period of time, as in *a late sitting of parliament*.   **3** recent, as in *the latest news*.   **4** no longer alive, as in *the late king*.
lateness *noun*

lately *adverb*
recently.

latent *adjective* (*say* **lay**-tuhnt)
existing but not yet active, developed, or visible, as in *His latent talent made him a great swimmer*.

lateral *adjective*
to do with the sides of something.
lateral thinking, thinking of unusual ways to solve problems or achieve things.

lathe *noun* **lathes** (*say* layth)
a machine for holding and turning pieces of wood or metal while they are shaped.

lather *noun* **lathers**
a thick, usually soapy froth.

lather *verb* **lathers, lathering, lathered**
to cover with a lather of soap, sunblock, shaving cream, etc.

Latin *noun*
the language of the ancient Romans.

latitude *noun* **latitudes**
1 the distance a place is from the equator, measured in degrees.   **2** freedom, as in *Her parents gave her great latitude in spending her pocket money*.

latter *noun*
the latter, the second of two people or things just mentioned, as in *Mike and Steve came in. The latter looked worried*.

latter *adjective*
1 later, as in *September is in the latter part of the year*.   **2** recent, as in *The most important invention of latter years has been the computer*.
latterly *adverb*

lattice *noun* **lattices**
a criss-cross framework often used to support plants.

laugh *verb* **laughs, laughing, laughed**
to make sounds that show you are happy or that you think something is very funny.

laugh *noun* **laughs**
1 an act or sound of laughing.
2 (*colloquial*) something that makes you laugh, as in *Drama lessons are a good laugh*.

a
b
c
d
e
f
g
h
i
j
k
l
m
n
o
p
q
r
s
t
u
v
w
x
y
z

laughable

laughable *adjective*
deserving to be laughed at; amusing.

laughter *noun*
the act, sound or way of laughing, as in *They heard laughter*.

launch *verb* **launches, launching, launched**
1 to send a ship into the water. **2** to send a rocket into space. **3** to start something new.
launching pad or **launch pad**, a platform or place from which rockets are sent into space.

launch *noun* **launches**
1 the launching of a ship, rocket, etc. **2** a large motor boat.

laundry *noun* **laundries**
1 a place where clothes are washed. **2** the clothes to be washed; the washing.

laurel *noun* **laurels**
an evergreen bush with smooth, shiny leaves.

lava *noun*
hot liquid rock that flows from a volcano, or the solid rock formed when it cools.

lavender *noun*
1 a bush with pale purple flowers that smell very sweet. **2** a pale purple colour.

lavish *adjective*
1 generous, as in *She was lavish with her gifts*. **2** plentiful, as in *a lavish meal*.

law *noun* **laws**
1 a rule or set of rules that everyone must obey; the area of knowledge to do with these laws, as in *She studies law at university*. **2** a scientific statement of something that always happens, as in *the law of gravity*.
-in-law, used to distinguish someone who became your relative by marriage, as in *George became my brother-in-law when he and my sister were married*.

lawcourt *noun* **lawcourts**
a place where people decide whether someone has broken the law.

lawful *adjective*
allowed or accepted by the law.
lawfully *adverb*

lawless *adjective*
not obeying the law; without laws, as in *a lawless band of bushrangers; a lawless country*.
lawlessly *adverb*, **lawlessness** *noun*

lawn *noun* **lawns**
an area of mown grass in a garden or park.

lawn-mower *noun* **lawn-mowers**
a machine for cutting grass or lawns.

lawsuit *noun* **lawsuits**
a dispute, claim, etc. considered in a lawcourt.

lawyer *noun* **lawyers**
an expert on law; someone whose job is to help people with the law and who can represent them in court.

lax *adjective*
1 careless, as in *He was lax in his homework*. **2** not strict, as in *The lax teacher has few rules*.

laxative *noun* **laxatives**
a medicine that causes your bowels to empty.

lay *verb* **lays, laying, laid**
1 to put something down in a particular place or in a particular way. **2** to arrange things, especially for a meal, as in *He laid the table*. **3** to produce an egg. **4** to place, as in *He laid the blame on his sister*.
lay off, to stop employing someone for a while; (*colloquial*) to stop doing something, as in *200 workers have been laid off. Lay off telling me what to do!*
lay on, to supply or provide something.
lay out, to arrange or prepare something; to knock someone unconscious, as in *We laid out the papers for the conference. The boxer laid out his opponent after two rounds*.

> **Usage** Do not confuse **lay** with **lie**, which means to be in or get into a flat position, or to stay. Remember that **lay** can also be the past tense of **lie**, as in *The dog lay in front of the fire; he had been lying there all night*.

lay past tense of **lie** *verb*.

lay-by *noun*
1 a way of buying something by making a deposit followed by regular payments until the article has been paid in full. **2** in some areas, particularly Western Australia, a place where vehicles can stop beside a main road.

layer *noun* **layers**
a single thickness or coating, as in *The damaged wall needed three layers of paint*.

layout *noun* **layouts**
the arrangement of parts of something according to a plan, as in *The students prepared a layout for the magazine*.

lazy *adjective* **lazier, laziest**
not wanting to work; doing little work.
lazily *adverb*, **laziness** *noun*

l.b.w. short for **leg before wicket**.

lead *verb* **leads, leading, led** (*say* leed)
1 to guide a person or animal, especially by going in front. 2 to be in charge of something. 3 to be winning in a race or contest. 4 to be a way of reaching a particular place, as in *This road leads to the beach*. 5 to live or experience, as in *She leads a full life*.
lead to, to result in, as in *Their carelessness led to the accident*.

lead *noun* **leads** (*say* leed)
1 leading; guidance, as in *Give us a lead*. 2 a leading place or position, as in *Victoria is in the lead*. 3 the amount ahead, as in *The Brisbane Broncos had a lead of ten points*. 4 a strap or cord for leading a dog. 5 an electric wire, as in *Don't trip over that lead*.

lead *noun* **leads** (*say* led)
1 a soft, heavy, grey metal. 2 the writing substance in the middle of a pencil.

leader *noun* **leaders**
1 someone who leads; a chief. 2 an important article in a newspaper.
leadership *noun*

leaf *noun* **leaves**
1 the flat, usually green part of a plant growing out from its stem, branch or root. 2 a page of a book. 3 a very thin sheet of metal, as in *gold leaf*. 4 a flap that makes a table larger.
turn over a new leaf, make a fresh start.
leafless *adjective*, **leafy** *adjective*

leaflet *noun* **leaflets**
a piece of paper printed with information, instructions, etc.

league *noun* **leagues** (*say* leeg)
1 a group of teams that play matches against each other. 2 a group of countries that have agreed to work together for a particular reason.
in league with, working or plotting together.

leak *noun* **leaks**
1 a hole, crack, etc. through which liquid or gas escapes by accident. 2 the revealing of some secret information.
leaky *adjective*

leak *verb* **leaks, leaking, leaked**
1 to let something out through a hole, crack, etc.; to get out in this way. 2 to reveal secret information.
leakage *noun*

lean *adjective* **leaner, leanest**
1 without fat, as in *lean meat*. 2 thin, as in *a lean person*.

lean *verb* **leans, leaning, leaned** or **leant**
1 to bend your body towards or over something. 2 to put or be in a sloping position. 3 to rest against something. 4 to rely or depend on someone.

lean-to *noun* **lean-tos**
a building or shed with its roof leaning against the side of a larger building.

leap *verb* **leaps, leaping, leapt** or **leaped**
1 to make a vigorous jump. 2 to increase or advance suddenly.

leap *noun* **leaps**
1 a vigorous jump. 2 a sudden increase or advance, as in *a leap in prices*.

leap year *noun* **leap years**
a year when February has twenty-nine days and which occurs every four years.

learn *verb* **learns, learning, learnt** or **learned**
to find out about something; to get knowledge or skill.

learned *adjective* (*say* **ler**-nuhd)
clever; having a lot of knowledge gained from study, as in *the learned judge*.

learner *noun* **learners**
someone who is learning something, especially how to drive a car.

learning *noun*
knowledge obtained from study.

lease *noun* **leases**
an agreement to let someone pay to use a building or land for a fixed period.
a new lease of life, a chance to go on being active or useful.

leash *noun* **leashes**
a strap or cord for leading a dog.

least *adjective*
smallest; less than all the others, as in *the least expensive bike*.
at least, not less than what is mentioned; anyway, as in *It will take at least two days to mend your bicycle. He doesn't mind—at least he says he doesn't*.

least *noun*
the smallest amount.

leather *noun* **leathers**
a strong material made from animals' skins.
leathery *adjective*

leave *verb* **leaves, leaving, left**
1 to go away from a person, place, or group. 2 to let something stay where it is or remain as it is, as in *I've left my book at home*. 3 to give something to be passed on or collected, as in *He left me his property in his will. Leave a message*.

a
b
c
d
e
f
g
h
i
j
k
l
m
n
o
p
q
r
s
t
u
v
w
x
y
z

leave

leave out, not to include something or someone.

leave *noun*
1 permission, as in *You have leave to go.*
2 permission to be away from work; the time when you are allowed to be away from work; holiday.
take leave of, to say goodbye or farewell.

leaves plural of **leaf.**

lecture *noun* **lectures**
1 a talk about a subject to an audience or a class. 2 a long talk criticising bad behaviour, as in *The principal lectured the students about their bad manners.*

lecture *verb* **lectures, lecturing, lectured**
to give a lecture.
lecturer *noun*

led past tense and past participle of **lead** *verb.*

ledge *noun* **ledges**
a narrow shelf.

lee *noun*
the sheltered side or part of something, away from the wind.

leech *noun* **leeches**
a small, blood-sucking worm that lives in water.

leek *noun* **leeks**
a white vegetable, like an onion, with broad leaves.

leer *verb* **leers, leering, leered**
to look unpleasantly or evilly at someone.

leeward *adjective*
facing away from the wind, as in *the leeward side of the ship.*

left *adjective*
1 on or near the left hand. 2 in favour of changes which would share wealth more equally, as in *the left wing of the political party.*

left *noun*
the left side, as in *We drive on the left.*

left past tense and past participle of **leave** *verb.*

left hand *noun* **left hands**
the hand that most people use less than the other, on the same side of the body as the heart, as in *When they eat, most people hold the fork in their left hand and the knife in their right hand.*
left-hand *adjective*

left-handed *adjective*
using the left hand more than the right hand.

left-overs *plural noun*
food not eaten by the end of a meal.

leg *noun* **legs**
1 one of the parts of a human's or animal's body on which it stands, walks, and runs.
2 the part of a piece of clothing that covers a leg. 3 one of the supports of a chair or other piece of furniture. 4 one part of a journey, race, etc., as in *the last leg of the marathon.*
leg before wicket, when a batter in cricket is out because of obstructing the ball with his or her body.
on your last legs, exhausted.

legacy *noun* **legacies**
something given to someone in a will.

legal *adjective*
1 allowed by the law. 2 to do with the law or lawyers, as in *legal fees.*
legality *noun*, **legally** *adverb*

legalise or **legalize** *verb* **legalises, legalising, legalised**
to make something lawful.

legend *noun* **legends** (*say* lej-uhnd)
1 an old story handed down from the past. 2 famous so as to be talked about often, as in *Joan Sutherland is a legend in her own lifetime.*
legendary *adjective*

legible *adjective*
clear enough to read, as in *Your tiny writing is hardly legible.*
legibility *noun*, **legibly** *adverb*

legion *noun* **legions**
1 a division of the ancient Roman army.
2 a group of soldiers, or men who used to be soldiers.

legislation *noun*
a law or group of laws.
legislator *noun*, **legislative** *adjective*

Legislative Assembly *noun* **Legislative Assemblies**
1 the lower house of the parliaments of Victoria, New South Wales and Western Australia. 2 the only house of the parliaments of Queensland, the Northern Territory and the Australian Capital Territory.

Legislative Council *noun*
the upper house of the parliaments of all Australian states except Queensland.

legislature *noun*
the law-making organisation of a state or nation.
legislate *verb*

legitimate *adjective* (*say* luh-**jit**-uh-muht)
lawful.
legitimacy *noun*, **legitimately** *adverb*

leisure *noun*
a time that is free from work, when you can do what you like.
leisurely *adjective* and *adverb*

lemon *noun* **lemons**
1 a yellow fruit with a sour taste. 2 a pale yellow colour.

lemonade *noun* **lemonades**
a fizzy drink made from lemons, sugar and water.

lend *verb* **lends, lending, lent**
to let someone have something of yours for a short time, as in *She lent me her bike.*
lend a hand, to help someone.

length *noun* **lengths**
1 how long something is. 2 a piece of rope, wire, cloth, etc. cut from a larger piece.
at length, finally; in detail, as in *He spoke at length on the economy.*

lengthen *verb* **lengthens, lengthening, lengthened**
to make something longer; to become longer.

lengthy *adjective* **lengthier, lengthiest**
long; too long, as in *a lengthy speech.*

lenient *adjective* (*say* **lee**-nee-uhnt)
merciful; not severe, as in *The judge was lenient to the first offender.*
lenience *noun*, **leniently** *adverb*

lens *noun* **lenses**
1 a curved piece of glass or plastic used to focus images of things, or to concentrate light. 2 the transparent part of the eye immediately behind the pupil.

Lent *noun*
the period of about six weeks before Easter.

lent past tense and past participle of **lend**.

lentil *noun* **lentils**
a kind of small bean.

leopard *noun* **leopards** (*say* **lep**-erd)
a large, spotted, wild animal of the cat family.

leotard *noun* **leotards** (*say* **lee**-uh-tahd)
a close-fitting garment of stretch material worn by athletes, dancers, etc.

leper *noun* **lepers**
someone who has leprosy.

leprechaun *noun* **leprechauns**
(*say* **lep**-ruh-kawn)
in Irish folklore, an elf who looks like a little old man.

leprosy *noun*
an infectious disease that makes parts of the body waste away.
leprous *adjective*

lerp *noun*
a whitish, sweet, edible waxy substance produced by baby insects and found on some eucalypts.

Origin This word comes from the Aboriginal language Wemba-Wemba: **lerep**. See the Aboriginal Languages map at the back of this dictionary.

lesbian *noun* **lesbians**
a woman who has sexual feelings for another woman.

less *adjective* **lesser, least**
smaller; not so much, as in *The noise eventually became less. Eat less meat.*

less *adverb*
to a smaller extent, as in *It is less important.*

less *preposition*
minus; deducting, as in *She earned $100, less tax.*

lessen *verb* **lessens, lessening, lessened**
to make something smaller or not so much; to become smaller or not so much.

lesson *noun* **lessons**
1 the time when someone is teaching you. 2 something that you have to learn. 3 a section of writing from the Bible read aloud in church.

lest *conjunction*
so that something should not happen; to prevent something, as in *He ran away lest he should be seen.*

let *verb* **lets, letting, let**
1 to allow someone to do something. 2 to allow something to happen. 3 to allow someone to use a house, building, etc. in return for payment. 4 to leave, as in *Let it go.*
let down, to let the air or gas out of something; to disappoint someone.
let off, to explode something; to excuse someone from a punishment or duty.
let on, (*colloquial*) to tell a secret, as in *I'll tell you the secret, but don't let on!*
let's, (*colloquial*) shall we; I suggest that we, as in *Let's go away for the weekend.*

lethal *adjective*
deadly, as in *a lethal gas.*
lethally *adverb*

lethargy *noun* (*say* **leth**-uh-jee)
the state of being without any energy, as in *Her long illness caused lethargy.*

a
b
c
d
e
f
g
h
i
j
k
l
m
n
o
p
q
r
s
t
u
v
w
x
y
z

letter

letter *noun* **letters**
1 one of the symbols used for writing words, such as *a*, *b*, or *c*. 2 a written message sent to another person.

letter-box *noun* **letter-boxes**
a box into which letters are delivered or posted.

lettering *noun*
letters drawn or painted.

lettuce *noun* **lettuces**
a green vegetable used in salads.

leukaemia *noun* **leukemia**
(*say* loo-**kee**-mee-uh)
a disease in which there are too many white cells in the blood.

levee *noun* **levees**
1 a bank built to prevent a river from flooding. 2 a bank of earth and sand built up naturally by a river.

level *noun* **levels**
1 height, as in *eye level*. 2 a device that shows if something is horizontal. 3 a flat or horizontal surface. 4 a standard or position, as in *She has reached level 3 in gymnastics*.
on the level, (*colloquial*) honest.

level *adjective*
1 flat; horizontal, as in *level ground*.
2 equal; alongside a person or thing, as in *He was level with the others*.
level crossing, a place where a road crosses a railway at the same level.

level *verb* **levels, levelling, levelled**
1 to make something flat or horizontal.
2 to make something equal, as in *an attempt to level incomes*. 3 to aim a gun.

lever *noun* **levers**
a bar that is pushed or pulled to lift something heavy, force something open, or make a machine work.
leverage *noun*

levy *verb* **levies, levying, levied**
to put on or impose a compulsory payment.

levy *noun* **levies**
a fee or tax which must be paid.

lexical *adjective*
to do with the words of a language.

liable *adjective*
1 likely to do or get something, as in *Parking on double lines makes you liable for a fine*. 2 responsible in a legal way.
liability *noun*

liaison *noun* **liaisons** (*say* lee-**ay**-zuhn)
1 communication and co-operation between people or groups. 2 a person who is a link or go-between.

liar *noun* **liars**
someone who tells lies.

libel *noun* **libels** (*say* **luy**-buhl)
a published statement which harms a person's reputation.

Usage Do not confuse **libel** with **slander** which is a spoken, not written, statement harming a person's reputation

liberal *adjective*
1 generous, as in *a liberal donation*. 2 not strict; tolerant, as in *a liberal approach to children's television viewing*.
Liberal Party, the political party.
liberality *noun*, **liberally** *adverb*

liberate *verb* **liberates, liberating, liberated**
to set free.
liberation *noun*

liberty *noun* **liberties**
freedom.
take liberties, to take advantage.

librarian *noun* **librarians**
someone who looks after or works in a library.
librarianship *noun*

library *noun* **libraries**
1 a place where books are kept for people to use or borrow. 2 a collection of books, films, records, etc.

lice plural of **louse.**

licence *noun* **licences**
an official permit allowing someone to do, use, or own something, as in *a driving licence*.

Usage Do not confuse **licence**, which is a noun, with **license**, which is a verb and is the next word in this dictionary.

license *verb* **licenses, licensing, licensed**
to give a licence to someone; to permit, as in *We are licensed to sell alcoholic drinks*.
licensee *noun*

lichen *noun* **lichens** (*say* **luy**-kuhn)
a dry-looking plant that grows on rocks, walls, trees, etc.

lick *verb* **licks, licking, licked**
1 to move your tongue over something.
2 to pass lightly over, as in *Flames licked the walls of the old house*. 3 (*colloquial*) to defeat easily, as in *The West Coast Eagles licked Collingwood*.

lick *noun* **licks**
1 the act of moving your tongue over something.   2 a light or scant covering, as in *The lick of paint failed to cover the spots.*

licorice or **liquorice** *noun* (*say* lik-uh-rish or lik-uh-ris)
a black substance from the root of a plant and used in medicine and as a sweet.

lid *noun* **lids**
1 a cover for a box, pot, etc.   2 an eyelid.

lie *verb* **lies, lying, lay, lain**
1 to be in or get into a flat position, especially to rest with your body flat as it is in bed, as in *He lay on the grass. The cat has lain here all night.*   2 to stay; to be, as in *The castle was lying in ruins. The valley lay before us.*
lie low, to keep yourself hidden.

Usage Do not confuse **lie** *verb* with **lay** *verb*, which means to put something down in a particular place, to arrange things, or to produce an egg.

lie *noun* **lies**
something that is deliberately not true.

lie *verb* **lies, lying, lied**
to say something that is not true.

lieutenant *noun* **lieutenants**
(*say* lef-**ten**-uhnt)
an officer in the army or navy.

life *noun* **lives**
1 the time between birth and death.   2 the state of being alive.   3 living things, as in *Is there life on Mars?*   4 liveliness, as in *full of life.*   5 the story of what a person has done, as in *the life of Ned Kelly.*
life expectancy, the length of time that a particular person, animal, or plant is likely to live, as in *Women have a longer life expectancy than men.*

lifeboat *noun* **lifeboats**
a boat for rescuing people at sea.

life cycle *noun* **life cycles**
the series of stages that living things go through as they develop, ending back at the first stage, as in *The life cycle of a butterfly is: egg, caterpillar, pupa, butterfly, egg.*

life insurance *noun*
insurance which pays someone money if the holder of the insurance dies.

life-jacket *noun* **life-jackets**
a jacket of material that will float, used to support someone's body in water.

lifeless *adjective*
1 without life.   2 unconscious.

lifelike *adjective*
looking exactly like a real person or thing.

lifelong *adjective*
lasting throughout someone's life.

lifesaver *noun* **lifesavers**
someone who checks that people swim at the safe part of a beach and who rescues swimmers in difficulty.

lifespan *noun* **lifespans**
how long a person, an animal, or a plant lives.

lifestyle *noun* **lifestyles**
the way of life of a person or a group of people, as in *an expensive lifestyle.*

lifetime *noun* **lifetimes**
the time for which someone is alive.

lift *verb* **lifts, lifting, lifted**
1 to pick up something; to raise someone or something.   2 to rise.   3 (*colloquial*) to steal.   4 to remove or get rid of, as in *The ban was lifted.*

lift *noun* **lifts**
1 the act of lifting.   2 a device for taking people or goods up and down inside a building.   3 a free ride in someone else's car, truck, etc.

lift-off *noun* **lift-offs**
the vertical take-off of a rocket.

light *noun* **lights**
1 what makes things visible, the opposite of darkness, as in *There was not enough light to see the garden.*   2 something that provides light or a flame, especially an electric light, as in *Switch on the light.*   3 additional knowledge, as in *Can you throw any light on her disappearance?*

light *verb* **lighting, lit** or **lighted**
1 to give light to something, as in *The streets were lit by neon signs.*   2 to start something burning or to begin to burn, as in *Have you lit the fire? The fire won't light.*
light up, to make something light or bright; to become light or bright; to turn lights on, especially at dusk.

light *adjective* **lighter, lightest**
1 full of light; not dark.   2 pale, as in *light blue.*   3 not heavy; weighing little.   4 not large; not strong, as in *a light wind.*   5 not serious; not needing great thought, as in *light reading.*
lightly *adverb*

lighten

lighten *verb* lightens, lightening, lightened
to make something lighter; to become lighter.

Usage Do not confuse **lightening** (which means making something lighter, or becoming lighter) with **lightning**, which means a flash of bright light in the sky during a thunderstorm.

lighter *noun* lighters
a device for lighting something like a cigarette or a fire.

light-headed *adjective*
slightly giddy.

light-hearted *adjective*
cheerful; free from worry; not serious.
light-heartedly *adverb*, **light-heartedness** *noun*

lighthouse *noun* lighthouses
a tower with a bright light at the top to warn ships that there are rocks or other dangers nearby.

lighting *noun*
lamps, or the light they provide.

lightning *noun*
a flash of bright light in the sky during a thunderstorm.
lightning-conductor, a metal wire or rod fixed on a building to divert lightning into the earth.

Usage Do not confuse **lightning** with **lightening**, which means making something lighter, or becoming lighter.

light-year *noun* light-years
the distance that light travels in one year (about 10 million million kilometres).

like *verb* likes, liking, liked
to think someone or something is pleasant or satisfactory.
should like or **would like**, to want, as in *I should like to see him.*
likeable *adjective*

like *adjective* and *adverb*
similar, as in *They have like tastes in food. They are as like as two peas.*

like *preposition*
1 resembling; similar to; in the manner of, as in *He cried like a baby.* **2** such as, for example, as in *We need things like knives and forks.* **3** typical of, as in *It was like her to forgive him.*

likely *adjective* likelier, likeliest
probable; expected to happen or to be true.
not likely!, (*colloquial*) that is impossible; I refuse.

likeness *noun* likenesses
a resemblance.

likewise *adverb*
similarly.

liking *noun* likings
the condition of liking someone or something, as in *She has a great liking for chocolate.*
to be to one's liking, to appeal to one's taste.

lilac *noun* lilacs
1 a bush with sweet-smelling purple or white flowers. **2** a pale purple colour.

lilt *noun*
a pleasant rhythm.
lilting *adjective*

lily *noun* lilies
a trumpet-shaped flower grown from a bulb.

limb *noun* limbs
1 a leg, arm, or wing. **2** the branch of a tree.

limber *verb* limbers, limbering, limbered
limber up to stretch and warm up to prepare for athletic activity, as in *They limbered up before aerobics.*

lime *noun*
a white, chalky powder used in making cement or as a fertiliser.

lime *noun* limes
a green fruit rather like a lemon.
lime-juice *noun*

lime *adjective*
a greenish-yellow colour.

limelight *noun*
great public interest or attention, as in *After the newspaper wrote about us, our school was in the limelight for several weeks.*

limerick *noun* limericks (*say* **lim**-uh-rik)
a comical poem with five lines.

limestone *noun*
a chalky, soft rock from which lime is made.

limit *noun* limits
1 a line or point that you cannot or should not pass, as in *A speed limit exists on most roads. There are limits to how much work we can do.* **2** an edge of something, as in *The white line marks the limit of the road on either side.*

limit *verb* limits, limiting, limited
to restrict something or someone, as in *The government has limited petrol supplies.*
limitation *noun*

limited *adjective*
restricted; small.

limp *verb* **limps, limping, limped**
to walk with difficulty because something is wrong with your leg or foot.

limp *noun* **limps**
a limping movement.

limp *adjective* **limper, limpest**
not stiff or firm; without strength, as in *limp lettuces; a limp handshake.*

limpet *noun* **limpets**
a small shellfish that clings to rocks.

line *noun* **lines**
1 a long, thin mark. 2 a row or series of people or things. 3 a length of rope, string, wire, etc. 4 a railway; a length of railway track. 5 a system of ships, aircraft, buses, etc. 6 a way of working, behaving, etc.
lines, words spoken by an actor.
in line, forming a straight line; conforming.

line *verb* **lines, lining, lined**
1 to mark something with lines. 2 to make an edge or border for something, as in *The streets are lined with trees.*
line up, to form lines; to cause someone or something to form lines, as in *The children lined up. We lined up the empty cans on top of the wall.*

linen *noun*
1 cloth made from flax. 2 things made from linen, cotton, etc., as in *The bed and table linen dried in the sun.*

liner *noun* **liners**
a large ship, usually carrying passengers.

linesman or **lineswoman** *noun* **linesmen, lineswomen**
1 an official in football, tennis, etc. who decides whether the ball has crossed a line. 2 a person who repairs or installs power lines.

linger *verb* **lingers, lingering, lingered**
1 to be slow to leave, as in *A few guests lingered at the end of the party.* 2 to stay somewhere for a long time, as in *He would linger for hours at the beach.*

lingerie *noun* (*say* **lon**-zhuh-ree *or* **lon**-zhuh-ray)
women's underclothes or nightwear.

linguist *noun* **linguists**
an expert in languages.
linguistic *adjective*

linguistics *noun*
the study of a language and its structure.

lining *noun* **linings**
a layer covering the inside of something, as in *The coat's lining was silk.*

link *noun* **links**
1 one of the rings in a chain.
2 a connection.

link *verb* **links, linking, linked**
to join things together.
linking verb, (*in grammar*) a type of verb that links parts of a clause.
link up, to become connected.

lintel *noun* **lintels**
a horizontal piece of wood or stone etc. above a door or other opening.

lion *noun* **lions**
a large, strong, flesh-eating animal with a golden brown coat found in Africa and India.

lioness *noun* **lionesses**
a female lion.

lip *noun* **lips**
1 one of the two edges of your mouth.
2 the edge of something hollow such as a cup or a crater. 3 a projecting part at the top of a jug, saucepan, etc. shaped for pouring.

lip-read *verb* **lip-reads, lip-reading, lip-read**
to understand what someone is saying by watching the movements of his or her lips, not by hearing his or her voice.

lipstick *noun* **lipsticks**
a stick of waxy substance used for colouring lips.

liquid *noun* **liquids**
a substance that can flow like water or oil.

liquid *adjective*
1 flowing freely, as in *The liquid mixture poured easily.* 2 to do with liquids, as in *liquid measure.*

liquidate *verb* **liquidates, liquidating, liquidated**
1 to pay off or settle a debt. 2 to close down a business and divide its value among those who are owed money.
3 to get rid of, especially by killing.

liquor *noun* **liquors** (*say* **lik**-uh)
alcoholic drink.

lisp *verb* **lisps, lisping, lisped**
a fault in speech in which *s* and *z* are pronounced like *th*.

list *noun* **lists**
a number of things or names written down or printed one after another.

list *verb* **lists, listing, listed**
1 to write down or print things one after another. 2 to lean over to one side; tilt, as in *The ship was listing badly.*

listen

listen *verb* **listens, listening, listened**
to pay attention in order to hear something.
listener *noun*

listless *adjective*
too tired to be active or enthusiastic.
listlessly *adverb*, **listlessness** *noun*

lit past tense and past participle of **light** *verb*.

literacy *noun* (*say* **lit**-uh-ruh-see)
the ability to read and write.

literal *adjective*
1 meaning exactly what it says. 2 precise,
as in *a literal translation*.
literally *adverb*

literary *adjective* (*say* **lit**-er-er-i)
to do with books; interested in literature.

literate *adjective* (*say* **lit**-uh-ruht)
able to read and write.

literature *noun*
1 books or writings, especially those
considered to have been written well.
2 printed material about a subject, as in *Get
some literature about coach tours*.

lithe *adjective* (*say* luyth)
flexible or supple, as in *a lithe gymnast*.

lithosphere *noun*
the solid crust of the earth, not the
hydrosphere or the atmosphere.

litmus *noun*
a blue substance used to show whether
something is an acid or an alkali.
litmus-paper *noun*

litre *noun* **litres** (*say* **lee**-tuh)
a metric measure of liquid.

litter *noun*
1 rubbish or untidy things left lying about.
2 all the young animals born to the same
mother at one time.

litter *verb* **litters, littering, littered**
to make a place untidy with rubbish or
things left lying about.

little *adjective* **less** or **littler**, **least** or **littlest**
1 small, as in *a little boy*. 2 not much, as in
We have little time. 3 a small amount of
something, as in *Have a little sugar*.
little by little, gradually.
little lunch, playlunch; the snack eaten at the
mid-morning break; the break itself.

live *verb* **lives, living, lived**
(rhymes with *give*)
1 to be alive. 2 to have your home in a
particular place, as in *She is living in
Fremantle*. 3 to pass your life in a certain
way, as in *He lived as a saint*.

live on, to use something as food; to depend
upon something, as in *The islanders lived
mainly on fish. The whole town lives on the
tourist trade*.

live *adjective*
(rhymes with *hive*)
1 alive. 2 carrying electricity. 3 broadcast while it is actually happening.
4 recorded with an audience present.

livelihood *noun* **livelihoods**
(*say* **luyv**-lee-huud)
the way in which you earn a living.

lively *adjective* **livelier, liveliest**
full of life or action; vigorous and cheerful,
as in *The band gave a lively performance. Her
lively personality makes her good company*.
liveliness *noun*

liver *noun* **livers**
1 a large organ in the body that produces
bile and helps keep the blood clean.
2 this organ from a cow, pig, lamb, etc.,
used as food.

lives plural of **life**.

livestock *noun*
farm animals.

livid *adjective*
1 very angry. 2 a bluey-grey colour, as in
the livid bruise.

living *noun*
1 the state of being alive. 2 the way a
person lives, as in *a good standard of
living*. 3 a way of earning money or
providing enough food to support yourself,
as in *He earned his living as a teacher*.

living-room *noun* **living-rooms**
the room in your house where you relax or
entertain; the lounge room.

lizard *noun* **lizards**
a four-legged reptile with rough or scaly
skin and usually a long tail.

llama *noun* **llamas** (*say* **lah**-muh)
a South American animal with woolly fur.

load *noun* **loads**
1 something to be carried. 2 the quantity
that can be carried. 3 (*colloquial*) a large
amount, as in *It's a load of nonsense*.

load *verb* **loads, loading, loaded**
1 to put a load in or on something. 2 to
put a weight into a thing, as in *loaded dice*.
3 to give someone large amounts of
something, as in *They loaded him with gifts*.
4 to put a bullet or shell into a gun. 5 to
put a film into a camera.

lodge

loading *noun* **loadings**
an additional amount paid over the normal salary, as in *At Christmas a holiday loading is paid.*

loaf *noun* **loaves**
bread in the shape in which it was baked.

loaf *verb* **loafs, loafing, loafed**
to waste time, as in *He is loafing at school and will certainly fail.*
loafer *noun*

loam *noun*
rich, fertile soil.
loamy *adjective*

loan *noun* **loans**
something that has been lent to someone.

loan *verb* **loans, loaning, loaned**
to lend, especially money.

loath *adjective*
(rhymes with *both*)
unwilling, as in *I was loath to go.*

Usage Do not confuse **loath** with **loathe**, which is a verb and is the next word in this dictionary.

loathe *verb* **loathes, loathing, loathed**
(rhymes with *clothe*)
to hate, as in *She loathed bad manners.*
loathsome *adjective*

loaves plural of **loaf** *noun*.

lob *verb* **lobs, lobbing, lobbed**
to throw or hit something high up into the air.

lobby *noun* **lobbies**
an entrance-hall.

lobby *verb* **lobbies, lobbying, lobbied**
to try and win support for a particular cause, as in *She will lobby for the conservation group.*
lobbyist *noun*

lobe *noun* **lobes**
the rounded part at the bottom of an ear.

lobster *noun* **lobsters**
a large shellfish with eight legs and two claws; a crayfish.

local *adjective*
1 to do with a particular place or district, as in *local government*. 2 affecting a particular area, as in *a local anaesthetic*.
local history, events that happened in the past in a particular place; the study of these events.
locally *adverb*

local *noun* **locals**
(*colloquial*) someone who lives in a particular district.

local government *noun*
a group of elected people who govern a particular place or district.

locality *noun* **localities**
1 a district. 2 a location, as in *Where is the exact locality of the accident?*

locate *verb* **locates, locating, located**
1 to discover where something is, as in *I have located the fault*. 2 to put in a certain place or area, as in *The cinema is located in the mall.*

location *noun* **locations**
the place where something is.
on location, filmed in natural surroundings, not in a studio.

loch *noun* **lochs**
a Scottish word for lake, as in *Loch Ness*.

lock *noun* **locks**
1 a fastening that is opened with a key. 2 part of a canal or river between gates where boats are raised or lowered to a different level. 3 the distance that a vehicle's front wheels can turn. 4 a position in a rugby team, the second row of the scrum. 5 a short length of hair.
lock-up, a cell at a police station.

lock *verb* **locks, locking, locked**
1 to fasten or secure with a lock. 2 to become fixed in one place; to jam.
lock up the land, to close land, forests, etc. to development.

locker *noun* **lockers**
a small cupboard where belongings can be stored safely.

locket *noun* **lockets**
a small case worn on a chain around someone's neck, often holding a photograph.

locus *noun* **loci**
(*in Mathematics*) the line made by a moving point or by points placed according to a particular rule.

locust *noun* **locusts**
a kind of grasshopper that flies in large swarms which eat all the plants in an area.

lodge *noun* **lodges**
a building in the snowfields used to accommodate skiers.
the Lodge, the prime minister's residence in Canberra.

lodge *verb* **lodges, lodging, lodged**
1 to board at someone's house. 2 to become fixed in a position, as in *The splinter*

loft

lodged in my finger. **3** to put in a certain place, as in *He lodged a complaint with his boss.*

loft *noun* **lofts**
the room or space under the roof of a house.

lofty *adjective* **loftier, loftiest**
1 tall, as in *lofty trees.* **2** noble; proud, as in *lofty ideals.*
loftily *adverb,* **loftiness** *noun*

log *noun* **logs**
1 a large piece of a tree that has fallen or been cut down; firewood. **2** a detailed record kept of a ship's voyage, aircraft's flight, etc.

log *noun* **logs** short for **logarithm.**

log *verb* **logs, logging, logged**
(*in Computing*)
log in or **log on,** to gain access to a computer system, usually by inputting a secret word.
log out or **log off,** to finish using a computer system.

logarithm *noun* **logarithms**
one of a series of numbers set out in tables, used to help you do arithmetic.

logbook *noun* **logbooks**
1 a book in which a log of a ship's voyage, etc. is kept. **2** a booklet or card listing details of a motor vehicle.

logic *noun*
thinking in an orderly way.
logical *adjective,* **logically** *adverb*

logo *noun* **logos**
a symbol that stands for a company or other organisation, as in *The Shell logo is like a sea shell.*

loiter *verb* **loiters, loitering, loitered**
to stand about with nothing to do.
loiterer *noun*

loll *verb* **lolls, lolling, lolled**
1 to sit or lie in an untidy, lazy way. **2** to hang out loosely, as in *His tongue lolled during the fit.*

lolly *noun* **lollies**
a sweet.

lone *adjective*
solitary, as in *a lone pine.*

lonely *adjective* **lonelier, loneliest**
1 unhappy because you are on your own. **2** far from other inhabited places; not often used or visited, as in *a lonely road.*
loneliness *noun*

long *adjective* **longer, longest**
1 big when measured from one end to the other, as in *a long river.* **2** taking a lot of time, as in *a long holiday.* **3** from one end to the other, as in *A cricket pitch is 20 metres long.*
long division, dividing one number by another and writing down all your calculations.
long jump, an athletic contest of jumping as far as you can with one leap.
long paddock, the grassy sides of a public road used to graze stock during droving or a drought.
long-sighted, not being able to see things clearly unless they are at a distance.

long *adverb* **longer, longest**
1 for a long time, as in *Have you been waiting long?* **2** a long time before or after, as in *They left long ago.*
as long as or **so long as,** provided that; on condition that.

long *verb* **longs, longing, longed**
long for something, to want something very much.

longitude *noun* **longitudes**
(*say* **long**-guh-tyood)
the distance east or west, measured in degrees, from an imaginary line that passes through Greenwich, London.
longitudinal *adjective*

long-life *adjective*
able to last or remain usable for a long time, as in *long-life milk.*

long-term *adjective*
to do with a long period of time, as in *Our long-term plan is to replace the car, but for now we're going to repair it.*

long-winded *adjective*
using more words than necessary when writing or speaking.

look *verb* **looks, looking, looked**
1 to use your eyes; to turn your eyes towards something. **2** to face in a particular direction. **3** to seem; to appear, as in *You look sad.*
look after, to protect; to attend to someone's needs, as in *Look after my bag, will you? Can you look after Granny for the afternoon?*
look down on, to despise.
look for something, to try to find something.
look forward to something, to wait for something eagerly or expectantly.
look out, to be careful.
look up to, to admire or respect.

look *noun* **looks**
1 the act of looking. **2** appearance; what something seems to be.

lookout *noun* **lookouts**
1 a place from which you watch for something. 2 someone whose job is to keep watch. 3 watching; being watchful, as in *Keep a lookout for snakes as you walk through the bush.*

loom *noun* **looms**
a machine for weaving cloth.

loom *verb* **looms, looming, loomed**
to appear large and threatening, as in *An iceberg loomed before us through the fog.*

loop *noun* **loops**
1 the shape made by a curve crossing itself; a piece of string, ribbon, wire, etc. made into this shape. 2 (*in Computing*) part of a computer program or flow chart which repeats itself.

loop *verb* **loops, looping, looped**
to make into a loop.

loophole *noun* **loopholes**
1 a narrow opening. 2 a way of avoiding a law, rule, etc.

loose *adjective* **looser, loosest**
1 not tight; not firm, as in *a loose tooth.* 2 not tied up or shut in, as in *The dog got loose.* 3 not packed in a container, as in *loose lollies.* 4 not exact, as in *loose translation.*
at a loose end, with nothing to do.
loosely *adverb*, **looseness** *noun*

Usage Do not confuse the adjective **loose** with **lose**, a verb which means to be without something, to be beaten, or to become slow.

loosen *verb* **loosens, loosening, loosened**
to make something less tight; to untie or release something.

loose-leaf *adjective*
with each leaf or page removable, as in *a loose-leaf folder.*

loot *noun*
1 stolen things. 2 (*colloquial*) gifts received at a celebration, as in *party loot.*

loot *verb* **loots, looting, looted**
to rob a place or an enemy, especially in a time of war or disorder.
looter *noun*

lop *verb* **lops, lopping, lopped**
to cut away branches; to cut off.

lope *verb* **lopes, loping, loped**
to move with ease taking long steps.

lopsided *adjective*
with one side lower than the other; uneven.

lord *noun* **lords**
1 a nobleman, especially one who is allowed to use the title 'Lord' in front of his name. 2 a master or ruler, as in *The lion is the lord of the jungle.*
Lord Mayor, the mayor of a large city.
the Lord, God.
lordly *adjective*, **lordship** *noun*

lore *noun* **lores**
a set of traditional facts or beliefs, as in *folklore.*

lorikeet *noun* **lorikeets**
any of various kinds of small, brightly coloured parrots found in north and eastern Australia.

lorry *noun* **lorries**
a truck.

lose *verb* **loses, losing, lost**
1 to be without something you once had, especially because you cannot find it, as in *I've lost my hat.* 2 to be beaten in a contest or game, as in *We lost last Friday's match.* 3 to become slow, as in *My watch loses two minutes every day.*
be lost or **lose your way,** not to know where you are.
get lost!, (*colloquial*) go away!

Usage Do not confuse **lose** with the adjective **loose**, which means something less tight.

loser *noun* **losers**
1 a person or thing that loses, as in *The loser of the match lost points.* 2 (*colloquial*) a person considered a failure.

loss *noun* **losses**
1 losing something. 2 something you have lost.
at a loss, puzzled; unable to do something.
a dead loss, (*colloquial*) a useless person or thing.

lot *noun* **lots**
something for sale at an auction.
a lot or **lots,** a large amount; plenty.
draw lots, to choose one person or thing from a group by a method that depends on chance.
the lot, everything.

lotion *noun* **lotions**
a liquid that you put on your skin to heal, clean or protect it.

lottery *noun* **lotteries**
a way of raising money by selling numbered tickets and giving prizes to people who have the winning numbers.

lotto

lotto *noun*
a game of chance where a person selects numbers and wins money if all or several of those numbers are drawn.

lotus *noun* **lotuses**
a kind of tropical water lily.

loud *adjective* **louder, loudest**
1 noisy; easily heard.   2 bright; gaudy, as in *loud colours*.
loudly *adverb*, **loudness** *noun*

loudspeaker *noun* **loudspeakers**
a device that changes electrical impulses into sound increasing the volume.

lounge *verb* **lounges, lounging, lounged**
to sit or stand lazily.

lounge *noun* **lounges**
1 a room in your home where you relax and entertain; the living room.   2 a couch.

louse *noun* **lice**
1 one of various small insects that suck the blood of animals or the juices of plants.
2 (*colloquial*) a person that you hate.

lousy *adjective* **lousier, lousiest**
1 full of lice.   2 (*colloquial*) very bad or ungenerous, as in *It is a lousy day. He is lousy with his money.*

lout *noun* **louts**
a bad-mannered young man.
loutish *adjective*

love *noun* **loves**
1 a feeling of liking someone or something very much; great affection or kindness.
2 sexual feelings and great affection between two people.   3 a person that you like very much.   4 in games, a score of nothing.
in love, feeling strong love for another person.
make love, to have sexual intercourse.

love *verb* **loves, loving, loved**
to like someone or something very much.
lovable *adjective*, **lover** *noun*, **lovingly** *adverb*

lovely *adjective* **lovelier, loveliest**
1 beautiful.   2 (*colloquial*) very pleasant or enjoyable.
loveliness *noun*

low *adjective* **lower, lowest**
not high.
lowest common denominator, the smallest denominator into which two or more other denominators can be divided, as in *12 is the lowest common denominator of the fractions* $^1/_3$ *and* $^1/_4$.
lowest common multiple, the smallest

number that contains an exact amount of two or more other numbers, as in *35 is the lowest common multiple of 5 and 7.*
lowness *noun*

low *verb* **lows, lowing, lowed**
to make a sound like a cow.

lower *verb* **lowers, lowering, lowered**
1 to make something less, or less high; to become less, or less high.   2 to bring something down, as in *He lowered the flag.*

lower-case *adjective*
(*in Printing*) not large; not in capital letters, as in *All the letters in this sentence are lower-case except the first.*

lowly *adjective* **lowlier, lowliest**
humble.
lowliness *noun*

loyal *adjective*
always true to your friends, group, country, etc.; faithful.
loyally *adverb*, **loyalty** *noun*

lozenge *noun* **lozenges**
a small sweet for sore throats.

Ltd. short for **limited.**

lubricate *verb* **lubricates, lubricating, lubricated**
to put oil or grease on something so that it moves smoothly.
lubricant *noun*, **lubrication** *noun*

lucerne *noun*
a plant rather like clover used for fodder.

lucid *adjective* (*say* **loo**-suhd)
1 clear, as in *Though he is very old, his mind is quite lucid.*   2 easy to understand, as in *a lucid explanation.*
lucidity *noun*, **lucidly** *adverb*

luck *noun*
1 the way things happen that have not been planned.   2 good things happening to you.

lucky *adjective* **luckier, luckiest**
having or bringing good luck.
lucky dip, a box or tub containing articles of various values, from which you pick one at random.
luckily *adverb*

lucrative *adjective*
profitable; producing much money, as in *a lucrative business.*

ludicrous *adjective* (*say* **loo**-duh-kruhs)
so silly that he, she, or it makes people laugh.
ludicrously *adverb*

lying

lug *verb* **lugs, lugging, lugged**
to drag, as in *She lugged the case up the stairs.*

luggage *noun*
suitcases, bags, boxes, etc. used by travellers.

lukewarm *adjective*
1 slightly warm. 2 not very enthusiastic, as in *lukewarm support.*

lull *verb* **lulls, lulling, lulled**
to soothe or calm something; to send someone to sleep.

lull *noun* **lulls**
a short period of quiet or rest.

lullaby *noun* **lullabies**
a song that is sung to send a baby to sleep.

lumber *verb* **lumbers, lumbering, lumbered**
1 to move along clumsily or noisily, as in *The elephants lumbered past.* 2 (*colloquial*) to leave someone with a problem, unpleasant job, etc.
lumbering *noun*

luminous *adjective* (*say* **loo**-muh-nuhs)
that shines or glows in the dark.
luminosity *noun*

lump *noun* **lumps**
1 a solid piece of something, as in *a lump of sugar.* 2 a swelling.
lumpy *adjective*

lump *verb* **lumps, lumping, lumped**
to put or deal with things together, as in *Several age groups were lumped together to compete in the school team.*

lunacy *noun* **lunacies** (*say* **loo**-nuh-see)
madness.

lunar *adjective*
to do with the moon.
lunar month, the period between new moons; four weeks.

lunatic *noun* **lunatics** (*say* **loo**-nuh-tik)
a mad person.

lunch *noun* **lunches**
a meal eaten in the middle of the day.
big lunch, lunch eaten at school.
little lunch, play-lunch; the snack eaten at the mid-morning break; the break itself.
lunchtime *noun*

luncheon *noun* **luncheons**
lunch.

lunge *verb* **lunges, lunging, lunged**
to thrust or move forward suddenly.

lungs *plural noun*
the two organs inside your body which fill with air when you breathe.

lurch *verb* **lurches, lurching, lurched**
1 to stagger, as in *The passengers lurched forward as the bus stopped suddenly.* 2 to lean suddenly to one side, as in *The table lurched to the left as one of its legs gave way.*

lurch *noun* **lurches**
1 a staggering movement. 2 a sudden leaning movement.
leave someone in the lurch, to desert someone, leaving him or her in difficulties.

lure *verb* **lures, luring, lured**
1 to tempt a person or animal into a trap, as in *The cheese is supposed to lure mice into the mousetrap.* 2 to attract a person or an animal, as in *Thousands of people have come to the city, lured by promises of wealth.*

lure *noun* **lures**
1 an object used to catch fish.
2 something that attracts, as in *the lure of money.*

lurid *adjective* (*say* **loo**-ruhd)
1 having very bright colours; gaudy.
2 shocking, as in *the lurid details of the murder.*

lurk *verb* **lurks, lurking, lurked**
to wait where you cannot be seen.

luscious *adjective*
tasting or smelling very pleasant.

lush *adjective* **lusher, lushest**
growing abundantly, as in *lush grass.*
lushly *adverb*, **lushness** *noun*

lust *noun* **lusts**
powerful desire.
lustful *adjective*

lustre *noun* **lustres** (*say* **lus**-tuh)
brightness; brilliance.
lustrous *adjective*

lute *noun* **lutes**
an old-fashioned musical instrument rather like a guitar.

luxury *noun* **luxuries**
1 something expensive that you enjoy but do not really need. 2 having many such things, as in *a life of luxury.*
luxurious *adjective*

lychee *noun* **lychees**
a small fruit with sweet, white flesh in a thin, rough skin.

lycra *noun*
(*trademark*) a stretch material used especially for sports clothing.

lying present participle of **lie** *verb* and **lie** *verb*.

lynch

lynch *verb* **lynches, lynching, lynched**
to execute someone, usually by hanging, without a proper trial, as in *The mob lynched the suspected thief.*

lyre *noun* **lyres**
an ancient musical instrument like a small harp.
lyre-bird, a bird able to mimic other sounds, the male of which has a beautiful lyre-shaped tail.

lyric *noun* **lyrics** (*say* li-rik)
a short poem expressing feelings and emotions.
lyric or **lyrics,** the words of a song.
lyrical *adjective*

Mm

m short for **metre**, **metres**, or **millions**.

macabre *adjective* (*say* muh-**kah**-buh *or* muh-**kah**-bruh)
horrible, gruesome, as in *macabre murders*.

macadamia *noun* **macadamias**
the edible nut from a tree grown in the eastern rainforest.

macaroni *noun*
flour paste made into tubes and used as food.

machete *noun* **machetes** (*say* muh-**shet**-ee)
a broad, heavy knife often used for cutting back thick growth.

machine *noun* **machines**
something with several parts that work together to do a job, as in *a washing-machine*.

machine-gun *noun* **machine-guns**
a gun that can keep firing bullets quickly one after another.

machinery *noun*
1 machines. 2 mechanism, as in *The lift's machinery is faulty*. 3 a system for doing something, as in *the machinery of local government*.

macho *adjective*
behaving in a very masculine way.

mackerel *noun* **mackerel**
an edible marine fish.

mad *adjective* **madder**, **maddest**
1 having something wrong with your mind; not sane or sensible. 2 very keen, as in *He's mad about football*. 3 (*colloquial*) very annoyed, as in *The teacher was mad with the rude students*.
like mad, (*colloquial*) with great speed, energy, enthusiasm, etc.
madly *adverb*, **madman** *noun*, **madness** *noun*

madam *noun*
a word sometimes used when speaking or writing politely to a woman, instead of her name, as in '*Can I help you, madam?*' said the salesperson.
[from French **ma dame** = my lady]

madden *verb* **maddens**, **maddening**, **maddened**
1 to make someone mad. 2 to make someone angry.

made past tense and past participle of **make** *verb*.

magazine *noun* **magazines**
1 a paper-covered publication that comes out regularly. 2 the part of a gun that holds the cartridges. 3 a store for ammunition, explosives, etc. 4 a device that holds film for a camera or slides for a slide-projector.

maggot *noun* **maggots**
the larva of some kinds of fly.
maggoty *adjective*

magic *noun*
the power to do wonderful things or clever tricks that people cannot usually do.
magic square, a pattern of numbers arranged in a square, for example 1 to 9 written in three rows and three columns, in a special order so that all the rows, columns, and diagonal lines of numbers add up to the same total.
magical *adjective*, **magically** *adverb*

magician *noun* **magicians**
a person who practises magic and does magic tricks.

magistrate *noun* **magistrates**
a judge in a local court.

magma

magma *noun*
melted material beneath the earth's crust.

magnanimous *adjective*
generous and forgiving.

magnesium *noun*
a silvery-white metal that makes a very bright flame when it burns.

magnet *noun* **magnets**
a piece of metal that can attract iron or steel and that points north and south when it is hung in the air.
magnetism *noun*

magnetic *adjective*
having or using the powers of a magnet.
magnetic field, the area affected by the force from a magnet.
magnetic tape, a plastic strip coated with a substance that acts like a magnet, for recording sound.
magnetically *adverb*

magnetise or **magnetize** *verb* **magnetises, magnetising, magnetised**
1 to make something into a magnet. 2 to influence someone by your attractiveness, as in *Felicity magnetised the audience as soon as she came on to the stage.*

magnificent *adjective*
1 looking grand or important.
2 excellent, as in *a magnificent meal.*
magnificence *noun*, **magnificently** *adverb*

magnify *verb* **magnifies, magnifying, magnified**
to make something look bigger than it really is.
magnification *noun*, **magnifier** *noun*, **magnifying glass** *noun*

magnitude *noun* **magnitudes**
how large or important something is.

magnolia *noun* **magnolias**
a tree with large white or pale mauve flowers.

magpie *noun* **magpies**
a black and white bird with a large beak commonly found throughout Australia.

mahogany *noun* (*say* muh-**hog**-uh-nee)
a reddish-brown wood used for furniture.

maid *noun* **maids**
1 a female servant. 2 (*old-fashioned use*) a girl.

maiden *noun* **maidens**
(*old-fashioned use*) a girl.

maiden *adjective*
not married, as in *a maiden aunt.*
maiden name, a woman's name before she got married.

maiden over, a cricket over in which no runs are scored.
maiden voyage, a ship's first voyage.

mail *noun*
1 letters, parcels, etc. sent by post. 2 a boat or train which carries mail, as in *People in Moree rely upon the North West Mail.*
3 armour made of metal rings joined together, as in a *coat of mail.*
mail order, ordering goods to be sent by post.

mail *verb* **mails, mailing, mailed**
to send something by post.

maim *verb* **maims, maiming, maimed**
to injure someone so that part of his or her body is useless.

main *adjective*
most important; largest, as in *The main thing is to be accurate. They are the main suppliers of fruit in this district.*
main clause, a clause which is a sentence and can be used by itself.

main or **mains** *noun*
the main pipe or cable in a system carrying water, gas, or electricity to a building.

mainframe *noun* **mainframes**
(*in Computing*) a large computer that is shared by many users.

mainland *noun*
the main part of a country, not the islands around it, as in *Tasmanians call the rest of Australia the mainland.*

mainly *adverb*
most importantly; almost completely; usually, as in *We are mainly a printing company, but we do some bookbinding as well. The team was picked mainly from the girls. She is at home mainly in the afternoon.*

mainstream *noun* **mainstreams**
the major trend or tendency in an area, as in *Her work represents the mainstream of modern painting.*

maintain *verb* **maintains, maintaining, maintained**
1 to keep something in good condition.
2 to have or state a belief, as in *I maintain that animals should not be killed or hunted.* 3 to provide money for someone.

maintenance *noun*
money payable to a spouse or former spouse after separation or divorce, as in *The mother relied on maintenance from her ex-husband to educate their children.*

maize *noun*
a tall kind of corn with large seeds.

majestic *adjective*
imposing; dignified.
majestically *adverb*

majesty *noun* **majesties**
1 being imposing and dignified, as in *the majesty of the Blue Mountains*. **2** the title used in speaking about or to a king or queen, as in *Her Majesty the Queen. Yes, Your Majesty.*

major *adjective*
1 more important; main, as in *major roads*. **2** of the musical scale that has a semitone between the 3rd and 4th notes and between the 7th and 8th notes.

major *noun* **majors**
an army officer higher in rank than a captain.

majority *noun* **majorities**
(*say* muh-**jo**-ruh-tee)
1 the greater part of a group of people or things, as in *The majority of the class wanted a quiz*. **2** the difference between a larger and a smaller number of votes, as in *She had a majority of 25 over her opponent*. **3** the age at which the law says you are an adult.

make *verb* **makes, making, made**
1 to get something new, usually by putting things together, as in *They are making a raft out of logs*. **2** to cause something to happen, as in *The bang made him jump*. **3** to get or earn, as in *She makes a lot of money*. **4** to score, as in *He has made 20 runs so far*. **5** to reach, as in *The swimmer just made the shore*. **6** to estimate or reckon, as in *What do you make the time?* **7** to equal; to amount to, as in *4 and 6 makes 10*. **8** to give, as in *Make me an offer*. **9** to tidy or arrange for use, as in *Make the beds*. **10** to cause something to be successful or happy, as in *Her visit made my day*.
make do, to manage with something that is not what you really want, as in *Without a stove, he will make do with a camp oven*.
make for, to go towards.
make off, to leave quickly.
make out, to manage to see, hear, or understand something; to pretend, as in *We could barely make out the inscription. She made out that she was ill.*
make up, to build something or put something together; to invent a story, etc.; to give someone something to make him or her feel better after losing something; to put on make-up; to become friends again after a fight.
make up your mind, to decide.

make *noun* **makes**
1 how something is made. **2** a brand of goods; something made by a particular firm, as in *What make of car is that?*

make-believe *noun*
the act of pretending or imagining things.

maker *noun* **makers**
the person or firm that has made something.

makeshift *adjective*
used because you have nothing better, as in *a makeshift table*.

make-up *noun* **make-ups**
1 substances for making your skin look beautiful or different. **2** a person's character.

malaria *noun* (*say* muh-**lair**-ree-uh)
a feverish disease spread by mosquitoes.

male *adjective*
to do with the sex that does not give birth to offspring.
male chauvinist, a man who thinks that men are more clever, brave, etc. than women.

male *noun* **males**
a male person or animal.

malevolent *adjective* (*say* muh-**lev**-uh-luhnt)
intending to harm other people, as in *malevolent tyrant*.
malevolence *noun*, **malevolently** *adverb*

malice *noun*
a desire to harm other people.
malicious *adjective*, **maliciously** *adverb*

malignant *adjective*
1 dangerous or fatal, as in *a malignant tumour*. **2** harmful; feeling or showing intense nastiness, as in *He gave his enemy a malignant look.*

mall *noun* **malls**
1 an area without traffic where people can walk and shop. **2** a shopping centre.

mallee *noun*
a small, scrubby gum tree with several trunks or stems growing from a large single root.
mallee country, dry areas of Australia where mallee scrub grows.
mallee root, the large root of the mallee, valued as firewood.

mallet *noun* **mallets**
a large hammer, usually made of wood.

malnutrition *noun*
physical weakness caused by not having enough food to eat.
malnourished *adjective*

malt

malt *noun*
dried barley used in brewing, making vinegar, etc.
malted *adjective*

mammal *noun* **mammals**
any animal of which the female can feed her babies with her own milk, as in *Humans, lions, and whales are mammals.*
mammalian *adjective*

mammoth *noun* **mammoths**
an extinct kind of large, hairy elephant.

mammoth *adjective*
huge.

man *noun* **men**
1 a grown-up male human being.
2 a person. 3 all the people in the world.
4 one of the pieces used in a board-game like chess or draughts.

man *verb* **mans, manning, manned**
to supply people to work something, as in *Man the pumps!*

manage *verb* **manages, managing, managed**
1 to be able to do something difficult.
2 to be in charge of a shop, factory, etc.
manageable *adjective*, **management** *noun*, **manager** *noun*, **manageress** *noun*, **managerial** *adjective*

mandarin *noun* **mandarin**
a small citrus fruit with soft, orange skin.

mandate *noun* **mandates**
authority given to someone to carry out a certain task or policy.

mane *noun* **manes**
the long hair along the back of the neck of a horse, lion, etc.

manger *noun* **mangers** (*say* **mayn**-juh)
a trough for animals to feed from.

mangle *verb* **mangles, mangling, mangled**
to crush, cut, or destroy.

mango *noun* **mangoes**
a sweet, yellowish, tropical fruit.

manhandle *verb* **manhandles, manhandling, manhandled**
to treat someone roughly.

manhole *noun* **manholes**
a hole, usually with a cover, through which a worker can get into a sewer, boiler, etc. to inspect or repair it.

mania *noun* **manias**
violent madness.
maniac *noun*, **manic** *adjective*

manifesto *noun* **manifestos**
a statement of a group's or person's policy or principles.

manipulate *verb* **manipulates, manipulating, manipulated**
1 to handle something skilfully, as in *The crane-driver manipulated the load with great accuracy.* 2 to arrange something or control someone cleverly or cunningly.
manipulation *noun*, **manipulator** *noun*

mankind *noun*
all the people in the world.

manly *adjective* **manlier, manliest**
1 strong or brave. 2 suitable for a man, as in *manly clothes.*
manliness *noun*

manna *noun*
white, sugary edible substance which seeps from many gum trees.

manner *noun* **manners**
the way that something happens or is done.
manners, how you behave with other people; behaving politely.

mannerism *noun* **mannerisms**
a gesture, a way of speaking, acting, etc. that you do from habit, as in *Her obvious mannerism is to play with her hair when she speaks.*

manoeuvre *noun* **manoeuvres**
(*say* muh-**noo**-vuh)
1 a clever action done to deceive or beat someone. 2 a difficult or skilful action, as in *Parking the caravan was an awkward manoeuvre.*

manoeuvre *verb* **manoeuvres, manoeuvring, manoeuvred**
1 to make a clever action to deceive or beat someone, as in *politicians manoeuvring for places in the Cabinet.* 2 to make a difficult or skilful action, as in *Watch the ships manoeuvring.*
manoeuvrable *adjective*

man on the land *noun*
the owner of property in the country.

manor *noun* **manors**
a large, English country house and its land.

mansion *noun* **mansions**
a large, impressive house.

manslaughter *noun* (*say* **man**-slaw-tuh)
killing someone without meaning to do so.

mantelpiece *noun* **mantelpieces**
a shelf above a fireplace.

mantle *noun* **mantles**
a cloak.

manual *adjective*
done with your hands, as in *manual work.*
manually *adverb*

manual *noun* manuals
a handbook.

manufacture *verb* manufactures, manufacturing, manufactured
to make things with machines.
manufacturer *noun*

manure *noun*
fertiliser, especially made from animal waste.

manuscript *noun* manuscripts
something written or typed but not printed.

many *adjective* more, most
large in number.

many *noun*
a large number of people or things, as in *Many were fed at the barbecue.*

Maori *noun* Maoris (*say* **mow**-ree)
one of the original race of people who lived in New Zealand.

map *noun* maps
a diagram of part or all of the earth's surface, showing towns, mountains, rivers, etc.
on the map, famous or important.

map *verb* maps, mapping, mapped
to make a map of an area.
map out, to arrange or organise something.

maple *noun* maples
a tree with broad leaves which grows in colder climates.

mapping *noun* mappings
(*in Mathematics*) a relationship between two sets of numbers, or an object and its image, that changes one into the other.

mar *verb* mars, marring, marred
to spoil, as in *The rain marred our sports carnival.*

marathon *noun* marathons
a long-distance race for runners, usually 42 kilometres long.

marauder *noun* marauders
someone who attacks a place and steals things from it.
marauding *adjective*

marble *noun* marbles
1 a small glass ball used in games. 2 a hard kind of limestone that is polished and used for building or sculpture.

March *noun*
the third month of the year.

march *verb* marches, marching, marched
1 to walk like soldiers, with regular steps. 2 to make someone walk somewhere.

march *noun* marches
1 the action of marching. 2 a piece of music suitable for marching.

mare *noun* mares
a female horse or donkey.

margarine *noun* margarines
(*say* mah-juh-**reen**)
a substance that looks like butter, made from animal or vegetable fats.

margin *noun* margins
1 the empty space between the edge of a page and the writing or pictures. 2 the small difference between two scores, prices, etc., as in *She won by a narrow margin.*
marginal *adjective*, **marginally** *adverb*

marijuana or **marihuana** *noun*
(*say* ma-ruh-**wah**-nuh)
a drug made from the dried leaves of the Indian hemp plant.

marina *noun* marinas (*say* muh-**ree**-nuh)
a harbour for yachts, motor boats, etc.

marinate *verb* marinates, marinating, marinated
to soak food in an oily, spiced liquid before cooking to improve the flavour.
marinade *noun*

marine *adjective* (*say* muh-**reen**)
to do with the sea, as in *marine fish; marine laws.*

marine *noun* marines (*say* muh-**reen**)
a soldier trained to serve on land and sea.

marionette *noun* marionettes
a puppet worked by strings or wires.

maritime *adjective*
to do with the sea or shipping, as in *maritime museum.*

mark *noun* marks
1 a spot, dot, line, stain, etc. on something. 2 a number, letter, etc. put on a piece of work to show how good it is. 3 a distinguishing feature of something. 4 the place from which you start a race. 5 (*in Australian Rules football*) a catch; the player, as in *Ablett is a brilliant high mark.*
to make one's mark, to make an impression.
on your mark, to get ready to start a race etc.

mark *verb* marks, marking, marked
1 to put a mark on something. 2 to give a number, letter, etc. to a piece of work to show how good it is; to correct a piece of work. 3 to pay attention to something, as in *Mark my words!* 4 to be a special feature of, as in *Happiness marks birthdays.*
mark time, to march on one spot, without

marked

moving forward; to wait, as in *The soldiers marked time. We're just marking time—when will we get down to work?*

marked *adjective*
1 having a mark which can be seen, as in *the marked wall*. 2 clearly noticeable, as in *a marked improvement*.

market *noun* markets
1 a place where things are bought and sold, usually from stalls in the open air.
2 a demand for goods, as in *There is hardly any market for our wool now.*
on the market, available to buy, as in *The house is on the market.*

market *verb* markets, marketing, marketed
to sell something.
marketable *adjective*

marksman or **markswoman** *noun* marksmen or markswomen
an expert in shooting at a target.
marksmanship *noun*

marlin *noun*
a long-nosed marine fish.

marloo *noun* marloos
a Western Australian name for the red kangaroo.

Origin This word comes from an Aboriginal Western Desert language: **marlu**. See the Aboriginal Languages map at the back of this dictionary.

marmalade *noun*
jam made from oranges or lemons.

maroon *verb* maroons, marooning, marooned
(*say* muh-**roon**)
to abandon someone in a place far away from other people.

maroon *adjective* (*say* muh-**rohn** or muh-**roon**)
brownish or dark red.

marquee *noun* marquees (*say* mah-**kee**)
a very large tent.

marriage *noun* marriages
1 the state of being married.
2 a wedding.

marron *noun*
a large, freshwater crayfish from Western Australia.

Origin This word comes from the Aboriginal language Nyungar: **marran**. See the Aboriginal Languages map at the back of this dictionary.

marrow *noun* marrows
1 a large, green or yellow hard-skinned vegetable. 2 the soft substance inside bones.

marry *verb* marries, marrying, married
1 to become the husband or wife of someone. 2 to make two people into husband and wife.

marsh *noun* marshes
a low-lying area of very wet ground.
marshy *adjective*

marshal *noun* marshals
1 an official who supervises a contest, ceremony, etc. 2 a high-ranking officer, as in *Field Marshal.*

marshmallow *noun* marshmallows
a soft, spongy sweet.

marsupial *noun* marsupials
(*say* mah-**soo**-pee-uhl)
an animal such as a kangaroo or wallaby which carries its young in a pouch for a time after birth.

martial *adjective*
to do with war.
martial arts, fighting sports such as karate and judo.
martial law, government by the armed forces.

Martian *noun* Martians
a creature in stories that comes from the planet Mars.

martyr *noun* martyrs (*say* **mah**-tuh)
someone who is killed or suffers because of his or her beliefs.
martyrdom *noun*

marvel *noun* marvels
a wonderful thing.

marvel *verb* marvels, marvelling, marvelled
to be filled with wonder or astonishment.

marvellous *adjective*
excellent; wonderful.
marvellously *adverb*

marzipan *noun*
a soft, sweet food made from ground almonds and sugar.

mascara *noun*
a cosmetic used for darkening the eyelashes.

mascot *noun* mascots
a person, animal, or object that is believed to bring good luck.

masculine *adjective*
1 related to, or suitable for men, as in

masculine voice. **2** (*in grammar*) having a grammatical form suitable for the names of males or for words linked with these, as in *a masculine noun.*
masculinity *noun*

mash *verb* **mashes, mashing, mashed**
to crush something into a soft mass, as in *mashed potato.*

mask *noun* **masks**
a covering worn over your face to disguise or protect it.

mask *verb* **masks, masking, masked**
1 to cover your face with a mask. **2** to hide something, as in *the student masked his disappointment by laughing.*

mason *noun* **masons**
someone who builds or works with stone.
Mason, a member of a secret society called the Freemasons.

masonry *noun*
the stone parts of a building.

masquerade *noun* **masquerades**
(*say* mas-kuh-**rayd**)
1 a false show; pretence. **2** a masked ball.

mass *noun* **masses**
1 a large amount, as in *masses of flowers.*
2 a lump; a heap. **3** (*in Science*) the amount of matter in an object. **4** a religious service in the Roman Catholic church, the most important part being the Communion.
mass media, radio, television, newspapers, etc. giving information to many people.
mass production, producing goods in large quantities.

massacre *verb* **massacres, massacring, massacred** (*say* **mas**-uh-kuh)
to kill a large number of people.

massage *verb* **massages, massaging, massaged** (*say* **mas**-ahzh *or* muh-**sahzh**)
to rub and press the body to make it less stiff or less painful.
masseur *noun*, **masseuse** *noun*

massive *adjective*
huge; large and heavy, as in *a massive problem. Ships' engines are massive machines.*
massively *adverb*

mast *noun* **masts**
a tall pole that holds up a ship's sail, a flag, or an aerial.

master *noun* **masters**
1 a man who teaches in a school, especially one who is head of a department.
2 someone who is in charge of something.
3 a great artist, composer, sportsperson,

etc. **4** something from which copies are made.
Master, a word used before a boy's name when addressing a letter to him.
master-class, a class given by a famous musician, etc.

master *verb* **masters, mastering, mastered**
1 to learn a subject or skill thoroughly.
2 to defeat or overcome something, as in *She succeeded in mastering her fear of heights.*

masterly *adjective*
very clever.

master-mind *noun* **master-minds**
1 a very clever person. **2** someone who organises a scheme, crime, etc.

masterpiece *noun* **masterpieces**
1 an excellent piece of work.
2 someone's best piece of work.

masturbate *verb* **masturbates, masturbating, masturbated**
to excite sexually by stimulating the genitals.

mat *noun* **mats**
1 a small piece of material that partly covers a floor. **2** a small piece of cork, rubber, etc. put on a table to protect the surface from hot or wet cups or plates.

matador *noun* **matadors**
someone who fights and kills the bull in a bullfight.

match *noun* **matches**
1 a small, thin stick with a small amount of chemical at one end that gives a flame when rubbed on something rough. **2** a game or contest between two teams or players. **3** one person or thing that is equal or similar to another. **4** a marriage.
matchbox *noun*, **matchstick** *noun*

match *verb* **matches, matching, matched**
1 to be equal or similar to another person or thing. **2** to put someone in competition with someone else.

mate *noun* **mates**
1 a friend or companion. **2** one of a pair of animals that have come together to have offspring. **3** one of the officers on a ship.

mate *verb* **mates, mating, mated**
to come together so as to have offspring; to put animals together so that they will have offspring.

material *noun* **materials**
1 anything used for making something else. **2** cloth.

a
b
c
d
e
f
g
h
i
j
k
l
m
n
o
p
q
r
s
t
u
v
w
x
y
z

materialise

materialise or **materialize** *verb*
materialises, materialising, materialised
to become visible, appear in a physical
shape, as in *The ghost didn't materialise.*

materialistic *adjective*
liking possessions, money, and comfort
rather than things of the mind such as
religion or art.
materialist *noun*

maternal *adjective*
to do with a mother or mothers; motherly,
as in *maternal instincts; a maternal old lady.*
maternally *adverb*

maternity *noun*
having a baby; motherhood.

mateship *noun*
the feeling shared by close friends.

matey *adjective*)
(*colloquial*) friendly, as in *He is very matey
with the boss.*

mathematician *noun* mathematicians
(*say* math-uhmuh-**tish**-uhn)
an expert in mathematics.

mathematics *noun*
the study of numbers, measurements, and
shapes.
mathematical *adjective*, **mathematically**
adverb

maths *noun*
short for mathematics.

matilda *noun* matildas
a bushman's bundle; a swag.

matinée *noun* matinées (*say* **mat**-uh-nay)
an afternoon performance at a theatre or
cinema.

matrimony *noun* (*say* **mat**-ruh-muh-nee)
marriage.
matrimonial *adjective*

matrix *noun* matrices
(*in Mathematics*) a set of numbers or
quantities arranged in rows and columns.

matron *noun* matrons
1 a middle-aged woman who is married.
2 the head nurse in a hospital. **3** a
woman nurse and housekeeper at a school,
etc.

matt *adjective*
not shiny, as in *matt paint.*

matted *adjective*
tangled, as in *matted hair.*

matter *noun*
a physical substance which makes up
things, as in *vegetable matter; reading matter.*

matter *noun* matters
something you need to think about or do,
as in *a serious matter.*
a matter of fact, something true.
no matter, it is not important.
what's the matter?, what is wrong?

matting *noun*
mats; rough material for covering a
floor.

mattress *noun* mattresses
a stuffed, or air- or water-filled cushion
used on a bed.

mature *adjective*
fully grown or developed; grown-up, as in
a mature tree; a mature attitude.
maturely *adverb*, **maturity** *noun*

maul *verb* mauls, mauling, mauled (*say* mawl)
1 to tear the flesh off. **2** to handle
roughly.

mauve *adjective* (*say* mohv)
pale purple.

maximum *noun* maxima
the greatest possible number or amount, as
in *10 out of 10 is the maximum.*
maximum and minimum thermometer, a
device that shows the highest and the
lowest temperature that has occurred over
a period of time.

maximum *adjective*
greatest, as in *maximum speed.*

May *noun*
the fifth month of the year.

may *verb, past tense* **might**
1 to be allowed to, as in *May I have a sweet?*
2 will possibly; has possibly, as in *He may
come tomorrow. He might have missed the
train.*

maybe *adverb*
perhaps.

mayday *noun* maydays
an international radio-signal calling for
help.

mayonnaise *noun* (*say* may-uh-**nayz**)
a creamy sauce made from eggs, oil,
vinegar, etc.

mayor *noun* mayors
the person in charge of the council in a
town or city.
mayoral *adjective*, **mayoress** *noun*

maze *noun* mazes
a complicated and puzzling network of
paths or lines to follow.

me *pronoun*
a word used for *I*, usually when it is the
object of a sentence or comes straight after
a preposition, as in *She spoke to me.*

meadow *noun* **meadows**
a paddock.

meagre *adjective* (*say* **mee**-guh)
not big enough; not sufficient.

meal *noun* **meals**
1 a time when food is eaten.   2 the food eaten at breakfast, lunch, dinner, etc.
mealtime *noun*

mean *verb* **means, meaning, meant**
1 to try to convey something; to indicate; to be the same as something, as in *'Maybe' means 'perhaps'*.   2 to intend, as in *I meant to tell him, but I forgot.*

mean *adjective* **meaner, meanest**
1 not generous; selfish, as in *a mean, miserly man*.   2 unkind; spiteful, as in *a mean trick*.
meanly *adverb*, **meanness** *noun*

mean *adjective*
average, as in *the mean temperature*.

meander *verb* **meanders, meandering, meandered** (*say* mee-**an**-duh)
1 to wander, as in *They meandered through the town, looking in all the shop windows*.
2 to take a winding course, as in *The river meandered across the plain*.

meanie *noun* **meanies**
(*colloquial*) a nasty person.

meaning *noun* **meanings**
what something means.
meaningful *adjective*, **meaningless** *adjective*

means *plural noun*
1 a way of doing something; a method.
2 money; resources, as in *He hadn't got the means to pay for a meal*.
by all means, certainly.
by means of something, using something; with something.
by no means, not at all.

meantime *noun*
in the meantime, in the period of time between two events, as in *The taxi will be here in half an hour; in the meantime, let's pack our bags.*

meantime *adverb*
meanwhile.

meanwhile *adverb*
while something else is taking place, as in *I cleaned the stove; meanwhile, Bruce mended my bike.*

measles *noun*
an infectious disease that causes small red spots on the skin.

measly *adjective* **measlier, measliest**
(*colloquial*) very small or poor, as in *What a measly ice-cream!*

measure *verb* **measures, measuring, measured**
1 to find out how big something is.   2 to be a certain size.
measure out, to mark or give a particular amount.
measurable *adjective*, **measurement** *noun*

measure *noun* **measures**
1 a unit used for measuring, as in *A kilometre is a measure of length*.   2 a device used for measuring, as in *tape measure*.
3 the size of something, as in *a measure of sugar*.   4 something done for a particular purpose; a law, as in *the police took measures to stop vandalism*.

meat *noun* **meats**
animal flesh used as food.
meaty *adjective*

mechanic *noun* **mechanics**
someone who makes, uses, or mends machines.

mechanical *adjective*
1 to do with machines.   2 automatic; done without thought.
mechanically *adverb*

mechanics *noun*
1 the study of force and movement.   2 the study or use of machines.

mechanism *noun* **mechanisms**
1 the moving parts of a machine.   2 the way something works, as in *He described the mechanism of a combine harvester*.

medal *noun* **medals**
a piece of metal shaped like a coin, star, or cross, given to someone for being brave or for achieving something.

medallist *noun* **medallists**
someone who has won a medal, as in *He was a gold medallist in the Olympics.*

meddle *verb* **meddles, meddling, meddled**
to interfere.
meddler *noun*, **meddlesome** *adjective*

media *plural noun* (*say* **mee**-dee-uh)
the means of communicating information to large numbers of people through radio, television, newspapers, etc., as in *The media gave much coverage to the Sydney 2000 Olympics.*

median *adjective*
in the middle.
median strip, a grassed or concrete area dividing a road; a plantation.

median *noun* **medians**
(*in Mathematics*) the middle number in a set of numbers that have been arranged in order, as in *The median of 2, 3, 5, 8, 9, 14, and 15 is 8.*

mediate

mediate *verb* **mediates, mediating, mediated**
to come between people or groups who disagree about something to try to settle the quarrel or dispute.
mediator, the person who mediates.

medical *adjective*
to do with the treatment of illness.
medically *adverb*

Medicare *noun*
the national system of basic health care, partly paid for by a levy on incomes.

medicine *noun* **medicines**
1 a substance, usually swallowed, used to try to cure or prevent illness. 2 the treatment of illness.
medicinal *adjective*

medicine man *noun* **medicine men**
the man in the tribe believed to have powers of healing, especially among Aborigines.

medieval *adjective* (*say* med-ee-**eev**-uhl)
of the Middle Ages.

mediocre *adjective* (*say* mee-dee-**oh**-kuh)
not very good.
mediocrity *noun*

meditate *verb* **meditates, meditating, meditated**
to think deeply and seriously.
meditation *noun*, **meditative** *adjective*

Mediterranean *adjective*
(*say* med-uh-tuh-**ray**-nee-uhn)
to do with the Mediterranean Sea or the countries round it, as in *a Mediterranean climate.*

medium *noun* **media** or **mediums**
1 a thing in which something exists, moves, or is expressed, as in *Newspapers and television are media for advertising.*
2 someone who claims to communicate with the dead.

medium *adjective*
average; of middle size, as in *medium height.*

meek *adjective* **meeker, meekest**
humble; quiet and obedient.
meekly *adverb*, **meekness** *noun*

meet *verb* **meets, meeting, met**
1 to come together from different places; to come face to face, as in *We all met in Hobart. I met him at the station.* 2 to get to know someone, as in *I met her at a friend's party.*
3 to pay a bill, solve a problem, etc., as in *Will he be able to meet all his debts?*
4 to come into contact with, to touch, as in *The wires met and caused a fire.*

meet *noun* **meets**
a gathering of competitors in a sport, as in *the athletics meet.*

meeting *noun* **meetings**
a time when people come together for a discussion, contest, etc.

megaphone *noun* **megaphones**
a funnel-shaped device for making someone's voice sound louder.

melancholy *adjective*
sad; gloomy, as in *a melancholy mood.*

Melburnian *noun* **Melburnians**
(*say* mel-**ber**-nee-uhn)
someone born or living in Melbourne.

mellow *adjective* **mellower, mellowest**
1 not harsh; soft and rich in flavour, colour or sound. 2 friendly.

melodious *adjective*
sounding sweet; pleasant to hear.

melodrama *noun* **melodramas**
a play full of excitement and emotion.
melodramatic *adjective*

melody *noun* **melodies**
a tune, especially a pleasing tune.
melodic *adjective*

melon *noun* **melons**
a large, sweet, juicy fruit with yellow or green skin.

melt *verb* **melts, melting, melted**
1 to make something liquid by heating; to become liquid by heating. 2 to go away or disappear slowly.

member *noun* **members**
1 someone who belongs to a society or group. 2 (*in Mathematics*) an object or number that belongs to a set.

Member of Parliament *noun*
someone who has been chosen by the people to act on behalf of them in an elected government.
membership *noun*

membrane *noun* **membranes**
a thin skin or covering.

memo *noun* **memos** (*say* **me**-moh *or* **mee**-moh)
short for memorandum.

memoirs *plural noun*
a book about events that someone has lived through or people that he or she has known.

memorable *adjective*
worth remembering; easy to remember, as in *a memorable event. He has a memorable name.*
memorably *adverb*

merit

memorandum *noun* **memorandums**
a written note, especially to remind
yourself of something.

memorial *noun* **memorials**
something to remind people of a person or
an event, as in *a war memorial*.

memorise or **memorize** *verb* **memorises,
memorising, memorised**
to get something into your memory so that
you do not forget it.

memory *noun* **memories**
1 the ability to remember things.
2 something that you remember.
3 the part of a computer where information
is stored.
in memory of, as a memorial to a person or
an event.

menace *verb* **menaces, menacing, menaced**
to threaten someone with harm or danger.
menacingly *adverb*

menace *noun* **menaces**
1 something menacing.   **2** an annoying
person or thing.

menagerie *noun* **menageries**
(*say* muh-**naj**-uh-ree)
a small zoo.

mend *verb* **mends, mending, mended**
to make a damaged thing as useful as it
was before.
mender *noun*

menstruation *noun*
the natural flow of blood from a woman's
womb, normally happening every 28 days.
menstrual *adjective*, **menstruate** *verb*

mental *adjective*
1 to do with the mind.   **2** (*colloquial*) mad.
mentally *adverb*

mentality *noun* **mentalities**
a person's mental ability or attitude, as in
*The teacher classed the student's mentality as
average. He hasn't the right mentality to handle
children.*

mention *verb* **mentions, mentioning,
mentioned**
to speak about someone or something,
especially when you are talking about
something else.

menu *noun* **menus** (*say* **men**-yoo)
1 a list of the food that is available in a
restaurant or served at a meal.   **2** (*in
Computing*) a list of possible actions,
displayed on a screen, from which you
choose what you want a computer to do.

mercenary *adjective*

working only for money or some other
reward; thinking only of money or reward,
as in *Her interest in the sport was purely
mercenary.*

mercenary *noun* **mercenaries**
a soldier paid to fight for a foreign country.

merchandise *noun*
goods for buying or selling.

merchant *noun* **merchants**
someone involved in trade, as in *wine
merchant.*

merciful *adjective*
kind to someone instead of punishing him
or her.
mercifully *adverb*

merciless *adjective*
not at all merciful; cruel.
mercilessly *adverb*

mercury *noun*
a heavy, silvery metal that is usually liquid,
as in *Some thermometers contain mercury.*

mercy *noun* **mercies**
1 kindness or pity shown in not punishing
or harming a wrongdoer or enemy etc.
2 something to be thankful for, as in *Thank
God for small mercies.*

mere *adjective*
not more than; no better than, as in *He's a
mere child.*
the merest, very small, as in *The merest trace
of colour.*

merely *adverb*
only; simply, as in *She was merely joking.*

merge *verb* **merges, merging, merged**
to combine.

merger *noun* **mergers**
making two businesses or companies into
one.

meridian *noun* **meridians**
(*say* muh-**rid**-ee-uhn)
a line on a map or globe from one pole to
the other, as in *the Greenwich meridian.*

meringue *noun* **meringues** (*say* muh-**rang**)
a crisp cake made from the whites of eggs
mixed with sugar and baked.

merino *noun* **merinos**
a variety of sheep with long, fine wool.

merit *noun* **merits**
something that deserves praise.
merits, the qualities of a person or thing, as
in *Judge it on its merits.*
meritorious *adjective*

merit *verb* **merits, meriting, merited**
to deserve, as in *He merits a reward.*

a
b
c
d
e
f
g
h
i
j
k
l
m
n
o
p
q
r
s
t
u
v
w
x
y
z

mermaid

mermaid *noun* **mermaids**
a mythical creature that looks like a woman but has a fish's tail instead of legs.

merry *adjective* **merrier, merriest**
happy; cheerful.
merrily *adverb*, **merriment** *noun*

merry-go-round *noun* **merry-go-rounds**
a revolving machine on which people, especially children, ride for amusement.

mesh *noun* **meshes**
1 one of the spaces in a net, sieve, or other criss-cross structure. 2 material made like a net; a network, as in *wire mesh*.

mess *noun* **messes**
1 an untidy or dirty condition or thing. 2 a difficult or confused situation, as in *He made a mess of the job*. 3 a place where soldiers or sailors eat their meals.

mess *verb* **messes, messing, messed**
mess about, to behave stupidly or idly.
mess up, to make a mess of something.

message *noun* **messages**
a question or piece of information sent from one person to another.

messenger *noun* **messengers**
someone who carries a message.

Messiah *noun* (*say* muh-**suy**-uh)
1 the person that the Jews expect to come and set them free. 2 according to Christians, Jesus.

messy *adjective* **messier, messiest**
1 untidy or dirty. 2 difficult or complicated.
messily *adverb*, **messiness** *noun*

met past tense and past participle of **meet** *verb*.

metal *noun* **metals**
a hard substance that melts when it is hot, as in *Iron, steel, gold, and tin are all metals*.
metallic *adjective*

metallurgy *noun* (*say* **met**-uh-ler-jee *or* muh-**tal**-uh-jee)
the study of metals; the craft of making and using metals.
metallurgical *adjective*, **metallurgist** *noun*

metamorphic *adjective*
(*say* met-uh-**maw**-fik)
formed or changed by heat or pressure, as in *metamorphic rocks*.

metamorphosis *noun* **metamorphoses**
a complete change, especially of the kind made by some living things, such as a caterpillar changing into a butterfly.

metaphor *noun* **metaphors** (*say* **met**-uh-faw)
using a word or words to suggest something different from their literal meaning, as in '*Food for thought*' and '*a heart of stone*' are metaphors.
metaphorical *adjective*, **metaphorically** *adverb*

meteor *noun* **meteors** (*say* **mee**-tee-aw)
a piece of rock or metal that moves through space and burns up when it gets near the earth.
meteoric *adjective*

meteorite *noun* **meteorites**
(*say* **mee**-tee-uh-ruyt)
a meteor that has landed on the earth.

meteorology *noun*
(*say* mee-tee-uh-**rol**-uh-jee)
the study of the weather.
meteorological *adjective*, **meteorologist** *noun*

meter *noun* **meters**
a machine for measuring something, especially for measuring how much of something has been used, as in *a gas meter*.

Usage Do not confuse **meter** with **metre**, which means a unit of length or a rhythm.

methane *noun*
a colourless gas produced when plants rot away, found mainly in mines and marshes.

method *noun* **methods**
1 a way of doing something. 2 behaviour that shows good organisation, as in *There is method in everything he does*.

methodical *adjective* (*say* muh-**thod**-i-kuhl)
done carefully; well organised, as in *methodical work; a methodical person*.
methodically *adverb*

meths *noun*
(*colloquial*) methylated spirit.

methylated spirit or **spirits** *noun*
a liquid fuel that is a kind of alcohol.

meticulous *adjective*
working very carefully or precisely.
meticulously *adverb*

metre *noun* **metres** (*say* **mee**-tuh)
1 the main metric unit of length. 2 a particular type of rhythm in poetry.

Usage Do not confuse **metre** with **meter**, which means a machine for measuring something.

metric *adjective*
1 to do with the metric system. 2 to do with poetic metre.

metric system, a measuring system based on decimal units, as in *In the metric system, the metre is the unit of length, the kilogram is the unit of mass, and the litre is the unit of capacity.*
metrically *adverb*

metronome *noun* **metronomes**
(*say* met-ruh-nohm)
a device that makes a regular clicking noise to help you keep in time when practising music.

metropolitan *adjective*
to do with a major city, as in *metropolitan transport.*

mew *verb* **mews, mewing, mewed**
to make a sound like a cat.

MHA **MHAs**
short for Member of the House of Assembly.

MHR *noun* **MHRs**
short for Member of the House of Representatives.

mia-mia *noun* **mia-mias** (*say* muy-uh-muy-uh *or* mee-uh-mee-uh)
a temporary shelter erected by a traveller in the bush.

Origin This word comes from the Aboriginal language Nyungar: **maya** or **maya-maya**. See the Aboriginal Languages map at the back of this dictionary.

miaow *verb* **miaows, miaowing, miaowed**
(*say* mee-ow)
to mew.

mice plural of **mouse.**

microbe *noun* **microbes** (*say* muy-krohb)
a very tiny creature, especially one that causes disease or fermentation.

microchip *noun* **microchips**
a silicon chip.

microcomputer *noun* **microcomputers**
a small computer that uses a microprocessor as its central processing unit.

microcosm *noun* **microcosms**
(*say* muy-kruh-koz-uhm)
a world in miniature; something seen as resembling something else on a very small scale.

microfilm *noun* **microfilms**
film on which something is photographed in a miniature size.

microphone *noun* **microphones**
an electrical device that picks up sound waves which are then made stronger, broadcast, or recorded.

microscope *noun* **microscopes**
(*say* muy-kruh-skohp)
a device with lenses that make tiny objects appear larger.

microscopic *adjective*
(*say* muy-kruh-skop-ik)
1 too small to be seen without a microscope; tiny. 2 using a microscope, as in *a microscopic examination.*

microsurgery *noun*
surgical operations on very tiny parts of the body, using microscopes and special small instruments.

microwave *noun* **microwaves**
1 energy moving in very short waves.
2 a microwave oven.
microwave oven, a kind of oven which heats things by using energy in very short waves.

mid *adjective*
in the middle of, as in *The holiday is from mid-December to mid-January.*

midday *noun*
noon.

middle *noun* **middles**
1 the place or part of something that is at the same distance from all its sides or edges or from both its ends. 2 someone's waist.

middle *adjective*
placed in the middle.
middle age, the time between youth and old age.
Middle Ages, the period in history from about AD 500 to about 1483.
Middle East, the countries roughly from Egypt to Iran.

middle-aged *adjective*
to do with people between youth and old age.

middle class *noun* **middle classes**
the class of people between the upper class and the working class.
middle-class *adjective*

midget *noun* **midgets**
an unusually short person.

Midlands *plural noun*
the middle part of Tasmania.

midnight *noun*
twelve o'clock at night.

midriff *noun* **midriffs**
the front of the body just above the waist.

midst *noun*
the middle of something.

midway

midway *adverb*
half-way.

midwife *noun* **midwives**
someone trained to help when a baby is being born.
midwifery *noun*

might past tense of **may** *verb*.

might *noun*
strength; great power.

mighty *adjective* **mightier, mightiest**
very strong or powerful.
mightily *adverb*, **mightiness** *noun*

migraine *noun* **migraines** (*say* **muy**-grayn *or* me-grayn)
a severe kind of headache.

migrant *noun* **migrants** (*say* **muy**-gruhnt)
a person or animal that goes to live in another country.

migrate *verb* **migrates, migrating, migrated** (*say* muy-**grayt**)
to go to live in another country, as in *Many people have migrated to Australia.*
migration *noun*, **migratory** *adjective*

mike *noun* **mikes**
(*colloquial*) a microphone.

mild *adjective* **milder, mildest**
gentle.
mildly *adverb*, **mildness** *noun*

mildew *noun*
a destructive growth appearing on damp cloth, paper, leather, walls, etc.

mile *noun* **miles**
a measure of distance, equal to about 1.6 kilometres.

mileage *noun*
the distance travelled, especially by a vehicle per litre of fuel.

milestone *noun* **milestones**
an important event in a life, history, etc.

militant *adjective*
prepared or wanting to fight or be aggressive.
militancy *noun*

militarism *noun*
belief in, or use of, military methods.
militarist *noun*, **militaristic** *adjective*

military *adjective*
to do with soldiers or the armed forces.

milk *noun*
a white liquid that female mammals produce in their bodies to feed to their babies, as in *People drink the milk of cows and goats.*

milk shake, a drink of milk blended with a flavouring.

milk tooth, one of your first teeth which fall out and are replaced by the teeth you have for the rest of your life.

milk *verb* **milks, milking, milked**
to get the milk from a cow or other animal.

milkman *noun* **milkmen**
a person who delivers milk to people's houses.
milko, (*colloquial*) the milkman.

milky *adjective* **milkier, milkiest**
like milk; white.
Milky Way, a faintly shining band of light that you can sometimes see in the sky, that comes from the stars in our galaxy.

mill *noun* **mills**
1 a building with machinery for grinding grain to make flour. **2** a factory where raw materials like paper, steel, wool, etc. are processed. **3** a small grinding machine, as in *a pepper-mill.*

millennium *noun* **millenniums** or **millennia** (*say* muh-**len**-ee-uhm)
a period of a thousand years.

millet *noun*
a kind of cereal with tiny seeds.

milligram *noun* **milligrams**
one thousandth of a gram.

millilitre *noun* **millilitres**
one thousandth of a litre.

millimetre *noun* **millimetres**
one thousandth of a metre.

million *noun* **millions**
the number 1,000,000; a thousand thousands.
millionth *adjective*

millionaire *noun* **millionaires**
an extremely rich person.

mime *verb* **mimes, miming, mimed**
to tell someone something, act a story, or pretend to do something by using actions, not words.

mimic *verb* **mimics, mimicking, mimicked**
to imitate someone, especially so as to make fun of him or her.
mimicry *noun*

minaret *noun* **minarets**
a tall, thin tower on a mosque, with a balcony where the man who calls Muslims to prayer stands.

mince *verb* **minces, mincing, minced**
to cut food into very small pieces.
not to mince your words, not to alter what you say just for the sake of politeness.

mince *noun*
minced meat.

mind *noun* minds
1 the power to think, feel, understand, and remember; your thoughts and feelings. 2 someone's opinion, as in *Have you changed your mind?*
mind's eye, imagination.

mind *verb* minds, minding, minded
1 to look after someone or something, as in *He was minding the baby.* 2 to be careful; to watch out for something, as in *Mind! I'm carrying a saucepan full of hot water. Mind the doors!* 3 to be sad or upset about something; to object to something, as in *I don't mind missing the party.*

mind-boggling *adjective*
(*colloquial*) unbelievable; startling.

mindless *adjective*
1 done without thinking; stupid, as in *The film is full of mindless violence.* 2 boring, especially because it is too simple, as in *the mindless job of packing fruit.*

mine *pronoun*
belonging to me, as in *That book is mine.*

mine *noun* mines
1 a place where coal, metal, jewels, etc. are dug out of the ground. 2 an explosive hidden under the ground or in the sea to destroy people and things that come close to it.

mine *verb* mines, mining, mined
1 to dig something from a mine. 2 to lay explosive mines in a place.

miner *noun* miners
1 someone who works in a mine. 2 a type of Australian bird with a yellow beak and legs, as in *the noisy miner.*

mineral *noun* minerals
1 a hard substance that can be dug out of the ground, as in *Iron ore and coal are minerals.*
mineral water, water from a spring; a drink made to resemble this.

minestrone *noun* (*say* min-uh-**stroh**-nee)
an Italian soup made from vegetables, pasta, beans, rice, etc.

mingle *verb* mingles, mingling, mingled
to mix or blend; *Salt water and fresh water mingle in the estuary. The host mingled with his guests.*

mingy *adjective* mingier, mingiest (*say* **min**-jee)
(*colloquial*) mean; stingy.

miniature *adjective* (*say* **min**-uh-chuh)
1 tiny, as in *A piccolo looks like a miniature*

flute. 2 copying something on a very small scale, as in *a miniature sailing-ship.*

minibus *noun* minibuses
a vehicle like a small bus with seats for several people.

minim *noun* minims
a musical note equal to half a semibreve, written ♩.

minimum *noun* minima
the smallest possible amount or number, as in *The teacher wants a minimum of noise.*
minimal *adjective*, **minimise** or **minimize** *verb*

minister *noun* ministers
1 someone in charge of a government department, as in *The Minister for Health decided to close the hospital.* 2 a member of the clergy.

ministry *noun* ministries
1 a government department. 2 the work of a minister in the church.

mink *noun* minks
1 a small animal rather like a weasel. 2 this animal's valuable brown fur.

minor *adjective*
1 less important; not very important, as in *a minor operation.* 2 of the musical scale that has a semitone between the 2nd and 3rd notes.

minority *noun* minorities (*say* muy-**no**-ruh-tee or muh-**no**-ruh-tee)
1 the smaller part of a group of people or things, as in *There was a minority of votes against the decision.* 2 a small group that is different from others, as in *ethnic minorities.*

minstrel *noun* minstrels
a wandering musician in the Middle Ages.

mint *noun*
1 a green plant with sweet-smelling leaves used for flavouring. 2 a sweet flavoured with peppermint.
mint sauce, chopped mint-leaves in vinegar, used as a sauce on roast lamb.

mint *noun* mints
a place where coins are made.
in mint condition, as new.

minus *preposition*
reduced by subtracting; less, as in *Eight minus two equals six (8 − 2 = 6).*

minute *noun* minutes (*say* **min**-uht)
1 one sixtieth of an hour. 2 (*colloquial*) a short time, as in *I'll be ready in a minute!*
minutes, a summary of what has been said at a meeting.

minute

minute *adjective* (*say* muy-**nyoot**)
1 tiny, as in *a minute insect*. 2 very detailed, as in *a minute examination*.
minutely *adverb*

miracle *noun* **miracles**
a wonderful or magical happening that is unexpected.
miraculous *adjective*, **miraculously** *adverb*

mirage *noun* **mirages** (*say* muh-**rahzh**)
something that a person imagines he or she sees but which is not there at all, as in *The lake he thought he saw in the desert was a mirage.*

mirrnyong *noun* **mirrnyongs** (*say* **mern**-yong)
a mound of ashes, shells, etc. gathered in a place used by Aborigines for cooking.

Origin This word probably comes from a Victorian Aboriginal language.

mirror *noun* **mirrors**
a glass or metal device or surface that reflects things clearly.
mirror image, a reflection or copy in which the right and left sides of the original are reversed.

mirth *noun*
another word for laughter or cheerfulness.

misbehave *verb* **misbehaves, misbehaving, misbehaved**
to behave badly or naughtily.
misbehaviour *noun*

miscarriage *noun* **miscarriages**
the birth of a baby too early, so that it dies.

miscellaneous *adjective*
(*say* mis-uh-**lay**-nee-uhs)
being of different kinds, as in *a miscellaneous collection of toys.*
miscellany *noun*

mischief *noun*
naughty or troublesome behaviour.
mischievous *adjective*

miser *noun* **misers**
someone who stores money away and spends as little as he or she can.
miserly *adjective*

miserable *adjective*
unhappy; wretched, as in *He felt miserable. What miserable weather!*
miserably *adverb*

misery *noun* **miseries**
unhappiness; suffering.
to put out of its misery, to release a person or thing from suffering or suspense.

misfit *noun* **misfits**
someone who does not fit in well with other people or with his or her surroundings.

misfortune *noun* **misfortunes**
1 an unlucky event; an accident. 2 bad luck.

misguided *adjective* (*say* mis-**guy**-duhd)
mistaken in thought or action.

mishap *noun* **mishaps** (*say* **mis**-hap)
an unfortunate accident.

mislay *verb* **mislays, mislaying, mislaid**
to lose something for a short time.

mislead *verb* **misleads, misleading, misled**
to give someone a wrong idea or impression; to deceive, as in *I was misled into thinking he was reliable.*

misprint *noun* **misprints**
a mistake in printing.

misrepresent *verb* **misrepresents, misrepresenting, misrepresented**
to give a false account or idea of.
misrepresentation *noun*

Miss *noun* **Misses**
a word used before the name of a girl or unmarried woman when speaking or writing politely to or about her, as in *Dear Miss Jones.*

miss *verb* **misses, missing, missed**
1 to fail to hit, reach, catch, see, hear, or find something. 2 to be sad because someone or something is not with you, as in *I missed my mother when she was in hospital.* 3 to notice that something has gone, as in *I did not miss my gloves until I needed them next.*

miss *noun* **misses**
not hitting, reaching, or catching something, as in *Was that shot a hit or a miss?*

missile *noun* **missiles**
a weapon fired or thrown at a target.

missing *adjective*
1 lost, as in *a missing dog.* 2 not in the proper place, as in *The scissors are missing; where have you put them?*

mission *noun* **missions**
1 an important job that someone is sent to do or that someone feels he or she must do. 2 a place or building where missionaries work.

missionary *noun* **missionaries**
someone who goes to another country to spread a religion.

misspell *verb* **misspells, misspelling**, *past tense* and *past participle* **misspelt** or **misspelled**
to spell a word wrongly.

mist *noun* **mists**
1 damp cloudy air like a thin fog.
2 condensed water-vapour on a window, mirror, etc.

mistake *noun* **mistakes**
something wrong; an incorrect action or idea.
by mistake, by being careless, forgetful, etc.

mistake *verb* **mistakes, mistaking, mistook, mistaken**
to misunderstand; to choose or identify wrongly.

mister *noun*
1 Mr. 2 (*colloquial*) sir, as in *Can you tell me the time, mister?*

mistletoe *noun*
a plant of the northern hemisphere with green leaves and white berries in winter.

mistreat *verb* **mistreats, mistreating, mistreated**
to treat someone badly or unfairly.
mistreatment *noun*

mistress *noun* **mistresses**
1 a female teacher in charge of a particular subject or department at a school, as in *a sports mistress.* 2 a female head of a large household; a woman in authority. 3 the female owner of a pet. 4 a woman who has a sexual relationship with a man who is married to someone else.

mistrust *verb* **mistrusts, mistrusting, mistrusted**
not to trust someone or something.

misty *adjective* **mistier, mistiest**
1 full of mist. 2 not clear.
mistily *adverb*, **mistiness** *noun*

misunderstand *verb* **misunderstands, misunderstanding, misunderstood**
to get a wrong idea or impression of something, as in *You misunderstood what I said.*
misunderstanding *noun*

misuse *verb* **misuses, misusing, misused** (*say* mis-**yooz**)
to use something wrongly; to treat something badly, as in *You are misusing that word. Someone has been misusing that bicycle; its frame is cracked.*

misuse *noun* (*say* mis-**yoos**)
the wrong use of something, as in *The misuse of the computer caused great damage.*

mite *noun* **mites**
1 a tiny insect. 2 a small child.

mitre *noun* **mitres** (*say* **muy**-tuh)
1 the tall, tapering hat worn by a bishop.
2 a joint of two tapering pieces of wood, cloth, etc.

mitten *noun* **mittens**
a glove without separate parts for the fingers.

mix *verb* **mixes, mixing, mixed**
1 to stir or shake different things together to make one thing; to combine. 2 to get together with other people, as in *She mixes well.*
mix up, to confuse.
mixer *noun*

mixed *adjective*
for or containing various kinds of people or things, especially males and females, as in *a mixed school* or people of different races or religions, as in *a mixed community.*

mixture *noun* **mixtures**
something made of different things mixed together.

mix-up *noun* **mix-ups**
a confused situation, especially one that ruins a plan, as in *Owing to a mix-up in the bookings we did not get a room at the hotel.*

mm short for **millimetre** or **millimetres.**

moan *noun* **moans**
1 a long low sound, usually of suffering.
2 a grumble.

moan *verb* **moans, moaning, moaned**
1 to make a long low sound. 2 to grumble.

moat *noun* **moats**
a deep ditch around a castle, usually full of water.

mob *noun* **mobs**
1 a dangerous crowd of people. 2 an Aboriginal extended family or community.

mob *verb* **mobs, mobbing, mobbed**
to crowd around someone.

mobile *adjective*
1 able to be moved, as in *a mobile toilet.*
2 able to change easily, as in *mobile expressions on her face.*
mobile home, a large caravan usually permanently parked and used as a house.
mobile phone, a portable telephone for use in a car, etc.
mobility *noun*

mobile *noun* **mobiles**
something decorative made to be hung from a frame, ceiling, etc. so that it moves about in the air.

mobilise or **mobilize** *verb* **mobilises, mobilising, mobilised**
to assemble people or things ready for a particular purpose, especially for war.
mobilisation *noun*

a
b
c
d
e
f
g
h
i
j
k
l
m
n
o
p
q
r
s
t
u
v
w
x
y
z

moccasin

moccasin *noun* moccasins
(*say* **mok**-uh-suhn)
a soft leather shoe often worn as a slipper.

mock *verb* mocks, mocking, mocked
to make fun of someone or something.
mockery *noun*

mock *adjective*
not real; imitation, as in *mock cream*.

mock-up *noun* mock-ups
a model of something, as in *They made a mock-up of the rocket*.

mode *noun* modes
1 the way that something is done, as in *a new mode of transport*. 2 what is fashionable, as in *These jackets are the latest mode*.

model *noun* models
1 a small copy of an object, as in *He makes models of aircraft*. 2 a particular version or design of something, as in *We saw the new models at the motor show*. 3 someone who poses for an artist or photographer.
4 someone whose job is to display clothes by wearing them. 5 an excellent person or thing, as in *a model of neatness*.

model *verb* models, modelling, modelled
1 to make a small copy of something.
2 to make something by following a pattern, as in *The building is modelled on an Egyptian temple*. 3 to work as an artist's model or a fashion model.

model *adjective*
1 miniature, as in *a model railway*. 2 being a good example for people to follow, as in *She was a model pupil*.

modem *noun* modems
(*in Computing*) a device that allows computers to exchange information, using the same wires as the telephone system.

moderate *adjective* (*say* **mod**-uh-ruht)
that is not too little and not too much; medium.
moderately *adverb*, **moderation** *noun*

moderate *verb* moderates, moderating, moderated (*say* **mod**-uh-rayt)
to make something less strong or severe.

modern *adjective*
to do with the latest ideas, fashions, etc., as in *a modern house*.
modernity *noun*

modernise or **modernize** *verb* modernises, modernising, modernised
to make something modern; to change something to suit modern tastes.
modernisation *noun*

modest *adjective*
1 being humble about yourself.
2 moderate, as in *Their needs were modest*.
modestly *adverb*, **modesty** *noun*

modify *verb* modifies, modifying, modified
to change something slightly.
modification *noun*

module *noun* modules (*say* **mod**-yool)
1 an independent part of a spacecraft, building, etc. 2 a part of a course of learning, as in *This term I'm doing a Maths module*. 3 a unit used in measuring.

moist *adjective* moister, moistest
damp.
moisture *noun*

moisten *verb* moistens, moistening, moistened
(*say* **moi**-suhn)
to make something moist; to become moist.

molar *noun* molars (*say* **moh**-luh)
one of the wide teeth at the back of your mouth.

mole *noun* moles
1 a small, dark grey, furry animal that digs holes under the ground. 2 a small dark spot on someone's skin.

molecule *noun* molecules
(*say* **mol**-uh-kyool)
1 a very small particle of matter. 2 (*in Science*) the smallest part into which you can divide a substance without changing its chemical nature; a group of atoms.
molecular *adjective*

molehill *noun* molehills
a small pile of earth thrown up by a mole.
make a mountain out of a molehill, to give something too much importance.

molest *verb* molests, molesting, molested
1 to annoy or pester someone in an unfriendly or violent way. 2 to touch someone's sexual parts in a way which upsets or hurts him or her, which is against the law.

mollusc *noun* molluscs
an animal with a soft body and usually a hard shell, as in *Snails, slugs, and oysters are molluscs*.

molten *adjective*
melted.

moment *noun* moments
1 a very short period of time, as in *Wait a moment*. 2 a particular time, as in *He arrived at the last moment*. 3 (*in Science*) a turning effect produced by a force acting at a distance on an object.
at the moment, now.

momentary *adjective* (*say* **moh**-muhn-tuh-ree *or* **moh**-muhn-tree)
lasting for only a moment.
momentarily *adverb*

momentous *adjective* (*say* muh-**ment**-uhs)
very important.

momentum *noun* (*say* muh-**ment**-uhm)
movement; the amount or force of movement.

monarch *noun* **monarchs**
a king, queen, emperor, or empress.
monarchist, one who believes in government where the monarch is the head of state.
monarchy *noun*

monastery *noun* **monasteries**
(*say* **mon**-uhs-tuhr-ree *or* **mon**-uhs-tree)
a building where monks live and work.
monastic *adjective*

Monday *noun* **Mondays**
the second day of the week.

Mondayitis *noun*
(*colloquial*) an imaginary disease involving a reluctance to go to work after the weekend.

money *noun*
coins and notes used by people to buy things.
in the money (*colloquial*) having or winning a lot of money.

mongoose *noun* **mongooses**
a small animal rather like a large weasel, that can kill snakes.

mongrel *noun* **mongrels** (*say* **mung**-gruhl)
a dog of mixed breeds.

monitor *noun* **monitors**
1 a pupil who is given a special job to do at school. **2** a device used for checking how something is working. **3** (*in Computing*) a screen on which a computer displays information. **4** a large lizard of Australia, Asia and Africa.

monk *noun* **monks**
a member of a religious community of men.

monkey *noun* **monkeys**
1 an animal rather like a human, with long arms and a tail. **2** a mischievous person, especially a child.

monolingual *adjective*
speaking only one language; dealing with only one language, as in *Australia is not a monolingual community. This is a monolingual dictionary.*

monolith *noun* **monoliths**
a single block of stone, especially one shaped like a pillar, as in *The Twelve Apostles off the Victorian coast are monoliths.*

monologue *noun* **monologues**
(*say* **mon**-uh-log)
a long speech by one person or performer.

monopoly *noun* **monopolies**
doing all the business, trade, etc. in one thing; controlling the supply of something, as in *The government has a monopoly in supplying electricity.*
monopolise *verb*

monorail *noun* **monorails**
a railway that uses only one rail.

monotonous *adjective*
(*say* muh-**not**-uhn-uhs)
boring because it does not change, as in *monotonous work.*
monotonously *adverb,* **monotony** *noun*

monotreme *noun* **monotremes**
(*say* **mon**-uh-treem)
an egg-laying mammal, as in *The only monotremes in Australia are the platypus and echidna.*

monsoon *noun* **monsoons**
a strong wind in and around the Indian Ocean, bringing heavy rain in summer.
monsoon season, the rainy season accompanying the summer monsoon.

monster *noun* **monsters**
a large, frightening creature.

monster *adjective*
huge.

monstrous *adjective*
1 like a monster; huge. **2** very shocking or cruel, as in *a monstrous crime.*
monstrosity *noun*

month *noun* **months**
one of the twelve parts into which a year is divided.

monthly *adjective*
happening every month; done every month, as in *a monthly event.*

monument *noun* **monuments**
a statue, building, column, etc. put up as a memorial of some person or event.

monumental *adjective*
great; huge, as in *a monumental achievement.*

moo *verb* **moos, mooing, mooed**
to make the sound of a cow.

mood *noun* **moods**
the way someone feels, as in *She's in a good mood.*

a
b
c
d
e
f
g
h
i
j
k
l
m
n
o
p
q
r
s
t
u
v
w
x
y
z

moody

moody *adjective* **moodier, moodiest**
1 gloomy. 2 likely to become bad-tempered suddenly.
moodily *adverb*, **moodiness** *noun*

moon *noun* **moons**
the object which orbits the earth and shines in the sky at night; a similar object which orbits another planet.
moonless *adjective*, **moonlight** *noun*, **moonlit** *adjective*

moor *noun* **moors**
open, uncultivated, high land with scrubby bushes but no trees, found in Britain, as in *the Yorkshire moors*.

moor *verb* **moors, mooring, moored**
to secure a boat, etc. to a fixed object, as in *Yachts were moored to the pier*.
moorings *plural noun*

moorhen *noun* **moorhens**
a small water-bird, as in *The Tasmanian native hen and the Mallee fowl are moorhens*.

mop *noun* **mops**
a piece of soft material on the end of a stick, used for cleaning floors or dishes.

mop *verb* **mops, mopping, mopped**
to clean something with a mop.
mop up, to clear away the remains of something.

mope *verb* **mopes, moping, moped**
to be sad.

mopoke *noun* **mopokes**
a type of owl found in Australia and New Zealand.

moraine *noun* **moraines**
a mass of stones, earth, etc. carried down by a glacier.
end moraine, a terminal moraine.
lateral moraine, a moraine left at the sides of a glacier.
terminal moraine, a moraine left at the lower end of a glacier.

moral *adjective*
1 connected with right and wrong, as in *Whether it is wrong to hunt whales is a moral question*. 2 being or doing good, as in *Clergy are expected to lead moral lives*.
morality *noun*, **morally** *adverb*

moral *noun* **morals**
a lesson taught by a story or event.
morals, standards of behaviour; a capacity for being or doing good.

morale *noun* (*say* muh-**rahl**)
confidence or courage, as in *The team's morale was boosted by several victories*.

more *adjective*
larger in number or amount.

more *noun*
a larger number or amount, as in *I want more*.

more *adverb*
1 again, as in *I'll tell you once more*. 2 to a greater extent, as in *You must work more*.
more or less, almost; approximately, as in *I've more or less finished the work. The repairs cost $100 more or less*.

moreover *adverb*
also; in addition.

morgue *noun* **morgues** (*say* mawg)
a mortuary.

morning *noun* **mornings**
the part of the day before noon or before lunchtime.

moron *noun* **morons**
(*colloquial*) a stupid person.
moronic *adjective*

morphine *noun* (*say* **maw**-feen)
a drug made from opium, used to relieve pain.

Morse code *noun*
a code using dots and dashes to represent letters and numbers, as in *Radio operators often use Morse code to send messages*.

morsel *noun* **morsels**
a small piece of food.

mortal *adjective*
1 that which will die, as in *All humans are mortal*. 2 that which causes death, as in *a mortal wound*. 3 very serious, extreme, as in *mortal enemy*.
mortally *adverb*

mortality *noun*
the number of people who die over a particular period of time, as in *a low rate of infant mortality*.

mortar *noun*
1 a mixture of sand, cement, and water used in building to stick bricks together. 2 a container in which substances are pounded with a pestle.

mortgage *noun* **mortgages** (*say* **maw**-gij)
an agreement to borrow money to buy a house.

mortuary *noun* **mortuaries**
a place where dead bodies are kept before they are buried or cremated; a morgue.

mosaic *noun* **mosaics** (*say* moh-**zay**-ik)
a picture or design made from small coloured pieces of glass, stone, paper, etc.

mosque *noun* **mosques** (*say* mosk)
a building where Muslims worship.

mosquito *noun* **mosquitoes**
(*say* muhs-**kee**-toh)
an insect that sucks blood.
mossie, (*colloquial*) short for mosquito.

moss *noun* **mosses**
a non-flowering plant that grows in damp places.
mossy *adjective*

most *adjective*
largest in number or amount.

most *noun*
the largest number or amount.

most *adverb*
1 more than any other, as in *I liked that teacher most.* **2** very; extremely, as in *It was most amusing.*

mostly *adverb*
mainly.

motel *noun* **motels** (*say* moh-**tel**)
a roadside hotel which provides accommodation in self-contained units for motorists and parking for their cars.

moth *noun* **moths**
an insect rather like a butterfly that usually flies around at night and is attracted to light.

mother *noun* **mothers**
a female parent.
Mother's Day, the second Sunday in May, when people often give presents to their mothers.
motherhood *noun*, **motherless** *adjective*

mother-in-law *noun* **mothers-in-law**
the mother of your husband or wife.

motherly *adjective*
kind or tender like a mother.

motion *noun* **motions**
movement.
go through the motions, to do or say something without sincere enthusiasm, or in a way that shows you are only doing it because you have to.
motionless *adjective*

motivate *verb* **motivates, motivating, motivated**
to make someone keen to achieve something, as in *She is good at motivating her team.*

motive *noun* **motives**
what makes a person do something.

motor *noun* **motors**
a machine that provides power.

motor bike *noun* **motor bikes**
(*colloquial*) a motor cycle.

motor boat *noun* **motor boats**
a boat driven by a motor.

motor cycle *noun* **motor cycles**
a motor vehicle with two wheels.
motor-cyclist *noun*

motorist *noun* **motorists**
someone who drives a motor car, especially for pleasure.

mottled *adjective*
marked with spots or patches of colour.

motto *noun* **mottoes**
a short saying used as a guide for behaviour, as in *His motto was 'Do your best'.*

mould *noun* **moulds**
1 a container for making things like jelly or plaster set in the shape that is wanted. **2** a furry growth that appears on some moist surfaces, especially on something decaying, as in *There is mould on this cheese.*
mouldy *adjective*

mould *verb* **moulds, moulding, moulded**
to make something have a particular shape or character.

moult *verb* **moults, moulting, moulted**
(*say* mohlt)
to lose feathers or hair, as in *Our cat is moulting.*

mound *noun* **mounds**
a pile of earth, stones, etc.; a small hill.

mount *verb* **mounts, mounting, mounted**
1 to get on to a horse or bicycle so that you can ride it. **2** to rise, as in *The cost of insurance is mounting.* **3** to put something firmly in place for use or display, as in *Mount your photos in an album.*

mount *noun* **mounts**
1 something in or on which an object is mounted. **2** an animal on which you are riding.

mount *noun*
a mountain, as in *Mount Kosciuszko.*

mountain *noun* **mountains**
a very high hill.
mountainous *adjective*

mountain bike *noun* **mountain bikes**
a bicycle with a strong frame, wide tyres, and many gears, designed for use on rough ground.

mountaineer *noun* **mountaineers**
someone who climbs mountains.
mountaineering *noun*

mourn

mourn *verb* **mourns, mourning, mourned**
to be sad, especially because someone has died.
mourner *noun*

mournful *adjective*
sad.
mournfully *adverb*

mouse *noun* **mice**
1 a small animal with a long tail and a pointed nose. 2 (*in Computing*) a device that you move around on your desk, etc. to control the movements of a computer's cursor and to choose what you want the computer to do.
mousetrap *noun*, **mousy** *adjective*

moussaka *noun* (*say* muu-**sah**-kuh)
a Greek dish of mincemeat, eggplant, etc. with a cheese sauce.

mousse *noun* **mousses** (*say* moos)
1 a sweet flavoured dessert made with beaten egg whites and cream and served cold. 2 a frothy, creamy substance used especially for holding hair in a particular style.

moustache *noun* **moustaches**
(*say* muh-**stahsh**)
hair growing above a man's upper lip.

mouth *noun* **mouths**
1 the part of the face that opens for eating and speaking. 2 the place where a river enters the sea. 3 an opening or outlet.
mouth-to-mouth resuscitation, the process of breathing into another person's lungs through the mouth to revive him or her.
mouthful *noun*

mouth-organ *noun* **mouth-organs**
a musical instrument played by blowing and sucking.

mouthpiece *noun* **mouthpieces**
the part of a musical instrument or other device that you put to your mouth.

movable *adjective*
able to be moved.

move *verb* **moves, moving, moved**
1 to take or go from one place to another. 2 to affect someone's emotions, as in *Their story moved us deeply.*
moving picture, a series of photographs shown quickly one after the other to give the appearance of movement.

move *noun* **moves**
1 a movement. 2 someone's turn in a game.
get a move on, (*colloquial*) to hurry up.
on the move, moving; making progress, as in *Large numbers of people are on the move.*

movement *noun* **movements**
1 the action of moving or being moved. 2 a group of people working for a particular cause. 3 one of the main parts of a piece of music, as in *a symphony in four movements.*

movie *noun* **movies**
a film for viewing in a cinema or on video.

moving *adjective*
causing someone to feel strong emotion, especially sadness or pity.

mow *verb* **mows, mowing, mowed, mown**
to cut grass.
mow down, to knock down or kill people or animals in large numbers.
mower *noun*

MP **MPs** short for **Member of Parliament.**

Mr *noun* **Messrs** (*say* **mis**-tuh)
a word used before the name of a man when speaking or writing politely to or about him.

Mrs *noun* **Mrs** or **Mesdames** (*say* **mis**-uhz)
a word used before the name of a married woman when speaking or writing politely to or about her.

Ms *noun* (*say* miz)
a word used before the name of a woman when speaking or writing to or about her.

much *adjective*
existing in a large amount, as in *much work.*

much *noun*
a large amount of something.

much *adverb*
greatly; considerably, as in *much to my surprise.*

muck *noun*
1 dirt; filth. 2 a mess, as in *You have made a muck of it.*
mucky *adjective*

muck *verb* **mucks, mucking, mucked**
muck about or **muck around**, (*colloquial*) to mess about.
muck up, (*colloquial*) to mess up.

mucus *noun* (*say* **myoo**-kuhs)
the thick, slimy substance which develops in your nose and throat when you have a heavy cold.

mud *noun*
wet, soft earth.
muddy *adjective*

mud crab *noun* **mud crabs**
a very large swimming crab found along the muddy shores of estuaries in northern Australia and highly rated as food.

muddle *verb* muddles, muddling, muddled
1 to mix things up.   2 to confuse someone.
muddler *noun*

muddle *noun* muddles
a confusion or mess.

mudguard *noun* mudguards
a device to stop mud and water being
thrown up by the wheels of a vehicle.

muesli *noun* (*say* **myooz**-lee *or* **mooz**-lee)
a breakfast food made of cereals, nuts,
dried fruit, etc.

muffin *noun* muffins
1 a light, flat, round spongy cake, eaten
toasted and buttered.   2 a small cake
containing fruit, nuts, etc.

muffle *verb* muffles, muffling, muffled
1 to cover or wrap something up to protect
it or keep it warm.   2 to deaden the sound
of something, as in *a muffled scream*.

mug *noun* mugs
1 a large cup, usually used without a
saucer.   2 (*colloquial*) a fool; someone who
is easily cheated.

mug *verb* mugs, mugging, mugged
to attack and rob someone in the street.
mugger *noun*

muggy *adjective* muggier, muggiest
unpleasantly warm and damp, as in *muggy
weather*.

Mulba *noun*
an Aborigine in the Pilbara region of
Western Australia.

Origin This word comes from the
Aboriginal language Panygima: **marlba**.
See the Aboriginal Languages map at the
back of this dictionary.

mule *noun* mules
an animal that is the offspring of a donkey
and a horse.

mulga *noun*
a type of wattle with a distinctive brown
and yellowish timber, found in dry inland
Australia.
mulga country, country where the mulga
vegetation grows.

mulgara *noun*
a small, flesh-eating marsupial that lives in
burrows in the sandy regions of drier
Australia.

Origin This word comes from
Wangganguru, an Aboriginal language of
South Australia. See the Aboriginal
Languages map at the back of this
dictionary.

multicultural *adjective*
to do with several cultural or ethnic groups
within a society, as in *Australia is a
multicultural society*.

multinational *noun* multinationals
an organisation which operates in several
countries.

multiple *adjective*
having or involving many parts or
elements.
multiple-choice test, a test in which you are
given several possible answers and have to
choose the right one.

multiple *noun* multiples
a number that can be divided exactly by
another number, as in *30 and 50 are
multiples of 10*.

multiply *verb* multiplies, multiplying, multiplied
1 to add a number to itself a given number
of times, as in *Five multiplied by four equals
twenty* $(5 \times 4 = 20)$.   2 to increase quickly
in number or amount, as in *The rabbits were
multiplying*.
multiplication *noun*

multiracial *adjective* (*say* mul-tee-**ray**-shuhl)
consisting of people of many different
races, as in *a multiracial society*.

multitude *noun* multitudes
a very large number of people or things.
multitudinous *adjective*

mum *noun* mums
(*colloquial*) mother.

mum *adjective*
silent.
mum's the word, say nothing.

mumble *verb* mumbles, mumbling, mumbled
to speak so that you are not easy to hear.
mumbler *noun*

mummy *noun* mummies
1 a dead body preserved for burial as was
the custom in ancient Egypt.   2 (*colloquial*)
mother.
mummify *verb*

mumps *noun*
an infectious disease that makes your neck
swell up.

munch *verb* munches, munching, munched
to chew something noisily; to make a loud
chewing sound.
munchies, (*colloquial*) snacks between
meals.

mundane *adjective*
dull, boring, as in *a mundane job*.

municipal

municipal *adjective* (*say* myoo-**nis**-uh-puhl or myoo-nuh-**sip**-uhl)
to do with a town or city, as in *a municipal library*.

municipality *noun* **municipalities**
a town or district having its own local government.
municipal *adjective*

munjon or **munjong** *noun* **munjons**
1 an Aborigine who has had little contact with white society. **2** an Aborigine brought up in white society and unfamiliar with the traditional way of life.

Origin This word comes from the Aboriginal language Yindjibarndi: **manyjangu** = stranger. See the Aboriginal Languages map at the back of this dictionary.

mural *noun* **murals**
a picture painted on a wall.

murder *verb* **murders, murdering, murdered**
to kill someone deliberately.
murderer *noun*, **murderess** *noun*

murder *noun* **murders**
1 the deliberate killing of someone.
2 (*colloquial*) something very difficult or unpleasant, as in *The exam was murder*.
murderous *adjective*

murky *adjective* **murkier, murkiest**
dark and gloomy.

murmur *noun* **murmurs**
1 a low continuous sound, as in *the murmur of the sea*. **2** the sound of softly spoken words, as in *A murmur of conversation was coming from next door*.

murmur *verb* **murmurs, murmuring, murmured**
1 to make a low continuous sound. **2** to speak softly; to say something softly.

Murri *noun*
an Aborigine, especially one from Queensland.

Origin This word comes from the Aboriginal language Kamilaroi: **mari** = Aboriginal person. See the Aboriginal Languages map at the back of this dictionary.

muscle *noun* **muscles**
one of the parts inside the body that cause movement.
muscular *adjective*

muscle *verb* **muscles, muscling, muscled**
muscle in on something, to insist on being involved in an activity in which you are not welcome, as in *He kept trying to muscle in on our conversation*.

museum *noun* **museums**
a place where interesting objects, especially old things, are displayed for people to see.

mushroom *noun* **mushrooms**
a fast-growing, edible fungus with a dome-shaped top.
mushie, (*colloquial*) mushroom.

mushroom *verb* **mushrooms, mushrooming, mushroomed**
to grow or appear suddenly like mushrooms, as in *Blocks of flats mushroomed in the city*.

music *noun*
1 pleasant or interesting sounds made by instruments or by the voice. **2** printed or written instructions for making this kind of sound.

musical *adjective*
1 to do with music, as in *musical instruments*. **2** good at music; interested in music, as in *Are you musical?*
musically *adverb*

musical *noun* **musicals**
a play or film containing a lot of music.

musician *noun* **musicians**
someone who plays a musical instrument.

musket *noun* **muskets**
an old type of rifle.
musketeer *noun*

Muslim or **Moslem** *noun* **Muslims**
(*say* **muuz**-lim)
someone who follows the religious teachings of Muhammad.

muslin *noun*
thin, fine cotton cloth.

mussel *noun* **mussels**
a type of edible shellfish found in two black shells joined together.

must *verb*
1 to have to; to be forced or obliged to do something, as in *I must go home soon*. **2** to be sure to; to be definitely, as in *You must be joking!*

must *noun* **musts**
(*colloquial*) a thing that should not be missed, as in *Cleaning your teeth is a must*.

mustard *noun*
a yellow paste or powder used to give food a hot taste.
keen as mustard, extremely keen.

muster *verb* **musters, mustering, mustered**
to assemble or gather together.

musty *adjective* **mustier, mustiest**
smelling or tasting mouldy or stale.
mustiness *noun*

mutation *noun* **mutations**
a change in the form or shape of something.

mute *adjective*
1 unable to speak, as in *She had been mute from birth.* **2** silent, as in *They stood and stared in mute astonishment.*
muted *adjective*, **mutely** *adverb*

mute *noun* **mutes**
1 a person who cannot speak. **2** a device fitted to a musical instrument to make it quieter.

mutilate *verb* **mutilates, mutilating, mutilated**
to damage something by breaking or cutting off part of it.
mutilation *noun*

mutineer *noun* **mutineers**
(*say* myoo-tuh-**neer**)
someone who takes part in a mutiny.

mutiny *noun* **mutinies** (*say* **myoo**-tuh-nee)
a rebellion by sailors or soldiers against their officers, as in *mutiny on the Bounty.*
mutinous *adjective*, **mutinously** *adverb*

mutiny *verb* **mutinies, mutinying, mutinied**
(*say* **myoo**-tuh-nee)
to take part in a mutiny.

mutter *verb* **mutters, muttering, muttered**
to murmur or grumble.

mutton *noun*
meat from a sheep.

mutton-bird *noun* **mutton-birds**
the brownish-black sea bird breeding in south-eastern Australia, especially on the Bass Strait islands.
mutton-bird eater, (*colloquial*) a non-Aboriginal Tasmanian.

mutual *adjective* (*say* **myoo**-tyoo-uhl *or* **myoo**-choo-uhl)
exchanged equally; shared, as in *mutual help.*
mutually *adverb*

muzzle *noun* **muzzles**
1 an animal's nose and mouth. **2** a cover put over an animal's nose and mouth so that it cannot bite. **3** the open end of a gun.

my *adjective*
to do with me; belonging to me.

myrtle *noun* **myrtles** (*say* **mer**-tuhl)
the tall tree of Victoria and Tasmania with small, shiny, dark green leaves and valuable timber.

myself *pronoun*
me and nobody else, as in *I'm ashamed of myself.*
by myself, on my own; alone, as in *I cooked the dinner all by myself. I walked along the beach by myself.*

mystery *noun* **mysteries**
something strange or puzzling.
mysterious *adjective*, **mysteriously** *adverb*

mystify *verb* **mystifies, mystifying, mystified**
to puzzle someone very much.
mystification *noun*

myth *noun* **myths**
1 a legend. **2** an untrue story or belief, as in *the myth that progress will lead to a perfect world.*
mythological *adjective*, **mythology** *noun*

myxomatosis *noun*
(*say* mik-suh-muh-**toh**-suhs)
a very infectious and usually fatal disease which affects rabbits.

Nn

nab *verb* nabs, nabbing, nabbed
(*colloquial*) to catch; to grab.

nag *verb* nags, nagging, nagged
to keep on criticising or finding fault, as in
The boy was nagged about his untidy room.

nag *noun* nags
(*colloquial*) a horse.

nail *noun* nails
1 the hard covering on the end of a finger
or toe. **2** a small, sharp piece of metal
used to fix pieces of wood together.

naïve *adjective* (*say* nuy-**eev**)
1 innocent; not experienced, as in *a naïve
young child.* **2** too ready to believe what
you are told; showing a lack of experience,
as in *He was naïve enough to believe the silly
story.*
naïvely *adverb*, **naïvety** *noun*

naked *adjective* (*say* **nay**-kuhd)
not wearing clothes; without any covering,
as in *The earth had blown away, leaving naked
rock.*
the naked eye, your eye when it is not
helped by a telescope, microscope, etc.
nakedly *adverb*, **nakedness** *noun*

name *noun* names
what you call a person or thing.
nameless *adjective*

name *verb* names, naming, named
1 to give someone or something a name.
2 to say what something or someone is
called, as in *Can you name these plants?*

namely *adverb*
that is to say, as in *Only one boy was absent,
namely Harry Smith.*

nanny *noun* nannies
1 a woman whose job is to look after small
children. **2** (*colloquial*) a grandmother.

nanny-goat *noun* nanny-goats
a female goat.

nap *noun* naps
a short sleep.

napkin *noun* napkins
1 a serviette. **2** a nappy.

nappy *noun* nappies
a piece of absorbent material put around a
baby's bottom, as in *The baby's dirty nappy
was changed.*

narcotic *noun* narcotics (*say* nah-**kot**-ik)
a drug that makes you sleepy or
unconscious.

nardoo *noun*
a clover-like fern growing on or near water
whose seeds are ground into flour and
used as food by Aborigines.

Origin This word comes from many
Aboriginal languages including
Yandruwandha. See the Aboriginal
Languages map at the back of this
dictionary.

nardoo cake, a cake made with nardoo
flour and water and baked.

narrate *verb* narrates, narrating, narrated
to tell a story; to give an account of
something, as in *She narrated her adventures
of her travels in the Antarctic.*
narration *noun*, **narrator** *noun*

narrative *noun* narratives
an oral, written or visual text that tells a
story.

narrow *adjective* narrower, narrowest
1 not wide. **2** with only a small margin
of safety, as in *a narrow escape.*
narrowly *adverb*

narrow-minded *adjective*
not liking or understanding other people's ideas.

nashi *noun*
a type of apple-like Japanese pear.

nasturtium *noun* **nasturtiums**
(*say* nuh-**ster**-shuhm)
an edible garden flower with round leaves and bright orange, yellow, or red flowers.

nasty *adjective* **nastier, nastiest**
not pleasant; unkind.
nastily *adverb*, **nastiness** *noun*

nation *noun* **nations**
1 a large number of people who live in the same part of the world and have the same language, customs, etc. 2 a country and the people who live there.

national *adjective*
1 to do with a whole country, as in *the national news*. 2 typical of a particular country, as in *the national dress of Greece*.
nationally *adverb*

nationalise or **nationalize** *verb*
nationalises, nationalising, nationalised
to put something under government control.
nationalisation *noun*

nationalism *noun*
1 a patriotic feeling or love of your own country. 2 a desire for your country to be independent and free.

nationalist *noun* **nationalists**
someone who loves and supports his or her country very much; someone who wants his or her nation to be independent.

nationality *noun* **nationalities**
the nation someone belongs to, as in *What is his nationality?*

nationwide *adjective* and *adverb*
extending over the whole of a country, as in *a nationwide fall in house prices. The fashion spread nationwide.*

native *noun* **natives**
someone born in a particular place, as in *Julia is a native of New Zealand.*

native *adjective*
1 natural; belonging to someone from birth, as in *native ability*. 2 to do with the country where you were born, as in *my native language*.

native title *noun*
a title to land by the indigenous people based on their traditions and customs.

nativity *noun* **nativities** (*say* nuh-**tiv**-uh-tee)
someone's birth.
the Nativity, the birth of Jesus.

natural *adjective*
1 made or done by nature, not by people or machines. 2 normal; not surprising. 3 of a musical note that is not sharp or flat.
natural gas, gas that is found under the ground or the sea, not made from coal.
natural history, the study of plants and animals.
naturally *adverb*

natural *noun* **naturals**
1 a natural note in music; a sign (♮) that shows a note is natural. 2 someone who is naturally good at something, as in *She's a natural at juggling.*

naturalist *noun* **naturalists**
someone who studies plants and animals.

naturalise or **naturalize** *verb* **naturalises, naturalising, naturalised**
1 to make someone a full citizen of a country. 2 to make something fit into a place where it is not normally found.
naturalisation *noun*

nature *noun* **natures**
1 everything in the universe that was not made by people. 2 the qualities or characteristics of a person or thing, as in *She has a loving nature.* 3 a kind or sort of thing, as in *He likes things of that nature.*
nature trail, a path in the bush where you can walk and see things connected with natural history.
nature strip, (in some parts of Australia, especially Victoria) the publicly-owned land, usually lawn, between the front boundary of a property and the street; a verge.

naughty *adjective* **naughtier, naughtiest**
not behaving as you should; disobedient or rude.
naughtily *adverb*, **naughtiness** *noun*

nausea *noun* (*say* **naw**-zee-uh *or* naw-see-uh)
a feeling that you want to vomit.

nautical *adjective*
to do with ships or sailors.

naval *adjective*
to do with the navy.

nave *noun* **naves**
the main central part of a church.

navel *noun* **navels**
the small round hollow in the centre of your stomach where the umbilical cord was detached.
navel orange, a type of orange that has a hollow at the top similar to a navel.

navigate

navigate *verb* navigates, navigating, navigated
1 to steer a ship on the sea, up a river, etc. 2 to make sure that an aircraft or vehicle is going in the right direction. **navigable** *adjective*, **navigation** *noun*, **navigator** *noun*

navy *noun* navies
1 a fleet of ships and the people trained to use them. 2 the dark blue colour of naval uniforms; navy blue.

NB short for take note.
[from the Latin *nota bene* = note well]

near *adverb* and *adjective* nearer, nearest
not far away, as in *The end is near. The learner driver had a near miss.*
nearness *noun*

near *preposition*
not far away from something, as in *She lives near the town.*

near *verb* nears, nearing, neared
to come close to something, as in *They were nearing the harbour.*

nearby *adjective* and *adverb*
at a place not far away, as in *a nearby town. They live nearby.*

nearly *adverb*
1 almost, as in *It was nearly midnight.* 2 closely, as in *nearly related.*
not nearly, far from; not at all, as in *There is not nearly enough food.*

neat *adjective* neater, neatest
1 tidy; simple and pleasant to look at. 2 cleverly done, as in *a neat piece of work.*
neatly *adverb*, **neatness** *noun*

necessary *adjective*
1 needed very much; essential. 2 unavoidable.
necessarily *adverb*, **necessity** *noun*

necessitate *verb* necessitates, necessitating, necessitated
to make necessary, as in *Her dreadful injuries necessitated surgery.*

neck *noun* necks
1 the part of your body that joins your head to your shoulders. 2 a narrow part of something, especially of a bottle.
stick your neck out, to say or do something that you know could get you into trouble, as in *He stuck his neck out and complained about his boss.*

necklace *noun* necklaces
an ornament worn around your neck.

nectar *noun*
a sweet liquid collected by bees from flowers.

nectarine *noun* nectarines
a smooth-skinned variety of peach.

need *verb* needs, needing, needed
1 to be without something that you should have. 2 to have to do something, as in *I needed to get a haircut.*

need *noun* needs
1 something that you need. 2 a situation in which something is necessary, as in *There is no need to cry.*
in need, needing money, help, comfort, etc.
needless *adjective*, **needlessly** *adverb*

needle *noun* needles
1 a very thin, pointed piece of metal used for sewing. 2 something long, thin, and sharp, as in *a knitting-needle.* 3 the pointer of a meter or compass.

needle *verb* needles, needling, needled
(*colloquial*) to annoy, irritate, as in *They needled him about his stutter.*

needy *adjective* needier, neediest
very poor.

negative *adjective*
1 saying 'no', as in *a negative answer.* 2 not definite or helpful, as in *gloomy, negative thoughts.* 3 less than nought, as in *a negative number.* 4 to do with the kind of electric charge carried by electrons.
negatively *adverb*

negative *noun* negatives
1 something that means 'no'. 2 a photograph or film from which prints are made.

neglect *verb* neglects, neglecting, neglected
not to look after or attend to something; to fail to do something, as in *He neglected his homework.*
neglectful *adjective*

negligent *adjective*
not taking proper care or paying enough attention, as in *The security staff had been negligent and had not locked all the doors.*
negligence *noun*

> **Usage** Do not confuse **negligent** with **negligible**, which is the next word in this dictionary.

negligible *adjective* (*say* neg-luh-juh-buhl)
not big enough or important enough to bother about, as in *The damage to my bike was negligible.*

negotiate *verb* negotiates, negotiating, negotiated (*say* nuh-**goh**-shee-ayt)
1 to try to reach agreement about something by discussion.

neutron

2 to get over or through an obstacle or difficulty.
negotiation *noun,* **negotiator** *noun*
negotiable *adjective*

neigh *verb* **neighs, neighing, neighed**
to make a high-pitched cry like a horse.

neighbour or **neighbor** *noun* **neighbours**
someone who lives next door or near to you.
neighbouring *adjective,* **neighbourly** *adjective*

neighbourhood or **neighborhood** *noun*
neighbourhoods
the surrounding district.
neighbourhood watch, a community-based program to help prevent crime.

neither *adjective* and *pronoun* (*say* **nuy**-*th*uh or **nee**-*th*uh)
not either, as in *Neither of them likes cabbage.*

neither *conjunction*
neither ... nor, not one thing and not the other, as in *I neither know nor care.*

neon *noun* (*say* **nee**-on)
a gas that glows when electricity passes through it, as in *Neon lights use neon in a glass tube.*

nephew *noun* **nephews**
the son of a brother or sister.

nerd *noun* **nerds**
(*colloquial*) a foolish, weak, or uninteresting person.

nerve *noun* **nerves**
1 one of the fibres inside your body that carry messages to and from your brain, so that your body can feel and move.
2 courage; calmness in a dangerous situation, as in *Don't lose your nerve.*
3 (*colloquial*) impudence, as in *He had the nerve to ask for more.*
get on someone's nerves, to annoy him or her.
nerves, nervousness, as in *I was suffering from nerves before my exam.*

nerve-racking *adjective*
causing anxiety, as in *The teenager spent a nerve-racking time awaiting exam results.*

nervous *adjective*
1 easily upset or agitated; timid. **2** to do with the nerves, as in *the nervous system.*
nervous breakdown, a kind of mental illness in which someone feels very worried and sad, and unable to face life.
nervously *adverb,* **nervousness** *noun*

nest *noun* **nests**
1 the place where a bird lays its eggs. **2** a warm place where some small animals keep their babies.

nest *verb* **nests, nesting, nested**
to make or have a nest, as in *The magpies were nesting in the gums.*

nestle *verb* **nestles, nestling, nestled**
to curl up comfortably.

net *noun* **nets**
1 something made of pieces of thread, cord, wire, etc. joined together in a criss-cross pattern with holes between.
2 material of this kind. **3** (*in Mathematics*) a pattern drawn on paper, etc. that can be cut out and folded to make a three-dimensional object.

net or **nett** *adjective*
remaining after all necessary deductions have been made, as in *After tax was deducted, his net pay was $350 a week.*

netball *noun*
a game similar to basketball played by two teams of seven players.

nettle *noun* **nettles**
a wild plant with leaves that sting.

network *noun* **networks**
1 a criss-cross arrangement. **2** a system with many connections or parts, as in *a television network.*

neurone *noun* **neurones**
(*in Science*) one of the cells making up the fibres that carry messages to and from your brain.

neurotic *adjective* (*say* nyoo-**rot**-ik)
being extremely sensitive or obsessive about something, as in *He showed neurotic behaviour in checking locks unnecessarily.*

neuter *adjective* (*say* **nyoo**-tuh)
(*in grammar*) not masculine or feminine.

neuter *verb* **neuters, neutering, neutered**
(*say* **nyoo**-tuh)
to operate on an animal so that it cannot have offspring, as in *We had our tom cat neutered.*

neutral *adjective* (*say* **nyoo**-truhl)
1 not supporting either side in a war or quarrel. **2** not distinct or distinctive, as in *neutral colours.* **3** having gears that are not connected to the driving parts of an engine.
neutrality *noun,* **neutrally** *adverb*

neutralise or **neutralize** *verb* **neutralises, neutralising, neutralised**
to take away the effect of something, as in *An alkaline substance will neutralise an acid.*

neutron *noun* **neutrons**
a particle of matter with no electric charge.
neutron bomb, a nuclear bomb that kills people but does little damage to buildings.

never *adverb*
at no time; not ever; not at all.

never-never *noun*
1 the far interior of Australia; the remote outback. 2 (*colloquial*) hire purchase.

nevertheless *conjunction* and *adverb*
in spite of this; although that is a fact, as in *He was sick, nevertheless he played in the match. She won but was nevertheless sad.*

new *adjective* **newer, newest**
1 not old; just bought, made, received, etc. 2 different; unfamiliar.
new moon, the moon when it appears as a thin crescent.
newly *adverb*, **newness** *noun*

newcomer *noun* **newcomers**
someone who has recently arrived in a place.

news *noun*
1 information about recent events. 2 a broadcast report about recent events.

newsagent *noun* **newsagents**
a shopkeeper who sells newspapers and magazines.

newsletter *noun* **newsletters**
a printed report sent regularly to members of an organisation such as a club, giving information of interest to them.

newspaper *noun* **newspapers**
a daily or weekly publication of large sheets of printed paper folded together, containing news reports, articles, advertisements, etc.

newsworthy *adjective*
considered important enough to be reported in the news.

New Testament *noun*
the Bible's second part, which describes the life and teachings of Jesus.

next *adjective*
the nearest; following immediately after.
next door, in the house on one side or the other of yours.

next *adverb*
in the nearest place; at the nearest time, as in *What comes next?*

nib *noun* **nibs**
the pointed metal part at the end of a pen that uses ink.

nibble *verb* **nibbles, nibbling, nibbled**
to take tiny bites at something.

nibblies *noun*
(*colloquial*) snacks, as in *They had potato chips for nibblies.*

nice *adjective* **nicer, nicest**
1 pleasant; friendly; kind. 2 delicate; precise, as in *There is a nice difference between stealing and borrowing.*
nicely *adverb*, **niceness** *noun*

niche *noun* **niches** (say neesh or nich)
1 a shallow recess, especially in a wall. 2 a comfortable or suitable position in life or employment.

nick *noun* **nicks**
1 a small cut or notch. 2 (*colloquial*) the condition of something, as in *The car's in good nick.*
in the nick of time, only just in time.

nick *verb* **nicks, nicking, nicked**
1 to make a notch in something.
2 (*colloquial*) to steal something.

nickel *noun*
a silvery-white metal.

nickname *noun* **nicknames**
a name given to someone instead of his or her real name, as in *The poet A.B. Paterson's nickname was Banjo.*

nicotine *noun* (say **nik**-uh-teen *or* nik-uh-**teen**)
a poisonous substance found in tobacco.

niece *noun* **nieces**
the daughter of a brother or sister.

nifty *adjective* **niftier, niftiest**
(*colloquial*) clever or smart, as in *a nifty invention.*

niggle *verb* **niggles, niggling, niggled**
to fuss over details or very small faults.

night *noun* **nights**
the time when it is dark, between sunset and sunrise.
night-time *noun*

nightfall *noun*
the time just after sunset.

nightingale *noun* **nightingales**
a small, reddish-brown European bird that sings sweetly.

nightly *adjective*
happening every night.

nightmare *noun* **nightmares**
a frightening dream.
nightmarish *adjective*

nil *noun*
nothing, as in *Our team's score was nil.*

nimble *adjective* **nimbler, nimblest**
moving quickly or easily.
nimbly *adverb*

non-fiction

nimbus *noun* **nimbi** or **nimbuses**
a rain-cloud.

nine *noun* **nines**
the number 9, one more than eight.
ninth *adjective* and *noun*

nineteen *noun* **nineteens**
the number 19, one more than eighteen.
nineteenth *adjective* and *noun*

ninety *noun* **nineties**
the number 90, nine times ten.
ninetieth *adjective* and *noun*

nip *verb* **nips, nipping, nipped**
1 to pinch or bite someone or something
quickly. 2 (*colloquial*) to go quickly, as in
I'll just nip into the supermarket.

nip *noun* **nips**
1 a quick pinch or bite. 2 a cold feeling,
as in *There's a nip in the air.*

nipple *noun* **nipples**
the small, protruding part of the breast and
in women the part from which a baby
sucks milk.

nippy *adjective* **nippier, nippiest**
(*colloquial*) 1 cold. 2 quick.

nit *noun* **nits**
a louse or its egg.
nit-picking, finding tiny faults or making
unimportant criticisms.

nitrate *noun* **nitrates**
a chemical compound that includes oxygen
and nitrogen.

nitric *adjective* (*say* **nuy**-trik)
to do with nitrogen; containing nitrogen.
nitric acid, a very strong colourless acid.

nitrogen *noun* (*say* **nuy**-truh-juhn)
a gas that makes up about four-fifths of the
air we breathe.

nitty-gritty *noun*
(*colloquial*) the most important details or the
true facts about something, as in *When you
get down to the nitty-gritty, you can travel long
distances on almost any kind of bicycle.*

no *adjective* and *adverb*
not any, as in *She had no money.*

no *interjection*
a word used to deny or refuse something.

no-ball *noun* **no-balls**
(*in cricket*) a ball not allowed by the rules
and which automatically gives the batsman
a run.

noble *adjective* **nobler, noblest**
1 to do with high rank; being an aristocrat.
2 having a good, generous nature, as in *The
nurse was respected for her noble character.*

3 stately; impressive, as in *a noble building.*
nobility *noun,* **nobly** *adverb*

nobody *pronoun*
no person; not anyone, as in *Nobody knows.*

nobody *noun* **nobodies**
an unimportant person, as in *He's a nobody.*

nocturnal *adjective* (*say* nok-**ter**-nuhl)
1 active at night, as in *Possums are nocturnal
animals.* 2 to do with the night, as in *A
nocturnal stillness lay over the countryside.*

nod *verb* **nods, nodding, nodded**
1 to move your head up and down as a
way of agreeing with someone or as a
greeting. 2 to be drowsy.

no-hoper *noun* **no-hopers**
(*colloquial*) a person who is a failure.

noise *noun* **noises**
a loud sound, especially one that is
unpleasant or unwanted.
noiseless *adjective,* **noiselessly** *adverb*

noisy *adjective* **noisier, noisiest**
making a lot of noise.
noisily *adverb,* **noisiness** *noun*

nomad *noun* **nomads** (*say* **noh**-mad)
1 a member of a tribe moving from place to
place for hunting and gathering or for
pasture. 2 any wanderer.
nomadic *adjective*

no-man's-land *noun*
unoccupied land, especially between two
armies at war.

nominal *adjective*
existing in name only; not real or actual, as
in *nominal ruler.*

nominate *verb* **nominates, nominating,
nominated**
to propose that someone should be a
candidate in an election.
nomination *noun*

nondescript *adjective*
having no special or distinctive qualities
and therefore difficult to describe.

none *pronoun*
not any; not one, as in *None of us went.*

none *adverb*
not at all, as in *He's none too awake this
morning.*
none the less or **nonetheless,** nevertheless.

non-existent *adjective*
not existing, as in *a non-existent ghost.*

non-fiction *noun*
writings that are not fiction; books about
real things and true events.

a
b
c
d
e
f
g
h
i
j
k
l
m
n
o
p
q
r
s
t
u
v
w
x
y
z

non-flammable

non-flammable *adjective*
unable to be set alight, as in *Children's pyjamas should be made of non-flammable material.*

non-renewable *adjective*
coming from or being a fuel such as coal, gas, or oil that cannot be replaced once it is used, as in *non-renewable energy.*

nonplussed *adjective* (*say* non-**plust**)
confused, puzzled.

nonsense *noun*
1 something that does not mean anything. 2 absurd or stupid ideas or behaviour.
nonsensical *adjective*

non-stick *adjective*
having a special coating to which food will not stick, as in *a non-stick frying-pan.*

non-stop *adjective*
not stopping, as in *non-stop chatter.*

noodles *plural noun*
a type of pasta made in long, narrow strips.

nook *noun* **nooks**
a corner or recess; a secluded place.

noon *noun*
twelve o'clock in the middle of the day.

no one *pronoun*
no person; not anyone.

noose *noun* **nooses**
a loop in a rope that gets smaller when the rope is pulled.

nor *conjunction*
and not, as in *He cannot do it; nor can I.*

norm *noun* **norms**
a standard or average type, amount, level, etc.

normal *adjective*
1 usual; typical, as in *It's normal to take a holiday.* 2 sane, as in *He's not normal.*
normality *noun*, **normally** *adverb*

north *noun*
the direction to the left of a person facing the east.

north *adjective*
1 coming from the north, as in *a north wind.* 2 situated in the north, as in *the north coast.*
the North, the northern part of Australia.
northerly *adjective*, **northern** *adjective*, **northerner** *noun*

north *adverb*
towards the north.
northward *adjective* and *adverb*, **northwards** *adverb*

nose *noun* **noses**
1 the part of the face that is used for breathing and smelling. 2 the front part of something.

nose *verb* **noses, nosing, nosed**
1 to push the nose near or into something, as in *We heard wombats nosing around our tent.* 2 to pry, as in *I don't want him nosing around here.* 3 to go forward cautiously, as in *The ship nosed through the ice.*

nostalgia *noun* (*say* nos-**tal**-juh)
an affectionate feeling for the past, especially for a happy time, as in *Many people look back with nostalgia to their childhood.*
nostalgic *adjective*

nostril *noun* **nostrils**
one of the two openings in your nose.

nosy *adjective* **nosier, nosiest**
(*colloquial*) always trying to find out things, especially about other people's business.
nosily *adverb*, **nosiness** *adjective*

not *adverb*
a word used to change the meaning of something to its opposite.

notable *adjective*
remarkable; famous, as in *a notable happening; notable scientists.*
notably *adverb*

notch *noun* **notches**
a small cut or mark, usually V-shaped.

note *noun* **notes**
1 something written down as a reminder or help. 2 a short letter. 3 notice, as in *Take note of what I say.* 4 a single sound in music. 5 a sound or tone that indicates something, as in *a note of anger in his voice.* 6 a banknote, as in *a ten dollar note.*

note *verb* **notes, noting, noted**
1 to write down something as a reminder or help. 2 to notice or pay attention to someone or something.

notebook *noun* **notebooks**
a book in which you write down things.

noted *adjective*
well-known, famous, as in *a noted artist.*

nothing *noun*
not anything.

notice *noun* **notices**
1 something written or printed and displayed for people to see. 2 attention, as in *It escaped my notice.* 3 a warning that something is going to happen.

notice *verb* **notices, noticing, noticed**
to see something; to become aware of something.
noticeable *adjective*, **noticeably** *adverb*

noticeboard *noun* **noticeboards**
a piece of wood or other material on which notices are displayed.

notify *verb* **notifies, notifying, notified**
to inform or give formal notice about something, as in *Bruce was notified that he was the successful applicant.*

notion *noun* **notions**
an idea, especially an uncertain idea, as in *The notion that the earth is flat was disproved long ago.*

notorious *adjective* (*say* nuh-**taw**-ree-uhs)
well-known for doing something bad, as in *notorious Ned Kelly.*
notoriety *noun*, **notoriously** *adverb*

nougat *noun* (*say* **noo**-gah)
a chewy sweet made from nuts, sugar, etc.

nought *noun* **noughts** (*say* nawt)
1 the figure 0. 2 nothing.

noun *noun* **nouns**
a word that is the name of a thing or a person, as in *Nouns are words like 'cat', 'courage', 'Hilary', 'Australia', and 'tent'.*
noun phrase, a group of words that includes a noun and is smaller than a clause, as in *'The large dog' is a noun phrase.*

nourish *verb* **nourishes, nourishing, nourished**
to feed someone enough good food to keep him or her alive and well.
nourishment *noun*

novel *adjective*
unusual, as in *a novel idea.*

novel *noun* **novels**
a story of fiction of book length.

novelist *noun* **novelists** (*say* **nov**-uh-list)
someone who writes novels.

novelty *noun* **novelties**
1 newness, as in *The novelty of the birthday gift soon wore off.* 2 a new or unusual thing or occurrence, as in *Swimming in the sea was a novelty for the children from the bush.* 3 a small toy or trinket, as in *The Christmas stocking was filled with novelties.*

November *noun*
the eleventh month of the year.

novice *noun* **novices**
a beginner; someone inexperienced.

now *adverb*
1 without any delay, as in *Do it now!* 2 at the present time, as in *She will be at home by now. They are here now.*
for now, until a later time, as in *Goodbye for now.*
now and again or **now and then**, occasionally; sometimes.

now *conjunction*
since; as, as in *I do remember, now you mention it.*

now *noun*
this moment, as in *I haven't seen him up to now.*

nowadays *adverb*
at the present time.

nowhere *adverb*
not anywhere; in or to no place.

noxious *adjective* (*say* **nok**-shuhs)
harmful, as in *Paterson's Curse is a noxious weed.*

nozzle *noun* **nozzles**
the part at the end of a hose or pipe from which something flows.

nuclear *adjective* (*say* **nyoo**-klee-uh)
1 to do with a nucleus, especially of an atom. 2 having or using the energy that is created by reactions in the nuclei of atoms, as in *nuclear energy; a nuclear weapon.*
nuclear family, a couple and their child or children seen as a basic social unit.

nucleus *noun* **nuclei** (*say* **nyoo**-klee-uhs)
1 the part in the centre of something, around which other things are grouped, as in *The queen bee is the nucleus of the hive.*
2 the central part of an atom or cell.

nude *adjective*
not wearing any clothes.
nudism *noun*, **nudist** *noun*, **nudity** *noun*

nudge *verb* **nudges, nudging, nudged**
to touch or push someone with your elbow.

nugget *noun* **nuggets**
1 a small lump of something, especially gold. 2 a small piece of something good or valuable, as in *Her book contains many nuggets of information.*

nuisance *noun* **nuisances**
a person or thing that annoys you.

null and void *adjective*
not valid, as in *The will was declared null and void because it was not witnessed.*

nulla-nulla *noun* **nulla-nullas**
a wooden club, used by Aborigines in fighting and hunting.

> **Origin** This word comes from the Aboriginal language Dharuk: **ngala-ngala**. See the Aboriginal Languages map at the back of this dictionary.

numb *adjective*
unable to feel or move.
numbly *adverb*, **numbness** *noun*

numbat

numbat *noun* **numbats**
a small, termite-eating marsupial with a long pointed snout and red to grey-brown fur, as in *The rare numbat is the faunal emblem of Western Australia.*

number *noun* **numbers**
1 a numeral. 2 a quantity of something. 3 one issue of a magazine or newspaper. 4 a song or piece of music.
number plate, a metal plate on a vehicle showing its registration number.

number *verb* **numbers, numbering, numbered**
1 to count something. 2 to amount to, as in *The crowd numbered 10,000.* 3 to mark something with numbers.

numeral *noun* **numerals**
a figure or word that tells you how many of something there are.

numerate *adjective*
having a good basic knowledge of mathematics.

numerator *noun* **numerators**
the number above the line in a fraction, as in *In $\frac{1}{4}$ the 1 is the numerator.*

numerical *adjective*
to do with numbers, as in *numerical value.*
numerically *adverb*

numerous *adjective*
many, as in *numerous kinds of cat.*

nun *noun* **nuns**
a member of a religious community of women.
nunnery *noun*

Nunga *noun*
an Aborigine from the southern part of South Australia.

Origin This word comes from the Aboriginal language Nhangka: **nhanga**. See the Aboriginal Languages map at the back of this dictionary.

nuptial *adjective* (*say* **nup**-shuhl)
to do with marriage or weddings.

nurse *noun* **nurses**
someone whose job is to look after people who are ill or hurt.

nurse *verb* **nurses, nursing, nursed**
1 to look after someone who is ill. 2 to hold someone or something carefully in your arms, as in *He was nursing a puppy.* 3 to feed a baby.

nursery *noun* **nurseries**
1 a place where very young children are looked after or play. 2 a place where young plants are grown and usually sold.
nursery rhyme, a simple poem or song that young children like.

nursing home *noun* **nursing homes**
a privately run hospital or home for invalids, old people, etc.

nurture *verb* **nurtures, nurturing, nurtured**
to train or educate a child, etc.

nut *noun* **nuts**
1 a fruit with a hard shell. 2 the edible part of this kind of fruit. 3 a hollow piece of metal for screwing on to a bolt. 4 (*colloquial*) the head.
nutcase, a crazy person.
nutty *adjective*

nutcrackers *plural noun*
a device like pincers for cracking the shells of nuts.

nutmeg *noun* **nutmegs**
a hard seed that is made into a powder and used as a spice.

nutrient *noun* **nutrients** (*say* **nyoo**-tree-uhnt)
something nourishing.

nutrition *noun* (*say* nyoo-**trish**-uhn)
1 food that keeps people well. 2 the study of what food keeps people well.
nutritional *adjective*

nutritious *adjective* (*say* nyoo-**trish**-uhs)
nourishing, as in *a nutritious meal.*

nutshell *noun* **nutshells**
the shell of a nut.
in a nutshell, briefly.

nuzzle *verb* **nuzzles, nuzzling, nuzzled**
to rub gently against something with the nose.

nylon *noun*
a lightweight synthetic cloth or fibre.

nymph *noun* **nymphs**
a mythical goddess or girl living in rivers, trees, etc.

Nyoongah or **Noongah** *noun*
(*say* **nyuung**-guh)
an Aborigine from the south-west of Western Australia.

Origin This word comes from the Aboriginal language Nyungar: **Nyungar**. See the Aboriginal Languages map at the back of this dictionary.

Oo

oak *noun* oaks
a large tree with seeds called acorns.

oar *noun* oars
a pole with a flat part at one end, used for rowing a boat.

oasis *noun* oases (*say* oh-**ay**-suhs)
a place with water and trees in a desert.

oath *noun* oaths
1 a solemn promise.   2 a swear-word.

oatmeal *noun*
a substance made by grinding oats.

oats *plural noun*
a cereal used to make food for humans and animals, as in *Porridge is made from oats.*

obedient *adjective*
obeying; willing to obey.
obedience *noun*, **obediently** *adverb*

obelisk *noun* obelisks
a four-sided, often tapered, stone pillar erected as a monument or landmark.

obese *adjective* (*say* oh-**bees**)
very fat.
obesity *noun*

obey *verb* obeys, obeying, obeyed
to do what you are told to do.

obituary *noun* obituaries
(*say* uh-**bich**-uh-ree)
a report that someone has died, usually with a short account of his or her life.

object *noun* objects (*say* ob-jekt)
1 something that can be seen or touched.
2 the aim or purpose of something, as in *Her object is to win the swimming trophy.*
3 (*in grammar*) something towards which the action of a verb is directed, as in *'Him' is the object in 'I chased him'.*

object *verb* objects, objecting, objected
(*say* uhb-**jekt**)
to say that you do not like something or that you disagree, as in *She objected to my speech.*
objection *noun*, **objector** *noun*

objectionable *adjective*
unpleasant; not liked, as in *What do you find objectionable about him? This chemical has an objectionable smell.*

objective *adjective*
1 having a real existence outside someone's mind, as in *No objective evidence has yet been found to prove his claims.*   2 not influenced by your own beliefs or ideas, as in *A judge needs to have an objective approach.*
objectivity *noun*

objective *noun* objectives
what you are trying to reach or do.

obligation *noun* obligations
a duty.
obligatory *adjective*

oblige *verb* obliges, obliging, obliged
to help and please someone.
obliged to do something, forced to do something.

oblique *adjective* (*say* uh-**bleek**)
1 slanting.   2 not straight or direct, as in *an oblique question.*
obliquely *adverb*

obliterate *verb* obliterates, obliterating, obliterated
to blot out, destroy, or leave no clear traces of something.

oblivious *adjective*
forgetful, not remembering, as in *He was oblivious of his earlier mistakes.*

a
b
c
d
e
f
g
h
i
j
k
l
m
n
o
p
q
r
s
t
u
v
w
x
y
z

oblong

oblong *noun* oblongs
a rectangle that is longer than it is wide.

obnoxious *adjective*
offensive, nasty.

oboe *noun* oboes (*say* oh-boh)
a high-pitched woodwind instrument.

obscene *adjective* (*say* ob-**seen** *or* uhb-**seen**)
offensive to people's feelings, especially because of being connected with sex, violence, or cruelty.
obscenely *adverb*, obscenity *noun*

obscure *adjective*
1 not clear. 2 not famous.
obscurely *adverb*, obscurity *noun*

observance *noun* observances
obeying a law; keeping a custom.

observant *adjective*
quick at noticing things.
observantly *adverb*

observation *noun* observations
1 observing; watching. 2 a remark, as in *He made a few observations about the weather.*

observatory *noun* observatories
(*say* uhb-**zer**-vuh-tree)
a building equipped with telescopes for looking at the stars, planets, etc.

observe *verb* observes, observing, observed
1 to watch someone or something carefully. 2 to notice something. 3 to obey a law or keep a custom. 4 to make a remark, as in *She observed that I did not like ice in my drinks.*
observer *noun*

obsessed *adjective*
always thinking about something, as in *He is obsessed with his work.*
obsession *noun*

obsolete *adjective*
not used any more; out of date, as in *an obsolete word; obsolete machinery.*
obsolescence *noun*

obstacle *noun* obstacles
something that gets in your way or makes it difficult for you to do something.

obstinate *adjective*
not ready to change your ideas or ways, even though they may be wrong.
obstinacy *noun*, obstinately *adverb*

obstreperous *adjective*
unruly and noisy, as in *The obstreperous children tired their mother.*

obstruct *verb* obstructs, obstructing, obstructed
to stop something from getting past; to get in someone's way.
obstruction *noun*, obstructive *adjective*

obtain *verb* obtains, obtaining, obtained
to buy, take, or be given something.
obtainable *adjective*

obtuse *adjective*
slow to understand; stupid.

obtuse angle *noun*
an angle between 90 and 180 degrees.

obvious *adjective*
very easy to see or understand.
obviously *adverb*

occasion *noun* occasions
1 the time when something happens, as in *On this occasion, we will not take any action.* 2 a special event, as in *The wedding was a grand occasion.*

occasional *adjective*
happening from time to time, but not often and not regularly.
occasionally *adverb*

occult *noun* occults
the knowledge and study of supernatural or magical forces, powers, etc.

occupant *noun* occupants
someone who occupies a place.

occupation *noun* occupations
a job or hobby, as in *His occupation is that of a baker.*

occupy *verb* occupies, occupying, occupied
1 to live in a place. 2 to fill a space or position. 3 to capture territory in a war. 4 to keep someone's mind busy and interested.
occupation *noun*

occur *verb* occurred, occurring, occurred
1 to happen; to take place. 2 to be found; to exist. 3 to come into your mind, as in *An idea occurred to me.*
occurrence *noun*

ocean *noun* oceans
1 the sea. 2 a large sea, as in *the Pacific Ocean.*

ochre *noun* ochres (*say* oh-kuh)
earth used as yellow, brown, or red colouring; the pale brownish-yellow colour.

o'clock *adverb*
by the clock, as in *Lunch is at one o'clock.*

octagon *noun* octagons
a flat shape with eight sides.
octagonal *adjective*

official

octave *noun* **octaves**
the distance between one musical note and the next note of the same name above or below it; these two notes played together.

October *noun*
the tenth month of the year.

octopus *noun* **octopuses**
a marine creature with eight arms (called *tentacles*).

odd *adjective* **odder, oddest**
1 strange or unusual, as in *odd beliefs*. 2 not an even number, as in *Five and nine are odd numbers*. 3 left over; spare, as in *an odd sock*.
odd job, varied, occasional tasks.
oddity *noun*, **oddly** *adverb*, **oddness** *noun*

oddments *plural noun*
small things of various kinds.

odds *plural noun*
1 the chances that something will happen. 2 the proportion of money that you will win if a bet is successful, as in *When the odds are 10 to 1, you will win $10 if you bet $1*.
odds and ends, small things of various kinds.

ode *noun* **odes**
a song or poem which praises something, as in *Ode to Autumn*.

odious *adjective*
hateful, as in *His odious behaviour made many enemies*.

odometer *noun* **odometers**
(*say* oh-**dom**-uh-tuh)
an instrument for measuring the distance travelled by a car, truck, etc.

odour *noun* **odours**
a smell.
odorous *adjective*

oesophagus *noun* **oesophagi** or **oesophaguses** (*say* uh-**sof**-uh-guhs)
the tube from your throat to your stomach.

of *preposition*
1 belonging to; coming from, as in *a native of Italy*. 2 away from, as in *two miles north of the town*. 3 about; concerning, as in *news of peace*. 4 from; out of, as in *built of stone*.

off *adverb*
1 not on; away, as in *His hat blew off*. 2 not working or happening, as in *The heating is off*. 3 behind or at the side of a stage, as in *There were noises off*.

off *preposition*
1 not on; away or down from, as in *He fell off his chair*. 2 not taking or wanting, as in *She is off her food*.

offbeat *adjective*
1 out of time with the rhythm. 2 odd, eccentric, as in *The teenager wore offbeat clothes*.

off colour *adjective*
1 unwell. 2 in poor taste.

offcut *noun* **offcuts**
a piece of timber, paper, etc. remaining after cutting.

offence *noun* **offences**
a crime, as in *When was the offence committed?*
give offence, to hurt someone's feelings, as in *I didn't mean to give offence*.
take offence, to be upset by what someone has said or done.

offend *verb* **offends, offending, offended**
1 to hurt someone's feelings; to be unpleasant to someone. 2 to break a law; to do wrong.
offence *noun*, **offender** *noun*

offensive *adjective*
1 hurting someone's feelings or being unpleasant to someone, as in *offensive remarks about her big ears*. 2 used for attacking; aggressive, as in *offensive weapons; offensive behaviour*.
offensively *adverb*

offer *verb* **offers, offering, offered**
1 to hold out something so that someone can take it if he or she wants it. 2 to say that you are willing to do something. 3 to say what you are willing to give for something.
offering *noun*

offer *noun* **offers**
1 the action of holding out something or saying you are willing to do something. 2 an amount of money that you are willing to pay for something.

offhand *adjective*
rude or casual.

office *noun* **offices**
1 a room or building where people do typing, accounts, business, etc. 2 an important job or position, as in *the office of Lord Mayor*.

officer *noun* **officers**
1 someone who is in charge of other people, especially in the armed forces; an official. 2 a policeman.

official *adjective*
1 done or said by someone with authority, as in *an official order to evacuate the building*.

official

2 connected with a job of authority or trust, as in *She has considerable official responsibilities.*
officially *adverb*

official *noun* **officials**
someone who does a job of authority or trust.

> **Usage** Do not confuse the adjective **official** with **officious**, which is the next word in this dictionary.

officious *adjective* (*say* uh-**fish**-uhs)
too ready to order people about.
officiously *adverb*

off-peak *adjective*
to do with times other than those of greatest demand, as in *off-peak electricity; off-peak travel.*

off-putting *adjective*
having an unpleasant or discouraging manner.

offshoot *noun* **offshoots**
something that has developed from something else, as in *Kanga cricket is an offshoot of traditional cricket.*

offshore *adjective* and *adverb*
1 blowing away from the seashore, as in *an offshore breeze.* **2** on the sea at or to some distance from the shore, as in *offshore drilling for oil; an oil spill offshore.*

offside *adjective*
(*in Sport*) in a position where you cannot move the ball without breaking the rules of the game.

offsider *noun* **offsiders**
a partner, assistant or friend.

offspring *noun* **offspring**
a child or young animal.

often *adverb* **oftener, oftenest**
many times; in many cases.

ogre *noun* **ogres**
a cruel giant; a frightening person.
ogress *noun*

oh *interjection*
a cry of surprise, pain, delight, etc.

ohm *noun* **ohms**
(rhymes with *home*)
a unit of electrical resistance.

oil *noun* **oils**
1 a thick, slippery liquid that does not mix with water. **2** a kind of petroleum used as fuel.
oil rig, a structure to support the equipment for drilling an oil well.

oil-tanker, a large ship made specially to carry oil.
oil well, a hole drilled in the ground or under the sea from which you get oil.

oil *verb* **oils, oiling, oiled**
to put oil on something to make it work smoothly.

oil-painting *noun* **oil-paintings**
a painting done with oil-colours.

oilskin *noun* **oilskins**
a waterproof piece of clothing worn especially by fishermen.

oily *adjective* **oilier, oiliest**
1 like oil; covered in oil. **2** unpleasantly keen to please, as in *She didn't like his oily manner.*

ointment *noun* **ointments**
a cream for putting on sore skin and cuts.

okay or **OK** *adjective*
all right; satisfactory, as in *I am okay now.*

okay *adverb*
satisfactorily, well, as in *She's doing okay, she just received a bonus.*

old *adjective* **older, oldest**
1 not new; born or made a long time ago. **2** to do with a particular age, as in *I'm ten years old.*

olden *adjective*
to do with the past, as in *the olden days.*

old-fashioned *adjective*
1 to do with something that was usual a long time ago, as in *old-fashioned clothes; old-fashioned engine.* **2** having attitudes or beliefs that were usual in past times, as in *He's rather old-fashioned, and never asks his children what they would like to do.*

Old Testament *noun*
the Bible's first part, which is the holy book of the Jewish and Christian religions.

oleander *noun* **oleanders**
a poisonous, evergreen Mediterranean shrub with pink or white flowers.

olive *noun* **olives**
1 an evergreen tree with a small, bitter fruit. **2** the fruit of this tree.
olive branch, something that shows you want to make peace.

Olympic *adjective* (*say* uh-**lim**-pik)
to do with the Olympic Games or the Olympics, a series of international sports contests held every four years in different countries.

ombudsman *noun* **ombudsmen**
(*say* **om**-buhdz-muhn)
an official who investigates people's complaints against government departments.

omelette *noun* **omelettes** (*say* **om**-luht)
eggs beaten together and fried, often with a filling or flavouring.

omen *noun* **omens**
a sign that something is going to happen.

ominous *adjective*
threatening; suggesting that trouble is coming.
ominously *adverb*

omit *verb* **omits, omitting, omitted**
1 to miss something out.   2 to fail to do something.
omission *noun*

omnipotent *adjective*
having great or total power, as in *Christians believe God is omnipotent.*
omnipotence *noun*

omnivorous *adjective*
eating plants as well as the flesh of animals.

on *preposition*
1 at or over the top or surface of something, as in *Sit on the floor.*   2 at the time of, as in *on my birthday.*   3 about; concerning, as in *a talk on butterflies.*   4 towards; near, as in *They advanced on the town.*

on *adverb*
1 so as to be on something, as in *Put your hat on.*   2 forwards, as in *Move on.*
3 working; in action, as in *Is the heater on?*

once *adverb*
1 at one time, as in *I once lived in Wollongong.*
2 ever, as in *They never once offered to pay.*

once *conjunction*
as soon as, as in *We can get out once I open this door.*

oncoming *adjective*
moving towards you, as in *the oncoming traffic.*

one *noun* **ones**
1 a person on his or her own; a thing on its own, as in *One of my friends is ill.*   2 the number 1, representing a person or thing alone, as in *One and one make two.*
one another, each other.

onerous *adjective*
being a burden; difficult, as in *The work was less onerous than in her previous demanding job.*

oneself *pronoun*
one's own self; yourself, as in *One should not always think of oneself.*

one-sided *adjective*
showing or considering only one person's point of view, as in *He's given you a very one-sided story of what happened.*

one-way *adjective*
where traffic may only go in one direction, as in *a one-way street.*

ongoing *adjective*
continuing to exist; making progress, as in *an ongoing problem; an ongoing project.*

onion *noun* **onions**
a round vegetable with a strong flavour, as in *Onions make you cry when you peel them.*

onlooker *noun* **onlookers**
a spectator.

only *adverb*
no more than, as in *There are only three cakes.*
not only ... but also, both ... and, as in *He not only thanked me but also paid me.*
only too, extremely, as in *I'm only too happy to help.*

only *adjective*
being the one person or thing of a kind, as in *He's the only person we can trust.*
only child, a child who has no brothers or sisters.

only *conjunction*
(*colloquial*) but then; however, as in *I want to come, only I'm busy that night.*

onomatopoeia *noun*
a word that sounds like what it is describing, as in *'sizzle', 'hiss', 'clang'.*
onomatopoeic *adjective*

onset *noun*
the beginning of something, as in *the onset of bad weather, war, or pain.*

onshore *adjective*
blowing towards the seashore, as in *an onshore breeze.*

onside *adjective*
to do with a player in a field game who is not offside.

onslaught *noun* **onslaughts**
a fierce attack.

onward or **onwards** *adverb*
forwards.

ooze *verb* **oozes, oozing, oozed**
to flow out slowly, especially through a narrow opening, as in *Blood oozed from his wound.*

a
b
c
d
e
f
g
h
i
j
k
l
m
n
o
p
q
r
s
t
u
v
w
x
y
z

opal

opal *noun* **opals**
a semiprecious stone usually of a milky or bluish colour and sometimes showing changing colours.

opaque *adjective* (*say* oh-**payk**)
unable to be seen through or let light through.

open *adjective*
1 not shut, as in *an open door*. **2** not enclosed, as in *open land*. **3** not folded; spread out, as in *with open arms*. **4** honest; not secret or secretive, as in *an open meeting*. **5** not settled or finished, as in *an open question*. **6** not restricted to a certain group, as in *The competition was open to both amateurs and professionals*.
open-air, outdoors, as in *open-air theatre*.

open *verb* **opens, opening, opened**
1 to make something open; to become open. **2** to start, as in *The jumble sale opens at 2 p.m.*
opener *noun*

open-cut *adjective*
(*in mining*) to do with the removal of minerals, etc. from the surface, not from underground shafts.

opening *noun* **openings**
1 a space or gap in something. **2** the beginning of something, as in *Don't miss the opening of the sale!* **3** an opportunity, as in *There is an opening for an experienced salesperson in our new shop*.

openly *adverb*
not secretly; publicly.

open-minded *adjective*
ready to listen to other people's ideas and opinions; not having fixed ideas.

opera *noun* **operas**
a play in which all or most of the words are sung.
operatic *adjective*

operate *verb* **operates, operating, operated**
1 to make something work. **2** to work; to be in action. **3** to do a surgical operation on someone.

operation *noun* **operations**
1 making something work; working.
2 something done by a surgeon to someone to deal with a disease or injury.
3 a planned military activity.

operator *noun* **operators**
someone who works something, especially a telephone switchboard.

opinion *noun* **opinions**
what you think of something; a belief.

opinion poll, an estimate of what people think, made by questioning a certain number of them.

opium *noun*
a drug made from poppies, used to calm people and to make them unable to feel pain.

opponent *noun* **opponents**
someone who is against you in a contest, war, or argument.

opportunity *noun* **opportunities**
a time when you can do something that you cannot do at other times.

oppose *verb* **opposes, opposing, opposed**
to be against someone or something.

opposite *adjective*
1 completely different, as in *They went in opposite directions*. **2** facing; on the other side, as in *She lives on the opposite side of the road to me*.

opposite *noun* **opposites**
something opposite, as in *'Happy' is the opposite of 'sad'*.

opposition *noun*
opposing something; resistance.
the Opposition, the political party or parties in parliament that oppose the government.

oppress *verb* **oppresses, oppressing, oppressed**
1 to govern or treat someone cruelly or unjustly. **2** to trouble someone with worry or sadness, as in *She felt oppressed by her daughter's problems*.
oppression *noun*, **oppressive** *adjective*, **oppressor** *noun*

opt *verb* **opts, opting, opted**
to choose, as in *We opted to go overseas*.
opt for something, to choose something, as in *I opted for the cash prize*.
opt out, to decide not to join in.

optic *adjective*
to do with the eyes, as in *optic nerve*.

optical *adjective*
to do with sight, as in *optical glasses*.
optical illusion, something you think you see that is not really there.
optically *adverb*

optician *noun* **opticians** (*say* op-**tish**-uhn)
someone who tests your eyesight and supplies glasses.

optimism *noun*
expecting that things will turn out right.
optimist *noun*, **optimistic** *adjective*

option *noun* options
1 choice, as in *You have no option but to pay.* 2 something that is or can be chosen, as in *Your options are to travel by bus or by train.*

optional *adjective*
to do with having a choice; not compulsory.
optionally *adverb*

opulent *adjective* (*say* **op**-yuh-luhnt)
1 showing wealth, as in *an opulent house.* 2 abundant, as in *a plant with green and opulent foliage.*
opulence *noun*, **opulently** *adverb*

or *conjunction*
a word used to show that there is a choice or alternative, as in *Do you want a bun or a biscuit?*

oral *adjective*
1 spoken, as in *an oral comprehension test.* 2 using your mouth, as in *an oral vaccine.*
orally *adverb*

Usage Do not confuse **oral** with **aural**, which means to do with hearing.

orange *noun* oranges
1 a round, juicy fruit with a thick, reddish-yellow peel. 2 a reddish-yellow colour.

orang-utan *noun* orang-utans
(*say* uh-rang-uh-**tan** *or* uh-**rang**-uh-tan)
a large kind of ape.

orator *noun* orators (*say* o-ruh-tuh)
someone who makes speeches.
oration *noun*, **oratorical** *adjective*, **oratory** *noun*

oratorio *noun* oratorios
(*say* o-ruh-**taw**-ree-oh)
a piece of music for voices and orchestra, usually on a religious subject.

orbit *noun* orbits
the path taken by something moving around a planet or other body in space.

orbit *verb* orbits, orbiting, orbited
to move around a planet or other body in space, as in *The satellite orbited the earth.*

orchard *noun* orchards
a place where a lot of fruit trees grow.

orchestra *noun* orchestras
a large group of people playing musical instruments together.
orchestral *adjective*

orchid *noun* orchids (*say* **aw**-kuhd)
a plant having a beautiful, brightly-coloured, waxy flower.

ordain *verb* ordains, ordaining, ordained
1 to appoint a person at a special ceremony to perform as a priest or minister in the Christian church. 2 to declare with authority, as in *The principal ordained that the school should close.*

ordeal *noun* ordeals
a very hard or painful experience.

order *noun* orders
1 a command. 2 a request for something to be supplied. 3 the condition in which everything is in its right place; neatness, as in *His bedroom was in perfect order after it was cleaned.* 4 the way things are arranged, as in *numerical order.* 5 the condition or state of something, as in *The equipment has been kept in good order. The police maintained law and order.* 6 a division into a particular group or kind, as in *an order of nuns; ability of the highest order.*
in (or out of) order, in the right (or wrong) sequence, position, etc.

order *verb* orders, ordering, ordered
1 to tell someone to do something. 2 to ask for something to be supplied to you.
order about, to keep giving someone commands.

orderly *adjective*
1 arranged tidily or well; methodical, as in *an orderly desk. She is an orderly person.* 2 well-behaved; obedient.
orderliness *noun*

ordinal number *noun* ordinal numbers
a number that shows where something comes in a series; 1st, 2nd, 3rd, etc. (compare *cardinal number*).

ordinary *adjective*
normal; not special in any way.
ordinarily *adverb*

ore *noun* ores
rock with metal in it, as in *iron ore.*

oregano *noun*
a herb used in cooking to flavour food.

organ *noun* organs
1 a large musical instrument with one or more keyboards. 2 a part of the body with a particular function, as in *the digestive organs.*

organic *adjective*
1 made by or found in living things. 2 not using artificial chemicals to kill pests on plants or to make plants grow bigger, as in *organic agriculture.*

a
b
c
d
e
f
g
h
i
j
k
l
m
n
o
p
q
r
s
t
u
v
w
x
y
z

organisation

organisation or **organization** *noun* organisations
1 an organised group of people, as in *the scout organisation*. 2 the getting of people together to do something; planning something; putting something in order; the systematic arrangement of something.

organise or **organize** *verb* organises, organising, organised
1 to get people together to do something. 2 to plan something, as in *She organised the picnic*. 3 to put something in order.
organiser *noun*

organism *noun* organisms
a living animal or plant.

organist *noun* organists
someone who plays the organ.

oriental *adjective*
to do with an Asian country.

orientate *verb* orientates, orientating, orientated
to place something or face in a certain direction.

orienteering *noun* (*say* aw-ree-en-**teer**-ring *or* o-ree-en-**teer**-ring)
the sport of finding your way across rough country with a map and compass.

origami *noun* (*say* o-ruh-**gah**-mee)
folding pieces of paper to make decorative shapes.

origin *noun* origins
the start of something; the point where something began.

original *adjective*
1 existing from the start; earliest, as in *Aborigines were Australia's original inhabitants*. 2 new; not a copy or an imitation, as in *an original design*. 3 producing new ideas, as in *an original thinker*.
originality *noun*, originally *adverb*

originate *verb* originates, originating, originated
to start; to create something.
origination *noun*, originator *noun*

ornament *noun* ornaments
a thing put in or on something to make it look pretty; a decoration.
ornamental *adjective*, ornamentation *noun*

ornate *adjective*
highly decorated; showy.

ornithology *noun* (*say* aw-nuh-**thol**-uh-jee)
the scientific study of birds.
ornithological *adjective*, ornithologist *noun*

orphan *noun* orphans
a child whose parents are dead.

orphanage *noun* orphanages
a home for orphans.

orthodontist *noun* orthodontists
a person who corrects faults in the teeth and jaws.

orthodox *adjective*
having correct or generally accepted beliefs, as in *orthodox medicine*.
Orthodox Church, the Christian Churches of Eastern Europe.
orthodoxy *noun*

oscillate *verb* oscillates, oscillating, oscillated
to move to and fro.
oscillation *noun*

ostentatious *adjective* (*say* os-ten-**tay**-shuhs)
to do with too much display or showiness, as in *After winning the lotto he built an ostentatious house*.

ostracise or **ostracize** *verb* ostracises, ostracising, ostracised (*say* os-truh-suyz)
to exclude or to send away, as in *The class ostracised the bully*.

ostrich *noun* ostriches
a large, long-legged African bird that can run fast but cannot fly.

other *adjective*
not the same as this, as in *The other dress was better*.
every other day, every second day, as in *He comes here every other day; this week he'll be here on Tuesday, Thursday, and Saturday*.
other than, except, as in *They have no belongings other than what they are carrying*.
the other day or the other week, a few days or weeks ago.

otherwise *adverb*
1 if you do not; if things happen differently, as in *Write it down, otherwise you'll forget it*. 2 in other ways, as in *It rained a lot but otherwise the holiday was good*.

otter *noun* otters
a furry, long-tailed animal that lives near water.

ouch *interjection*
a cry of pain.

ought *verb*
should; must; to have a duty to, as in *You ought to stop fighting*.

ounce *noun* ounces
an old-fashioned unit of weight equal to about 30 grams.

our *adjective*
belonging to us, as in *our house*.

ours *pronoun*
belonging to us, as in *This house is ours*.

ourselves *pronoun*
us and nobody else, as in *We washed ourselves.*

oust *verb* **ousts, ousting, ousted** (*say* owst)
to drive out or expel.

out *adverb*
1 not in; away from a place. 2 not burning, as in *The fire is out.* 3 loudly, as in *She cried out.*
out of, from a place; without something.
out of date, old-fashioned; not used any more.
out of the way, no longer an obstacle; distant; unusual, as in *Now that the exams are out of the way I can relax. They live in a small, out-of-the-way country town. The film was nothing out of the way.*
out to, determined to, as in *I am out to beat him.*

outback *noun*
the remote inland areas of the country.

outbreak *noun* **outbreaks**
the sudden start of a disease, war, show of anger, etc.

outburst *noun* **outbursts**
the bursting out of steam, laughter, anger, etc.

outcast *noun* **outcasts**
someone who has been rejected by his or her family, friends, or society.

outcome *noun* **outcomes**
the result of something.

outcrop *noun* **outcrops**
a piece of rock, etc. from a lower level that sticks out on the surface of the ground.

outcry *noun* **outcries**
a strong protest from many people, as in *There was an outcry over the rise in rail fares.*

outdated *adjective*
out of date.

outdoor *adjective*
to do with activities or things used outdoors, as in *outdoor sports; outdoor furniture.*

outdoors *adverb*
in the open air, as in *It is cold outdoors.*

outer *adjective*
nearer the outside; external.
outer space, the universe beyond the earth's atmosphere.

outer *noun*
the usually uncovered area for non-members at a racecourse or sports ground.

outfit *noun* **outfits**
1 clothes that are worn together. 2 a set of things needed for doing something, as in *a cricket outfit.* 3 (*colloquial*) a group of people seen as an organisation, as in *The computing outfit were an efficient group.*

outgoing *adjective*
1 friendly. 2 departing, as in *The outgoing principal was farewelled.*

outgrow *verb* **outgrows, outgrowing, outgrew, outgrown**
1 to grow out of clothes, habits, etc. 2 to grow faster or taller than someone else.

outhouse *noun* **outhouses**
1 a small building attached to or near a larger building. 2 an outdoor toilet.

outing *noun* **outings**
a trip to somewhere and back, made for pleasure.

outlaw *noun* **outlaws**
a lawless person; a robber, especially one who roams about.

outlay *noun* **outlays**
the time or money that is spent on something.

outlet *noun* **outlets**
1 a way for something to come out, as in *The tank has an outlet at the bottom.* 2 a way of getting rid of something, as in *Running is a good outlet for his energy.* 3 a place to sell goods, as in *We need to find fresh outlets for our products.*

outline *noun* **outlines**
1 the line around the outside of something; a line showing the shape of a thing, as in *the dark outline of trees against the setting sun.* 2 a summary.

outline *verb* **outlines, outlining, outlined**
1 to draw a line to show the shape of something. 2 to summarise or describe something.

outlook *noun* **outlooks**
1 a view. 2 the way that someone looks at and thinks about things. 3 what seems likely to happen in the future.

outlying *adjective*
far from a town or city; distant, as in *outlying suburbs; outlying islands.*

outnumber *verb* **outnumbers, outnumbering, outnumbered**
to be greater in number than something else.

outpatient *noun* **outpatients**
someone who visits a hospital for treatment but does not stay there.

outpost

outpost *noun* **outposts**
a distant settlement.

output *noun* **outputs**
1 the amount produced, especially by a factory, etc. **2** (*in Computing*) information sent out by a computer.

outrage *noun* **outrages**
something very shocking or cruel.
outrageous *adjective*

outright *adverb*
1 completely, as in *We won outright.* **2** not gradually, as in *They were able to buy their house outright.*

outset *noun*
at or **from the outset,** at or from the beginning of something.

outside *noun* **outsides**
the surface or edges of a thing; the part farthest from the middle.

outside *adjective*
placed in or coming from the outside.
outside broadcast, a broadcast that is not made from a studio.

outside *adverb*
on or to the outside; outdoors, as in *Come outside.*

outside *preposition*
on or to the outside of something, as in *The milk is outside the door.*

outsider *noun* **outsiders**
1 someone who is not a member of a particular group of people. **2** a horse or person unlikely to win a race or contest.

outskirts *plural noun*
the parts on the outside edge of an area; the suburbs.

outspoken *adjective*
speaking frankly; not tactful.

outstanding *adjective*
1 extremely good or distinguished, as in *an outstanding athlete.* **2** not yet dealt with, as in *outstanding debts.*

outward *adjective*
1 going outwards. **2** on the outside, as in *She displayed outward calm though she was nervous inside.*
outwardly *adverb*

outwards *adverb*
towards the outside.

outweigh *verb* **outweighs, outweighing, outweighed**
to be more important than something else, as in *The benefits of the plan outweigh its drawbacks.*

outwit *verb* **outwits, outwitting, outwitted**
to get an advantage over someone by being clever.

oval *adjective*
shaped like an egg or a number 0.

oval *noun* **ovals**
1 an oval shape. **2** a sports field, not necessarily oval in shape.

ovary *noun* **ovaries**
1 part of a female body where egg-cells (*ova*) are produced. **2** the part of a flowering plant that produces seeds.

ovation *noun* **ovations**
an enthusiastic response, especially with clapping and cheering, to a performance.

oven *noun* **ovens**
a closed space in which things are cooked or heated.

over *adverb*
1 sideways; into a different position, as in *He fell over.* **2** finished, as in *Playtime is over.* **3** left; remaining, as in *3 into 7 goes 2 and 1 over.* **4** through; thoroughly, as in *Think it over.* **5** too much, as in *Don't get over-excited.*
all over, everywhere; finished, as in *You've spilt paint all over! The work's all over now.*
over and over, repeatedly; many times.

over *preposition*
1 above; covering, as in *I knocked his hat over his eyes.* **2** across, as in *They ran over the road.* **3** more than, as in *There are over 3,000 kinds of wildflowers in Western Australia.*

over *noun* **overs**
in cricket, a series of balls bowled by one person, as in *There are usually 6 balls in an over.*

overall *adjective* and *adverb*
including everything.

overalls *plural noun*
a piece of clothing worn over other clothes to protect them.

overbearing *adjective*
bullying, domineering, as in *His overbearing manner made him very unpopular.*

overboard *adverb*
over the side of a boat into the water, as in *She jumped overboard.*

overcast *adjective*
covered with cloud, as in *The sky is grey and overcast.*

overcoat *noun* **overcoats**
a warm outdoor coat.

overcome *verb* overcomes, overcoming, overcame, overcome
1 to gain a victory over someone; to succeed in a struggle against something. 2 to make someone helpless, as in *The fumes overcame her.*

overdo *verb* overdoes, overdoing, overdid, overdone
1 to do something too much. 2 to cook food for too long.

overdose *noun* overdoses
too large a dose of a drug or medicine.

overdue *adjective*
past the due time for payment, arrival, return, etc.

overflow *verb* overflows, overflowing, overflowed
1 to flow over its edges or banks, as in *The river overflowed.* 2 to be so full that the liquid in it spills out, as in *The sink is overflowing.*
overflow *noun*

overgrown *adjective*
covered with weeds or unwanted plants.

overhang *verb* overhangs, overhanging, overhung
to stick out beyond and above something else, as in *The second storey of the old house overhung the first.*

overhaul *verb* overhauls, overhauling, overhauled
1 to examine something thoroughly and repair it if necessary. 2 to overtake someone or something.

overhead *adjective* and *adverb*
above your head; in the sky, as in *overhead power lines. A few clouds floated by overhead.*
overhead projector, a type of projector having a flat plastic sheet on which you draw or write, and throwing a large image of the drawing, writing, etc. on to a screen.

overheads *plural noun*
the expenses of running a business.

overhear *verb* overhears, overhearing, overheard
to hear something accidentally.

overjoyed *adjective*
filled with great joy.

overland *adjective* and *adverb*
over the land, not by sea, as in *overland journey; travelling overland from Melbourne to Perth.*
overlander *noun*

overlap *verb* overlapped, overlapping, overlapped
to lie across part of something, as in *The tiles overlapped each other.*

overload *verb* overloads, overloading, overloaded
to load with too much baggage, work, demand, etc.

overlook *verb* overlooks, overlooking, overlooked
1 not to notice something. 2 not to punish an offence. 3 to have a view over something.

overnight *adverb* and *adjective*
to do with or during a night, as in *We stayed overnight in a bushman's hut. There will be an overnight stop in Paris.*

overpass *noun* overpasses
a road that passes over another by means of a bridge.

overpower *verb* overpowers, overpowering, overpowered
to overcome.
overpowering, very strong.

overrate *verb* overrates, overrating, overrated
to value too highly, as in *The film was overrated by the impressionable audience.*

overrun *verb* overruns, overrunning, overran, overrun
1 to spread harmfully over an area, as in *The place is overrun with mice.* 2 to go on longer than it should, as in *The broadcast overran by ten minutes.*

overseas *adverb*
abroad, as in *They travelled overseas.*

oversee *verb* oversees, overseeing, oversaw, overseen
to supervise in an official way.
overseer *noun*

oversight *noun* oversights
a mistake made by not noticing something.

overt *adjective*
open, not secret, as in *The unpopular clerk treated the public with overt rudeness.*

overtake *verb* overtakes, overtaking, overtook, overtaken
to pass a moving vehicle or person.

overthrow *verb* overthrows, overthrowing, overthrew, overthrown
to make something fall or fail; to defeat.

overtime *noun*
time spent working outside the normal hours.

overture

overture *noun* **overtures**
a piece of music played at the start of a concert, opera, ballet, etc.
overtures, a friendly attempt to start a discussion with someone.

overturn *verb* **overturns, overturning, overturned**
1 to make something turn or fall over.
2 to turn over, as in *The car overturned.*

overview *noun* **overviews**
a general survey.

overwhelm *verb* **overwhelms, overwhelming, overwhelmed**
to overcome someone; to weigh down or bury something under a huge mass of something, as in *The bushfire overwhelmed several country towns.*

overwork *verb* **overworks, overworking, overworked**
1 to work too hard.   2 to use something too much, as in *Don't overwork the word 'nice'—find a more interesting word instead.*

overwrought *adjective*
overexcited, nervous, as in *The child became overwrought at test time.*

ovulate *verb* **ovulates, ovulating, ovulated**
to produce eggs or discharge them from the ovary.

ovum *noun* **ova** (*say* **oh**-vuhm)
a female cell in plants and animals that can develop into offspring.

owe *verb* **owes, owing, owed**
1 to have a duty to pay or give something to someone, especially money that you have borrowed, as in *I owed her a dollar.*
2 to have something because of someone else, as in *They owed their lives to the pilot's skill.*
owing to, because of.

owl *noun* **owls**
a nocturnal bird of prey with large eyes and a hooked beak, as in *Owls usually hunt at night.*

own *adjective*
belonging to yourself.
get your own back, (*colloquial*) to get revenge.
on your own, by yourself; alone, as in *I did it all on my own. I sat on my own in the empty church.*

own *verb* **owns, owning, owned**
to have something that belongs to you.
own up, (*colloquial*) to confess, as in *Has anyone owned up to the theft yet?*

owner *noun* **owners**
the person who owns something.
ownership *noun*

ox *noun* **oxen**
a neutered bull kept for its meat and for pulling carts.

oxide *noun* **oxides**
a compound of oxygen and another element.

oxidise or **oxidize** *verb* **oxidises, oxidising, oxidised**
to cause something to combine with oxygen; to combine with oxygen.
oxidation *noun*

oxygen *noun*
one of the gases in the air that people need to stay alive.

oyster *noun* **oysters**
an edible shellfish whose shell sometimes contains a pearl.

Oz *noun*
(*colloquial*) Australia.

ozone *noun*
a colourless gas that is a form of oxygen.
ozone-friendly, not harmful to the ozone layer, as in *an ozone-friendly cleaning fluid.*
ozone layer, a layer of ozone in the atmosphere high above the earth, that absorbs harmful radiation from the sun.

Pp

pace *noun* **paces**
1 one step in walking or marching.
2 speed, as in *She ran at a fast pace.*

pace *verb* **paces, pacing, paced**
to walk with slow or regular steps.
pace off or **pace out**, to measure a distance in paces.

pacemaker *noun* **pacemakers**
1 someone who sets the speed for someone else in a race. 2 a device to keep someone's heart beating.

pacifist *noun* **pacifists** (*say* **pas-uh-fuhst**)
someone who believes that war is always wrong.
pacifism *noun*

pacify *verb* **pacifies, pacifying, pacified** (*say* **pas-uh-fuy**)
to make someone or something peaceful or calm.
pacification *noun*

pack *noun* **packs**
1 a bundle or collection of things. 2 a set of playing-cards. 3 a haversack. 4 a group of hounds, wolves, or other animals.
5 a group of people, especially a group of Brownies or Cubs.

pack *verb* **packs, packing, packed**
1 to put things into a suitcase, bag, box, etc. in order to move them or store them.
2 to fill a place, as in *The hall was packed with students.*
packer *noun*

package *noun* **packages**
1 a parcel or packet. 2 a package deal.
package deal, a number of goods or services offered or accepted together, as in *a word-processing software package.*
package holiday or **package tour**, a holiday with everything arranged by travel agents.

packet *noun* **packets**
a small parcel.

pact *noun* **pacts**
an agreement.

pad *noun* **pads**
1 a piece of soft material used to protect or shape something. 2 a device to protect your legs in cricket or other games. 3 a flat surface from which helicopters, spacecraft, etc. take off. 4 a number of sheets of paper joined together along one edge so that you can tear off a sheet when you need it.

pad *verb* **pads, padding, padded**
1 to put a piece of soft material on or in something to protect or shape it. 2 to walk softly.
pad out, to make a book, story, etc. longer, usually when this is not necessary.

padding *noun*
1 soft material used to protect or shape something. 2 something used to make a book, story, etc. longer.

paddle *verb* **paddles, paddling, paddled**
1 to walk about in shallow water. 2 to move a boat along with a short oar.

paddle *noun* **paddles**
1 a time spent walking in shallow water.
2 a time spent moving a boat with a short oar. 3 a short oar.

paddock *noun* **paddocks**
A large piece of land surrounded by a fence mainly used for grazing animals or growing crops.

paddy *noun* **paddies**
a field where rice is grown.

a
b
c
d
e
f
g
h
i
j
k
l
m
n
o
p
q
r
s
t
u
v
w
x
y
z

padlock

padlock *noun* **padlocks**
a lock with a metal loop that you can use to fasten something shut.

paediatrics *plural noun* (*say* pee-dee-**at**-riks)
the branch of medicine dealing with children and their diseases.

pagan *noun* **pagans** (*say* **pay**-guhn)
a non-religious person.

page *noun* **pages**
1 a piece of paper that is part of a book, magazine, etc.; one side of this piece of paper. 2 a boy who acts as a servant or attendant.

page *verb* **pages, paging, paged**
to call someone in a hotel, airport, etc. especially by making an announcement over the public address system.

pageant *noun* **pageants** (*say* **paj**-uhnt)
1 a play or entertainment about historical events and people. 2 a procession of people in costume.
pageantry *noun*

pagoda *noun* **pagodas** (*say* puh-**goh**-duh)
a temple, especially a tower with many tiers, found in India and East Asia.

paid past tense and past participle of **pay** *verb*.

pain *noun* **pains**
1 an unpleasant feeling caused when part of your body is injured or diseased. 2 a feeling of deep unhappiness, as in *His mother's death caused him great pain*.
pains, careful effort or trouble, as in *He took pains to do the job properly*.
painless *adjective*

painful *adjective*
able to cause pain.
painfully *adverb*

painkiller *noun* **painkillers**
a drug that reduces pain.

painstaking *adjective*
making a careful effort.

paint *noun* **paints**
a substance put on something to colour or cover it.
paintbox *noun*, **paintbrush** *noun*

paint *verb* **paints, painting, painted**
1 to put paint on something. 2 to make a picture with paints; to make a picture of someone or something in this way.

painter *noun* **painters**
1 someone who paints. 2 a rope used to tie up a boat.

painting *noun* **paintings**
1 a painted picture, as in *These paintings of Ned Kelly are by Sidney Nolan*. 2 using paints to make a picture, as in *She likes painting*.

pair *noun* **pairs**
1 two things or people that go together or are the same kind, as in *a pair of shoes*. 2 something made of two joined parts, as in *a pair of scissors*.

pal *noun* **pals**
(*colloquial*) a friend, mate.

palace *noun* **palaces**
the official home of a monarch, president, archbishop, etc.

palatable *adjective*
pleasant to taste; acceptable.

palate *noun* **palates** (*say* **pal**-uht)
1 the roof of your mouth. 2 a person's sense of taste, as in *She has a refined palate*.

Usage Do not confuse **palate** with **palette**, which means a board on which an artist mixes colours.

Palawa *noun*
an Aborigine from Tasmania.

Origin This word comes from a Tasmanian Aboriginal language: **Palawa** = native. See the Aboriginal Languages map at the back of this dictionary.

pale *adjective* **paler, palest**
1 almost white, as in *a pale face*. 2 not bright in colour; faint, as in *a pale blue sky*.
palely *adverb*, **paleness** *noun*

palette *noun* **palettes** (*say* **pal**-uht)
a board on which an artist mixes colours.

Usage Do not confuse **palette** with **palate**, which means the roof of your mouth, or your sense of taste.

paling *noun* **palings**
the long narrow piece of timber used in building a fence.

pallid *adjective*
pale, especially because of illness.
pallor *noun*

palm *noun* **palms**
1 the inner part of your hand, between your fingers and your wrist. 2 a tropical tree with large leaves and no branches.
Palm Sunday, the Sunday before Easter.

palmist *noun* **palmists**
someone who claims to be able to tell, by looking at your hand, what will happen to you in the future.
palmistry *noun*

palpitate *verb* **palpitates, palpitating, palpitated**
1 to tremble, as in *She palpitated with fear*. **2** (*of the heart*) to beat faster due to exercise, illness, etc.

pampas *plural noun*
the grassy plains of South America.
pampas-grass, a tall plant with sharp-edged leaves and feathery flowers.

pamper *verb* **pampers, pampering, pampered**
to be too kind towards a person or animal, letting him or her have or do whatever he or she wants.

pamphlet *noun* **pamphlets**
a thin book with a cover of paper or thin cardboard.

pan *noun* **pans**
a pot or dish with a flat base.

pan *verb* **pans, panning, panned**
to separate gold and other metals from gravel by washing in a pan.

pancake *noun* **pancakes**
a thin flat cake of fried batter.

pancreas *noun* (*say* **pang**-kree-uhs)
the gland near the stomach which helps digestion.

panda *noun* **pandas**
a large, furry, black-and-white animal found in China.

pandemonium *noun*
a loud noise or disturbance.

pane *noun* **panes**
a sheet of glass in a window.

panel *noun* **panels**
1 a long, flat piece of wood, metal, etc. that is part of a door, wall, or piece of furniture. **2** a group of people appointed to discuss or decide something, as in *a panel of judges*.

pang *noun* **pangs**
a sudden feeling of guilt, sadness, or other emotion.

panic *noun*
sudden uncontrollable fear.
panicky *adjective*

panic *verb* **panics, panicking, panicked**
to be filled with sudden uncontrollable fear.

panorama *noun* **panoramas**
a view or picture of a wide area.
panoramic *adjective*

pansy *noun* **pansies**
a small, brightly-coloured garden flower.

pant *verb* **pants, panting, panted**
to take short, quick breaths, usually after running or working hard.

panther *noun* **panthers**
a leopard.

pantihose *noun*
women's tights made from stretch material like lycra, nylon, etc.

pantomime *noun* **pantomimes**
a Christmas entertainment based on a fairy tale.

pantry *noun* **pantries**
a cupboard or small room where food is kept.

pants *plural noun*
1 women's underpants. **2** trousers or slacks.

paper *noun* **papers**
1 a thin substance used for writing or printing on, wrapping up things, etc. **2** a newspaper. **3** a document.

paperback *noun* **paperbacks**
a book with thin flexible covers.

papier mâché *noun*
(*say* pap-puh-**mash**-ay)
paper made into pulp and used to make models, ornaments, etc.
[from the French = **chewed paper**]

papyrus *noun* **papyri** (*say* puh-**puy**-ruhs)
1 a kind of paper made of reeds, used in Ancient Egypt. **2** something written on a piece of this paper. **3** the kind of reed from which this paper was made.

parable *noun* **parables**
a story told to teach people something, especially one of the stories told by Jesus.

parabola *noun* **parabolas**
(*say* puh-**rab**-uh-luh)
a curve like the path of an object thrown into the air and falling down again.
parabolic *adjective*

parachute *noun* **parachutes**
an umbrella-shaped device on which people or things can float slowly down to the ground from an aircraft.
parachuting *noun*, **parachutist** *noun*

parade *noun* **parades**
1 a procession that displays people or things. **2** an assembly of troops for inspection, etc.

parade *verb* **parades, parading, paraded**
1 to move in a procession. **2** to assemble for inspection, drill, etc.

paradise

paradise *noun*
1 heaven; a heavenly place. 2 the Garden of Eden.

paradox *noun* **paradoxes** (*say* pa-ruh-doks)
a statement which goes against common sense, but which may still be true, as in *'More haste, less speed' is a paradox.*
paradoxical *adjective*, **paradoxically** *adverb*

paragraph *noun* **paragraphs**
a division of a piece of writing, starting on a new line, as in *Paragraphs usually contain several sentences.*

parakeet *noun* **parakeets**
a small usually long-tailed parrot.

parallel *adjective*
to do with lines that are the same distance apart for their whole length, as in *Railway lines are parallel.*

parallelogram *noun* **parallelograms**
a four-sided figure with its opposite sides parallel to each other.

paralyse *verb* **paralyses, paralysing, paralysed**
1 to make someone unable to feel anything or move. 2 to make something unable to move.

paralysis *noun* (*say* puh-**ral**-uh-suhs)
being unable to move or feel anything.
paralytic *adjective*

paranoid *adjective*
neurotic, full of fear about something that does not exist, as in *She showed paranoid behaviour in refusing to enter lifts.*

parapet *noun* **parapets**
a low wall along the edge of a balcony, bridge, roof, etc.

paraphernalia *noun*
(*say* pa-ruh-fuh-**nay**-lee-uh)
numerous pieces of equipment, small possessions, etc.

Usage **paraphernalia** was originally a plural noun, but is usually treated as singular.

paraphrase *verb* **paraphrases, paraphrasing, paraphrased**
to give the meaning of a piece of writing in other words.

parasite *noun* **parasites**
an animal or plant that lives in, or on another, from which it gets its food.
parasitic *adjective*

parasol *noun* **parasols**
a lightweight umbrella used to shade yourself from the sun.

paratrooper *noun* **paratroopers**
a soldier who is trained to be dropped by parachute into battle or enemy territory.

parcel *noun* **parcels**
something wrapped up to be posted or carried.

parched *adjective*
very dry or thirsty, as in *parched earth; parched after the marathon.*

parchment *noun*
a heavy, paper-like substance made from animal skins, used for writing on.

pardon *verb* **pardons, pardoning, pardoned**
to forgive or excuse someone.
pardon me, I apologise.
pardonable *adjective*, **pardonably** *adverb*

pardon *noun*
1 forgiveness. 2 used as an exclamation to mean 'I didn't hear or understand what you said', or 'I apologise'.

parent *noun* **parents**
one of a couple who together produced a child or a young creature.
parentage *noun*, **parental** *adjective*, **parenthood** *noun*

parenthesis *noun* **parentheses**
(*say* puh-**ren**-thuh-suhs)
1 something extra inserted in a sentence between brackets or dashes. 2 one of a pair of brackets used in the middle of a sentence.

parish *noun* **parishes**
a district that has its own church.
parishioner *noun*

park *noun* **parks**
1 a large garden for public use. 2 a place where vehicles may be left for a time.

park *verb* **parks, parking, parked**
to leave a vehicle somewhere for a time.

parka *noun* **parkas**
a warm, waterproof jacket with a hood attached.

parking-meter *noun* **parking-meters**
a device that shows how long a vehicle has been parked in a street, as in *When you park your car, you put a coin in the parking-meter.*

parliament *noun* **parliaments**
a group of people that meets regularly and makes a country's laws.
parliamentary *adjective*

parody *noun* **parodies**
a play, poem, etc. that makes fun of people or things by imitating them.

parole *noun* (*say* puh-**rohl**)
the release of a prisoner before his or her sentence is finished, on condition that he or she behaves well, as in *He was on parole.*

parrot *noun* **parrots**
a brightly-coloured bird with a short hooked bill, having the ability to mimic the human voice.

parse *verb* **parses, parsing, parsed** (*say* pahz)
to work out what part of speech each word is in a given sentence.

parsley *noun*
a green plant used to flavour and decorate food.

parsnip *noun* **parsnips**
a whitish vegetable shaped like a carrot.

parson *noun* **parsons**
a member of the clergy.
parsonage *noun*

part *noun* **parts**
1 anything that belongs to something bigger; a piece. 2 the character played by an actor or actress; the words spoken by a character in a play.

part of speech *noun*
the categories or classes to which words are assigned according to their purpose in specific texts, as in *In English some parts of speech are: common noun, pronoun, verb, adjective, adverb, preposition and conjunction.*

part *verb* **parts, parting, parted**
1 to separate people or things. 2 to divide hair so that it goes in two different directions.

part with *noun*
to give away or get rid of something.

part-exchange *noun* **part-exchanges**
giving something you own as well as some money to get something else.

partial *adjective*
to do with a part; not complete, as in *a partial eclipse.*
partial to something, fond of something.
partially *adverb*

participate *verb* **participates, participating, participated**
to take part or have a share in something.
participant *noun*, **participation** *noun*

participle *noun* **participles**
a word formed from a verb and used as part of the verb or as an adjective, as in *Participles are words like 'going', 'gone', 'sailed', and 'sailing'.*

particle *noun* **particles**
1 a tiny piece, as in *particles of dust.* 2 (*in Science*) one of the tiny simple parts, such as electrons, neutrons, and protons, of which all matter is made.

particular *adjective*
1 only this one and no other; special; individual. 2 fussy; hard to please.
in particular, especially; chiefly.
particularly *adverb*

particular *noun* **particulars**
a detail; a single fact.

parting *noun* **partings**
leaving; separation.

partition *noun* **partitions**
1 a thin dividing wall. 2 dividing something into parts.

partly *adverb*
not completely; somewhat.

partner *noun* **partners**
one of a pair of people who do something together, especially in business, dancing, or playing a game.
partnership *noun*

partridge *noun* **partridges**
a European or Asian game-bird with brown feathers.

part-time *adjective* and *adverb*
working for only some of the normal hours.
part-timer *noun*

party *noun* **parties**
1 a time when people get together to enjoy themselves, as in *my birthday party.* 2 a group of people working or travelling together, as in *a search party.* 3 an organised group of people with similar political beliefs, as in *the Labor Party.* 4 a person who is involved in an action or legal case, as in *the guilty party.*

pascal *noun* **pascals**
a unit of pressure equal to one newton per square metre.

pass *verb* **passes, passing, passed**
1 to go by. 2 to move or go, as in *They passed over the bridge.* 3 to give something to someone; to hand over, as in *Please pass the salt.* 4 to be successful in an examination. 5 to spend time. 6 to approve or accept, as in *The law was passed.*
pass away, to die.
passable *adjective*

pass *noun* **passes**
1 going by something. 2 the transfer of the ball to a team-mate in football, basketball, etc. 3 a permit to go in or out of a place. 4 a narrow way between hills.

passage

passage *noun* **passages**
1 a corridor. 2 a way through something, as in *The police forced a passage through the crowd.* 3 a journey by sea or air. 4 a section of a piece of writing or music. 5 passing, as in *the passage of time.*
passageway *noun*

passenger *noun* **passengers**
someone who is driven in a car or train, flown in an aircraft, etc.

passion *noun* **passions**
1 strong emotion. 2 great enthusiasm.
the Passion, Jesus's suffering on the Cross.
passionate *adjective,* **passionately** *adverb*

passionfruit *noun*
a small fruit having purple skin with edible seeds and pulp.

passive *adjective*
not active; not resisting or fighting.
passively *adverb*

passive verb *noun*
a verb that affects the subject, not the object of a sentence, as in *The verb is passive in 'She was chased by a dog'.*

Passover *noun*
a Jewish religious festival, celebrating the escape of the Jews from Egypt.

passport *noun* **passports**
an official document that you must have if you want to travel abroad.

password *noun* **passwords**
a secret word or phrase used to distinguish friends from enemies, or to gain access to a computer system.

past *noun*
the time before now.

past *adjective*
to do with the time before now.

past *preposition*
1 beyond, as in *Go past the school.* 2 after, as in *It is past midnight.*
past it, (*colloquial*) too old to be able to do something.

past participle *noun*
a form of a verb used after *has, have, was, were,* etc. to describe an action that happened at a time before now, as in *'Done', 'overtaken',* and *'written'* are past participles.

past tense *noun*
a form of a verb used by itself to describe an action that happened at a time before now, as in *'Went' is the past tense of 'go'.*

pasta *noun*
a paste of flour, water, and often eggs, made into various shapes and used as food.

paste *noun* **pastes**
a soft and moist or gluey substance.

paste *verb* **pastes, pasting, pasted**
to stick something with paste.

pastel *noun* **pastels**
1 a crayon that is like a slightly greasy chalk. 2 a light, delicate colour.

pasteurise or **pasteurize** *verb* **pasteurises, pasteurising, pasteurised**
(*say* pahs-chuh-ruyz)
to purify milk by heating it.
pasteurisation *noun*

pastime *noun* **pastimes**
something done to pass time pleasantly.

pastoralist *noun* **pastoralists**
the owner of a large grazing property or properties.

pastry *noun* **pastries**
1 a mixture of flour, fat, and water rolled flat and baked. 2 something made of this kind of mixture.

pasture *noun* **pastures**
land covered with grass that cattle, sheep, horses, etc. can eat.

pasty *noun* **pasties** (*say* pahs-tee *or* pas-tee)
a sort of pie with a vegetable and meat filling.

pasty *adjective* **pastier, pastiest** (*say* pays-tee)
pale or white, as in *a pasty face.*

pat *verb* **pats, patting, patted**
to tap something or someone gently with your open hand or with something flat.

pat *noun* **pats**
a patting movement or sound.
a pat on the back, congratulations or praise.

patch *noun* **patches**
1 a piece of material put over a hole or damaged place. 2 an area that is different from its surroundings, as in *a black cat with a white patch on her chest.* 3 a small area of land. 4 a small piece of something, as in *There are patches of ice on the road.*

patch *verb* **patches, patching, patched**
to put a piece of material on something as a repair.
patch up, to repair something roughly; to settle a quarrel, as in *He's patched up his rusty old car again. We tried to patch up our disagreement.*

patchwork *noun*
joining small pieces of different cloth together; a piece of material made in this way, as in *a bedspread made of patchwork.*

pawn

patchy *adjective* **patchier, patchiest**
1 occurring in small distinct areas, as in *There may be patchy rain.* 2 not of the same quality throughout, as in *His work has been patchy in the past.*

pâté *noun* **pâtés** (*say* **pat**-ay *or* **pah**-tay)
a paste of mashed and spiced liver, meat, fish, etc.

patent *noun* **patents** (*say* **pay**-tuhnt)
official authority to make something you have invented and to stop other people copying it.
patent *adjective*

patent *adjective* (*say* **pay**-tuhnt)
obvious, as in *Her statement is a patent lie.*
patent leather, glossy leather.
patently *adverb*

patent *verb* **patents, patenting, patented**
(*say* **pay**-tuhnt *or* **pat**-uhnt)
to get a patent for an invention, etc.

paternal *adjective*
to do with or being like a father.

path *noun* **paths**
1 a narrow way to walk or ride along.
2 the line along which something moves, as in *the path of the meteor.*

pathetic *adjective*
1 sad; pitiful, as in *The orphan looked pathetic.* 2 sadly or comically weak or useless, as in *He made a pathetic attempt to climb the tree.*
pathetically *adverb*

pathologist *noun* **pathologist**
a doctor who specialises in studying the symptoms of disease.

patience *noun* (*say* **pay**-shuhns)
1 being patient. 2 a card-game for one person.

patient *adjective* (*say* **pay**-shuhnt)
1 able to wait for a long time without getting angry. 2 able to bear pain or trouble.
patiently *adverb*

patient *noun* **patients** (*say* **pay**-shuhnt)
someone who is ill or who is getting treatment from a doctor or dentist.

patio *noun* **patios** (*say* **pat**-ee-oh)
a paved area next to a house.

patriot *noun* **patriots**
(*say* **pay**-tree-uht *or* **pat**-ree-uht)
someone who loves and supports his or her country.
patriotic *adjective*, **patriotism** *noun*

patrol *verb* **patrols, patrolling, patrolled**
to move around a place or a thing so as to guard it and see that all is well.

patrol *noun* **patrols**
1 a patrolling group of people, ships, aircraft, etc. 2 a group of Scouts or Guides.
on patrol, patrolling.

patron *noun* **patrons** (*say* **pay**-truhn)
someone who supports a person or cause with money or encouragement.
patron saint, a saint who is thought to protect a particular place, person, etc.
patronage *noun*

patronise or **patronize** *verb* **patronises, patronising, patronised**
1 to be a regular customer of a shop, restaurant, etc. 2 to treat as a lesser person, as in *The older students patronised the kindergarten class.*

patter *noun* **patters**
1 a series of light tapping sounds. 2 the quick talk of a comedian, conjurer, salesman, etc.

pattern *noun* **patterns**
1 a decorative group of lines or shapes. 2 a thing that you copy in order to make something, as in *a dress pattern.*

pause *noun* **pauses**
a short stop before continuing.

pause *verb* **pauses, pausing, paused**
to make a short stop before continuing.

pave *verb* **paves, paving, paved**
to make a hard surface for a road, path, etc.
pave the way, to prepare for something.

pavement *noun* **pavements**
a paved path for pedestrians beside a road; a footpath.

pavilion *noun* **pavilions**
1 a summer house or decorative shelter in a park. 2 a large tent at a show, sporting event, etc.

pavlova *noun* **pavlovas**
a dessert having a large soft-centred meringue cake topped with whipped cream and fruit, often passionfruit.
[from the name of the Russian ballerina Anna *Pavlova*]

paw *noun* **paws**
an animal's foot.

paw *verb* **paws, pawing, pawed**
to touch someone or something with a paw; to touch someone or something clumsily with a hand.

pawn *noun* **pawns**
1 one of the least valuable pieces in chess. 2 a person who is controlled by someone else.

a
b
c
d
e
f
g
h
i
j
k
l
m
n
o
p
q
r
s
t
u
v
w
x
y
z

pawn

pawn *verb* **pawns, pawning, pawned**
to leave something with a pawnbroker so as to borrow money from him or her, as in *I pawned my watch.*

pawnbroker *noun* **pawnbrokers**
a shopkeeper who lends money to people in return for objects that they hand over to him or her and which are sold if the money is not paid back.

pawpaw *noun* **pawpaws**
an oval-shaped tropical fruit with soft orange flesh; the tree bearing this fruit.

pay *verb* **pays, paying, paid**
1 to give money in return for something, as in *Have you paid for your lunch?* 2 to be profitable, as in *It pays to advertise.* 3 to give or make, as in *He paid me a compliment.* 4 to suffer for something you have done, as in *I'll make you pay for this!*
Pay As You Earn, the regular deduction of income tax from weekly or monthly earnings.
pay back, to pay money that you owe; to get revenge on someone, as in *I've paid back my debts. She is determined to pay him back for cheating her.*

pay *noun*
wages, as in *Have you had your pay?*

pay-back *noun* **pay-backs**
(*Aboriginal English*) an act of revenge in traditional Aboriginal law.

PAYE short for **Pay As You Earn.**

payment *noun* **payments**
1 the action of paying. 2 money paid.

PC short for **personal computer.**

PE short for **physical education.**

pea *noun* **peas**
a tiny, round, green vegetable that grows inside a pod.

peace *noun*
1 a time when there is no war, violence, or disorder. 2 quietness; calm.

peaceful *adjective*
1 having peace, as in *a peaceful country.* 2 liking or working for peace, as in *a peaceful man.*
peacefully *adverb*

peach *noun* **peaches**
a round, soft, juicy fruit with a large stone.

peacock *noun* **peacocks**
a large bird with a long, brightly-coloured tail that it can spread out like a fan.

peak *noun* **peaks**
1 the top of a mountain. 2 the highest or best point of something, as in *at the peak of*

his career. 3 the part of a cap that sticks out in front.
peak hour, the time of the most intense traffic.
peaked *adjective*

peal *verb* **peals, pealing, pealed**
to make a loud ringing sound.

> **Usage** Do not confuse the verb **peal** with the verb **peel,** which means to remove a peel or covering, or to lose a covering or skin.

peal *noun* **peals**
a loud ringing sound.

> **Usage** Do not confuse the noun **peal** with the noun **peel,** which is the skin of fruit or vegetables.

peanut *noun* **peanuts**
a small, round nut that grows in a pod in the ground.
peanut butter, roasted peanuts crushed into a paste.

pear *noun* **pears**
a pale green or brownish juicy fruit that gets narrower near the stalk.

pearl *noun* **pearls**
a small, shiny, white ball found in the shells of some oysters and used as a jewel.
pearly *adjective*

peasant *noun* **peasants**
a person who belongs to a farming community, especially in poor areas of the world.
peasantry *noun*

peat *noun*
rotted plant material that can be dug out of the ground and used as fertiliser.

pebble *noun* **pebbles**
a small round stone.
pebbly *adjective*

pecan *noun* **pecans** (*say* pee-kan *or* pee-kuhn)
a pinkish-brown, smooth nut with an edible centre.

peck *verb* **pecks, pecking, pecked**
1 to bite or eat something with the beak, as in *The hens were pecking at the corn.* 2 (*colloquial*) to give someone a quick kiss.

peck *noun* **pecks**
1 a short, sharp bite with the beak. 2 (*colloquial*) a quick kiss, as in *She gave him a peck on the cheek.*

peckish *adjective*
(*colloquial*) hungry.

peculiar *adjective*
strange; unusual.
peculiar to, restricted to, as in *a custom that is peculiar to one tribe*.
peculiarity *noun*, **peculiarly** *adverb*

pedal *noun* **pedals**
part of a machine worked by a person's foot, as in *A bicycle has two pedals*.

pedal *verb* **pedals, pedalling, pedalled**
to push or turn the pedal or pedals of a device; to move something by using pedals, as in *You pump air for the organ by pedalling. She pedalled her bicycle right across the Nullarbor*.

peddle *verb* **peddles, peddling, peddled**
to sell things from door to door.

pedestal *noun* **pedestals**
the base that supports a statue, pillar, etc.
put someone on a pedestal, to admire someone greatly or think that he or she is perfect.

pedestrian *noun* **pedestrians**
someone who is walking.

pedigree *noun* **pedigrees**
a list of a person's or animal's ancestors, especially to show how purely an animal has been bred.

pedlar *noun* **pedlars**
someone who goes from house to house selling small things; a door-to-door salesperson.

peel *noun* **peels**
the skin of some fruit and vegetables.

Usage Do not confuse the noun **peel** with the noun **peal**, which means a loud ringing sound.

peel *verb* **peels, peeling, peeled**
1 to remove the peel or covering from something. 2 to lose a covering or skin, as in *My skin is peeling*.

Usage Do not confuse the verb **peel** with the verb **peal**, which means to make a loud ringing sound.

peep *verb* **peeps, peeping, peeped**
1 to look quickly or secretly. 2 to look through a narrow opening. 3 to show slightly or briefly, as in *The moon peeped out through the clouds*.
peep-hole *noun*

peer *verb* **peers, peering, peered**
to look at something closely or with difficulty.

peer *noun* **peers**
1 a person of your own age or rank.
2 a nobleman.
peer group, a group of people of the same age, status, etc.

peg *noun* **pegs**,
1 a clip or pin for fixing things in place or for hanging things on. 2 a clothes-peg.

peg *verb* **pegs, pegging, pegged**
1 to fix something with pegs, as in *We pegged out the tent*. 2 to keep something at a fixed amount, as in *The price was pegged at $4*.
peg out, (*colloquial*) to die.

Pekingese or **Pekinese** *noun* **Pekingese** or **Pekinese** (*say* pee-kuh-**neez**)
a small breed of dog with short legs and long silky hair.

pelican *noun* **pelicans**
a large bird with a pouch in its long beak for storing fish.

pellet *noun* **pellets**
a tiny ball of metal, food, wet paper, etc.

pelt *verb* **pelts, pelting, pelted**
1 to throw a lot of things at someone, as in *We pelted him with snowballs*. 2 to move very quickly. 3 to rain very hard, as in *The rain pelted down*.

pelt *noun* **pelts**
an animal skin, especially with the fur or hair on it.

pelvis *noun* **pelvises**
the large, wide, curved group of bones at the base of the spine at the level of the hips.

pen *noun* **pens**
1 an instrument for writing, etc. with ink. 2 an enclosure for cattle or other animals.
pen-friend, someone that you write to regularly but usually do not meet.

penalise or **penalize** *verb* **penalises, penalising, penalised**
1 to punish someone. 2 to give a penalty against someone in a game.

penalty *noun* **penalties**
1 a punishment. 2 an advantage given to one side in a game when a member of the other side breaks a rule. 3 a goal scored as the result of a penalty.

penance *noun* **penances**
a punishment willingly done to show you are sorry for doing wrong.

pencil *noun* **pencils**
a device for drawing or writing, made of a thin stick of graphite or coloured chalk inside a cylinder of wood or metal.

a
b
c
d
e
f
g
h
i
j
k
l
m
n
o
p
q
r
s
t
u
v
w
x
y
z

pencil

pencil *verb* **pencils, pencilling, pencilled**
to draw or write with a pencil.

pendant *noun* **pendants**
an ornament hung round your neck on a long chain or string.

pendulum *noun* **pendulums**
a rod with a weight on the end so that it swings to and fro, as in *Some clocks are worked by pendulums*.

penetrate *verb* **penetrates, penetrating, penetrated**
to make or find a way through or into something.
penetration *noun*

penguin *noun* **penguins**
an Antarctic sea bird that cannot fly but uses its wings as flippers for swimming.

penicillin *noun*
a drug obtained from fungi, that kills bacteria.

peninsula *noun* **peninsulas**
a long piece of land that is almost surrounded by water.
peninsular *adjective*

penis *noun* **penises**
the part of the body with which a male urinates or has sexual intercourse.

penitence *noun*
regret that you have done wrong.
penitent *adjective*

penitentiary *noun* **penitentiaries**
(*say* pen-uh-**ten**-shuh-ree)
a jail or prison.

penknife *noun* **penknives**
a small folding knife.

pennant *noun* **pennants**
1 a triangular or tapering flag.   2 a flag awarded for success in sports, as in *Geelong unfurled the Premiership pennant in 1964*.

penniless *adjective*
having no money; very poor.

penny *noun* **pennies** or **pence**
a coin worth a hundredth of a pound in the currency of Britain. Before 1966, the penny was part of Australian currency.

pension *noun* **pensions**
a regular payment made by a government to people above a certain age, widows, etc.

pensioner *noun* **pensioners**
someone who receives a pension.

pensive *adjective*
thoughtful and quiet, sometimes in a sad way, as in *The war film made the soldier pensive*.

pentagon *noun* **pentagons**
a flat shape with five sides.

people *plural noun*
1 men, women, and children.   2 the men, women, and children who live in a country.

pepper *noun* **peppers**
1 a hot-tasting powder used to flavour food.   2 a bright green or red vegetable; a capsicum.
peppery *adjective*

peppermint *noun* **peppermints**
1 a kind of mint used for flavouring.   2 a sweet flavoured with this mint.

per *preposition*
for each; in each, as in *The charge is $2 per person*.
per cent, for or in every hundred, as in *A pay-rise from $100 to $110 is a 10 per cent (10%) increase*.

per annum *adverb*
each year, as in *$15,000 per annum*.

per capita *adjective* and *adverb*
for each person, as in *The daily water consumption was thirty litres per capita*.

perceive *verb* **perceives, perceiving, perceived**
to notice something.
perceptible *adjective*, **perceptibly** *adverb*, **perception** *noun*

per cent *noun*
short for percentage.

percentage *noun* **percentages**
1 the proportion out of every hundred of something, as in *Out of $300 he spent $60, a percentage of 20*.   2 a part or a proportion of something, as in *A large percentage of teenagers enjoy pop music*.

perceptive *adjective*
quick to notice things.

perch *noun* **perch**
a marine or freshwater fish that can be eaten.

perch *noun* **perches**
a place where a bird sits or rests.

perch *verb* **perches, perching, perched**
to sit or stand on the edge of something or on something small.

percolator *noun* **percolators**
a device for making coffee.

percussion *noun*
musical instruments played by hitting or shaking, as in *Drums, cymbals, and chime bars are percussion instruments*.
percussive *adjective*

perennial *adjective*
1 lasting or recurring for many years, as in *a perennial problem.* 2 flowering for many years, as in *perennial plants.*
perennially *adverb*

perfect *adjective* (*say* **per**-fuhkt)
1 so good that it cannot be made any better; without any faults. 2 complete, as in *a perfect stranger.*
perfection *noun*, **perfectly** *adverb*

perfect *verb* **perfects, perfecting, perfected** (*say* per-**fekt**)
to make something so good that it cannot be made any better.

perfect *noun*
a form of verb that describes a completed action or event in the past, as in *In English, the perfect includes the word 'has' or 'have', as in 'The letter has arrived'.*

perforate *verb* **perforates, perforating, perforated**
to make tiny holes in something, especially so that it can be torn easily.
perforation *noun*

perform *verb* **performs, performing, performed**
1 to do something in front of an audience, as in *They performed 'Macbeth' in the school hall.* 2 to do something you have to do or ought to do, as in *The surgeon performed the operation.*
performance *noun*, **performer** *noun*

perfume *noun* **perfumes**
1 a liquid with a very sweet smell.
2 a sweet smell.

pergola *noun* **pergolas** (*say* per-**goh**-luh *or* per-guh-luh)
a timber frame over which plants are trained to grow.

perhaps *adverb*
it may be; possibly.

peril *noun* **perils**
danger, as in *She was in great peril.*
perilous *adjective*, **perilously** *adverb*

perimeter *noun* **perimeters**
(*say* puh-**rim**-uh-tuh)
1 the distance around the edge of something.
2 a boundary, as in *A fence marks the perimeter of the airfield.*

period *noun* **periods**
1 a length of time. 2 the time every month when a woman or girl menstruates.
periodic *adjective*, **periodically** *adverb*

period *adjective*
to do with a particular period of history, as in *period furniture.*

periodical *noun* **periodicals**
a magazine published regularly.

periscope *noun* **periscopes**
a device using mirrors to let you see something on a higher level than where you are or around a corner.

perish *verb* **perishes, perishing, perished**
1 to die. 2 to rot, as in *The tyres have perished.*
perishable *adjective*

perjury *noun* (*say* **per**-juh-ree)
the act of deliberately telling a lie when under oath in court.

perky *adjective* **perkier, perkiest**
lively; cheerful.

permanent *adjective*
lasting for ever or for a very long time.
permanence *noun*, **permanently** *adverb*

permission *noun*
permitting something; a statement that something is permitted.

permissive *adjective*
letting people do what they wish; tolerant, as in *permissive parents; a permissive society.*
permissively *adverb*, **permissiveness** *noun*

permit *verb* **permits, permitting, permitted** (*say* puh-**mit**)
to say that someone may do something; to let someone do something.
permissible *adjective*

permit *noun* **permits** (*say* per-**mit**)
a written or printed statement that something is permitted.

perpendicular *adjective*
1 upright, as in *a perpendicular cliff-face.* 2 at a right angle to the base or to another line, as in *a perpendicular line.*

perpetual *adjective*
continual; permanent.
perpetually *adverb*, **perpetuate** *verb*

perplex *verb* **perplexes, perplexing, perplexed**
to puzzle someone very much.
perplexity *noun*

persecute *verb* **persecutes, persecuting, persecuted**
to be continually cruel to someone, especially because you disagree with his or her beliefs.
persecution *noun*, **persecutor** *noun*

persevere *verb* **perseveres, persevering, persevered**
to go on despite difficulties.
perseverance *noun*

a
b
c
d
e
f
g
h
i
j
k
l
m
n
o
p
q
r
s
t
u
v
w
x
y
z

persist

persist *verb* persists, persisting, persisted
1 to keep on doing something, as in *She persists in slamming doors.* **2** to go on despite difficulties, as in *At first his experiments were unsuccessful, but he persisted.*
persistence *noun*, **persistent** *adjective*, **persistently** *adverb*

person *noun* persons
1 a man, woman, or child. **2** (*in grammar*) the parts of a verb and the pronouns that refer to someone who is speaking (the *first person*), someone who is spoken to (the *second person*), or someone who is spoken of (the *third person*), as in *'I write' is the first person singular of 'to write'; 'they write' is the third person plural.*

personal *adjective*
1 belonging to, done by, or concerning a particular person, as in *The film star made a personal appearance at the gala.* **2** private, as in *We have personal business to discuss.*
personal computer, a small computer designed to be used by one person.
personally *adverb*

Usage Do not confuse **personal** with **personnel**, which means the people employed in a place.

personality *noun* personalities
1 a person's nature and characteristics, as in *She has a friendly personality.* **2** a well-known person, as in *television personalities.*

personnel *noun* (*say* per-suh-**nel**)
the people employed in a particular place.

Usage Do not confuse **personnel** with **personal**, which means belonging to, done by, or concerning a person.

perspective *noun* perspectives
the impression of depth and space in a picture or scene.
in perspective, in a way that gives a balanced view of things, as in *Look at your problems in perspective.*

perspire *verb* perspires, perspiring, perspired
to give off moisture through the pores of your skin.
perspiration *noun*

Usage **perspire** and **perspiration** have the same meaning as **sweat** (verb and noun), but are thought by some people to be politer words than **sweat**.

persuade *verb* persuades, persuading, persuaded
to get someone to agree with something.
persuasion *noun*, **persuasive** *adjective*

perturb *verb* perturbs, perturbing, perturbed
to disturb or make anxious, as in *She was perturbed by the bad news.*

perverse *adjective* (*say* puh-**vers**)
obstinately being unreasonable or wicked.
perversely *adverb*, **perversity** *noun*

pervert *verb* perverts, perverting, perverted (*say* puh-**vert**)
1 to make something go wrong. **2** to make someone behave in a way that most people find unacceptable.
perversion *noun*

pervert *noun* perverts (*say* per-**vert**)
someone who behaves in a way that most people find unacceptable, especially in sexual matters.

pessimism *noun*
expecting that things will not happen as you want.
pessimist *noun*, **pessimistic** *adjective*

pest *noun* pests
a destructive or annoying animal or person.

pester *verb* pesters, pestering, pestered
to annoy someone with frequent questions, requests, etc.

pesticide *noun* pesticides
a chemical used to kill insects and grubs, especially on plants.

pestle *noun* pestles
a club-shaped instrument for pounding substances in a mortar.

pet *noun* pets
1 a tame animal kept for companionship and amusement. **2** a person treated as a favourite, as in *teacher's pet.*

petal *noun* petals
one of the separate coloured parts of a flower, as in *Daisies have a lot of white or yellow petals.*

peter *verb* peters, petering, petered
to come to an end, as in *The mine was closed when the gold petered out.*

petition *noun* petitions
a written request for something, usually signed by a large number of people.

petrify *verb* petrifies, petrifying, petrified
to make someone so terrified, surprised, etc. that he or she cannot act or move.

petrochemical *noun* petrochemicals
a chemical substance made from petroleum or natural gas.

petrol *noun*
a liquid made from petroleum, used to drive the engines of cars, planes, etc.

petrol pump, a device for putting petrol into the tank of a motor vehicle.

petrol station, a place where petrol is sold.

petroleum *noun* (*say* puh-**troh**-lee-uhm)
an oil found underground that is purified to make petrol, diesel oil, paraffin, etc.

petticoat *noun* **petticoats**
a piece of women's clothing worn under a skirt or dress; a slip.

petty *adjective* **pettier, pettiest**
small and unimportant, as in *petty regulations.*
pettily *adverb,* **pettiness** *noun*

pew *noun* **pews**
one of the long wooden seats in a church.

pewter *noun*
a grey alloy of tin and lead.

pH *noun*
a measure of the acidity or alkalinity of a solution, as in *Pure water has a pH of 7; acids have a pH between 0 and 7, and alkalis have a pH between 7 and 14.*

pharmacy *noun* **pharmacies**
(*say* **fah**-muh-see)
1 the preparation and handing out of drugs used in medicine. 2 a chemist's shop.

phase *noun* **phases**
a stage in the progress or development of something.

phase *verb* **phases, phasing, phased**
to carry out something in stages, as in *The building of the school was phased over three years.*
phase in, to start something gradually.
phase out, to stop something gradually.

pheasant *noun* **pheasants** (*say* **fez**-uhnt)
a game-bird with a long tail.

phenomenal *adjective*
(*say* fuh-**nom**-uh-nuhl)
amazing.
phenomenally *adverb*

phenomenon *noun* **phenomena**
an event or fact, especially one that is remarkable or unusual, as in *Thunder and lightning are strange phenomena.*

phial *noun* **phials** (*say* **fuy**-uhl)
a small glass bottle, especially one used for liquid medicine.

philately *noun* (*say* fuh-**lat**-uh-lee)
collecting postage stamps, as in *My hobby is philately.*
philatelic *adjective,* **philatelist** *noun*

philosophical *adjective*
1 to do with philosophy. 2 not upset by suffering, misfortune, etc., as in *He was philosophical about his illness.*
philosophically *adverb*

philosophy *noun* **philosophies**
(*say* fuh-**los**-uh-fee)
1 the study of truths about life, morals, etc. 2 a way of thinking; a system of beliefs.
philosopher *noun*

phobia *noun* **phobias** (*say* **foh**-bee-uh)
a great or unusual fear of something.

phoenix *noun* **phoenixes** (*say* **fee**-niks)
a mythical bird that was said to burn itself to death on a fire and be born again from the ashes.

phone *noun* **phones**
a telephone.

phone *verb* **phones, phoning, phoned**
to telephone.

phonecard *noun* **phonecards**
a special plastic card that you can use instead of coins to make a call on a public phone.

phone-in *noun* **phone-ins**
a broadcast program in which listeners or viewers telephone the studio and take part in the program.

phonetics *plural noun* (*say* fuh-**net**-iks)
the study of sounds used in speaking.

phoney or **phony** *adjective* **phonier, phoniest**
(*say* **foh**-nee)
false; not real, as in *They realised the counterfeit money was phoney.*

phosphorescent *adjective*
shining or glowing in the dark, as in *phosphorescent glow-worms.*
phosphorescence *noun*

phosphorus *noun*
a yellowish substance that glows in the dark.
phosphoric *adjective*

photo *noun* **photos**
a photograph.

photocopier *noun* **photocopiers**
a machine that makes photocopies.

photocopy *noun* **photocopies**
a copy of a document, page, etc. made by photography.

photo-finish *noun* **photo-finishes**
a very close finish of a race, photographed so that the winner can be decided.

a
b
c
d
e
f
g
h
i
j
k
l
m
n
o
p
q
r
s
t
u
v
w
x
y
z

photograph

photograph *noun* photographs
a picture made on film, using a camera.
photographic *adjective*, **photography** *noun*

photograph *verb* photographs,
photographing, photographed
to take a photograph of someone or
something.
photographer *noun*

photosynthesis *noun*
the process by which plants use sunlight to
turn carbon dioxide and water into
complex substances, giving off oxygen.

phrase *noun* phrases
1 a small group of words; (*in grammar*) a
group of words that is smaller than a
clause. **2** a short part of a tune.

phrase *verb* phrases, phrasing, phrased
to put something into words.

physical *adjective*
1 to do with your body, as in *physical
health*. **2** to do with things that can be
touched or seen, as in *The physical
characteristics of the earth include sand and
sea*.
physical education, gymnastics or other
exercises that you do to keep healthy.
physical geography, the branch of
geography that deals with natural features
such as rivers and mountains.
physically *adverb*

physician *noun* physicians
a doctor.

physics *noun*
the study of energy, movement, heat, light,
sound, etc.
physicist *noun*

physiology *noun* (*say* fiz-ee-**ol**-uh-gee)
the study of the bodies of people and other
living things.
physiological *adjective*, **physiologist** *noun*

physiotherapy *noun*
(*say* fiz-ee-oh-**the**-ruh-pee)
the treatment of disease, injury, etc. by
methods such as massage, heat treatment
and exercise.

physique *noun* physiques (*say* fuh-**zeek**)
the structure of someone's body, as in *The
swimmer had a muscular physique*.

pi *noun* (*say* puy)
a number roughly equal to 3.14159, shown
by the symbol π and used in calculating the
circumference and area of circles, as in *The
diameter of a circle multiplied by pi gives the
circumference*.

pianist *noun* pianists
someone who plays the piano.

piano *noun* pianos
a large musical instrument with a
keyboard.

piccolo *noun* piccolos
a small flute.

pick *verb* picks, picking, picked
1 to choose, as in *Pick someone to dance
with*. **2** to take something from where it
is, as in *She picked some flowers*. **3** to steal
from someone's pocket. **4** to open a lock
without using a key. **5** to pull bits off or
out of something.
pick holes in something, to find faults in
something.
pick on, to keep criticising or bothering a
particular person.
pick up, to take something upwards from
where it is; to collect a thing; to take
someone with you in a vehicle; to manage
to hear something; to improve, as in *I picked
up a piece of litter. Can you pick up the parcel
from their office? I'll drive over and pick you
up. This radio can pick up messages from
planes. Will the economy pick up?*

pick *noun*
1 a choice, as in *Take your pick*. **2** the best
part of something, as in *We got there first
and had the pick of the crop*.

pick *noun* picks
a pickaxe.

pickaxe *noun* pickaxes
a heavy pointed tool with a long handle,
for breaking up hard ground, concrete, etc.

picket *noun* pickets
1 a group of strikers who try to persuade
other people not to work. **2** a pointed
stake driven into the ground to form a
fence.

picket *verb* pickets, picketing, picketed
to stand outside a factory, office, etc. to
prevent people from going to work and
persuade them to join the strike.

pickle *noun* pickles
a strong-tasting food made of vegetables,
etc. preserved in vinegar.

pickle *verb* pickles, pickling, pickled
to preserve something in vinegar or salt
water.

pickpocket *noun* pickpockets
someone who steals from people's pockets.

picnic *noun* picnics
1 a meal eaten in the open air away from
home. **2** (*colloquial*) an easy thing to do,

as in *The clever student found the exam a picnic.*

picnic *verb* **picnics, picnicking, picnicked**
to have a picnic.
picnicker *noun*

pictorial *adjective*
with or using pictures.
pictorially *adverb*

picture *noun* **pictures**
1 a painting, drawing, or photograph.
2 a film at the cinema; a movie.
3 something or someone beautiful.
in the picture, knowing the facts about something.

picture *verb* **pictures, picturing, pictured**
1 to show someone or something in a picture. 2 to imagine someone or something.

picturesque *adjective* (*say* pik-chuh-**resk**)
1 attractive or charming, as in *a picturesque village.* 2 vivid, as in *a picturesque account of the battle.*

pidgin *noun* (*say* **pij**-uhn)
a simplified language containing words from two or more languages, used between people not having a common language.

pie *noun* **pies**
meat or fruit covered with pastry and baked.
pie chart, a way of showing how some quantity is divided up, using a circle divided into sectors to represent the parts of the quantity.

piece *noun* **pieces**
1 a part of something; a bit. 2 something written, composed, etc., as in *a piece of music.* 3 one of the objects used on a board to play a game, as in *a chess-piece.*
in one piece, not broken.
piece by piece, gradually; one part at a time.

piece *verb* **pieces, piecing, pieced**
to join pieces together to make something, as in *The detective pieced together what had really happened.*

piecemeal *adverb*
piece by piece.

pier *noun* **piers**
1 a long structure built out into the sea for people to walk on. 2 a pillar supporting a bridge.

pierce *verb* **pierces, piercing, pierced**
to make a hole in or through something or someone; to make or find a way through or into something, as in *The torch pierced the darkness of the cave.*

piercing *adjective*
very strong or very loud, as in *a piercing shriek.*

pig *noun* **pigs**
1 a fat animal with short legs and a blunt snout, kept by farmers for its meat.
2 (*colloquial*) someone who is greedy, dirty, or unpleasant.
piggy *adjective* and *noun*

pigeon *noun* **pigeons** (*say* **pij**-uhn)
a common, easily-tamed bird with a small head and large chest.
homing pigeon, a pigeon that can be taught to fly home from far away.

pigeon-hole *noun* **pigeon-holes**
a small compartment where you can put papers, letters, etc., especially for someone to collect.

piggyback *noun* **piggybacks**
a ride on someone's back.

pigheaded *adjective*
obstinate.

piglet *noun* **piglets**
a young pig.

pigment *noun* **pigments**
a substance that colours something.

pigsty *noun* **pigsties**
1 a building for pigs. 2 (*colloquial*) a very untidy room or place.

pigtail *noun* **pigtails**
a single plait of hair at the back of your head.

pike *noun* **pikes**
1 a type of large, fierce fish with a long, pointed head and sharp teeth found in Australian waters. 2 a weapon with a pointed metal head on a long wooden pole used in earlier times.

pikelet *noun* **pikelets**
a small pancake eaten with butter.

pilchard *noun* **pilchards**
a small marine fish.

pile *noun* **piles**
1 a number of things on top of one another. 2 (*colloquial*) a large amount of something, especially money.

pile *verb* **piles, piling, piled**
to put things on top of one another.
pile up, to become numerous, as in *Jobs were piling up.*

pilfer *verb* **pilfers, pilfering, pilfered**
to steal small things.

pilgrim *noun* **pilgrims**
someone who goes on a journey to a holy place.

a
b
c
d
e
f
g
h
i
j
k
l
m
n
o
p
q
r
s
t
u
v
w
x
y
z

pilgrimage

pilgrimage *noun* **pilgrimages**
a journey to a holy place.

pill *noun* **pills**
a small pellet of medicine.
the pill, a special kind of pill taken by a woman to prevent her from becoming pregnant.

pillage *verb* **pillages, pillaging, pillaged**
to rob in a rough and violent way.

pillion *noun* **pillions**
the seat on a motor cycle behind the driver's seat.

pillow *noun* **pillows**
a cushion for a person to rest his or her head on, especially in bed.

pilot *noun* **pilots**
1 someone who flies an aircraft.
2 someone who helps to steer a ship through narrow or dangerous places.

pilot *verb* **pilots, piloting, piloted**
to be a pilot of an aircraft or ship.

pimple *noun* **pimples**
a small, round swelling on the skin.
pimply *adjective*

pin *noun* **pins**
1 a short piece of metal with a sharp point and a rounded head, used to fasten pieces of paper, cloth, etc. together. 2 a pointed device for fixing or marking something.
pins and needles, a tingling feeling.

pin *verb* **pins, pinning, pinned**
1 to fasten something with a pin. 2 to keep a person or thing in one place, as in *He was pinned under the wreckage.*

PIN *noun*
short for PIN number, the personal identification number issued by a bank which enables its customers to make electronic transactions.
[an acronym from the first letters of the words *Personal Identification Number*]

pinafore *noun* **pinafores**
a dress without sleeves and a low neck, worn over a blouse or jumper, as in *The school uniform was a navy pinafore over a white blouse.*

pincer *noun* **pincers**
the claw of a shellfish such as the lobster or crayfish.

pincers *plural noun*
a tool for gripping and pulling things, especially for pulling out nails.

pinch *verb* **pinches, pinching, pinched**
1 to squeeze something tightly between two things, especially between your finger and thumb. 2 (*colloquial*) to steal.

pinch *noun* **pinches**
1 a firm squeezing movement. 2 the amount you can pick up between the tips of your finger and thumb, as in *a pinch of salt.*
at a pinch, if it is necessary.

pincushion *noun* **pincushions**
a small pad in which needles and pins are stuck to keep them ready for use.

pine *noun* **pines**
an evergreen tree with leaves shaped like needles, as in *Huon pine.*

pine *verb* **pines, pining, pined**
1 to long for someone or something. 2 to become weak or ill through sorrow or yearning.

pineapple *noun* **pineapples**
a large, juicy, tropical fruit with yellow flesh and tough, prickly skin.

ping-pong *noun*
table tennis.

pink *adjective* **pinker, pinkest**
pale red.

pinnacle *noun* **pinnacles**
1 a high, pointed mountain peak, or a tall pointed turret on the roof of a church, castle, etc. 2 the highest or most successful point of something, as in *Being appointed principal was the pinnacle of her career.*

pint *noun* **pints**
a liquid measurement equal to 600 millilitres.

pioneer *noun* **pioneers**
one of the first people to go to a place, do something, find out about a subject, etc.

pious *adjective*
very religious.
piously *adverb*

pip *noun* **pips**
1 a seed of an apple, orange, pear, etc. 2 a short, high-pitched sound, as in *She heard the 6 pips of the time-signal on the radio.*

pipe *noun* **pipes**
1 a tube for carrying water, gas, etc. from one place to another. 2 a short tube with a small bowl at one end, used to smoke tobacco. 3 a tubular musical instrument.
the pipes, bagpipes.

pipe *verb* pipes, piping, piped
1 to send something along pipes or wires.
2 to play music on a pipe or the bagpipes.
pipe down, (*colloquial*) be quiet.
piping hot, very hot.

pipeline *noun* pipelines
a pipe for carrying oil, water, etc. a long distance.

piranha *noun* piranhas (*say* puh-**rah**-nuh)
a small, flesh-eating fish found in South American rivers.

pirate *noun* pirates
a sailor who attacks and robs other ships.
piracy *noun*, **piratical** *adjective*

pirate *verb* pirates, pirating, pirated
to take or reproduce the work, ideas, etc. of others without permission, as in *They pirated his computer program.*

pistil *noun* pistils
the part of a flower that produces the seed.

pistol *noun* pistols
a small gun for use with one hand.

piston *noun* pistons
a disc that moves up and down inside a cylinder in an engine, pump, etc.

pit *noun* pits
1 a deep hole or hollow.   2 a coalmine.
3 the part of a race circuit where racing cars are refuelled, repaired, etc.
the pits, the very worst of something.

pit *verb* pits, pitting, pitted
1 to make deep holes, hollows, scars, etc. in something, as in *a face pitted by acne.*
2 to put someone in competition with someone else, as in *He was pitted against their strongest player.*

pitch *verb* pitches, pitching, pitched
1 to throw.   2 to put up a tent.   3 to fall heavily, as in *He tripped over the doorstep and pitched headlong.*   4 to move up and down on a rough sea.   5 to set something at a particular height, as in *We must pitch the standard so that only the best candidates pass the test.*
pitched battle, a battle between troops in prepared positions.
pitch in, to start working or eating vigorously.

pitch *noun* pitches
1 a piece of ground marked out for cricket, football, or another game.   2 the height of a voice or musical note.   3 intensity; strength, as in *Excitement was at a high pitch.*

pitch *noun*
a black, sticky substance like tar.
pitch-black or **pitch-dark,** very black or dark; with no light at all.

pitcher *noun* pitchers
1 a large jug, usually with two handles.
2 the player who throws the ball to the batter in games like softball, etc.

pitchfork *noun* pitchforks
a large fork with two prongs for lifting hay, grass, etc.

pitfall *noun* pitfalls
an unsuspected danger or difficulty.

pitiful *adjective*
1 causing pity, as in *a pitiful sight.*
2 inadequate; arousing contempt, as in *a pitiful attempt to make us laugh.*
pitifully *adverb*

pitiless *adjective*
having or showing no pity.
pitilessly *adverb*

pitta *noun*
a flat, hollow, unleavened bread which can be split and filled.

pittance *noun*
a very small sum of money.

pity *noun*
1 the feeling of being sorry that someone is in pain or trouble, as in *I feel pity for the homeless people.*   2 something that you are sorry about, as in *It's a pity we can't meet.*
take pity on someone, to help someone who is in trouble.

pity *verb* pitied, pitying, pitied
to feel pity for someone.

pivot *noun* pivots
a point on which something turns or balances.

pixie or pixy *noun* pixies
a small fairy.

pizza *noun* pizzas (*say* **peet**-suh)
a layer of dough covered with cheese, vegetables, etc. and baked.

pizzicato *adverb* and *adjective*
(*say* pit-suh-**kah**-toh)
plucking the strings of a musical instrument.

placard *noun* placards
a large notice or advertisement for everyone to read; a notice, especially one carried by a protester.

place *noun* places
1 a particular part of space, especially where something belongs; a position or area.   2 a seat, as in *Save me a place.*

place

330

from place to place, from one place to another; travelling around.
in place, in the proper position.
in place of, instead of.
out of place, not in the proper position; unsuitable, as in *Her shoulder was out of place. That tatty jacket would look out of place in a restaurant.*
place-name, the name of a town, city, etc.
take place, to happen.

place *verb* **places, placing, placed**
to put something in a particular place.

placid *adjective*
calm; peaceful.
placidity *noun*, **placidly** *adverb*

plague *noun* **plagues**
1 a dangerous illness that spreads very quickly.   2 a large number of pests, as in *a plague of mice in the Mallee.*

plague *verb* **plagues, plaguing, plagued**
to pester or annoy someone, as in *They were plagued with inquiries.*

plaid *noun* **plaids** (*say* plad)
cloth with a tartan or checkered pattern.

plain *adjective* **plainer, plainest**
1 not decorated.   2 not pretty.   3 easy to understand or see.   4 frank; straightforward.
plain clothes, civilian clothes worn instead of a uniform.
plainly *adverb*, **plainness** *noun*

plain *noun* **plains**
a large area of flat country, with few or no trees.

plaintiff *noun* **plaintiffs**
a person who brings a complaint against someone else to a lawcourt.

plaintive *adjective*
sounding sad, as in *a plaintive cry.*
plaintively *adverb*

plait *noun* **plaits** (*say* plat)
a length of hair, rope, etc. with several strands twisted together.

plait *verb* **plaits, plaiting, plaited** (*say* plat)
to make something into a plait.

plan *noun* **plans**
1 a way of doing something, thought out in advance.   2 a drawing showing what something should look like.   3 a map of a town or district.

plan *verb* **plans, planning, planned**
to think out a way of doing something.
planner *noun*

plane *noun* **planes**
1 (*colloquial*) an aeroplane.   2 a flat or level surface.   3 a tool for making wood smooth.

plane *verb* **planes, planing, planed**
to smooth wood with a plane.

planet *noun* **planets**
a large object that orbits the sun or other stars, as in *The main planets of the solar system are Mercury, Venus, Earth, Mars, Jupiter, Saturn, Uranus, Neptune, and Pluto.*
planetary *adjective*

plank *noun* **planks**
a long, flat piece of wood.

plankton *noun*
tiny creatures that float in the sea, lakes, etc.

plant *noun* **plants**
1 something that grows out of the ground, as in *Flowers, bushes, trees, and vegetables are plants.*   2 a factory or its equipment.

plant *verb* **plants, planting, planted**
1 to put something in the ground to grow.
2 to put something firmly in place, as in *He planted his feet and took hold of the rope.*
3 (*colloquial*) to put something where it will be found, usually to cause someone trouble, as in *Someone planted a packet of drugs on him.*
planter *noun*

plantain *noun* **plantains**
a tropical tree with a fruit like a banana.

plantation *noun* **plantations**
1 an area of land where cotton, tea, etc. is cultivated.   2 an area planted with trees.

plaque *noun* **plaques** (*say* plahk *or* plak)
1 a metal or porcelain plate fixed on a wall as a memorial or an ornament.   2 a substance that forms a thin layer on your teeth, allowing bacteria to gather.

plasma *noun* (*say* plaz-muh)
the colourless liquid part of blood which carries the corpuscles.

plaster *noun* **plasters**
1 a small covering that sticks to the skin around a wound.   2 a mixture of lime, sand, water, etc. used to cover walls and ceilings.
plaster of Paris, a white paste used for making moulds and cast shapes.

plaster *verb* **plasters, plastering, plastered**
1 to cover a surface with plaster.   2 to cover something thickly, as in *The toddlers plastered the floor with mud.*
plasterer *noun*

plastered *adjective*
(*colloquial*) drunk.

plastic *noun* **plastics**
a strong, light, synthetic substance that can be moulded into different shapes.

plastic *adjective*
made of plastic, as in *a plastic bag*.
plastic surgery, work done by a surgeon to alter or mend parts of someone's body.

plasticine *noun*
a soft, coloured, easily shaped substance used for making models.

plate *noun* **plates**
1 a dish that is flat or almost flat. 2 a flat sheet of metal, glass, etc. 3 one of the large areas of rock that make up the earth's crust. 4 an illustration on a separate page in a book.
plateful *noun*

plate *verb* **plates, plating, plated**
to coat metal with a thin layer of gold, silver, tin, etc.

plateau *noun* **plateaux** (*say* **plat**-oh)
a flat area of high land.

platform *noun* **platforms**
1 the raised area along the side of the line at a railway station. 2 a small stage in a hall. 3 the policies of a political party, as in *They fought the election on a platform of economic reform.*

platinum *noun*
a silver-coloured metal that does not lose its brightness.

platonic *adjective* (*say* pluh-**ton**-ik)
to do with love that is not sexual.

platoon *noun* **platoons**
a small unit of soldiers.

platter *noun* **platters**
a large flat dish or plate, especially for serving food.

platypus *noun* **platypuses**
an Australian web-footed mammal, with thick brown fur, a duck-like bill, leathery skin and a broad flat tail.

plausible *adjective* (*say* **plawz**-uh-buhl)
reasonable or probable.

play *verb* **plays, playing, played**
1 to take part in a game or other amusement. 2 to make music or sound with a musical instrument, record-player, etc. 3 to perform a part in a play or film.
play about, play around, or **play up,** to be naughty.
player *noun*

play *noun* **plays**
1 a story acted on a stage or broadcast on radio or television. 2 playing; having fun.

playback *noun* **playbacks**
playing something that has been recorded.

playful *adjective*
wanting to play; full of fun; not serious.
playfully *adverb*, **playfulness** *noun*

playground *noun* **playgrounds**
a place out of doors where children can play.

playgroup *noun* **playgroups**
a group of children who are too young to go to school, who play together regularly, with adults to take care of them.

playing-card *noun* **playing-cards**
one of a set of cards used for playing games.

play-lunch *noun* **play-lunches**
1 the snack taken by children to school to eat during the mid-morning break; little lunch. 2 the break itself.

playmate *noun* **playmates**
someone that you play games with.

playwright *noun* **playwrights**
someone who writes plays.

plaza *noun* **plazas**
an open square in a city or town.

plea *noun* **pleas**
1 a request or appeal. 2 a statement made by or for a person charged with an offence, in a lawcourt, as in *a plea of not guilty.*

plead *verb* **pleads, pleading, pleaded**
to make a request or appeal.
plead guilty, to admit in a lawcourt that you are guilty.

pleasant *adjective*
able to please or attract you, as in *pleasant weather; a pleasant face.*
pleasantly *adverb*

please *verb* **pleases, pleasing, pleased**
1 to make someone happy or satisfied, as in *Nothing pleases him.* 2 used when you want to make a request polite, as in *Shut the door, please. Please may I have a slice of cake?* 3 to wish; to choose, as in *Do as you please.*

pleasure *noun* **pleasures**
being pleased; something that pleases you.
with pleasure, gladly; willingly.
pleasurable *adjective*

pleat *noun* **pleats**
a fold made in the cloth of a garment.
pleated *adjective*

plectrum

plectrum *noun* **plectrums**
a thin flat piece of plastic, etc. used for plucking the strings of a guitar, etc.

pledge *noun* **pledges**
a solemn promise.

plentiful *adjective*
large in amount.
plentifully *adverb*

plenty *noun*
a lot of something; more than enough, as in *We have plenty of chairs. You don't need to bring any food—we have plenty.*

pliable *adjective*
1 easy to bend, as in *a pliable stick.* 2 easy to influence, as in *He is so pliable that he will do anything his friends suggest.*
pliant *adjective*

pliers *plural noun*
a tool for gripping something or for breaking wire.

plight *noun* **plights**
a difficult situation.

plod *verb* **plods, plodding, plodded**
1 to walk slowly and heavily. 2 to work slowly but steadily.
plodder *noun*

plop *noun* **plops**
the sound of something dropping into water.

plot *noun* **plots**
1 a piece of land, usually small. 2 a secret plan. 3 what happens in a story, play, film, etc.

plot *verb* **plots, plotting, plotted**
to make a secret plan.
plotter *noun*

plough *noun* **ploughs** (*say* plow)
a device used on farms for turning over the soil.

plough *verb* **ploughs, ploughing, ploughed** (*say* plow)
1 to turn over soil with a plough. 2 to go through something with difficulty, as in *He ploughed through the book.*
ploughman *noun*

plover *noun* **plovers** (*say* **plu**-vuh)
a long-legged, often migratory, wading bird.

pluck *verb* **plucks, plucking, plucked**
1 to pull the feathers off a bird. 2 to pick a flower or fruit. 3 to pull something up or out, as in *She plucked out the splinter.* 4 to pull a string and let it go again.
pluck up courage, to overcome your fear.

pluck *noun*
bravery.
pluckily *adverb*, **plucky** *adjective*

plug *noun* **plugs**
1 something used to stop up a hole. 2 the part by which an electric wire is fitted into a socket. 3 (*colloquial*) a piece of publicity for something.

plug *verb* **plugs, plugging, plugged**
1 to stop up a hole. 2 (*colloquial*) to publicise something.
plug in, to put an electric plug into a socket.

plum *noun* **plums**
a soft, juicy fruit with a stone in the middle.

plumage *noun* (*say* **ploo**-mij)
feathers.

plumb *verb* **plumbs, plumbing, plumbed**
1 to measure how deep something is. 2 to reach the bottom of something.

plumber *noun* **plumbers**
someone who fits and mends water-pipes in a building.

plumbing *noun*
1 the work of a plumber. 2 the water-pipes and water-tanks in a building.

plume *noun* **plumes**
1 a large feather. 2 something shaped like a feather, as in *a plume of smoke.*
plumed *adjective*

plummet *verb* **plummets, plummeting, plummeted**
to fall or plunge rapidly.

plump *adjective* **plumper, plumpest**
rounded; slightly fat, as in *The baby has short, plump arms and legs. You're getting a bit plump—how much exercise do you get?*

plunder *verb* **plunders, plundering, plundered**
to rob a place or an enemy, especially in a time of war or disorder.
plunderer *noun*

plunge *verb* **plunges, plunging, plunged**
1 to jump suddenly into water. 2 to put something suddenly into a liquid, as in *Plunge the jars into boiling water.* 3 to move suddenly and dramatically, as in *He plunged down the stairs.*

plural *noun* **plurals**
the form of a word meaning more than one person or thing, as in *'Buns', 'children', 'mice', and 'teeth' are plurals.*

plural *adjective*
to do with the plural; meaning more than one, as in *'Mice' is a plural noun.*

plus *preposition*
with the next number added, as in *2 plus 2 equals 4 (2 + 2 = 4).*

plutonium *noun (say* ploo-**toh**-nee-uhm)
a radioactive element used in nuclear weapons and reactors.

plywood *noun*
board made from thin sheets of wood glued together.

p.m. short for Latin *post meridiem* which means 'after midday'.

pneumatic *adjective (say* nyoo-**mat**-ik)
1 filled with air, as in *pneumatic tyres.*
2 using compressed air, as in *a pneumatic drill.*

pneumonia *noun (say* nyoo-**moh**-nee-uh *or* nyoo-**mohn**-yuh)
a lung disease.

poach *verb* **poaches, poaching, poached**
1 to cook fish, or an egg without its shell, in or over boiling water. 2 to hunt animals or fish illegally on someone else's land.
poacher *noun*

pocket *noun* **pockets**
part of a garment shaped like a small bag, for keeping things in.
pocket bread, pitta bread.
pocket money, a small amount of money given to a child to spend as he or she likes.
your pocket, what you can afford, as in *prices to suit your pocket.*
pocketful *noun*

pocket *adjective*
small enough to carry in your pocket, as in *a pocket calculator.*

pod *noun* **pods**
a long seed-container on a pea or bean plant.

poddy *noun* **poddies**
a young animal, especially a calf, which is being hand-fed.

poem *noun* **poems**
a piece of poetry.

poet *noun* **poets**
someone who writes poetry.

poetry *noun*
writing arranged in short lines, often with a particular rhythm.
poetic *adjective,* **poetical** *adjective*

point *noun* **points**
1 the sharp end of something, as in *Don't hold that knife by the point.* 2 a dot or mark, as in *the decimal point.* 3 a particular place

or time, as in *She gave up at this point.* 4 a detail; a characteristic, as in *He has some good points.* 5 purpose; advantage, as in *There's no point in hurrying.*
point of view, how you see things or think of things.
points, a device for changing a railway train from one track to another.
the point, the main thing, as in *Come to the point.*

point *verb* **points, pointing, pointed**
1 to show where something is, especially by holding out your finger towards it.
2 to aim something, as in *She pointed the gun at him.*
point out, to show or explain something.
point the bone, (*in Aboriginal custom*) to cast a bad spell on a person so that he or she will die.

point-blank *adjective*
at point-blank range, from a very short distance away, as in *The shot was fired at point-blank range.*

pointed *adjective*
1 with a sharp end, as in *a pointed stick.*
2 clearly directed at someone or his behaviour, as in *a pointed remark.*
pointedly *adverb*

pointer *noun* **pointers**
1 a stick, rod, mark, etc. used to point at something. 2 a breed of dog that points with its muzzle at birds which it has found by their smell. 3 an indication or hint, as in *She gave us a few pointers on finding bargains.*

pointless *adjective*
with no purpose or meaning.
pointlessly *adverb*

poise *noun*
1 balance. 2 a dignified, self-confident appearance.

poise *verb* **poises, poising, poised**
to balance.

poison *noun* **poisons**
a substance that can kill or harm you.
poisonous *adjective*

poison *verb* **poisons, poisoning, poisoned**
1 to give poison to someone. 2 to put poison in something.
poisoner *noun*

poke *verb* **pokes, poking, poked**
to push something or someone hard with a stick, a finger, etc.
poke out, to stick out.

poker

poker *noun* **pokers**
a metal rod for poking a fire.

poker *noun*
a card-game in which the players bet on who has the best cards.

poky *adjective* **pokier, pokiest**
small and cramped, as in *The filing cabinet did not fit into the poky office.*

polar *adjective*
to do with or near the North or South Pole, as in *polar ice cap.*

polar bear *noun* **polar bears**
a white Arctic bear.

pole *noun* **poles**
1 a long, round piece of wood or metal.
2 the North Pole or the South Pole, one of the two points at the ends of the earth's axis. 3 one end of a magnet.

pole-vault *noun* **pole-vaults**
a jump over a high bar done with the help of a long pole.

police *noun*
the people whose job is to catch criminals and make sure that the law is kept.
police station, the office of the local police force.
policeman *noun*, **policewoman** *noun*

policy *noun* **policies**
1 the aims and ideals of a person or group. 2 a plan of action, as in *Honesty is the best policy.*

polio *noun* (*say* **poh**-lee-oh) short for **poliomyelitis.**

poliomyelitis *noun*
(*say* poh-lee-oh-muy-uh-**luy**-tuhs)
a disease that may make someone's body unable to move.

polish *verb* **polishes, polishing, polished**
(*say* **pol**-ish)
to make a surface shiny or smooth.
polish off, (*colloquial*) to finish something quickly.

polish *noun* **polishes** (*say* **pol**-ish)
1 a substance used in polishing.
2 a shine.

polished *adjective*
1 shiny. 2 well practised or rehearsed, as in *a polished performance.*

polite *adjective* **politer, politest**
having good manners; respectful and thoughtful towards other people.
politely *adverb*, **politeness** *noun*

political *adjective*
connected with the governing of a country.
politically *adverb*

politician *noun* **politicians**
someone involved in politics, especially a member of parliament.
pollie, (*colloquial*) politician.

politics *noun*
political matters.

polka *noun* **polkas**
a lively dance.
polka dots, an even pattern of round dots on cloth.

poll *noun* **polls**
1 voting at an election. 2 an opinion poll.

pollen *noun*
the yellow powder found inside flowers, which fertilises the ova to make new seeds.
pollen count, a measurement of how much pollen there is in the air, given as a warning for people who are allergic to pollen.

pollinate *verb* **pollinates, pollinating, pollinated**
to fertilise a plant or tree with pollen.

pollute *verb* **pollutes, polluting, polluted**
to make a place or thing dirty or impure.
pollution *noun*

polo *noun*
a game rather like hockey, with players on horseback using mallets with long handles.
polo-neck, a high, round, turned-over collar.

poltergeist *noun* **poltergeists**
(*say* **pol**-tuh-guyst)
a noisy, mischievous ghost that damages things.

polygon *noun* **polygons**
a 2D or 3D figure with many sides and angles.

polyhedron *noun* **polyhedra**
a solid figure with many faces.

polystyrene *noun* (*say* pol-ee-**stuy**-reen)
a kind of plastic used for insulating, packing, etc.

polythene *noun* (*say* **pol**-uh-theen)
a lightweight plastic used to make bags, wrappings, etc.

pomegranate *noun* **pomegranates**
a fruit with a tough skin, reddish flesh and many seeds.

pommy *noun* **pommies**
(*colloquial*) an English person, especially a recent immigrant to Australia.
Pommyland, England.

pomp *noun*
splendid, dignified display or ceremony.

pompous *adjective*
thinking too much of your own importance.
pomposity *noun*, **pompously** *adverb*

poncho *noun* **ponchos**
a piece of cloth with a hole in the middle for your head, worn as a cloak.

pond *noun* **ponds**
a small lake.

ponder *verb* **ponders, pondering, pondered**
to think seriously about something.

ponderous *adjective*
1 heavy. 2 not fluent; not easy to read or listen to, as in *He writes in a ponderous style.*
ponderously *adverb*

pony *noun* **ponies**
a small horse.

pony-tail *noun* **pony-tails**
a bunch of long hair tied at the back of the head.

poodle *noun* **poodles**
a breed of dog with long, curly hair.

pool *noun* **pools**
1 a pond. 2 a puddle. 3 a swimming-pool. 4 a fund of money. 5 a group of things shared by several people. 6 a game played on a billiards table.
the pools, a way of gambling on the results of football matches.

poor *adjective* **poorer, poorest**
1 having very little money, as in *a poor family.* 2 bad; inadequate, as in *poor work.* 3 unfortunate, as in *Poor fellow!*

poorly *adverb*
not adequately, as in *poorly dressed.*

pop *noun* **pops**
a small explosive sound.

pop *verb* **pops, popping, popped**
1 to make a small explosive sound. 2 (*colloquial*) to go or put quickly, as in *I'm just popping out to the shop. She popped the pie in the oven.*

pop *noun*
modern popular music.

popcorn *noun*
Indian corn heated till it bursts, making light, fluffy balls which are flavoured and eaten.

Pope *noun* **Popes**
the leader of the Roman Catholic Church; the Pontiff.

poplar *noun* **poplars**
a tall, slender tree with a straight trunk.

poppy *noun* **poppies**
a red flower.
Poppy Day, the day on which a red poppy is worn to remember those who died in wars; Remembrance Day.

popular *adjective*
liked by a lot of people.
popular culture, music, fashions, pastimes, television programs, shows, etc. that a lot of people like.
popularity *noun*, **popularise** *verb*, **popularly** *adverb*

populated *adjective*
having people living there, as in *The interior is thinly populated.*

population *noun* **populations**
the people who live in a particular place.

populous *adjective*
inhabited by a lot of people.

porcelain *noun* (*say* **paw**-suh-luhn)
a fine kind of china.

porch *noun* **porches**
a small roofed area outside the door of a building.

porcupine *noun* **porcupines**
a small animal covered with long prickles.

pore *noun* **pores**
a tiny opening in the skin through which sweat passes.

pore *verb* **pores, poring, pored**
pore over, to study something closely.

Usage Do not confuse **pore** with **pour**, which means to make liquid flow out of a container, to flow, to rain heavily, or to come or go in large amounts.

pork *noun*
meat from a pig.

pornography *noun* (*say* paw-**nog**-ruh-fee)
obscene pictures, writings, etc.
pornographer *noun*, **pornographic** *adjective*

porous *adjective*
allowing liquid or air to pass through, as in *Sandy soil is porous.*
porosity *noun*

porpoise *noun* **porpoises** (*say* **paw**-puhs)
a marine mammal of the whale family with a blunt rounded snout.

porridge *noun*
oatmeal boiled in water to make a thick paste that you can eat.

port *noun* **ports**
1 a harbour. 2 a city or town with a harbour.

a
b
c
d
e
f
g
h
i
j
k
l
m
n
o
p
q
r
s
t
u
v
w
x
y
z

port *noun*
the left side of a ship or aircraft when you are facing forward.

port *noun*
a strong red Portuguese wine.

port *noun* ports
a suitcase, schoolbag, etc.; portmanteau.

portable *adjective*
able to be carried, as in *a portable tape recorder.*

porter *noun* porters
someone whose job is to carry other people's luggage, as in *hotel porter.*

portfolio *noun* portfolios
1 a case or folder for carrying loose sheets of paper, drawings, etc. 2 the office or duties of a government minister, as in *The prime minister gave his financial expert the Treasury portfolio.*

porthole *noun* portholes
a small round window in the side of a ship or aircraft.

portion *noun* portions
a part or share given to someone.

portly *adjective* portlier, portliest
rather fat, as in *a portly old gentleman.*
portliness *noun*

portmanteau word *noun*
a word combining the sounds and meaning of two other words, as in *motel = motor + hotel; brunch = breakfast + lunch.*

portrait *noun* portraits
a picture of a person.

portray *verb* portrays, portraying, portrayed
1 to make a portrait of someone. 2 to describe or show something, as in *The play portrays the king as a kind man.*
portrayal *noun*

pose *verb* poses, posing, posed
1 to put your body into a particular position. 2 to put someone into a particular position to be painted or photographed. 3 to pretend, as in *The thief posed as a Telstra technician official.* 4 to present a question or problem, as in *Wet weather always poses a problem to motorists.*

pose *noun* poses
1 a position in which someone can paint a picture or take a photograph of you. 2 a pretence; unnatural behaviour to impress people.

poser *noun* posers
someone who behaves in an unnatural way to impress people.

posh *adjective* posher, poshest
(*colloquial*) 1 very smart, as in *a posh hotel.* 2 to do with a high social class, as in *She spoke with a posh accent.*

position *noun* positions
1 the place where something is or should be. 2 the way in which someone or something is placed or arranged, as in *in a sitting position.* 3 a situation or condition, as in *I am in no position to help you.* 4 a regular job.

positive *adjective*
1 sure; definite, as in *I am positive that my book was in my desk.* 2 saying 'yes', as in *a positive answer.* 3 more than nought, as in *positive numbers.* 4 to do with the kind of electric charge that lacks electrons.
positively *adverb*

possess *verb* possesses, possessing, possessed
to own something.
possessed, mad; controlled by an evil spirit.
possessor *noun*

possession *noun* possessions
1 something that you own. 2 owning something, as in *They gained possession of a piece of land.* 3 being controlled by an evil spirit, as in *demoniac possession.*

possessive *adjective*
wanting to get and keep things for yourself.

possessive case *noun*
shows ownership, as in *The children's books: This sentence shows that the books are owned by the children.*

possible *adjective*
able to exist, happen, be done, or be used.
as possible, as can happen; as can be done, as in *Come as quickly as possible.*
possibility *noun*

possibly *adverb*
1 in any way, as in *That cannot possibly be right.* 2 perhaps, as in *I will arrive at six o'clock, or possibly earlier.*

possum *noun* possums
a long-tailed, nocturnal marsupial that lives in trees.

post *noun* posts
1 an upright piece of wood, concrete, metal, etc., usually fixed in the ground. 2 the post marking the start or finish of a race, as in *He was left at the post.* 3 the carrying of letters, parcels, etc. 4 letters, parcels, etc. carried by post; the mail. 5 a collection or delivery of mail, as in *The last*

post is at 4 p.m. **6** a regular job. **7** the place where a sentry stands. **8** a place occupied by soldiers, traders, etc.

post *verb* **posts, posting, posted**
1 to put up a notice, poster, etc. **2** to send a letter, parcel, or card to someone. **3** to put a letter, card, etc. into a post-box.

postage *noun*
the cost of sending something by post.
postage stamp, a small piece of paper that you must stick on a letter, parcel, etc. before it is posted.

postal *adjective*
to do with the post.
postal order, a document bought from a post office, used for sending money by post.

postbox *noun* **postboxes**
a public box for posting mail.

postcard *noun* **postcards**
a piece of card that you can write a message on and post.

postcode *noun* **postcodes**
a group of letters and numbers included in an address to help sorting, as in *My postcode is 2601.*

poster *noun* **posters**
a large notice for everyone to read.

posthumous *adjective* (*say* pos-chuh-muhs)
to do with something occurring after someone's death, as in *The child accepted her father's posthumous award for bravery.*

postman or **postwoman** *noun* **postmen, postwomen**
someone who delivers letters, parcels, etc.

post-mortem *noun* **post-mortems**
an examination of a dead person to find out why he or she died.

post office *noun* **post offices**
a place where you can buy stamps, postal orders, etc., post letters, send parcels, etc.

postpone *verb* **postpones, postponing, postponed**
to decide that something will happen later than you originally intended.
postponement *noun*

postscript *noun* **postscripts**
something extra added at the end of a letter or book and introduced by 'PS'.

posture *noun* **postures**
the way that someone stands, sits, or walks.

posy *noun* **posies**
a small bunch of flowers.

pot *noun* **pots**
a round container.
go to pot, (*colloquial*) to be ruined.

pot *verb* **pots, potting, potted**
to put something into a pot.
potted, (*colloquial*) shortened, as in *a potted version.*

pot *noun*
(*colloquial*) another name for marijuana.

potassium *noun*
a soft, silvery-white, metallic substance that is essential for living things.

potato *noun* **potatoes**
a starchy vegetable that grows underground.
potato scallop, a slice of potato battered and fried, as in *In Victoria potato scallops are called potato cakes.*

potato chip *noun* **potato chips**
a very thin, fried slice of potato, usually sold in a packet; a crisp.

potent *adjective*
powerful.
potency *noun,* **potently** *adverb*

potential *adjective*
capable of happening or being used some time in the future, as in *potential energy.*
potentiality *noun,* **potentially** *adverb*

potential *noun*
the ability to do something, especially in the future.

pothole *noun* **potholes**
1 a deep natural hole in the ground.
2 a hole in a road.

potholing *noun*
exploring underground potholes.
potholer *noun*

potion *noun* **potions** (*say* poh-shuhn)
a drink containing medicine, poison, or something magical.

potoroo *noun*
a small, long-nosed, nocturnal, plant-eating marsupial that lives in areas of dense ground vegetation of south-eastern Australia.

Origin This word comes from Dharuk, an Aboriginal language of New South Wales. See the Aboriginal Languages map at the back of this dictionary.

potter *verb* **potters, pottering, pottered**
to work in a leisurely or casual way.

potter *noun* **potters**
someone who makes pottery.

pottery

pottery *noun* **potteries**
 1 pots, cups, plates, etc. made of baked clay. 2 a place where a potter works.

potty *noun* **potties**
 (*colloquial*) a pot used as a toilet, especially for a young child.

pouch *noun* **pouches**
 1 a small bag. 2 a pocket-like part of the body in which marsupials carry their young, as in *Kangaroos keep their babies in pouches.*

poultry *noun*
 birds kept for their eggs and meat, as in *Chickens, geese, and turkeys are poultry.*

pounce *verb* **pounces, pouncing, pounced**
 to jump suddenly on someone or something.

pound *noun* **pounds**
 1 a unit of money used in Australia until 1966 and still the currency of Britain. 2 a unit of weight equal to just under half a kilogram. 3 a place where stray animals or vehicles which have been officially removed are kept until claimed.

pound *verb* **pounds, pounding, pounded**
 1 to hit something often, especially so as to crush it, as in *Pound the chalk into a fine powder.* 2 to hit something or someone heavily, as in *The boxer pounded his opponent.* 3 to make a dull, heavy sound, as in *We could hear large guns pounding in the distance.*

pour *verb* **pours, pouring, poured**
 1 to make a liquid flow out of a container. 2 to flow. 3 to rain heavily, as in *It was pouring.* 4 to come or go in large amounts, as in *Letters poured in.*

Usage Do not confuse the phrase **pour over** with **pore over**, which means to study something closely.

pout *verb* **pouts, pouting, pouted**
 to stick out your lips when you are not pleased.

poverty *noun*
 the state of being poor.

powder *noun* **powders**
 1 tiny pieces of something dry, like flour or dust. 2 a dust-like coloured substance used as make-up on the face.
 powdery *adjective*

powder *verb* **powders, powdering, powdered**
 1 to make something into powder. 2 to put powder on, as in *I am powdering my face.*

power *noun* **powers**
 1 strength; great force, energy, or might, as in *the engine's power; the power of the sun.* 2 ability; authority, as in *the power of speech; a ruler's power.* 3 a powerful country. 4 electricity or other energy. 5 (*in Mathematics*) the result obtained by multiplying a number by itself one or more times, as in *27 is the third power of 3 (3 × 3 × 3 = 27).*
 powered *adjective*

powerful *adjective*
 very strong or important.
 powerfully *adverb*

powerless *adjective*
 not able to control what is happening; not able to prevent something from happening.

power point *noun* **power points**
 a socket in the wall, etc. for connecting an electrical device.

power station *noun* **power stations**
 a building where electricity is produced.

practicable *adjective*
 possible to do or use, as in *a practicable plan.*

Usage Do not confuse **practicable** with **practical**, which is the next word in this dictionary.

practical *adjective*
 1 able to do or make useful things, as in *She is very practical and can do all kinds of repairs about the house.* 2 likely to be useful, as in *a practical idea.* 3 concerned with doing or making things, as in *He has had practical experience.*
 practical joke, an amusing trick played on someone.

practically *adverb*
 1 in a practical way, as in *As an organised person she works practically.* 2 almost, as in *It's practically ready now.*

practice *noun* **practices**
 1 doing something again and again so as to get better at it, as in *Have you done your piano practice?* 2 actually doing something rather than thinking or talking about it, as in *It works well in practice.* 3 the business of a doctor or lawyer.

Usage Do not confuse **practice**, which is a noun, with **practise**, which is a verb and is the next word in this dictionary.

practise *verb* **practises, practising, practised**
 1 to do something again and again so as to get better at it. 2 to do something,

especially regularly, as in *He practises what he preaches.*   **3** to work as a doctor, lawyer, etc.

practitioner *noun* **practitioners**
a person practising a profession, especially medicine, as in *medical practitioner.*

prairie *noun* **prairies**
a large area of flat grass-covered land in North America.

praise *verb* **praises, praising, praised**
to say that someone or something is very good.

praise *noun* **praises**
words that praise someone or something.

pram *noun* **prams**
a small vehicle with four wheels, to carry a baby.

prance *verb* **prances, prancing, pranced**
to jump about in a lively or happy way.

prank *noun* **pranks**
a practical joke.

prattle *verb* **prattles, prattling, prattled**
to chatter in a childish or silly way.

prawn *noun* **prawns**
a small shellfish that can be eaten.

pray *verb* **prays, praying, prayed**
1 to talk to God.   **2** to ask earnestly, as in *He prayed to be set free.*

Usage Do not confuse **pray** with the noun **prey**, which means an animal hunted and eaten by another animal.

prayer *noun* **prayers**
the act of praying; what you say when you pray.

praying mantis *noun* **praying mantises**
a slender hunting insect that holds its four legs like hands folded in prayer.

preach *verb* **preaches, preaching, preached**
to give a talk about religion or about right and wrong.
preacher *noun*

preamble *noun* **preambles**
an introduction that comes before something that is written or spoken.

precarious *adjective* (*say* pruh-**kair**-ree-uhs)
not secure or safe.
precariously *adverb*

precaution *noun* **precautions**
something done to prevent future trouble or danger.

precede *verb* **precedes, preceding, preceded**
to come or go in front of someone or something.
precedence *noun*

precedent *noun* **precedents**
(*say* **prees**-uh-duhnt *or* **pres**-uh-duhnt)
a previous case, decision, etc. which can be taken as a guide for future action, as in *They set a precedent when he was given the job without an interview.*

precious *adjective*
very valuable.

precipice *noun* **precipices**
the steep face of a mountain, cliff, etc.

précis *noun* **précis** (*say* **pray**-see)
a statement of the main points of a piece of writing.

precise *adjective*
1 exact, as in *Are your measurements precise?*   **2** clearly stated, as in *precise instructions.*
precisely *adverb*, **precision** *noun*

Usage Do not confuse **precise** with **concise**, which means brief, or giving a lot of information in a few words.

predator *noun* **predators** (*say* **pred**-uh-tuh)
an animal that hunts other animals, as in *The kookaburra is one of the snake's predators.*
predatory *adjective*

predecessor *noun* **predecessors**
(*say* **pree**-duh-ses-uh)
1 an ancestor.   **2** someone who did the job that you do now.

predicament *noun* **predicaments**
a difficult, unpleasant, or embarrassing situation.

predict *verb* **predicts, predicting, predicted**
to say what is going to happen before it happens.
predictable *adjective*, **prediction** *noun*

predominate *verb* **predominates, predominating, predominated**
to be largest in size or number, or most important, as in *Girls predominate in our class.*
predominance *noun*, **predominant** *adjective*

preface *noun* **prefaces** (*say* **pref**-uhs)
an introduction at the beginning of a book.

prefect *noun* **prefects**
1 a school pupil who is given certain duties to perform.   **2** (in some countries) a high-ranking official.

prefer

prefer *verb* **prefers, preferring, preferred**
to like one person or thing more than another.
preference *noun*

preferable *adjective* (*say* **pref**-uh-ruh-buhl)
preferred; that you want or like more, as in *Living close to work is preferable to making long journeys every day.*
preferably *adverb*

prefix *noun* **prefixes**
a word or syllable joined to the front of a word to change to or add to its meaning, as in *dis*order, *out*stretched, and *un*happy.

pregnant *adjective*
(of a female) having an unborn baby growing inside her body.
pregnancy *noun*

prehistoric *adjective*
existing a very long time ago, before written records were kept.
prehistory *noun*

prejudice *noun* **prejudices**
1 making up your mind without examining the facts fairly. 2 behaviour or unfair treatment that results from a prejudice.
prejudiced *adjective*

preliminary *adjective*
coming before or preparing for something.

prelude *noun* **preludes** (*say* **prel**-yood)
1 an introduction or lead-up to a play, poem, event, etc. 2 a short piece of music.

premature *adjective*
to do with occurring before the usual or proper time.

premier *noun* **premiers** (*say* **prem**-ee-uh)
1 the leader of a State government. 2 (*in plural*) the sporting team which wins the contest.
premiership *noun*

Usage Do not confuse **premier** with **première**, which is the next word in this dictionary.

première *noun* **premières** (*say* prem-ee-**air**)
the first public performance of a play or showing of a film.

premises *plural noun*
a building with its land.
on the premises, in a particular building.

premium *noun* **premiums**
(*say* **pree**-mee-uhm)
an amount paid regularly to an insurance company.
at a premium, above the normal price; valued highly.

premonition *noun* **premonitions**
a feeling that something, often unpleasant, is about to happen.

preoccupied *adjective*
with your thoughts completely occupied by something.
preoccupation *noun*

preparation *noun* **preparations**
1 the action of getting something ready.
2 a thing done in order to get ready for something, as in *We were making last-minute preparations.*

preparatory *adjective*
(*say* pruh-**pa**-ruh-tuh-ree *or* pruh-**pa**-ruh-tree)
in preparation for something, as in *preparatory organisation for the concert.*

prepare *verb* **prepares, preparing, prepared**
to get ready.
be prepared to do something, to be ready or willing to do something.

preposition *noun* **prepositions**
a word put in front of a noun or pronoun to show how the noun or pronoun is connected with another word, as in *In the sentence 'I stayed at the seaside from Monday to Friday with my friends', 'at', 'from', 'to', and 'with' are prepositions.*

preposterous *adjective*
utterly absurd.

preschool *noun* **preschools**
the year of education before formal schooling begins.

prescribe *verb* **prescribes, prescribing, prescribed**
1 to give someone a doctor's order for a particular medicine. 2 to say what must be done.

prescription *noun* **prescriptions**
a doctor's written instruction to a chemist for the supply and use of a medicine.

presence *noun*
being at a place, as in *Your presence is expected.*
in the presence of someone, at the place where someone is.

present *adjective* (*say* **prez**-uhnt)
1 in a particular place; here, as in *Nobody else was present.* 2 existing now, as in *the present King.*

present participle *noun*
a form of a verb used after *am, are, is,* etc. to describe an action that is happening now, or used after *was, were,* etc. to describe an action that went on for some time in the

present tense *noun*
a form of a verb used on its own to describe something that is happening now, as in *The verbs in 'I go' and 'he sees' are in the present tense.*

present *noun (say* prez-uhnt)
the time now, as in *Our teacher is away at present.*

present *verb* **presents, presenting, presented** (*say* pruh-**zent**)
1 to give something to someone, especially with a ceremony. **2** to put on a play or other entertainment. **3** to show something or someone, as in *We are here to present our latest products.*
presentation *noun*, **presenter** *noun*

present *noun* **presents** (*say* prez-uhnt)
something that you give to someone.

presentable *adjective*
fit to be presented to other people.

presently *adverb*
soon, as in *I shall be with you presently.*

preserve *verb* **preserves, preserving, preserved**
to keep something safe or in good condition.
preservation *noun*, **preservative** *noun*

preside *verb* **presides, presiding, presided** (*say* pruh-**zuyd**)
to be in charge of a meeting, council, etc., as in *The mayor presided over the council.*

president *noun* **presidents**
1 the person in charge of a society, business, etc. **2** the head of a republic, as in *Roosevelt and Kennedy were American presidents.*
presidency *noun*, **presidential** *adjective*

press *verb* **presses, pressing, pressed**
1 to push hard on something; to squeeze something. **2** to make something flat and smooth. **3** to urge someone to do or give something; to make a demand, as in *They pressed him for details. We must press for better conditions.*

press *noun* **presses**
1 the action of squeezing or pushing on something. **2** a device for flattening and smoothing things. **3** a device or firm that does printing.
the press, newspapers, journalists.
press conference, an interview with a group of journalists.

press-up *noun* **press-ups**
an exercise in which you lie face downwards and press down with your hands to lift your body.

pressure *noun* **pressures**
1 continuous pushing or squeezing. **2** the force with which something pushes against or squeezes something. **3** an action that persuades or forces you to do something, as in *If you keep up the pressure, your opponent will make mistakes.*

pressurise or **pressurize** *verb* **pressurises, pressurising, pressurised**
1 to keep a place, vehicle, etc. at the same air pressure all the time, as in *This aircraft is pressurised.* **2** to try to force someone to do something.

prestige *noun (say* pres-**teezh**)
1 good reputation, as in *a politician of great prestige.* **2** honour that comes from being successful, rich, etc., as in *He wanted the prestige of owning an expensive car.*
prestigious *adjective*

presumably *adverb*
probably; according to what you may presume.

presume *verb* **presumes, presuming, presumed**
1 to suppose, as in *I presumed that he was dead.* **2** to dare, as in *I wouldn't presume to advise you.*
presumption *noun*

presumptuous *adjective*
too bold or confident.

pretend *verb* **pretends, pretending, pretended**
1 to behave as if something untrue or imaginary is true. **2** to claim something dishonestly, as in *They pretended that they had not been told what to do.*
pretence *noun*, **pretender** *noun*

pretentious *adjective (say* pre-**ten**-shuhs)
making an exaggerated claim of importance, wealth, etc.

pretty *adjective* **prettier, prettiest**
pleasant to look at or hear; attractive.
prettily *adverb*, **prettiness** *noun*

pretty *adverb*
(*colloquial*) quite; moderately, as in *It's pretty cold outside.*

prevail *verb* **prevails, prevailing, prevailed**
1 to be most frequent or general, as in *a prevailing tendency.* **2** to be successful in a battle, contest, or game.
prevailing wind, the most common wind in a particular place, as in *On the east coast the prevailing wind is a southerly.*
prevalent *adjective*

prevent

prevent *verb* **prevents, preventing, prevented**
to stop something from happening; to make something impossible.
prevention *noun*, **preventive** *adjective*

preview *noun* **previews**
a showing of a film, play, etc. before it is shown to the public.

previous *adjective*
coming before this; preceding, as in *the previous week*.
previously *adverb*

prey *noun* (*say* pray)
an animal hunted and eaten by another animal.
bird of prey, a bird that lives by killing and eating other animals.

Usage Do not confuse **prey** with the verb **pray**, which means to talk to God or to ask earnestly.

prey *verb* **preys, preying, preyed** (*say* pray)
prey on, to hunt and kill an animal for food; to make someone anxious or nervous, as in *Owls prey on mice and other small animals. The worry about not earning enough money began to prey on her mind.*

price *noun* **prices**
1 the amount of money for which something is sold. **2** what you have to give or do to get something, as in *What is the price of peace?*
at any price, at any cost.

price *verb* **prices, pricing, priced**
to decide the price of something.

priceless *adjective*
1 very valuable. **2** (*colloquial*) very amusing, as in *a priceless remark.*

prick *verb* **pricks, pricking, pricked**
1 to make a tiny hole in something.
2 to hurt someone with a pin, needle, etc.
prick up your ears, to start listening suddenly.

prickle *noun* **prickles**
a thin, sharp thing like a thorn.
prickly *adjective*

pride *noun* **prides**
1 being proud. **2** something that makes you feel proud, as in *pride in his garden.*

priest *noun* **priests**
1 a member of the clergy. **2** someone who conducts religious ceremonies; a religious leader.
priestess *noun*, **priesthood** *noun*

prig *noun* **prigs**
a self-righteous person.
priggish *adjective*

prim *adjective* **primmer, primmest**
not liking anything rough or rude.
primly *adverb*, **primness** *noun*

primary *adjective*
first; most important.
primary colours, the colours from which all other colours can be made by mixing: red, yellow, and blue for paint, and red, green, and violet for light.
primary school, a school for children aged 5 to 12.
primarily *adverb*

primate *noun* **primates**
an animal of the group that includes human beings, apes, and monkeys.

prime *adjective*
1 chief; most important, as in *the prime cause*. **2** excellent, as in *prime beef.*

prime *noun* **primes**
the best part of a person's life, as in *He was in the prime of life.*

prime minister *noun* **prime ministers**
the leader of a government.

prime number *noun*
a number that can only be divided exactly by 1 or itself, as in 2, 3, 5, 7, 11 and 37.

primer *noun* **primers**
1 paint used for the first coat on an unpainted surface. **2** a textbook dealing with the first or simplest stages of something.

primeval *adjective* (*say* pruy-**mee**-vuhl)
to do with the earliest times of the world; ancient.

primitive *adjective*
1 occurring at an early stage of development or civilisation, as in *Primitive humans were hunters rather than farmers.*
2 not complicated or sophisticated, as in *a primitive technology.*

prince *noun* **princes**
1 the son of a king or queen. **2** a man or boy in a royal family.
princely *adjective*

princess *noun* **princesses**
1 the daughter of a king or queen. **2** a woman or girl in a royal family. **3** the wife of a prince.

principal *adjective*
chief; most important, as in *The principal city of New South Wales is Sydney.*
principally *adverb*

principal *noun* **principals**
the head of a college or school.

problem

Usage Do not confuse **principal** with **principle**, which is the next word in this dictionary.

principle *noun* **principles**
general truth, belief, or rule, as in *He taught me the principles of geometry.*
in principle, in general, not in details.

print *verb* **prints, printing, printed**
1 to put words or pictures on paper with a machine. 2 to write with letters that are not joined together. 3 to make a photograph from a negative.
printed circuit, an electric circuit made by pressing thin metal strips on to a board.

print *noun* **prints**
1 printed words or pictures. 2 a mark made by something pressing on a surface, as in *Her thumb left a print on the glass.*
3 a photograph made by shining light through a negative on to sensitive paper.

printer *noun* **printers**
1 someone whose job is to put words or pictures on paper with a machine; a company that does this work.
2 (*in Computing*) a machine that puts information stored in a computer on to paper.

printout *noun* **printouts**
sheets of printed paper produced by a computer.

priority *noun* **priorities** (*say* pruy-o-ruh-tee)
1 something that is more urgent or important than other things, as in *Repairing the roof is a priority.* 2 the right to be considered before other things, as in *People in need of urgent medical help will have priority.*

prise *verb* **prises, prising, prised**
to force something open, as in *They prised the box open.*

prism *noun* **prisms**
1 a piece of glass that breaks up light into the colours of the rainbow. 2 (*in Mathematics*) a three-dimensional object with parallel ends that are equal triangles or polygons.
prismatic *adjective*

prison *noun* **prisons**
a place where criminals are kept as a punishment.
prisoner *noun*

private *adjective*
1 belonging to or used by a particular person or people, as in *a private road.* 2 to be kept secret or confidential, as in *a private*

letter. 3 away from people, as in *a private place for a swim.*
privacy *noun,* **privately** *adverb*

private *noun* **privates**
a soldier of the lowest rank.
in private, in secret; where only particular people can see, hear, or take part.

privatise or **privatize** *verb* **privatises, privatising, privatised**
to transfer a business, organisation, etc. from government to private ownership.

privet *noun*
a bushy, evergreen European shrub used for hedges and now a serious pest in the Australian bush.

privilege *noun* **privileges**
a special advantage for one person or group of people.
privileged *adjective*

prize *noun* **prizes**
1 something won in a game, competition, etc.; an award. 2 something captured from an enemy.

prize *verb* **prizes, prizing, prized**
to value something highly, as in *She prizes her garden more than anything else.*

pro *noun* **pros**
(*colloquial*) someone doing a regular job for money; a professional, as in *Take lessons from a golf pro.*

probable *adjective*
likely to be true; likely to happen.
probability *noun,* **probably** *adverb*

probation *noun*
testing a person's character or behaviour; finding out if a person is suitable for a job, club, etc.
on probation, being supervised by a probation officer.
probation officer, an official who supervises the behaviour of a convicted criminal who is not in prison.
probationary *adjective*

probe *noun* **probes**
1 a long, thin device used to explore wounds, etc. 2 an investigation, especially one done by a journalist.

probe *verb* **probes, probing, probed**
1 to explore something with a probe.
2 to investigate something.

problem *noun* **problems**
something difficult to answer, understand, or overcome.

a
b
c
d
e
f
g
h
i
j
k
l
m
n
o
p
q
r
s
t
u
v
w
x
y
z

procedure

procedure *noun* procedures
1 a way of doing something. 2 (*in Computing*) a separate part of a computer program, performing an operation that is needed frequently in the program.

proceed *verb* proceeds, proceeding, proceeded (*say* pruh-**seed**)
to go on; to continue.

proceedings *plural noun*
1 things that happen. 2 a lawsuit.

proceeds *plural noun* (*say* proh-seedz)
the money made from a sale, show, etc.

process *noun* processes
a series of actions for doing something or for making something with machines.

process *verb* processes, processing, processed
to use a process to change or deal with something, as in *This cheese has been processed*.

procession *noun* processions
a number of people, vehicles, etc. moving steadily forwards.

proclaim *verb* proclaims, proclaiming, proclaimed
to announce something officially or publicly.
proclamation *noun*

procrastinate *verb* procrastinates, procrastinating, procrastinated
to put off or delay.

procreate *verb* procreates, procreating, procreated (*say* proh-kree-ayt)
to produce offspring by sexual intercourse.

prod *verb* prods, prodding, prodded
to push something or someone hard with a stick, finger, etc.

prodigal *adjective*
wasteful; extravagant.
prodigality *noun*, **prodigally** *adverb*

prodigy *noun* prodigies (*say* prod-uh-jee)
1 a very gifted or able person, especially a child. 2 a marvellous or extraordinary thing.

produce *verb* produces, producing, produced (*say* pruh-**dyoos**)
1 to make or create something. 2 to bring something out so that it can be seen. 3 to organise the performance of a play or the making of a film, video, etc.
producer *noun*

produce *noun* (*say* prod-yoos)
things produced, especially by farming.

product *noun* products
1 something produced, as in *the products of this factory*. 2 the result of multiplying two numbers, as in *12 is the product of 4 and 3*.

production *noun* productions
1 the action of making or creating, as in *a factory engaged in car production*. 2 a thing or amount made or created, as in *Steel production has increased*. 3 a play or film, as in *The production was made by Film Australia*.

productive *adjective*
1 producing a lot of things, as in *a productive farm*. 2 useful, as in *a productive idea*.
productivity *noun*

profess *verb* professes, professing, professed
to declare or claim, often falsely, as in *The salesperson professed surprise at the faulty goods*.

profession *noun* professions
a job for which you need special knowledge and training, as in *The professions include being a doctor, nurse, member of the clergy, or lawyer*.

professional *adjective*
1 to do with a profession, as in *She used professional advice from an architect for her extensions*. 2 doing a regular job for money, as in *a professional footballer*.
professionally *adverb*

professional *noun* professionals
1 someone doing a regular job for money, as in *an amateur footballer who became a professional*. 2 someone who works in a profession.

professor *noun* professors
the highest-ranking academic position in a university.
professorial *adjective*

proficient *adjective* (*say* pruh-**fish**-uhnt)
skilled; doing something properly, as in *She is proficient at welding. If you practise, you will soon be proficient*.
proficiency *noun*, **proficiently** *adverb*

profile *noun* profiles
1 a side view of someone's face. 2 a short description of a person's life or character.

profit *noun* profits
1 the extra money got by selling something for more than it cost to buy or make. 2 an advantage or benefit.

profit *verb* profits, profiting, profited
to get a profit.
profitable *adjective*, **profitably** *adverb*

pronounce

profound *adjective* profounder, profoundest
1 very deep or great. 2 showing or needing great knowledge or thought, as in *That was a profound comment!*
profoundly *adverb*, profundity *noun*

profuse *adjective* (*say* pruh-**fyoos**)
large in amount, as in *profuse wealth*.
profusely *adverb*, profusion *noun*

progeny *noun* (*say* **proj**-uh-nee)
offspring; descendants.

program *noun* programs
a coded series of actions for a computer to carry out.

program *verb* programs, programming, programmed
to prepare or control a computer by means of a program.
programmer *noun*

program or **programme** *noun* programs
1 a show, play, talk, etc. on radio or television. 2 a list of an organised series of events; a leaflet or pamphlet giving details of an entertainment, contest, etc.

progress *noun* (*say* **proh**-gres *or* **pro**-gres)
1 forward movement; an advance, as in *The procession made slow progress.*
2 development or improvement, as in *As progress continues, computers are becoming smaller and more powerful.*

progress *verb* progresses, progressing, progressed (*say* pruh-**gres**)
1 to move forwards. 2 to develop or improve, as in *Has civilisation progressed in the last century?*
progression *noun*, progressive *adjective*

prohibit *verb* prohibits, prohibiting, prohibited
to forbid, as in *Smoking is prohibited.*
prohibition *noun*

project *noun* projects (*say* **proh**-jekt *or* **pro**-jekt)
1 a planned task in which you find out as much as you can about something and write about it. 2 a plan.

project *verb* projects, projecting, projected (*say* pruh-**jekt**)
1 to stick out. 2 to show a picture on a screen.
projection *noun*

projector *noun* projectors
a machine for showing films or photographs on a screen.
projectionist *noun*

prolific *adjective*
producing a plentiful amount, as in *Rabbits are prolific breeders.*

prologue *noun* prologues (*say* **proh**-log)
an introduction or preface.

prolong *verb* prolongs, prolonging, prolonged
to make something last longer.

promenade *noun* promenades (*say* prom-uh-**nahd**)
1 a place suitable for walking, especially beside the seashore. 2 a slow, relaxed walk.

prominent *adjective*
1 sticking out. 2 important.
prominence *noun*, prominently *adverb*

promise *noun* promises
1 saying that you will definitely do or not do something. 2 an indication of future success, as in *She shows promise.*

promise *verb* promises, promising, promised
to say that you will definitely do or not do something, as in *He promised that he would be there on time.*
promising, likely to be good or successful, as in *a promising pupil.*

promontory *noun* promontories (*say* **prom**-uhn-tuh-ree *or* **prom**-uhn-tree)
a piece of high land sticking out into the sea.

promote *verb* promotes, promoting, promoted
1 to move someone to a higher rank or position. 2 to help the progress or sale of something. 3 to organise a public entertainment.
promoter *noun*, promotion *noun*

prompt *adjective* prompter, promptest
without delay, as in *a prompt reply.*
promptly *adverb*, promptness *noun*

prompt *verb* prompts, prompting, prompted
1 to cause or encourage someone to do something. 2 to remind an actor of the words of a play, etc. if he or she forgets them.
prompter *noun*

prone *adjective*
lying face downwards.
prone to, likely to do or suffer something, as in *He is prone to jealousy.*

prong *noun* prongs
one of the pointed spikes at the end of a fork.

pronoun *noun* pronouns
a word used instead of a noun, as in *Pronouns are words like 'he', 'her', 'it', 'them', and 'those'.*

pronounce *verb* pronounces, pronouncing, pronounced
1 to say a sound or word in a particular

a
b
c
d
e
f
g
h
i
j
k
l
m
n
o
p
q
r
s
t
u
v
w
x
y
z

pronunciation

way, as in *'Too' and 'two' are pronounced the same.* **2** to declare formally, as in *I now pronounce you man and wife.*
pronounced, obvious; definite.
pronouncement *noun*

pronunciation *noun* **pronunciations**
(*say* pruh-nun-see-**ay**-shuhn)
how you pronounce something.

proof *noun* **proofs**
1 a fact which shows that something is true. **2** a printed copy of something made for checking before other copies are printed.

proof *adjective*
giving protection against something, as in *a waterproof parka.*

proofread *verb* **proofreads, proofreading, proofread**
to read and correct.

prop *noun* **props**
1 a support, especially made of a long piece of wood or metal. **2** a movable object, such as a piece of furniture, used on stage during a play in a theatre.

prop *verb* **props, propping, propped**
to support something by leaning it on something else, as in *The ladder was propped up against the wall.*

propaganda *noun*
publicity intended to make people believe something.

propagate *verb* **propagates, propagating, propagated**
1 to breed; reproduce, as in *The roses were propagated by cuttings.* **2** to spread a belief, ideas, etc., as in *Christian ideas were propagated by missionaries.*

propel *verb* **propels, propelling, propelled**
to move something forward.
propellant *noun*

propeller *noun* **propellers**
a device with blades that spin around to drive an aircraft or ship.

proper *adjective*
1 suitable; right, as in *Is that screwdriver the proper size?* **2** respectable, as in *prim and proper.* **3** (*colloquial*) complete; great, as in *He's in a proper mess.*
properly *adverb*

proper noun *noun*
the name of a person, place, animal, organisation, country or thing that starts with a capital letter, as in *John Smith, Australia, Koori, Australian Capital Territory, Murray River.*

property *noun* **properties**
1 things that belong to someone.
2 buildings or land belonging to someone. **3** a characteristic or quality, as in *Rubber has elastic properties.*

prophecy *noun* **prophecies** (*say* prof-uh-see)
something that someone has said will happen, before it actually happens; saying what will happen in the future.

Usage Do not confuse **prophecy** with **prophesy,** which is a verb and is the next word in this dictionary.

prophesy *verb* **prophesies, prophesying, prophesied** (*say* **prof**-uh-suy)
to say that something will happen, before it actually happens, as in *She prophesied that a war would break out.*

prophet *noun* **prophets**
1 someone who can tell what is going to happen, before it happens. **2** a great religious teacher.
prophetic *adjective*

proportion *noun* **proportions**
1 a fraction; a share. **2** a ratio. **3** the correct relationship between the size, amount, or importance of two things.
proportions, size; importance, as in *a ship of large proportions.*
proportional *adjective*, **proportionally** *adverb*, **proportionate** *adjective*

propose *verb* **proposes, proposing, proposed**
1 to suggest an idea or plan. **2** to ask someone to marry you.
proposal *noun*

proprietor *noun* **proprietors**
(*say* pruh-**pry**-uht-er)
the owner of a shop or business.

propriety *noun* **proprieties**
proper or correct behaviour.

propulsion *noun*
the act of driving or pushing forward.

proscribe *verb* **proscribes, proscribing, proscribed**
to forbid, as in *The government proscribed the legalisation of drugs.*

prose *noun*
writing that is not in verse.

prosecute *verb* **prosecutes, prosecuting, prosecuted**
to make someone go to a lawcourt to be tried for a crime.
prosecution *noun*, **prosecutor** *noun*

prospect *noun* **prospects** (*say* **pros**-pekt)
1 a possibility; a hope, as in *no prospects of*

proximity

success. **2** a wide view, as in *A vast prospect lay before us as we stood on the hill.*

prospect *verb* prospects, prospecting, prospected (*say* **pros**-spekt *or* pruh-**spekt**)
to search for gold or some other mineral.
prospector *noun*

prosper *verb* prospers, prospering, prospered
to be successful; to do well.

prosperous *adjective*
successful; rich.
prosperity *noun*

prostitute *noun* prostitutes
someone who takes part in sexual acts for money.

protect *verb* protects, protecting, protected
to keep someone or something safe.
protection *noun*, **protective** *adjective*, **protector** *noun*

protectorate *noun* protectorates
a nation that is controlled and protected by another.

protégé *noun* protégés (*say* **proh**-tuh-zhay *or* **pro**-tuh-zhay)
a person who is protected or guided by another.

protein *noun* proteins (*say* **proh**-teen)
a substance in food that is necessary for growth and good health.

protest *noun* protests (*say* **proh**-test)
something you say or do because you disagree with what someone else is saying or doing.

protest *verb* protests, protesting, protested (*say* pruh-**test**)
to make a protest.
protester *noun*

Protestant *noun* Protestants (*say* **prot**-uhs-tuhnt)
a Christian who does not belong to the Roman Catholic or Orthodox Churches.

proton *noun* protons
a particle of matter with a positive electric charge.

protoplasm *noun* (*say* **proh**-toh-plaz-uhm)
a colourless substance of which animal and vegetable cells are made.

prototype *noun* prototypes (*say* **proh**-tuh-tuyp)
the first example of something, used as a model for the manufacture of others.

protracted *adjective*
drawn out, as in *The meeting was protracted and many left.*

protractor *noun* protractors
a device for measuring angles.

protrude *verb* protrudes, protruding, protruded
to stick out.
protrusion *noun*

proud *adjective* prouder, proudest
1 very pleased with yourself or with someone else who has done well, as in *I am proud of my sister.* **2** too satisfied because of who you are or what you have done, as in *He's too proud to talk to us.*
proudly *adverb*

prove *verb* proves, proving, proved
1 to show that something is true. **2** to turn out to be, as in *My pen proved to be useless.*

proverb *noun* proverbs
a short, well-known saying that states a truth, as in *'A stitch in time saves nine'* and *'Many hands make light work'* are proverbs.
proverbial *adjective*

provide *verb* provides, providing, provided
1 to supply something. **2** to prepare for something, as in *They have provided for all possible disasters.*
provided or **providing,** on condition; on condition that, as in *You can come with us providing that you pay for yourself.*

province *noun* provinces
1 a part of a country. **2** an area of learning, as in *Classical music is his province.*
provincial *adjective*

provision *noun* provisions
1 providing something, as in *the provision of free meals for old people.* **2** a statement in a document, as in *the provisions of the treaty.*
provisions, supplies of food and drink.

provisional *adjective*
arranged or agreed on temporarily, but possibly to be altered later, as in *After the revolution a provisional government was established.*

provoke *verb* provokes, provoking, provoked
1 to make someone angry. **2** to arouse or stimulate something, as in *His statement provoked a great deal of criticism.*
provocation *noun*, **provocative** *adjective*

prowess *noun* (*say* **prow**-es *or* prow-**es**)
1 skill; expertise. **2** bravery.

prowl *verb* prowls, prowling, prowled
to move quietly or cautiously.
prowler *noun*

proximity *noun*
nearness in space, time, etc.

prudent

prudent *adjective* (*say* **proo**-duhnt)
careful; not reckless.
prudence *noun*, **prudently** *adverb*

prune *noun* **prunes**
a dried plum.

prune *verb* **prunes, pruning, pruned**
to cut off unwanted parts of a tree, bush, etc.

pry *verb* **pries, prying, pried**
to try often or in an annoying way to find out things about other people's business.

PS short for **postscript.**

psalm *noun* **psalms** (*say* sahm)
a religious song, especially one of those in the Book of Psalms in the Bible.

pseudonym *noun* **pseudonyms**
(*say* **syoo**-duh-nim)
a false name used by an author.

psychiatrist *noun* **psychiatrists**
(*say* suy-**kuy**-uh-truhst)
a person trained to treat mental illness.
psychiatric *adjective*, **psychiatry** *noun*

psychic *adjective* (*say* **suy**-kik)
1 supernatural. 2 having or using telepathy or supernatural powers.

psychologist *noun* **psychologists**
(*say* suy-**kol**-uh-juhst)
someone who studies how the mind works.
psychological *adjective*, **psychology** *noun*

pub *noun* **pubs**
(*colloquial*) an hotel.

puberty *noun* (*say* **pyoo**-buh-tee)
the time when a young person begins to mature sexually.

public *adjective*
belonging or open to everyone; used or known by everyone.
public servant, a person employed by the State or Federal governments.
public transport, transport owned and operated by the government.
public works, buildings, roads, etc. constructed by a country's government for its people.
publicly *adverb*

public *noun*
all the people; everyone.
in public, openly; where anyone can see, hear, or take part.

publication *noun* **publications**
1 printing and selling books, etc.
2 a book, etc. that is printed and sold.

publicity *noun*
information or activity to make people interested in someone or something; advertising.

publicise or **publicize** *verb* **publicises, publicising, publicised** (*say* **pub**-luh-suyz)
to give publicity to something.

publish *verb* **publishes, publishing, published**
1 to print and sell books, etc. 2 to announce something in public.
publisher *noun*

puck *noun* **pucks**
the hard rubber disc used in ice-hockey.

pucker *verb* **puckers, puckering, puckered**
to wrinkle.

pudding *noun* **puddings**
a type of cooked dessert, as in *lemon pudding.*

puddle *noun* **puddles**
a small pool, usually of rainwater.

puff *noun* **puffs**
1 a small amount of breath, wind, smoke, steam, etc. 2 a soft pad for putting powder on the skin. 3 a small cake filled with cream.

puff *verb* **puffs, puffing, puffed**
1 to blow out puffs of smoke, steam, etc.
2 to breathe with difficulty. 3 to inflate or swell something, as in *He puffed out his chest.*
puffy *adjective*

puffin *noun* **puffins**
a northern hemisphere sea bird with a large striped beak.

pull *verb* **pulls, pulling, pulled**
1 to get hold of something and make it come towards you or follow behind you.
2 to move, as in *The train pulled into the station.*
pull a face, to make a strange face.
pull off, to achieve something.
pull out, not to do something that you had arranged to do, as in *Half the competitors pulled out just before the race.*
pull someone's leg, to play a trick on someone; to tease someone.
pull through, to recover from an illness.
pull up, (of a vehicle) to stop, as in *A car pulled up and two men got out.*
pull yourself together, to become calm or sensible.

pulley *noun* **pulleys**
a wheel with a groove around it to take a rope, used for lifting heavy things.

pullover *noun* pullovers
a knitted garment for the top half of your body; a jumper.

pulp *noun* pulps
a soft, wet mass of something, especially for making paper.

pulp *verb* pulps, pulping, pulped
to be reduced to pulp, as in *They pulped the old books. The oranges were pulped for jam.*

pulpit *noun* pulpits
a small enclosed platform where the preacher stands in a church.

pulse *noun* pulses
1 a regular movement of blood in your arteries that shows how fast your heart is beating. 2 a regular vibration.

pulverise or **pulverize** *verb* pulverises, pulverising, pulverised
to crush something so that it becomes a powder.

pumice *noun* (*say* **pum**-uhs)
a kind of soft, sponge-like stone rubbed on things to clean or polish them.

pump *noun* pumps
1 a device that pushes air or liquid into or out of something, or along pipes. 2 a lightweight shoe.

pump *verb* pumps, pumping, pumped
to move air or liquid with a pump.
pump iron, (*colloquial*) to exercise with weights.
pump up, to fill something with air or gas.

pumpkin *noun* pumpkins
a very large, round fruit with a hard skin, cooked as a vegetable.

pun *noun* puns
a joke made by using words that sound similar, as in *Deciding where to bury him was a grave decision.*
punning *noun*

punch *verb* punches, punching, punched
1 to hit someone with your fist. 2 to make a hole in something; to make a hole, as in *The guard checked and punched our tickets. I punched a few more holes in my belt.*

punch *noun* punches
1 a hit with the fist. 2 a device for making holes in paper, metal, or other substances. 3 force or vigour. 4 a drink of wine or spirits mixed with water, fruit juices, spices, etc., and served chilled or hot.
punch line, words that give the climax of a joke or story.
punch-up, (*colloquial*) a fight.

punctual *adjective*
exactly on time; not arriving late.
punctuality *noun*, **punctually** *adverb*

punctuate *verb* punctuates, punctuating, punctuated
to put punctuation in a piece of writing.

punctuation *noun*
marks such as commas, full stops, and brackets put into a piece of writing to make it easier to read.

puncture *noun* punctures
a hole in a tyre.

pungent *adjective* (*say* **pun**-juhnt)
sharp or strong in taste or smell, as in *Bleach has a pungent smell.*

punish *verb* punishes, punishing, punished
to make someone suffer because he or she has done wrong.
punishment *noun*

punk *noun* punks
1 someone who likes punk rock. 2 (*colloquial*) a rough, dirty, or worthless person.
punk rock, a kind of loud, simple, rock music.

punt *noun* punts
1 a flat-bottomed boat. 2 (*Australian Rules Football*) a kick which a player gives to a dropped football before it hits the ground.

punt *verb* punts, punting, punted
to bet on something, as in *He punts on the horses.*

punter *noun* punters
(*colloquial*) a person who gambles or who places a bet.

puny *adjective* punier, puniest (*say* **pyoo**-nee)
small and weak.

pup *noun* pups
a puppy.

pupa *noun* pupae (*say* **pyoo**-puh)
an insect in the stage between larva and maturity; a chrysalis.

pupil *noun* pupils
1 someone who is being taught by a teacher. 2 the opening in the centre of the eye.

puppet *noun* puppets
1 a kind of doll that can be made to move by fitting it over your hand or by working it with strings or wires. 2 a leader or ruler who is controlled by other people.

puppy *noun* puppies
a young dog.

purchase

purchase *verb* **purchases, purchasing, purchased**
to buy.
purchaser *noun*

purchase *noun* **purchases**
1 something you have bought. 2 the action of buying something, as in *Please keep the receipt as proof of purchase.*

pure *adjective* **purer, purest**
1 not mixed with anything else, as in *pure olive oil.* 2 clean or clear, as in *a pure, cold mountain stream.*
purely *adverb*, **purity** *noun*

purée *noun* **purées**
food which has been mashed or blended to form a thick, smooth sauce, as in *tomato purée.*

purgatory *noun* (*say* per-guh-tree *or* per-guh-tuh-ree)
1 the place where Roman Catholics believe the souls of dead people are sent to suffer for their sins before they enter heaven. 2 a place or state of temporary suffering, as in *He saw homework as purgatory.*

purge *verb* **purges, purging, purged**
to get rid of unwanted people or things.

purify *verb* **purifies, purifying, purified**
to make something pure.
purification *noun*, **purifier** *noun*

Puritan *noun* **Puritans**
a Protestant in the 16th or 17th century who wanted simpler religious ceremonies and strict moral behaviour.
puritan, a person with very strict morals.
puritanical *adjective*

purple *adjective* **purpler, purplest**
deep reddish-blue.

purpose *noun* **purposes**
what you intend to do; a plan or aim.
on purpose, intentionally; not by chance.
purposeful *adjective*, **purposeless** *adjective*

purposely *adverb*
on purpose.

purr *verb* **purrs, purring, purred**
to make a gentle murmuring sound like a cat when it is pleased.

purse *noun* **purses**
a small bag to hold money.

pursue *verb* **pursues, pursuing, pursued**
1 to chase someone or something. 2 to continue with something; to work at something, as in *We cannot pursue the investigation any further. She pursued her studies at college.*
pursuer *noun*

pursuit *noun* **pursuits**
1 the act of chasing, as in *the police pursuit of the thief.* 2 something you spend time doing; a regular activity, as in *Sailing is his main pursuit.*

pus *noun*
a thick yellowish substance produced in boils, etc. or in infected wounds.

push *verb* **pushes, pushing, pushed**
to use force to move something away from you; to press something.
push off, (*colloquial*) to go away.
push on, (*colloquial*) to continue.

push *noun* **pushes**
a pushing movement.
at a push, in a crisis; if necessary.
the push, (*colloquial*) dismissal from a job.

puss or **pussy** *noun* **pusses** or **pussies**
(*colloquial*) a cat.

put *verb* **puts, putting, put**
1 to move something into a place. 2 to cause someone or something to be in a particular condition, as in *Put the light out.* 3 to express something in words, as in *She put it tactfully.*
put off, to postpone something; to stop someone wanting something, as in *We'll have to put off the outdoor concert if it rains. Eating too much ice-cream last week seems to have put her off ice-cream for good.*
put out, to stop a fire burning, light shining, etc.
put up, to raise something; to give someone a place to sleep, as in *Put up a tent. Can we put him up for the night?*
put up with, to tolerate.

putrid *adjective*
rotten or foul, as in *The garbage bin had a putrid smell.*

putt *verb* **putts, putting, putted**
to hit a golf ball gently towards the hole.
putter *noun*, **putting-green** *noun*

putty *noun*
a soft paste that sets hard, used especially for fitting windows in their frames.

puzzle *noun* **puzzles**
1 a difficult question; a problem. 2 a game where you have to solve a problem or do something difficult.

puzzle *verb* **puzzles, puzzling, puzzled**
1 to give someone a problem. 2 to think deeply about something.

pygmy or **pigmy** *noun* **pygmies**
(*say* **pig**-mee)
1 a member of a dwarf people, as in *the*

pygmies of the Amazon. **2** a very small person, animal, or thing, as in *pygmy possum.*

pyjamas *plural noun*
a loose jacket and trousers worn in bed.

pylon *noun* **pylons**
a metal tower that supports electric cables.

pyramid *noun* **pyramids**
1 a structure with a square base and four sloping sides coming to a point. **2** an ancient Egyptian monument shaped like this.

Pythagoras' theorem *noun*
the statement that a square drawn on the longest side (*hypotenuse*) of a right-angled triangle is equal in area to the squares on the other two sides added together.

python *noun* **pythons**
a large snake that crushes its prey.

a
b
c
d
e
f
g
h
i
j
k
l
m
n
o
p
q
r
s
t
u
v
w
x
y
z

Qq

quack *noun* quacks
1 the sound made by a duck. 2 a person without proper medical qualifications who acts as a doctor. 3 (*colloquial*) the doctor.

quad *noun* quads
1 (*colloquial*) a quadrangle. 2 (*colloquial*) a quadruplet.

quadrangle *noun* quadrangles
a rectangular courtyard.

quadrant *noun* quadrants
a quarter of a circle.

quadrilateral *noun* quadrilaterals
a four-sided figure.

quadruple *adjective*
1 four times as much or as many. 2 having four parts.

quadruple *verb* quadruples, quadrupling, quadrupled
to make something four times as much or as many; to become four times as much or as many.

quadruplet *noun* quadruplets
one of four children born to the same mother at one time.

quail *noun* quails
a small game-bird.

quail *verb* quails, quailing, quailed
to feel or show fear.

quaint *adjective* quainter, quaintest
attractive in an unusual or old-fashioned way.

quake *verb* quakes, quaking, quaked
to tremble; to shake.

Quaker *noun* Quakers
a member of a Christian religious group founded by George Fox in the 17th century.

qualify *verb* qualifies, qualifying, qualified
1 to be suitable for a job; to make someone suitable for a job, as in *With her experience, she qualifies immediately for the work. His degree qualifies him to become a graphic designer.* 2 to alter a statement, etc., usually making it less strong.
qualification *noun*

quality *noun* qualities
1 how good or bad something is. 2 what something is like, as in *The paper had a shiny quality.*

qualm *noun* qualms
a feeling of doubt or nervousness about something.

quantity *noun* quantities
how much there is of something; how many things there are of one sort.

quarantine *noun* (*say* kwo-ruhn-teen)
a period when a person or animal is kept apart from others to prevent a disease from spreading.

quarrel *noun* quarrels
a strong or angry argument.
quarrelsome *adjective*

quarrel *verb* quarrels, quarrelling, quarrelled
to have a strong or angry argument with someone.

quarry *noun* quarries
1 a place where stone, slate, etc. is dug out of the ground. 2 an animal that is being hunted.

quarter *noun* quarters
1 one of four equal parts into which something is divided or can be divided. 2 three months.

quiver

at close quarters, close together, as in *They fought at close quarters.*
quarters, a place to live.

quartet *noun* quartets (*say* kwaw-**tet**)
1 a group of four musicians.   2 a piece of music for four musicians.

quartz *noun* (*say* kwawts)
a hard mineral.

quaver *verb* quavers, quavering, quavered
to tremble, as in *His voice quavered with fear.*

quaver *noun* quavers
1 a trembling sound.   2 a musical note equal to half a crotchet, written ♪.

quay *noun* quays (*say* kee)
a wharf or pier where ships load and unload.

queasy *adjective*
feeling slightly sick.

queen *noun* queens
1 a woman who is the crowned ruler of a country.   2 a king's wife.   3 a female bee or ant, etc., that produces eggs.   4 an important piece in chess.   5 a playing-card with a picture of a crowned woman on it.
queen mother, a king's widow who is the mother of the present king or queen.

queer *adjective* queerer, queerest
1 strange.   2 ill, as in *I feel queer.*
3 (*colloquial offensive*) an insulting word meaning homosexual.

quench *verb* quenches, quenching, quenched
1 to satisfy your thirst.   2 to put out a fire.

query *noun* queries (*say* **kweer**-ree)
1 a question.   2 a question mark.

quest *noun* quests
a search, as in *talent quest.*

question *noun* questions
1 something you ask, as in *I cannot answer your question.*   2 a problem or subject requiring a solution, as in *Parliament debated the question of immigration.*
in question, that is being discussed.
out of the question, impossible.

question *verb* questions, questioning, questioned
1 to ask someone questions.   2 to be doubtful about something.
questionable *adjective*, questioner *noun*

question mark *noun* question marks
the punctuation mark '?' put at the end of a question.

questionnaire *noun* questionnaires
(*say* kwes-chuhn-**air** *or* kes-chuhn-**air**)
a list of questions.

queue *noun* queues (*say* kyoo)
a line of people or vehicles waiting for something.

queue *verb* queues, queueing *or* queuing, queued (*say* kyoo)
to wait in a queue.

quibble *verb* quibbles, quibbling, quibbled
to argue over unimportant matters.

quiche *noun* quiches (*say* keesh)
a large tart filled with savoury things such as eggs, cheese, onion, and tomato.

quick *adjective* quicker, quickest
1 rapid.   2 done in a short time.
3 lively; clever, as in *quick-witted.*
4 (*old-fashioned use*) alive, as in *the quick and the dead.*
quicken *verb*

quicksand *noun* quicksands
loose, wet sand that can quickly swallow up people, animals, etc.

quiet *adjective* quieter, quietest
1 silent.   2 not loud, as in *a quiet voice.*
3 without much movement, as in *a quiet sea.*

quieten *verb* quietens, quietening, quietened
to make something or someone quiet; to become quiet.

quill *noun* quills
1 a large feather.   2 a pen made from a large feather.

quilt *noun* quilts
a thick, soft cover for a bed.

quinine *noun*
a bitter medicine used as a tonic and to reduce fever, as in *Quinine is used to treat malaria.*

quintet *noun* quintets
1 a group of five musicians.   2 a piece of music for five musicians.

quit *verb* quits, quitting, quitted *or* quit
1 to leave or abandon something.
2 (*colloquial*) to stop doing something, as in *Quit pulling my leg!*
quitter *noun*

quite *adverb*
1 completely; truly, as in *I am quite all right.*   2 somewhat; rather, as in *He's quite a good swimmer.*

quiver *verb* quivers, quivering, quivered
to tremble, as in *He was quivering with excitement.*

a
b
c
d
e
f
g
h
i
j
k
l
m
n
o
p
q
r
s
t
u
v
w
x
y
z

quiver

quiver *noun* **quivers**
a container for arrows.

quiz *noun* **quizzes**
a series of questions, especially as an entertainment or competition.

quoit *noun* **quoits** (*say* koit)
a ring thrown at a peg in the game of quoits.

quokka *noun* **quokkas** (*say* **kwo**-kuh)
the small, short-tailed wallaby of south-western Western Australia, having long, greyish-brown fur.

Origin This word comes from Nyungar, an Aboriginal language of Western Australia. See the Aboriginal languages map at the back of this dictionary.

quoll *noun* **quolls** (*say* kwol)
a native cat.

quota *noun* **quotas** (*say* **kwoh**-tuh)
1 a share, as in *Each school was given its quota of equipment.* 2 a limited amount that is allowed, as in *The council has exceeded its quota of employees.*

quotation *noun* **quotations**
1 the act of repeating words that were first written or spoken by someone else.
2 words from someone's book, speech, etc., repeated by someone else.
quotation marks, inverted commas.

quote *verb* **quotes, quoting, quoted**
1 to repeat words that were first spoken or written by someone else. 2 to give a price on something, as in *The plumber gave a reasonable quote to repair the drain.*

quotient *noun* **quotients** (*say* **kwoh**-shuhnt)
the result of dividing one number by another, as in *When 15 is divided by 5, the quotient is 3.*

Rr

rabbi *noun* rabbis (*say* **rab**-uy)
a Jewish religious leader.

rabbit *noun* rabbits
a furry animal with long ears, as in *Rabbits live in burrows.*

rabble *noun*
a disorderly crowd; a mob.

rabid *adjective* (*say* **rab**-uhd)
1 furious; violent. 2 affected with rabies.
rabidly *adverb*

rabies *noun* (*say* **ray**-beez)
a disease that makes dogs go mad.

race *noun* races
1 a competition to be the first to reach a particular place. 2 a group of people with the same ancestors, characteristics, or skin-colour.
race relations, the way in which people of different races live together in the same community.
racial *adjective*

race *verb* races, racing, raced
1 to have a race against someone. 2 to move very fast, as in *The train raced along the track.*
racer *noun*

racecourse *noun* racecourses
a ground for horse-racing.

racism *noun* (*say* **rays**-iz-uhm)
1 believing that your own race of people is better than others. 2 hostility between different races of people.
racist *noun* and *adjective*

rack *noun* racks
1 a framework used as a shelf or container.
2 an ancient device for torturing people by stretching them.

racket *noun* rackets
1 a loud noise. 2 (*colloquial*) a scheme for obtaining money, etc. by dishonest means.

racquet *noun* racquets
an implement for hitting the ball in tennis, badminton, etc., made of strings stretched across a wooden or metal frame.

radar *noun* (*say* **ray**-dah)
a system that uses radio waves to find the position of objects which you cannot see because of darkness, fog, distance, etc.

radiant *adjective*
1 bright; shining, as in *the radiant sun.*
2 looking very happy.
radiance *noun*, **radiantly** *adverb*

radiate *verb* radiates, radiating, radiated
1 to give out heat, light, or other energy.
2 to be arranged like the spokes of a wheel.

radiation *noun*
1 heat, light, or other energy given out by something. 2 radioactivity.

radiator *noun* radiators
1 a device that gives out heat, especially a metal container through which steam or hot water flows. 2 the device that cools the engine of a vehicle.

radical *adjective*
1 thorough, going right to the roots of something, as in *radical changes.*
2 wanting change in the world, as in *a radical politician.*
radical *noun*, **radically** *adverb*

radio *noun* radios
1 an apparatus for receiving broadcast sound programs. 2 sending or receiving sound by means of electrical waves.

radioactive *adjective*
giving out atomic energy.
radioactivity *noun*

a
b
c
d
e
f
g
h
i
j
k
l
m
n
o
p
q
r
s
t
u
v
w
x
y
z

radish

radish *noun* **radishes**
a small, hard, round, red vegetable, eaten raw in salads.

radium *noun*
a radioactive element.

radius *noun* **radii**
1 a straight line from the centre of a circle to the circumference. 2 the distance between the centre and the circumference of a circle.

raffia *noun*
a fibre from palm tree leaves which is used in weaving baskets, hats, etc.

raffle *noun* **raffles**
a way of raising money by selling numbered tickets which may win prizes.

raft *noun* **rafts**
a floating platform of logs, barrels, etc. fastened together.

rafter *noun* **rafters**
one of the long, sloping pieces of wood that hold up a roof.

rag *noun* **rags**
1 a torn or old piece of cloth.
2 (*colloquial*) an insulting name for a newspaper.

rage *noun* **rages**
great or violent anger.
all the rage, (*colloquial*) very fashionable or popular.

rage *verb* **rages, raging, raged**
1 to be very angry. 2 to be violent or noisy. 3 (*colloquial*) to thoroughly enjoy oneself, as in *We raged till dawn*.

ragged *adjective* (*say* **rag**-uhd)
1 torn or frayed, as in *ragged clothes*.
2 wearing torn or old clothes, as in *a ragged man*. 3 not smooth, as in *a ragged performance*.

ragtime *noun*
an old-fashioned kind of jazzy music.

raid *noun* **raids**
a sudden attack.

raid *verb* **raids, raiding, raided**
to attack a place suddenly; to make a surprise visit to a place where there may be law-breakers, as in *The police raided a nightclub*.
raider *noun*

rail *noun* **rails**
1 a bar or rod, as in *a towel-rail*. 2 a long metal bar that is part of a railway track.
by rail, on a train.

railings *plural noun*
a fence made of rails.

railway *noun* **railways**
1 the parallel metal bars that trains travel on. 2 a system of transport using rails, as in *The railways are used to transport coal*.

rain *noun*
drops of water that fall from the sky.
rainforest, a thick tropical forest with heavy rainfall.
rain gauge, a device for measuring how much rain has fallen.
raindrop *noun*, **rainwater** *noun*, **rainy** *adjective*

rain *verb* **rains, raining, rained**
to come down or send something down like rain.
it is raining, rain is falling.
rain cats and dogs, to rain heavily.

rainbow *noun* **rainbows**
an arched band of colours seen in the sky when the sun shines through rain, as in *The colours in a rainbow are red, orange, yellow, green, blue, indigo, and violet*.

rainbow serpent *noun*
the most important spirit in Aboriginal mythology connected especially with the creation of the earth.

raincoat *noun* **raincoats**
a waterproof coat.

rainfall *noun*
the amount of rain that falls in a particular place or time.

raise *verb* **raises, raising, raised**
1 to move something to a higher place or upright position. 2 to manage to get the money or people needed for something, as in *They raised $1,000 for the appeal. He raised an army in just ten days*. 3 to bring up young children or animals. 4 to make or cause, as in *He raised a laugh with his joke*. 5 to end a siege.

raise *noun*
an increase in a wage or salary.

raisin *noun* **raisins**
a dried grape.

rake *noun* **rakes**
a gardening tool with a row of short spikes fixed to a long handle.

rake *verb* **rakes, raking, raked**
1 to move or smooth something with a rake. 2 to search, as in *I raked around in my desk but couldn't find the letter*.
rake in, (*colloquial*) to make money or profit.

rally *verb* **rallies, rallying, rallied**
1 to bring people together, or to come together, for a united effort, as in *The general rallied his troops. The community*

rallied to help farmers in the drought. **2** to revive; to recover, as in *The team rallied when they realised they could win.*

rally *noun* **rallies**
1 a large meeting. **2** a competition to test skill in driving, as in *the London to Sydney Rally.* **3** a series of strokes and return strokes in tennis, etc. before a point is scored.

RAM short for *random-access memory*, a type of computer memory which can have information put into it or taken out of it by the user, but which does not keep the information if the computer is switched off.

ram *noun* **rams**
a male sheep.

ram *verb* **rams, ramming, rammed**
to push one thing hard against another.

Ramadan *noun* (*say* **ram**-uh-dan *or* ram-uh-**dan**)
the ninth month of the Muslim year, when Muslims fast during the daytime.

ramble *noun* **rambles**
a long walk in the country.

ramble *verb* **rambles, rambling, rambled**
1 to go for a long walk in the country; to wander, as in *I rambled through town, looking at the shops.* **2** not to keep to a subject, as in *The speaker kept rambling.*
rambler *noun*

ramp *noun* **ramps**
a slope between two levels.

rampage *verb* **rampages, rampaging, rampaged** (*say* ram-**payj**)
to rush about wildly or destructively.

ran past tense of **run** *verb.*

ranch *noun* **ranches**
a large cattle station, especially in America.
rancher *noun*

random *noun*
at random, by chance; without any choice, purpose, or plan.

random *adjective*
done or taken at random, as in *a random sample.*
random breath test, a measurement of the amount of alcohol in the breath of a motorist chosen randomly from a line of traffic.

rang past tense of **ring** *verb.*

range *noun* **ranges**
1 a line or series of things, as in *a range of mountains.* **2** the size of the difference between first and last, or between highest and lowest in a group, as in *There is a large range of ages in my family.* **3** a number of different things, as in *a wide range of goods.* **4** the distance that a gun can shoot, an aircraft can fly, etc. **5** a place with targets for shooting-practice. **6** a large area of land. **7** an electric or gas stove.

range *verb* **ranges, ranging, ranged**
1 to exist between two limits; to extend, as in *Prices ranged from $1 to $50.* **2** to arrange, as in *Hundreds of people ranged themselves along the streets, hoping to see the parade go by.* **3** to wander; to move over a wide area, as in *Hens ranged all over the farm.*

ranger *noun* **rangers**
1 someone who looks after a national park, etc. **2** in some areas, particularly Western Australia, a person employed by the local council to attend to parking, litter, etc.

rank *noun* **ranks**
1 a line of people or things, as in *a taxi rank.* **2** a position in a series of people or things, especially in society or in the armed forces, as in *He was promoted to the rank of captain.*

ransack *verb* **ransacks, ransacking, ransacked**
to search a place thoroughly, leaving things untidy.

ransom *noun* **ransoms**
money paid so that a captive can be set free.
hold someone to ransom, to keep someone as a captive and demand a ransom.

rant *verb* **rants, ranting, ranted**
to speak loudly or violently.

rap *noun* **raps**
1 a slight blow. **2** a knock or sharp, tapping sound. **3** a kind of pop music in which the words are spoken rhythmically, not sung.

rap *verb* **raps, rapping, rapped**
to knock quickly and loudly.

rape *noun* **rapes**
the act of forcing another person to have sexual intercourse against his or her will.

rapid *adjective*
moving or working at speed.
rapidity *noun,* **rapidly** *adverb*

rapids *plural noun*
part of a river where the water flows very quickly.

rapt *adjective*
1 to be fully absorbed in your own thoughts.
2 to be carried away by strong feelings.

rapture

rapture *noun* **raptures**
a great delight or pleasure, as in *He was in rapture over the film.*

rare *adjective* **rarer, rarest**
unusual; not often found or experienced, as in *She died of a rare disease.*
rarely *adverb*, **rarity** *noun*

rare *adjective*
underdone, as in *rare steak.*

rascal *noun* **rascals**
a dishonest or mischievous person.

rash *adjective* **rasher, rashest**
acting or done quickly without proper thought, as in *She made a rash decision when she was under pressure at work.*

rash *noun* **rashes**
a red patch or red spots on the skin.

rasher *noun* **rashers**
a slice of bacon.

rasp *verb* **rasps, rasping, rasped** (*say* rahsp *or* rasp)
to scrape or rub roughly; to make a grating sound.

raspberry *noun* **raspberries**
a small, soft, red fruit.

rat *noun* **rats**
1 an animal like a large mouse. 2 a nasty or treacherous person.
ratbag, (*colloquial*) an irritating or eccentric person.
rat race, (*colloquial*) a continuous competition for success in your career, business, etc.

rate *noun* **rates**
1 speed, as in *The train moved at a great rate.* 2 cost; charge, as in *What is the rate for a letter to New Zealand?* 3 quality; standard, as in *She was first-rate in athletics.*
at any rate, anyway.
at this rate or **at that rate,** if this is typical or true.
rates, a tax paid by householders to the local government.

rate *verb* **rates, rating, rated**
1 to value something, as in *Drivers rated the new car very highly.* 2 to regard someone in a particular way, as in *He rated me among his friends.*

rather *adverb*
1 slightly; somewhat, as in *It was rather dark.* 2 preferably; more willingly, as in *I would rather not come.* 3 more truly, as in *He lay down, or rather fell, on the bed.*

rating *noun* **ratings**
an assessment based on how much of a particular quality, etc. someone or something has, as in *The swimmer was given an excellent fitness rating.*

ratio *noun* **ratios** (*say* **ray**-shee-oh)
the relationship between two numbers; how often one number goes into another, as in *In a group of 2 girls and 10 boys, the ratio of girls to boys is 1 to 5.*

ration *noun* **rations** (*say* **rash**-uhn)
an amount allowed to one person, as in *You have had your ration of sweets for today.*

ration *verb* **rations, rationing, rationed** (*say* **rash**-uhn)
to share something out in fixed amounts.

rational *adjective* (*say* **rash**-uh-nuhl)
reasonable; sane, as in *a rational method. No rational person would do such a stupid thing.*
rationalise *verb*, **rationally** *adverb*

rattle *verb* **rattles, rattling, rattled**
1 to make a series of short, sharp, hard sounds, as in *Dried peas rattle inside a tin.* 2 (*colloquial*) to make someone nervous and confused.

rattle *noun* **rattles**
1 a series of short, sharp, hard sounds.
2 a baby's toy that makes this kind of sound.

rave *verb* **raves, raving, raved**
to talk or behave madly or very enthusiastically.

raven *noun* **ravens**
1 a large black bird with a hoarse cry. 2 shiny black, as in *raven hair.*

ravenous *adjective* (*say* **rav**-uh-nuhs)
very hungry.
ravenously *adverb*

ravine *noun* **ravines** (*say* ruh-**veen**)
a very deep, narrow gorge.

ravioli *noun*
small pasta envelopes containing minced meat, vegetables, etc., usually eaten with a sauce.

raw *adjective* **rawer, rawest**
1 not cooked, as in *a raw steak.* 2 in the natural state; not processed, as in *raw materials.* 3 without experience, as in *raw beginners.* 4 with the skin removed, as in *a raw wound.* 5 cold and damp, as in *a raw wind.*
raw deal, (*colloquial*) unfair treatment.

ray *noun* **rays**
a thin line of light, heat, or other energy.

reassure

raze *verb* **razes, razing, razed**
to completely destroy; to tear down, as in *During the fire the building was razed to the ground.*

razor *noun* **razors**
a device with a very sharp blade, especially one used for shaving.

reach *verb* **reaches, reaching, reached**
1 to get to a place or thing. 2 to stretch out your hand to get or touch something.

reach *noun* **reaches**
1 the distance you can reach with your hand. 2 a distance that you can easily travel, as in *My uncle lives within reach of the sea.* 3 a straight stretch of a river or canal.

react *verb* **reacts, reacting, reacted**
to have a reaction.

reaction *noun* **reactions**
an action or feeling caused by another person or thing.

reactor *noun* **reactors**
an apparatus for producing nuclear power.

read *verb* **reads, reading, read**
to look at something written and printed, and understand it or say it aloud, as in *Have you read this book? I read it last year.*
readable *adjective*

reader *noun* **readers**
1 someone who reads. 2 a book that helps you learn to read.

readily *adverb*
1 willingly, as in *She readily agreed to help.* 2 quickly; without any difficulty, as in *The system can be installed readily by anyone who can use a screwdriver.*

reading *noun* **readings**
1 the act of reading a book, magazine, etc. 2 an amount shown on a measuring instrument, as in *Check the barometer readings every day.*

ready *adjective* **readier, readiest**
1 able or willing to do something or to be used at once; prepared. 2 quick, as in *ready answers.*
at the ready, ready for use or action.
readiness *noun*

real *adjective*
1 existing; true; not imaginary.
2 genuine; not a copy.

real estate *noun*
land and what is built on it.

realism *noun*
seeing or showing things as they really are.
realist *noun*, **realistic** *adjective*, **realistically** *adverb*

reality *noun* **realities**
1 what is real. 2 something real, as in *Cold and hunger are the realities of homelessness.*

realise or **realize** *verb* **realises, realising, realised**
to understand something clearly; to accept something as true.
realisation *noun*

really *adverb*
truly; certainly; in fact.

realm *noun* **realms** (*say* relm)
1 a kingdom. 2 an area of knowledge, interest, activity, etc.

reap *verb* **reaps, reaping, reaped**
1 to cut and gather a grain crop. 2 to obtain as a result of something done, as in *The reaped great benefit from their training.*
reaper *noun*

reappear *verb* **reappears, reappearing, reappeared**
to appear again.
reappearance *noun*

rear *noun* **rears**
1 the back of something. 2 a person's bottom.

rear *adjective*
placed or found at the back, as in *a car with a rear engine.*

rear *verb* **rears, rearing, reared**
1 to bring up young children or animals.
2 to rise up on the hind legs, as in *The horse reared up in fright.*

rearrange *verb* **rearranges, rearranging, rearranged**
to arrange something differently.
rearrangement *noun*

reason *noun* **reasons**
1 a cause for something; an explanation.
2 reasoning; common sense, as in *Listen to reason.*

reason *verb* **reasons, reasoning, reasoned**
to think in an organised way.

reasonable *adjective*
1 sensible; logical. 2 fair; moderate, as in *reasonable prices.*
reasonableness *noun*, **reasonably** *adverb*

reasoning *noun*
thinking in an orderly way.

reassure *verb* **reassures, reassuring, reassured**
to remove someone's doubts or fears.
reassurance *noun*

a
b
c
d
e
f
g
h
i
j
k
l
m
n
o
p
q
r
s
t
u
v
w
x
y
z

rebel

rebel *verb* **rebels, rebelling, rebelled**
(*say* ruh-**bel**)
to refuse to obey someone in authority,
especially the government.
rebellion *noun*, **rebellious** *adjective*

rebel *noun* **rebels** (*say* **reb**-uhl)
someone who refuses to obey someone in
authority.

rebound *verb* **rebounds, rebounding,
rebounded**
to bounce back after hitting something.

rebuild *verb* **rebuilds, rebuilding, rebuilt**
to build something again; to put something
together again.

rebuke *verb* **rebukes, rebuking, rebuked**
to express strong disapproval.

recall *verb* **recalls, recalling, recalled**
1 to ask someone to come back. 2 to
remember someone or something.

recap *verb* **recaps, recapping, recapped**
(*colloquial*) to state again the main points of
something that has been said.

recapture *verb* **recaptures, recapturing,
recaptured**
to capture something or someone again.

recede *verb* **recedes, receding, receded**
to go back, as in *The floods receded.*

receipt *noun* **receipts** (*say* ruh-**seet**)
1 a written statement that money has been
received. 2 receiving something.

receive *verb* **receives, receiving, received**
1 to get something that is given or sent to
you. 2 to greet a visitor formally, as in
The president was received at the Lodge.

receiver *noun* **receivers**
1 someone who receives something.
2 someone who buys and sells stolen
goods. 3 an official who takes charge of a
bankrupt person's property. 4 a radio or
television set. 5 the part of a telephone
that you hold to your ear.

recent *adjective*
made or happening a short time ago.
recently *adverb*

receptacle *noun* **receptacles**
something for holding what is put into it; a
container.

reception *noun* **receptions**
1 the sort of welcome that someone gets, as
in *We were given a friendly reception.* 2 a
formal party, as in *a wedding reception.* 3 a
place in a hotel, office, etc. where visitors
are welcomed, registered, etc.

receptionist *noun* **receptionists**
someone employed at the reception of a
hotel, office, etc.

recess *noun* **recesses**
1 an alcove. 2 a time when work or
business is stopped for a while, as in *At
morning recess the school child ate her little
lunch.*

recession *noun* **recessions**
a reduction in trade or in the wealth
created by a country's industry.

recipe *noun* **recipes** (*say* **res**-uh-pee)
instructions for preparing or cooking food.

reciprocal *adjective* (*say* ruh-**sip**-ruh-kuhl)
given and received by the same person, or
by two people at once; mutual, as in *a
reciprocal greeting.*

reciprocal *noun* **reciprocals**
the number by which you must multiply a
number to obtain the answer 1, as in *0.5 is
the reciprocal of 2 (0.5 x 2 = 1).*

recital *noun* **recitals** (*say* ruh-**suy**-tuhl)
a concert by a small number of performers.

recite *verb* **recites, reciting, recited**
to say something aloud that you have
learnt.
recitation *noun*

reckless *adjective*
doing things without thinking or caring
about what might happen.
recklessly *adverb*, **recklessness** *noun*

reckon *verb* **reckons, reckoning, reckoned**
1 to calculate; to count. 2 to have an
opinion; to think.

reclaim *verb* **reclaims, reclaiming, reclaimed**
1 to make something usable again, as in
reclaimed land. 2 to claim or get
something back.
reclamation *noun*

reclamation *noun*
making something usable again, as in *land
reclamation.*

recline *verb* **reclines, reclining, reclined**
to lean or lie back.

recognise or **recognize** *verb* **recognises,
recognising, recognised**
1 to know who someone is because you
have seen him or her before; to realise that
you know something you have seen
before. 2 to accept something; to agree
with something, as in *We recognise that we
may have acted unfairly.*
recognition *noun*, **recognisable** *adjective*

red-back

recoil *verb* recoils, recoiling, recoiled
to move backwards suddenly, as in *He recoiled in horror. Guns recoil as they are fired.*

recollect *verb* recollects, recollecting, recollected
to remember something.
recollection *noun*

recommend *verb* recommends, recommending, recommended
1 to say that something is good, as in *I recommend the crayfish—it's excellent.* **2** to praise someone, saying that he or she would be a good person to do a particular job. **3** to advise doing something, as in *We recommend that you read the instructions thoroughly before you use the lawn-mower.*
recommendation *noun*

recompense *verb* recompenses, recompensing, recompensed
to repay or reward someone, as in *The owner was recompensed for damage to his house. She was recompensed for her efforts by winning first prize.*

reconcile *verb* reconciles, reconciling, reconciled
1 to restore peace or friendship between people, countries, etc. **2** to persuade someone to put up with something, as in *He became reconciled to wearing glasses.*
reconciliation *noun*

reconstruction *noun* reconstructions
1 building something up again, as in *the reconstruction of war-damaged buildings.* **2** an object or a collection of things, buildings, etc. made to look like things that existed in the past; the acting out of an event that took place in the past, as in *a reconstruction of the Eureka Stockade.*

record *noun* records (*say* **rek**-awd)
1 a description of things that have happened. **2** the best performance in a sport or most remarkable event of its kind, as in *Christopher broke the record for swimming 50 metres.* **3** a flat, round piece of plastic that makes music or other sounds when it is played on a record-player, as in *Compact discs have replaced records.*

record *verb* records, recording, recorded (*say* ruh-**kawd**)
1 to put music or other sounds on a tape or disc. **2** to describe things that have happened.

recorder *noun* recorders
1 a tape recorder. **2** a wooden musical instrument played by blowing into one end. **3** someone who records something.

record-player *noun* record-players
a device for reproducing sound from records.

recount *verb* recounts, recounting, recounted
to give an account of something, as in *Alice recounted her overseas trip to the class.*

recover *verb* recovers, recovering, recovered
1 to get better after being ill. **2** to get something back that you had lost.
recovery *noun*

recreation *noun* recreations
a game, hobby, or other enjoyable pastime done in your spare time.
recreation ground, a public playground for children.

recruit *noun* recruits
someone who has just joined the armed forces or a business, team, etc.

rectangle *noun* rectangles
a shape with four straight sides and four right angles.
rectangular *adjective*

rectify *verb* rectifies, rectifying, rectified
to correct, as in *She rectified the mistakes in her spelling.*

rectum *noun* rectums
the last part of the large intestine, ending at the anus.

recur *verb* recurs, recurring, recurred
to happen again.
recurring decimal, a decimal fraction in which the same numbers are repeated over and over.
recurrence *noun*, **recurrent** *adjective*

recycle *verb* recycles, recycling, recycled
to treat waste material so that it can be used again, as in *Waste paper can be recycled to make cardboard.*
recycling *noun*

red *adjective* redder, reddest
1 being the colour of blood, a cherry, a stop-light, etc. **2** (*colloquial*) to do with Communists; favouring Communism.
red herring, a thing that misleads someone or diverts his or her attention.
red tape, excessive rules and forms in official business.
redden *verb*, **reddish** *adjective*

red *noun* reds
1 red colour. **2** (*colloquial*) a Communist.
in the red, in debt.
see red, to become suddenly angry.

red-back *noun* red-backs
a small, poisonous, black spider having a pea-sized body with a red streak.

a
b
c
d
e
f
g
h
i
j
k
l
m
n
o
p
q
r
s
t
u
v
w
x
y
z

redeem

redeem *verb* **redeems, redeeming, redeemed**
1 to save someone from sin, faults, etc.
2 to get something back by paying for it.
redeemer *noun*, **redemption** *noun*

red-handed *adjective*
in the act of committing a crime, as in *He was caught red-handed.*

redhead *noun* **redheads**
a person with reddish-brown hair.

reduce *verb* **reduces, reducing, reduced**
1 to make something smaller or less. 2 to force someone into a situation, as in *She was reduced to borrowing the money.*
reduction *noun*

redundant *adjective*
not needed, especially for a particular job.
redundancy *noun*

reed *noun* **reeds**
1 a plant that grows in or near water. 2 a thin strip that vibrates to make the sound in a clarinet, saxophone, oboe, etc.
reedy *adjective*

reef *noun* **reefs**
a line of rocks near the surface of the sea.

reef-knot *noun* **reef-knots**
a symmetrical double knot for tying two cords together.

reek *verb* **reeks, reeking, reeked**
to have a strong, unpleasant smell.

reel *noun* **reels**
1 a round device on which cotton, fishing-line, etc. is wound. 2 a roll or spool of film. 3 a lively Scottish dance.

reel *verb* **reels, reeling, reeled**
1 to stagger, as in *The drunk reeled along the road.* 2 to be dizzy, as in *My head was reeling.*
reel off, to say something quickly.

refer *verb* **refers, referring, referred**
to pass a question, problem, etc. to someone else.
refer to, to mention; to look in a book, etc. for information; to be connected with, as in *Are you referring to me? Refer to a dictionary to find the meanings of words. The word 'equilateral' refers to a triangle with sides of equal length.*

referee *noun* **referees**
someone who makes sure that people keep to the rules of a game.

referee *verb* **referees, refereeing, refereed**
to act as a referee.

reference *noun* **references**
1 a mention of something. 2 a place in a book, file, etc. where information can be found. 3 a letter describing what work someone has done, how well he or she did it, etc.
in or **with reference to**, concerning; in connection with.
reference book, a book that gives information.

referendum *noun* **referendums** or **referenda** (*say* ref-uh-**ren**-duhm)
a vote on a particular question by all the people in a country.

refill *noun* **refills**
a thing used to replace something that has been used up, as in *My lighter needs a refill.*

refine *verb* **refines, refining, refined**
to purify.
refined, cultured; with good manners.
refinement *noun*, **refinery** *noun*

reflect *verb* **reflects, reflecting, reflected**
1 to send back light from a shiny surface; to send back sound from a surface. 2 to show an image of something, as in a mirror. 3 to think seriously about something.
reflection *noun*, **reflective** *adjective*, **reflector** *noun*

reflective *adjective*
1 sending back light, as in *The cyclist wore a reflective waistcoat.* 2 suggesting or showing serious thought, as in *The music has a reflective quality.*

reflex *noun* **reflexes** (*say* ree-fleks)
a movement or action done without any conscious thought.
reflex angle, an angle between 180 and 360 degrees.

reflexive *adjective* (*say* ruh-**flek**-siv)
(*in grammar*) referring to an action whose subject and object are the same, as in *In 'He washed himself', the verb is reflexive.*

reform *verb* **reforms, reforming, reformed**
to improve a person or thing by getting rid of faults.
reformer *noun*

reform *noun* **reforms**
changing something to get rid of faults and to improve it; a change made for this reason.

refract *verb* **refracts, refracting, refracted**
to cause a ray of light, a wave of sound, or a wave of heat to change its direction.
refraction *noun*

refrain *verb* **refrains, refraining, refrained**
to keep yourself from doing something, as in *Please refrain from talking.*

refrain *noun* **refrains**
the chorus of a song.

refresh *verb* **refreshes, refreshing, refreshed**
to make a tired person feel fresh and strong
again.
refresh your memory, to remind yourself, as
in *I knew the route, but glanced at the map to
refresh my memory.*

refreshments *plural noun*
drinks and snacks.

refrigerate *verb* **refrigerates, refrigerating,
refrigerated**
to freeze or keep something cold so as to
keep it in good condition.
refrigeration *noun*

refrigerator *noun* **refrigerators**
a cabinet or room in which food is stored at
a low temperature.

refuel *verb* **refuels, refuelling, refuelled**
to supply a ship, aircraft, etc. with fuel.

refuge *noun* **refuges**
a place where you are safe from pursuit or
danger.

refugee *noun* **refugees** (*say* ref-**yoo**-jee)
someone who has had to leave his or her
home or country because of war,
persecution, disaster, etc.

refund *verb* **refunds, refunding, refunded**
(*say* ruh-**fund** *or* ree-fund)
to pay money back.

refund *noun* **refunds** (*say* **ree**-fund)
money paid back, as in *I want a refund for
this faulty toaster.*

refuse *verb* **refuses, refusing, refused**
(*say* ruh-**fyooz**)
to say that you will not do or accept
something, as in *She refuses to help.*
refusal *noun*

refuse *noun* (*say* **ref**-yoos)
rubbish.

refute *verb* **refutes, refuting, refuted**
to prove that a person or statement, etc. is
wrong, as in *The survey results were refuted
after much investigation.*

regain *verb* **regains, regaining, regained**
1 to get something back. 2 to reach a
place again.

regard *verb* **regards, regarding, regarded**
1 to look at someone or someone closely.
2 to think of someone or something in a
certain way, as in *I regard her as a friend.*

regard *noun* **regards**
1 a gaze. 2 consideration; respect.
regards, kind wishes.

with regard to, on the subject of; about, as in
*With regard to the athletics carnival there will
be no running until the rain has cleared.*

regarding *preposition*
on the subject of; about.

regardless *adjective*
paying no attention to something, as in *Get
it, regardless of the cost.*

regatta *noun* **regattas** (*say* ruh-**gat**-uh)
a meeting for boat or yacht races.

regime *noun* **regimes** (*say* ray-**zheem**)
1 a method or system of government or
management. 2 a particular government,
as in *The new regime introduced higher taxes.*

regiment *noun* **regiments**
an army unit consisting of two or more
battalions.
regimental *adjective*

region *noun* **regions**
1 a part of a country. 2 a part of the
world.
regional *adjective*

register *noun* **registers**
a book in which information is recorded, as
in *a marriage register.*

register *verb* **registers, registering, registered**
1 to list in a register; to record information
officially, as in *Is this car registered?* 2 to
indicate; to show, as in *The earthquake
registered 6 on the Richter scale.* 3 to pay
extra for a letter or parcel to be sent with
special care.
registration *noun*

registration number *noun* **registration
numbers**
the set of numbers and letters that appears
on a plate in front of and behind a motor
vehicle, as in *My motor cycle's registration
number was ACT 6.*

regret *noun* **regrets**
the feeling of being sorry or sad about
something.
regretful *adjective*, **regretfully** *adverb*

regret *verb* **regrets, regretting, regretted**
to feel sorry or sad about something.
regrettable *adjective*, **regrettably** *adverb*

regular *adjective*
1 always happening at certain times, as
in *regular meals.* 2 even; symmetrical,
as in *regular teeth.* 3 normal; correct, as in
the regular procedure.
regularity *noun*, **regularly** *adverb*

regulate *verb* **regulates, regulating, regulated**
to adjust or control something.
regulator *noun*

regulation

regulation *noun* **regulations**
  1 the adjusting or controlling of something.
  2 a rule or law.

rehabilitate *verb* **rehabilitates, rehabilitating, rehabilitated**
  to assist the return to a normal state, as in *After his car accident he was rehabilitated by physiotherapy. The company rehabilitated the land it had mined.*

rehearse *verb* **rehearses, rehearsing, rehearsed**
  to practise something before it is performed.
  rehearsal *noun*

reign *verb* **reigns, reigning, reigned**
  1 to be king or queen.   2 to be the most noticeable or important thing, as in *Silence reigned.*

reign *noun* **reigns**
  the time when someone is king or queen.

rein *noun* **reins**
  a strap used to guide a horse.

reindeer *noun* **reindeer**
  a kind of deer that lives in cold countries of the northern hemisphere.

reinforce *verb* **reinforces, reinforcing, reinforced**
  to strengthen.
  reinforced concrete, concrete with metal bars or wires embedded in it.

reinforcement *noun* **reinforcements**
  a thing that strengthens something.
  reinforcements, extra troops, ships, etc. sent to strengthen a force.

reject *verb* **rejects, rejecting, rejected**
  (*say* ruh-**jekt**)
  1 to refuse to accept a person or thing, as in *She rejected my offer of help.*   2 to get rid of something, as in *Any faulty parts are rejected at the factory.*
  rejection *noun*

reject *noun* **rejects** (*say* **ree**-jekt)
  a thing that is got rid of, especially because of being faulty or poorly made.

rejoice *verb* **rejoices, rejoicing, rejoiced**
  to be very happy.

relate *verb* **relates, relating, related**
  1 to connect or compare one thing with another.   2 to tell a story.
  related, belonging to the same family, as in *He and I are related.*

relation *noun* **relations**
  1 someone in your family.   2 the way that one thing is connected or compared with another.

relationship *noun* **relationships**
  1 the way people or things are connected with each other.   2 the way people get on with one another, as in *There is a good relationship between the teachers and the children.*   3 a connection, especially because of love, between two people.

relative *noun* **relatives**
  someone in your family.

relative *adjective*
  1 connected or compared with something.
  2 compared with the average, as in *They live in relative comfort.*

relative pronoun *noun*
  one of the words 'who', 'what', 'which', or 'that', placed in front of a clause to connect it with an earlier clause, as in *In 'the man who came to lunch', the relative pronoun is 'who'.*
  relatively *adverb*

relax *verb* **relaxes, relaxing, relaxed**
  1 to become less stiff or less strict.   2 to rest something.
  relaxation *noun*

relay *verb* **relays, relaying, relayed**
  to pass on a message or broadcast.

relay *noun* **relays**
  1 one of a series of groups, as in *The firemen worked in relays.*   2 a relay race.   3 a device for passing on a broadcast.
  relay race, a race between two teams in which each competitor covers part of the distance.

release *verb* **releases, releasing, released**
  1 to set free; to unfasten.   2 to give off, as in *Cars release fumes.*   3 to make a film, record, etc. available to the public.

release *noun* **releases**
  1 the act of being released, as in *The bird welcomed its release from the cage.*
  2 something released, especially a new film, record, etc.   3 a device that unfastens something, as in *The seat-belt has a quick release.*

relegate *verb* **relegates, relegating, relegated**
  (*say* **rel**-uh-gayt)
  to put something into a lower group or position than before; to put a team into a lower division.
  relegation *noun*

relent *verb* **relents, relenting, relented**
  to be less angry or more merciful than you were going to be.

relentless *adjective*
  never stopping, as in *relentless rain; relentless pressure.*
  relentlessly *adverb*

renewable energy

relevant *adjective* (*say* **rel**-uh-vuhnt)
connected with what is being discussed or
dealt with, as in *It was relevant to consider
the weather when deciding on a date for the
athletics carnival.*
relevance *noun*, **relevantly** *adverb*

reliable *adjective*
able to be trusted or depended on.
reliability *noun*, **reliably** *adverb*

relic *noun* **relics**
something that has survived from the past,
as in *The cannon was a relic from the First
World War.*

relief *noun* **reliefs**
1 the ending or lessening of pain, trouble,
boredom, etc.   2 something that causes
the ending or lessening of pain, etc.   3 a
person or thing that takes over or helps
with a job.   4 a method of moulding,
carving, etc. in which the design stands out
from the surface, as in *The model shows hills
and valleys in relief.*

relieve *verb* **relieves, relieving, relieved**
to end or lessen someone's pain, trouble,
boredom, etc.

religion *noun* **religions**
what people believe about God or gods,
and how they worship.
religious *adjective*, **religiously** *adverb*

relish *verb* **relishes, relishing, relished**
to enjoy greatly, as in *She relished her success
in the competition.*

reluctant *adjective*
not wanting to do something; not keen.
reluctance *noun*, **reluctantly** *adverb*

rely *verb* **relies, relying, relied**
rely on or **upon,** to trust someone or
something to help or support you.
reliance *noun*, **reliant** *adjective*

remain *verb* **remains, remaining, remained**
1 to continue in the same place or
condition.   2 to be left over, as in *A lot of
food remained after the party.*
remainder *noun*

remains *plural noun*
1 something left over.   2 ruins; relics.
3 a corpse.

remark *verb* **remarks, remarking, remarked**
to say something that you have thought or
noticed.

remark *noun* **remarks**
something said.

remarkable *adjective*
so unusual that you notice or remember it.
remarkably *adverb*

remedial *adjective* (*say* ruh-**mee**-dee-uhl)
to do with improving a person's health,
skills, etc., as in *Remedial exercise assisted the
stroke victim. The student needed remedial
reading to improve language skills.*

remedy *noun* **remedies**
a cure; a medicine.

remember *verb* **remembers, remembering,
remembered**
1 to keep something in your mind.   2 to
bring something into your mind when you
want to, as in *Can you remember his telephone
number?*
remembrance *noun*

remind *verb* **reminds, reminding, reminded**
to help or make someone remember
something.
reminder *noun*

reminisce *verb* **reminisces, reminiscing,
reminisced** (*say* rem-uh-**nis**)
to think or talk about things you remember.
reminiscence *noun*, **reminiscent** *adjective*

remnant *noun* **remnants**
a small piece of something left over.

remorse *noun*
deep regret for having done wrong.
remorseful *adjective*, **remorseless** *adjective*

remote *adjective* **remoter, remotest**
1 far away; isolated.   2 unlikely; slight, as
in *a remote chance.*
remote control, controlling something from
a distance, usually by means of radio or
electricity.
remotely *adverb*, **remoteness** *noun*

remove *verb* **removes, removing, removed**
to take something away or off.

render *verb* **renders, rendering, rendered**
1 to put someone in a particular condition,
as in *She was rendered speechless by the
shock.*   2 to give or perform something, as
in *a reward for services rendered.*

rendezvous *noun* **rendezvous**
(*say* **ron**-day-voo)
a meeting with someone; a place or
appointment to meet someone.
[from the French **rendezvous** = present
yourselves]

renew *verb* **renews, renewing, renewed**
to make something as it was before or
replace it with something new.
renewal *noun*

renewable energy *noun*
energy from the sun, including wind
power, water power, and energy from
plants.

a
b
c
d
e
f
g
h
i
j
k
l
m
n
o
p
q
r
s
t
u
v
w
x
y
z

renovate

renovate *verb* renovates, renovating, renovated
to restore to good condition; repair.

renown *noun*
fame, as in *a man of great renown*.
renowned *adjective*

rent *noun* rents
a regular payment for the use of something, especially a house, that belongs to another person.

rent *verb* rents, renting, rented
to pay money for the use of something.

repair *verb* repairs, repairing, repaired
to mend something.

repair *noun* repairs
1 mending something; the result of mending something, as in *The car is in for repair*. 2 condition, as in *His car is in good repair*.

repay *verb* repays, repaying, repaid
to pay back, as in *She has repaid her debt*.
repayment *noun*

repeat *verb* repeats, repeating, repeated
to say or do the same thing again.
repeatedly *adverb*, **repetition** *noun*, **repetitive** *adjective*

repeat *noun* repeats
something that is repeated, especially a radio or television program.

repel *verb* repels, repelling, repelled
1 to drive or force someone or something away, as in *Unlike poles of magnets attract each other, and like poles repel each other*. 2 to disgust someone.
repellent *adjective*

repent *verb* repents, repenting, repented
to be sorry for what you have done.
repentance *noun*, **repentant** *adjective*

repertoire *noun* repertoires
(*say* rep-uh-twah)
the variety of works that a performer, artist, etc. knows or is prepared to perform, as in *The clown had a variety of tricks in her repertoire*.

replace *verb* replaces, replacing, replaced
1 to put something back in its place. 2 to take the place of another person or thing. 3 to put a new thing in the place of an old one, as in *Replace the old engine with a new one*.
replacement *noun*

replay *noun* replays
1 a sporting match played again after a draw. 2 the playing or showing again of a recording.

replica *noun* replicas (*say* rep-li-kuh)
an exact copy.

reply *noun* replies
something said or written to deal with a question, letter, etc.; an answer.

reply *verb* replies, replying, replied
to give a reply; to answer, as in *She replied to my letter. He replied immediately*.

report *verb* reports, reporting, reported
1 to describe something that has happened or something you have studied. 2 to make a complaint or accusation against someone. 3 to go to someone and say that you have arrived.

report *noun* reports
1 a description or account of something. 2 a regular statement of how someone has worked or behaved, especially at school. 3 an explosive sound, as in *the report of a gun*.

reporter *noun* reporters
someone whose job is to collect news for a newspaper, radio, television, etc.

repossess *verb* repossesses, repossessing, repossessed
to claim back goods which someone has taken but has not fully paid for.

represent *verb* represents, representing, represented
1 to be a picture, model, or symbol of something or someone. 2 to be an example of something. 3 to help someone by speaking or acting for him or her, as in *She was represented in court by her lawyer*.
representation *noun*, **representative** *noun*

repress *verb* represses, repressing, repressed
1 to keep something down or under, as in *The dictator tried to repress all opposition*. 2 to prevent someone or something from being free or enjoying life, as in *The slaves were repressed*.
repression *noun*, **repressive** *adjective*

reprieve *noun* reprieves (*say* ruh-**preev**)
postponing or cancelling a punishment, especially the death penalty.

reprimand *noun* reprimands
a rebuke especially from a person in charge, as in *The teacher reprimanded the selfish student*.

reprisal *noun* reprisals (*say* ruh-**pruy**-zuhl)
an act of revenge.

reproach *verb* reproaches, reproaching, reproached
to tell someone off; to find fault with someone.

reproduce *verb* reproduces, reproducing, reproduced
1 to copy something.   2 to have offspring.
reproduction *noun*, reproductive *adjective*

reptile *noun* reptiles
a group of cold-blooded, scaly animals that creep or crawl, as in *Snakes, lizards, crocodiles, and tortoises are reptiles.*
reptilian *adjective*

republic *noun* republics
a country ruled by a president and government that are chosen by the people.

republican *adjective*
to do with a country ruled by a president and a government that has been chosen by the people.

republican *noun* republicans
a person who supports a republican system of government.

repulsive *adjective*
disgusting.
repulsion *noun*

reputable *adjective* (*say* rep-yuh-tuh-buhl)
able to be trusted, as in *The reputable tradesman had many clients.*

reputation *noun* reputations
what people think about a person or thing, as in *He has a reputation for being honest.*

request *verb* requests, requesting, requested
to ask politely for something.

request *noun* requests
1 the action of asking for something.
2 what someone asks for.

require *verb* requires, requiring, required
1 to need or want, as in *We require some paper.*   2 to make someone do something, as in *Drivers are required to register their cars.*
requirement *noun*

reread *verb* rereads, rereading, reread
to read something again.

rescue *verb* rescues, rescuing, rescued
to save someone from danger, capture, etc.
rescue *noun*, rescuer *noun*

research *noun* researches
careful study or investigation, as in *The scientists continued research into a cure for cancer.*
researcher *noun*

resemblance *noun* resemblances
being similar, as in *There is a resemblance between the brothers.*

resemble *verb* resembles, resembling, resembled
to look or sound like another person or thing.

resent *verb* resents, resenting, resented
to feel indignant or angry about something.
resentful *adjective*, resentment *noun*

reservation *noun* reservations
1 an arrangement that something such as a motel room, theatre tickets, etc. will be kept for you.   2 a doubt; a feeling of unease, as in *I had reservations about buying such an old car.*

reserve *verb* reserves, reserving, reserved
to keep or order something for a particular person or for a special use.
reserved, shy; not sociable.

reserve *noun* reserves
1 a person or thing kept ready to be used if necessary.   2 an area of land kept for a special purpose, as in *This island is a nature reserve.*

reservoir *noun* reservoirs (*say* rez-uh-vwah)
a place, especially an artificial lake, where water is stored.

reshuffle *noun* reshuffles
a rearrangement, especially an exchange of jobs between people in a group, as in *The prime minister announced a cabinet reshuffle.*

reside *verb* resides, residing, resided
to live in a particular place.
resident *noun*

residence *noun* residences
where someone lives.
residential *adjective*

resign *verb* resigns, resigning, resigned
to give up your job or position.
resign yourself to something, to accept something without complaining or arguing.
resignation *noun*

resin *noun* resins (*say* rez-uhn)
a sticky substance that comes from plants or is made artificially.
resinous *adjective*

resist *verb* resists, resisting, resisted
to try to stop someone or something; to fight back against someone or something.
resistant *adjective*

resistance *noun* resistances
fighting or taking action against someone or something, as in *The new taxes met with public resistance. The troops came up against armed resistance.*
resistor *noun*

resolute *adjective* (*say* rez-uh-loot *or* rez-uh-lyoot)
determined; firm.
resolutely *adverb*

resolution

resolution *noun* **resolutions**
1 determination or firmness, as in *The captain showed resolution in carrying out her duties.* 2 something that you have decided.

resolve *verb* **resolves, resolving, resolved**
1 to make a decision. 2 to overcome disagreements, doubts, etc.

resort *noun* **resorts**
a place where people go for holidays.
the last resort, the only thing you can do when all else has failed.

resound *verb* **resounds, resounding, resounded**
to fill a place with sound; to echo.

resource *noun* **resources**
something that can be used, as in *The land is rich in natural resources.*

resourceful *adjective*
being skilful at dealing with difficult situations, problems, etc., as in *The resourceful cook could make a delicious meal from basic ingredients.*

respect *noun* **respects**
1 admiration for someone's good qualities, achievement, etc. 2 consideration; concern, as in *Have respect for people's feelings.* 3 a detail or aspect, as in *In some respects, he is like his sister.*
with respect to something, concerning something.

respect *verb* **respects, respecting, respected**
1 to admire someone for his or her good qualities, achievement, etc. 2 to have consideration or concern for someone.

respectable *adjective*
1 having good manners, character, appearance, etc. 2 having a good size or standard, as in *Your assignment gained a respectable mark.*
respectability *noun,* **respectably** *adverb*

respectful *adjective*
showing respect; polite.
respectfully *adverb*

respective *adjective*
to do with each one, as in *We went to our respective rooms.*
respectively *adverb*

respiration *noun*
breathing.
respirator *noun,* **respiratory** *adjective*

respond *verb* **responds, responding, responded**
1 to reply. 2 to react.

response *noun* **responses**
1 a reply. 2 a reaction.

responsible *adjective*
1 looking after something and likely to take the blame if anything goes wrong. 2 to do with being trusted. 3 important, as in *a responsible job.* 4 causing something, as in *His carelessness was responsible for their deaths.*
responsibility *noun,* **responsibly** *adverb*

rest *verb* **rests, resting, rested**
1 to sleep, relax, not work, etc. 2 to support something; to be supported, as in *Rest the ladder against the wall. The ladder is resting against the wall.*

rest *noun* **rests**
a time of sleep, relaxation, freedom from work, etc.
restful *adjective*

rest *noun*
the part that is left; the others, as in *I shall go; the rest can stay here.*

restaurant *noun* **restaurants**
a place where you can buy a meal and eat it.

restless *adjective*
unable to rest or keep still.
restlessly *adverb,* **restlessness** *noun*

restore *verb* **restores, restoring, restored**
1 to put something back as it was, as in *Some Aboriginal groups are trying to restore their traditional languages. I have restored the clock to its place on the mantelpiece.* 2 to repair something, as in *She restores furniture as a hobby.*
restoration *noun*

restrain *verb* **restrains, restraining, restrained**
to hold someone or something back; to keep something under control.
restraint *noun*

restrict *verb* **restricts, restricting, restricted**
to keep a person or thing within certain limits.
restriction *noun,* **restrictive** *adjective*

result *noun* **results**
1 a thing that happens because something else has happened. 2 the score or situation at the end of a game, competition, race, etc. 3 the answer to a sum or problem.

result *verb* **results, resulting, resulted**
1 to happen as a result, as in *What resulted from their action?* 2 to have a particular result, as in *The game resulted in a draw.*
resultant *adjective*

resume *verb* **resumes, resuming, resumed**
to start again after stopping for a while.
resumption *noun*

369 — review

resuscitate *verb* **resuscitates, resuscitating, resuscitated**
to revive someone who has been unconscious, as in *The lifesaver resuscitated the drowning child.*

retail *noun*
the sale of goods in small quantities to the public.

retain *verb* **retains, retaining, retained**
1 to keep something. 2 to hold something in place.

retaliate *verb* **retaliates, retaliating, retaliated**
to attack in return for an insult, injury, etc., as in *After receiving a punch, the footballer retaliated with a deliberate high tackle.*

retard *verb* **retards, retarding, retarded**
to delay, as in *A faulty engine retarded his progress.*

retina *noun* **retinas** (*say* **ret**-uh-nuh)
a layer at the back of your eyeball that is sensitive to light.

retire *verb* **retires, retiring, retired**
1 to give up work, usually because you are getting old. 2 to retreat; to withdraw. 3 to go to bed.
retirement *noun*

retiring *adjective*
shy.

retort *verb* **retorts, retorting, retorted**
to reply quickly or angrily.

retrace *verb* **retraces, retracing, retraced**
to go back over something.

retreat *verb* **retreats, retreating, retreated**
to go back so as to avoid death or danger.

retrench *verb* **retrenches, retrenching, retrenched**
to sack an employee in order to reduce costs.
retrenchment *noun*

retrieve *verb* **retrieves, retrieving, retrieved**
to get something back; to find something.
retrievable *adjective*, **retrieval** *noun*

retriever *noun* **retrievers**
a dog that can find and bring back birds and other animals that have been shot.

return *verb* **returns, returning, returned**
1 to come or go back to a place. 2 to give or send something back.
returnable *adjective*

return *noun* **returns**
1 the act of coming or going back, as in *a return home.* 2 something given or sent back. 3 profit, as in *He gets a good return on his savings.* 4 a return ticket.

return game or **return match**, a second game between two teams.
return ticket, a ticket for a journey to a place and back again.

reunion *noun* **reunions**
a meeting of people who have not met for some time.

rev *verb* **revs, revving, revved**
(*colloquial*) to make an engine run quickly.

rev *noun* **revs**
(*colloquial*) a revolution of an engine.

Revd. or **Rev.** short for **Reverend**.

reveal *verb* **reveals, revealing, revealed**
to let something be seen or known.
revelation *noun*

revenge *noun*
the act of harming someone because he or she has harmed you or your friends.

revenue *noun* **revenues** (*say* **rev**-uh-nyoo)
a government's annual income.

revere *verb* **reveres, revering, revered** (*say* ruh-**veer**)
to respect someone or something deeply or religiously.

Reverend *noun* **Reverends**
the title of a member of the clergy, as in *the Reverend John Smith.*

> **Usage** Do not confuse **Reverend** with **reverent**, which is an adjective and is the next word in this dictionary.

reverent *adjective*
feeling or showing awe or respect, especially towards God or holy things.
reverence *noun*

reverse *noun*
1 the opposite way or side. 2 reverse gear.
in reverse, going in the opposite direction.
reverse gear, the gear used to drive a vehicle backwards.

reverse *verb* **reverses, reversing, reversed**
1 to turn something round. 2 to go backwards in a vehicle.
reversal *noun*, **reversible** *adjective*

review *noun* **reviews**
1 an inspection or survey. 2 a published description and opinion of a book, film, play, etc.

> **Usage** Do not confuse **review** with **revue**, which means an entertainment made up of several short performances.

a b c d e f g h i j k l m n o p q r s t u v w x y z

review

review *verb* reviews, reviewing, reviewed
1 to inspect or survey something. 2 to publish a description and opinion of a book, film, play, etc.
reviewer *noun*

revise *verb* revises, revising, revised
1 to get ready for a test, etc. by studying work that you have already done. 2 to correct or change something, such as a plan or piece of writing.
revision *noun*

revive *verb* revives, reviving, revived
1 to bring someone or something back to life or strength; to come back to life or strength. 2 to start using or performing something again, as in *They revived the old custom of having a baked lunch on Sunday.*
revival *noun*

revolt *verb* revolts, revolting, revolted
1 to rebel. 2 to disgust or horrify someone.

revolution *noun* revolutions
1 a rebellion that overthrows the government. 2 a complete change. 3 one turn of a wheel, engine, etc.

revolutionary *adjective*
to do with a revolution, as in *Computers have brought a revolutionary change to communications.*

revolutionise or **revolutionize** *verb*
revolutionises, revolutionising, revolutionised
to change something completely.

revolve *verb* revolves, revolving, revolved
to go round in a circle.

revolver *noun* revolvers
a pistol that has a revolving store for bullets so that it can be fired several times without having to be loaded again.

revue *noun* revues
an entertainment made up of several short performances such as songs, short amusing plays, or stories.

Usage Do not confuse **revue** with the noun **review**, which means an inspection, or a description of a book, film, or play.

reward *noun* rewards
something given to a person because he or she has done something, behaved well, etc.

reward *verb* rewards, rewarding, rewarded
to give someone a reward.

rewind *verb* rewinds, rewinding, rewound
to wind back a film, videotape, etc.

rewrite *verb* rewrites, rewriting, rewrote, rewritten
to write something again or differently.

rheumatism *noun* (*say* **roo**-muh-tiz-uhm)
a disease that causes pain and stiffness in joints and muscles.
rheumatic *adjective*

rhinoceros *noun* rhinoceroses or rhinoceros
(*say* ruy-**nos**-uh-ruhs)
a large, heavy animal from Africa or Asia, with either one or two horns on its nose.

rhododendron *noun* rhododendrons
(*say* roh-duh-**den**-druhn)
an evergreen shrub with large clusters of trumpet-shaped flowers.

rhombus *noun* rhombuses
a flat shape with four straight equal sides and with no right angles between them.

rhubarb *noun*
a plant with pink or green stalks cooked as a dessert food.

rhyme *noun* rhymes
1 similar sounds in the endings of words, as in *bat* and *mat, batter* and *matter.* 2 a short rhyming poem.

rhyme *verb* rhymes, rhyming, rhymed
1 to have rhymes, especially at the ends of lines, as in *This verse doesn't rhyme.* 2 to sound similar to other words, as in *Bat rhymes with hat.*

rhythm *noun* rhythms
a regular pattern of beats, sounds, or movements, as in eg *Most poetry and music has rhythm.*
rhythmic *adjective*, **rhythmical** *adjective*, **rhythmically** *adverb*

rib *noun* ribs
one of the curved bones above your waist.

ribbon *noun* ribbons
a strip of nylon, silk, or other material, as in *Her hair was tied up with a ribbon.*

rice *noun*
white seeds from a kind of grass, used as food.

rich *adjective* richer, richest
1 having a lot of money or property. 2 full of goodness, quality, strength, etc., as in *Bananas are rich in vitamins.* 3 costly; luxurious, as in *rich furnishings.*
richly *adverb*, **richness** *noun*

riches *plural noun*
wealth.

Richter scale *noun* (*say* rik-tuh **skayl**)
the scale of 0 to 10 that measures how strong or severe an earthquake is.
[from the name of the scientist C.F. *Richter*]

rickety *adjective*
unsteady; likely to fall down.

rigour

rickshaw *noun* **rickshaws**
a two-wheeled carriage pulled by one or more people, as in *Rickshaws are used in some Asian countries.*

ricochet *verb* **ricochets, ricocheting, ricocheted** (*say* **rik**-uh-shay)
to bounce off something, as in *The bullets ricocheted off the wall.*

rid *verb* **rids, ridding, rid**
to make a person or place free from something unwanted, as in *He rid the town of rats.*
get rid of, to cause someone or something to go away; to get free of something, as in *I wish I could get rid of these spots.*

riddance *noun*
good riddance, a phrase used to show that you are glad that something or someone has gone, as in *'The wasps have gone away.' 'Good riddance!'*

riddle *noun* **riddles**
a puzzling question, especially as a joke, as in *Here is a riddle. What is the difference between an old car and a school? The old car breaks down and the school breaks up.*

ride *verb* **rides, riding, rode, ridden**
1 to sit on a horse, bicycle, etc. and be carried along on it, as in *I have never ridden a pony.* 2 to travel in a car, bus, train, etc., as in *We rode to school on a bus.*
rider *noun*

ride *noun* **rides**
a journey on a horse, bicycle, etc. or in a vehicle.

ridge *noun* **ridges**
a long, narrow part of something higher than the rest of it, as in *There are special tiles for the ridge of a roof.*

ridicule *verb* **ridicules, ridiculing, ridiculed**
to make fun of someone or something.

ridiculous *adjective*
so silly as to make people laugh.
ridiculously *adverb*

rife *adjective*
commonly occurring; widespread, as in *Colds are rife in winter.*

rifle *noun* **rifles**
a long gun that you hold against your shoulder when you fire it, as in *Rifles have grooved barrels and they fire bullets.*

rift *noun* **rifts**
1 a crack or split. 2 a disagreement between friends.

rig *verb* **rigs, rigging, rigged**
to provide a ship with rigging, sails, etc.
rig up, to make something quickly.

rigging *noun*
the ropes that support a ship's masts and sails.

right *adjective*
1 on the side opposite the left. 2 correct, as in *Is this sum right?* 3 fair; virtuous, as in *Is it right to cheat?* 4 a political party or group in favour of private ownership of land, wealth, etc., as in *The right wing of the political party supported the sale of government railways.*
she'll be right, (*colloquial*) all will be well.
rightly *adverb*, **rightness** *noun*

right *noun* **rights**
1 the side opposite the left, as in *In America, cars drive on the right.* 2 what is fair or just; something that people ought to be allowed, as in *They protested for their rights.*

right *verb* **rights, righting, righted**
1 to make something upright, as in *They righted the overturned boat.* 2 to make something correct; to avenge something, as in *The fault might right itself. Conservationists hope to right the wrongs of pollution.*

right *adverb*
1 on or towards the right-hand side, as in *Turn right.* 2 completely, as in *Turn right around.* 3 exactly, as in *She stood right in the middle.* 4 straight; directly, as in *Go right ahead.*
right away, immediately.

right angle *noun* **right angles**
an angle of 90 degrees, as in *The angles in a square are right angles.*

righteous *adjective*
being or doing good; obeying the law.
righteously *adverb*, **righteousness** *noun*

rightful *adjective*
deserved; proper, as in *his rightful place.*
rightfully *adverb*

right hand *noun* **right hands**
the hand that most people use more than the other.
right-hand *adjective*

right-handed *adjective*
using the right hand more than the left hand.

rigid *adjective* (*say* **rij**-uhd)
1 firm; stiff, as in *a rigid support.* 2 strict; harsh, as in *rigid rules.*
rigidity *noun*, **rigidly** *adverb*

rigour or **rigor** *noun* **rigours**
strictness or harshness, as in *The gymnast's diet was followed with great rigour. The rigours of the Antarctic made life difficult.*

a b c d e f g h i j k l m n o p q **r** s t u v w x y z

rim

rim *noun* **rims**
the outer edge of a wheel or other round object.

rind *noun* **rinds**
the skin on bacon, cheese, or fruit.

ring *noun* **rings**
1 a circle. 2 a thin circular piece of metal worn on a finger. 3 the space where a circus performs. 4 the place where a boxing-match or other contest is held.

ring *verb* **rings, ringing, ringed** or **rang, rung**
1 to put a ring around something, as in *Ring the answer that you think is the right one.* 2 to cause a bell to sound, as in *Have you rung the bell?* 3 to make a clear, musical sound like a bell. 4 to telephone, as in *She rang her brother last night.*

ringbark *verb* **ringbarks, ringbarking, ringbarked**
to kill a tree by cutting a ring of bark from around the trunk.

ringleader *noun* **ringleaders**
someone who leads other people in rebellion, mischief, crime, etc.

ringlet *noun* **ringlets**
a curly and usually long piece of hair.

ringmaster *noun* **ringmasters**
the person who is in charge of what happens in the circus ring.

rink *noun* **rinks**
a place made for skating.

rinse *verb* **rinses, rinsing, rinsed**
to wash something in clean water.

riot *noun* **riots**
wild or violent behaviour by a crowd of people.
riotous *adjective*

riot *verb* **riots, rioting, rioted**
to run wild and behave violently.

rip *verb* **rips, ripping, ripped**
to tear something roughly.
rip off, (*colloquial*) to cheat someone; to steal something, as in *That cost too much, you've been ripped off! Someone's ripped off my bike.*

rip *noun* **rips**
1 a tear or cut in a material, as in *The yacht's sail had a huge rip.* 2 a stretch of rough water caused by meeting currents.
rip-off, (*colloquial*) a swindle.

ripe *adjective* **riper, ripest**
ready to be harvested or eaten.
ripeness *noun*

ripen *verb* **ripens, ripening, ripened**
to make something ripe; to become ripe.

ripper *adjective*
(*colloquial*) excellent, great, as in *a ripper party.*

ripple *noun* **ripples**
a small wave on the surface of water.

ripple *verb* **ripples, rippling, rippled**
to form small waves.

rise *verb* **rises, rising, rose, risen**
1 to go upwards, as in *Prices have risen.* 2 to get up, as in *They all rose for the national anthem.* 3 to rebel, as in *They rose against the government.* 4 to swell up by the action of yeast, as in *Let the dough rise.*

rise *noun* **rises**
1 an increase, especially in wages. 2 an upward slope.
give rise to something, to cause something.

risk *noun* **risks**
a chance of danger or loss.
risky *adjective*

risk *verb* **risks, risking, risked**
to take the chance of damaging or losing something.

rissole *noun* **rissoles**
a fried cake of minced food.

rite *noun* **rites**
a ceremony, particularly a religious one, as in *funeral rite.*

ritual *noun* **rituals**
a regular ceremony or series of actions.
ritualistic *adjective*, **ritually** *adverb*

rival *noun* **rivals**
a person or thing that competes with another, or tries to do the same thing.
rivalry *noun*

rival *verb* **rivals, rivalling, rivalled**
to compete with, or try to do the same thing as someone or something.

river *noun* **rivers**
a large natural stream of water flowing to the sea or a lake, etc.

rivet *noun* **rivets**
a strong metal pin for holding pieces of metal together.

rivet *verb* **rivets, riveting, riveted**
1 to fasten something with rivets. 2 to fix, as in *She stood riveted to the spot.* 3 to fascinate, as in *The children were riveted by his story.*

road *noun* **roads**
a level way with a hard surface made for traffic to go along.
roadside *noun*, **roadway** *noun*

road train *noun* road trains
a truck that hauls several long trailers which often carry livestock.

roam *verb* roams, roaming, roamed
to wander, as in *They roamed about the city.*

roar *noun* roars
a loud, deep sound of the kind that a lion makes.

roar *verb* roars, roaring, roared
to make a loud, deep sound like a lion.
a roaring trade, brisk selling of something.

roast *verb* roasts, roasting, roasted
1 to cook something in an oven or over a fire. 2 to make someone or something very hot; to be very hot.

roast *noun* roasts
roast meat, as in *We are having a roast for dinner.*

rob *verb* robs, robbing, robbed
to steal something from someone, as in *He robbed me of my watch.*
robber *noun*, **robbery** *noun*

robe *noun* robes
a long, loose piece of clothing.

robin *noun* robins
1 any of several small Australian birds, some having a brightly coloured breast.
2 a small European bird with a red breast; a robin redbreast.

robot *noun* robots (*say* roh-bot)
a machine that can move and behave in some ways like a person.

rock *noun* rocks
1 a large stone. 2 a large mass of stone.
3 a backwards-and-forwards or side-to-side movement. 4 rock music.
rock-plant, a plant suitable for a rockery.
rocky *adjective*

rock *verb* rocks, rocking, rocked
to move gently backwards and forwards or from side to side.

rock-bottom *adjective*
very low, as in *All the goods were sold off at rock-bottom prices.*

rocker *noun* rockers
1 a rocking-chair. 2 one of the curved bars that supports a rocking-chair.
off your rocker, (*colloquial*) mad.

rockery *noun* rockeries
part of a garden where flowers grow between rocks.

rocket *noun* rockets
1 a firework that shoots high into the air. 2 a pointed tube propelled into the

air by hot gases, especially as a spacecraft or weapon.
rocketry *noun*

rocking-chair *noun* rocking-chairs
a chair which can be rocked by the person sitting in it.

rock melon *noun* rock melons
a melon with a sweet-smelling, orange-coloured flesh; a cantaloupe.

rock painting *noun* rock paintings
a traditional, usually ancient, Aboriginal painting on the wall of a cave, rock, etc.

rod *noun* rods
a long, thin stick or bar, especially one with a line attached for fishing.

rode past tense of **ride** *verb*.

rodent *noun* rodents
an animal that has large front teeth for gnawing things, as in *Rats, mice, and guinea pigs are rodents.*

rodeo *noun* rodeos (*say* roh-**day**-oh *or* roh-dee-oh)
a display or contest of cowboy-type skills in riding, controlling cattle, etc.

roe *noun* (*say* roh)
1 the mass of eggs inside a female fish.
2 the sperm of a male fish.

rogue *noun* rogues
a dishonest or mischievous person.
roguery *noun*, **roguish** *adjective*

role *noun* roles
a performer's part in a play, film, etc.

role-play *noun*
a kind of acting in which people play the part of other people, used especially in teaching languages.

roll *verb* rolls, rolling, rolled
1 to move along by turning over and over, like a ball or wheel. 2 to move something along in this way. 3 to form something into the shape of a cylinder or ball. 4 to flatten something by moving a rounded object over it. 5 to sway from side to side, as in *Some ships roll more than others.* 6 to make a long vibrating sound, as in *The drums rolled.*

roll *noun* rolls
1 a cylinder made by rolling something up. 2 a small amount of bread individually baked. 3 a list of names.
4 a long vibrating sound, as in *a roll on the drums.*
on a roll, to be experiencing success or progress, as in *The cricket team is on a roll.*

a
b
c
d
e
f
g
h
i
j
k
l
m
n
o
p
q
r
s
t
u
v
w
x
y
z

roller

roller *noun* **rollers**
1 a cylinder-shaped object, especially one used for flattening things. 2 a long sea-wave. 3 a small cylinder on which hair is rolled for curling.

rollerblade *noun* **rollerblades**
a roller-skate with four wheels on one track.

roller-skate *noun* **roller-skates**
a device with wheels that you can fit on your feet, making you able to move quickly and smoothly over the ground.
roller-skating *noun*

rolling-pin *noun* **rolling-pins**
a heavy cylinder rolled over pastry to flatten it.

ROM short for *read-only memory*, a type of computer memory which holds information that can be accessed but not changed by the user, and which keeps the information whether the computer is switched on or not.

Roman *adjective*
to do with Rome.
Roman candle, a firework that sends out coloured balls of flame.
Roman Catholic, a member of the Church that has the Pope as its head.
Roman numerals, letters that represent numbers (compare *Arabic figures*), as in *In Roman numerals, I = 1, V = 5, X = 10, etc.*

romance *noun* **romances**
experiences, feelings, stories, etc. connected with love.

romantic *adjective*
1 to do with romance, as in *a romantic film*. 2 connected with emotions or imagination, as in *The artist painted a romantic scene of the bush*.
romantically *adverb*

romp *verb* **romps, romping, romped**
to play in a lively way.

roof *noun* **roofs**
1 the part that covers the top of a building, shelter, or vehicle. 2 the upper part of your mouth.

rook *noun* **rooks**
a piece in chess shaped like a castle.

room *noun* **rooms**
1 a part of a building with its own walls and ceiling. 2 enough space for someone or something, as in *Is there room for me?*
roomful *noun*

roomy *adjective* **roomier, roomiest**
with plenty of room or space.

roost *noun* **roosts**
the place where a bird rests.

root *noun* **roots**
1 the part of a plant that grows under the ground. 2 a source or basis of something, as in *Money is the root of all evil.* 3 a number in relation to the number it produces when multiplied by itself, as in *9 is the root, or square root, of 81.*
take root, to grow roots; to become established, as in *The plant took root. The custom never took root in other countries.*

root *verb* **roots, rooting, rooted**
1 to take root. 2 to fix someone in a particular spot, as in *Fear rooted him to the spot.*
root out, to get rid of something.

rope *noun* **ropes**
threads or strands twisted together.
show someone the ropes, to show someone how to do something.

rose *noun* **roses**
a sweet-smelling flower with a thorny stem.

rose past tense of **rise** *verb.*

rosella *noun* **rosellas**
a brightly-coloured, long-tailed type of parrot.
[from *Rose Hill*, the original name for Parramatta in New South Wales]

rosemary *noun*
an evergreen fragrant shrub used as a herb.

rosette *noun* **rosettes**
a large circular badge.

roster *noun* **rosters**
a list of people who take turns to do a particular job, as in *He added his name to the cleaning roster.*

rosy *adjective* **rosier, rosiest**
1 pink. 2 hopeful, as in *rosy future.*

rot *verb* **rots, rotting, rotted**
to go soft or bad so that it is useless; to decay, as in *This wood has rotted.*

rot *noun*
1 decay. 2 (*colloquial*) nonsense.

rotate *verb* **rotates, rotating, rotated**
1 to go round like a wheel. 2 to arrange something in a series; to happen in a series, as in *Rotate the jobs so that everybody has to take a turn at everything. The job of chairperson rotates.*
rotary *adjective*, **rotation** *noun*

rotisserie *noun* **rotisseries** (*say* roh-**tis**-uh-ree)
a rotating spit for roasting or barbecuing.

rotten *adjective*
1 rotted, as in *rotten fruit*. 2 (*colloquial*) nasty; very bad, as in *rotten weather*.
rottenness *noun*

rottweiler *noun* **rottweilers**
a large breed of dog with short black and tan hair, often kept to protect people or buildings.

rotund *adjective*
round and plump, as in *The athlete grew rotund when he stopped exercising*.

rough *adjective* **rougher, roughest**
1 not smooth; uneven, as in *a rough surface*. 2 not gentle, as in *a rough boy*. 3 not exact; done quickly, as in *a rough guess*.
roughly *adverb*, **roughness** *noun*

roughage *noun*
fibre in food, which helps you to digest the food.

roughen *verb* **roughens, roughening, roughened**
to make something rough; to become rough.

round *adjective* **rounder, roundest**
1 shaped like a circle or ball. 2 full; complete, as in *a round dozen*. 3 that returns to where it started, as in *a round trip*.

round *noun* **rounds**
1 a series of visits or calls made by a doctor, postman, etc. 2 one stage in a competition, as in *The winners go on to the next round*. 3 a shot or series of shots from a gun; a piece of ammunition. 4 a song in which people sing the same words but start at different times.

round *adverb*
1 in a circle or curve; by a longer route, as in *Go round to the back of the house*. 2 in all or various directions, as in *Hand the cakes round*. 3 in a new direction, as in *Turn your chair round*. 4 to someone's house, office, etc., as in *Come round at lunchtime*.

round *preposition*
1 on all sides of something, as in *a fence round the field*. 2 in a curve or circle about something, as in *The earth moves round the sun*. 3 to all or various parts of something, as in *Show them round the house*.
round the bend or **round the twist**, (*colloquial*) mad.

round *verb* **rounds, rounding, rounded**
1 to make something round; to become round. 2 to travel round, as in *The ship rounded the Tasman Peninsula*.
round down, to decrease a number to the nearest lower number, as in *123.4 may be rounded down to 123*.
round off, to finish something.
round up, to gather people, cattle, etc. together; to increase a number to the nearest higher number, as in *123.7 may be rounded up to 124*.

roundabout *noun* **roundabouts**
a road junction where traffic has to go around a circle.

rounders *noun*
a game in which players try to hit a ball and run through a round of bases.

rouse *verb* **rouses, rousing, roused**
to make someone awake, active, or excited.

rouseabout *noun* **rouseabouts**
an unskilled worker or a person who does odd jobs on a farm, in a shearing shed, etc.

rout *verb* **routs, routing, routed** (*say* rowt)
to defeat and chase away an enemy.

rout *noun* **routs** (*say* rowt)
a disorganised retreat from a battle.

route *noun* **routes** (*say* root)
the way you have to go to get to a place.

routine *noun* **routines** (*say* roo-teen)
a regular way of doing things.

rove *verb* **roves, roving, roved**
to wander; to travel.
rover *noun*

row *noun* **rows**
(rhymes with *go*)
a line of people or things.

row *noun* **rows**
(rhymes with *cow*)
1 a great noise or disturbance. 2 a quarrel; a noisy argument or scolding.

row *verb* **rows, rowing, rowed**
(rhymes with *go*)
to use oars to make a boat move.
rower *noun*, **rowing-boat** *noun*

rowdy *adjective* **rowdier, rowdiest**
noisy and disorderly.
rowdily *adverb*, **rowdiness** *noun*, **rowdyism** *noun*

rowlock *noun* **rowlocks** (*say* rol-uhk)
a device on the side of a boat to hold an oar in place.

royal *adjective*
to do with a king or queen.
royally *adverb*, **royalty** *noun*

rub *verb* **rubs, rubbing, rubbed**
to move something backwards and forwards while pressing it on something else, as in *He rubbed his hands together*.

rubber

rub it in, to repeatedly remind a person about his or her weakness, failure, etc.
rub out, to make something disappear by rubbing it.

rubber *noun* **rubbers**
1 a strong elastic substance used for making tyres, balls, hoses, etc.   2 a piece of this substance for rubbing out pencil marks.
rubbery *adjective*

rubbish *noun*
1 things that are not wanted or needed.
2 nonsense.

rubble *noun*
broken pieces of brick or stone.

rubella *noun* (*say* roo-**bel**-uh)
the medical name for German measles.

ruby *noun* **rubies**
a red jewel.

rucksack *noun* **rucksacks**
a bag carried on your back especially by a hiker.

rudder *noun* **rudders**
a flat, hinged device at the back of a ship or aircraft, used for steering.

ruddy *adjective* **ruddier, ruddiest**
red and healthy-looking, as in *a ruddy face.*

rude *adjective* **ruder, rudest**
1 not polite.   2 obscene; indecent.
rudely *adverb,* **rudeness** *noun*

ruffian *noun* **ruffians**
a violent, brutal person.

ruffle *verb* **ruffles, ruffling, ruffled**
to disturb the smoothness of something or the calmness of someone, as in *The bird ruffled its feathers. Your question seems to have ruffled her.*

rug *noun* **rugs**
1 a thick piece of material that partly covers a floor.   2 a thick blanket.

Rugby or **Rugby football** *noun*
a kind of football game using an oval ball that the players are allowed to kick or carry, as in *There are 13 players on each side in Rugby League but 15 in Rugby Union.* [from *Rugby* school in England where the game was first played]

rugged *adjective* (*say* **rug**-uhd)
1 rough; uneven, as in *a rugged face.*
2 rocky, as in *a rugged coast.*

ruin *verb* **ruins, ruining, ruined**
to spoil something completely; to destroy something.

ruin *noun* **ruins**
1 a building that has almost all fallen down.   2 the action of ruining; destruction.
ruinous *adjective*

rule *noun* **rules**
1 something that people have to obey; a way that people must behave.
2 governing, as in *Vietnam used to be under French rule.*
as a rule, usually.

rule *verb* **rules, ruling, ruled**
1 to govern; to reign.   2 to make a decision, as in *The referee ruled that it was a foul.*   3 to draw a straight line with a ruler or some other straight edge.

ruler *noun* **rulers**
1 someone who governs.   2 a strip of wood, plastic, or metal with straight edges, used for measuring and drawing straight lines.

rum *noun* **rums**
a strong alcoholic drink made from sugar or molasses.

rumble *verb* **rumbles, rumbling, rumbled**
to make a deep, heavy sound like thunder.

rummage *verb* **rummages, rummaging, rummaged**
to turn things over or move them about while looking for something, as in *She rummaged in the wardrobe.*

rummy *noun*
a card-game in which players try to form sequences or sets of cards.

rumour *noun* **rumours**
something that a lot of people are saying, although it may not be true.

rump *noun* **rumps**
the hind part of an animal.

rumpus *noun*
(*colloquial*) a disturbance, row, etc, as in *The dog caused a rumpus when it ran into the classroom.*

run *verb* **runs, running, ran, run**
1 to use your legs to move quickly.   2 to go or travel; to flow, as in *Tears ran down his cheeks.*   3 to produce a flow of liquid, as in *Your nose is running.*   4 to work or function, as in *The engine was running smoothly.*   5 to manage or organise, as in *She runs a book shop.*
run a risk, to take a chance.
run away, to leave a place quickly or secretly.

run into, to hit someone or something with a vehicle; to meet someone without expecting it.

run out, to have used up your stock of something, as in *We have run out of sugar*.

run over, to knock someone down with your car, bicycle, etc.

run *noun* **runs**
1 a time spent running, as in *Go for a run*. 2 a point scored in cricket or baseball. 3 a series of damaged stitches in a stocking or other piece of clothing. 4 a continuous series of events, as in *She had a run of good luck*. 5 a place for animals with a fence round it, as in *a run for a dog*.

on the run, running away.

runaway *noun* **runaways**
someone who has run away.

rung *noun* **rungs**
one of the short crossbars on a ladder.

rung past participle of **ring** *verb*.

run-in *noun* **run-ins**
a quarrel.

runner *noun* **runners**
1 a person or animal that runs, especially in a race. 2 a rod, groove, roller or blade on which a thing slides, as in *drawer runners*. 3 a person who carries messages from the coach of a team to the players on the field. 4 running shoes; sneakers.

runner bean, a kind of climbing bean.

runner-up, someone who comes second in a race or competition.

runny *adjective* **runnier, runniest**
flowing or moving like liquid.

runway *noun* **runways**
an airstrip.

rural *adjective*
to do with the country area, as in *rural schools, rural industry*.

rush *verb* **rushes, rushing, rushed**
1 to hurry. 2 to attack or capture someone or something by a sudden, quick action.

rush *noun* **rushes**
1 a hurry. 2 a plant with a thin stem that grows in wet or marshy places.

rush hour, the time when traffic is busiest.

rust *noun*
1 a red or brown substance formed on metal that is exposed to air and dampness. 2 the process of forming this substance.

rusty *adjective*

rust *verb* **rusts, rusting, rusted**
1 to cause a red or brown substance to form on metal that is exposed to air and dampness, as in *Salt water rusts steel quickly*. 2 to become covered with this substance, as in *The chain on my bicycle has rusted*.

rustle *verb* **rustles, rustling, rustled**
1 to make a gentle sound like dry leaves being blown by the wind. 2 to steal horses or cattle.

rustle up, (*colloquial*) to provide, at short notice, a meal, helpers, etc.

rustler *noun*

rut *noun* **ruts**
1 a deep groove in the ground made by wheels. 2 a boring habit or way of life, as in *We are getting into a rut*.

rutted *adjective*

ruthless *adjective*
pitiless; merciless; cruel.

ruthlessly *adverb*, **ruthlessness** *noun*

rye *noun*
a cereal used to make bread, biscuits, etc.

a
b
c
d
e
f
g
h
i
j
k
l
m
n
o
p
q
r
s
t
u
v
w
x
y
z

Ss

Sabbath *noun* Sabbaths
a weekly day for rest and prayer, Saturday for Jews, Sunday for Christians.

sabotage *noun* (*say* **sab**-uh-tah*zh*)
deliberate damage or disruption to hinder an enemy, employer, etc.
saboteur *noun*

sabre *noun* sabres (*say* **say**-buh)
a heavy sword with a curved blade.

sac *noun* sacs
part of an animal or plant that is shaped like a bag.

saccharin *noun* (*say* **sak**-uh-ruhn)
a sweet substance used as a substitute for sugar.

sachet *noun* sachets
a small, sealed packet of something such as shampoo.

sack *noun* sacks
a large bag made of strong material.
the sack, being dismissed from a job, as in *They gave me the sack.*

sack *verb* sacks, sacking, sacked
to dismiss someone from a job.

sacred *adjective*
treated with religious respect; connected with religion, as in *sacred places.*

sacred site *noun* sacred sites
an important spiritual place for Aborigines.

sacrifice *noun* sacrifices
1 giving or doing something that you think will please a god.   2 giving up a thing that you value so that something good may happen.   3 something given or done to please a god or to make something good happen.
sacrificial *adjective*

sacrifice *verb* sacrifices, sacrificing, sacrificed
to give something as a sacrifice.

sad *adjective* sadder, saddest
unhappy.
sadly *adverb*, **sadness** *noun*

sadden *verb* saddens, saddening, saddened
to make someone unhappy.

saddle *noun* saddles
1 a seat designed to be put on the back of a horse or other animal.   2 the seat of a bicycle.

saddle *verb* saddles, saddling, saddled
to put a seat on a horse's back.

sadist *noun* sadists (*say* **say**-dist *or* **sad**-ist)
someone who likes hurting other people.
sadism *noun*, **sadistic** *adjective*

safari *noun* safaris (*say* suh-**fah**-ree)
an expedition to see or hunt wild animals.

safe *adjective* safer, safest
1 free from danger; protected, as in *The bus crashed, but the passengers are safe. The child felt safe in his mother's arms.*   2 not causing danger, as in *Drive at a safe speed.*
safely *adverb*

safe *noun* safes
a strong cupboard or box in which valuable things can be locked safely.

safeguard *noun* safeguards
a protection.

safety *noun*
being safe; protection.
safety-pin, a curved pin made with a clip to protect the point.

saffron *noun*
a deep yellow food colouring and flavouring made from a flower.

sag *verb* **sags, sagging, sagged**
to go down in the middle because something heavy is pressing on it, as in *The chair sagged under his weight.*

saga *noun* **sagas**
a long story, especially one that tells Norwegian or Icelandic legends.

sage *noun*
a herb used to flavour food.

said past tense and past participle of **say**.

sail *noun* **sails**
1 a large piece of strong cloth attached to a mast to make a boat move.   2 a short voyage.   3 an arm of a windmill.

sail *verb* **sails, sailing, sailed**
1 to travel in a ship.   2 to start a voyage, as in *We sail at noon.*   3 to control a boat.   4 to be moved along by means of a sail or sails, as in *This boat sails beautifully.*
sailing-boat, a boat or ship moved by sails.

sailboard *noun* **sailboards**
a type of boat like a surfboard with a mast and sail, used for windsurfing.

sailor *noun* **sailors**
1 a member of a ship's crew.   2 someone who travels in a sailing-boat.

saint *noun* **saints**
a holy or very good person.
saintly *adjective*

sake *noun*
for its own sake, because you like doing it, as in *I'm learning about music for its own sake, not because I want to become a teacher of music.*
for someone's sake, so as to help or please someone, as in *She went to great trouble for his sake.*
for something's sake, in order to get something that you want, as in *He'll do anything for the sake of money. I check the tyres every day, for safety's sake.*

salad *noun* **salads**
a mixture of vegetables eaten cold and often raw.

salami *noun* **salamis**
a highly seasoned, originally Italian, sausage.

salary *noun* **salaries**
a regular wage, especially for non-manual work.

sale *noun* **sales**
1 the selling of something.   2 a time when things are sold at reduced prices.
for sale or **on sale,** able to be bought.

salesperson *noun* **salespersons**
someone whose job is to sell things.

saline *adjective*
salty; containing salt.

saliva *noun* (*say* suh-**luy**-vuh)
the natural liquid in a person's mouth.

salmon *noun* **salmon**
a large fish with pink flesh that can be eaten.

salon *noun* **salons**
the place where a hairdresser or a beauty specialist works.

saloon *noun* **saloons**
a room where people can sit, drink, etc., as in *The saloon in the hotel was comfortably furnished.*

salt *noun*
the white substance that gives sea-water its taste and is used for flavouring food.
salty *adjective*

saltbush *noun* **saltbushes**
a plant which grows in dry areas and is eaten by livestock.

salt-water crocodile *noun* **salt-water crocodiles**
a large crocodile found in the coastal areas of northern Australia, as in *The salt-water crocodile is often called a 'saltie'.*

salute *noun* **salutes**
1 the act of greeting someone respectfully or politely.   2 the firing of guns as a sign of respect for someone.

salute *verb* **salutes, saluting, saluted**
to raise your hand to your forehead as a sign of respect or greeting, especially in the armed forces.

salvage *verb* **salvages, salvaging, salvaged**
to save or rescue something, especially a damaged ship, so that it can be used again.

salvation *noun*
the act of saving someone or something.

same *adjective*
not different, as in *We are the same age.*

samosa *noun* **samosas**
a small case of crisp pastry filled with a mixture of vegetables and spices, with or without meat.

sample *noun* **samples**
a small amount that shows what something is like, as in *They are giving away samples of cheese. The doctor took a blood sample.*

sample *verb* **samples, sampling, sampled**
1 to take a sample of something, as in *Scientists sampled the lake water.*   2 to try part of something, as in *She sampled the cake.*

a
b
c
d
e
f
g
h
i
j
k
l
m
n
o
p
q
r
s
t
u
v
w
x
y
z

sanction

sanction *verb* **sanctions, sanctioning, sanctioned**
to support or agree to, as in *The principal sanctioned the use of the school oval for weekend cricket.*

sanctuary *noun* **sanctuaries**
a safe place, as in *a bird sanctuary.*

sand *noun* **sands**
the tiny grains of rock that you find on beaches and in deserts.
sands, a sandy area.

sand *verb* **sands, sanding, sanded**
to smooth or polish something with sandpaper or some other rough material.
sander *noun*

sandal *noun* **sandals**
a lightweight shoe with straps that go around your foot.

sandalwood *noun*
the scented wood of a tree found in South Asia and Australia.

sandbag *noun* **sandbags**
a bag filled with sand, used to protect a place, especially from floods.

sandpaper *noun*
strong paper with sand glued to it, rubbed on rough surfaces to make them smooth.

sandshoes *plural noun*
canvas shoes with a rubber sole used mainly for sport.

sandstone *noun*
rock made of compressed sand.

sandwich *noun* **sandwiches**
two slices of bread with a filling of meat, cheese, Vegemite, etc. between them.
[from the name of the British nobleman, the Earl of *Sandwich*, who invented it]

sandy *adjective* **sandier, sandiest**
1 having much sand. 2 yellowish-red, as in *sandy hair.*

sane *adjective* **saner, sanest**
not mad; with a healthy mind.
sanely *adverb*

sang past tense of **sing.**

sanitary *adjective*
free from germs and dirt.

sanity *noun*
having a healthy mind.

sank past tense of **sink** *verb.*

sap *noun*
the liquid inside a plant.

sap *verb* **saps, sapping, sapped**
to weaken someone's strength or energy.

sapling *noun* **saplings**
a young tree.

sapphire *noun* **sapphires**
a bright blue jewel.

sarcasm *noun*
the act of mocking someone or something, especially by saying the opposite of what you mean, as in *Saying 'Great shot!' when Jane missed the ball was a piece of sarcasm.*
sarcastic *adjective,* **sarcastically** *adverb*

sardine *noun* **sardines**
a small marine fish, usually sold in tins.

sari *noun* **saris** (*say* **sah**-ree)
a long length of cloth worn as a dress, especially by Indian women and girls.

sarong *noun* **sarongs** (*say* suh-**rong**)
a long strip of cloth, tucked around the waist or under the armpits and worn by people in some Asian countries and some Pacific islands.

sash *noun* **sashes**
a strip of cloth worn around the waist or over one shoulder.
sash window, a window that slides up and down.

sat past tense and past participle of **sit.**

satay *noun* **satays** (*say* **sah**-tay *or* **sat**-ay)
small pieces of meat, grilled on a skewer and usually served with a spiced sauce.

satchel *noun* **satchels**
a bag worn over your shoulder or on your back, especially for carrying books to and from school.

satellite *noun* **satellites**
a moon or a spacecraft that moves in an orbit around a planet.
satellite dish, a dish-shaped aerial for receiving television signals sent by satellite.
satellite television, a television system in which programs are sent by means of an artificial satellite.

satin *noun*
smooth cloth that is very shiny on one side.

satire *noun* **satires**
1 the use of humour or exaggeration to make fun of someone or something. 2 a play, poem, etc. that does this.
satirical *adjective,* **satirist** *noun,* **satirise** *verb*

satisfaction *noun*
1 the feeling of being satisfied. 2 giving someone what he or she needs or wants.
3 something that makes you contented, as in *Helping people is the greatest satisfaction of his job.*

381   **scale**

satisfactory *adjective*
good enough; sufficient.
satisfactorily *adverb*

satisfy *verb* **satisfies, satisfying, satisfied**
1 to give someone what he or she needs or wants. 2 to convince yourself or someone else, as in *I am satisfied that you have done your best.*

saturate *verb* **saturates, saturating, saturated**
1 to soak something, as in *My clothes are saturated with rain.* 2 to make something accept as much as possible of a substance or a product, as in *The market has been saturated with second-hand cars.*
saturation *noun*

Saturday *noun* **Saturdays**
the seventh day of the week.

sauce *noun* **sauces**
a thick liquid used to flavour food.

saucepan *noun* **saucepans**
a metal cooking pot with a handle.

saucer *noun* **saucers**
a small curved plate on which a cup is put.

sauna *noun* **saunas** (*say* **saw**-nuh)
a place where you can sit in a very hot, steamy room, and afterwards take hot or cold showers.

saunter *verb* **saunters, sauntering, sauntered**
to walk in a leisurely way.

sausage *noun* **sausages**
a tube of skin or plastic stuffed with minced meat and other ingredients.
sausage-meat, minced meat of the kind used in sausages.
sausage roll, sausage-meat in a small, short roll of pastry.

savage *adjective*
wild and fierce; cruel.
savagely *adverb,* **savagery** *noun*

savage *verb* **savages, savaging, savaged**
to attack and bite someone fiercely, as in *He had been savaged by a mad dog.*

savannah or **savanna** *noun* **savannahs**
(*say* suh-**van**-uh)
a grassy plain, with few trees, in a hot country.

save *verb* **saves, saving, saved**
1 to free a person or thing from danger.
2 to keep something, especially money, so that it can be used later. 3 to put information on to a computer disc so that it can be kept. 4 to stop a ball going into your goal.
saver *noun*

saveloy *noun* **saveloys**
a thick, seasoned, red pork sausage.

savings *plural noun*
money saved.

saviour *noun* **saviours**
a person who saves someone.
our Saviour or **the Saviour,** Jesus.

savoury *adjective*
tasty but not sweet.

saw *noun* **saws**
a tool with sharp teeth for cutting wood, metal, etc.

saw *verb* **saws, sawing, sawn, sawed**
to cut something with a saw, as in *Have you sawn that plank yet? I sawed it in half yesterday.*

saw past tense of **see.**

saxophone *noun* **saxophones**
a wind instrument with a reed in the mouthpiece, used especially for playing jazz music.

say *verb* **says, saying, said**
1 to make words with your voice. 2 to give an opinion.

saying *noun* **sayings**
a well-known phrase; a proverb.

scab *noun* **scabs**
1 a hard crust that forms over a cut or graze. 2 (*colloquial*) someone who works while other workers are on strike.

scabbard *noun* **scabbards**
a cover for the blade of a sword or dagger.

scaffold *noun* **scaffolds**
1 a platform on which criminals were executed. 2 a scaffolding.

scaffolding *noun*
1 a structure of poles and planks for workmen to stand on, especially when building or repairing a house. 2 the poles used to build this structure.

scald *verb* **scalds, scalding, scalded**
1 to burn yourself with very hot liquid.
2 to clean something with boiling water.

scale *noun* **scales**
1 a series of units, steps, or marks for measuring something, as in *This ruler has one scale in centimetres and another in inches.* 2 a series of musical notes going up or down in a fixed pattern.
3 proportion; ratio, as in *The scale of this map is one centimetre to the kilometre.* 4 the relative size or importance of something, as in *They were making yoghurt on a large scale.* 5 one of the thin overlapping parts

a
b
c
d
e
f
g
h
i
j
k
l
m
n
o
p
q
r
s
t
u
v
w
x
y
z

scale

on the outside of fish, snakes, etc.   6 the coating that forms on the inside of kettles, etc., especially caused by the action of heat on hard water.
scaly *adjective*

scale *verb* **scales, scaling, scaled**
to climb up something.

scalene triangle *noun*
a triangle with no equal sides.

scales *plural noun*
a weighing-machine, as in *bathroom scales.*

scallop *noun* **scallops** (*say* **skol**-uhp)
1 an edible shellfish with two fan-shaped shells.   2 an ornamental edging of semicircular curves on clothes, pastry, etc.

scalp *noun* **scalps**
the skin on top of your head.

scalp *verb* **scalps, scalping, scalped**
to cut off someone's scalp.

scalpel *noun* **scalpels**
a surgeon's small sharp knife.

scamper *verb* **scampers, scampering, scampered**
to run quickly, as in *The rabbits scampered for safety.*

scan *verb* **scans, scanning, scanned**
1 to look at every part of something.   2 to look at a large area quickly.   3 to analyse the rhythm of a line of poetry; to have a poetic rhythm, as in *This line doesn't scan.*
4 to sweep a radar or electronic beam over an area in search of something; to examine part of the body using an electronic beam.
scan *noun*

scandal *noun* **scandals**
1 a disgraceful action.   2 gossip that damages someone's reputation.
scandalous *adjective*

Scandinavian *adjective*
to do with Scandinavia, as in *The Scandinavian countries are Norway, Sweden, Denmark, and Finland.*

scanner *noun* **scanners**
1 a device used to examine the body or part of it, using an electronic beam.   2 a machine for copying a document.

scant *adjective*
barely enough, as in *The student gave scant attention to his spelling.*

scapegoat *noun* **scapegoats**
someone who is blamed or punished for other people's mistakes, sins, etc.

scar *noun* **scars**
the mark left on your skin by a cut or burn after it has healed.

scar *verb* **scars, scarring, scarred**
to make a scar or scars on skin.

scarce *adjective* **scarcer, scarcest**
not available in sufficient amounts; not seen or found very often, as in *Wheat was scarce because of the drought.*
make yourself scarce, (*colloquial*) to go away or keep out of the way.
scarcity *noun*

scarcely *adverb*
hardly.

scare *verb* **scares, scaring, scared**
to frighten.

scarecrow *noun* **scarecrows**
a figure of a man dressed in old clothes, set up to frighten birds away from crops.

scarf *noun* **scarves**
a strip of material worn around your neck or head.

scarlet *adjective*
bright red.
scarlet fever, an infectious disease which produces a scarlet rash.

scary *adjective* **scarier, scariest**
(*colloquial*) frightening.

scathing *adjective* (*say* **skay**-thing)
very scornful, as in *The coach made a scathing remark on the team's poor performance.*

scatter *verb* **scatters, scattering, scattered**
1 to throw things in various directions.
2 to move quickly in various directions, as in *The crowd scattered when the police arrived.*

scene *noun* **scenes**
1 the place where something happens, as in *the scene of the crime.*   2 part of a play or film.   3 a view.   4 a place represented on the stage by scenery; scenery.   5 an angry or noisy outburst, as in *She made a scene about the money.*

scenery *noun*
1 the natural features of an area, as in *They admired the scenery.*   2 painted screens, curtains, etc. put on a stage to make it look like another place.

scent *noun* **scents** (*say* sent)
1 a perfume.   2 an animal's smell, that other animals can follow.
scented *adjective*

sceptic *noun* **sceptics** (*say* **skep**-tik)
someone who is not inclined to believe things.
sceptical *adjective*, **scepticism** *noun*

Usage Do not confuse **sceptic** with **septic,** which is an adjective meaning infected with germs.

383 **scramble**

schedule *noun* **schedules** (*say* **shed**-yool *or* **sked**-yool)
a list of details, things to be done, and especially times.
on schedule, on time; not arriving late.

scheme *noun* **schemes**
1 a plan. 2 a secret plan.

scheme *verb* **schemes, scheming, schemed**
to make secret plans.
schemer *noun*

scholar *noun* **scholars**
1 someone who studies a lot or knows a lot. 2 a student, as in *a diligent scholar.*
scholarly *adjective*

scholarship *noun* **scholarships**
1 money given to someone to help pay for his or her education. 2 the knowledge that scholars have; learning or studying.

school *noun* **schools**
1 a place where children are educated. 2 the children who go there, as in *The whole school had a holiday.* 3 the time when children are taught things, as in *School begins at 9 o'clock.*
school-leaver, someone who is old enough to leave school, or who has just left school.
schoolboy *noun,* **schoolchild** *noun,* **schoolgirl** *noun*

School of the Air *noun*
a government education program using a two-way radio system to enable children in the outback to take part in lessons with a teacher.

schooner *noun* **schooners** (*say* **skoo**-nuh)
a sailing-ship with at least two masts.

science *noun*
the study of objects and happenings which can be observed and tested; knowledge gained in this way.
science fiction, stories about the future.
scientific *adjective,* **scientifically** *adverb*

scientist *noun* **scientists**
an expert in science; someone who studies science.

scissors *plural noun*
a cutting device made of two movable blades joined together.

scoff *verb* **scoffs, scoffing, scoffed**
to make fun of someone; to jeer, as in *Many people scoffed at the inventor. Don't scoff.*

scold *verb* **scolds, scolding, scolded**
to tell someone off angrily or noisily.

scone *noun* **scones** (*say* skon)
a small cake, usually eaten with butter, cream, and jam.

scoop *noun* **scoops**
1 a deep spoon for serving ice-cream, mashed potato, etc. 2 a deep shovel. 3 an important piece of news published by only one newspaper.

scoop *verb* **scoops, scooping, scooped**
to serve something with a deep spoon; to move something with a deep shovel.

scooter *noun* **scooters**
1 a kind of motor cycle with a small engine and small wheels. 2 a toy with two wheels and a narrow platform that you ride on.

scope *noun* **scopes**
1 opportunity; possibility, as in *Her job gives her scope for development.* 2 the range of something, as in *Chemistry is outside the scope of the syllabus for this class.*

scorch *verb* **scorches, scorching, scorched**
to make something go brown by heating or burning it, as in *He scorched the shirt he was ironing. The sun scorched the dry land.*
scorching, (*colloquial*) very hot.

scorcher *noun* **scorchers**
(*colloquial*) a very hot day.

score *noun* **scores**
1 the number of points or goals made in a game. 2 twenty, as in *He reached the age of fourscore (= 80).*

score *verb* **scores, scoring, scored**
1 to get a goal or point in a game. 2 to keep a count of the score in a game. 3 to scratch a surface. 4 music for a film, play, etc. especially for a musical.
scorer *noun*

scorn *noun*
treating a person or thing as worthless or laughable.
scornful *adjective,* **scornfully** *adverb*

scorpion *noun* **scorpions**
a kind of spider with a poisonous sting in its tail.

scoundrel *noun* **scoundrels**
a wicked person.

scour *verb* **scours, scouring, scoured**
1 to rub something until it is clean and bright. 2 to search an area thoroughly.

scout *noun* **scouts**
someone sent out to collect information, spy on an enemy, etc.

scowl *verb* **scowls, scowling, scowled**
to look bad-tempered.

scramble *verb* **scrambles, scrambling, scrambled**
1 to move quickly and awkwardly, as in

a
b
c
d
e
f
g
h
i
j
k
l
m
n
o
p
q
r
s
t
u
v
w
x
y
z

scramble

We scrambled up the steep slope.   **2** to cook eggs by mixing them up and heating them in a saucepan.

scramble *noun* **scrambles**
   1 the action of moving quickly with difficulty, as in *a tough scramble over the rocks.*   **2** a struggle to get something, as in *There was a mad scramble for the best seats.*   **3** a motor-cycle race across rough country.

scrap *noun* **scraps**
   1 a small piece of something, as in *a scrap of cloth.*   **2** rubbish, especially unwanted metal.   **3** (*colloquial*) a fight.
   scrapbook, a book in which you stick newspaper cuttings, souvenirs, etc.

scrap *verb* **scraps, scrapping, scrapped**
   to get rid of something you do not want.

scrape *verb* **scrapes, scraping, scraped**
   1 to rub something with something rough, hard, or sharp, as in *He was scraping the frying-pan.*   **2** to move along or get past, touching or almost touching something, as in *The car scraped past.*   **3** to use effort or care to get something, as in *They scraped together enough money for a holiday.*
   scraper *noun*

scrape *noun* **scrapes**
   1 a scraping movement or sound.   **2** a mark made by scraping something.   **3** an awkward situation.

scrappy *adjective* **scrappier, scrappiest**
   made of scraps or bits; not complete.

scratch *verb* **scratches, scratching, scratched**
   1 to damage a surface by rubbing something sharp over it.   **2** to rub the skin with fingernails or claws because it itches.

scratch *noun* **scratches**
   1 a mark made by scratching.   **2** the act or sound of scratching.
   start from scratch, to begin at the very beginning.
   up to scratch, up to the proper standard.
   scratchy *adjective*

scratchie *noun* **scratchies**
   an instant lottery ticket whose surface you scratch to find if a prize has been won.

scrawl *verb* **scrawls, scrawling, scrawled**
   to scribble, especially big letters or marks.

scream *noun* **screams**
   1 a loud cry of pain, fear, etc.
   2 (*colloquial*) something very amusing.

scream *verb* **screams, screaming, screamed**
   to give a scream.

screech *verb* **screeches, screeching, screeched**
   to make a harsh, high-pitched sound, as in *The brakes screeched as the train came to a stop.*

screen *noun* **screens**
   1 a flat surface on which films or television programs are shown.   **2** a movable wall or covered framework used to hide something, divide a room, or protect something from excessive heat, light, etc.   **3** something that gives shelter or protection, as in *a smokescreen.*

screen *verb* **screens, screening, screened**
   1 to show a film or television program.   **2** to hide, divide, or protect something with a movable wall or covered framework.   **3** to test someone to see if he or she has a disease, as in *The hospital can screen people for cancer.*

screw *noun* **screws**
   a metal pin with a spiral ridge around it.

screw *verb* **screws, screwing, screwed**
   1 to fix something with screws.   **2** to move or fix something by turning it, as in *Screw the lid on to the jar. I screwed in the light bulb.*

screwdriver *noun* **screwdrivers**
   a tool for turning a screw.

scribble *verb* **scribbles, scribbling, scribbled**
   1 to write untidily or carelessly.   **2** to make meaningless marks.
   scribbler *noun*

script *noun* **scripts**
   1 the words of a play or broadcast.
   2 handwriting; something handwritten.

scripture *noun* **scriptures**
   a sacred book, especially the Bible.

scroll *noun* **scrolls**
   a roll of paper or parchment with writing on it.

scrotum *noun* **scrotums** or **scrota**
   (*say* **skroh**-tuhm)
   the pouch of skin behind the penis, containing the testicles.

scrounge *verb* **scrounges, scrounging, scrounged**
   (*colloquial*) to get something without paying for it, as in *He scrounged a meal from us.*
   scrounger *noun*

scrub *verb* **scrubs, scrubbing, scrubbed**
   1 to rub something with a hard brush, as in *He scrubbed the floor.*   **2** (*colloquial*) to cancel something, as in *We'll have to scrub the show.*

search

scrub *noun* **scrubs**
1 the action of scrubbing, as in *The floor needs a good scrub.* 2 a bush area with low stunted trees or bushes growing in poor soil.

scruffy *adjective* **scruffier, scruffiest**
shabby and untidy.

scrum or **scrummage** *noun* **scrums** or **scrummages**
a group of players from each side in Rugby football pushing against each other and trying to win the ball.

scrutinise or **scrutinize** *verb* **scrutinises, scrutinising, scrutinised**
to examine or look at something closely.
scrutiny *noun*

scuba diving *noun*
swimming underwater, breathing air from tanks carried on your back.
[from the first letters of the words *self-contained underwater breathing apparatus*]

scuffle *noun* **scuffles**
a confused struggle or fight.

scullery *noun* **sculleries**
in the past, a small room in some houses where the washing-up was done.

sculptor *noun* **sculptors**
someone who makes sculptures.

sculpture *noun* **sculptures**
1 something carved or shaped out of stone, clay, metal, etc. 2 the art or work of a sculptor.

scum *noun*
1 froth or dirt on the top of a liquid.
2 (*colloquial and offensive*) people who are thought to be worthless.

scungies *plural noun*
sporting briefs.

scurry *verb* **scurries, scurrying, scurried**
to run with short steps; to hurry.

scurvy *noun*
a disease caused by lack of fresh fruit and vegetables.

scuttle *verb* **scuttles, scuttling, scuttled**
1 to sink your own ship deliberately. 2 to run with short, quick steps.

scythe *noun* **scythes**
a tool with a long curved blade for cutting, as in *He used a scythe to cut the cane.*

sea *noun* **seas**
1 the salt water that covers most of the earth's surface. 2 a very large area of water, as in *the Timor Sea.* 3 a large area of something, as in *a sea of faces.*

at sea, on the sea; very puzzled, as in *He's completely at sea in his new job.*

sea anemone *noun* **sea anemones**
a marine creature looking like a small mass of jelly with short tentacles around its mouth.

seabed *noun*
the bottom of the sea.

seafaring *adjective* and *noun*
travelling or working on the sea.
seafarer *noun*

seafood *noun*
fish or shellfish from the sea eaten as food.

seagull *noun* **seagulls**
a sea bird with long wings.

sea horse *noun* **sea horses**
a small fish with a head rather like a horse's head.

seal *noun* **seals**
1 a fish-eating, marine mammal with sleek fur and flippers. 2 a design pressed into wax, lead, etc. 3 something designed to close an opening. 4 a small decorative sticker.

seal *verb* **seals, sealing, sealed**
to close something by sticking two parts together; to close tightly, as in *She sealed the envelope.*

sea level *noun*
the level of the sea half-way between high and low tide, as in *The mountain rises 1,000 metres above sea-level.*

sea lion *noun* **sea lions**
a kind of large seal having a white mane of hair on the back of its neck.

seam *noun* **seams**
1 the line where two edges of cloth, wood, etc. join together. 2 a layer of coal, gold, etc. in the ground.

seaman *noun* **seamen**
a sailor.
seamanship *noun*

seaplane *noun* **seaplanes**
an aeroplane that can land on water.

search *verb* **searches, searching, searched**
1 to look very carefully for something.
2 to examine a person, place, etc. thoroughly.
searcher *noun*

search *noun* **searches**
a very careful look for someone or something.
search-party, a group of people looking for someone or something.
search warrant, official permission allowing the police to search a house, etc.

a
b
c
d
e
f
g
h
i
j
k
l
m
n
o
p
q
r
s
t
u
v
w
x
y
z

searching

searching *adjective*
thorough, as in *Ask some searching questions.*

searchlight *noun* **searchlights**
a light with a strong beam that can be turned in any direction.

seasick *adjective*
sick because of the movement of a ship.
seasickness *noun*

season *noun* **seasons**
1 one of the four main parts of the year, as in *The seasons are spring, summer, autumn, and winter.* 2 a period when something happens, as in *the football season.*
season ticket, a ticket that can be used as often as you like throughout a period of time.
seasonal *adjective*

season *verb* **seasons, seasoning, seasoned**
to flavour food with herbs and spices.
seasoning *noun*

seat *noun* **seats**
something for sitting on.
seatbelt, a belt to hold someone securely in a seat.

seat *verb* **seats, seating, seated**
to have seats for a particular number of people, as in *The theatre seats 3,000.*
seat yourself, to sit down.

seaweed *noun* **seaweeds**
plants that grow in the sea.

secateurs *plural noun* (*say* **sek**-uh-tuhz *or* sek-uh-**terz**)
a tool like a large pair of scissors for pruning plants.

secluded *adjective*
away from large numbers of people; not crowded, as in *a secluded beach.*
seclusion *noun*

second *adjective*
next after the first.
have second thoughts about something, to wonder whether the first decision you made about something was really right, as in *I'm having second thoughts about going overseas; I'm not sure if I've got enough money.*
second nature, behaviour that has become a habit, as in *Lying is second nature to him.*
secondly *adverb*

second *noun* **seconds**
1 a person or thing that is second.
2 someone who helps a fighter in a boxing-match, duel, etc. 3 something that is not of the best quality. 4 a very short period of time, as in *60 seconds = 1 minute.*

second *verb* **seconds, seconding, seconded**
to support a proposal, motion, etc.

secondary *adjective*
coming second; not original or essential, as in *of secondary importance.*
secondary industry, industry which produces manufactured goods, as in *Secondary industries process primary products like minerals and natural fibres.*

secondary school *noun* **secondary schools**
a school providing education after primary school and before any tertiary course.

second-hand *adjective* and *adverb*
1 bought or used after someone else has used it, as in *a second-hand car.* 2 that sells used goods, as in *a second-hand shop.*

secret *adjective*
kept or meant to be kept private, unknown, or hidden.
secret agent, a spy.
secrecy *noun,* **secretly** *adverb*

secret *noun* **secrets**
something that must be kept private, unknown, or hidden.
in secret, secretly.

secretary *noun* **secretaries** (*say* **sek**-ruh-tree *or* sek-ruh-tuh-ree)
someone whose job is to type letters, answer the telephone, and make business arrangements for a person, organisation, etc.
secretarial *adjective*

secrete *verb* **secretes, secreting, secreted** (*say* suh-**kreet**)
1 to hide something. 2 to form a substance in the body, as in *Saliva is secreted in the mouth.*
secretion *noun*

secretive *adjective* (*say* **seek**-ruh-tiv)
liking or trying to keep things secret.
secretively *adverb,* **secretiveness** *noun*

sect *noun* **sects**
a group of people who have different opinions, beliefs, etc. from the majority of people.

section *noun* **sections**
a part of something.
sectional *adjective*

sector *noun* **sectors**
part of an area.

secular *adjective*
not concerned with religion, as in *secular education.*

secure *adjective* **securer, securest**
1 firm, as in *Is that ladder secure?* 2 not likely to be lost, as in *a secure job.*
3 protected, as in *The bank vault is a very secure place.* 4 tightly shut or fixed, as in *Check that all the doors and windows are secure before leaving.*
securely *adverb*, **security** *noun*

secure *verb* **secures, securing, secured**
1 to make something secure. 2 to get hold of something, as in *She secured two tickets for the show.*

sedan *noun* **sedans** (*say* suh-**dan**)
a car with four doors, as in *Sedans usually seat four to five people.*

sedate *adjective* (*say* suh-**dayt**)
calm and dignified.
sedately *adverb*

sedative *noun* **sedatives** (*say* sed-uh-tiv)
a medicine that makes someone calm.
sedation *noun*

sediment *noun*
solid matter that floats in liquid or sinks to the bottom of it.

sedimentary *adjective*
(*say* sed-uh-**ment**-uh-ree *or* sed-uh-**men**-tree)
formed from particles that have settled on a surface, as in *sedimentary rocks.*

see *verb* **sees, seeing, saw, seen**
1 to use your eyes to get to know things, recognise people, etc., as in *Have you seen my brother?* 2 to meet or visit someone, as in *See me in my office.* 3 to understand, as in *She saw what I meant.* 4 to imagine, as in *Can you see yourself as a teacher?* 5 to experience something, as in *The old farmer had seen many droughts.* 6 to attend to something; to make sure, as in *See that the windows are shut.* 7 to escort or lead someone, as in *I'll see you to the door.*
see through, not to be deceived by something or someone; to continue with something until it is finished, as in *I saw through his pretence. We will see the job through.*
see to, to attend to something.

seed *noun* **seeds**
a tiny part of a plant that can grow in the ground to make a new plant.

seedling *noun* **seedlings**
a very young plant.

seek *verb* **seeks, seeking, sought**
1 to try to find a person or thing, as in *We sought him everywhere.* 2 to try to get something, as in *She is seeking fame.*

seem *verb* **seems, seeming, seemed**
to give the impression of being something, as in *He seems clever but he is a fool.*
seemingly *adverb*

seen past participle of **see.**

seep *verb* **seeps, seeping, seeped**
to flow slowly through, into, or out of something, as in *Water was seeping into the tunnel.*
seepage *noun*

see-saw *noun* **see-saws**
a plank balanced in the middle so that people can sit at each end and make it go up and down.

seethe *verb* **seethes, seething, seethed**
1 to boil or bubble. 2 to be very angry or excited, as in *She seethed with anger.*

segment *noun* **segments**
a part that is cut off or can be separated from the rest of something, as in *a segment of an orange.*
segmented *adjective*

segregate *verb* **segregates, segregating, segregated** (*say* seg-ruh-gayt)
to separate people of different races, religions, etc.
segregation *noun*

seismograph *noun* **seismographs**
a device for detecting the shock-waves of earthquakes.

seize *verb* **seizes, seizing, seized** (*say* seez)
to take hold of someone or something suddenly or eagerly.
seize up, to become jammed or stuck.
seizure *noun*

seldom *adverb*
not often, as in *I seldom cry.*

select *verb* **selects, selecting, selected**
to choose a person or thing.
selection *noun*, **selective** *adjective*, **selector** *noun*

select *adjective*
small and carefully chosen; exclusive, as in *a select group of friends.*

self *noun* **selves**
a person as an individual; a person's particular nature, interests, etc., as in *She is her old self again.*

self-centred *adjective*
selfish; thinking about yourself too much.

self-confidence *noun*
confidence in what you can do.
self-confident *adjective*

self-conscious

self-conscious *adjective*
embarrassed or shy because you are wondering what other people are thinking of you.
self-consciously *adverb*, **self-consciousness** *noun*

self-contained *adjective*
1 having all the things that a home needs, as in *a self-contained granny flat*.   2 not needing the company of other people, as in *She is very self-contained*.

self-control *noun*
the ability to control your own behaviour or feelings.
self-controlled *adjective*

self-defence *noun*
1 a way of fighting back if you are attacked, as in *Karate is a kind of self-defence*.   2 the act of defending yourself against attack, as in *She stabbed the man in self-defence*.

self-employed *adjective*
working independently and not for an employer.

selfish *adjective*
only interested in yourself and what you want, as in *The selfish boy ate all the sweets*.
selfishly *adverb*, **selfishness** *noun*

selfless *adjective*
not selfish, as in *He devoted years of selfless work to helping the elderly*.

self-raising *adjective*
to do with flour that makes cakes, etc. rise as they are cooking.

self-respect *noun*
the feeling that you are behaving, thinking, etc. in the proper way.

self-righteous *adjective*
convinced that you are better than other people; thinking too much of your own goodness.

self-service *adjective*
where customers serve themselves with goods and pay a cashier for what they have taken, as in *a self-service garage*.

self-sufficient *adjective*
providing for all your own needs without help from others.
self-sufficiency *noun*

sell *verb* **sells, selling, sold**
to give goods or property in exchange for money, as in *I sold my bike yesterday*.
sell out, to sell all your stock of something; (*colloquial*) to be disloyal to something you believed in, as in *There are no more pineapples*

—*the shop has sold out. He sold out his principles when he accepted a bribe.*

semaphore *noun*
a system of signalling with your arms, usually holding flags.

semen *noun* (*say* **see**-muhn)
white liquid produced by males, containing the male sex cells.

semibreve *noun* **semibreves**
(*say* **sem**-ee-breev)
the longest musical note normally used, written ○ and equal to four crotchets.

semicircle *noun* **semicircles**
half a circle.
semicircular *adjective*

semicolon *noun* **semicolons**
a punctuation mark (;), marking a more definite break than a comma.

semi-detached *adjective*
joined to the side of one other house; a duplex, as in *a semi-detached house*.

semi-final *noun* **semi-finals**
a match played to decide who will take part in the final.
semi-finalist *noun*

semitone *noun* **semitones**
half a tone in music.

semi-trailer *noun* **semi-trailers**
a truck with a cabin and engine at the front pulling a long trailer with wheels at the back.

Senate *noun* (*say* **sen**-uht)
1 the Upper House of the Federal Parliament.   2 the most important council in Ancient Rome.
senator *noun*

send *verb* **sends, sending, sent**
to make a person or thing go somewhere.
send for, to ask for someone or something to come to you.
send someone mad, to make someone become mad.
send up, (*colloquial*) to make fun of.

senile *adjective* (*say* **see**-nuyl *or* se-**nuyl**)
mentally or physically weak because of old age.

senior *adjective*
1 older.   2 more important, as in *a senior officer in the navy*.
senior citizen, a person who is above the age when people usually retire.
seniority *noun*

senior *noun* **seniors**
someone who is older or more important than you are.

sensation *noun* **sensations**
  1 a feeling, as in *a sensation of warmth*. 2 a very exciting event; the excitement caused by it, as in *The news caused a great sensation*.
  sensational *adjective*, **sensationally** *adverb*

sense *noun* **senses**
  1 the ability to see, hear, smell, touch, or taste. 2 the ability to feel or appreciate something; awareness, as in *a sense of humour*. 3 the power to think, make wise decisions, etc., as in *He hasn't got the sense to come in out of the rain*. 4 meaning, as in *'Bore' has several senses*.
  make sense, to have a meaning; to be reasonable.
  senses, sanity, as in *He is out of his senses*.

sense *verb* **senses, sensing, sensed**
  1 to feel; to be vaguely aware of something, as in *He sensed the warmth of the sun. I sensed that she did not like me*. 2 to detect something, as in *This device senses radioactivity*.
  sensor *noun*

senseless *adjective*
  1 stupid; not sensible. 2 unconscious.

sensible *adjective*
  1 wise; having or showing common sense. 2 practical, not just fashionable, as in *sensible shoes*.
  sensibly *adverb*

sensitive *adjective*
  1 easily hurt or affected by the sun, chemicals, etc., as in *sensitive skin*. 2 easily offended, as in *She is very sensitive about her height*. 3 affected by light, as in *sensitive photographic paper*.
  sensitively *adverb*, **sensitivity** *noun*, **sensitise** *verb*

sensual *adjective*
  to do with feelings or senses, as in *Touching velvet is a sensual experience*.

sent past tense and past participle of **send**.

sentence *noun* **sentences**
  1 a group of words that belong together, starting with a capital letter and ending with a full stop, a question mark, or an exclamation mark. 2 the punishment given to a criminal in a lawcourt.

sentence *verb* **sentences, sentencing, sentenced**
  to give someone a sentence in a lawcourt, as in *The judge sentenced him to a year in prison*.

sentiment *noun* **sentiments**
  1 a feeling; an emotion. 2 sentimental behaviour, as in *The film was full of sentiment*.

sentimental *adjective*
  arousing or showing emotion, especially weak or foolish emotion, as in *That love story is too sentimental*.
  sentimentality *noun*, **sentimentally** *adverb*

sentinel *noun* **sentinels**
  a sentry.

sentry *noun* **sentries**
  a soldier guarding something.

separate *adjective* (*say* **sep-uh-ruht** *or* **sep-ruht**)
  1 not joined to anything; on its own.
  2 not together; not with other people, as in *They lead separate lives*.
  separately *adverb*

separate *verb* **separates, separating, separated** (*say* **sep-uh-rayt**)
  1 to take things or people away from others; to become separate. 2 to stop living together as a married couple.
  separable *adjective*, **separation** *noun*

September *noun*
  the ninth month of the year.

septic *adjective*
  infected with germs, as in *a septic cut*.

Usage Do not confuse **septic** with **sceptic**, which is a noun meaning someone who is not inclined to believe things.

sequel *noun* **sequels** (*say* **see-kwuhl**)
  1 a book, film, etc. that continues the story of an earlier one. 2 something that results from an earlier event.

sequence *noun* **sequences** (*say* **see-kwuhns**)
  1 a series of things. 2 the order in which things happen.

sequin *noun* **sequins** (*say* **see-kwuhn**)
  one of the tiny bright discs sewn on clothes to decorate them.

serene *adjective* **serener, serenest**
  calm; peaceful.
  serenely *adverb*, **serenity** *noun*

serf *noun* **serfs**
  a person, in feudal times, who was not allowed to leave the land on which he worked.

sergeant *noun* **sergeants** (*say* **sah-juhnt**)
  a soldier or policeman who is in charge of a few other soldiers or policemen.

serial *noun* **serials**
  a story, film, etc. that is presented in separate parts.

series *noun* **series**
  a number of things following each other or connected with each other.

serious

serious *adjective*
1 not funny; important, as in *a serious talk*. 2 thoughtful; solemn, as in *His face was serious*. 3 very bad, as in *a serious accident*.
seriously *adverb*, **seriousness** *noun*

sermon *noun* **sermons**
a talk about religion or right and wrong, especially one given by a priest, etc.

serpent *noun* **serpents**
1 a snake. 2 a sly or cunning person.

serum *noun* **sera** or **serums**
clear liquid that separates from blood when it clots and used especially in vaccines.

servant *noun* **servants**
a person whose job is to work in someone else's house.

serve *verb* **serves, serving, served**
1 to work for someone or something.
2 to sell things to people in a shop. 3 to give food to people at a meal. 4 to be suitable for some purpose. 5 (*in tennis*) to start play by hitting the ball towards your opponent.
it serves you right, you deserve it.

serve *noun* **serves**
the start of play in tennis when you hit the ball towards your opponent.

service *noun* **services**
1 the act of helping, as in *She did a good service for me.* 2 something that helps people, supplies what they want, etc., as in *There is a good bus service.* 3 a gathering to worship God; a religious ceremony, as in *a church service.* 4 providing people with goods, food, etc., as in *quick service.* 5 a public department or organisation, as in *He works in the public service as a lawyer.* 6 a set of plates, crockery, etc. for a meal, as in *a dinner service.* 7 the servicing of a vehicle, machine, etc. 8 (*in tennis*) a serve.
the services, the armed forces.

service *verb* **services, servicing, serviced**
to repair or maintain a vehicle, machine, etc.

serviette *noun* **serviettes**
a piece of cloth or paper used to keep your clothes or hands clean at a meal; a napkin.

session *noun* **sessions**
1 a time spent doing one thing, as in *Tennis lessons cost $6 a session.* 2 a meeting, especially of a lawcourt or a parliament.

set *verb* **sets, setting, set**
1 to put or place, as in *Set the vase on the table.* 2 to fix or prepare, as in *Have you set the alarm?* 3 to become solid or hard, as in

The jelly has set. 4 to go down towards the horizon, as in *The sun was setting.* 5 to start, as in *The news set me thinking.* 6 to give someone a task, problem, etc., as in *Has the teacher set your homework?*
set about, to start doing something; (*colloquial*) to attack someone.
set off, to begin a journey; to start something happening.
set out, to begin a journey; to display or declare something, as in *We set out at 7 a.m. She set out her reasons for resigning.*
set sail, to start a voyage.
set up, to place something in position; to establish something, as in *I've set up the ironing-board. We want to set up a playgroup.*

set *noun* **sets**
1 a group of people or things that belong together. 2 an apparatus for receiving radio or television programs. 3 (*in Mathematics*) a collection of things that have something in common, such as being odd numbers or letters of the alphabet. 4 one of the main sections of a tennis match.
5 the setting, stage furniture, etc. for a play, film, etc.

set-back *noun* **set-backs**
something that slows down progress, as in *The mountain climbers suffered a setback when a snowstorm hit Mount Kosciuszko.*

set square *noun* **set squares**
a triangular device for drawing parallel lines, also used to draw right angles and other angles (usually 30 degrees, 45 degrees, or 60 degrees).

settee *noun* **settees**
a sofa.

setting *noun* **settings**
1 the land, buildings, etc. around something. 2 a set of cutlery or crockery for one person.

settle *verb* **settles, settling, settled**
1 to decide or solve something, as in *That settles the problem.* 2 to make or become comfortable, calm, etc., as in *He settled down in the armchair.* 3 to go and live somewhere, as in *They settled in Darwin.*
4 to sink; to come to rest on something, as in *The dust was settling on the books.* 5 to pay a bill or debt, as in *She settled the bill.*
settlement *noun*, **settler** *noun*

set-up *noun* **set-ups**
the way that something is organised or arranged.

seven *noun* **sevens**
the number 7, one more than six.
seventh *adjective* and *noun*

seventeen *noun* **seventeens**
the number 17, one more than sixteen.
seventeenth *adjective* and *noun*

seventy *noun* **seventies**
the number 70, seven times ten.
seventieth *adjective* and *noun*

sever *verb* **severs, severing, severed**
to cut something; to break.

several *adjective*
more than two but not a lot.

severe *adjective* **severer, severest**
1 strict; not gentle or kind, as in *Their teacher was severe.* 2 very bad; violent, as in *a severe cold.*
severely *adverb*, **severity** *noun*

sew *verb* **sews, sewing, sewed,** *past participle* **sewn** or **sewed** (*say* so)
1 to use a needle and cotton to join pieces of cloth, etc. together. 2 to work with a needle and thread.

sewage *noun* (*say* soo-ij)
waste matter carried away in drains.

sewer *noun* **sewers** (*say* soo-uh)
a drain that carries waste matter away.

sewerage *noun*
the drainage system that carries sewage.

sewing-machine *noun* **sewing-machines**
a machine for sewing things.

sex *noun* **sexes**
1 one of the two groups, male or female, that people and animals belong to. 2 the instinct that causes members of the two sexes to be attracted to one another. 3 sexual intercourse.

sexism *noun*
unfair or offensive treatment of people of a particular sex, especially women.
sexist *noun* and *adjective*

sextet *noun* **sextets**
1 a group of six musicians. 2 a piece of music for six musicians.

sexual *adjective*
to do with sex or the sexes; to do with activities connected with sexual intercourse.
sexual intercourse, the coming together of two people for pleasure, to make a baby, or for both these reasons.
sexuality *noun*, **sexually** *adverb*

sexy *adjective* **sexier, sexiest**
1 (*colloquial*) attractive to people of the opposite sex. 2 to do with sex, as in *a sexy film.*

shabby *adjective* **shabbier, shabbiest**
1 very old and worn, as in *shabby clothes.*
2 mean; unfair, as in *a shabby trick.*
shabbily *adverb*, **shabbiness** *noun*

shack *noun* **shacks**
a roughly-built hut or cabin; a small holiday house.

shade *noun* **shades**
1 an area sheltered from bright light. 2 a device that decreases or shuts out bright light. 3 a colour; how light or dark a colour is. 4 a slight difference, as in *This word has several shades of meaning.*

shade *verb* **shades, shading, shaded**
1 to shelter something from bright light. 2 to make part of a drawing darker than the rest.

shadow *noun* **shadows**
1 the dark shape that falls on a surface when something is between it and the light. 2 an area of shade.
shadowy *adjective*

shadow *verb* **shadows, shadowing, shadowed**
1 to cast a shadow on something. 2 to follow someone secretly.

shady *adjective* **shadier, shadiest**
1 able to give shade, as in *a shady tree.*
2 situated in the shade, as in *a shady spot.* 3 not completely honest, as in *a shady deal.*

shaft *noun* **shafts**
1 a thin pole or rod, as in *the shaft of an arrow.* 2 a deep, narrow hole; a vertical space, as in *a mine shaft.* 3 a ray of light.

shaggy *adjective* **shaggier, shaggiest**
1 having long, untidy hair. 2 untidy, as in *The swagman had a shaggy appearance.*
shaggy-dog story, a very long and usually boring story or joke.

shake *verb* **shakes, shaking, shook, shaken**
1 to move quickly up and down or from side to side, as in *Have you shaken the bottle?* 2 to shock or upset, as in *The news shook her.* 3 to tremble, as in *His voice was shaking.*
shake hands, to clasp someone's hand, usually his or her right hand, when you meet or part or as a sign that you agree.

shake *noun* **shakes**
1 the action of shaking. 2 (*in New Zealand*) an earthquake.
no great shakes, ordinary; of no particular value.

shaky *adjective* **shakier, shakiest**
1 likely to fall down. 2 shaking, as in *a shaky old man.*
shakily *adverb*, **shakiness** *noun*

shall

shall *verb* past tense **should**
used with other verbs to refer to the future, as in *We shall arrive tomorrow. We told them we should arrive the next day.*

shallot *noun* **shallots**
an onion-like plant with a small bulb, used to flavour food.

shallow *adjective* **shallower, shallowest**
not deep, as in *shallow water.*

sham *noun* **shams**
something that is not genuine; someone who is not what he or she pretends to be.

shamble *verb* **shambles, shambling, shambled**
to walk or run in a lazy or awkward way.

shambles *noun*
(*colloquial*) a mess, muddle.

shame *noun*
1 a feeling of great sorrow or guilt because you have done wrong. **2** something that you regret, as in *He thought it a shame that he missed winning first prize.*
shameful *adjective*, **shamefully** *adverb*, **shameless** *adjective*, **shamelessly** *adverb*

shampoo *noun* **shampoos**
liquid soap for washing hair.

shandy *noun* **shandies**
a mixture of beer with lemonade or some other soft drink.

shan't short for *shall not.*

shanty *noun* **shanties**
1 a sailor's traditional song. **2** a roughly-built hut.
shanty town, a group of shanties, usually outside a large town, where poor people live.

shape *noun* **shapes**
1 the outline of something; the way that something looks, as in *Books are rectangular in shape.* **2** the proper form or condition of something, as in *Get your essay into shape. Dry the pullover flat so that it does not go out of shape.*
shapeless *adjective*

shape *verb* **shapes, shaping, shaped**
to give a particular shape to something.

shapely *adjective* **shapelier, shapeliest**
with an attractive shape.

share *noun* **shares**
1 one of the parts into which something is divided between several people or things.
2 part of a company's money, lent by someone who is given a small part of the profits in return.

share *verb* **shares, sharing, shared**
1 to divide something between several people or things, as in *She shared out the toffees.* **2** to use something that someone else is also using, as in *May I share your book? She shared her room with me.* **3** to tell someone something, as in *I wanted to share the news with you.*

shark *noun* **sharks**
a large, fierce, marine fish with sharp teeth and a prominent dorsal fin.

sharp *adjective* **sharper, sharpest**
1 with an edge or point that can cut or make holes, as in *a sharp knife.* **2** quick to learn or notice things, as in *sharp eyes.*
3 sudden; severe, as in *a sharp bend in the road.* **4** slightly sour, as in *This stewed apple tastes sharp.* **5** clearly defined, as in *a good sharp picture on TV.* **6** above the proper musical pitch.
sharply *adverb*, **sharpness** *noun*

sharp *adverb*
1 sharply, as in *Turn sharp right.*
2 punctually; exactly, as in *at six o'clock sharp.*

sharp *noun* **sharps**
the note that is a semitone above a particular musical note; the sign (♯) that indicates this.

sharpen *verb* **sharpens, sharpening, sharpened**
to give something a good cutting edge or a fine point, as in *She sharpened her pencil.*
sharpener *noun*

shatter *verb* **shatters, shattering, shattered**
1 to break suddenly into tiny pieces. **2** to destroy, as in *Our hopes were shattered.* **3** to make someone very weak or upset, as in *We were shattered by the news.*

shave *verb* **shaves, shaving, shaved**
1 to cut hair from the surface of your skin with a razor. **2** to cut or scrape a thin slice off something, as in *The door needed shaving to make it fit the opening.*
shaver *noun*

shave *noun* **shaves**
the act of cutting hair from the surface of your skin.
close shave, (*colloquial*) a narrow escape.

shavings *plural noun*
thin strips shaved off a piece of wood.

shawl *noun* **shawls**
a piece of cloth or knitted material worn around your shoulders or head, or wrapped around a baby.

sherbet

she *pronoun*
the female person or animal being talked about.

sheaf *noun* **sheaves**
a bundle of things laid lengthways together and usually tied, as in *a sheaf of wheat; a sheaf of flowers*.

shear *verb* **shears, shearing, sheared, shorn** or **sheared**
1 to cut the wool off a sheep, etc. 2 to cut with scissors or shears.
shear off, to break off.
shearer *noun*

Usage Do not confuse **shear** with **sheer**, which is an adjective meaning complete, vertical, or very thin.

shears *plural noun*
a tool like a very large pair of scissors for trimming bushes, shearing sheep, etc.

sheath *noun* **sheaths**
1 a cover for the blade of a sword or dagger. 2 a cover that fits something closely.

sheathe *verb* **sheathes, sheathing, sheathed**
1 to put a sword into its sheath. 2 to put a protective covering on something.

shed *noun* **sheds**
a simply-made building used for storing things, sheltering animals, etc.; a hut.

shed *verb* **sheds, shedding, shed**
to let something fall or flow, as in *The caterpillar has shed its skin. We shed tears*.

she'd short for *she had, she should*, or *she would*.

sheen *noun*
a shine on a surface.

sheep *noun* **sheep**
a grass-eating animal kept by farmers for its wool and meat.

sheep-dog *noun* **sheep-dogs**
a dog trained to guard and round up sheep.

sheepish *adjective*
shy; embarrassed.
sheepishly *adverb*

sheer *adjective* **sheerer, sheerest**
1 complete; thorough, as in *sheer stupidity*.
2 perpendicular; vertical, as in *a sheer drop*.
3 very thin; transparent, as in *sheer pantihose*.

Usage Do not confuse **sheer** with **shear**, which is a verb meaning to cut wool off a sheep.

sheet *noun* **sheets**
1 a large piece of lightweight cloth put on a bed. 2 a whole flat piece of paper, glass, or metal. 3 a wide area of water, snow, flame, etc.

sheikh *noun* **sheikhs**
the leader of an Arab tribe or village.

shelf *noun* **shelves**
1 a board fixed to a wall or fitted in a piece of furniture so that books, ornaments, etc. may be put on it. 2 a flat, level surface that sticks out from a cliff, etc.
shelf-life, the time for which a stored item remains usable.

shell *noun* **shells**
1 the hard cover around or over a nut, egg, snail, tortoise, etc. 2 a long, round metal case containing explosives, shot from a large gun. 3 the walls or framework of a building, ship, etc.

shell *verb* **shells, shelling, shelled**
1 to take something out of its shell. 2 to fire explosive shells at a building, ship, town, etc.
shell out, (*colloquial*) to pay money for something.

she'll short for *she will*.

shellfish *noun* **shellfish**
a marine animal that has a hard cover over its body, as in *Oysters, prawns, and scallops are examples of shellfish*.

shelter *noun* **shelters**
1 a place that protects people from rain, wind, danger, etc. 2 being protected, as in *We found shelter from the rain*.

shelter *verb* **shelters, sheltering, sheltered**
1 to protect or cover, as in *The hill shelters the house from the wind*. 2 to find a shelter, as in *They sheltered under the trees*.

shelve *verb* **shelves, shelving, shelved**
1 to put something on a shelf or shelves.
2 to reject or postpone a plan, etc. 3 to slope, as in *The ocean floor shelves away from the beach*.

shepherd *noun* **shepherds**
someone whose job is to look after sheep.

shepherd *verb* **shepherds, shepherding, shepherded**
1 to guide and guard, as in *The father shepherded his young children through the large crowd*. 2 (*in Australian Rules Football*) to guard a team-mate who has the ball by blocking opponents, etc.

sherbet *noun* **sherbets**
a fizzy sweet powder or drink.

a
b
c
d
e
f
g
h
i
j
k
l
m
n
o
p
q
r
s
t
u
v
w
x
y
z

sheriff

sheriff *noun* **sheriffs**
an officer who has a number of duties in the Supreme Court.

sherry *noun* **sherries**
a kind of strong sweet or dry wine.

she's short for *she is* and (before a verb in the past tense) *she has*, as in *She's gone to the pictures.*

shield *noun* **shields**
1 a large piece of metal, wood, etc. used to protect the body, as in *Soldiers used to hold shields in front of them when they were fighting.* 2 a protection, as in *The car was fitted with a sun shield.*

shield *verb* **shields, shielding, shielded**
to protect, as in *I was shielded from the wind.*

shift *verb* **shifts, shifting, shifted**
to move or change.

shift *noun* **shifts**
1 a change of position, condition, etc. 2 a group of workers who start work as another group finishes; the time when they work, as in *the night shift.* 3 a loose-fitting dress.

shifty *adjective* **shiftier, shiftiest**
deceitful, as in *He had a shifty look after he had stolen the money.*

shilling *noun* **shillings**
a silver coin used before decimal currency was introduced and equal to about 10 cents.

shimmer *verb* **shimmers, shimmering, shimmered**
to shine with a quivering light, as in *The sea shimmered in the sunlight.*

shin *noun* **shins**
the front of your leg between your knee and your ankle.

shine *verb* **shines, shining, shone** or, in 'polish' sense, **shined**
1 to give out or reflect light; to be bright. 2 to polish, as in *Have you shined your shoes?* 3 to be excellent, as in *He does not shine in maths.*

shine *noun*
1 brightness, as in *the shine of polished brass.* 2 the act of polishing, as in *Give your shoes a good shine.*
shiny *adjective*

shingle *noun* **shingles**
a thin rectangular piece of wood, slate, etc. used on roofs.

ship *noun* **ships**
a large boat, especially one that goes to sea.

ship *verb* **ships, shipping, shipped**
to send something on a ship.

shipment *noun* **shipments**
an amount of goods shipped, as in *The department store received a large shipment of shoes for the sale.*

shipwreck *noun* **shipwrecks**
1 the wrecking of a ship. 2 the remains of a wrecked ship.
shipwrecked *adjective*

shiralee *noun* **shiralees**
a swag.

shire *noun* **shires**
a local government district in the country.

shirk *verb* **shirks, shirking, shirked**
to avoid doing something that you ought to do.

shirt *noun* **shirts**
a garment worn on the top half of your body, as in *Most shirts have sleeves, a collar, and buttons down the front.*

shiver *verb* **shivers, shivering, shivered**
to tremble with cold or fear.
shivery *adjective*

shoal *noun* **shoals**
1 a large number of fish swimming together. 2 a sandbank visible at low tide.

shock *noun* **shocks**
1 a sudden unpleasant surprise. 2 a violent knock or jolt. 3 an effect caused by electric current passing through your body.

shock *verb* **shocks, shocking, shocked**
1 to give someone a shock. 2 to fill someone with disgust or outrage.

shoddy *adjective* **shoddier, shoddiest**
having poor quality, as in *a shoddy piece of work.*

shoe *noun* **shoes**
a strong covering of leather, canvas, etc. for the foot.
in someone's shoes, in someone's place, as in *I'm glad I'm not in her shoes.*
on a shoestring, with only a small amount of money.
shoelace *noun*

shone past tense and past participle of **shine** *verb.*

shook past tense of **shake** *verb.*

shoot *verb* **shoots, shooting, shot**
1 to fire a gun, rocket, etc. 2 to hurt or kill someone or an animal by using a gun. 3 to move or send something very quickly,

as in *The car shot past.* **4** to kick or hit a ball at a goal. **5** to film or photograph something, as in *The film was shot in Tasmania.* **6** to send out new growth, as in *The healthy shrub shot up in spring.*
shooting star, a meteor.

shoot *noun* **shoots**
a young branch or growth of a plant.

shop *noun* **shops**
a building where people buy things; a store.

shop *verb* **shops, shopping, shopped**
to go and buy things at shops.
shopper *noun*

shoplifter *noun* **shoplifters**
someone who steals from shops.
shoplifting *noun*

shopping *noun*
1 buying goods at shops, as in *I like shopping.* **2** what someone has bought, as in *Will you carry my shopping, please?*
shopping centre, a group of different shops in one place, often in the same large building.

shore *noun* **shores**
1 the seashore. **2** the land along the edge of a lake, etc.

shorn past tense of **shear.**

short *adjective* **shorter, shortest**
1 not long; occupying a small distance or time, as in *a short walk.* **2** not tall, as in *a short person.* **3** not sufficient; scarce, as in *Water is short.* **4** bad-tempered, as in *He was rather short with me.*
short circuit, a fault in an electrical circuit when current flows along a shorter route than the normal one.
short cut, a route or method that is quicker than the usual one.
short for, a shorter form of something, as in *Vicki is short for Victoria.*
short sight, not being able to see things clearly unless they are close.
short wave, a radio wave with a wavelength between 10 and 100 metres.
shortish *adjective,* **shortness** *noun*

short *adverb*
suddenly, as in *She stopped short.*

shortage *noun* **shortages**
the situation when something is scarce or insufficient.

shortbread *noun*
a rich, sweet kind of biscuit.

shortcoming *noun* **shortcomings**
a fault or failure, as in *He has many shortcomings.*

shorten *verb* **shortens, shortening, shortened**
to make something shorter; to become shorter.

shorthand *noun*
a set of special signs for writing words down as quickly as people say them.

shortly *adverb*
1 soon. **2** briefly.

shorts *plural noun*
trousers reaching to the knees or higher.

short-sighted *adjective*
unable to see distant things clearly.

shot *noun* **shots**
1 the firing of a gun. **2** something fired from a gun. **3** lead pellets fired from small guns. **4** a person judged by his or her skill in shooting, as in *He is a good shot.* **5** a heavy metal ball thrown in the shot-put. **6** a stroke in tennis, cricket, etc. **7** a photograph or filmed sequence. **8** an attempt, as in *Have a shot at this crossword.*

shot past tense and past participle of **shoot** *verb.*

shotgun *noun* **shotguns**
a gun for firing many small lead pellets over a short distance.

shot-put *noun*
an athletic contest in which a heavy metal ball is thrown.

should *verb*
1 past tense of **shall.** **2** to have a duty or wish to; ought to, as in *You should come. I should like to come.* **3** used in speaking of something that will happen if something else happens first, as in *You should win as long as you get a good start.*

shoulder *noun* **shoulders**
the part of your body between your neck and your arm.
shoulder-blade, one of the two large flat bones near the top of your back.

shoulder *verb* **shoulders, shouldering, shouldered**
1 to put or rest something on your shoulder or shoulders, as in *The window-cleaner shouldered his ladder and walked over to his truck.* **2** to accept responsibility or blame.

shout *verb* **shouts, shouting, shouted**
1 to speak or call very loudly. **2** to buy or give as a treat.

shout *noun* **shouts**
1 a loud cry or call. **2** something bought or given as a treat.

a
b
c
d
e
f
g
h
i
j
k
l
m
n
o
p
q
r
s
t
u
v
w
x
y
z

shove

shove *verb* **shoves, shoving, shoved** (*say* shuv)
to push hard.

shovel *noun* **shovels** (*say* shuv-uhl)
a curved spade for lifting and moving
earth, sand, etc.

shovel *verb* **shovels, shovelling, shovelled**
to move or clear something with a shovel.

show *verb* **shows, showing, showed, shown**
1 to let something be seen, as in *She showed
me her new bike.* 2 to make something
clear to someone, as in *He has shown me how
to do it.* 3 to guide or lead someone, as in
Show him in. 4 to be visible, as in *That
scratch won't show.*
show off, to try to impress people.

show *noun* **shows**
1 a display or exhibition, as in *a flower
show.* 2 an entertainment. 3 (*colloquial*)
something that happens or is done, as in
Good show! 4 an annual exhibition of
animals, produce, etc. with entertainment,
etc. in a city or town, as in *the Melbourne
Show.*
show bag, a bag of sample goods available
at annual shows, etc; a sample bag.

shower *noun* **showers**
1 a brief fall of rain. 2 a lot of small
things coming or falling like rain, as in *a
shower of stones.* 3 a cubicle in which a
person stands under a spray of water to
wash; the act of washing in a shower.
showery *adjective*

shower *verb* **showers, showering, showered**
1 to fall like rain; to send a lot of
something, as in *His father showered money
on him.* 2 to wash under a shower.

showjumping *noun*
a competition in which riders make horses
jump over fences and other obstacles.
showjumper *noun*

showroom *noun* **showrooms**
a large room where goods, especially cars,
furniture, or electrical equipment, are
displayed for people to look at and to buy.

showy *adjective* **showier, showiest**
likely to attract attention; bright or highly
decorated.
showily *adverb*, **showiness** *noun*

shrank past tense of **shrink.**

shrapnel *noun*
pieces of metal scattered from an exploding
shell.

shred *noun* **shreds**
a tiny strip or piece torn or cut off
something.

shred *verb* **shreds, shredding, shredded**
to tear or cut something into shreds.
shredder *noun*

shrew *noun* **shrews**
1 a small animal rather like a mouse. 2 a
bad-tempered woman.

shrewd *adjective* **shrewder, shrewdest**
having common sense and good judgment.
shrewdly *adverb*, **shrewdness** *noun*

shriek *noun* **shrieks**
a shrill scream.

shrill *adjective* **shriller, shrillest**
sounding very high, strong, and loud, as in
a shrill, angry voice.
shrillness *noun*, **shrilly** *adverb*

shrimp *noun* **shrimps**
a small prawn.

shrine *noun* **shrines**
a sacred place, as in *the Melbourne Shrine of
Remembrance.*

shrink *verb* **shrinks, shrinking, shrank, shrunk**
1 to make or become smaller, as in *This
dress has shrunk.* 2 to move back or avoid
something because of fear, embarrassment,
etc., as in *He shrank from meeting strangers.*
shrinkage *noun*

shrivel *verb* **shrivels, shrivelling, shrivelled**
to make something wrinkled and dry; to
become wrinkled and dry.

shroud *noun* **shrouds**
1 a sheet in which a corpse is wrapped.
2 one of the ropes that support a ship's
mast.

shroud *verb* **shrouds, shrouding, shrouded**
1 to wrap a corpse in a sheet. 2 to cover
or conceal something, as in *The countryside
was shrouded in mist.*

shrub *noun* **shrubs**
a small tree-like plant.

shrubbery *noun* **shrubberies**
an area full of shrubs.

shrug *verb* **shrugs, shrugging, shrugged**
to raise your shoulders slightly as a sign
that you do not care, do not know, etc.

shrunk past participle of **shrink.**

shudder *verb* **shudders, shuddering,
shuddered**
to shake because you are cold or
frightened.

shuffle *verb* **shuffles, shuffling, shuffled**
1 to drag your feet along the ground as
you walk. 2 to mix up playing-cards
before you deal them.

shunt *verb* **shunts, shunting, shunted**
to move a railway train from one place to another.

shut *verb* **shuts, shutting, shut**
1 to move a door, lid, cover, etc. in order to block up an opening; to close something, as in *She shut the door and drove off.* 2 to become closed, as in *The door shut suddenly.*
shut down, to stop operating.
shut up, to shut securely; (*colloquial*) to stop talking.

shutter *noun* **shutters**
1 a cover or screen that can be closed over a window. 2 the device in a camera that opens and closes to let light fall on the film.

shuttle *noun* **shuttles**
1 the part of a loom that is sent to and fro, carrying a thread. 2 a vehicle that goes backwards and forwards between two places, as in *Take the shuttle between the airport terminals.* 3 a space shuttle.

shuttlecock *noun* **shuttlecocks**
1 a small rounded piece of cork or plastic with a ring of feathers fixed to it, used in the game of badminton. 2 the game played with a shuttlecock.

shy *adjective* **shyer, shyest**
1 afraid to meet or talk to other people.
2 timid, as in *Deer are often shy.*
shyly *adverb,* **shyness** *noun*

Siamese *adjective*
to do with Siam (now called Thailand).
Siamese cat, a cat with blue eyes and short fur.
Siamese twins, twins whose bodies are joined together.

sick *adjective* **sicker, sickest**
1 ill. 2 vomiting or likely to vomit, as in *I feel sick.*
sick of, tired of; fed up with.
sickness *noun*

sicken *verb* **sickens, sickening, sickened**
1 to start feeling ill. 2 to disgust someone; to annoy someone very much.

sickie *noun* **sickies**
(*colloquial*) a day taken off work for which you are paid, usually when you are not really ill.

sickly *adjective* **sicklier, sickliest**
1 unhealthy; looking weak or pale, as in *a sickly child.* 2 able to make you feel sick, as in *a sickly smell.*

side *noun* **sides**
1 a flat surface which bounds an object, as in *A cube has six sides.* 2 a part or area, as in *shiny side of the gift wrapping; left side of the road.* 3 the outer part of something that is not the front, back, top or bottom, as in *side of the house; side of the mountain.* 4 a group of people playing, arguing, or fighting against another group, as in *She is on my side.* 5 the right or left part of a person or animal, as in *She stood at my side. I have a pain in my side.*

sideboard *noun* **sideboards**
a long, heavy piece of furniture with drawers and cupboards, and a flat top where things can be put.

sideshow *noun* **sideshows**
an entertainment forming part of a large show.

sidestep *verb* **sidesteps, sidestepping, sidestepped**
1 to avoid by stepping sideways.
2 to avoid, as in *He sidestepped the question of debt.*

sideways *adverb* and *adjective*
1 to or from the side, as in *Crabs walk sideways.* 2 with one side facing forward, as in *We sat sideways in the bus.*

siege *noun* **sieges** (*say* seej)
1 the action of surrounding a place in order to attack it or to prevent people from leaving it. 2 being surrounded and attacked, as in *The castle was under siege.*

sieve *noun* **sieves** (*say* siv)
a device made of metal or plastic mesh, or a metal or plastic sheet with many holes in it, used to separate lumps from liquid, etc.

sift *verb* **sifts, sifting, sifted**
1 to put something through a sieve.
2 to examine or select facts, evidence, etc.

sigh *noun* **sighs**
a sound made by breathing out heavily when you are sad, tired, relieved, etc.

sigh *verb* **sighs, sighing, sighed**
to make a sigh.

sight *noun* **sights**
1 the ability to see, as in *She is losing her sight.* 2 something that you see, as in *I laughed at the sight of him in that hat.* 3 something worth seeing, as in *See the sights of Sydney.* 4 a device that helps you to aim a gun.
at sight or **on sight,** as soon as you see someone or something.

sight *verb* **sights, sighting, sighted**
to see or observe something.

sightseer

sightseer *noun* **sightseers**
someone who goes round looking at interesting places; a tourist.
sightseeing *noun*

sign *noun* **signs**
1 a board, notice, etc. that tells or shows people something, as in *a road sign*.
2 something that conveys a meaning, significance, etc., as in *There are signs of rust*. 3 a gesture or signal, as in *She made a sign to them to be quiet*. 4 a mark, symbol, etc. which represents something, as in *a dollar sign; A cross is a sign of Christ*.
sign language, a set of hand movements used for communicating with deaf people.

sign *verb* **signs, signing, signed**
1 to write your signature on something.
2 to make a sign or signal.
sign up, to employ or enlist a person; to become employed, as in *The Canberra Raiders signed up a new recruit. He signed up with the army*.

signal *noun* **signals**
a device, gesture, sound, etc. that tells people something, as in *a railway signal*.

signal *verb* **signals, signalling, signalled**
to wave, shout, etc. to someone to attract his or her attention or to tell him or her what to do.
signaller *noun*

signalman *noun* **signalmen**
a person who controls railway signals.

signature *noun* **signatures**
your name written by yourself.
signature tune, a special tune used to introduce a particular program, performer, etc.

significance *noun*
1 importance, as in *They attach a lot of significance to legends*. 2 what something means or is understood to mean, as in *What is the significance of her remark?*
significant *adjective*, **significantly** *adverb*

signify *verb* **signifies, signifying, signified**
to mean something, as in *The bell signified the end of the school day*.

signpost *noun* **signposts**
a sign at a road junction showing the names and distances of the places that are down each road.

silence *noun* **silences**
absence of sound or talk; lack of noise.

silence *verb* **silences, silencing, silenced**
to make a person or thing silent.

silent *adjective*
without any sound; not talking.
silently *adverb*

silhouette *noun* **silhouettes** (*say* sil-oo-**et** *or* sil-uh-**wet**)
a dark outline seen against a light background.

silicon *noun*
an element found in many rocks and used in the making of glass, etc.
silicon chip, a tiny electronic device made of a small piece of silicon with many very small electric circuits on it.

silk *noun*
1 fine thread made by silkworms.
2 smooth, shiny cloth made from this thread.
silken *adjective*, **silky** *adjective*

silkworm *noun* **silkworms**
a kind of caterpillar that covers itself with a case of fine threads when it is ready to turn into a moth.

sill *noun* **sills**
a ledge underneath a window or door.

silly *adjective* **sillier, silliest**
stupid or foolish.
silliness *noun*

silver *noun*
1 a precious shiny white metal. 2 things like cutlery, coins and jewellery made of this metal or a metal that looks like it. 3 the colour of silver.
silver birch, a birch tree with silvery bark.
silverfish, a small, silvery, wingless insect which destroys clothes, books, etc.
silver medal, a medal made of silver, awarded as the second prize.
silver wedding, the 25th anniversary of a wedding.
silvery *adjective*

similar *adjective*
1 being the same kind, as in *The two cars are exactly similar*. 2 nearly the same as another person or thing, as in *Your dress is similar to mine, but its collar is different*.
similarity *noun*, **similarly** *adverb*

simile *noun* **similes** (*say* **sim**-uh-lee)
saying that one thing is like another, as in *'He is as brave as a lion' is a simile*.

simmer *verb* **simmers, simmering, simmered**
to boil very gently.
simmer down, to calm down.

simple *adjective* **simpler, simplest**
1 easy, as in *a simple question*. 2 not complicated, as in *a simple idea*. 3 plain, as

in *a simple dress.* **4** stupid, as in *I'm not so simple.* **5** having only one part, as in *a simple sentence.*
simplicity *noun*

simplify *verb* **simplifies, simplifying, simplified**
to make something simple or easy to understand.
simplification *noun*

simplistic *adjective*
too simple to be accurate.

simply *adverb*
1 in a simple way, as in *She dresses simply.*
2 completely, as in *She looks simply lovely.*
3 only; merely, as in *It is simply a question of money.*

simulate *verb* **simulates, simulating, simulated**
1 to reproduce the conditions for something, as in *a simulated flight.* **2** to pretend.
simulation *noun*, **simulator** *noun*

simulcast *noun* **simulcasts**
a program on television and radio at the same time.

simultaneous *adjective*
(*say* sim-uhl-**tay**-nee-uhs)
happening at the same time, as in *At midnight on New Year's Eve there are simultaneous celebrations all over the country.*
simultaneously *adverb*

sin *noun* **sins**
the breaking of a religious or moral law; a very bad action.

sin *verb* **sins, sinning, sinned**
to break a religious or moral law; to do a very bad deed.
sinner *noun*

sin-bin *noun* **sin-bins**
a place where a player in hockey, football, etc. is sent for a set time because a rule has been broken.

since *conjunction*
1 from the time when, as in *Where have you been since I last saw you?* **2** as; because, as in *Since you have been naughty, you must stay indoors.*

since *preposition*
from the time when, as in *I have been here since Christmas.*

since *adverb*
from that time; before now, as in *He has not been seen since.*

sincere *adjective* **sincerer, sincerest**
truly felt or meant; genuine, as in *sincere good wishes.*
sincerely *adverb*, **sincerity** *noun*

sine *noun* **sines**
in a right-angled triangle, a number linked with one of the acute angles, equal to the length of the side opposite the angle divided by the length of the longest side (the *hypotenuse*).

sinew *noun* **sinews**
strong tissue that joins a muscle to a bone.

sinful *adjective*
wicked; very bad.
sinfully *adverb*, **sinfulness** *noun*

sing *verb* **sings, singing, sang, sung**
1 to make music with your voice. **2** to make a humming or whistling sound, as in *A bullet went singing past his head.*
singer *noun*

singe *verb* **singes, singeing, singed** (*say* sinj)
to burn something slightly; to burn the edge of something.

single *adjective*
1 only one; separate. **2** designed for one person, as in *a single bed.* **3** not married. **4** for the journey to a place but not back again, as in *a single ticket.*
single file, a line of people one behind the other.
singly *adverb*

single *noun* **singles**
1 a single person or thing. **2** a single ticket. **3** a record played at 45 revolutions per minute, usually with one tune on each side.
singles, a game, especially of tennis, with one player on each side.

single *verb* **singles, singling, singled**
single out, to pick out or distinguish someone or something from other people or things.

singlet *noun* **singlets**
a sleeveless vest usually worn under clothes.

singular *noun* **singulars**
the form of a word that refers to only one person or thing, as in *The singular of 'children' is 'child'.*

singular *adjective*
1 of the singular; referring to only one.
2 extraordinary, as in *a woman of singular courage.*
singularly *adverb*

sinister *adjective*
that looks or seems evil or unpleasant.

sink *noun* **sinks**
a large basin with taps where you do the washing-up.

a
b
c
d
e
f
g
h
i
j
k
l
m
n
o
p
q
r
s
t
u
v
w
x
y
z

sink

sink *verb* **sinks, sinking, sank** or **sunk, sunk**
1 to go under water, as in *The liner has sunk.* 2 to make something go under water, as in *They sank the ship.* 3 to go or fall down, as in *He sank to his knees.*
sink in, to penetrate; to become understood, as in *Let the face-cream sink in. The news was so unexpected that it only sank in gradually.*

sinus *noun* **sinuses** (*say* **suy**-nuhs)
a hollow in the bones of your skull, connected with your nose, as in *My sinuses are blocked.*

sip *verb* **sips, sipping, sipped**
to drink a very small amount at a time.

siphon *verb* **siphons, siphoning, siphoned**
to move a liquid from a container at a high level into a lower container by letting the liquid run down a U-shaped pipe, drawing more liquid after it.
siphon *noun*

sir *noun*
a word sometimes used when speaking or writing politely to a man, instead of his name, as in *Can I help you, sir?*

siren *noun* **sirens**
a device that makes a loud hooting or screaming sound, usually to warn people about something.

sister *noun* **sisters**
1 a woman or girl who has the same parents as another person. 2 a nurse who is in charge of other nurses in a hospital. 3 a nun. 4 a word used in Aboriginal English to describe an Aboriginal woman who might or might not be a relative.
sisterly *adjective*

sister-in-law *noun* **sisters-in-law**
the sister of your husband or wife.

sit *verb* **sits, sitting, sat**
1 to rest on your buttocks, as you do when you are on a chair. 2 to take up this kind of position; to put someone in this kind of position, as in *Sit down on that chair. Jane's father picked her up and sat her on his shoulders.* 3 to take an examination, test, etc., as in *We sit our end-of-year exam this afternoon.* 4 to be situated; to stay, as in *The house sits on top of a hill. The books are still sitting on my shelves—I haven't had time to read them yet.* 5 to be in a session, as in *Parliament is sitting this week.*
sitter *noun*

site *noun* **sites**
1 the place where something has been built or will be built, as in *a building site.* 2 the place where something happens or happened, as in *a camping site; the site of the Anzac landing.*

situated *adjective*
in a particular place or situation, as in *The town is situated in a valley.*

situation *noun* **situations**
1 a place or position; where something is. 2 the conditions affecting a person or thing. 3 a job; employment.

six *noun* **sixes**
the number 6, one more than five.
sixth *adjective* and *noun*

sixteen *noun* **sixteens**
the number 16, one more than fifteen.
sixteenth *adjective* and *noun*

sixty *noun* **sixties**
the number 60, six times ten.
sixtieth *adjective* and *noun*

size *noun* **sizes**
1 how big a person or thing is. 2 the measurement something is made in, as in *a size eight shoe.*

size *verb* **sizes, sizing, sized**
size up, (*colloquial*) to form an opinion or judgment about something.

sizeable *adjective*
fairly large.

sizzle *verb* **sizzles, sizzling, sizzled**
to make a crackling and hissing sound, as in *The sausages sizzled in the frying-pan.*

skate *noun* **skates**
1 a boot with a steel blade attached to the sole, used for sliding smoothly over ice. 2 a roller-skate.

skate *verb* **skates, skating, skated**
to move with skates on your feet.
skater *noun*

skateboard *noun* **skateboards**
a small board with wheels, on which you balance with both feet while it moves quickly over the ground.

skeleton *noun* **skeletons**
the framework of bones that is or was inside a person's or animal's body.
skeletal *adjective*

sketch *noun* **sketches**
1 a quick or rough drawing. 2 a rough outline.

sketch *verb* **sketches, sketching, sketched**
to make a quick or rough drawing; to draw someone or something in this way.

skew *adjective*
slanting or set askew, as in *That wall chart is skew.*

skewer *noun* **skewers**
a pointed piece of metal or wood, used to hold meat together for cooking.

ski *noun* **skis** (*say* skee)
a long piece of wood, plastic, etc. fastened to each of your feet for moving quickly over snow.
ski-lift, a set of seats or handles fixed to a moving cable, pulling skiers up to the top of a slope.

ski *verb* **skis, skiing, skied** or **ski'd** (*say* skee)
to move on skis.
skier *noun*

skid *verb* **skids, skidding, skidded**
to slide accidentally.

skilful *adjective*
having, or showing skill.
skilfully *adverb*

skill *noun* **skills**
the ability to do something very well.
skilled *adjective*

skim *verb* **skims, skimming, skimmed**
1 to move quickly over a surface. 2 to remove something from the surface of a liquid, especially to take the cream off milk.
skim milk, milk with the cream removed.

skin *noun* **skins**
1 the outer covering of a person's or animal's body. 2 the outer covering of a fruit or vegetable. 3 a thin, firm layer that has formed on the surface of a liquid.

skin *verb* **skins, skinning, skinned**
to take the skin off something.

skin-diver *noun* **skin-divers**
someone who swims under water without a diving-suit, usually with an aqualung and flippers.
skin-diving *noun*

skink *noun* **skinks**
any small, usually smooth-scaled lizard.

skinny *adjective* **skinnier, skinniest**
very thin.

skip *verb* **skips, skipping, skipped**
1 to jump or move along by hopping from one foot to the other. 2 to jump over a skipping-rope. 3 to miss out or ignore something, as in *Skip the boring details!*

skip *noun* **skips**
1 a skipping movement. 2 a large, usually open metal container used for collecting and taking away rubbish, especially waste from building work.

skipper *noun* **skippers**
the captain of a ship, team, etc.

skipping-rope *noun* **skipping-ropes**
a piece of rope, usually with a handle at each end, that is turned over your head and under your feet as you jump.

skirt *noun* **skirts**
a woman's or girl's piece of clothing that hangs down from her waist.

skirt *verb* **skirts, skirting, skirted**
to go around the edge of something.

skirting or **skirting-board** **skirtings** or **skirting-boards** *noun*
a board around the bottom of the wall of a room.

skit *noun* **skits**
a play, poem, etc. that makes fun of something by imitating it, as in *He wrote a skit on a well-known fairytale.*

skite *noun* **skites**
a person who boasts.

skittle *noun* **skittles**
a piece of wood or plastic shaped like a bottle, that people try to knock down with a ball.

skivvy *noun* **skivvies**
a close-fitting, high-necked, long-sleeved top.

skull *noun* **skulls**
the framework of bones in a person's head.

skunk *noun* **skunks**
1 a black, furry, American animal that can make an unpleasant smell. 2 (*colloquial*) a mean or horrible person.

sky *noun* **skies**
the area above our heads when we are out of doors; the space containing the sun, moon, and stars.

skylark *noun* **skylarks**
a small brown bird from the northern hemisphere, that sings as it hovers high in the air.

skylight *noun* **skylights**
a window in a roof.

skyscraper *noun* **skyscrapers**
a very tall building.

slab *noun* **slabs**
1 a thick, flat piece of something. 2 a roughly-cut plank used for building, especially in the bush.

slack *adjective* **slacker, slackest**
1 not pulled tight, as in *The rope was slack.* 2 lazy; not busy or working hard.
slackly *adverb*, **slackness** *noun*

slacken

slacken *verb* **slackens, slackening, slackened**
1 to make something slack; to become slack. 2 to make something slower; to become slower, as in *Their speed slackened*.

slacks *plural noun*
trousers.

slain past participle of **slay**.

slalom *noun* **slaloms** (*say* **slah**-luhm *or* **slay**-luhm)
a ski-race down a winding obstacle course.

slam *verb* **slams, slamming, slammed**
1 to shut something loudly. 2 to hit something violently, as in *He slammed the ball into the net*.

slander *noun*
a false spoken statement which harms a person's reputation.

Usage Do not confuse **slander** with **libel** which is a written, not spoken, false statement.

slang *noun*
a kind of colourful language not used in formal writing or speaking.
slangy *adjective*

slant *verb* **slants, slanting, slanted**
1 to slope; to lean. 2 to present news, information, etc. from a particular point of view.

slant *noun* **slants**
1 a sloping or leaning position, as in *The caravan's floor was at a slant*. 2 a way of presenting news, information, etc. from a particular point of view.

slap *verb* **slaps, slapping, slapped**
1 to give someone a slap. 2 to put something forcefully or carelessly, as in *We slapped paint on the walls*.

slap *noun* **slaps**
a hit with the palm of the hand or with something flat.

slapstick *noun*
noisy, lively comedy, with people hitting each other, falling over, etc.

slash *verb* **slashes, slashing, slashed**
1 to make large cuts in something. 2 to reduce prices, etc.

slash *noun* **slashes**
1 a large cut. 2 a sloping line (/) used to separate words or letters, especially in some computer commands.

slat *noun* **slats**
a thin strip of wood, plastic, etc.

slate *noun* **slates**
1 a kind of grey rock that is easily split into flat plates. 2 a piece of this rock used as part of a roof.
slaty *adjective*

slaughter *verb* **slaughters, slaughtering, slaughtered**
1 to kill an animal for food. 2 to kill many people or animals.
slaughter *noun*

slave *noun* **slaves**
a person who has to work for someone else without being paid.
slavery *noun*

slave *verb* **slaves, slaving, slaved**
to work very hard.

slay *verb* **slays, slaying, slew, slain**
(*old-fashioned or poetical use*) to kill.

sled or **sledge** *noun* **sleds** or **sledges**
a vehicle for travelling over snow, running on strips of metal or wood instead of wheels.

sledgehammer *noun* **sledgehammers**
a very large, heavy hammer.

sleek *adjective* **sleeker, sleekest**
smooth and shiny, as in *sleek hair*.

sleep *noun*
1 the condition in which the eyes are closed, the body is relaxed, and the mind is unconscious, as in *You need some sleep*. 2 a time when you are in this condition, as in *Have a sleep*.
sleepless *adjective*

sleep *verb* **sleeps, sleeping, slept**
1 to have a sleep. 2 to provide beds for, as in *The flat sleeps four only*.

sleeper *noun* **sleepers**
1 someone who is asleep. 2 one of the wooden or concrete beams on which a railway line rests.

sleeping-bag *noun* **sleeping-bags**
a warm padded bag for sleeping in, especially when you are camping.

sleepwalker *noun* **sleepwalkers**
someone who walks around while he or she is asleep.
sleepwalking *noun*

sleepy *adjective* **sleepier, sleepiest**
feeling like sleeping; wanting to sleep.
sleepily *adverb*, **sleepiness** *noun*

sleet *noun*
a mixture of rain and snow or hail.

sleeve *noun* **sleeves**
1 the part of a piece of clothing that covers your arm. 2 a cover for a record.
sleeveless *adjective*

sleigh *noun* **sleighs** (*say* slay)
a sledge, especially a large one pulled by horses.

slender *adjective* **slenderer, slenderest**
1 slim, thin, as in *She has a slender build.*
2 slight, small, as in *They had a slender chance of winning.*

slept past tense and past participle of **sleep** *verb.*

slew past tense of **slay.**

slice *noun* **slices**
a thin, flat piece cut off something.

slice *verb* **slices, slicing, sliced**
to cut something into thin, flat pieces.

slick *adjective* **slicker, slickest**
quick and clever or cunning.

slick *noun* **slicks**
a large patch of oil floating on water.

slide *verb* **slides, sliding, slid**
1 to move smoothly over a flat, polished, or slippery surface. 2 to move quickly or secretly, as in *The thief slid behind the curtains.*

slide *noun* **slides**
1 a sliding movement. 2 a smooth slope or a slippery surface where children can slide for fun. 3 a type of photograph that lets light through and that can be displayed on a screen by means of a projector.
4 a small glass plate on which things are examined under a microscope.

slight *adjective* **slighter, slightest**
very small; not serious or important.
slightly *adverb*

slim *adjective* **slimmer, slimmest**
1 thin and graceful. 2 small; hardly enough, as in *a slim chance.*

slim *verb* **slims, slimming, slimmed**
to try to make yourself thinner.
slimmer *noun*

slime *noun*
unpleasant, wet, slippery stuff, as in *There was slime on the pond.*
slimy *adjective*

sling *noun* **slings**
1 a piece of cloth tied around your neck to support an injured arm. 2 a device for throwing stones.

sling *verb* **slings, slinging, slung**
1 (*colloquial*) to throw something, especially violently or carelessly, as in *They slung stones at us.* 2 to hang something up; to support something so that it hangs loosely, as in *He had slung the bag round his neck.*

slink *verb* **slinks, slinking, slunk**
to move in a stealthy or guilty way, as in *He slunk off to bed.*

slip *verb* **slips, slipping, slipped**
1 to slide without meaning to; to fall over, as in *The wet glass slipped from her hand. She slipped on the banana skin.* 2 to move quickly and quietly, as in *They slipped away from the party.* 3 to forget, as in *The date slipped my mind.*
slipped disc, part of someone's spine that causes pain because it is out of place.
slip up, to make a mistake.

slip *noun* **slips**
1 an accidental slide or fall. 2 a mistake. 3 a petticoat. 4 a small piece of paper.

slipper *noun* **slippers**
a soft, comfortable shoe to wear indoors.

slippery *adjective*
smooth, wet, etc. so that it is difficult to stand on, hold, etc.

slit *noun* **slits**
a long cut or narrow opening in something.

slit *verb* **slits, slitting, slit**
to make a long cut or a narrow opening in something.

slither *verb* **slithers, slithering, slithered**
to slide; to slip as you move along.

sliver *noun* **slivers** (*say* sli-vuh)
a thin strip of wood, glass, etc.

slob *noun* **slobs**
(*colloquial*) an insulting word to describe a lazy, fat, or untidy person.

slog *verb* **slogs, slogging, slogged**
1 to hit something hard or wildly, as in *He slogged the ball right past the fielders.* 2 to work hard, as in *She just kept slogging on until the work was done.* 3 to walk with effort, as in *We slogged through the mud.*

slogan *noun* **slogans**
a phrase used to advertise something or to sum up the aims of an organisation, campaign, etc., as in *Their slogan was 'Save the Bilby'.*

slop *verb* **slops, slopping, slopped**
to spill liquid over the edge of a container.

slope *verb* **slopes, sloping, sloped**
to go gradually downwards or upwards; not to be horizontal or vertical.

slope *noun* **slopes**
1 a surface that is not horizontal or vertical. 2 the amount by which one edge of a surface is higher or lower than the opposite edge.

a
b
c
d
e
f
g
h
i
j
k
l
m
n
o
p
q
r
s
t
u
v
w
x
y
z

sloppy 404

sloppy *adjective* **sloppier, sloppiest**
1 careless, as in *sloppy work*. 2 runny, as in *This porridge is sloppy*. 3 sentimental, as in *a sloppy story*.
sloppily *adverb*, **sloppiness** *noun*

sloppy joe *noun* **sloppy joes**
a loose oversized jumper.

slosh *verb* **sloshes, sloshing, sloshed**
1 to splash, as in *The bus sloshed through the puddles at the edge of the road*. 2 to slop liquid; to pour liquid carelessly.

slot *noun* **slots**
a narrow opening to put things in, especially money.

sloth *noun* **sloths**
(rhymes with *both*)
1 laziness. 2 a long-haired South American animal that lives in trees and moves slowly.

slouch *verb* **slouches, slouching, slouched**
to move, stand, or sit in a lazy way, especially with your head and shoulders bent forwards.

slouch hat *noun* **slouch hats**
a hat with the left brim turned up, worn by a soldier.

slovenly *adjective* (*say* **sluv**-uhn-lee)
careless; untidy.

slow *adjective* **slower, slowest**
1 not quick; taking more time than usual. 2 showing a time earlier than the correct time, as in *That clock is slow*.
slowly *adverb*, **slowness** *noun*

slow *verb* **slows, slowing, slowed**
to go slower.

slowcoach *noun* **slowcoaches**
(*colloquial*) someone who moves or works slowly.

sludge *noun*
thick sticky mud, oil, etc.

slug *noun* **slugs**
1 a small animal like a snail without its shell. 2 a pellet for firing from a gun.

slug *verb* **slugs, slugging, slugged**
1 to hit hard. 2 to charge too much, as in *They were slugged $50 for the tasteless lunch*.

slum *noun* **slums**
an area of old, dirty, crowded houses.

slumber *noun*
sleep.

slump *verb* **slumps, slumping, slumped**
to fall heavily or suddenly.

slump *noun* **slumps**
a sudden fall in prices, trade, etc.

slung past tense and past participle of **sling** *verb*.

slunk past tense and past participle of **slink**.

slush *noun*
snow that is melting.
slushy *adjective*

sly *adjective* **slyer, slyest**
cunning; mischievous.
slyly *adverb*, **slyness** *noun*

smack *verb* **smacks, smacking, smacked**
to slap someone, especially as a punishment.

smack *noun* **smacks**
a slap, especially as a punishment.

small *adjective* **smaller, smallest**
not big; less than the normal size.

smallpox *noun*
a serious infectious disease, common in the past, that causes a fever and produces spots which leave scars on the skin.

smart *adjective* **smarter, smartest**
1 neat; dressed well. 2 clever. 3 fast, as in *She ran at a smart pace*. 4 sharp or painful, as in *a smart slap across the face*.
smarten *verb*, **smartly** *adverb*, **smartness** *noun*

smart *verb* **smarts, smarting, smarted**
to feel a stinging pain.

smash *verb* **smashes, smashing, smashed**
1 to break into pieces noisily and violently; to break something in this way. 2 to hit or move with great force, as in *The runaway truck smashed into a wall*.

smash *noun* **smashes**
1 the act or sound of smashing. 2 a collision, especially one involving trains or cars, etc.
smash hit, (*colloquial*) an extremely successful or popular show, film, song, etc.

smear *verb* **smears, smearing, smeared**
1 to rub something dirty or greasy on a surface. 2 to try to damage someone's reputation.
smear *noun*

smell *noun* **smells**
1 something that you can smell, especially something unpleasant. 2 the ability to smell things, as in *the sense of smell*.
smelly *adjective*

smell *verb* **smells, smelling, smelt**
1 to use your nose to sense something, as in *I bent down and smelt the rose*. 2 to give out something that you can detect with your nose, as in *This cheese smells*.

smelt *verb* **smelts, smelting, smelted**
to melt ore so as to get metal from it.
smelter *noun*

smile *verb* smiles, smiling, smiled
to have a pleased or amused expression on your face; to look at someone while you have this kind of expression on your face.

smile *noun* smiles
a pleased or amused expression on your face.

smithereens *plural noun*
small fragments, as in *Smash it to smithereens.*

smock *noun* smocks
a loose garment like a very long shirt, usually worn to protect your clothes.

smog *noun*
a mixture of smoke and fog.

smoke *noun*
1 the grey or blue gas that rises from a fire. 2 (*colloquial*) a cigarette, as in *He wants a smoke.*
the big smoke, (*colloquial*) a large city.
smokeless *adjective*, **smoky** *adjective*

smoke *verb* smokes, smoking, smoked
1 to give out smoke, as in *The fire is smoking.* 2 to breathe in the smoke of a cigarette, cigar, or pipe. 3 to preserve fish or meat with smoke, as in *smoked salmon.*
smoker *noun*

smooth *adjective* smoother, smoothest
1 having a surface without any lumps, marks, roughness, etc. 2 moving without bumps or jolts. 3 not harsh; flowing easily, as in *a smooth voice.*
smoothly *adverb*, **smoothness** *noun*

smooth *verb* smooths, smoothing, smoothed
to make something smooth.

smorgasbord *noun* smorgasbords
a meal at which there is a variety of dishes from which to choose.

smother *verb* smothers, smothering, smothered
1 to prevent someone from breathing.
2 to cover something thickly, as in *a cake smothered in icing.* 3 to put out a fire by covering it.

smoulder *verb* smoulders, smouldering, smouldered
to burn slowly without a flame.

smudge *noun* smudges
a dirty mark made by rubbing something.

smuggle *verb* smuggles, smuggling, smuggled
to bring something into a country secretly and illegally.
smuggler *noun*

smut *noun* smuts
1 a small piece of soot or dirt. 2 obscene things.
smutty *adjective*

snack *noun* snacks
a small meal.

snag *noun* snags
1 an unexpected difficulty; an obstacle.
2 (*colloquial*) a sausage.

snail *noun* snails
a small soft animal with a shell, as in *Snails move very slowly.*

snake *noun* snakes
a long reptile without legs, as in *Some snakes give poisonous bites.*
snake in the grass, a secret enemy.
snaky *adjective*

snap *verb* snaps, snapping, snapped
1 to break suddenly with a sharp noise.
2 to bite suddenly or quickly, as in *The dog snapped at me.* 3 to say something quickly and angrily. 4 to move or do something quickly, as in *She snapped her fingers. It's time you snapped into action!*

snap *noun* snaps
1 the act or sound of snapping. 2 a card-game in which players shout 'Snap!' when they see two similar cards.

snare *noun* snares
a trap for catching animals.

snarl *verb* snarls, snarling, snarled
to growl; to say something angrily.

snatch *verb* snatches, snatching, snatched
to grab, as in *He snatched the bag from me.*

sneak *verb* sneaks, sneaking, sneaked
1 to move quietly and secretly.
2 (*colloquial*) to tell someone in authority that someone else has misbehaved.

sneak *noun* sneaks
(*colloquial*) a mean natured person; a tell-tale.
sneakily *adverb*, **sneaky** *adjective*

sneakers *plural noun*
a soft-soled shoe made from leather, canvas, etc.

sneer *verb* sneers, sneering, sneered
to speak or behave in a scornful way.

sneeze *verb* sneezes, sneezing, sneezed
to push air through your nose suddenly and uncontrollably, as in *She was sneezing a lot because of her cold.*
not to be sneezed at, (*colloquial*) valuable; important.

sneeze

sneeze *noun* sneezes
the action or sound of sneezing.

sniff *verb* sniffs, sniffing, sniffed
1 to make a noise by drawing air in through your nose. 2 to smell something.

sniff *noun* sniffs
1 the action or sound of drawing air in through your nose. 2 the action or sound of smelling something.

sniffle *verb* sniffles, sniffling, sniffled
to sniff continually or slightly, as in *His cold caused him to sniffle.*

sniffle *noun*
the act of sniffling.
the sniffles, a head cold causing sniffling.

snigger *verb* sniggers, sniggering, sniggered
to give a quiet, unpleasant laugh.

snip *verb* snips, snipping, snipped
to cut a small piece or pieces off something.

snipe *verb* snipes, sniping, sniped
to shoot at people from a hiding-place.
sniper *noun*

snivel *verb* snivels, snivelling, snivelled
to cry or complain in a whining way.

snob *noun* snobs
someone who despises people who have not got wealth, power, or particular tastes or interests.
snobbery *noun*, **snobbish** *adjective*

snooker *noun*
a game like billiards played with long sticks (called *cues*) and 22 coloured balls on a cloth-covered table.

snoop *verb* snoops, snooping, snooped
to keep trying to find out secretly about someone else's business.
snooper *noun*

snore *verb* snores, snoring, snored
to breathe very noisily while sleeping.

snorkel *noun* snorkels
a tube that supplies air to someone swimming under water.

snort *verb* snorts, snorting, snorted
to make a loud noise by forcing air out of your nose.

snout *noun* snouts
an animal's nose, or nose and jaws, of the kind that stick out in front of its head, as in *The pig raised its snout.*

snow *noun*
frozen drops of water falling from the sky as small white flakes.
snowflake *noun*

snow *verb* snows, snowing, snowed
it is snowing, snow is falling.

snowball *noun* snowballs
snow pressed into the shape of a ball for throwing at someone.

snowfields *plural noun*
country where snow falls, especially areas used for skiing, tobogganing, etc.

snow gum *noun* snow gums
a gum tree having a smooth, usually whitish trunk growing naturally in mountain areas.

snowman *noun* snowmen
a figure made of snow.

snowstorm *noun* snowstorms
a storm with snow falling.

snowy *adjective* snowier, snowiest
1 with snow falling, as in *snowy weather*.
2 covered with snow, as in *snowy hills*.
3 brilliantly white, as in *snowy sheets*.

snub *verb* snubs, snubbing, snubbed
to treat someone in a scornful or unfriendly way.

snub-nosed *adjective*
with a short, thick nose.

snuff *noun*
powdered tobacco that is taken into someone's nose by sniffing.

snug *adjective* snugger, snuggest
warm and comfortable.
snugly *adverb*

snuggle *verb* snuggles, snuggling, snuggled
to curl up in a warm, comfortable place, as in *She snuggled up in bed.*

so *adverb*
1 in this or that way; in such a way; to such an extent, as in *Why are you so cross?*
2 very, as in *This film is so boring*. 3 also, as in *I was wrong but so were you.*
and so on, and other similar things, as in *They took food, water, spare clothing, and so on.*
or so, or about that number.
so as to, in such a way as to; for the purpose of.
so far, up to now.
so far, so good, everything has gone well up to now.
so-so (*colloquial*) only moderately good or fair.
so what?, (*colloquial*) what does that matter?; I don't care.

so *conjunction*
therefore; for that reason, as in *They threw me out, so I came here.*

soft

soak *verb* **soaks, soaking, soaked**
to make someone or something very wet.
soak up, to take in or absorb, as in *The sponge soaked up the water. The child soaked up knowledge.*

soak *noun* **soaks**
1 the act of soaking, as in *She had a long soak in a bubble bath.* **2** a hollow, usually in sandy soil where water collects, on or below the surface of the ground; a waterhole.

so-and-so *noun* **so-and-so's**
1 (*colloquial*) a person or thing that need not be named, as in *Old so-and-so told me.* **2** (*colloquial*) an unpleasant person, as in *He's a real so-and-so.*

soap *noun* **soaps**
1 a substance used with water for washing and cleaning things. **2** (*colloquial*) a soap opera.
soap opera, (*colloquial*) a television serial about the day-to-day life of a group of imaginary people.
soapy *adjective*

soar *verb* **soars, soaring, soared**
1 to rise or fly high in the air. **2** to rise very high, as in *Prices were soaring.*

sob *verb* **sobs, sobbing, sobbed**
to make gasping noises as you cry.

sober *adjective* **soberer, soberest**
1 not drunk. **2** calm and serious, as in *a sober expression.* **3** not bright or showy, as in *sober colours.*
soberly *adverb,* **sobriety** *noun*

so-called *adjective*
named in what may be the wrong way, as in *This so-called mechanic couldn't mend a toy car!*

soccer *noun*
a form of football played by sides of eleven with a round ball which players must not touch with their hands or arms, as in *The Socceroos play soccer for Australia.*

sociable *adjective* (*say* **soh**-shuh-buhl)
liking to be with other people; friendly.
sociability *noun,* **sociably** *adverb*

social *adjective* (*say* **soh**-shuhl)
1 living in a community, as in *We are social beings.* **2** to do with society, as in *the dance was a happy social event.* **3** helping the people in a community, as in *a social worker.* **4** helping people to meet one another, as in *a social club.*
socially *adverb*

social *noun* **socials**
a party, dance, gathering, etc., as in *a school social.*

socialism *noun*
a particular belief that in a social system all the wealth and industry should be owned and controlled by the people.

socialist *noun* **socialists**
someone who believes that wealth should be equally shared and that the main industries and resources should be controlled by the government.
socialist *adjective*

society *noun* **societies**
1 a community; people living together in a group or nation. **2** a group of people organised for a particular purpose, as in *a dramatic society.* **3** people of the higher classes and their way of life, as in *The way you behave would not be accepted in society.* **4** mixing with others; companionship, as in *I enjoyed her society.*

sociology *noun* (*say* soh-see-**ol**-uh-jee)
the study of society or societies.
sociological *adjective,* **sociologist** *noun*

sock *noun* **socks**
a small, soft piece of clothing that covers your foot and the lower half of your leg.
pull your socks up, (*colloquial*) to try to do better.

sock *verb* **socks, socking, socked**
(*colloquial*) to hit something forcefully; to punch someone, as in *He socked me on the jaw.*

socket *noun* **sockets**
a device or hole into which something fits, especially the place where an electric plug or bulb is put to make a connection.

soda *noun*
1 crystals dissolved in water and used for cleaning (*washing-soda*); powder used in cooking (*baking-soda*). **2** soda-water.
soda-water, fizzy water used in drinks.

sodium *noun* (*say* **soh**-dee-uhm)
a soft, silvery-white, metallic substance.

sofa *noun* **sofas**
a long soft seat with sides and a back; a lounge or couch.
sofa bed, a sofa that can be converted into a bed.

soft *adjective* **softer, softest**
1 not hard or firm; easily pressed or cut into a new shape. **2** smooth; not rough or stiff. **3** gentle; not loud, as in *a soft voice.*

a
b
c
d
e
f
g
h
i
j
k
l
m
n
o
p
q
r
s
t
u
v
w
x
y
z

soften

soft drink, a drink that does not contain alcohol.
softly *adverb*, **softness** *noun*

soften *verb* **softens, softening, softened**
to make something softer; to become softer.
softener *noun*

software *noun*
(*in Computing*) things like programs and manuals, which are not part of the machinery (the *hardware*) of a computer.

soggy *adjective* **soggier, soggiest**
very wet and heavy.

soil *noun*
the earth that plants grow in.

soil *verb* **soils, soiling, soiled**
to make something dirty; to stain.

solar *adjective*
to do with the sun, as in *solar heating*.
solar panel, a device that collects energy, especially heat, from the sun.
solar power, energy from the sun.
solar system, the sun and the planets that revolve around it.

sold past tense and past participle of **sell.**

solder *noun*
a soft alloy that is melted to join wires, etc. together.
solder *verb*

soldier *noun* **soldiers**
a member of an army.

sole *noun* **soles**
the bottom part of a shoe or foot.

sole *adjective*
single; only, as in *She was the sole survivor.*
solely *adverb*

solemn *adjective*
serious; dignified, as in *a solemn face.*
solemnity *noun*, **solemnly** *adverb*

solicitor *noun* **solicitors**
a kind of lawyer who advises people, prepares legal documents and instructs barristers who argue the case in court.

solid *adjective*
1 not hollow; with no space inside.
2 able to keep its shape; not a liquid or gas.
solidity *noun*, **solidly** *adverb*

solid *noun* **solids**
a solid thing; a solid substance.

solidify *verb* **solidifies, solidifying, solidified**
to become solid; to make something become solid.

soliloquy *noun* **soliloquies**
(*say* **suh-lil-uh-kwee**)
a speech in which an actor is alone and speaks his or her thoughts aloud.

solitary *adjective*
1 alone; on your own, as in *He lived a solitary life.* **2** single, as in *A solitary bird sang.*

solitude *noun*
being on your own.

solo *noun* **solos**
something sung, played, danced, or done by one person, as in *She sang a solo.*
soloist *noun*

solstice *noun* **solstices**
either of the two times in the year when the sun is at its furthest point north or south of the equator, the **summer solstice**, about 22 December, or the **winter solstice**, about 21 June.

soluble *adjective*
1 able to be dissolved, as in *a soluble detergent.* **2** able to be solved, as in *Is the problem soluble?*
solubility *noun*

solution *noun* **solutions**
1 something dissolved in a liquid. **2** the answer to a problem or puzzle.

solve *verb* **solves, solving, solved**
to find the answer to a problem or puzzle.

solvent *noun* **solvents**
a liquid in which other substances can be dissolved, as in *Some solvents can be used to remove stains.*

solvent *adjective*
not in debt.

sombre *adjective*
gloomy; dark.

some *adjective*
1 a few, as in *some sweets.* **2** a certain amount of, as in *some cake.* **3** a; an unknown, as in *Some fool left a pin on this chair!*

some *pronoun*
a certain or unknown number or amount, as in *Some of them were late.*

somebody *pronoun*
someone.

somehow *adverb*
in some way, as in *We must find money somehow.*

someone *pronoun*
a person.

somersault *noun* **somersaults**
(*say* **sum-uh-solt**)
a movement in which you turn head over heels in the air or on the ground, before landing on your feet.

something *pronoun*
a certain or unknown thing.

sometime *adverb*
at some time, as in *I saw her sometime last year*.

sometimes *adverb*
at some times, as in *Sometimes we walk to school*.

somewhat *adverb*
to some extent; to a certain amount, as in *He was somewhat annoyed*.

somewhere *adverb*
in or to some place.

son *noun* **sons**
a boy or man who is someone's child.

song *noun* **songs**
1 a tune for singing.   2 singing, as in *the song of the birds*.
a song and dance, (*colloquial*) a great fuss.

sonic *adjective*
to do with sound or sound waves.
sonic boom, a bang caused by an aircraft flying faster than the speed of sound.

sonnet *noun* **sonnets**
a kind of poem with 14 lines.

sook *noun* **sooks**
a timid, shy person; a crybaby.

soon *adverb* **sooner, soonest**
1 in a short time from now.   2 not long after, as in *She became ill, but was soon better*.   3 early; quickly, as in *You spoke too soon*.   4 willingly, as in *I'd just as soon stay at home*.
sooner or later, at some time in the future.

soot *noun*
the black powder left by smoke in a chimney, on a building, etc.
sooty *adjective*

soothe *verb* **soothes, soothing, soothed**
1 to make someone calm.   2 to ease a pain, ache, etc.

sophisticated *adjective*
(*say* suh-**fis**-tuh-kay-tuhd)
1 not simple or innocent; cultured; civilised, as in *sophisticated people*.
2 complicated, as in *a sophisticated machine*.
sophistication *noun*

sopping *adjective*
very wet; soaked.

soppy *adjective* **soppier, soppiest**
(*colloquial*) sentimental; silly.

soprano *noun* **sopranos** (*say* suh-**prah**-noh)
a woman or boy with a high singing voice.

sorbet *noun* **sorbets** (*say* **saw**-bay)
a frozen dessert made from fruit, egg whites, etc.

sorcerer *noun* **sorcerers**
a man who can do magic.
sorcery *noun*

sorceress *noun* **sorceresses**
a woman who can do magic.

sore *adjective* **sorer, sorest**
1 painful; smarting.   2 annoyed, as in *He was sore about losing his job*.
sorely *adverb*, **soreness** *noun*

sore *noun* **sores**
a painful place on the body.

sorrow *noun* **sorrows**
sadness; regret.
sorrowful *adjective*, **sorrowfully** *adverb*

sorry *adjective* **sorrier, sorriest**
1 feeling sorrow, as in *I'm sorry I forgot to send you a birthday card*.   2 feeling pity, as in *She felt sorry for the lost child*.

sort *noun* **sorts**
a group of things or people that are similar; a kind, as in *What sort of fruit do you like?*
sort of, (*colloquial*) rather; to some extent, as in *I sort of expected a present*.

sort *verb* **sorts, sorting, sorted**
to arrange things into groups, kinds, etc., as in *I must sort these books into piles*.

SOS *noun*
an urgent appeal for help, as in *The sinking ship sent out an SOS*.

sought past tense and past participle of **seek**.

soul *noun* **souls**
the invisible part of a person that is believed to go on living after he or she dies.

sound *noun* **sounds**
something that can be heard.
sound barrier, the resistance of the air to objects moving at speeds near the speed of sound.
sound effect, a sound made artificially for use in a play, film, broadcast, etc.

sound *verb* **sounds, sounding, sounded**
1 to make a sound; to give a particular impression by the sound that is made, as in *A bell sounded. He sounds angry. The car sounds as if it is about to fall to pieces*.   2 to test the depth of water beneath a ship.
sound out, to try to find out what someone thinks or feels.

sound *adjective* **sounder, soundest**
1 not damaged; in good condition.
2 healthy.   3 reasonable; correct, as in *His*

a
b
c
d
e
f
g
h
i
j
k
l
m
n
o
p
q
r
s
t
u
v
w
x
y
z

sound system

ideas are sound. **4** reliable; secure, as in *a sound investment.* **5** thorough; deep, as in *a sound sleep.*
soundly *adverb*, **soundness** *noun*

sound system *noun* **sound systems**
equipment which reproduces sound, as in *My new sound system includes a cassette deck and compact disc player.*

soundtrack *noun* **soundtracks**
the sound that goes with a cinema film.

soup *noun* **soups**
a liquid food made from vegetables, meat, etc.

sour *adjective* **sourer, sourest**
with a sharp taste like vinegar or lemons.
sourly *adverb*, **sourness** *noun*

source *noun* **sources**
the place where something comes from; the place where a river begins.

south *noun*
the direction to the right of a person facing east.

south *adjective*
1 coming from the south, as in *a south wind.* **2** situated in the south, as in *the south coast.*
southerly *adjective*, **southern** *adjective*, **southerner** *noun*

south *adverb*
towards the south.
southward *adjective* and *adverb*, **southwards** *adverb*

Southern Cross *noun*
a group of stars in the shape of a cross, as in *The Southern Cross appears on our flag.*

souvenir *noun* **souvenirs** (*say* soo-vuh-**neer**)
something that you keep because it reminds you of a person, place, or event.

sovereign *noun* **sovereigns** (*say* **sov**-ruhn)
a king or a queen.

Soviet *adjective* (*say* **soh**-vee-uht *or* **sov**-ee-uht)
to do with the states dominated by Russia before 1991.

sow *verb* **sows, sowing, sowed, sown** or **sowed** (rhymes with *go*)
to put seeds into the ground so that they will grow into plants, as in *Have you sown those beans? I sowed them yesterday.*
sower *noun*

sow *noun* **sows**
(rhymes with *cow*)
an adult female pig.

soya bean *noun* **soya beans**
a kind of bean from which edible oil, flour, milk, etc. are made.

spa *noun* **spas**
1 a place where mineral springs flow.
2 a warm bath or outdoor pool that has underwater jets of water which massage you.

space *noun* **spaces**
1 the whole area outside the earth, where the stars and planets are. **2** an area or volume, as in *There is plenty of space for your luggage.* **3** an empty area; a gap, as in *The door had spaces at the top and bottom, letting in a draught.* **4** a period of time, as in *They moved house twice in the space of a year.*

space *verb* **spaces, spacing, spaced**
to arrange things with gaps or periods of time between them.

spacecraft *noun* **spacecraft**
a vehicle for travelling in space.

spaceship *noun* **spaceships**
a spacecraft.

space shuttle *noun* **space shuttles**
a type of spacecraft that can travel into space and return to earth many times.

space station *noun* **space stations**
an artificial satellite used as a base for exploring space or for doing scientific experiments, etc.

spacious *adjective*
roomy.
spaciously *adverb*, **spaciousness** *noun*

spade *noun* **spades**
1 a tool with a long handle and a wide blade for digging. **2** a playing-card with a black shape, like an upside-down heart on a short stem, printed on it.

spaghetti *noun* (*say* spuh-**get**-ee)
a type of pasta made in long, thin pieces, as in *Spaghetti looks like long pieces of string when it is cooked.*

span *noun* **spans**
1 the length from one end of something to the other, especially the distance between the tips of your thumb and little finger when your hand is spread out. **2** a part of a bridge between supports. **3** a period of time.

span *verb* **spans, spanning, spanned**
to reach from one side or end of something to the other, as in *A bridge spanned the river.*

spaniel *noun* **spaniels**
a breed of dog with long ears and silky fur.

spanner *noun* **spanners**
a tool for tightening or loosening a nut.

spar *noun* **spars**
a strong pole, especially one used on a ship.

spar *verb* **spars, sparring, sparred**
to practise boxing, as in *The fighters were sparring in the ring.*

spare *adjective*
1 not used but kept ready in case it is needed; extra, as in *a spare tyre.* 2 thin; lean.
spare time, time not needed for work or other important purposes.

spare *verb* **spares, sparing, spared**
1 to afford; to give someone something, as in *Can you spare a penny?* 2 to be merciful towards someone; not to harm a person or thing, as in *Spare my feelings.* 3 to use or treat economically, as in *No expense will be spared.*

spark *noun* **sparks**
1 a tiny flash. 2 a tiny, glowing piece of something hot.

sparkle *verb* **sparkles, sparkling, sparkled**
to shine with a lot of tiny flashes of bright light.

sparkler *noun* **sparklers**
a firework that sparkles.

spark-plug *noun* **spark-plugs**
a device that makes a spark to explode the fuel in an internal-combustion engine.

sparrow *noun* **sparrows**
a small, brownish-grey bird introduced to Australia, as in *You often see sparrows in the garden.*

sparse *adjective* **sparser, sparsest**
small in number or amount, as in *a sparse population; sparse vegetation.*
sparsely *adverb*, **sparseness** *noun*

spastic *noun* **spastics**
someone who was born with a disability that makes it difficult for him or her to control his or her muscles.

spat past tense and past participle of **spit** *verb.*

spatter *verb* **spatters, spattering, spattered**
to splash; to scatter something in small drops or pieces, as in *My bike's front wheel has spattered mud all over my shoes.*

spawn *noun*
the eggs of frogs, fish, and other water-animals.

speak *verb* **speaks, speaking, spoke, spoken**
1 to say something, as in *Have you spoken to* him? *I spoke to him this morning.* 2 to be able to talk in a particular language, as in *Do you speak German?*
speak up, to say something more clearly or loudly.

speaker *noun* **speakers**
1 a person who is speaking; someone who makes a speech. 2 a loudspeaker.
the Speaker, the person who is in charge of debates in a house of parliament.

spear *noun* **spears**
a long pole with a sharp point, used as a weapon.

special *adjective*
1 different from other people or things; unusual. 2 for a particular person or purpose.

special *noun* **specials**
an item bought at a reduced price.

specialise or **specialize** *verb* **specialises, specialising, specialised**
to give particular attention to one subject or thing, as in *She is specialising in biology.*
specialisation *noun*

specialist *noun* **specialists**
an expert in a particular subject.

speciality *noun* **specialities**
1 something that you specialise in. 2 a special product, especially a food, that you find in a particular place, as in *Spring rolls are the speciality of the local Vietnamese restaurant.*

specially *adverb*
especially, as in *I came specially to see you.*

species *noun* **species** (*say* **spee**-seez *or* **spee**-sheez)
a group of animals or plants that are very similar, as in *Men and women belong to the same species.*

specific *adjective*
1 definite; precise. 2 referring to a particular thing, as in *The money was given for a specific purpose.*
specifically *adverb*

specify *verb* **specifies, specifying, specified**
to name or list things precisely, as in *The recipe specified brown sugar, not white.*
specification *noun*

specimen *noun* **specimens**
1 a small amount of something that shows what the rest is like, as in *This painting is a specimen of her work.* 2 an example of one kind of plant, animal, or thing, as in *a fine specimen of an oak.*

speck

speck *noun* **specks**
1 a tiny piece of something. 2 a tiny mark or spot.

speckled *adjective*
covered with small spots.

spectacle *noun* **spectacles**
1 an impressive or exciting sight or display. 2 something that you see, especially something ridiculous.
spectacles, a pair of lenses in a frame to help someone see; glasses.

spectacular *adjective*
impressive to see.

spectator *noun* **spectators**
a person who watches a game or show, or who watches anything without joining in.

spectre *noun* **spectres** (*say* **spek**-tuh)
a ghost.

spectrum *noun* **spectra**
1 the bands of colours like those you see in a rainbow. 2 a wide range of things, ideas, etc., as in *The questionnaire covered a very broad spectrum of topics.*

speech *noun* **speeches**
1 the act or power of speaking. 2 a talk given to a group of people.

speechless *adjective*
unable to speak, especially because of surprise or anger.

speech marks *noun*
the punctuation marks used to show direct speech (the words actually spoken), as in *Emma said, 'Let's go home'. 'Let's go home' is what Emma said.*

speed *noun* **speeds**
1 quickness; swiftness. 2 the rate at which something moves.
at speed, quickly.
speedily *adverb*, **speedy** *adjective*

speed *verb* **speeds, speeding, sped** or **speeded**
to go very fast; to go too fast, as in *Drivers who speed can be fined.*

speedboat *noun* **speedboats**
a fast motor boat.

speedometer *noun* **speedometers**
(*say* spee-**dom**-uh-tuh)
a device that measures a vehicle's speed; the speedo.

spell *verb* **spells, spelling, spelt** or **spelled**
to put the right letters in the right order to make a word or name, as in *How is your name spelt?*

spell *noun* **spells**
1 a period of time, as in *a cold spell.* 2 a period when something is done or happens, as in *a spell of work.* 3 a period of rest from work. 4 a saying that is supposed to have magic power.

spell checker or **spelling checker** *noun* **spell checkers**
a computer program to check that words have been spelt correctly.

spelling *noun* **spellings**
the way in which letters are put together to form words; how well someone does this, as in *Use the dictionary to check your spelling.*

spend *verb* **spends, spending, spent**
1 to use money to pay for things. 2 to pass time, as in *He spent a year in prison.* 3 to use up, as in *She spends all her energy on gardening.*

spendthrift *noun* **spendthrifts**
a person who wastes money.

sperm *noun* **sperms** or **sperm**
1 the male sex cell that joins with an ovum to produce offspring. 2 the liquid that contains these cells.
sperm whale, a large whale whose head contains a waxy oil.

sphere *noun* **spheres**
a globe; the shape of a ball.
spherical *adjective*

spice *noun* **spices**
a substance used to flavour food, as in *Spices like pepper and ginger are usually dried parts of plants.*
spicy *adjective*

spider *noun* **spiders**
a small animal with eight legs that often spins webs to catch insects.

spied past tense and past participle of **spy** *verb*.

spike *noun* **spikes**
a pointed piece of metal; a sharp point.
spikes, special running shoes with metal points which grip the ground and prevent athletes from slipping.
spiky *adjective*

spill *verb* **spills, spilling, spilt** or **spilled**
1 to let something fall out of a container, as in *You have spilt the milk.* 2 to fall out of a container, as in *The coins came spilling out.*

spin *verb* **spins, spinning, spun**
1 to turn round and round quickly; to make something turn in this way. 2 to make pieces of wool, cotton, etc. into thread by twisting them. 3 to make a web

splinter

or cocoon out of threads, as in *The spider spun a web*.
spin out, to make something last a long time.

spinach *noun*
a dark green, leafy vegetable.

spin bowler *noun* **spin bowlers**
a bowler in cricket who makes the ball spin, as in *Shane Warne is an excellent spin bowler*.

spindle *noun* **spindles**
1 a thin rod on which you wind thread.
2 a pin or bar that turns around, or a fixed pin or bar with something turning around it.

spindly *adjective* **spindlier, spindliest**
long or tall and thin.

spine *noun* **spines**
1 the line of bones down the middle of the back. 2 a needle-like growth on an animal or plant. 3 the back part of a book where the pages are joined together.
spinal *adjective*, **spiny** *adjective*

spine-chilling *adjective*
frightening but exciting, as in *a spine-chilling ghost story*.

spinning-wheel *noun* **spinning-wheels**
a machine for spinning thread out of wool, cotton, etc.

spinifex *noun* **spinifexes**
a spiny grass found mainly in dry areas or on coastal sand dunes.

spinnaker *noun* **spinnakers**
the large triangular sail used on a racing yacht.

spin-off *noun* **spin-offs**
something useful produced when something else is developed or done, as in *This chemical was a spin-off from space research*.

spinster *noun* **spinsters**
a woman who has not married.

spiny anteater *noun* **spiny anteaters**
an echidna.

spiral *adjective*
winding round and round like the shape of a spring, the thread of a screw, or the jam in a Swiss roll.

spire *noun* **spires**
a tall, pointed part on top of a church tower.

spirit *noun* **spirits**
1 the soul. 2 a being such as a ghost, an angel, a fairy, etc. that is thought by some

people to exist but that cannot be seen, heard, touched, etc. in the same way that humans and animals can. 3 courage; liveliness. 4 how someone feels or thinks, as in *She was in good spirits*. 5 an alcoholic liquid; a strong alcoholic drink.

spiritual *adjective*
1 to do with the human soul. 2 to do with religion, as in *spiritual leader*.
spiritually *adverb*

spiritual *noun* **spirituals**
a religious song originally sung by black Americans.

spiritualism *noun*
the belief that the spirits of dead people can communicate with living people.
spiritualist *noun*

spit *verb* **spits, spitting, spat**
1 to send drops of liquid forcibly out of your mouth, as in *He spat into the basin*.
2 to rain lightly, as in *It's only spitting*.

spit *noun* **spits**
1 a long, thin spike put through meat to hold it while it is roasted. 2 a narrow strip of land sticking out into the sea.

spite *noun*
a desire to hurt or annoy someone.
in spite of, although something has happened or is happening, as in *They went out in spite of the rain*.
spiteful *adjective*

splash *verb* **splashes, splashing, splashed**
1 to make liquid fly about, as you do when you jump into water. 2 to fly about in drops, as in *The water poured out of the hose and splashed all over me*. 3 to make someone wet by sending drops of liquid towards them, as in *The bus splashed us as it went past*.

splash *noun* **splashes**
the act or sound of splashing.
make a splash, to make a big display or effect, as in *Her wedding made quite a splash in the small town*.

splashdown *noun* **splashdowns**
the landing of a spacecraft in the sea.

splendid *adjective*
magnificent; very satisfying.
splendidly *adverb*, **splendour** *noun*

splint *noun* **splints**
a straight piece of wood, metal, etc. that is tied to a broken arm or leg to hold it firm.

splinter *noun* **splinters**
a small, sharp piece of wood, glass, etc. broken off a larger piece.

a
b
c
d
e
f
g
h
i
j
k
l
m
n
o
p
q
r
s
t
u
v
w
x
y
z

split

split *verb* **splits, splitting, split**
1 to cut or break something into parts; to divide something. 2 (*colloquial*) to leave somewhere, to go, as in *Let's split!*
split up, to divide or separate.

split *noun* **splits**
1 the splitting or dividing of something. 2 a place where something has split.
the splits, a movement where you stretch out your legs in opposite directions along the floor, at right angles to the top half of your body.

splutter *verb* **splutters, spluttering, spluttered**
1 to make a quick series of spitting sounds, as in *The smoke from the bonfire made him cough and splutter.* 2 to speak quickly but not clearly, as in *Stop spluttering; I can't hear what you're saying!*

spoil *verb* **spoils, spoiling, spoilt** or **spoiled**
1 to make something less useful, pleasant, good, etc., as in *The rain spoilt our holiday.* 2 to make someone selfish by always giving in to his or her wishes, as in *Don't spoil your child.* 3 to go bad, as in *Fruit often spoils in the heat.*

spoilsport *noun* **spoilsports**
a person who spoils other people's fun.

spoke *noun* **spokes**
one of the rods or bars that go from the centre of a wheel to the rim.

spoke past tense of **speak**.

spoken past participle of **speak**.

spokesperson *noun* **spokespersons**
someone who speaks on behalf of a group of people.

sponge *noun* **sponges**
1 a lump of absorbent rubber-like material containing lots of tiny holes, used in washing, cleaning, etc. 2 a sea-creature from which you get this kind of material. 3 a soft, lightweight cake or pudding.
spongy *adjective*

sponge *verb* **sponges, sponging, sponged**
1 to wash something with a sponge. 2 (*colloquial*) to get money or help from someone without intending to return it, as in *He was sponging on his relatives.*
sponger *noun*

sponsor *noun* **sponsors**
someone who provides money, help, etc. for a person or thing, especially someone who gives money to a charity in return for something done by another person.
sponsorship *noun*

spontaneous *adjective*
(*say* spon-**tay**-nee-uhs)
happening or done naturally; not forced, as in *A spontaneous cheer greeted the local team.*
spontaneity *noun,* **spontaneously** *adverb*

spooky *adjective* **spookier, spookiest**
(*colloquial*) frighteningly strange; haunted by ghosts.

spool *noun* **spools**
a round device on which cotton, string, film, etc. is wound.

spoon *noun* **spoons**
a metal or wooden device consisting of a small bowl with a handle, used for lifting food to your mouth or for stirring or measuring.
spoonful *noun*

sport *noun* **sports**
1 a game that exercises your body, especially a game played out of doors, as in *Football, netball, swimming, and tennis are all sports.* 2 games of this sort, as in *Are you keen on sport?* 3 (*colloquial*) someone who plays or behaves fairly and unselfishly, as in *Come on, be a sport.*
sports car, a low, fast motor car, usually with two seats.

sporting *adjective*
1 to do with sport; interested in sport. 2 behaving fairly and unselfishly.
a sporting chance, a reasonable chance.

sportsman *noun* **sportsmen**
1 a man who takes part in sport. 2 a person who behaves fairly and unselfishly.
sportsmanship *noun*

sportswoman *noun* **sportswomen**
a woman who takes part in sport.

spot *noun* **spots**
1 a small mark that is usually round. 2 a pimple. 3 a small amount of something. 4 a place.
on the spot, immediately; in a difficult situation, as in *We can repair your bike on the spot. Her question really put us on the spot.*
spotless *adjective,* **spotty** *adjective*

spot *verb* **spots, spotting, spotted**
1 to mark with spots. 2 to notice; to watch for, as in *You can spot the tourists at the Opera House.*
spotter *noun*

spotlight *noun* **spotlights**
a strong light that can shine on one small area.

spout *noun* **spouts**
1 a pipe or a shaped opening from which liquid can pour. 2 a jet of liquid.

spout *verb* spouts, spouting, spouted
1 to send out a jet of liquid; to come out in a jet. 2 (*colloquial*) to speak for a long time or in a pompous way.

spouting *noun*
pipes which carry rainwater from the roof.

sprain *verb* sprains, spraining, sprained
to injure an ankle, wrist, etc. by twisting it.

sprang past tense of **spring** *verb*.

sprawl *verb* sprawls, sprawling, sprawled
1 to sit or lie with your arms and legs spread out. 2 to spread out loosely or untidily.

spray *noun* sprays
1 tiny drops of liquid scattered on something. 2 a device for spreading liquid in many tiny drops. 3 a small bunch of flowers.

spray *verb* sprays, spraying, sprayed
to scatter tiny drops of liquid all over something.

spread *verb* spreads, spreading, spread
1 to lay or stretch something out to its full size, as in *The seagull spread its wings*. 2 to make something cover a surface, as in *He spread jam on his toast*. 3 to make or become widely known, felt, heard, etc., as in *Spread the news*.

spread *noun* spreads
1 the breadth or extent of something, as in *the spread of daisies in spring*. 2 something put on bread, rolls, etc. to add extra flavour, as in *Favourite spreads include Vegemite, peanut butter, and jam*. 3 (*colloquial*) a huge meal. 4 a cover for a bed; a bedspread.

spreadsheet *noun* spreadsheets
a computer program that allows you to set out tables of figures, and to do calculations that involve all the figures at once.

sprightly *adjective* sprightlier, sprightliest
lively; energetic.

spring *verb* springs, springing, sprang, sprung
1 to move upwards suddenly. 2 to arise, as in *The trouble has sprung from carelessness*. 3 to start suddenly, as in *The engine sprang into life*. 4 to make something happen without warning, as in *They sprang a surprise on us*.

spring *noun* springs
1 a springy coil of metal, as in *This mattress contains springs*. 2 a sudden upward movement. 3 a place where water rises out of the ground. 4 the season of the year when most plants start to grow, between winter and summer.

springboard *noun* springboards
a springy board from which people jump or dive.

spring-clean *verb* spring-cleans, spring-cleaning, spring-cleaned
to clean a house thoroughly, especially in spring.

spring roll *noun* spring rolls
a fried pancake filled with vegetables, meat, etc.

springy *adjective* springier, springiest
able to return to its original position when you bend it and let it go.

sprinkle *verb* sprinkles, sprinkling, sprinkled
1 to make tiny drops or pieces fall on something, as in *Sprinkle the seedlings with water. He sprinkled sugar on his cereal*. 2 to rain lightly.

sprinkler *noun* sprinklers
a device for watering the garden or putting out fires.

sprint *verb* sprints, sprinting, sprinted
to run very fast for a short distance.
sprinter *noun*

sprout *verb* sprouts, sprouting, sprouted
to start to grow; to produce leaves.

spruce *noun* spruces
a cone-shaped conifer tree with dense foliage.

spruce *adjective* sprucer, sprucest
neat; smart.

sprung past participle of **spring** *verb*.

spud *noun* spuds
(*colloquial*) a potato.

spun past tense and past participle of **spin**.

spunk *noun*
1 (*colloquial*) courage. 2 (*colloquial*) an attractive person.
spunky *adjective*

spur *noun* spurs
1 a sharp device worn on the heel of a rider's boot to urge a horse to go faster. 2 (*in Geography*) a ridge that sticks out from a mountain.
on the spur of the moment, without planning.

spur *verb* spurs, spurring, spurred
to urge a horse to go faster; to encourage someone.

spurt *verb* spurts, spurting, spurted
1 to gush out or up, as in *Blood spurted from the cut*. 2 to speed up suddenly, as in *He spurted to catch the leader*.

spurt

spurt *noun* **spurts**
1 a jet, especially of liquid. 2 an act of speeding up suddenly, as in *He put on a spurt and overtook the runner in front of him.*

spy *noun* **spies**
someone who works secretly to find out things about another country, person, etc.

spy *verb* **spies, spying, spied**
1 to be a spy; to watch secretly, as in *He was spying on us.* 2 to see; to notice, as in *She spied a house in the distance.*

squabble *verb* **squabbles, squabbling, squabbled**
to quarrel about something unimportant.

squad *noun* **squads**
a small group of people working or being trained together.

squadron *noun* **squadrons**
part of an air force, army, or navy.

squalid *adjective*
dirty and unpleasant, as in *squalid houses.*
squalidly *adverb*, **squalor** *noun*

squall *noun* **squalls**
a sudden strong wind.
squally *adjective*

squander *verb* **squanders, squandering, squandered**
to waste money, time, etc.

square *noun* **squares**
1 a square shape or object. 2 an open area surrounded by buildings, as in *Civic Square.* 3 the result of multiplying a number by itself, as in *9 is the square of 3.*
4 a person who is old-fashioned in his or her looks or taste.

square *adjective* **squarer, squarest**
1 with four straight equal sides and four right angles; forming a right angle; having right angles, as in *a square piece of paper.*
2 to do with units that describe the size of an area, as in *A square metre is the size of a square with each side one metre long.*
3 equal; even; paid-up. 4 honest; fair.
5 old-fashioned.
square meal, a good, satisfying meal.
square root, the number that gives a particular number if it is multiplied by itself, as in *The square root of 64 is 8.*
squarely *adverb*, **squareness** *noun*

square *verb* **squares, squaring, squared**
1 to make something square. 2 to multiply a number by itself, as in *5 squared is 25.* 3 to match; to be consistent, as in *His story doesn't square with yours.*

squash *verb* **squashes, squashing, squashed**
1 to press something so that it loses its shape; to crush something. 2 to move something or yourself into a place where there is very little room, as in *We all squashed into Monica's small car. I'll try to squash another jumper into my suitcase.*

squash *noun* **squashes**
1 a crowd; a crowded situation, as in *There was a tremendous squash outside the football ground. Both of us can sleep in my tent, though it'll be a squash.* 2 a drink made from crushed fruit. 3 a game played with racquets and a small ball on a special indoor court. 4 a kind of marrow with white flesh.

squat *verb* **squats, squatting, squatted**
1 to sit on your heels. 2 to live in an unoccupied house without permission.

squat *adjective* **squatter, squattest**
short and fat, as in *a squat man.*

squatter *noun* **squatters**
1 a sheep farmer using a large area of land. 2 a person who occupies a place that they do not own.

squaw *noun* **squaws**
an American Indian woman or wife.

squawk *verb* **squawks, squawking, squawked**
to make a loud, harsh cry.

squeak *noun* **squeaks**
a tiny, shrill sound such as a mouse makes.
squeakily *adverb*, **squeaky** *adjective*

squeal *noun* **squeals**
a long, shrill sound.

squeeze *verb* **squeezes, squeezing, squeezed**
1 to press something from opposite sides, especially so as to get liquid out of it.
2 to force a way into or through a place, gap, etc., as in *We squeezed into the car.*
squeezer *noun*

squeeze *noun* **squeezes**
1 the act of squeezing. 2 a hug.
3 a time when money is difficult to get, borrow, etc.
a tight squeeze, (*colloquial*) a difficult situation.
squeeze-box, another name for an accordion.

squelch *verb* **squelches, squelching, squelched**
to make a sound like someone treading in thick mud.

squid *noun* **squid** or **squids**
an edible marine animal with ten arms.

squint *verb* **squints, squinting, squinted**
1 to have eyes that do not move together but look in different directions. 2 to peer; to look with half-shut eyes at something.

squire *noun* **squires**
1 an English country gentleman, especially the main landowner. 2 a knight's attendant in the Middle Ages.

squirm *verb* **squirms, squirming, squirmed**
to wriggle; to twist your body about.

squirrel *noun* **squirrels**
a small animal of the northern hemisphere that lives in trees and eats nuts, as in *Squirrels have very thick tails.*

squirt *verb* **squirts, squirting, squirted**
to send something out or come out in a fast-moving jet of liquid, as in *He squirted his friend with a water pistol.*

St short for **Saint.**

St short for **Street.**

stab *verb* **stabs, stabbing, stabbed**
to pierce or wound someone with something sharp, as in *She stabbed him with a knife.*

stabilise or **stabilize** *verb* **stabilises, stabilising, stabilised**
to make something stable; to become stable, as in *Prices have stabilised.*

stabiliser *noun* **stabilisers**
a device that helps keep a ship or vehicle steady.

stable *adjective* **stabler, stablest**
steady; firmly fixed.
stability *noun*, **stably** *adverb*

stable *noun* **stables**
a building where horses are kept.

stack *noun* **stacks**
1 a neat pile. 2 a large amount of something, as in *a stack of money.* 3 a tall chimney, especially a factory chimney.

stack *verb* **stacks, stacking, stacked**
to pile things up.

stadium *noun* **stadiums**
a sports ground surrounded by seats for spectators.

staff *noun* **staffs**
1 the people who work in an office, shop, etc. 2 the teachers in a school, college, etc. 3 a thick stick for walking with.

stag *noun* **stags**
a male deer.

stage *noun* **stages**
1 a platform for performances in a theatre or hall. 2 the point that someone or something has reached.

stage *verb* **stages, staging, staged**
1 to present a performance on a stage. 2 to organise, as in *They staged a show for charity.*

stagecoach *noun* **stagecoaches**
a large, horse-drawn coach of a kind that used to travel regularly along the same route.

stagger *verb* **staggers, staggering, staggered**
1 to walk unsteadily. 2 to amaze or confuse someone, as in *I was staggered at the price.* 3 to arrange events so that they do not all happen at the same time.

stagnant *adjective*
1 not flowing or fresh, as in *a stagnant pond.* 2 dull and sluggish, as in *His life was stagnant after the accident.*

stain *verb* **stains, staining, stained**
1 to make a dirty mark on something. 2 to colour something, as in *The juice stained my dress.*

stain *noun* **stains**
a dirty mark on something, often caused by liquid.

stainless *adjective*
without stains.
stainless steel, steel that does not rust easily.

stair *noun* **stairs**
a flat place to put your foot when walking up or down to a different level inside a building.

staircase *noun* **staircases**
a series of stairs.

stake *noun* **stakes**
1 a thick pointed stick to be driven into the ground. 2 the thick post to which people used to be tied to execute them by burning. 3 an amount of money bet on something.
at stake, something at risk, to be won or lost.

stalactite *noun* **stalactites**
a stony spike hanging from the roof of a cave, as in *Stalactites look like icicles.*

stalagmite *noun* **stalagmites**
a stony spike rising from the floor of a cave.

stale *adjective* **staler, stalest**
not fresh; musty, as in *stale bread; stale air.*

stalk *noun* **stalks**
1 the main part of a plant above the ground. 2 a thin branch that holds a leaf, fruit, or flower.

a b c d e f g h i j k l m n o p q r **s** t u v w x y z

stalk

stalk *verb* **stalks, stalking, stalked**
1 to hunt stealthily. 2 to walk in a stiff or dignified way.

stall *noun* **stalls**
1 a table or small open-fronted shop where things are sold, usually in the open air.
2 a place for one animal in a stable or shed.
the stalls, the seats on the ground floor of a theatre.

stall *verb* **stalls, stalling, stalled**
to stop suddenly, as in *The car engine stalled.*

stallion *noun* **stallions**
a male horse.

stamen *noun* **stamens** (*say* **stay**-muhn)
the part of a flower that bears pollen.

stamina *noun* (*say* **stam**-uh-nuh)
the ability to endure physical or mental strain over a long time.

stammer *verb* **stammers, stammering, stammered**
to keep repeating the sounds at the beginning of words when you speak.

stamp *verb* **stamps, stamping, stamped**
1 to bang your foot heavily on the ground. 2 to put a postage stamp on something; to put marks on something by means of a stamp.
stamped addressed envelope, an envelope with an unused postage stamp and your own address on it.

stamp *noun* **stamps**
1 a postage stamp. 2 the act of banging your foot on the ground. 3 a small block with raised letters, etc. for printing words or marks on something; the words or marks printed with this.

stampede *noun* **stampedes**
a sudden rush by animals or people.

stand *verb* **stands, standing, stood**
1 to be on your feet without moving, as in *She stood there like a statue.* 2 to get or put upright; to place, as in *Stand the vase on the table.* 3 to stay; to remain unchanged, as in *My offer still stands.* 4 to tolerate or endure something, as in *I can't stand the heat.* 5 to be a candidate for an office, position, etc., as in *She stood for the position of president.*
it stands to reason, it is reasonable or obvious.
stand by, to be ready for action.
stand down, to withdraw from a position; to end a person's job especially because of a strike.
stand for, to represent; (*colloquial*) to

tolerate, as in *The flag stands for one's country. She won't stand for any disobedience.*
stand in, to act as a deputy for someone.
stand out, to stick out.
stand up for, to support or defend.

stand *noun* **stands**
1 something made for putting things on, as in *a music-stand.* 2 a stall where things are sold or displayed. 3 a grandstand.
4 resistance to attack, as in *She was determined to make a stand for her rights.*

standard *noun* **standards**
1 the level of quality something has, as in *a high standard of work.* 2 a thing used to measure or judge something else, as in *The metre is the standard for length.* 3 a flag.
standard lamp, a lamp on a pole that stands on the floor.
standard of living, the sort of things that you can afford.

standard *adjective*
to do with the ordinary kind; fitting an accepted standard, as in *standard English.*
standardise *verb*

standstill *noun* **standstills**
a stop; an end to activity.

stank past tense of **stink** *verb*.

stanza *noun* **stanzas**
a group of lines in a poem.

staple *noun* **staples**
a U-shaped piece of metal with sharp ends used for holding pieces of paper together, or fastening material, wire, etc. in place.
stapler *noun*

staple *adjective*
main; normal, as in *Rice is their staple food.*

star *noun* **stars**
1 one of the objects in space that you see at night as small points of light. 2 one of the main performers in a film, show, etc.; a famous entertainer. 3 a shape with five or six points.
starry *adjective*

star *verb* **stars, starring, starred**
to be a star in a film, show, etc.; to make someone the star of a film, show, etc., as in *She has starred in dozens of shows at the Opera House. The film 'The Wizard of Oz' starred Judy Garland.*

starboard *noun*
the right-hand side of a ship or aircraft when you are facing forward.

starch *noun* **starches**
1 a white carbohydrate in bread, potatoes,

status

etc. **2** this or a similar substance used to stiffen clothes.
starchy *adjective*

stare *verb* stares, staring, stared
to look continuously at someone or something without moving your eyes.

starfish *noun* starfish or starfishes
a small marine animal shaped like a star with five points.

starling *noun* starlings
a noisy, black or brown speckled bird, introduced into Australia.

start *verb* starts, starting, started
1 to take the first steps in doing something. **2** to make something happen; to set something going. **3** to make a sudden movement, as in *He started at the sound of rattling chains.*
starter *noun*

start *noun* starts
1 the act of starting; the beginning. **2** an advantage that someone has or is given at the beginning of something, as in *We gave the young ones 10 minutes start.*

starter *noun* starters
1 a device for an engine, vehicle etc. **2** (usually in *plural*) the first course of a meal. **3** the person who gives the signal to start a race. **4** a competitor in a race.

starting-pistol *noun* starting-pistols
a pistol fired to signal the start of a race.

startle *verb* startles, startling, startled
to surprise or alarm a person or animal.

starve *verb* starves, starving, starved
1 to suffer or die because you have not got enough food. **2** to make someone suffer or die in this way, as in *The prisoners had been starved to death.* **3** to deprive a person or thing of something important, as in *She was starved of love.* **4** (*colloquial*) to be very hungry, as in *Where's my dinner? I'm starving!*
starvation *noun*

state *noun* states
1 the condition of a person or thing. **2** a nation. **3** a division of a country, as in *New South Wales is a state.* **4** a government and its officials. **5** (*colloquial*) an excited or upset condition, as in *Don't get in a state about the test.*
state school, a school that is mainly managed and paid for by the government.

state *verb* states, stating, stated
to say something clearly or formally.

statement *noun* statements
1 a sentence that says something that is either true or false, as in *'Zebras have black and white stripes' is a statement.* **2** words that someone uses to say something officially, as in *The witness made a statement in court.*

statesman *noun* statesmen
someone who is important or skilled in governing a state.
statesmanship *noun*

static *adjective*
not moving; not changing.
static electricity, electricity which is present in something but does not flow as a current.

station *noun* stations
1 a set of buildings where people get on or off trains or buses. **2** a building for police, firemen, or other workers who serve the public. **3** a place from which radio or television broadcasts are made. **4** a large sheep or cattle farm, as in *The grazier had 2000 cattle on his station.*

station *verb* stations, stationing, stationed
to put a person somewhere for a particular purpose, as in *He was stationed to guard the ship.*

stationary *adjective*
not moving, as in *The car was stationary.*

Usage Do not confuse **stationary** with **stationery**, which is the next word in this dictionary.

stationery *noun*
paper, envelopes, and other things used for writing, office work, etc.

station-wagon *noun* station-wagons
a car which has a rear door and extra space for luggage behind the back seat.

statistic *noun* statistics
a piece of information expressed as a number, as in *The statistics show that the population has doubled.*
statistics, the science or study of information that is expressed as numbers.
statistical *adjective*, **statistically** *adverb*, **statistician** *noun*

statue *noun* statues
a model made of stone, metal, etc. to look like a person, animal, etc.

status *noun*
1 a person's position or rank in relation to other people, as in *What is her status in the company?* **2** a good position in society; prestige.

a
b
c
d
e
f
g
h
i
j
k
l
m
n
o
p
q
r
s
t
u
v
w
x
y
z

stave

stave *noun* **staves**
1 a set of five horizontal, parallel lines on which music is written. 2 the curved piece of wood that forms the side of a cask, barrel, etc.

stave *verb* **staves, staving,** *past tense* and *past participle* **staved** or **stove**
to make a hole or dent in something, as in *The collision stove in the front of the ship*.
stave off, to keep something away, as in *They staved off hunger by drinking a lot of water*.

stay *verb* **stays, staying, stayed**
1 to remain. 2 to spend time in a place as a visitor.

stay *noun*
a time of living in a certain place, as in *We had a short stay at Bateman's Bay*.

steady *adjective* **steadier, steadiest**
1 not shaking or moving; firm. 2 regular; continuous, as in *a steady pace*.
steadily *adverb*, **steadiness** *noun*

steady *verb* **steadies, steadying, steadied**
to make something steady.

steady *noun* **steadies**
(*colloquial*) a regular girlfriend or boyfriend.

steak *noun* **steaks**
a thick slice of meat or fish, usually grilled or fried.

steal *verb* **steals, stealing, stole, stolen**
1 to take and keep something that does not belong to you, as in *The money was stolen*.
2 to move stealthily, as in *He stole out of the room*.

steal *noun* **steals**
(*colloquial*) an easy task or a good bargain.

stealthy *adjective* **stealthier, stealthiest**
secret and quiet, as in *stealthy movements*.
stealth *noun*, **stealthily** *adverb*, **stealthiness** *noun*

steam *noun*
1 the vapour that comes from boiling water. 2 (*colloquial*) energy; power, as in *He ran out of steam*.
steamy *adjective*

steam *verb* **steams, steaming, steamed**
1 to give out steam. 2 to move using the power of steam, as in *The boat steamed down the river*. 3 to cook with steam, as in *I steamed the vegetables*. 4 to cover something or be covered with mist or condensation, as in *The windows steamed up*.
steamed up, (*colloquial*) excited or angry, as in *He's got all steamed up about the broken window*.

steam-engine *noun* **steam-engines**
an engine driven by steam.

steamroller *noun* **steamrollers**
a heavy vehicle with wide metal wheels, driven by steam and used to flatten surfaces when making roads.

steed *noun* **steeds**
(*old-fashioned or poetical use*) a horse.

steel *noun*
a strong metal made from iron.
steely *adjective*

steep *adjective* **steeper, steepest**
rising or sloping sharply.
steeply *adverb*, **steepness** *noun*

steeple *noun* **steeples**
a church tower with a spire.

steeplechase *noun* **steeplechases**
1 a horse-race over hedges and fences.
2 a race on foot across country.

steer *verb* **steers, steering, steered**
to make a car, ship, bicycle, etc. go in the direction you want.

steer *noun* **steers**
a young bull kept for its beef.

steering-wheel *noun* **steering-wheels**
a wheel for steering a car, truck, etc.

stegosaurus *noun* **stegosauruses**
(*say* steg-uh-**saw**-ruhs)
a plant-eating dinosaur with a double row of bony plates along the spine.

stem *noun* **stems**
1 a stalk. 2 the thin part of a wine-glass. 3 (*in grammar*) the main part of a word, to which different endings are attached, as in *'Caller', 'called', and 'calling' all have the same stem*.

stench *noun* **stenches**
a very unpleasant smell.

stencil *noun* **stencils**
a piece of card, metal, etc. with pieces cut out of it, used to produce a picture, design, etc.

step *noun* **steps**
1 a movement made by your foot when walking, running, or dancing. 2 the sound of a person putting down his or her foot when walking. 3 a stair, usually out of doors. 4 one of a series of actions.
watch your step, be careful.

step *verb* **steps, stepping, stepped**
to tread or walk.
step on it, (*colloquial*) to hurry.
step up, to increase something.

stepladder *noun* **stepladders**
a folding ladder with flat steps that stands up without being leant against anything.

steppe *noun* **steppes**
a grassy plain with few trees, especially in Russia.

stepping-stone *noun* **stepping-stones**
one of a line of stones put in a river or stream to help people walk across.

stereo *noun* **stereos**
1 stereophonic sound or recording.   2 a stereophonic radio or record-player, etc.

stereo *adjective*
stereophonic.

stereophonic *adjective*
(*say* ste-ree-uh-**fon**-ik *or* steer-ree-uh-**fon**-ik)
to do with sound that comes from two different directions at the same time.

sterile *adjective*
1 not fertile.   2 free from germs.
sterility *noun*, **sterilise** *verb*, **sterilised** *adjective*

sterling *adjective*
1 to do with British money, as in *pound sterling*.   2 to do with a coin or precious metal which is genuine, as in *sterling silver*.   3 having solid worth; genuine, reliable, as in *She was known for her sterling work with orphans*.

stern *noun* **sterns**
the back part of a ship.

stern *adjective* **sterner, sternest**
severe; strict; grim.
sternly *adverb*, **sternness** *noun*

stethoscope *noun* **stethoscopes**
(*say* steth-uh-skohp)
a device used by doctors for listening to patients' heartbeats, breathing, etc.

stew *verb* **stews, stewing, stewed**
to cook slowly in liquid.

stew *noun* **stews**
meat cooked slowly in liquid with vegetables.
in a stew, (*colloquial*) very worried or agitated.

steward *noun* **stewards**
1 someone whose job is to look after the passengers of a ship or aircraft.   2 an official who looks after a public place, hotel, club, etc., as in *The showground stewards will show you where to park*.

stick *noun* **sticks**
1 a long, thin piece of wood.   2 a walking-stick.   3 the implement used to hit the ball in hockey, polo, etc.   4 a long, thin piece of something, as in *a stick of toffee*.
the sticks, a remote country area; the outback.

stick *verb* **sticks, sticking, stuck**
1 to push a thing into something; to put carelessly, as in *She stuck a pin in her finger*.   2 to fasten or join; to glue.   3 to become fixed or jammed; not to be able to move, as in *The door keeps sticking*.   4 (*colloquial*) to stay, as in *We must stick together*.
stick around, (*colloquial*) to remain.
stick out, to come or push out from a surface; to be higher than the surrounding area; to be very noticeable.
stick up for, (*colloquial*) to support or defend someone or something.
stuck with, (*colloquial*) unable to avoid a person, job, etc.

sticker *noun* **stickers**
a label or sign that you can stick on something.

stick insect *noun* **stick insects**
an insect whose body looks like a twig.

sticky *adjective* **stickier, stickiest**
1 able or likely to stick to things.   2 (*colloquial*) unpleasant; nasty, as in *He came to a sticky end*.
stickily *adverb*, **stickiness** *noun*

stickybeak *noun* **stickybeaks**
(*colloquial*) an inquisitive person who sticks his or her nose (beak) into other people's business.

stiff *adjective* **stiffer, stiffest**
1 difficult to bend or move.   2 difficult, as in *a stiff climb*.   3 formal; not friendly.   4 strong, severe, etc., as in *a stiff drink; stiff punishment*.   5 (*colloquial*) unlucky, as in *a bit stiff in being beaten*.
stiffly *adverb*, **stiffness** *noun*

stiff *noun* **stiffs**
(*colloquial*) a dead body.

stiffen *verb* **stiffens, stiffening, stiffened**
to make something stiff; to become stiff.

stifle *verb* **stifles, stifling, stifled**
1 to make it difficult or impossible for someone to breathe, as in *The heat stifled us*.   2 to suppress something, as in *She stifled a yawn*.

stile *noun* **stiles**
an arrangement of steps allowing people, but not animals, to climb over a fence or wall.

still

still *adjective* **stiller, stillest**
1 not moving. 2 silent, as in *In the night, the streets are still.*
stillness *noun*

still *adverb*
1 up to this or that time; even now, as in *Are you still there? He was still there.*
2 even; yet, as in *He wanted still more food.*

still *conjunction*
however, as in *He has been unfair; still, he is your father.*

still *noun* **stills**
equipment for distilling alcohol, water, etc.

stilted *adjective*
stiff and unnatural, as in *Her nerves made her speak in a stilted way.*

stilts *plural noun*
a pair of poles on which you can walk high above the ground.

stimulant *noun* **stimulants**
(*say* **stim**-yuh-luhnt)
something that stimulates the body, especially a drug or an alcoholic drink.

stimulate *verb* **stimulates, stimulating, stimulated**
to excite or interest someone; to make something more lively or active, as in *We hope that the new book will stimulate interest in dinosaurs.*
stimulation *noun*

stimulus *noun* **stimuli**
something that stimulates or produces a reaction.

sting *noun* **stings**
1 the part of an insect or plant that can cause pain. 2 a painful area or wound caused by an insect or plant.

sting *verb* **stings, stinging, stung**
1 to hurt someone with a sting, as in *She was stung by a bee.* 2 to feel a sharp or throbbing pain, as in *My back is stinging from sunburn.* 3 (*colloquial*) to charge someone an excessive price; to swindle someone, as in *They stung him for $10.*
stinging-nettle *noun*

stingy *adjective* **stingier, stingiest** (*say* **stin**-jee)
mean; not generous.

stink *verb* **stinks, stinking, stank** or **stunk, stunk**
to have a very unpleasant smell.

stink *noun* **stinks**
1 a stench. 2 (*colloquial*) a fuss.

stir *verb* **stirs, stirring, stirred**
1 to move a liquid or soft mixture round and round, especially with a spoon. 2 to move slightly; to start to move.

3 (*colloquial*) to deliberately cause trouble, as in *He stirred the new teacher.*
stir up, to excite or arouse, as in *They stirred up trouble.*

stir *noun* **stirs**
1 an act of moving something round and round. 2 a fuss or disturbance, as in *The news caused a stir.*

stirrup *noun* **stirrups**
one of the D-shaped metal rings on a strap which hang from a horse's saddle, for riders to put their feet into.

stitch *noun* **stitches**
1 a loop of thread made in sewing or knitting. 2 a sudden pain in your side caused by running.

stoat *noun* **stoats**
an animal of the northern hemisphere rather like a weasel, with brown fur turning white in winter.

stock *noun* **stocks**
1 a number of things kept ready to be sold or used, as in *stock of ski wear; stock of food.* 2 livestock. 3 a line of ancestors.
4 liquid made by stewing meat, vegetables, etc. 5 a garden flower with a sweet smell. 6 a kind of share in a company's capital.
Stock Exchange, a place where stocks and shares are bought and sold.
Stock Market, a Stock Exchange; the stocks and shares sold there.

stock *verb* **stocks, stocking, stocked**
1 to keep a number of things ready to be sold or used. 2 to provide a place with things to be sold or used, as in *The explorers stocked their base camp with tinned food.*

stockade *noun* **stockades**
a fence made of large upright stakes.

stocking *noun* **stockings**
a long woven covering for the leg and foot, made from nylon, lycra, silk, etc.

stockman *noun* **stockmen**
a person employed to look after livestock, especially cattle.

stockpile *noun* **stockpiles**
a large stock of things kept in reserve.

stocks *plural noun*
a wooden framework in which people's legs used to be locked as a punishment.

stocky *adjective* **stockier, stockiest**
short and solid or strong, as in *a stocky man.*

stodgy *adjective* **stodgier, stodgiest**
1 thick and heavy; not easy to digest, as in *a stodgy pudding.* 2 boring, as in *a stodgy book.*

stove

stoke *verb* **stokes, stoking, stoked**
to put fuel in a furnace or on a fire.

stole *noun* **stoles**
a wide piece of material worn around your shoulders.

stole past tense of **steal**.

stolen past participle of **steal**.

stomach *noun* **stomachs**
1 the part of the body where food starts to be digested. 2 the abdomen.

stone *noun* **stones**
1 a hard, solid mineral which is not metal. 2 a piece of this mineral. 3 a jewel, as in *precious stone*. 4 the hard seed in the middle of a cherry, plum, peach, etc. 5 an old-fashioned unit of weight equal to about 6 kilograms, as in *The old lady said she weighed 7 stone*.

stone *verb* **stones, stoning, stoned**
1 to throw stones at someone. 2 to take the stones out of fruit, as in *Stone the cherries*.

stoned *adjective*
(*colloquial*) very drunk or drugged.

stone-deaf *adjective*
completely deaf.

stony *adjective* **stonier, stoniest**
1 full of stones. 2 like stone. 3 not answering or sympathising, as in *a stony silence*.

stood past tense and past participle of **stand** *verb*.

stool *noun* **stools**
a small seat without a back.

stoop *verb* **stoops, stooping, stooped**
to bend your body forwards.

stop *verb* **stops, stopping, stopped**
1 to finish something. 2 to cease moving or working; to stay. 3 to prevent or obstruct something. 4 to fill a hole or gap.
stoppage *noun*

stop *noun* **stops**
1 stopping; an end. 2 a place where a bus, train, etc. stops regularly.

stopper *noun* **stoppers**
something that fits into the top of a bottle, jar, etc. to close it.

stop press *noun*
late news printed in a newspaper after printing has started.

stopwatch *noun* **stopwatches**
a watch that can be started or stopped as you wish, used for timing races, etc.

storage *noun*
the storing of goods, furniture, etc.

store *noun* **stores**
1 a place where things are stored. 2 things kept for future use. 3 a shop, as in *department store, general store*.
in store, that is going to happen, as in *There is a treat in store for you*.

store *verb* **stores, storing, stored**
to keep things until they are needed.

storey *noun* **storeys**
one whole floor of a building; all the rooms on the same level.

Usage Do not confuse **storey** with **story**, which means words that tell of real or imaginary events.

stork *noun* **storks**
a large wading bird with very long legs and a long beak.

storm *noun* **storms**
1 a very strong wind with much rain, snow, etc. 2 a violent attack or outburst, as in *a storm of protest*.
storm in a teacup, a great fuss over something unimportant.
stormy *adjective*

storm *verb* **storms, storming, stormed**
1 to move or behave violently or angrily, as in *He stormed out of the room*. 2 to attack a place suddenly, as in *They stormed the castle*.

storm bird *noun* **storm birds**
any of several Australian birds whose movements or cries are said to signal a storm's arrival.

story *noun* **stories**
1 words that tell of real or imaginary events. 2 (*colloquial*) a lie, as in *Don't tell stories!*

Usage Do not confuse **story** with **storey**, which means one whole floor of a building or all the rooms on the same level.

stout *adjective* **stouter, stoutest**
1 rather fat. 2 thick and strong, as in *She carried a stout stick*. 3 brave, as in *The defenders put up a stout resistance*.
stoutly *adverb*, **stoutness** *noun*

stout *noun* **stouts**
a strong dark beer made from malt or barley.

stove *noun* **stoves**
a device that produces heat for warming a room or cooking.

a
b
c
d
e
f
g
h
i
j
k
l
m
n
o
p
q
r
s
t
u
v
w
x
y
z

stove

stove past tense and past participle of **stave** *verb*.

stow *verb* **stows, stowing, stowed**
to pack or store something away.
stow away, to hide on a ship or aircraft so as to escape, or to travel without paying.

stowaway *noun* **stowaways**
someone who stows away on a ship or aircraft.

straddle *verb* **straddles, straddling, straddled**
to sit or stand with one leg on one side of something, and the other leg on the other side; to stand across something, as in *The rider straddled his horse. The town straddles the NSW–Victorian border.*

straggle *verb* **straggles, straggling, straggled**
1 to grow or move in an untidy way, as in *Lantana straggled across the path. A line of children straggled across the playing-field.*
2 to lag behind; to wander on your own.
straggler *noun*, **straggly** *adjective*

straight *adjective* **straighter, straightest**
1 going continuously in one direction; not curving or bending.   2 tidy; in proper order.   3 honest; frank, as in *Give me a straight answer.*

Usage Do not confuse **straight** with **strait**, which is a noun meaning a narrow stretch of water connecting two seas.

straightaway *adverb*
at once; immediately.

straighten *verb* **straightens, straightening, straightened**
to make something straight; to become straight.

straightforward *adjective*
1 easy to understand or do; not complicated.   2 honest; frank.

strain *verb* **strains, straining, strained**
1 to stretch, push, or pull hard or too hard.   2 to make a great effort.   3 to put something through a sieve to separate liquid from the lumps or other things in it, as in *Strain the tea to get rid of the tea-leaves.*

strain *noun* **strains**
1 an injury caused by straining.
2 something that uses up your strength, patience, etc.; exhaustion, as in *The strain of overwork made her ill. He found it a strain being totally responsible for the baby.*   3 a breed or stock of animals, plants, etc., as in *That strain of dog is very rare.*

strainer *noun* **strainers**
a sieve, especially a small one for straining tea.

strait *noun* **straits**
a narrow stretch of water connecting two seas, as in *the Torres Strait.*

Usage Do not confuse **strait** with **straight**, which is an adjective meaning going continuously in one direction, tidy, or honest.

strand *noun* **strands**
1 one of the threads or wires twisted together to make a rope, cable, etc.
2 a lock of hair.

stranded *adjective*
being in difficulty, especially without money, transport, etc., as in *The teenagers were stranded when they missed the last train home.*

strange *adjective* **stranger, strangest**
unusual; not known or experienced before.
strangely *adverb*, **strangeness** *noun*

stranger *noun* **strangers**
1 a person that you do not know.   2 a person who is in a place he or she does not know, as in *She's a stranger in this city.*

strangle *verb* **strangles, strangling, strangled**
to kill someone by pressing his or her throat so as to prevent breathing.
strangler *noun*, **strangulation** *noun*

strap *noun* **straps**
a flat strip of leather, cloth, etc. for fastening things together or holding them in place.

strap *verb* **straps, strapping, strapped**
to fasten something with a strap or straps.

strapping *adjective*
tall and sturdy.

strategy *noun* **strategies**
1 a plan or policy to achieve something.
2 planning a war, campaign, etc.
strategic *adjective*, **strategist** *noun*

stratum *noun* **strata** (*say* strah-tuhm)
one of a series of layers or levels, as in *You can see several strata of rock in the cliffs.*

straw *noun* **straws**
1 dry cut stalks of wheat, corn, etc.   2 a narrow tube for drinking through.

strawberry *noun* **strawberries**
a small, red, juicy fruit which has a surface studded with seeds.

stray *verb* **strays, straying, strayed**
to wander; to get lost.

stray *adjective*
lost or away from the usual place, as in *a stray cat; a stray hair on the jacket.*

streak *noun* **streaks**
a long thin line or mark.
streaky *adjective*

streak *verb* **streaks, streaking, streaked**
1 to mark with streaks. 2 to move very quickly. 3 (*colloquial*) to run naked through a public place for a bet, dare, etc.
streaker *noun*

stream *noun* **streams**
1 a narrow river; a creek. 2 liquid flowing in one direction. 3 a number of things moving in the same direction. 4 a group in a school containing children of similar ability.

stream *verb* **streams, streaming, streamed**
1 to move in or like a river, as in *Traffic streamed across the junction*. 2 to produce a flow of liquid, as in *Blood was streaming from her cut hand*. 3 to arrange schoolchildren in groups according to their ability.

streamer *noun* **streamers**
a long strip of paper.

streamline *verb* **streamlines, streamlining, streamlined**
1 to give something a smooth shape that helps it to move easily through air or water. 2 to organise something so that it works more efficiently.

street *noun* **streets**
1 a road in a city or town. 2 the people who live or work in a particular street.

strength *noun* **strengths**
1 how strong a person or thing is.
2 something that makes a person or thing useful, effective, etc., as in *Her greatest strength is her good memory*.

strengthen *verb* **strengthens, strengthening, strengthened**
to make something or someone strong or stronger; to become strong or stronger.

strenuous *adjective*
needing or using great effort, as in *Rock climbing is strenuous exercise*.
strenuously *adverb*

stress *noun* **stresses**
1 strain, especially worry and nervous tension. 2 emphasis, especially the extra force with which you pronounce part of a word or phrase.

stress *verb* **stresses, stressing, stressed**
1 to put a strain on someone. 2 to put extra force on part of a word or phrase.
3 to emphasise something, as in *I must stress that this is an exceptional case*.

stretch *verb* **stretches, stretching, stretched**
1 to pull something so that it becomes longer, wider, or tighter. 2 to become longer or wider when pulled. 3 to extend, as in *The cattle station stretched for miles*.
stretch one's legs, to go for a walk, especially after sitting for a long time.
stretch out, to lie down and extend your arms and legs fully.

stretch *noun* **stretches**
1 the act of pulling something, making it longer, wider, or tighter; the condition of being able to become longer or wider when pulled, as in *This material has a lot of stretch in it*. 2 a continuous period of time or area of land, as in *a stretch of five years imprisonment; a stretch of desert*.

stretcher *noun* **stretchers**
a framework with handles at each end, on which a sick or injured person is carried.

strew *verb* **strews, strewing, strewed, strewn or strewed**
to scatter something, as in *Flowers were strewn over the path*.

stricken *adjective*
overcome; strongly affected by something, as in *stricken with fear*.

strict *adjective* **stricter, strictest**
1 demanding obedience or good behaviour, as in *a strict teacher*.
2 complete; exact, as in *the strict truth*.
strictly *adverb*, **strictness** *noun*

stride *verb* **strides, striding, strode, stridden**
to walk with long steps.

stride *noun* **strides**
1 a long step when walking or running.
2 a steady way of working, as in *Get into your stride*.

strides *plural noun*
(*colloquial*) trousers.

strife *noun*
conflict; fighting or quarrelling.
in strife, in trouble.

strike *verb* **strikes, striking, struck**
1 to hit, as in *The school was struck by lightning*. 2 to attack suddenly, as in *Chickenpox struck the school*. 3 to light a match by rubbing it against something rough. 4 to sound, as in *The clock struck 12*. 5 to stop working until the people in charge agree to improve wages, conditions, etc. 6 to find oil, gold, etc. by drilling, mining, etc. 7 to affect someone in some way, as in *The film struck me as truthful*.
striker *noun*

a
b
c
d
e
f
g
h
i
j
k
l
m
n
o
p
q
r
s
t
u
v
w
x
y
z

strike

strike *noun* **strikes**
1 a hit.   2 refusing to work, as a way of making a protest.   3 a find of oil, gold, etc. underground.
on strike or **out on strike**, having stopped working, as a protest.

striking *adjective*
impressive; very interesting.

string *noun* **strings**
1 thin rope; a piece of thin rope.   2 a piece of stretched wire, nylon, etc. used in a musical instrument to make sounds.   3 a line or series of things, as in *a string of buses*.
strings, the instruments in an orchestra that have strings; violins, cellos, etc.

string *verb* **strings, stringing, strung**
1 to tie with string.   2 to thread on a string, as in *I helped Kylie string her pearls.*
3 to remove the tough fibre from beans.
4 to put strings into a racket, a guitar, etc.
string out, to spread out in a line; to extend or make something last longer, as in *The runners began to string out as the race went on. Can't we string out the work until the weekend?*

stringed *adjective*
having strings, as in *The violin and cello are stringed instruments.*

stringy *adjective* **stringier, stringiest**
1 like string.   2 containing tough fibres.

stringybark *noun* **stringybarks**
any of the many gum trees having thick, rough bark.

strip *verb* **strips, stripping, stripped**
1 to take a covering off something.   2 to undress.   3 to deprive someone of something, as in *He has been stripped of his property.*

strip *noun* **strips**
a long, narrow piece of something, as in *a strip of leather; a strip of land.*

stripe *noun* **stripes**
1 a long, narrow band of colour, as in *Tigers have stripes; leopards have spots.*
2 something worn on the sleeve of a uniform to show your rank.
striped *adjective*, **stripy** *adjective*

strive *verb* **strives, striving, strove, striven**
to try hard; to struggle.

strobe *noun* **strobes**
a light that flashes on and off continuously.

strode past tense of **stride** *verb*.

stroke *noun* **strokes**
1 a hit; a movement or action, as in *a stroke of lightning; a stroke of good luck.*   2 a

sudden illness that often causes someone to be unable to move or feel anything.   3 a special way of swimming, as in *butterfly stroke.*

stroke *verb* **strokes, stroking, stroked**
to move your hand gently along something.

stroll *verb* **strolls, strolling, strolled**
to walk slowly.
stroll *noun*

stroller *noun* **strollers**
a folding chair on wheels in which a small child can be pushed along.

strong *adjective* **stronger, strongest**
1 having great power, energy, or effect, as in *a strong horse; a strong wind.*   2 not easily broken or damaged, as in *a strong chain.*   3 with a lot of flavour or smell, as in *strong tea.*
strongly *adverb*

stronghold *noun* **strongholds**
a fortress.

strove past tense of **strive**.

struck past tense and past participle of **strike** *verb*.

structure *noun* **structures**
1 something that has been built or put together.   2 the way that something is built or made.
structural *adjective*, **structurally** *adverb*

struggle *verb* **struggles, struggling, struggled**
1 to move your arms, legs, etc. in fighting or trying to get free.   2 to make strong efforts to do something.

struggle *noun* **struggles**
the act or time of struggling, as in *The struggle to win the trophy was fierce. Unemployment is a time of struggle for many families.*

strum *verb* **strums, strumming, strummed**
to sound a guitar by running your finger across its strings.

strung past tense and past participle of **string** *verb*.

strut *noun* **struts**
a bar of wood or metal that strengthens a framework.

strut *verb* **struts, strutting, strutted**
to walk proudly or stiffly.

stub *noun* **stubs**
a short piece of something left after the rest has been used up or worn down, as in *a cigar stub.*

stub *verb* **stubs, stubbing, stubbed**
  1 to knock your toe against something hard.   2 to put out a cigarette, cigar, etc. by pressing it against something hard.

stubble *noun*
  1 the short stalks of wheat, corn, etc. left in the ground after a harvest.   2 short, stiff hairs on a man's chin.

stubborn *adjective*
  not ready to change your ideas or ways, even though they may be wrong; resisting strongly, as in *as stubborn as a mule*.
  stubbornly *adverb*, **stubbornness** *noun*

stubby or **stubbie** *noun* **stubbies**
  a small squat bottle of beer.

stuck past tense and past participle of **stick** *verb*.

stuck-up *adjective*
  (*colloquial*) unpleasantly proud; despising people who have not got wealth, power, or particular tastes or interests.

stud *noun* **studs**
  1 a small curved lump or knob as in *Football boots have studs on the bottom*.
  2 short nail with a thick head.   3 a farm for breeding horses and cattle.

student *noun* **students**
  someone who studies, especially at college or university.

studio *noun* **studios**
  1 a place where radio or television broadcasts are made.   2 a place where cinema or television films are made.   3 the room where a painter, photographer, etc. works.

studious *adjective*
  keen on studying.
  studiously *adverb*

study *verb* **studies, studying, studied**
  1 to spend time learning about something.   2 to look at something very carefully.

study *noun* **studies**
  1 knowledge or learning about a subject, as in *The detailed study on Australian plants was published. She completes her university studies next year*.   2 a room used for reading, writing, and learning.

stuff *noun*
  1 a substance or material.   2 things; possessions, as in *Do you want to move your stuff off the table?*

stuff *verb* **stuffs, stuffing, stuffed**
  1 to fill something tightly, especially with stuffing, as in *She stuffed the turkey*.   2 to

push something inside another thing, as in *He stuffed the paper into his pocket*.

stuffing *noun* **stuffings**
  1 material used to fill the inside of something.   2 a flavoured mixture put inside poultry, etc. before cooking.

stuffy *adjective* **stuffier, stuffiest**
  1 badly ventilated; without fresh air.
  2 formal and boring.
  stuffily *adverb*, **stuffiness** *noun*

stumble *verb* **stumbles, stumbling, stumbled**
  1 to lose your balance; to fall over something.   2 to speak or act in a hesitant or uncertain way.
  stumble across or **stumble on,** to find something accidentally.

stump *noun* **stumps**
  1 the bottom of a tree-trunk left in the ground when the tree is cut down.   2 one of the three upright sticks put at each end of a cricket-pitch.

stump *verb* **stumps, stumping, stumped**
  1 (*in cricket*) to get a batter out by touching the stumps with the ball when he or she is not standing in the correct place.   2 to be too difficult for someone, as in *The question stumped him*.

stun *verb* **stuns, stunning, stunned**
  1 to knock someone unconscious.   2 to shock or confuse someone, as in *She was stunned by the news*.

stung past tense and past participle of **sting** *verb*.

stunk past tense and past participle of **stink** *verb*.

stunt *verb* **stunts, stunting, stunted**
  to slow down the growth or development of a person or thing, as in *Poor food can stunt a child's growth*.

stunt *noun* **stunts**
  1 something done to attract attention, as in *a publicity stunt*.   2 a dangerous feat, especially one performed in making a film.

stupendous *adjective*
  amazing; tremendous.

stupid *adjective* **stupider, stupidest**
  without reason or common sense; not clever or thoughtful.
  stupidity *noun*, **stupidly** *adverb*

sturdy *adjective* **sturdier, sturdiest**
  strong and vigorous or solid.
  sturdily *adverb*, **sturdiness** *noun*

stutter *verb* **stutters, stuttering, stuttered**
  to keep repeating the sounds, especially consonants, at the beginning of words when you speak.

sty *noun* **sties**
1 a pigsty.   2 a red swelling on an eyelid.

style *noun* **styles**
the way that something is done, made, said, or written, as in *She always dressed in a modern style. The story was written in an old-fashioned style.*

stylish *adjective*
fashionable; smart.
stylishly *adverb*

stylus *noun* **styluses**
1 the device like a needle that travels in the grooves of a record to reproduce the sound.   2 a pointed writing tool.

sub short for **submarine**.

subconscious *noun* (*say* sub-**kon**-shuhs)
the part of the mind that is not fully conscious but influences actions etc.

subdivide *verb* **subdivides, subdividing, subdivided**
to divide again after the first division, as in *The council subdivided the land to build townhouses.*

subdue *verb* **subdues, subduing, subdued**
1 to bring under control; to overcome.
2 to make quieter or gentler.

subject *noun* **subjects** (*say* **sub**-jekt)
1 the person or thing that is being talked or written about.   2 something that is being studied.   3 (*in grammar*) the person or thing that is doing the action stated by the verb in a sentence, as in *In 'she hit him', the subject is 'she'*.   4 someone who is ruled by a particular king, government, etc.

subject *adjective* (*say* **sub**-jekt)
ruled by a king, government, etc.; not independent.
subject to, having to obey; liable to; depending upon, as in *The lords were all subject to the king in the Middle Ages. Ferries are subject to delays in storms. Our decision is subject to your approval.*

subject *verb* **subjects, subjecting, subjected** (*say* suhb-**jekt**)
to make a person or thing undergo something, as in *They subjected him to torture.*

subjective *adjective*
influenced by your own beliefs or ideas, as in *His account of the events is rather subjective.*

submarine *noun* **submarines**
a ship that can travel under water.

submerge *verb* **submerges, submerging, submerged**
to go under water; to put something or someone under water.
submergence *noun*, **submersion** *noun*

submit *verb* **submits, submitting, submitted**
1 to surrender; to let someone rule or control you.   2 to give something to someone for his or her opinion, decision, etc., as in *The students submitted their projects to the teacher for marking.*
submission *noun*, **submissive** *adjective*

subordinate *adjective*
(*say* suh-**baw**-duh-nuht)
less important; lower in rank.
subordinate clause, a clause which cannot be used by itself, but which makes a sentence when it is joined to a *main clause*, as in *'When I went to the beach'* is the subordinate clause in the sentence *'When I went to the beach I swam.'*

subordinate *verb* **subordinates, subordinating, subordinated**
(*say* suh-**baw**-duh-nayt)
to treat something as less important than another thing.
subordination *noun*

subscribe *verb* **subscribes, subscribing, subscribed**
to pay money, especially to pay regularly so as to be a member of a club or have the use of a telephone, etc.
subscriber *noun*, **subscription** *noun*

subsequent *adjective*
following; later, as in *Subsequent events proved that she was right.*
subsequently *adverb*

subside *verb* **subsides, subsiding, subsided**
1 to sink, as in *The house has subsided over the years.*   2 to become quiet or normal, as in *The noise subsided.*
subsidence *noun*

subsidy *noun* **subsidies**
money paid to keep prices low, to help an industry, etc.
subsidise *verb*

substance *noun* **substances**
1 something that you can touch or see; something used for making things.   2 the essential part of something, as in *The substance of his argument was true.*

substantial *adjective*
1 large; considerable.   2 strong; solid.
substantially *adverb*

suffocate

substitute *verb* substitutes, substituting, substituted
to use someone or something instead of another person or thing, as in *In this recipe you can substitute oil for butter.*
substitution *noun*

substitute *noun* substitutes
a person or thing used instead of another.

subtitle *noun* subtitles
1 a secondary or additional title of a book, etc. 2 the caption on a film which translates a foreign language.

subtle *adjective* subtler, subtlest (*say* **sut**-uhl)
1 slight or faint but pleasant; delicate, as in *a subtle perfume.* 2 clever; ingenious, as in *a subtle joke.*
subtly *adverb*, **subtlety** *noun*

subtract *verb* subtracts, subtracting, subtracted
to take one amount from another, as in *If you subtract 2 from 7, you get 5.*
subtraction *noun*

suburb *noun* suburbs
an area of houses on the edge of a city or large town, as in *A suburb usually has its own shopping centre and school.*
suburban *adjective*, **suburbia** *noun*

subway *noun* subways
an underground passage for pedestrians.

succeed *verb* succeeds, succeeding, succeeded
1 to do or get what you wanted or intended. 2 to come after another person or thing, especially to become king or queen after another king or queen, as in *She succeeded him as manager.*

success *noun* successes
1 doing or getting what you wanted or intended. 2 a person or thing that does well, as in *The plan was a great success.*

successful *adjective*
having success.
successfully *adverb*

succession *noun* successions
1 a series of people or things. 2 the act of following other people or things.

successive *adjective*
following one after another.
successively *adverb*

successor *noun* successors
a person or thing that follows another, as in *The principal retired and handed over to her successor.*

such *adjective*
1 of the same kind, as in *sweets such as*

these. 2 so great; so much of, as in *It gave me such a fright!*
such-and-such, particular but not named, as in *It was at such-and-such a time.*

suck *verb* sucks, sucking, sucked
1 to take in liquid or air through your mouth, as in *I sucked milk through a straw.* 2 to move something around inside your mouth, as in *She sucked a sweet.* 3 to draw in; to absorb, as in *A vacuum cleaner sucks up dirt.*

suckle *verb* suckles, suckling, suckled
to feed from the breast or udder, as in *The mother suckled her baby. The cow suckled her calf.*

suction *noun*
1 producing a vacuum so that liquid, air, etc. is drawn in. 2 the action that causes something to be sucked in; the force that holds two surfaces together when some of the air has been removed from between them, as in *Vacuum cleaners work by suction.*

sudden *adjective*
happening or done quickly and unexpectedly.
suddenly *adverb*, **suddenness** *noun*

suds *plural noun*
froth on soapy water.

sue *verb* sues, suing, sued
to start a claim in a lawcourt to get money from someone, as in *I sued him for damages.*

suede *noun* (*say* swayd)
soft, velvety leather.

suet *noun*
hard fat from cattle and sheep, used in cooking.

suffer *verb* suffers, suffering, suffered
1 to feel pain or sadness. 2 to have to put up with something unpleasant, as in *She suffered their nasty comments.*

sufficient *adjective*
enough, as in *Have we sufficient food?*
sufficiency *noun*, **sufficiently** *adverb*

suffix *noun* suffixes
a word or syllable joined to the end of a word to change or add to its meaning, as in forget*ful*, lion*ess*, and rust*y*.

suffocate *verb* suffocates, suffocating, suffocated
1 to make it impossible or difficult for someone to breathe. 2 to have difficulty in breathing. 3 to kill someone or something by cutting off the supply of oxygen; to die from lack of oxygen.
suffocating *adjective*, **suffocatingly** *adverb*, **suffocation** *noun*

a
b
c
d
e
f
g
h
i
j
k
l
m
n
o
p
q
r
s
t
u
v
w
x
y
z

sugar

sugar *noun*
a sweet food obtained from various plants.
sugar beet, a plant with a root from which sugar is made.
sugar cane, a tropical grass with tall stems from which sugar is made.
sugary *adjective*

suggest *verb* **suggests, suggesting, suggested**
1 to give someone an idea that you think is useful. 2 to give an idea or impression of something, as in *Your smile suggests that you agree with me.*
suggestion *noun*

suicide *noun* **suicides**
1 deliberately killing yourself, as in *He committed suicide.* 2 a person who suicides.
suicidal *adjective*

suit *noun* **suits**
1 a jacket and pair of trousers or skirt, sometimes with a waistcoat, that are meant to be worn together. 2 a set of clothes for a particular purpose, as in *a spacesuit.*
3 one of the four sets in a pack of playing-cards, as in *The four suits are spades, hearts, diamonds, and clubs.* 4 a lawsuit.

suit *verb* **suits, suiting, suited**
to be suitable or convenient for someone or something.

suitable *adjective*
satisfactory or right for a particular person, purpose, or occasion, as in *suitable clothes for a hot day; a suitable time to meet.*
suitability *noun,* **suitably** *adverb*

suitcase *noun* **suitcases**
a case with a lid and a handle, for carrying clothes and other things on journeys, holidays, etc.

suite *noun* **suites** (*say* sweet)
1 a set of furniture. 2 a set of rooms.
3 a set of short musical pieces or dances.

suitor *noun* **suitors**
a man who is trying to get a woman's love.

sulk *verb* **sulks, sulking, sulked**
to be silent and bad-tempered, as in *He sulked when he thought he was overlooked.*
sulkily *adverb,* **sulkiness** *noun,* **sulky** *adjective*

sullen *adjective*
sulky and gloomy.
sullenly *adverb,* **sullenness** *noun*

sulphur or **sulfur** *noun*
a yellow chemical used in industry and medicine.

sulphuric *adjective*
containing sulphur.
sulphuric acid, a strong, colourless acid.

sultan *noun* **sultans**
the ruler of a Muslim country.

sultana *noun* **sultanas**
1 a sultan's wife, mother, daughter.
2 a raisin without seeds. 3 a small, green, seedless grape.

sultry *adjective*
hot and humid, as in *Queensland has sultry weather in summer.*

sum *noun* **sums**
1 the amount you get when you add numbers together. 2 a problem in arithmetic. 3 an amount of money.

sum *verb* **sums, summing, summed**
sum up, to give a summary of something, especially at the end of a discussion or talk.

summarise or **summarize** *verb*
summarises, summarising, summarised
to make or give a summary of something.

summary *noun* **summaries**
a statement of the main points of something said or written.

summer *noun* **summers**
the warm season between spring and autumn.

summit *noun* **summits**
the highest point, the top, as in *summit of the mountain.*
summit meeting, a meeting between the most important people from various governments, organisations, etc.

summons *noun* **summonses**
a command to someone to appear in a lawcourt.

sun *noun*
1 the star from which the earth gets warmth and light. 2 warmth and light from this star.

sunbake *verb* **sunbakes, sunbaking, sunbaked**
to be or sit in the sun, especially to tan the body.

sunburn *noun*
redness of your skin caused by being in the sun too long.
sunburned *adjective,* **sunburnt** *adjective*

sundae *noun* **sundaes** (*say* **sun**-day)
a mixture of ice-cream with fruit, nuts, cream, etc.

Sunday *noun* **Sundays**
the first day of the week.
Sunday school, a place where children go for religious teaching on Sundays.

supper

sundial *noun* sundials
a device that shows the time by a shadow made by the sun.

sunflower *noun* sunflowers
a very tall plant with large yellow flowers grown for its seeds which produce an oil used in cooking.

sung past participle of **sing**.

sun-glasses *plural noun*
dark glasses to protect your eyes from the sun or glare.
sunnies, (*colloquial*) sunglasses.

sunk past tense and past participle of **sink** *verb*.

sunlight *noun*
light from the sun.
sunlit *adjective*

sunny *adjective* sunnier, sunniest
1 with the sun shining, as in *a sunny day*.
2 full of sunshine, as in *a sunny room*.

sunrise *noun* sunrises
dawn, as in *They left at sunrise*.

sun-roof *noun* sun-roofs
a panel in a car's roof that can be opened to let in air and sunlight.

sunset *noun* sunsets
the time when the sun sets.

sunshine *noun*
warmth and light that come from the sun.

Sunshine State *noun*
Queensland.

sunspot *noun* sunspots
a dark patch on the surface of the sun.

sunstroke *noun*
an illness caused by being in strong sun for too long.

suntan *noun* suntans
a brown colour of the skin caused by the sun.
suntanned *adjective*

super *adjective*
(*colloquial*) excellent.

superb *adjective*
magnificent; excellent.
superbly *adverb*

superficial *adjective*
1 on the surface, as in *a superficial cut*.
2 not deep or thorough, as in *She has only superficial knowledge of the subject*.
superficiality *noun*, **superficially** *adverb*

Usage Do not confuse **superficial** with **superfluous**, which is the next word in this dictionary.

superfluous *adjective*
not necessary; no longer needed.

superintend *verb* superintends, superintending, superintended
to be in charge of something or someone and look after it, him, or her.

superintendent *noun* superintendents
1 someone who is in charge of something or someone.   2 a high-ranking police officer.

superior *adjective*
1 higher or more important than someone else.   2 better than another person or thing.   3 conceited; proud, as in *I dislike his superior attitude*.
superiority *noun*

superior *noun* superiors
someone of higher rank or position than another person.

superlative *noun* superlatives
the form of an adjective or adverb that expresses the greatest degree of something, as in *Superlatives are words like 'best', 'highest', 'soonest', and 'worst'*.

supermarket *noun* supermarkets
a large self-service shop that sells food and other goods.

supernatural *adjective*
having no natural explanation; strange, as in *Ghosts are supernatural*.

supernatural *noun*
the supernatural, things that have no natural explanation, such as ghosts, angels, fairies, etc.

supersede *verb* supersedes, superseding, superseded
to take the place of, as in *This latest computer supersedes the first one*.

supersonic *adjective*
faster than the speed of sound.

superstition *noun* superstitions
a belief or action that is not based on reason or evidence, as in *It is a superstition that it is unlucky to walk under a ladder*.
superstitious *adjective*, **superstitiously** *adverb*

supervise *verb* supervises, supervising, supervised
to be in charge of something or someone and look after it, him, or her, as in *He supervised the building of the dam*.
supervision *noun*, **supervisor** *noun*

supper *noun* suppers
a snack or light meal eaten in the late evening.

a
b
c
d
e
f
g
h
i
j
k
l
m
n
o
p
q
r
s
t
u
v
w
x
y
z

supple

supple *adjective* **suppler, supplest**
bending easily; flexible, not stiff.
suppleness *noun*

supplement *noun* **supplements**
1 a part added to a book, etc. to improve it or bring it up to date. 2 a magazine, usually in colour, sold as part of a newspaper, as in *the colour supplement.*
supplementary *adjective*

supply *verb* **supplies, supplying, supplied**
to give or sell someone what he or she needs or wants.
supplier *noun*

supply *noun* **supplies**
1 a stock of something; things kept ready to be used when needed. 2 the act of providing what is needed, as in *The supply of food to the refugees was handled by Care Australia.*

support *verb* **supports, supporting, supported**
1 to hold something so that it does not fall down. 2 to give help, strength, or encouragement to someone or something.
supporter *noun*

support *noun* **supports**
1 the action of holding something; the action of helping or encouraging someone. 2 a thing that holds something; a person or thing that helps or encourages someone.

suppose *verb* **supposes, supposing, supposed**
to think; to guess that something is true.
supposed to, expected or ordered to do something.
supposedly *adverb*, **supposition** *noun*

suppress *verb* **suppresses, suppressing, suppressed**
1 to stop something happening, as in *The police suppressed the demonstrators' protest march.* 2 to keep something secret, as in *The information in the report was suppressed.*
suppression *noun*, **suppressor** *noun*

supreme *adjective*
highest; greatest; most important.
supremacy *noun*, **supremely** *adverb*

Supreme Court *noun* **Supreme Courts**
the highest court of law in an Australian State.

sure *adjective* **surer, surest**
1 confident about something; convinced. 2 certain to happen, as in *The telephone is sure to ring any moment now.* 3 completely true, as in *One thing is sure; she is not here at the moment.* 4 reliable, as in *Visiting places is a sure way of getting to know them.*
make sure, to find something out or make something happen.

sure *adverb*
(*colloquial*) certainly, as in *You sure were lucky.*
for sure, (*colloquial*) definitely.
sure enough, (*colloquial*) certainly; in fact, as in *I thought that he would be late, and sure enough he was.*
sure thing, something that is certain to happen.

surely *adverb*
1 certainly; definitely. 2 it must be true; I believe, as in *Surely I met you last year.*

surf *noun*
1 waves breaking on the shore or reefs. 2 a swim in the surf, especially the riding of waves.
surfboard, a long narrow board used in surfing.

surf *verb* **surfs, surfing, surfed**
1 to swim in the surf. 2 to ride waves on a surfboard, etc.

surface *noun* **surfaces**
1 the outside of something. 2 one of the sides of something, especially the top part.
surface area, the area of all the outside of something, as in *The surface area of a cube is six times the square of one side.*

surface *verb* **surfaces, surfacing, surfaced**
1 to give a firm covering layer to a road, path, etc. 2 to come up to the surface of the sea, etc., as in *The submarine surfaced.*

surfie or **surfy** *noun* **surfies**
(*colloquial*) a surfer, especially one dedicated to surfboard-riding.

surfing *noun*
the sport of riding the surf on a board or as a body surfer.
surfer *noun*

surge *verb* **surges, surging, surged**
1 to move forwards or upwards like waves. 2 to increase suddenly.
surge *noun*

surgeon *noun* **surgeons**
a doctor who deals with disease or injury by cutting or repairing the affected parts of the body.

surgery *noun* **surgeries**
1 the place where a doctor, dentist, etc. sees his or her patients. 2 the time when this place is open. 3 the work of a surgeon.

surgical *adjective*
dealing with disease or injury by cutting the affected parts of the body, as in *a surgical operation.*
surgically *adverb*

433 **swallow**

surly *adjective* **surlier, surliest**
bad tempered or unfriendly.

surname *noun* **surnames**
your last name, which is the same as your family's name.

surpass *verb* **surpasses, surpassing, surpassed**
to do or be better than others.

surplice *noun* **surplices**
a loose white garment sometimes worn by clergy and members of the choir, etc.

Usage Do not confuse **surplice** with **surplus**, which is the next word in this dictionary.

surplus *noun* **surpluses**
an amount left over after you have spent or used what you need.

surprise *noun* **surprises**
1 something that you did not expect.
2 the feeling you have when something happens that you did not expect.

surprise *verb* **surprises, surprising, surprised**
1 to be something that someone did not expect. 2 to catch or attack someone unexpectedly.
surprisingly *adverb*

surrender *verb* **surrenders, surrendering, surrendered**
1 to stop fighting someone and agree to obey him or her. 2 to give up something to someone.

surround *verb* **surrounds, surrounding, surrounded**
to be all around a person or thing.

surroundings *plural noun*
the things or conditions around a person or place.

survey *noun* **surveys** (*say* **ser**-vay)
1 a general look at something, as in *a survey of Australian history*. 2 a detailed inspection or examination of an area, building, etc.

survey *verb* **surveys, surveying, surveyed**
(*say* suh-**vay** or ser-**vay**)
1 to take a general look at something.
2 to make a detailed inspection of an area, a building, etc.
surveyor *noun*

survive *verb* **survives, surviving, survived**
to stay alive; to live after someone else dies or after a disaster.
survival *noun*, **survivor** *noun*

suspect *verb* **suspects, suspecting, suspected**
(*say* suh-**spekt**)
1 to think that someone is not to be trusted or has done a crime. 2 to think that

something unpleasant is happening or will happen.

suspect *noun* **suspects** (*say* **sus**-pekt)
someone who is thought to have done something wrong.

suspend *verb* **suspends, suspending, suspended**
1 to postpone something. 2 to deprive someone of his or her job or position for a time, as in *He was suspended from the team*. 3 to hang something up.

suspense *noun*
an anxious or uncertain feeling while waiting for an event, information, etc.

suspension *noun* **suspensions**
suspending something or someone; being suspended.
suspension bridge, a bridge supported by cables.

suspicion *noun* **suspicions**
1 suspecting someone; being suspected.
2 a feeling that is not definite or certain.

suspicious *adjective*
1 feeling suspicion, as in *I gave a suspicious glance at the open drawer*. 2 able to cause suspicion, as in *There were suspicious footprints leading up to the open window*.
suspiciously *adverb*

sustain *verb* **sustains, sustaining, sustained**
1 to keep someone alive. 2 to keep something happening, as in *Can he sustain this effort?* 3 to support something, as in *The floor should be able to sustain the weight of the new machinery*.

swag *noun* **swags**
1 a swagman's belongings, usually carried on the back in a rolled-up blanket; a matilda. 2 a bed-roll, as in *The bushwalkers carried a swag for camping out overnight*. 3 (*colloquial*) a large number, as in *She received a swag of presents at Christmas*.

swagger *verb* **swaggers, swaggering, swaggered**
to walk or behave in a conceited way.

swagman *noun* **swagmen**
a person in the olden days who travelled on foot looking for work in the outback, as in *Once a jolly swagman camped by a billabong*.

swallow *verb* **swallows, swallowing, swallowed**
to make something go down your throat.
swallow up, to cover or hide something.

swallow *noun* **swallows**
a small migratory bird with a forked tail and pointed wings.

a
b
c
d
e
f
g
h
i
j
k
l
m
n
o
p
q
r
s
t
u
v
w
x
y
z

swam

swam past tense of **swim** *verb*.

swamp *noun* **swamps**
a marsh.
swampy *adjective*

swamp *verb* **swamps, swamping, swamped**
1 to flood something. **2** to overwhelm someone or something, as in *The switchboard has been swamped with people phoning in to complain.*

swan *noun* **swans**
a large white or black bird with a long neck, as in *Swans live on or near water.*

swank *verb* **swanks, swanking, swanked**
(*colloquial*) to swagger or boast.
swank *noun*

swap or **swop** *verb* **swaps, swapping, swapped**
to exchange, as in *I swapped my comic for his sweets.*

swarm *noun* **swarms**
a large number of bees, birds, etc. clustering or moving about together.

swarm *verb* **swarms, swarming, swarmed**
1 to move in a large cluster. **2** to be crowded with people, insects, etc., as in *The town is swarming with tourists in summer.*

swastika *noun* **swastikas** (*say* **swos**-tik-uh)
a sign formed by a cross with its ends bent at right angles, as in *The swastika was the symbol of the Nazis.*

swat *verb* **swats, swatting, swatted** (*say* swot)
to hit or crush a fly or other insect.
swatter *noun*

sway *verb* **sways, swaying, swayed**
to move from side to side.

swear *verb* **swears, swearing, swore, sworn**
1 to make a solemn promise, as in *She swore to tell the truth.* **2** to make someone give a solemn promise, as in *He was sworn to secrecy.* **3** to use curses or rude words.
swear-word *noun*

sweat *verb* **sweats, sweating, sweated** (*say* swet)
to give off moisture through the pores of your skin, especially when you are hot or doing exercise.

sweat *noun* (*say* swet)
moisture that is given off through the pores of your skin.
sweaty *adjective*

sweater *noun* **sweaters** (*say* **swet**-uh)
a jumper or pullover.

sweatshirt *noun* **sweatshirts**
a type of jumper made of thick cotton.

sweep *verb* **sweeps, sweeping, swept**
1 to clean or clear with a broom, brush, etc., as in *He swept the floor.* **2** to move, remove, or change something quickly, as in *The flood has swept away the bridge.* **3** to move along quickly, smoothly, or proudly, as in *She swept out of the room.*
sweeper *noun*

sweep *noun* **sweeps**
a sweeping action or movement, as in *Give this room a sweep.*

sweet *adjective* **sweeter, sweetest**
1 tasting of sugar or honey. **2** very pleasant, as in *a sweet smell.* **3** kind, pretty, or lovable, *a sweet little house. She is a sweet child.*
sweetly *adverb*, **sweetness** *noun*

sweet *noun* **sweets**
1 a small shaped piece of sweet food made of sugar, chocolate, etc.; a lolly, as in *a bag of sweets.* **2** a dessert; the sweet course in a meal, as in *The sweet on the menu is cheesecake.*
sweet corn, a kind of maize with sweet yellow seeds.

sweeten *verb* **sweetens, sweetening, sweetened**
to make something sweet.
sweetener *noun*

sweetheart *noun* **sweethearts**
the person that you love very much.

sweet pea *noun* **sweet peas**
a climbing plant with sweet-smelling flowers.

swell *verb* **swells, swelling, swelled**, *past participle* **swollen** or **swelled**
to get bigger or louder, as in *My ankle has swollen. The noise swelled as the procession got nearer.*

swell *noun* **swells**
the rise and fall of the surface of the sea.

swelling *noun* **swellings**
a swollen place on your body.

swelter *verb* **swelters, sweltering, sweltered**
to be uncomfortably hot.

swept past tense and past participle of **sweep** *verb*.

swerve *verb* **swerves, swerving, swerved**
to move suddenly to one side, as in *The car swerved to avoid the cyclist.*

swift *adjective* **swifter, swiftest**
quick; moving quickly and easily.
swiftly *adverb*, **swiftness** *noun*

symbolise

swift *noun* **swifts**
a swift-flying, migratory bird having long wings and black feathers with white markings.

swill *noun*
the food and liquid given to pigs.

swim *verb* **swims, swimming, swam, swum**
1 to move yourself through the water; to be in the water for pleasure, as in *I swam in the sea yesterday*. 2 to cross something by moving yourself through water, as in *She has swum the Channel*. 3 to be covered with or full of liquid, as in *Her eyes were swimming with tears*. 4 to feel dizzy, as in *His head swam*.
swimmers, clothing worn for swimming; bathers.
swimming-pool, an area of water designed for people to swim in.
swimmer *noun*

swim *noun* **swims**
a time spent swimming, as in *Let's go for a swim*.

swindle *verb* **swindles, swindling, swindled**
to get money or goods from someone dishonestly; to trick or cheat someone.
swindler *noun*

swindle *noun* **swindles**
a trick to get money or goods from someone dishonestly.

swine *noun* **swine** or **swines**
1 a pig. 2 (*colloquial*) an unpleasant person; a difficult thing.

swing *verb* **swings, swinging, swung**
1 to move to and fro; to move in a curve, as in *The door swung open*. 2 to turn quickly or suddenly, as in *He had swung the car around to avoid the bus*.

swing *noun* **swings**
1 a swinging movement. 2 a seat hung on chains, ropes, etc. so that it can move backwards and forwards. 3 the amount that votes, opinions, etc. change from one side to the other.
in full swing, full of activity; working fully.

swipe *verb* **swipes, swiping, swiped**
1 (*colloquial*) to give someone or something a hard hit. 2 (*colloquial*) to steal something.

swirl *verb* **swirls, swirling, swirled**
to move around quickly in circles; to move something in this way.

swish *verb* **swishes, swishing, swished**
to make a hissing or rustling sound.

switch *noun* **switches**
1 a device that you press or turn to start or stop something working, especially something that works by electricity.
2 a sudden change of policy, methods, etc.

switch *verb* **switches, switching, switched**
1 to turn an electric current on or off.
2 to change something suddenly.

switchboard *noun* **switchboards**
a panel with switches for connecting telephone lines.

swivel *verb* **swivels, swivelling, swivelled**
to turn round.

swollen past participle of **swell** *verb*.

swoon *verb* **swoons, swooning, swooned**
to faint, as in *She swooned with terror*.

swoop *verb* **swoops, swooping, swooped**
1 to dive or come down suddenly, as in *The eagle swooped on its prey*. 2 to make a sudden attack or raid, as in *The police swooped on the gangsters' hide-out*.

sword *noun* **swords** (*say* sawd)
a weapon like a knife with a very long blade.

swore past tense of **swear**.

sworn past participle of **swear**.

swot *verb* **swots, swotting, swotted**
(*colloquial*) to study hard.

swum past participle of **swim** *verb*.

swung past tense and past participle of **swing** *verb*.

Sydney-sider *noun* **Sydney-siders**
a person born in or living in the city of Sydney.

syllable *noun* **syllables**
a word or part of a word that has one separate sound when you say it, as in *'El-e-phant' has three syllables; 'cat' has one syllable*.
syllabic *adjective*

syllabus *noun* **syllabuses** (*say* sil-uh-buhs)
a list of things to be studied by a class, for an examination, etc.

symbol *noun* **symbols**
a thing that represents or suggests something, as in *The cross is a symbol of Christianity*.
symbolic *adjective*, **symbolical** *adjective*, **symbolically** *adverb*, **symbolism** *noun*

symbolise or **symbolize** *verb* **symbolises, symbolising, symbolised**
to be a symbol of something, as in *Red symbolises danger*.

a
b
c
d
e
f
g
h
i
j
k
l
m
n
o
p
q
r
s
t
u
v
w
x
y
z

symmetrical

symmetrical *adjective (say* suh-**met**-ri-kuhl)
two halves which are exactly the same but
the opposite way round, as in *Wheels and
butterflies are symmetrical.*
symmetrically *adverb,* **symmetry** *noun*

sympathise or **sympathize** *verb*
sympathises, sympathising, sympathised
1 to show or feel sympathy with others, as
in *I sympathised with her ideas.* 2 to feel
sorry for someone, as in *I sympathised with
the small boy, because he looked so sad.*
sympathiser *noun*

sympathy *noun* **sympathies**
1 the sharing or understanding of other
people's feelings, opinions, etc. 2 the
feeling of being sorry for someone's
unhappiness, pain, or bad luck.
sympathetic *adjective,* **sympathetically** *adverb*

symphony *noun* **symphonies**
a long piece of music for an orchestra.
symphony orchestra, a large orchestra.
symphonic *adjective*

symptom *noun* **symptoms**
one of the things that show that someone is
ill, as in *Red spots are a symptom of measles.*
symptomatic *adjective,* **symptomatically**
adverb

synagogue *noun* **synagogues**
(say **sin**-uh-gog)
a building where Jews worship.

synchronise or **synchronize** *verb*
synchronises, synchronising, synchronised
(say **sing**-kruh-nuyz)
1 to make things happen at the same
time. 2 to make watches or clocks show
the same time.
synchronisation *noun*

syncopate *verb* **syncopates, syncopating,
syncopated** *(say* **sin**-kuh-payt)
to change the rhythm of a piece of music by
putting stress off the beat.
syncopation *noun*

syndicate *noun* **syndicates**
a group of people or businesses who
combine to work together for the benefit of
everyone in the group.

synonym *noun* **synonyms**
(say **sin**-uh-nim)
a word that means the same or almost the
same as another word, as in *'Sufficient' and
'enough' are synonyms.*
synonymous *adjective*

synthesis *noun* **syntheses**
combining parts, substances, etc. into a
whole thing or system.

synthesise or **synthesize** *verb* **synthesises,
synthesising, synthesised**
to make a whole thing out of parts.

synthesiser or **synthesizer** *noun*
synthesisers
an electronic musical instrument that can
make a large variety of sounds.

synthetic *adjective*
artificially made; not natural.
synthetically *adverb*

syringe *noun* **syringes**
a device for sucking in and squirting out a
liquid.

syrup *noun* **syrups**
a thick, sticky, sweet liquid.
syrupy *adjective*

system *noun* **systems**
1 a set of parts, things, or ideas that work
together. 2 a well-organised way of doing
something, as in *There is system in everything
she does.*
systematic *adjective,* **systematically** *adverb*

Tt

tab *noun* **tabs**
a small flap or strip of material attached to an item of clothing, bag, etc. used to hang or identify it.

tabby *noun* **tabbies**
a cat with grey or brown streaks in its fur.

table *noun* **tables**
1 a piece of furniture with a flat top supported by legs. 2 a list of facts arranged in order, especially a list of the results of multiplying a number by other numbers, as in *multiplication tables*.

tablecloth *noun* **tablecloths**
a cloth spread over a table.

tablespoon *noun* **tablespoons**
a large spoon used for serving or measuring food.
tablespoonful *noun*

tablet *noun* **tablets**
1 a pill. 2 a flat piece of stone, wood, etc. with words carved or written on it.

table tennis *noun*
a game played on a table divided in the middle by a net, over which a small ball is hit with bats.

taboo *adjective* (*say* tuh-**boo**)
totally unacceptable, as in *Sexism in the playground is taboo.*

tabouli *noun* (*say* tuh-**boo**-lee)
a salad made from chopped parsley, onions, tomato and cracked wheat.

tack *noun* **tacks**
1 a short nail with a flat top, as in *Nail down that carpet with tacks.* 2 (*in sailing*) the direction or temporary change of direction, especially to take advantage of a wind.

tack *verb* **tacks, tacking, tacked**
1 to fix something with small nails.
2 to sew something quickly with long stitches. 3 to sail a zigzag course against the wind.
tack on, to add something extra.

tackle *noun*
1 equipment, especially for fishing.
2 the ropes, blocks, hooks, etc. used for lifting weights, sails, etc. 3 the act of tackling in football, etc.

tackle *verb* **tackles, tackling, tackled**
1 to try to do something that needs doing. 2 to try to get the ball from someone else in a game of football, hockey, etc., or to bring down an opponent in a football game.

tacky *adjective* **tackier, tackiest**
1 sticky; not quite dry, as in *The paint is still tacky.* 2 (*colloquial*) cheap or shabby, as in *a tacky ornament made of imitation gold; a tacky jumper.*

taco *noun* **tacos** (*say* **tay**-koh *or* **ta**-koh)
a round piece of fried corn bread filled with spicy meat, cheese, etc.

tact *noun*
skill in not offending people.

tactful *adjective*
having or showing skill in not offending people.
tactfully *adverb*

tactics *plural noun*
ways of organising people or things to do something, especially organising troops in a battle.
tactical *adjective*, **tactically** *adverb*

tactless *adjective*
likely to offend people; having no tact.
tactlessly *adverb*

a
b
c
d
e
f
g
h
i
j
k
l
m
n
o
p
q
r
s
t
u
v
w
x
y
z

tadpole

438

tadpole *noun* **tadpoles**
a tiny creature, with an oval head and a long tail, that lives in water and turns into a frog or toad.

tag *noun* **tags**
1 a label. 2 the metal or plastic part at the end of a shoelace, etc.

tag *verb* **tags, tagging, tagged**
1 to fix a label on something. 2 to join or to attach something extra, as in *An extra room was tagged onto the drawings for the new house*.
tag along, to go along with other people.

tag *noun*
a game in which one child chases others.

tail *noun* **tails**
1 the part that sticks out from the rear end of the body of an animal or bird. 2 the part at the end or rear of something, as in *an aircraft's tail*. 3 the side of a coin opposite the head.

tail *verb* **tails, tailing, tailed**
to follow a person or thing.

tailor *noun* **tailors**
someone whose job is to make clothes.
tailoring *noun*

taipan *noun* (*say* **tuy**-pan)
a long-fanged, venomous, brownish snake of northern Australia and New Guinea.

Origin This word comes from the Aboriginal language Wik-Mungkan: **dhayban**. See the Aboriginal Languages map at the back of this dictionary.

take *verb* **takes, taking, took, taken**
1 to get hold of something, as in *He took a biscuit*. 2 to carry away; to remove, as in *The money was taken yesterday*. 3 to guide or accompany someone, as in *Are you taking us to the zoo?* 4 to capture, as in *They took many prisoners*. 5 to have; to use, as in *Do you take sugar?* 6 to occupy, as in *Take a seat*. 7 to need; to require, as in *It takes a lot of effort to succeed at school*. 8 to understand; to believe, as in *I take it that you wish to leave*. 9 to find out; to make a note of, as in *Take his name*. 10 to subtract, as in *Take two from ten*. 11 to accept; to endure, as in *Can't you take a joke?* 12 to make; to get, as in *She took a photo of Uluru*.
take in, to deceive or cheat someone.
take off, to remove something; to begin a flight.
take over, to take control of something.
take part, to share in doing something.
take place, to happen.

take up, to start something; to occupy a place, time, etc., as in *I've taken up yoga. That car takes up a lot of space*.

take-away *noun* **take-aways**
a place where you can buy cooked food to take away with you; the food itself.

takings *plural noun*
money that has been received, especially by a shopkeeper.

talc or **talcum powder** *noun*
a perfumed powder put on the skin to dry it or make it smell pleasant.

tale *noun* **tales**
a story.

talent *noun* **talents**
a natural ability to do something well, as in *She has a talent for singing*.
talented *adjective*

talk *verb* **talks, talking, talked**
to speak; to have a conversation.
talk down to, to talk to someone as though he or she were unimportant or unintelligent.
talker *noun*

talk *noun* **talks**
1 a conversation or discussion.
2 a lecture.

talkative *adjective*
talking a lot, as in *a talkative boy*.

tall *adjective* **taller, tallest**
1 higher than the average, as in *a tall gum tree*. 2 measured from the bottom to the top, as in *The bookcase is two metres tall*.
tall story, a story that is hard to believe.

tally *verb* **tallies, tallying, tallied**
1 to correspond or agree with something else, as in *Does your list tally with mine?*
2 to count or record, as in *Tally up the votes for the school captain*.

talon *noun* **talons**
the claw of a bird of prey.

tambourine *noun* **tambourines**
a round musical instrument like a small drum with metal discs fixed around the edge so that it jingles when you shake or hit it.

tame *adjective* **tamer, tamest**
1 not wild or dangerous, as in *The kangaroos are very tame*. 2 dull; uninteresting, as in *The football match was very tame*.
tamely *adverb*, **tameness** *noun*

tame *verb* **tames, taming, tamed**
to make an animal used to humans and not afraid of or dangerous to them.
tamer *noun*

tamper *verb* tampers, tampering, tampered
tamper with something, to interfere with something; to change something so that it will not work properly.

tampon *noun* tampons
a plug of cotton used to absorb the flow of blood from the vagina during the menstrual period.

tan *noun* tans
1 a suntan. 2 a yellowish-brown colour.

tan *verb* tans, tanning, tanned
1 to make your skin brown with suntan.
2 to make the skin of a dead animal into leather.

tandem *adverb*
one behind another, as in *They ran in tandem down the narrow bush track.*
tandem bike, a bicycle with two or more seats one behind the other.

tangent *noun* tangents (*say* **tan**-juhnt)
1 (*in Mathematics*) a straight line that touches the outside of a curve or circle. 2 a change from a previous action or thought, as in *She was discussing cooking but suddenly went off at a tangent to describe her holiday.*

tangerine *noun* tangerines (*say* tan-juh-**reen**)
a kind of small orange.

tangle *verb* tangles, tangling, tangled
to make something twisted or muddled; to become twisted or muddled, as in *My fishing-line has tangled.*

tank *noun* tanks
1 a large container for a liquid or gas.
2 a heavy armoured vehicle used in war.

tankard *noun* tankards
a large, heavy mug for drinking from.

tanker *noun* tankers
a large ship or road vehicle for carrying oil, liquid gas, etc.

tantalise or **tantalize** *verb* tantalises, tantalising, tantalised
to torment someone by showing him or her something that he or she cannot have.

tantrum *noun* tantrums
an outburst of bad temper.

tap *noun* taps
1 a device for controlling the flow of a liquid or gas. 2 a quick, light hit, as in *I gave him a tap on the shoulder.* 3 tap-dancing.

tap *verb* taps, tapping, tapped
1 to take liquid out of something, as in *Tap the barrel.* 2 to fix a device to a telephone wire, etc. so that you can hear someone else's conversation. 3 to hit a person or thing quickly and lightly.

tap-dancing *noun*
dancing in which you wear hard shoes that make tapping sounds on the floor.
tap-dance *noun*, **tap-dancer** *noun*

tape *noun* tapes
1 a narrow strip of cloth, paper, plastic, etc. 2 a narrow plastic strip coated with a magnetic substance and used for making recordings. 3 a strip of adhesive plastic, etc., as in *sticky tape; masking tape.* 4 a strip of marked tape or flexible metal for measuring.

tape *verb* tapes, taping, taped
1 to fix, cover, or surround something with tape. 2 to record sound on magnetic tape.

tape-measure *noun* tape-measures
a long strip marked in centimetres for measuring lengths; a tape.

taper *noun* tapers
a long thin candle.

taper *verb* tapers, tapering, tapered
to get narrower towards one end.

tape recorder *noun* tape recorders
a device for recording sound on magnetic tape and playing it back.
tape recording *noun*

tapestry *noun* tapestries (*say* **tap**-uh-stree)
a piece of strong cloth with pictures or patterns woven on it.

tar *noun*
a thick, black, sticky liquid made from coal or wood and used in making roads.
tarry *adjective*

tar *verb* tars, tarring, tarred
to coat something with tar.

tarantula *noun* tarantulas
(*say* tuh-**ran**-chuh-luh)
1 a large, hairy, tropical spider 2 a large, black spider found in southern Europe.

target *noun* targets
something that you aim at and try to hit or reach.

tarmac *noun*
1 a mixture of tar and broken stone, sometimes used to seal roads, paths, etc. 2 the runway at an airport made of this material.

tarnish *verb* tarnishes, tarnishing, tarnished
1 to lose brightness; to cause something to lose its brightness, as in *Dampness tarnishes some metals.* 2 to spoil something, as in *The scandal tarnished his reputation.*

a
b
c
d
e
f
g
h
i
j
k
l
m
n
o
p
q
r
s
t
u
v
w
x
y
z

tarpaulin 440

tarpaulin *noun* **tarpaulins**
a large piece of waterproof canvas.

tart *noun* **tarts**
a pastry case containing fruit or jam.

tart *adjective* **tarter, tartest**
sour or bitter, as in *tart lemons; a tart reply.*

tartan *noun* **tartans**
Scottish woollen cloth with a criss-cross pattern, as in *Each Scottish clan has its own design of tartan.*

task *noun* **tasks**
a piece of work to be done.
take someone to task, to tell someone off for doing wrong.

tassel *noun* **tassels**
a bundle of threads tied together at the top and used to decorate something, as in *Dressing-gown cords often have tassels at each end.*

taste *noun* **tastes**
1 the flavour something has when you taste it, as in *This milk has a strange taste.* **2** the ability to taste things. **3** the ability to appreciate beautiful things, as in *Her choice of clothes shows her good taste.* **4** a tiny amount of food, as in *Can I have a taste of your chocolate cake?*
tasteful *adjective,* **tastefully** *adverb,* **tasteless** *adjective,* **tastelessly** *adverb*

taste *verb* **tastes, tasting, tasted**
1 to eat a little bit of food or sip a drink to see what it is like. **2** to have a particular flavour.

tasty *adjective* **tastier, tastiest**
having a taste that you like.

tatters *plural noun*
rags; badly torn pieces, as in *My coat was in tatters.*

tattoo *verb* **tattoos, tattooing, tattooed**
to make a picture or pattern on someone's skin using a needle and some dye.

tattoo *noun* **tattoos**
1 a picture or pattern made on someone's skin with a needle and some dye. **2** a drumming sound, as in *He beat a tattoo on the table with his fingers.* **3** an entertainment consisting of military music, marching, etc.

taught past tense and past participle of **teach.**

taunt *verb* **taunts, taunting, taunted**
to jeer at or insult someone, especially by making fun of his or her weaknesses.

taut *adjective* **tauter, tautest**
stretched tightly.
tautly *adverb,* **tautness** *noun*

tavern *noun* **taverns**
a place where alcohol and food are bought and eaten.

tawny *adjective* **tawnier, tawniest**
brownish-yellow.

tax *noun* **taxes**
money that people have to pay to the government.
taxpayer *noun*

tax *verb* **taxes, taxing, taxed**
1 to charge someone a tax, as in *He was taxed on his income.* **2** to charge a tax when someone buys, owns, or uses something, as in *The government taxes alcohol, tobacco and petrol.* **3** to make heavy demands on, as in *A marathon taxes a runner's strength.*
taxable *adjective,* **taxation** *noun*

taxi or **taxi-cab** *noun* **taxis** or **taxi-cabs**
a car with a driver which you can hire for journeys, as in *Most taxis have meters to record the fare.*

taxi *verb* **taxis, taxiing, taxied**
to move along the ground or on the water before or after flying, as in *The plane taxied out to the runway.*

tea *noun* **teas**
1 a drink made by pouring hot water on the dried leaves of an evergreen shrub. **2** the dried leaves of this shrub. **3** a meal eaten in the evening.
teacup *noun,* **tea-leaf** *noun*

teach *verb* **teaches, teaching, taught**
1 to educate someone. **2** to give lessons in a particular subject, as in *She taught history last year.*

teacher *noun* **teachers**
someone who teaches others, especially in a school.

teak *noun*
a hard strong wood from a south-east Asian tree, as in *teak furniture.*

team *noun* **teams**
1 a group of people who play on the same side in a game. **3** a number of animals harnessed together to do work.

Usage Do not confuse **team** with **teem,** which is a verb meaning to be full of something or to rain very hard.

teapot *noun* **teapots**
a pot in which tea is made.

tear *verb* **tears, tearing, tore, torn** (*say* tair)
1 to pull something apart, away, or into pieces. **2** to become torn, as in *Tissue paper tears easily.* **3** to move very quickly, as in *He tore down the street.*

441 · · · **telephonist**

tear *noun* **tears** (*say* tair)
a hole or split made by pulling something
apart or away.

tear *noun* **tears** (*say* teer)
a drop of water that comes from your eye
when you cry.
in tears, crying.
tear-gas, a gas that makes your eyes water
painfully.
tearful *adjective*, **tearfully** *adverb*

tease *verb* **teases, teasing, teased**
to amuse yourself by annoying someone or
saying humorous things about him or her.

teaspoon *noun* **teaspoons**
1 a small spoon. 2 the amount that this
spoon holds.
teaspoonful *noun*

teat *noun* **teats**
1 the part of a female animal through
which her babies suck milk. 2 the rubber
top of a baby's feeding-bottle.

tea-tree *noun* **tea-trees**
. a shrub with strong-scented leaves and
white, pink, or red flowers.

technical *adjective*
1 to do with machinery or the way that
things work. 2 to do with a particular
subject and its methods, as in *The technical
language of physics is used by engineers.*
technical college, a college where technical
subjects are taught.
technically *adverb*, **technician** *noun*

technique *noun* **techniques** (*say* tek-**neek**)
the method of doing something skilfully.

technology *noun* **technologies**
1 the study of machinery and the way
things work. 2 the machinery, methods,
and ideas used in a particular activity, as in
computer technology.
technological *adjective*, **technologically**
adverb, **technologist** *noun*

teddy bear *noun* **teddy bears**
a soft, furry, toy bear.

tedious *adjective* (*say* **tee**-dee-uhs)
boring; annoyingly slow or long.
tediously *adverb*, **tediousness** *noun*, **tedium**
noun

tee *noun* **tees**
1 a cleared space from which a golf ball is
hit at the start of play for each hole. 2 a
wooden or plastic holder from which a ball
is hit, as in *A tee is used in the games of golf
and teeball.*
tee off, to play a ball from a tee.
tee up, (*colloquial*) to arrange.

teem *verb* **teems, teeming, teemed**
1 to be full of something, as in *The river was
teeming with fish.* 2 to rain very hard.

Usage Do not confuse **teem** with **team**,
which is a noun meaning a group of people
who play or work together.

teenage *adjective*
to do with teenagers.
teenaged *adjective*

teenager *noun* **teenagers**
a person between 13 and 19 years old.

teens *plural noun*
the time of your life between the ages of 13
and 19, as in *He started playing chess in his
teens.*

teeth plural of **tooth.**

teetotaller *adjective*
someone who never drinks alcoholic drink.
teetotal *adjective*

telecast *noun* **telecasts**
a television broadcast.

telecommunications *plural noun*
sending news, messages, etc. over long
distances by telephone, telegraph, fax,
television, etc.

telegram *noun* **telegrams**
a message sent by telegraph, usually
delivered as words on paper.

telegraph *noun* **telegraphs**
a way of sending messages by using
electric current along wires or by radio.
telegraph pole, a pole that supports
telephone wires.
telegraphic *adjective*, **telegraphy** *noun*

telepathy *noun* (*say* tuh-**lep**-uh-thee)
communication from one person's mind to
another without speaking, writing, or
gestures.
telepathic *adjective*

telephone *noun* **telephones**
a device using electric wires, radio, etc. to
enable someone to speak to another person
who is some distance away.
on the telephone, using a telephone to
speak to someone; having a telephone in
your house, office, etc.

telephone *verb* **telephones, telephoning,
telephoned**
to speak or try to speak to someone on the
telephone.

telephonist *noun* **telephonists**
(*say* tuh-**lef**-uh-nist)
someone who operates a telephone
switchboard.

a
b
c
d
e
f
g
h
i
j
k
l
m
n
o
p
q
r
s
t
u
v
w
x
y
z

telescope

telescope *noun* **telescopes**
a tube with lenses at each end, through which you can see distant things more clearly, as in *Portable telescopes have sections that slide inside one another.*
telescopic *adjective*

teletext *noun*
a system for getting information from a database and displaying it on a screen, using a special television set.

televise *verb* **televises, televising, televised**
to send out a program by television.

television *noun* **televisions**
1 a system using radio waves to reproduce a picture on a screen. **2** a television set. **3** televised programs.

tell *verb* **tells, telling, told**
1 to pass on a story, news, instructions, etc. to someone by speaking, as in *He told us a joke.* **2** to reveal a secret, as in *Promise you won't tell.* **3** to recognise, as in *Can you tell the difference between butter and margarine?* **4** to count, as in *There are ten of them all told.*
tell off, (*colloquial*) to speak severely to someone who has done wrong.
tell tales, to report that someone else has done wrong.

teller *noun* **tellers**
a person working at the counter of a bank.

telling *adjective*
meaningful, as in *It was a telling reply.*

tell-tale *noun* **tell-tales**
a person who reveals secrets about another; a sneak.

tell-tale *adjective*
showing or telling something, as in *The thief left tell-tale prints on the window.*

temper *noun* **tempers**
1 the mood you are in, as in *Your good behaviour has put him in a good temper.* **2** an angry mood, as in *Now she's in a temper.*
lose your temper, to become very angry.

temperament *noun* **temperaments**
a person's or animal's nature or character, as in *a nervous temperament.*

temperate *adjective*
neither extremely hot nor extremely cold; mild; moderate, as in *Sydney has a temperate climate.*

temperature *noun* **temperatures**
1 the measure of how hot or cold someone or something is. **2** an unusually high body-temperature.

tempest *noun* **tempests**
(*old-fashioned use*) a violent storm.
tempestuous *adjective*

temple *noun* **temples**
1 a building where a god is worshipped. **2** part of your head between your forehead and your ear.

tempo *noun* **tempos**
the speed or rhythm of something, especially of a piece of music.

temporary *adjective*
lasting, or intended to last, for only a short time, as in *a temporary classroom.*
temporarily *adverb*

tempt *verb* **tempts, tempting, tempted**
1 to try to make someone do wrong or do something he or she would not normally do. **2** to attract someone to do something, as in *I am tempted to try the chocolate cake.*
temptation *noun*, **tempter** *noun*, **temptress** *noun*

ten *noun* **tens**
the number 10, one more than nine.
tenth *adjective* and *noun*

tenacious *adjective* (*say* te-**nay**-shuhs)
1 keeping a firm hold on something, as in *The child had a tenacious grip of her favourite toy.* **2** persistent, as in *The tenacious player finally scored a goal.*
tenacity *noun*

tenant *noun* **tenants**
someone who rents a house, building, piece of land, etc.
tenancy *noun*

tend *verb* **tends, tending, tended**
1 to be inclined or likely to do something, as in *Prices are tending to rise.* **2** to look after something, as in *She was tending her garden.*

tendency *noun* **tendencies**
wanting or being likely to do something; a habit, as in *She has a tendency to be lazy.*

tender *adjective* **tenderer, tenderest**
1 not tough or hard; easy to chew, as in *tender meat.* **2** delicate; sensitive, as in *tender plants.* **3** gentle; loving, as in *a tender smile.*
tenderly *adverb*, **tenderness** *noun*

tender *verb* **tenders, tendering, tendered**
to give; to offer, as in *She tendered her resignation.*

tender *noun* **tenders**
an offer, usually in writing, to carry out work or supply goods at a stated price.

tendon *noun* **tendons**
strong tissue that joins a muscle to a bone.

tendril *noun* **tendrils**
the part of a climbing plant that twists around something to support itself.

443 **test**

tennis *noun*
a game played with racquets and a ball on a court with a net across the middle.

tenor *noun* **tenors**
a male singer with a high voice.

tenpin bowling *noun*
a game in which you knock down sets of ten skittles with a ball.

tense *adjective* **tenser, tensest**
1 tightly stretched. 2 nervous; excited or exciting.
tensely *adverb*, **tension** *noun*

tense *noun* **tenses**
a form of a verb that shows when something happens, as in *The past tense of 'come' is 'came'.*

tent *noun* **tents**
a portable shelter made of weatherproof cloth supported by a pole or poles.

tentacle *noun* **tentacles**
a long, snake-like part of an animal's body, as in *An octopus has eight tentacles.*

tentative *adjective*
hesitant; not definite, as in *The shy student made a tentative suggestion about the school play. A tentative estimate of building costs was made.*

tepid *adjective*
only just warm, as in *tepid water.*

term *noun* **terms**
1 the period of weeks when a school or college is open. 2 a definite period, as in *a term of imprisonment.* 3 a word or expression, as in *'Decimal point' is a mathematical term.* 4 a condition offered or agreed, as in *terms of surrender.*
to be on good, bad, etc. terms, to be in a good, bad, etc. relationship with someone, as in *They are on good terms.*

terminal *noun* **terminals**
1 the place where something ends; a terminus. 2 a building where air passengers arrive or depart. 3 a place where a wire is connected to a battery, etc. 4 a device by which you can make contact with a computer.

terminate *verb* **terminates, terminating, terminated**
to end; to stop.
termination *noun*

terminus *noun* **termini**
the station at the end of a railway or bus route.

termite *noun* **termites**
a small, ant-like insect which destroys timber.

terrace *noun* **terraces**
1 a row of houses joined together. 2 a level area on a slope or hillside. 3 a raised flat place next to a house or in a garden.

terrain *noun* **terrains**
a piece of land and its natural features, as in *The Kimberley has rugged terrain.*

terrapin *noun* **terrapins**
a kind of tortoise that lives in water.

terrible *adjective*
awful.
terribly *adverb*

terrier *noun* **terriers**
one of various breeds of strong, lively, usually small dog.

terrific *adjective*
(*colloquial*)
1 very great, as in *a terrific speed.* 2 (*colloquial*) very good; excellent, as in *a terrific idea.*
terrifically *adverb*

terrify *verb* **terrifies, terrifying, terrified**
to make a person or animal very frightened.

territory *noun* **territories**
an area of land, especially an area that belongs to a country, person or animal.
the Territory, the Northern Territory.
territorial *adjective*

terror *noun* **terrors**
great fear.

terrorise or **terrorize** *verb* **terrorises, terrorising, terrorised**
to fill someone with terror.

terrorist *noun* **terrorists**
someone who uses violence for a political cause.
terrorism *noun*

tertiary education *noun* (say **ter**-shuh-ree)
education, in a university, etc., that follows secondary education.

tessellation *noun* **tessellations**
an arrangement of shapes, usually of the same shape and size, to cover a surface without gaps or overlapping, as in *Hexagons can form a tessellation, but octagons cannot.*

test *noun* **tests**
1 a short set of questions to check someone's knowledge, especially in school. 2 a series of questions, experiments, etc. to get information about someone or something, as in *a computer aptitude test. They gave her a test for diabetes.* 3 (*colloquial*) a Test match.

a
b
c
d
e
f
g
h
i
j
k
l
m
n
o
p
q
r
s
t
u
v
w
x
y
z

test

test *verb* **tests, testing, tested**
to make a test on a person or thing.

testament *noun* **testaments**
a written statement.
Testament, one of the two main parts of the Bible, the *Old Testament* or the *New Testament*.

testicle *noun* **testicles**
one of the two glands in the scrotum where semen is produced.

testify *verb* **testifies, testifying, testified**
to give evidence; to swear that something is true.

testimonial *noun* **testimonials**
1 a certificate which describes a person's character, abilities, etc.   2 a presentation given to a person to express appreciation, as in *At his retirement dinner he was given a fine silver tray as a testimonial.*

testimony *noun* **testimonies**
evidence; what someone testifies.

Test match *noun* **Test matches**
a match between teams from different countries, especially in cricket and Rugby.

test-tube *noun* **test-tubes**
a glass tube, closed at one end, used for experiments in chemistry.
test-tube baby, a baby that develops from an egg which is fertilised outside the womb.

tetanus *noun* (*say* **tet**-uh-nes)
an infectious disease, often fatal, which affects the nervous system, causing extreme stiffness of the muscles.

tether *verb* **tethers, tethering, tethered**
to tie an animal so that it cannot move far.

tether *noun* **tethers**
a rope for tying an animal.
at the end of your tether, unable to endure something any more.

text *noun* **texts**
1 the words of a book, speech, etc.
2 a short extract from the Bible.

textbook *noun* **textbooks**
a book that teaches you about a subject.

textiles *plural noun*
kinds of cloth; fabrics.

texture *noun* **textures**
the way that the surface of something feels, as in *Silk has a smooth texture.*

than *conjunction*
compared with another person or thing, as in *Fred is taller than Jim.*

thank *verb* **thanks, thanking, thanked**
to tell someone you are grateful for something he or she has given you or done for you.
thank you, words that you say when thanking someone.

thankful *adjective*
feeling glad that someone has done something for you.
thankfully *adverb*

thanks *plural noun*
1 saying that you are glad that someone has done something for you.   2 a short way of saying 'Thank you'.
thanks to, because of, as in *Thanks to you, we succeeded.*

that *adjective* and *pronoun*
the one there, as in *Whose is that book? That is mine.*

that *conjunction*
1 with the result, as in *He was such a liar that nobody believed him.*   2 used to introduce a fact, thought, wish, hope, etc., as in *I hope that you are well. Do you know that it is one o'clock?*

that *pronoun*
which; who, as in *This is the record that I wanted.*

thatch *verb* **thatches, thatching, thatched**
to make a roof with straw, reeds, or palm leaves.

thaw *verb* **thaws, thawing, thawed**
to melt; to stop being frozen, as in *The ice has thawed. How long will it take for the frozen fish to thaw?*

the *adjective* (called the *definite article*)
a particular one; that or those, as in *the car, not a car.*

theatre *noun* **theatres**
1 a place where people go to see plays or shows.   2 a special room where surgical operations are done, as in *operating theatre.*

theatrical *adjective*
to do with plays or acting.
theatrically *adverb*

thee *pronoun*
(*old-fashioned use*) you, as in *I gave thee my commands.*

theft *noun* **thefts**
stealing, as in *the theft of the jewels.*

their *adjective*
belonging to them, as in *Their coats are over there.*

445   **thin**

theirs *pronoun*
belonging to them, as in *Those cakes are theirs, not ours.*

them *pronoun*
a word used for *they* when it is used after a verb, as in *We can hand them around. We went on holiday with them.*

theme *noun* **themes**
1 a subject. 2 a short piece of music, as in *The theme for the film 'Jaws' helps to create fear.*
theme park, a place with exciting things to do and machines to ride on, all connected with a particular subject, as in *a colonial theme park.*

themselves *plural noun*
them and nobody else.
by themselves, on their own; alone, as in *They built the house by themselves. Victoria and Christopher were standing by themselves.*

then *adverb*
1 after that; next, as in *Then there were nine.*
2 at that time, as in *She was happy then.*
3 in that case; therefore, as in *It isn't here. It must be lost, then.*

then *noun*
that time, as in *Have you seen him since then?*

theology *noun*
the study of religion.
theologian *noun,* **theological** *adjective*

theorem *noun* **theorems**
a statement in mathematics that can be proved or needs to be proved.

theory *noun* **theories**
1 an idea or set of ideas suggested to explain something. 2 the principles of a subject; the non-practical part of a subject or process, as in *In theory, this printer should run automatically, but in practice it needs to be adjusted by hand.*
theoretical *adjective,* **theoretically** *adverb*

therapy *noun* **therapies**
a way of treating an illness of the mind or the body, usually without using surgery or artificial medicines, as in *She had speech therapy for her stutter.*
therapist *noun*

there *adverb*
1 in or to that place. 2 a word that you say to call attention to someone or something, as in *There's a good boy!*

thereabouts *adverb*
near there, as in *They live in Subiaco or thereabouts.*

therefore *adverb*
for that reason; and so.

thermal *adjective*
to do with heat; using or operated by heat, as in *a thermal power station.*

thermometer *noun* **thermometers**
a device for measuring temperature.

thermos *noun* **thermoses**
a vacuum flask used to keep food or drink hot or cold, as in *They took a thermos of tea to the footy.*

thermostat *noun* **thermostats**
a device that automatically keeps temperature steady.
thermostatic *adjective,* **thermostatically** *adverb*

thesaurus *noun* **thesauri** or **thesauruses**
a book giving sets of words arranged according to their meanings, as in *Use a thesaurus to find another word for 'enough'.*

these *adjective* and *pronoun*
the people or things here.

they *pronoun*
the people or things that someone is talking about.

they'd short for *they had, they should,* or *they would.*

they'll short for *they will.*

they're short for *they are.*

they've short for *they have.*

thick *adjective*
1 measuring a lot from one side to the other, as in *a thick book.* 2 measured from one side to the other, as in *a wall 10 centimetres thick.* 3 crowded; dense, as in *thick scrub.* 4 not pouring easily, as in *a thick chocolate sauce.* 5 (*colloquial*) stupid, as in *He was as thick as two planks.*
thickly *adverb,* **thickness** *noun*

thicken *verb* **thickens, thickening, thickened**
to make something thicker; to become thicker.

thicket *noun* **thickets**
a group of trees and shrubs growing close together.

thief *noun* **thieves**
someone who steals things.
thieve *verb*

thigh *noun* **thighs**
the part of your leg above your knee.

thimble *noun* **thimbles**
a metal or plastic cover to protect the end of your finger when you are sewing.

thin *adjective* **thinner, thinnest**
1 not fat; not thick. 2 made of thin material, as in *thin curtains.* 3 not dense,

a
b
c
d
e
f
g
h
i
j
k
l
m
n
o
p
q
r
s
t
u
v
w
x
y
z

thin

as in *thin hair.* **4** runny, as in *thin paint; thin gravy.*
thinly *adverb*, **thinness** *noun*

thin *verb* **thins, thinning, thinned**
1 to make something less thick or less crowded, as in *Thin the seedlings once they are 2 centimetres high.* **2** to become less thick or less crowded, as in *The crowds had thinned by the late afternoon.*

thine *adjective*
(*old-fashioned use*) yours.

thing *noun* **things**
an object; anything that can be touched, seen, thought about, etc.

think *verb* **thinks, thinking, thought**
1 to use your mind. **2** to have an idea or opinion, as in *I think that's a good plan.*
thinker *noun*

third *adjective*
next after the second.
Third World, the developing countries of Asia, Africa and Latin America, as in *A lot of poverty still exists in the Third World.*
thirdly *adverb*

third *noun* **thirds**
one of three equal parts into which something is divided or could be divided.

thirst *noun*
the feeling that you want to drink.
thirsty *adjective*

thirteen *noun* **thirteens**
the number 13, one more than twelve.
thirteenth *adjective* and *noun*

thirty *noun* **thirties**
the number 30, three times ten.
thirtieth *adjective* and *noun*

this *adjective* and *pronoun*
the one here, as in *Is this the man? This is the one.*

thistle *noun* **thistles**
a wild plant with prickly leaves and purple flowers.

thong *noun* **thongs**
1 a narrow strip of leather. **2** a usually rubber sandal with a thong between the big and second toe.

thorn *noun* **thorns**
a small pointed growth on the stem of a plant, as in *Roses have thorns.*

thorny *adjective* **thornier, thorniest**
1 full of thorns; prickly. **2** difficult; causing argument or disagreement, as in *a thorny problem.*

thorough *adjective*
1 done properly and carefully, as in *thorough work.* **2** absolute; complete, as in *a thorough mess.*
thoroughly *adverb*, **thoroughness** *noun*

those *adjective* and *pronoun*
the ones there, as in *Where are those cards? Those are the ones I want.*

thou *pronoun*
(*old-fashioned use*) you, as in *Thou art a friend of Robin Hood, I hear.*

though *conjunction*
and yet; in spite of the fact that, as in *It is not true, though he believes it.*

though *adverb*
(*colloquial*) however; all the same, as in *She said she would come; she didn't, though.*

thought *noun* **thoughts**
1 something that you think; an idea or opinion, as in *a good thought for raising money.* **2** thinking, as in *Give the problem some thought.*

thought past tense and past participle of **think.**

thoughtful *adjective*
1 thinking a lot, as in *thoughtful and intelligent in approach.* **2** thinking of other people and what they would like, as in *a thoughtful, kind person.*
thoughtfully *adverb*, **thoughtfulness** *noun*

thoughtless *adjective*
not thinking of other people and what they would like; reckless.
thoughtlessly *adverb*, **thoughtlessness** *noun*

thousand *noun* **thousands**
the number 1,000, ten hundreds.
thousandth *adjective* and *noun*

thrash *verb* **thrashes, thrashing, thrashed**
1 to keep hitting a person or animal very hard. **2** to defeat a person, team, etc. **3** to move your arms and legs wildly.

thread *noun* **threads**
1 a long piece of cotton, wool, nylon, etc. used for sewing, weaving, etc. **2** a long, thin strand, as in *She pulled a thread in her jumper.* **3** the spiral ridge around a screw or bolt.

thread *verb* **threads, threading, threaded**
1 to put thread through the eye of a needle. **2** to put beads, pearls, etc. on a piece of cotton, nylon, etc.

threat *noun* **threats**
1 a warning that you will punish or harm someone if he or she does not do what you want. **2** a danger, as in *the threat of bushfires in summer.*

threaten *verb* threatens, threatening, threatened
1 to make threats to someone. 2 to be a danger to someone or something.

three *noun* threes
the number 3, one more than two.

three-dimensional *adjective*
with depth as well as height and width.

thresh *verb* threshes, threshing, threshed
to beat wheat, corn, etc. so as to get the grain out of it.

threshold *noun* thresholds
1 the stone, board, etc. under the doorway of a house, building, etc.; the entrance.
2 the beginning of something, as in *We are on the threshold of a new discovery in science.*

threw past tense of **throw** *verb*.

thrift *noun*
carefulness with money.
thriftily *adverb*, thrifty *adjective*

thrill *noun* thrills
1 a sudden excited feeling. 2 something that gives you a sudden excited feeling, as in *Winning the premiership gave him a thrill.*

thrill *verb* thrills, thrilling, thrilled
to give someone a sudden excited feeling.

thriller *noun* thrillers
an exciting story, usually about crime.

thrive *verb* thrives, thriving, throve, thrived
to prosper; to grow strongly.

throat *noun* throats
1 the front of the neck. 2 the tube in the neck that takes food and air into the body.

throb *verb* throbs, throbbing, throbbed
to beat or vibrate with a strong rhythm.

throne *noun* thrones
1 a special chair for a king or queen.
2 the position of being king or queen, as in *Henry VIII came to the throne when he was a young man.*

throng *noun* throngs
a crowd of people.

throttle *noun* throttles
a device to control the flow of fuel to an engine.

throttle *verb* throttles, throttling, throttled
to choke or strangle someone.

through *preposition*
1 from one end or side to the other, as in *Climb through the window.* 2 because of; by means of, as in *We sold our car through an advertisement.*

through *adverb*
1 from one end or side to the other, as in *Can we get through?* 2 completed or finished, as in *He's through his exams. I'm through with this job.*

through *adjective*
going somewhere by the most direct route, or without stopping, as in *a through road.*

throughout *preposition* and *adverb*
all the way through.

throw *verb* throws, throwing, threw, thrown
1 to make a person or thing move through the air; to put something somewhere casually or carelessly, as in *'Who has thrown that stick into the water?' 'He threw it.'* 2 to move your body about wildly. 3 to shape a pot on a potter's wheel.
throw away, to get rid of something.
throw off, to get rid of; to shed.
throw up, (*colloquial*) to vomit.

throw *noun* throws
a throwing action or movement.

throwing stick *noun* throwing sticks
a boomerang.

thrush *noun* thrushes
a small or medium-sized bird with a sweet song.

thrust *verb* thrusts, thrusting, thrust
to push hard, as in *He thrust his hands into his pockets.*

thud *noun* thuds
the dull sound of something heavy falling on to something softer.

thug *noun* thugs
a violent and brutal person, as in *The thug robbed and bashed the old man.*

thumb *noun* thumbs
the short, thick finger at the side of each hand.
under someone's thumb, controlled or ruled by him or her.

thump *verb* thumps, thumping, thumped
1 to hit something heavily. 2 to punch someone. 3 to make a dull, heavy sound.

thunder *noun*
1 the loud noise that follows lightning.
2 a loud, heavy noise.
thunderous *adjective*, thunderstorm *noun*

Thursday *noun* Thursdays
the fifth day of the week.

thus *adverb*
in this way, as in *She did it thus.*

thy *adjective*
(*old-fashioned use*) your.

thyme

thyme *noun*
a herb with sweet-smelling leaves, used to flavour food.

tick *noun* **ticks**
1 a small mark, usually ✓, made next to something when checking it.   2 the high, short, sharp sounds that a traditional clock or watch makes when it is working; one of these sounds.   3 (*colloquial*) a moment, as in *I'll be with you in a tick*.   4 a very small blood-sucking creature which buries itself in the flesh of animals and people, as in *My dog almost died from a tick*.

tick *verb* **ticks, ticking, ticked**
1 to mark something with a tick, as in *She ticked the correct answers*.   2 to make the sound of a traditional clock or watch, as in *His watch was still ticking*.
tick off, (*colloquial*) to speak severely to someone who has done wrong.

ticket *noun* **tickets**
a piece of paper or card that allows you to see a show, travel on a bus or train, etc.

tickle *verb* **tickles, tickling, tickled**
1 to keep touching someone's skin lightly so as to make him or her laugh or feel irritated.   2 to have a tickling or itching feeling, as in *My throat is tickling; perhaps I'm catching a cold*.   3 to excite or amuse someone, as in *The mother was tickled by the baby's behaviour*.

ticklish *adjective*
1 likely to laugh or wriggle when tickled, as in *Are you ticklish?*   2 awkward; difficult, as in *a ticklish situation*.

tidal *adjective*
to do with the tide or tides.
tidal wave, an unusually large sea-wave.

tide *noun* **tides**
the rising or falling of the sea which usually happens twice a day.

tide *verb* **tides, tiding, tided**
tide over, to provide someone with what he or she needs, especially money, during a time of shortage, as in *Here's $5 to tide you over until you get the rest of your pocket money*.

tidy *adjective* **tidier, tidiest**
looking clean and orderly, as in *a tidy room*.
tidily *adverb*, **tidiness** *noun*

tie *verb* **ties, tying, tied**
1 to fasten something with string, ribbon, etc.   2 to make a knot or bow in something.   3 to finish a game or competition with an equal score or position.
tied up, very busy, as in *I'm tied up until late this afternoon*.

tie *noun* **ties**
1 a thin strip of material tied around the collar of a shirt.   2 the situation where there is an equal score or position in a game or competition.   3 one of the matches in a competition, as in *Davis Cup tie*.

tier *noun* **tiers**
a row or layer of something that has other layers above or below it, as in *tiers of seats; a wedding cake with three tiers*.
tiers, in Tasmania and South Australia, a mountain range.

tiger *noun* **tigers**
a large wild animal of the cat family, with yellow fur and black stripes.

tiger country *noun*
country that is remote and difficult to reach, as in *The north-west of Australia has areas of tiger country*.

tiger snake *noun* **tiger snakes**
the highly venomous, striped snake.

tight *adjective* **tighter, tightest**
1 fitting very closely; firmly fastened.
2 mean, as in *He is tight with money*.
3 (*colloquial*) drunk; intoxicated.
tightly *adverb*, **tightness** *noun*

tighten *verb* **tightens, tightening, tightened**
to make something tighter; to become tighter.

tightrope *noun* **tightropes**
a tightly stretched rope above the ground, for acrobats to balance on.

tights *plural noun*
a piece of clothing made from stretch material covering the body below the waist.

tigress *noun* **tigresses**
a female tiger.

tile *noun* **tiles**
a thin piece of baked clay or other hard material used to cover roofs, walls, or floors.
tiled *adjective*

till *preposition* and *conjunction*
until.

till *noun* **tills**
a drawer or box for money in a shop; a cash register.

till *verb* **tills, tilling, tilled**
to cultivate land.

tiller *noun* **tillers**
a long handle used to turn a boat's rudder.

tilt *verb* tilts, tilting, tilted
1 to slope or lean. 2 to make something slope; to tip, as in *The caravan suddenly tilted sideways*.

timber *noun* timbers
wood for building or making things.

time *noun* times
1 years, months, weeks, days, hours, minutes, and seconds; the way that these pass by. 2 a particular moment or period; an occasion. 3 a period suitable or available for something, as in *Is there time for another cup of tea?* 4 the rhythm and speed of a piece of music.
times, multiplied by, as in *5 times 3 is 15 (5 × 3 = 15)*.
at times or **from time to time,** occasionally.
in time, not late; eventually, as in *In time, water can wear away rock*.
on time, not late.
time after time or **time and again,** often; on many occasions.
time-limit, a limited amount of time for doing something; the time by which something must be done.

time *verb* times, timing, timed
1 to measure how long something takes. 2 to note the time when something happens or starts. 3 to arrange the time when something happens.
timer *noun*

timetable *noun* timetables
1 a list of the times when buses, trains, etc. depart and arrive. 2 a list showing the time of school lessons in each subject.

timid *adjective* timider, timidest
fearful; easily frightened.
timidity *noun*, **timidly** *adverb*

timpani *plural noun* (*say* **tim**-puh-nee)
kettledrums.

tin *noun* tins
1 a soft, white metal. 2 a metal container for food.
tin-opener, a tool for opening tins.

tin *verb* tins, tinning, tinned
to put something into tins, as in *The tomatoes were tinned at the cannery*.

tingle *verb* tingles, tingling, tingled
to have a slight stinging or tickling feeling, as in *Her ears were tingling with the cold*.

tinker *noun* tinkers
(*old-fashioned use*) someone who travelled around mending pots and pans.

tinker *verb* tinkers, tinkering, tinkered
to try to mend or improve something unskilfully.

tinkle *verb* tinkled, tinkling
to make a gentle ringing sound.

tinnie or **tinny** *noun* tinnies
(*colloquial*) a can of beer.

tinny *adjective* tinnier, tinniest
1 having poor quality, not made properly, as in *His tinny car was always being repaired*. 2 having a thin metallic sound, as in *a tinny whistle*.

tinsel *noun*
strips of glittering material used for decorations.

tint *noun* tints
a shade of colour, especially a pale one.
tinted *adjective*

tiny *adjective* tinier, tiniest
very small.

tip *noun* tips
the part right at the end of something, as in *tip of the finger; tip of the iceberg*.

tip *verb* tips, tipping, tipped
1 to turn something upside down; to move something on to one edge. 2 to leave rubbish somewhere. 3 to make a small present of money especially for a service given. 4 to name as the likely winner of a race, contest, etc.
tip off, to give someone a hint or piece of special information or warning.

tip *noun*
1 a slight push or tilt. 2 a place where rubbish is left.

tip *noun* tips
1 a small present of money given to someone who has helped you. 2 a small piece of advice or information, as in *a tip for the winner of the Melbourne Cup*.

tiptoe *verb* tiptoes, tiptoeing, tiptoed
to walk on your toes very quietly or carefully.

tire *verb* tires, tiring, tired
to make someone tired; to become tired.

tired *adjective*
weary; ready for sleep.
tired of, bored with, as in *I am tired of doing the housework*.

tiresome *adjective*
1 annoying, as in *The flies buzzed around my face constantly, which was tiresome*. 2 boring, as in *a long, tiresome speech*.

tissue *noun* tissues
1 very thin, soft paper; a piece of this. 2 the substance of which an animal or plant is made.
tissue-paper *noun*

tit *noun* **tits**
a kind of small bird, as in *scrub tit*.

title *noun* **titles**
1 the name of a book, film, piece of music, etc. 2 a word that shows a person's position or profession, such as *Sir, Lady, Dr,* and *Mrs*.

titter *verb* **titters, tittering, tittered**
to laugh in a silly way.

to *preposition*
1 towards, as in *They set off to Adelaide*. 2 as far as; so as to reach, as in *I am wet to the skin*. 3 compared with; rather than, as in *She prefers cats to dogs*. 4 touching, as in *He fell to the ground. She put a brush to her hair*.

to *adverb*
to or in the proper or closed position or situation, as in *Push the door to*.
to and fro, backwards and forwards.

toad *noun* **toads**
an animal like a big frog, as in *Cane toads are found in Queensland*.

toadfish *noun* **toadfishes**
a usually poisonous fish which inflates its body.

toadstool *noun* **toadstools**
a fungus that looks like a mushroom, as in *Most toadstools are poisonous*.

toast *noun* **toasts**
1 toasted bread. 2 drinking to honour a person or thing; the person or thing honoured in this way.

toast *verb* **toasts, toasting, toasted**
1 to cook something by heating it under a grill, in front of a fire, etc. 2 to have a drink as a way of honouring a person or thing.
toaster *noun*

tobacco *noun*
the dried leaves of certain plants prepared for smoking in cigarettes, cigars, or pipes.

tobacconist *noun* **tobacconists**
someone who keeps a shop that sells tobacco and other things for smoking.

toboggan *noun* **toboggans**
a small sled.
tobogganing *noun*

today *adverb*
on this day; nowadays, in the present time, as in *I saw him today. Today we do not allow children to work in factories and mines*.

today *noun*
this day; the present time, as in *Today is Monday*.

toddler *noun* **toddlers**
a young child just learning to walk.

toe *noun* **toes**
1 one of the five separate parts at the end of each foot. 2 the part of a shoe or sock that covers the toes.

toffee *noun* **toffees**
a sticky sweet made from butter and sugar.
toffee-apple, an apple coated with toffee and fixed on a small stick.

tofu *noun* (*say* toh-foo)
a jelly-like substance made from soya beans, used in Asian cooking.

toga *noun* **togas**
a long, loose piece of clothing worn by men in Ancient Rome.

together *adverb*
1 with another person or thing; with each other, as in *They went to school together*. 2 so as to join one with another, as in *Tie the ends together*.

togs *plural noun*
(*colloquial*) a swimming costume; bathers.

toil *verb* **toils, toiling, toiled**
1 to work hard. 2 to move slowly and with difficulty.

toilet *noun* **toilets**
1 a bowl connected to the plumbing of a building, used to get rid of urine and other waste matter. 2 the room containing one of these bowls. 3 the process of washing, shaving, dressing, etc.

token *noun* **tokens**
1 a card, piece of plastic, etc. used instead of money to pay for something, as in *a record token*. 2 a sign or signal of something, as in *A white flag is a token of surrender*.

told past tense and past participle of **tell**.

tolerant *adjective*
able to tolerate things, especially other people's beliefs, behaviour, etc.
tolerance *noun,* **tolerantly** *adverb*

tolerate *verb* **tolerates, tolerating, tolerated**
to allow something; not to oppose something.
tolerable *adjective,* **tolerably** *adverb,* **toleration** *noun*

toll *noun* **tolls**
a payment charged for using a bridge, road, etc.

toll *verb* **tolls, tolling, tolled**
to ring a bell slowly.

topical

tom *noun* **toms**
a male cat.
tom-cat *noun*

tomahawk *noun* **tomahawks**
an axe originally used by Native Americans.

tomato *noun* **tomatoes**
a soft, round, usually red fruit with seeds inside it, as in *Tomatoes are eaten raw in salads*.

tomb *noun* **tombs** (*say* toom)
a place where a corpse is buried; a grave.
tombstone *noun*

tomboy *noun* **tomboys**
an energetic, adventurous girl who enjoys activities usually associated with boys.

tomorrow *noun* and *adverb*
the day after today, as in *Tomorrow is Saturday. Come tomorrow*.

tom-tom *noun* **tom-toms**
a primitive drum beaten with the hands, as in *The rock band included a tom-tom*.

ton *noun* **tons**
1 an old-fashioned unit of weight equal to about 1,016 kilograms.   2 (*colloquial*) a large amount, as in *tons of money*.
3 (*colloquial*) a speed of 100 kilometres per hour; a score of 100, as in *This motor bike can do a ton. Allan Border hit a ton*.

tone *noun* **tones**
1 a sound, especially in music.   2 one of the five larger intervals between two notes in a musical scale.   3 a shade of a colour.
4 the quality or character of something, as in *Swearing lowers the tone of the classroom*.
tonal *adjective*, **tonally** *adverb*

tongs *plural noun*
a tool that is used for picking up things, as in *salad tongs*.

tongue *noun* **tongues**
1 the long, soft part that moves about inside the mouth.   2 a language.   3 the strip of material under the laces of a shoe.
4 the part inside a bell that makes it ring.
tongue-tied, too shy to speak.
tongue-twister, something that is very difficult to say.

tonic *noun* **tonics**
something that makes a person healthier or stronger.
tonic water, a kind of clear fizzy drink.

tonight *adverb* and *noun*
this evening or night.

tonne *noun* **tonnes**
a unit of weight equal to 1,000 kilograms.

tonsillitis *noun*
a disease that makes your tonsils sore.

tonsils *plural noun*
two small masses of soft flesh at the back of your throat.

too *adverb*
1 also, as in *I know the answer too*.   2 more than is wanted, allowed, safe, etc., as in *Don't drive too fast*.

took past tense of **take**.

tool *noun* **tools**
a device that you use to help you do a particular job, as in *Hammers and saws are tools*.

tooth *noun* **teeth**
1 one of the hard, white, bony parts that grow in your gums, used for biting and chewing.   2 one of a row of sharp parts, as in *the teeth of a saw*.
fight tooth and nail, to fight very fiercely.
toothache *noun*, **toothbrush** *noun*, **toothed** *adjective*

toothpaste *noun* **toothpastes**
a creamy paste for cleaning your teeth.

top *noun* **tops**
1 the highest part of something.   2 the upper surface of something.   3 the covering or stopper of a jar, bottle, etc.
4 a piece of clothing for the upper part of a person's body.   5 a toy that spins round and round.

top *adjective*
highest in position, degree or importance, as in *top shelf; top speed; top job*.

top *verb* **tops, topping, topped**
1 to put a top on something, as in *a cake topped with icing*.   2 to be at the top of something.
top up, to fill a container to the top.

top end or **Top End** *noun*
the northern part of the Northern Territory, as in *Darwin is in the top end*.
top ender, a person born in or living in the northern part of the Northern Territory.

top hat *noun* **top hats**
a tall, stiff, black or grey hat worn with formal clothes.

topic *noun* **topics**
a subject to write, talk, or learn about.

topical *adjective*
to do with things that are happening now, as in *a topical film*.
topicality *noun*, **topically** *adverb*

a b c d e f g h i j k l m n o p q r s t u v w x y z

topless *adjective*
without clothes on the top half of your body.

topple *verb* **topples, toppling, toppled**
1 to overturn something; to remove someone from power, as in *The army had toppled the president.* 2 to fall over, as in *That pile of books is about to topple.*

top secret *adjective*
extremely secret, as in *top secret military research.*

topsy-turvy *adverb* and *adjective*
upside-down; muddled.

torch *noun* **torches**
1 a small portable electric lamp.
2 burning material tied to a stick, giving light.

tore past tense of **tear** *verb.*

toreador *noun* **toreadors**
a bullfighter.

torment *verb* **torments, tormenting, tormented**
1 to make someone or an animal feel great pain. 2 to keep annoying someone deliberately.
torment *noun,* **tormentor** *noun*

torn past participle of **tear** *verb.*

tornado *noun* **tornadoes** (*say* taw-**nay**-doh)
a violent storm or whirlwind.

torpedo *noun* **torpedoes**
a long, tubular bomb sent under water to destroy ships and submarines.

torrent *noun* **torrents**
a very strong stream or fall of water.
torrential *adjective*

tortoise *noun* **tortoises** (*say* **tor**-tuhs)
a slow-moving animal with a shell over its body.

torture *verb* **tortures, torturing, tortured**
to make someone feel great pain, especially in order to make him or her tell a secret.
torture *noun,* **torturer** *noun*

toss *verb* **tosses, tossing, tossed**
1 to throw, especially up into the air. 2 to spin a coin so as to decide something from the way it lies after falling. 3 to move around, as in *The restless sleeper tossed in her bed. He tossed the salad.*

total *adjective*
complete; including everything.
totally *adverb*

total *noun* **totals**
the amount you get by adding everything together.

total *verb* **totals, totalling, totalled**
1 to add up, as in *Total the scores of all the players.* 2 to make a particular total, as in *Sales totalled over $50,000 this month.*

totalitarian *adjective*
(*say* toh-tal-uh-**tair**-ree-uhn)
to do with a government with only one political party.

totter *verb* **totters, tottering, tottered**
to walk unsteadily; to wobble, as in *The toddler tottered across the room. The chair on which I was standing tottered, and I nearly fell off.*

touch *verb* **touches, touching, touched**
1 to feel something with your hand or fingers. 2 to come into contact with something; to hit something gently. 3 to be next to something so that there is no space in between. 4 to interfere with something, as in *Leave the engine alone; don't touch anything.* 5 to reach, as in *The temperature touched 40 degrees.* 6 to affect someone's emotions, as in *We were touched by his sad story.*
touch down, to land, as in *The aircraft touched down.*
touch up, to improve something by making small changes or additions.

touch *noun* **touches**
1 the act of touching, as in *I felt a touch on my arm.* 2 the ability to understand or identify by touching, as in *The blind man relied on his sense of touch.* 3 a small amount of something; a small action or piece of work, as in *the finishing touches.* 4 communication with someone, as in *We have lost touch with them.*
touch-and-go, uncertain; risky.

touchy *adjective* **touchier, touchiest**
easily or quickly offended, as in *He was touchy about his weight.*

tough *adjective* **tougher, toughest** (*say* tuff)
1 strong; hard to break or damage, as in *tough shoes.* 2 hard to chew, as in *tough meat.* 3 firm; stubborn; rough or violent, as in *tough criminals.* 4 difficult, as in *a tough job.*
toughly *adverb,* **toughness** *noun*

toughen *verb* **toughens, toughening, toughened**
1 to become or to make something stronger or more difficult to break, as in *The glass in the door was specially toughened.* 2 to make someone, or become, more resistant to discomfort or suffering, as in *His time in the army toughened him.*

tour *noun* **tours**
a journey visiting several places.

tourist *noun* **tourists**
someone making a tour or visit for pleasure.
tourism *noun*

tournament *noun* **tournaments**
a series of contests, as in *a chess tournament*.

tourniquet *noun* **tourniquets**
(*say* **taw**-nuh-kay *or* **tooh**-nuh-kay)
a bandage tied tightly around a limb to stop the flow of blood, as in *A tourniquet was used on his leg when he was bitten by a venomous snake.*

tow *verb* **tows, towing, towed**
(rhymes with *go*)
to pull a vehicle, boat, etc. along behind you, as in *They towed our car to a garage.*

toward or **towards** *preposition*
1 in the direction of, as in *She walked towards the sea.* 2 in relation to, as in *He behaved badly towards his children.* 3 as a contribution to, as in *Put the money towards a new bike.*

towel *noun* **towels**
a piece of soft cloth used for drying things.
throw in the towel, admit defeat; lose hope; give up.
towelling *noun*

tower *noun* **towers**
1 a tall, narrow building, as in *Black Mountain Tower.* 2 a tall, flat-topped part of a building, as in *the church tower.*

tower *verb* **towers, towering, towered**
to be very high, as in *The skyscrapers towered above the city.*

town *noun* **towns**
1 a place where many people live, smaller than a city but larger than a village, as in *country town.* 2 the people who live in the town, as in *The whole town disapproved of the new road toll.* 3 the central business or shopping area used by people in the surrounding suburbs, as in *He works in town.*

town hall *noun* **town halls**
a building with offices for the local council and usually a hall for public events.

toxic *adjective*
poisonous, as in *toxic fumes.*

toy *noun* **toys**
something to play with.
toyshop *noun*

trace *verb* **traces, tracing, traced**
1 to find someone or something after a search; to follow the marks left by a person or thing. 2 to copy a picture, map, etc. by drawing over it on tracing-paper.

trace *noun* **traces**
1 a mark left by a person or thing; a sign, as in *There was no trace of the thief.* 2 a very small amount of something, as in *They found traces of poison in his stomach.*

track *noun* **tracks**
1 a path made by people or animals. 2 marks left by a person or thing. 3 a set of rails for trains, trams, etc. 4 a road or area of ground prepared for racing. 5 a section of a record, tape, or compact disc containing a single song, etc.
keep track of, to know where something is, what someone is doing, etc.

track *verb* **tracks, tracking, tracked**
1 to follow the marks left by a person or animal. 2 to follow or observe something as it moves, as in *The astronomer tracked the path of the satellite.*
tracker *noun*

track suit *noun* **track suits**
a warm, loose, two-piece set of clothing worn especially by athletes.

tract *noun* **tracts**
1 an area of land. 2 a series of connected parts in the body, as in *the digestive tract.* 3 a short pamphlet or essay, often about religion.

traction *noun*
1 the ability to grip the ground, as in *The car's wheels lost traction in the mud.* 2 a medical treatment in which an injured arm, leg, etc, is pulled gently for a long time.

tractor *noun* **tractors**
a motor vehicle used on farms for pulling heavy machines or loads.

trade *noun* **trades**
1 buying, selling, or exchanging things, as in *Trade is usually good at Christmas.* 2 a job; an occupation, especially a skilled craft, as in *plumbing trade; the trade of an electrician.*
trade mark, a sign or name used by only one manufacturer.

trade *verb* **trades, trading, traded**
to buy, sell, or exchange things.
trade in, to give a thing to pay part of the cost of something new, as in *He traded in his motor bike for a car.*

a
b
c
d
e
f
g
h
i
j
k
l
m
n
o
p
q
r
s
t
u
v
w
x
y
z

trade union

trade on, to take advantage of, as in *he's trading on my good nature.*
trader *noun*, **tradesman** *noun*

trade union *noun* **trade unions**
an organisation of workers in a trade, profession, etc. formed to protect their interests.
trade-unionism *noun*, **trade-unionist** *noun*

tradition *noun* **traditions**
1 the passing down of beliefs, customs, habits, etc. from one generation to another. **2** something passed on in this way, as in *Australia has a strong sporting tradition.*

traditional *adjective*
passed down from one generation to another; of a kind that has existed for a long time, as in *a traditional rocking-chair; A traditional Aboriginal society lives as they did before white settlement.*
traditionally *adverb*

traffic *noun*
1 vehicles, ships, people, etc. moving on a road, in the air or at sea, as in *The traffic was heavy at peak hour. The pedestrian traffic moved slowly at the Royal Show.* **2** trade, especially illegal, as in *the drug traffic.*
traffic-light, a light that controls traffic.

tragedy *noun* **tragedies**
1 a serious play about sad events, as in *Shakespeare's 'Hamlet' is a tragedy.* **2** a very sad event, as in *Her death was a tragedy.*
tragic *adjective*, **tragically** *adverb*

trail *noun* **trails**
1 a path through rough country or bush. **2** the scent and marks left behind a person or animal as it moves. **3** a part dragging behind a thing or person, as in *a trail of smoke.*

trail *verb* **trails, trailing, trailed**
1 to follow the scent or marks left by a person or animal. **2** to drag something behind you; to be dragged along in this way. **3** to follow someone at a distance or at a slower speed, as in *A few walkers trailed behind the others.* **4** to hang down or float loosely, as in *The bride's long train trailed behind her.*

trailer *noun* **trailers**
1 a vehicle that is pulled along by a car or truck. **2** a short film advertising a film or television program that will soon be shown.

train *verb* **trains, training, trained**
1 to give someone skill or practice in something. **2** to practise, as in *She was*

training for the race. **3** to make something grow in a particular direction, as in *Roses can be trained on a lattice.* **4** to aim a gun, as in *He trained his rifle on the bridge.*
trainer *noun*

train *noun* **trains**
1 a group of railway carriages or trucks joined together and pulled by an engine.
2 a number of people or animals making a journey together, as in *a camel train.* **3** a series, as in *a train of events.* **4** a long part of a dress that trails on the ground. **5** a group of supporters, as in *The cricket captain had a train of keen followers.*

trainee *noun* **trainees**
a person receiving training for something, as in *She was a trainee at the hairdressing salon.*

trait *noun* **traits**
a feature or quality which distinguishes someone from others, as in *Her traits of generosity and honesty made her popular.*

traitor *noun* **traitors**
someone who betrays his or her country or friends.
traitorous *adjective*

tram *noun* **trams**
an electric passenger vehicle that runs along rails set in the road.

tramp *verb* **tramps, tramping, tramped**
1 to walk with heavy footsteps. **2** to walk for a long distance.

tramp *noun* **tramps**
1 someone without a home or job who walks from place to place. **2** a long walk. **3** the sound of heavy footsteps.

trample *verb* **tramples, trampling, trampled**
to tread heavily on something; to crush something with your feet.

trampoline *noun* **trampolines**
(*say* **tram**-puh-leen)
a large piece of strong, stretched material joined to a frame by springs, used for bouncing up and down on.

trance *noun* **trances**
1 an unconscious condition like sleep.
2 a state of extreme happiness or rapture, as in *Her favourite pop star sent her into a trance.*

tranquil *adjective*
peaceful; quiet; calm.
tranquillity *noun*, **tranquilly** *adverb*

tranquilliser or **tranquillizer** *noun*
tranquillisers
a drug used to make someone feel calm.

transaction *noun* transactions
a piece of business.
transact *verb*

transfer *verb* transfers, transferring, transferred (*say* trans-**fer**)
to move a person or thing to another place.
transference *noun*

transfer *noun* transfers (*say* trans-fer)
1 the moving of a person or thing to another place. 2 a piece of paper with a picture or design that can be applied to a surface by soaking or heating the paper.

transform *verb* transforms, transforming, transformed
to make a great change in a person or thing, as in *The caterpillar is transformed into a butterfly.*
transformation *noun*

transformer *noun* transformers
a device to change the voltage of electric current.

transfusion *noun* transfusions
putting blood from one person into another person's body.

transistor *noun* transistors
1 a tiny electronic device that controls a flow of electricity. 2 a portable radio that uses transistors to strengthen the signal it receives.

transit *noun*
the carrying of goods or people by vehicle from one place to another, as in *The transit from Hobart to Melbourne is often done by sea.*
in transit, the process of passing through from one place to another, as in *His luggage was lost in transit.*

transition *noun* transitions
a change from one thing to another.
transitional *adjective*

transitive *adjective*
to do with a verb which takes a direct object as in *'saw' is a transitive verb in the sentence 'I saw the sea.'*
transitively *adverb*

translate *verb* translates, translating, translated
to put something into another language, as in *This Japanese book has been translated into English.*
translation *noun*, **translator** *noun*

translucent *adjective*
allowing light to shine through, but which you cannot see through, as in *Glass bricks are translucent but not transparent.*

transmission *noun* transmissions
1 the passing or sending of something, as in *the transmission of disease by famine; the transmission of news by radio.* 2 the gears, clutch, etc. that transmit power from the engine to the wheels of a vehicle.

transmit *verb* transmits, transmitting, transmitted
1 to broadcast something. 2 to send or pass from one person or place to another.
transmitter *noun*

transparency *noun* transparencies
1 being transparent, as in *the transparency of glass.* 2 a type of photograph that lets light through and that can be displayed on a screen by means of a projector.

transparent *adjective*
able to be seen through, as in *transparent material; a transparent lie.*

transplant *verb* transplants, transplanting, transplanted
to move a plant, part of a human body, etc. from one place to another.
transplant *noun*, **transplantation** *noun*

transport *verb* transports, transporting, transported (*say* trans-**pawt**)
to take people, animals, or things from one place to another.
transportation *noun*, **transporter** *noun*

transport *noun* (*say* trans-pawt)
1 the action of moving people, animals, or things from one place to another, as in *the transport of sheep to the abattoir.* 2 vehicles, ships, or planes.

trap *noun* traps
1 a device to catch animals or people.
2 a plan to capture, detect, or cheat someone. 3 a two-wheeled carriage pulled by a horse.

trap *verb* traps, trapping, trapped
1 to catch a person or animal in a trap.
2 to catch or catch out a person by means of a trick, etc., as in *The dishonest salesperson trapped the young buyer into spending his money.*
trapper *noun*

trapdoor *noun* trapdoors
a door in a floor, ceiling, or roof.

trapdoor spider *noun*
a large burrowing spider which digs a nest in the shape of a tube, hiding the entrance at the top with a flap which opens and shuts like a trapdoor.

trapeze *noun* trapezes
a bar hanging from two ropes, used by acrobats, gymnasts, etc.

trapezium

trapezium *noun* **trapeziums**
a four-sided figure that has only two parallel sides, which are of different length.

trash *noun*
1 rubbish; nonsense.   2 people regarded as worthless.
trashy *adjective*

trauma *noun* **traumas** or **traumata**
(*say* **traw**-muh)
1 a physical wound or injury.   2 the deep emotional shock which follows a stressful event, as in *She suffered trauma when her son died.*

travel *verb* **travels, travelling, travelled**
to move from one place to another.

travel *noun*
the act of travelling, especially to foreign countries.
travel agent, someone whose job is to arrange travel and holidays for people.

traveller *noun* **travellers**
someone who is making a journey or who often makes journeys.
traveller's cheque, a cheque for a fixed amount of money that is sold by banks and that can be exchanged for money in foreign countries.

trawler *noun* **trawlers**
a fishing-boat that pulls a large net behind it.

tray *noun* **trays**
a flat piece of wood, metal, or plastic, usually with raised edges, used for carrying food, cups, plates, etc.

treacherous *adjective*
1 not loyal.   2 dangerous, as in *treacherous seas.*
treacherously *adverb,* **treachery** *noun*

treacle *noun*
a thick, sweet, sticky liquid.

tread *verb* **treads, treading, trod, trodden**
to walk or put your foot on something, as in *Who has trodden on the flowers? He trod on them.*
tread water, to stay upright in the water by moving your arms and legs.

tread *noun* **treads**
1 a sound or way of walking.   2 the part of a staircase or ladder that you put your foot on.   3 the pattern around the outside of a tyre.

treason *noun*
the act of betraying your own country.

treasure *noun* **treasures**
1 valuable things, like jewels or money.
2 a precious thing.

treasure hunt, a search for hidden valuable things; a game in which you try to find something that is hidden.

treasure *verb* **treasures, treasuring, treasured**
to think that something is very precious.

treasurer *noun* **treasurers**
the person in charge of the money of a club, association, etc.
the Treasurer, the politician responsible for managing the country's finance, as in *The Treasurer presented her budget to parliament.*

treasury *noun* **treasuries**
a place where treasure is stored.
the Treasury, the government department in charge of a country's money.

treat *verb* **treats, treating, treated**
1 to behave towards someone or something in a certain way; to deal with something, as in *She treats her dog badly. How should we treat this problem?*   2 to give medical attention to a person or animal, as in *He was treated for rheumatism.*   3 to pay for someone else's food, drink, or entertainment, as in *I'll treat you to an ice-cream.*   4 to change by a certain process, as in *The oil slick was treated with detergent.*
treatment *noun*

treat *noun* **treats**
1 something special that gives someone pleasure.   2 the action of paying for someone else's food, drink, or entertainment, as in *You're not to pay; this is my treat.*

treaty *noun* **treaties**
an agreement between two or more countries.

treble *adjective*
three times as many; three times as much.

treble *noun* **trebles**
1 a boy with a high singing voice.   2 an amount that is three times the usual size.

tree *noun* **trees**
a tall plant with leaves, branches, and a thick wooden stem.

trek *verb* **treks, trekking, trekked**
to make a long journey, often on foot and usually in a remote part of the world, as in *We spent our holidays trekking in the Kimberleys.*
trek *noun*

trellis *noun* **trellises**
a framework of crossing wooden or metal bars, used to support climbing plants.

tremble *verb* **trembles, trembling, trembled**
to shake gently, especially with fear.

trinity

tremendous *adjective*
1 very large. 2 excellent.
tremendously *adverb*

tremor *noun* **tremors**
a shaking or trembling movement, as in *The earth tremor was strongest in the Newcastle area. The nervous performer had a tremor in her voice.*

trench *noun* **trenches**
a long hole dug in the ground; a ditch.
the trenches, ditches dug by troops as shelter from enemy fire, as in *During the First World War terrible fighting occurred in the trenches.*

trend *noun* **trends**
the general direction in which something is going; a tendency.

trendy *adjective* **trendier, trendiest**
(colloquial) fashionable; trying to be up to date.
trendily *adverb*, **trendiness** *noun*

trespass *verb* **trespasses, trespassing, trespassed**
to go on someone's land or property without permission.
trespasser *noun*

trestle *noun* **trestles**
one of a set of supports on which you place a board to make a table.
trestle-table, a table made in this way.

trial *noun* **trials**
1 trying something to see how well it works. 2 an examination of the charges against someone in a lawcourt.
by trial and error, by trying out different methods until you find one that works.
on trial, being tried out; being examined in a lawcourt.

triangle *noun* **triangles**
1 a flat shape with three straight sides and three corners. 2 a chiming percussion instrument made from a metal rod bent into this shape.
triangular *adjective*

tribe *noun* **tribes**
1 a community or a group of families which shares the same customs, language and living area and which has a recognised leader or leaders. 2 a large group with something in common, as in *a tribe of students.*
tribal *adjective*, **tribesman** *noun*

tributary *noun* **tributaries**
a river or stream that flows into a larger one or a lake.

tribute *noun* **tributes**
a speech, gift, etc. to show that you like or respect someone.

triceratops *noun* (*say* truy-se-ruh-tops)
a dinosaur with three sharp horns on the forehead and a wavy-edged collar round the neck.

trick *noun* **tricks**
1 something done to deceive or fool someone. 2 a clever action or special knack, as in *She performed magic tricks. He has the trick of making perfect pies.* 3 an illusion, as in *The light can play tricks on your eyes.*

trick *verb* **tricks, tricking, tricked**
to deceive or fool someone.
trickery *noun*, **trickster** *noun*

trickle *verb* **trickles, trickling, trickled**
to flow slowly and in small quantities, as in *Tears trickled down her face.*

trickle *noun* **trickles**
a small amount of flowing liquid; a very small amount, as in *The flood of customers dropped to a trickle by 5 o'clock.*

tricky *adjective* **trickier, trickiest**
difficult; needing skill, as in *a tricky job.*

tricycle *noun* **tricycles**
a vehicle like a bicycle with three wheels.

tried past tense and past participle of **try** *verb.*

trifle *noun* **trifles**
1 a pudding made of sponge-cake covered with custard, jelly, fruit, cream, etc. 2 a very small amount of something. 3 something that has little importance or value.

trigger *noun* **triggers**
the lever that you pull to fire a gun.

trigger *verb* **triggers, triggering, triggered**
to set off, as in *The smoke triggered the fire alarm.*

trillion *noun* **trillions**
a million millions (1,000,000,000,000).

trim *verb* **trims, trimming, trimmed**
1 to cut the edges or unwanted parts off something. 2 to decorate a piece of clothing, as in *The dress was trimmed with lace.* 3 to arrange sails to suit the wind.

trim *adjective* **trimmer, trimmest**
neat, tidy, and attractive, as in *the trim lawns of the well-kept garden.*

trinity *noun*
a group of three, as in *The clover leaf is a common symbol of a trinity.*
the Trinity, God regarded as Father, Son, and Holy Spirit.

a
b
c
d
e
f
g
h
i
j
k
l
m
n
o
p
q
r
s
t
u
v
w
x
y
z

trio

trio *noun* **trios**
1 three people or things. 2 a group of three musicians. 3 a piece of music for three musicians.

trip *verb* **trips, tripping, tripped**
1 to fall over something. 2 to make someone fall over. 3 to move with quick, gentle steps.

trip *noun* **trips**
1 a journey, often a short one, as in *a trip to the beach.* 2 the act of falling over something; the act of making someone fall over.

tripe *noun*
1 part of the stomach of cattle, especially an ox, used as food. 2 (*colloquial*) nonsense.

triple *adjective*
consisting of three parts.
triple jump, an event in athletics in which you run up to a line on the ground and then do a hop, a step, and a jump.

triplet *noun* **triplets**
one of three children or animals born at the same time from the same mother.

tripod *noun* **tripods** (*say* **truy**-pod)
a support with three legs, as in *Fix the camera on a tripod.*

triumph *noun* **triumphs**
1 a great success; a victory. 2 a celebration of a victory.
triumphal *adjective*, **triumphant** *adjective*, **triumphantly** *adverb*

trivial *adjective*
not important; not valuable.
triviality *noun*, **trivially** *adverb*

trod past tense of **tread** *verb*.

trodden past participle of **tread** *verb*.

troll *noun* **trolls**
a kind of cave-dwelling dwarf in fairy stories.

trolley *noun* **trolleys**
1 a small table on wheels, as in *drinks trolley.* 2 a low truck running on rails, as in *coal trolley.* 3 a kind of large basket on wheels, used in supermarkets.

trombone *noun* **trombones**
a large brass musical instrument with a sliding tube.

troop *noun* **troops**
a group of people or animals, as in *a troop of musicians, soldiers; a troop of elephants.*

troop *verb* **troops, trooping, trooped**
to move along in large numbers.

troops *plural noun*
a large group of soldiers, as in *The troops returned from war.*

trophy *noun* **trophies**
a prize or souvenir for a victory or success, as in *Silver cups were given to the winners as trophies.*

tropic *noun* **tropics**
a line of latitude about $23^1/_2°$ north of the equator (*Tropic of Cancer*) or about $23^1/_2°$ south of the equator (*Tropic of Capricorn*).
the tropics, the hot regions between these two latitudes.
tropical *adjective*

trot *verb* **trots, trotting, trotted**
to run but not to canter or gallop, as in *The horse trotted along.*

trot *noun* **trots**
a trotting run.
on the trot, (*colloquial*) one after another; continually busy, as in *He worked ten days on the trot.*

trouble *noun* **troubles**
something that upsets, worries, or bothers you; something difficult or unpleasant.
take trouble, to take great care in doing something.

trouble *verb* **troubles, troubling, troubled**
1 to cause trouble to someone. 2 to make an effort to do something, as in *Nobody ever troubled to check our tickets.*

troublesome *adjective*
causing trouble.

trough *noun* **troughs** (*say* trof)
1 a long, narrow box for cattle, horses, etc. to eat or drink from. 2 an area of low pressure between two areas of high pressure, as in *The low trough on the weather map was a sign of rain.*

trousers *plural noun*
a piece of clothing worn over the lower half of your body, with two parts to cover your legs.

trout *noun* **trout**
a freshwater fish highly valued as food.

trowel *noun* **trowels**
1 a tool for digging small holes, lifting plants, etc. 2 a tool with a flat blade for spreading cement, mortar, etc.

truant *noun* **truants**
a child who stays away from school without permission.
play truant, to stay away from school without permission.
truancy *noun*

truce *noun* **truces**
an agreement to stop fighting for a while.

truck *noun* **trucks**
1 a large powerful motor vehicle with a back section for carrying goods. 2 an open railway wagon for carrying freight. **truckie,** (*colloquial*) someone who drives a truck for a living.

trudge *verb* **trudges, trudging, trudged**
to walk slowly and heavily.

true *adjective* **truer, truest**
1 real; correct; factual, as in *a true story.* 2 loyal; faithful, as in *a true friend.* **truly** *adverb*

trump *verb* **trumps, trumping, trumped**
to outdo or defeat, as in *In the card game I trumped his jack with an ace. His offer was trumped by someone with more money.* **trump up,** to make a false accusation, etc., as in *His enemies trumped up charges of theft against him.*

trumpet *noun* **trumpets**
a brass musical instrument.
trumpeter *noun*

truncheon *noun* **truncheons**
a short, thick stick carried by a policeman.

trundle *verb* **trundles, trundling, trundled**
to move along noisily or awkwardly; to move something in this way.

trunk *noun* **trunks**
1 the main stem of a tree. 2 an elephant's long nose. 3 a large box for carrying or storing clothes, etc. 4 the human body except for the head, legs, and arms.

trust *noun*
1 the feeling that a person or thing can be trusted. 2 responsibility; being trusted. **trustful** *adjective,* **trustfully** *adverb*

trust *verb* **trusts, trusting, trusted**
1 to believe that a person or thing is good, truthful, or strong. 2 to hope, as in *I trust that you are well.*

trustee *noun* **trustees**
a person legally appointed to manage business property for another.

trustworthy *adjective*
able to be trusted; reliable.

truth *noun* **truths**
something that is true; the quality of being true or honest.
truthful *adjective,* **truthfully** *adverb,* **truthfulness** *noun*

try *verb* **tries, trying, tried**
1 to attempt. 2 to use or do something to see if it works, as in *Try sleeping on your back.* 3 to attempt to find out, in a lawcourt, whether someone is guilty or not. 4 to annoy someone, as in *You really do try me with your constant complaining.* **try it on,** (*colloquial*) to see how annoying, cheeky, etc. you can be without getting into trouble.
try on, to put on clothes to see if they fit.
try out, to use or do something to see if it works.

try *noun* **tries**
1 an attempt. 2 in Rugby football, putting the ball down on the ground behind your opponents' goal so as to score points.

T-shirt *noun* **T-shirts**
a short-sleeved casual top.

tuan *noun*
a small, gliding possum.

Origin This word comes from Wathawurung, an Aboriginal language of Victoria. See the Aboriginal Languages map at the back of this dictionary.

tub *noun* **tubs**
1 an open, flat-bottomed, usually round container, as in *a garden tub.* 2 (*colloquial*) a bath.

tuba *noun* **tubas** (*say* **tyoo**-buh)
a large brass musical instrument with a deep sound.

tube *noun* **tubes**
1 a long, thin, hollow piece of metal, plastic, rubber, glass, etc. 2 a long, hollow container, as in *a tube of toothpaste.* **tubing** *noun*

tubular *adjective*
shaped like a tube.

tuck *verb* **tucks, tucking, tucked**
to push the loose end of something into a tidy place.
tuck in, (*colloquial*) to make a person, usually a child, comfortable and secure in bed; to eat heartily, as in *The child's father came to tuck her in and kiss her goodnight. The hungry children tucked into the pies.*

tuck *noun* **tucks**
a flat fold stitched in a garment.
tuck shop, a canteen, especially in a school, selling snacks, lunches, drinks, etc.

a b c d e f g h i j k l m n o p q r s t u v w x y z

tucker

tucker *noun*
(*colloquial*) food.
tucker bag, a bag or box for food, especially one carried by a swagman, etc.

Tudor *noun* **Tudors**
a member of a royal family that ruled England from 1485 to 1603, as in *Henry VIII and Elizabeth I were Tudors.*
Tudor *adjective*

Tuesday *noun* **Tuesdays**
the third day of the week.

tuft *noun* **tufts**
a bunch of threads, grass, hair, feathers, etc. held or growing together.

tug *verb* **tugs, tugging, tugged**
to pull hard.

tug *noun* **tugs**
1 a hard or sudden pull.   2 a powerful boat used for towing ships.
tug of war, a contest between two teams pulling a rope from opposite ends.

tulip *noun* **tulips**
a colourful, cup-shaped flower that grows from a bulb, and flowers in spring.

tumble *verb* **tumbles, tumbling, tumbled**
to fall over or down.

tumbler *noun* **tumblers**
a drinking-glass with no stem or handle.

tummy *noun* **tummies**
(*colloquial*) the stomach.

tumour or **tumor** *noun* **tumours** (*say* **tyoo**-muh)
a diseased growth or swelling on or in the body.

tumult *noun* **tumults** (*say* **tyoo**-mult)
an uproar.
tumultuous *adjective*

tuna *noun* **tuna** or **tunas** (*say* **tyoo**-nuh)
a large, edible marine fish found in tropical and warm waters.

tundra *noun*
a vast, level, treeless Arctic region with scant vegetation.

tune *noun* **tunes**
a short piece of music; a pleasant series of musical notes.
in tune, at the correct musical pitch.
tuneful *adjective*, **tuneless** *adjective*

tune *verb* **tunes, tuning, tuned**
1 to put a musical instrument in tune.
2 to adjust a radio or television set so as to receive a particular program.   3 to adjust an engine so that it runs smoothly.
tuner *noun*

tunic *noun* **tunics** (*say* **tyoo**-nik)
1 a long or close-fitting jacket worn by soldiers, etc.   2 a sleeveless dress, especially one worn by a girl as part of a school uniform.

tunnel *noun* **tunnels**
a long hole made under the ground or through a hill, especially for a railway.

tunnel *verb* **tunnels, tunnelling, tunnelled**
to make a tunnel.

turban *noun* **turbans**
a covering for your head made by wrapping a long strip of cloth around it.

turbine *noun* **turbines**
a motor that is driven by a flow of water or gas.

turbo *noun* **turbos**
a turbocharger; a car fitted with a turbocharger.

turbocharger *noun* **turbochargers**
a device driven by a turbine fitted to a vehicle's exhaust, supplying the vehicle's engine with air under pressure.

turbulent *adjective*
violent; not controlled, as in *turbulent waves.*
turbulence *noun*

turf *noun* **turfs** or **turves**
1 short grass and the soil it is growing on.   2 a piece of grass and soil cut out of the ground.
the turf, the racecourse; horseracing and its followers.

turkey *noun* **turkeys**
a large bird used for its meat.

turmoil *noun* **turmoils**
a great disturbance; confusion.

turn *verb* **turns, turning, turned**
1 to move around; to move to a new direction.   2 to become, as in *He turned pale.*   3 to change, as in *The frog turned into a prince.*   4 to make something change, as in *She turned the milk into cheese.*   5 to move a switch, tap, etc. to control something, as in *Turn on the radio.*
turn down, to reduce the volume, flow, etc.; to reject something.
turn out, to happen; to put out; to produce or make, as in *Wait and see how things turn out. They were turned out of the house for failing to pay rent. How many shirts did you turn out?*
turn up, to appear or arrive; to increase the volume, flow, etc., as in *The lost purse turned up. He always turns up when you least expect him. Turn up the heating.*

turn *noun* **turns**
1 the act of turning, as in *the turn of the wheel*. **2** a place where a road bends; a junction. **3** the proper time for something to happen, as in *It's your turn to wash up*. **4** (*colloquial*) a party. **5** (*colloquial*) an attack of illness; a nervous shock, as in *It gave me a nasty turn*.
good turn, a helpful action.
in turn, first one and then the other; following one after another.

turnip *noun* **turnips**
a plant with a large, round, white root used as a vegetable.

turnout *noun* **turnouts**
the number of people attending a meeting, voting at an election, etc.

turnover *noun* **turnovers**
1 a small pie made of pastry folded over fruit, jam, etc. **2** the amount of money taken in a business.

turnstile *noun* **turnstiles**
a revolving gate that lets through one person at a time.

turntable *noun* **turntables**
the revolving part of a record-player that you put the record on.

turpentine *noun* (*say* **ter**-puhn-tuyn)
1 an oil used to make paint thinner and to clean paintbrushes; turps. **2** a tall tree with thick bark, fluffy, creamy flowers and a sap which acts as a preservative.

turquoise *noun* (*say* **ter**-kwoiz)
1 sky-blue or greenish-blue. **2** a greenish-blue jewel.

turret *noun* **turrets**
1 a small tower in a castle. **2** a revolving structure containing a gun.

turrum *noun*
a large game fish found in northern Australian coastal waters.

turtle *noun* **turtles**
a marine or freshwater reptile which has a hard shell covering its body and flippers or webbed toes used in swimming.

tusk *noun* **tusks**
a long pointed tooth that sticks out of the mouth of an elephant, walrus, or boar.

tutor *noun* **tutors**
a teacher, especially one who teaches one person at a time.

tuxedo *noun* **tuxedos** or **tuxedoes**
a dinner jacket.

TV short for **television.**

tweed *noun*
a thick, rough, woollen cloth.

tweezers *plural noun*
a small tool for gripping or picking up small things like stamps and hairs.

twelve *noun* **twelves**
the number 12, one more than eleven.
twelfth *adjective* and *noun*

twenty *noun* **twenties**
the number 20, one more than nineteen.
twentieth *adjective* and *noun*

twice *adverb*
1 two times; on two occasions. **2** double the amount.

twiddle *verb* **twiddles, twiddling, twiddled**
to turn something around or over and over in an idle way, as in *He just twiddled his thumbs*.

twig *noun* **twigs**
a short, thin branch.

twilight *noun*
the light from the sky when the sun is below the horizon; the time when this occurs.

twin *noun* **twins**
1 one of two children or animals born at the same time from one mother. **2** one of two things that are exactly alike.

twine *noun*
strong, thin string.

twinge *noun* **twinges**
a short, sharp pain.

twinkle *verb* **twinkles, twinkling, twinkled**
to sparkle.

twirl *verb* **twirls, twirling, twirled**
to turn around and around quickly; to cause something to turn in this way.

twist *verb* **twists, twisting, twisted**
1 to turn something around so as to face the other way, as in *He twisted my ear*. **2** to turn around or from side to side, as in *The river twisted along the valley*. **3** to bend out of its proper shape, as in *My bicycle's front wheel is twisted. Her ankle twisted when she fell*.
to twist one's arm, (*colloquial*) to persuade forcefully.

twist *noun* **twists**
a twisting movement or action.
round the twist, (*colloquial*) mad, crazy.

twitch *verb* **twitches, twitching, twitched**
to jerk; to move suddenly and quickly, as in *The rabbit was twitching its nose*.

twitter

twitter *verb* **twitters, twittering, twittered**
to make quick chirping sounds, as in *The sparrows twittered.*

two *noun* **twos**
the number 2, one more than one.
in two minds, undecided.
put two and two together, to work out from the known facts.
two-piece, consisting of two separate parts, as in *a two-piece suit.*

two-dimensional (2D) *adjective*
shapes that have only two dimensions such as length and width.

two-faced *adjective*
insincere; deceitful.

two-up *noun*
a gambling game in which two coins are tossed in the air and bets placed on a showing of two heads or two tails, as in *Aussie Rules and two-up are dinkum Australian sports.*

type *noun* **types**
1 a kind or class, as in *There are many different types of cars. He is not the sporting type.* 2 letters, figures, etc. designed and made for use in printing, as in *The headlines were in bold type.*

type *verb* **types, typing, typed**
to write something with a typewriter; to use a typewriter.
typist *noun*

typewriter *noun* **typewriters**
a machine with keys that you press to print letters or figures on a sheet of paper.
typewritten *adjective*

typhoid *noun* (*say* **tuy**-foid)
a serious, often fatal, disease caused by eating or drinking food or water containing the deadly bacteria.

typhoon *noun* **typhoons**
a violent windy storm.

typical *adjective*
1 belonging to a particular type of person or thing, as in *a typical outback building has a verandah.* 2 usual in a particular person or thing, as in *She worked with typical thoroughness.*
typically *adverb*

tyranny *noun* **tyrannies** (*say* **ti**-ruh-nee)
a cruel or unjust way of ruling people.
tyrannical *adjective*, **tyrannous** *adjective*

tyrannosaurus *noun* **tyrannosauruses**
(*say* tuy-ran-uh-**saw**-ruhs)
a dinosaur with very short front legs and a long, well-developed tail.

tyrant *noun* **tyrants** (*say* **tuy**-ruhnt)
someone who rules people cruelly or unjustly.

tyre *noun* **tyres**
a circle of rubber around the rim of a wheel, as in *Tyres are usually hollow tubes filled with air.*

Uu

udder *noun* **udders**
the part of a cow, goat, etc. from which milk is taken.

UFO *noun* **UFOs**
(short for **unidentified flying object**) a flying object that cannot be explained, and is thought to be a spacecraft from a planet other than Earth.

ugly *adjective* **uglier, ugliest**
1 not beautiful; unpleasant to look at, as in *an ugly house.* **2** threatening; dangerous, as in *an ugly crowd at the demonstration.*
ugliness *noun*

ulcer *noun* **ulcers**
a sore on the surface of the body or on one of its organs, as in *a mouth ulcer.*

ultimate *adjective*
last; final, as in *the ultimate weapon.*
ultimately *adverb*

ultraviolet *adjective*
(of light) beyond the violet end of the spectrum.

Uluru *noun*
the official Australian name for what was formerly called 'Ayers Rock' in Central Australia.

Usage This word comes from Luritja, an Aboriginal language of the Northern Territory. See the Aboriginal Languages map at the back of this dictionary.

umbilical cord *noun* **umbilical cords**
the tube connecting the unborn baby to its mother's womb.

umbrella *noun* **umbrellas**
a mushroom-shaped piece of material stretched over a folding frame, used to protect yourself from rain, snow, or sun.

umpire *noun* **umpires**
the person who sees that the rules are obeyed in various sports, as in *The cricket umpire declared the batter out.*

unable *adjective*
not able, as in *She was unable to hear.*

unanimous *adjective* (say yoo-**nan**-uh-muhs)
agreed to by all, as in *a unanimous decision.*
unanimity *noun*, **unanimously** *adverb*

unassuming *adjective*
modest or not thinking highly of yourself.

unavoidable *adjective*
not able to be prevented; bound to happen.
unavoidably *adverb*

unbearable *adjective*
not able to be endured; unpleasant; painful.
unbearably *adverb*

unbelievable *adjective*
unlikely; extraordinary or amazing, as in *an unbelievable excuse for lateness; the swimmer's unbelievable time.*
unbelievably *adverb*

uncanny *adjective* **uncannier, uncanniest**
1 strange and rather frightening, as in *uncanny sounds in the dark.* **2** difficult to explain, as in *The computer forecast the results of the election with uncanny accuracy.*

uncertain *adjective*
1 not certain, as in *He is uncertain about what to do.* **2** not reliable, as in *uncertain weather.*
uncertainly *adverb*, **uncertainty** *noun*

uncle *noun* **uncles**
1 the brother of your father or mother; your aunt's husband. **2** (in Aboriginal English) any male of the same age as your parents.

a
b
c
d
e
f
g
h
i
j
k
l
m
n
o
p
q
r
s
t
u
v
w
x
y
z

uncomfortable

uncomfortable *adjective*
1 not comfortable, as in *The lumpy bed was uncomfortable.* 2 not at ease, as in *He was uncomfortable acting as the boss.*
uncomfortably *adverb*

unconscious *adjective*
1 not conscious. 2 not aware, as in *I was unconscious of doing anything wrong.*
unconsciously *adverb*, **unconsciousness** *noun*

uncontrollable *adjective*
not able to be controlled or stopped.
uncontrollably *adverb*

uncountable *adjective*
unable to be counted; immense, as in *uncountable wealth.*

uncouth *adjective* (say un-**kooth**)
being rough in appearance, manners, etc., as in *His uncouth behaviour made him unwelcome at the party.*

uncover *verb* uncovers, uncovering, uncovered
1 to take the cover or top off something. 2 to reveal something, as in *The police have uncovered a huge fraud.*

undecided *adjective*
not settled or certain, as in *They were undecided about the date of the concert.*

under *preposition*
1 lower than; below, as in *under the desk.* 2 less than, as in *under 5 years old.* 3 ruled or controlled by, as in *under his command.* 4 in the process of; undergoing, as in *The road is under repair.* 5 using; moving by means of, as in *under its own steam.*
under way, in progress, happening.

under *adverb*
in or to a lower place, as in *The diver went under.*

underarm *adverb*
with the arm below shoulder level, as in *He bowled underarm.*

underclothes *plural noun*
underwear.
underclothing *noun*

underdeveloped *adjective*
not fully developed, immature; not rich; not yet modernised, as in *an underdeveloped country.*

underdog *noun* underdogs
1 a person who is in a position of inferiority, as in *The dedicated charity worker always cared for the underdog.* 2 the loser or expected loser in a game, etc., as in *They were surprised when the underdogs won.*

undergo *verb* undergoes, undergoing, underwent, undergone
to experience or suffer something; to pass through something, as in *She underwent great pain after the injury. The coffee beans undergo a process of drying and roasting.*

undergraduate *noun* undergraduates
a student at a university who has not yet taken a degree.

underground *adverb* and *adjective*
1 under the ground. 2 done or working in secret.

undergrowth *noun*
bushes and other plants growing under tall trees.

underhand *adjective*
secretive and deceitful.

underlie *verb* underlies, underlying, underlay, underlain
1 to be or lie under something. 2 to be the basis or explanation for something, as in *Hard work underlies the team's success this season.*

underline *verb* underlines, underlining, underlined
1 to draw a line under a word. 2 to show something clearly, as in *John's accident underlines what I was saying about being careful.*

undermine *verb* undermines, undermining, undermined
to make something less strong, secure or likely to succeed, as in *Her injury undermined her chances of winning.*

underneath *preposition* and *adverb*
below; under.

underpants *plural noun*
underwear worn under trousers.

underpass *noun* underpasses
a place where one road or path goes under another.

understand *verb* understands, understanding, understood
1 to know what something means, what it is, or how it works, as in *She understood the scientific theory.* 2 to learn; to have heard, as in *I understand he has measles.*
understandable *adjective*, **understandably** *adverb*

understanding *noun*
1 the power to understand or think; intelligence. 2 agreement; harmony. 3 sympathy; tolerance.

understanding *adjective*
sympathetic and tolerant, as in *He was very understanding when I was ill.*

undertake *verb* undertakes, undertaking, undertook, undertaken
to agree or promise to do something.
undertaking *noun*

undertaker *noun* undertakers
someone whose job is to arrange funerals.

underwear *noun*
clothes worn next to the skin, under other clothes.

underworld *noun*
1 the people in society who live by organised crime, as in *The underworld makes great profits from illegal drugs.* 2 in legends, the place for the spirits of the dead; hell.

undesirable *adjective*
not wanted; not liked.

undeveloped *adjective*
not developed, as in *undeveloped land; undeveloped personality; undeveloped film.*

undo *verb* undoes, undoing, undid, undone
1 to unfasten something, as in *I undid the knot. Your shoe is undone.* 2 to destroy the effect of something, as in *He has undone our good work.*

undoubted *adjective*
definite; certain.
undoubtedly *adverb*

undress *verb* undresses, undressing, undressed
to take your clothes off; to take someone's clothes off.

unearth *verb* unearths, unearthing, unearthed
1 to dig up something, as in *The archaeologist unearthed rare coins.* 2 to find something by searching, as in *She unearthed her lost passport.*

unearthly *adjective*
supernatural; strange and frightening, as in *The campers heard the unearthly sound of a dingo's howl at night.*

uneasy *adjective*
uncomfortable; worried.
uneasily *adverb*, **uneasiness** *noun*

unemployed *adjective*
without a job.
unemployment *noun*

unemployment benefit *noun* unemployment benefits
a government payment made to an unemployed person.

uneven *adjective*
1 not level, as in *an uneven running track.* 2 not regular, as in *an uneven row of teeth.*
unevenly *adverb*, **unevenness** *noun*

unexpected *adjective*
not expected; surprising.
unexpectedly *adverb*, **unexpectedness** *noun*

unfair *adjective*
not fair; unjust.
unfairly *adverb*, **unfairness** *noun*

unfamiliar *adjective*
not known.

unfasten *verb* unfastens, unfastening, unfastened
to open something that has been fastened.

unfavourable or **unfavorable** *adjective*
not helpful; not approving, as in *an unfavourable answer; unfavourable weather.*
unfavourably *adverb*

unfinished *adjective*
incomplete.

unfold *verb* unfolds, unfolding, unfolded
1 to open; to spread something out. 2 to make something known slowly; to become known slowly, as in *The story unfolds.*

unforeseen *adjective*
not expected.

unforgettable *adjective*
not able to be forgotten.

unforgivable *adjective*
not able to be excused, as in *an unforgivable crime.*

unfortunate *adjective*
1 unlucky. 2 regrettable, as in *The unfortunate mistake caused much sorrow.*
unfortunately *adverb*

unfreeze *verb* unfreezes, unfreezing, unfroze, unfrozen
to stop being frozen; to cause something to stop being frozen.

unfriendly *adjective*
not friendly, hostile.
unfriendliness *noun*

ungrateful *adjective*
not feeling or showing gratitude.
ungratefully *adverb*

unhappy *adjective* unhappier, unhappiest
1 not happy, miserable. 2 unfortunate, as in *an unhappy remark.*
unhappily *adverb*, **unhappiness** *noun*

unhealthy *adjective* unhealthier, unhealthiest
not in good health.

unheard

unheard *adjective*
not heard, as in *Her call for help was unheard.*
unheard-of, never known or done before;
extraordinary.

unicorn *noun* **unicorns** (*say* yoo-nuh-**kawn**)
an imaginary animal like a horse with a
long, straight horn growing out of the front
of its head.

uniform *noun* **uniforms**
the special clothes worn by members of an
army, organisation, school, etc.
uniformed *adjective*

uniform *adjective*
always the same; not changing, as in *Egg
cartons are of uniform size and shape.*
uniformity *noun*, **uniformly** *adverb*

unify *verb* **unifies, unifying, unified**
to make several things, especially
countries, into one thing; to join together.
unification *noun*

unimportant *adjective*
not important.
unimportance *noun*

uninhabited *adjective*
having nobody living there, as in
uninhabited desert.

unintentional *adjective*
not deliberate.
unintentionally *adverb*

uninterested *adjective*
not interested; not wanting to know about
something.

Usage Do not confuse **uninterested** with
disinterested, which means not prejudiced
or not favouring one side more than the
other.

uninteresting *adjective*
not interesting.

union *noun* **unions**
1 the joining of things together; a united
thing. 2 a trade union.

unique *adjective* (*say* yoo-**neek**)
being the only one of its kind; very unusual,
as in *Your teeth are unique. A unique tropical
flower was found.*
uniquely *adverb*, **uniqueness** *noun*

unisex *adjective*
for either men or women; designed to suit
men or women, as in *a unisex bicycle. A
T-shirt is a unisex piece of clothing.*

unison *noun* (*say* yoo-nuh-**suhn**)
in unison, making the same sound together;
agreeing.

unit *noun* **units**
1 an amount used in measuring or counting,
as in *Centimetres are units of length, and cents
are units of money.* 2 an individual thing,
person, or group regarded as single and
complete, as in *kitchen unit; Dedicated
medical staff formed the heart unit.* 3 a type
of accommodation, as in *home unit.*

unite *verb* **unites, uniting, united**
to form into one thing; to join together.

unity *noun* **unities**
the state of being united or in complete
agreement, as in *There was unity among the
students on the need for a better tuckshop.*

universal *adjective*
concerning or including everyone and
everything.
universal joint, a joint which allows
movement in all directions.
universally *adverb*

universe *noun*
everything that exists; the whole of space
and the stars, etc. in it.

university *noun* **universities**
a place where people go to study for
degrees after they have left school.

unjust *adjective*
not fair; not just.
unjustly *adverb*

unkind *adjective* **unkinder, unkindest**
not kind; cruel, as in *an unkind remark.*
unkindly *adverb*, **unkindness** *noun*

unknown *adjective*
not known or unfamiliar, as in *The stranger
is unknown to me.*

unleaded *adjective*
not containing lead, as in *This car runs on
unleaded petrol.*

unless *conjunction*
except when; if not, as in *We shall not go
unless we have to. You cannot come into this
club unless you are a member.*

unlike *preposition*
differently from, as in *Unlike me, she enjoys
sport.*

unlike *adjective*
not similar; different, as in *The two children
are unlike.*

unlikely *adjective* **unlikelier, unlikeliest**
not likely to happen or be true, as in *The
drought is unlikely to break for some time. He
told an unlikely tale about space aliens.*

unwind

unload *verb* unloads, unloading, unloaded
to take off the things carried by a car, truck, boat, etc.

unlock *verb* unlocks, unlocking, unlocked
to open a door, box, etc. with a key.

unlucky *adjective* unluckier, unluckiest
not lucky; unfortunate.
unluckily *adverb*

unmistakable *adjective*
obvious; definite, as in *There was an unmistakable likeness between mother and daughter.*
unmistakably *adverb*

unnatural *adjective*
not natural, usual or normal, as in *High temperatures are unnatural in May.*

unnecessary *adjective*
not necessary.
unnecessarily *adverb*

unnerve *verb* unnerves, unnerving, unnerved
to make nervous or anxious, as in *The large crowd unnerved the speaker.*

unoccupied *adjective*
empty; vacant, as in *an unoccupied house.*

unpleasant *adjective*
not pleasant; nasty, as in *unpleasant weather; an unpleasant person.*
unpleasantly *adverb*, **unpleasantness** *noun*

unplug *verb* unplugs, unplugging, unplugged
to disconnect an electrical device by taking its plug out of the socket.

unpopular *adjective*
not popular; disliked.
unpopularity *noun*

unravel *verb* unravels, unravelling, unravelled
1 to undo or cause to become undone, as in *The jumper unravelled.* 2 to explain or work out the answer, as in *The detective unravelled the mystery of the murder.*

unreal *adjective*
1 not real; imaginary. 2 (*colloquial*) incredibly good, as in *an unreal pop concert.*

unroll *verb* unrolls, unrolling, unrolled
to open something that has been rolled up.

unruly *adjective* unrulier, unruliest
(*say* un-**roo**-lee)
difficult to control; behaving badly.
unruliness *noun*

unscrew *verb* unscrews, unscrewing, unscrewed
to undo something that has been screwed up.

unseemly *adjective*
indecent; improper, as in *unseemly behaviour.*

unseen *adjective*
not seen; invisible.

unselfish *adjective*
being aware of other people's wishes and interests.
unselfishly *adverb*, **unselfishness** *noun*

unskilled *adjective*
1 (of a person) not having special training for a job. 2 (of a job) not needing workers with special training.

unspeakable *adjective*
too awful to be described; objectionable, as in *unspeakable crime.*

unsteady *adjective* unsteadier, unsteadiest
not steady.
unsteadily *adverb*, **unsteadiness** *noun*

unsuitable *adjective*
not suitable, as in *His casual clothes were unsuitable for the wedding.*
unsuitably *adverb*

untie *verb* unties, untying, untied
to undo something that has been tied.

until *preposition* and *conjunction*
1 up to a particular time, as in *The shop is open until 8 o'clock.* 2 up to the time when, as in *We will help them until they are able to look after themselves.*

untold *adjective*
1 not able to be counted or measured, as in *untold wealth.* 2 not told, as in *untold story.*

untrue *adjective*
not true; false.

untruthful *adjective*
not telling the truth.
untruthfully *adverb*

unused *adjective* (*say* un-**yoozd**)
not used, as in *an unused stamp.*

unusual *adjective*
not usual; strange or rare.
unusually *adverb*

unwanted *adjective*
not wanted.

unwell *adjective*
not well; ill.

unwieldy *adjective*
awkward or hard to manage because of size, shape, etc.

unwilling *adjective*
not willing; reluctant.
unwillingly *adverb*, **unwillingness** *noun*

unwind *verb* unwinds, unwinding, unwound
(rhymes with *find*)
1 to unroll something; to become unrolled. 2 (*colloquial*) to relax.

unzip

unzip *verb* **unzips, unzipping, unzipped**
to undo something that has a zip.

up *adverb*
1 in or to a standing or upright position. **2** in or to a high or higher place. **3** completely, as in *Eat up your carrots.* **4** out of bed, as in *It's time to get up.* **5** finished, as in *Your time is up.* **6** (*colloquial*) happening, as in *Something is up.* **7** (*colloquial*) ahead or leading, as in *The Adelaide Crows were three goals up at half-time.*
up against, (*colloquial*) faced with difficulties, dangers, etc.
up and down, backwards and forwards; to and fro.
up and coming, (*colloquial*) making good progress and likely to succeed.
up for, available for or being considered for a job, etc.
up to, until; busy with; capable of; needed from, as in *We'll be at home up to 9 p.m. What's she up to at the moment? He's up to winning the race. It's up to you to do it.*
up to date, suiting what is now needed, known, or fashionable; modern.

up *preposition*
in or to a higher position on something, as in *Climb up the mountain.*

up-country *noun*
country which is inland and away from a major centre of population.

upgrade *verb* **upgrades, upgrading, upgraded**
to improve something, especially a machine, by replacing some or all of it with something better or more modern, as in *Alec has just upgraded his sound equipment by adding a CD player.*

upheaval *noun* **upheavals**
a sudden or violent change or disturbance.

uphill *adjective*
1 sloping upwards. **2** difficult, as in *an uphill job.*

uphold *verb* **upholds, upholding, upheld**
to support a decision, statement, or belief, as in *The headmistress upheld the teacher's version of the story.*

upholster *verb* **upholsters, upholstering, upholstered**
to provide furniture with covers, padding, springs, etc.
upholstery *noun*

upkeep *noun*
the cost of looking after something and keeping it in good condition.

uplift *verb* **uplifts, uplifting, uplifted**
to raise an object, spirits, etc., as in *Her spirits were uplifted by the choir.*

up-market *adjective* and *adverb*
(*colloquial*) to do with more expensive products, as in *The Mercedes is an up-market car. The wealthy couple shop up-market.*

upon *preposition*
on.

upper *adjective*
higher in place or rank, as in *upper lip; upper class.*

upper case *adjective*
(*in Printing*) large; in capital letters, as in *'ABC' is in upper-case letters.*

upright *adjective*
1 erect; vertical. **2** honest.

uprising *noun* **uprisings**
a situation in which people refuse to obey someone in authority, especially the government; a rebellion.

uproar *noun*
a loud noise or disturbance.

upset *verb* **upsets, upsetting, upset** (*say* up-set)
1 to make someone unhappy. **2** to knock something over; to overturn.

upset *noun* **upsets** (*say* **up**-set)
1 a slight illness, as in *a stomach upset.*
2 an unexpected result or setback, as in *Their plans suffered an upset when the holiday was cancelled.*

upshot *noun* **upshots**
a result of something happening, as in *The upshot of it was that they were both given a detention.*

upside down *adjective*
1 turned over so that the top is at the bottom, as in *an upside down picture.*
2 very untidy; in disorder, as in *The child's bedroom was upside down.*

upside down *adverb*
1 so that the top is at the bottom, as in *I turned the box upside down.* **2** into disorder, as in *The robbers turned the house upside down.*

upstairs *adverb* and *adjective*
to or on a higher floor, as in *They went upstairs. The upstairs room was a study.*

upstart *noun* **upstarts**
someone who quickly reaches a position of power even though he or she is relatively young or inexperienced.

upstream *adjective*
in the direction opposite to the way a river or stream flows.

uptight *adjective*
(*colloquial*) upset; annoyed; nervous.

upward *adjective*
moving or directed upwards, as in *an upward glance*.

upward or **upwards** *adverb*
towards a higher place; up.

uranium *noun* (*say* yoo-**ray**-nee-uhm)
a valuable metal used as a source of atomic energy.

urban *adjective*
to do with a town or city, as in *urban population*.

urbanise or **urbanize** urbanises, urbanising, urbanised
to change a place into a town-like area.
urbanisation *noun*

urchin *noun* urchins
a poor or mischievous boy.

urge *verb* urges, urging, urged
1 to try to make someone do something.
2 to drive people or animals forward.

urge *noun* urges
a sudden strong desire or wish, as in *She felt an urge to dive into the cool water.*

urgent *adjective*
needing immediate attention.
urgency *noun*, **urgently** *adverb*

urinate *verb* urinates, urinating, urinated
(*say* **yoo**-ruh-nayt)
to pass urine out of the body.
urination *noun*

urine *noun* (*say* **yoo**-ruhn *or* **yoo**-ruyn)
waste liquid that collects in the bladder and is passed out of the body.
urinary *adjective*

urn *noun* urns
1 a large metal container in which water is heated. 2 a kind of vase.

us *pronoun*
a word used for *we* when it follows a verb, as in *We thanked him and he thanked us.*

usable *adjective*
able to be used.

usage *noun* usages (*say* **yoo**-sij)
the way that something is used, especially the way that a language is used.

use *verb* uses, using, used (*say* yooz)
to do a job with something, as in *Have you used my pen? I am using it now.*

use-by date, a date marked on a package of food, showing how long the food can be kept.
used to, (*say* **yoost**-too) did in the past.
use up, to use all of something.
user *noun*

use *noun* uses (*say* yoos)
1 the act of using something; being used, as in *the use of gas as a fuel; daily use of the car.* 2 the purpose or value of something, as in *That money is no use to us.*

used *adjective* (*say* yoozd)
second-hand, as in *a used car.*

useful *adjective*
able to be used a lot; helpful, as in *a useful dictionary; a useful tip.*
usefully *adverb*, **usefulness** *noun*

useless *adjective*
not useful; having no purpose.
uselessly *adverb*, **uselessness** *noun*

user-friendly *adjective*
designed to be easy to use for someone who does not have technical knowledge, as in *a user-friendly computer system.*

usher *noun* ushers
someone who shows people to their seats in a theatre, church, etc.

usual *adjective*
normally happening; expected, as in *He sat in his usual chair. It is usual to go to school on Monday.*
usually *adverb*

utensil *noun* utensils (*say* yoo-**ten**-suhl)
a device used in the house, especially in the kitchen.

uterus *noun* uteri
the womb.

utilise or **utilize** *verb* utilises, utilising, utilised
to use something.
utilisation *noun*

utmost *adjective*
greatest, as in *Change the fuse with the utmost care.*

utter *verb* utters, uttering, uttered
to say something; to make a sound with your mouth, as in *She uttered a scream.*
utterance *noun*

utter *adjective*
complete; absolute, as in *He is an utter fool.*
utterly *adverb*

U-turn *noun* U-turns
turning a vehicle around so that it faces in the opposite direction, as in *At some intersections you cannot do a U-turn.*

Vv

vacant *adjective*
1 empty; available.   2 not thoughtful; not intelligent, as in *a vacant stare*.
vacancy *noun*, **vacantly** *adverb*

vacation *noun* **vacations**
(*say* vuh-**kay**-shuhn *or* vay-**kay**-shuhn)
1 a fixed holiday period, especially between the terms at a university, school, etc.   2 a holiday.

vaccinate *verb* **vaccinates, vaccinating, vaccinated** (*say* **vak**-suh-nayt)
to inject someone with a vaccine to immunise against a disease, as in *They were vaccinated against smallpox*.
vaccination *noun*

vaccine *noun* **vaccines** (*say* **vak**-seen)
a type of medicine injected into people to protect them from disease.

vacuum *noun* **vacuums**
a completely empty space; a space without any air in it.
vacuum cleaner, a device that sucks up dust and dirt.

vagina *noun* **vaginas** (*say* vuh-**juy**-nuh)
the passage in the female body between the outside of the body and the womb.

vague *adjective* **vaguer, vaguest**
not definite; not clear.
vaguely *adverb*, **vagueness** *noun*

vain *adjective* **vainer, vainest**
1 too proud of yourself, especially of how you look.   2 useless, as in *They made vain attempts to save her*.
in vain, with no result; uselessly.
vainly *adverb*

valentine *noun* **valentines**
1 a card or gift sent on St Valentine's Day (14 February) to someone you love.   2 the person you send a valentine to.

valiant *adjective*
courageous.
valiantly *adverb*

valid *adjective*
able to be accepted or used; legal, as in *Her injury was a valid excuse for not competing in the game. This passport is not valid.*
validity *noun*

valley *noun* **valleys**
an area of low land between hills.

valour *noun*
bravery, especially in fighting.

valuable *adjective*
1 worth a lot of money.   2 very useful or important, as in *a valuable lesson; valuable advice*.

valuables *plural noun*
things that are worth a lot of money.

value *noun* **values**
1 the amount of money that something could be sold for.   2 how useful or important something is.

value *verb* **values, valuing, valued**
1 to think that something is valuable, as in *I value my mother's ring*.   2 to estimate the value of a thing, as in *The estate agent valued our house*.
valuation *noun*, **valuer** *noun*

valve *noun* **valves**
1 a device used to control the flow of gas or liquid through a pipe or tube, as in *We have valves in our body to control the flow of blood*.   2 the half shell of an oyster, mussel, etc.

vampire *noun* **vampires**
a mythical creature that sucks people's blood.

vegetarian

van *noun* **vans**
a covered vehicle for carrying people and goods, as in *The large family needed a van instead of a sedan. The furniture van delivered the couch.*

vandal *noun* **vandals**
someone who deliberately breaks or spoils things, as in *Vandals broke the seats in the park.*
vandalism *noun*

Van Diemen's Land *noun*
The name given to Tasmania by its discoverer, Abel Tasman in 1642.
[from the name of the governor of the Dutch East Indies Anthony *Van Diemen*]

vane *noun* **vanes**
1 a pointer that shows which way the wind is blowing, as in *a weather vane.* 2 a blade or surface that moves, or is moved by, air or water, as in *Windmills and propellers have vanes.*

vanilla *noun*
a liquid used to flavour sweet food, as in *vanilla ice-cream, vanilla slice.*

vanish *verb* **vanishes, vanishing, vanished**
to disappear.

vanity *noun*
being too proud of yourself.

vanquish *verb* **vanquishes, vanquishing, vanquished**
to gain a victory over someone; to defeat.

vapour *noun* **vapours**
a visible gas produced by heat; steam or mist.

variable *adjective*
likely to change; able to be changed, as in *variable weather, variable pressure.*

variable *noun* **variables**
(*in Mathematics*) a quantity that can have various values, represented by a symbol, as in *In the formula to find the circumference of a circle, $c = 2\pi r$, c and r are variables.*

variation *noun* **variations**
1 an alteration or change, as in *variation in demand for cars.* 2 something that has a different form from the normal or usual one, as in *It is the same television program with a few variations for each city.*

varied *adjective*
being of different kinds, as in *a varied selection of cakes.*

variety *noun* **varieties**
1 a number of different kinds of things, as in *There was a variety of sweets.* 2 a particular kind of something, as in *rare varieties of butterflies.* 3 change; a situation where things are not always the same, as in *a life full of variety.*

various *adjective*
1 different kinds, as in *for various reasons.*
2 several, as in *He uses various names.*

varnish *noun* **varnishes**
a transparent paint that gives a hard, shiny surface.

vary *verb* **varies, varying, varied**
1 to change; to keep changing, as in *The weather varies from day to day.* 2 to be different, as in *These cars are the same, though the colours vary.*

vase *noun* **vases** (*say* vahz)
a vessel used as an ornament or container for flowers.

vasectomy *noun* **vasectomies**
(*say* vuh-**sek**-tuh-mee)
an operation which prevents a man from fathering a child.

vast *adjective*
very large; very wide.
vastly *adverb*, **vastness** *noun*

vat *noun* **vats**
a very large container for liquid.

vault *noun* **vaults**
1 a vaulting jump. 2 an arched roof.
3 an underground room especially one where people are buried or valuables are stored, as in *cathedral vault; bank vault.*

vault *verb* **vaults, vaulting, vaulted**
to jump over something, especially with the help of your hands or a pole.

VCR short for **video cassette recorder.**

VDU short for **visual display unit.**

veal *noun*
calf's flesh used as food.

vector *noun* **vectors**
(*in Mathematics*) a quantity that has size and direction.

veer *verb* **veers, veering, veered**
to swerve; to change direction.

vegan *noun* **vegans** (*say* **vee**-guhn)
someone who neither uses nor eats any products from animals.

vegetable *noun* **vegetables**
a plant that can be used as food, for example potato, pumpkin, or bean.

vegetarian *noun* **vegetarians**
(*say* vej-uh-**tair**-ree-uhn)
someone who does not eat meat.

a
b
c
d
e
f
g
h
i
j
k
l
m
n
o
p
q
r
s
t
u
v
w
x
y
z

vegetation

vegetation *noun*
plants that are growing.

vehicle *noun* **vehicles**
a device for carrying people or things on land or in space, as in *Cars, trucks, buses, and trams are all vehicles.*

veil *noun* **veils** (*say* vayl)
a piece of thin material to cover your face or head.

veil *verb* **veils, veiling, veiled** (*say* vayl)
to conceal or disguise, as in *She veiled her sadness with a smile.*

vein *noun* **veins**
1 one of the tubes in the body through which blood flows towards the heart.
2 a line or streak on a leaf, rock, insect wing, etc. 3 a long deposit of a mineral in the middle of rock.

Velcro *trademark*
a fastener consisting of two strips of fabric which cling when pressed together.

velocity *noun* **velocities** (*say* vuh-**los**-uh-tee)
speed, as in *wind velocity, velocity of light.*

velvet *noun*
a kind of thick, soft material, as in *She wore a velvet skirt.*
velvety *adjective*

venereal *adjective* (*say* vuh-**neer**-ree-uhl)
venereal disease, a disease that is passed on by having sexual intercourse with an infected person, as in *Venereal disease is often referred to as VD.*

venetian blind *noun* **venetian blinds**
a type of blind for a window, made of thin, horizontal slats which you can move to control the amount of light that comes through.

vengeance *noun*
revenge.
with a vengeance, very strongly or effectively.

venison *noun*
deer's flesh used as food.

venom *noun*
1 the poison of snakes. 2 hatred; a very bitter feeling towards someone.
venomous *adjective*

vent *noun* **vents**
an opening in something, especially to let out smoke, gas, etc.
give vent to, to express your feelings openly, as in *He gave vent to his anger.*

ventilate *verb* **ventilates, ventilating, ventilated**
to let air move freely in and out of a place.
ventilation *noun*

ventriloquist *noun* **ventriloquists**
(*say* ven-**tril**-uh-kwist)
an entertainer who makes his or her voice seem to come from a dummy, or from another place.
ventriloquism *noun*

venture *noun* **ventures**
something you decide to do that is dangerous or adventurous.

venture *verb* **ventures, venturing, ventured**
to do something or go somewhere which is dangerous, as in *They ventured into the crocodile's nesting area.*

verandah or **veranda** *noun* **verandahs**
(*say* vuh-**ran**-duh)
a long, open place with a roof and floor along one or more sides of a house which gives shelter and shade.

verb *noun* **verbs**
a word that says what someone or something is doing, feeling, etc., as in *Verbs are words like 'bring', 'eat', 'sit', 'suffer', 'enjoy', 'seem', 'be', 'have', and 'need'.*

verdict *noun* **verdicts**
the decision made by a judge or jury.

verge *noun* **verges**
1 the edge or border, as in *The toddler was on the verge of tears.* 2 the strip of grass at the edge of a road, footpath, etc.; a nature strip.

verify *verb* **verifies, verifying, verified**
to find or show the truth of something.
verification *noun*

vermin *noun*
animals, birds, or insects that damage crops or food, or carry diseases, as in *Rabbits are considered as vermin by some farmers.*

verruca *noun* **verrucas** (*say* vuh-**roo**-kuh)
a wart on the sole of someone's foot.

versatile *adjective* (*say* **ver**-suh-tuyl)
able to do or be used for many different things, as in *a versatile actor; a versatile pocketknife.*
versatility *noun*

verse *noun* **verses**
1 poetry. 2 a group of lines in a poem or song. 3 one of the numbered parts of a chapter in the Bible.

version *noun* **versions**
1 someone's account of something that has happened, as in *His version of the accident is different from mine.* 2 something translated or rewritten, as in *a new version of the Bible.* 3 a particular form of a thing, as in *a new version of this car.*

video

versus *preposition*
against; competing with, as in *Australia versus England*.

vertebra *noun* **vertebrae**
(*say* **ver**-tuh-bruh)
one of the bones that form the backbone.

vertebrate *noun* **vertebrates**
(*say* **ver**-tuh-bruht)
an animal with a backbone.

vertex *noun* **vertices**
1 the highest point; top, apex. 2 the meeting point of lines that form an angle in a triangle, polygon, etc., as in *A cube has eight vertices*.

vertical *adjective*
at a right angle to a flat surface; directed or moving straight up; upright.
vertically *adverb*

very *adverb*
extremely, as in *Ice is very cold*.

very *adjective*
exact; actual, as in *That's the very thing we need!*

vessel *noun* **vessels**
1 a boat; a ship. 2 a container. 3 a tube inside an animal or plant, carrying blood or some other liquid.

vest *noun* **vests**
1 a piece of underwear worn on the top half of your body; a singlet. 2 a waistcoat.

vestry *noun* **vestries**
a room in a church where the priest, etc. or the choir get ready for a service.

vet *noun* **vets**
a veterinary surgeon.

veteran *noun* **veterans**
a person with long experience, especially as a soldier.
veteran car, a car made before 1916.

veterinary *adjective* (*say* **vet**-uh-ruhn-ree *or* **vet**-uhn-ree)
concerned with the diseases of animals.
veterinary surgeon, a person trained to heal sick animals.

veto *noun* **vetoes** (*say* **vee**-toh)
a refusal to let something happen; the right to prohibit something.

vex *verb* **vexes, vexing, vexed**
to annoy someone; to cause someone worry.
vexation *noun*, **vexatious** *adjective*

VHF short for **very high frequency**.

via *preposition* (*say* **vuy**-uh)
going through; stopping at, as in *This train goes to Melbourne via Albury*.

viaduct *noun* **viaducts** (*say* **vuy**-uh-dukt)
a long bridge with many arches.

vibes *plural noun*
(*colloquial*) vibrations, especially the good or bad feelings you get by being in a place, as in *This dark cellar gives me bad vibes*.

vibrate *verb* **vibrates, vibrating, vibrated**
to move quickly to and fro; to make a quivering sound.
vibration *noun*

vice *noun* **vices**
1 evil; wickedness. 2 a bad habit or bad feature of someone, as in *His only vice is eating between meals*. 3 a device for holding something in place while you work on it.

vice-president *noun* **vice-presidents**
a deputy for a president.

viceregal *adjective*
to do with the governor-general or a State governor.

vice versa *adverb* (*say* vuys **ver**-suh *or* vuy-see **ver**-suh)
the other way round, as in 'We talk about them and vice versa' means 'We talk about them and they talk about us'.

vicinity *noun* **vicinities**
the neighbourhood; the surrounding district, as in *There are shops in the vicinity of their house*.

vicious *adjective* (*say* **vish**-uhs)
cruel; dangerously wicked or strong.
viciously *adverb*, **viciousness** *noun*

victim *noun* **victims**
a person who suffers from injury, disease, destruction, etc., as in *a road victim; the murderer's victim*.

victor *noun* **victors**
the winner of a battle or contest.

Victorian *adjective*
1 to do with the State of Victoria, as in *Victorian drivers*. 2 to do with the time when the English Queen Victoria reigned (1837–1901).

victory *noun* **victories**
success in a battle, contest, or game.
victorious *adjective*

video *noun* **videos** (*say* **vid**-ee-oh)
1 the recording on tape of pictures and sound. 2 a video recorder. 3 a television program or a film recorded on a video cassette, as in *Have you got a video of 'Storm Boy'?*
video cassette, a sealed case containing videotape.

video
474

video cassette recorder, a machine for recording pictures and sound on videotape.
video game, a game in which you use joysticks, etc. to move around pictures produced by a computer program and shown on a VDU screen.
video recorder, a video cassette recorder.

video *verb* **videoes, videoing, videoed**
to record something on videotape.

videotape *noun* **videotapes**
magnetic tape suitable for video recording.

view *noun* **views**
1 what you can see from one place, as in *What a lovely view!* 2 someone's opinion, as in *She has strong views about teaching.*
in view or **on view,** that you can see.
in view of, because of.
with a view to, with the intention of.

view *verb* **views, viewing, viewed**
to look at something; to consider something, as in *They viewed the paintings. He views smoking as a nasty habit.*
viewer *noun*

vigilant *adjective* (*say* **vij**-uh-luhnt)
watchful.
vigilance *noun,* **vigilantly** *adverb*

vigorous *adjective*
full of energy, healthy, growth, or strength, as in *a vigorous sportsperson; a vigorous creeping plant.*
vigorously *adverb*

vigour or **vigor** *noun*
energy; liveliness; strength.

Viking *noun* **Vikings** (*say* **vuy**-king)
one of the Scandinavian pirates or traders that sailed to various parts of Europe between the 8th and 10th centuries.

vile *adjective* **viler, vilest**
disgusting, as in *a vile smell.*

village *noun* **villages**
1 a small country settlement. 2 a shopping centre in a suburb, as in *Manuka village.*

villain *noun* **villains**
a wicked person.
villainous *adjective,* **villainy** *noun*

villein *noun* **villeins** (*say* **vil**-uhn)
a person in feudal times ruled by the lord or attached to a manor as a tenant, as in *In the Middle Ages villeins had little freedom.*

vindictive *adjective*
wanting to have revenge; spiteful.

vine *noun* **vines**
a plant on which grapes grow.

vinegar *noun*
a sour liquid used to flavour food, as in *Vinegar is used in salad dressing.*

vineyard *noun* **vineyards** (*say* **vin**-yahd *or* **vin**-yuhd)
an area of land where vines are grown to produce grapes.

vintage *noun* **vintages**
1 all the grapes that are harvested in one season; wine made from these grapes.
2 the period in history from which something comes, as in *This furniture is of 1960s vintage.*
vintage car, a car made between 1917 and 1930.

vinyl *noun* (*say* **vuy**-nuhl)
a kind of plastic.

viola *noun* **violas** (*say* vee-**oh**-luh)
a stringed instrument rather like a violin but slightly larger and with a lower pitch.

violate *verb* **violates, violating, violated**
1 to break something like a promise or a law. 2 to treat a person or place without respect, as in *The vandals violated the church.*
violation *noun,* **violator** *noun*

violence *noun*
force that does harm or damage.
violent *adjective,* **violently** *adverb*

violet *noun* **violets**
1 a small plant that usually has purple flowers. 2 a bluish-purple colour.

violin *noun* **violins**
a musical instrument with four strings played by a bow.
violinist *noun*

VIP short for **very important person.**

viper *noun* **vipers**
a small poisonous snake; an adder.

virgin *noun* **virgins**
a person who has not yet had sexual intercourse.
the Virgin, Mary, the mother of Jesus.
virginity *noun*

virgin *adjective*
not yet used or explored, as in *virgin bush.*

virtual *adjective*
actual; as good as the real thing, as in *His silence was a virtual admission that he was guilty.*
virtually *adverb*

virtue *noun* **virtues**
1 goodness; excellence. 2 a particular kind of goodness, as in *Honesty is a virtue.*
virtuous *adjective,* **virtuously** *adverb*

virus *noun* **viruses** (*say* **vuy**-ruhs)
a microscopic creature that can cause disease.

visa *noun* **visas**
an official mark put on someone's passport by officials of a foreign country to show that the holder of the passport has permission to enter that country.

visible *adjective*
able to be seen, as in *The ship was visible on the horizon.*
visibility *noun*, **visibly** *adverb*

vision *noun* **visions**
1 the power to see, as in *He has excellent vision and doesn't need glasses.* **2** something that you see or imagine, especially in a dream. **3** imagination; understanding, as in *a leader with vision.*

visit *verb* **visits, visiting, visited**
to go to see a person or place; to stay somewhere for a while.
visit *noun*, **visitor** *noun*

visor *noun* **visors** (*say* **vuy**-zuh)
1 the part of a helmet that closes over your face. **2** a shield for the eyes, especially one at the top of a vehicle windscreen.

visual *adjective*
to do with seeing, as in *the visual appeal of bright colours.*
visual aids, pictures, films, etc. used by teachers or people giving talks.
visual display unit, a screen on which a computer displays information.
visually *adverb*

visualise or **visualize** *verb* **visualises, visualising, visualised**
to imagine something.

vital *adjective*
1 to do with or essential to life, as in *The surgeon transplanted a vital organ. Water is vital for life.* **2** extremely important; necessary, as in *It is vital that we meet the deadline.* **3** full of life, as in *The healthy boy had a vital appearance.*
vitally *adverb*

vitality *noun*
liveliness; energy.

vitamin *noun* **vitamins** (*say* **vuy**-tuh-muhn *or* **vit**-uh-muhn)
a substance in food that you need to stay healthy.

vivid *adjective*
bright; clear; lively, as in *She gave a vivid description of the storm.*
vividly *adverb*, **vividness** *noun*

vivisection *noun*
surgical experiments on live animals, or other painful treatment of them, done as part of scientific research.

vixen *noun* **vixens**
a female fox.

vocabulary *noun* **vocabularies** (*say* vuh-**kab**-yoo-luh-ri)
1 a list of words used in a particular book, language, etc. **2** the words that a person knows and uses.

vocal *adjective*
1 of or to do with your voice, as in *The sound of your voice is made by your vocal cords.* **2** expressing one's feelings freely in speech, as in *He is very vocal about his rights.*
vocally *adverb*

vocalist *noun* **vocalists**
a singer.

vocation *noun* **vocations**
a strong feeling that you are suitable for a particular career, especially one in the church or as a teacher.

vocational *adjective*
to do with skills needed for a particular job, as in *vocational training.*

vodka *noun* **vodkas**
a strong alcoholic drink especially popular in Russia.

vogue *noun* (*say* vohg)
fashion, as in *Suntans are now out of vogue.*

voice *noun* **voices**
1 the sound of speaking or singing. **2** the power to speak or sing, as in *She lost her voice.*

voice *verb* **voices, voicing, voiced**
to say something, as in *He voiced his objections to the plan.*

void *adjective*
empty or vacant, as in *The uncaring parent was void of feeling. The position of caretaker has been void for some time.*

volcano *noun* **volcanoes**
a mountain or hill from which molten lava, steam, ashes, etc. erupt, as in *The volcano becomes active occasionally, causing destruction to the villages below.*
volcanic *adjective*

volley *noun* **volleys**
1 a number of bullets or shells fired at the same time. **2** in tennis and some other games, hitting back the ball before it bounces.

volleyball

volleyball *noun*
a game in which two teams hit a large ball to and fro over a net with their hands.

volt *noun* **volts**
a unit for measuring the strength of an electric current.
voltage *noun*

volume *noun* **volumes**
1 the amount of space filled by something. 2 an amount, as in *The volume of work has increased.* 3 the power of sound; how loud something is, as in *Turn down the volume!* 4 a book, especially one of a set, as in *Shakespeare's plays in 3 volumes.*

voluntary *adjective*
done or working without payment, as in *voluntary work. The youth club has several voluntary workers.*
voluntarily *adverb*

volunteer *noun* **volunteers**
someone who volunteers to do something.

volunteer *verb* **volunteers, volunteered, volunteering**
1 to offer to do something that you do not have to do. 2 to give something willingly or freely, as in *Several people generously volunteered their time.*

vomit *verb* **vomits, vomiting, vomited**
to bring food back from the stomach through the mouth.

vote *noun* **votes**
1 a formal expression of choice or opinion by a ballot, show of hands, etc., as in *The vote for the class captain was close.* 2 the right to vote, especially for a government.

vote *verb* **votes, voting, voted**
1 to show which person or thing you prefer by putting up your hand, making a mark on paper, etc. 2 to say what you would prefer to do, as in *I vote we go away this weekend.*
voter *noun*

voucher *noun* **vouchers**
a piece of paper showing that you have paid something or that you can receive something, as in *This gift voucher can be exchanged for clothes.*

vow *noun* **vows**
a solemn promise.

vow *verb* **vows, vowing, vowed**
to make a vow, as in *She vowed never to smoke again.*

vowel *noun* **vowels**
any of the letters *a, e, i, o, u,* and sometimes *y.*

voyage *noun* **voyages**
a journey by ship, plane, or spacecraft, especially a long journey.
voyager *noun*

vulgar *adjective*
rude; without good manners.
vulgar fraction, a fraction shown by numbers above and below a line, not a decimal fraction, *as in $^3/_{10}$ is a vulgar fraction.*
vulgarity *noun,* **vulgarly** *adverb*

vulnerable *adjective*
easily wounded or harmed, as in *Elderly people living alone are vulnerable to attacks by robbers.*

vulture *noun* **vultures**
a large bird that eats dead flesh.

vulva *noun* **vulvas**
the outer parts of the female genitals.

a
b
c
d
e
f
g
h
i
j
k
l
m
n
o
p
q
r
s
t
u
v
w
x
y
z

wad *noun* **wads**
a pad or bundle of soft material, pieces of paper, etc., as in *a wad of cottonwool; a wad of banknotes*.

waddle *verb* **waddles, waddling, waddled**
to walk like a duck, with short steps, rocking from side to side.

waddy or **waddie** *noun* **waddies**
(*say* **wod**-ee)
an Aboriginal war-club made of wood.

> **Origin** This word comes from an Aboriginal language of New South Wales Dharuk: **wadi** = tree, stick, club. See the Aboriginal Languages map at the back of this dictionary.

wade *verb* **wades, wading, waded**
to walk through water.

wafer *noun* **wafers**
1 a very thin kind of biscuit, often eaten with ice-cream. 2 a thin disc of bread made without yeast, used in the Sacrament of the Eucharist in some Christian churches.

wag *verb* **wags, wagging, wagged**
1 to move quickly to and fro; to move something in this way, as in *The dog wagged its tail*. 2 to be absent without permission, as in *The boys wagged school to go to the mall*.

wage *noun* or **wages** *plural noun*
the fixed regular payment given to an employee, especially one who does manual work.

wage *verb* **wages, waging, waged**
to carry on a war or campaign.

wager *noun* **wagers** (*say* **way**-juh)
a bet.

waggle *verb* **waggles, waggling, waggled**
(*colloquial*) to wag, as in *He waggled his finger*.

wagon *noun* **wagons**
1 a cart with four wheels used for pulling heavy loads. 2 an open railway truck. 3 (*colloquial*) a station wagon.

wagtail *noun* **wagtails**
a kind of bird with a long tail that moves up and down constantly when the bird is standing still; the willy wagtail.

wail *verb* **wails, wailing, wailed**
to make a long, sad cry; to moan or howl, as in *The wind wailed through the gum trees*.

waist *noun* **waists**
the usually narrow part in the middle of your body, below the ribs and above the hips.

waistcoat *noun* **waistcoats**
a close-fitting jacket without sleeves, usually worn under a loose jacket.

wait *verb* **waits, waiting, waited**
1 to remain in a place or situation until something happens. 2 to be a waiter.
waiting-list, a list of people waiting for something to become available.
waiting-room, a room for people who are waiting for something, such as seeing a doctor or dentist.

waiter *noun* **waiters**
a man whose job is to serve people with food in a restaurant or hotel.

waitress *noun* **waitresses**
a woman whose job is to serve people with food in a restaurant or hotel.

waive

waive *verb* **waives, waiving, waived**
not to insist on having something, as in *She waived her right to travel first class.*

Usage Do not confuse **waive** with **wave,** which means to move your hand to and fro, to move to and fro, or to make hair curved or curly.

wake *verb* **wakes, waking, woke, woken**
1 to stop sleeping, as in *Wake up! I woke when I heard the bell. Has he woken up yet?*
2 to make someone stop sleeping, as in *You have woken the baby.*

wake *noun* **wakes**
1 the trail left on the water by a ship.
2 what is left when something is gone, or when something unusual has happened, as in *The storm left a lot of damage in its wake.*
in the wake of, following.

waken *verb* **wakens, wakening, wakened**
to wake.

walk *verb* **walks, walking, walked**
to move along on your feet at an ordinary speed.
walk off with, to steal; to win easily.
walker *noun*

walk *noun* **walks**
1 a journey on foot. 2 the way that someone walks, as in *He has a funny walk.* 3 a path or route for walking, as in *There are some lovely walks near here.*
walk of life, your job or occupation.
walk-over, an easy victory.

walkabout *noun*
a journey on foot by an Aborigine in order to live in the traditional way.

walkie-talkie *noun* **walkie-talkies**
a small portable radio transmitter and receiver, as in *The firefighters used walkie-talkies to keep in contact in the bush.*

walking-stick *noun* **walking-sticks**
a stick carried or used as a support when you walk.

walkman *noun* **walkmans**
(*trademark*) a portable stereo cassette-player.

wall *noun* **walls**
1 one of the sides of a building or room.
2 a barrier of bricks or stone surrounding a garden, courtyard, etc.
up the wall, (*colloquial*) mad.
walled *adjective*

wallaby *noun* **wallabies**
any of several marsupials similar to a kangaroo but smaller, as in *rock wallaby; red-necked wallaby.*

Origin This word comes from the Aboriginal language Dharuk: **walabi** or **waliba.** See the Aboriginal Languages map at the back of this dictionary.

wallaroo *noun* **wallaroos**
a large stocky kangaroo living in rocky or hilly country.

Origin This word comes from the Aboriginal language Dharuk: **walaru.** See the Aboriginal Languages map at the back of this dictionary.

wallet *noun* **wallets**
a small, flat, folding case for holding banknotes, documents, credit cards, etc.

wallop *verb* **wallops, walloping, walloped**
(*colloquial*) 1 to thrash; beat. 2 to defeat easily, as in *Australia walloped England in the Ashes series.*

wallow *verb* **wallows, wallowing, wallowed**
1 to roll about in water, mud, etc. 2 to indulge in a situation or emotional state, as in *wallow in luxury; wallow in self pity.*

wallpaper *noun* **wallpapers**
paper used to cover the walls of rooms.

walnut *noun* **walnuts**
1 a kind of edible nut that grows on a northern hemisphere tree. 2 the patterned wood of this tree used for furniture, as in *walnut table.*

walrus *noun* **walruses**
a large Arctic marine animal with two long tusks.

waltz *noun* **waltzes**
a dance with three beats to a bar.
waltz off with, (*colloquial*) to steal or win easily, as in *He waltzed off with the raffle money. Blue House waltzed off with the swimming trophy.*

wan *adjective*
pale from being ill or tired, as in *a wan complexion.*

wand *noun* **wands**
a short, thin stick, especially used by a conjurer.

wander *verb* **wanders, wandering, wandered**
1 to go about without trying to reach a particular place. 2 to get lost, as in *Do not wander in the bush.*
wanderer *noun*

wane *verb* **wanes, waning, waned**
to become less or smaller, as in *His popularity was waning.*

a b c d e f g h i j k l m n o p q r s t u v **w** x y z

479   **wash**

wangle *verb* wangles, wangling, wangled
(*colloquial*) to get or arrange something by
trickery or persuasion.

want *verb* wants, wanting, wanted
1 to feel that you would like to have
something.   2 to need something.
3 to be without something; to lack.
4 to be poor, as in *Waste not, want not*.

want *noun* wants
1 a desire or need.   2 a lack of something,
as in *The plant died from want of water*.

wanted *adjective*
to do with someone sought by the police,
as in *He was a wanted man*.

war *noun* wars
1 fighting between nations or armies; a
long period of such fighting.   2 a serious
struggle or effort, as in *the war on poverty*.

waratah *noun* waratahs
a shrub with very large red flowers; the
floral emblem of New South Wales.

Origin This word comes from the
Aboriginal language Dharuk: **Warrada**. See
the Aboriginal Languages map at the back
of this dictionary.

warble *verb* warbles, warbling, warbled
to sing gently, like some birds.

warbler *noun* warblers
a kind of small bird with a very melodic
song.

ward *noun* wards
1 a room for patients in a hospital.
2 a child looked after by a guardian.
3 an area of a town or city represented by
an elected councillor.

ward *verb* wards, warding, warded
ward off, to keep something away, as in *He
took vitamin C to ward off a cold*.

warden *noun* wardens
1 the person who is in charge of or given
responsibility for something; a supervisor,
as in *warden of a university college*.

warder *noun* warders
someone in charge of prisoners in a prison.

wardrobe *noun* wardrobes
1 a cupboard to hang clothes in.   2 a stock
of clothes or costumes, especially those
worn by actors.

warehouse *noun* warehouses
a large building where goods are stored.

wares *plural noun*
goods offered for sale, as in *A variety of
wares can be found at the markets*.

warfare *noun*
making war; fighting, as in *guerrilla warfare*.

warhead *noun* warheads
the explosive head of a missile.

warm *adjective* warmer, warmest
1 fairly hot; not cold.   2 enthusiastic;
kind, as in *a warm welcome*.   3 (*colloquial*)
close to the right answer, or to something
hidden, as in *Try again; you're getting warm!*
warmly *adverb*, **warmth** *noun*

warm *verb* warms, warming, warmed
to make something or someone warm; to
become warm.

warn *verb* warns, warning, warned
to tell someone about a danger or future
event.
warning *noun*

warp *verb* warps, warping, warped
(*say* wawp)
1 to bend or twist because of dampness,
heat, etc., as in *The rain warped the
boards*.   2 to distort something; to make
something unnatural, as in *The unhappy
child had a warped view of school*.

warrant *noun* warrants
a document that entitles you to do
something, especially to arrest someone or
search a place.

warranty *noun* warranties (*say* **wo**-ruhn-tee)
a guarantee or assurance that a product
will be repaired or replaced if faults are
found.

warren *noun* warrens
a piece of ground where there are many
rabbit burrows.

warrigal *noun* warrigals
a dingo.

Origin This word comes from the
Aboriginal language Dharuk: **warrigal** =
wild dingo. See the Aboriginal Languages
map at the back of this dictionary.

warrior *noun* warriors
someone who fights in battles; a soldier.

wart *noun* warts
a small, hard lump on the skin.

wary *adjective* warier, wariest (*say* **wair**-ree)
cautious; careful.
warily *adverb*, **wariness** *noun*

was 1st and 3rd person singular past tense of
be.

wash *verb* washes, washing, washed
1 to clean something with water.   2 to
flow, as in *Waves washed over the deck*.   3 to

a
b
c
d
e
f
g
h
i
j
k
l
m
n
o
p
q
r
s
t
u
v
w
x
y
z

wash

carry along by means of moving liquid, as in *The sailor was washed overboard*.
4 (*colloquial*) to be accepted or believed, as in *That story won't wash*.
wash up, to wash dishes and cutlery after a meal.
washable *adjective*

wash *noun* **washes**
1 the action of washing. **2** clothes ready to be washed or just washed, as in *Put your dirty socks in the wash*. **3** the disturbed water or air behind a moving ship or aircraft.

washer *noun* **washers**
1 a small ring of metal, rubber, etc. placed between two surfaces, especially under a bolt or screw. **2** a small cloth for washing the face; a face-washer.

washing *noun*
clothes that need washing, are being washed, or have been washed; the wash.

washing-machine *noun* **washing-machines**
a machine for washing clothes, linen, etc.

washing-up *noun*
the act of washing dishes after a meal, etc.; dishes that need to be washed or are being washed, as in *Will you do the washing-up? The sink is full of washing-up*.

wash-out *noun* **wash-outs**
(*colloquial*) a complete failure, a non-event, as in *The poorly planned social was a wash-out. The match was a wash-out because of very heavy rain*.

wasn't short for *was not*.

wasp *noun* **wasps**
a flying insect that can sting.

waste *verb* **wastes, wasting, wasted**
1 to use more of something than you need to; to use something without getting much value from it. **2** to make no use of something, as in *You are wasting a lot of your talent*. **3** to make something weak or useless; to become weak or useless, as in *The illness had wasted his muscles*.
wastage *noun*

waste *adjective*
1 not wanted; thrown away, as in *waste paper*. **2** not used or usable; not cultivated, as in *waste ground*.
waste-paper basket, a container for waste paper.

waste *noun* **wastes**
1 the act of wasting something, as in *It's a waste of time*. **2** things that are not wanted

or used; rubbish. **3** an area of desert or frozen land, as in *the wastes of the Nullarbor*.
wasteful *adjective*, **wastefully** *adverb*, **wastefulness** *noun*

watch *verb* **watches, watching, watched**
1 to look at a person or thing for some while. **2** to be on guard or ready for something to happen, as in *His job is to watch the school at night. Watch your step on those stairs*. **3** to take care of a person or thing, as in *The mother watched over the sleeping child*.
watcher *noun*

watch *noun* **watches**
1 a device like a small clock, usually worn on your wrist. **2** the act of watching, as in *He was on watch in the hope of catching the thieves*. **3** a period of duty on a ship.

watchful *adjective*
alert; careful.
watchfully *adverb*, **watchfulness** *noun*

water *noun*
1 a transparent, colourless liquid that is a compound of hydrogen and oxygen found in seas, rivers, rain, etc. **2** urine, as in *The doctor asked if I had passed water*.

water *verb* **waters, watering, watered**
1 to sprinkle something with water, as in *Have you watered the plants?* **2** to give water to an animal. **3** to produce water, tears, or saliva, as in *The smell of bacon makes my mouth water*.
water down, to dilute.

water-colour *noun* **water-colours**
1 a paint that can be mixed with water. **2** a painting done with this kind of paint.

watercress *noun*
a small leafy plant with a spicy taste, used in salads.

water cycle *noun*
the circulation of water through the air, rivers, and seas, including evaporation and rain.

waterfall *noun* **waterfalls**
a place where a river or stream flows over a cliff or large rock.

waterfront *noun* **waterfronts**
the part of a town next to a river, lake, harbour, etc.

watering-can *noun* **watering-cans**
a container with a long spout, for watering plants.

watering-hole *noun* **watering-holes**
1 a waterhole from which animals regularly drink. **2** (*colloquial*) a hotel or bar.

weak

waterlogged *adjective*
completely soaked or filled with water.

watermelon *noun* **watermelons**
a large dark-green melon with red flesh and watery juice.

water polo *noun*
a ball game played by two teams each with seven swimmers.

waterproof *adjective*
able to keep water out, as in *a waterproof coat*.

watershed *noun* **watersheds**
1 the line of separation between waters flowing to different rivers, basins, or seas. 2 the turning point in a situation, as in *The end of primary school was a watershed in her life.*

water-ski *noun* **water-skis**
each of a pair of skis for skimming the surface of the water while being towed by a motor boat.

watertight *adjective*
1 not able to let water in, as in *watertight container*. 2 not able to be changed or questioned, as in *a watertight agreement*.

waterway *noun* **waterways**
any river, channel, lake, etc. that ships, boats, etc. navigate.

watery *adjective*
1 to do with water, as in *The pipe made gurgling watery noises*. 2 moist or tearful, as in *watery eyes*. 3 containing a lot of water, as in *watery soup, watery milk*.

watt *noun* **watts**
a unit of electric power.

wattle *noun* **wattles**
any plant of the *Acacia* family which has blossom ranging in colour from white to deep-gold, as in *Wattle is our unofficial national floral emblem*.
wattle and daub, a network of rods and twigs plastered with clay or mud and used as a building material, as in *wattle and daub hut*.

wave *verb* **waves, waving, waved**
1 to move your hand to and fro, usually to say hello or goodbye to someone. 2 to move something to and fro or up and down. 3 to make hair curved or curly.

Usage Do not confuse **wave** with **waive,** which means not to insist on having something.

wave *noun* **waves**
1 a moving ridge on the surface of water, especially on the sea. 2 a curving piece of hair; a curl. 3 a sudden build-up of something strong, as in *a wave of anger*. 4 (*in Science*) one of the to-and-fro movements in which sound, light, etc. travel. 5 the act of waving your hand, as in *She gave a wave as she drove off*.

wavelength *noun* **wavelengths**
1 the size of a radio wave or electric wave. 2 a particular way of thinking or approach, as in *As the two friends shared common interests they were always on the same wavelength*.

waver *verb* **wavers, wavering, wavered**
1 to be unsteady or uncertain, as in *They wavered between two choices*. 2 to move unsteadily, as in *He wavered as the force of the wind hit him*.
waverer *noun*

wavy *adjective* **wavier, waviest**
full of waves or curves.

wax *noun* **waxes**
a slippery substance that melts easily, as in *Wax is used for making candles, crayons, and polish*.
waxy *adjective*

wax *verb* **waxes, waxing, waxed**
to cover or treat with wax, as in *He waxed his surfboard*.
wax and wane, (of the moon) to grow bigger and then smaller.

wax plant *noun* **wax plants**
a small to medium-sized shrub with attractive waxy flowers of various colours, growing in Western Australia, as in *The Geraldton wax plant is a famous Australian wildflower*.

waxworks *plural noun*
an exhibition of models of persons, etc. made of wax.

way *noun* **ways**
1 a road or path. 2 a route; the direction or distance to a place, as in *Show me the way to Wagga*. 3 how something is done; a method, as in *This is the best way to make bread*. 4 a condition or state, as in *Things are in a bad way*.
no way, (*colloquial*) that is impossible; that is not true.

we *pronoun*
a word someone uses to talk about himself or herself and another person or other people.

weak *adjective* **weaker, weakest**
not strong; easy to break, bend, defeat, etc.
weakly *adverb*, **weakness** *noun*

weaken

weaken *verb* **weakens, weakening, weakened**
to become weak or weaker; to make something or someone become weak or weaker.

weakling *noun* **weaklings**
a weak person or animal.

wealth *noun*
1 a lot of money or property.   2 a large quantity, as in *This book has a wealth of illustrations.*

wealthy *adjective* **wealthier, wealthiest**
having a lot of money or property.

weapon *noun* **weapons**
something used to hurt other people in a battle or fight.

wear *verb* **wears, wearing, wore, worn**
1 to be dressed in something, as in *I wore that dress last night.*   2 to have something attached to your clothes, as in *He often wears that badge.*   3 to damage something by rubbing or using it; to become damaged like this, as in *Your sleeve has worn thin.*
4 to last, as in *This cloth wears well.*
wear off, to become less; to disappear.
wear out, to become weak or useless; to make something or someone become weak or useless.
wearer *noun*

wear *noun*
1 clothes, as in *men's wear.*   2 gradual damage done by rubbing or using something, as in *School uniforms suffer from wear and tear.*

weary *adjective* **wearier, weariest**
not wanting to make any more effort; tired.
wearily *adverb*, **weariness** *noun*

weasel *noun* **weasels**
a small, fierce, flesh-eating European animal with a slender body.

weather *noun*
the rain, snow, wind, sunshine, etc. at a particular time or place.
under the weather, (*colloquial*) feeling ill or depressed.
weather forecast, a report saying what the weather is expected to be like in the near future.

weather *verb* **weathers, weathering, weathered**
1 to become dried, worn, etc. because of being exposed to the sun, rain, etc., as in *The rocks have weathered over the centuries.*
2 to wear down buildings, rocks, etc., as in *The wind and rain have weathered the cliffs.*   3 to come through something successfully, as in *They weathered the storm.*

weatherboard *noun* **weatherboards**
1 one of the overlapping horizontal boards on a wall, as in *That house is made from weatherboard.*   2 a house built from weatherboards, as in *They live in a weatherboard.*

weathering *noun*
the action of the weather on materials, especially rock, exposed to it, as in *The rocks have taken on strange shapes through weathering.*

weather-vane *noun* **weather-vanes**
a revolving pointer on a roof, etc. to show the direction of the wind.

weave *verb* **weaves, weaving, wove, woven**
1 to make something by passing threads or strips over and under other threads or strips, as in *This basket was woven from straw.*   2 to twist and turn, as in *He wove through the traffic.*
weaver *noun*

web *noun* **webs**
1 a cobweb.   2 something like a net, as in *caught up in a web of lies.*

web-footed *adjective*
having toes joined by pieces of skin, as in *Ducks are web-footed.*

wed *verb* **weds, wedding,** *past tense and past participle* **wedded** or **wed**
to marry.

we'd short for *we had, we should,* or *we would.*

wedding *noun* **weddings**
the ceremony when a man and woman get married.

wedge *noun* **wedges**
a piece of wood, metal, etc. that is thick at one end and thin at the other.
the thin end of the wedge, (*colloquial*) a situation which does not seem serious now, but which will quickly get worse.

wedge *verb* **wedges, wedging, wedged**
to put or keep something firmly in place, especially with a wedge, as in *He wedged the door open with a block of wood.*

Wednesday *noun* **Wednesdays**
the fourth day of the week, coming after Tuesday.

weed *noun* **weeds**
a wild plant that grows where it is not wanted.

weed *verb* **weeds, weeding, weeded**
to remove weeds from the ground.

weedy *adjective* **weedier, weediest**
1 full of weeds.   2 weak; thin.

week *noun* **weeks**
a period of seven days, especially from Sunday to the following Saturday.

weekday *noun* **weekdays**
any day except Saturday and Sunday.

weekend *noun* **weekends**
Saturday and Sunday.

weekender *noun* **weekenders**
a house used only for holidays or at the weekend, as in *We have a weekender at the coast.*

weekly *adjective* and *adverb*
done or happening once a week.

weep *verb* **weeps, weeping, wept**
to cry; to shed tears.
weeping willow, a kind of willow tree that has drooping branches.

weigh *verb* **weighs, weighing, weighed** (*say* way)
1 to find out how heavy something is. **2** to have a certain weight, as in *The melon weighs two kilograms.*
weigh down, to hold something down; to depress or trouble someone.
weigh up, to estimate something; to consider something.

weight *noun* **weights**
1 how heavy something is. **2** a piece of metal of known heaviness, used on scales to weigh things. **3** a heavy object, as in *I used a stone as a weight to keep my papers from blowing away.*
weights, discs, etc. of a certain heaviness, fixed to the ends of a bar, handgrip, etc. lifted as a sport or for exercise.

weightless *adjective*
seeming to have little weight or no weight at all, as in *Astronauts are weightless in space.*

weightlifting *noun*
lifting heavy weights as a sport or for exercise.

weighty *adjective* **weightier, weightiest**
1 heavy. **2** important, as in *A court judge considers weighty matters.*

weir *noun* **weirs** (*say* weer)
a dam across a river to raise the level of water upstream or regulate its flow.

weird *adjective* **weirder, weirdest** (*say* weerd)
very strange; not natural.
weirdly *adverb*, **weirdness** *noun*

weirdo *noun* **weirdos**
(*colloquial*) an odd or eccentric person.

welcome *adjective*
1 pleased to see or receive, as in *a welcome gift.* **2** allowed or free to do or take something, as in *You are welcome to use my bicycle.*

welcome *verb* **welcomes, welcoming, welcomed**
to show that you are pleased when a person or thing arrives.

weld *verb* **welds, welding, welded**
to join two pieces of metal or plastic together by heat or pressure.
welder *noun*

welfare *noun*
people's health, happiness, or comfort.

welfare state *noun* **welfare states**
the system where the government agrees to protect the well-being of its citizens especially those unable to take care of themselves; a country practising this system.

well *noun* **wells**
a deep hole dug or drilled to get water or oil out of the ground.

well *adverb*
1 in a good or right way, as in *He swims well.* **2** reasonably; probably, as in *It may well be our last chance.*
well off, fairly rich; fortunate.

well *adjective* **better, best**
1 in good health, as in *She is not well.* **2** good; satisfactory, as in *All is well.*

we'll short for *we shall* or *we will.*

well-being *noun*
the state of being well, contented, healthy, etc.

well-known *adjective*
known by many people.

well-mannered *adjective*
having good manners.

well-meaning *adjective*
having good intentions which are not always effective.

went past tense of **go** *verb*.

wept past tense and past participle of **weep**.

were plural and 2nd person singular past tense of **be**.

we're short for *we are.*

werewolf *noun* **werewolves**
in stories, a person who sometimes changes into a wolf.

west *noun*
the direction in which the sun sets.
the West, Western Australia; a name that used to be given to the countries of Europe, Australia, America, etc. that were not Communist, as in *Perth is in the West; the elected leaders of the West.*

a
b
c
d
e
f
g
h
i
j
k
l
m
n
o
p
q
r
s
t
u
v
w
x
y
z

west

west *adjective*
1 coming from the west, as in *a west wind*.
2 situated in the west, as in *the west coast*.
westerly *adjective*

west *adverb*
towards the west.
westward *adjective* and *adverb*, **westwards** *adverb*

western *adjective*
situated in or towards the west, as in *western rock lobster; western Tasmania*.

western *noun* **westerns**
a film or story about cowboys, American Indians, etc. in the American west.

westie *noun* **westies**
(*colloquial*) 1 an insulting name for a person who lives in the western suburbs of Sydney. 2 (*colloquial*) a person who lacks style, manners, and taste.

wet *adjective* **wetter, wettest**
1 covered or soaked in water or other liquid. 2 not dry, as in *wet paint*.
3 rainy, as in *wet weather*. 4 (*colloquial*) lacking spunk or zest; feeble, as in *a wet party*.
the wet, the season of tropical rains in tropical and northern Australia.
wet blanket, (*colloquial*) someone who is gloomy and who prevents other people from enjoying themselves.
wet suit, a suit made from a kind of rubber and worn by skin-divers, windsurfers, etc. to keep them warm.
wetness *noun*

wet *verb* **wets, wetting, wetted**
to make something wet.

we've short for *we have*.

whack *verb* **whacks, whacking, whacked**
to hit someone or something hard, especially with a stick.

whale *noun* **whales**
a very large marine mammal which breathes through a blowhole on the head and has a streamlined body and horizontal tail.
a whale of a, (*colloquial*) very great or good, as in *We had a whale of a time at the party*.

whaler *noun* **whalers**
a person or ship that hunts whales.
whaling *noun*

wharf *noun* **wharfs** (*say* worf)
a quay where ships are loaded or unloaded.
wharfie, (*colloquial*) a wharf labourer.

what *adjective*
1 used to ask the amount or kind of something, as in *What food have you got?*
2 used to say how strange or great a person or thing is, as in *What a fool you are!*

what *pronoun*
the thing that; which thing or things, as in *What did you say? This is what I said*.
what's what, (*colloquial*) what is important or useful, as in *She knows what's what*.

whatever *pronoun*
no matter what; anything or everything that, as in *Whatever happens, I'll be there. Do whatever you like*.

whatever *adjective*
to do with any kind or amount, as in *Get whatever help you can*.

wheat *noun*
the grain of a cereal plant from which flour is made.

wheel *noun* **wheels**
1 a round device that turns on an axle.
2 a horizontal revolving disc on which clay is made into a pot.

wheel *verb* **wheels, wheeling, wheeled**
1 to push along a bicycle, cart, etc. 2 to move in a curve or circle, as in *The column of soldiers wheeled to the right*.

wheelbarrow *noun* **wheelbarrows**
a small handcart with one wheel and two handles used for carrying garden loads etc.

wheelchair *noun* **wheelchairs**
a chair on wheels for someone who cannot walk easily, which can be moved and steered by the person in it or by someone pushing it.

wheeze *verb* **wheezes, wheezing, wheezed**
to make a whistling or gasping noise as you breathe, as in *A person with asthma wheezes*.

whelk *noun* **whelks**
a shellfish that looks like a snail.

when *adverb*
at what time, as in *When can you come to tea?*

when *conjunction*
1 at the time that, as in *The bird flew away when I moved*. 2 because; considering that, as in *Why do you smoke when you know it is dangerous?*

whenever *conjunction*
at any time; every time, as in *Whenever I see him, he's asleep*.

where *adverb* and *conjunction*
1 in or to what place, as in *Where is he? Where have you put the glue?* 2 in or to that place, as in *Leave the book where it is.*

whereabouts *adverb*
roughly where, as in *'Whereabouts are the Bernier and Dorre Islands?' 'They're off the coast of Western Australia.'*

whereas *conjunction*
but, as in *Some people like sailing whereas others hate it.*

whereupon *adverb*
after that; and then, as in *She arrived whereupon they left for the party.*

wherever *adverb* and *conjunction*
in or to whatever place; no matter where, as in *The child followed wherever the mother went.*

whether *conjunction*
used to introduce more than one possibility, as in *I don't know whether she is here or not.*

whey *noun* (*say* way)
the watery liquid left when milk forms curds.

which *adjective*
what particular, as in *Which way did he go?*

which *pronoun*
the thing spoken about; what person or thing, as in *Which is your teacher?*

whichever *pronoun* and *adjective*
that or those which; any which, as in *Take whichever book you like.*

whiff *noun* whiffs
a puff or slight smell of smoke, gas, etc.

while *conjunction*
1 during the time that; as long as, as in *Whistle while you work.* 2 but; although, as in *She was dressed in black, while I was in white.*

while *noun*
a period of time, as in *We have waited all this while.*

while *verb* whiles, whiling, whiled
while away, to pass time, as in *We whiled away the time by playing cards.*

whilst *conjunction*
while.

whim *noun* whims (*say* wim)
a sudden fancy.

whimper *verb* whimpers, whimpering, whimpered
to make feeble crying sounds, as in *The dog whimpered while I bathed its injured leg.*

whine *verb* whines, whining, whined
1 to make a long, high, piercing sound, as in *The electric drill whined.* 2 to complain in a feeble, miserable voice, as in *'It's just not fair', he whined.*

whinge *verb* whinges, whingeing, whinged (*say* winj)
to grumble or whine.

whinny *verb* whinnies, whinnying, whinnied
to neigh gently or happily.

whip *noun* whips
a cord or strip of leather fixed to a handle and used for hitting people or animals.

whip *verb* whips, whipping, whipped
1 to hit a person or animal with a whip. 2 to beat cream, eggs, etc. into a froth. 3 to move or take something suddenly, as in *He whipped out a gun.* 4 (*colloquial*) to steal something, as in *He whipped off the money left on the table.*
whip up, to excite, stir up, or make quickly.

whirl *verb* whirls, whirling, whirled
to turn or spin very quickly; to cause something to move in this way.

whirlpool *noun* whirlpools
a strong current of water going around in a circle and often drawing floating objects towards it.

whirlwind *noun* whirlwinds
a very strong wind that whirls around or blows in a spiral; a willy willy.

whirr *verb* whirrs, whirring, whirred
to make a continuous buzzing sound.

whisk *verb* whisks, whisking, whisked
1 to move something very quickly, as in *A waiter whisked away my plate as soon as I had finished my meal.* 2 to stir something briskly.

whisk *noun* whisks
1 a device for whisking eggs, cream, etc. 2 a quick sweeping movement, as in *With a whisk of its tail, the cat ran off.*

whisker *noun* whiskers
a hair growing on the face of a person or animal.

whisky *noun* whiskies
a kind of very strong alcoholic drink.

whisper *verb* whispers, whispering, whispered
1 to speak very softly. 2 to talk secretly.

whisper *noun* whispers
a whispering voice or sound.

whist *noun*
a card-game usually for four people.

whistle

whistle *noun* **whistles**
1 a clear, shrill sound. 2 a device that makes a shrill sound when you blow into it.

whistle *verb* **whistles, whistling, whistled**
to make a shrill or musical sound by blowing through your lips.
whistler *noun*

white *adjective* **whiter, whitest**
1 having the very lightest colour, like snow or milk. 2 with light-coloured skin.
white coffee, coffee with milk or cream.
white elephant, something useless.
white-hot, extremely hot.
white lie, a harmless lie.
whiteness *noun*, **whitish** *adjective*

white *noun* **whites**
white colour.
White, a white person.

white ant *noun* **white ants**
a wood-eating insect; a termite.

whiteboard *noun* **whiteboards**
a kind of 'blackboard' made of white plastic, and written on with a felt pen rather than with chalk.

whiten *verb* **whitens, whitening, whitened**
to make something white; to become white.

whiz *verb* **whizzes, whizzing, whizzed**
1 to move very quickly. 2 to sound like something rushing through the air.

whiz-kid *noun* **whiz-kids**
(*colloquial*) a brilliant or very successful young person, as in *a nine-year-old computer whiz-kid*.

who *pronoun*
1 which person; which people, as in *Who threw that?* 2 the person or people spoken about, as in *the boys who did it*.

whoever *pronoun*
the person who; any person who, as in *Whoever comes is welcome*.

whole *adjective*
complete; not broken or damaged.
whole number, a number without any fractions.

whole *noun* **wholes**
a complete thing.
on the whole, considering everything; mainly.

wholemeal *adjective*
made from the whole grain of wheat, etc., as in *wholemeal bread*.

wholesale *adjective* and *adverb*
1 sold in large quantities, usually to shopkeepers. 2 on a large scale; including everybody or everything, as in *wholesale destruction*.

wholesome *adjective*
good for health; healthy, as in *wholesome food*.

wholly *adverb*
completely; entirely.

whom *pronoun*
a word used for *who* when it is the object of a sentence, or comes straight after a preposition, as in *the lawyer whom I consulted. Whom did you see? To whom did you give the parcel?*

whoop *noun* **whoops** (*say* woop)
a loud excited cry, as in *Bill gave a whoop of delight*.

whoopee *interjection* (*say* **wuup**-ee)
a joyful exclamation, as in *It's a holiday! Whoopee!*

whooping cough *noun* (*say* **hoop**-ing-kof)
an illness that makes you cough and gasp, especially suffered by children.

who's short for *who has* or *who is*, as in *Who's coming for a swim?*

whose *adjective* and *pronoun*
1 belonging to what person, as in *Whose bike is that?* 2 of which; of whom, as in *The house whose roof is red. The boy whose mother died.*

why *adverb*
for what reason or purpose.

wick *noun* **wicks**
a strip or twist of thread giving fuel to a flame in a candle, lamp, etc.
get on a person's wick, (*colloquial*) to annoy a person.

wicked *adjective* **wickeder, wickedest**
very bad or cruel; doing things that are wrong or spiteful, as in *a wicked deed. He was a wicked and dangerous man.*
wickedly *adverb*, **wickedness** *noun*

wickerwork *noun*
things made of reeds or cane woven together.

wicket *noun* **wickets**
1 the set of three stumps with two bails on top of them in cricket. 2 the part of a cricket ground between or near the wickets.
wicket-keeper, the fielder in cricket who stands behind the batter's wicket.

wide *adjective* **wider, widest**
1 measuring a lot from one side to the · other, as in *a wide river*. 2 from one side to

winch

the other, as in *The room is 4 metres wide.*
3 covering a great area, as in *wide knowledge.*
widely *adverb*, **wideness** *noun*

wide *adverb* **wider, widest**
1 completely; fully, as in *wide awake.*
2 far from the target, as in *His shot went
wide.* **3** over a large area, as in *She
travelled far and wide.*

widen *verb* **widens, widening, widened**
to make something wider; to become
wider.

widespread *adjective*
existing in many places; common.

widow *noun* **widows**
a woman whose husband has died.

widower *noun* **widowers**
a man whose wife has died.

width *noun* **widths**
how wide something is.

wield *verb* **wields, wielding, wielded**
(*say* weeld)
to hold something and use it, as in *He
wielded a sword.*

wife *noun* **wives**
the woman that a man has married, as in
Henry VIII had six wives.

wig *noun* **wigs**
a covering of false hair worn on someone's
head.

wiggle *verb* **wiggles, wiggling, wiggled**
to move from side to side.

wigwam *noun* **wigwams**
the tent of a Native American.

wild *adjective* **wilder, wildest**
1 not tame; not looked after by people, as
in *a wild dog.* **2** not grown by people; not
cultivated, as in *wild blackberries.* **3** not
controlled; violent, as in *wild behaviour.*
in the wild, natural areas far from where
people live, as in *Kangaroos exist in large
numbers in the wild.*
Wild West, the western parts of America in
the 19th Century, when Europeans were
settling there.
wildly *adverb*, **wildness** *noun*

wilderness *noun* **wildernesses**
an uncultivated and still wild region of
forest, scrub, bush, desert, etc.
wilderness area, an area of land largely
undisturbed by people where native plants
and animals flourish in their natural
environment, as in *The wilderness areas of
Tasmania are popular with bushwalkers.*

wildflower *noun* **wildflowers**
the flower of a native plant, as in
Wildflowers flourish in Western Australia.

wildlife *noun*
animals, birds, snakes, etc. living in their
natural habitat, as in *There are several
endangered species in our wildlife.*

wilful *adjective*
1 obstinate, as in *a wilful child.*
2 deliberate, as in *wilful disobedience.*
wilfully *adverb*, **wilfulness** *noun*

will *verb* past tense **would**
shall; is or are going to, as in *She will like
this.*

will *noun* **wills**
1 the power to use your mind to decide
and control what you do. **2** what
someone chooses or wants, as in *The
people's will must be done.* **3** a legal
document saying what is to be done with
someone's possessions after he or she dies.

willing *adjective*
ready and happy to do what is wanted.
willingly *adverb*, **willingness** *noun*

willow *noun* **willows**
a tree with thin, flexible branches, as in
Willows often grow near water.

willy willy *noun* **willy willies**
a whirlwind or dust-storm.

Origin This word comes from either one of
two Aboriginal languages Yindjibarndi:
wili-wili or Wemba-wemba: **wilang-wilang**.
See the Aboriginal Languages map at the
back of this dictionary.

wilt *verb* **wilts, wilting, wilted**
1 to lose freshness and to droop; to cause a
plant to do this, as in *The plants have wilted.*
2 to lose strength, as in *The team began to
wilt after half-time.*

wily *adjective* **wilier, wiliest**
crafty; cunning.

wimp *noun* **wimps**
(*colloquial*) a feeble, easily frightened
person.

win *verb* **wins, winning, won**
1 to do best in a contest, game, battle, etc.
2 to get something by using effort, skill,
luck, etc., as in *She won the prize.*

wince *verb* **winces, wincing, winced**
to make a slight movement because you are
in pain, unhappy, etc.

winch *noun* **winches**
a device for lifting or pulling things, using
a rope or cable that goes around a wheel.

a
b
c
d
e
f
g
h
i
j
k
l
m
n
o
p
q
r
s
t
u
v
w
x
y
z

wind

wind *noun* **winds**
(rhymes with *tinned*)
1 a current of air. **2** gas in the stomach or bowels that makes you uncomfortable. **3** breath used for a purpose. **4** the wind instruments of an orchestra.
get or **have the wind up,** (*colloquial*) to be scared.
wind instrument, a musical instrument that you blow into.
wind power, energy from the wind.

wind *verb* **winds, winding, wound**
(rhymes with *find*)
1 to turn or go in twists, curves, or circles. **2** to wind up a watch or clock.
wind up, to make a watch, clock, etc. work by turning a key; to close a business; (*colloquial*) to end in a place or condition, as in *I have wound up my watch. The company has been wound up. He wound up in jail.*

wind-break *noun* **wind-breaks**
a thing, especially a row of trees or shrubs that breaks the force of the wind.

windfall *noun* **windfalls**
1 a fruit blown down from a tree. **2** a piece of unexpected good luck, especially getting a sum of money.

windmill *noun* **windmills**
a mill with four long arms called *sails* which are turned by the wind.

window *noun* **windows**
1 an opening in a wall, roof, etc. to let in light and air, usually filled with glass; this piece of glass. **2** (*in Computing*) an area on a VDU screen used for a particular purpose, as in *You can display different pieces of text in separate windows.*
window-shopping, looking at things in shop-windows but not buying anything.

windpipe *noun* **windpipes**
the tube through which air reaches the lungs.

windscreen *noun* **windscreens**
the window at the front of a motor vehicle.

windsurfing *noun*
the sport of riding on water on a sailboard.
windsurfer *noun*

windward *adjective*
facing the wind, as in *the windward side of the ship.*

windy *adjective* **windier, windiest**
with much wind, as in *a windy night.*

wine *noun* **wines**
an alcoholic drink made from grapes or other plants.

wing *noun* **wings**
1 one of the parts of a bird or insect that it uses for flying. **2** one of the long, flat parts that support an aircraft in the air. **3** part of a building that extends from the main part. **4** a section within a political party having different ideas, as in *the right wing of the Labor Party.* **5** the side part of a playing-area in football, hockey, etc.; a player in this position.
on the wing, flying.
wings, the sides of a theatre stage.
winged *adjective*, **wingless** *adjective*

wingspan *noun* **wingspans**
the distance across the wings of an insect, a bird, or an aeroplane.

wink *verb* **winks, winking, winked**
1 to close and open your eye quickly. **2** to flicker or twinkle, as in *a sky full of stars that winked and twinkled.*

wink *noun* **winks**
1 the act of winking. **2** (*colloquial*) a short period of sleep, as in *I didn't sleep a wink.*

winner *noun* **winners**
1 a person who wins something. **2** someone or something very successful, as in *Her book is a winner.*

winnings *plural noun*
money won by betting, in a game, etc.

winter *noun* **winters**
the coldest season of the year, between autumn and spring.
wintry *adjective*

wipe *verb* **wipes, wiping, wiped**
to dry or clean something by rubbing it.
wipe out, to destroy someone or something; to remove something, as in *wipe out a debt.*
wiper *noun*

wipe-out *noun* **wipe-outs**
(*in Surfing*) a fall from a surfboard.

wire *noun* **wires**
a very thin length of metal, especially used to carry electric current.

wire *verb* **wired, wiring, wired**
1 to connect objects with wires so that electricity can flow between them. **2** to fasten, strengthen, etc. with wire, as in *She wired the creeping rose to the wall.*

wireless *noun* **wirelesses**
(*old-fashioned use*) radio.

wiring *noun*
the system of wires carrying electricity in a building or in an electrical device.

wizard

wiry *adjective* **wirier, wiriest**
1 like wire, as in *Terriers have wiry hair.*
2 lean and strong, as in *a tanned, wiry man.*

wisdom *noun*
1 being wise. 2 wise sayings or writings.
wisdom tooth, a molar that may grow at the back of your jaw much later than the other teeth.

wise *adjective* **wiser, wisest**
knowing or understanding many things.
none the wiser, knowing no more about something than before, as in *He tried to explain his theory to me, but I'm afraid I'm none the wiser.*
wisely *adverb*

wish *verb* **wishes, wishing, wished**
1 to think or say that you would like something. 2 to say that you hope someone will get something, as in *We wish you a merry Christmas.*

wish *noun* **wishes**
1 something you want. 2 the act of wishing, as in *Make a wish. We send you our best wishes.*

wishbone *noun* **wishbones**
a forked bone from a bird like a chicken, as in *Two people break the wishbone and the person who gets the bigger piece can make a wish.*

wisp *noun* **wisps**
a thin piece of hair, straw, smoke, etc.
wispy *adjective*

wistful *adjective*
sadly longing for something, as in *A wistful look appeared on her face when she thought of her loss.*
wistfully *adverb,* **wistfulness** *noun*

wit *noun* **wits**
1 intelligence; cleverness. 2 a clever kind of humour; the ability to be cleverly humorous. 3 a witty person.
keep your wits about you, to stay alert.

witch *noun* **witches**
1 a woman who claims to have magic powers to use for good or bad purposes.
2 an ugly, mean, usually old woman.
witch-doctor, a person in primitive tribes believed to have magic powers which can heal or hurt people.

witchcraft *noun*
the use of magic, especially to make bad things happen.

witchetty grub *noun* **witchetty grubs**
a large edible grub.

Origin This word probably comes from the Aboriginal language Adnyamathanha: a combination of **wityu** = hooked stick used to catch these grubs and **varti** = grub or insect. See the Aboriginal Languages map at the back of this dictionary.

with *preposition*
1 having, as in *the child with freckles.* 2 in the company of; accompanied by, as in *I came with a friend.* 3 using, as in *Hit it with a hammer.* 4 against, as in *They fought with each other.* 5 because of, as in *He shook with laughter.* 6 towards; concerning, as in *Be patient with me.*

withdraw *verb* **withdraws, withdrawing, withdrew, withdrawn**
1 to take away or back; to remove, as in *She withdrew money from the bank.* 2 to retreat; to leave, as in *They withdrew from the club.*
withdrawal *noun*

wither *verb* **withers, withering, withered**
to dry up; to wilt, as in *The grapes had withered on the vine. The seedlings will wither unless you water them.*

withhold *verb* **withholds, withholding, withheld**
to refuse to give something to someone, as in *He withheld his permission.*

within *preposition* and *adverb*
inside; not beyond something, as in *Stay within the school boundaries.*

without *preposition*
not having; free from, as in *They were without food. They would like a life without worry.*

withstand *verb* **withstands, withstanding, withstood**
to resist or hold out against a person or thing, as in *He withstood the child's demands for more sweets. Her courage made her able to withstand the pain.*

witness *noun* **witnesses**
1 a person who sees something happen, as in *There were no witnesses to the accident.*
2 someone who gives evidence in a lawcourt.

witty *adjective* **wittier, wittiest**
clever and amusing.
wittily *adverb,* **wittiness** *noun*

wizard *noun* **wizards**
1 a man who can do magic things. 2 an amazing person, as in *He's a wizard on the computer.*
wizardry *noun*

a
b
c
d
e
f
g
h
i
j
k
l
m
n
o
p
q
r
s
t
u
v
w
x
y
z

wobble

wobble *verb* **wobbles, wobbling, wobbled**
to move unsteadily from side to side; to shake, as in *The jelly was wobbling*.
wobbly *adjective*

woe *noun* **woes**
sorrow; misfortune.
woeful *adjective*, **woefully** *adverb*

wog *noun* **wogs**
1 (*colloquial*) an insulting word for a foreigner or migrant, especially a person from southern Europe. **2** (*colloquial*) a germ which causes illness or infection, as in *There is a stomach wog going around the school*.

wok *noun* **woks**
a deep, round-bottomed frying-pan used in Asian cookery.

woke past tense of **wake** *verb*.

woken past participle of **wake** *verb*.

wolf *noun* **wolves**
a wild animal, like a large, fierce dog, from the northern hemisphere.

woman *noun* **women**
a grown-up human female.

womb *noun* **wombs** (*say* woom)
the part of a female's body where babies develop before they are born.

wombat *noun* **wombats**
a heavy burrowing marsupial which has short legs and eats plants.

Origin This word comes from the Aboriginal language Dharuk: **wambad, wambaj, or wambag**. See the Aboriginal Languages maps at the back of this dictionary.

won past tense and past participle of **win**.

wonder *noun* **wonders**
1 a feeling of surprise and admiration. **2** something that makes you feel surprised and admiring; a marvel.
no wonder, it is not surprising.

wonder *verb* **wonders, wondering, wondered**
1 to feel that you want to know or decide about something, as in *I wonder what to do next*. **2** to feel surprise and admiration at something, as in *The tourists stood and wondered at Katherine Gorge*.

wonderful *adjective*
1 astonishing. **2** excellent.
wonderfully *adverb*

Wongi *noun*
an Aborigine from the Kalgoorlie region in Western Australia.

Origin This word comes from the Aboriginal Western Desert language: **wanggayi**. See the Aboriginal Languages maps at the back of this dictionary.

won't short for *will not*.

wood *noun* **woods**
1 the substance of which trees are made. **2** a lot of trees growing together.

wooden *adjective*
1 made of wood, as in *a wooden chair*. **2** stiff; awkward, as in *His movements were wooden*.

woodpecker *noun* **woodpeckers**
a bird that makes holes in trees with its beak, to find insects to eat.

woodwind *noun*
wind instruments that are usually made of wood or plastic, such as the clarinet and oboe.

woodwork *noun*
1 making things with wood. **2** things made out of wood.

woody *adjective* **woodier, woodiest**
1 like wood, as in *the woody taste of some wine*. **2** full of trees, as in *a woody landscape*.

wool *noun*
1 the thick, soft hair of sheep, goats, etc. **2** thread or cloth made from this hair.

woollen *adjective*
made of wool.

woolly *adjective* **woollier, woolliest**
1 covered with wool. **2** woollen or like wool, as in *woolly jumper; woolly clouds*. **3** not clear; vague, as in *He had woolly ideas*.
woolliness *noun*

woomera *noun* **woomeras**
an implement used by the Aborigines to help throw a spear.

Origin This word comes from the Aboriginal language Dharuk: **wamara**. See the Aboriginal Languages maps at the back of this dictionary.

word *noun* **words**
1 a letter or group of letters that means something when you write it. **2** a sound or group of sounds that means something when you say it. **3** a promise, as in *He cannot keep his word*. **4** a command; an order, as in *Run when I give the word*. **5** a message; information, as in *We sent word that we had arrived safely*.

word processor *noun* **word processors**
a computer system designed specially to allow you to store, alter, arrange, and print pieces of writing.

wordy *adjective* **wordier, wordiest**
using too many words, as in *a wordy speech*.

wore past tense of **wear** *verb*.

work *noun* **works**
1 something that you have to do that needs effort or energy, as in *Weeding is hard work*. 2 a person's job, as in *Has Bruce gone to work yet?* 3 something produced by work, as in *The teacher marked our work*. 4 something that needs to be done by effort, as in *There is a lot of repair work to be done*.
at work, working; functioning.
the works, (*colloquial*) all that is available, as in *a party with the works*.
work of art, a painting, sculpture, etc.
works, a factory; the moving parts of a machine.

work *verb* **works, working, worked**
1 to do work. 2 to have a job; to be employed, as in *She works in a bank*. 3 to act or operate correctly or successfully, as in *Is the lift working?* 4 to make something act or operate, as in *Can you work the lift?* 5 to bring about, as in *The cream worked miracles on the sunburn*.
work out, to find an answer by working or calculating; to have a particular result; to exercise.

workable *adjective*
able to be used or done, as in *a workable plan*.

worker *noun* **workers**
1 someone who works, especially for an employer. 2 a person who works very hard, as in *She is known to be a hard worker*. 3 a bee, ant, etc. that does the work in a hive or colony.

working class *noun* **working classes**
those who work for wages, especially in industry.
working-class *adjective*

workmanship *noun*
the amount of skill in doing a task, or the result in the product of such skill, as in *the carpenter's workmanship; The workmanship in the sculpture was remarkable*.

workout *noun* **workouts**
a session of physical exercise or training.

worksheet *noun* **worksheets**
a sheet of paper with a set of questions

about a subject for students, often intended to be used with a textbook, as in *The science museum has produced a series of worksheets for pupils studying dinosaurs*.

workshop *noun* **workshops**
1 a place where things are made or mended. 2 a place or meeting organised for discussion or activity, as in *a dance workshop; a writing workshop*.

world *noun* **worlds**
1 the planet that we live on, with all its peoples; the earth. 2 the universe. 3 everything to do with a particular subject or activity, as in *the world of sport*.
world war, a war in which countries all over the world are involved, especially the *First World War* (1914–18) and the *Second World War* (1939–45).

worldwide *adjective* and *adverb*
over the whole of the world, as in *Global warming could bring a worldwide rise in temperature. Electricity is used worldwide*.

worm *noun* **worms**
1 a small, thin, wriggling animal without legs, especially an earthworm. 2 an unimportant or disliked person.

worm *verb* **worms, worming, wormed**
to move by wriggling or crawling.

worn past participle of **wear** *verb*.

worry *verb* **worries, worrying, worried**
1 to trouble someone; to make someone think of something bad that may happen. 2 to think of something bad that may happen. 3 (of an animal) to hold something in its teeth and shake it, as in *The dog was worrying the rat*.
worrier *noun*

worry *noun* **worries**
something that disturbs or causes anxiety, as in *The worry of illness upset her. Unemployment is their main source of worry*.

worse *adjective* and *adverb*, comparative of **bad** and **badly**.
more bad or more badly; less good or less well, as in *She is bad, but I am worse. Which team played worse?*

worsen *verb* **worsens, worsening, worsened**
to make something worse; to become worse.

worship *noun*
worshipping; religious ceremonies or services, as in *the worship of money; worship on Sundays*.

worship

worship *verb* **worships, worshipping, worshipped**
1 to idolise or adore, as in *She worships the ground he walks on.* 2 to give praise or respect to God or a god.
worshipper *noun*

worst *adjective* and *adverb*, superlative of **bad** and **badly.**
most bad or most badly; least good or least well, as in *It was the worst game of the season. Of all the students he performed worst.*

worth *adjective*
1 having a certain value, as in *This stamp is worth $100.* 2 deserving; good enough for, as in *That book is worth reading.*

worth *noun*
1 the equal of money in a product, as in *$10 worth of petrol.* 2 value, as in *a book of little worth.*

worthless *adjective*
with no value; useless.

worthwhile *adjective*
important or good enough to do; useful.

worthy *adjective* **worthier, worthiest**
deserving respect or support; good, as in *The jumble sale is for a worthy cause.*
worthy of, deserving something; good enough for something, as in *The student's good work was worthy of a prize.*
worthily *adverb*, **worthiness** *noun*

would *verb*
1 past tense of **will.** 2 to be willing or likely to do something, as in *He would come if he could.*

wouldn't short for *would not.*

wound *noun* **wounds** (*say* woond)
an injury done to a body or to someone's feelings.

wound *verb* **wounds, wounding, wounded** (*say* woond)
to give someone a wound or offence, as in *They were wounded in battle. Her rudeness wounded her mother.*

wound (*say* wownd) past tense and past participle of **wind** *verb.*

wove past tense of **weave.**

woven past participle of **weave.**

wrap *verb* **wraps, wrapping, wrapped**
to put paper, cloth, etc. around something.

wrath *noun*
(rhymes with *cloth*)
(*old-fashioned use*) anger.
wrathful *adjective*, **wrathfully** *adverb*

wreath *noun* **wreaths** (*say* reeth)
flowers, branches, etc. bound together to make a circle, as in *Christmas wreaths.*

wreathe *verb* **wreathes, wreathing, wreathed** (*say* reeth)
1 to surround or decorate something with a wreath. 2 to cover, as in *Her face was wreathed in smiles.*

wreck *noun* **wrecks**
a very badly damaged ship, car, building, etc.

wreck *verb* **wrecks, wrecking, wrecked**
to damage something, especially a ship, so badly that it cannot be used again.
wrecker *noun*

wreckage *noun*
the pieces of a wreck.

wren *noun* **wrens**
a very small bird, the male having brightly coloured, especially blue, feathers.

wrench *noun* **wrenches**
1 a violent twist, pull or tear, as in *the wrench of a tooth from the mouth.* 2 the pain felt at parting, as in *Leaving home was a great wrench.* 3 a tool for gripping and turning bolts, nuts, etc.

wrench *verb* **wrenches, wrenching, wrenched**
to pull or twist something suddenly or violently, as in *He wrenched the door open.*

wrest *verb* **wrests, wresting, wrested**
to wrench away from a person's grasp, as in *The policewoman wrested the pistol from the bank robber.*

wrestle *verb* **wrestles, wrestling, wrestled**
1 to struggle with someone and try to throw him or her to the ground. 2 to struggle with a difficulty, problem, etc.
wrestler *noun*, **wrestling** *noun*

wretch *noun* **wretches**
someone who is unhappy, poor, or disliked.

wretched *adjective* (*say* **rech**-uhd)
1 unhappy; miserable; poor, as in *a wretched beggar.* 2 not satisfactory or pleasant, as in *This wretched car won't start. Wretched weather caused them to cancel the party.*

wriggle *verb* **wriggles, wriggling, wriggled**
to twist and turn your body around.
wriggler *noun*, **wriggly** *adjective*

wring *verb* **wrings, wringing, wrung**
1 to squeeze or twist a wet thing to get the water out of it, as in *Have you wrung out your swimsuit?* 2 to squeeze or twist something, as in *I'll wring your neck!*
wringing wet, very wet; soaked.

wrinkle *noun* **wrinkles**
a small crease or line in the skin or on a surface.

wrinkle *verb* **wrinkles, wrinkling, wrinkled**
to make wrinkles.

wrist *noun* **wrists**
the thin part of your arm where it joins your hand.
wrist-watch, a watch that you wear on your wrist.

write *verb* **writes, writing, wrote, written**
1 to put words or signs on paper or some other surface so that people can read them, as in *Who wrote these words on the wall?*
2 to be the author or composer of something, as in *'Snugglepot and Cuddlepie' was written by May Gibbs.* 3 to send a letter to someone.
write off, to damage a vehicle so badly that it is not worth repairing.
writing *noun*

writer *noun* **writers**
a person who writes books, etc.; an author.

writhe *verb* **writhes, writhing, writhed**
(*say* ruyth)
to twist your body about because you are in pain or discomfort.

wrong *adjective*
1 not fair; not moral, as in *Is it wrong to swear?* 2 incorrect, as in *Your answer is wrong.* 3 not working properly, as in *There's something wrong with the engine.*
wrongly *adverb*

wrong *noun* **wrongs**
something that is bad or unjust, as in *In her heart she knew she had done no wrong.*
in the wrong, having done or said something wrong.

wrote past tense of **write.**

wrought iron *noun* (*say* rawt **uy**-uhn)
a tough type of iron which can be easily formed into different shapes, as in *The old colonial house had wrought iron trimmings.*

wrung past tense and past participle of **wring.**

wry *adjective* **wryer, wryest**
twisted; showing disgust or disappointment, as in *a wry smile.*

wuss *noun*
(*colloquial*) a timid, sooky person; a wimp, as in *The boy who was too afraid to dive in the pool was called a wuss.*

Xmas *noun* **Xmases** (*say* **kris**-muhs *or* **eks**-muhs)
(*colloquial*) Christmas.

X-ray *noun* **X-rays**
1 a ray that can pass through something solid. 2 a photograph of the inside of something, especially part of the body, made by means of these rays.

X-ray *verb* **X-rays, X-raying, X-rayed**
to make an X-ray photograph of something.

xylophone *noun* **xylophones**
(*say* **zuy**-luh-fohn)
a musical instrument made of bars of different lengths, that you hit with small hammers.

Yy

yabber *verb* yabbers, yabbering, yabbered
(*colloquial*) to talk or chat.
[probably from an Aboriginal language]
yabber *noun*

yabby *noun* yabbies
a small, edible freshwater crayfish.

Origin This word comes from the
Aboriginal language Wemba wemba: **yabij**.
See the Aboriginal Languages map at the
back of this dictionary.

yabbying, fishing for yabbies, as in *The
children went yabbying in the dam.*

yacht *noun* yachts (*say* yot)
a sailing-boat used for racing or cruising.
yachting *noun*, **yachtsman** *noun*,
yachtswoman *noun*

yachtie *noun* yachties
(*colloquial*) a person very keen about
yachting.

yak *noun* yaks
a long-haired Tibetan ox with a hump.

yak *noun*
(*colloquial*) a long conversation about
unimportant matters.
yak *verb*

yakka *noun*
(*colloquial*) work, as in *Digging ditches is
hard yakka.*

Origin This word comes from the
Aboriginal language Yagara: **yuga**. See the
Aboriginal Languages map at the back of
this dictionary.

yam *noun* yams
a vegetable like a potato that grows in
tropical climates, as in *People from New
Guinea eat yams.*

Yammagi *noun*
an Aborigine from the Gascoyne-Murchison
region in Western Australia.

Origin This word comes from the
Aboriginal language Watjari: **yamaji** =
person, man. See the Aboriginal Languages
map at the back of this dictionary.

yank *verb* yanks, yanking, yanked
(*colloquial*) to pull something strongly and
suddenly.
yank *noun*

Yank *noun* Yanks
(*colloquial*) a name for an American.

yap *verb* yaps, yapping, yapped
to make a shrill barking sound, as in *a
yapping dog.*

yard *noun* yards
1 the garden or land around a house, as in
We played cricket in the back yard. **2** an
enclosed area in which sheep, cattle, etc.
are kept, as in *stock yard.* **3** an enclosed
area in which business or work is carried
out, as in *timber yard, ship yard.* **4** a
measure of length equal to about 91
centimetres.

yarn *noun* yarns
1 thread used for knitting, weaving,
embroidery, etc. **2** (*colloquial*) a chat; a
long rambling story, as in *a yarn with
friends; grandfather's yarns about the olden
days.*

yawn *verb* yawns, yawning, yawned
1 to open your mouth wide and breathe in
deeply when you are tired or bored. **2** to
form a wide opening, as in *The chasm
yawned beneath them.*

a
b
c
d
e
f
g
h
i
j
k
l
m
n
o
p
q
r
s
t
u
v
w
x
y
z

yawn

yawn *noun* **yawns**
the action of yawning.

ye *pronoun*
(*old-fashioned use*) you, as in *O ye of little faith!*

year *noun* **years**
the time that the earth takes to go right around the sun; twelve months.
yearly *adjective* and *adverb*

yearn *verb* **yearns, yearning, yearned**
to long for something, as in *She yearned for the holidays to come.*

yeast *noun*
a substance used in making bread, beer, wine, etc.

yell *noun* **yells**
a loud cry; a shout.

yellow *adjective* **yellower, yellowest**
1 yellow in colour. 2 (*colloquial*) cowardly.
yellow fever, a tropical disease that makes your skin yellow.
Yellow Pages, a special telephone directory giving addresses and numbers of businesses, arranged according to what services they provide.
yellowish *adjective*

yellow *noun*
the colour of lemons or wattle.

yelp *verb* **yelps, yelping, yelped**
to make a shrill bark or cry.

yes *interjection*
a word used for agreeing to something.

yesterday *noun* and *adverb*
the day before today.

yet *adverb*
1 up to now; by this time, as in *Has the postman called yet?* 2 eventually, as in *I'll get even with him yet.* 3 in addition; even; still, as in *She became yet more excited.*

yet *conjunction*
nevertheless, as in *It is strange, yet it is true.*

yeti *noun* **yetis** (*say* **yet**-ee)
a huge animal thought to live in the Himalayas.

yield *verb* **yields, yielding, yielded**
1 to surrender; to give in, as in *He yielded to persuasion.* 2 to produce a crop, profit, etc., as in *These trees yield good apples.*

yield *noun* **yields**
an amount produced by something, as in *What is the yield of wheat per hectare?*

yobbo *noun* **yobbos**
(*colloquial*) a hooligan, as in *The yobbos painted graffiti on the wall.*

yodel *verb* **yodels, yodelling, yodelled**
to sing or shout with your voice often going from low to high notes, as in *The Swiss mountaineer was yodelling.*
yodeller *noun*

yoga *noun* (*say* **yoh**-guh)
a method of meditation and self-control.

yoghurt *noun* (*say* **yoh**-guht *or* **yog**-uht)
a food with a sour taste made from milk treated with a bacteria, as in *Yoghurt is often flavoured with fruit.*

yoke *noun* **yokes**
a curved piece of wood put across the necks of animals pulling a cart.

yolk *noun* **yolks**
(rhymes with *coke*)
the yellow part of an egg.

Yolngu *noun*
an Aborigine from Arnhem Land in the Northern Territory.

Origin This word comes from the Aboriginal language Yolngu: **Yuulngu**. See the Aboriginal Languages map at the back of this dictionary.

Yom Kippur *noun*
an important religious day for Jews.

yonder *adverb* and *adjective*
(*old-fashioned use*) that is over there, as in *There is a church over yonder.*

you *pronoun*
1 the person or people someone is speaking to, as in *Who are you?* 2 people; everyone; anyone, as in *You can never be too sure.*

you'd short for *you had, you should,* or *you would.*

you'll short for *you will.*

young *adjective* **younger, youngest**
born not long ago; that has existed for a short time; not old.

young *noun*
children or young animals, as in *The magpie defended its young.*

youngster *noun* **youngsters**
a child or young person.

your *adjective*
belonging to you; to do with you.

you're short for *you are.*

yours *pronoun*
belonging to you; the things belonging to you, as in *This pen is yours. I've found this pen of yours.*
yours faithfully, yours sincerely, yours truly, formal ways of ending a letter before you sign it.

yourself *pronoun* (**yourselves**)
you and no one else.
by yourself, on your own.

youth *noun* **youths**
1 being young; the period when you are young, as in *The preschoolers were filled with the innocence of youth. She was a swimmer in her youth.* **2** a young person, especially a young man, as in *a youth of 16.* **3** young people, as in *a youth club.*
youth hostel, a chain of cheap accommodation, especially for young people on holiday.
youthful *adjective*

you've short for *you have.*

yowie *noun*
an ape-like monster which is supposed to live in parts of eastern Australia.

Origin This word comes from the Aboriginal language Yuwaalaraay: **Yuwi** = dream spirit. See the Aboriginal Languages map at the back of this dictionary.

yo-yo *noun* **yo-yos**
a round wooden or plastic toy that moves up and down on a string which you hold.

yuck or **yuk** *interjection*
an expression of disgust.

yuppie *noun* **yuppies**
(*colloquial*) a young, usually middle-class person with a professional job, who earns a lot of money and spends it on expensive things.

Yura *noun*
an Aborigine, especially from South Australia.

Origin This word comes from the Aboriginal language Adnyamathanya. See the Aboriginal Languages map at the back of this dictionary.

Zz

zany *adjective* **zanier, zaniest**
funny in a crazy kind of way.

zap *verb* **zaps, zapping, zapped**
(*colloquial*)
1 to attack or destroy something forcefully; to shoot someone. **2** to change quickly, as in *He zapped through the ads on the videotape.*

zeal *noun*
keenness, especially in doing what you believe to be right.
zealous *adjective*, **zealously** *adverb*

zebra *noun* **zebras** (*say* zeb-ruh)
an animal like a horse with black and white stripes, as in *Zebras are found in Africa.*
zebra crossing, part of a road marked with broad white stripes for pedestrians to cross.

zero *noun* **zeros**
nought; the figure 0; nothing.
zero hour, the time when something is planned to start.

zest *noun*
1 enthusiasm. **2** great enjoyment or interest, as in *The risk added zest to the adventure.*

zigzag *noun* **zigzags**
a line or route full of sharp turns from one side to the other.

zigzag *verb* **zigzags, zigzagging, zigzagged**
to move in a zigzag, as in *The learner driver zigzagged down the road.*

zinc *noun*
a greyish-white metal used in making brass and galvanised sheet iron.

zip *noun* **zips**
1 a device with two rows of small teeth that fit together to join two pieces of material. **2** a sharp sound like a bullet going through the air. **3** liveliness; energy, as in *The fit runner was full of zip.*

zip *verb* **zips, zipping, zipped**
1 to fasten something with a zip. **2** to move quickly with a sharp sound.

zodiac *noun* (*say* zoh-dee-ak)
(*in Astrology*) an area of the sky divided into twelve equal parts called signs, as in *Pisces and Sagittarius are signs of the zodiac.*

zombie *noun* **zombies**
1 a dead body brought back to life by witchcraft. **2** (*colloquial*) someone who seems to be doing things without thinking, as if he or she were very tired.

zone *noun* **zones**
a district; an area, as in *a parking zone.*

zoo *noun* **zoos**
a public garden or park where wild animals are kept so that people can look at them.

zoology *noun* (*say* zoo-**ol**-uh-jee *or* zoh-**ol**-uh-jee)
the scientific study of animals.
zoological *adjective*, **zoologist** *noun*

zoom *verb* **zooms, zooming, zoomed**
to move very quickly, especially upwards, as in *The rocket zoomed into the air.*

zoom lens *noun* **zoom lenses**
a camera lens that can be adjusted quickly to focus on things that are close up or far away.

zucchini *noun* **zucchinis** (*say* zoo-**kee**-nee *or* zuh-**kee**-nee)
a small, usually green, variety of vegetable marrow.

zzz *noun*
(*colloquial*) a sleep.

Appendix 1 Some common prefixes

Prefix	Meaning	Example
ant(i)-	against	anti-aircraft
arch-	chief	archbishop
auto-	self	autobiography
com-; con-	together; with	compare; connect
contra-	against	contradict
de-	removing something	debug
dis-	not; taking away	dishonest; disarm
em-; en-	in; into	embark; encircle
ex-	that used to be	ex-husband
extra-	more; outside	extra-special; extraterrestrial
fore-	before	foresee
il-; im-; in-; ir-;	not	illegal; impossible; irresponsible
il-; im-; in-	in; into	illuminate; import; inside
inter-	between	international
mis-	wrong	misbehave
mono-	one	monorail
multi-	many	multicultural
non-	not	nonsense
over-	too much	overdo
poly-	many	polygon
post-	after	postpone
pre-	before	prehistoric
pro-	supporting	pro-government
re-	again	reappear
semi-	half	semicircle
sub-	below	submarine
super-	over; beyond	supersonic
tele-	at a distance	television
trans-	across	transport
ultra	beyond	ultraviolet
un-	not	uncertain

Appendix 2 Some common suffixes

Suffix	Meaning	Example
-able; -ible; -uble	able (to be . . .)	eatable; edible; soluable
-ant; -ent	a doer	attendant; student
-dom	condition, rank; territory	freedom; kingdom
-ee	one who is . . .	employee
-er	a doer	baker; miner
-er	more	harder; higher
-esque	in the style of	picturesque
-ess	used to make feminine forms of words	lioness
-est	most	hardest; highest
-fold	times	threefold; fourfold
-ful	full of	trustful
-hood	state of	childhood; manhood
-ic	belonging to	historic
-ise; -ize	used to make verbs	publicise; publicize
-ish	rather like	reddish; boyish
-ism	belief; system of thought	Hinduism; Catholicism
-ist	a doer	artist
-itis	inflammation of	tonsillitis
-less	lacking; free from	useless; smokeless
-let	small	piglet
-ly	used to make adverbs and adjectives	bravely; kindly
-ment	used to make nouns	amusement
-ness	state of being	kindness
-oid	like	cuboid
-or	a doer	sailor; tailor
-ous	used to make adjectives	dangerous
-ship	state of being	friendship
-some	full of	troublesome
-ty	showing condition	cruelty; loyalty
-ward(s)	in a particular direction	homeward(s)

Appendix 3 Floral emblems of Australian States and Territories

New South Wales	Waratah
Queensland	Cooktown Orchid
South Australia	Sturt's Desert Pea
Tasmania	Blue Gum
Victoria	Common Heath
Western Australia	Kangaroo Paw
Australian Capital Territory	Bluebell
Northern Territory	Sturt's Desert Rose

Appendix 4 English terms

abstract noun p. 2
acronym p. 5
adjective p. 6
adverb p. 7
allegory p. 11
alliteration p. 12
ampersand p. 14
anagram p. 14
antonym p. 17
apostrophe p. 18
autobiography p. 26
bracket p. 49
capital letter p. 61
clause p. 75
collective noun p. 79
colon p. 80
comma p. 81
common noun p. 82
comparative p. 83
complement p. 83
comprehension p. 84
concrete noun p. 86
conjunction p. 87
consonant p. 89
context p. 90
conundrum p. 91
direct speech p. 119
discussion p. 121
ditto marks p. 124
drama p. 128
exclamation mark p. 147
explanation p. 149
exposition p. 149
fable p. 152
fiction p. 159
figurative
  language p. 160

free verse p. 173
full stop p. 176
future tense p. 177
gender p. 181
grammar p. 189
grammatical p. 189
haiku p. 197
homograph p. 210
homonym p. 210
homophone p. 210
indirect question p. 224
indirect speech p. 224
infinitive p. 226
information report p. 226
interjection p. 231
inverted commas p. 233
limerick p. 258
linguistics p. 259
literacy p. 260
literary p. 260
literature p. 260
lyric p. 266
metaphor p. 278
narrative p. 292
non-fiction p. 297
noun p. 299
onomatopoeia p. 306
paragraph p. 316
paraphrase p. 316
parse p. 317
part of speech p. 317
passive verb p. 318
past participle p. 318
past tense p. 318
phrase p. 326
plural p. 332
poetry p. 333

possessive case p. 336
prefix p. 340
preposition p. 340
present participle p. 340
present tense p. 341
procedure p. 344
pronoun p. 345
prose p. 346
proverb p. 347
rhythm p. 370
semicolon p. 388
simile p. 398
singular p. 399
soliloquy p. 408
sonnet p. 409
speech marks p. 412
stanza p. 418
statement p. 419
subject p. 428
subtitle p. 429
suffix p. 429
superlative p. 431
supplement p. 432
syllable p. 435
synonym p. 436
tense p. 443
text p. 444
thesaurus p. 445
verb p. 472
verse p. 472
vocabulary p. 475
vowel p. 476

Appendix 5 Mathematical terms

acre p. 5
acute angle p. 5
add p. 5
addition p. 5
algebra p. 11
algorithm p. 11
angle p. 15
apex p. 18
arc p. 20
arithmetic p. 21
bracket p. 49
calculator p. 59
cardinal number p. 62
circumference p. 73
cone p. 86
congruent p. 87
count p. 95
cross section p. 100
cube p. 101
cubic p. 101
cuboid p. 102
decade p. 108
decagon p. 108
decahedron p. 108
decimal p. 108
decimal fraction p. 108
decimal number p. 108
decimal point p. 108
degree p. 111
denominator p. 113
diameter p. 117
divide p. 124
dodecagon p. 125
dodecahedron p. 125
ellipse p. 137

equation p. 142
equidistant p. 142
equilateral p. 142
equilateral triangle p. 143
equivalent p. 143
faces p. 152
factor p. 152
fraction p. 172
graph p. 190
half p. 197
halve p. 198
hectare p. 204
hemisphere p. 205
heptagon p. 205
hexagon p. 206
horizontal p. 211
hypotenuse p. 216
isosceles p. 235
kilogram p. 245
lengthen p. 255
locus p. 261
logarithm p. 262
mathematics p. 274
matrix p. 274
measure p. 275
median p. 275
multiple p. 289
multiply p. 289
numeral p. 300
numerate p. 300
numerator p. 300
numerical p. 300
obtuse angle p. 302
octagon p. 302
ordinal number p. 307

oval p. 310
parallel p. 316
parallegogram p. 316
pentagon p. 322
perimeter p. 323
perpendicular p. 323
pi p. 326
polygon p. 334
polyhedron p. 334
prime number p. 342
quadrant p. 352
quadrilateral p. 352
quadruple p. 352
quarter p. 352
quotient p. 354
reciprocal p. 360
rhombus p. 370
scalene triangle p. 382
sine p. 399
square p. 416
statistic p. 419
subtract p. 429
sum p. 430
symmetrical p. 436
tally p. 438
tangent p. 439
theorem p. 445
three-dimensional p. 447
triangle p. 457
trillion p. 457
two-dimensional p. 462
vertex p. 473
vertical p. 473
volume p. 476

Appendix 6 Computers and technology

ampere p. 14
amplifier p. 14
anemometer p. 15
bar-code p. 31
BASIC p. 33
cassette p. 63
CD p. 65
CD-ROM p. 65
CFC p. 67
compact disc p. 82
compact disc
  player p. 82
computer p. 85
computerise p. 85
database p. 106
debug p. 108
DOS p. 126
electromagnet p. 137
electron p. 137
electronic p. 137
E-mail p. 138
floppy disc p. 165
Geiger counter p. 181
gyroscope p. 196

hacker p. 197
hard disc p. 200
high fidelity p. 207
interactive p. 231
intercom p. 231
interface p. 231
in vitro p. 234
isotope p. 235
joystick p. 240
mainframe p. 268
metallurgy p. 278
microcomputer p. 279
microfilm p. 279
microscope p. 279
microsurgery p. 279
microwave p. 279
modem p. 284
neutron p. 295
odometer p. 303
pacemaker p.313
pasteurise p. 318
petrochemical p. 324
RAM p. 357
renewable energy p. 365

Richter scale p. 370
rocket p. 373
ROM p. 374
satellite p. 380
seismograph p. 387
silicon p. 398
space shuttle p. 410
strobe p. 426
submarine p. 428
switchboard p. 435
technology p. 441
thermostat p. 445
transformer p. 455
transistor p. 455
turbocharger p. 460
VCR p. 471
VDU p. 471
VHF p. 473
video p. 473
videotape p. 474
wavelength p. 481
word processor p. 491
X-ray p. 494
zoom lens p. 498

Appendix 7 Aboriginal words

Alcheringa p. 10
Anangu: Western Desert language p. 15
Bama: North Queensland Aboriginal
  languages p. 30
barramundi: Queensland language p. 32
bilby: Yuwaalaraay p. 39
bindi-eye: Kamilaroi and
  Yuwaalaraay p. 40
bogong: Ngarigo p. 45
boodie: Nyungar p. 46
boomerang: Dharuk p. 46
brolga: Kamilaroi p. 52
bunyip: Wemba-wemba p. 55
churinga: Aranda p. 72
coolamon: Kamilaroi p. 92
coolibah: Yuwaaliyaay p. 92
corella: Wiradhuri p. 93
corroboree: Dharuk p. 94
currawong: Yagara p. 103
dalgite: Nyungar p. 105
didgeridoo p. 117
dingo: Dharuk p. 119
gidgee: Yuwaalaraay p. 183
gilgie or jilgie: Nyungar p. 183
humpy: Yagara p. 214
kangaroo: Guugu Yimidhirr p. 243
kookaburra: Wiradhuri p. 247
Koori: Awabakal p. 247
kowari: Diyari p. 247
kurrajong: Dharuk p. 247
kylie: Nyungar p. 247
marloo: Western Desert language p. 272
marron: Nyungar p. 272
mia-mia: Nyungar p. 279

mirrnyong: Victorian Aboriginal
  language p. 282
Mulba: Panyjima p. 289
mulgara: Wangganguru p. 289
munjon: Yindjibarndi p. 290
Murri: Kamilaroi p. 290
nardoo: Yandruwandha p. 292
nulla-nulla: Dharuk p. 299
Nunga: Nhangka p. 300
Nyoongah or Noongah: Nyungar p. 300
Palawa: Tasmanian Aboriginal
  language p. 314
potoroo: Dharuk p. 337
quokka: Nyungar p. 354
taipan: Wik-Mungkan p. 438
tuan: Wathawurung p. 459
Uluru: Luritja p. 463
waddy: Dharuk p. 477
waratah: Dharuk p. 479
warrigal: Dharuk p. 479
willy willy: Yindjibarndi or
  Wemba-wemba p. 487
witchetty grub: Adnyamathanha p. 489
wombat: Dharuk p. 490
Wongi: Aboriginal Desert
  language p. 490
woomera: Dharuk p. 490
yabby: Wemba-wemba p. 495
yakka: Yagara p. 495
Yammagi: Watjari p. 495
Yolngu: Yolngu p. 496
yowie: Yuwaalaraay p. 497
Yura: Adnyamathanha p. 497

Appendix 8 Human body

abdomen p. 1
acne p. 4
Adam's apple p. 5
adenoids p. 6
alimentary canal p. 11
ankle p. 16
appendix p. 18
artery p. 22
asthma p. 24
back p. 28
bladder p. 41
blood p. 43
body p. 45
bone p. 46
bony p. 46
bosom p. 47
breast p. 50
bulimia p. 54
cartilage p. 63
cataract p. 64
cervix p. 67
cheek p. 69
cholesterol p. 71
colon p. 80
coronary p. 93
corpuscle p. 94
cuticle p. 104
cyst p. 104

diaphragm p. 117
ear p. 133
exhale p. 148
feet p. 157
finger p. 161
finger nail p. 161
fingerprint p. 161
foetus p. 167
foot p. 168
forehead p. 169
genitals p. 181
hair p. 197
head p. 202
heart p. 203
hormone p. 211
intercourse p. 231
intestine p. 232
iris p. 234
kidney p. 245
menstruation p. 277
molar p. 284
mole p. 284
mouth p. 288
muscle p. 290
nerve p. 295
neurone p. 295
nipple p. 297
nose p. 298

nostril p. 298
oesophagus p. 303
ovary p. 310
pelvis p. 321
penis p. 322
period p. 323
pimple p. 328
plasma p. 330
pore p. 335
pregnant p. 340
protoplasm p. 347
puberty p. 348
pupil p. 349
pus p. 350
rectum p. 361
saliva p. 379
scrotum p. 384
semen p. 388
sinew p. 399
sinus p. 400
sperm p. 412
stomach p. 423
sweat p. 434
teeth p. 441
testicle p. 444
vagina p. 470

Appendix 9 Civics and citizenship

administration p. 6
alderman p. 10
arbitration p. 20
autocracy p. 26
ballot p. 30
bureaucracy p. 55
by-election p. 57
candidate p. 60
capitalism p. 61
census p. 66
citizenship p. 73
citizenship
    ceremony p. 73
civic p. 73
commonwealth p. 82
community p. 82
constitution p. 89
culture p. 102
debate p. 108
democracy p. 112
diplomacy p. 119
education p. 135
election p. 136
electorate p. 136
embassy p. 138
federal p. 157
federation p. 157
Gallup poll p. 179
govern p. 188

government p. 188
governor p. 189
Governor-General p. 189
House of
    Representatives p. 213
indigenous p. 224
jurisdiction p. 241
justice p. 241
kingdom p. 245
law p. 252
law court p. 252
lawful p. 252
lawless p. 252
lawyer p. 252
legal p. 254
legalise p. 254
legislation p. 254
Legislative
    Assembly p. 254
Legislative
    Council p. 254
legislature p. 254
local government p. 261
mayor p. 274
member of
    parliament p. 276
MHA p. 279
MHR p. 279
MP p. 288

multiracial p. 289
municipal p. 290
municipality p. 290
nationalise p. 293
nationalism p. 293
nationalist p. 293
nationality p. 293
naturalise p. 293
neighbourhood p. 295
parliament p. 316
petition p. 324
political p. 334
politician p. 334
politics p. 334
poll p. 334
premier p. 340
president p. 341
prime minister p. 342
referendum p. 362
revenue p. 369
Senate p. 388
socialism p. 407
society p. 407
state p. 419
Supreme Court p. 432
vote p. 476
welfare state p. 483

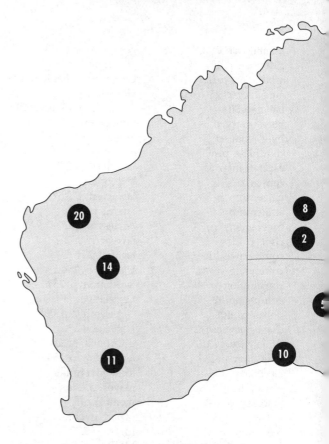

Map showing the Ab[original languages]
referred to in t[he text]

Aboriginal Languages:

1. Adnyamathanha
2. Aranda
3. Awabakal
4. Dharuk
5. Diyari
6. Guugu Yimidhirr
7. Kamilaroi
8. Luritja
9. Ngarigo
10. Nhangka
11. Nyungar
12. Wangganguru
13. Wathawurung
14. Watjari
15. Wemba-wemba
16. Wik-Mungkan
17. Wiradhuri
18. Yagara
19. Yandruwandha
20. Yindjibarndi
21. Yolngu
22. Yuwaalaraay and Yuwaaliyaay

Original languages
this dictionary

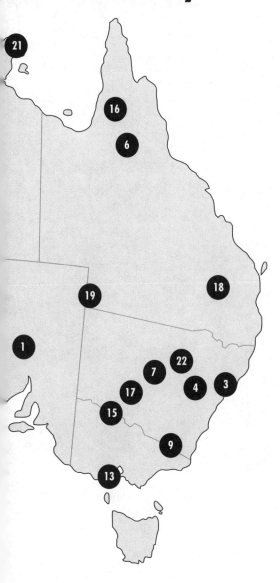